ALMANACH

DE

GOTHA

---•---

ANNUAL

GENEALOGICAL *and*
DIPLOMATIC REFERENCE
Volume I (Parts I & II)
240 Years

2003
MMIII

ONE HUNDRED AND EIGHTY SIXTH EDITION

LONDON
ALMANACH DE GOTHA LTD

ALMANACH DE GOTHA
ORIGINAL GENEALOGICAL REFERENCE
1763-2003
into a fourth century of publishing

Almanach de Gotha Limited™
9 Cork Street
London W1S 3LL (The United Kingdom)

Telephone 0208 404 2489 (*or* From Overseas) + 44 208 404 2489
Facsimile   0208 404 2629 (*or* From Overseas) + 44 208 404 2629

e-mail:Gotha1763@aol.com

website   www.AlmanachDeGotha.com

© Standard Edition; *186th Edition* Almanach de Gotha™
Established 1763

First Impression (*186th Edition*) 1st January 2003

ISBN 0 9532142 4 9

Publisher & Managing Editor John Kennedy

Associate Editor John E James

Printed & Bound By Compass Press Limited

British Library **CIP** catalogue entry for this book is available from the **BRITISH LIBRARY**.

Société des Amis de l'Almanach de Gotha

(*President*)

His Majesty King Juan Carlos I of Spain

(*Chairman*)

His Majesty King Michael I of Romania

(*Deputy Chairmen*)

HI&RH Archduke Lorenz of Austria, Prince of Belgium

HH Prince Eduard, Duke of Anhalt

(Director)

Mr John Kennedy

Comité de patronage

HM King Leka of Albania

HI&RH The Archduke Dr Otto von Habsburg,

HIH Crown Prince Osman of Turkey,

HIH The Prince Napoléon,

HI&RH Prince Dom Pedro Orleans-Bragança,

HI&RH The Archduke Felix of Austria,

HI&RH The Archduke Rudolf of Austria,

HI&RH The Archduke Sigismund of Austria, GD of Tuscany,

HRH Prince Vittorio Emanuele of Savoy, The Prince of Naples,

HRH Dom Duarte, Duke of Bragança,

HRH Crown Prince Nicholas of Montenegro,

HRH The Duke of Aosta,

HH Nicholas Romanov, Prince of Russia,

HH Duke Borwin of Mecklenburg-Strelitz,

HRH Prince George of Yugoslavia,

HRH Prince Franz Wilhelm of Prussia,

HSH Prince Pierre d'Arenberg.

MARIE
Reine de Hannovre.

GEORGE
Roi de Hannovre.

8

ALMANAC de GOTHA

Pour l'année

estd. 1763 – 240 Years

Gotha and London

2003 (186th Edition)

PREFACE

This new 2003 Edition of the Gotha updates the last of Volume I, published in 2000, which was followed in 2001 by the revival of Volume II *(The Princely & Ducal Houses)*.

Gotha listings begin with this famous red covered book containing entries for the Sovereign Houses of Europe and South America. For those who require a detailed account of the abbreviations contained in this Volume, or an explanation of the format, these can be found in *Appendix I (page 975)*.

The Almanach de Gotha has, since 1763, provided an up to date reference point for births, marriages and deaths in each of the families making up the reigning and formerly reigning sovereign houses of Europe and South America.

Our thanks must again go the *Research Committee*, who are listed after *Appendix VI (page 1023)*. They have given generously of their time. We also owe our gratitude to family members who have checked and updated their own entries and who remain a constant point of contact.

In the end it is fitting to express our appreciation to those readers who have added the Gotha to their libraries. Without this patronage the publication had no future, with it we shall continue with our well established and respected tradition.

JOHN KENNEDY
MANAGING EDITOR & PUBLISHER
LONDON, 1 JANUARY 2003
WWW.ALMANACHDEGOTHA.COM

Part One Families *(1st Part)*

CONTENTS

Part One Families *(1st Part)*

Part One & Part Two Families *(1st & 2nd Part)*

Part Two Families *(2nd Part)*

Part Two Families *(2nd Part)*

Almanach

de

Gotha

2003
MMIII
186th Edition

(Volume I)

PART ONE
(Première Partie)

Genealogies of the Sovereign

Houses of Europe & South America

ALMANAC
de
GOTHA
Pour l'année

Estd. 1763 – 240 Years
Gotha and London
2003

ALBANIA
(HOUSE OF ZOGU)

Islamic: This family, originally named Zogolli "Son of the Bird",
came from Zogaj, a mountainous region of Kosovo. *Circa* the end of
the 15th centur Zogu the Great emigrated from northern Albania to
Mati in central Albania, where he led an uprising against the Turkish
Governor Gazi Bey, who was killed. Zogu, who was a Christian,
converted to Islam and his grandson, Zogu the Small, was recognised
as Hereditary Governor of Mati by Turkey. His son Abdullah Bey
Zogu (✝ AH 1039) made an armed attempt to gain Albania's
independence, in which he lost his life. Ahmed Bey Zogu (*b* 8 Oct
1895; ✝ 9 April 1961), *succ* his father as Hereditary Governor of Mati
to the exclusion of his half-brother Xhelal 1911, became Prime
Minister of Albania 3 Dec 1922 - 10 June 1924 (when he was overthrown
by Bishop Fan Noli), and 6 - 21 Jan 1925, President of Albania 21 Jan
1925 - 1 Sept 1928, was proclaimed King of the Albanians by the
Albanian National Assembly 1 Sept 1928, and left the country
following the Italian invasion and occupation 8 April 1939.
Arms: Gu, a double-headed eagle sa. *Mantling:* Gu, fringed and tasselled
or, doubled erm and surmounted by the Cap of Scander-Beg, thereon
a goat's head sinster ppr.
After the establishment of the Monarchy the Albanian National
Assembly conferred the title of Queen Mother on King Zog's mother
and the titles of Prince and Princess (with the qualification of
Highness) on his half-brother and his sisters. The Sons and daughters
of a King or Crown Prince or Heir Apparent bear the title of Prince
or Princess of Albania with the qualification of Royal Highness; the
daughters of Kings or Heirs Apparent assume their husband's rank
and style upon marriage, losing all dynastic title and position.

LEKA I, KING OF THE ALBANIANS, proclaimed King at
Paris by the Albanian National Assembly in exile, *b* at Tirana 5
April 1939, son of Zog I, King of the Albanians, formerly Ahmed Bey
Zogu (*b* 8 Oct 1895; ✝ 9 April 1961) and Countess Geraldine Apponyi
de Nagy-Appony (*b* 6 Aug 1915; *m* 27 April 1938; ✝ 22 Oct 2002), *m*
at Biarritz 7 Oct 1975, Susan (*b* at Waverly, Sydney, NSW, Australia
28 Jan 1941), dau of *Alan* Robert Cullen-Ward and *Phyllis* Dorothia
Murray Prior.
[*Oborri Mbretëror Shqiptar, Rr, Lekë Dukagjini 11, Tirana, Albania*]

Son
Leka Anwar Zog Reza Baudouin Msiziwe, Crown Prince of the
Albanians, *b* at Sandton, South Africa 26 March 1982.
[*P.O. Box 70303, 2021 Bryanston, Republic of South Africa*].

Half-Brother of Father

Issue of Xhemal Zogu Pasha, Hereditary Governor of Mati (*b ca* 1860; ✝ 1911) and his first wife, Melek Zogu (*b* 1860; *m* 1880; ✝ 1884).

Xhelal Bey Zogu, from 1 Sept 1928, HH Prince Xhelal Zogu, *b* at Burgajet 14 May 1881; ✝ at Istanbul 26 Feb 1944; *m* 1stly at Burgajet April 1908 (*m* diss by div 1912), Ruhijé (*b* at Dibra 9 March 1881; ✝ at Cannes 6 Dec 1956), dau of Salih Agolli Doshishti and Gylijé Allaj.He *m* 2ndly at Burel 2 Aug 1931, Ikbal (*b* at Pekkini; ✝ at Burel 3 May 1932), dau of Izzet Bey Pekkini, and by her had further issue,

    1. *Elvira, b* at Burel 3 May 1932; *m* at Alexandria, Egypt 10 June 1955 (officially seperated 9 Jan 1986), Ibrahim Hadidi (*b* at Alexandria, Egypt 9 October 1934).

    [*6 rue Nag Hamadi, Ibrahimieh, Alexandria, Egypt*].

Prince Xhelal *m* 3rdly at Burel 2 Aug 1932 (*m* diss by div 9 Feb 1933), Faika Minxhalliu (*b* at Delvine 1897; ✝ at Kruja 9 Dec 1935), and had further issue,

    2. *Skender, b* at Davos, Switzerland 3 June 1933; *m* at Compiègne 10 Nov 1962, Jacqueline (*b* at Bucquoy, Pas de Calais 7 Aug 1932; ✝ at Senlis 14 Dec 2001), dau of Georges Cosme and Lucienne Prouvost, and has issue,

    [*39 avenue Maréchal Joffre, 60500 Chantilly, France*].

        1. *Virginie* Alexandra Geraldine, *b* at Compiègne 25 Jan 1963; *m* at St Jean de Luz 6 June 1987, Raphael de Urresti (*b* at St Jean de Luz 18 Oct 1959).

        [*43 rue Perronet, 92400 Neuilly-sur-Seine, France*].

Prince Xhelal *m* 4thly at Burel May 1933, Hyrijet (*b* at Elbasan 1916; ✝ at Alexandria 17 Oct 1993), dau of Emin Bey Allaj and Ulkijé Binbashi, and had further issue, among whom,

    3. *Melita, b* at Burel 18 June 1935; *m* at Alexandria 22 Feb 1958, Abdel Aziz Khadr, (*b* at Alexandria, Egypt 20 Oct 1927; ✝ at Cairo 22 Jan 2002).

    [*36 Shaheed Said Afifi, Golf City, Misr el Gedida, Cairo*].

    4. *Vera, b* at Durazzo 3 Feb 1938; *m* at Cairo 24 Dec 1955 (diss by div at Cairo 4 Nov 1961), Essawi Khadr (*b* at Mahallah, Egypt 12 Jan 1936).

    [*Centre Culturel Francois, 30 rue Nahi Demiel, BP 760, Alexandria*].

    5. *Mirgin, b* at Durazzo 3 Sept 1937; *m* at Cannes 23 Nov 1959, Maryse (*b* at Cannes 17 Jan 1934), dau of Joseph Ferrando

and Aline Lavenne, and has issue,
[*45 ave.du Feric, St Pancras, 06000, Nice*].

    1. *Alexandre, b* at Paris 10 Jan 1963; *m* at Paris 2 Oct 1993, *Emanuelle* (*b* at Beaufort 25 Aug 1969), dau of José Munoz and *Minni* Claude
    [*605 Ave de Cannes, Mourous, Sartoux, France*].

        1. *Erina b* at Nice 9 Jan 1994.
        2. *Anna, b* at Nice 16 June 1995.
        3. *Flora, b* at Grasse 13 Dec 1996.

    2. *Michel, b* at Cannes 16 Sept 1966.
    [*13 rue 3 Septembre, 06320 Cap d'Ail, France*].

ANDORRA
(PRINCE-BISHOPRIC OF URGELL)

Catholic: The present sovereign Andorran state has enjoyed a separate identity and socio-political independence for more than 1000 years, but it is at the same time one of Europe's youngest independent states, the current Constitution having effect from March 14 1993, the country remaining until that date suzerain (*señorío feodal*) and not sovereign.

The original inhabitants of the Valleys of Andorra were also related to the Basques of northern Spain and southern France and the name Andorra is supposedly of Basque derivation. Andorra was part of the Roman Empire. Andorra was and remained Christian during the Moors' conquest and according to tradition was liberated by the Emperor Charlemagne. Its six parishes are mentioned shortly afterwards in ecclesiastical diocesan records concerning the Act of Consecration in 839 of the Cathedral of La Seu d'Urgell. Andorran rights belong both to the Head of State of France as such (Co-Prince of Andorra) and to the Bishopric as such of Urgell, normally exercised by the Incumbent of that See (also Co-Prince of Andorra). In some instances, the Holy See has authorized other Bishops to exercise these rights, as was the case in the nineteenth century (Third Carlist War) when the Archbishop of Albi in France temporarily replaced the impeded Bishop of Urgell as Co-Prince.

The *Carta de Fundació d Andorra*, which asserts the autonomy of the country, is usually ascribed to Charlemagne albeit without sufficient historical proof. The Emperor's son, Louis the Pious, upheld this Charter which has often been cited against claims made by France and Spain. The Carolingian Empire falling victim to territorial dispute, Andorra came under the rule of the Count of Urgell. In 1133 "in order to save his soul", that Count ceded his

Andorran lands (which always belonged to the *comunidades* and never to the feudal lords) to the Bishop of Urgell. A struggle ensued between that Bishop and the Count of Foix which was resolved through the intervention of the King of Aragon by the Treaty of *pareatges* on September 8 1278, signed by Roger Bernard, Count of Foix, and Pedro d'Urtx, Bishop of Urgell. The Bishop's authority was recognized and certain rights granted to the Count of Foix. This Treaty, followed by further agreements in 1289, definitively established the suzerain autonomy and virtual independence of the country. The joint suzerainty of the Bishop of Urgell and the Count of Foix (whose rights upon the extinction of his line passed to the French Crown and hither to that Head of State) is the basis of the present Constitution which has granted sovereignty and complete independence to the Principality.

The twin Heads of State, who are Co-Princes of Andorra, until the new Constitution formally represented in the Country by Veguers (Vicars), are now represented by Delegates. The Co-Princes of Andorra each bear that title with the qualification of Excellency. According to the Andorran principle that "charges have no wives", the consort of the President of the French Republic is not considered to be the Co-Princess consort of Andorra.

JACQUES CHIRAC, (CO) PRINCE OF ANDORRA,

durante munere Præsidis Reipublicæ Gallicæ ad personam, President of the Republic of France (1995-), *b* at Paris 29 November 1932 (son of François Chirac and Marie-Louise Valette), Grand Cross of the National Order of Merit; Cross of Military Valour; Grand Cross of Merit Sovereign Military Order of Malta; French Agriculture and Rural Development Minister, 1973-74; French Interior Minister, 1974; Prime Minister of the Republic of France (1974-6; 1986-8); Mayor of Paris (1977-95); Member National Assembly (1967); Military Service 1954-57 (Wounded in action - Algeria); *educ* Lycée Carnot; Lycée Louis-le-Grand (with honors in 1950); Institut d' études politiques and Harvard University (1953); Ecole Nationale d'Administration (ENA); *m* at Paris 16 March 1956 Bernadette (*b* at Paris 19 May 1933) dau of Jean Chodron de Courcel and Marguerite-Marie de Brondeau d' Urtiéres.
[*Elysees Palace, 55 rue de Faubourg St Honoré Paris 7500, France*].

JOAN MARTÍ y Alanís BISHOP OF URGELL (CO) PRINCE-BISHOP OF ANDORRA,

durante munere Episcopi Urgellensis ad personam, b at Mila, Archdiocese of Tarragona, 29 Nov 1928 (son of Ramon Martís and Emilia Alanís), Grand Cross Order of Isabella the Catholic; ordained 17 June 1951, ecclesiastical

student at the seminary of Tarragona; degree in classical studies at the Univ of Salamanca, parish priest of Montblanch, Tarragona (1956-66), dir. San Pablo Diocesan School, Tarragona (1966); episcopal vicar of teaching and of Doctrine of Faith (1969), appointed Bishop of the See of Urgel, Lérida and Co-Prince of Andorra by His late Holiness Pope Paul VI 25 Nov 1970, consecrated 31 Jan 1971.
[*Pati Palau 1-5, 25700 La Seu d'Urgell, Spain*]

ANHALT
(HOUSE OF ASCANIA)

The ruling house of the former sovereign Duchy of Anhalt traces its origin to a Count Esico who flourished in the Schwabengau and Hartgau 1039-59. His descendants acquired the county of Ballenstedt and, *ca* 1100, that of Ascania. In 1180 Bernhard, Count of Ascania and Anhalt obtained the title of Duke of Saxony with the territories of Lauenburg and Wittenberg, but lost the former to King Waldemar II of Denmark. Bernhard (✝ 1212) and his younger son Albert recovered Lauenburg in 1227. On his death in 1260 his two sons founded the ducal lines of Saxe-Lauenburg (extinct 1689) and Saxe-Wittenberg (extinct 1422). Meanwhile, the descendants of Duke Bernhard's elder son, Heinrich I, continued to reign in Anhalt and acquired the title of Prince in 1218. During the subsequent 350 years many divisions and sub-divisions of territory took place, but in 1570 all the possessions of the family were reunited in the person of Prince Joachim Ernst (1536-1586). In 1603 his sons decided on a new partition and founded the lines of Anhalt-Dessau (the only one still extant), Anhalt-Bernburg (extinct 19 March 1863), Anhalt-Köthen (extinct 13 April 1665), succeeded by the line of Plotzkau (extinct 23 Nov 1847) and Anhalt-Zerbst (extinct 3 March 1793). The order of primogeniture was introduced into the principalities during the first quarter of the 18th century and confirmed 12 April 1729. The title of Duke was conferred on the line of Anhalt-Bernburg by Imperial Decree 8 April 1806, and assumed by the lines of Anhalt-Dessau and Anhalt-Köthen in 1807 (published June 1807). The Duchies were reunited into the Duchy of Anhalt in 1863. The dynasty ceased to reign 12 Nov 1918, when the Prince Regent Aribert abdicated in the name of Duke Joachim Ernst.

Arms:- Per pale, dexter, a demidiated eagle gu, beaked and membered or, sinister, barry, sa and or, over all a wreath of rue in bend, vert. The shield is ensigned with a Royal Crown. *Supporters:-* Two bears rampant reguardant ppr crowned or.

Members of the family bear the title of Prince or Princess of Anhalt with the qualification of Highness. The Princes also bear the additional titles of Duke of Saxony, Count of Ascania.

EDUARD Julius Ernst August Erdmann, **DUKE OF ANHALT,** Duke of Saxony, Engern and Westphalia, Count of Ascania, Lord of Zerbst, Bernburg and Gröbzig, etc, *b* at Schloß Ballenstedt 3 Dec 1941, son of Joachim Ernst, Duke of Anhalt (*b* 11 Jan 1901; ✠ 18 Feb 1947; *succ* his father under the regency of his uncle Aribert who abdicated on his behalf 12 Nov 1918) and his second wife, Edda Marwitz von Stephani (*b* 20 Aug 1905; *m* 15 Oct 1929; ✠ 22 Feb 1986; *m* 1stly 18 Nov 1926, Maximilian, Ritter and Edler von Rogister; that *m* diss by div at Berlin 4 March 1927); *m* at Munich 21 July 1980 (civ) and at St-Scharl, Switzerland 7 June 1986 (relig), Corinna (*b* at Würzburg 19 Aug 1961), dau of Günther Krönlein and Anneliese Benz.

[*Jagdschloß Röhrkopf, D-06493, Ballenstedt, Germany; Unterdiessen 86944, Germany*].

Daughters

1. Princess *Julia* Katharina, *b* at Bad Tölz 14 Dec 1980.
2. Princess Julia *Eilika* Nicole, *b* at Munich 3 January 1985.
3. Princess Julia *Felicitas* Leopoldine Friederike Franziska, *b* at Munich 14 May 1993.

Brother and Sisters

1. Princess Marie Antoinette Elisabeth *Alexandra* Irmgard Edda Charlotte, *b* at Schloß Ballenstedt 14 July 1930; ✠ at Memmingen 22 March 1993; *m* 1stly at Lahr 24 May 1957 (*m* diss by div at Munich 8 April 1968), Karl-Heinz Guttmann (*b* at Mingstimehlen, Schloßberg 13 March 1911). She *m* 2ndly at Visselhövede 20 (civ) and 21 (relig) Dec 1974 (*m* diss by div 3 Dec 1976), Dr *Max* Theodor Andreas Riederer (*b* at Munich 3 Feb 1917).
2. Princess *Anna Luise* Marie Friederike Elisabeth Alice, *b* at Schloß Ballenstedt 26 March 1933, *m* at Los Angeles, California USA 5 Aug 1966 (*m* diss by div at Berlin 1 June 1970), *Thomas* Beverly Birch (*b* at New York 27 Sept 1927).
[*Jagdschloß Röhrkopf, D-06493, Ballenstedt, Germany*].
3. Leopold **Friedrich** Franz Sieghard Hubertus Erdmann, **Duke of Anhalt,** *b* at Schloß Ballenstedt 11 April 1938; ✠ at Munich 9 Oct 1963.
4. Princess *Edda* Adelheid Antoinette Emma Elisabeth, *b* at Schloß Ballenstedt 30 Jan 1940, *m* at Garmisch-Partenkirchen 20 Dec 1973,

Albert Darboven (*b* at Darmstadt 15 April 1936).
[*c/o J.J. Darboven, Pinkertweg 13, 22113 Hamburg, Germany*].

Brother of Father

Issue of Eduard, Duke of Anhalt (*b* 18 April 1861; ✠ 13 Sept 1918) and Princess Luise of Saxe-Altenburg (*b* 11 Aug 1873; *m* 6 Feb 1895; ✠ 14 April 1953) amongs whom,

1. Prince *Eugen* Friedrich Ernst August Heinrich Adolf Aribert, *b* at Dessau 17 April 1903; ✠ at La Tour de Pielz, Switzerland 2 Sept 1980; *m* at Munich 2 Oct 1935, Anastasia Marie Therese Karoline, (*b* at Straubing 25 July 1901; ✠ at Vevey 19 Feb 1970), dau of Max Jungmeier and Anastasia Steiner, and has issue,

    1. Princess *Anastasia Luise* Alexandra Elisabeth Jutta Sybille Marie-Auguste Henriette, *b* at Regensburg 22 Dec 1940, *m* at La Tour-de-Peilz 22 June (civ) and at Vevey, Switzerland 23 June (relig) 1962, Maria Emanuel, Margrave of Meissen, Prince of Saxony, Head of the Royal House of Saxony (*b* at Prufening, nr Regensburg 31 Jan 1926).
    [*Ascania Nova, Avenue de Sully 102, 1814 La-Tour-de-Peilz, VD Switzerland*].

AUSTRIA
(House of Habsburg-Lorraine)

Catholic: The Founder of the House of Habsburg was Guntrum the Rich, Lord of Muri (✠ after 973); his son Lanzelin (✠ 991), Count of Altenburg (a fortified castle, today in ruins, in the Swiss Canton of Argau) 952; his descendants acquired the following dignities: Count of Habespurg (Habichtsburg) 1020 - 1450; King of Germany 29 Sept 1273 - 1291, 1298 - 1308, 1314 - 1330 and 1438 to 1740; Holy Roman Emperor 1452 - 1403, 1530 -1556, elected Holy Roman Emperor 10 Feb 1508 - 1519 and 1558 - 20 Oct 1740; Duke of Austria and Duke of Styria 27 Dec 1282; Count of Kyburg (in the Swiss Canton of Zurich) 1264 - 1400; Duke of Carinthia and Lord of Krain 2 May 1335 (1364, Duke); Count of Tyrolia 1363; Lord of Trieste 1382; Archduke of Austria 1453; Count of Görz, of Gradisca and Margrave of Istria 12 April 1500; Margrave of Upper Lusatia and Lower Lusatia (1438 - 1457) 24 Oct 1526 - 1740; King of Hungary (1438 - 1457, 24 Oct 1526 - 1780 - after 1687 the title became hereditary); King of Croatia, King of Dalmatia, King of Slavonia, King of Jerusalem and Prince of Transylvania 5 Nov 1527; Grand Voivode of Serbia 1718 to 1739;

Duke of Parma and of Piacenza (1735 - 1748); Karl VI (✠ 20 Oct
1740), became Holy Roman Emperor, 13 Sept 1745; Count of
Hohenems (1759), Feldkirch (1365) and Bregenz (1451, 1523),
Sonnenberg (1483, 1511), in Vorarlberg (11 March 1765), his dau
and heiress, Maria Theresia (b 13 May 1717; ✠ 29 Nov 1780),
Archduchess of Austria, Apostolic Queen of Hungary and of Bohemia,
Grand Duchess of Transylvania (1765), Queen of Galicia (Halicz)
and Lodomerie (Wlodimierz in the Russian Grand Duchy of
Wolhynie), Duchess of Auschwitz (Oswieczim) and Zator (Galicia)
5 Aug 1772; Dame of Bukovinia 7 May 1775, married 8 Dec 1736,
Franz III Stephan (b 1708; ✠ 1765), Duke of Lorraine (1729 - 1736),
Grand Duke of Tuscany; the House of Lorraine was founded by
Hugo, Count in Alsace (✠ 940); whose immediate ancestors were
Eberhard I, Count in Alsace (✠ 966); Adalbert (II) (✠ 1032/33), also
a Count in Alsace, Count in Saargau (1005), Count of Metz (1020);
Gerhard IV (✠ 1070) became Duke of Upper Lorraine in 1048; Simon
I (✠ 1139) became Duke of all Lorraine 1115 (- 1736); Duke of Teschen
(Austrian Silesia) 12 May 1722; Grand Duke of Tuscany (Etruria in
central Italy) as compensation for the loss of Lorraine 7 July 1737;
elected King of the Romans and King of Germany 1745 - 1806.

The Lines below descend from the sons of Leopold II (b 5 May 1747;
✠ 1 March 1792), Emperor of Austria, etc (from 30 Sept 1790),
Grand Duke of Tuscany as Leopoldo I (18 Aug 1765 to 7 March
1791), who was the son of Emperor Franz I and Empress Maria
Theresia.

Arms:- (of the Head of the House): Tierced per pale: dexter, or, a
lion rampant gu, armed langued and crowned az (Habsburg); per
pale, gu, a fess arg (Austria); and sinister, or, on a bend gu, three
alerions arg (Lorraine). The Shield is ensigned by a Royal Crown
without a cap and surrounded by the Collar of the Order of the
Golden Fleece.

(of the Austrian Empire): A double-headed eagle sa, armed and
membered gu, each head regally crowned holding in the dexter claw
a sword and sceptre, and in the sinister an orb, all ppr, per pale:
dexter, or, a lion rampant gu, armed, langued and crowned az
(Habsburg): per pale, gu, a fess arg (Austria); and sinister, or, on a
bend gu, three alerions arg (Lorraine). The whole is ensigned with
the Imperial Crown of Austria. For family Members of the Order of
the Golden Fleece, the Shield is surrounded by the Collar of the
Order.

(of the Kingdom of Hungary): Per pale, dexter, barry of eight gu and
arg (Hungary A): sinister, gu, a conventionalised mountain of three
peaks in base vert, crowned or and issuant therefrom a patriarchal
cross arg (Hungary M). The shield is ensigned with the Sacred
Crown of Hungary (Cross bent dexter) and surrounded by the Collar
of the Order of Saint Stephen. Supporters:- On each side an angel
proper close-girt and winged arg.

LINE I: Emperors of Austria and Kings of Hungary
This line descends from Franz II, King of Hungary, King of Bohemia, Archduke of Austria (b 12 Feb 1768; succ his father 1 March 1792; ✠ 2 March 1835), last Holy Roman Emperor and King of Germany 7 July 1792 - 6 Aug 1806; Grand Duke of Krakow 24 Oct 1795; Duke of Frioul (Margraviate since 850) and Lord of Cattaro (Kotor -Dalmatia/Montenegro) 1797; Emperor of Austria 11 Aug 1804 as Franz I; King of Illyria, Elector of Salzburg (Bishophric 785; Archbishophric 798), Duke of Raguse and of Zara (Dalmatia), Prince of Triente and of Brixen 10 June 1815; Duke of Salzburg and of Bukovinia 1849; Emperor of Austria and King of Hungary 21 Dec 1867. By declaration abolition of Sovereign rights of the House of Habsburg-Lorraine in Austria 3 April 1919; by declaration loss of the Hungarian throne 5 Nov 1921. Members of the Imperial Family bear the titles of Archduke or Archduchess of Austria, Prince or Princess of Hungary and Bohemia, with the qualification of Imperial and Royal Highness. Since 30 Nov 1990 the descendants of marriages not recognised as being of equal status bear the title of Count or Countess von Habsburg unless another title has been conferred upon them.

Franz Joseph **OTTO** Robert Maria Anton Karl Max Heinrich Sixtus Xaver Felix Renatus Ludwig Gaetan Pius Ignatius, **ARCHDUKE OF AUSTRIA**, formerly Crown Prince of Austria and Hungary, Dr of Pol and Soc Sciences, mem Acad of Moral and Pol Sciences Institut de France in Paris, previously Head and Sovereign Order of the Golden Fleece, Kt of Hon Teutonic Order, German Bundesverdienstkreuz, Bavarian Verdienstorden, Carlos III and Orden de Africa of Spain, Papal Gregorius Order, etc, Bailiff Gd Cross Hon and Dev Sovereign Military Order of Malta, former Member of the European Parliament (Munich & Uper Bavaria), has since June 1961 used the style of Dr Otto von Habsburg, b at Villa Wartholtz, in Reichenau 20 Nov 1912, son of Karl I, Emperor of Austria, King of Hungary, etc (b 17 Aug 1887; ✠ 1 April 1922) and Princess Zita of Bourbon-Parma (b 9 May 1892; m 21 Oct 1911; ✠ 14 March 1989); m at Nancy 10 May 1951, Princess Regina Helene Elisabeth Margarete (b at Würzburg 6 Jan 1925), Supreme Lady Protectress Star Cross Order, Dame Gd Cross Hon and Dev Sovereign Military Order of Malta, dau of Georg III, Duke of Saxe-Meiningen and Countess Klara-Marie von Korff genannt Schmising-Kerssenbrock, and has issue,
[*Hindenburgstraße 15, 82343 Pöcking, nr Starnberg, Upper Bavaria, Germany*].

Sons and Daughters

1. Archduchess *Andrea* Maria, *b* at Würzburg 30 May 1953, Dame Star Cross Order; *m* at Pöcking 9 July (civ) and 30 July 1977, Karl Eugen, Hereditary Count (Erbgraf) von Neipperg (*b* at Schwaigern 20 Oct 1951), Dipl Eng agr.

[*74193 Schwaigern, Württemberg, Germany*].

2. Archduchess *Monika* Maria Roberta Antonia Raphaela, *b* at Würzburg 13 Sept 1954, Dame Star Cross Order; *m* at Pöcking 21 June 1980, Don Luis Gonzaga de Casanova-Cárdenas y Baron, Duke de Santangelo, Marquess de Elche, Count de Lodosa, Grandee of Spain (*b* at Madrid 24 April 1950), Farmer.

[*Castillo de la Rápita, 25680 Vallfogona de Balaguer, Prov. Lérida, Spain*].

3. Archduchess *Michaela* Maria Madeleine Kiliana Elisabeth, *b* at Würzburg 13 Sept 1954 (twin with Archduchess Monika); *m* 1stly at Anton, Panama 12 Jul 1982 (civ) and at Anton, Panama 14 Jan (relig) 1984 (*m* diss by div 1993), Eric Alba Teran d'Antin (*b* at Mexico City 21 May 1920), Financier. She *m* 2ndly at Naples, Florida, 22 Oct 1994 (*m* diss by div 1998), Count *Hubertus* Joseph Alfons Carl Maria von Kageneck (*b* at Haus Bumenscheidt, nr. Wittlich 10 Aug 1940).

[*Av Cataluna 62, B 1-2 Tarragona, Spain*].

4. Archduchess *Gabriela* Maria Charlotte Felicitas Elisabeth Antonia, *b* at Luxembourg 14 Oct 1956, Academic Artist; *m* at Pöcking 30 Aug (civ) and at St Odile 5 Sept (relig) 1978 (*m* diss by div 1996 and annulled 1998), Christian Meister (*b* at Starnberg 1 Sept 1954), Lawyer.

[*Am Waldweg 21, 82541 Münsing-Seeheim, Germany*].

5. Archduchess *Walburga* Maria Franziska Helene Elisabeth, *b* at Berg am Starnberger See 5 Oct 1958, Dr of Law, Dame Star Cross Order; Dame Hon. and Dev. Sovereign Military Order of Malta; *m* at Budapest 5 Dec 1992, Carl Axel *Archibald*, Count Douglas (*b* at Stockholm 27 Nov 1949), Farmer.

[*Ekensholm, 64032 Malmköping, Sweden*].

6. Archduke *Karl* Thomas Robert Maria Franziskus Georg Bahnam, *b* at Starnberg 11 Jan 1961, Head of the Sovereign Order of the Golden Fleece, Kt of Hon Teutonic Order, Capt (*reserve*) Austrian Airforce, former Member of the European Parliament (Austria); *m* at Mariazell 31 Jan 1993, Baroness Francesca (*b* at Lausanne 7 June 1958), Chairman of Art Restoration for Cultural Heritage, dau of Hans Heinrich, Baron von Thyssen-Bornemisza de Kászon and Fiona

Campbell-Walter, and has issue,
[*Casa Austria, 5081 Anif, Austria*]
    1. Archduchess *Eleonore* Jelena Maria del Pilar Iona, *b* at Salzburg 28 Feb 1994.
    2. Archduke *Ferdinand* Zvonimir Maria Balthus Keith Michael Otto Antal Bahnam Leonhard, *b* at Salzburg 21 June 1997.
    3. Archduchess *Gloria* Maria Bogdana Paloma Regina Fiona Gabriela, *b* at Salzburg 15 October 1999.
7. Archduke *Paul Georg* Maria Joseph Dominikus, *b* at Starnberg 16 Dec 1964, Kt Order of the Golden Fleece; Ambassador at large (Hungary) and Television Manager; Dir MTM Communications, Hungary; *m* at St Stephen's Basilica, Budapest18 Oct 1997 (relig), Duchess Eilika (*b* at Bad Segeberg 22 Aug 1972), dau of Duke Johann of Oldenburg and Countess Ilka zu Ortenburg, and has isue,
[*IV Károly Király út 1, 2038 Sóskút, Hungary*].
    1. Archduchess Zsofia (*Sofia*) Mária Tatjana Monika Erzsébet Katalin, *b* at Telki, Hungary, 12 Jan 2001.
    2. Archduchess *Ildiko* Maria Walburga, *b* at Budapest, 6 June 2002.

Brothers and Sisters

1. Archduchess *Adelheid* Maria Josepha Sixta Antonia Roberta Ottonia Zita Charlotte Luise Immakulata Pia Theresia Beatrix Franziska Isabella Henriette Maximiliana Genoveva Ignatia Marcus d'Aviano, *b* at Hetzendorf 3 Jan 1914; ✝ at Pöcking, Upper Bavaria 2 Oct 1971, Dr of Pol and Soc Sciences, Dame Star Cross Order.
2. Archduke *Robert* Karl Ludwig Maximilian Michael Maria Anton Franz Ferdinand Joseph Otto Hubert Georg Pius Johannes Marcus d'Aviano, *b* at Schönbrunn 8 Feb 1915; ✝ at Basel 7 Feb 1996, Archduke of Austria-Este, his father took the name and arms of **AUSTRIA ESTE** (*to descend by primogeniture*) by transmission with Imp approval 31 Oct 1914, subsequently resigned by him to Archduke Robert 16 April 1917, Kt Order of the Golden Fleece, Bailiff Gd Cross Hon and Dev Sovereign Military Order of Malta, Kt Supreme Order of St Annunziata, etc; *m* at Bourg-en-Bresse 28 Dec (civ) and at Brou 29 Dec (relig) 1953, Princess Margherita (*b* at Capodimonte, Naples 7 April 1930), Diplome de l'Ecole du Louvre, Hautes Etudes Sorbonne, Dame Star Cross Order, Dame of Hon and Dev Sovereign Military Order of Malta, dau of Prince Amedeo of Savoy, 3rd Duke of Aosta, (1938-42) Viceroy of Ethiopia, Gov-Gen East Africa, Gen Italian Air Force, Senator of the Kingdom, Phd

(*Law*) etc; and Princess Anne of France, and had issue,
[*Obere Turmatt 4, 6370 Stans, Switzerland*].

1. Archduchess *Maria Beatrix* Anna Felicitas Zita Charlotte
Adelheid Christina Elisabeth Gennara, *b* at Boulogne-sur-
Seine 11 Dec 1954, Ph.D Economics and Business
Administration, Dame Star Cross Order; *m* at St Martin am
Inn, Upper Austria 31 March (civ) and at Chartres 26 April
(relig) 1980, Riprand, Count von and zu Arco Zinneberg (*b* at
Munich 25 July 1955), Proprietor of Moos, nr Plattling in
Bavaria, St Martin in Upper Austria, and Vysochi Chimec in
Bohemia; Chairman, American Asset Corporation.
[*Schloß Moos, 94554 Moos, Germany; Schloß Sankt Martin,
4973 Sankt Martin im Innkreis, Austria.*].

2. Archduke *Lorenz* Otto Carl Amedeo Thadeus Maria Pius
Andreas Marcus d'Aviano, Duke of Este, *b* at Boulogne-sur-
Seine 16 Dec 1955, Archduke of Austria-Este, -*cr* Prince of
Belgium by Royal Decree 27 Nov 1995; Kt Order of the Golden
Fleece, Kt Hon and Dev Sovereign Military Order of Malta,
etc, Banker, Mag rer oec; *m* at Brussels 22 Sept 1984, Princess
Astrid of Belgium, President Belgian Red Cross, Colonel and
Member of the Belgiun Senate (*b* at Château Belvedere, nr
Laeken 5 June 1962), dau of Albert II, King of the Belgians
and Donna Paola Ruffo di Calabria of the Princes Ruffo, and
has issue,
[*Palais de Bruxelles, 1000 Bruxelles, Belgium*].

1. Archduke *Amédéo* Maria Josef Carl Pierre Philippe
Paola Marcus d'Aviano of Austria-Este and Prince of
Belgium, (*created Prince of Belgium 1991, following
constitutional changes in that country repealing the
laws of succession by male primogeniture*), *b* at Woluwe
St Lambert, Belgium 21 Feb 1986.

2. Archduchess *Maria Laura* Zita Beatrix Gerhard of
Austria and Princess of Belgium, (*created Princess of
Belgium 1991, following constitutional changes in that
country repealing the laws of succession by male
primogeniture*), *b* at Woluwe St Lambert 26 Aug 1988.

3. Archduke *Joachim* Carl Maria Nikolaus Isabelle
Marcus d'Aviano of Austria-Este and Prince of
Belgium, (*Prince of Belgium from birth as a result of
constitutional changes in 1991 in that country repealing
the laws of succession by male primogeniture*), *b* at

Woluwe St Lambert 9 Dec 1991.

4. Archduchess *Luisa Maria* Anna Martina Pilar of
Austria and Princess of Belgium (*Princess of Belgium
from birth as a result of constitutional changes in
1991 in that country repealing the laws of succession
by male primogeniture*), *b* at Brussels 11 Oct 1995.

3. Archduke *Gerhard* Thadeus Anton Marcus d'Aviano Maria
Umberto Otto Carl Amadeus of Austria-Este, *b* at Boulogne-
sur-Seine 30 Oct 1957, Lic Pol and Soc Sciences.
[*Vorstadt 10, 6800 Feldkirch, Austria*].

4. Archduke *Martin* Carl Amadeo Maria Bruno Marcus
d'Aviano of Austria-Este, *b* at Boulogne-sur-Seine 19 Dec
1959, Dipl Ing agr.
[*Azienda Agricola del Castello, via Marconi 14-16, 27020
Sartirana Lomellina, Italy*].

5. Archduchess *Isabella* Marie Laura Helena Antonia Zita
Gennara, *b* at Boulogne-sur-Seine 2 March 1963, Lic. Rer.
Int.Pol., Dame Star Cross Order, *m* at Luxembourg-Ville 19
March (civ) and at Stams-Tirol, Austria 27 April (relig) 1997,
Count Andrea, Czarnocki-Lucheschi (*b* at Lausanne 21 April
1960), Businessman.
[*1 Rue du Château, 8805 Rambrouch, Luxembourg*].

3. Archduke *Felix* Friedrich August Maria vom Siege Franz Josef
Peter Karl Anton Robert Otto Pius Michael Benedikt Sebastian
Ignatius Marcus d'Aviano, *b* at Schönbrunn 31 May 1916,
Industrialist, Chairman and Dir of several corporations, Prince of
Bar, Kt Order of the Golden Fleece, Kt of Hon and Dev Sovereign
Military Order of Malta, etc, *m* at Beaulieu-sur Mer, France 18 Nov
(civ) and 19 Nov (relig) 1952, Princess and Duchess Anna-Eugenia
(*b* at Dillingen 6 July 1925 † at San Angel, Mexico DF 6 Jun 1997), Dr
of Vet Surg, Dame Star Cross Order, dau of Robert, Prince and Duke
of Arenberg and Princess (Fürstin) Gabriele von Wrede, and has
issue,
[*Reyna 193, San Angel, Mexico City 01060 D.F., Mexico*].

1. Archduchess *Maria del Pilar* Sophie Valerie Charlotte
Zita Johanna Marcus d'Aviano Caspara, *b* at Mexico City 18
Oct 1953; *m* at Pöcking 30 May (civ) and at Guttenberg 8
June (relig) 1980, Vollrad-Joachim, Ritter and Edler von
Poschinger (*b* at Munich 2 Jan 1952), Dipl Forestry.
[*Gut Waltersteig, 82547 Eurasburg-Herrnhausen, Germany*].

2. Archduke Carl *Philipp* Maria Otto Lukas Marcus d'Aviano

Melchior, *b* Mexico City 18 Oct 1954, MBA, Commercial
Counsellor, Mexican Foreign Commerce; *m* 1stly at Munich 4
Sept 1994 (*m* diss by div and annuled 1997) Martina, (*b* at
Vienna 18 June 1955), dau of Walter. Donath and Gabriele
Urban, and has issue,

    1. *Julian* Lorenz Peter, *b* at Montreal 29 May 1994.
Archduke Carl *Philipp, m* 2ndly at Pau 12 May 1998, *Annie-
Claire* Christine (*b* at Pau 15 Feb 1959), dau of *Henri* Gustave
Lacrambe and Fanny Pruvost de Montrichard, and has issue,
[*Reyna 193, San Angel, Mexico City 01060 D.F., Mexico*].

      2. *Louis-Damian* Henri Maria Marco d'Aviano Melchor,
      b at Montreal 23 Sept 1998.

3. Archduchess *Kinga* Barbara Maria Carlota Jakobea Markus
d'Aviano Balthasara, *b* at Schloß Guttenberg, Bavaria, 13
Oct 1955, Historian; *m* at Ahorn 3 June (civ) and at Perk,
Belgium 8 June (relig) 1985, Wolfgang, Baron von Erffa (*b* at
Coburg 6 Sept 1948), Dr. jur., Diplomat, Publicist.
[*Brandenburgische Straße 48, 15566 Schoeneiche Bei Berlin,
Germany*].

4. Archduke Raimund (*Ramon*) Joseph Carl Ludwig Maria
Gabriel Markus d'Aviano Gaspar *b* at Mexico City 28 Jan
1958, MBA Business; *m* at Bad Soden 29 April 1994 (civ) and
at Königstein 1 May 1994 (relig), Bettina (*b* at Frankfurt-am-
Main 25 Sept 1969), Dipl Travel Agent, dau of Dr rer pol
Heinrich Goetz and Helga Hager.
[*Freiligrathstraße 11, 65812 Bad Soden/Ts., Germany*].

    1. Archduke *Felix* Carl Maria Jürgen Melchior *b* at
    Bad Soden/Ts., 12 Dec 1996.

    2. Archduchess *Sophia* Maria Alexandra Gaspera *b* at
    Bad Soden/Ts., 12 March 1998.

    3. Archduchess *Maria Teresa* Beatrice Nicole
    Balthasara *b* at Bad Soden/Ts., 8 May 2000.

5. Archduchess *Myriam* Adelheid Hugoline Carola Omnes
Sancti Markus d'Aviano Melchiora, *b* at Mexico City 21 Nov
1959; *m* at Mexico City 22 June (civ) and 24 June (relig) 1983,
Jaime Corcuera Acheson (*b* at Mexico City 12 Jan 1955),
Banker.
[*Hidalgo 20, San Angel, Mexico City 01000, D.F., Mexico*].

6. Archduke *István* Franz-Leopold Johannes Maria Rudolph
Theresius Markus d'Aviano Balthasar, *b* at Mexico City 22
Sept 1961, Industrialist; *m* at Budapest 18 June (civ) and at

Tihany, Hungary 11 Sept (relig) 1993, Paola (*b* at Budapest 4 June 1971), Dipl Eng Architect, dau of Dr Lászlo Imre Temesváry and Dr Maria Csilla Rozenszki, and has issue,

[*1 Rue du Chateau, 8805 Rambrouch, Luxembourg*].

    1. Archduke *Andras* Francesco László Felix Carl Alexander Maria Marcus d'Aviano Caspar, *b* at Luxemburg 22 Dec 1994.

    2. Archduke *Pal* Johannes Maria Marcus d'Aviano Melchor, *b* at Luxemburg 10 Jan 1997.

    3. Archduchess *Marguerite* Alexandra Maria Csilla Eugina Catharina Marcus d'Aviano Balthasara *b* at Luxemburg 25 March 1999.

7. Archduchess *Viridis* Aloisa Marie-Eleonore Elisabeth Markus d'Aviano Caspara, *b* at Mexico City 23 Sept 1961 (twin with Archduke István), Translator; *m* at Frières, Aisne, France 8 Sept (civ) and at Beuerberg, nr Eurasburg 14 Oct (relig) 1990, Carl Harold William Dunning-Gribble (*b* at Paris 29 May 1961), Lord of the Manor of Marnhull, Banker.

[*23 Rue René Beon, 78100 St Germain en Laye, France*].

4. Archduke *Carl Ludwig* Maria Franz Joseph Michael Gabriel Antonius Robert Stephan Pius Gregor Ignatius Markus d'Aviano, *b* at Baden, nr Vienna 10 March 1918, Lic jur, Dr of Pol and Soc Sciences, Dir several industrial Co's, Kt Order of the Golden Fleece, Kt of Hon and Dev Sovereign Military Order of Malta, etc; *m* at the Château de Beloeil, Belgium 17 Jan 1950, Princess Yolande (*b* Madrid 6 May 1923), Dame Star Cross Order, dau of Eugène, 12th Prince de Ligne and Philippine de Noailles of the Dukes de Mouchy, and has issue,

[*57 route Gouvernementale, 1150 Brussels, Belgium*].

    1. Archduke *Rudolf* Maria Carl Eugen Anna Antonius Markus d'Aviano, *b* at Château de Beloeil 17 Nov 1950, INSEAD, Dir several Co's, Bailiff Gd Cross of Justice Constantinian Order of St George; *m* at Brussels 3 July 1976, Baroness *Hélène* (*b* Schaerbeek 24 March 1954), Dame Star Cross Order, Dame Gd Cross of Justice Constantinian Order of St George, dau of Guy, Baron de Villenfagne de Vogelsanck et du Saint-Empire and Baroness Renée (Marina) de Crombrugghe de Looringhe, and has issue,

[*Château de Torny, 1748 Torny-le-Grand, Switzerland*].

    1. Archduke *Carl Christian* Marie Guy Eugene Marcus d'Aviano, *b* at Fontainebleau 9 May 1977.

2. Archduchess *Priscilla* Marie Zita Sybille, *b* at Montreal, Quebec, Canada 5 June 1979.

3. Archduke *Johannes* Marie Alexander Bertrand Guy Pius Marcus d'Aviano, *b* at Brussels 1 June 1981.

4. Archduchess *Thomas* Marie Carl Frédéric François Marcus d'Aviano, *b* at Brussels 13 Oct 1983.

5. Archduchess *Marie-des-Neiges* Constanza Laurence Françoise Thérese Anne, *b* at Geneva 17 July 1986.

6. Archduke *Franz-Ludwig* Marie Martin Pie Michael Gabriel Rafael Marcus d'Aviano, *b* at Geneva 5 Oct 1988.

7. Archduke *Michael* Joseph Maria Carl-Christian Raphael Gabriel Marcus d'Aviano, *b* at Fribourg, Switzerland 15 Sept 1990.

8. Archduke *Josef* Maria Christian Andreas Michael Rafaël Gabriel Marcus d'Aviano, *b* at Fribourg, Switzerland 14 Nov 1991.

2. Archduchess *Alexandra* Maria Anna Philippa Othonia, *b* at Château de Beloeil 10 July 1952; *m* at Brussels 15 Sept 1984, Hector Riesle (*b* at Antofagasta, Chile 16 Feb 1943), Dr of Law, Ambassador, Kt Gd Cross of Honour and Devotion Sovereign Military Order of Malta, Kt Gd Cross of Justice Constantinian Order of St George, Kt Gd Cross Order of Pius IX.

[*San Damian 490, Las Condes, Santiago 6772312, Chile*].

3. Archduke *Carl Christian* Maria Anna Rudolph Anton Marcus d'Aviano, *b* at Château de Beloeil 26 Aug 1954, Bank Dir, Kt Order of the Golden Fleece; *m* at Luxemburg 6 Feb 1982, Princess Marie Astrid (*b* at Château Betzdorf 17 Feb 1954), dau of Jean, Grand Duke of Luxembourg and Princess Josephine Charlotte of Belgium, and has issue,

[*2 Chemin des Cabrits, 1254 Jussy, Switzerland*].

1. Archduchess *Marie Christine* Anne Astrid Zita Charlotte, *b* at Brussels 31 July 1983.

2. Archduke *Imre* Emmanuel Simeon Jean Carl Marcus d'Aviano, *b* at Geneva 8 Dec 1985.

3. Archduke *Christoph* Henri Alexander Maria Marcus d'Aviano, *b* at Geneva 2 Feb 1988.

4. Archduke *Alexander* Hector Marie Karl Leopold Marcus d'Aviano, *b* at Meyrin, Kt Genf 26 Sept 1990.

5. Archduchess *Gabriella* Maria Pilar Yolande

Joséphine-Charlotte, *b* at Geneva 26 March 1994.

4. Archduchess Maria *Constanza* Anna Rosario Roberta, *b* at Château de Beloeil 19 Oct 1957, Dame Star Cross Order; *m* at Château de Beloeil 18 June (civ) and at Brussels 10 Sept (relig) 1994, Prince Franz-Josef von Auersperg-Trautson (*b* at Salzburg 11 Dec 1954), Kt Sovereign Military Order of Malta.

[*Weitwörth 21, 5110 Oberndorf, nr Salzburg, Austria*].

5. Archduke *Rudolph* Syringus Peter Karl Franz Joseph Robert Otto Antonius Maria Pius Benedikt Ignatius Laurentius Justiniani Markus d'Aviano, *b* at Villa Prangins, nr Nyon, Switzerland 5 Sept 1919, Lic sc pol et oec, Dir of companies, Kt Order of the Golden Fleece, Kt of Hon and Dev Sovereign Military Order of Malta, Bailiff Gd Cross Constantinian Order of St George etc; *m* 1stly at Tuxedo Park, New York, USA 22 June 1953, Countess Xenia (*b* Paris 11 June 1929; ✠*k* in a motor accident between Soignies and Mons, Belgium 20 Sept 1968), dau of Count Sergej Czernichew-Besobrazow and Countess Elisabeth Cheremetjeff, and has issue, among whom,

[*6 Corniche verte, 1150 Brussels, Belgium*].

1. Archduchess *Maria-Anna* Charlotte Zita Elisabeth Regina Therese, *b* at Brussels-Uccle 19 May 1954, Magister rer oec; *m* at Brussels 24 Nov (civ) and at Brussels-Uccle 25 Nov (relig) 1981, Piotr Dmitrievitch, Prince Galitzine (*b* at Mendoza, Argentina 25 March 1955), Engineer, Chief Representative of Mannesmann AG in Russia.

[*Ul. Akademika Pilygima, Dom 14 Korp 3, KV 976, 117393 Moscow, Russia*].

2. Archduke *Carl Peter* Otto Serge Joseph Paul Leopold Heinrich, *b* at Katana, Prov of Kivu, Belgian Congo 5 Nov 1955, Lic. law, industrial consultant, *m* at Freren 27 March (civ) and at Ellingen, Bavaria 2 May (relig) 1998, Princess Alexandra (*b* at Munich 12 May 1970), Medical Doctor, dau of Carl 6th Prince (Fürst) von Wrede and Ingeborg Hamberger.

[*80a rue Principale, 5367 Schuttrange, GD Luxembourg*].

1. Archduchess *Antonia* Maria Zita Josepha Kaspara Markus d'Aviano, *b* at Munich 31 Dec 2000

3. Archduke *Simeon* Carl Eugen Joseph Leopold, *b* at Katana, Prov of Kivu, Belgian Congo 29 June 1958, Bailiff Gd Cross Constantinian Order of St George, Lic. rer soc oec; *m* at La Toledana, Ciudad Real 13 July 1996, Princess Maria (*b* at Madrid 5 April 1967), dau of Prince Don Carlos of Bourbón

Two Sicilies, Infante of Spain, Duke of Calabria and Princess Anne Orléans, Princess of France, and has issue,
[*Im Gässle 16, 9490 Vaduz, Liechtenstein*].

    1. Archduke *Johannes* Rudolf Antonio Maria, *b* at Hohenems, Austria 29 Oct 1997.

    2. Archduke *Ludwig* Christian Franziskus Maria *b* at Grabs, Switzerland, 16 Nov 1998.

    3. Archduchess *Isabelle* Rocio Maravillas Lourdes, *b* at Grabs, Switzerland 14 Sept 2000.

Archduke Rudolph *m* 2ndly at Ellingen, Bavaria 15 Oct 1971, Princess Anna Gabriele (*b* at Pähl, nr Wilzhofen 11 Sept 1940), Dame Star Cross Order, dau of Carl, 5th Prince (Fürst) von Wrede and Countess Sophie Schaffgotsch genannt Semperfrei von and zu Kynast and Greiffenstein, Baroness zu Trachenberg, and by her has further issue,
[*6 Corniche verte, 1150 Brussels, Belgium*].

    5. Archduchess *Catharina* Maria Johanna Zita Sophie Caspara, *b* at Weissenburg, Bavaria 14 Sept 1972, Lic.sc.Pol and International Relations, *m* at Brussels 4 Dec 1998 (civ) and at Gent (relig) 9 Jan 1999, Count Massimiliano Secco d'Aragona (*b* at Brussels 19 July 1967) financier.
    [*24 via San Gaetanino, 25125, Brescia, Itlay*].

6. Archduchess *Charlotte* Hedwig Franziska Josepha Maria Antonia Roberta Ottonia Pia Anna Ignatia Markus d'Aviano, *b* Villa Prangins 1 March 1921; ✝ at Munich 23 July 1989, Dame Star Cross Order, Dame Gd Cross Sovereign Military Order of Malta; *m* at Pöcking am Starnberger See 21 July (civ) and 25 July (relig) 1956, as his 2nd wife, Duke Georg Alexander of Mecklenburg-Strelitz (*b* at Oranienbaum, nr St Petersburg 4 Oct 1899; ✝ at Sigmaringen 6 July 1963).

7. Archduchess *Elisabeth* Charlotte Alphonsa Christina Theresia Antonia Josepha Roberta Ottonia Franziska Isabella Pia Markus d'Aviano et omnes sancti, *b* posthumously at El Pardo, nr Madrid 31 May 1922; ✝ at Waldstein 6 Jan 1993, Dr rer pol, Dame Star Cross Order; *m* at Lignères, France 12 Sept 1949, Prince Heinrich von and zu Liechtenstein (*b* at Graz 5 Aug 1916; ✝ at Graz 17 April 1991), Dr of Phil.

Brother of Father

Issue of Archduke Otto (*b* 21 April 1865; ✝ 1 Nov 1906) and Princess Maria Josepha of Saxony (*b* 31 May 1867; *m* 2 Oct 1886; ✝ 28 May

1944), having had issue, among whom,

1. Archduke *Maximilian* Eugen Ludwig Friedrich Philipp Ignatius Joseph Maria, *b* at Vienna 13 April 1895; ✝ at Nice 19 Jan 1952, Kt Qrder of the Golden Fleece; *m* at Laxenburg 29 Nov 1917, Princess Franziska (*b* at Teplitz 21 June 1897; ✝ at Salzburg 12 July 1989), Dame Star Cross Order, dau of Konrad, Prince zu Hohenlohe-Waldenburg-Schillingsfürst von Ratibor and Corvey, and Countess Franziska von Schönborn-Buchheim, and had issue,

    1. Archduke *Ferdinand* Karl Max Franz Otto Konrad Maria Joseph Ignatius Nikolaus, *b* at Vienna 6 Dec 1918, Kt Order of the Golden Fleece; *m* at Munich 6 April (civ) and at Seefeld am Pilsensee, Bavaria 10 April (relig) 1956, Countess Helen (*b* at Winhöring 20 May 1937), Dame Star Cross Order, dau of Carl Theodor, Count zu Toerring-Jettenbach and Princess Elisabeth of Greece and Denmark, and has issue, [*20 Friston Street, London SW6 3AT; 5081 Anif Eisgraben 245 bei Salzburg, Austria*].

        1. Archduchess *Elisabeth* Cecilia Helen Antonia, *b* at Essen 15 March 1957; ✝ at Myalla, Cooma, Australia 18 May 1983; *m* at Maria Plain, nr Salzburg 9 Oct 1982, James Litchfield (*b* at Sydney 15 Nov 1956). [*Myalla, Cooma, Australia*].

        2. Archduchess *Sophie* Franziska Maria Germaine, *b* at Boulogne-sur-Seine 19 Jan 1959; *m* at Salzburg 31 Jan (civ) and 11 Feb (relig) 1990, Mariano Hugo, Prince (Fürst) zu Windisch-Graetz (*b* at Trieste 27 July 1055) Industrialist, Kt Order of the Golden Fleece. [*Palazzo Taverna, Via Monte Giordano 36, 00186 Rome, Italy; Il Palazzo, 81017, Sant Angolo d Alife, Prov Caserta, Italy*].

        3. Archduke *Maximilian* Heinrich Ferdinand, *b* at Boulogne-sur-Seine 8 Feb 1961; *m* at May 1999, Princess *Margita Octavia* Alexandra Silvia Felizitas Irmgard Madeleine (*b* at Frankfurt-am-Main 7 Nov 1966), dau of Prince *Christian Albrecht* Franz Nikolaus Heinrich Wolfgang, zu Isenburg und Büdingen in Wächtersbach and Baroness Monika von Plessen. [*Ronda de Poniente 8, Parque Empresial, 28760 Tres Cantos, Madrid, Spain*].

    2. Archduke *Heinrich* Karl Maria, *b* at Munich 7 Jan 1925,

Bank Dir, Kt Sovereign Military Order of Malta, Kt Order of the Golden Fleece; *m* at Lippborg, nr Beckum, Münster, Westphalia 23 Sept (civ) and at Münster 17 Oct (relig) 1961, Countess Ludmilla (*b* at Assen, Beckum, Westphalia 20 June 1939), Dame Star Cross Order, dau of Christoph Bernhard, Count von Galen, Proprietor of Assen and Countess Sophie Kinsky von Wchinitz and Tettau, and has issue,
[*Dolderstraße 79, 8032 Zurich, Switzerland*].

    1. Archduke *Philipp* Joachim Franz Max Clemens Gallus, *b* at Zurich 16 Oct 1962, Investment Manager, Kt Sovereign Military Order of Malta.
[*22a Prince of Wales Drive, London, SW11 4SF*].

    2. Archduchess *Marie-Christine* Franziska Sophie, *b* at Zurich 14 March 1964; *m* at Salzburg 10 Feb 1996, Clemens Guggenberg von Riedhofen , Herr and Landmann in Tirol (*b* at Innsbruck 19 May 1962).
[*5 Rosenau Crescent, London, SW11 4RY*].

    3. Archduke *Ferdinand* Karl Augustinus Maria, *b* at Zurich 28 May 1965; *m* at Berlin-Zehlendorf 20 May (civ) and at Friedenskirche, Potsdam 22 May (relig) 1999, Countess *Katharina* Isabelle(*b* at Hamburg 21 Apr 1968), dau of Count Andreas von Hardenberg and Baroness Isa von Hahn.
[*C/o John Kennedy, Almanach de Gotha, London, W1S 3LL*].

      1. Archduke *Jakob* Maximilian, *b* at Berlin 22 January 2002.

    4. Archduke *Konrad* Erwein Felix Regula Maria, *b* at Zurich 11 Sept 1971.
[*1c Brompton Cottages, Hollywood Rd, London SW10*].

Brother of Grandfather

Issue of Archduke Karl Ludwig (*b* 30 July 1833; ✠ 19 May 1896 and his second wife, Princess Doña Maria Annunciata of Bourbon-Two Sicilies (*b* 24 March 1843; *m* 16/21 Oct 1862; ✠ 4 May 1871), having had issue, among whom,

Son

Archduke Franz Ferdinand Karl Ludwig Joseph Maria, (*b* at Graz 18 Dec 1863; assassinated at Sarajevo 28 June 1914), Archduke of Austria-Este 20 Nov 1875, became Heir Presumptive of the Austrian

Empire on the death of his cousin, Crown Prince Rudolf, 30 Jan 1889; *m* (morganatically) at Reichstadt, Bohemia 1 July 1900, Countess Sophie (*b* at Stuttgart 1 March 1868; assassinated at Sarajevo 28 June 1914), *cr* Princess von Hohenberg with the qualification of Princely Grace 1 July (Diploma 8 Aug) 1900, granted the qualification of Serene Highness 8 June 1908; *cr* Duchess von Hohenberg with the qualification of Highness (ad personam) 4 Oct 1909, dau of Bohuslaw, Count Chotek von Chotkowa and Wognin and Countess Wilhelmine Kinsky von Wchinitz and Tettau, and had issue (see HOHENBERG - Part III).

LINE II: Grand Dukes of Tuscany

Founded by Archduke Ferdinand (*b* 6 May 1769; ✝ 18 June 1824; *succ* his father as Grand Duke of Tuscany on his father's accession to the Throne of Austria in 1790), reigned as Ferdinando III, Grand Duke of Tuscany from 7 March 1791. In accordance with the terms of the Treaty of Vienna (1735), Tuscany was given to François, Duke of Lorraine (later Holy Roman Emperor as Franz I) on the death of the last Medici Grand Duke Gian Gastone 9 July 1737. He was *succ* in Tuscany by his 2nd surv son Leopold, who reigned as Grand Duke Leopoldo I until 1790, when he *succ* his brother, Joseph II as Emperor of Austria. The Grand Duchy of Tuscany was reunited with the Kingdom of Sardinia by Royal Decree of Victor Emmanuel II dated 22 March 1860. (Protested by Ferdinando IV, Dresden 26 March 1860).

Members of the Grand Ducal family bear the titles of Archduke or Archduchess of Austria, Prince or Princess of Hungary and Bohemia, Prince or Princess of Tuscany, with the qualification of Imperial and Royal Highness. Since 30 Nov 1990 the descendants of marriages not recognised as being of equal status bear the title of Count or Countess von Habsburg unless another title has been conferred upon them.

SIGISMUND Otto Maria Josef Gottfried Heinrich Erik Leopold Ferdinand, **ARCHDUKE OF AUSTRIA, GRAND DUKE OF TUSCANY**, etc, Head of the Grand Ducal House of Tuscany, *b* at Lausanne, Switzerland 21 April 1966, BSc Computer Science, Software Engineer, Grand Master Sacred Mil Order of St Stephen Pope and Martyr, Grand Master Order of Merit of St Joseph of Tuscany, Kt of Hon and Dev Sovereign Military Order of Malta, son of Leopold Franz, former Head of the Grand Ducal House of Tuscany (*b* 25 Oct 1942; renounced his rights as Head of the Grand Ducal House of Tuscany - see below) and Laetitia de Belzunce (*b* 2 Sept 1941); *m* at London 11 Sept 1999, *Elyssa* Juliet (*b* at Glasgow 11 Sept 1973) dau of Sir Archibald Edmonstone (7th) Baronet Edmonstone and Juliet Deakin.

[*Hartwood House, West Calder, West Lothian, EH55 8LE, Scotland*].

Son

1. Archduke *Leopold* Amadeo Peter Ferdinand Archibald Henri Joseph, Hereditary Grand Duke, *b* at Glasgow 9 May 2001.

Father

Leopold Franz Peter Ferdinand Maria Joseph Gottfried Georg Karl Otto Rudolf Michael, **Archduke of Austria, etc, former Head of the Grand Ducal House of Tuscany,** *b* at Schloß Leutstetten 25 Oct 1942, Engineer, Kt Grand Cross Sacred Mil Order of St Stephen Pope and Martyr, Kt Grand Cross Order of Merit of St Joseph of Tuscany, Kt Grand Cross Order of St Maurice and St Lazarus, (*renounced his rights as Head of the Grand Ducal House of Tuscany 18 June 1993*); *m* 1stly at St Gilgen 19 June (civ) and at Menetou-Salon, Cher 28 July (relig) 1965 (*m* diss by div at Salzburg 27 May 1981), Laetitia (*b* at Broumana, Lebanon 2 Sept 1941), dau of Henri, Marquess de Belzunce and Marie-Thérèse de la Poëze d'Harambure, adopted dau of Erik Engelbert, Duke d'Arenberg; *m* 2ndly 18 June 1993 (*m* diss by div at St Gilgen 13 July 1998), Marta (*b* at San Salvador de Jujuy, Argentina 13 March 1947), dau of Antonio Fernando Perez-Fernandez and Marta Dolores Valverde de Soria.
[*Gschwand 70, 5342 Abersee, Austria*].

Brother

Archduke *Guntram* Maria Josef, *b* at Montevideo 21 July 1967, BA Econ; *m* at Cuernavaca, Mexico 13 April (civ) and 19 May (relig) 1995, Debora (*b* at San Salvador, El Salvador 21 Jan 1970), dau of Orlando de Sola and Marion Liebes.
[*Administration Privé, Case Postale 558, ave. Général Guisan 44, CH-1009 Pully (VD), Switzerland*].

    1. Countess *Anna* Faustina, *b* Montivideo 28 December 2001.

Grandmother

Archuchess *Dorothea* Therese Marie Franziska, Princess of Tuscany, etc, *b* at Leutstetten 25 May 1920, Dame Grand Cross Sacred Mil Order of St Stephen Pope and Martyr, Dame of Hon Bavarian Orders of St Theresia and St Elisabeth, dau of Prince Franz of Bavaria and Princess Isabella of Croÿ; *m* at Sarvar, Hungary 2 Aug (civ) and 3 Aug (relig) 1938, Archduke Gottfried of Austria,

Prince of Tuscany, former Head of the Grand Ducal House of Tuscany (b at Linz 14 March 1902; W at Bad Ischl 21 Jan 1984). [*Fürsten Allee 8, 5020 Salzburg, Austria*].

Sisters of Father

Issue of Archduke Gottfried, Head of the Grand Ducal House of Tuscany (b 14 March 1902; ✝ 21 Jan 1984) and Princess Dorothea of Bavaria (b 25 May 1920; m 2/3 Aug 1938).

1. Archduchess *Elisabeth* Maria Dorothea Josefa Thereseia Ludmilla, b at Schloß Achberg 22 Oct 1939; m at Salzburg 26 April 1965, Friedrich, Edler von Braun (b at Regensburg 26 Dec 1934), Reg Dir. [*Pollingerstraße 10, 5340 St Gilgen Austria*].

2. Archduchess *Alice* Marie Christine Margarete Antoinetta Josefa Rosa Helene Adelgunde Eleonora, b at Schloß Leutstetten 29 April 1941; m at Maria Plain, nr Salzburg 7 May 1970, Don Vittorio, Baron Manno (b at Cuneo, Italy 31 July 1938), Dr Phys. [*St Lorenz 470, 5310 Mondsee, Austria*].

3. Archduchess *Marie Antoinette* Christine Josefa Rosa Margarethe Pia Angela Theresia Gabriele Isabella Ludmilla Zita Ruperta, b at St Gilgen 16 Sept 1950; m at St Gilgen 13 April (civ) and at Salzburg 29 May (relig) 1974, Hans Walter Nattermann (b at Munich 7 March 1938), Baron von Proff zu Irnich by adoption 28 Nov 1952, Reg Dir. [*Cuvilliéstraße 21, 81679 Munich, Germany*].

Brothers of Grandfather

Issue of Archduke Peter Ferdinand (b 12 May 1874; *succ* his brother Archduke Joseph Ferdinand, 25 Aug 1942; ✝ 8 Nov 1948) and Princess Doña Maria Cristina of Bourbon-Two Sicilies (b 10 April 1077, m 8 Nov 1900, ✝ 4 Oct 1947) having had issue, among whom,

Son

Archduke *Georg* Maria Rainer Joseph Peter Hubert Gottfried Eustach Rupert Ignaz, b at Parsch, nr Salzburg 22 Aug 1905; ✝ at Altshausen, Württemberg 21 March 1952, Kt Order of the Golden Fleece; m at St Gilgen 29 April 1936, Countess Marie Valerie (b at Wallsee 28 June 1913), Dame Star Cross Order, dau of Georg, Count von Waldburg-Zeil-Hohenems and Archduchess Elisabeth of Austria, and had issue, among whom,
[*Schwarzenberg Promenade 28, 5026 Salzburg, Austria*].

   1. Archduke *Radbot* Ferdinand Maria Johann Georg Gottfried Otto Josef Anton Raphael Willibald Linus, b at Muri, Aargau,

Switzerland 23 Sept 1938, Dir; Kt Grand Cross Sacred Mil
Order of St Stephen Pope and Martyr, *m* at Croutoy, Dept
Oise, France 4 Aug 1972, Caroline (*b* at Paris 3 May 1952),
dau of Claude Proust and Marie Thérese Defaucamberge,
and has issue,
[*Dr-Petter-Straße 20a, 5020 Salzburg, Austria; Via Barbara
Tortolini 29, 00197 Rome, Italy*].

    1. Count *Leopold* Karl Radbot Gregor, *b* at Vienna 17
June 1973.
    [*Dianagaße 5/4, 1030, Vienna, Austria*].
    2. Count *Maximilian* Karl Maria Radbot, *b* at Vienna
12 Aug 1976.
    [*Lerchenfelderstraße 66/88, 1080, Vienna, Austria*].
    3. Countess *Eleonore* Katharina Caroline Marie, *b* at
Vienna 6 Oct 1979.
    [*15 Rue de Vézelay, 75008 Paris, France*]

2. Archduchess *Walburga* Rosa Marie Christine Elisabeth
Helene Caroline Ita Stephanie Michaela Appollinaria, *b* at
Muri 23 July 1942, Dame Star Cross Order; *m* at Ettal, Upper
Bavaria 17 Feb 1969, Dom Carlos Tasso de Saxe-Coburgo e
Bragança of the Barons Taxis von Bordogna and Valnigra (*b*
at Gmunden, Upper Austria 16 July 1931), Farmer.
[*Staudach 49, 9546 Bad Kleinkirchheim, Austria*].

3. Archduchess *Katharina* Marie Christine Josefa Clementine
Elisabeth Walburga Theresia Gertrud Georgine Agnes
Gabriele, *b* at Muri 24 April 1948, Dipl Graphics; *m* at Cortona
22 May 1983, Roland Huber (*b* at Eggelsberg 26 June 1950),
Restaurateur.
[*Bergheimerstraße 10, 5020 Salzburg, Austria*].

4. Archduchess *Agnes* Maria Gertrud Elisabeth Josepha Pia
Theresia Walburga Raphaela, *b* at Muri 20 April 1950,
Kindergarten Teacher; *m* at Salzburg 23 Sept (civ) and 23
Oct (relig) 1976, Peter, Baron von Fürstenberg, Proprietor of
Gimborn and Eibach (*b* at Heppingen 31 Aug 1945), Farmer.
[*Schloß Gimborn, 51709 Marienheide, Germany*].

5. Archduke *Georg* Maria Otto Josef Leopold Philipp Michael
Vitus Augustinus, *b* posthumously at Syrgenstein, Allgäu 28
Aug 1952, Adverting Executive.
[*Schwarzenberg Promenade 28, 5026 Salzburg, Austria*].

Brothers of Great-Grandfather

Issue of Ferdinand IV, last Grand Duke of Tuscany (*b* 10 June 1835; *succ* his father on his abdication 1859; ✧ at Salzburg 17 Jan 1908) who lost his throne when Tuscany was united to the Kingdom of Sardinia by decree of King Vittorio Emanuele II 22 March 1860, and his second wife, Princess Alicia of Bourbón-Parma (*b* 27 Dec 1849; *m* 11 Jan 1868; ✧ 16 Jan 1935), having had issue, among whom,

Sons

1. **Joseph Ferdinand** Salvator Maria Franz Leopold Anton Albert Johann Baptist Karl Ludwig Rupert Maria Auxiliatrix, **Archduke of Austria, Grand Duke of Tuscany, Head of the Grand Ducal House of Tuscany**, etc, *b* at Salzburg 24 May 1872; ✧ at Vienna 25 Aug 1942, *succ* his father as Head of the Grand Ducal House of Tuscany 1908, Kt Order of the Golden Fleece; *m* 1stly at Maria Plain, nr Salzburg 2 May 1921 (*m* diss by div 16 Oct 1928), Rosa (*b* at Linz 27 Feb 1878; ✧ at Salzburg 9 Dec 1929; she *m* 1stly at Linz 16 Jan 1897, Adolf Jockel who ✧ 12 April 1921; that *m* diss by div at Josephstadt, Bohemia 11 March 1902), dau of Anton Kaltenbrunner and Karolina Reith. He *m* 2ndly at Vienna 27 Jan 1929, Gertrud, (*who used the title of Princess of Florence*) (*b* at Brünn 13 April 1902; ✧ at Salzburg 15 Feb 1997), dau of Aloys Tomanek, Edler von Beyerfels and Klothilde Dörfl, and, by her, had issue,

    1. Countess *Claudia* Maria Theresia, *b* at Vienna 6 April 1930, (*uses the title Princess of Florence*).
    [*Reichenhaller Straße 3/1/2, 5020 Salzburg, Austria*].

    2. Count *Maximilian* Franz Joseph Karl Otto Heinrich, *b* at Vienna 17 March 1932, MA, Employee Austrian Bundeskammer; *m* at London 3 Sept 1961, Doris (*b* at Blundell Sands, Lancashire 24 Dec 1929), dau of Harold Edward Williams and Elizabeth Kenny, and has issue,
    [*Laudongasse31, 1080 Vienna, Austria*].

        1. Countess *Maria Camilla*, *b* at Wimbledon 29 May 1962, Advertising Assistant.
        [*Reichenhallerstraße 3B, 5020 Salzburg, Austria*].

2. Archduke *Heinrich* Ferdinand Salvator Maria Joseph Leopold Karl Ludwig Pius Albert Rupert Katharina von Rici, *b* at Salzburg 13 Feb 1878; ✧ at Salzburg 21 May 1969, Major-Gen Austrian Army, Kt Order of the Golden Fleece; *m* at Munich-Nymphenburg 29 Nov 1919, Maria Karoline (*b* at Staudach, nr Stams, Tyrolia 6 Dec 1883;

✠ at Salzburg 25 March 1981), dau of Johann-Georg Ludescher and Barbara Prantl, and had issue, among whom,

1. Count *Heinrich*, *b* at Munich 27 Aug 1908; ✠ at Mürzzuschlag 13 June 1968, Dr Eng, Forester; *m* at St Johann im Pongau 13 May 1939, Helvig (Helle) (*b* at Copenhagen 10 Feb 1910; ✠ at St Andrä im Lavanttal, Kärnten 26 March 1990), Dipl Engineer, dau of Gudmund Schütte and Elsa Pichler, and had issue,

1. Count *Ulrich* Ferdinand Gudmund, *b* at Wolfsberg, Kärnten 3 Oct 1941, Dr nat techn Dipl Eng; *m* at Pustritz im Lavanttal 29 Oct 1964, Friederike (*b* at Vienna 31 March 1942), dau of Carl von Klinkowström and Elisabeth Unterhuber, and has issue, amongst whom,

[*Klagenfurterstraße 1, 9400 Wolfsberg, Kärnten, Austria*].

1. Count *Eugen*, *b* at Vienna 31 Dec 1964, Dipl Eng Pulp and Paper; *m* at St Paul Lavanttal 27 May 1995, Gabriele (*b* at Wolfsberg 22 March 1969), dau of Andreas Greschonig and Eleonore Wetschnig, and has issue,

[*Proleberstraße 12, 8712 Niklasdorf, Austria*].

1. Countess *Julia* Maria, *b* at Leoben 6 Sept 1999.

2. Count *Clemens* (*b* Vienna 28 Aug 1967); *m* Lavanttal 12 Oct 1996 *Gislinde* (*b* 8 Sep 1966), dau of .. Angerer and ..

2. Count *Clemens*, *b* at Vienna 28 Aug 1967, Dipl Eng Landscape Design; *m* at St Paul Lavanttal 12 Oct 1996, Gislinde (*b* at Wolfsberg 8 Sept 1996), dau of Hermann Angerer and Gislinde Skoff, and has issue,

[*Hauptstraße 72, 8301 Lassnitzhöhe Austria*].

1. Countess *Anna-Lea* Timna, *b* at Wolfsberg 7 July 1996.

2. Count *Benedikt* Ferdinand Lenrad, *b* at Graz 12 Nov 2000.

3. Count *Philipp*, *b* at Vienna 14 Dec 1968, Student Architecture.

[*Klagenfurterstraße 1, 9400 Wolfsberg, Kärnten, Austria*].

2. Countess *Helvig* Helle, *b* at Wolfsberg 29 Dec 1942,
Dipl Business, Mag rer soc oec, Dame of Hon and Dev
Sovereign Military Order of Malta; *m* at Salzburg 25
Aug (civ) and at St Paul im Lavanttal, 28 Oct (relig)
1972, Andreas, Baron Jordis von Lohausen (*b* at Graz
21 Sept 1940), Kt of Hon and Dev Sovereign Military
Order of Malta, Businessman.

[*Hof Blumenstein, Pausingerstraße 6, 5020 Salzburg,
Austria*].

3. Count *Christoph* Heinrich, *b* at Wolfsberg 22 Oct
1944, Dipl Eng, Forester; *m* at St Martin, nr
Freudenberg 19 May 1973, Ebba (*b* at Schloß
Freudenberg 17 Dec 1949), dau of Reinhold von
Mohrenschildt and Margarethe Kauffmann, and has
issue,

[*9433 St. Andrä 14 im Lavanttal, Kärnten, Austria*].

    1. Count *Dominik* Heinrich Reinhold, *b* at
    Klagenfurt 27 Feb 1974, Dipl Eng Forestry.

    2. Count *Maximilian* Christoph, *b* at Klagenfurt
    9 March 1975

    3. Count *Constantin* Oktavian, *b* at Klagenfurt
    2 Dec 1976.

    4. Count *Ferdinand* Karl, *b* at Klagenfurt 1
    Feb 1980.

    5. Countess *Elmerice* Karoline Sidonie
    Elisabeth, *b* at St Veit an der Glan 6 Sept
    1984.

2. Count *Uthmar*, *b* at Munich 7 Aug 1910; ✝ at Salzburg 5
Feb 1988, Dr Dipl Eng Forestry; *m* at Salzburg 19 Dec 1944,
Helene (*b* at Altenmarkt, nr Salzburg 3 July 1920; ✝ at
Salzburg 27 Oct 1994), dau of Johannes Moser and Helene
Gruber, and had issue,

    1. Countess *Ulrike* Margarethe, *b* at Salzburg 29 Dec
    1945; *m* at Salzburg 22 Nov 1969, (*m* diss by div 20
    Aug 1997) Luitpold, Prince von and zu Liechtenstein
    (*b* at Würzburg 11 April 1940), Dipl Engineer Forestry.
    [*Khunngaße 6-8/4/9, 1030 Vienna, Austria*].

    2. Countess *Elisabeth* Maria, *b* at Salzburg 20 Jan 1948,
    Dipl Eng Argriculture; *m* at Hariensee 10 July 1971,
    Stephan Schenker, Dipl Eng Agriculture (*b* at
    Mariensee 8 Nov 1946), Dipl Eng Forestry.

[2870, Aspang, Mariensee 62, Austria].
3. Count *Albrecht* Clemens, *b* at Salzburg 24 Oct 1951, Designer; *m* at Mondsee 18 July 1997, *Birgit* Elisabeth Franziska (*b* at Berndorf, nr Salzburg 14 May 1960), dau of Dr *Roland* Wilhelm Walter Guttenberg and *Franziska* Maria Gmachl.
[Schloß Flederbach, Aignerstraße 13, 5020 Salzburg, Austria].
       1. Count *Clemens* Roland, *b* at Salzburg 17 July 1992.

Brothers of Great-Great-Grandfather

Issue of Leopoldo II, Grand Duke of Tuscany (*b* 3 Oct 1797; *succ* his father 18 June 1824; abdicated 21 July 1859, ✝ 29 Jan 1870) and his second wife, Princess Doña Marie Antonia of Bourbon-Two Sicilies (*b* 19 Dec 1814; *m* 7 June 1833; ✝ 7 Nov 1898), having had issue, among whom,

Son

Archduke *Karl Salvator* Maria Joseph Johann Baptist Philipp Jakob Januarius Ludwig Gonzage Rainer, *b* at Florence 30 April 1839; ✝ at Vienna 18 Jan 1892, Field Marshal Austrian Army, Kt Order of the Golden Fleece; *m* at Rome 19 Sept 1861, Princess Doña Maria Immakulata of Bourbon-Two Sicilies (*b* at Naples 14 April 1844; ✝ at Vienna 18 Feb 1899), Dame Star Cross Order, dau of Ferdinand II, King of Two Sicilies and Archduchess Theresia of Austria, and had issue, among whom,

Sons

1. Archduke *Leopold Salvator* Maria Joseph Ferdinand Franz von Assisi Karl Anton von Padua Johann Baptist Januarius Aloys Gonzaga Rainer Wenzel Gallus, *b* at Alt-Bunzlau, Bohemia 15 Oct 1863; ✝ at Vienna 4 Sept 1931, Dr techn hc, Protector of the Bohemian Academy of the Sciences in Prague, Kt Order of the Golden Fleece; *m* at Frohsdorf 24 Oct 1889, Princess Blanka (*b* at Graz 7 Sept 1868; ✝ at Viareggio 25 Oct 1949), Dame Star Cross Order, dau of Karl, Prince of Bourbón, Duke of Madrid and Princess Margareta of Bourbón-Parma, and had issue, among whom,
       1. Archduke *Leopold* Maria Alphons Blanka Karl Anton Beatrix Raphael Michael Joseph Peter Ignatz, *b* at Agram 30 Jan 1897; ✝ at Willimantic, Connecticut, USA 14 March 1958 (became a naturalised citizen of the USA 1953 as Leopold

Lorraine); *m* 1stly at Vienna 12 April 1919 (*m* diss by div ....
1931), Baroness Dagmar (*b* at Agram 15 July 1898; ✠ at
Lausanne 15 Nov 1967), created Baroness von Wolfenau by
the Head of the family 12 Feb 1922 but did not use this title,
dau of Wladimir, Baron Nicolic-Podrinski and Baroness Ella
Scotti. He *m* 2ndly, Alice (*b* New York State 20 Jan 1894; ✠
at New York 25 Aug 1960), dau of Alexander Lynden Coburn
and Ann Desmore Gibson, and had issue by his first wife,

> 1. Countess *Gabrielle*, *b* at Vienna 15 Feb 1921; *m* at
> Geneva 25 Sept (civ) and at Aubonne, Vaud 28 Sept
> (relig) 1948 (*m* diss by div 1958), Jean von der Mühll
> (*b* at Riehen, nr Basel 17 Nov 1918), Dr (Law).
> [*Weidgaße 7 8330 Pfäffikon, Switzerland*].

2. Archduke *Anton* Maria Franz Leopold Blanka Karl Joseph
Ignaz Raphael Michael Margareta Nicetas, *b* at Vienna 20
March 1901; ✠ at Salzburg 22 Oct 1987, Kt Order of the
Golden Fleece; *m* at Sinaia, Romania 26 July 1931 (*m* diss by
div 1954), Princess Ileana (*b* at Bucharest 23 Dec 1908/5 Jan
1909; ✠ at Ellwood City, Pennsylvania 21 Jan 1991; *m* 2ndly
at Newton, Mass, USA 19 June 1954, Stefan Nicolas Issarescu;
that *m* diss by div at 1965), Mother Superior as Mother
Alexandra, dau of Ferdinand I, King of Romania and Princess
Marie of Saxe-Coburg and Gotha, Princess of Great Britain
and Ireland, and had issue,

> 1. Archduke *Stefan*, *b* at Mödling 15 Aug 1932, ✠ at
> Brighton, MI, 12 Nov 1998; *m* at Milton, Mass 28 Aug
> 1954, Jerrine (*b* at Boston, Massachusetts 19 June
> 1931), dau of Charles Soper and Agnes McNeil, and
> has issue,
>
> [*684 Pine Eagles Drive, Brighton, MI 48116, U.S.A.*].
>
>> 1. Count *Christopher*, *b* at Boston 26 Jan 1957;
>> *m* 1stly at Mount Tamalpais, California 1 May
>> 1987 (*m* diss by div 11 July 1994), Elizabeth
>> (*b* at Peoria, Illinois 22 Jan 1967), dau of Larry
>> Lee Popejoy and Regina Irene Keller, and has
>> issue,
>>
>>> 1. Countess Saygan Genevieve, *b* at Mill
>>> Valley, California 31 Oct 1987.
>>> 2. Count Stefan Christopher, *b* at
>>> Southfield, Michigan 19 Jan 1990.
>
> Count Christopher *m* 2ndly at Clarkston,

Michigan 15 Oct 1994, Catherine (b at Pontiac,
Michigan 5 Sept 1958), dau of Anthony Ripley
and Anna Marie Brunner, and has further issue,
[*2057 White Lake Road, Highland, MI 48356,
USA*]

    3. Countess Maria Antonia, at
Commerce, Michigan 1 Oct 1997

2. Countess *Ileana, b* at Detroit, Michigan 4
Jan 1958; *m* at Farmington Hills, Michigan 23
June 1979, David Scott Snyder (*b* at Pontiac,
Michigan 18 Nov 1956).
[*1085 Hickory Hill, Rochester Hills, MI 48309,
USA*]

3. Count *Peter, b* at Detroit, Michigan 19 Feb
1959; *m* 1stly at Farmington Hills, Michigan 27
June 1981 (*m* diss by div 1985; annulled 1988),
Shari Suzzanne (*b* at Highland Park, Michigan
1 Sept 1960), dau of William Marshal Reid and
Barbara Lou Miller. He *m* 2ndly at Union Lake,
Michigan 17 June 1989, Lauren Ann (*b* at
Detroit, Michigan 9 May 1956), dau of Martin
Klaus and Vera Krug, and has issue by
adoption,
[*6370 Meadowfield, West Bloomfield, MI 48324,
USA*]

    1. *Oksana* Nicole, *b* at Saratov, Russia 8
May 1991 (formerly Oksana Andreevna
Zheleznova - until 8 Dec 1997).

    2. *Alexander* Stefan, *b* at Volsk, Russia
30 Jan 1996 (formerly Alexander
Romanovitch Yemelyanov - until 10
March 1998).

    3. *Tatiana* Julia, *b* at Saratov, Russia 28
Feb 1997 (formerly Julia Nikolaeyna
Makarova - until 8 Dec 1997)

4. Countess *Constantza, b* at Detroit 2 Oct
1960; *m* at Franklin, Michigan 16 Jan 1987 (*m*
diss by div 31 Oct 1995), Mark Lee Matheson (*b*
at Grosse Point, Michigan 15 Feb 1958). She *m*
2dly at Marietta, Georgia, 8 Nov 1997, Michael
Bain (*b* at Rockwood, Tennessee 4 Jan 1962).

[*405 Harbor Way, Woodstock, GA 30189, USA*]

5. Count *Anton, b* at Detroit 7 Nov 1964; *m* at Aurora, Ohio 5 Oct 1991, Ashley Byrd (*b* at Nashville, Tennessee 23 Aug 1966), dau of Rev Dr William Douglas Carrell and Paula Maxine Anderson.

[*4588 High Street, Mantua, OH 44255, USA*]

2. Archduchess *Alexandra, b* at Sonnberg, Lower Austria 21 May 1935; *m* 1stly at Mondsee 31 Aug (civ) and at Salzburg 3 Sept (relig) 1962 (*m* diss by div at Frankfurt-am-Main 6 April 1972 and annulled at Rome 7 Feb 1973), Eugen Eberhard, Duke of Württemberg (*b* at Carlsruhe, OSilesia 2 Nov 1930), Dipl Econ, Banker. She *m* 2ndly at Mondsee 22 Aug (civ) and at Salzburg 29 Dec (relig) 1973, Victor, Baron von Baillou (*b* at Vienna 27 June 1931), Dr of Law.

[*Mönchsberg 33, 5020 Salzburg, Austria*].

3. Archduke *Dominic, b* at Sonnberg 4 July 1937, Industrial Designer; *m* at Houston, Texas 11 June 1960 (*m* diss by div at New York 6 May 1999), Engel (*b* at Houston 31 March 1937), dau of Ernst von Voss and Mildred McKibben. He *m* 2ndly at North Salem, New York 14 Aug 1999, *Emmanuella* (*b* at Atula, Israel, 14 Jan 1948), dau of Yadidia Mlynarski and Raissa Mossieva Fogel, and has issue,

[*70 Cat Ridge Road, North Salem, NY 10560, USA*].

  1. Count *Sándor, b* at Vienna 13 Feb 1965, *m* at Berndorf 15 May 2000, *Priska* Vilcsek (*b* at Hofheim, Taunus, 18 March 1959), dau of Herbert Vilcsek and Elsa Hohofer, and has issue.

  [*Alkersdorf 1, 2560 Hernstein, Austria*].

    1. Count *Constantin, b* at Vienna 11 July 2000.

  2. Count *Gregor, b* at Vienna 20 Nov 1968.

  [*5670 West Olympic Blvd., Los Angeles, 90036 California, USA*].

4. Archduchess *Maria Magdalena, b* at Sonnberg 2 Oct 1939, Dame of Hon Sovereign Military Order of Malta; *m* at Mondsee 27 Aug (civ) and 29 Aug (relig) 1959, Hans Ulrich, Baron von Holzhausen (*b* at

Windischgarsten, Austria 1 Sept 1929).

[*Johann Wolfstraße 6, 5020 Salzburg, Austria*].

5. Archduchess *Elisabeth, b* at Sonnberg 15 Jan 1942; *m* at Mondsee 3 Aug 1964, Friedrich Sandhofer (*b* at Salzburg 1 Aug 1934), MD, Prof.

[*Gärtnerstraße 2, 5020 Salzburg, Austria*].

3. Archduke *Franz Josef Karl* Leopold Blanka Adelgunde Ignatius Rafael Michael Vero, *b* at Vienna 4 Feb 1905; ✠ at Hernstein, Lower Austria 9 May 1975, Forester, Farmer, Pilot; *m* 1stly at London 22 July 1937 (*m* diss by div), Marta Aloisia (*b* at Vienna 30 Sept 1906; ✠ at Vienna 9 March 1987; *m* 1stly Franz, Edler von Kahler, that *m* annulled), dau of Andreas Rudolf Baumer and Anna di Locatelli. He *m* 2ndly at Zurich 21 Jan 1962, Maria Elena (*b* at Trieste 7 Sept 1925; ✠ at Baden 20 Aug 1994), dau of Egon Seunig and Nella Penelope Gialdini, and by her had issue,

> 1. Countess *Patricia* Federica Maria Valeria Nella, *b* at Vienna 23 April 1963, Student of Philosophy.
>
> [*Franz-Josef-Hof, 2560 Berndorf, Austria*]

4. Archduke *Karl Pius* Maria Adelgonde Blanka Leopold Ignaz Raphael Michael Salvator Kyrill Angelus Barbara, *b* at Vienna 4 Dec 1909; ✠ at Barcelona 24 Dec 1953; *m* at Vienna 10 May 1938 (*m* diss by div at Reno, Nevada, USA .. Dec 1950), Christa (*b* at Vienna 4 Dec 1914; *m* 2ndly at Waterbury, Connecticut, USA 20 Dec 1950, György Sándor, Pianist), dau of Géza Satzger de Bálványos and Maria Alexandrine Friedmann, and had issue,

> 1. Countess *Alejandra* Blanca, *b* at Viareggio 20 Jan 1941; *m* at Barcelona 1 Feb 1960, Don José Maria Riera y de Leyva (*b* at Almeria 13 Nov 1934).
>
> [*Lauria 53, 08032 Barcelona, Spain*].
>
> 2. Countess Maria *Immaculata* Pia, *b* at Barcelona 3 July 1945; *m* at Great Falls, Virginia 18 Dec 1969 (*m* diss by div 6 June 1994), John Howard Dobkin (*b* at Hartford, Connecticut 19 Feb 1942), Museum Director.
>
> [*445 West 18th Street, New York, N.Y. 10011, U.S.A.*].

2. Archduke *Franz Salvator* Maria Joseph Ferdinand Karl Leopold Anton von Padua Johann Baptist Januarius Aloys Gonzaga Rainer Benedikt Bernhard, *b* at Alt-Münster, Upper Austria 21 Aug 1866; ✠ at Vienna 20 April 1939, Hon Dr of Med, Gen Austrian Cavalry

(Ret), Kt Order of the Golden Fleece, Bailiff Gd Cross Hon and Dev Sovereign Military Order of Malta; *m* 1stly at Ischl 31 July 1890, Archduchess Marie Valerie (*b* at Ofen 22 April 1868; ✠ at Schloß Wallsee, Lower Austria 6 Sept 1924), Dame Star Cross Order, dau of Franz Joseph I, Emperor of Austria, etc and Duchess Elisabeth in Bavaria. He *m* 2ndly at Vienna 28 April 1934, Baroness Melanie (*b* at Seisenegg, Lower Austria 20 Sept 1898; ✠ at Amstetten 10 Nov 1984), dau of Philipp, Baron von Risenfels and Baroness Agathe Redl von Rottenhausen and Rasztina, and had issue from his first wife, among whom,

Sons

1. Archduke *Hubert Salvator* Rainer Maria Joseph Ignatius, *b* at Schloß Lichtenegg 30 April 1894; ✠ at Schloß Persenbeug, Lower Austria 24 March 1971, Dr of Law, Kt Order of the Golden Fleece, Kt of Hon Teutonic Order; *m* at Anholt 25 Nov (civ) and 26 Nov (relig) 1926, Princess Rosemary (*b* at Potsdam 13 April 1904; ✠ at 3 May 2001), Dame Star Cross Order, Dame Spanish Order of Maria-Luisa, dau of Emmanuel, Hereditary Prince (Erbprinz) zu Salm-Salm and Archduchess Maria Christina of Austria, and had issue,

    1. Archduke *Friedrich* Salvator Franz Carl Rainer Gabriel Matthäus Vincentius Hubert Maria Joseph Ignatius, *b* at Vienna 27 Nov 1927; ✠ at Amstetten, Lower Austria 26 March 1999; Engineer, Kt Order of the Golden Fleece, Grand Master Papal Order of Sylvester; *m* at Vienna 13 June (civ) and 18 June (relig) 1955, Countess Margarete (*b* at Csicso, Komorn, Hungary 13 May 1926), Dame Star Cross Order, dau of Alexander, Count Kálnoky von Köröspatak, Proprietor of Csicso and Princess Maria Theresia von Schönburg-Hartenstein, and has issue,

    [*Schloß Rorregg, 3683 Ysperthal, Lower Austria, Austria*].

        1. Archduke *Leopold* Salvator Hubert Maria Rainer Judas Thaddäus Alexander Maximilian Stephan Franziskus Pius Alois, *b* at Vienna 16 Oct 1956, Forester.

        [*Schloß Rorregg, 3683 Ysperthal, NÖsterreich, Austria*].

        2. Archduchess Maria *Bernadette* Christa Agnes Josepha Raphaela, *b* at Vienna 10 Feb

1958; *m* at Salzburg 24 June (civ) and at Schloß Persenbeug 9 July (relig) 1983, Rupert Wolff (*b* at Salzburg 16 May 1957), Dr of Law, Lawyer. [*Kreuzberg Promenade 35B, 5020 Salzburg, Austria*].

3. Archduke *Alexander* Salvator Maria Josef Raphael Pius, *b* at Vienna 12 April 1959, Mag rer soc oec; *m* at Nieder-Fladnitz 5 June 1993 (relig), Countess Maria-Gabriele (*b* at Vienna 14 April 1969), dau of Georg, Count von Waldstein-Wartenberg and Countess Maria-Theresia Spiegelfeld.
[*Wickenburg Gasse 3/17, 1080 Vienna, Austria; Schloß, 3680, Persenbeug, Austria*].

    1. Archduchess *Annabella* Maria Kofi Mariella, *b* at Vienna 5 Sept 1997.

    2. Archduchess *Tara*, *b* at Vienna 6 Feb 2000.

    3. Archduke *Constantin* Salvator Maria Raphael Alexander, *b* at Amstetten 4 January 2002.

4. Archduchess *Katharina* Mathilde Aloisia Maria Elisabeth Raphaela, *b* at Rorregg 1 Nov 1960; *m* at Westminster, London 9 April (civ) and at Schloß Persenbeug 18 June (relig) 1988, Niall Andreas Brooks (*b* at Neuchatel, Switzerland 7 Jan 1960), Writer.
[*Briar Cottage, 30 Stoke Gabriel Road, Galmpton TQ5 ONQ, Devon*].

2. Archduchess *Agnes* Christina Franziska Karoline Theresia Raphaela Johanna Magdalena Huberta Josepha Ignatia, *b* at Schloß Persenbeug 14 Dec 1928, Dame Star Cross Order; *m* at Schloß Persenbeug 17 Feb 1949, Karl Alfred, Prince von and zu Liechtenstein (*b* at Frauenthal 16 Aug 1910; ✞ at Hainburg 17 Nov 1985), Dipl Forestry Eng.
[*Porzellangasse 48/D/23, 1090 Vienna, Austria*].

3. Archduchess *Maria Margaretha* Elisabeth Franziska Josepha Valeria Emmanuela Michaela Philippa Rosa Huberta Ignatia, *b* at Vienna 29 Jan 1930, Dame Star Cross Order.

[*SODC, via dei Bresciani 2, 00186 Rome, Italy*].

4. Archduchess Maria Ludowika (*Maria Roland*)
Isabella Alfonsa Anna Thadea Ferdinanda Katharina
Huberta Marie Josepha Ignatia, *b* at Schloß Persenbeug
31 Jan 1931; ✛ at Vienna 17 April 1999.

5. Archduchess Maria Adelheid (*Alix*) Theodora
Antonia Bartholomea Leopolda Amalia Mathilde
Markus d'Aviano Huberta Josepha Ignatia, *b* at Schloß
Persenbeug 28 July 1933.

[*1 rue de Gascogne, 65100 Lourdes, France*].

6. Archduchess Elisabeth (*Sissy*) Mathilde Karoline
Alberta Jacobea Martina Helena Lucia Maria Josepha
Huberta Ignatia, *b* at Schloß Persenbeug 18 March
1935; ✛ in a motor accident at Ybbs 9 Oct 1998, *m* at
Schloß Persenbeug 6 July 1957, Heinrich, Prince von
Auersperg-Breunner (*b* at Ainödt 21 May 1931).

[*Schloß Wald, 3144 Wald, Lower Austria, Austria;
Estancia "Los Leones", RA-6614 Rivas FCNGSM,
Prov. Buenos Aires, Argentina*].

7. Archduke *Andreas Salvator* Gabriel Gottfried Petrus
Paulus Augustinus Severinus Maria Josephus Hubertus
Ignatius, *b* at Schloß Persenbeug 28 April 1936,
Import-Export Businessman, Kt Order of the Golden
Fleece, Kt Order of Calatrava, Grand Master
International Order of St Hubertus; *m* at San Lorenzo
de Escorial, nr Madrid 22 April 1986 (*m* diss by div at
Madrid 16 Nov 2000; annulled 14 March 2002), Maria
de la Piedad (*b* at Madrid 13 Jan 1953), Mag phil et
art, dau of Eugenio Espinosa de los Monteros y Dato
and Maria de la Piedad Rosillo y Martos. He *m* 2ndly
at Vienna 9 Feb 2001, Countess *Valerie* (*b* at
Grieskirchen 12 January 1967), dau of Christoph,
Count Podstatzky-Lichtenstein and of Lydia
Weinheim.

[*Keinergasse 20, III., 1030 Vienna, Austria*].

    1. Count *Tadeus Salvator*, *b* at Vienna 30 March
2001.

8. Archduchess *Josepha* Hedwig Georgia Henrietta
Barbara Agathe Stephana Mathia Koloman Maria
Huberta Ignatia, *b* at Schloß Persenbeug 2 Sept 1937;
m at Persenbeug 3 Sept 1969, Clemens, Count von

Waldstein, Herr von Wartenberg (*b* at Vienna 17 June 1935; ✟ at Horn 20 April 1996), Dr of Law, Dipl Engineer, Forester.

[Schloß Carlslust, 2081 Niederfladnitz 101, NÖsterreich, Austria].

9. Archduchess *Valerie* Isabelle Maria Anna Alfonsa Desideria Brigitte Sophia Thomasia Huberta Josepha Ignatia, *b* at Vienna 23 May 1941; *m* at Salem 23 Sept (civ) and at Persenbeug 30 Sept (relig) 1966, Maximilian (Max), Margrave of Baden (*b* at Salem 3 July 1933).

[88682 Schloß Salem, Baden, Germany].

10. Archduchess *Maria Alberta* Dominika Benedikta Dorothea Felicitas Beatrix Simon Josaphat Huberta Josepha Ignatia, *b* at Schloß Persenbeug 1 June 1944; *m* at Persenbeug 10 May 1969, Alexander, Baron von Kottwitz-Erdödy (*b* at Göttingen 24 Sept 1943), Forestry Engineer.

[Kaltes Eck, 7512 Kohfidisch, Austria].

11. Archduke *Markus* Emanuel Salvator Franziskus de Paula Stanislaus Gregorius Josephat Florian Maria Joseph Hubert Ignatius, *b* at Schloß Persenbeug 2 April 1946, Mag jur, Museum Director; *m* at Vienna 30 Dec 1982 (civ) and at Stift Wilhering, Upper Austria 25 Feb 1983 (relig), Hildegard (*b* at Linz 6 Aug 1955), Teacher, dau of Friedrich Jungmayr and Eleonore Ritzberger, and has issue,

[Kaservilla, 4820 Bad Ischl, Austria].

    1. Count *Valentin* Salvator Markus, *b* at Salzburg 30 July 1983.

    2. Count *Maximilian* Salvator, *b* at Salzburg 28 Dec 1984.

    3. Countess *Magdalena* Maria Sophie Rosemary, *b* at Salzburg 7 March 1987.

12. Archduke *Johann* Maximilian Salvator Benedictus Ambrosius Pius Lukas Wolfgang Maria Joseph Hubert Ignatius, *b* at Schloß Persenbeug 18 Sept 1947, Administrator; *m* at Altmünster 28 May 1977, Annemarie (*b* at Gmunden 15 June 1950), dau of Johann Stummer and Maria Stadler, and has issue,

[Seestraße 49, 4801 Traunkirchen, Austria].

   1. Countess *Caroline* Anna Maria Michaela,
   b at Bad Ischl 12 Feb 1978.
   2. Countess *Stephanie* Rosa Marie Christine,
   b at Bad Ischl 10 July 1979.
   3. Countess *Isabelle* Johanna Maria Margarethe,
   b at Bad Ischl 3 Nov 1981.

13. Archduke *Michael* Salvator Konrad Johannes
Aloisius Franziskus Xaverius Barnabas Antonius Maria
Josephus Hubertus Ignatius, *b* at Schloß Persenbeug
2 May 1949, Ph.D., Dr of Phil, Historian, Hon Mayor
of the State of Cognac in France, Kt Order of the
Golden Fleece; *m* at Persenbeug 12 Nov (civ) and at
Kaiservilla, Bad Ischl 21 Nov (relig) 1992, Eva-Antonia
(*b* at Linz 25 Feb 1961), dau of Norbert von Hofmann
and Doña Maria-Manuela Fernández-Dulcet y Frias
de Remisa, and has issue.
[*Schloß, 3680 Persenbeug, Austria; Frankenberg
Gasse7, 1040 Vienna, Austria*].

   1. Archduchess *Maria-Christina* Carmen
   Manuela Michaela Rosemary Almudena
   Theodora Therese Esther Rocio, *b* at Vienna 9
   Nov 1997.

2. Archduke *Theodor Salvator* Petrus Realinus Maria Josef
Ignatius, *b* at Schloß Wallsee, nr Amstetten 9 Oct 1899; ✠ at
Amstetten 8 April 1978, Dipl Agr, Kt Order of the Golden
Fleece, Bailiff Gd Cross Hon and Dev Sovereign Military
Order of Malta; *m* at Schloß Zeil 28 July 1926, Countess Maria
Theresia (*b* at Neutrachburg 18 Oct 1901; ✠ at Munich 17
July 1967), Dame Star Cross Order, dau of Georg, Prince
(Fürst) von Waldburg zu Zeil and Trauchburg and Altgräfin
Maria Therese zu Salm-Reifferscheidt-Raitz, and had issue,
   1. Archduke *Franz Salvator* Georg Josef Maria
   Thaddäus, *b* at Schloß Wallsee 10 Sept 1927, Engineer,
   Kt Order of the Golden Fleece, Kt of Hon Sovereign
   Military Order of Malta; *m* 1stly at Hochburg, nr Ach,
   Austria 28 April 1962, Princess Anna-Amelie (*b* at
   Frankfurt an der Oder 22 Jan 1936; ✠ at
   Frankenmarkt, Austria 7 Oct 1966), dau of Georg,
   Prince von Schönburg-Waldenburg and Countess
   Pauline zu Castell-Castell. He *m* 2ndly at Wallsee 2
   May 1980, Hedwig (*b* at Innsbruck 12 March 1938 ✠

at Wallsee 28 Oct 2000), dau of Heinrich Lichem-Löwenburg and Margaretha Kroyer, and by her has issue,

[*3313 Schloß Wallsee, Austria*]

        1. Archduchess *Margaretha* Valerie, *b* at Amstetten 10 Feb 1981; *m* at Taferl 4 Aug 2001, Andreas Baumgartner (*b* at Scheibbs 1 Nov 1977)

        2. Archduchess *Marie Valerie, b* at Amstetten 16 March 1982.

2. Archduchess *Theresa* Monika Valerie Elisabeth Ludovika Walburga Anna, *b* at Schloß Wallsee 9 Jan 1931, Dame Star Cross Order, Dame of Hon Bavarian Orders of St Theresia and St Elisabeth; *m* at Schloß Wallsee 17 Oct 1955, Rasso, Prince of Bavaria (*b* at Leutstetten 24 May 1926).

[*Wittelsbacherpark 11, 82340 Feldafing, Germany*].

3. Archduchess Maria *Immaculata* Mathilde Elisabeth Gabriele Walburga Huberta, *b* at Schloß Wallsee 7 Dec 1933; *m* at Koslar 14 May (civ) and at Schloß Wallsee 9 June (relig) 1959, Reinhart, Count von and zu Hoensbroech, Proprietor of Kellenberg, nr Jülich (*b* at Kellenberg 15 Oct 1926), Farmer, Forester.

[*Schloß Kellenberg, 52428 Jüllich-Barmen, Germany*].

4. Archduke *Carl Salvator* Otto Maximilian Johannes Maria, *b* at Schloß Wallsee 23 June 1936, Kt Order of the Golden Fleece; *m* at Uttenheim 25 July 1970, Baroness Edith (*b* at Bruneck, Bozen 10 June 1943), dau of Lothar Wenzl, Baron von Sternbach, Proprietor of Stock in Uttenheim, Bozen and Lucy Schnetzer, and has issue,

[*Mühlweg 1, 3353 Seitenstetten, Austria*].

        1. Archduke *Matthias* Josef, *b* at Linz 30 April 1971; *m* at Seitenstetten, Austria 11 May (civ) 1995 and 11 May (relig) 1996 (diss by div 12 May 1998), Sabine (*b* at Vienna 22 March 1973), dau of Otto Karl Binder and Elisabeth Braun. He *m* 2ndly at Vienna 10 Sept (civ) 1999 and 23 Sept (relig) 2000, Eva (*b* at Vienna 16 March 1968), dau of Herbert Anderle and Caharlotte..., and has issue.

[Maxingstraße 22/6/2, 1130 Vienna, Austria]
      1. Count *Nikolaus* Petrus Salvator, *b* at
Vienna 5 Aug 2000.
2. Archduchess *Hedwig* Walburga, *b* at Linz 31
Aug 1972; *m* at Seitenstethem 9 Sept 1995,
Georg Feldscher, *b* at Vienna 26 Aug 1968.
[Favoritenstraße 25/10, 1040 Vienna, Austria]
3. Archduke *Johannes* Florian, *b* at Linz 10
Feb 1974.
[Mühlweg 1, 3353 Seitenstetten, Austria].
4. Archduke *Bernhard* Wolfgang, *b* at Linz 11
June 1977.
[Mühlweg 1, 3353 Seitenstetten, Austria].
5. Archduchess *Veronika* Anna, *b* at Linz 3
Jan 1982.
[Mühlweg 1, 3353 Seitenstetten, Austria].
6. Archduke *Benedikt* Stephan, *b* at Linz 16
Sept 1983.
[Mühlweg 1, 3353 Seitenstetten, Austria].
3. Archduke *Clemens* Salvator Leopold Benedikt Antonius
Maria Joseph Ignatius, *b* at Schloß Wallsee 6 Oct 1904; ✠ at
Salzburg 20 Aug 1974, Kt Order of the Golden Fleece, assumed
the title Count von Altenburg 2 April 1931 and, with the
approval of the Head of the Imperial Family, that of Prince
von Altenburg 15 Dec 1949; *m* at Vienna 20 Feb 1930, Countess
Elisabeth (*b* at Nisko, Galicia 28 Oct 1906; ✠ at Salzburg 9
July 2000), dau of Friedrich, Count Rességuier de Miremont
and Countess Christiane von Wolkenstein, Baroness von
Trostburg and Neuhauss, and had issue, who bear the title of
Princes or Princesses von Altenburg,
      1. Princess Maria *Valerie* Christiane Elisabeth
Clementine Franziska Josepha Marcella, *b* at Vienna
16 Jan 1931; *m* at St Gilgen, nr Salzburg 19 July (civ)
and at Unterach am Attersee, Upper Austria 20 July
(relig) 1959, Mario, Count von Ledebur-Wicheln (*b* at
St Moritz 28 July 1931).
*[Leumatt 38, 6006 Luzern, Switzerland;
Johannesgasse 15, 1010 Vienna, Austria]*.
2. Prince *Clemens* Maria Franz Salvator Friedrich
Christian Joseph Johannes a Mata, *b* at Vienna 8 Feb
1932, Kt Order of the Golden Fleece; *m* at St Gilgen

16 Oct (civ) and at Unterach 17 Oct (relig) 1964,
Laurence (*b* at Neuilly 3 June 1942), dau of Henry
Costa, Marquess de St Genix de Beauregard and
Geneviève Poupart de Neuflize, and has issue,
[*Lenzgarten Weg 7, 5026 Salzburg-Aigen, Austria*].

  1. Prince *Philipp* Maria Paul, *b* at Salzburg 15
  March 1966.
  [*Freyung 6/9/2, 1010 Vienna, Austria*].
  2. Princess *Henriette* Marie Caroline, *b* at
  Salzburg 16 Nov 1972; *m* at Salzburg 6 Nov
  (civ) and 7 Nov (relig) 1998, Count *Guillaume*
  du Bessey de Contenson (*b* at Paris 16 May
  1969).
  [*Chaussée de Waterloo 868/870, 1180 Brussels,
  Belgium*]

3. Prince *Georg* Adam Maria Friedrich Leopold Joseph
Michael, *b* at Vienna 23 Sept 1933; *m* at Salzburg 9
Feb (civ) and at St Gilgen 17 Feb (relig) 1963, Maria
Roswitha (*b* at Prague 2 March 1941), dau of Anton
Wickl and Maria Machaczek, and has issue,
[*Wirtsgütlstraße 2, 4754 Andrichsfurth, Upper Austria,
Austria*].

  1. Prince Georg *Aegidius* Clemens Ferdinand
  Maria, *b* at Salzburg 4 Jan 1964, Kt. Hon and
  Dev Sovereign Military Order of Malta.
  [*Straß 2, 4754 Andrichsfurth, Upper Austria*].
  2. Princess *Maria Katharina* Elisabeth Barbara
  Louise Josefine Carola Felicitas, *b* at Vienna 7
  May 1967; *m* at St Gilgen 9 June (civ) and 12
  June (relig) 1993, *Ivo* von Deskovic (*b* at
  Klosterneuburg 15 Oct 1962),
  [*Hofzeile 27 1190 Vienna, Austria*].
  3. Prince *Stephan* Georg Max Joseph Aegidius
  Ferdinand Maria, *b* at Salzburg 20 Aug 1971;
  m at Frohnleiten Steiermark 6 May (civ) and
  24 June (relig) 2000, Baroness Katharina (*b* at
  Vienna 19 March 1974), dau of Baron Franz
  von Mayr-Helnhoe-Saurau and Countess
  Erzsbet Andrassy of Czik-Szent-Király und
  Kraszna-Horka.
  [*Gonzagagasse 17, 1010 Vienna, Austria*]

1.Princess *Maria* Elisabeth, *b* at Vienna
24 March 2001.

4. Prince *Peter* Friedrich Christian Clemens Maria
Leopold Joseph Matthäus, *b* at Vienna 18 Sept 1935;
m at Retz, NÖsterreich 30 Sept (civ) and at
Nieder-Flatnitz 2 Oct (relig) 1965, Countess Juliane
Waldstein-Forni (*b* at Buchberg am Kamp,
NÖsterreich 22 May 1940), dau of Eugen, Count von
Waldstein-Wartenberg and Princess Elisabeth von
Croÿ,(adopted by Count Franz Josef Forni) and has
issue,
[*Schönbrunngasse 49, 8010 Graz, Austria*].

    1. Prince *Friedrich* Eugen Clemens Petrus
    Maria, *b* at Munich 9 July 1966; *m* at Hadersdorf
    Am Kamp 16 June (civ) and at Etsdorf Am
    Kamp 8 July (relig) 2000, Countess Gabriele (*b*
    at Vienna 7 Oct 1965), dau of Count Georg von
    Walters zu Wolfsthal and Countess Agathe
    Hrin von and zu Stubenberg.
    [*Meravigliagasse 3, 1060 Vienna, Austria*].
    2. Princess *Hemma* Juliane Maria Elisabeth
    Clementine, *b* at Munich 22 May 1969, Vienna
    29 July (civ) and at Graz 14 Sep(relig) 1996,
    Count
    Nikolaus Ségur-Cabanac (*b* at Vienna 19 Nov
    1963), Dr. med., Dr. rer.soc.oec.
    [*Dreimarksteingasse 6, 1190 Vienna, Austria*].
    3. Prince *Leopold* Maximilian Vinzenz Petrus
    Maria, *b* at Graz 17 March 1971.
    [*Schönbrunngasse 49, 8010 Graz, Austria*].
    4. Princess *Franziska* Christiane Maria Elisabeth
    Juliane, *b* at Graz 17 May 1972.
    [*Zimmermann-Platz 1/17, 1090 Vienna,
    Austria*].
    5. Princess *Maria Elisabeth* Luise Juliane, *b* at
    Graz 5 Dec 1973.
    [*Schönbrunngasse 49, 8010 Graz, Austria*].

5. Prince *Christoph* Theodor Johannes Leopold Joseph
Maria Vitalis, *b* at Wallsee 28 April 1937; *m* at Mona,
nr Braidwood, New South Wales 7 Feb 1970, Kirsty (*b*
at Braidwood 8 Nov 1946), [*Macquariedale Residence,*

Po Box 274, Braidwood 2622, N.S.W., Australia], dau
of Jan Farquart Mackay and Janette Walker, and has
issue,
[*Po Box 266, Braidwood 2622, N.S.W., Australia*].

   1. Prince *Sebastian* Christoph, *b* at Perth 9
July 1971; *m* at Sydney 28 Sept 1997, Megan
Elizabeth (*b* at Sydney 24 Nov 1971), dau of
Don Rees and Joy Dunkley, and has issue,
[*2/21 Grevillea Road, Katherine NT, Australia*]

      1. Prince Henry Jork *b* at Katherine NT
5 June 2000.

   2. Princess *Matilda* Elisabeth, *b* at Canberra
12 Nov 1975.
[*Macquariedale Residence, Po Box 274,
Braidwood 2622, N.S.W., Australia*]

   3. Princess *Francesca* Kirsty, *b* at Canberra 4
April 1979.
[*Macquariedale Residence, Po Box 274,
Braidwood 2622, N.S.W., Australia*]

6. Princess *Elisabeth* Christiane Maria Walburga Anna
Magdalena, *b* at Vienna 11 Dec 1938.
[*Franz Bergerstraße 3, 5020 Salzburg, Austria*].

7. Prince *Franz Josef* Georg Clemens Maria Leopold
Salvator, *b* at Ischl 15 March 1941; *m* at Klagenfurt 3
May 1969, Baroness Christa (*b* at St Veit an der Glan,
Kärnten 29 Jan 1945), dau of Thomas, Baron von
Haerdtl and Ilse von Burger-Scheidlin, and has issue,
[*Aspeding 1, 4691 Breitenschützing, Upper Austria,
Austria*].

   1. Princess Maria *Caecilia* Elisabeth Theresa
Margarete, *b* at Gmunden 2 April 1970.
[*Aspeding 1, 4691 Breitenschützing, Upper
Austria, Austria*]

   2. Prince *Augustin* Franz Josef Maria Clemens
Georg Salvator, *b* at Gmunden 27 Oct 1971.
[*Opernring 4/ Stge 2, 1010 Vienna, Austria*]

   3. Princess *Amalia* Maria Elisabeth, *b* at
Vöcklabruck 13 Jan 1979.
[*Aspeding 1, 4691 Breitenschützing, Upper
Austria, Austria*].

   4. Princess *Elisabeth* Maria Caecilia Amalia

Katharina, *b* at Vöcklabruck 9 June 1983.
[*Aspeding 1, 4691 Breitenschützing, Upper Austria, Austria*].

8. Prince *Nikolaus* Gottfried Salvator Maria Joseph Leopold Johannes Vianney, *b* at Ischl 22 May 1942; *m* at Salzburg 28 April 1973; (*m* diss by div at Salzburg 13 Jan 2000), Suzanne Madeleine (*b* at Washington 9 Nov 1946), dau of Franz Robinow and Madeleine Suzanne Lebkircher, and has issue,
[*Reinholdgasse 9, 5026 Salzburg-Aigen, Austria*].

    1. Prince Florian Max, b at Munich 17 Jan 1974.
    [*326 Whyte Avenue, Brooklyn, 11211 NY, New York, U.S.A*]

    2. Princess *Anna* Elisabeth, *b* at Salzburg 28 March 1977.
    [*430 East 65 Street, Apartment 4K, 1021 NY, New York, U.S.A*]

9. Prince *Johannes* Maria Karl Salvator Leopold Ignatius Florian, *b* at Gmunden 21 Jan 1949; *m* at Vienna 26 Aug 1978, Eugenie (*b* at Vienna 22 Sept 1953), dau of Herbert Fundulus and Countess Evamarie von Schönfeldt, and has issue,
[*Landstrasser Hauptstraße 6, 1030 Vienna, Austria*].

    1. Princess Maria *Agnes*, *b* at Vienna 15 June 1979.
    [*Landstrasser Hauptstraße 6, 1030 Vienna, Austria*].

    2. Princess Maria *Josepha*, *b* at Vienna 20 March 1981.
    [*Landstrasser Hauptstraße 6, 1030 Vienna, Austria*].

    3. Princess *Clara* Maria Johanna, *b* at Vienna 12 Sept 1983.
    [*Landstrasser Hauptstraße 6, 1030 Vienna, Austria*].

    4. Prince Franz *Clemens,* *b* at Vienna 25 Sept 1985.
    [*Landstrasser Hauptstraße 6, 1030 Vienna, Austria*].

4. Archduchess *Mathilde* Maria Antonia Ignatia, *b* at Ischl 9

Aug 1906; ✠ at Salzburg 18 Oct 1991; *m* at Hall, Tirol 9 April
(civ) and 10 April (relig) 1947, Ernst Hefel (*b* at Schruns,
Vorarlberg 25 Nov 1888; ✠ at Salzburg 21 March 1974) Dr jur
and phil.

LINE III: Dukes of Teschen

**Founded by Archduke Karl (*b* 5 Sept 1771; ✠ 30 April 1847), *cr* Duke
of Teschen 10 Feb 1822, Grand Master Teutonic Order in Austria 27
July 1801-25, Gov-Gen of The Netherlands 1793, Field Marshal of
the Empire 1796, Gov-Gen of the Kingdom of Bohemia 1800-09, Min
of War Austrian Empire 1805-09, Gen Field Marshal, Kt Order of
the Golden Fleece, Kt Gd Cross Mil Order of Maria Theresia, Kt Gd
Eagle Legion of Honour, etc; leader of the Austrian forces against
Napoleon. The line below descends from his second son.**

**Members of the Imperial Family bear the titles of Archduke or
Archduchess of Austria, Prince or Princess of Hungary, with the
qualification of Imperial and Royal Highness. Since 30 Nov 1990 the
descendants of marriages not recognised as being of equal status
bear the title of Count or Countess von Habsburg unless another
title has been conferred upon them.**

Son

Archduke *Karl Ferdinand,* *b* at Vienna 29 July 1818; ✠ at
Gross-Seelowitz, Moravia 20 Nov 1874, Gen Austrian Army, Kt Order
of the Golden Fleece; *m* at Vienna 18 April 1854, Archduchess
Elisabeth (*b* at Ofen 17 Jan 1831; ✠ at Vienna 14 Feb 1903; *m* 1stly
at Vienna 4 Oct 1847, Archduke Ferdinand of Austria-Este, Prince
of Modena who ✠ 15 Dec 1849), dau of Archduke Joseph of Austria,
Palatine of Hungary and Duchess Marie Dorothea of Württemberg,
and had issue, among whom,

Sons

1. Archduke *Friedrich* Maria Albrecht Wilhelm Karl, Duke von
Teschen, *succ* as 3rd Duke von Teschen on the death of his uncle,
Albrecht, 2nd Duke (✠ 18 Feb 1895), *b* at Gross-Seelowitz 4 June
1856; ✠ at Mosonmagyarovar, Hungary 30 Dec 1936, Imp and Royal
Field Marshal, Royal Prussian Gen-Field Marshal, etc, Kt Order of
the Golden Fleece; *m* at Château L'Hermitage, Belgium 8 Oct 1878,
Princess Isabella (*b* at Dülmen 27 Feb 1856; ✠ at Budapest 5 Sept
1931), Dame Star Cross Order, dau of Rudolf, 11th Duke von Croÿ
and Princess Natalie de Ligne, and had issue, among whom,

Son

1. Archduke *Albrecht* Franz Josef Karl Friedrich Georg Hubert

Maria, 4th Duke von Teschen, *b* at Weilburg, nr Baden 24 July 1897; ✠ at Buenos Aires 23 July 1955, Col Royal Hungarian Army, Bailiff Gd Cross Hon and Dev Sovereign Military Order of Malta; *m* 1stly at Brighton 16 Aug 1930, Irene (*b* at Szabadka 22 12 1897; *m* 1stly 1917, Ludwig Rudnay de Rudnó et Divék-Ujfalu who ✠ 13 Oct 1944; that *m* diss by div), dau of Johann Lelbach and Ilma Skultéty. He *m* 2ndly at Budapest 7 May (civ) and at Pannonhalma 9 May (relig) 1938 (*m* diss by div at Morales, Mexico 1951), Katalin (Catherine) (*b* at Szelevény 1 Nov 1909), dau of Béla Bocskay de Felsö-Bánya and Eszter Farkas [*4553 California Street, San Francisco, CA 94118, USA*], and had issue (*who bear the surname of Habsburg-Lorraine, Princesses of Hungary*),

    1. Princess *Sarolta* (Charlotte) Izabella Mária Krisztine Eszter Katalin Pia, *b* at Budapest 3 March 1940; *m* at La Tour de Peilz 19 July (civ) and 20 July (relig) 1967, Ferdinand Joseph Wutholen (*b* at Graz 9 Feb 1927). [*6 Chemin du Milieu, 1245 Collonge-Bellerive, Switzerland*].

    2. Princess *Ildiko* Katalin Izabella Henriette Alice Mária, *b* at Budapest 19 Feb 1942; *m* 1stly at San Francisco 26 Feb 1963 (*m* diss by div at 9 Feb 1978), Joseph J Calleja (*b* at San Francisco 31 Oct 1939). She *m* 2ndly at Fresno 2 Feb 1982, Terry Fortier (*b* at Alameda 11 Feb 1939).
[*27510 Corrall Hollow, Tracy, CA 95376, U.S.A*].

Archduke *Albrecht* *m* 3rdly at Asuncion, Paraguay, Lydia Strausz-Dorner (*b* ....) and had issue (*who bears the surname of Habsburg-Lorraine, Prince of Hungary*),

    3. Prince Rudolf Stefan *b* 1951

2. Archduke *Karl Stephan* Eugen Victor Felix Maria, *b* at Gross-Seelowitz 5 Sept 1860; ✠ at Zywiec, Poland (formerly Saybusch, Galicia) 7 April 1933, Admiral Austrian Navy, Protector of the Academy of Sciences at Kraków, Kt Order of the Golden Fleece; *m* at Vienna 28 Feb 1886, Archduchess Maria Theresia (*b* at Alt Bunzlau 18 Sept 1862; ✠ at Zywieć 10 May 1933), Dame Star Cross Order, dau of Archduke Karl Salvator of Austria and Princess Doña Immaculata of Bourbon-Two Sicilies, and had issue, among whom,

Sons

    1. Archduke *Karl Albrecht* Nikolaus Leo Gratianus, *b* at Pola

18 Dec 1888; ✠ at Östervik, nr Stockholm 17 March 1951, Col
Austrian Army, Polish Col, Kt Order of the Golden Fleece;
m at Zywiec, Poland 8 Nov 1920, Alice (*b* at Tullgarn 18 Dec
1889; ✠ at Saltsjobaden 26 Nov 1985; *m* 1stly at Stockholm
21 Nov 1911, Ludwig, Count Badeni who ✠ at Vienna 11 Nov
1916), used the title of Princess von Altenburg by written
authorisation of the Head of the Imperial Family 15 Dec 1949,
dau of Major Oscar Ankarcrona (of Swedish nobility), Master
of the Royal Swedish Hunt and Elisabeth (Beth) Carleson (of
Swedish nobility), and had issue (who bear the surname of
Habsburg and the title of Prince or Princess von Altenburg),

    1. Prince *Karl*-Stefan Maximilian Ferdinand Narcissus
Maria, *b* at Balice 29 Oct 1921, Banker; *m* at Geneva
18 Sept 1952, Marie-Louise (*b* at Stockholm 10 Nov
1910 ✠ at Stockholm 27 May 1998), dau of August af
Petersens, Proprietor of Erstavik in Södermanland and
Victoria (Vera) Ankarcrona (of Swedish nobility), and
has issue, among whom,
[*Östervik 4, 13349 Saltsjöbaden, Sweden*].

        1. Princess *Maria-Christina* Ninfa Renata
Margarita Isabella Clara Eugenia Anselma,
b at Stockholm 21 April 1953.
[*Östervik 4, 13349 Saltsjöbaden, Sweden*].

    2. Princess *Maria-Christina* Immaculata Elisabeth
Renata Alice Gabriela, *b* at Zywiec 8 Dec 1923, Dame
of Hon and Dev Sovereign Military Order of Malta.
[*Rossweidstraße 3, 7270 Davos Platz, Switzerland*].

    3. Princess *Renata* Maria Theresia Alice Elisabeth,
b at Zywiec, Poland (formerly Saybusch, Galicia) 13
April 1931; *m* at Stockholm 26 June 1957, Eduardo de
Zulueta y Dato of the Marqueses de Alava (*b* at Paris
4 Dec 1923), Ambassador.
[*O'Donnell 15, 28009 Madrid, Spain*].

2. Archduke *Leo Karl* Maria Kyrill Method, *b* at Pola 5 July
1893; ✠ at Bestwina 28 April 1939, Imp and Roy Capt Cavalry,
Kt Order of the Golden Fleece; *m* at Vienna 4 Oct 1922,
Countess Maria-Klothilde (*b* at Vienna 6 Nov 1893; ✠ at
Vienna 7 Dec 1978), Dame Star Cross Order, dau of Karl de
Thuillières, Count de Montjoye-Vaufrey et de la Roche and
Countess Irene O'Donell von Tyrconell, and had issue, among
whom,

1. Archduchess *Mechtildis* Maria Irene Fidelis, *b* at Leszno, nr Posen, Poland (*formerly Lissa*) 14 Aug 1924; ✣ at Vienna 18 Feb 2000, Dame Star Cross Order; *m* at Vienna 29 April 1948, Manfred, Count and Marquess Piatti (*b* at Schloß Loosdorf, nr Mistelbach, Lower Austria 22 July 1924).
[*Malterser-Hospiz, Bürgerspitalgasse 1, 1060, Vienna, Austria*].

2. Archduchess *Elisabeth* Irene Maria Fidelis, *b* at Vienna 13 March 1927, Dr of Med, Dipl Business.
[*Schikanedergasse2, 1040 Vienna, Austria*].

3. Archduke *Leo*-Stefan Maria Carl Wolfgang Rudolf Fidelis, *b* at Zywiec, Poland (formerly Saybusch, Galicia) 12 June 1928; *m* 1stly at Vienna 31 March 1962 (*m* diss by div at Vienna 19 Aug 1969), *Gaby* (Gabriele) (*b* at Warnsdorf, Bohemia 15 June 1935; ✣ at Munich 20 Oct 1975), dau of Julius Kunert and Gertraud Eger, and had issue,

    1. Countess Marie *Isabella* Klara, *b* at Reading, Pennsylvania, USA 21 Dec 1962; *m* at Tettang 5 Oct 1990 (*m* diss by div at Tettang 23 March 2001), Andreas Fehr (*b* at Zurich 30 May 1957).
    [*Harrathof, 2822 Erlach AD Pitten, Austria*]

    2. Count *Albrecht* Stanislaus Bernhard Matthias Manfred, *b* at St Gallen 6 Sept 1963; *m* at Immenstadt 19 May 1990 (*m* diss by div at Stuttgart 3 April 1993), Nadja (*b* at Immenstadt 15 May 1969), dau of Gerd Würfel and Karen Würfel; He *m* 2ndly at Stuttgart 11 March 1994, *Carmen* (*b* at Stuttgart 15 May 1968), dau of Rolf Eckstein and Gerda Schäfer, and has issue,
    [*Robert-Leichtstraße 175, 70569 Stuttgart, Germany*]

        1. Countess Jessica-Tatjana, *b* at Sigmaringen 11 June 1994.

    3. Count *Hubertus* Karl Stefan Severin Gottfried Sigmund, *b* at Salzburg 24 Feb 1967.
    [*Frauenkau 2, 87730 Bad Grönebach-Zell, Allgau, Germany*]

Archduke *Leo*-Stefan *m* 2ndly at Salzburg 21 Sept

1973, Heidi (*b* at Salzburg 16 Oct 1942), dau of Herbert Aigner and Stephanie Mosl, and has further issue, [*Astäett 42, 5221 Lochen, Upper Austria, Austria*].

4. Count *Philipp* Bernhard, *b* at Salzburg 17 June 1974.
[*Astäett 59, 5221 Lochen, Upper Austria, Austria*].

5. Countess *Anna* Katharina Andrea, *b* at Salzburg 27 Jan 1977.
[*Siezenheimenstraße 57, 5020 Salzburg, Austria*]

6. Countess *Valerie* Elisabeth, *b* at Salzburg 27 March 1982.
[*Astäett 42, 5221 Lochen, Upper Austria, Austria*].

7. Count *Leo* Stefan Manfred, *b* at Salzburg 30 May 1985.
[*Astäett 42, 5221 Lochen, Upper Austria, Austria*].

5. Archduke *Hugo Carl* Maria Leo Fidelis, *b* at Zywiec, Poland (formerly Saybusch, Galicia) 27 Sept 1930; ✣ at Vienna 26 Oct 1981, Dir of Güssinger Mineralwasser-AG; *m* at Vienna 23 Sept 1972, Eleonore (*b* at Vienna 10 Dec 1943), dau of Gottfried Kristen and Elfriede Lihotzky.
[*Doblhoffgasse3, 1010 Vienna, Austria*].

LINE IV: Former Palatines of Hungary

Founded by Archduke Joseph, Palatine of Hungary, Gov and Capt-Gen of Hungary, Gen-Field Marshal Austrian Army (*b* 9 March 1776; ✣ 13 Jan 1847). The line below descends from his third son. Members of the Imperial Family bear the titles of Archduke or Archduchess of Austria, Prince or Princess of Hungary, with the qualification of Imperial and Royal Highness. Since 30 Nov 1990 the descendants of marriages not recognised as being of equal status bear the title of Count or Countess von Habsburg unless another title has been conferred upon them.

Son

Archduke *Joseph* Karl Ludwig, *b* at Pressburg 2 March 1833; ✣ at Fiume 13 June 1905, Gen Austrian Army, Cmdr-in-Chief Hungarian Honvéd Army; *m* at Coburg 12 May 1864, Princess Marie Adelheid

Clotilde (*b* at Neuilly-sur-Seine 8 July 1846; ✠ at Alcsút, Hungary 3 June 1927), dau of Prince August of Saxe-Coburg and Gotha, Duke of Saxony and Princess Clémentine of Bourbón-Orléans, and had issue, among whom,

Son

Archduke *Joseph* August Viktor Klemens Maria, *b* at Alcsút 9 Aug 1872; ✠ at Rain, nr Straubing 6 July 1962, President of the Hungarian Academy of the Sciences, Hon Dr of Sciences Univ of Budapest, Hon MD Univ of Kolozsvar, and Hon Dr of Tech Sciences Univ of Budapest, Field Marshal Austrian Army, Kt Order of the Golden Fleece, Bailiff Gd Cross Hon and Dev Sov Order of Malta, Cmdr Austrian Mil Order of Maria Theresia, Kt Orders of the Black Eagle, for Merit, Gd Cross Orders of St Stefan of Hungary and of Leopold; *m* at Munich 15 Nov 1893, Princess Auguste (*b* at Munich 28 April 1875; ✠ at Regensburg 25 June 1964), dau of Prince Leopold of Bavaria and Archduchess Gisela of Austria, and had issue, among whom,

1. Archduke *Joseph Franz* Leopold Anton Ignatius Maria, *b* at Brünn 28 March 1895; ✠ at Carcavelos, Portugal 25 Sept 1957, Dr of Law, Lt-Col Royal Hungarian Army, Kt Order of the Golden Fleece, Kt Gd Cross Sovereign Military Orders of Malta and of the Holy Sepulchre, etc; *m* at Sibyllenort 4 Oct 1924, Princess Anna (*b* at Lindau 4 May 1903; ✠ at Munich 8 Feb 1976), dau of Friedrich August III, King of Saxony and Archduchess Luise of Austria-Tuscany, and had issue, among whom,

1. Archduchess Margarethe (*Margit*), *b* at Budapest 17 Aug 1925; ✠ at Stockholm 3 May 1979; *m* at Tihany 17 Aug 1943, Alexander Erba Odescalchi, Prince di Monteleone, etc (*b* at Budapest 23 March 1914), titles confirmed by Victor Emanuel III, King of Italy 30 Aug 1943, Dr of Law, Lt Royal Hungarian Army, Writer, son of Lt-Field Marshal Joseph Cech and Princess Amelia Erba-Odescalchi of the Princes di Monteleone. [*Friherreg.146, 165-58 Hässelby, Sweden*].

2. Archduchess Helene (*Ilona*), *b* at Budapest 20 April 1927, Dame Gd Cross Hon and Dev Sovereign Military Order of Malta; *m* at Sigmaringen 20 Feb (civ) and 30 April (relig) 1946 (*m* diss by div at Freiburg im Breisgau 12 Dec 1974), George Alexander, Duke of Mecklenburg

(*b* at Nice 27 Aug 1921; ✝ at Mirow 26 Jan 1996).
[*Fasanenstraße 9, 79110 Freiburg Lehn, Germany*]

3. Archduke *Joseph* Arpád Benedikt Ferdinand Franz
Maria Gabriel, *b* at Budapest 8 Feb 1933, Dipl rer pol,
Kt Order of the Golden Fleece, Kt of Hon and Dev
Sovereign Military Order of Malta; *m* at Bronnbach 25
Aug (civ) and 12 Sept (relig) 1956, Princess Maria (*b*
at Munich 6 Nov 1935), Dame Star Cross Order, Dame
of Hon Sovereign Military Order of Malta, dau of Karl,
Prince (Fürst) zu Löwenstein-Wertheim-Rosenberg
and Carolina Rignon of the Counts Rignon, and has
issue,
[*Avenida General Carmona 3, 2765 Estoril, Portugal;
Knöbelstraße 28, 80538 Munich, Germany*].

     1. Archduchess *Monika-Ilona* Maria Carolina
Stephanie Elisabeth Immacolata Benedicta
Dominica, *b* at Munich 14 Sept 1958; *m* at
Székesehérvár 18 May 1996, Charles-Henry
Rambure (*b* at Tours, France 23 April 1968).
[*Château de Ringy, Routes des deux Luions,
37360 Joue-Les-Tours, Dept Imde-Et-Loir,
France*].

     2. Archduke *Joseph* Karl Maria Arpád Stephan
Pius Ignatius Aloysius Cyrillus, *b* at Munich 18
March 1960, Businessman, Kt Order of the
Golden Fleece; *m* at Munich 28 Dec 1990 (civ)
and at Vienna 20 April 1991 (relig), Princess
(Fürstin) Margarete (*b* at Vienna 19 June 1963),
dau of Albrecht, Fürst von Hohenberg and
Countess Leontine von Cassis-Faraone, and has
issue,
[*Tauberstraße 19, 14193 Berlin, Germany*].

       1. Archduchess *Johanna*, *b* at London
21 May 1992.

       2. Archduke *Joseph* Albrecht, *b* at
Hanover 26 July 1994.

       3. Archduke *Paul* Leo, *b* at Hanover 13
Jan 1996.

       4. Archduchess *Elisabeth*, *b* at Hanover
22 Sept 1997.

    3. Archduchess *Maria Christine* Regina

Stephanie Immaculata Carolina Monika Ägidia, *b* at Munich 1 Sept 1961; *m* at Estoril, Portugal 22 May 1988, Raymond Willem van der Meide (*b* at Geelong, Australia 22 June 1959), BSc.

[*24 Palmerston Road, Woodston, Peterborough PE2 9DG*].

4. Archduke *Andreas*- Augustinius Maria Arpád Aloys Konstantin Pius Ignatius Peter, *b* at Munich 29 April 1963; *m* at Johannisberg 2 Oct 1994, Countess Maria-Christiana (*b* at Mainz 18 Dec 1968), dau of Johann-Christian, Count von Hatzfeldt-Wildenburg-Dönhoff and Countess Maria de Mumm, and has issue,

[*Knöbelstraße 28, 80538 Munich , German*].

    1. Archduke *Frederic* Cyprien, *b* at Frankfurt-am-Main 18 July 1995.

    2. Archduke *Pierre* Nicholas, *b* at Frankfurt-am-Main 8 May 1997.

    3. Archduchess *Celina* Maria Christiana, *b* at Frankfurt-am-Main 14 Nov 1998.

    4. Archduchess Florina, *b* at Frankfurt-am-Main 15 Aug 2000.

5. Archduchess *Alexandra* Lydia Pia Immacolata Josepha Petra Paula Maria, *b* at Munich 29 June 1965; *m* at Lisbon 19 June 1999, Wilhelmus de Wit (*b* at Utrecht 6 Nov 1965).

[*Kastanielann 16, 5342 XM OSS, The Netherlands*].

6. Archduke *Nicolaus* Franziskus Alexander Nuno Josef Arpád Pius Ruppert Donatus Virgil Maria, *b* at Munich 27 Nov 1973; *m* at Madrid 13 July 2002, Eugenia (*b* at Saint Sabastian 24 April 1973), dau of don *Ignacio* de Calonje y Velásquez and of *María* Eugenia Gurrea y Saavedra.

[*Avenida General Carmona 3, 2676-207 Estoril, Portugal*].

7. Archduke *Johannes* Jacobus Josef Arpád

Ulrich Pius Stephan Ignatius Hermann Maria, *b* at Munich 21 May 1975.
[*Avenida General Carmona 3, 2676-207 Estoril, Portugal*].

4. Archduke Stephan (*István*) Dominik Anton Umberto, *b* at Budapest 1 July 1934, Kt of Hon and Dev Sovereign Military Order of Malta; *m* at Birnau 15 May 1971, Maria (*b* at Klein-Uretschlag, Bohemia 27 April 1942), dau of Gustav Anderl and Maria Reidinger, and has issue,
[*Starnbergerstraße 7, 82343 Pöcking, Kr. Starnberg, Germany*].

   1. Count *Leonhard* Stefan Antonius, *b* at Starnberg 17 March 1972, Dipl. Engineer, *m* at Munich 8 Dec 2000, Manuela (*b* at Munich 8 June 1964) dau of Wolfgang Bach and Ingrid Lösel
   [*Starnbergerstraße 7, 82343 Pöcking, Kr. Starnberg, Germany*].

   2. Countess *Christina* Maria Elisabeth, *b* at Starnberg 25 Feb 1975.
   [*Starnbergerstraße 7, 82343 Pöcking, Kr. Starnberg, Germany*].

5. Archduchess Maria *Kynga* Beatrix, *b* at Budapest 27 Aug 1938; *m* 1stly at Regensburg 15 July 1959 (*m* diss by div at Regensburg 11 Jan 1974), Ernst (Ernö) Kiss (*b* at Könlo, Hungary 12 July 1922). She *m* 2ndly at Munich 30 March 1988, Joachim Krist (*b* at Schwientochlowitz, Upper Silesia 3 April 1919), Dr of Med.
[*Pagodenburgstr. 2, 81247 Munich, Germany*].

6. Archduke *Géza* Ladislaus Euseb Gerhard Rafael Albert Maria, *b* at Budapest 14 Nov 1940, Dr of Phil, Kt Sovereign Military Order of Malta; *m* 1stly at Freiburg im Breisgau 7 July 1965 (*m* diss by div at New York 23 Sept 1991 and annulled 6 July 1993), Monica (*b* at Frankfurt-am-Main 1 Dec 1939), dau of Walther Decker and Maria Schwarzmann, and has issue,

   1. Count *Franz* Ferdinand, *b* at Geneva 8 May 1967; *m* at Tete, Mozambique 12 Jan 1995

Theresa Joao Manuel Carlos, (*b* at Ilha Mozambique 3 Feb 1973), dau of .... and ..... and has issue.
[*P.O. Box 84, Tete 50100 Mozambique, Africa*]
    1. Countess *Ana* Monica *b* at Tete, Mozambique 24 Nov 1995.
    2. Count Philip Paolo, *b* at Harare, Zimbabwe 9 Aug 1997

2. Count *Ferdinand* Leopold Joseph, *b* at Geneva 14 July 1969; *m* at Nairobi, Kenya 28 Aug 1999, Marie Nyanut (*b* at Wau, Sudan 1 July 1969), dau of Cirillo Ring Maciar and Victoria Adhar Adop, and has issue,.
[*Diocese of El Obeid, Blessed Bakhita House, Po Box 21102, Nairobi, Kenya*]
    1. Countess *Luisa* Aluzl, *b* at Nairobi, Kenya 18 Aug 2000.

3. Count *Maximilian* Philip, *b* at Geneva 7 July 1974.
[*24 The Scores, St Andrews, Fife, KY16 9AS, Scotland*].

Archduke Géza *m* 2ndly at New York 20 Dec 1991 (civ) and 1 Dec 1993 (relig), Elizabeth Jane (*b* 13 July 1966), dau of John Kunstadter and Geraldine Sapolsky, and has further issue
[*12 Governors Road, Bronxville, NY 10708, U.S.A.*].
    1. Countess *Isabella* Maria Luisa, *b* at New York 24 Sept 1990.

7. Archduke *Michael* Koloman Pius Matthias Ludwig Emerich Mārtın, *b* at Budapest 5 May 1942, Businessman Textiles, Kt Order of the Golden Fleece, Kt of Hon and Dev Sovereign Military Order of the Malta; *m* at Bronnbach an der Tauber 4 March (civ) and 14 April (relig) 1966, Princess Christiana (*b* at Würzburg 18 Sept 1940), Dame Star Cross Order, Dame of Hon Sovereign Military Order of Malta, dau of Karl, Prince (Fürst) zu Löwenstein-Wertheim-Rosenberg and Carolina Rignon of the Counts Rignon, and has issue,
[*Hintzerstraße 9/16, 1030 Vienna, Austria*].
    1. Archduke *Eduard* Karl Joseph Michael

Marcus Antonius Koloman Volkhold Maria, *b* at Munich 12 Jan 1967, Dr of Phil; *m* at Frauenkirchen 1 July 1995, Baroness Maria Theresia (*b* at Vienna 11 Feb 1967), dau of Gordian, Baron von Gudenus and Countess Anna Maria von Meran.

[*Frankenstraße 29, 50354 Hürth, Germany*].

    1. Archduchess *Anna-Carolina*, *b* at Munich 11 June 1996.

    2. Archduchess Teresa, *b* at Munich 2 Sept 1997.

    3 Archduke *Paul* Benedikt, *b* at Munich 25 Aug 2000.

2. Archduke *Paul* Rudolph Joseph Michael Antal Petrus Maria, *b* at Munich 19 Oct 1968, Semianarist of the Cath Rel Order of the Legionaries of Christ.

[*via Aurelia 677, 00165 Rome, Italy*]

3. Archduchess *Margherita* Anastasia Maximiliana Michaela Christiana Anna Carolina Maria, *b* at Munich 26 July 1972, Dame Star Cross Order, *m*, at Wildon 7 Feb 1997 (civ) and at Budapest.18 April 1998 (relig), Benedikt, Count von Piatti (*b* at Vienna 21 Jan 1966).

[*Renngasse14/36, 1010 Vienna, Austria*]

BADEN
(HOUSE OF ZÄHRINGEN)

Evangelical: Founded by Berchtold, Count in Breisgau 962-68, whose great-grandson Berchtold I the Bearded (✝ 1078), having been promised the Duchy of Swabia by the Emperor Heinrich III, received in its place in 1061 the Duchy of Carinthia and Margraviate of Verona, although he never obtained effective possession. His yr son Berchtold II (✝ 12 April 1111) and his descendants bore the title of Duke and eventually assumed the title of Duke of Zähringen in 1100 from the name of a castle in the district of Freiburg im Breisgau. His line became extinct 1218. Berchtold I's elder son Hermann I (✝ at the Abbey of Cluny 26 April 1074) took the title of Margrave of Verona but was in fact only Count of Breisgau. His son Hermann II

(✝ 7 Oct 1130) called himself Margrave of Baden from 27 April 1112, having inherited Baden-Baden (the ancient Aurelia Aquensis) from his mother Judith, Countess of Calw (✝ at Salerno 27 Sept 1091); Margrave of Baden 27 April 1112; acquisition of Hachberg (Hochberg, a fortified castle, today a ruin, north of Freiburg im Breisgau) circa 1155, Durlach and Ettlingen 1219, Pforzheim circa 1236, Eberstein (fortified castle near Baden-Baden) 1281; Investiture of the Margraviate of Baden 1362; acquired the Lordship of Lahr and Malberg 1442; inherited Sausenberg 1503; institution of the right of primogeniture and a rule banning all further division of the territories introduced 17 Nov 1615; qualification of Durchlaucht (Serene Highness) confirmed 11 April 1664. The line of Baden-Baden became extinct 21 Oct 1771 and its territories passed to the Durlach line. The Margrave Karl Friedrich became successively Elector (1803) and Grand Duke (1806) of Baden; qualification of Grand Ducal Highness authorised for all descendants in the male line 15 Aug 1844; Friedrich II (b 9 July 1857; succ 28 Sept 1907; ✝ 9 Aug 1928) abdicated 22 Nov 1918.

Arms:- Or, a bend gu. The Shield is ensigned with a Royal Crown.
Supporters:- Two griffins reguardant, wings elevated and expanded or.

The Head of the Grand Ducal family and his wife bear the title of Margrave and Margravine of Baden with the qualification of Royal Highness while cadet members of the family bear the title of Prince or Princess of Baden with the qualification of Grand Ducal Highness.

Maximilian (**MAX**) Andreas Friedrich Gustav Ernst August Bernhard, **MARGRAVE OF BADEN,** Duke of Zähringen, *b* at Schloß Salem 3 July 1933, son of Berthold, Margrave of Baden, etc (*b* 24 Feb 1906; ✝ 27 Oct 1963) and Princess Theodora of Greece and Denmark (*b* 30 May 1906; *m* 17 Aug 1931; ✝ 16 Oct 1969); *m* at Salem 23 Sept (civ) and and at Schloß Persenbeug, Lower Austria 30 Sept (relig) 1966, Archduchess Valerie (*b* at Vienna 23 May 1941), dau of Archduke Hubert Salvator of Austria and Princess Rosemary zu Salm-Salm.

[*88682 Schloß Salem, Baden, Germany*].

Sons and Daughter

1. Princess *Marie-Louise* Elisabeth Mathilde Theodora Cecilie Sarah Charlotte, *b* at Schloß Salem 3 July 1969, *m* at Salem 15 Sept (civ) and 25 Sep (relig) 1999 Richard Baker (*b* at Biddeford, Maine 30 March 1936).
2. *Bernhard* Max Friedrich August Gustav Louis Kraft, Hereditary Prince of Baden, *b* at Schloß Salem 27 May 1970; *m* at Salem 2 June (civ) and there 23 June (relig) 2001, Stephanie (*b* at .....1967) dau of

Christian Kaul and ......, and has issue,
     1. Prince *Leopold* Bernhard Max Michael Ernst-August Friedrich Guillaume, *b* at Ravensburg 18 May 2002.
3. Prince *Leopold* Max Christian Ludwig Clemens Hubert, *b* at Schloß Salem 1 Oct 1971.
4. Prince *Michael* Max Andreas, *b* at Schloß Salem 11 March 1976.

Brother and Sister

1. Princess *Margarita* Alice Thyra Viktoria Marie Louise Scholastica, *b* at Schloß Salem 14 July 1932; *m* there 6 June 1957 (*m* diss by div at London 13 Nov 1981 since when she reverted to her maiden name), Prince Tomislav of Yugoslavia (*b* at Belgrade 19 Jan 1928; ✝ at Oplenac 12 July 2000; *m* 2ndly at Bourneville, *nr* Birmingham 16 Oct 1982, Linda Bonney), son of Alexander I, King of Yugoslavia and Princess Marie of Romania.
[*4 Pencombe Mews, Denbigh Road, London, W11 2RZ*].
2. Prince *Ludwig* Wilhelm Georg Ernst Christoph, *b* at Karlsruhe 16 March 1937, Forester; *m* at Salem 21 Sept (civ) and at Wald, Lower Austria 21 Oct (relig) 1967, Princess Anna Maria (Marianne) (*b* at Zseliz, Bars, Hungary 15 Dec 1943), dau of Karl, Prince von Auersperg-Breunner and Countess Henriette von Meran, and has issue,
[*Schloßstraße 1, 69439 Zwingenberg, Baden, Germany*].
     1. Princess *Sophie* Thyra Josephine Georgine Henriette, *b* at Heidelberg 8 July 1975.
     [*Schloßstraße 1, 69439 Zwingenberg, Baden, Germany*].
     2. Prince *Berthold* Ernst-August Emich Rainer, *b* at Heidelberg 8 Oct 1976.
     [*Schloßstraße 1, 69439 Zwingenberg, Baden, Germany*].
     3. Princess *Aglaë* Margaretha Tatiana Mary, *b* at Heidelberg 3 March 1981.
     [*Schloßstraße 1, 69439 Zwingenberg, Baden, Germany*].

BAVARIA
(HOUSE OF WITTELSBACH)

Catholic: Founded by Margrave Luitpold (✝ 5 July 907), cousin and General of the Carolingian Emperor Arnulf; Duke of Bavaria 907-38; Count Palatine of Scheyern (a fortified castle, today a ruin, near Pfaffenhofen, Upper Bavaria) 940 - 1124; transferred to Kelheim 1112 and Wittelsbach (near Aichach, Upper Bavaria 1115; Otto V was invested with the Duchy of Bavaria 16 Sept 1180; Count Palatine of the Rhine (bei Rhein) 1214; Elector Palatine 15 May 1275; the dignity of Elector Palatine passed to the Dukes of Bavaria 25 Feb 1623; reestablished 24 Oct 1648; Carl Theodor, Elector Palatine, acquired the Electorate of Bavaria 30 Dec 1777. The Lines below descend from two sons of Christian I, Count Palatine of Birkenfeld-Bischweiler (b 5 Sept 1598; ✠ 6 Sept 1654).

Arms: Quarterly: 1st sa a lion rampant or, armed, langued and crowned gu (Palatine of the Rhine); 2nd parted per fesse dancetté gu and arg (Franconia); 3rd bendy sinister of six arg and gu a pale or (Burgau); 4th arg a lion az, armed and langued gu, crowned or (Veldenz); and over all an escutcheon of pretence, paly, bendy, arg and az. *Supporters:-* Two lions reguardant crowned or, armed and langued gu. *Motto:-* In Trau Vast. The achievement is borne on a mantle purpure, fringed and tasselled or, doubled ermine and surmounted by the Royal Crown of Bavaria.

LINE I: (Royal)

Founded by Christian II, Count Palatine of Birkenfeld-Bischweiler (b 22 June 1637; ✠ 26 April 1717); Count Palatine of Birkenfeld 31 March 1671; Count Palatine Zweibrücken 1731; Elector Palatine of Bavaria 16 Feb 1799; King of Bavaria 26 Dec 1805; abdication of the dynasty 7/8 Nov 1918.

Members of the Royal Family bear the title of Prince or Princess of Bavaria with the qualification of Royal Highness.

FRANZ Bonaventura Adalbert Maria, **DUKE OF BAVARIA,** b at Munich 14 July 1933, Senior Representative of the House of Stuart, of the Dukes of Modena, and of the Kings of Cyprus and Jerusalem, Grand Master Order of Saint Hubert, and of the Order of Saint George for the Defence of the Immaculate Conception, of the Orders of Maximilian Joseph, Saint Michael, Theresia, Saint Elizabeth and Saint Anne, Bailiff Gd Cross Hon & Dev Sov Mil Order of Malta, Kt Order of the Golden Fleece, son of Albrecht, Duke of Bavaria (b 3 May 1905; ✠ 8 July 1996) and Countess Maria (Marita) Draskovich de Trakostjan (b 8 March 1904; m 3 Sept 1930; ✠ 10 June 1969).
[*Schloß Nymphenburg 11, 80638 Munich, Germany*].

Brother and Sisters

1 Princess Marie Gabrielle Antonia José, b at Munich 30 May 1931, Dame of Hon Bavarian Orders of Theresia and St Elisabeth; m at Reichenhofen 31 Aug (civ) and at Nymphenburg 23 Oct (relig) 1957, Georg, 7th Prince (Fürst) von Waldburg zu Zeil and Trauchburg (b at Würzburg 5 June 1928), Dipl Econ.
[*Schloß Zeil, 88299 Leutkirch im Allgäu, Germany*].

2. Princess Marie *Charlotte* Juliane, *b* at Munich 30 May 1931 (twin with Princess Gabriele), Dame of Hon Bavarian Orders of St Theresia and St Elisabeth; *m* at Berg 1 Sept (civ) and at Nymphenburg 3 Sept (relig) 1955, Paul, 4th Prince (Fürst) von Quadt zu Wykradt and Isny (*b* at Isny 28 Nov 1930).
[*Herrenberger Weg 26, 88316 Isny im Allgäu, Germany*].

3. Prince *Max Emanuel* Ludwig Maria, *b* at Munich 21 Jan 1937, since 18 March 1965 has borne the title of Duke in Bavaria as adopted heir of Duke Ludwig Wilhelm in Bavaria (*b* 1884; ✝ 1968 - see below), Kt Bavarian Order of St Hubert; *m* at Kreuth 10 Jan (civ) and at Munich 24 Jan (relig) 1967, Countess Elizabeth Christina (*b* at Stockholm 31 Dec 1940), elder dau of Carl Ludvig, Count Douglas, (Royal Swedish Ambassador) and Ottora Maria Haas-Heye, and has issue, (Princesses of and Duchesses in Bavaria),
[*Schloß Wildenwart, 83112 Frasdorf, Germany*].

      1. Princess and Duchess *Sophie* Elizabeth Marie Gabrielle, *b* at Munich 28 Oct 1967; *m* at Vaduz, Liechtenstein 3 July 1993, Alois Philipp Maria, Hereditary Prince of Liechtenstein, Count of Rietberg (*b* at Zurich 11 June 1968).
      [*Schloß, 9490 Vaduz, Liechtenstein*].

      2. Princess and Duchess *Marie* Caroline Hedwig Eleonore, *b* at Munich 23 June 1969; *m* at Schloß Altshausen 28 June (civ) and Schloß Tegernsee 27 July (relig) 1991, Philipp Albrecht, Duke of Württemberg (*b* at Friedrichshafen am Bodensee 1 Nov 1964), Dr of Phil, Art Historian.
      [*Ditmarstraße 33, 60487 Frankfurt-am-Main, Germany*].

      3. Princess and Duchess *Helene* Eugenie Maria Donatha Mechtilde, *b* at Munich 6 May 1972.

      4. Princess and Duchess *Elizabeth* Marie Charlotte Franziska, *b* at Munich 4 Oct 1973.

      5. Princess and Duchess *Maria Anna* Henriette Gabriele Julie, *b* at Munich 7 May 1975.

Half-Sisters of Father

Issue of Crown Prince Rupprecht (*b* 18 May 1869; ✝ 2 Aug 1955) and his second wife, Princess Antonia (Antionette) of Luxembourg (*b* 7 Oct 1899, *m* 7 April 1921 ✝ 31 July 1954), having had issue, among whom,

1. Princess *Irmingard* Marie Josefa, *b* at Berchtesgaden 29 May 1923, Dame of Hon Bavarian Orders of St Theresia and St Elisabeth; *m*

Leutstetten 19 July (civ) and at Nymphenburg 20 July (relig) 1950, Prince Ludwig of Bavaria (*b* at Nymphenburg 22 June 1913 - see below).

[*Schloß Leutstetten, Wangener Straße 6, 82319 Starnberg, Germany*].

2. Princess *Editha* Marie Gabrielle Anna, *b* at Schloß Hohenburg 16 Sept 1924, Dame of Hon Bavarian Orders of St Theresia and St Elisabeth; *m* 1stly at Milan 12 Nov 1946, Tito Tommaso Maria Brunetti (*b* at Florence 18 Dec 1905; ✠ nr Piacenza 13 July 1954), Engineer. She *m* 2ndly at Tegernsee, 29 Dec 1959, Prof Gustav Christian Schimert (*b* at Budapest 28 Nov 1910; ✠ at Munich 16 May 1990), MD, Prof of Circulatory Research Univ of Munich.

[*Schumannstraße 8/II, 81679 Munich, Germany*].

3. Princess *Gabrielle* Adelgunde Marie Theresia Antonia *b* at Berchtesgaden 10 May 1927, Dame of Hon Bavarian Orders of St Theresia and St Elisabeth; *m* at Leutstetten 17 June (civ) and at Nymphenburg 18 June (relig) 1953, Carl, 14th Duke von Croÿ (*b* at Düsseldorf 11 Oct 1914), Lic jur.

[*Schloß Merfeld, 48249 Dülmen, Westfalen, Germany*].

4. Princess *Sophie* Marie Therese, *b* at Starnberg 20 June 1935, Dame of Hon Bavarian Orders of St Theresia and St Elisabeth, Dame of Hon Sov Order of Malta; *m* at Berchtesgaden 18 Jan (civ) and 20 Jan (relig) 1955, Jean-Engelbert, 12th Duke of Arenberg (*b* at The Hague 14 July 1921), MA, Dr of Law, Pres and Director of several companies.

[*Avenue des Acacias 10, 1006 Lausanne, Switzerland; 88 Rue de la Foret, Champlon-Famenne, 6900 Grand Marchè, Belgium*].

Brother of Grandfather

Issue of Ludwig III, King of Bavaria (*b* 7 Jan 1845, ✠ 18 Oct 1921) and Archduchess Maria-Theresia of Austria-Este, Princess of Modena who *succ* her paternal uncle, Francesco V, Duke of Modena as representative and Heir-Gen of Charles I, King of England and as such was regarded by British legitimists as "Queen Mary IV and III" (*b* 2 July 1849; *m* 20 Feb 1868; ✠ 3 Feb 1919), having had issue, among whom,

Son

Prince *Franz* Maria Luitpold, *b* at Leutstetten 10 Oct 1875; ✠ at Samerhof 25 Jan 1957, Royal Bavarian Major-Gen, Kt Bavarian Orders of St Hubert and St George, Kt Order of the Black Eagle (Prussia),

etc; *m* at Schloß Weilburg, Baden, nr Vienna 8 July 1912, Princess
Isabella (*b* at Château de l'Hermitage 7 Oct 1890; ✠ at Starnberg 30
March 1982), Gd Mistress of the Bavarian Order of St Elisabeth and
Dame of Hon Bavarian Order of St Theresia, dau of Carl Alfred,
Duke von Croÿ and Princess and Duchess Ludmilla d'Arenberg, and
had issue,

 1. Prince *Ludwig* Karl Maria Anton Joseph, *b* at Nymphenburg
22 June 1913, Kt Order of St Hubert, Kt Order of the Golden
Fleece; *m* at Nymphenburg, Princess Irmingard (*b* at
Berchtesgaden 29 May 1923), dau of Crown Prince Rupprecht
of Bavaria and Princess Antonia of Luxemburg and Nassau
(see above), and has issue,
[*Schloß Leutstetten, Wangener Straße 6, 82319 Starnberg,
Germany*].

  1. Prince *Luitpold* Rupprecht Heinrich, *b* at
Leutstetten 14 April 1951, Kt Order of St Hubert; *m*
at Starnberg 25 June (civ) and at Erling-Andechs 26
June (relig) 1979, Katrin Beatrix (*b* at Munich 19 Sept
1951), dau of Gerd Wiegand and Ellen Schumacher,
and has issue,
[*Schloß Kaltenberg, 82269 Geltendorf, Germany*].

   1. Princess *Auguste* Marie Philippa, *b* at
Landsberg am Lech 11 Oct 1979.
   2. Princess *Alice* Isabelle Marie, *b* at Landsberg
am Lech 25 June 1981.
   3. Prince *Ludwig* Heinrich, *b* at Landsberg am
Lech 14 June 1982.
   4. Prince *Heinrich* Rudolf, *b* at Landsberg am
Lech 23 Jan 1986.
   5. Prince *Karl* Rupprecht, *b* at Munich 10
March 1987.

 2. Princess *Maria* Elisabeth Franziska Josepha Therese, *b* at
Nymphenburg 9 Sept 1914, Dame of Hon Bavarian Orders of
St Theresia and St Elisabeth; *m* at Leustetten 17 Aug (civ)
and at Nymphenburg (relig) 19 Aug 1937, Prince Peter
Heinrich (Pedro Henrique) of Orleans and Bragança (*b* at
Boulogne-sur-Seine 13 Sept 1909; ✠ at Vassouras, Brazil 5
July 1981).
[*Rua Custódio Serrao 36, 206 Jardin Botanico, 22470 Rio de
Janeiro, Brazil*].

 3. Princess *Adelgunde* Maria Antonia Elisabeth Josefa, *b* at

Nymphenburg 9 June 1917, Dame of Hon Bavarian Orders of St Theresia and St Elisabeth; *m* at Leutstetten 23 May (civ) and 2 June (relig) 1948, Zdenko, Baron von Hoenning-O'Carroll (*b* at Sünching 6 Aug 1906; ✠ at Sünchingm 8 May 1996 *m* 1stly Princess Margit of Lobkowicz *b* at Pilsen-Zàmecek 4 July 1913 ✠ at Sünching 13 Feb 1946).

[Samerhof, Wangenerstraße 19, 82319 Starnberg-Leutstetten, Germany].

4. Princess *Eleonore* Therese Marie Josephe Gabriele, *b* at Nymphenburg 11 Sept 1918, Dame of Hon Bavarian Orders of St Theresia and St Elisabeth; *m* at Leutstetten 2 Aug (civ) and at Nymphenburg 14 Aug (relig) 1951, Konstantin, Count von Waldburg zu Zeil and Trauchburg (*b* at Schloß Zeil 15 March 1909; ✠ at Feldafing 27 Feb 1972).

[Dünzelbach 89, 82272 Moorenweis, Germany].

5. Princess *Dorothea* Therese Marie Franziska, *b* at Leutstetten 25 May 1920, Dame of Hon Bavarian Orders of St Theresia and St Elisabeth; *m* at Sárvár, Hungary 2 Aug (civ) and 3 Aug (relig) 1938, Archduke Gottfried of Austria, Prince of Tuscany, Head of the Grand Ducal House of Tuscany (*b* at Linz 14 March 1902; ✠ at Bad Ischl 21 Jan 1984).

[Fürsten Allee 8, 5020 Salzburg, Austria].

6. Prince *Rasso* Maximilian Rupprecht, *b* at Leutstetten 24 May 1926, Kt Orders of St Hubert and of the Golden Fleece, Grand Prior Order of St George; *m* at Schloß Wallsee, nr Amstetten 17 Oct 1955, Archduchess Theresia (*b* at Schloß Wallsee 9 Jan 1931), Dame Star Cross Order, Dame of Hon Bavarian Orders of St Theresia and St Elisabeth, dau of Archduke Theodor of Austria, Prince of Tuscany and Countess Maria Theresia von Waldburg zu Zell and Trauchburg, and has issue,

[Wittelsbacherpark 11, 82340 Feldafing, Germany]

1. Princess *Maria-Theresia* (Marie-Theres) Anna Walburga Irmingard, *b* at Hohenschwangau 10 Sept 1956; *m* at Andechs, nr Starnberg, Bavaria 23 July 1977, Thomas (Tamás), Count Kornis von Göncz-Ruszka (*b* at Budapest 4 Oct 1949), Businessman.

[Berzsenyi utca 18, 9545 Jánosháza, Kom. Eisenburg, Hungary].

2. Prince *Franz-Josef* Michael Maria Ignatius, *b* at Leutstetten 21 Sept 1957, Benedictine Monk at the

Erzabtei St Ottilien, known as Pater Florian.
[*86941 St. Ottilien, Germany*].

3. Princess *Elisabeth* Maria Immaculata Anastasia, *b* at Leutstetten 22 Jan 1959; *m* at Horn, Lower Austria 9 May (civ) and at Eberau, Burgenland 25 May (relig) 1986, Andreas, Count von Kuefstein (*b* at Vienna 9 Aug 1954), Farmer.
[*Schloß Greillenstein, 3592 Röhrenbach, Austria*].

4. Prince *Wolfgang* Rupprecht Maria Theodor, *b* at Leutstetten, 28 Jan 1960, Grand Prior Order of St George, Kt Order of St Hubert; *m* at Starnberg 16 Nov (civ) 1990 and at the Convent of the Augustines of Vorau, Styria 6 April (relig) 1991, Countess Beatrice (*b* at Vienna 29 May 1964), dau of Georg, Count zu Lodron-Laterano and Castelromano and Baroness Alice von Steeb, and has issue,
[*Baümlstraße 8, 80638 Munich, Germany*].

     1. Prince *Tassilo* Maria Georg Eugen Heinrich Rasso, *b* at Munich 19 June 1992.

     2. Prince *Richard* Maria Philipp Stephan Maximilian, *b* at Munich 19 Nov 1993.

     3. Prince *Philipp* Maria Max Emanuel Rupprecht Zeno, *b* at Munich 25 May 1996.

5. Princess *Benedikta* Maria Gabrielle, *b* at Starnberg 13 March 1961; *m* at Wettenhausen 9 June (civ) and at Wettenhausen, Kammeltal 11 June (relig) 1989, Rudolf, Baron von Freyberg-Eisenberg (*b* at Munich 7 Feb 1958).
[*Schloß, 89356 Haldenwang, Germany; Via Alessi 9, 95124 Catania, Sicily, Italy*]

6. Prince *Christoph* Ludwig Maria, *b* at Leutstetten 5 May 1962, Grand Prior Order of St George, Kt Order of St Hubert; *m* at Munich 18 Aug (civ) and at Lehnhausen 20 Aug (relig) 1994, Countess Guida (*b* at Lehnhausen 14 Oct 1962), dau of Count Huno von Plettenberg and Baroness Therese von Lüninck.
[*Trendlstraße 17, 82340 Feldafing, Germany*].

     1. Prince *Corbinian* Maria Hunold Rasso Nikolaus, *b* at Starnberg 9 Jan 1996.

     2. Prince *Stanislaus* Maria Hermann Theodor Philipp, *b* at Starnberg 24 May 1997.

3. Prince *Marcello* Maria Aloysius Franz Hubertus, *b* at Starnberg 20 Oct 1998

7. Princess *Gisela* Maria Karolina Adelgunde, *b* at Leutstetten 10 Sept 1964; *m* at Mexico City 3 April (civ) and at Andechs 28 Sept (relig) 1987, Alexander Gessaphe who bears the title of Prince von Sachsen-Gessaphe (*b* at Munich 12 Feb 1953), eldest son of Roberto Gessaphe and Princess Maria Anna Josepha of Saxony, as a result of adoption 1 June 1999 by Maria Emanuel, Margrave of Meißen, Duke of Saxony he bears the name Prince of Saxony, Duke of Saxony. [*Tieckstraße 17, 01099 Dresden, Germany*].

Brother of Great-Grandfather

Issue of Luitpold, Prince of Bavaria (*b* 12 March 1821; ✠ 12 Dec 1912), Prince Regent (9 June 1886 - 12 Dec 1912) for his nephews King Ludwig II and King Otto I, Gen-Field Marshal Bavarian Army, Insp-Gen Bavarian Army, etc (*b* 12 March 1821; ✠ 12 Dec 1912) and Archduchess Augusta of Austria-Tuscany (*b* 1 April 1825; *m* 15 April 1844; ✠ 26 April 1864), having had issue, among whom,

Sons

1. Prince *Leopold* Maximilian Joseph Maria Arnulf, *b* at Munich 9 Feb 1846; ✠ at Munich 28 Sept 1930, Royal Bavarian and Royal Prussian Gen-Field Marshal, Kt Gd Cross Bavarian Mil Order of Max Joseph, Kt Order of the Golden Fleece; *m* at Vienna 20 April 1873, Archduchess Gisela (*b* at Laxenburg 12 July 1856; ✠ at Munich 27 July 1932), Dame Star Cross Order, dau of Franz Joseph I, Emperor of Austria and Duchess Elisabeth in Bavaria, and had issue, among whom,

Son

Prince *Konrad* Luitpold Franz Joseph Maria, *b* at Munich 22 Nov 1883; ✠ at Hinterstein 6 Sept 1969, Royal Bavarian Major (Ret), Kt Bavarian Order of St George, Kt Orders of the Black Eagle, of the Golden Fleece and of Annunciata; *m* at Chateau d'Aglié, Piedmont 8 Jan 1921, Princess Bona Margherita (*b* at Chateau d'Aglié 1 Aug 1896; ✠ at Rome 2 Feb 1971), Dame Star Cross Order, Dame of Hon Bavarian Orders of St Theresia and of St Elisabeth, dau of Prince Tommaso of Savoy, 2nd Duke of Genoa and Princess Isabella of Bavaria, having had issue, among whom,

1. Prince *Eugen* Leopold Adelaide Thomas Maria, *b*
at Munich 16 July 1925; ✚ at Grasse, Dept
Alpes-Maritimes, France 1 Jan 1997, Kt Order of St
Hubert, Gd Prior Order of St George, Kt of Hon
Sovereign Military Order of Malta; *m* at Munich 16
Nov (civ) and at Innsbruck 21 Nov (relig) 1970,
Countess Helene (*b* at Vienna 4 April 1921; *m* 1stly at
Hochosterwitz 15 Aug 1953, Prince Konstantin of
Bavaria who ✚ at Hechingen 30 July 1969), Dame of
Hon Bavarian Orders of St Theresia and St Elisabeth,
Dame Star Cross Order, dau of Franz, Prince (Fürst)
von Khevenhüller-Metsch and Princess Anna zu
Fürstenberg.
[*Jagdhaus, 87541 Hinterstein, Germany; Bäumlstasse
13, 80638 Munich, Germany*].

1. Prince *Adalbert* Wilhelm Georg Ludwig, *b* at Munich 19 July 1828;
✚ at Nymphenburg 21 Sept 1875, Major-Gen Bavarian Army, Kt
Orders of St Hubert and St George, Kt Gd Cross Order of Carlos III
of Spain, etc; *m* at Madrid 25 Aug 1856, Infanta Amalia Felipe (*b* at
Madrid 12 Oct 1834; ✚ at Schloß Nymphenburg 27 Aug 1905), dau
of Infante Don Francisco de Paula of Spain, Duke of Cadiz, and had
issue, among whom,

Son
1. Prince *Ludwig Ferdinand* Maria Karl Heinrich Adalbert
Franz Philipp Andreas Konstantin, *b* at Madrid 22 Oct 1859;
✚ at Schloß Nymphenburg 23 Nov 1949, MD, Gen of Cavalry
Bavarian Army, sometime Inspector-Gen Royal Spanish Mil
Med Corps and Hon Surgeon Royal Spanish Academy; *m* at
Madrid 2 April 1883, Infanta Maria de la Paz (*b* at Madrid 23
June 1862; ✚ at Schloß Nymphenburg 4 Dec 1946), dau of
Isabel II, Queen of Spain and Infante Don Francisco de Asis
of Spain, titular King of Spain, and had issue, among whom,

1. Prince *Ferdinand Maria* Ludwig Franz von Assisi
Isabellus Adalbert Ildefons Martin Bonifaz Joseph
Isidro, *b* at Madrid 10 May 1884; ✚ at Madrid 5 April
1958, Infante of Spain, naturalised in Spain 20 Oct
1905; renounced his rights as a member of the Royal
House of Bavaria (1914) following the outbreak of
World War I and on his assumption of Spanish
citizenship but received *ad personam* the right, title,
rank and arms of a Prince of Bavaria 3 Aug 1914, Kt

Spanish Order of the Golden Fleece, etc; *m* 1stly at Madrid 12 Jan 1906, Infanta Maria Teresa (*b* at Madrid 12 Nov 1882; ✞ there 23 Sept 1912), Dame Star Cross Order, Dame Order of Maria Luisa, Dame of Hon Bavarian Orders of St Theresia & St Elisabeth, dau of Alfonso XII, King of Spain and Archduchess Maria Christina of Austria. He *m* 2ndly at Fuentarrabia 1 Oct 1914, Maria Luisa (*b* at Madrid 3 Dec 1870; ✞ there 22 April 1955), *cr* Duquesa de Talavera de la Reina and Grandee of Spain by King Alfonso XIII 25 June / 2 Sept 1914, and Infanta of Spain with the qualification of Royal Highness 17 May 1927, dau of Luis de Silva y Fernández de Córdova, 10th Count de Pié de Concha, 17th Marquess de Zahara, etc and Maria de los Dolores Fernández de Henestrosa y Fernández de Córdoba, and had issue by his first wife (see SPAIN).

2. Prince *Adalbert* Alfons Maria Ascension Antonius Hubertus Joseph omnes sancti, *b* at Nymphenburg 3 June 1886; ✞ at Munich 29 Dec 1970, PhD, Kt Order of the Golden Fleece (Spanish), Bailiff Gd Cross Constantinian Order of St George, sometime Federal German Ambassador to Spain; *m* at Salzburg 12 June 1919, Countess Augusta (*b* at Znaim 20 June 1899; ✞ at Munich 21 Jan 1978), dau of Otto, Count von Seefried, Proprietor of Buttenheim and Princess Elisabeth of Bavaria, and had issue, amongst whom,

    1. Prince *Konstantin* Leopold Ludwig Adalbert Georg Thadeus Josef Petrus Johannes Antonius Franz von Assisi Assumption et omnes sancti, *b* at Munich 15 Aug 1920; ✞*k* in a flying accident at Hechingen 30 July 1969, Writer and Editor; *m* 1stly at Sigmaringen 30 Aug (civ) and 31 Aug (relig) 1942 (*m* diss by div at Munich 14 July 1948 and annulled 24 March 1950), Princess Maria Adelgunde (*b* at Sigmaringen 19 Feb 1921; *m* 2ndly at Baden-Baden 25 March 1950, Werner Hess, *b* at Baden-Baden 20 Sept 1907, Dr of Med, *m* diss by div at Baden-Baden 28 Dec 1962; *m* 3rdly at Frauenfeld 9 Feb 1973, Hans Huber, *b* at Frauenfeld 12 May 1909),

[Binkeweg 9, 79224 Umkirch, Germany], dau of Friedrich, Prince of Hohenzollern and Princess Margarete of Saxony, and had issue,

1. Prince *Leopold* Rupprecht Ludwig Ferdinand Adalbert Friedrich Maria et omnes sancti, *b* at Schloß Umkirch, nr Freiburg im Breisgau 21 June 1943, Businessman, Kt Order of St Hubert; *m* (non-dynastic) at Berg, nr Starnberg 21 Oct (civ) and at Aufkirchen, nr Starnberg 19 Nov (relig) 1977, Ursula (*b* at Velbert, Rheinland 20 Sept 1947), dau of Willi Möhlenkamp and Ingeborg Brauckmann, and has issue, *[Seestraße 1-3, 82335 Berg nr Starnberg, Germany; Schackstraße 1, 80539 Munich, Germany]*.

    1. Prince *Manuel* Maria Alexander Leopold Jerg, *b* at Starnberg 27 Dec 1972, Dipl-Biology.

    2. Princess *Maria* del *Pilar* Birgitta Adelgunde Charlotte, *b* at Starnberg 3 May 1978.

    3. Princess Maria *Felipa* Karin Marion Gabriele, *b* at Starnberg 1 Feb 1981.

    4. Prince *Konstantin* Eugen Alexander Max-Emanuel Maria Ludwig-Ferdinand Leopold, *b* at Munich 8 Nov 1986.

2. Prince *Adalbert* Friedrich Johannes Maria et omnes sancti, *b* at Krauchenwies 27 Dec 1944, Data Processor, Kt Order of St Hubert; *m* 1stly (civ) at Munich 9 May 1978 (*m* diss by div at Munich 11 Nov 1983), (non-dynastic) Marion (*b* at Celle 14 Oct 1945; *m* 1stly at Frankfurt-am-Main 24 April 1967, Hubertus von Biela; that *m* diss by div at Frankfurt-am-Main 3

April 1970; she *m* 3rdly at Las Vegas
1983, Rainer Hasslacher), dau of
Wilhelm Malkowsky and Margot
Massengeil. He *m* 2ndly at Munich 21
Feb (civ) and at the Church of St
Leonhard, nr Schliersee 1 March (relig)
1986, (non-dynastic) Sandra (*b* at
Munich 19 June 1966), dau of Frank
Burckhardt, and Heidi Schiemeck and
has issue,
[*Schumannstraße 2, 81679 Munich,
Germany*].

> 1. Princess Bernadette Desirée,
> *b* at Munich 27 June 1986.
> 2. Prince *Hubertus* Florian
> Konstantin Clemens, *b* at
> Munich 29 August 1989.

Prince Konstantin *m* 2ndly at St. George am
Lingsee 14 Aug (civ) and at Hochosterwitz 15
Aug (relig) 1953, Countess Helene (*b* at Vienna
4 April 1921; *m* 2ndly Munich 16 Nov (civ) and
at Innsbruck 21 Nov (relig) 1970, Prince Eugen
of Bavaria - see above), dau of Franz Eduard,
8th Prince (Fürst) von Khevenhüller-Metsch
and Princess Anna zu Fürstenberg, and by
her had further issue,
[*Jagdhaus, 87541 Hindelang-Hinterstein;
Bäumlstraße 13, 80638 Munich, Germany*].

> 3. Princess *Ysabel* Helene Anna
> Augusta Maria de la Paz Ludovica-
> Fernanda, *b* at Munich 20 July 1954,
> Painter, Dame of Bavarian Orders of St
> Theresia and St Elisabeth; *m* at
> Canberra, Australia 19 Feb (civ) and at
> Munich 30 May (relig) 1976, Alfred,
> Count Hoyos, Baron zu Stichsenstein
> (*b* at Salzburg 17 July 1951), Artist.
> [*Hochwies, 3351 Weistrach, Austria*].

2. Prince *Alfons* Maria Franz von Assisi Klemens Maz
Emanuel, *b* at Munich 24 Jan 1862; ✝ at 8 Jan 1933, Gen
Royal Bavarian Cavalry; *m* at Nymphenburg 15 April 1891,

Princess Louise (*b* at Bushy House, nr Teddington, Surrey 9 July 1869; ✠ at Munich 4 Feb 1952), Dame Star Cross Order, dau of Prince Ferdinand of Orleans, Duke d'Alençon and Duchess Sophie in Bavaria, and had issue, among whom,

1. Princess *Elisabeth* Maria Anna Henriette Josepha Sophie Amalia Ferdinanda Ludovika Antonia Theresia Kreszentia Ala Ghislaine, *b* at Munich 10 Oct 1913, Dame Bavarian Orders of St Elisabeth and St Theresia; *m* 1stly at Nymphenburg 6 May 1939, Franz Joseph, Count von Kageneck (*b* at Berlin 8 Jan 1915; ✠*k* in action at Staritza, nr Kalinin 29 Dec 1941). She *m* 2ndly at Frankfurt an der Oder 9 May (civ) and at Garmisch-Partenkirchen 6 June (relig) 1944 (*m* diss by div at Munich 13 Aug 1953), Ernst Küstner (*b* at Hanau am Main 18 June 1920), Businessman.
[*Naumburgerstraße 25, 80993 Munich, Germany*].

LINE II: (Ducal)
(✠ Extinct ✠)

Founded by Johann Karl (*b* 17 Oct 1638; ✠ 21 Feb 1704).
Members of the Ducal Family bear the title of Duke or Duchess in Bavaria with the qualification of Royal Highness.

✠ **LUITPOLD** Emanuel Ludwig Maria, **DUKE IN BAVARIA,** *b* at Schloß Biederstein 30 June 1890; *dunm* at Kreuth 16 Jan 1973, son of Karl Theodor, Duke in Bavaria (*b* 9 Aug 1839; ✠ 29 Nov 1909) and his second wife, Infanta Maria Josefa of Portugal (*b* 19 March 1857; *m* 29 April 1874; ✠ 11 March 1943), *succ* his brother, Ludwig Wilhelm, Duke in Bavaria (*b* 17 Jan 1884; ✠ 5 Nov 1968). Succ by his Kinsman Max, Prince of Bavaria 18 March 1965 (see above) who had been adopted by his brother, Ludwig Wilhelm, Duke in Bavaria.

BELGIUM
(HOUSE OF SAXE-COBURG AND GOTHA)

Catholic: Prince Leopold of Saxe-Coburg and Gotha, Duke of Saxony (*b* 16 Dec 1790; ✠ 10 Dec 1865) was elected as King of the Belgians by the National Congress of Belgium 4 June 1831 and reigned as Leopold I, King of the Belgians from 21 July 1831.

Arms: Sa, a lion rampant or, armed and langued gu. *Supporters:* Two lions proper each holding a banner paly of three, sa, or and gu, bordered or. *Motto:* L'Union fait la force. The shield is surrounded by the Order of Leopold. The achievement is borne on a mantle purpure, fringed and tasselled or, doubled erm and surmounted by the Royal Crown.

Male primogeniture by the standards of Salic Law was abolished in 1991 by constitutional changes applying only to the descendants of Albert II, King of the Belgians. For such descendants succession in the direct line is by order of birth. Members of the Family bear the title of Prince or Princess of Belgium with the qualification of Royal Highness.

ALBERT II Felix Humbert Theodor Christian Eugène Marie, **KING OF THE BELGIANS,** *b* at Château de Stuyvenberg 6 June 1934, Dr h c University of Löwen, Gent, Brussels, Mons and St Louis (Philippines), Grand Master Order of Leopold, Kt Order of the Golden Fleece (*Austria and Spain*), Bailiff Gd Cross Hon and Dev Sovereign Military Order of Malta, *succ* his brother, Baudouin I, King of the Belgians (see below), son of Leopold III, King of the Belgians (*b* 3 Nov 1901; ✠ 25 Sept 1983; abdicated in favour of his eldest son 16 July 1951) and Princess Astrid of Sweden (*b* 17 Nov 1905; *m* 4/10 Nov 1926; ✠ 29 Aug 1935); *m* at Brussels 2 July 1959, Donna Paola (*b* at Forte dei Marmi, Italy 11 Sept 1937), Gd Cross Sovereign Military Order of Malta, dau of Don Fulco, Prince Ruffo di Calabria, Duke di Guardia Lombarda and Luisa Gazelli of the Counts di Rossana e di San Sebastiano.

[*Château de Belvédère, 1020 Laeken, Belgium*].

Sons and Daughter

1. Prince *Philippe* Leopold Louis Marie, Duke of Brabant, *b* at Château de Belvédère, nr Laeken 14 April 1960, Col. Belgian Army and Airforce, Gd Cross Sovereign Military Order of Malta; *m* at Hotel de Ville, Brussels (civ) and St Michael's Cathedral, Brussels (relig) 4 Dec 1999, *Mathilde* (*b* at Villers-la-Bonne-Eau, nr Bastogne 20 Jan 1973), *cr*. Princess of Belgium in her own right by Royal Decree 8 Nov 1999, dau of Count Patrick d'Udekem d'Acoz and Countess Anne Marie Komorowski.

[*Palais de Bruxelles, 1000 Brussels, Belgium*].

    1. Princess *Elisabeth* Thérèrese Marie Hélène, *b* at Anderlecht 25 Oct 2001.

2. Princess *Astrid* Josephine-Charlotte Fabrizia Elisabeth Paola Marie, *b* at Château de Belvédère 5 June 1962, President Belgian

Red Cross; *m* at Brussels 22 Sept 1984, Archduke *Lorenz* Otto Carl
Amedeo Thadeus Maria Pius Andreas Marcus d'Aviano, of Austria
and Archduke of Austria-Este, Duke of Este, Kt Order of the Golden
Fleece, Kt Hon and Dev Sovereign Military Order of Malta, Banker
(*b* at Boulogne-sur-Seine 16 Dec 1955), -*cr* Prince of Belgium by
Royal Decree 27 Nov 1995

[*Palais de Bruxelles, 1000 Brussels, Belgium*].

> 1. Prince *Amédéo* Maria Josef Carl Pierre Philippe
> Paola Marcus d'Aviano, (Prince of Belgium from 1991,
> following constitutional changes repealing the laws of
> succession by male primogeniture), Archduke of
> Austria-Este *b* at Woluwe St Lambert, Belgium 21
> Feb 1986.
> 2. Princess *Maria Laura* Zita Beatrix Gerhard,
> (Princess of Belgium from 1991, following constitutional
> changes repealing the laws of succession by male
> primogeniture), Archduchess of Austria *b* at Woluwe
> St Lambert 26 Aug 1988.
> 3. Prince *Joachim* Carl Maria Nikolaus Isabelle Marcus
> d'Aviano, (Prince of Belgium from birth), Archduke
> of Austria-Este *b* at Woluwe St Lambert 9 Dec 1991.
> 4. Princess *Luisa Maria* Anna Martine Pilar, (Princess
> of Belgium from birth), Archduchess of Austria *b* at
> Brussels 11 Oct 1995.

3. Prince *Laurent* Benoit Baudouin Marie, *b* at Château de Belvédère
19 Oct 1963.

[*Palais de Bruxelles, 1000 Brussels, Belgium*].

Brother and Sister

1. Princess *Joséphine Charlotte* Ingeborg Elisabeth Maria Josepha
Margarethe Astrid, *b* at Brussels 11 Oct 1927; *m* at Luxembourg 9
April 1953, Jean, Grand Duke of Luxembourg, Duke of Nassau (*b* at
Schloß Berg, Luxembourg 5 Jan 1921).

[*Schloß Berg, 7710 Colmar-Berg, Luxembourg*].

2. **Baudouin I** Albert Karl Leopold Axel Marie Gustav, **King of the
Belgians,** *b* at Château de Styvenberg 7 Sept 1930; ✠ at Motril,
Spain 31 July 1993, *succ* on his father's abdication 16 July 1951; *m* at
Brussels 15 Dec 1960, Doña Fabiola (*b* at Madrid 11 June 1928), dau
of Don Gonzalo Mora y Fernández, Count de Mora, Marquess of
Casa Riera and Doña Blanca de Aragón y Carillo de Albornoz.

[*Palais de Bruxelles, 1000 Brussels, Belgium*].

Half-Brother and Sisters
Issue of Leopold III, King of the Belgians (*see above*); *m* 2ndly at Laeken 11 Sept (civ) and 6 Dec (relig) 1941, Mary *Lilian b* at London 28 Nov 1916; ✣ at Waterloo 7 June 2002, (*who bore the title of Princess of Belgium with the qualification of Royal Highness and was created Princess Rethy*), dau of Henri Baels and Anne Marie de Visscher,and has issue (*who are non-dynastic in terms of the order of sucession to the Throne of Belgium*).

3. Prince *Alexandre* Emanuel Henry Albert Marie Leopold, *b* at Laeken 18 July 1942; *m* at Woodbridge, Suffolk 14 Mar 1991 Léa (*b* at Brussels 2 Dec 1951), dau of *Sigismund* Wellner Wolman and Lisa von Stein des Tilleuls
[*Avenue Rhode, 1640, St Genese, Belgium*].
4. Princess *Marie-Christine* Daphné Astrid Elisabeth Léopoldine, *b* at Laeken 6 Feb 1951; *m* at Coral Gables, Miami, Florida 23 May 1981 (*m* diss by div 9 July 1981), Paul Druker (*b* at Montreal 18 April 1938), Pianist. She *m* 2ndly at Westwood, Los Angeles, California 28 Sept 1989, Jean-Paul Gourgues (*b* at Bordeaux, France ..).
[*Domaine d'Argenteuil, 1410 Waterloo, Belgium*].
5. Princess Marie-*Esmeralda* Adelaid Lilian Anne Léopoldine, *b* at Laeken 30 Sept 1956, Journalist, *m* at.London 5 April 1998, Salvador Moncada, pharmacologist (*b* at El Savador 3 Dec 1944).
[*16 Park Village East, London NW1 7PX*].

Brother and Sister of Father
Issue of Albert I, King of the Belgians (*b* 8 April 1875; ✣ 17 Feb 1934) and Duchess Elisabeth in Bavaria (*b* 25 July 1876; *m* 2 Oct 1900; ✣ 23 Nov 1965), and has issue among whom

1. Prince *Charles* Théodore Henri Antoine Meinrad, Count of Flanders, Prince Regent of the Kingdom of Belgium 20 Sept 1944 - 20 July 1950, *b* at Brussels 10 Oct 1903; ✣ at Ostende 1 June 1983; *m* at Paris 14 Sept (relig only) 1977, Jacqueline (*b* at La Réole, Gironde 16 Feb 1921; *m* 1stly 18 Dec 1943, Georges Schaack who ✣ 24 Jan 1977), dau of Alfred Peyrebrune and Marie Madeleine Triaut,

BONAPARTE
(IMPERIAL HOUSE OF FRANCE)

Catholic:- Founded by François Bonaparte who ✝ at Ajaccio 1540.
Two descendants of Carlo Bonaparte (*b* at Ajaccio 29 March 1746; ✝
24 Feb 1785) became Emperors of the French. The branch below
descends from a younger brother of Napoleon I, Emperor of the
French from 18 May 1804 to 11 April 1814, and 1 March 1815 to 22
June 1815 (*b* at Ajaccio 15 Aug 1769; ✝ at St Helena 5 May 1821),
Jérome Bonaparte, King of Westphalia 8 July 1807 - 26 Oct 1813, *cr*
Prince of Montfort by King Friedrich I of Württemberg 31 July
1816, Gov-Gen of the Invalides and Marshal of France 1850, declared
Heir Presumptive of the (Second) Empire 18 Dec 1852 (in accordance
with Article III of Senatus-Consult of 7 Nov 1852), confirmed as
Prince français and Imperial Highness 23 Dec 1852 (*b* 15 Nov 1784; ✝
24 June 1860).
Arms:- Az, an antique eagle holding a thunderbolt or. The
achievement is borne on a mantle purpure, semée of bees or, fringed
and tasselled or, doubled erm and surmounted by the Imperial
Crown.
Members of the family bear the name of Napoléon and the title of
Prince or Princesse Français with the qualification of Imperial
Highness.

CHARLES Marie Jérôme Victor Napoléon, **PRINCE
NAPOLÉON,** *b* at Boulogne-sur- Seine 19 Oct 1950, son of Louis,
Prince Napoléon (*b* 23 Jan 1914; ✝ 3 May 1997) and Alix de Foresta
(*b* 4 April 1926; *m* 16 Aug 1949); *m* 1stly at Paris 19 Dec (civ) 1978 (*m*
diss by div at Nanterre 2 May 1989), Princess Béatrice (*b* at St
Raphaël, Dept Var 16 June 1950), [*31 Avenue du Parc Saint-James,
92200 Neuilly-sur-Seine, France*],dau of Don Ferdinand, Prince of
Bourbon-Two Sicilies, Duke of Castro and Chantal de Chevron-Villette
of the Counts Chevron-Villette. He *m* 2ndly 30 Oct 1996, Françoise
(*b* at Ortiporrio, Haute-Corse 26 March 1958; *m* 1stly at Casaglione,
Corsica 15 July 1978, Erik Langrais, *m* diss by div at Aix-en-Provence
24 July 1990), dau of Paul Louis Valliccionni and Padoue Piacentini.
[*129 rue Blomet, 75015 Paris, France*].

Son and Daughter - 1st Marriage

1. Princess *Caroline,* *b* at Paris 24 Oct 1980.
[*31 Avenue du Parc Saint-James, 92100 Neuilly-sur-Seine, France*].
2. Prince *Jean-Christophe* Louis Ferdinand Albéric, *b* at St Raphaël
11 July 1986.
[*31 Avenue du Parc Saint-James, 92100 Neuilly-sur-Seine, France*].

Daughter - 2nd Marriage

3. Princess *Sophie* Cathérine, *b* at Paris 18 April 1992.

Mother

Alix, Princess Napoléon, *b* at Marseille 4 April 1926, dau of Count Alberic de Foresta and Genevieve Frédet; *m* at Linières-Bouton, Dept Maine-et-Loire 16 Aug 1949, Louis, Prince Napoléon (*b* at Brussels 23 Jan 1914; ✢ at Prangins 3 May 1997), Cmdr Legion of Honour, Gd Officer Order of Léopold, Croix de guerre françaises et belges.
[*Villa de Prangins, 1197 Prangins, Kt. Vaud, Switzerland; 23 Rue Albéric Magnard, 75016 Paris, France*].

Brother and Sisters

2. Princess *Catherine* Elisabeth Alberique Marie, *b* at Boulogne-sur-Seine 19 Oct 1950 (twin with Prince Charles), *m* 1stly at Nyon, Vaud 4 June (civ) and 5 June (relig) 1974 (*m* diss by div 1981 and religiously annulled 1982), Nicolo San Martino d'Aglie di San Germano, Marquess di San Germano (*b* at Campiglione 3 July 1948). She *m* 2ndly at Paris 13 Oct 1982, Jean-Claude Dualé (*b* at Medjez-el-Bab, Tunisia 3 Nov 1936), Directeur de Société.
[*1 Square Racan, 75016 Paris, France*].

3. Princess *Laure* Clémentine Geneviève, *b* at Paris 8 Oct 1952, Sales Assistant; *m* at Grenoble, Dept Isère 23 Dec 1982, Jean-Claude Pierre Lecomte (*b* at Ax-les-Thermes 15 March 1948).
[*6 Rue Brocherie, 38000 Grenoble, France*].

4. Prince *Jérôme* Xavier Marie Joseph Victor, *b* at Boulogne-sur-Seine 14 Jan 1957, Librarian.
[*Villa de Prangins, 1197 Prangins, Kt. Vaud, Switzerland*].

BOURBON-ORLÉANS
(ROYAL HOUSE OF FRANCE)

Catholic:- Founded by Robert the Strong, Duke of France, Count of Paris, of Orléans and of Anjou (✢ in combat against the Norsemen 866); two of his sons became Kings of France: Eudes 888 - 898, and Robert I 922 - 923; Hugues Capet, grandson of Robert I, became King of France in 987; Bourbon was acquired by Robert of France, Count of Clermont, younger son of King Louis IX (St Louis) (*b* 1250; ✢ 1318), through marriage to Béatrice, daughter and heiress of Jean de Bourgogne (✠ 1268) and Agnes de Dampierre Bourbon; Bourbon was created a Duchy in favour of Louis, son of Robert, 27 Dec 1327. Through the extinction of the senior male lines, the branch of Bourbon came to the throne in the person of Henri III of Navarre (*b* 13 Dec 1553; ✠ 14 May 1610; Duke of Vendôme and of Beaumont, Comte de la Marche, d'Albret, de Foix, etc, who became King of France as Henri IV 2 Aug 1589; the remaining lines still extant descend from two sons of King Louis XIII (*b* 27 Sept 1601; ✠ 14 May 1643).

The line of Bourbon-Orléans was founded by Philippe, Duc d'Anjou (*b* 21 Sept 1640; ✠ 9 June 1701), later Duc d'Orléans (1660), of Valois (1693), of Chartres (1661), of Nemours (1672) and of Montpensier, Prince de Joinville, etc. The Dukes of Orléans bore the title of Premier Prince "du Sang". Louis Philippe, Duke of Orléans, Royal Highness (22 May 1824), reigned as King of the French 9 Aug 1830 to 24 Feb 1848; his grandson, Philippe (VII), Count of Paris (1838 - 1894) inherited the dignity of the Head of the House of France through the renunciation of King Philippe V of Spain, on the extinction of the premier line of the House of Bourbón 24 Aug 1883. *Arms:-* Az, three fleurs-de-lys or, a label argent. *Supporters:-* Two angels vested of a dalmatic crown of the arms of France, each holding a banner of the arms of France, all ppr. The Head of the House uses the plain Arms of France. *Crest:-* The oriflamme of Saint Denis. *War Cry:-* Montjoie, Saint Denis. *Mottoes:-* Lilia non laborant neque nent; Ex omnibus floribus elegi mihi lilium. The shield is encircled by the collars of the Orders of Saint Michael and of The Holy Ghost. The achievement is borne on a mantle az, semée of fleurs-de-lys or, doubled erm, fringed and tasselled or and surmounted by the Royal Crown of France.

Members of the Royal House of France bear the title of Prince or Princess of Bourbon-Orléans with the qualification of Royal Highness. Some members of the Royal Family also bear differing titles granted by the Head of the Royal House. *(See Appendix V).*

HENRI VII Philippe Pierre Marie, **COUNT OF PARIS, DUKE OF FRANCE,** regarded by the majority of French monarchists and royalists as Henri VII, King of France and Navarre, *b* at the Manoir d'Anjou, Woluwé-Saint-Pierre, nr Brussels 14 June 1933, Consul for Int'l Commercial Exchange, Lt French Army, Bailiff Gd Cross Constantinian Order of St George, son of Henri VI, Count of Paris (*b* 5 July 1908; ✠ 19 June 1999) and Princess Isabelle of Orléans and Bragança (*b* 13 Aug 1911; *m* 8 April 1931); *m* 1stly at Dreux 5 July 1957 (legally *sep* at Paris 23 Feb 1977; *m* diss by div at Paris 3 Feb 1984), Duchess Marie Thérèse (*b* at Schloß Altshausen 12 Nov 1934), Dame of Justice Gd Cross Constantinian Order of St George, granted the title of Duchess of Montpensier *ad personam* at Paris 22

Feb 1984 [*10 rue Duras, 75008 Paris, France*], dau of Philipp, Duke of Württemberg and Archduchess Rosa of Austria. He *m* 2ndly at Bordeaux 31 Oct 1984, Micaela (*b* at Vichy, Allier 30 April 1938; *m* 1stly at Saint-Cloud 12 June 1961, Jean Robert Francis-Boeuf; that *m* diss by div at Paris 24 May 1966), granted the title of Princess of Joinville, dau of Luis Maximiliano Cousiño y Sebire and Antonia Maria Micaela Quinones de Léon y Banuelos, Marchioness de San Carlos, and has issue by his first wife,
[*74 rue des Cévennes, 75015 Paris, France*].

Sons and Daughters

1. Princess *Marie* Isabelle Marguerite Anne Genevieve, *b* at Boulogne-Billancourt 3 Jan 1959; *m* at Dreux, Dept Eure et Loire 22 July (civ) and at Friedrichshafen 29 July (relig) 1989, Gundakar, Prince von and zu Liechtenstein (*b* at Vienna 1 April 1949), Mag rer soc et oec. [*Herrenhub, 3051 St. Christophen, Lower Austria; Caixa Postal 117, 78400-000 Diamantino, Mato Grosso, Brazil*].

2. Prince *François* Henri Louis Marie, *b* at Boulogne-Billancourt 7 Feb 1961, Count of Clermont.
[*10 rue Duras, 75008 Paris, France*].

3. Princess *Blanche* Elisabeth Rose Marie, Mademoiselle de Valois, *b* at Ravensburg, Württemberg 10 Sept 1962.
[*10 rue Duras, 75008 Paris, France*].

4. Prince *Jean* Carl Pierre Marie, *b* at Boulogne-Billancourt, 19 May 1965, Duke of Vendôme.
[*10 rue Duras, 75008 Paris, France*].

5. Prince *Eudes* Thibaut Joseph Marie, Duke of Angoulême, *b* at Paris 18 March 1968; *m* at Dreux 19 June 1999, Countess Marie-Liesse (*b* at Paris 25 June 1969), dau of Count *Louis* Meriadek Alain Marie Jean de Rohan-Chabot and *Isabelle* Marie Laurence Mathilde de Beauffremont Courtenal, Princess de Marnay of the Dukes of Beauffremont.

    1. Princess *Thérèse, b* at Cannes 23 April 2001.

Brothers and Sisters

1. Princess *Isabelle* Marie Laure Victoire, *b* at the Manoir d'Anjou 8 April, 1932, Dame Star Cross Order, Dame of Hon and Dev Sovereign Military Order of Malta; *m* at Louveciennes, Yvelines 9 Sept (civ) and at Dreux 10 Sept (relig) 1964, Friedrich Karl, Count von Schönborn-Buchheim (*b* at Schloß Schönborn 30 March 1938).
[*Schloß Weyerburg, 2031 Eggendorf im Thales, NÖsterr.,*

Austria].

2. Princess *Hélène* Astrid Leopoldine Marie, *b* at the Manoir d'Anjou 17 Sept 1934, Dame of Hon and Dev Sovereign Military Order of Malta; *m* at Louveciennes 16 Jan (civ) and at Dreux 17 Jan (relig) 1957, Évrard, Count van Limburg Stirum (*b* at the Château d'Huldenberg, Saint-Joris Weert, Brabant, Belgium 31 Oct 1927; ✝ at Brussels 5 March 2001), Bailiff Gd Cross Sovereign Military Order of Malta.

[*Schloßpark 4, 3040 Huldenberg, Brabant, Belgium*].

3. Prince *François* Gaston Michel Marie, *b* at the Manoir d'Anjou 15 Aug 1935; ✝*k* in action at Taouriat, Algeria 11 Oct 1960, *cr* Duke of Orléans posthumously by his father, Sub-Lt 7th Bn Chasseurs Alpins, served in Algeria, awarded posthumously the Croix de la valeur militaire and medaille commemorative d'Algerie, Kt Legion of Honour.

4. Princess *Anne* Marguerite Brigitte Marie, *b* at the Manoir d'Anjou 4 Dec 1938, Dame Gd Cross Constantinian Order of St George; *m* at Louveciennes 11 May (civ) and at Dreux 12 May (relig) 1965, Don Carlos, Infante of Spain, Prince of Bourbon-Two Sicilies, Duke of Calabria, (*b* at Lausanne, Switzerland 16 Jan 1938), Banker.

[*José Ortega y Gasset 26, 28006 Madrid, Spain*].

5. Princess *Diane* Françoise Maria, *b* at Petrópolis, Brazil 24 March 1940, Dame Gd Cross Constantinian Order of St George; *m* at Altshausen, Württemberg 18 July (civ) and 21 July (relig) 1960, Carl, Duke of Württemberg, Head of the Royal House (*b* at Schloß Friedrichshafen 1 Aug 1936).

[*7963 Schloß Altshausen, Kr. Ravensburg, Germany; 7990 Schloß Friedrichshafen, Württ., Germany*].

6. Prince *Michel* Joseph Benoit Marie, Count of Évreux; *b* at Rabat, Morocco 25 June 1941; *m* (declared non-dynastic by his father) at the French Consulat General, Casablanca 17 Nov (civ) and at the Church of Notre-Dame des Flots, Aïn-Diab, nr Casablanca 18 Nov (relig) 1967 (separated Madrid 1994), Béatrice (*b* at Neuilly-sur-Seine 24 Oct 1941), dau of Count Bruno Pasquier de Franclieu and Jacqueline Térisse, and has issue,

[*Calle de Alfonso XII 50, 28014 Madrid, Spain*].

    1. Princess *Clotilde* Jacqueline Charlotte Marie, *b* at Casablanca 28 Dec 1968; *m* at Neuilly-sur-Seine 26 June (civ) and at Villamanrique de la Condesa, Spain 18 Sept (relig) 1993, Edouard Crépy (*b* at Croix, Nord 19 Jan 1969).

    2. Princess *Adelaide* Jeanne Marie, *b* at Paris XV 11 Sept

1971; *m* at Fontainebleau 27 April (civ) and at Villamanrique de la Condessa, Seville 1 June (relig) 2002, Pierre-Louis Dailly (*b* at ......).

3. Prince *Charles-Philippe* Marie Louis, *b* at Paris XV 3 March 1973.

4. Prince *François* Charles Frederic Bruno Marie, *b* at Madrid 10 Feb 1982.

7. Prince *Jacques* Jean Yaroslaw Marie, Duke of Orléans, *b* at Rabat, Morocco 25 June 1941 (twin with Prince Michel), *m* at Ansouis, Vaucluse 2 Aug (civ) and 3 Aug (relig) 1969, Gersende (*b* at Château d'Ansouis 29 July 1942) dau of Foulques de Sabran Pontevès, 6th Duke de Sabran and Roselyne Mancat-Amat de Vallombrosa, and has issue,

[*3 Place Vauban, 75007 Paris, France*].

1. Princess *Diane* Marie Laure, *b* at Neuilly-sur-Seine 24 June 1970.

2. Prince *Charles-Louis* Henri Foulques Benoît Elzéar Jean Marie, Duke of Chartres, *b* at Neuilly-sur-Seine 11 July 1972; *m* at Dreux 20 June (civ) and at Athens 28 June (relig) 1997, Iléana (*b* at Athens 22 Sept 1970), dau of Konstantinos Manos and Sybille Chrissoveloni.

    1. Prince *Philippe*, *b* at Buenos Aires 3 Nov 1998.

    2. Princess *Louise*, *b*.at Paris 6 Dec 1999

    3. Princess *Hélène*, *b* at Paris 24 Jan 2001.

3. Prince *Foulques* Thibaut Robert Jacques Géraud Jean Marie, Duke of Aumale, Count of Eu, *b* at Paris XVIII 9 July 1974.

8. Princess *Claude* Marie Agnès Catherine, *b* at Larache, Morocco 11 Dec 1943, Dame Gd Cross Constantinian Order of St George; *m* 1stly at Sintra, Portugal 22 July 1964 (legally *sep* at Florence 20 July 1976; *m* diss by div at Port au Prince, Haiti 26 April 1982 and annulled at Rome 9 Jan 1987), Prince Amedeo of Savoy, 5th Duke of Aosta (*b* at the Palazzo della Cisterna, Florence 27 Sept 1943). She *m* 2ndly at Port au Prince 27 April 1982 (that *m* diss by div), Arnaldo R La Cagnina (*b* at Rome 26 June 1929), Art Publisher.

9. Princess *Chantal* Alice Clotilde Marie, *b* at Pamplona, Navarre 9 Jan 1946, *m* at Dreux 28 July 1972, Baron François-Xavier de Sambucy de Sorgue (*b* at Montmajour, Bouches-du-Rhône 20 Aug 1943), Engineer.

10. Prince *Thibaut* Louis Denis Humbert Marie, Count de La Marche, *b* at Ranholas, nr Sintra, Portugal 20 Jan 1948; ✝ at Bamangui,

Central Africa 23 March 1983; *m* (declared non-dynastic by his father) at Edinburgh 23 Sept 1972, Marion (*b* at Santiago, Chile 4 Sept 1941), dau of James Gordon-Orr and Mercédès Devia, and had issue, among whom,
[*Ferme de l'Ecu, 29 rue de la Porte-Saint-Martin, 78770 Thoiry, France*].

> 1. Prince *Robert* Benoit Paul Henri James Marie, Count de La Marche, petit fils de france, *b* at Edinburgh 6 Sept 1976.

Mother

Isabelle, Dowager Countess of Paris, Dame Star Cross Order, *b* at Château d'Eu 13 Aug 1911, dau of Prince Dom Pedro de Alcantara of Orléans and Bragança, Prince of Grão Para and Countess Elisabeth Dobrzensky von Dobrzenicz; *m* at at Palermo 8 April 1931, Henri (VI) Robert Ferdinand Marie Louis Philippe, Count of Paris (*b* at the Château de Nouvion en Thiérache, Aisne 5 July 1908; ✝ at Dreux 19 June 1999).
[*121 bis rue de Miromesnil, 75008 Paris, France*].

BOURBON PARMA

In 1545 Pope Paul III (Alessandro Farnese) ceded the towns of Parma and Piacenza to his natural son Pier Luigi Farnese (✝ 10 Sept 1547) and the Emperor Karl V raised them into a Duchy the same year. The Farnese male line became extinct on the death of Antonio Francesco 20 Jan 1731. His niece and heiress Doña Isabella Farnese, wife of Felipe V, King of Spain, transmitted her rights to her son Don Carlos (later King Carlos III of Spain) who became Duke of Parma and Piacenza in 1731 (giving up the Duchy by the Treaty of Vienna of 1736 but retaining the title and rights of succession to the Farnese inheritance, which included the Grand Magistery of the Constantinian Order). By the Treaty of Aix-la-Chapelle of 1748, Isabel's second son Don Felipe (Filippo) (*b* 15 March 1720; ✝ 18 July 1765) was established as Duke of Parma, Plaisance and Guastalla (this former Gonzaga Duchy an addition to the State). Following the deposition of the Grand Duke of Tuscany, the Grand Duchy territories with the Duchy of Parma combined into the Kingdom of Etruria 1801 - 1807 for the reigning Duke Carlo Lodovico (*b* 22 Dec 1799; ✝ 16 April 1884), a minor, under the Regency of his mother, Infanta Doña Maria Luisa, as part of the Napoleonic settlement with Spain; given the Duchy of Lucca in 1815 in compensation the loss of Parma (accorded to the former Empress Marie-Louise of the French for her lifetime), but deposed 15 Oct 1847; reacquired the Duchy of Parma 17 Dec 1847; annexed to the Kingdom of Sardinia in 1859; formal protestation of the annexation was made by the Duchess Regent, on behalf of her son Don Roberto I, 20 June 1860. For the early ancestry of the Bourbons - see FRANCE and SPAIN.

Arms:- Quarterly of ten: 1st, or, six fleurs-de-lys az, three, two and one (Farnese); 2nd, arg, a cross patée gu, between four eagles displayed sa, beaked and membered gu (Gonzaga for Guastalla); 3rd, az, a lion bendy gu and arg, crowned or (Rossi di San Secondo); 4th, or, six torteaux, one, two, two and one, the chiefmost absconded by a heurte charged with three fleurs-de-lys or, the other five gu (Medici); 5th, per fesse gu and or, and over all a bush without leaves, sa (Malaspina); 6th, arg, an eagle sa, beaked and membered gu, crowned or, charged on the breast with an escutcheon gu, a cross arg (Savoy); 7th, gu a fess arg (Correggio); 8th, checky gu and arm, or a chief or, a double-headed eagle sa, beaked and membered gu (Pallavicini); 9th, gu, a cross or, between four letters B or (Paleologue); 10th, grand-quarters, 1st and 4th, paly of six or and arg and over all a fesse arg 2nd and 3rd, or, three bars wavy az (Landi); over all an inescutcheon of pretence, counter quarter, 1st and 4th, gu, a castle or, masoned sa, port and fenestration az (Castile); 2nd and 3rd arg, a lion rampant gu, armed, langued and crowned or (Leon), and over all an escutcheon of pretence, az, three fleurs-de-lys or, a bordure gu, charged with eight scallops arg (Bourbón-Anjou). The shield is encircled with the collar of the Order of Constantine of Parma and ensigned by the Royal Crown. *Motto:-* Deus et dies.

Members of the Ducal Family bear the title of Prince or Princess of Bourbón Parma with the qualification of Royal Highness.

Don Hugues **CARLOS HUGO** Xavier Marie Sixte Louis Robert Jean Georges Benoit Michel, **DUKE OF PARMA** and Piacenza, Prince and Head of the Royal House of Bourbón Parma, Grand Master Constantinian Order of St George, Grand Master Royal Order of St Lodovico, *b* at Paris XVI 8 April 1930, assumed Carlist leadership 8 April 1975, naturalised in Spain as Carlos-Hugo de Borbón-Parma y Borbón by Royal Decree 5 Jan 1979, son of Xavier, Duke of Parma, etc (*b* 25 May 1889; ✝ 7 May 1977) and Madeleine de Bourbón-Busset (*b* at Paris 25 March 1898; *m* 12 Nov 1927; ✝ 1 Sept 1984); *m* at the French Consulate, Rome (civ) and at the Borghese Chapel, Church of Santa Maria Maggiore, Rome 29 April 1964 (*m* diss by div at Utrecht 26 May 1981), Princess Irene (*Schloß Soestdijk, Baarn, Prov. Utrecht, Netherlands*) (*b* at Soestdijk Palace, Baarn, Utrecht 5 Aug 1939), converted to Catholicism at Rome 3 Jan 1964, dau of Bernhard, Prince of Lippe-Biesterfeld, Prince of the Netherlands and Juliana, Queen of the Netherlands.

[*Las Nozias, Bl. 12-2B, Claveles 43, 28220 Majadahonda, Prov. Madrid, Spain*].

Sons and Daughters

1. Prince Don *Carlos* Xavier Bernardo Sixto Maria, Grand Chancellor Constantinian Order of St George, Grand Cross and Senator Royal Order of St Lodovico, *b* at Nimeguen, Netherlands 27 Jan 1970, *cr* Prince of Piacenza by his father 2 Sept 1996.

2. Prince Don *Jaime* Bernardo, Grand Chancellor Royal Order of St Lodovico, Grand Cross and Senator Constantinian Order of St George, *b* at Nimeguen 13 Oct 1972, *cr* Count of Bardi by his father 2 Sept 1996.

3. Princess Doña *Marguerite* Marie Beatrice Grand Cross and Senator Constantinian Order of St George, Grand Cross and Senator Royal Order of St Lodovico, *b* at Nimeguen 13 Oct 1972 (twin with Prince Jacques), *cr* Countess of Colorno by her father 2 Sept 1996; *m* at Amsterdam 19 June (civ) and at Auch, France 22 Sept (relig) 2001, Edwin Karel Willem de Roy van Zuydewijn (*b* at Amsterdam 19 June 1966).
[*Château de Barthas, St. Georges, Gers, France*].

4. Princess Doña Marie-*Carolina* Christine Grand Cross and Senator Constantinian Order of St George, Grand Cross and Senator Royal Order of St Lodovico, *b* at Nimeguen 23 June 1974, *cr* Marchioness of Sala by her father 2 Sept 1996.

Brother and Sisters

1. Princess Doña Marie *Françoise* Antoinette Jeanne Madeleine, *b* at Paris 19 Aug 1928, Dame Gd Cross Hon and Dev Sovereign Military Order of Malta, Dame Com Order of the Holy Sceptre; *m* at Besson, Allier 11 Dec 1959 (civ) and at Paris 7 Jan 1960 (relig), Eduard, Prince of Lobkowicz (*b* at New York 12 June 1926), Bailiff Gd Cross Hon and Dev Sovereign Military Order of Malta.
[*30 avenue Marceau, 75008 Paris, France; Manoir d'Ujezd, Grainville Ymauville, 76110 Goderville, France*].

2. Princess Doña *Marie-Thérèse* Cécile Zita Charlotte, Grand Cross and Senator Constantinian Order of St George, Grand Cross and Senator Royal Order of St Lodovico, *b* at Paris 28 July 1933, Dr soc.
[*Las Norias, Claveles 43, Bloque 12-2B, 28220 Majadahonda, Prov. Madrid, Spain*].

3. Princess Doña *Cécile* Marie Antoinette Madeleine Jeanne Agnes Françoise, Grand Cross and Senator Constantinian Order of St George, Grand Cross and Senator Royal Order of St Lodovico, Dame Gd Cross Hon and Dev Sovereign Military Order of Malta, *b* at Paris

12 April 1935.

[*45 rue Notre Dame des Champs, 75006 Paris, France*].

4. Princess Doña *Marie-des-Neiges* Madeleine Françoise, Grand Cross and Senator Constantinian Order of St George, Grand Cross and Senator Royal Order of St Lodovico, *b* at Paris 29 April 1937, Dr Biologist.

[*El Pinar del Plantillo, Calle Ateanea 2, 28220 Majadahonda, Prov. Madrid, Spain*].

5. Prince Don *Sixte Henri* Hugues François Xavier, *b* at Pau, Béarn 22 July 1940.

[*38 bis rue Fabert, 75007 Paris, France*].

Half-Brother and Brothers of Father

Issue of Don Roberto I, Duke of Parma (*b* 9 July 1848; ✝ 16 Nov 1907) and Princess Doña Maria Pia delle Grazie of Bourbon-Two Sicilies (*b* 2 Aug 1849; *m* 5 April 1869; ✝ 29 Sept 1882), having had issue, among whom,

Sons

1. Don **Elias I (Élie I)** Roberto Carlo Maria Pio Giuseppe, **Duke of Parma and Piacenza,** *b* at Biarritz 23 July 1880; ✝ at Friedberg, Austria 27 June 1959, acted as head of the Ducal Family from the death of his father in 1907; *m* at Vienna 25 May 1903, Archduchess Maria Anna (*b* at Linz 6 Jan 1882; ✝ at Laussanne 25 Feb 1940), dau of Archduke Friedrich of Austria, Duke of Teschen and Princess Nathalie von Croÿ, and had issue, among whom,

    1. Don **Roberto II (Robert II)** Ranieri Alexis Luigi Enrico Deodato Elias Pio Maria, **Duke of Parma and Piacenza,** *b* at Weilburg, nr Baden, Lower Austria 7 Aug 1909; *dunm* at Vienna 22 Nov 1974.

    2. Princess Doña Alice (*Alicia*) Maria Teresa Francesca Luisa Pia Anna Valeria, *b* at Vienna 13 Nov 1917, Dame Gd Cross Constantinian Order of St George; *m* there 16 April 1936, Prince Don Alfonso of Bourbon-Two Sicilies, Duke of Calabria, Infant of Spain (*b* at Madrid 30 Nov 1901; ✝ there 3 Feb 1964).

[*Hermanos Pinzón 4, 28016 Madrid, Spain*].

    3. Princess Doña Maria Cristina (*Marie Christine*) Albertina Enrichetta Luisa Pia Carlotta, *b* at Vienna 7 June 1925, Dame Gd Cross Constantinian Order of St George.

[*Metternichgasse 7, 1030 Vienna, Austria*].

Don Roberto I, Duke of Parma *m* 2ndly, Infanta Maria Antonia of
Portugal (*b* 28 Nov 1862; *m* 15 Oct 1884; ✠ 14 May 1959), and by her
had further issue, among whom,

    2. Prince Don Sisto (*Sixte*) Ferdinando Maria Ignazio Alfonso
Roberto Michael Francesco Carlo Luigi Saverio Guiseppe
Antonio Pio Taddeo Giovanni Sebastiano Paolo Biagio
Estanislao Bernedetto Bernardo Marco, *b* at Wartegg 1 Aug
1886; ✠ at Paris 14 March 1934, author of historical works; *m*
at Paris 12 Nov 1919 Hedwige (*b* at Paris 15 Feb 1896; ✠ at
Paris 7 May 1986), dau of Armand de la Rochefoucauld, Duke
de Bisaccia, 5th Duke de Doudeauville and Princess Louise
Radziwill, and had issue,

        1. Princess Doña *Isabelle* Marie Antoinette Louise
Hedwige, *b* at Paris 14 March 1922; *m* there 23 June
1943 (*m* diss by div at Paris 22 June 1966), Roger,
Count de La Rochefoucauld of the Dukes d'Estissac (*b*
at Paris 8 Oct 1915; ✠*k* in a flying accident nr St
Germain-les-Paroisses, Dept Ain 13 April 1970).
*[107 avenue Henri-Martin, 75016 Paris, France;
Château de Bonnetable, 72110 Bonnetable, France]*.

    3. Prince Don Renato (*René*) Carlo Maria Giuseppe, *b* at
Schwartzau 17 Oct 1894; ✠ at Hellerup 30 July 1962; *m* at
Copenhagen 9 June 1921, Princess Margrethe (*b* at
Bernstorffshoj 17 Sept 1895; ✠ at Brødrehøj 18 Sept 1992),
dau of Prince Valdemar of Denmark and Princess Marie of
Bourbón-Orléans, and had issue,

        1. Prince Don *Jacques* Marie Antoine Robert Valdemar
Charles Felix Sixte Ansgar, *b* at Longwy, France 9
June 1922; ✠ nr Roskilde, Denmark 5 Nov 1964; *m* at
Ledreborg 9 June 1947, Countess Birgitte (*b* at
Ledreborg 29 June 1922), dau of Joseph, Count
Holstein-Ledreborg and Countess Christina Hamilton,
and had issue,

           1. Prince Don *Philippe* Georg Karl *b* at Hellerup,
nr Copenhagen 22 Jan 1949; *m* at Ledreborg 5
May 1979 (non-dynastic), Annette (*b* at Køge,
Seeland, Denmark 24 April 1955), dau of Carl
Christian Smith and Lise Andersen, and has
issue,
[Kisserupvej 5, 4320 Lejre, Denmark].

1. *Jacques* Carl Christian Marie, *b* at
Roskilde 3 Jan 1986.
2. *Joseph* Axel Alain Erik Marie, *b* at
Roskile 6 June 1989.

2. Princess Doña *Lorraine* Charlotte Tatjana Ebba
Jeanne Maria Antonia Josephine Renée, *b* at Roskilde
27 July 1951.
[*Fredshoj, 4320 Lejre, Denmark*].

3. Prince Don *Alain* Jean Knud Bernard Félix Marie
René Joseph, *b* at Roskilde 15 May 1955.
[*Hvalsøvej 375, 4330 Hvalse, Denmark*].

2. Princess Doña *Anne* Antoinette Françoise Charlotte, *b* at
Paris 18 Sept 1923, converted to Eastern Orthodoxy; *m* at
Athens 10 June 1948, Michael I, King of Romania (*b* at Sinaia
25 Oct 1921).
[*77 chemin Louis Degallier, 1290 Versoix, Kt. Genf,
Switzerland*].

3. Prince Don *Michel* Marie Xavier Valdemar Georges Robert
Charles Aymard, *b* at Paris 4 March 1926, Factory Director;
m at Paris 9 June 1951 (*m* diss by div at Paris 22 June 1966),
Princess Yolande (*71 blvd Saint Antoine, 78000 Versailles,
France*) (*b* at Paris 26 April 1928), dau of Prince Joseph de
Broglie-Revel and Marguerite (Daisy) de la Cour Balleroy,
and has issue, among whom,
[*Le Buisson, 69 boulevard St. Antoine, 78000 Versailles,
France*].

1. Prince Don *Eric* Marie Joseph René Michel Pierre,
b at Copenhagen 28 Aug 1953; *m* at Ledreborg 8 Aug
1980 (*m* diss by div 2000), Countess Lydia (*b* at Roskilde
22 Feb 1955), dau of Knud, Count (Lensgreve) Holstein-
Ledreborg, af Ledreborg and Princess Marie Gabrielle
of Luxemburg, Bourbón Parma and of Nassau, and has
issue,
[*69 boulevard St. Antoine, 78000 Versailles, France*].
1. Princess Doña *Antonia* Monique Charlotte
Marie, *b* at Roskilde 10 June 1981.
2. Princess Doña *Marie Gabrielle* Yolande
Camilla Philippine, *b* at Paris 23 Dec 1982.
3. Princess Doña *Alexia* Thérèse Sybille Eric
Charles Marie, *b* at Palm Beach, Florida 7
March 1985.

    4. Prince Don *Michel* Knud John Joseph Marie, *b* at Lejre, nr Roskilde 12 Feb 1989.

    5. Prince Don *Henri* Luitpold Antoine Victor Marie Joseph, *b* at Roskilde 14 Oct 1991.

2. Princess Doña *Sybil* Marie Josèphe Anne Victoire, *b* at Paris 10 Nov 1954; *m* at Versilles 5 Dec 1997, Craig Richards (*b* at Wales 22 Apri 1962).

3. Princess Doña *Victoire* Maria Pia Josèphe Philippe Isaure, *b* at Boulogne-Billancourt 8 Nov 1957, ✝ at Neuilly sur Seine 24 Jan 2001; *m* Paris 25 Feb (civ) and at Beaumont le Roger, Eure 26 Feb (relig) 1974 (*m* diss by div at Paris Dec 1988), Alexis, Baron von Gecmen-Waldeck (*b* at Prague 11 July 1943), Businessman.

5. Prince Don Charles (*Charles Emmanuel*) Marie Joseph Jacques Hély, *b* at Paris 3 June 1961; *m* at Dampierre 25 May 1991 (relig), Constance (*b* at Paris 18 July 1971), dau of Baron Yves de Ravinel and Countess Alexe de Castellane, and has issue,
[*69 boulevard St. Antoine, 78000 Versailles, France*].

    1. Prince Don *Amaury* Yves Michel Marie Joseph, *b* at Boulogne-Billancourt, Paris 30 Oct1991.

    2. Princess Doña *Charlotte* Alexe Yolande Marie Joseph, *b* at Boulogne-Billancourt, Paris 18 July 1993.

    3. Princess Doña *Elizabeth,* *b* at Boulogne-Billancourt, Paris 12 June 1996.

    4. Princess Doña *Zita,* *b* at Boulogne-Billancourt, Paris 1 April 1999.

4. Prince Don *André* Marie, *b* at Paris 6 March 1928, Dipl Econ; *m* at Paris 2 May (civ) and at Villefranche, nr Nice 9 May (relig) 1960, Marina (*b* at Paris 5 Sept 1935), dau of Paul Gacry and Yvonne Dessaules, and has issue,
[*Hameau de Plateau 91410, Roinville S/Dourdan, France*].

    1. Sophie (*Tania*) Marie Margarethe Carole Yvonne de Bourbon, *b* 13 Nov 1961; *m* at La Bussiere, Vienna 8 July (civ) and at Buisson, Lozère, France 9 Aug (relig) 1988, Gilbert (*Gaya*) Silly (dit Bécaud) (*b* at Paris 3 Jan 1971).

    2. *Astrid* Marie de Bourbon, *b* at Paris 29 Sept 1964.

3. *Axel* Andre Pierre Marie de Bourbon, *b* 19 Sept 1968; *m* at St Sauver-de-Peyre 17 Aug (civ) and at Loiret 14 Sept (relig) 1996, Raphaële (*b* at Paris 9 June 1971), dau of Jean Paul Bonnes and Ghisliane de Montangon, and has issue,

[7 rue Jean Formige, 75015, Paris, France]

    1. *Côme* de Bourbon, *b* at Neuilly 7 May 1997.

    2. *Alix* de Bourbon, *b* at Paris 26 March 2002.

7. Prince Don Luigi (*Louis*) Carlo Maria Leopoldo Roberto, *b* at Schwarzau 5 Dec 1899; ✠ at Mandelieu 4 Dec 1967, Kt of Hon and Dev Sovereign Military Order of Malta; *m* at Rome 23 Jan 1939, Princess Maria (*b* at Rome 26 Dec 1914; ✠ at Mandelieu 4 Dec 2001), Dame Star Cross Order, Dame of Hon and Dev Sovereign Military Order of Malta, dau of Vittorio Emanuele III, King of Italy and Princess Elena of Montenegro, and had issue,

1. Prince Don Guido (*Guy*) Sisto Luigi Roberto Vittorio, *b* at Cannes 7 Aug 1940; ✠ at Paris 9 March 1991; *m* (non-dynastic) at Cannes 10 July (civ) and 11 July (relig) 1964 (*m* diss by div at Nanterre, Hauts de Seine 17 Sept 1981), Brigitte (*b* at Cannes 13 Aug 1943; ✠ at Lausanne 25 Feb 1993), dau of Victor Peu-Duvallon and Maria (Nina) Munzinger, and has issue,

    1. *Louis* Victor-Emmanuel Sixte Robert, *b* at Paris 25 June 1966; *m* at Prangins, Switzerland 11 May 1990, Ariane Nicolet (*b* at Tramelan, Switzerland 16 Jan 1966), and has issue,

        1. *Delphine*, *b* at Lausanne 11 July 1992.

        2. *Guy*, *b* at Genolier, Vaud 6 Feb 1995.

2. Prince Don Remigio (*Remy*) Francesco Saverio Luigi Roberto Vittorio, *b* at Cannes 14 July 1942; *m* at Saint-Prix, Val d'Oise 8 Feb (civ) and at Paris 10 Feb (relig) 1973 (*m* diss by div at Paris 21 March 1983), Laurence (*10 rue du Dr. Calmette, Les Oliviers, 06110 Le Cannet, France*) (*b* at Paris VIII 18 Jan 1951), dau of Christian Dufresne d'Arganchy and Geneviève Normand, and has issue,

[Mas Saint Rémy, 00210 Mandelieu, Alpes Maritimes]

    1. *Tristan* Louis Christian Theirry Marie, *b* at Cannes 30 June 1974.

    2. *Aude* Marie Geneviéve Jeanne, *b* at Cannes 26 Jan 1977.

3. Princess Doña Jeanne de *Chantal* Marie Hélène Antoinette

Charlotte, *b* at Cannes 24 Nov 1946; *m* 1stly at Mandelieu 1
July (civ) and at Cannes 23 Sept (relig) 1977 (*m* diss by div at
Paris 26 Nov 1986), Panayotis Skinas (*b* at Athens 8 March
1937), Art Expert. She *m* 2ndly at Sainte-Thorette, Cher 24
Sept 1988, François Henri des Georges (*b* at Nice 4 March
1941).

4. Prince Don *Jean* Bernard Remy, *b* at Cannes 15 Oct 1961,
Bank Assistant; *m* at Antibes, Alpes Maritimes 25 March
(civ) and at Juan-les-Pins, Alpes Maritimes 26 March (relig)
1988 (*m* diss by div at Grasse 9 June 1998), Virginie (*b* at
Saint-Chamond, Dept Loire 31 Aug 1964), Book-keeper, dau
of Guy Roatta and Andrée Obeniche, and has issue,
[*Mas Saint-Rémy, 06210 Mandelieu, Alpes Maritimes, France*].

    1. *Arnaud* Pascual Dominique Louis Marie Alphonse,
    b at Cannes 26 Oct 1989.

    2. *Christophe*, *b* at Mandelieu 4 July 1991.

8. Prince Don Gaetano (*Gaëtan*) Maria Giuseppe Pio, *b* at Pianore
11 June 1905; ✠ at Mandelieu 9 March 1958; *m* at Paris 29 April
1931 (*m* diss by div at Budapest 30 Aug 1940 and at Paris 24 Jan
1950), Princess Margarete (*b* at Beloeil, Belgium 8 Nov 1909), dau of
Alexander, Prince von Thurn and Taxis, 1st Duke di Castel-Duino,
and Princess Marie de Ligne, and had issue,
[*Hotel Atlantico, 55042 Forte dei Marmi, Prov. Lucca, France*].

    1. Princess Doña *Diane* Marguerite, *b* at Paris 22 May 1932,
    m 1stly in London 15 March (civ) and at Krauchenwies, nr
    Sigmaringen 16 April (relig) 1955 (*m* diss by div at Stuttgart
    19 Jan 1961 and annulled 17 Jan 1980), Prince Franz Joseph
    of Hohenzollern (*b* at Schloß Umkirch 15 March 1926; ✠ at
    Sigmaringen 13 March 1996; *m* 1stly at Regensburg 15 July
    1950, Princess Fernanda von Thurn and Taxis; that *m* diss by
    div at Freiburg im Breisgau 30 Oct 1951 and annulled 7 Dec
    1954). She *m* 2ndly at Stuttgart 21 March 1961, Hans Joachim
    Oehmichen (*b* at Barnitz, Meissen 4 April 1920; ✠ at Bad
    Krozingen 11 July 1995).
    [*Graser Weg 3, 79189 Bad Kronzingen, Germany*].

———◆◆◆———

BOURBON-TWO SICILIES

**Founded by Infante Ferdinando of Spain (*b* 12 Jan 1751; ✠ 4 Jan
1825), to whom his father, Carlos III, King of Spain (see SPAIN)
abdicated as King of Naples and Sicily 6 Oct 1759, in the Pragmatic**

Decree which required that the Crowns of Spain and the Two Sicilies not be united in the same person, but which gave reciprocal rights to both thrones to all his male descendants. Ferdinand reigned as Ferdinando IV, King of Naples and Ferdinando III, King of Sicily, and from 8 Dec 1816 as Ferdinando I of the Kingdom of the Two Sicilies. The dynasty ceased to reign when the Kingdom of the Two Sicilies was annexed to the new Kingdom of Italy 17 Dec 1860. King Francesco II (*b* 16 Jn 1836; ✝ 27 Dec 1894; *succ* 22 May 1859) protested against the annexation 12 Dec 1860 and held the fortress of Gaeta until 13 Feb 1861, when he was obliged to surrender. For the early ancestry of the Bourbóns - see FRANCE and SPAIN.

Arms:- Per pale: Dexter, per pale: dexter, Quarterly of six: 1st and 6th, or, six fleurs-de-lys az, one, two, two and one (Farnese of Parma); 2nd and 4th, gu, a fesse arg (Austria); 3rd and 5th, bendy of six or and az, a bordure gu (Burgundy Ancient); all debruised of an escutcheon arg charged with five escutcheons az in cross, each bearing five plates in saltire arg, all within a bordure gu, charged with seven castles or (Portugal). Sinister, on a fesse gu, a fesse arg (Austria); In chief, Quarterly: 1st and 4th, gu a castle or, masoned sa, port and fenestration az (Castile); 2nd and 3rd, arg, a lion rampant gu, armed langued and crowned or (Leon); ente en pointe: arg, a pomegranate gu, stalked and leaved vert (Granada). In base, per fesse: in chief per bend-sinister in dexter-chief, bendy of six or and az, a bordure gu (Burgundy Ancient); in sinister base, or, a lion sa, armed and langued gu (Flanders); in base az, nine fleurs-de-lys, three, three and three or, debruised of a label throughout of five points gu (Anjou). Sinister per pale: dexter per fess: in chief, per fess, or, four pallets gu (Aragon) impaling per saltire, palewise, or, four pallets gu (also for Aragon) and fessewise arg, an eagle displayed sa beaked and membered gu, crowned or (Sicily). In base az, eight fleurs-de-lys or, three, two and three, within a bordure compony arg and gu (Burgundy Modern). In base, per fesse: in chief, in bend; in dexter base, arg, an eagle displayed gu, beaked, membered, crowned and trefle or (Tyrol); and in sinister chief, sa, a lion rampant or, armed and langued gu (Brabant). In base, arg a cross potent between four crosses humetty or (Jerusalem). Sinister, or, six torteaux, the chief most absconded by a heurte charged with three fleurs-de-lys or, the other five gu (Medicis of Tuscany). Over all an escutcheon of pretence az, three fleurs-de-lys or, a bordure gu (Bourbón-Anjou). The whole ensigned with the Royal Crown of the Two Sicilies and surrounded by the Collars of the Orders of St Januarius, St Ferdinand and of Merit, the Constantinian Order of St George and the Golden Fleece.

The children and grandchildren in the male line of the King (or Head of the House) bear the title of Prince or Princess Royal of the Two Sicilies while all other cadets born of dynastic marriages bear the title of Prince or Princess of the Two Sicilies, all with the qualification of Royal Highness. These titles are customarily abbreviated to Prince or Princess of Bourbon-Two Sicilies.

Since the death of Ferdinando, Duke of Calabria, Prince and Head of the Royal House of Bourbon-Two Sicilies (27 Jan 1960 - see below), a dispute arose over the Headship of the Royal House of Bourbon-Two Sicilies with two competing claims:

Prince and Infante Don **CARLOS** Maria Alfonso Marcelo, *b* at Lausanne 16 Jan 1938, assumed the title of **DUKE OF CALABRIA** by declaration of 5 March 1964 and Headship of the Royal House of the Two Sicilies following the death of his father on 3 Feb 1964, having also been *cr* Duke of Noto by his father 17 March 1960, *cr* Infante of Spain by King Juan Carlos I of Spain 16 Dec 1994, Grand Magistery Sacred Mil Constantinian Order of St George, Royal Order of St Januarius, Kt Order of the Golden Fleece, Gd Cmdr Order of Alcántara, Gd Cross Naval Merit (Spain), Gd Cross Argricultural Merit (Spain), Gd Cross Order of the Holy Septre, Gd Cross Order of the White Eagle (Karageorgevitch), Gd Cross Order of Vila Viçosa (Bragança), Pres of Council of four Spanish Mil Orders of Santiago, Calatrava, Alcántara and Montesa, Pres Spanish br United World College, Pres Confederación Española de Fundaciones, Pres Spanish br WWF for Nature (ADENA), etc, son of Prince and Infante Alfonso, Duke of Calabria (*b* 30 Nov 1901; ✠ 3 Feb 1964) and Princess Doña Alice of Bourbon Parma (*b* 13 Nov 1917; *m* 16 April 1936); *m* at Louveciennes, Yvelines 11 May (civ) and Dreux 12 May (relig) 1965, Princess Anne (*b* at Woluwé-Saint-Pierre, nr Brussels 4 Dec 1938), Dame Gd Cross Constantinian Order of St George, dau of Henri, Count of Paris, Head of the Royal House of France and Princess Isabella of Orléans and Bragança.
[*José Ortega y Gasset 26, 28006 Madrid, Spain*].

Son and Daughters

1. Princess Doña *Cristina* Isabella Maria Luisa, *b* at Madrid 15 March 1966, Dame Gd Cross Constantinian Order of St George; *m* at La Toledana, Cuidad Real 15 July 1994, Pedro Lopez-Quesada y Fernanda-Urrutia (*b* at Madrid 26 July 1964), Gd Cross Constantinian Order of St George.
2. Princess Doña *María Paloma* Diana Irene, *b* at Madrid 5 April 1967; *m* at La Toledana, Ciudad Real 13 July 1996, Archduke Simeon of Austria (*b* at Katana, Belgian Congo 29 June 1958), Bailiff Gd Cross Constantinian Order of St George, Lic. rer soc oec.
[*Hanenberg 11, 6833 Weiler, Vorarlberg, Austria*].
3. Prince Don *Pedro* Giovanni Maria Alejo Saturnino y Todos los

Santos, assumed the title of Duke of Noto, *b* at Madrid 16 Oct 1968, Kt Order of St Januarius, Grand Prefect and Bailiff Gd Cross with collar Constantinian Order of St George, Kt Order of Alcántara; *m* at Club Puerta de Hierro, Madrid 30 March 2001, Doña Sofia Landaluce y Melgarejo (*b* at Madrid 23 Nov 1973), dau of Don José Manuel Landaluce Dominguez and Doña Blanca Melgarejo González, and has issue,

    1. Don *Jaime* de Borbón y Landaluce, *b* at Madrid ... Jan 1993.

4. Princess Doña *Inès* Maria Alice Anna Isabella, *b* at Madrid 20 April 1971, Dame Gd Cross Constantinian Order of St George; *m* at Toledo 13 Oct 2001, Michele Carrelli-Palombi, (*b* at Rome 17 Sept 1965).

5. Princess Doña *Victoria* Maria Aline Carolina de la Santisima Trinidad y de Todos los Santos, *b* at Madrid 24 May 1976, Dame Gd Cross Constantinian Order of St George.

Mother

Doña *Alice,* Duchess of Calabria, *b* at Vienna 13 Nov 1917, dau of Elias I, Duke of Parma and Archduchess Maria Anna of Austria, Dame Gd Cross Constantinian Order of St George, Dame Order of Maria Luisa; *m* at Vienna 16 April 1936, Prince and Infante Don Alfonso of Bourbon-Two Sicilies, lay claim to the Headship of the Royal House of the Two Sicilies on the death of his uncle Ferdinand, Duke of Calabria, Count of Caserta, Head of the Royal House of Bourbon-Two Sicilies (✠ 7 Jan 1960 - see below) and assumed the title of Duke of Calabria Jan 1960 (*b* at Madrid 30 Nov 1901; ✠ at Madrid 3 Feb 1964), Grand Master of the Constantinian Order of St George and of St Januarius, Kt Order of the Golden Fleece, Gd Cross Order of Carlos III, Gd Cross Order of Isabel the Catholic, Gd Cross Order of Leopold (Belgium), Gd Cross Order of the Saviour (Greece), Kt Order of Alcántara.

[*Hermanos Pinzón 4, 28016 Madrid, Spain*].

Sisters

1. Princess Doña *Teresa* Maria Francesca Dorotea, *b* at Lausanne 6 Feb 1937, *cr* Duchess of Salerno by her father (17 March 1960 until her marriage), Dame Gd Cross Constantinian Order of St George; *m* at Madrid 16 April 1961, Don Iñigo Moreno y de Arteaga, 12th Marquess de Laula (*b* at Madrid 18 April 1934), Kt Order of St Januarius, Bailiff Gd Cross Constantinian Order of St George, Kt of

Hon and Dev Sovereign Military Order of Malta, Kt Order of
Santiago.
[*Juan Ramón Jiménez 55, 28036 Madrid, Spain*].
2. Princess Doña *Inès* Maria Alicia, *b* at Ouchy 18 Feb 1940, *cr*
Duchess of Syracuse by her father (17 March 1960 until her
marriage), Dame Gd Cross Constantinian Order of St George; *m*
1stly at Madrid 21 Jan 1965 (judicial separation 1978), Don Luis
Morales y Aguado (*b* at Grenada 8 Oct 1933; ✝ at Elche de la Sierra
9 Nov 2000). She *m* 2ndly at Toledo 13 Oct 2001, Nobile Michele
Carrelli Palombi (*b* at ......).
[*Juan Bravo 28, 28006 Madrid, Spain*].

Half-Brother and Sisters of Father

Issue of Prince Don *Carlos* of Bourbon-Two Sicilies, naturalised a
Spanish subject and granted the title of Infante of Spain 7 Feb 1901
(*b* 10 Nov 1870; ✝ 11 Nov 1949) and his second wife, Princess Louise
of Bourbón-Orleans, Infanta of Spain, (*b* 24 Feb 1882; *m* 16 Nov 1907;
✝ 18 April 1958), and had further issue (granted the title of Princes
of Bourbon with the honours and placements of Infantes of Spain by
Royal Decree of King Alfonso XIII 3 Aug 1908), among whom.

1. Princess Doña Maria de la *Esperanza* Amelia Raniera, *b* at Madrid
14 June 1914, Dame Gd Cross Constantinian Order of St George,
Dame Gd Cross Order of Maria Luisa; *m* at Seville 18 Dec 1944,
Prince Dom Pedro Gastão of Orleans and Bragança, Prince of Grão
Pará (*b* at Château d'Eu, Seine Maritime 19 Feb 1913).
[*Palácio do Grão Pará, Avenida da Epitacio Pessoa 130, Petrópolis,
Rio de Janeiro, Brazil; Villamanrique de la Condesa, Seville, Spain*].

Brother and Sisters of Grandfather

Issue of Don Alfonso, Count of Caserta, Prince and Head of the
Royal House of Bourbon-Two Sicilies (*b* 28 March 1841; ✝ 26 May
1934) and Princess Doña Antonietta of Bourbon-Two Sicilies (*b* 16
March 1851; *m* 8 June 1868; ✝ 12 Sept 1938).

1. Prince Don **RÉNIER** Marie Benoit Joseph Labre Gaétan Franco
Xavier Barbe Nicholas Toussaint, (lay claim to the Headship of the
Royal House of the Two Sicilies after 7 Jan 1960) and assumed the
title of **DUKE OF CASTRO** on the death of his brother
Ferdinando (see above), *b* at Cannes 3 Dec 1883; ✝ at Domaine de
La Combe, Roquebrune-sur-Argens 13 Jan 1973, naturalised French

as Rénier de Bourbón 1904, Kt Order of the Golden Fleece (resigned 1962), Kt Order of Annunziata, Kt Order of St Hubert, Bailiff Gd Cross Hon and Dev Sovereign Military Order of Malta, Gd Cross Order of Carlos III, Kt Order of Alcántara, Hon Capt Spanish Army; *m* at Drúzbaki, Zips, Czechoslovakia 12 Sept 1923, Countess Karolina (*b* at Cracow 22 Sept 1896; ✠ at Marseilles 9 May 1968), dau of Count Andrzej Zamoyski and Princess Doña Maria Carolina of Bourbon-Two Sicilies, and had issue,

  1. Princess Doña Maria *Carmen* Carolina Antonietta, *b* at Podzamcze, Poland 13 July 1924, Dame Gd Cross Constantinian Order of St George.
  [*Domaine de La Combe, 83520 Roquebrune-sur-Argens, France*].

  2. Prince Don **FERDINANDO** Maria Andrea Alfonso Marco, assumed the title of **DUKE OF CASTRO** on the death of his father, Kt Order of Annunziata, Kt Order of St Hubert (Bavaria), Bailiff Gd Cross Hon and Dev Sovereign Military Order of Malta, Gd Cross Order of the Crown of Württemberg, *b* at Podzamcze, Poland 28 May 1926, Kt Gd Cross Sovereign Military Order of Malta; *m* at Giez, Dept Haute-Savoie 23 July 1949, Chantal (*b* at Le Cannet des Maures, Dept Var 10 Jan 1925), Dame of Justice Gd Cross Constantinian Order of St George, Dame of Hon Sovereign Military Order of Malta and Bavarian Order of St Theresa, dau of Joseph Pierre de Chevron-Villette of the Counts de Chevron-Villette and Marie de Colbert, and has issue,
  [*Domaine de La Combe, 83520 Roquebrune-sur-Argens, France*].

    1. Princess Doña *Béatrice* Marie Caroline Louise Françoise, *b* at St Raphaël, Var 16 June 1950; *m* at Paris 19 Dec 1978 (*m* diss by div at Nanterre, Hauts de Seine 2 May 1989), Charles, Prince Napoléon (*b* at Boulogne-sur-Seine 19 Oct 1950), Dr ScEc.
    [*34 boulevard Victor Hugo, 92700 Colombes, France*].

    2. Princess Doña *Anna* Marie Caroline Carmen, *b* at St Raphaël 24 April 1957, Dame of Justice Gd Cross Constantinian Order of St George; *m* at Roquebrune-sur-Argens, Dept Var 7 Sept (civ) and 9 Sept (relig) 1977 (*m* diss by div), Jacques Cochin of the Barons Cochin (*b* at Vichy, Allier 23 March 1951).
    [*51 rue Babylone, 75007 Paris, France*].

3. Prince Don (Charles) **Carlo** Maria Bernardo
Gennaro, *b* at St Raphaël 24 Feb 1963, assumed the
title of **Duke of Calabria**, Gd Cross Hon and Dev
Sovereign Military Order of Malta, Gd Cross Order of
Sts Maurice and Lazarus, Gd Cross Order of Merit
(Italy), appointed by his father Grand Chancellor
Sacred Military Constantinian Order of St George; *m*
at the Cathedral Sainte-Devote, Monte-Carlo 31 Oct
1998, Camilla (*b* at Rome 5 April 1971), dau of Camillo
Crociani and Edoarada Vessel.

[*Via Margana 42, 00186 Rome, Italy*].

4. Prince Don *Filippo* Maria Alfonso Antonio Ferdinando Francesco
di Paola Luigi Enrico Alberto Taddeo Francesco Saverio Uberto, *b*
at Cannes 10 Dec 1885; ✠ at St John, New Brunswick, Canada 9
March 1949; *m* 1stly at Neuilly-sur-Seine 10 Jan (civ) and 15 Jan
(relig) 1916 (*m* diss by div at Grasse, Dept Alpes-Maritimes 3 Nov
1925 and relig annulled at Rome 31 May 1926), Princess Marie Louise
(*b* at Neuilly 31 Dec 1896; ✠ at New York 8 March 1973; *m* 2ndly at
Chichester, Sussex 12 Dec 1928, Walter Kingsland, who ✠ at New
York 20 July 1961), dau of Prince Emanuel of Bourbon-Orléans,
Duke de Vendôme and Alençon and Princess Henriette of Belgium.
He *m* 2ndly at Paris 10 Jan 1927 (non-dynastic), Odette (*b* at Paris
22 Nov 1902; ✠ at Le Kremlin-Bicêtre, Val de Marne 19 June 1968;
m 1stly at Paris 18 Feb 1925, Dino Ceretti; that *m* annulled at Milan
15 Nov 1926 and at Rome 6 Dec 1926), dau of Fernand Labori and
Marguerite O'Key, and had issue by his first wife,

1. Prince Don *Gaëtano* Marie Alphonse Raol, *b* at Cannes 16
April 1917; ✠ at Harare, Zimbabwe 27 Dec 1984, a naturalised
British subject 24 Feb 1939, Officer RN (ret), Farmer; *m* at
Paddington, London 16 Feb 1946 (non-dynastic), Olivia (*b* at
Dumfries, Scotland 16 July 1917; ✠ at Harare 24 May 1987),
dau of Lt-Cmdr Charles Arthur Yarrow, RN and Gladys
Winifred Foulkes, and has issue,

1. Prince Don (*ad Personam*) *Adrian* Philip, *b* at
Warrington, Lancashire 7 April 1948; *m* at Harare,
Zimbabwe 20 March 1976, Linda Rose (*b* at Harare 3
Feb 1950), dau of Leonard George Idensohn and Doreen
Deyzel, and has issue,

1. Philip Charles, *b* at Harare 5 May 1977.

2. Michelle Lara, *b* at Harare 12 Feb 1979.

[*11 Pentland Close, Highlands, Harare, Zimbabwe*]

2. Prince Don (*ad Personam*) *Gregory* Peter, *b* at Warrington, Lancashire 2 Jan 1950; *m* at Rusape, Zimbabwe 15 May 1971 (*m* diss by div at Brisbane, Queensland 7 June 1986), Maureen Marjorie (*b* at Bulawayo 19 April 1951), dau of Allen Robert Powell and Olive Elizabeth Olsen. He *m* 2ndly at Brisbane, Australia 30 Aug 1986, Carrie Anne (*b* at Cessnock, Australia 2 Feb 1945), dau of Samuel Thornley and Edna Perkins, and has issue from his first marriage, [*Unit 6/29 Stopford Street, Wooloowin, 4030 Queensland, Australia*].

> 1. *Christan*, *b* at Vancouver, BC, Canada 11 April 1974; m at Marondera, Zimbabwe 26 April 1997, Brigette (*b* at...), dau of David Dick and Eileen...
>
> 2. *Raymond*, *b* at Harare 8 Nov 1978.

5. Prince Don *Gabriele* Maria Giuseppe Carlo Ignazio Antonio Alfonso Pietro Giovanni Gerardo di Majella et omnes sancti, *b* at Cannes 11 Jan 1897; ✠ at Itú, São Paolo, Brazil 22 Oct 1975, naturalised in Spain, *cr* Prince of Borbon with the qualification of Royal Highness and the honours and treatment of Infant of Spain (Royal Decree 19 Aug 1920), Kt Order of the Golden Fleece, Kt Order of St Januarius, Bailiff Gd Cross Constantinian Order of St George, Gd Cross Order of Carlos III, Kt Order of Alcántara, Kt of Hon and Dev Sovereign Military Order of Malta, Capt Spanish Army; *m* 1stly at Paris 25 Aug 1927, Princess Marguerite (*b* at Warsaw 17 Aug 1902; ✠ at Cannes 8 March 1929), dau of Adam Ludwik, 12th Prince Czartoryski and Countess Ludwika Krasinska, and had issue,

> 1. Prince Don *Antonio* Maria Giuseppe Alfonso Adam et omnes sancti, *b* at Cannes 20 Jan 1929, Dipl Eng; *m* at Altshausen, Württemberg 18 July (civ) and 19 July (relig) 1958, Duchess Elisabeth (*b* at Stuttgart 2 Feb 1933), Dame of Justice Gd Cross Constantinian Order of St George, dau of Philipp Albrecht, Duke of Württemberg und Archduchess Rosa of Austria-Tuscany, and has issue,
> [*70 chaussée de Louvain, 1410 Waterloo, Belgium*].
>
> > 1. Prince Don *Francesco* Filippo Maria Giuseppe Gabriele, *b* at Ravensburg, Württemberg 20 June 1960, Kt Order of St Januarius; *m* at Geneva 17 June 2002, Countess Alexandra (*b* at Zürich 2 June 1967; *m* 1stly Dom Pedro de Mello de Vasconcelos e Souza, *b* at Sao

Sebastiao da Pedreira 9 Aug 1965, *m* diss by div 20
Feb 1995), dau of Count Franz-Clemens of Schönborn-
Wiesentheid and Princess Tatiana Gortchakoff.
[*21 chemin de la Fontanetaz, 1009 Pully,
Switzerland*].

2. Princess Doña *Maria Carolina* Giovanna Rosa
Cecilia, *b* at Friedrichshafen am Bodensee 18 July
1962; *m* at Tübingen 6 May 1988 (civ) and 26 Aug 1989
(relig), Dr Andreas Baumbach (*b* at Tübingen 30 April
1963).
[*Gechtstraße 49, 72074 Tübingen, Germany*].

3. Prince Don *Gennaro* Maria Pio Casimiro, *b* at
Ravensburg 27 Jan 1966, Kt Order of St Januarius.
[*70 chaussée de Louvain, 1410 Waterloo, Belgium*].

4. Princess Doña *Maria Annunziata* Urraca Margarita
Elisabeth, *b* at Friedrichshafen am Bodensee 18 Feb
1973.

Prince Don Gabriele *m* 2ndly at Cracow 15 Sept 1932, Princess
Cecylia (*Cécile*) (*b* at Poreba Wielka, Myslenice, Poland 28 June
1907; ✠ at Sao Paulo 20 Sept 2001), Dame Gd Cross Constantinian
Order of St George, dau of Kasimir, Prince Lubomirski and Countess
Theresia Granów-Wodzicka, and by her had further issue, among
whom,

2. Princess Doña *Maria Margherita* Teresa Antonieta Alfonsa
Casimira, *b* at Warsaw 16 Nov 1934, Dame Gd Cross
Constantinian Order of St George; *m* at San Miguel de Jerez
de la Frontera, Prov Cadiz 11 June 1962, Don Luís de Gonzaga
Maldonaldo y Gordon (*b* at Madrid 17 Nov 1932).
[*Calle Azalea 76, El Soto de la Moraleja, Alcobendas, 28100
Madrid, Spain*].

3. Princess Doña Maria *Immacolata*, *b* at Warsaw 25 June
1937, Dame Gd Cross Costantinian Order of St George; *m* at
San Carlos, Ibiza 29 June 1970 (*m* diss by div at Madrid 25
Oct 1979 and relig annulled at Madrid 24 April 1980), Don
Miguel García de Saéz y Tellecea (*b* at Pamplona, Spain 6
Sept 1921; ✠ at Madrid 12 March 1982).
[*Avenida de la Vega 18, 28108 Alcobendas, Madrid, Spain*].

4. Prince Don *Casimiro* Maria Alfonso Gabriele, *b* at Warsaw
8 Nov 1938, Branch Dir, Bailiff Gd Cross Constantinian Order
of St George, Kt Order of St Januarius; *m* at Jacarézinho,
Brazil 29 Jan 1967, Princess Maria Cristina (*b* at Château

Miramar, nr Trieste 12 Sept 1933), Dame Gd Cross
Constantinian Order of St George, dau of Prince Amedeo of
Savoy, Duke of Aosta and Princess Anne of France, and has
issue,

[*Rua Atlantica 256, Jardim América, 01440-000 São Paulo,
Brazil*].

> 1. Prince Don *Luigi* Alfonso, *b* at Rio de Janeiro 28
> Nov 1970; *m* at Sao Paulo 22 Oct 1998, Christina (*b* at
> Sao Paulo 20 May 1969), dau of Rubens Apovian and
> Laudelina Pereira, and has issue,
>
>> 1. Princess Doña *Anna* Sophia, b at ... April
>> 1999.
>
> 2. Princess Don *Anna* Cecilia, *b* at São Paulo 24 Dec
> 1971.
>
> 3. Princess Doña *Elena* Sofia, *b* at São Paulo 9 Sept
> 1973, took religious orders and lives in Madrid.
>
> 4. Prince Don *Alessandro* Enrico, *b* at São Paulo 9
> Aug 1974.

Brother of Great-Great-Grandfather

Issue of Don Francesco I, King of the Two Sicilies (*b* 19 Aug 1777; ✠
8 Nov 1830) and his second wife, Infanta Doña Maria Isabella of
Spain (*b* 6 July 1785; *m* 6 July/6 Oct 1802; ✠ 13 Sept 1848; *m* 2ndly
15 Jan 1839, Don Francesco, Count del Balzo), having had issue,
among whom,

Son

Prince Don *Luigi* Carlo Maria Giuseppe, Count d'Aquila, *b* at Naples
19 July 1824; ✠ at Paris 5 March 1897, Imperial Highness (*jure
uxoris* 28 April 1844), Hon Adm Brazilian Navy, Vice-Adm and Pres
of the Council of Admiralty of the Two Sicilies, Adjt-Gen of the King
of the Two Sicilies, etc; *m* at Rio de Janeiro 28 April 1844, Januária,
Princess Imperial of Brazil (*b* at Rio de Janeiro 11 March 1822; ✠ at
Nice 13 March 1901), having had issue, among whom,

Son

Prince Don *Luigi* Maria Ferdinando Pietro di Alcantara Francesco
d'Assisi Gennaro Francesco di Paula Alfonso Luigi di Gonzaga
Camillo de Hellis Alexis Raimondo Torillo Sebastiano Filomeno,
Count de Aquila, *b* at Naples 18 July 1845; ✠ at Nice 27 Nov 1909,
cr **Count of Roccaguglielma** by Francesco II 31 Jan 1872; *m*
(non-dynastic in Two Sicilies, Spain and Brazil, and without

permission of the King thereby forfeiting Two Sicilies succession rights and titles) at New York 22 March (civ) and 28 May (relig) 1869, María *Amelia* Isabel (*b* at Havana, Cuba 19 June 1847; ✠ at Paris 1 March 1914), dau of Juan Bellow Hamel y Nathans and Enriquetta Penot y Gilbau, and had issue (who by decision of King Francesco II were deprived of all rights and titles of the House of Bourbon and given the name Roccaguglielma 31 Jan 1872), among whom,

Son

Don *Louis* Marie Alphonse Christino Janvier Pierre d'Alcantara Désiré Charles Jean Baptiste Michel Gabriel Raphaël Gonzague, **2nd Count of Roccaguglielma** (title confirmed Italy 16 Feb 1898), *b* at Paris 21 May 1873; ✠ at Château d'Arkia, nr Ustaritz, France 17 July 1940, styled in his Birth Act as Royal and Imperial Highness, later as HRH Prince Louis de Bourbon, naturalised with the name "de Bourbón" France 29 Nov 1931; *m* 1stly at Nice 20 Jan 1898 (*m* diss by div 1910), *Enrica* Maria (*b* at Naples 23 Feb 1880; ✠ at Viareggio 27 Dec 1947; *m* 2ndly at Lucca 15 Nov 1910, Tullio Campriani who ✠ 14 Feb 1936), dau of Emilio Weiss, 1st Count and 1st Viscount de Valbranca and Caterina Lucernari). He *m* 2ndly at Beaulieu-sur-Mer 5 Jan 1932, Adeline Marie Antoinette (*b* at Saint-Servan-sur-Mer 3 Dec 1875; ✠ at la Tour de Peilz, Switzerland 23 Feb 1959), dau of Napoleon Marie Landegren and Adèle Eudoxie Dexasy, and had issue, among whom,

Son

1. Don *Luigi* Maria Carlo Emilio Gennaro Pietro d'Alcantara Ferdinando Giuseppe Francesco d'Assisi Alfonso Michele Raffaele Gabriele Gonzaga, **3rd Count of Roccaguglielma**, *b* at Castello di Narni, nr Perugia 18 Oct 1898 (as Prince Luigi Borbone, styled HRH Prince Louis de Bourbon, Count of Roccaguglielma); ✠ at Paris 12 April 1967; *m* at Paris 25 (civ) and 26 (relig) Sept 1925, Marie Louise (*b* at Boucq, Meurthe-en-Moselle 30 March 1894; ✠ at Boucq 12 May 1941), dau of Gaspard, Marquess de Clermont-Tonnerre and Henriette Piat de Braux, and had issue,

> 1. Doña *Marie Christine* Amelie Januaria Léopoldine Louise Jeanne Thérèse Caroline Henriette Françoise Isabelle Elisabeth Gabrielle Victoire, *b* at Paris 15 March 1933, styled HRH Princess Marie Christine de Bourbon-Sicilies and recognised as Highness by Prince Ferdinando, Duke of Castro;

m at Neuilly-sur-Seine 24 Sept (civ) and 26 Sept (relig) 1957, Michel Gaston Denizot (*b* at Paris 17 May 1923; *m* 1stly Claire Odette Marie Lefebvre).

2. Don *Carlo* Maria Ferdinando Ranieri d'Alcantara, 4th **Count of Roccaguglielma**, *b* at Vaccoli, nr Lucca 8 Nov 1905; ✝ at Rome 12 Dec 1968, styled Prince Charles de Bourbon-Sicilies; *m* at Viareggio, Lucca 25 April 1925, Fanny Greco di Chiaramonte (*b* at Buenos Aires 6 Oct 1905; ✝ at Montevideo, Uruguay 21 May 1977), dau of Ageislao Greco di Chiaramonte and Valentina Diaz, and had issue,

1. Doña *Isabella* Maria Francesca, b at Viareggio 17 April 1926; *m* 1stly at Buenos Aires 2 Aug 1954 (*m* diss by div Feb 1969), José Manuel Guttierrez (*b* at Buenos Aires 16 April 1921). She *m* 2ndly 7 July 1969, Isidoro Mariano Vejo Rodríguez, ex-Government Minister in Uruguay (*b* at Rivera, Uruguay 31 Jan 1915).

BRAZIL
(HOUSE OF ORLÉANS-BRANGANÇA)

On 22 April 1500 Pedro Alvares Cabral, the commander of a Portuguese fleet en route to India, landed in the South American continent and took possession of the area in the name of King Dom Manoel I, calling it firstly Vera Cruz, then Santa Cruz (Holy Cross) and later Brazil after the tree of the *Pau-Brasil* species. The title of Prince of Brazil was first bestowed on the heir apparent to the Portuguese Throne 27 Oct 1645. The Portuguese Royal family retreated to the colony of Brazil to escape Napoleon's invading armies in 1807. On his return to Portugal in 1821, King Dom João VI left his eldest son Dom Pedro as Prince Regent of Brazil. However the country was demanding independence from Portugal and Dom Pedro was created Emperor of Brazil 7 Sept 1822 (Brazilian National Day), reigning as Emperor Dom Pedro I, following his coronation on 1 Dec 1822 at the Imperial Cathedral, Rio de Janeiro. On the death of his father he also succeeded to the throne of Portugal which he abdicated in favour of his six year old daughter, who became Queen Dona Maria. His son succeeded to the throne of Brazil as Emperor Pedro II and was deposed 15 Nov 1889. For the early ancestry of the BRAGANÇA and BOURBÓN Families see FRANCE and PORTUGAL. The contract of marriage between Isabel, Princess Imperial of Brazil and Prince Gaston d'Orléans, Count d'Eu dated 15 Oct 1864, the latter renounced any position or employment outside Brazil (by implication his Orleanist French rights, although such renunciation contravened the laws of the ancient French Monarchy).

This was revised by the terms of a Pact between the Duke of Orléans (then Head of the Branch of Bourbón-Orléans) and the Count and Countess of Eu dated 26 April 1909, by which the Family of Orléans and Bragança, the Imperial House of Brazil, would retain its rights of succession to the throne of France, but take last place in the order of primogeniture.

Arms:- Vert, an armillary sphere or, placed upon the Cross of the Order of Christ (gu fimbriated or, charged with a cross arg), encircled by an annulet az, fibriated on both sides arg, charged with nineteen mullets arg. Over all an escutcheon of pretence, az, three fleurs-de-lys or, charged with a label or three points arg. The shield is ensigned with the Imperial Crown of Brazil. Surrounding the shield are two branches crossed, tied in a bow with a ribbon gu, dexter, a branch of a coffee plant seeded ppr; and sinister, a branch of a tobacco plant flowered ppr.

Members of the Imperial House bear the qualification of Imperial and Royal Highness, with the additional style "of Brazil", except where those members have renounced their rights (*). Non-Imperial dynasts are accorded the rank of Royal Highness of Orléans and Bragança. The younger daughters of the Emperors Pedro I and Pedro II bore the title of Princess of Brazil with the qualification of Highness. Other descendants of the Princess Imperial Dona Isabel bear the title of Prince or Princess of Orléans and Bragança with the qualification of Royal Highness.

The succession to the Imperial Crown of Brazil, as a consequence of the renunciation by Prince Dom Pedro of Orléans and Bragança (30 Oct 1908), falls to Prince Luis Gastão, his great nephew (see below), who is Heir to the Imperial Throne. Prince Dom Pedro's surviving son, Dom Pedro:- *see Line II below* , is the senior male descendant (by primogeniture) by descent from the late Princess Imperial and is regarded as Head of the Princely line of Orléans and Bragança.

LINE I (Imperial Succession)

This line is second in descent by primogeniture; through Prince Dom Luiz of Orléans-Bragança (*b* 26 Nov 1878; ✠ 26 March 1920) and Princess Dona Maria Pia of Bourbon-Two Sicilies (*b* at Cannes 12 Aug 1878; *m* 3 Nov (civ) and 4 Nov (relig) 1908; ✠ at Mandelieu 20 June 1973); the younger brother of Prince Dom Pedro of Orléans-Bragança :- *see Line II below* (*b* 15 Oct 1875; ✠ 29 Jan 1940), who had renounced his rights to the Imperial Crown of Brazil for himself and his descendants under Article 117 of the Constitution of 25 May 1824). The brothers were both the issue of Isabel, Princess Imperial of Brazil (*b* 29 July 1846; ✠ 14 Nov 1921, Regent of the Empire of Brazil 25 May 1871 - 31 March 1872, 20 March - 28 Sept 1876 and 30 June 1887 - 22 Aug 1888) and Prince Gaston of Orléans, Count d'Eu (*b* 28 April 1842; *m* 15 Oct 1864 ✠ 28 Aug 1922).

PRINCE DOM LUIZ GASTÃO Maria Jose Pio, *b* at Mandelieu, Alpes Maritimes, France 6 June 1938, son of Prince *Pedro Henrique* of Orléans-Bragança, (*b* 13 Sept 1909; ✠ 5 July 1981) and Princess Maria of Bavaria (*b* 9 Sept 1914; *m* 19 Aug 1937); *succ* his father as heir to the Imperial Throne of Brazil with the qualification of Imperial and Royal Highness; Gd Cross Order of Dom Pedro I, Imperial Order of the Rose, Kt Gd Cross Constantinian Order of St George.
[*R. Itápolis, 873 Pacaembu, 01245-000, São Paulo SP, Brazil*].

Mother

Princess *Maria* Elisabeth Franziska Josepha Theresia, The Princess Mother of Brazil, *b* at Schloß Nymphenburg 9 Sept 1914, eldest dau of Prince Franz of Bavaria and Princess Isabella of Croÿ; *m* at Schloß Nymphenburg 19 Aug 1937, Prince *Pedro Henrique*, (*b* at Boulogne-Billancourt 13 Sept 1909; ✠ at Vassouras, Brazil 5 July 1981) who had succeeded his grandmother.
[*Rua Custódio Serrão 36, Apt. 202, 22470 Lagoa, Rio de Janeiro, Brazil*].

Brothers and Sisters

1. *Prince Dom *Eudes* Maria Ranieri Pedro José, *b* at Mandelieu 8 June 1939, renounced his rights of succession to the Brazilian throne for himself and his descendants 3 June 1966, Officer Brazilian Navy, Kt Gd Cross Order of Dom Pedro I, Imperial Order of the Rose, Kt Gd Cross Constantinian Order of St George, Kt Order of Merit Admiral Tamandare, Member of the Royal and Ancient Golf Club of St Andrews, Fife, Scotland; *m* 1stly at São Paulo 8 May 1967, (*m* dis by div 1976), Ana Maria (*b* at São Paulo 20 Nov 1945), dau of Luiz de Moraes e Barros and Maria do Carmo Cerqueira César, and by her has issue,
[*Rua Prof. Abelardo Lobo 50, Apt. 2, 22470 Lagoa, Rio de Janeiro, Brazil*].

    1. *Prince Dom *Luiz Philippe* Maria José Miguel Gabriel Rafael Gonzaga, *b* at Rio de Janeiro 3 April 1969.
    [*Rua Pe. João Manuel, 329/12A, Cerquiera César, 01426 São Paulo, Brazil*].

    2. *Princess Dona Ana Luiza Maria Josefa Micaela Gabriela Rafaela Gonzaga, *b* at Rio de Janeiro 19 June 1971; *m* at Idaiatuba, State of São Paulo 18 May 1996, *Paulo* Ibrahim Mansour (*b* at São Paulo 5 Feb 1962).
    [*Rua Cojuba, 136/1, Itam Bibi 04533-040 São Paulo, Brazil*].

Prince Eudes *m* 2ndly (civ) at Rio de Janeiro.... 1976, Mercedes (*b* at Petrópolis 26 Jan 1955), dau of Guy Provenca Neves da Rocha and Lia Viega Williemsens, and by her has further issue,

    3. *Eudes, b* at Rio de Janeiro 17 Dec 1977.

    4. *Maria Francisca, b* at Rio de Janeiro 18 Aug 1979

    5. *Maria Antonia, b* at Rio de Janeiro 18 Aug 1979.

    (twin with Maria Francisca).

    6. *Guy, b* at Rio de Janeiro 8 Oct 1985.

2. Prince Dom *Bertrand* Maria José Pio Januario, The Prince Imperial, *b* at Mandelieu 2 Feb 1941, Pilot, Jurist, Kt Gd Cross Order of Dom Pedro I and Imperial Order of the Rose, Kt Gd Cross Constantinian Order of St George.

[*Rua Alagoas 350/2, 01242 São Paulo SP, Brazil*].

3. Princess Dona *Isabel* Maria Josefa Henriqueta Francisca, *b* at La Bourboule, Puy-de-Dôme, France 5 April 1944.

[*Rua Custódio Serrão 36, Apt. 202, 22470 Lagoa, Rio de Janeiro, Brazil*].

4. *Prince Dom *Pedro* de Alcantara Henrique Maria Miguel Gabriel Rafael Gonzaga, *b* at Pétropolis 1 Dec 1945, renounced his rights of succession to the Brazilian throne for himself and his descendants 28 Dec 1972, Kt Gd Cross Order of Dom Pedro I and Imperial Order of the Rose; *m* at Rio de Janeiro 4 July 1974, Maria de Fatima (*b* at Rio de Janeiro 14 July 1952), dau of Orlando de Lacerda Rocha and Silvia Maria de Andrada Baptista de Oliveira, and has issue,

[*Praia de Botafogo, 28/901, 22250-040 Rio de Janeiro, Brazil*].

    1. *Princess Dona *Maria Pia* Josefa Micaela Gabriela Rafaela Gonzaga, *b* at Rio de Janeiro 23 Aug 1975; *m* at Rio de Janeiro 25 Aug 2001, Rodrigo Octávio Broglia Mendes (*b* at Rio de Janeiro 7 Nov 1974).

    2. *Princess Dona Maria *Carolina* Josefa Micaela Gabriela Rafaela Gonzaga, *b* at Rio de Janeiro 19 Sept 1978.

    3. *Prince Dom *Gabriel* (Maria) José Miguel Rafael Gonzaga, *b* at Rio de Janeiro 1 Dec 1980.

    4. *Princess Dona *Maria de Fátima Isabel* Josefa Micaela Gabriela Rafaela Gonzaga, *b* at Rio de Janeiro 13 May 1988.

    5. *Princess Dona Maria *Manuela* Josefa Micaela Gabriela Rafaela Gonzaga, *b* at Rio de Janeiro 26 May 1989.

5. *Prince Dom *Fernando* Diniz Maria José Miguel Gabriel Rafael Gonzaga, *b* at Pétropolis 2 Feb 1948, Economist, Industrialist, renounced his rights to the Brazilian throne for himself and his descendants 24 Feb 1975, Kt Gd Cross Order of Dom Pedro I and

Imperial Order of the Rose; *m* at Rio de Janeiro 19 March 1975, Maria de Graça (*b* at Rio de Janeiro 27 June 1952), dau of Walter Baere de Araújo and Maria Madalena de Siqueira Carvalho, and has issue,

[*Rua Candido Gaffré 161/101, 22291 Rio de Janeiro, Brazil*].

> 1. *Princess Dona *Isabel* Maria *Eleonora* Josefa Francisca Micaela Gabriela Rafaela Gonzaga, *b* at Rio de Janeiro 30 Jan 1978.
>
> 2. *Princess Dona *Maria da Glória Cristina* Josefa Joana Elenora Micaela Gabriela Rafaela Gonzaga, *b* at Rio de Janeiro 11 Nov 1982.
>
> 3. *Princess Dona *Luiza Carolina* Maria de Fatima Josefa Julia Micaela Gabriela Rafaela Gonzaga, *b* at Rio de Janeiro 27 Oct 1984.

6. Prince Dom *António* João Maria José Jorge Miguel Gabriel Rafael Gonzaga, *b* at Rio de Janeiro 24 June 1950, Engineer, Kt Gd Cross Order of Dom Pedro I and Imperial Order of the Rose; *m* at Beloeil, Belgium 25 Sept (civ) and 26 Sept (relig) 1981, Princess Christine (*b* at Beloeil 11 Aug 1955), dau of Antoine, Prince de Ligne and Princess Alix of Luxembourg, Bourbon-Parma and Nassau, and has issue,

[*Rua Sant Moritz 65, Morin, 25630-50, Petrópolis, Rio de Janeiro, Brazil*].

> 1. Prince Dom *Pedro Luiz* Maria José Miguel Rafael Gabriel Gonzaga, *b* at Rio de Janeiro 12 Jan 1983.
>
> [*Rua Sant Moritz 65, Morin, 25630-50, Petrópolis, Rio de Janeiro, Brazil*].
>
> 2. Princess Dona *Amélia* Maria de Fátima Josefa Antonia Michaela Gabriela Rafaela Gonzaga, *b* at Brussels 15 March 1984.
>
> [*Rua Sant Moritz 65, Morin, 25630-50, Petrópolis, Rio de Janeiro, Brazil*].
>
> 3. Prince Dom *Rafael* Antonio Maria José Francisco Miguel Gabriel Gonzaga, *b* at Rio de Janeiro 24 April 1986.
>
> [*Rua Sant Moritz 65, Morin, 25630-50, Petrópolis, Rio de Janeiro, Brazil*].
>
> 4. Princess Dona *Maria Gabriela* Josefa Fernanda Jolanda Michaela Rafaela Gonzaga, *b* at Rio de Janeiro 8 June 1989.
>
> [*Rua Sant Moritz 65, Morin, 25630-50, Petrópolis, Rio de Janeiro, Brazil*].

7. Princess Dona Eleonora Maria Josefa Rose Felipe Michaela Gabriela Rafaela Gonzaga, *b* at Jacarezinho, Paraná 20 May 1953, lic hist; *m*

at Rio de Janeiro 10 March 1981, Michel, Prince de Ligne (*b* at Beloeil 26 May 1951).
[*Château de Beloeil, B-7970, Beloeil, Belgium*].

8. *Prince Dom *Francisco* Maria Jose Rasso Miguel Gabriel Rafael Gonzaga, *b* at Jacarezinho, Paraná 6 April 1955, renounced his rights to the Brazilian throne for himself and his descendants 11 Dec 1980, Kt Gd Cross Order of Dom Pedro I and Imperial Order of the Rose; *m* at Rio de Janeiro 28 Dec 1980, Claudia Regina (*b* at Rio de Janeiro 11 July 1954), dau of Eurico Borges Godinho and Nilza Martins, and has issue,
[*Ave Francisco Bhering 169/201, Arpoador 22080-050, Rio de Janeiro, Brazil*].

    1. *Princess Dona *Maria Elisabeth* Josefa Angela Michaela Gabriela Rafaela Gonzaga, *b* at Rio de Janeiro 1 March 1982.
    2. *Princess Dona *Maria Thereza* Cristiana Josefa Albertina Michaela Gabriela Rafaela Gonzaga, *b* at Rio de Janeiro 31 Jan 1984.
    3. *Princess Dona *Maria Eleonora* Josefa Antonia Michaela Gabriela Rafaela Gonzaga, *b* at Rio de Janeiro 31 Jan 1984 (twin with Princess Maria Thereza).

9. *Prince Dom *Alberto* Maria José João Miguel Gabriel Rafael Gonzaga, *b* at Jundiai do Sul, Paraná 23 June 1957, renounced his rights to the Brazilian throne for himself and his descendants 22 Dec 1982, Kt Gd Cross Order of Dom Pedro I and Imperial Order of the Rose; *m* at Rio de Janeiro 11 Jan 1983, Maritza (*b* at Rio de Janeiro 29 April 1961), dau of Jaddo Barbosa Bockel and Miriza Bulcão Ribas, and has issue,
[*Rua Dr Lugi Capriglione 215, Itanhangá 22641-050, Rio de Janeiro, Brazil*].

    1. *Prince Dom *Pedro* Alberto Maria José Francisco Miguel Gabriel Rafael Gonzaga, *b* at Rio de Janeiro 31 May 1988.
    2. *Princess Dona *Maria Beatriz* Isabel Guilhermina Michaela Gabriela Rafaela Gonzaga, *b* at Rio de Janeiro 27 July 1990.
    3. *Princess Dona *Ana Thereza* Maria Francisca Michaela Gabriela Rafaea Gonzaga, *b* at Rio de Janeiro 7 April 1995.
    4. *Prince Dom *Antonio* Alberto Maria José Henrique Miguel Gabriel Rafael Gonzaga, *b* at Rio de Janeiro 28 May 1997.

10. *Princess Dona *Maria Teresa* Aldeguna Luiza Josefa Michaela Gabriela Rafaela Gonzaga, *b* at Jundiai do Sul, Paraná 14 July 1959; *m* at Rio de Janeiro 4 Nov 1995, Johannes Hessel de Jong (*b* at Frisa 5 March 1953).

[*58 Eaton Square, London SW1W 9BG*].

11. Princess Dona *Maria Gabriela* Dorotea Isabel Josefa Michaela Gabriela Rafaela Gonzaga, *b* at Jundiai do Sul, Paraná 14 July 1959 (twin with Princess Dona Maria Teresa), Radio and Television Technician.

[*Rua Custódio Serrão 36, Apt. 202, 22470 Lagoa, Rio de Janeiro, Brazil*].

Line II (Princely Line - Senior Line by Primogeniture)

DOM PEDRO de Alcantara Gastão João Maria Felipe Lourenço Humberto Miguel Gabriel Rafael Gonzaga, **PRINCE OF ORLÉANS AND BRAGANCA**, Prince of Grão Para, *b* at Château d'Eu 19 Feb 1913, son of Prince Pedro of Orléans-Bragança (*b* 15 Oct 1875; ✝ 29 Jan 1940; who had renounced his rights to the Imperial Crown of Brazil for himself and his descendants *(under Article 117 of the Constitution of 25 May 1824)* at Cannes 30 Oct 1908) and Countess Elisabeth Dobrzenska von Dobrzcnicz (*b* 7 Dec 1875; *m* 14 Nov 1908; ✝ 11 June 1951); assumed the Headship of the Princely House of Orléans and Bragança following the death of his father; Gd Cross Imperial Order of Christ, Gd Cross Order of Dom Pedro I, Imperial Order of the Rose, Imperial Order of the Southern Cross; Kt Gd Cross Constantinian Order of St George, Royal Order of St Sauvior of Greece, Gd Cross Hon and Dev Sovereign Military Order of Malta, Kt Order Real Maestranza de Caballeria de Sevilla, Kt Order Real Maestranza de Zaragoza; *m* at Seville 18 Dec 1944, Princess Maria de la *Esperanza* (*b* at Madrid 14 June 1914), Dame Gd Cross Constantinian Order of St George, dau of Don Carlo, Prince of Bourbon-Two Sicilies, Infante of Spain and Princess Louise of Bourbon-Órleans, Infanta of Spain, and has issue,

[*Palácio do Grão Pará, Avenida Epitácio Pessoa 130, 25600 Petrópolis, Rio de Janeiro, Brazil; Palácio Villamanrique, 41850 Villamanrique de la Condesa, Prov. Sevilla, Spain*].

Sons and Daughters

1. Prince Dom *Pedro* de Alcantara Carlos João Lourenço Miguel Rafael Gabriel Gonzaga, *b* at Rio de Janeiro 31 Oct 1945, Gd Cross Order of Dom Pedro I, Imperial Order of the Rose, Imperial Order of Christ, Gd Cross Constantinian Order of St George; *m* 1stly at Petrópolis 2 Sept 1975, Rony (*b* at São Paolo 20 March 1938; ✝ at Petrópolis 14 Jan 1979), dau of Alfredo Kuhn and Maria das Graças

Mercedes de Souza, and by her has issue,

    1. Prince Dom *Pedro* Tiago Maria Miguel Gabriel Rafael Gonzaga, *b* at Petrópolis 12 Jan 1979.

Prince Dom Pedro *m* 2ndly at Fazenda São Geraldo, Paraiba do Sul, Brazil 16 July 1981, Patricia Alexandra (*b* at Petrópolis 22 Nov 1964), dau of Frank Brascombe and Maria Braumeyer, and by her has further issue,

[*Palácio do Grão Pará, Avenida Epitácio Pessoa 130, 25600 Petrópolis, Rio de Janeiro, Brazil*].

    2. Prince Dom *Felipe* Rodrigo Alexandre Francisco Cristóvão Miguel Gabriel Gonzaga, *b* at Brasilia 31 Dec 1982.

2. Princess Dona *Maria da Gloria* Henriqueta Dolores Lucia Michaela Rafaela Gabriela Gonzaga, *b* at Pétropolis 13 Dec 1946; *m* 1stly at Villamanrique de la Condesa 1 July 1972 (*m* diss by div at Virginia, USA 19 Feb 1985), Alexander, Crown Prince of Yugoslavia (*b* in London 17 July 1945; *m* 2ndly at London 20 (civ) 21 (relig) Sept 1985, Catherine Clairy Batis). She *m* 2ndly at Seville 24 Oct 1985 (relig), Don Ignacio de Medina y Fernández de Córdoba, Duke de Segorbe, Count Moriana del Rio Count de Ampurias, Grandee of Spain, (*b* at Seville 23 Feb 1947), Grandee of Spain.

[*Callejón de Dos Hermanas 4, 41004 Sevilla, Spain*].

3. Prince Dom *Afonso Duarte* Francisco Marcos Miguel Rafael Gabriel Gonzaga, *b* at Petrópolis 25 April 1948, Kt Gd Cross Order of Dom Pedro I, Imperial Order of the Rose, Imperial Order of Christ, Gd Cross Constantinian Order of St George; *m* at Seville 3 Jan 1973 (*m* diss by div at.....1998), Maria (*b* at Seville 13 May 1954), dau of Isidro Parejo and Maria Vitória Gurruchaga, and has issue,

[*Palácio do Grão Pará, Avenida Epitácio Pessoa 130, 25600 Petrópolis, Rio de Janeiro, Brazil*].

    1. Princess Dona *Maria*, *b* at Seville 14 Jan 1974.

    2. Princess Dona *Julia*, *b* at Petrópolis 18 Sept 1977.

4. Prince Dom *Manuel* Alvaro Rainiero Miguel Gabriel Rafael Gonzaga, *b* at Petrópolis 17 June 1949, Kt Gd Cross Order of Dom Pedro I, Imperial Order of the Rose, Imperial Order of Christ, Kt Order Real Maestranza de Caballeria de Sevilla, Kt Order of Montesa, Kt Gd Cross Constantinian Order of St George; *m* at Malaga 12 Dec 1977 (*m* diss by div 1995), Margarita (*b* at Malaga 10 Dec 1945), dau of Oskar Haffner and Lida Lamcha, and has issue,

[*Palácio Villamanrique, 41850 Villamanrique de la Condesa, Prov. Sevilla, Spain*].

    1. Princess Dona *Luiza* Christina, *b* at 25 July 1978.

2. Prince Dom *Manuel* Afonso, *b* at Seville 7 March 1981.

5. Princess Dona *Cristina Maria do Rosario* Leopoldina Michaela Gabriela Rafaela Gonzaga, *b* at Petrópolis 16 Oct 1950; *m* 1sty there 16 May 1980 (m diss by div at 1992), Jean, Prince Sapieha-Rozanski (*b* at Warsaw 26 Aug 1935); *m*.2ndly at Rio de Janeiro Oct 1992 (*m* diss by div Dec 1996), Jao Carlos Calmon de Brito (*b* at ......).
[*Palácio do Grão Pará, Avenida Epitácio Pessoa 130, 25600 Petrópolis, Rio de Janeiro, Brazil*].

6. Prince Dom *Francisco* Humberto Miguel Rafael Gabriel Gonzaga, *b* at Petrópolis 9 Dec 1956; *m* there 28 Jan 1978, Christina (*b* at Rio de Janeiro 14 Jan 1953), dau of Gaubert Schmidt and Alice Peçanha, and has issue,
[*Palácio do Grão Pará, Avenida Epitácio Pessoa 130, 25600 Petrópolis, Rio de Janeiro, Brazil*].

    1. Prince Dom *Francisco* Theodoro, *b* at Petrópolis 25 Sept 1979.

Prince Dom Francisco *m* 2ndly (civ) at Petrópolis .... 1980, ...
(*b* at.....), dau of Pires and has further issue,

    2. Princess Dona *Maria* Isabel at Petrópolis ....1982.

    3. Princess Dona Gabriel, *b* at Petrópolis ...... 1989.

Brother and Sisters

1. Princess Dona Isabel (*Isabelle*) Maria Amélia Luiza Vitoria Teresa Joana Michaela Gabriela Rafaela Gonzaga, *b* at Château d'Eu 13 Aug 1911, Dame Star Cross Order; *m* at Palermo 8 April 1931, Henri, Prince of France, Count of Paris, Head of the Royal House of France (*b* at the Château de Nouvion en Thiérache, Aisne 5 July 1908; ✠ at Dreux 19 June 1999).
[*121 Bis Rue de Miromesnil, 75008 Paris, France*].

2. Princess Dona Maria *Francisca* Amelia Luiza Vitoria Teresa Elisabeth Michaela Gabriela Rafaela Gonzaga, *b* at Château d'Eu 8 Sept 1914; ✠ at Lisbon 15 Jan 1968; *m* at Rio de Janeiro 13 Oct (civ) and at Petrópolis 15 Oct (relig) 1942, Dom Duarte Nuno, Infante of Portugal, Duke of Dragança, Head of the Royal House of Portugal (*b* at Seebenstein, Lower Austria 23 Sept 1907; ✠ at Lisbon 24 Dec 1976).

3. Prince Dom *João* Maria Felipe Miguel Gabriel Rafael Gonzaga, *b* at Boulogne-Billancourt, Hauts-de-Seine, France 15 Oct 1916, Gd Cross Order of Dom Pedro I, Imperial Order of the Rose, Gd Cross Constantinian Order of St George, Major Brazilian Air Force, Vice-Pres Pan-Air do Brasil (ret); *m* 1stly at Sintra, Portugal 29

April 1949 (*m* diss by div 1971), Sherifa Fatima (*b* at Cairo 19 April 1923; ✠ at Rio de Janeiro 14 March 1990; *m* 1stly, Prince Nabil Hassan Toussoun who was ✠*k* in a motor accident 15 Sept 1966; *m* 3rdly, Eduardo Bahout who ✠ at Rio de Janeiro 29 Jan 1980), dau of Ismail Chirine Bey and Aisha Mussalam. He *m* 2ndly at Petrópolis 29 April (relig) and at Rio de Janeiro 11 May (civ) 1990, Tereza (*b* at Uba, Minas, Gerais 11 Jan 1929; *m* 1stly, Carlos Eduardo Souza Campos; that *m* diss by div), dau of José Leite and Blanca César, and had issue by his first wife,

[*Rua Fresca 4, 23970 Parati, Rio de Janeiro, Brazil*],

    1. Prince Dom *João* Henrique, *b* at Rio de Janeiro 20 April 1954, Photographer; *m* at Rio de Janeiro 26 June 1986, Stella Christina (*b* at Rio de Janeiro 20 June 1958), dau of Hersias Morado Lutterbach and Stella Carmen Correa Pinto, and has issue,

    [*Avenida Ataulfo de Paiva 135, Sala 1210, 22440 Leblon, Rio de Janeiro, Brazil*].

        1. Prince Dom *João* Philippe, *b* at Rio de Janeiro 27 Nov 1986.

        2. Princess Dona Maria *Cristina, b* at Rio de Janeiro 26 Dec 1989.

4. Princess Dona *Teresa* Maria Teodora Michaela Gabriela Raphaela Gonzaga, *b* at Boulogne-Billancourt 18 June 1919; *m* at Sintra 7 Oct 1957, Ernesto Martorell y Caldero (*b* at Lisbon 1921; ✠ at Madrid 10 Jan 1985).

[*Rua Dom Afonso Henriques 41, Estoril, Portugal*].

<hr>

BULGARIA
(HOUSE OF SAXE-COBURG AND GOTHA)

Prince Ferdinand of Saxe-Coburg and Gotha (*b* 26 Feb 1861; ✠ 10 Sept 1948) was elected Prince of Bulgaria 7 July 1887. He proclaimed himself King (Tsar) of the Bulgarians 5 Oct 1908 and was recognised by the Great Powers 27 April 1909. He abdicated in favour of his elder son 3 Oct 1918. His grandson, King Simeon II left the country without having abdicated 16 Sept 1946. For the early ancestry of this family - see SAXE-COBURG and GOTHA.

Arms:- Gu, a lion rampant, crowned or, armed and langued vert.
Supporters:- Two lions or, armed and langued vert and crowned or.
Motto:- Vierno I Postovenstvo. The shield is ensigned by the Royal Crown of Bulgaria and encircled by the Collar of the Order of Saints

Cyril and Methodius.

Members of the Royal Family bear the title of Prince or Princess of Bulgaria and Duke or Duchess of Saxony with the qualification of Royal Highness.

SIMEON II, KING OF THE BULGARIANS, PRIME MINISTER OF BULGARIA, *b* at Sofia 16 June 1937, reigned

under the Regency of his uncle Prince Kyril, Prime Min Filov and Gen Mihov, left the country without having abdicated, following a communist rigged plebiscite 16 Sept 1946, King Simeon returned to Bulgaria from his enforced exile in 1996, returning permanently on 6 April 2001. King Simeon was sworn in as Prime Minister on 24 July 2001 following a landslide victory in that countrys General Election; Gd Master Order of St Cyril and St Methodius, son of Boris III, King of the Bulgarians (*b* 30 Jan 1894; ✝ 28 Aug 1943) and Princess Giovanna (Ioanna) of Italy (*b* 13 Nov 1907; *m* 25 Oct 1930; ✝ 26 Feb 2000); *m* at Lausanne 20 Jan (civ) and at Vevey 21 Jan (relig) 1962, Margarita (*b* at Madrid 6 Jan 1935), dau of Don Manuel Gomez-Acebo y Modet of the Marquesses de Cortina and Mercedes Cejuela y Fernández, and has issue,

[*Vrana Palace, Sofia, Bulgaria; Avenida del Valle 3, 28003 Madrid, Spain*].

Sons and Daughter

1. *Kardám*, Crown Prince of Bulgaria, Prince of Tirnovo, *b* at Madrid 2 Dec 1962, Master's Degree Water Resources and Economy Penn State College; *m* at Madrid 11 July 1996, Miriam (*b* at Madrid 2 Sept 1963), dau of Don Bernardo de Ungría y Goiburu and Maria del Carmen López Oleaga, and has issue,

[*Avenida Alberto Alcocer 5, 28036 Madrid, Spain*].

    1. Prince *Boris*, *b* at Madrid 12 Oct 1997.

    2. Prince *Beltran*, *b* at Madrid 22 March 1999.

2. *Kyril*, Prince of Preslav, *b* at Madrid 11 July 1964, BA Physics cum laude Princeton University; *m* at Palma de Mallorca, Balearic Islands, Spain 15 Sept 1989, Rosario (*b* at Palma de Mallorca 22 Oct 1968), BA Fine Arts Richmond University in London, dau of Miguel Nadal Bestard and Isabel Puigdorfila Villalonga, and has issue,

[*72 Redcliffe Square, London, SW10 9NB*].

    1. Princess *Mafalda* Cecilia Preslavska, *b* at London 27 July 1994.

    2. Princess *Olympia* Preslavska, *b* at London 14 Dec 1995.

    3. Prince *Tassilo*, *b* at London 20 Jan 2002.

3. *Kubrat*, Prince of Panagiúrishte, *b* at Madrid 5 Nov 1965, Dr of Med Univ of Navarra, Surgeon, Kt Gd Cross Order of St Alexander; *m* at Madrid 2 July 1993, Carla (*b* at Madrid 3 Jan 1969), Law Degree Madrid University, dau of Jaime Royo-Villanova Payá and Carmen Urrestarazu Orueta, and has issue,
[*Calle Joaquin Lorenzo 100, 28035 Madrid, Spain*].

    1. Prince *Mirko* Panagjurski, *b* at Madrid 26 April 1995.

    2. Prince *Lucas* Panagjurski, *b* at Madrid 15 July 1997.

    3. Prince *Tirso* Panagjurski, *b* at Madrid 3 June 2002.

4. *Konstantin-Assen*, Prince of Vídin, *b* at Madrid 5 Dec 1967, MBA Business Adminsitration Columbia University; *m* at Madrid 7 July 1994, María (*b* at Madrid 13 May 1970), Degree in Business Administration Washington University, dau of Alvaro García de la Rasilla y Pineda and María de Gortázar e Ybarra.

    1. Prince *Umberto*, *b* at 25 Nov 1999.

    2. Princess *Sofia*, *b* at 25 Nov 1999.

5. Princess *Kalina*, *b* at Madrid 19 Jan 1972, Artist; *m* at Borovets, Bulgaria 26 Oct 2002, Antonio '*Kitin*' Muñoz y Valcárcel (*b* at Sidi Ifni, Morocco 19 Nov 1958).
[*Avenida del Valle 3, 28003 Madrid, Spain*].

Sister

Princess *Marie-Luisa*, *b* at Sofia 13 Jan 1933; *m* 1stly at Amorbach 14 Feb (civ) and at Cannes 20 Feb (relig) 1957 (*m* diss by div at Frankfurt-am-Main 4 Dec 1968), Karl, Prince zu Leiningen (*b* at Coburg 2 Jan 1928; ✝ at Vered Hagalil, Israel 28 Sept 1990). She *m* 2ndly at Toronto, Ontario, Canada 16 Nov 1969, Bronislaw Chrobok (*b* at Kattowitz 27 Aug 1933), Investment Banker.
[*236 Woodland Road, Madison, N.J. 07940, U.S.A.*]

DENMARK
(HOUSE OF GLÜCKSBORG)

Lutheran:- Christian, Prince of Slesvig-Holsten-Sønderborg-Glücksborg, later King Christian IX, King of Denmark, son of Duke Wilhelm of Schleswig-Holstein-Sonderburg-Glücksburg (*b* 4 Jan 1785; ✝ 17 Feb 1831), was designated as successor to his kinsman, King Frederik VII (*b* 6 Oct 1808; ✝ 15 Nov 1863) of the senior branch of the House of Holstein-Oldenburg (see Oldenburg for the early origins of this family), by a Treaty dated 8 May 1852 and the Danish Law of Succession of 31 July 1853. A new law of succession to the Throne, allowing for the succession of females and limiting it to the descendants of King Christian X was passed 27 March 1953.

Arms:- A cross pattée throughout arg fimbriated gu (Dannebrog); between 1st and 4th or, semée of hearts gu, three lions passant az, crowned or (Denmark); 2nd, or, two lions passant az (Schleswig); 3rd, per fesse, in chief, ax, three crowns or (Sweden); and in base per pale, dexter, az, a ram arg (Faroes); sinister, az, a polar bear seiant ramor, two bars gu (Oldenburg). *Supporters:-* Two wild men or savages wreathed around the loins and temples with ivy and bearing spiked clubs all ppr brog and the Elephant. The achievement is borne on a mantle gu, fringed and tasselled or, doubled erm and surmounted by the Royal Crown of Denmark.

Members of the Royal Family bear the title of Prince or Princess of Denmark with the qualification of Royal Highness for the children of the Monarch and Highness for cadet members, following the Cabinet Order of 23 Sept 1774.

MARGRETHE II Alexandrine Thorhildur Ingrid, **QUEEN OF DENMARK**, *b* at Copenhagen 16 April 1940, dau of King Frederik IX (*b* 11 March 1899; ✝ 14 Jan 1972) and Princess Ingrid of Sweden (*b* 28 March 1910; *m* 24 May 1935; ✝ 7 Nov 2000); *succ* her father; *m* at Copenhagen 10 June 1967, Henri (Henrik) de Laborde de Monpezat (*b* at Talence, Gironde, France 11 June 1934), *cr* Prince of Denmark with the qualification of Royal Highness by King Frederik IX 1 June 1967, Kt Order of the Elephant, Chancellor Royal Danish Orders. [*Amalienborg Palace, 1257 Copenhagen, Denmark; Fredensborg Castle, 3480 Fredensborg , Denmark; Marselisborg Castle, 8000 Aarhus, Denmark*].

Sons

1. *Frederik* André Henrik Christian, Crown Prince of Denmark, *b* at Copenhagen 26 May 1968
[*Amalienborg Palace, 1257 Copenhagen, Denmark*].
2. Prince *Joachim* Holger Valdemar Christian, *b* at Copenhagen 7 June 1969; *m* at Fredensborg Castle 18 Nov 1995, Alexandra (*b* at Hong Kong 30 June 1964), dau of Richard Manley and Christa Novotny. [*Amalienborg Palace, 1257 Copenhagen, Denmark*].

    1.Prince *Nikolai* William Alexander Frederik, *b* at Copenhagen 28 Aug 1999.
    2.Prince *Felix* Henrik Valdemar Christian, *b* at.Copenhagen 22 July 2002.

Sisters

1. Princess *Benedikte* Astrid Ingeborg Ingrid, *b* at Amalienborg 29

April 1944; *m* at Fredensborg 3 Feb 1968, Richard, 6th Prince (Furst) zu Sayn-Wittgenstein-Berleburg (*b* at Giessen 29 Oct 1934).
[*Schloß Berleburg, 57319 Bad Berleburg, Westfalen, Germany*]
2. Princess *Anne-Marie* Dagmar Ingrid, *b* at Copenhagen 30 Aug 1946, *m* at Athens 18 Sept 1964, Constantine II, King of the Hellenes (*b* at Psychiko 2 June 1940).
[*4 Linnell Drive, Hampstead Way, London N.W.11*].

Brother of Father

Issue of King Christian X (*b* 26 Sept 1870; *succ* 14 May 1912; ✠ 20 April 1947) and Duchess Alexandrine of Mecklenburg-Schwerin (*b* 24 Dec 1879; *m* 26 April 1898; ✠ 28 Dec 1952), having had issue, among whom,

Prince *Knud* Christian Frederik Michael, *b* at Sorgenfri 27 July 1900; ✠ at Genofte 14 June 1976, Hereditary Prince of Denmark (from 5 June 1953), Adm Danish Navy, Heir Presumptive to the Danish Throne 1947-53; *m* at Fredensborg 8 Sept 1933, his 1st cousin, Princess Caroline-Mathilde (*b* at Jaegersborghus 27 April 1912; ✠ at Sorgenfri 12 Dec 1995), dau of Prince Harald of Denmark and Princess Helena of Schleswig-Holstein-Sonderburg-Glücksburg, and had issue,

> 1. Princess *Elisabeth* Caroline-Mathilde Alexandrine Helena Olga Thyra Feodora Estrid Margarethe Désirée, *b* at Copenhagen 8 May 1935.
> [*2840 Holte, Denmark*].
> 2. Prince *Ingolf* Christian Frederik Knud Harald Gorm Gustav Viggo Valdemar Aage, *b* at Sorgenfri 17 Feb 1940, *renounced his rights of succession for himself and his descendants along with the title of Prince of Denmark and the qualification of Royal Highness and received the title of Count af Rosenborg 4 Jan 1968*; *m* 1stly at Lyngby 13 Jan 1968, Inge (*b* at Copenhagen 21 Jan 1938; ✠ at Egeland 21 July 1996), dau of Georg Terney and Jenny Kamilla Hansen; *m* 2ndly at Egtved 7 March 1998, Sussie (*b* at Copenhagen 20 Feb 1950) dau of Fritz Walther Pedersen and Ruth Hjorhøy.
> [*Egeland, Ø.Starup, 6040 Egtved, Denmark*].
> 3. Prince *Christian* Frederik Franz Knud Harald Carl Oluf Gustav Georg Erik, *b* at Sorgenfri 22 Oct 1942; *renounced his rights of succession for himself and his descendants along with the title of Prince of Denmark and the qualification of*

Royal Highness and received the title of Count af Rosenborg;
m at Lyngby 27 Feb 1971, Anne-Dorthe (*b* at Copenhagen 3
Oct 1947), dau of Edgard Wilhelm (*Villy*) Maltoft-Nielsen
and Bodil Marie Elisabeth Maltoft-Nielsen, and has issue,
[*Sorgenfri Slot, 2800 Lyngby, Denmark*].

> 1. Countess *Josephine* Caroline Elisabeth, *b* at
> Frederikssund 29 Oct 1972; *m* at Lyngby 3 Oct 1998,
> *Thomas* Christian Schmidt (*b* at Copenhagen 22 April
> 1970).
> [*Frederiksholms Kanal 26D, 1200 Copenhagen,
> Denmark*].
> 2. Countess *Camilla* Alexandrine Kristine Anastasia
> Caroline Amalie (twin with Countess Josephine), *b* at
> Frederikssund 29 Oct 1972; *m* at Søllerød 20 May
> 1995, Mikael Rosanes (*b* at Copenhagen 8 Feb 1952).
> [*Virumgade 24, 2830 Virum, Denmark*].
> 3. Countess *Feodora* Mathilde Helena, *b* at
> Frederikssund 27 Feb 1975.
> [*Frederiksholms Kanal 26D, 1200 Copenhagen,
> Denmark*].

Brothers of Grandfather
Issue of King Frederik VIII (*b* 3 June 1843; ✠ 14 May 1912) and
Princess of Louise of Sweden (*b* 31 Oct 1851; *m* 28 July 1869; ✠ 20
March 1926), having had issue, among whom,

Sons
1. Prince Christian Frederik *Carl* George Valdemar Axel, who
became **HAAKON VII, KING OF NORWAY** -(*see Norway*).
2. Prince *Harald* Christian Frederik, *b* at Charlottenlund Slot 8 Oct
1876; ✠ at Copenhagen 30 March 1949, Lt-Gen Danish Army,
Chancellor Royal Danish Orders; *m* at Glücksburg 28 April 1909,
Princess Helena (*b* at Grünholz 1 June 1888; ✠ at Hellerup 30 June
1962), dau of Friedrich-Ferdinand, Duke of Schleswig-Holstein-
Sonderburg-Glücksburg and Princess Karoline of Schleswig-Holstein-
Sonderburg-Augustenburg, and had issue, among whom,

> 1. Prince *Oluf* Christian Carl Axel, *b* at Copenhagen 10 March
> 1923; ✠ at Copenhagen 19 Dec 1990; *renounced his rights of
> succession for himself and his descendants along with the
> title of Prince of Denmark and the qualification of Royal
> Highness and received the title of Count af Rosenborg 13 Jan*

1948, Wing Cmdr Royal Danish Air Force, Kt Order of the
Elephant; *m* 1stly at Copenhagen 4 Feb 1948 (*m* diss by div
at 20 Jan 1977), Annie Helene *Dorrit* (*b* at Copenhagen 8
Sept 1926) [*Helleruplund Allé 27, 2900 Hellerup, Denmark*],
dau of Gunnar Puggaard-Müller and Gerda Annie Nielsen.
He *m* 2ndly at Lyngby 17 Sept 1982 (*m* diss by div at Lyngby
19 Dec 1983), *Lise* Wolf-Jürgensen (*b* at Frederiksberg 30
June 1935), [*Krokusvej 11, 4840 Nørre Alslev*] and had issue
from his first wife,

> 1. Count *Ulrik* Harald Gunnar Oluf, *b* at Copenhagen
> 17 Dec 1950; *m* at Copenhagen 4 April 1981, Tove (*b*
> at Copenhagen 14 Dec 1950), dau of Axel Waigner
> Larsen and Karen Dorothea Nielsen, and has issue,
> [*Blomstervænget 30, 2800 Kgs. Lyngby, Denmark*].
>
>> 1. Countess *Katharina,* Dortha Helene *b* at
>> Gentofte 1 May 1982.
>> [*Blomstervænget 30, 2800 Kgs. Lyngby,
>> Denmark*].
>> 2. Count *Philip, b* at Gentofte 8 May 1986.
>
> 2. Countess *Charlotte* Helene Annie Dorrit, *b* at
> Ordrup 11 April 1953; *m* 1stly at Ordrup 12 Nov 1977
> (*m* diss by div 25 July 1979), Jens Philipsen (*b* at
> Vilborg 29 Sept 1954). She *m* 2ndly at Lyngby 11
> April 1981, Torben Gyldenfeldt Wulff (*b* at Lyngby 15
> Sept 1954).
> [*Christian X's Allé 70, 2800 Lyngby, Denmark*]

Brother of Great-Grandfather
Issue of King Christian IX of Denmark (see above) and Princess
Louise of Hesse-Cassel (*b* 7 Sept 1817; *m* 26 May 1842; ✝ 29 Sept
1898), having had issue, among whom,

Sons
1. Prince Christian *Wilhelm* Ferdinand Adolf Georg, who was elected
GEORGE I, KING OF THE HELLENES -(*see Greece*).
2. Prince *Valdemar, b* at Bernstorff Slot 27 Oct 1858; ✝ at
Copenhagen 14 Jan 1939, Adm Danish Navy; *m* at Paris 20 Oct (civ)
and at Château d'Eu 22 Oct (relig) 1885, Princess Marie (*b* at Ham,
Surrey 13 Jan 1865; ✝ at Copenhagen 4 Dec 1909), dau of Prince
Robert of Bourbón-Orléans, Duke de Chartres and Princess Marie
Amélie of Bourbón-Orléans, and had issue, who were granted the

qualification of Royal Highness 5 Feb 1904,

    1. Prince *Axel* Christin Georg, *b* at Copenhagen 12 Aug 1888; ✝ there 14 July 1964, Adm Danish Navy, Mem Int'l Olympic Committee from 1932, Dir Scandinavian Airlines System, Kt Orders of the Elephant of Denmark, the Seraphim of Sweden and the Black Eagle of Prussia; *m* at Stockholm 22 May 1919, Princess Margaretha (*b* at Stockholm 25 June 1899; ✝ at Tranemosegaard, Rønnede, Island of Zealand 4 Jan 1977), dau of Prince Carl of Sweden, Duke of Västergötland and Princess Ingeborg of Denmark, and had issue, among whom,

        1. Prince *Flemming* Valdemar Carl Axel, *b* at Stockholm 9 March 1922; ✝ at Antibes 19 June 2002; *renounced his rights of succession for himself and his descendants along with the title of Prince of Denmark and the qualification of Royal Highness and received the title of Count af Rosenborg 14 June 1949*; Cmdr Royal Danish Navy; *m* at Copenhagen 24 May 1949, Alice Ruth (*b* at Copenhagen 8 Oct 1924), dau of Kai Nielsen and Edith Fischer, and has issue,
[*Skovvangen 34, 2920 Charlottenlund, Denmark*].

            1. Count (*Axel*) Valdemar Georg Flemming Kai, *b* at Copenhagen 24 Jan 1950; *m* 1stly at Oxholm, North Jutland 24 May 1975 (*m* diss by div 1986), *Jane* (*b* at Höräp 17 Sept 1950), dau of Major Steen Glarborg and Kirsten Vibeke Hansen, and has issue,

                1. Countess *Julie*, *b* at Aalborg 10 May 1977.
[*Gothersgade 158, 1123 Copenhagen, Denmark*].

                2. Count *Carl Johan*, *b* at Copenhagen 15 Nov 1979.
[*Louise Park 12, 2960 Rungsted, Denmark*].

            Count (*Axel*) Valdemar Georg Flemming Kai, *m* 2ndly at Hørsterkøb 10 Dec 1988, Jutta (*b* at Copenhagen 9 Nov 1958), dau of Villy Beck and Tove Beck, and has further issue,
[*Louise Park 12, 2960 Rungsted, Denmark*].

                3. Countess *Desirée* Christina, *b* at Copenhagen 25 Dec 1990.

4. Count *Alexander*, *b* at Copenhagen 4
Nov 1993.

2. Count *Birger* Valdemar Georg Flemming
Kai Axel, *b* at Copenhagen 24 Jan 1950 (twin
with Count Axel); *m* 1stly at Skovshoved 19
Oct 1974 (*m* diss by div 1978), Minna Benedicte
(*b* at Helleruplund 3 July 1949), dau of Niels
Benedict Tillisch and Countess Dagmar Knuth
[*Buddingevej 80, 1. tv, 2800 Kgs. Lyngby,
Denmark*]. He *m* 2ndly at 28 Nov 1981 (*m* diss
by div 1990), Susanne (*b* at Copenhagen 13
Feb 1951; W at Thisted 22 Oct 1999), dau of
Svend Erik Kristensen and Gurli Soerensen,
and has issue from his first wife,
[*Hjortevangen 3, 2920 Charlottenlund,
Denmark*].

1. Countess *Benedikte* Margaretha
Dagmar, *b* at Marstal 20 July 1975.
[*Ulrikkenborg Allé 25, 2800 Kgs.
Lyngby, Denmark*].

3. Count *Carl Johan* Valdemar Georg
Flemming Kai Axel, *b* at Copenhagen 30 May
1952; *m* at Skovshoved 3 Sept 1982 (*m* diss by
div at Copenhagen 9 Oct 1986), Dorrit (*b* at
Copenhagen 23 Oct 1956), dau of Paul Zander
Olsen and Anne Berta Terning, [*Borups Allé
109, 2000 Frederiksberg, Denmark*] and has
issue,

1. Countess *Caroline*, *b* at Copenhagen
31 March 1984.

He *m* 2ndly at Venice 19 Nov 1994, *Collette*
Vivian (*b* at New York 9 May 1967), dau of
Michael Cabral and Dorris Jamieson, and has
further issue,
[*14a Hollywood Road, London SW10 9HY*].

2. Countess *Josephine* Coco, *b* at London
24 June 1999.

4. Countess *Désirée* Märtha Ingeborg, *b* at
Copenhagen 2 Feb 1955; *m* 1stly at Kongsted
23 May 1981 (*m* diss by div 30 July 1987), *Fergus*
Stuartson Smith (*b* at Rochester U.S.A. 17

Sept 1949). She *m* 2ndly at Gentofte 6 Feb 1988, Peter Rindom (*b* at Copenhagen 10 Oct 1955).

[*Schimmelmanns Bej 32, 2920 Charlottenlund, Denmark*].

2. Prince *Erik* Frederik Christian Alexander, *b* at Copenhagen 8 Nov 1890; ✝ at Copenhagen 10 Sept 1950; *renounced his rights of succession for himself and his descendants along with the title of Prince of Denmark and the qualification of Royal Highness and received the title of HH Prince Erik, Count af Rosenborg 2 Dec 1923*; *m* at Ottawa, Canada 11 Feb 1924 (*m* diss by div 1937), Lois Frances (*b* at Ottawa 2 Aug 1897; ✝ at Copenhagen 26 Feb 1941), dau of John Frederick Booth and Frances Hunsiker, and had issue, among whom,

1. Count *Christian* Edward Valdemar Jean Frederik Peter, *b* at Bjergbygaard 16 July 1932; ✝ at Overton, England 24 March 1997; *m* at Stouby 10 Aug 1962 (*m* diss by div 15 Jan 1996), Karin (*b* at Stouby 12 Aug 1938), [*Skovridervej 18, 4171 Glumsø, Denmark*], dau of Folmer Lüttichau and Ingeborg Carl, and had issue,

1. Count *Valdemar* Erik Flemming Christian, *b* at Skovshoved 9 July 1965; *m* at Bordeaux 29 June 1996, *Charlotte* Diane Isabelle (*b* at Cognac 23 April 1967), dau of Roland Cruse and Annette Ingemann.

[*Solvaenget 4, 2100 Copenhagen, Denmark*].

1. Count *Nicolai* Christian Valdemar, *b* at Gentofte 6 Nov 1997.

2. Countess *Marie* Geraldine Charlotte, *b* at Copenhagen 7 May 1999.

2. Countess Marina Isabelle Ingeborg Karin, *b* at Skovshoved 28 March 1971.

[*Willemoesgade 22, 2100 Copenhagen, Denmark*]

GREAT BRITAIN AND NORTHERN IRELAND
(HOUSE OF WINDSOR)

Anglican:- William I the Conqueror (*b* 1027/1028; ✝ 9 Sept 1087) *succ* his father as Duke of Normandy 1035 and obtained the crown of England by conquest 14 Oct 1066; the English Crown has passed through the female line several times and was joined to the Scottish Crown after the death of Queen Elizabeth I (*b* 7 Sept 1533; ✝ 24 March 1603) who was *succ* by James VI, King of Scots as James I, King of England, Scotland, etc (*b* 19 June 1566; ✝ 27 March 1625), great-grandson of Margaret, elder dau of Henry VII, King of England. His son, Charles I, King of England, Scotland, etc (*b* 19 Nov 1600) was accused of treason and beheaded 30 Jan 1649; the Crown was restored in 1660 to his son, Charles II, King of England, etc (*b* 29 May 1630; ✝ 6 Feb 1685); the House of Guelf (see Hanover) succeeded to the Crown in accordance with the terms of the Act of Settlement of 12 June 1701 but, due to the Salic Law, the Crown of England was separated from that of Hanover on the death of King William IV; his niece, Victoria, Queen of the United Kingdom of Great Britain and Ireland, etc (*b* 24 May 1819; *succ* 20 June 1837; ✝ 22 Jan 1901) was proclaimed Empress of India 1 Jan 1877; married her cousin, Prince Albert of Saxe-Coburg and Gotha, *cr* Prince Consort by Patent 26 June 1857 (*b* 26 Aug 1819; *m* 10 Feb 1840; ✝ 14 Dec 1861) (see Saxe-Coburg and Gotha). George V, King of the United Kingdom of Great Britain and Ireland, etc assumed by Royal Proclamation 17 July 1917 the name of Windsor for his House and Family; the Crown again passed through the female line to Elizabeth II, Queen of the United Kingdom of Great Britain and Northern Ireland who married Philip Mountbatten, Duke of Edinburgh, formerly Prince Philip of Greece and Denmark (see Greece), and declared in Council 9 April 1952 that she and her children shall be styled and known as the House and Family of Windsor. On 8 Feb 1960 a declaration in Council stated that descendants of the Queen shall bear the surname of Mountbatten-Windsor, other than those bearing Royal Attributes and female descendants who marry into other families.

Arms:- Quarterly: 1st and 4th, gu, three lions passant guardant in pale or (England); 2nd, or, a lion rampant within a double tressure flory counter-flory gules (Scotland); 3rd, az, a harp or, stringed arg (Ireland); the whole encircled with the Garter. Crests:- Upon the Royal helmet the Crown ppr, thereon a lion statant guardant or, royally crowned, also proper (England); on an Imperial Crown ppr a lion sejant affrontée gu imperially crowned or, holding in the dexter paw a sword, and in the sinister a sceptre erect also ppr (Scotland). Supporters:- Dexter, a lion rampant guardant or, crowned as the crest; Sinister, a unicorn argent, armed, crined and unguled or, gorged with a coronet composed of crosses patées and fleurs-de-lis, a chain affixed thereto, passing between the fore-legs and reflexed over the back, of the last. Mottoes:- Dieu et mon droit (England); In defens; Nemo me impune lacessit (Scotland).

The Children and Grandchildren of a Sovereign in the male line bear the title of Prince or Princess of the Kingdom of Great Britain and Northern Ireland with the style of Royal Highness. The recent custom has been for the children of a Sovereign to be distinguished by the prefix "The" before the title of Prince or Princess. The great-grandchildren in the male line of a Sovereign bear the surname of Windsor and the prefix of Lord or Lady before their Christian names unless they happen to hold an hereditary honour or bear a courtesy title.

ELIZABETH II Alexandra Mary, **QUEEN OF THE UNITED KINGDOM OF GREAT BRITAIN and NORTHERN IRELAND** and of Her Other Realms and Territories, Head of the Commonwealth, Defender of the Faith, Sovereign of all the British Orders of Knighthood, appt'd a Lady of the Most Noble Order of the Garter 1947, crowned at Westminster Abbey 2 June 1953, Lord High Adm of the United Kingdom 1964, has many foreign Orders and before her accession rec'd several Hon Degrees and Freedoms, *b* at 17 Bruton Street, London 21 April 1926, dau of King George VI (*b* 14 Dec 1895; ✢ 6 Feb 1952) and Lady Elizabeth Bowes-Lyon, (*b* 4 Aug 1900; *m* 26 April 1923; ✢ 31 March 2002); *m* at Westminster Abbey 20 Nov 1947, *Philip* Mountbatten, formerly Prince *Philip* of Greece and Denmark (*b* at Mon Repos, Corfu 10 June 1921), *cr* Duke of Edinburgh, Earl of Merioneth and Baron Greenwich, of Greenwich, Co London and granted the style of Royal Highness 19 Nov 1947, having relinquished the name and the titles of Prince of Greece and Denmark and assumed the surname of Mountbatten on becoming a naturalised British subject 28 Feb 1947, granted the style and dignity of a Prince of the UK of Great Britain and Northern Ireland 22 Feb 1957, KG (1947), KT (1952), OM (1968), Gd Master and 1st or Principal Kt Order of the British Empire (1953), PC (1951) and PC Canada (1957), has many foreign Orders, Hon Degrees, Freedoms and Fellowships, took his seat in the House of Lords 21 July 1947; lost the right to sit in the House of Lords by virtue of the House of Lords Act 1999 (Chapter 34) of 11 Nov 1999, Adm of the Fleet, Field Marshal in the Army, and Marshal of the RAF 1953, Capt Gen Royal Marines 1953, Col Gren Guards from 1975, Chairman, President or Patron of many charitable organisations, etc.

[*Buckingham Palace, London, SW1A 1AA; Windsor Castle, Berkshire SL4 1NJ; Balmoral Castle, Ballater AB35 5TB,*

Aberdeenshire, Scotland; Sandringham House, Norfolk PE35 6EN].

Sons and Daughter

1. Prince *Charles* Philip Arthur George, Prince of Wales and Earl of Chester (since 26 July 1958), Duke of Cornwall, Duke of Rothesay, Earl of Carrick, Baron of Renfrew, Lord of the Isles and Prince and Great Steward of Scotland (since 6 Feb 1952), *b* at Buckingham Palace 14 Nov 1948; invested as Prince of Wales at Caernarvon Castle 1 July 1969, KG (1958, installed 1968), KT (1977), GCB and Great Master Order of the Bath from 1975, Kt of the Order of Australia (AK) from 1981, Extra Companion of the Queen's Service Order (QSO) from 1983, took his seat in the House of Lords 11 Feb 1970; lost the right to sit in the House of Lords by virtue of the House of Lords Act 1999 (Chapter 34) of 11 Nov 1999, PC (1977), Col-in-Chief The Royal Dragoon Guards, The 22nd (Cheshire) Regiment, Royal Regiment of Wales (24th/41st Foot) 1969, The Parachute Regiment, The Royal Gurkha Rifles, Army Air Corps, The Royal Canadian Dragoons, Lord Strathcona's Horse (Royal Canadians), Royal Regiment of Canada (10th Royal Grenadiers), Royal Winnipeg Rifles, Royal Australian Armoured Corps, The Royal Pacific Islands Regiment, Air Reserve Group of Air Command (of Canada), Dept Col-in-Chief The Highlanders (Seaforth, Gordons and Camerons), Col Welsh Guards from 1975, Royal Hon Col The Queen's Own Yeomanry, Air Cdre-in-Chief Royal New Zealand Air Force, Royal Hon Air Cdre RAF Valley, entered Royal Navy 1971, Major General, Army, Vice Admiral RN (*Apptd* 14 Nov 2002), Major-General, Army, and Air Vice Marshal, RAF 1998, Elder Brother Trinity House from 1974, etc, Gd Cross Order of the White Rose of Finland (1969), Gd Cordon Supreme Order of the Chrysanthemum of Japan (1971), Gd Cross Order of the House of Orange of the Netherlands (1972), Gd Cross Order of the Oak Crown of Luxembourg (1972), Kt Order of the Elephant of Denmark (1974), Gd Cross Order of Ojaswi Rajanya of Nepal (1975), Kt Order of the Seraphim of Sweden (1975), Gd Cross Order of the Southern Cross of Brazil (1978), Collar of the Republic of Egypt (1981), Gd Cross Order of Orange Nassau of the   Netherlands (1982), Gd Cross Order of the St Olav of Norway (1978), Officer Order of the Star of Ghana (1977), Gd Cross of the Legion of Honour of France (1984), Gd Cross Order of Carlos III of Spain, Gd Cross of the Lion of Malawi (1985), Gd Cordon of Khalifiyyeh Order of Bahrain (1986), Gd Cordon of Order of Merit of Saudi Arabia (1986), Collar of Merit of Qatari

Order (1986), Gold Medal of Mubarak the Great of Kuwait (1993), Most Esteemed Family Order of Brunei (1996), and several other foreign Orders and Hon Freedoms and Fellowships, has acted as Counsellor of State on several occasions, *educ* Gordonstoun, Geelong Grammar School, Melbourne, Trinity College Cambridge (BA 1970, MA 1975), and Univ Coll of Wales, Aberystwyth; *m* at St Paul's Cathedral, London 29 July 1981 (*m* diss by div at London 28 Aug 1996), Lady *Diana* Frances (*b* at Park House, Sandringham 1 July 1961; ✠ at Paris 31 Aug 1997), dau of Edward John Spencer, 8th Earl Spencer and Hon Frances Ruth Burke Roche of the Barons Fermoy, and has issue,

[*St. James's Palace, London, SW1A 1BS; Highgrove House, Doughton, Tetbury, Gloucestershire GL8 8TN*].

    1. Prince *William* Arthur Philip Louis, *b* at St Mary's Hospital, Paddington, London 21 June 1982.

    2. Prince *Henry* Charles Albert David, *b* at St Mary's Hospital, Paddington, London 15 Sept 1984.

2. Princess *Anne* Elizabeth Alice Louise, *b* at Clarence House, London 15 Aug 1950, Princess Royal since 13 June 1987, Lady of the Garter (LG) granted dispensation of KG (1994), GCVO (1974), Lady of the Thistle (LT) from 2000, Rear-Adm Chief Cmmdt for Women in the Royal Navy, Col-in-Chief The King's Royal Hussars, the Worcestershire and Sherwood Foresters Regiment (29th/45th Foot), Royal Scots (The Royal Regiment), 8th Canadian Hussars (Princess Louise's), Royal Newfoundland Regiment, Canadian Forces Communications and Electronics Branch, Grey and Simcoe Foresters (Royal Canadian Armoured Corps), Royal Regina Rifle Regiment, Royal Australian Corps of Signals, Royal New Zealand Corps of Signals, Royal New Zealand Nursing Corps, Col Blues and Royals (Royal Horse Guards and 1st Dragoons), Affiliated Col-in-Chief The Queen's Gurkha Signals, The Queen's Own Gurkha Transport Regiment, Royal Hon Col University of London Officers' Training Corp, Royal Hon Air Cdre RAF Lyneham, University of London Air Squadron, Comdt First Aid Nursing Yeomary (Princess Royal's Volunteer Corps), Cmdt-in-Chief Ambulance and Nursing Cadets, St John Ambulance Brigade, Pres Save the Children Fund, received Freedom of the City of London 1976, Chancellor of London University from 1981, Equestrian, won European Championships at Burghley 1971, Member British Three-Day-Event Team Olympic Games at Montreal 1976, Dame of Justice Order of St John of Jerusalem (1971), Austrian Order of Merit (1969), Order of the White

Rose of Finland (1969), Order of the Precious Crown 1st Class of Japan (1971), Darjah Utama Bakti Chemerland of Singapore (1972), Most Esteemed Family Order of Brunei (1972), and Grand Cross Order of the Oak Crown of Luxembourg (1972), Riband of the Order of the Aztec Eagle of Mexico (1973), Gd Cross of St Olav of Norway, has acted as Counsellor of State on several occasions, *educ* Benenden; *m* 1stly at Westminster Abbey 14 Nov 1973 (*m* diss by div 23 April 1992), Capt *Mark* Anthony Peter Phillips, CVO, ADC, 1st Queen's Dragoon Guards (*b* at Tetbury, Gloucestershire 22 Sept 1948). She *m* 2ndly at Crathie Church, nr Balmoral 12 Dec 1992, Cdre *Timothy* James Hamilton Laurence (*b* at Camberwell, London 1 March 1955), MVO, RN, and has issue, by her first husband, a son and dau. (*see appendix*).

[*Gatcombe Park, Minchinhampton, Stroud, Gloucestershire GL6 9AT*].

3. Prince *Andrew* Albert Christian Edward, Duke of York, Earl of Inverness, Baron Killyleagh (since 23 July 1986), *b* at Buckingham Palace 19 Feb 1960, CVO (1979), took his seat in the House of Lords 11 Feb 1987; lost the right to sit in the House of Lords by virtue of the House of Lords Act 1999 (Chapter 34) of 11 Nov 1999, Entered the Royal Navy 1979, Diplomacy Section of the Naval Staff Directorate 27 April 1999, Cdr 27 April 1999, Personal ADC to the Queen 1984, served as helicopter pilot in HMS Invincible in the South Atlantic Campaign 1982, Gd Cross of St Olaf of Norway; Adm Sea Cadet Corps, Col-in-Chief The Staffordshire Regiment (The Prince of Wales's) (1989), The Royal Irish Regiment (27th (Inniskilling), 83rd, 87th and The Ulster Defence Regiment) (1992), The Queen's York Rangers (First Americans) (1997), The London Regiment (1997), The Duke of York's Own Royal New Zealand Army Logistic Regiment (1996) and Royal Hon Air Cdre RAF Lossiemouth *educ* Gordonstoun, Lakefield College, Ontario and Dartmouth; *m* at Westminster Abbey 23 July 1986 (*m* diss by div at London 30 May 1996), *Sarah* Margaret (*b* at London 15 Oct 1959), dau of Major Ronald Ivor Ferguson and Susan Mary Wright, and has issue,

[*Buckingham Palace, London, SW1A 1AA; Sunninghill Park, Ascot, Berkshire SL5 7TH*].

    1. Princess *Beatrice* Elizabeth Mary, *b* at Portland Hospital, London 8 Aug 1988.

    2. Princess *Eugenie* Victoria Helena, *b* at Portland Hospital, London 23 March 1990.

4. Prince *Edward* Antony Richard Louis, Earl of Wessex, Viscount

Severn (since 19 June 1999), *b* at Buckingham Palace 10 March 1964, Silver Jubilee Medal (1977), Commander Royal Victorian Order (CVO) (1989), New Zealand 1990 Commemoration Medal (1990), Royal Brunei Silver Jubilee Medal (1992), lost the right to sit in the House of Lords by virtue of the House of Lords Act 1999 (Chapter 34) of 11 Nov 1999; has acted as Counsellor of State on several occasions, *educ* Gordonstoun, Jesus College Cambridge (BA 1986/MA 1990), House Tutor Wanganui Collegiate School (New Zealand) 1982/3, entered Royal Marines 1983, resigned 1987, Patron Classworks Theatre Cambridge, Pres Children's Film Unit, Patron City of Birmingham Symphony Orchestra, Trustee Duke of Edinburgh's Award, Trustee Duke of Edinburgh's Award International Foundation, Pres Commonwealth Games Federation, Pres Globe Theatre, Saskatchewan, Canada, Patron Haddo Arts Trust, Patron London Mozart Players, Patron National Youth Theatre of Great Britain, Patron Ocean Youth Trust, Patron National Youth Orchestra of Scotland, Patron The Royal Exchange Theatre Company, Patron Scottish Badminton Union, *m* at Windsor Castle 19 June 1999, *Sophie* Helen (*b* at Oxford 20 Jan 1965), dau of Christopher Bournes Rhys-Jones and Mary O'Sullivan.
[*Buckingham Palace, London, SW1A 1AA; Bagshot Park, Bagshot, Surrey GU19 5PJ*].

Sister

1. Princess *Margaret* Rose, *b* at Glamis Castle, Angus 21 Aug 1930; ✠ at London 9 Feb 2002; *m* at Westminster Abbey 6 May 1960 (*m* diss by div at London 5 July 1978), Antony Armstrong-Jones (*b* at London 7 March 1930; *m* 2ndly Lucy Mary Davies, that *m* diss by div Sept 2000), *cr* Earl of Snowdon (1961), GCVO (1969); life Peerage (1999).

Brothers of Father

Issue of King George V (*b* 3 June 1865; *succ* 6 May 1910; ✠ 20 Jan 1936) and Princess Mary of Teck (*b* 26 May 1867; *m* 6 July 1893; ✠ 24 March 1953), having had issue, among whom,

Sons

1. Prince *Henry* William Frederick Albert, Duke of Gloucester, Earl of Ulster and Baron Culloden (since 31 March 1928), *b* at York Cottage 31 March 1900; ✠ at Barnwell, Northampton 10 June 1974, KG (1921), KT (1933), KP (1934), Great Master and GCB (1942), GCMG (1935), GCVO (1922), had Royal Victorian Chain (1932), PC (1925), Field Marshal in the Army 1955, Marshal of the RAF 1958,

Personal ADC from 1929, Gov-Gen of Australia 1944-47, Lord High
Commissioner to General Assembly Church of Scotland 1949 and
1963, Master of Trinity House 1942-69, High Steward of King's Lynn
and of Windsor and Ranger of Epping Forest, Chairman King George's
Jubilee Trust, Gd Prior and Bailiff Gd Cross Order of St John of
Jerusalem 1930, Grand Pres League of Mercy, etc, had many foreign
Orders, *educ* Eton, RMC and Trinity College, Cambridge; *m* at
Buckingham Palace 6 Nov 1935, Lady *Alice* Christabel (*b* at London
25 Dec 1901), GCB (1975), CI (1937), GCVO (1948), GBE (1937),
GCStJ (1936), Star and Badge of Gd Cross Order of the Crown of
Roumania (1938), Gd Cordon Order of Al Kamal of Egypt (1950),
and Star and Badge Order of the Queen of Sheba of Ethiopia (1958),
Col-in-Chief KOSB, Dep Col-in-Chief The King's Royal Hussars and
Royal Anglican Regiment, Air Chief Marshal (1990), Air Chief Cmdt
Women RAF (1994), etc, dau of Charles Montagu-Douglas Scott, 7th
Duke of Buccleuch and (9th Duke of) Queensberry, KT, GCVO and
Lady Margaret Bridgeman of the Earls of Bradford, and had issue,
[*Kensington Palace, London W8 4PU*].

    1. Prince *William* Henry Andrew Frederick, *b* at Barnet,
Herts 18 Dec 1941; ✝*k* in a flying accident at Wolverhampton
28 Aug 1972, FRGS, acted as Counsellor of State on several
occasions from 1963, Cmdt-in-Chief St John Ambulance
Brigade 1968, Member Guild Air Pilots and Air Navigators,
joined Commonwealth Relations Office 1965, 3rd Sec Tokyo
1965-68, 2nd (Commercial) Sec Lagos 1968- 70, Hon Freeman
Mercers' (1963), Merchant Taylors' (1971) and Grocers'
Liveryman (1972), *educ* Eton and Magdalene College,
Cambridge.

    2. Prince *Richard* Alexander Walter George, 2nd Duke of
Gloucester, etc, *b* at Northampton 26 Aug 1944, KG (1997)
GCVO (1974), took his seat in the House of Lords 23 Oct
1974; lost the right to sit in the House of Lords by virtue of the
House of Lords Act 1999 (Chapter 34) of 11 Nov 1999, MRIBA,
has acted as Counsellor of State on several occasions from
1966, Architect, Col-in-Chief The Gloucester, Berkshire and
Wiltshire Regiment, The Royal Logistics Corps, Deputy
Col-in-Chief Royal Monmouthshire Royal Engineers (Militia),
Honorary Air Marshal (1996), Royal Honorary Air Cdre RAF
Odiham, No 501 (County of Gloucester) Squadron Royal
Auxiliary Air Force, Gd Prior and Bailiff Gd Cross Order of
St John of Jerusalem from 1975, Liveryman Vintners' Co 1965,

Pres Institute of Advanced Motorists from 1971, Vice-Pres LEPRA, Patron-in-Chief New Islington and Hackney Housing Association, etc, author of "On Public View", "The Face of London", etc, BA 1966, MA 1968, DipArch 1969, *educ* Eton and Magdalene College, Cambridge; *m* at Barnwell Parish Church, Northamptonshire 8 July 1972, Birgitte Eva Van Deurs, (*b* at Odense, Island of Funen, Denmark 20 June 1946), GCVO (1989), Dame of Justice Order of St John of Jerusalem (1975), Freeman City of London 1973, Col-in-Chief Royal Australian Army Educational Corps, Royal New Zealand Army Educational Corps, Royal Army Dental Corps, Deputy Col-in-Chief Adjutant General's Corps (1992), yr dau of Asger Preben Wissing Henriksen, of Odense, Denmark, by his former wife Vivian Van Deurs (now Mrs Marx-Nielsen), and has issue,

[*Kensington Palace, London W8 4PU*].

> 1. *Alexander* Patrick Gregers Richard, Earl of Ulster, *b* at St Mary's Hospital, Paddington, London 24 Oct 1974, Captain, The King's Royal Hussars,; *m* at Queen's Chapel, St. James's Palace 22 June (civ and relig) 2002, Claire Alexandra Booth (*b* at Sheffield 29 Dec 1977), Dr of Medicine, dau of Robert Booth and Barbara Hitchen.
>
> 2. Lady *Davina* Elizabeth Alice Benedikte, *b* at St Mary's Hospital, Paddington, London 19 Nov 1977.
>
> 3. Lady *Rose* Victoria Birgitte Louise, *b* at St Mary's Hospital, Paddington, London 1 March 1980.

2. Prince *George* Edward Alexander Edmund, Duke of Kent, Earl of St Andrews and Baron Downpatrick (since 12 Oct 1934), *b* at Sandringham House, Norfolk 20 Dec 1902; ✝*k* in a flying accident on active service at Morven, Scotland 25 Aug 1942, KG (1923), KT (1935), PC (1937), GCMG (1934), GCVO (1924), had Royal Victorian Chain, Lt Royal Navy 1926, Cmdr 1934, Capt 1937, Rear-Adm 1939, Major-Gen in the Army as Personal ADC to his brother King George VI 1937-42, Hon LLD Edinburgh (1929), Sheffield (1930) and St Andrews (1936), Hon DCL Durham (1935), Barrister-at-Law and Bencher of Lincoln's Inn 1932, Lord High Commissioner Gen Assembly Church of Scotland 1935, Col-in-Chief Queen's Own Royal West Kent Regiment 1935 and The Royal Fusiliers City of London Regiment 1937, G/Capt RAF 1937, Hon Air Commodore/No 500 (Co of Kent) (Bomber) Squadron AAF 1938,

nominated Gov-Gen and C-in-C Commonwealth of Australia 1938 (but did not proceed), served in World War II in Intelligence Division, Admiralty 1939-40 and with Trg Cmd RAF 1940-42, Bailiff Gd Cross Order of St John of Jerusalem, had many Foreign Orders; *m* at Westminster Abbey 29 Nov 1934, Princess Marina (*b* at Athens 30 Nov 1906; ✠ at Kensington Palace 27 Aug 1968; *bur* Frogmore), CI, GCVO, GBE, MusD Wales, Hon DCL Univ of Kent at Canterbury, Chancellor of Univ of Kent at Canterbury 1966, Gd Cross Order of St John of Jerusalem (Cmdt-in-Chief of Nursing Corps and Div for Wales), Chief Cmdt WRNS, Hon Cmdt WRANS, Col-in-Chief The Queen's Regiment, The Devonshire and Dorset Regiment, the Essex and Kent Scottish (Canadian Army), and Corps of REME, Pres Alexandra Rose Day, Gd Cross Orders of St Olga and St Sophia (Greece), of the Sun (Peru) and of the Order of the Aztec Eagle 1st Class (Mexico), represented The Queen at Independence Celebrations of Ghana 1957, Botswana 1966 and Lesotho 1966, dau of Prince Nicholas of Greece and Denmark and Grand Duchess Helene Vladimirovna of Russia, and had issue,

  1. Prince *Edward* George Nicholas Paul Patrick, 2nd Duke of Kent, etc, *b* at 3 Belgrave Square, London 9 Oct 1935, KG (1985), Grand Master and GCMG (1967), GCVO (1960), took his seat in the House of Lords 9 Dec 1959; lost the right to sit in the House of Lords by virtue of the House of Lords Act 1999 (Chapter 34) of 11 Nov 1999, Field Marshal in the Army, Hon Air Chief Marshal, Col-in-Chief The Royal Regiment of Fusiliers, The Devonshire and Dorset Regiment, Lorne Scots (Peel, Dufferin and Hamilton Regiment), Deputy Col-in-Chief The Royal Scots Dragoon Guards (Carabiniers and Greys), Col Scots Guards, Royal Hon Air Cdre RAF Leuchars, Personal ADC to HM The Queen from 1966, Vice-Chairman British Overseas Trade Board (1976-2000), Chancellor Surrey Univ from 1977, Hon DCL Durham (1961), Hon Liveryman Clothworkers' Co, Liveryman of the Salters Co, and Hon Freeman Mercers' Co, Gd Master and Gd Lodge of England from 1967 (Freemason 1964), Pres RAF Benevolent Fund, etc, has acted as Counsellor of State on several occasions from 1957, Kt Orders of St George and St Constantine, 1st Class (Greece), of Tri Shakti Patta 1st Class with Chain (Nepal), Gd Band Order of the Star of Africa (Liberia), and of Al Nahda 1st Class (Jordan), *educ* Eton, RMA Sandhurst; *m* at York Minster 8 June 1961, *Katharine* Lucy Mary (*b* at

Hovingham Hall, York 22 Feb 1933), GCVO (1977), Honorary
Major-General in the Army, Col-in-Chief Prince of Wales's
Own Regiment of Yorkshire, Deputy Col-in-Chief Royal
Dragoon Guards, Adjutant General's Corps and Royal Logistic
Corps, Chancellor Leeds Univ, etc, only dau of Col Sir William
Arthington Worsley, 4th Bt and Joyce Morgan Brunner of
the Baronets Brunner, and has issue,
[*York House, St James's Palace, London SW1A 1BQ*].

    1. *George* Philip Nicholas, Earl of St Andrews, *b* at
    Coppins, Iver, Bucks 26 June 1962, on 9 Jan 1988, by
    effect of the Act of Settlement 1700 (12 & 13 Will III
    c 2) he became legally dead, for the purposes of
    succession, upon marrying a Catholic, and was removed
    from the line of succession to the British Throne, *educ*
    Eton and Downing College, Cambridge; *m* at Leith,
    Scotland 9 Jan 1988, Sylvana Palma (*b* at Placentia,
    Terre-Neuve, Canada 28 May 1957; *m* 1stly at
    Vancouver, Canada 25 Dec 1977, John Paul Jones;
    that *m* diss by div 1981), dau of Maximilian Karl
    Tomaselli and Josiane Preschez, and has issue,

        1. *Edward* Edmund Maximilian George, Lord
        Downpatrick, *b* at St Mary's Hospital,
        Paddington, London 2 Dec 1988.
        2. Lady *Marina-Charlotte* Alexandra
        Katharine Helen, *b* at Cambridge 30 Sept 1992.
        3. Lady *Amelia* Sophia Theodora Mary
        Margaret, *b* at Cambridge 24 Aug 1995.
    2. Lady *Helen* Marina Lucy, *b* at Coppins, 28 April
    1964; *m* at St George's Chapel, Windsor 18 July 1992,
    Timothy Verner Taylor (*b* at Yelverton 8 Aug 1963),
    and has issue.
    3. Lord *Nicholas* Charles Edward Jonathan, *b* at
    Coppins 25 July 1970.
2. Princess *Alexandra* Helen Elizabeth Olga Christabel, *b* at
3 Belgrave Square, London 25 Dec 1936, GCVO (1960),
Col-in-Chief The King's Own Royal Border Regiment, The
Queen's Own Rifles of Canada, The Canadian Scottish
Regiment (Princess Mary's), Deputy Col-in-Chief The Queen's
Royal Lancers, The Light Infantry, Royal Honorary Air Cdre
RAF Cottesmore, Deputy Royal Honorary Col The Royal
Yeomanry, Patron QARNNS, Patron and Air Chief

Commandant PMRAFNS, etc, Chancellor Lancaster Univ, and (1st) of Univ of Mauritius from 1974, Hon LLD Queensland (1961), has Hon Freedom Clothworkers' Co, Pres Alexandra Rose Day etc, Gd Cross Orders of the Sun (Peru), of Merit (Chile), of the Southern Cross (Brazil), of the White Rose (Finland), and of the Oak Crown (Luxembourg), Orders of Aztec Eagle 1st Class (Mexico), and the Sacred Crown 1st Class (Japan); *m* at Westminster Abbey 24 April 1963, Rt Hon Sir Angus Ogilvy, KCVO, of the Earls of Airlie (*b* in London 14 Sept 1928), and has issue.
[*Thatched House Lodge, Richmond Park, Surrey TW10 5HP*].

3. Prince *Michael* George Charles Franklin, *b* at Coppins, Iver, Buckinghamshire 4 July 1942, KCVO (1992), on 30 June 1978, by effect of the Act of Settlement 1700 (12 & 13, Will III c 2) he became legally dead, for the purposes of succession, upon marrying a Catholic, and was removed from the line of succession to the British Throne, FIMI, Hon FIHT; Hon FRAeS, Holder of the Order of the Sun (Peru), Col-in-Chief Essex and Kent Scottish Regiment (Ontario), Major (retd) The Royal Hussars (Prince of Wales's Own), Hon Cdre Royal Naval Reserve, Grand Master of the Grand Lodge of Mark Master Masons, Commonwealth President of the Royal Life Saving Society, *educ* Eton and RMA Sandhurst; *m* at Vienna 30 June (civ) and at Lambeth Palace, London 30 Oct (relig) 1978, Baroness Marie-Christine (*b* at Karlsbad 15 Jan 1945; *m* 1stly at London 15 Sept 1971, Thomas Troubridge of the Baronets Troubridge; that *m* diss by div at London Aug 1977; annulled at Westminster May 1978; validated (Catholic) 27 July 1983), dau of Günther Hubertus, Baron von Reibnitz and Countess Marianne Szápáry von Muraszombath, Széchysziget and Szápár, and has issue,
[*Kensington Palace, London W8 4PU; Nether Lypiatt Manor, Stroud, Gloucestershire GL6 7LS*].

> 1. Lord *Frederick* Michael George David Louis, *b* at St Mary's Hospital, Paddington, London 6 April 1979, *educ* Eton and Magdalen College, Oxford.
>
> 2. Lady *Gabriella* (*Ella*) Marina Alexandra Ophelia, *b* at St Mary's Hospital, Paddington, London 23 April 1981.

GREECE
(House of Oldenburg)

Greek Orthodox: Prince Wilhelm of Denmark (*b* 24 Dec 1845) was elected King of Greece by the Greek National Assembly in virtue of a Protocol signed at London 5 June 1863 by England, France and Russia 6 June 1863. He accepted the crown and reigned as Georg I, King of the Hellenes from 31 Oct 1863 until his assassination on 18 March 1913. His son Constantine I, King of the Hellenes left the country 11 June 1917 after an ultimatum issued by France, and his second son Alexander I reigned until his accidental death on 5 Dec 1920. King Constantine returned to Greece on 19 Dec 1920, and abdicated in favour of his eldest son on 28 Sept 1922. King George II was deposed by a revolutionary Government and left the country 25 March 1924. He was restored to the Throne on 3 Nov 1935 until, once again, he was forced to leave the country by the German invasion of Greece on 23 April 1941, returning after a plebiscite voted in his favour 28 Sept 1946. On his death on 1 April 1947, he was succeeded by his youngest brother, King Paul I who was the father of the present King who left the country following the "Colonels Coup" 13 Dec 1967 and was deposed 1 June 1973, but remained nominally King until a plebiscite voted against his return 8 Dec 1974, when Greece was proclaimed a Republic.

For the early history of this family - see DENMARK and OLDENBURG.

Arms:- Az, a cross couped arg and over all an escutcheon of pretence, or, semée of hearts gu, three lions passant az crowned or (Denmark). The shield is ensigned with the Royal Crown and surrounded by the Riband of the Order of the Saviour. Supporters:- Two figures of Hercules vested with the skin of Nemian lion and each holding a club all ppr.

Members of the Royal House of Greece bear the title of Prince or Princess of Greece and Denmark with the qualification of Royal Highness.

CONSTANTINE II, KING OF THE HELLENES, *b* at Psychiko 2 June 1940, left the country following the "Colonels Coup" 13 Dec 1967, deposed 1 June 1973, but remained nominally King until a plebiscite voted against his return 8 Dec 1974, when Greece was proclaimed a republic, Order of the Redeemer, Order of the Elephant of Denmark, Order of Dannebrog, Order of the Golden Fleece, etc, son of Paul I, King of the Hellenes (*b* 14 Dec 1901; ✠ at 1964) and Princess Frederike of Hanover and Brunswick-Lüneburg, Princess of Great Britain and Ireland (*b* 18 April 1917; ✠ 6 Feb 1981); *m* at Athens 18 Sept 1964, Princess Anne-Marie (*b* at

Copenhagen 30 Aug 1946), Order of the Elephant of Denmark, dau of Frederik IX, King of Denmark and Princess Ingrid of Sweden.
[*65 Grosvenor Street, London W1X 9DB; 4 Linnell Drive, Hampstead Way, London, N.W.11.*].

Sons and Daughters

1. Princess *Alexia*, b at Mon Repos, Corfu 10 July 1965, Crown Princess of Greece from her birth until 20 May 1967; m at London 9 July 1999, Carlos Morales y Quintana.(b at Arrecife de Lanzarotte 31 Dec 1970).
2. Pavlos (*Paul*), Crown Prince of Greece, b at Tatoi 20 May 1967; m at London 1 July 1995, Marie Chantal (b at London 17 Sept 1968), dau of Robert Miller and Marie Chantal Pesantes, and has issue,

     1. Princess *Maria Olympia*, b at New York 26 July 1996.
     2. Prince *Constantine* Alexios, Hereditary Prince of Greece, b at New York 29 Oct 1998.
     3. Prince Achileas-Andreas, b at New York 12 Aug 2000.

3. Prince *Nikolaos*, b at Rome 1 Oct 1969, Banker.
4. Princess *Theodora*, b at Paddington, London 9 June 1983.
5. Prince *Philippos*, b at Paddington, London 26 April 1986.

Sisters

1. Princess *Sophie* (Sofia), b at Psychiko 2 Nov 1938; m at Athens 14 May 1962, Juan Carlos I, King of Spain (b at Rome 5 Jan 1938).
[*Palacio de la Zarzuela, 28048 El Pardo, Madrid, Spain*].
2. Princess *Irene*, b at Cape Town, South Africa 11 May 1942, Crown Princess of Greece from 6 March 1964 until 10 July 1965.
[*Palacio de la Zarzuela, 28048 El Pardo, Madrid, Spain*].

Sister of Father

Issue of Constantine I, King of the Hellenes (b 2 Aug 1868; ✠ 11 Jan 1923) and Princess Sophie of Prussia (b 14 June 1870; m 27 Oct 1889; ✠ 13 Jan 1932), among whom,

5. Princess *Katherine*, b at Athens 4 May 1913, granted the rank of a Duke's dau in Great Britain by HM King George VI 9 Sept 1947 and known in England as Lady Katherine Brandram, Dame Gd Cross Order of St Olga and Sophia of Greece; m at Athens 21 April 1947, Major Richard Brandram, MC, TD, RA (ret) (b at Bexhill-on-Sea, Sussex 5 Aug 1911; ✠ at Marlow, Bucks 28 March 1994).
[*Cook Cottage, Pond Lane, Marlow, Bucks.*].

Brothers of Grandfather

Issue of George I, King of the Hellenes (formerly Prince Wilhelm of Denmark (b 24 Dec 1845; succ 5 June 1963; ✠k 18 March 1913) and Grand Duchess Olga of Russia, Queen Regent of Greece Oct - Dec 1920 (b 3 Sept 1851; m 27 Oct 1867; ✠ 18 June 1926), having had issue, among whom,

Sons

1. Prince *Andrew*, b at Athens 2 Feb 1882; ✠ at Monte Carlo 3 Dec 1944, Gen Greek Army, GCVO, Kt Orders of the Elephant of Denmark, St Andrew of Russia, Annunziata of Italy, and Black Eagle of Prussia, author of "Towards Disaster - The Greek Army in Asia Minor in 1921" (translated into English by Princess Andrew); m at Darmstadt 7 Oct 1903, Princess Alice (b at Windsor Castle 25 Feb 1885; ✠ at Buckingham Palace, London 5 Dec 1969), dau of Prince Louis of Battenberg, later 1st Marquess of Milford Haven and Princess Victoria of Hesse-Darmstadt, and had issue, among whom,

    1. Princess *Sophie*, b at Corfu 26 June 1914; ✠ at Neuhaus bei Schliersee 24 Nov 2001; m 1stly at Kronberg, Taunus 15 Dec 1930, Prince Christoph of Hesse (b at Franfurt am Main 14 May 1901; ✠ka in the Appenines 7 Oct 1943), Major Luftwaffe. She m 2ndly at Salem 23 April (civ) and 24 April (relig) 1946, Prince Georg of Hanover, Duke of Brunswick-Lüneburg (b at Brunswick 25 March 1915), Dr of Law, Lt-Col (Res).

    [*Breitensteinstraße 1, 8166 Neuhaus, bei Schliersee, Upper Bavaria, Germany*].

    2. Prince *Philip*, b at Mon Repos, Corfu 10 June 1921, renounced his rights to the throne of Greece and was naturalised in Great Britain taking the surname of Mountbatten 28 Feb 1947, cr Duke of Edinburgh, Earl of Merioneth and Baron Greenwich in the Peerage of the United Kingdom 19 Nov 1947, granted the style and dignity of Prince of the United Kingdom of Great Britain and Northern Ireland 22 Feb 1957, KG (1947), KT (1952), OM (1968), GMBE (1953), PC (1951) and PC of Canada (1957) Adm of the Fleet, Field Marshal and Marshal of RAF, etc; m Westminster Abbey, London 20 Nov 1947, Elizabeth II, Queen of Great Britain and Northern Ireland (b at 17 Bruton St, London W1 21 April 1926), and has issue (see GREAT BRITAIN).

2. Prince *Christopher*, b at Pavlovsk 10 Aug 1888; ✠ at Athens 21

Jan 1940, Major-Gen Greek Army, Kt Orders of St Andrew of Russia, Elephant of Denmark, and Black Eagle of Prussia, author of "Memoirs of HRH Prince Christopher of Greece"; *m* 1stly at Vevey, Vaud, Switzerland 1 Feb 1920, Nonie-May (*Nancy*) May (Anastasia) (*b* at Cleveland, Ohio, USA 20 Jan 1873; ✝ in London 29 Aug 1923), widow of William Bateman Leeds, previously wife of George Ely Worthington, and dau of William Charles Stewart and Mary Holden Stewart. He *m* 2ndly at Palermo 11 Feb 1929, Princess Françoise (*b* at Paris 25 Dec 1902; ✝ there 25 Feb 1953), dau of Jean, Duke of Guise, Head of the Royal House of France and Princess Isabelle of France and, from his second wife, had issue,

    1. Prince *Michael*, *b* at Rome 7 Jan 1939, Kt Order of the Elephant of Denmark, Kt Order of the Redeemer, author of several books on Greek and European History; *m* at Athens 7 Feb 1965, Marina (*b* at Athens 17 July 1940), dau of Theodore Karella and Elly Chalikiopoulos, and has issue,

    [*9 Rue de Poitiers 75007 Paris, France;19 Bd de Suisse, 98000 Monte Carlo, Monaco*].

        1. Princess *Alexandra*, *b* at Athens 15 Oct 1968; *m* at Venice 27 June 1998, Nicolas Mirzayantz (*b* at Marseille 1 Jan 1963).

        [*19 Bd de Suisse, 98000 Monte Carlo, Monaco*].

        2. Princess *Olga* Isabelle, *b* at Athens 17 Nov 1971.

        [*19 Bd de Suisse, 98000 Monte Carlo, Monaco*].

HANOVER
(HOUSE OF GUELPH)

Evangelical: - Founded by Otbert I (✝ 975), Margrave and Count Palatine of Este (a district in the province of Padua, Italy); inherited important possessions of the Guelfs through the marriage of Azzo II, Margrave of Este (*b* after 997) to Kunigunde (Chuniza), dau of Welf II, Count of Altdorf 1055; Dukes of Bavaria 1070 - 1138 and 1156 - 1180; acquired important possessions of the Billing family through the marriage of Heinrich the Black, Duke of Bavaria to Wulfhild (✝ 29 Dec 1126), dau of Magnus, the last of the Billing (✝ 23 Aug 1106); inherited important possessions in Nordheim-Supplinburg-Brunswick through the marriage (1127) of Heinrich the Proud (✝ 20 Oct 1139) to Gertrude (✝ 18 April 1143), dau of Lothar II, last Count of Supplinburg (Supplinburg, near Helmstedt in the Duchy of Brunswick); Duks of Saxony 1137 - 1138 and 1142 - 1180; Lord of

Brunswick and of Lüneburg 1181; Duke of Brunswick-Lüneburg 21 Aug 1235; of Saxe Lauenberg (1697; Elector of Hanover 22 March 1692; King of Great Britain and Ireland 1 Aug 1714 through the marriage (30 Sept 1658) of Elector Ernst August (✝ 23 Jan 1698) to Sophie, dau of the Elector Palatine Friedrich V and Elisabeth, Princess of Great Britain and Ireland of the House of Stuart (b 13 Oct 1630; Proclaimed successor to the throne of Great Britain and Ireland 22 March 1701; W 8 June 1714); Duke of Bremen and of Verden 1719; Duke of Cumberland and Teviotdale (British Peerage) and Earl of Armagh (Irish Peerage) (struck off the Roll of Peers of the United Kingdom of Great Britain and Ireland, 28 March 1919, by the Order of the King in Council in pursuance of the Enemy Peers and Princes Forfeiture of British Titles, Order in Council 1919 (SR & O 1919/475) under the Titles Deprivation Act 1917 (7 & 8, Geo V c 47); Prince of Osnabruck of 1803; King of Hanover, acquired the Principality of Hildesheim, the State of Goslar, land around the Ems and the Principality of East Friesland 12 Aug 1814; the Kingdom of Hanover was annexed to Prussia 20 Sept 1866; protestation made at Vienna 23 Sept 1866. After the death of King George V of Hanover the Hereditary Prince, Ernst August took the title of Duke of Cumberland, Duke of Brunswick and Lüneburg 11 July 1878. After the extinction of the premier branch reigning in the Duchy of Brunswick (in the person of Duke Wilhelm - ✝ 18 Oct 1884), Duke Ernst August of Cumberland, Duke of Brunswick and Lüneburg declared his right of succession to the Duchy 18 Oct 1884, but was prevented from succeeding to the throne by a decision of the Federal Council of the German Empire 2 July 1885; New decision of the Federal Council prohibited the succession of any member of the House of Brunswick-Lüneburg to the throne of the Duchy 28 Feb 1007; Duke Ernst August of Cumberland renounced his rights in favour of his son Ernst August 24 Oct 1913; Reversal of the decision of Federal Council 27 Oct 1913; Accession of Prince Ernst August to the throne of the Duchy of Brunswick 1 Nov 1913; Abdication of the dynasty 8 Nov 1018.

Members of the Royal House of Hanover bear the titles of Prince or Princess of Hanover, Prince or Princess of Great Britain and Ireland, and Duke or Duchess of Brunswick and Lüneburg with the qualification of Royal Highness.

ERNST AUGUST Albert Paul Otto Rupprecht Oskar Berthold Friedrich-Ferdinand Christian-Ludwig, **PRINCE OF HANOVER**, Prince of Great Britain and Ireland, **DUKE OF BRUNSWICK AND LÜNEBURG;** in whom is vested the right to claim the suspended title of Duke of Cumberland and Teviotdale; on 23 Jan 1999, in the United Kingdom, by effect of the Act of Settlement 1700 (12 & 13 Will III c 2) he became legally dead, for the purposes of

succession, upon marrying a Catholic, and was removed from the line of succession to the British Throne, *b* at Hanover 26 Feb 1954, son of Ernst August, Duke of Brunswick and Lüneburg, etc (*b* 18 March 1914; ✠ 9 Dec 1987) and Princess Ortrud zu Schleswig-Holstein-Sonderburg-Glücksburg (*b* 19 Dec 1925; *m* 31 Aug (civ) and 4 Sept (relig) 1951; ✠ 6 Feb 1980); *m* 1stly (with the official permission of his father, Head of the Royal House of Hanover, 24 Aug 1981, according to Chapter 3 paragraphs 3 and 5 of the House Laws dated 19 Nov 1836) at Pattensen 28 Aug (civ) and at Schloß Marienburg 30 Aug (relig) 1981 (*m* diss by div at London 23 Oct 1997), Chantal (*b* at Zurich 2 June 1955), dau of Johann (Hans) Hochuli and Rosmarie Lembeck. He *m* 2ndly at Monaco 23 Jan 1999 (civ) Princess *Caroline* Louise Marguerite, (*b* at Monaco 23 Jan 1957; *m* 1stly at Monaco 28 June (civ) and 29 June (relig) 1978; *m* diss at Monaco 9 Oct 1980 and annulled at Rome 26 Feb 1992, confirmed 20 June 1992, Philippe Junot (*b* at Paris 19 April 1940). She *m* 2ndly at Monaco 29 Dec 1983 (civ), Stefano Casiraghi (*b* at Milan 8 Sept 1960; ✠ at Monaco 3 Oct 1990), dau of Prince *Rainier III*, Sovereign Prince of Monaco and Grace Kelly.
[*Villa Le Clos Saint-Pierre, Monaco; Hurlingham Lodge, Hurlingham Road, London SW6 3RD; Calenberg, 30978 Schulenburg an der Leine, Germany*].

Sons - 1st Marriage
1. Prince *Ernst August* Andreas Philipp Constantin Maximilian Rolf Stephan Ludwig Rudolph, *b* at Hildesheim 19 July 1983.
2. Prince *Christian* Heinrich Clemens Paul Frank Peter Welf Ernst-Wilhelm Friedrich Franz, *b* at Hildesheim 1 June 1985.

Daughter - 2nd Marriage
1. Princess *Alexandra* Charlotte Ulrike Maryam Virginia, *b* at Vöcklabruck, nr Salzburg 20 July 1999.

Step-Mother
Monika, Princess of Hanover and Duchess of Brunswick and Lüneburg, Princess of Great Britain and Ireland, *b* at Laubach 8 Aug 1929, dau of Georg Friedrich, Count zu Solms-Laubach and Princess Johanna of Solms-Hohensolms-Lich; *m* at Laubach, OHesse 16 July (civ) and 17 July (relig) 1981, as his 2nd wife, Ernst August, Prince of Hanover, Prince of Great Britain and Ireland, Duke of Brunswick and Lüneburg (*b* at Brunswick 18 March 1914; ✠ at Hanover 9 Dec 1987), Capt German Army, Dr of Law, Gd Master

Hanoverian Orders of St George, Guelf and Ernst August and Brunswick Order of Heinrich the Lion, Kt Order of the Elephant (Denmark), Kt Gd Cross Order of the Redeemer (Greece), established right to be a British subject in legal actions which went to the House of Lords 1955/6.

[*Calenberg, 30978 Schulenburg an der Leine, Germany; Königinvilla, 4810 Gmunden, Austria*].

Brothers and Sisters

1. Princess *Marie* Victoria Luise Hertha Friederike, *b* at Hanover 26 Nov 1952; *m* at Pattensen 4 June (civ) and at Schloß Marienburg 5 June (relig) 1982, Michael, Count von Hochberg, Baron zu Fürstenstein of the Princes of Pless (*b* at Züllichau 5 Dec 1943).
[*Hosegstieg 1, 22880 Wedel, Germany*].

2. Prince *Ludwig Rudolph* Georg Wilhelm Philipp Friedrich Wolrad Maximilian, *b* at Hanover 21 Nov 1955; ✠ at Gmunden 28 Nov 1988; *m* at Schloß Bleiburg, Carinthia, Austria 4 Oct 1987, Countess Isabella (*b* at Klagenfurt 12 Feb 1962; ✠ at Gmunden 28 Nov 1988), dau of Ariprand, Count von ThurnandValsassina-Como-Vercelli and Princess Marie von Auersperg, and had issue,

    1. Prince *Otto* Heinrich Ariprand Georg Johannes Ernst August Vinzenz Egmont Franz, *b* at Gmunden am Traunsee 13 Feb 1988.

3. Princess *Olga* Sophie Charlotte Anna, *b* at Hanover 17 Feb 1958.
[*Calenberg, 30978 Schulenburg an der Leine, Germany*].

5 Princess *Alexandra* Irene Margitha Elisabeth Bathildis, *b* at Hanover 18 Feb 1959; *m* at Amorbach, Odenwald 5 Oct (civ) and Gmunden, Austria 11 Oct (relig) 1981, Andreas, Prince zu Leiningen (*b* at Frankfurt-am-Main 27 Nov 1955).
[*Rethelstraße 3, 60596 Frankfurt-am-Main, Germany*].

6. Prince *Heinrich Julius* Christian Otto Friedrich Franz Anton Gunther, *b* at Hanover 29 April 1961; *m* at Teistungen 19 Jun 1999 Thyra (*b* at Oldenburg 14 Aug 1973), dau of Burghard von Westernhagen and Uta-Maria von Pape.
[*Calenberg, 30978 Schulenburg an der Leine, Germany*].

    1. Prince *Albert* Thilo Ludwig Arndt, *b* at Göttingen 14 Dec 1999.

Brothers and Sister of Father

Issue of Ernst August, Prince of Hanover, Duke of Brunswick, etc, (*b* at 17 Nov 1887; ✠ 30 Jan 1959) and Princess Viktoria Luise of

Prussia (*b* 13 Sept 1892; *m* 24 May 1913; ✠ 11 Dec 1980), among
whom,

1. Prince *Georg Wilhelm* Ernst August Friedrich Axel, Prince of
Great Britain and Ireland, etc, *b* at Brunswick 25 March 1915, late
Major 10th Cav Regt, sometime Headmaster of Salem School, Kt Gd
Cross Order of the Redeemer (Greece), Dr of Law; *m* at Salem,
Baden 23 April (civ) and 24 April (relig) 1946, Princess Sophie (*b* at
Corfu 26 June 1914; ✠ at Neuhaus 24 Nov 2001; *m* 1stly 15 Dec 1930,
Prince Christoph of Hesse who was ✠*k* in action 7 Oct 1943), dau of
Prince Andrew of Greece and Denmark and Princess Alice of
Battenberg, and has issue,
[*Breitensteinstraße 1, 83727 Neuhaus, nr Schliersee, Bavaria,
Germany*].

    1. Prince *Welf* Ernst August Andreas Philipp Georg Wilhelm
    Ludwig Berthold, *b* at Schloß Marienburg 25 Jan 1947; ✠ at
    Poona, India 10 Jan 1981; *m* at Essen 25 May 1969, (*m* diss by
    div 1979); Wibeke (*b* at Lubeck 26 Nov 1948), dau of Harry
    van Gunsteren and Ursula Schmidt-Prange, and had issue,

        1. Princess Tanja *Saskia* Victoria Louise, *b* at Duisburg
        24 July 1970; *m* at London 6 July 1990, Michael
        Naylor-Leyland of the Baronets Naylor-Leyland (*b* at
        London 14 July 1956).
        [*10 Wallgrave Road, London, SW5 0RL*].

    2. Prince *Georg* Paul Christian, *b* at Salem, Baden 9 Dec
    1949; *m* at Salem 20 Aug (civ) and at Schliersee 15 Sept
    (relig) 1973, Viktoria Anne (*b* at New York 6 March 1951),
    dau of Robert Bee and Countess Eleonore Fugger von
    Babenhausen, and has issue,
    [*Rahnhaz Weg 103, 8012 Ottobrunn, Germany*].

        1. Princess *Vera* Alice, *b* at Munich 5 Nov 1976.
        2. Princess *Nora* Sophia, *b* at Munich 15 Jan 1979.

    3. Princess *Frederike* Elisabeth Victoria Luise Alice Olga
    Theodora Helene, *b* at Salem, Baden 15 Oct 1954; *m* at
    Vancouver, British Columbia, Canada 17 Aug 1979, Jerry Cyr
    (*b* at Port Alberni, British Columbia 16 Jan 1951).

2. Prince *Christian* Oskar Ernst August Wilhelm Viktor Georg
Heinrich, *b* at Gmunden 1 Sept 1919; ✠ at Lausanne, Switzerland
10 Dec 1981, Capt 13th Cav, Kt Gd Cross Order of the Redeemer
(Greece); *m* at Salzburg 23 Nov (civ) and at Brussels 25 Nov (relig)
1963 (*m* diss by div 18 Dec 1979), Mireille (*b* at Chelsea, London SW3

10 Jan 1946), dau of Armand Dutry and Tinou Soinne, and had issue,

    1. Princess *Caroline-Luise* Mireille Irene Sophie, *b* at Wels, Upper Austria 3 May 1965.

    2. Princess *Mireille* Viktoria Luise, *b* at Brussels 3 June 1971.

3. Prince *Welf Heinrich* Ernst August George Christian Berthold Friedrich Wilhelm Louis Ferdinand, *b* at Gmunden 11 March 1923; ✠ at Frankfurt-am-Main 12 July 1997, Dr of Law, Kt Gd Cross of the Order of the Redeemer (Greece); *m* at Büdingen 20 Sept (civ) and 21 Sept (relig) 1960, Princess Alexandra (*b* at Frankfurt-am-Main 23 Oct 1937), only dau of Otto Friedrich, 3rd Prince (Fürst) zu Isenburg and Büdingen and Princess Felizitas Reuss.

[*Neuwiesenstraße 22, 60528 Frankfurt-Niederrad, Germany*].

HESSE
(HOUSE OF LORRAINE-BRABANT)

Founded by Count Gisbert who *m ca* 846 a dau of Emperor Lothar I (grandson of Charlemagne); their son Reginar I (✠ 915), Count in Hainaut and Hesbaye; his son Giselbert (✠ 939) married Gerberg of Saxony, dau of the German King, Heinrich I; acquired the Duchy of Lorraine (Lotharingia) in 928. Reginar II, Count of Hainaut, another son of Reginar I, was the father of Reginar III, whose sons were Reginar IV who *m ca* 998 Hedwig, dau of Hugues Capet, King of France and continued the line of the Counts of Hainaut (extinct 1093) and Lambert I the Bearded (✠ 1015), who married the heiress of Brabant and was ancestor of the Counts of Louvain, later created Dukes of Lower Lorraine, Margraves of Antwerp and Dukes of Limburg, who in 1191 assumed the title of Duke of Brabant. Henri II, Duke of Brabant married first Marie, dau of the German King Philipp of Hohenstaufen, by whom he was ancestor of the senior line of the House, reigning in The Netherlands, which became extinct in the male line in 1355 with Duke Johann III "the Triumphant" of Lorraine, Brabant and Limburg, and in the female line in 1406 with the dau of Jeanne of Bohemia and Luxemburg and whose possessions eventually passed to Burgundy; Duke Heinrich II *m* 2ndly Sophie, dau of Landgrave Ludwig IV of Thuringia and St Elisabeth of Hungary, heiress of her uncle, Heinrich Raspe, last Landgrave of Thuringia and Hesse, King of Germany (✠ without issue 1247); their son Heinrich I, ("the Infant of Hesse") became the first Landgrave of Hesse and was made a Prince of the Empire 1292; the House of Hesse descends from his marriage to his first wife, Adelaide of Brunswick; Count of Ziegenhain and Nidda 1450; Count of Katzenelnbogen and Dietz

(Rheinfels and Darmstadt) 1479; acquisition of Homburg 1504. The
lines below descend from two sons of Landgrave Philipp the
Magnanimous (*b* 13 Nov 1504; ✝ 31 March 1567).
Arms:- Az, a lion rampant queue fourchée barry arg and gu, crowned
or,. The shield is ensigned by the Royal Crown of Hesse. *Supporters:-*
Two lions queue fourchée crowned or.

Line I: LANDGRAVES OF HESSE

Founded by Wilhelm IV, Landgrave of Hesse-Cassel (*b* 24 June 1532;
✝ 25 Aug 1592), Count of Schaumburg 1648 after the extinction of
the Counts of Holstein-Schaumburg, Prince of Hersfeld 1648. The
two branches below descend from the two sons of Landgrave Wilhelm
VI (*b* 29 May 1629; ✝ 16 July 1663) and his wife, Hedwig Sophie of
Brandenburg (*b* 4 July 1623; ✝ 16 June 1683).

First Branch: HESSE-CASSEL

Evangelical: Founded by Friedrich, Landgrave of Hesse-Cassel (*b* 11
Sept 1747; ✝ 20 May 1837), younger brother of the ruling Landgrave
Wilhelm IX (b 3 June 1803, ✝ 27 Feb 1821) who became Wilhelm I
Elector of Hesse in 1803. The electoral branch became extinct on
the death of Elector Friedrich Wilhelm (b 20 Aug 1802, ✝ 6 Jan
1875), the throne having been lost to Prussian annexation in 1866.
The Landgravial branch became the senior branch of the family. By
adoption the present Landgrave succeeded to the Grandducal line
of Hesse and the Rhine (Hesse-Darmstadt) in 1968/1997.
The Head of the Family bears the title of Landgrave and his eldest
son that of Hereditary Prince, both with the qualification of Royal
Highness while cadet members of the family bear the title of Prince
or Princess of Hesse with the qualification of Highness.

MORITZ Friedrich Karl Emanuel Humbert **LANDGRAVE OF
HESSE**, *b* at Racconigi 6 Aug 1926, adopted by his kinsman, Ludwig,
last Prince of Hesse-and-by-Rhine (see below), son of Philipp,
Landgrave of Hesse, etc (*b* 6 Nov 1896; ✝ 25 Oct 1980) and Princess
Mafalda of Savoy (*b* 19 Nov 1902; *m* 23 Sept 1925; ✝ 27 Aug 1944); *m*
at Kronberg 1 June (civ) and 3 June (relig) 1964 (*m* diss by div at
Kiel 16 Oct 1974), Princess Tatiana (*b* at Giessen 31 July 1940), dau
of Gustav Albrecht, 5th Prince (Fürst) zu Sayn-Wittgenstein-
Berleburg and Margarete Fouché d'Otrante.
[*Schloß Friedrichshof, 61476 Kronberg, Taunus, Germany; Schloß
Panker, 24321 Gadendorf, Ostholstein, Germany; Schloß
Wolfsgarten, 63329 Egelsbach, Germany*].

Sons and Daughters

1. Princess *Mafalda* Margarethe, *b* at Kiel 6 July 1965; *m* 1stly at

Kronberg 8 July 1989 (*m* diss by div 1991), Don Enrico of the Counts Marone Cinzano (*b* at Turin 5 April 1963), Banker. She *m* 2ndly at Lütjenburg, Schleswig-Holstein 19 Dec 1991 (*m* diss by div at Rome 1 June 1999), Carlo Galdo (*b* at Naples 26 March 1954); She *m* 3rdly at Rome 14 July (civ) and at Palazzo Grotta Pallotta 28 Sept (relig) 2000, Count *Ferdinando* Brachetti-Peretti (*b* at Rome 13 Jan 1960).
[*Villa Polissena, Via San Filippo Martire 6, 00197 Rome, Italy*].

2. *Heinrich* Donatus Philipp Umberto, Hereditary Prince of Hesse, *b* at Kiel 17 Oct 1966.
[*Schloß Panker, 24321 Gadendorf, Germany*].

3. Princess *Elena* Elisabeth Madeleine, *b* at Kiel 8 Nov 1967.
[*Schloß Panker, 24321 Gadendorf, Germany*].

4. Prince *Philipp* Robin, *b* at Kiel 17 Sept 1970, Photographer.
[*Schloß Panker, 24321 Gadendorf, Germany*].

Brothers and Sister

1. Prince *Heinrich* Wilhelm Konstantin Victor Franz, *b* at Rome 30 Oct 1927; ✠ at Schloß Wolfsgarten Nov 1999.

2. Prince *Otto* Adolf, *b* at Rome 3 June 1937 ✠ at Hanover 3 Jan 1998, Prehistorian, Prof of Archaelogy Univ Venice; *m* 1stly at Munich 5 April (civ) and at Trostberg, Upper Bavaria 8 April (relig) 1965 (*m* diss by div at Munich 3 Feb 1969), Angela (*b* at Goslar 12 Aug 1940; *m* 1stly at Munich 31 July 1959, Hans Peter Schmeidler; that *m* diss by div at Munich 16 Feb 1961; *m* 3rdly 20/21 June 1969, Wilbrand von Roden; ✠ at Hanover 11 April 1991), dau of Major-Gen Bernd von Doering and Eleonore Wrede. He *m* 2ndly at Lastrup-Matrum 28 Dec 1988 (*m* diss by div at Munich 1994), Elisabeth (*b* at Rumburg, Czechoslovakia 31 Jan 1944; *m* 1stly at Munich 1960, Arrigo Wittler), dau of Wilhelm Bönker and Elisabeth Nagel.
[*San Marco 3300, 30124 Venice, Italy*].

3. Princess *Elisabeth* Margarethe Elena Johanna Maria Jolanda Polyxene, *b* at Rome 8 Oct 1940; *m* at Frankfurt-am-Main 26 Feb (civ) and 28 Feb (relig) 1962, Friedrich Carl, Count von Oppersdorff (*b* at Oberglogau, Upper Silesia 30 Jan 1925; ✠ at Gravensbruch 11 Jan 1985).
[*Fasanenstraße 24, 63263 Neu Isenburg-Gravensbruch, Germany*]

Brothers of Father

Issue of Friedrich Karl, Landgrave of Hesse, etc (*b* 1 May 1868; ✠ 28 May 1940; elected King of Finland 9 Oct 1918, withdrew acceptance 20 Dec 1918) and Princess Margarethe of Prussia (*b* 22 April 1872;

m 25 Jan 1893; ✠ 22 Jan 1954), among whom,

1. Prince *Wolfgang* Moritz, *b* at Rumpenheim 6 Nov 1896 (twin with Philipp, Landgrave of Hesse - see above); ✠ at Kronberg 12 July 1989; *m* 1stly at Salem, Baden 17 Sept 1924, Princess Marie Alexandra (*b* at Salem 1 Aug 1902; ✠ in an air raid on Frankfurt-am-Main 29 Jan 1944), dau of Prince Maximilian of Baden, Head of the Grand Ducal House and Princess Marie Louise of Great Britain and   Ireland, Duchess of Brunswick-Lüneburg. He *m* 2ndly at Frankfurt-am-Main 7 Sept 1948, Ottilie (*b* at Frankfurt-am-Main 24 June 1903; ✠ at Kronberg 4 Nov 1991), dau of Ludwig Moeller and Eleonore Steinmann. Prince Wolfgang adopted his nephew 7 July 1952,

    1. Prince *Karl* Adolf Andreas, *b* at Berlin 26 March 1937 (see below).

2. Prince *Richard* Wilhelm Leopold, *b* at Frankfurt-am-Main 14 May 1901; ✠ there 11 Feb 1969, having adopted his nephew 7 July 1952,

    1. Prince *Rainer* Christoph Friedrich, *b* at Kronberg 18 Nov 1939 (see below).

3. Prince *Christoph* Ernst August, *b* at Frankfurt-am-Main 14 May 1901 (twin with Prince Richard); ✠ *ka* in the Appennines 7 Oct 1943, Major Luftwaffe; *m* at Kronberg 15 Dec 1930, Princess Sophie (*b* at Corfu 26 June 1914; ✠ at Neuhaus 24 Nov 2001; *m* 2ndly at Salem 23 April (civ) and 24 April (relig) 1946, Prince Georg Wilhelm of Hanover), dau of Prince Andrew of Greece and Denmark and Princess Alice of Battenberg, and had issue,

    1. Princess *Christina* Margarethe, *b* at Kronberg 10 Jan 1933; *m* 1stly at Kronberg 1 Aug (civ) and at Kronberg-im-Taunus 2 Aug (relig) 1956 (*m* diss by div at London 31 May 1962), Prince Andrej of Yugoslavia (*b* at Bled, Slovinia 28 June 1929; ✠ at Irvine, California, USA 7 May 1990). He *m* 2ndly at Langton Green, nr Tunbridge Wells, Kent 18 Sept (civ) and at Amorbach 12 Oct (relig) 1963; that *m* diss by div at Frankfurt-am-Main 10 July 1972, Princess Kira zu Leiningen (*b* at Coburg 18 July 1930). He *m* 3rdly at Palm Springs, California 30 March 1974, Eva-Maria Andjelkovic (*b* at Vrnjacka Banja 26 Aug 1926; *m* 1stly Frank Lowe; that *m* diss by div 1973). She *m* 2ndly in London 3 Dec 1962 (*m* diss by div at London 3 Feb 1986), Robert Floris van Eyck (*b* at The Hague, 3 May 1916; ✠ at Ashford 19 Dec 1991), Painter. [*Ruetlistraße 34, 6442 Gersau, Switzerland*].

    2. Princess *Dorothea* Charlotte Karin, *b* at Panker 24 July

1934; m at Schliersee, Bavaria 31 March (civ) and at Munich
1 April (relig) 1959, Friedrich, Prince zu Windisch-Graetz (b
at Heiligenberg, Baden 7 July 1917; ✝ at Gersau, Switzerland,
29 May 2002), Businessman, Lt-Col German Army.
3. Prince *Karl* Adolf Andreas, b at Berlin 26 March 1937,
adopted by his uncle Prince Wolfgang (see above); m at The
Hague 26 March (civ) and 18 April (relig) 1966, Countess
Yvonne (b at Budapest 4 April 1944), only dau of Béla, Count
Szápary von Muraszombath, Széchysziget and Szápar and
Baroness Ursula von Richthofen, and has issue,
[*Simmernstraße 4, 80804 Munich, Germany*].
   1. Prince *Christoph*, b at Munich 18 June 1969.
   2. Princess *Irina* Verena, b at Munich 1 April 1971; m
   at Wolfsgarten nr Frankfurt-am-Main 22 May (relig)
   and at Berlin 30 April (civ) 1999, *Alexander* Georg
   Maria Ernst Heinrich István Ludwig Kisito Hubertus,
   Count and Lord von Schönburg-Glauchau (b at
   Mogadiscio, Somalia 15 Aug 1969), B.A., Journalist.
   [*Carl-von-Ossietzky-Straße 7, 14471 Potsdam,
   Germany*].
4. Prince *Rainer* Christoph Friedrich, b at Kronberg 18 Nov
1939, adopted by his uncle Prince Richard (see above),
Author.
[*Schloß Friedrichshof, 61476 Kronberg, Taunus, Germany*].
5. Princess *Clarissa* Alice, b posthumously at Kronberg 6
Feb 1944; m at Paris 20 July 1971 (m diss by div at Paris 21
June 1976), Claude Jean Derrien (b at Boulogne-sur-Seine 12
March 1944).
[*108 Rue Lepic, 75118 Paris, France*].

Second Branch: HESSE-PHILIPPSTHAL (-BARCHFELD)

The line of Hesse-Philippsthal was founded by Landgrave Philipp,
who built Schloß Philippsthal (b 14 Dec 1655; ✝ 18 June 1721). The
qualification of Highness was granted 18 July 1881; Hereditary
Member Prussian House of Lords 24 Oct 1881. Landgrave Philipp's
youngest son, Wilhelm (✝ 1761) founded the line of Hesse-
Philippsthal-Barchfeld and this line inherited when the main line
became extinct on the death of Ernst, Landgrave of Hesse-Philippsthal
(b 20 Dec 1846; ✝ 22 Dec 1925).
Members of the family bear the titles of Prince or Princess and
Landgrave and Landgravine of Hesse with the qualification of

Highness, as do their wives only if they are of equal birth.

WILHELM Chlodwig Friedrich Ernst Hermann Paul Philipp
Heinrich, **PRINCE and LANDGRAVE OF HESSE,** *b* at
Herleshausen 14 Aug 1933, Lt Col (ret), *succ* his grandfather Chlodwig,
Landgrave of Hesse 17 Nov 1954, son of Prince and Landgrave Wilhelm
of Hesse-Philippsthal-Barchfeld (*b* 1 March 1905; *ka* 30 April 1942)
and Princess Marianne of Prussia (*b* 23 Aug 1913; *m* 30 Jan 1933; ✛
1 March 1983); *m* at Friedrichshausen, Kr Einbeck 5 Aug 1961,
Oda-Mathilde (*b* at Friedrichshausen 12 Feb 1935), dau of Hilmar
von Garmissen, Proprietor of Friedrichshausen and Dassel, Kr
Einbeck and Baroness Oda von Houwald.
[*Bornbarg 7, 24361 Holzbunge, nr Rendsburg, Germany*].

Sons

1. *Wilhelm,* Hereditary Prince and Landgrave, *b* at Munich 1 Jan
1963, Dipl Engineer.
[*111 Gates Street, Binghampton, New York, NY 13903, USA*].
2. Prince and Landgrave *Otto, b* at Oldenburg 19 Jan 1965; *m* at Las
Vegas 8 Sept 1998, *Carla* Elisa (*b* at Düren 4 Sept 1974), dau of
Wolfgang Blickhauser and Segrun Sibille Esser, and has issue,
[*Franz Lisztstraße 18, 95615 Marktredwitz, Germany*].

    1. Prince and Landgrave *Max* Ernst-Ludwig, *b* at Marktredwitz
    26 Jan 1999.
    2. Princess and Landgravine *Elena* Marie-Sophie, *b* at
    Marktredwitz 11 March 2000.

Brother and Sister

1. Prince and Landgrave *Hermann* Ernst Ludwig Joachim Hans
Georg Hugo Alexander Wilhelm, *b* at Herleshausen 21 Aug 1935,
Farmer, Forester; *m* at Cassel 9 May 1962, Countess Monika (*b* at
Eisenach 11 July 1939), dau of Manfred, Count Strachwitz von
Gross-Zauche and Camminetz and Tosca von Baumbach, and has
issue,
[*Schloß Augustenau, 37293 Herleshausen, Germany*].

    1. Princess and Landgravine *Verena* Tosca Marianne, *b* at
    Eschwege 12 Feb 1972; *m* at Herleshausen 25 Feb (civ) and
    15 April (relig) 2000, *Felix* von Saucken (*b* at Hamburg 30
    Aug 1970).
    [*Schlüterstraße 63, 20146 Hamburg, Germany*].
    2. Prince and Landgrave *Alexis* Wilhelm Manfred, *b* at
    Eschwege 5 March 1977.

[Bahnhofstraße 10, 37293 Herleshausen, Germany].

2. Princess and Landgravine *Johanna*, *b* at Herleshausen 22 Nov 1937; *m* 1st at Herleshausen 30 Sept 1957 (*m* diss by div at Kassel 27 Nov 1961), Alfons Kuhn (*b* at Salzuflen 10 Dec 1924), teacher. She *m* 2ndly at Herleshausen 8 June 1963, Bruno Riek (*b* at Ahrensburg, Holstein 19 May 1927), Dipl Eng.

[Timmendorfer Straße 31, 22147 Hamburg-Rahlstedt, Germany].

Half-Brother of Grandfather

Issue of Prince Wilhelm Friedrich Ernst, Rear-Adm Prussian Navy (*b* 3 Oct 1831; ✛ 17 Jan 1890) and his 4th wife, Princess Auguste of Schleswig-Holstein-Sonderburg-Glücksburg (*b* 27 Feb 1844; ✛ 16 Sept 1932).

Son

Prince and Landgrave *Christian* Ludwig Friedrich Adolf Alexis Wilhelm Ferdinand, *b* at Schloß Luisenlund 16 June 1887; ✛ at Geneva, Switzerland 19 Oct 1971; *m* 1stly (morganatically) at Berlin 14 Jan 1915, *Elizabeth* Reid (*b* at Jackson, Tennessee, USA 17 Aug 1893; ✛ at Cannes 2 Feb 1957), *cr* Baroness von Barchfeld by the Grand Duke of Hesse-and-by-Rhine 14 Jan 1915, bore the name of Princess of Hesse (-Philippsthal-Barchfeld) from 14 Nov 1921, dau of Richard Rogers, Gov of Kentucky and Eunice Tomlin. He *m* 2ndly at Geneva 10 June (civ) and at Cannes 25 June (relig) 1958, Ann Pearl (*b* at Launceston, Tasmania, Australia 23 Aug 1906; ✛ at Cannes 14 March 1972; *m* 1stly at Sydney, Australia 29 Dec 1933 John Field who ✛ at Nice 13 April 1953), dau of Henry John Everett and Florence Smith, and had issue from his first wife (who bear the title of Princes and Princesses of Hesse-Philippsthal-Barchfeld without any qualification),

    1. Princess Elisabeth *Auguste* Eunice Bertha Caroline Luise Christiane, *b* at Berlin 2 Nov 1915; *m* at Suresnes 6 Aug 1949 (*m* diss by div at Paris 2 Nov 1956), Jacques Olivetti (*b* at Paris 25 July 1909). She has since reverted to her maiden name.

    [55 rue de l'Assomption, 75016 Paris, France].

    2. Prince Wilhelm *Richard Christian* Chlodwig Albert Carl Eduard Alexis, *b* at Sully, Vevey, Vaud, Switzerland 14 Oct 1917; ✛ at Tucson, Arizona, USA 18 Feb 1985, Stockbroker; *m* at Tucson 8 April 1953, Maria Lourdes (*b* at Hermosillo, Mexico 15 Oct 1926), dau of Carlos Lafontaine and Margarita

Araiza.
[*6025 San Bernardino, Tucson, Arizona 85715, U.S.A.*]
3. Prince *Valdemar* Christian Victor Heinrich Philipp, *b* at
Sully 20 Sept 1919, ✠ at Bad Homburg vor der Höhe 17
March 2002; *m* at Houston, Texas, USA 9 Feb 1952, Ellen
Jane (*b* at Atlanta, Georgia 25 Nov 1922; *m* 1stly at New York
22 May 1942, Anthony Taylor; that *m* diss by div at New York
.. April 1945), dau of Robert Hamilton and Jane Jerome, and
had issue,
[*Obere Terrassenstraße 7, 61348 Bad Homburg, Germany*].

    1. Prince *Alexander,* *b* at Houston, Texas, USA 31
    Aug 1956, Bank Director; *m* at Kronberg, Taunus 9
    Oct 1981, Brigitte Elisabeth (*b* at Worms 23 Jan 1950),
    dau of Dr Johann Heinrich Friedrich Göllner and
    Erika Anna Elisabeth Dehn, and has issue,
    [*Am Aufstieg 8, 61476 Kronberg, Germany*].

        1. Prince *Christian* Friedrich Wilhelm Johann
        Waldemar Alexander, *b* at Frankfurt-Höchst
        30 July 1984.

        1. Prince *Carl-Friedrich* Philipp Heinrich
        Richard Alexander, *b* at Frankfurt-Höchst 16
        Sept 1988.

    2. Prince *Henry* Christian, *b* at Frankfurt-am-Main 15
    March 1963, Banker.
    [*Obere Terrassenstraße 7, 61348 Bad Homburg,
    Germany*].

4. Princess Marie Louise *Olga* Elvira Victoria, *b* at Paris 30
Dec 1921; ✠ at Istanbul 14 Jan 1999; *m* at Lausanne,
Switzerland 13 June 1952, Michael Savich (*b* at Constantinople
25 July 1924), Dr of Med, Psychiatrist.
[*Ermin Vafi Korusu, Muallim Naci Cadessi 109-1, Ortaköy,
Istanbul, Turkey*].

Line II: GRAND DUKES OF ✠ HESSE-AND-BY-RHINE
formerly Hesse-Darmstadt
(✠ Extinct ✠)

**Lutheran: Founded by Georg I, Landgrave of the Upper County of
Katzelenbogen (*b* 10 Sept 1547; ✠ 7 Feb 1597); Inherited the bailliages
of Schotten, Stornfels and Homburg at the extinction of the Line of
Rheinfels (after the death of Georg I's brother, Landgrave Philipp
II, who died without descendants 20 Nov 1583) and parts of Upper
Hesse with Giessen at the extinction of the Line of Marburg (after**

the death of Landgrave Ludwig IV) 1604 and 1648, the County of Hanau-Lichtenberg 1736; loss of possessions on the left bank of the Rhine in 1801 were compensated by the donation of territories comprising parts of the Electorate of Mainz, the Bishopric of Worms and the Duchy of Westphalia (see Prussia) etc. in 1803; Grand Duke of Hesse 13 Aug 1806; compensated for the loss of the Duchy of Westphalia which was ceded to Prussia in 1814 (with effect from 30 June 1816) by the donation of Hesse Rhine, several parts of the Principality of Isenburg, etc. 10 June 1815; Grand Duke of Hesse and by Rhine, etc. 7 July 1816; the dynasty ceased to reign when the Republic of Hesse was proclaimed 9 Nov 1918.

Members of the family bore the title of Prince or Princess of Hesse and by Rhine with the qualification of Royal Highness for the Head of the House and his eldest son only while cadet members bore the qualification of Grand Ducal Highness.

✠ **LUDWIG V** Hermann Alexander Chlodwig, **PRINCE OF HESSE-AND-BY-RHINE**, *b* at Darmstadt 20 Nov 1908; ✠ at Frankfurt-am-Main 30 May 1968; *succ* his brother, Georg Donatus, Hereditary Grand Duke 16 Nov 1937, son of Ernst Ludwig, Grand Duke of Hesse-and-by-Rhine (*b* 25 Nov 1868; ✠ 9 Oct 1937) and Princess Eleonore zu Solms-Hohensolms-Lich (*b* 17 Sept 1871; *m* 2 Feb 1905; ✠ 16 Nov 1937); *m* at London 17 Nov 1937, Hon Margaret (*b* at Dublin 18 March 1913; ✠ at Schloß Wolfsgarten 26 Jan 1997), dau of Rt Hon Auckland Campbell Geddes, 1st Baron Geddes and Isabella Gamble Ross.

Adopted Son

MORITZ Friedrich Karl Emanuel Humbert, **LANDGRAVE OF HESSE**, *b* at Racconigi 6 Aug 1926 (see Line I, First Branch - above); adopted at Schloß Wolfsgarten 24 Dec 1960, registered at Langon 4 Dec 1961.

HOHENZOLLERN

Catholic: Founded by Burchardus of Zolorin (Hohenzollern, regency of Sigmaringen) (✠ *ca* 1061); Comes 1111; invested with the Burggraviate of Nuremberg by the Emperor through the marriage of Count Friedrich of Zollern (✠ *ca* 1200) to Sophie, dau of the last Burggrave of the House of the Counts of Raabs *ca* 1191; their two sons are the probable ancestors of the two Branches of this family; Konrad, probably the younger, took the Burggraviate and the counties of Raabs and Abensberg, becoming the ancestor of the Royal House of Prussia (see that family). The Princely Line of

Hohenzollern was founded by Friedrich, Count of Zollern, Burggrave of Nuremberg 1205 - 1251; in 1288 the line was divided into Zollern-Schalksburg (extinct 1408); the Lordship of Haigerloch was acquired in 1497; Count Karl I was invested with the counties of Sigmaringen and Veringen 24 Dec 1535; in 1576 his sons founded the lines of Hohenzollern-Haigerloch (extinct 7 March 1634), Hohenzollern-Hechingen (extinct 3 Sept 1869), and Hohenzollern-Sigmaringen (the only line still extant); Count Johann Georg of Hohenzollern-Hechingen and Count Johann of Hohenzollern-Sigmaringen (✠ 1638) were invested as Princes of the Holy Roman Empire (primogeniture) at Regensburg 29 March 1623; the Hechingen line was admitted to the College of Princes of the Empire 30 June 1653; the title of Burggrave of Nuremberg was assumed following a mutual succession pact concluded with the House of Brandenburg (Prussia) at Nuremberg 20/30 Nov 1695 (renewed 29 April 1707); the Princes of Hohenzollern-Hechingen and Hohenzollern-Sigmaringen joined the Confederation of the Rhine 12 July 1806 and the German Confederation 7 June 1815; both lines ceded their sovereign rights to Prussia 7 Dec 1849; the qualification of Highness was conceded to the Heads both lines by a Supreme Cabinet Order at Charlottenburg 20 March 1850; on the extinction of the Hechingen line, the Princes of Hohenzollern-Sigmaringen adopted the title of Prince of Hohenzollern only.

Arms:- Quarterly: arg and sa. The shield is encircled by the Order of the Princely House of Hohenzollern. The achievement is borne on a mantle gu, fringed and tasselled or, doubled ermine and surmounted by the Royal Crown. *Motto:-* Nihil Sine Deo.

Members of the Princely Family of Hohenzollern bear the title of Prince or Princess von Hohenzollern with the qualification of Serene Highness. with the qualification of Highness for the Head of the Family.

FRIEDRICH WILHELM Ferdinand Josef Maria Manuel Georg Meinrad Fidelis Benedikt Michael Hubert, **PRINCE (FÜRST) VON HOHENZOLLERN,** Burggrave of Nuremberg, Count of Sigmaringen and Veringen, Count of Berg, Lord of Haigerloch and Werstein, etc, Co-Grand Master Hohenzollern House Order, Bailiff Gd Cross Hon and Dev Sovereign Military Order of Malta, Bailiff Gd Cross with Collar Constantinian Order of St George, *b* at Umkirch 3 Feb 1924, son of Friedrich, Prince of Hohenzollern (*b* 30 Aug 1891; ✠ 6 Feb 1965) and Princess Margarete of Saxony (*b* 24 Jan 1900; ✠ 16 Oct 1962); *m* at Sigmaringen 5 Jan (civ) and at Amorbach 3 Feb (relig) 1951, Princess Margarita (*b* at Coburg 9 May 1932; ✠ at Überlingen 16 June 1996), Dame Gd Cross Sovereign Military Order of Malta, dau of Karl, 6th Prince (Fürst) zu Leiningen and Grand

Duchess Maria of Russia, and has issue,
[*Landhaus Josefslust, 72488 Sigmaringen, Germany*].

Sons

1. *Karl Friedrich* Emich Meinrad Benedikt Fidelis Maria Michael Gerold, Hereditary Prince of Hohenzollern, *b* at Sigmaringen 20 April 1952, lic rer pol, Capt German Army; *m* at Sigmaringen 17 May (civ) and at Beuron 16 June (relig) 1985, Countess Alexandra (*b* at Detmold 25 May 1960), dau of Clemens, Count Schenk von Stauffenberg and Countess Clementine Wolff Metternich zur Gracht, and has issue,
[*Schloß, 72488 Sigmaringen, Germany*].

    1. Prince *Alexander* Friedrich Antonius Johannes, *b* at New York 16 March 1987.

    2. Princess *Philippa* Marie Carolina Isabelle, *b* at New York 2 Nov 1988.

    3. Princess *Flaminia* Pia Eilika Stephanie, *b* at Munich 9 Jan 1992.

    4. Princess *Antonia* Elisabeth Georgina Tatiana, *b* at Munich 22 June 1995.

2. Prince *Albrecht* Johannes Hermann Meinrad Stephan, *b* at Umkirch 3 Aug 1954, Art Dealer.; *m* at Rome ... Sept 2001, Nathalie (*b* at...), dau of .... Rocabado de Viets and ....
[*Josefstraße 22, 72488 Sigmaringen, Germany*]

3. Prince *Ferdinand* Maria Fidelis Leopold Meinrad Valentin, *b* at Sigmaringen 14 Feb 1960, Dipl Eng Architect; *m* at Sigmaringen 10 May (civ) and at Csicsó, Slovakia 3 Aug (relig) 1996, Countess Ilona (*b* at Bruck an der Mur, Steiermark 9 March 1968), dau of Alois, Count Kálnoky de Köröspatak and Baroness Sieglinde von Oer, and has issue,
[*Wundstraße 62, 14057 Berlin, Germany*]

    1. Prince *Aloys* Freidrich, *b* at Berlin 6 April 1999.

Brothers and Sisters

1. Princess Benedikta *Maria Antonia Mathilde Anna*, Dame Star Cross Order, etc, *b* at Sigmaringen 19 Feb 1921; *m* there 4 Jan 1942, Heinrich, Count von Waldburg zu Wolfegg and Waldsee (*b* at Wolfegg 16 Sept 1911; ✝ 26 May 1972).
[*Karl-Anton-Platz 3, 72488 Sigmaringen, Germany*].

2. Princess *Maria Adelgunde* Alice Luise Josephine, *b* at Sigmaringen 19 Feb 1921 (twin with Princess Maria Antonia); *m* 1stly at

Sigmaringen 30 Aug (civ) and 31 Aug (relig) 1942 (*m* diss by div at Munich 14 July 1948 and ecclesiastically annulled 24 March 1950), Prince Konstantin of Bavaria [*b* at Munich 15 Aug 1920; ✠ at Hechingen 30 July 1969). She *m* 2ndly at Baden-Baden 25 March 1950 (*m* diss by div at Baden-Baden 28 Dec 1962), Dr Werner Hess (*b* at Baden-Baden 20 Sept 1907). She *m* 3rdly at Frauenfeld, Thurgau, Switzerland 9 Feb 1973, Hans Huber (*b* at Frauenfeld 12 May 1909), Col Swiss Army.

[*Binkeweg 9, 79224 Umkirch, Germany*].

3. Princess *Maria Theresia* Ludovika Cecilie Zita Elisabeth Hilda Agnes, *b* at Sigmaringen 11 Oct 1922.

[*Hugo Junkersstraße 19, 82031 Grünwald, Germany*].

4. Prince *Franz Joseph* Hubertus Maria Meinrad Michael, *b* at Umkirch 15 March 1926; ✠ at Sigmaringen 13 March 1996, Bailiff Gd Cross Sovereign Military Order of Malta, Bailiff Gd Cross with Collar Constantinian Order of St George (Naples); *m* 1stly at Regensburg 15 July 1950 (*m* diss by div at Freiburg 30 Oct 1951 and annulled by the Holy See 7 Dec 1954), Princess Maria Ferdinanda (*b* at Schloß Huas, nr Regensburg 19 Dec 1927), dau of Franz Joseph, 9th Prince (Fürst) von Thurn andTaxis and Infanta Elisabeth of Portugal. [*Keplerstraße 11, 81679 Munich, Germany*]. He *m* 2ndly at London 15 March (civ) and at Krauchenwies, Hohenzollern 16 April (relig) 1955 (*m* diss by div at Stuttgart 19 Jan 1961), Princess Diana (*b* at Paris 22 May 1932; *m* 2ndly at Stuttgart 21 March 1961, Hans Joachim Oehmichen), dau of Prince Don Gaetano of Bourbon-Parma and Princess Margarete von Thurn and Taxis.

[*Graserweg 3, 79189 Bad Krozingen, Germany*].

5. Prince *Johann Georg* Carl Leopold Eitel-Friedrich Meinrad Maria Hubertus Michael, *b* at Sigmaringen 31 July 1932, emeritus Dr of Phil, Director of the Bavarian State Picture Gallery at Munich; Chairman of the Hypo-Cultural Foundation at Munich, Bailiff Gd Cross Hon and Dev Sovereign Military Order of Malta, Bailiff Gd Cross Constantinian Order of St George (Naples); *m* at Stockholm 25 May (civ) and at Sigmaringen 30 May (relig) 1961, Princess *Birgitta* (*b* at Haga Slot 19 Jan 1937), dau of Prince Gustaf Adolf of Sweden, Duke of Västerbotten and Princess Sibylla of Saxe-Coburg and Gotha, and has issue,

[*Fliederweg 2, 82031 Grünwald, Germany*].

    1. Prince *Carl Christian* Friedrich Johannes Meinrad Maria Hubertus Edmund, *b* at Munich 5 April 1962; *m* at Munich 8 July (civ) and (relig) 1999, *Nicole* Helene(*b* at Munich 21 Jan

1968), dau of Nicholas Neschitsch and Margot Mayr.
[*Ickstattstraße 32, 80469, Munich, Germany*].

    1. Prince *Nickolas* Johann Georg Maria, *b* at Munich 22 Nov 1999.

  2. Princess *Desirée* Margarethe Victoria Louise Sybilla Katharina Maria, *b* at Munich 27 Nov 1963; *m* at Weitramsdorf 21 Sept (civ) and at Hechingen 6 Oct (relig) 1990, Heinrich, Hereditary Count (Erbgraf) zu Ortenburg (*b* at Bamberg 11 Oct 1956).
[*Schloßalle 11, 96479 Weitramsdorf, OFranken, Germany*].

3. Prince *Hubertus* Gustav Adolf Veit Georg Meinrad Maria Alexander, *b* at Munich 10 June 1966; *m* at Grünwald 10 July (civ) and at Mallorca 23 Sept (relig) 2000; *Ute* Maria (*b* at Trier 25 Feb 1964) dau of Wilhelm König and Marianne Wehlen.
[*Lerchenstaße 28, 80995 Munich, Germany*].

    1. Prince *Lennart*, *b* at Munich 10 Jan 2001 ✠ at Munich 14 Jan 2001

6. Prince *Ferfried* Maximilian Pius Meinrad Maria Hubert Michael Justinus, *b* at Schloß Umkirch 14 April 1943; *m* 1stly at Sigmaringen 21 Sept 1968 (*m* diss by div at Munich 25 Oct 1973), Angela (*b* at Berlin 11 Nov 1942; *m* 2ndly at Hollywood, CA, USA 2 Aug 1979, Fritz Wepper), dau of Major Ernst von Morgen and Countess Margarethe Schlitz genannt von Görtz, [*Hartthauserstraße 89, 81545 Munich, Germany*]. and has issue,

  1. Princess *Valerie Alexandra* Henriette Margarethe, *b* at Munich 14 April 1969; *m* at Feldkirchen-Westerham 8 July 1993, Peter Brenske (*b* at 1955).
[*Kleinstraße 45, 81379 Munich, Germany*].

  2. Princess *Stefanie* Michaela Sigrid Birgitta, *b* at Munich 8 May 1971; *m* at Hechingen.28.Sept 1996 (*m* diss by div at Munich 20 July 1999), Hieronymus, Count Wolff-Metternich (*b* at Gelsenkirchen-Horst 21 June 1955).
[*Hartthauserstraße 89, 81545 Munich, Germany*].

Prince Ferfried *m* 2ndly at Busingen 7 April 1977 (*m* diss by div at Munich 28 Nov 1987), Eliane (*b* at Luzern 4 May 1947), dau of Dr Hans Etter and Irmgard Zosso. He *m* 3rdly at Dresden 19 March 1999, *Maja* (*b* at ....8 Oct 1971), dau of .. Meinert and .., and had further issue by his 2nd wife,
[*Martinstraße 1, 12167 Berlin, Germany*].

    3. Princess *Henriette* Annabelle Gabriele Adrienne, *b* at

Zurich 26 March 1978.
[*In der Deisten 19, Zollikerberg 8125, Switzerland*].
4. Prince *Moritz* Johannes Axel Peter Meinrad, *b* at
Münsterlingen, Switzerland 5 Aug 1980.
[*In der Deisten 19, Zollikerberg 8125, Switzerland*].

Brother of Father

Issue of Wilhelm, Prince of Hohenzollern (*b* 7 March 1864; ✝ 22 Oct
1927) who was granted the qualification of Royal Highness ad
personam 23 Sept 1910, Gen of Infantry Prussian Army, and his first
wife, Princess Doña Maria Theresa Magdalena of Bourbon-Two Sicilies
(*b* 15 Jan 1867; *m* 27 June 1889; ✝ 1 March 1909), and had issue,
among whom,

Son

Prince *Franz Joseph* Maria Ludwig Karl Anton Thassilo, Prince of
Hohenzollern-Emden (which name was added as a compliment to
the cruiser Emden by decree of the German Min of the Interior 18
Nov 1933), *b* at Heilingendam, Mecklenburg 30 Aug 1891 (twin with
Prince Friedrich who *succ* as Prince of Hohenzollern); ✝ at Tübingen
3 April 1964, Rear-Adm Romanian Navy, Cmdr German Navy, etc;
m at Sibyllenort 25 May 1921, Princess Maria Alix (*b* at Wachwitz,
nr Dresden 27 Sept 1901; ✝ at Hechingen 11 Dec 1990), dau of
Friedrich August III, King of Saxony, and Archduchess Luise of
Austria-Tuscany, and had issue, among whom,

1. Prince *Meinrad* Leopold Maria Friedrich Christian
Ferdinand Albert, Bailiff Gd Cross Hon and Dev Sovereign
Military Order of Malta, *b* at Sigmaringen 17 Jan 1925, Lic
jur, Cmdr Naval Reserve, Managing Director MEDEA GmbH
Frankfurt-am-Main; *m* at Frankfurt-am-Main 25 Aug (civ)
and at Sigmaringen 11 Sept (relig) 1971, Baroness Edina (*b* at
Vienna 23 Aug 1938), dau of Alfred, Baron von Kap-Herr and
Editha von Bierski genannt Habicht, and has issue,
[*Oberfeld 2, 82418 Murnau-Hechendorf, Germany*].

   1. Princess *Stephanie-Antoinette* Alexandra Calixta
Maria-Theresia, *b* at Stuttgart 6 Dec 1974; *m* at
Ludwigsburg 4 Aug 1999, Sebastian Exner, *b* at
Ludwigsburg 23 Feb 1977.
[*Martin-Lutherstraße 4, 71636 Ludwigsburg,
Germany*]

2. Princess *Maria Margarete* Anna Viktoria Luise Josephine

Mathilde Theresia vom Kinde Jesu, *b* at Sigmaringen 2 Jan 1928; *m* at Hechingen 18 Dec 1965 (civ) and at Burg Hohenzollern 23 April 1966 (relig), Duke Carl Gregor of Mecklenburg (*b* at Remplin 14 March 1933).
[*Villa Silberburg, 72379 Hechingen, Germany*].
3. Prince *Emanuel* Joseph Maria Wilhelm Ferdinand Burkhard, *b* at Munich 23 Feb 1929; ✠ at Hechingen 8 Feb 1999; *m* at Burg Hohenzollern 25 May 1968 (*m* diss by div at Hechingen 1 July 1985), Princess Katharina (*b* at Breslau 30 Nov 1943), only dau of Prince Bernhard Friedrich of Saxe-Weimar-Eisenach, Duke of Saxony and Princess Felicitas zu Salm-Horstmar, and has issue,
[*Seitzstraße 8 RGB, 80538 Munich, Germany*].
    1. Princess *Eugenia* Maria Margarethe Adelheid Felicitas Luise Henrietta, *b* at Hechingen 13 March 1969; *m* 15 Nov 1991, Alexander Sautter (*b* at .....).
    [*Mühlweg 28, 72138 Kirchentellinsfurt, Germany*].
    2. Prince *Carl Alexander* Franz Joseph Wilhelm Ernst Meinrad, *b* at Hechingen 26 Oct 1970; *m* at Gebrazhofen, Baden April 1991 (*m* diss by div 1997), Angela (*b* at.........1942), dau of ......Stölze and ....
    [*Villa Eugenia, 72379 Hechingen, Germany*].

Brothers and Sisters of Grandfather

Issue of Leopold, Prince of Hohenzollern (*b* 22 Sept 1835; ✠ 8 June 1905) and Infanta Antonia of Portugal, Princess of Saxe-Coburg and Gotha (*b* 17 Feb 1845; *m* 12 Sept 1861; ✠ 17 Dec 1913), having had issue, among whom,

Sons

1. Prince *Ferdinand* Victor Albert Meinrad, **KING OF ROMANIA** (*succ his paternal uncle:- see ROMANIA*); *b* at Sigmaringen 24 Aug 1865 ✠ at Castle Pelesch, Sinaia 20 July 1927; *m* at Sigmaringen 10 Jan 1893, Princess Marie Alexandra Victoria (*b* at Eastwell Park, Kent; ✠ at Castle Pelesch, Sinaia 18 July 1938), dau of Prince Alfred, Duke of Saxe-Coburg and Gotha, Prince of Great Britain and Ireland, Duke of Edinburgh, Earl of Ulster, Earl of Kent (*elected King of Greece 1862 - but refused that Crown*) and Grand-Duchess Maria of Russia.
2. Prince *Karl Anton* Friedrich Wilhelm Ludwig, *b* at Sigmaringen 1 Sept 1868; ✠ at Namedy 21 Feb 1919, Lt-Gen Prussian Army; *m* at

Brussels 28 May 1894, his 1st cousin Princess Josephine Charlotte (*b* at Brussels 18 Oct 1872; ✠ at Namur, Belgium 6 Jan 1958), yst dau of Prince Philippe of Belgium, Count of Flanders and Princess Maria of Hohenzollern-Sigmaringen, and had issue, among whom,

Son

Prince *Albrecht* Ludwig Leopold Tassilo, *b* at Potsdam 28 Sept 1898; ✠ at Bühlerhöhe 30 July 1977, Bailiff Gd Cross Hon and Dev Sovereign Military Order of Malta; *m* at Potsdam 19 May 1921, Ilse Margot (*b* at Potsdam 28 June 1901; ✠ at Andernach 2 July 1988), dau of Lt-Gen Fritz von Friedeburg and Willy von Wenckstern, and had issue, among whom,

    1. Princess *Josephine Wilhelma* Karola Luise Maria Stephanie Marie-Antoinette Lini, *b* at Burg Namedy 15 Feb 1922; *m* there 3 June 1967, Harold, Count von Posadowsky-Wehner, Baron von Postelwitz (*b* at Kiel 25 Sept 1910; ✠ at Bonn 8 Sept 1990).
    [*Kolumbusring 31, 53176 Bonn, Germany*].
    2. Princess *Rose-Margarethe* (Margot) Adelgunde Clementine Mechtilde Maria Felicitas, *b* at Burg Namedy 19 Feb 1930; *m* there 15 Sept 1955, Edgar Pfersdorf (*b* at Wiesbaden 23 March 1920 ✠ at Neuss-Selicum 25 Feb 1997).
    [*Grünwaldstraße 12, 41466 Neuss-Selicum, Germany*].
    3. Prince *Godehard-Friedrich* Karl Anton Heinrich Albrecht Joseph Ernst Egon Hermann Johann Georg Rudolf Tassilo Benedikt, *b* at Koblenz 17 April 1939; ✠ at 21 May 2001; *m* at Munich 29 Aug 1971, Heide (*b* at Neunkirchen 2 May 1943), dau of Hellmut Hansen and Hedwig Simon, and has issue,
    [*Burg Namedy, 56626 Andernach, Germany*].
        1. Prince *Carlos* Patrick Godehard, *b* at Munich 2 Dec 1978.
        2. Princess *Anna* Corinna Dione, *b* at Bonn 19 Aug 1983.

———◆◆◆———

HOLSTEIN
(HOUSE OF OLDENBURG)

Lutheran: Founded by Christian, Count of Oldenburg (*b* 1426; ✠ 1481) who became King of Denmark as Christian I 20 Aug 1448, King of Norway 29 July 1450, King of Sweden 1457 - 1467, Duke of Slesvig since 1115 (united with Holstein since 15 Aug 1386) and Count of Holstein, through his mother Heilwige (✢ 1436), sister and heiress of Adolph VIII (✢ 4 Dec 1459), last Count of Holstein and Duke of Slesvig of the House of the Lords of Schauenburg in Westphalia 2 March 1460; elevation of the County of Holstein with Wagrien, Dithmarschen and Stormarn to a Duchy 14 Feb 1474; the Duchy of Holstein was ceded by King Johann of Denmark (b 1455; ✢ 1513) to his younger brother Frederik (b 1471; ✢ 1533) who became Duke of Holstein 10 Aug 1490 and also King of Denmark under the name of Frederik I 29 Jan 1523, after the deposition of his nephew, Christian II, King of Denmark (son of Johann) (b 2 July 1481; ✢ 25 Jan 1559); the Lines below were founded by two of his sons. For the early history of this family - see OLDENBURG.

Line I: HOLSTEIN-SONDERBURG

Founded by Christian III (b 12 Aug 1504; ✢ 1 Jan 1559), King of Denmark 1533, and of Norway 1536; his third son, Johann (b 25 March 1545; ✢ 9 Nov 1622) became Duke of Schleswig-Holstein-Sonderburg 1582; the branches below are descended from two sons of his son, Alexander (b 20 Jan 1573; ✢ 13 March 1627).

Branch I: ✢ SCHLESWIG-HOLSTEIN-SONDERBURG-AUGUSTENBURG
(✢ Extinct ✢)

Founded by Ernst Günther, Duke of Schleswig-Holstein-Sonderburg (b 14 Oct 1609; ✢ 18 Jan 1689) who built the castle of Augustenburg which he named after his wife; acquired the Lordship of Primkenau 1852; assumed the title of Duke of Schleswig-Holstein, etc at the extinction of the Royal Line of Denmark (continued through the younger son of Christian III, King of Denmark) 15 Nov 1863; title of Duke of Schleswig-Holstein recognised in Prussia 1 April 1885. This Branch became extinct in the male line on the death of Albert, Duke of Schleswig-Holstein (b 26 Feb 1869; ✢ 27 April 1931).
Members of the Ducal Family bore the title of Prince or Princess of Schleswig-Holstein-Sonderburg-Augustenburg with the qualification of Highness.

Branch II: SCHLESWIG-HOLSTEIN SONDERBURG-GLÜCKSBURG

Founded by August Philipp, Duke of Schleswig-Holstein-Beck (b 11 Nov 1612; ✢ 1675); Duke Wilhelm was invested with the Duchy of Glücksburg by the King of Denmark 6 July 1825; received the qualification of Highness in Denmark 19 Dec 1863; Hereditary Member Prussian House of Lords 6 Feb 1894. By virtue of an Oldenburg Law of 19 Oct 1904, the male descendants of Duke Frederik (✢ 27 Nov 1885) are affiliated to the Grand Ducal House of

Oldenburg through the collateral line and may succeed to that title should the direct line become extinct.

Arms:- Quarterly: 1st, gu, a lion rampant crowned or, holding in his paws the long-handled axe of St Olaf blade arg, handle or (Norway); 2nd, or, two lions passant az (Schleswig); 3rd, gu, an escutcheon per fesse arg and of the field, between three deminettle leaves and as many passion nails in pairle of the second (Holstein); 4th, gu, a swan arg, beaked, membered and royally gorged or (Stormarn); enté en pointe, gu, a knight in armour or on a horse and holding a sword arg and a shield az charged with a cross patée of the second (Ditmarsken); over all, an escutcheon of pretence, quarterly: 1st and 4th, or, two bars gu (Oldenburg); 2nd and 3rd, az, a cross patée or (Delmenhorst). The achievement is borne on a mantle purp, fringed and tasselled or, doubled erm and surmounted by a Royal Crown.

Members of the Ducal Family bear the title of Prince or Princess of Schleswig-Holstein-Sonderburg-Glücksburg with the qualification of Highness.

CHRISTOPH, PRINCE (PRINZ) ZU SCHLESWIG-HOLSTEIN-SONDERBURG-GLÜCKSBURG, *b* at Schloß Louisenlund 22 Aug 1949, Dipl Eng Agriculture, son of Peter, Duke (Herzog) of Schleswig-Holstein-Sonderburg-Glücksburg (*b* 30 April 1922; ✠ 30 Sept 1980) and Princess Marie-Alix of Schaumburg-Lippe (*b* 2 April 1923; *m* 9 Oct 1947; *m* at Glücksburg 23 Sept (civ) and 3 Oct (relig) 1981, Princess Elisabeth (*b* at Munich 28 July 1957), dau of Prince Alfred Karl of Lippe-Weissenfeld and Baroness Irmgard Wagner von Wehrborn.
[*Schloß Grünholz, 24351 Thumby, Germany*].

Sons and Daughter

1. Princess *Sophie b* at Eckernförde 9 Oct 1983.
2. Prince *Friedrich Ferdinand,* Hereditary Prince (Erbprinz) of Schleswig-Holstein-Sonderburg-Glücksburg *b* at Eckernförde 19 July 1985.
3. Prince *Constantin,* *b* at Eckernförde 14 July 1986.
4. Prince *Leopold,* *b* at Eckernförde 5 Sept 1991.

Mother

Marie-Alix, Dowager Duchess zu Schleswig-Holstein-Sonderburg-Glücksburg, *b* at Bückeburg 2 April 1923, dau of Prince Stephan of Schaumburg-Lippe and Duchess Ingeborg-Alix of Oldenburg; *m* at Glücksburg 9 Oct 1947, Peter, Duke of Schleswig-Holstein-Sonderburg-Glücksburg (*b* at Schloß Louisenlund 30 April 1922; ✠ at Bienebek 30 Sept 1980).

[*Gut Bienebek, 24351 Thumby, Germany*].

Brother and Sisters

1. Princess *Marita*, *b* at Schloß Louisenlund 5 Sept 1948; *m* at Glücksburg 23 May 1975, Wilfrid, Baron von Plotho (*b* at Bliestorf 10 Aug 1941), Banker.
[*Sonnenweg 14, 4313 Möhlin, nr Basel, Switzerland*].

2. Prince *Alexander*, *b* at Bienebeck 9 July 1953, Career Consultant; *m* at Munich 29 Aug (civ) and at San Cabeneta, Mallorca, Spain 3 Sept (relig) 1994, Barbara (*b* at Friedberg, Hesse 27 July 1961), dau of Fritz-Wilhelm Fertsch and Elke Gaidetzka, and has issue,
[*Gut Bienebek, 24351 Thumby, Germany; Brünschentwiete 70, 22559 Hamburg, Germany*].

    1. Princess *Elena*, *b* at Hamburg 25 Jan 1994.

    2. Prince *Julian Nicolaus*, *b* at Hamburg 20 Oct 1997.

3. Princess *Ingeborg*, *b* at Bienebek 9 July 1956; *m* at Hamburg 31 May (civ) and at Glücksburg 1 June (relig) 1991, Kurt *Nikolaus* Albert Broschek (*b* at Munich 30 May 1942).
[*Leinpfad 76, 22299 Hamburg, Germany*].

Sister of Father

Issue of Friedrich, Duke of Schleswig-Holstein-Sonderburg-Glücksburg (*b* 23 Aug 1891; ✠ 10 Feb 1965) and Princess Marie Melita zu Hohenlohe-Langenburg (*b* 18 Jan 1899; *m* 15 Feb 1916; ✠ 8 Nov 1967), among whom,

1. Princess *Marie-Alexandra* Caroline-Mathilde Viktoria Irene, *b* at Schloß Louisenlund 9 July 1927; ✠ at Friedrichshafen 14 Dec 2000; *m* at Grünholz 9 July (civ) and at Louisenlund 25 July (relig) 1970, Douglas Barton Miller (*b* at San Francisco, California 8 Dec 1929).
[*Schloßstraße 1, 88045 Friedrichshafen, Germany*].

Brother of Great-Grandfather

Issue of Friedrich, Duke of Schleswig-Holstein-Sonderburg-Glücksburg (*b* 23 Oct 1814; ✠ 27 Nov 1885) and Princess Adelheid of Schaumburg-Lippe (*b* 9 March 1821; *m* 16 Oct 1841; ✠ 30 July 1899), having had issue, among whom,

Son

Prince *Albert* Christian Adolf Karl Eugen, *b* at Kiel 15 March 1863; ✠ at Glücksburg 23 April 1948, Lt-Gen, Kt of St John of Jerusalem;

m 1stly at Meerholz 14 Oct 1906, Countess Ortrud (*b* at Meerholz 15 Jan 1879; ✠ at Gotha 28 April 1918), Dame of Hon Bavarian Order of St Theresia, dau of Karl, Count zu Isenburg and Büdingen in Meerholz, etc and Princess Agnes zu Isenburg and Büdingen in Büdingen, and had issue, among whom,

    1. Prince *Friedrich Ferdinand* Karl Ernst August Wilhelm Harald Kasimir Nicola, *b* at Gotha 14 May 1913; ✠ at Glücksburg 31 May 1989, Proprietor of Kunzendorf and Greif, Businessman; *m* at Willigrad, nr Schwerin 1 Sept 1943, Duchess Anastasia (*b* at Gelbensande, nr Ribnitz, Meckl 11 Nov 1922; ✠ at Hamburg 25 Jan 1979), dau of Friedrich Franz IV, Grand Duke of Mecklenburg-Schwerin and Princess Alexandra of Hanover, Princess of Great Britain and Ireland, Duchess of Brunswick and Lüneburg, and had issue,

        1. Princess *Elisabeth* Marie Alexandra, *b* at Schleswig 10 Sept 1945; *m* at Glücksburg 2 Jan (civ) and 5 Jan (relig) 1975, Ferdinand Heinrich, Prince zu Isenburg and Büdingen (*b* at Frankfurt-am-Main 19 Oct 1940; ✠ at Büdingen 8 March 1989), Businessman.
        [*Christinenhof, 63654 Büdingen, OHesse, Germany*].
        2. Princess *Irene* Olga Adelheid, *b* at Flensburg 11 Oct 1946.
        [*Kavalierhaus, 25821 Glücksburg, Germany*].
        3. Princess *Margaretha* Friederike Luise, *b* at Flensburg 10 Feb 1948, Painter, Graphic Artist.
        [*Kavalierhaus, 25821 Glücksburg, Germany*].
        4. Princess *Sibylla* Ursula Ortrud, *b* at Flensburg 11 Sept 1955, Nurse; *m* at Glücksburg 24 Oct (civ) and 25 Oct (relig) 1980, Dieter Franz (*b* at Kirchberg an der Jagst 26 March 1950).
        [*Alte Schule, Hemmelmark, 24360 Barkelsby, Germany*].

Prince Albert *m* 2ndly at Büdingen 15 Sept 1920, Princess Hertha (*b* at Büdingen 27 Dec 1883; ✠ at Glücksburg 30 May 1972), dau of Bruno, Prince (Fürst) zu Isenburg and Büdingen in Büdingen and Countess Bertha zu Castell-Rüdenhausen, and had further issue.

Line II: HOLSTEIN-GOTTORP

Founded by Adolph (*b* 25 Jan 1526; ✠ 1 Oct 1586), Duke of Holstein-Gottorp who received Hadersleben after the death of his older brother, Johann (*b* 1521; ✠ 2 Oct 1580); received sovereign status in the

Treaty of Copenhagen 12 May 1658; the branches below descend from two sons of the 6th Duke, Christian Albert (*b* 3 Feb 1641; ✝ 27 Dec 1694).

1st Branch: HOLSTEIN-GOTTORP

Founded by Frederik IV, Duke of Holstein-Gottorp (*b* 18 Oct 1671; ✝ 19 July 1702); Emperor of Russia 5 Jan 1762; the Duchy of Holstein-Gottorp was ceded to Denmark in exchange for Oldenburg 1773 (see RUSSIA).

2nd Branch: OLDENBURG

Founded by Duke Christian August (*b* 11 Jan 1673; ✝ 25 April 1726), Bishop of Lubeck 1706 (see OLDENBURG).

HOLY SEE

The Holy See - also called the Papal See or the Holy Apostolic See - is the See of Saint Peter, of Bethsaida in Galilee, Prince of the Apostles, personally established in Rome in the first century of Christianity, having received from Jesus Christ the *suprema potestas pontificia* to be transmitted to his Successors. He first resided in Antioch and further during 25 years in Rome, being its first Bishop, and suffered martyrdom for Christ in that City in A.D. 64 or 67, where his Sacred Tomb has always been venerated by Christians. (*See Appendix IV*).

Besides its dignity of Patriarch of the West, the Universal Primacy of the Petrine See within the Church founded by Christ, as well as its sovereignty have been recognised from earliest times, also before the fall of the Roman Empire. The successors of Saint Peter form the uninterrupted line of Popes until today [*see appendix*]. Christian sovereign families normally consider the Incumbent of the Holy See as the "Father of the Family of Kings", also since His Holiness represents the oldest Monarchy in Europe. Charlemagne, first Emperor of the Holy Roman Empire (800 - 1806), was crowned in Rome on Christmas Eve 799/800 by Pope Saint Leo III (795-816). Countless other Sovereigns have received their original or later investiture or anointing during their coronation from the Pope or his Legates. Besides the case of the Heads of the Holy Roman Empire, this was considered constitutionally necessary in many cases, independently of the feudal system. Emperor Napoleon I deemed this essential for his legitimacy when he wished Pope Pius VII (1800-1823) to preside over his coronation ceremony in Paris. Today, Sovereigns or Heads of State inform the Pope of their succession and other events concerning their families. Besides purely ecclesiastical conferring or confirmation of dignities, Sovereign Pontiffs, since the early Middle Ages, have granted nobility, also outside of their immediate civil or temporal jurisdiction.

From earliest times, *Apocrisiari* (Legates or Envoys) to the Emperors of the East are known. Bilateral and multilateral diplomatic relations of The Holy See now subordinately comprise those with the State of Vatican City, which as such does not have diplomatic representatives. The triple sovereignty of His Holiness the Pope in Person, of The Holy See and of the State of Vatican City, although united, is therefore understood as distinct in law and practice.

International law recognises the sovereignty (not being subject to anyone on earth) of the Pope, which is triple: personal, as Incumbent of the Holy See which itself is sovereign, and as Sovereign of the State of Vatican City. His Holiness personally sends Cardinal Legates and Cardinal Envoys (sometimes an Archbishop), Apostolic Nuncio's or Apostolic Delegates (always Archbishops) principally as the Incumbent of the Holy See, also receiving Letters of Credence of Ambassadors to The Holy See in that capacity *(ius legationis et fœderis)*, while the sovereign State of Vatican City is a member of some international organisations. Papal sovereignty was not linked to the States of the Church (the Pope being however their Sovereign *in iure* until the Treaties of the Lateran (11 February 1929, but *de facto* until 20 September 1870 after which date they were annexed to the then Kingdom of Italy) nor does it derive from the State of Vatican City, existing since 11 February 1929. The temporal interests of the Holy See are entrusted during the vacancy of the Holy See to the Cardinal Camerlengo of the Holy Roman Church *(Sanctæ Romanæ Ecclesiæ Camerarius)* who presides over the Apostolic Chamber *(Camera Apostolica)*. If impeded, his task in entrusted to the Vice-Camerlengo, and the College of Cardinals provide according to the Apostolic Constitution

Universi dominici gregis (**22 February 1996**) of Pope John Paul II.

As far as honours conferred by the Holy See are concerned, the Almanach de Gotha traditionally confined itself to the College of Cardinals since its members are Princes of the Church, considered equal to the sons of reigning monarchs. They are citizens of the State of Vatican City if residing in Rome. Created for life, every member of the College, which has existed for more than a thousand years, is considered as heir presumptive to the Papal See. A Cardinal may resign with Papal consent but only one case occurred in the 20th century.

The Holy See does not publish granting of lay titles and according to a ruling of Pope Saint Pius X (1903-1914) some hereditary honours must be confirmed at succession. The Bull *Urbem Romam* of Pope Benedict XIV (1740-1758), concerning Papal and Roman families and the Roman Patriciate and Nobility, is still in existence, *inter alia* granting *ipso iure* Roman Nobility to immediate relatives of Sovereign Pontiffs and their descendants in the male line.

The Papacy being the oldest monarchy in Christendom, the Sovereign (or Supreme) Pontiff is its first Monarch and hence customarily also called *Pater Principum et Regum* and addressed as *Most Holy Father* or *Your Holiness* or sometimes *Most August Pontiff*.

The Pope usually signs in Latin: *Ioannes Paulus PP. II*, on dogmatic or some solemn documents adding: *Catholicæ Ecclesiæ Episcopus*.

His Holiness Pope **JOHN PAUL II, SOVEREIGN PONTIFF**, Bishop of Rome, Vicar of Jesus Christ, Successor of the Prince of the Apostles, Supreme Pontiff of the Church Universal, Patriarch of the West, Primate of Italy, Archbishop and Metropolitan of the Roman Province, Sovereign of the State of Vatican City, *Servant of the servants of God (Karol Wojtyła)*, b at Wadowice 18 May 1920, then Princely Diocese of Kraków since 28 October 1925 [Princely] Metropolitan Archdiocese of Kraków (Poland); ordained 1 Nov 1946 in Kraków by His late Eminence Cardinal Prince Adam Sapieha-Kodenski, Metropolitan Prince-Archbishop of Kraków; Elected Titular Bishop of Ombi 4 July 1958 by His late Holiness Pope Pius XII and deputed Auxiliary of the [Princely] Archdiocese

of Kraków; Consecrated 28 September 1958 by His Excellency the
Most Reverend Eugene Baziak, Archbishop of Leopolis [Lviv, Lemberg]
of the Latins and then Apostolic Administrator of the [Princely]
Archdiocese of Kraków; Promoted to the [Princely] Metropolitan
See of Kraków 13 Jan 1964 by His late Holiness Pope Paul VI;
Created Cardinal by the same Supreme Pontiff with the Presbyteral
Title of Saint Cæsareus *in Palatio* in Consistory of 26 June 1967;
Elected Supreme Pontiff 16 October 1978; Solemnly enthroned as
Universal Shepherd of the Church 22 Oct 1978.

[*Vatican City*].

COLLEGE OF CARDINALS

Traditionally called The Sacred College, it consists of three Orders
and is the Pope's and Universal Church's Senate or *Sacrum
Laticlavium*, its Members being called *Patres Purpurati* who have
the principal duty of electing a new Pope in Conclave, not
necessarily a member of the College, cfr. Bulls *In nomine Domini* of
Pope Nicholas II (1059-1061), and *Licet de vitanda* of Pope
Alexander III (1159-1181); they are the principal counsellors of the
Pope within and outside of a Consistory, that being the assembly of
Cardinals about the Pope, recalling the *Consistorium Principis* of
the Roman Empire, cfr. Pope John VIII (872-882) *de iure Cardinalium*;
public Consistories are attended also by Bishops, Prelates, Princes
and Ambassadors to The Holy See. But for a few exceptions,
Cardinals are consecrated Bishops, using their episcopal titles only
if belonging to the Cardinalitial Order of Bishops or also to the
Cardinalitial Order of Priests but only when residential Ordinaries
or Emeriti of residential Sees. Titular Sees, none of which entail
territorial jurisdiction, formerly held, are always surrendered upon
cardinalitial creation and are mentioned as last episcopal title (*olim*)
only in case of Ordinations.

The ancient Roman Titles (*Tituli*) and Deaconries (*Diaconiæ*, these
being in origin both regional and palatine) on which the cardinalitial
dignity is based, were established in the first century and confirmed
by Pope Saint Evarist (97-105), further by Pope Saint Dionysius
(259-268) and Pope Saint Marcellus I (308-309), cfr. *Liber Pontificalis*,
Duchesne, Paris 1886, I, 126, 157, 164. Different Supreme Pontiffs
have later increased these Titles and Deaconries. Suburbicarian
Cardinals are since early centuries the first members of the College,
immediately followed by those who retain Eastern Patriarchal
dignity. Since the Lateran Treaties (1929), all Cardinals resident in

Rome are citizens of the State of Vatican City.

The Most Eminent and Most Reverend Lords [Cardinals]:
Listed according to Order and precedence; as Roman Princes (all considered equal to Princes of the blood royal of any country) they follow immediately after the reigning Sovereign Pontiff and rank with the Princes of reigning Houses, cfr. Pope Leo X, *Supernæ* 1514, *Cæremoniale Cardinalium* 1706, confirmed 1858 et al. Notwithstanding the three Orders in the College which are always strictly observed, they rank equal inter se while the Cardinal Dean is *primus inter pares*, immediately followed by the Cardinal Vice-Dean, formerly called Sub-Dean; they are styled as above, solemnly also as Most Eminent Prince or more usually His (Your) Eminence, also My Lord Cardinal, and His (Your) Most Eminent Beatitude if Eastern Patriarchs. Except for these, who are created Cardinals upon their Eastern patriarchal Title, Their Eminences each have a personal Roman Title or Deaconry of creation, or of later option (*ius optionis*), sometimes also a second one *in commendam*. If belonging to the highest Order and class, they are in possession of the Title of a Suburbicarian See, upon subsequent summons by the Sovereign Pontiff. Cardinals who are over the age of eighty maintain all privileges, are also convoked to Consistory and attend the General Assemblies before a papal election but do not enter a Conclave, albeit, the same as any baptized man, they do not lose the right of election to the Papacy. Cardinal Legates *a latere* represent the Sovereign Pontiff in Person and are never outranked, being during their mission on equality with Emperors and Kings, or other Heads of States, all addressed as "Brothers or Sisters", this being constantly recognized since Cardinal Roland, Legate at the Diet of Besançon in 1157. Cardinal Envoys are outranked only by Heads of State. According to Decrees issued by Popes Benedict XV (1914-1922) and Pius XII (1939-1958), secular titles of nobility from whatever *fons honorum* or *ab immemorabili*, whether hereditary, personal or held through tenure of certain Sees, although not abolished, normally are not to be used (except where by local law part of their name), including the dignity of secular Prince also of the Holy Roman Empire. Inimical persecution of a Cardinal, personal injury to or imprisonment are counted high treason (*crimen lesæ maiestatis*). The official signature is: -if a Cardinal Bishop: †Bernardinus S.R.E. Card. Gantin, Ep. Ostien et Prænestin - if a Cardinal Priest: Franciscus Tit. S. Eusebii S.R.E. [Prior] Presb. Card. König (adding the name

of a residential See only if actually held and acting as its Incumbent,
in which case the preceding † may be used) - if a Cardinal Deacon:
Pius S.R.E. [Proto]diac. Card. Laghi. The daily signature for all is:
[†] Bernardinus Card. Gantin.

Order of Cardinal Bishops
Class of Cardinals of Suburbicarian Churches

No one is now created directly into this Order and class; the
elevation to the Titles of these seven Sees in the immediate vicinity
of Rome is reserved to the Sovereign Pontiff, the former *ius optionis*
to this dignity having been abolished; their six Incumbents are
considered as *Collaterales Summi Pontificis* and chosen from among
those Cardinals who live in Rome and have hitherto belonged to the
Order of Priests; the Cardinal Dean is chosen with the Pope's   Assent
by the peers of his Order and class from among the same Order and
class of Cardinal Bishops and he adds the Suburbicarian Title of
Ostia to the one already retained. It is his duty in Conclave to
formally request a newly elected Pope whether he accepts his
election and if so which name His Holiness will assume; the Dean is
invested with the Sacred Pallium and in case the new Pope is not yet
consecrated, it is his task to do so immediately. The Cardinal Dean
has the right of access to His Holiness. In case of impediment, the
Cardinal Vice-Dean (chosen the same as the Dean) replaces him and
further the one in that Order and class longest created. According
to recent precedent, a Cardinal Dean may surrender his deanship to
the Sovereign Pontiff especially if leaving Rome.

1. Joseph *Ratzinger*, **Dean of the College of Cardinals** with   Papal
Assent of the reigning Supreme Pontiff given 30 November 2002,
formerly *Vice-Dean of the College of Cardinals* with Papal Assent of
the reigning Supreme Pontiff given 6 November 1998, Bishop of the
Suburbicarian Titles of *Ostia* since 30 November 2002 and of
Velletri-Segni 5 April 1993, created by His late Holiness Pope Paul
VI 27 June 1977 with the Presbyteral Title of Saint Mary of
Consolation *in regione Tiburtina*, surrendered upon advancement
to the Order of Bishops by the reigning Supreme Pontiff, *b* at Marktl
am Inn, Diocese of Passau (Germany) 16 April 1927, ordained 29
June 1951, formerly Archbishop of Munich and Freising 24 March
1977, consecrated 28 May 1977, resigned that Metropolitan See 25
November 1981, Prefect of the Congregation for the Doctrine of the
Faith, President of the Pontifical Biblical Commission and of the

International Biblical Commission.
[*Vatican City*].

2. Bernardin *Gantin*, until 30 November 2002 *Dean of the College of Cardinals* with Papal Assent of the reigning Supreme Pontiff given 5 June 1993, Bishop of the Suburbicarian Titles of *Ostia* 5 June 1993, relinquishing that Title on 30 November 2002, *and of Palestrina* 29 September 1986, **Dean Emeritus of the College of Cardinals**, created by His late Holiness Pope Paul VI 27 June 1977 with the Deaconry of the Sacred Heart of Christ the King, later raised to Presbyteral Title subsequently surrendered 29 September 1986 upon advancement to the Order of Bishops by the present Supreme Pontiff, *b* [of the Blood Royal of Abomey] at Toffo, Archdiocese of Cotonou (Benin, formerly Dahomey) 8 May 1922, ordained 14 January 1951, formerly Titular Bishop of Tipasa in Mauretania 11 December 1956, consecrated 3 February 1957, promoted to the Metropolitan See of Cotonou 5 January 1960, resigned that See 28 June 1971 upon appointment as Secretary of the Congregation for the Evangelisation of Peoples; Prefect Emeritus of the Congregation for Bishops and President Emeritus of the Pontifical Commission for Latin America. [*Cotonou, Benin*].

3. Angelo *Sodano*, Bishop of the Suburbicarian Title of *Albano* 10 Jan 1994, retaining in commendam the Presbyteral Title of *Saint Mary Nova*, created with that Title by His Holiness Pope John Paul II 28 June 1991, *b* at Isola d'Asti, [Princely] Diocese of Asti (Piedmont, Italy) 23 Nov 1927, ordained 23 Sept 1950, formerly Titular Archbishop of *Nova Cæsaris in Numidia* 30 Nov 1977, consecrated 15 Jan 1978, former Apostolic Nuncio, former Pro-Secretary of State 1 Dec 1990, Secretary of State of His Holiness 29 June 1991. [*Vatican City*].

4. Roger *Etchegaray*, Bishop of the Suburbicarian Title of *Porto-Santa Rufina* 24 June 1998, created by His Holiness Pope John Paul II 30 June 1979 with the Presbyteral Title of *Saint Leo I Pope* called *The Great*, surrendered upon advancement to the Order of Bishops by the reigning Supreme Pontiff, *b* at Espelette, Diocese of Bayonne, Lescar et Oloron (France) 25 Sept 1922, ordained 13 July 1947, formerly Titular Bishop of Gemellæ in Numidia 29 March 1969, consecrated 27 May 1969, promoted to the Archiepiscopal See of Marseilles 22 Dec 1970 and Prelate of the 'Mission de France' 25 November 1975, resigned both dignities 8 April 1984, President Emeritus of the Committee for the Great Jubilee of the Year 2000, President Emeritus of the Pontifical Councils for Justice and Peace,

and Cor Unum.

[*Vatican City*].

5. Alfonso *López Trujillo*, Bishop of the Suburbicarian Title of *Frascati* 17 Nov 2001, created with the Title of Saint Prisca by His Holiness Pope John Paul II 2 Feb 1983, *b* at Villahermosa, now Diocese of Líbano-Honda (Colombia) 8 Nov 1935, ordained 13 November 1960, formerly Titular Bishop of *Boseta in Proconsulari* 25 Feb 1971, consecrated 25 March 1971, formerly promoted to the Archiepiscopal Coadjutorship of Medellín 22 May 1978, succeeded to that Metropolitan See 2 June 1979, resigned 9 Jan 1991, Archbishop Emeritus of that See, President of the Pontifical Council for the Family.

[*Vatican City*].

6. Giovanni Battista *Re*, Bishop of the Suburbicarian Title of *Sabina-Poggio Mirteto*, created with the Title *The Twelve Holy Apostles*, surrendered upon advancement to the Order of Bishop by the reigning Supreme Pontiff, created by His Holiness Pope John Paul II 21 Feb 2001, *b* at Borno, [Ducal] Diocese of Brescia (Lombardy, Italy) 30 Jan 1934, ordained 3 March 1957, formerly Titular Archbishop of Vescovìo in the *Latium* 9 Oct 1987, consecrated 7 Nov 1987, Prefect of the Congregation for Bishops and President of the Pontifical Commission for Latin America.

[*Vatican City*].

Class of Cardinals of Eastern Patriarchal Sees

(*Styled His/Your Most Eminent Beatitude*)

7. Nasrallah Pierre *Sfeir, Patriarch of Antioch of the Maronites*, created with that Eastern Patriarchal Title by His Holiness Pope John Paul II 26 Nov 1994, *b* at Reyfoun, now Patriarchal Eparchy of Batrun and Sarba of the Maronites (Lebanon) 15 May 1920, ordained 7 May 1950, formerly Titular Bishop of Tarsus of the Maronites 19 June 1961, consecrated 16 July 1961, Patriarch of Antioch of the Maronites and of All the Orient since 19 April 1986, Ecclesiastical Communion granted by the reigning Sovereign Pontiff 7 May 1986.

[*Patriarcat Maronite, Bkerké, Lebanon*].

8. Stephanos II *Ghattas*, a member of the Congregation of the Mission [Lazarists], *Patriarch of Alexandria of the Copts*, created with that Eastern Patriarchal Title by His Holiness Pope John Paul II 21 February 2001, *b* at Cheikh Zein-el-Dine, Eparchy of Sohag of the Copts (Egypt) 16 Jan 1920, ordained 25 March 1944, formerly Eparch

of Luqsor of the Copts 8 May 1967, consecrated 9 June 1967,
Patriarch of Alexandria of the Copts 9 June 1986, Ecclesiastical
Communion granted by the reigning Sovereign Pontiff 23 June 1986.
[*Patriarcat Copte Catholique, B.P. 69, Pont-de-Koubbeh, 11712
Cairo, Egypt*].

9. Ignace Moussa I *Daoud, Patriarch Emeritus of Antioch of the
Syrians*, created with that Eastern Patriarchal Title by His Holiness
Pope John Paul II 21 Feb 2001, *b* at Meskané, Archeparchy of Homs
of the Syrians (Syria) 18 Sept 1930, ordained 17 Oct 1954, formerly
Eparch of Cairo of the Syrians 2 July 1977, consecrated 18 Sept 1977,
formerly Archeparch of Homs of the Syrians 1 July 1944, Patriarch of
Antioch of the Syrians 13 Oct 1998, Ecclesiastical Communion granted
by the reigning Sovereign Pontiff 20 Oct 1998, surrendered his
Patriarchate 8 June 2001 retaining Patriarchal rank, style and title,
Grand Chancellor of the Pontifical Oriental Institute.
[*Vatican City*].

Order of Cardinal Priests

Direct creation into this Order is normally reserved to Latin
Patriarchs as well as residential (Major) Archbishops and Bishops of
any rite but usually only if upon cardinalitial elevation they retain
their Sees by specific papal derogation. By exceptional Papal favour,
Titular Archbishops may be created into this Order for special
reasons, while relinquishing their titular Sees. The Cardinal Premier
Priest, or the senior of the Order who replaces him in Conclave, is
the official witness, together with the Cardinal Protodeacon, of the
new Pope's acceptance of office at the request of the Cardinal Dean
or the one who acts in that capacity.

10. Franz *König,* **Premier Priest** of the Title of *Saint Eusebius* by
seniority since 13 Nov 1991, created with that Title by Blessed Pope
John XXIII 15 Dec 1958, *b* at Rabenstein, Diocese of Sankt Pölten
(Austria) 3 Aug 1905, ordained 29 Oct 1933, formerly Titular Bishop
of Livias *in Palestine* 3 July 1952, consecrated 31 Aug 1952, formerly
[*Prince-*] Archbishop of Vienna 10 May 1956, Archbishop Emeritus
of that Metropolitan See since 16 Aug 1985, President Emeritus of
the then Pontifical Council for Dialogue with non Believers.
[*Wollzeile 2, 1010 Vienna, Austria*].

11. Corrado *Ursi,* Priest of the Title of *Saint Calixtus*, created by His
late Holiness Pope Paul VI 26 June 1967, *b* at Andria, same Diocese
(Apulia, Italy) 26 July 1908, ordained 25 July 1931, formerly Bishop

of Nardò 31 July 1951, consecrated 30 Sept 1951, promoted to the now Archiepiscopal then Metropolitan See of Acerenza 30 Nov 1960 and translated to the Metropolitan See of Naples 23 May 1966, Archbishop Emeritus of that last See since 9 May 1987.

[*Via Capodimonte 13, 80136 Naples, Italy*].

12. Stephen *Kim Sou-hwan*, Priest of the Title of *Saint Felix a Cantalicio ad Centumcellas*, created by His late Holiness Pope Paul VI 28 April 1969, until 8 May 1992 Head *ad actum in Conclavi* of the Cardinalitial Presbyteral Order, *b* at Taegu (Korea), now same Archdiocese, 8 May 1922, ordained 15 Sept 1951, formerly Bishop of Masan 15 Feb 1966, consecrated 31 May 1966, promoted to the Metropolitan See of Seoul 9 April 1968, resigned 30 May 1998, Archbishop Emeritus of that last See, former Apostolic Administrator of P'yong-yang.

[*Chung-gu Myong-dong 2-ga 1, Myong Dong, Jung Ku, Seoul 100-022, Korea*].

13. Eugênio *de Araújo Sales*, Priest of the Title of *Saint Gregory VII Pope*, created by His late Holiness Pope Paul VI 28 April 1969, *b* at Acari, now Diocese of Caicó (Brazil) 8 Nov 1920, ordained 21 Nov 1945, formerly Titular Bishop of Thibica *in Proconsulari* 1 June 1954, consecrated 15 Aug 1954, promoted to the Metropolitan and Primatial See of São Salvador da Bahia 29 October 1968, translated to the Metropolitan See of São Sebastião do Rio de Janeiro 13 March 1971, Archbishop Emeritus of that See, Ordinary Emeritus of all Catholic faithful of the Oriental Rites in Brazil without Ordinary of their own Rite, former Primate of Brazil.

[*C.P. 1362, 20241-150 Rio de Janeiro, RJ, Brazil*].

14. Johannes *Willebrands*, Priest of the Title of *Saint Sebastian ad Catacumbas*, created by His late Holiness Pope Paul VI with the Deaconry of Saints Cosmas and Damian *on the Roman Forum* 28 April 1969, later opting for his present Presbyteral Title, *b* at Bovenkarspel, Diocese of Haarlem (The Netherlands) 4 Sept 1909, ordained 26 May 1934, formerly Titular Bishop of Mauriana *in Mauretania Cæsariensi* 4 June 1964, consecrated 28 June 1964, formerly Archbishop of Utrecht 6 Dec 1975, resigned from that Metropolitan See 3 Dec 1983, President Emeritus of the Pontifical Council for the Promotion of the Unity of Christians.

[*c/o Aartsbisdom Utrecht, Maliebaan 40, 3508 SB Utrecht, The Netherlands*].

15. Luis *Aponte Martínez*, Priest of the Title of *Saint Mary Mother of Providence in Monte Viridi*, created by His late Holiness Pope

Paul VI 5 March 1973, *b* at Lajas, now Diocese of Mayagüez (Puerto Rico) 4 Aug 1922, ordained 10 April 1952, formerly Titular Bishop of Lares *in Proconsulari* 23 July 1960, consecrated 12 Oct 1960, succeeded to the residential See of Ponce 18 Nov 1963; promoted to the Metropolitan See of San Juan de Puerto Rico 4 Nov 1964, resigned 26 March 1999, Archbishop Emeritus of that See.

[*Apartado 1967, San Juan, PR 00902-1967, Puerto Rico*].

16. Raúl Francisco *Primatesta,* Priest of the Title of the *Blessed Virgin Mary of Dolours ad forum Bonaĕrense,* created by His late Holiness Pope Paul VI 5 March 1973, *b* at Capilla del Señor, now Diocese of Zárate-Campana (Argentina) 14 April 1919, ordained 25 Oct 1942, formerly Titular Bishop of Tanais *in Zechia* 14 June 1957, translated to the residential See of San Rafael 12 June 1961, promoted to the Metropolitan See of Córdoba 16 Feb 1965, resigned that See 1998, Archbishop Emeritus of that See.

[*Caseros 160 2 ° piso, 5000 Córdoba, Argentina*].

17. Salvatore *Pappalardo,* Priest of the Title of *Saint Mary Odigitria of the Sicilians,* created by His late Holiness Pope Paul VI 5 March 1973, *b* at Villafranca Sicula, now Archdiocese of Agrigento (Sicily, Italy) 23 Sept 1918, ordained 12 April 1941, formerly Titular Archbishop of Miletus *in Caria* 7 Dec 1965, consecrated 16 Jan 1966, former Apostolic Nuncio, translated to the Metropolitan See of Palermo 17 Oct 1970, resigned 4 April 1996, Archbishop Emeritus of that See.

[*Piazza Baida 1, 90136 Palermo, Italy*].

18. Marcelo *González Martín,* Priest of the Title of *Saint Augin,* created by His late Holiness Pope Paul VI 5 March 1973, *b* at Villanubla, Archdiocese of Valladolid (Spain) 16 Jan 1918, ordained 29 June 1941, formerly Bishop of Astorga 31 Dec 1960, consecrated 5 March 1961, formerly Titular Archbishop of Casæ Medianæ *in Numidia* 21 Feb 1966, succeeded to the Archiepiscopal See of Barcelona 7 Jan 1967, translated to the Metropolitan and Primatial See of Toledo 3 Dec 1971, resigned 23 June 1995, Archbishop Emeritus of Toledo and former Primate of all the Spains.

[*Ronda de Buenavista 7, 45005 Toledo, Spain*].

19. Maurice Michael *Otunga,* Priest of the Title of *Saint Gregory Barbarigo ad Aquas Salvias,* created by His late Holiness Pope Paul VI 5 March 1973, *b* at Chebukwa, now Diocese of Kakamega (Kenya) 1 Jan 1923, ordained 3 Oct 1950, formerly Titular Bishop of Tacapæ *in Tripolitania* 17 Nov 1956, consecrated 25 Feb 1957, translated to the residential See of Kisii 21 May 1960, formerly Titular Archbishop

of Polymartium *in the Latium* 15 Nov 1969, succeeded to the Metropolitan See of Nairobi 24 Oct 1971, resigned 21 April 1997, Archbishop Emeritus of that See.

[*P.O.B. 14231, Nairobi, Kenya*].

20. Paulo Evaristo *Arns,* a member of the Order of the Friars Minor of Saint Francis [*Franciscans*], Priest of the Title of *Saint Anthony of Padua in via Tuscolana,* created by His late Holiness Pope Paul VI 5 March 1973, *b* at Forquilhinha, now Diocese of Tubarão (Brazil) 14 Sept 1921, ordained 30 Nov 1945, formerly Titular Bishop of Respecta *in Numidia* 2 May 1966, consecrated 3 July 1966; promoted to the Metropolitan See of São Paulo 22 Oct 1970, resigned 15 April 1998, Archbishop Emeritus of that See.

[*C.P. 916, 0217-170 São Paulo, SP, Brazil*].

21. Pio *Taofinu'u,* a member of the Society of Mary [*Marists*], Priest of the Title of *Saint Honuphrius in Ianiculo,* created by His late Holiness Pope Paul VI 5 March 1973, *b* at Falealupo, now Archdiocese of Samoa-Apia (Principality of Western Samoa) 9 Dec 1923, formerly Bishop of Apia 11 Jan 1968, consecrated 29 May 1968, Archbishop Metropolitan of Samoa-Apia and Tokelau 10 Sept 1982, since 26 June 1992 of Samoa-Apia, Archbishop of that See, since 16 Nov 2002 Archbishop Emeritus of that See.

[*P.O.Box 532, Apia, Western Samoa*].

22. Opilio *Rossi,* Priest of the Title of *Saint Lawrence in Lucina,* created with the Deaconry of Saint Mary Liberatress by His late Holiness Pope Paul VI 24 May 1976, later opting for his present Presbyteral Title, *b* at New York (United States of America) 14 May 1910, ordained for the Diocesan Clergy now of Piacenza-Bobbio (Emilia-Romagna, Italy) 11 March 1933, formerly Titular Archbishop of Ancyra *in Galatia Prima* 21 Nov 1953, consecrated 27 Dec 1953, former Apostolic Nuncio, President Emeritus of the Pontifical Council for the Laity and President Emeritus of the Cardinalitial Commission for the Pontifical Sanctuaries of Pompei, Loreto and Bari.

[*Vatican City*].

23. Juan Carlos *Aramburu,* Priest of the Title of *Saint John the Baptist of the Florentines,* created by His late Holiness Pope Paul VI 24 May 1976, *b* at Reducción, now Diocese of Villa de la Concepción del Río Cuarto (Argentina) 11 Feb 1912, ordained 28 Oct 1934, formerly Titular Bishop of Platea *in Hellade Secunda* 7 Oct 1946, consecrated 15 Dec 1946, translated to the then residential Episcopal See of Tucumán 28 Aug 1953, promoted first

Archbishop Metropolitan of that See 13 March 1957, formerly Titular Archbishop of Turres in Byzacene 14 June 1967, succeeded to the Metropolitan and Primatial See of Buenos Aires 22 April 1975, resigned 10 July 1990, Archbishop Emeritus of that See and former Primate of Argentina.

[*La Pampa 4022, 1430 Buenos Aires, Argentina*].

24. Corrado *Bafile,* Priest of the Title of *Saint Mary in Porticu in Campitelli,* created by His late Holiness Pope Paul VI 24 April 1976 with that Deaconry, later raised to his present Presbyteral Title, *b* at L'Aquila, same Archdiocese (Abruzzo, Italy) 4 July 1903, ordained 11 April 1936, formerly Titular Archbishop of Antioch in Pisidia 13 Feb 1960, consecrated 19 March 1960, former Apostolic Nuncio, Prefect Emeritus of the Congregation for Causes of Saints.

[*Vatican City*].

25. Hyacinthe *Thiandoum,* Priest of the Title of *Saint Mary de Populo,* created by His late Holiness Pope Paul VI 24 May 1976, *b* at Poponguine, now Archdiocese of Dakar (Senegal) 2 Feb 1921, ordained 18 April 1949, Archbishop of Dakar 24 Feb 1962, consecrated 20 May 1962, resigned 2 June 2000, Archbishop Emeritus of that Metropolitan See.

[*P.B. 1098, Dakar-Fann, Senegal*].

26. Jaime Lachica *Sin,* Priest of the Title of *Saint Mary ad Montes,* created by His late Holiness Pope Paul VI 24 May 1976, *b* at New Washington, now Diocese of Kalibo (Philippines) 31 Aug 1928, ordained 3 April 1954, formerly Titular Bishop of Obba *in Proconsulari* 10 Feb 1967, formerly Titular Archbishop of Massa Lubrense *in Campania* 15 Jan 1972, consecrated 18 March 1967, succeeded to the Metropolitan See of Jaro 8 Oct 1972, translated to that of Manila 24 May 1976, Archbishop of that last Metropolitan See.

[*P.O.Box 132, 1099 Manila, Philippines*].

27. William Wakefield *Baum,* Priest of the Title of *The Holy Cross in via Flaminia,* created by His late Holiness Pope Paul VI 24 May 1976, *b* at Dallas, same Diocese (United States of America) 21 Nov 1926, ordained for the Diocesan Clergy of Kansas City-Saint Joseph 12 May 1951, formerly Bishop of Springfield-Cape Girardeau 18 Feb 1970, consecrated 6 April 1970, promoted to the Metropolitan See of Washington 5 March 1973, resigned 18 March 1980, Archbishop Emeritus of that See, Emeritus Major Penitentiary.

[*Vatican City*].

28. Aloisio *Lorscheider,* a member of the Order of the Friars Minor of Saint Francis [*Franciscans*], Priest of the Title of *Saint Peter in*

Monte Aureo, created by His late Holiness Pope Paul VI 24 May 1976, *b* at Estrela, Archdiocese of Porto Alegre (Brazil) 8 Oct 1924, ordained 22 Aug 1948, formerly Bishop of Santo Ángelo 3 Feb 1962, consecrated 20 May 1962, promoted to the Metropolitan See of Fortaleza 26 March 1973, translated to that of Aparecida 12 July 1995, Archbishop of that See.

[*C.P. 05, 12570-000 Aparecida, SP, Brazil*].

29. Giuseppe *Caprio*, Priest of the Title of *Saint Mary of the Victory*, created with the Deaconry of Saint Mary Help of Christians by His Holiness Pope John Paul II 30 June 1979, later opting for his present Presbyteral Title, *b* at Lapio, Archdiocese of Benevento (Campania, Italy) 15 Nov 1914, ordained 17 Dec 1938, formerly Titular Archbishop of Apollonia *in New Epyrus* 14 Oct 1961, consecrated 17 Dec 1961, former Apostolic Nuncio, President Emeritus of the Prefecture of the Economic Affairs of the Holy See, Grand Master Emeritus of the Equestrian Order of the Holy Sepulchre.

[*Vatican City*].

30. Marco *Cé*, Priest of the Title of *Saint Mark*, created by His Holiness Pope John Paul II 30 June 1979, *b* at Izano, Diocese of Crema (Lombardy, Italy) 8 July 1925, ordained 27 March 1948, formerly Titular Bishop of Vulturia *in Mauretania Cæsariensi* 22 April 1970, consecrated 17 May 1970, promoted to the Patriarchal Primatial and Metropolitan See of Venice 7 Dec 1978, since 1 July 2002 Patriarch Emeritus of Venice, former Metropolitan of the Tri-Veneto and former Primate of Dalmatia.

[*San Marco 318, 30124 Venezia, Italy*].

31. Ernesto *Corripio Ahumada*, Priest of the Title of *The Immaculate Conception of the Blessed Virgin Mary ad viam Tiburtinam*, created by His Holiness Pope John Paul II 30 June 1979, *b* at Tampico, same Diocese (Mexico) 29 June 1919, ordained 25 Oct 1942, formerly Titular Bishop of Zapara *in Macedonia* 27 Dec 1952, consecrated 19 March 1953, translated to the residential See of Tampico 25 Feb 1956, promoted to the Metropolitan See of Antequera 25 July 1967, translated to that of Puebla de los Ángeles 8 March 1976 and further to the Primatial and Metropolitan See of Mexico (City) 19 July 1977, resigned 29 Sept 1994, Archbishop Emeritus of that last See and former Primate of Mexico.

[*A. Nieto 40, Col. Tetlameya, 04730 México, D.F., Mexico*].

32. Gerald Emmett *Carter*, Priest of the Title of *Saint Mary in Transpontina*, created by His Holiness Pope John Paul II 30 June 1979, *b* at Montréal, same Archdiocese (Canada) 1 March 1912,

ordained 22 May 1937, formerly Titular Bishop of Altiburus *in Proconsulari* 1 Dec 1961, consecrated 2 Feb 1962, translated to the residential Episcopal See of London *in Ontario* 17 Feb 1964, promoted to the Metropolitan See of Toronto 27 April 1978, resigned 17 March 1990, Archbishop Emeritus of that See.

[*355 Church Street, Toronto, Ont. M5B 1Z8, Canada*].

33. Franciszek *Macharski*, Priest of the Title of *Saint John ante Portam Latinam*, created by His Holiness Pope John II 30 June 1979, *b* at Kraków, same Archdiocese, 20 May 1927, ordained 2 April 1950, promoted to the [Princely] Metropolitan See of Kraków 29 Dec 1978 in succession to the reigning Supreme Pontiff, Archbishop of that See.

[*ul. Franciszkańska 3, PL-31-004 Kraków, Poland*].

34. Aurelio *Sabattani*, Priest of the Title of *Saint Apollinaris ad Thermas Neronianas-Alexandrinas*, created by His Holiness Pope John Paul II with the Deaconry of Saint Apollinaris 2 Feb 1983, later raised to his present Presbyteral Title, *b* at Casal Fiumanese, Diocese of Imola (Emilia-Romagna, Italy) 18 Oct 1912, ordained 26 July 1935, formerly Titular Archbishop of Justiniana Prima in *Mediterranean Dacia* 24 June 1965, consecrated 25 July 1965, formerly Territorial Prelate of Loreto, resigned 30 Sept 1971, Prefect Emeritus of the Supreme Tribunal of the Apostolic Signature, Archpriest Emeritus of the Patriarchal Vatican Basilica of Saint Peter's, formerly Vicar General of His Holiness for the State of Vatican City and former President of the Fabric of Saint Peter's.

[*Vatican City*].

35. Michael Michai *Kitbunchu*, Priest of the Title of *Saint Lawrence in Panepernu*, created by His Holiness Pope John Paul II 2 Feb 1983, *b* at Samphran, now Archdiocese of Bangkok (Thailand) 25 Jan 1929, ordained 20 Dec 1959, Metropolitan Archbishop of Bangkok 18 Dec 1972, consecrated 3 June 1973, Archbishop of that See.

[*51 Oriental Avenue, Bangkok 10500, Thailand*].

36. Alexandre *do Nascimento*, Priest of the Title of *Saint Mark in Agro Laurentino*, created by His Holiness Pope John Paul II 2 Feb 1983, *b* at Malanje, now same Diocese (Angola) 1 March 1925, ordained 20 Dec 1952, formerly Bishop of Malanje 10 Aug 1975, consecrated 31 Aug 1975, promoted to the Metropolitan See of Lubango (formerly Sá da Bandeira) 3 Feb 1977, translated to the Metropolitan See of Luanda 16 Feb 1986, Archbishop of that See.

[*C.P. 87, 1230-C, Luanda, Angola*].

37. Godfried *Danneels*, Priest of the Title of *Saint Anastasia*, created

by His Holiness Pope John Paul II 2 Feb 1983, taking canonical possession of that Title in the presence of H.M. Queen Fabiola of the Belgians, *b* at Kanegem, Diocese of Bruges or Brugge (Belgium) 4 June 1933, ordained 17 Aug 1957, formerly Bishop of Antwerp 4 Nov 1977, consecrated 18 Dec 1977, promoted to the Metropolitan and Primatial See of Mechlin-Brussels 19 Dec 1979, Archbishop of that See and Primate of Belgium.

[*Wollemarkt 15, 2800 Mechelen, Belgium*].

38. Thomas Stafford *Williams,* Priest of the Title of *Jesus the Divine Master in regione vulgo Pineta Sacchetti, c*reated by His Holiness Pope John Paul II 2 Feb 1983, *b* at Wellington, same Archdiocese (New Zealand) 20 March 1930, ordained 20 Dec 1959, Archbishop of Wellington 30 Oct 1979, consecrated 20 Dec 1979, Archbishop of that Metropolitan See, Military Ordinary for New Zealand.

[*P. O. Box 1937, Wellington 6015, New Zealand*].

39. Carlo Maria *Martini,* a member of the Society of Jesus [*Jesuits*], Priest of the Title of *Saint Cecilia,* created by His Holiness Pope John Paul II 2 Feb 1983, *b* at Turin, same Archdiocese (Piedmont, Italy) 15 Feb 1927, ordained 13 July 1952, Archbishop of Milan and *Pontifex Ambrosianus* 29 Dec 1979, consecrated 6 Jan 1980, since 1 July 2002 Archbishop Emeritus of that Metropolitan See.

[*Piazza Fontana 2, 20122 Milano, Italy*].

40. Jean-Marie *Lustiger,* Priest of the Title of *Saint Louis of the French*, created by His Holiness Pope John Paul II 2 Feb 1983, *b* at Paris, same Archdiocese (France) 17 Sept 1926, ordained 17 April 1954, formerly Bishop of Orléans 10 Nov 1979, consecrated 8 Dec 1979, promoted to the Metropolitan See of Paris 31 Jan 1981, Archbishop of that See, Ordinary of all Catholic faithful of Oriental rites in France lacking an Ordinary of their own rite.

[*8 rue de la Ville-l'Évêque, 75384 Paris, France*].

41. Józef *Glemp,* Priest of the Title of *Saint Mary trans Tiberim*, created by His Holiness Pope John Paul II Feb 1983, *b* at Inowroclaw, [Princely] Archdiocese of Gniezno (Poland) 18 Dec 1929, ordained 25 May 1956, formerly Bishop of the then residential Episcopal now Metropolitan See of Warmia 4 May 1979, consecrated 21 April 1979, promoted to the Metropolitan Primatial [Princely] See of Gniezno 7 July 1981, uniting *ad personam pro illa vice* the Metropolitan See of Warsaw 25 March 1992, resigned the Metropolitan See of Gniezno 25 March 1992 retaining by specific Papal provision the [Princely] Primacy of Poland, Archbishop of Warsaw and Ordinary of all Catholic faithful of Oriental rites in Poland lacking an Ordinary of their own

rite, Primate of Poland.

[*ul. Miodowa 17-19, 00-246 Warszawa, Poland*].

42. Joachim *Meisner*, Priest of the Title of *Saint Pudentiana*, created by His Holiness John Paul II 2 Feb 1983, *b* at Breslau now Wroc aw, same [Princely] Archdiocese (then Germany, now Poland) 25 Dec 1933, ordained 22 Dec 1962, formerly Titular Bishop of Vina *in Proconsulari* 17 March 1975, consecrated 17 May 1975, translated to the then Episcopal now Metropolitan See of Berlin 22 April 1980, promoted to the [Princely] Metropolitan See of Cologne 20 Dec 1988, Archbishop of that See.

[*Kardinal-Frings-Strasse 10, 50668 Köln 1, Germany*].

43. Duraisamy Simon *Lourdusamy*, Priest of the Title of *Saint Mary de Gratiis ad Fornaces extra Portam Equitum*, created by His Holiness Pope John Paul II 25 May 1985 with the Deaconry of Saint Mary de Gratiis ad Fornaces, later raised to his present Presbyteral Title, *b* at Kalleri, Archdiocese of Pondicherry and Cuddalore (India) 5 Feb 1924, ordained 21 Dec 1951, formerly Titular Bishop of Sozusa *in Libya* 2 July 1962, consecrated 22 Aug 1962, formerly Titular Archbishop of Philippi *in Macedonia* 9 Nov 1964, succeeded to the Metropolitan See of Bangalore 11 Jan 1968, resigned 30 April 1971, Prefect Emeritus of the Congregation for the Oriental Churches.

[*Vatican City*].

44. Francis *Arinze*, Priest of the Title of *Saint John a Pinea*, created by His Holiness Pope John Paul II 25 May 1985 with the Deaconry of Saint John a Pinea, later raised to his present Presbyteral Title, *b* at Eziowelle, now Archdiocese of Onitsha (Nigeria) 1 Nov 1932, ordained 23 Nov 1958, formerly Titular Bishop of Fissiana *in Byzacene* 6 July 1965, consecrated 29 Aug 1965, promoted to the Metropolitan See of Onitsha 26 June 1967, resigned 27 May 1985, appointed that day President of the Pontifical Council for Inter-Religious Dialogue, since 1 Oct 2002 Prefect of the Congregation for Divine Cult and the Discipline of the Sacraments.

[*Vatican City*].

45. Juan Francisco *Fresno Larraín*, Priest of the Title of *Saint Mary Immaculate of Lourdes ad viam Bocceam*, created by His Holiness Pope John Paul II 25 May 1985, *b* at Santiago de Chile, same Archdiocese 26 July 1914, ordained 18 Dec 1937, formerly Bishop of Copiapó 15 June 1958, consecrated 15 Aug 1958, promoted to the Metropolitan See of La Serena 28 July 1967 and further translated to that of Santiago de Chile 3 May 1983, resigned 30 March 1990, Archbishop Emeritus of that See.

[*Casilla 13520, Santiago 21, Chile*].

46. Antonio *Innocenti*, Priest of the Title of *Saint Mary in Aquiro*, created by His Holiness Pope John Paul II 25 May 1985 with the Deaconry of Saint Mary in Aquiro, later raised to his present Presbyteral Title, *b* at Poppi, Diocese of Fiesole (Tuscany, Italy) 23 Aug 1915, ordained 17 July 1938, formerly Titular Archbishop of Æclanum *in Campania* 15 Dec 1967, consecrated 28 Feb 1968, former Apostolic Nuncio, Prefect Emeritus of the Congregation for the Clergy, President Emeritus of the Pontifical Commission for the Preservation of the Church's Artistic and Historic Patrimony and President Emeritus of the Pontifical Commission *Ecclesia Dei*.
[*Vatican City*].

47. Miguel *Obando Bravo*, a member of the Salesian Society of Saint John Bosco [*Salesians*], Priest of the Title of *Saint John the Evangelist in Spinaceto*, created by His Holiness Pope John Paul II 25 May 1985, *b* at La Libertad, Chontales, now Diocese of Juigalpa (Nicaragua) 2 Feb 1926, ordained 10 Aug 1958, formerly Titular Bishop of Putia in Byzacene 18 Jan 1968, consecrated 31 March 1968, promoted to the Metropolitan See of Managua 16 Feb 1970, Archbishop of that See.
[*Apartado 3058, Managua, Nicaragua*].

48. Paul Augin *Mayer*, a member of the Order of Saint Benedict [*Benedictines*], Priest of the Title of *Saint Anselm on the Aventine*, created by His Holiness Pope John Paul II with the Deaconry of Saint Anselm, later raised to his present Presbyteral Title 2 Feb 1983, *b* at Altötting, Diocese of Passau (Bavaria, Germany) 23 May 1911, ordained 25 Aug 1935, formerly Titular Archbishop of Satrianum *in Salernitana* 6 Jan 1972, consecrated 13 Feb 1972, Prefect Emeritus of the Congregation for Divine Cult and the Discipline of the Sacraments, President Emeritus of the Pontifical Commission *Ecclesia Dei*.
[*Vatican City*].

49. Ángel *Suquía Goycochea*, Priest of the Title of *The Great Mother of God*, created by His Holiness Pope John Paul II 25 May 1985, *b* at Zaldivia, Diocese of San Sebastián (Spain) 2 Oct 1916, ordained 7 July 1940, formerly Bishop of Almería 17 May 1966, consecrated 16 July 1966, translated to the residential Episcopal See of Málaga 28 Nov 1969, promoted to the Metropolitan See of Santiago de Compostela 13 April 1973 and translated to the Archiepiscopal now Metropolitan See of Madrid 12 April 1983, resigned 28 July 1994, Archbishop Emeritus of that See.

[*Javier Barcaiztegui 7-3 °, 20010 San Sebastián, Spain*].

50. Ricardo Jamin *Vidal*, Priest of the Title of *Saints Peter and Paul in via Ostiensi,* created by His Holiness Pope John Paul II 25 May 1985, *b* at Mogpoc, now Diocese of Boac (Philippines) 6 Feb 1931, ordained 17 March 1956, formerly Titular Bishop of Claternæ *in Æmilia* 10 Sept 1971, consecrated 30 Nov 1971, promoted to the Metropolitan See of Lipa 22 Aug 1973, translated to the Archiepiscopal Coadjutorship of Cebu 13 April 1981, succeeded to that Metropolitan See 24 Aug 1982, Archbishop of that See.
[*P.O.B. 52, 6000 Cebu City, Philippines*].

51. Henryk Roman *Gulbinowicz,* Priest of the Title of *The Immaculate Conception of Mary ad Saxa Rubra,* created by His Holiness Pope John Paul II 25 May 1985, *b* at Šukiškes, Archdiocese of Vilnius (Lithuania) 17 Oct 1928, ordained 18 June 1950, formerly Titular Bishop of Acci *in Hispania* 12 Jan 1970, consecrated 8 Feb 1970, promoted to the [Princely] Metropolitan See of Wroclaw (Poland) 3 Jan 1976, Archbishop of that See.
[*ul. Katedralna 11, 50-328 Wroc aw, Poland*].

52. Paulos *Tzadua,* Priest of the Title of the *Most Holy Name of Mary ad viam Latinam,* created by His Holiness Pope John Paul II 25 May 1968, *b* at Addifini, now Eparchy of Asmara (then Ethiopia now Eritrea) 25 Aug 1921, ordained 12 March 1944, formerly Titular Bishop of Abila in Palæstina 1 March 1973, consecrated 20 May 1973, promoted to the Metropolitan Archeparchy of Addis Abeba 24 Feb 1977, resigned 11 Sept 1998, Archbishop Emeritus of that See.
[*P.O.B. 21903, Addis Abeba, Ethiopia*].

53. Jozef *Tomko,* Priest of the Title of *Saint Sabina,* created with the Deaconry of Jesus the Good Shepherd in Montagnola by His Holiness Pope John Paul II 25 May 1985, later opting for his present Presbyteral Title, *b* at Udavské (now Slovakia) 11 March 1924, ordained 12 March 1949, formerly Titular Archbishop of Doclea *in Upper Dalmatia* 12 July 1979, consecrated 15 Sept 1979, Prefect Emeritus of the Congregation for the Evangelisation of Peoples and Grand Emeritus Chancellor of the Pontifical Urbanian University, President of the Pontifical Committee for International Eucharistic Congresses.
[*Vatican City*].

54. Andrzej Maria *Deskur,* Priest of the title of *Saint Cæsareus in Palatio,* created by His Holiness Pope John Paul II with the Deaconry of Saint Cæsareus 25 May 1985, later raised to his present Presbyteral Title, *b* at Sancygniów, Diocese of Kielce (Poland) 29

Feb 1924, ordained for the Archdiocesan Clergy of Kraków 20 Aug 1950, formerly Titular Bishop of Thenæ *in Byzacene* 17 June 1974, consecrated 30 June 1974, formerly promoted Archbishop of the same Titular See 15 Feb 1980, President Emeritus of the Pontifical Council for Social Communications.

[*Vatican City*].

55. Paul *Poupard*, Priest of the Title of *Saint Praxedis*, created by His Holiness Pope John Paul II with the Deaconry of Saint Eugene I Pope 25 May 1985, later opting for his present Presbyteral Title, *b* at Bouzillé, Diocese of Angers (France) 30 Aug 1930, ordained 18 Dec 1954, formerly Titular Bishop of Usula *in Byzacene* 2 Feb 1979, consecrated 6 April 1979, formerly promoted Archbishop of the same Titular See 27 June 1980, former Rector of the *Institut Catholique de Paris*, President of the Pontifical Council for Culture.

[*Vatican City*].

56. Louis-Albert *Vachon*, Priest of the Title of *Saint Paul of The Cross in Corviale*, created by His Holiness Pope John Paul II 25 May 1985, *b* at Saint-Frédéric-de-Beauce, Archdiocese of Québec (Canada) 4 Feb 1912, ordained 11 June 1938, formerly Titular Bishop of Mesarfelta *in Numidia* 4 April 1977, consecrated 14 May 1977, promoted to the Metropolitan and Primatial See of Québec 20 March 1981, resigned 17 March 1990, Archbishop Emeritus of that same See and former Primate of Canada.

[*1 rue des Remparts, Québec, Qué. G1R 5L7, Canada*].

57. Rosalio José *Castillo Lara*, a member of the Salesian Society of Saint John Bosco [*Salesians*], Priest of the Title of *Our Lady of Coromoto in Saint John of God*, created by His Holiness Pope John Paul II 25 May 1985 with the Deaconry of Our Lady of Coromoto, later raised to his present Presbyteral Title, *b* at San Casimiro, now Diocese of Maracay (Venezuela) 4 Sept 1922, ordained 4 Sept 1949, formerly Titular Bishop of Præcausa *in Byzacene* 26 March 1973, consecrated 24 May 1973, formerly promoted Archbishop of that same Titular See 26 May 1982, President Emeritus of the Pontifical Commission for the State of Vatican City, President Emeritus of the Administration of the Patrimony of The Holy See.

[*Vatican City*].

58. Friedrich *Wetter*, Priest of the Title of *Saint Stephen in Cœlio Monte*, created by His Holiness Pope John Paul II 25 May 1985, *b* at Landau, Diocese of Speyer (Bavaria, Germany) 20 Feb 1928, ordained 10 Oct 1953, formerly Bishop of Speyer 28 May 1968, consecrated 29 June 1968, promoted to the Metropolitan See of

Munich and Freising 28 Oct 1992, Archbishop of that See.
[*Postfach 100551, 80079 München, Germany*].

59. Silvano *Piovanelli*, Priest of the Title of *Our Lady of Graces in via Triumphali*, created by His Holiness Pope John Paul II 25 May 1985, *b* at Ronta di Mugello, [Princely] Archdiocese of Florence (Tuscany, Italy) 21 Feb 1924, ordained 13 July 1947, formerly Titular Bishop of Tubunæ in Mauretania 28 May 1982, consecrated 24 June 1982, promoted to the [Princely] Metropolitan See of Florence 18 March 1983, since 21 March 2001 Archbishop Emeritus of that.
[*Piazza San Giovanni 3, 50129 Firenze, Italy*].

60. Adrianus Johannes *Simonis,* Priest of the Title of *Saint Clement I Pope*, created by His Holiness Pope John Paul II 25 May 1985, *b* at Lisse, now Diocese of Rotterdam (The Netherlands) 26 Nov 1931, ordained 15 June 1957, formerly Bishop of Rotterdam 29 Dec 1970, consecrated 20 March 1971, promoted to the Archiepiscopal Coadjutorship of Utrecht 27 June 1983, succeeded to that Metropolitan See 3 Dec 1983, Archbishop of that See, Grand Chancellor of the Catholic University of Nijmegen.
[*P.B. 14019, 3508 SB Utrecht, The Netherlands*].

61. Édouard *Gagnon,* a member of the Company of Priests of Saint Sulpice [*Sulpicians*], Priest of the Title of *Saint Marcellus I Pope*, created by His Holiness Pope John Paul II with the Deaconry of Saint Helen the Empress *extra Portam Prænestinam* 25 May 1983, later opting for his present Presbyteral Title, *b* at Saint-Daniel, now Diocese of Gaspé (Canada), 15 Jan 1918, ordained 15 Aug 1940, formerly Bishop of Saint Paul in Alberta 19 Feb 1969, consecrated 25 March 1969, resigned that See 3 May 1972, formerly Bishop emeritus of that See, promoted Titular Archbishop of Justiniana Prima *in Mediterranean Dacia* 7 July 1983, President Emeritus of the Pontifical Committee for International Eucharistic Congresses, President Emeritus of the Pontifical Council for the Family.
[*116 rue Notre-Dame Ouest, Montréal, Q.C. H2Y 1T2, Canada*].

62. Alfons Maria *Stickler,* a member of the Salesian Society of Saint John Bosco [*Salesians*], Priest of the Title of *Saint George in Velabro*, created by His Holiness Pope John Paul II 25 May 1985 with the Deaconry of Saint George, later raised to his present Presbyteral Title, *b* at Neunkirchen, Archdiocese of Vienna (Austria) 23 Aug 1910, ordained 27 March 1937, formerly Titular Archbishop of Volsinium *in the Latium* 8 Sept 1983, consecrated 1 Nov 1983, Emeritus Archivist and Emeritus Librarian of the Holy Roman Church.
[*Vatican City*].

63. Bernard Francis *Law,* Priest of the Title of *Saint Susanna,*
created by His Holiness Pope John Paul II 25 May 1985, *b* at Torreón,
now same Diocese (Mexico) 4 Nov 1931, ordained for the Diocesan
Clergy of Jackson, then Natchez-Jackson (Mississippi, United States
of America) 21 May 1961, formerly Bishop of Springfield-Cape
Girardeau 22 Oct 1973, consecrated 5 Dec 1973, promoted to the
Metropolitan See of Boston 11 Jan 1984, Archbishop of that See.
[*2101 Commonwealth Avenue, Brighton, MA 02135, U.S.A.*].

64. Giacomo *Biffi,* Priest of the Title of *Saints John the Evangelist
and Petronius,* created by His Holiness Pope John Paul II 25 May
1985, *b* at Milan, same Archdiocese (Lombardy, Italy) 13 June 1928,
ordained 23 Dec 1950, formerly Titular Bishop of Fidenæ *in the
Latium* 7 Dec 1975, consecrated 11 Jan 1976, promoted to the
[Princely] Metropolitan See of Bologna 19 April 1984, Archbishop of
that See.
[*Via Altabella 6, 40126 Bologna, Italy*].

65. Eduardo *Martínez Somalo,* Priest of the Title of *The Most Holy
Name of Jesus,* created with that Deaconry by His Holiness Pope
John Paul II 28 June 1988, raised 9 Jan 1999 to his present Presbyteral
Title, *b* at Baños del Río, Diocese of Calahorra y La Calzada-Logroño
(Spain) 31 March 1927, ordained 19 March 1950, formerly Titular
Archbishop of Tagora *in Numidia* 12 Nov 1975, former Apostolic
Nuncio, consecrated 13 Dec 1975, Prefect of the Congregation for
Institutes of consecrated life and Societies of apostolic life, *Camerarius*
of the Holy Roman Church.
[*Vatican City*].

66. Achille *Silvestrini,* Priest of *Saint Benedict outside the Gate of
Saint Paul,* created with that Deaconry by His Holiness Pope John
Paul II 28 June 1988, raised 9 Jan 1999 to his present Presbyteral
Title, *b* at Brisighella, now Diocese of Faenza-Modigliana
(Emilia-Romagna, Italy) 25 Oct 1923, ordained 13 July 1946, formerly
Titular Archbishop of Novaliciana *in Mauretania Sitifensi* 4 May
1979, consecrated 27 May 1969, Prefect Emeritus of the
Congregation for the Oriental Churches and Grand Chancellor
Emeritus of the Pontifical Oriental Institute.
[*Vatican City*].

67. Angelo *Felici,* Priest of the Title of *Saints Blaise with the Ring
and Charles ad Catinarios,* created with that Deaconry by His
Holiness Pope John Paul II 28 June 1988, raised 9 Jan 1999 to his
present Presbyteral Title, *b* at Segni, now Suburbicarian Diocese of
Velletri-Segni (Latium, Italy) 26 July 1919, ordained 4 April 1942,

formerly Titular Archbishop of Cæsariana *in Numidia* 22 July 1964, former Apostolic Nuncio, consecrated 24 Sept 1967, Prefect Emeritus of the Congregation for Causes of Saints, President Emeritus of the Pontifical Commission *Ecclesia Dei*.

[*Vatican City*].

68. José *Freire Falcão*, Priest of the Title of *Saint Luke in via Prænestina*, created by His Holiness Pope John Paul II 28 June 1988, *b* at Ererê, now Diocese of Limoeiro do Norte (Brazil) 23 Oct 1925, ordained 19 June 1949, formerly Titular Bishop of Vardimissa *in Mauretania Cæsariensi* 24 April 1967, consecrated 17 June 1967, succeeded to the residential See of Limoeiro do Norte 19 Aug 1967, promoted to the Metropolitan See of Teresina 25 Nov 1971 and translated to that of Brasília 15 Feb 1984, Archbishop of that See.

[*QL 12-Cj12, Lote 1, Lago Sul, 71630-325 Brasília, Brazil*].

69. Michele *Giordano*, Priest of the Title of *Saint Joachim ad Prata Castelli Sancti Angeli*, created by His Holiness Pope John Paul II 28 June 1988, *b* at Sant'Arcangelo, now Diocese of Tursi-Lagonegro (Lucania, Italy) 26 Sept 1930, ordained 5 July 1953, formerly Titular Bishop of Lari Castellum *in Mauretania Cæsariensi* 23 Dec 1971, consecrated 5 Feb 1972, promoted contemporaneously to the then Metropolitan See of Matera, the residential See of Irsina and the Abbacy of Saint Michael the Archangel of Montescaglioso (Italy) 12 June 1974, translated to the Metropolitan See of Naples 9 May 1987, Archbishop of that See.

[*Largo Donnaregina 23, 80138 Napoli, Italy*].

70. Alexandre José Maria *dos Santos*, a member of the Order of Friars Minor of Saint Francis [*Franciscans*], Priest of the Title of *Saint Frumentius ad Prata Fiscalia*, created by His Holiness Pope John Paul II 28 June 1988, *b* at Zavala, now Diocese of Inhambane (Mozambique) 18 March 1924, ordained 25 June 1953, appointed 23 Dec 1974 to the Metropolitan See of Lourenço Marques, since 18 Sept 1976 called Maputo, consecrated 9 March 1975, Archbishop of Maputo.

[*C.P. 258, Maputo, Mozambique*].

71. Giovanni *Canestri*, Priest of the Title of *Saint Andrew the Apostle de Valle*, created by His Holiness Pope John Paul II 28 June 1988, *b* at Castelspina, Diocese of Alessandria (Piedmont, Italy) 30 Sept 1918, ordained 12 April 1941, formerly Titular Bishop of Tenedus *in Mytilene* 8 July 1961, consecrated 30 July 1961, translated to the residential Episcopal See of Tortona 7 June 1971, formerly Titular Archbishop of Monterano *(Forum Clodii) in the Latium* and

Vicegerent of Rome 8 Feb 1975, translated to the Metropolitan See of Cagliari 22 March 1984 and to that of Genoa 6 July 1987, resigned 20 April 1995, Archbishop Emeritus of that last See and former Transmarine Legate of the Holy See.
[Vatican City]

72. Antonio María *Javierre Ortas*, a member of the Salesian Society of Saint John Bosco *[Salesians]*, Priest of the Title of *Saint Mary the Liberatress ad collem Testaceum*, created with that Deaconry by His Holiness Pope John Paul II 28 June 1988, raised 9 Jan 1999 to his present Presbyteral Title, *b* at Siétamo, Diocese of Huesca (Spain) 21 Feb 1921, ordained 24 April 1949, formerly Titular Archbishop of Meta *in Numidia* 20 May 1976, consecrated 29 June 1976, Prefect Emeritus of the Congregation for Divine Cult and the Discipline of the Sacraments and Emeritus Librarian and Archivist Emeritus of the Holy Roman Church.
[Vatican City].

73. Simon Ignatius *Pimenta*, Priest of the Title of *Saint Mary Queen of the World in Turri vulgo Spaccata*, created by His Holiness Pope John Paul II 28 June 1988, *b* at Marol, Archdiocese of Bombay (India) 1 March 1920, ordained 21 Dec 1949, formerly Titular Bishop of Bocconia *in Numidia* 5 June 1971, consecrated 29 June 1971, promoted to the Archiepiscopal Coadjutorship of Bombay 26 Feb 1977, succeeded to that Metropolitan See 11 Sept 1978, resigned 8 Nov 1996, Archbishop Emeritus of that See.
[21 Nathalal Parekh Marg, Mumbai-400001, India].

74. Edward Bede *Clancy*, Priest of the Title of *Saint Mary in Vallicella*, created by His Holiness Pope John Paul II 28 June 1988, *b* at Lithgow, Diocese of Bathurst (Australia) 13 Dec 1923, ordained 23 July 1949, formerly Titular Bishop of Árd Carna *in Connacia Hibernica* 25 Oct 1973, consecrated 19 Jan 1974, promoted to the Archiepiscopal See of Canberra and Goulburn 24 Nov 1978, translated to the Metropolitan See of Sydney 12 Feb 1983, since 26 March 2001 Archbishop Emeritus of that See.
[Saint Mary's Cathedral, Sydney, NSW 2000, Australia].

75. James Aloysius *Hickey*, Priest of the Title of *Saint Mary Mother of the Redeemer ad Turrim Bellamonicam*, created by His Holiness Pope John Paul II 28 June 1988, *b* at Midland, now Diocese of Saginaw (United States of America) 11 Oct 1920, ordained 15 June 1946, formerly Titular Bishop of Taraqua *in Byzacene* 18 Feb 1967, consecrated 14 April 1967, translated to the residential See of Cleveland 31 May 1974, promoted to the Metropolitan See of

Washington 17 June 1980, resigned 21 Nov 2000, Archbishop Emeritus of that See.

[*P.O.B. 29260, Washington, DC 20017, U.S.A.*].

76. Edmund Casimir *Szoka*, Priest of the Title of *Saints Andrew the Apostle and Gregory Pope called the Great ad Clivum Scauri*, created by His Holiness Pope John Paul II 28 June 1988, *b* at Grand Rapids (United States of America) 14 Sept 1927, ordained 5 June 1954, formerly Bishop of Gaylord 11 June 1971, promoted to the Metropolitan See of Detroit 21 March 1981, resigned 28 April 1990, Archbishop Emeritus of that See, President Emeritus of the Prefecture of Economic Affairs of The Holy See, President of the Pontifical Commission and of the Government of the State of Vatican City.

[*Vatican City*].

77. László *Paskai*, a member of the Order of Friars Minor of Saint Francis [*Franciscans*], Priest of the Title of *Saint Teresa The Virgin*, created by His Holiness Pope John Paul II 28 June 1988, *b* at Szeged, now Diocese of Szeged-Csanád, 8 May 1927, ordained 3 March 1951, formerly Titular Bishop of Bavagaliana *in Byzacene* 2 March 1978, consecrated 5 April 1978, translated to the residential See of Veszprém 31 March 1979, promoted to the Archiepiscopal Coadjutorship of Kalocsa 5 April 1982, translated to the Metropolitan and Primatial See of Esztergom 3 March 1987, Esztergom-Budapest since 31 May 1993, Archbishop of that See and [Prince-] Primate of Hungary.

[*Úri utca 62, 1014 Budapest, Hungary*].

78. Christian Wiyghan *Tumi*, Priest of the Title of *The Holy Martyrs of Uganda*, created by His Holiness Pope John Paul II 28 June 1988, *b* at Kikaikelaki, now Diocese of Kumbo (Cameroon) 15 Oct 1930, ordained 17 April 1966, formerly Bishop of Yagoua 6 Dec 1979, consecrated 6 Jan 1980, promoted to the Archiepiscopal Coadjutorship of Garoua 19 Nov 1982, succeeded to that Metropolitan See 17 March 1984, translated to the Metropolitan See of Douala 31 Aug 1991, Archbishop of that See.

[*D.P. 179, Douala, Cameroon*].

79. Hans Hermann *Groër*, a member of the Order of Saint Benedict [*Benedictines*], Priest of the Title of *Saints Joachim and Anne in regione Tuscolana*, created by His Holiness Pope John Paul II 28 June 1988, *b* at Vienna, same Archdiocese (Austria) 13 Oct 1919, ordained 12 April 1942, formerly [Prince-]Archbishop of Vienna 15 July 1986, consecrated 14 Sept 1986, resigned 14 Sept 1995,

Archbishop Emeritus of that See.

[*Marienplatz 2, 2041, Maria Roggendorf, Austria*].

80. Jean *Margéot*, Priest of the Title of *Saint Gabriel The Archangel ad Aquam Transversam*, created by His Holiness Pope John Paul II 28 June 1988, *b* at Quatre-Bornes, Diocese of Port-Louis (Mauritius) 3 Feb 1916, ordained 17 Dec 1938, formerly Bishop of Port-Louis 6 Feb 1969, consecrated 4 May 1969, resigned 15 Feb 1993, Bishop Emeritus of that See.

[*13 rue Mgr Gonin, Port-Louis, Mauritius*].

81. Pio *Laghi*, Priest of the Eudoxian Title of *Saint Peter in Bonds*, created with the Deaconry of *Saint Mary Help of Christians in via Tuscolana* by His Holiness Pope John Paul II 28 June 1991, from 9 Jan 1999 until 27 Feb 2002 Protodeacon, on which day opted in Consistory for his present Presbyteral Title and advanced to that Cardinalitial Order *b* at Castiglione, now Diocese of Forlì-Bertinoro (Emilia-Romagna, Italy) 21 May 1922, ordained 20 April 1946, formerly Titular Archbishop of Mauriana *in Mauretania Cæsariensi* 24 May 1969, former Apostolic Nuncio, consecrated 22 June 1969, Prefect Emeritus of the Congregation for Catholic Education (Seminaries and Institutes of Study), Grand Chancellor Emeritus of the Pontifical Gregorian University, *Patronus* of the Sovereign Military Order of Malta of Saint John.

[*Vatican City*].

82. Edward Idriss *Cassidy*, Priest of *Saint Mary in via Lata*, created by His Holiness Pope John Paul II with that Deaconry 28 June 1991, advanced to the Cardinalitial Presbyteral Order in Consistory of 26 Feb 2002 *b* at Sydney, same Archdiocese (Australia) 5 July 1924, ordained 23 July 1949, formerly Titular Archbishop of Amantia *in New Epyrus* 27 Oct 1970, former Apostolic Nuncio, consecrated 15 Nov 1970, President Emeritus of the Pontifical Council for the Promotion of Unity of Christians.

[*16 Coachwood Drive, Warabrook, N.S.W. 2304, Australia*].

83. José Tomás *Sánchez*, Priest of *Saint Pius V Pope ad Villam Carpineam*, created by His Holiness Pope John Paul II with that Deaconry 28 June 1991, advanced to the Cardinalitial Presbyteral Order in Consistory of 26 Feb 2002 *b* at Pandan, now Diocese of Virac (Philippines) 17 March 1920, ordained 12 May 1946, formerly Titular Bishop of Lesvi *in Mauretania Sitifensi* 5 Feb 1968, consecrated 12 May 1968, succeeded to the residential Episcopal See of Lucena 25 Sept 1976, promoted to the Metropolitan See of Nueva Segovia 12 Jan 1982, relinquished that See upon appointment

as Secretary of the Congregation for the Evangelisation of Peoples 22 March 1986, Prefect Emeritus of the Congregation for the Clergy.
[*Vatican City*].

84. Virgilio *Noè*, Priest of The Queen of the Apostles, created with the Deaconry of *Saint John Bosco in via Tuscolana* by His Holiness Pope John Paul II 28 June 1991, advanced to the Presbyteral Cardinalitial Order 26 Feb 2002, opting in Consistory on that day for his present Presbyteral Title *b* at Zelata di Bereguardo, Diocese of Pavia (Lombardy, Italy) 30 March 1922, ordained 1 Oct 1944, formerly Titular Archbishop of Voncaria *in Mauretania Cæsariensi* 30 Jan 1982, consecrated 6 March 1982, Archpriest Emeritus of the Patriarchal Basilica of Saint Peter in the Vatican, Vicar General Emeritus of His Holiness for the State of Vatican City, President Emeritus of the Fabric of Saint Peter's.
[*Vatican City*].

85. Fiorenzo *Angelini*, Priest of *The Holy Spirit of the Saxons*, created by His Holiness Pope John Paul II with that Deaconry 28 June 1991, advanced to the Presbyteral Cardinalitial Order in Consistory of 26 Feb 2002, *b* at Rome (Italy) 1 Aug 1916, ordained 3 Feb 1940, formerly Commander of the Holy Spirit, Abbot of Monte Romano, Baron of La Manziana and Titular Bishop of Messene *in Peloponnesus* 27 June 1956, consecrated 29 July 1956, formerly Titular Archbishop of the same See 11 Feb 1985, first President now Emeritus of the Pontifical Council for the Pastoral Care of Health Operators.
[*Vatican City*].

86. Frédéric *Etsou-Nzabi-Bamungwabi*, a member of the Congregation of the Immaculate Heart of Mary called Missionaries of Scheut, Priest of the Title of *Saint Lucia ad Forum Armorum*, created by His Holiness Pope John Paul II 28 June 1991, *b* at Mazalonga, now Diocese of Lisala (Congo, formerly Zaïre) 3 Dec 1930, ordained 13 July 1958, formerly Titular Archbishop of Menefessi *in Byzacene* 8 July 1976, consecrated 7 Nov 1976, succeeded to the Metropolitan See of Mbandaka Dikoro 11 Nov 1977, translated to that of Kinshasa 7 July 1990, Archbishop of that See.
[*R P 8491, Kinshasa 1, Democratic Republic of Congo*].

87. Nicolás de Jesús *López Rodríguez*, Priest of the Title of *Saint Pius X Pope ad regionem Balduinæ*, created by His Holiness Pope John Paul II 28 June 1991, *b* at Barranca, now Diocese of La Vega (Dominican Republic) 31 Oct 1936, ordained 18 March 1991, formerly Bishop of San Francisco de Macorís 16 Jan 1978,

consecrated 25 Feb 1978, promoted to the Metropolitan and Primatial See of Santo Domingo 15 Nov 1981, Archbishop of that See and Primate of the Indies *seu Totius Americæ*, Military Ordinary for the Dominican Republic.

[*Calle Pellerano Alfau 1, Ciudad Colonial, Santo Domingo, Dominican Republic*].

88. Roger Michael *Mahoney*, Priest of the Title of the *Four Holy Crowned Martyrs*, created by His Holiness Pope John Paul II 28 June 1991, *b* at Hollywood, Archdiocese of Los Angeles (United States of America) 27 Feb 1936, ordained 1 May 1962, formerly Titular Bishop of Tamascani *in Mauretania Sitifensi* 7 Jan 1975, consecrated 19 March 1975, translated to the residential See of Stockton 15 Feb 1980, promoted to the Metropolitan See of Los Angeles 16 July 1985, Archbishop of that See.

[*3424 Wiltshire Boulevard, Los Angeles, CA 90010-2241, United States of America*].

89. Anthony Joseph *Bevilacqua*, Priest of the Title of the *Most Holy Redeemer and Saint Alphonsus in Exquiliis*, created by His Holiness Pope John Paul II 28 June 1991, *b* at Brooklyn, same Diocese (United States of America) 17 June 1923, ordained 11 June 1949, formerly Titular Bishop of Aquæ Albæ in Byzacene 4 Oct 1980, consecrated 24 Nov 1980, translated to the residential See of Pittsburgh 10 Oct 1983, promoted to the Metropolitan See of Philadelphia 11 Feb 1988, Archbishop of that See.

[*222 North 17th Street, Philadelphia, PA 19103-1299, United States of America*].

90. Giovanni *Saldarini*, Priest of the Title of the *Most Sacred Heart of Jesus ad Castrum Prætorium*, created by His Holiness Pope John Paul II 28 June 1991, *b* at Cantù, Archdiocese of Milan (Lombardy, Italy) 11 Dec 1924, ordained 31 May 1947, formerly Titular Bishop of Gaudiaba *in Numidia* 10 Nov 1984, consecrated 7 Dec 1984, promoted to the Metropolitan See of Turin 31 Jan 1989, resigned 19 June 1999, Archbishop Emeritus of that See.

[*Via dell'Arcivescovado 12, 10121, Torino, Italy*].

91. Cahal Brendan *Daly*, Priest of the Title of *Saint Patrick*, created by His Holiness Pope John Paul II 28 June 1991, *b* at Loughguile, Diocese of Down and Connor (Ireland) 1 Oct 1917, ordained 22 June 1941, formerly Bishop of Ardagh and Clonmacnoise 26 May 1967, consecrated 16 July 1967, translated to the residential Episcopal See of Down and Connor 24 Aug 1982, promoted to the Metropolitan Primatial See of Armagh 6 Nov 1990, resigned 1 Oct 1996,

Archbishop Emeritus of Armagh and former Primate of All Ireland.
[*Ara Cœli, Armagh, BT61 7QY, Northern Ireland*].

92. Camillo *Ruini*, Priest of the Title of *Saint Agnes outside the Walls*, created by His Holiness Pope John Paul II 28 June 1991, *b* at Sassuolo, now Diocese of Reggio Emilia-Guastalla (Emilia-Romagna, Italy), 19 Feb 1931, ordained 8 Dec 1954, formerly Titular Bishop of Nepte *in Byzacene* 16 May 1983, promoted Archbishop of the same Titular See 17 Jan 1991, Vicar General of His Holiness for the Italian portion of the City of Rome and its District and Archpriest of the Patriarchal Lateran Archbasilica of the Most Holy Saviour, Saint John the Baptist and Saint John the Evangelist 1 July 1991, Grand Chancellor of the Pontifical Lateran University, President Emeritus of the *Peregrinatio ad Petri Sedem.*
[*Vatican City*].

93. Ján Chryzostom *Korec*, a member of the Society of Jesus [*Jesuits*], Priest of the Title of *Saints Fabian and Venantius ad Villam Florelliam*, created by His Holiness Pope John Paul II 28 June 1991, *b* at Bošany, Diocese of Nitra (now Slovakia) 22 Jan 1924, ordained 1 Oct 1950, secretly consecrated 24 Aug 1951, Bishop of Nitra since 6 Feb 1990.
[*Biskupsky úrad, post. schranka 46A, SK-95050 Nitra, Slovakia*].

94. Henri *Schwery*, Priest of the Title of The *Holy Protomartyrs in via Aurelia Antiqua*, created by His Holiness Pope John Paul II 28 June 1991, *b* at Saint-Léonard, Diocese of Sion, Sitten (Valais or Wallis, Switzerland) 14 June 1932, ordained 7 July 1957, formerly Bishop of Sion 22 July 1977, consecrated 17 Sept 1977, resigned 1 April 1995, Bishop Emeritus of Sion or Sitten
[*Argnou, 1900 Ayent 2, Switzerland*].

95. Georg Maximilian *Sterzinsky*, Priest of the Title of *Saint Joseph in reytone Aurelia*, created by His Holiness Pope John Paul II 28 June 1991, *b* at Warlack, now Archdiocese of Warmia (Poland) 9 Feb 1936, ordained for the Diocesan Clergy of Erfurt (Germany) 29 June 1960, formerly Bishop of Berlin 28 May 1989, consecrated 9 Sept 1989, since 27 June 1994 first Metropolitan Archbishop of Berlin.
[*Wundtstrasse 48-50, 14057 Berlin, Germany*].

96. Miloslav *Vlk*, Priest of the Sessorian Title of *The Holy Cross in Jerusalem*, created by His Holiness Pope John Paul II 26 Nov 1994, *b* at Lišnice-Sepekov, Diocese of Ceské Budejovice (now Czech Republic) 17 May 1932, ordained 23 June 1968, formerly Bishop of Ceské Budejovice 14 Feb 1990, consecrated 31 March 1990, promoted to the [Princely] Metropolitan See of Prague 27 March

1991, Archbishop of that See.

[*Hradcanské nám. 16, 119 02 Praha 1, Czech Republic*].

97. Peter Seiichi *Shirayanagi*, Priest of the Title of *Saint Emerentiana ad Turrim Florentiam*, created by His Holiness Pope John Paul II 26 Nov 1994, *b* at Hachioji, now Archdiocese of Tokyo (Japan) 17 June 1928, ordained 21 Dec 1954, formerly Titular Bishop of Atenia *in Pisidia* 15 March 1966, promoted to the Titular Archiepiscopal See of Castro *in Tuscia* 15 Nov 1969, succeeded by Coadjutorship to the Metropolitan See of Tokyo 21 Feb 1970, resigned 17 Feb 2000, Archbishop Emeritus of that See.

[*16-15 Sekiguchi, 3-chôme, Bunkyo-ku, Tokyo 112, Japan*].

98. Adolfo Antonio *Suárez Rivera*, Priest of the Title of *Our Lady of Guadalupe in Monte Malo*, created by His Holiness Pope John Paul II 26 Nov 1994, *b* at San Cristóbal de las Casas then Chiapas, same Diocese (Mexico) 9 Jan 1927, ordained 8 March 1952, formerly Bishop of Tepic 14 May 1991, consecrated 15 Aug 1971, translated to the residential See of Tlalnepantla 8 May 1980 and promoted to the Metropolitan See of Monterrey 8 Nov 1983, Archbishop of that See.

[*Apartado postal 7, Loma Larga 2429 con Sierra Madre, 64000 Monterrey, NL, Mexico*].

99. Jaime Lucas *Ortega y Alamino*, Priest of the Title of *Saints Aquila and Priscilla*, created by His Holiness Pope John Paul II 26 Nov 1994, *b* at Jagüey Grande, Diocese of Matanzas (Cuba) 18 Oct 1936, ordained 2 Aug 1964, formerly Bishop of Pinar del Río 4 Dec 1978, consecrated 14 Jan 1979, promoted to the Metropolitan See of San Cristóbal de La Habana 20 Nov 1981, Archbishop of that See.

[*Apartado 594, La Habana 10100, Cuba*].

100. Julius Riyadi *Darmaatmadja*, a member of the Society of Jesus [*Jesuits*], Priest of the Title of *The Sacred Heart of Mary*, created by His Holiness Pope John Paul II 26 Nov 1994, *b* at Muntilan, now Archdiocese of Semarang (Indonesia) 20 Dec 1934, ordained 18 Dec 1969, formerly Archbishop of Semarang 19 Feb 1983, consecrated 29 June 1983, translated to the Metropolitan See of Jakarta 11 Jan 1996, Archbishop of that last See and Military Ordinary for Indonesia.

[*Keuskupan Agung, Jl. Katedral 7, Jakarta 10710, Indonesia*].

101. Emmanuel *Wamala*, Priest of the Title of *Saint Hugh*, created by His Holiness Pope John Paul II 26 Nov 1994, *b* at Kamaggwa, now Diocese of Masaka (Uganda) 15 Dec 1926, ordained 21 Dec 1957, formerly Bishop of Kiyinda-Mityana 17 July 1981, consecrated 22 Nov 1981, promoted to the Archiepiscopal Coadjutorship of Kampala 21 June 1988, succeeded to that Metropolitan See 8 Feb

1990, Archbishop of that See.

[*P.O.B. 14125, Kampala, Uganda*].

102. William Henry *Keeler*, Priest of the Title of *Saint Mary of the Angels*, created by His Holiness Pope John Paul II 26 Nov 1994, *b* at San Antonio, same Archdiocese (United States of America) 4 March 1931, ordained 17 July 1955, formerly Titular Bishop of Ulcinium *in Upper Dalmatia* 24 July 1979, consecrated 21 Sept 1979, translated to the residential Episcopal See of Harrisburg 10 Nov 1983, promoted to the Protometropolitan See of Baltimore 6 April 1989, Archbishop of that See.

[*320 Cathedral Street, Baltimore MD 21201, U.S.A*].

103. Jean-Claude *Turcotte*, Priest of the Title of *Our Lady of the Most Blessed Sacrament and the Holy Canadian Martyrs*, created by His Holiness Pope John Paul II 26 Nov 1994, *b* at Montréal, same Archdiocese (Canada) 26 June 1936, ordained 24 May 1959, formerly Titular Bishop of Suas *in Proconsulari* 14 April 1982, consecrated 29 June 1982, promoted to the Metropolitan See of Montréal 17 March 1990, Archbishop of that See.

[*1071 rue de la Cathédrale, Montréal P.Q., H2B 2V4, Canada*].

104. Ricardo María *Carles Gordó*, Priest of the Title of *Saint Mary of Consolation in via Tiburtina*, created by His Holiness Pope John Paul II 26 Nov 1994, *b* at Valencia, same Archdiocese (Spain) 24 Sept 1926, ordained 29 June 1951, formerly Bishop of Tortosa 6 June 1969, consecrated 3 Aug 1969, promoted to the Archiepiscopal See of Barcelona 23 March 1990, Archbishop of that See.

[*Carrer del Bisbe, 5, 08002 Barcelona, Spain*].

105. Adam Joseph *Maida*, Priest of the Title of *Saint Vitalis*, created by His Holiness Pope John Paul II 26 Nov 1994, *b* at East Vandergrift, now Diocese of Greensburg (United States of America) 18 March 1930, ordained 26 May 1956, formerly Bishop of Green Bay 7 Nov 1983, consecrated 25 Jan 1984, promoted to the Metropolitan See of Detroit 28 April 1990, Archbishop of that See.

[*75 East Boston Boulevard, Detroit MI 48202, U.S.A*.].

106. Vinko *Puljić*, Priest of the Title of *Saint Clare ad Vineam Claram*, created by His Holiness Pope John Paul II 26 Nov 1994, *b* at Prijecani, Diocese of Banja Luka (then Yugoslavia, now Bosnia and Herzegovina) 8 Sept 1945, ordained 29 June 1970, Archbishop of Vrhbosna or Sarajevo 19 Nov 1990, consecrated 6 Jan 1991, Metropolitan Archbishop of that See.

[*Kaptol 7, 71000 Sarajevo, Bosnia and Herzegovina*].

107. Armand Gaétan *Razafindratandra*, Priest of the Title of *Saints*

Sylvester and Martin in Montibus, created by His Holiness Pope
John Paul II 26 Nov 1994, *b* at Ambohimalaza, now Archdiocese of
Antananarivo (Madagascar) 7 Aug 1925, ordained 27 July 1954,
formerly Bishop of Mahajanga then Majunga 27 April 1978,
consecrated 2 July 1978, promoted to the Metropolitan See of
Antananarivo formerly Tananarive 3 Feb 1994, Archbishop of that
See.
[Archevêché, Andohalo, Antananarivo 01, Madagascar].
108. Paul Joseph *Pham Dinh Tung,* Priest of the Title of *Saint Mary
Queen of Peace ad litus Ostiense,* created by His Holiness Pope
John Paul II 26 Nov 1994, *b* at Binh Hoa, now Diocese of Phát Diêm
(Vietnam) 15 July 1919, ordained 6 June 1949, formerly Bishop of
Bac Ninh 5 April 1963, consecrated 15 Aug 1963, promoted to the
Metropolitan See of Hà Nôi 23 March 1994, Archbishop of that See.
[Tòa Tôg Giám Muc, 40 Phô Nhà Chung, Hà Nôi, Vietnam].
109. Juan *Sandoval Íñiguez,* Priest of the Title of *Our Lady of Guadalupe
and Saint Philip The Martyr in via Aurelia,* created by His   Holiness
Pope John Paul II 26 Nov 1994, *b* at Yahualica, now Diocese of San
Juan de los Lagos (Mexico) 28 March 1933, ordained 27 Oct 1957,
formerly Coadjutor Bishop of Ciudad Juárez 3 March 1988,
consecrated 30 April 1988, succeeded to that residential See 11 July
1992, promoted to the Metropolitan See of Guadalajara 21 April
1994, Archbishop of that See
[Morelos 244, 45500 San Pedro Tlaquepaque, Jal., Mexico].
110. Kazimierz *Swiatek,* Priest of the Title of *Saint Gerard Majella,*
created by His Holiness Pope John Paul II 26 Nov 1994, *b* at Walga,
now Apostolic Administration of Estonia 21 Oct 1914, ordained for
the Diocesan Clergy of Pinsk (Poland) 8 April 1939; appointed to the
Metropolitan See of Minsk-Mohilev (Belarus) 13 April 1991,
consecrated 21 May 1991, Archbishop of that See and Apostolic
Administrator of Pinsk.
[ul. Szewczenki 12/1, 225710 Pinsk, Belarus].
111. Ersilio *Tonini,* Priest of the Title of The *Most Holy Redeemer in
Valle Melaina,* created by His Holiness Pope John Paul II 26 Nov
1994, *b* at Centovera di San Giorgio Piacentino, now Diocese of
Piacenza-Bobbio (Emilia, Italy) 20 July 1914, ordained 18 April
1937, formerly Bishop of Macerata, Tolentino, and subsequently
contemporaneously of Recanati, Cingoli and Treia 28 April 1969,
consecrated 2 June 1969, promoted to the Protometropolitan See of
Ravenna and the therewith united residential Episcopal See of Cervia
22 Nov 1975, resigned 27 Oct 1990, Archbishop Emeritus of

Ravenna-Cervia.

[*Via Santa Teresa 8, 48100 Ravenna, Italy*].

112. Salvatore *De Giorgi*, Priest of the Title of *Saint Mary in Aracœli*, created by His Holiness Pope John Paul II 21 Feb 1998, *b* at Vernole, now Archdiocese of Lecce (Apulia, Italy) 6 Sept 1930, ordained 28 June 1953, formerly Titular Bishop of Tulana *in Proconsulari* 21 Nov 1973, consecrated 27 Dec 1973, succeeded by right of Coadjutorship to the residential Episcopal See of Oria 17 March 1978, promoted to the Metropolitan See of Foggia and simultaneously to the residential Episcopal Sees of Bovino and of Troia, all in Apulia, Italy, 4 April 1981; resigned Troia 30 Sept 1986, translated to the Metropolitan See of Tàranto 10 Oct 1987, relinquished that See 11 May 1990 upon his appointment as Secretary General of the Italian Catholic Action; translated to the Metropolitan See of Palermo, Sicily, Italy, 4 April 1996, Archbishop of that See.

[*Curia Arcivescovile, 90134 Palermo, Italy*].

113. Serafim *Fernandes de Araújo*, Priest of the Title of *Saint Louis Marie Grignion de Montfort*, created by His Holiness Pope John Paul II 21 Feb 1998, *b* at Araçuaí, now same Diocese (Brazil) 13 Aug 1924, ordained 12 March 1949, formerly Titular Bishop of Verinopolis *in Galatia*, consecrated 7 May 1959, promoted to the Archiepiscopal Coadjutorship of Belo Horizonte 22 Nov 1982, succeeded to that Metropolitan See 5 Feb 1986, Archbishop of that See.

[*Praça da Liberdade 263, Bairro Funcionários, 30140-010 Belo Horizonte, MG, Brazil*].

114. Antonio María *Rouco Varela*, *Priest of the Title of Saint Lawrence in Damasus*, created by His Holiness Pope John Paul II 21 Feb 1998, *b* at Villalba, now Diocese of Mondoñedo-Ferrol (Spain) 24 Aug 1936, ordained 28 March 1959, formerly Titular Bishop of Gergis *in Tripolitania* 17 Sept 1976, consecrated 31 Oct 1976, promoted to the Metropolitan See of Santiago de Compostela 9 May 1984 and to the Metropolitan See of Madrid 21 Feb 1998, Archbishop of that See.

[*Calle San Justo 2, 28005, Madrid, Spain*].

115. Aloysius Matthew *Ambrozic*, Priest of the Title of *Saints Marcellinus and Peter*, created by His Holiness Pope John Paul II 21 Feb 1998, *b* at Gabrje, [Princely] now Archdiocese of Ljubljana (now Slovenia) 27 Jan 1930, ordained 4 June 1955, formerly Titular Bishop of Valabria *in Galecia* 26 March 1976, consecrated 27 May 1976, promoted to the Archiepiscopal Coadjutorship of Toronto 22 May 1986, succeeded to that Metropolitan See 17 March 1990,

Archbishop of the same See.

[*1155 Yonge Street, Toronto, Ont. M4T 1W2, Canada*].

116. Dionigi *Tettamanzi*, Priest of the Title of *Saints Ambrose and Charles*, created by His Holiness Pope John Paul II 21 Feb 1998, *b* at Renate, Archdiocese of Milan (Lombardy, Italy) 14 March 1934, ordained 28 June 1957, formerly promoted to the Metropolitan See of Ancona-Osimo *in the Marches* 1 July 1989, consecrated 23 Sept 1989, resigned that See 6 April 1991, translated to the Metropolitan See of Genoa in Liguria 20 April 1995, further translated to the Metropolitan See of Milan 1 Sept 2002, Archbishop of that last See and Pontifex Ambrosianus.

[*Piazza Fontana 2, 20122 Milano, Italy*].

117. Polycarp *Pengo*, Priest of the Title of *Our Lady of La Salette*, created by His Holiness Pope John Paul II 21 Feb 1998, *b* at Mwazye, now Diocese of Sumbawanga (now Tanzania), 5 Aug 1944, ordained 20 June 1971, formerly Bishop of Nachingwea 11 Nov 1983, consecrated 6 Jan 1984, translated to the residential Episcopal See of Tunduru-Masasi 17 Oct 1986, promoted to the Archiepiscopal Coadjutorship of Dar-es-Salaam 22 Jan 1990, succeeded to that Metropolitan See 22 July 1992, Archbishop of that See.

[*Archbishop's House, P.O.B. 167, Dar-es-Salaam, Tanzania*].

118. Christoph *Schönborn*, a member of the Order of Preachers [*Dominicans*], Priest of the Title of *Jesus The Divine Worker*, created by His Holiness Pope John Paul II 21 Feb 1998, *b* (*Count Christoph* Maria Hugo Damian Peter Adalbert von Schönborn, second son of Maria Hugo-Damian Adalbert Josef Hubertus *Count von Schönborn*, 1916-1979, and of his wife Eleonore Baroness von Doblhoff 1920-) in Skalsko, Diocese of Litomerice (now Czech Republic) 22 Jan 1945, ordained 27 Dec 1970, formerly titular Bishop of Sutri *in the Latium* 11 July 1995, promoted to the Archiepiscopal Coadjutorship of Vienna 13 April 1995, succeeded to that [Princely] Metropolitan See 14 Sept 1995, Archbishop of that See.

[*Wollzeile 2, 1010 Wien, Austria*].

119. Norberto *Rivera Carrera*, Priest of the Title of *Saint Francis of Assisi ad ripam maiorem*, created by His Holiness Pope John Paul II 21 Feb 1998, *b* at Tepehuanes, Archdiocese of Durango (Mexico), 6 June 1942, ordained 3 July 1966, formerly Bishop of Tehuacán 5 Nov 1985; consecrated 21 Dec 1985, promoted to the Primatial Metropolitan See of Mexico [City] 13 June 1995, Archbishop of that See and Primate of Mexico.

[*Camelia 110, Col. Florida, 01030 México, D.F., México*].

120. Francis Eugene *George*, a member of the Congregation of the Missionary Oblates of Mary Immaculate, of Saint Charles Eugène de Mazenod [*Oblates*], Priest of the Title of *Saint Bartholomew on the Tiber Island*, created by His Holiness Pope John Paul II 21 Feb 1998, *b* at Chicago 16 Jan 1937, ordained 21 Dec 1963, formerly Bishop of Yakima 10 July 1990, consecrated 21 Sept 1990, promoted to the Metropolitan See of Portland in Oregon 30 April 1966, translated to that of Chicago 8 April 1997, Archbishop of that See. [*P.O.Box 1979, Chicago, Illinois 60690, U.S.A.*].

121. Paul *Shan Kuo-hsi*, a member of the Society of Jesus [*Jesuits*], Priest of the Title of *Saint Chrysogonus,* created by His Holiness Pope John Paul II 21 Feb 1998, *b* at Puyang, diocese of Taming (China) 3 Dec 1923, ordained 18 March 1955, formerly Bishop of Hwalien (Formosa) 15 Nov 1979, consecrated 14 Feb 1980, translated to the residential See of Kaohsiung (Formosa) 4 March 1991, Bishop of that See. [*125 Szu-Wei 3rd Road, Kaohsiung 80203, Taiwan*].

122. Adam *Kozlowiecki*, a member of the Society of Jesus [*Jesuits*], Priest of the Title of *Saint Andrew at the Quirinal,* created by His Holiness Pope John Paul II 21 Feb 1998, *b* at Huta Komorowska, Diocese of Sandomierz (Poland) 1 April 1911, ordained 24 June 1937, formerly Titular Bishop of Diospolis Inferior in Ægypto 4 June 1955, consecrated 11 Sept 1955, promoted to the Metropolitan See of Lusaka (Zambia) 25 April 1959, translated to the Titular Archiepiscopal See of Potenza Picena *in the Marches* 29 May 1969, surrendering that See upon cardinalitial creation. [*P.O. Box 50003, 15101 Ridgeway, Zambia*].

123. Marian *Jaworski*, Priest of the Title of *Saint Syxtus*, created and reserved *in pectore* by His Holiness Pope John Paul II 21 Feb 1998, published in Consistory of 21 Feb 2001, *b* at Lemberg, now Ukraine, 21 Aug 1926, ordained 25 June 1950, formerly titular Bishop of Lambæsis in Numidia 21 May 1984, consecrated 23 June 1984, promoted to the Metropolitan See of Lemberg [Lviv] of the Latins 16 Jan 1991, Archbishop of that See. [*Pl. Katedralny 1, 290008 Lviv, Ukraina*]

124. Jānis *Pujats*, Priest of the Title of *Saint Sylvia*, created and reserved *in pectore* by His Holiness Pope John Paul II 21 Feb 1998, published in Consistory of 21 Feb 2001, *b* at Nautreni, Archdiocese of Riga (Latvia) 14 Nov 1930, ordained 29 March 1951, Archbishop of Riga 8 May 1991, consecrated 1 June 1991, Archbishop of that Metropolitan See.

[Maza Pils iela 2/A, 1050 Riga, Latvia].

125. Antonio José *González Zumárraga,* Priest of the Title of *Saint Mary in Via,* created by His Holiness Pope John Paul II 21 Feb 2001, *b* at Pujili, now Diocese of Latacunga (Ecuador) 18 March 1925, ordained 29 June 1951, formerly Titular Bishop of Tagarata *in Proconsulari* 17 May 1969, consecrated 15 June 1969, translated to the residential See of Machala 30 Jan 1978, Archbishop Coadjutor of Quito 28 June 1980, succeeded to that Metropolitan See 1 June 1985, Archbishop of the same See.

[Apartado 17-01-00106, Quito, Ecuador].

126. Ivan *Dias,* Priest of the Title of *The Holy Spirit ad Ferratellam,* created by His Holiness Pope John Paul II 22 Feb 2001, *b* at Bombay [now Mumbai], same Archdiocese 14 April 1936, ordained 8 Dec 1958, formerly Titular Archbishop of Rusubisir *in Mauretania Cæsariensi* 8 May 1982, consecrated 19 June 1982, former Apostolic Nuncio, translated to the Metropolitan See of Bombay 8 Nov 1996, Archbishop of that same See.

[21 Nathalal Parekh Marg, Mumbai-4000001, India].

127. Geraldo Majella *Agnelo,* Priest of the Title of *Saint Gregory the Great in Maliana Nova,* created by His Holiness Pope John Paul II 21 Feb 2001, *b* at Juiz de Fora, now same Archdiocese (Brazil) 19 Oct 1933, ordained 29 June 1957, formerly Bishop of Toledo *in Brasilia* consecrated 6 Aug 1978, promoted to the Metropolitan See of Londrina 4 Oct 1982, relinquished that See 16 Sept 1991 on his appointment as Secretary of the Congregation of Divine Cult and the Discipline of the Sacraments, translated to the Primatial and Metropolitan See of São Salvador da Bahia 13 Jan 1999, Archbishop of that See and Primate of Brazil.

[Av. Cardeal da Silva, 26, Casa 412-Federação, 40220-140 Salvador, Bahia, Brazil].

128. Pedro *Rubiano Sáenz,* Priest of the Title of *The Transfiguration of Our Lord Jesus Christ,* created by His Holiness Pope John Paul II 21 Feb 2001, b at Cartago (Colombia) 13 Sept 1932, ordained 8 July 1956, formerly Bishop of Cúcuta 2 June 1971, consecrated 11 July 1971, Archbishop Coadjutor of Cali 26 March 1983, succeeded to that Metropolitan See 7 Feb 1985, translated to the Primatial and Metropolitan See of Bogotá 27 Dec 1994, Archbishop of that last See and Primate of Colombia.

[Carrera 7, n. 10-20, Santafé de Bogotá, Colombia]

129. Theodore Edgar *McCarrick,* Priest of the Title of *Saints Nereus and Achilleus,* created by His Holiness Pope John Paul II 21 Feb

2001, b at New York, same Archdiocese (United States of America) 7 July 1930, ordained 31 May 1958, formerly Titular Bishop of Rusubisir *in Mauretania Cæsariensi* 24 May 1977, consecrated 29 June 1977, translated to the residential See of Metuchen 19 Nov 1981, promoted to the Metropolitan See of Newark 30 May 1986, further translated to the Metropolitan See of Washington 21 Nov 2000, Archbishop of that same See.

[P.O. Box 29260, Washington, D.C., U.S.A.]

130. Desmond *Connell*, Priest of the Title of *Saint Sylvester in Capite*, created by His Holiness Pope John Paul II 21 Feb 2001, b at Dublin, same Archdiocese (Ireland) 24 March 1926, ordained 19 May 1951, Archbishop of Dublin and Primate of Ireland 21 Jan 1988, consecrated 6 March 1988, Archbishop of that same Metropolitan See and Primate of Ireland.

[Archbishop's House, Dublin 9, Ireland]

131. Audrys Juozas *Backis,* Priest of the Title of *The Nativity of Our Lord Jesus Christ in via Gallia*, created by His Holiness Pope John Paul II 21 Feb 2001, b at Kaunas (Lithuania), same Archdiocese, 1 Feb 1937, ordained 18 March 1961, formerly Titular Archbishop of Meta *in Numidia* 5 Aug 1988, consecrated 4 Oct 1988, former Apostolic Nuncio, translated to the Metropolitan See of Vilnius 14 Dec 1991, Archbishop of that same See.

[Šventaragio 4, 2001 Vilnius, Lithuania]

132. Francisco José *Errázuriz Ossa,* a member of the Fathers of Schönstatt, Priest of the Title of *Our Lady of the Peace*, created by His Holiness Pope John Paul II 21 Feb 2001, b at Santiago de Chile 5 Sept 1933, ordained 16 July 1961, formerly Titular Archbishop of Hólar *in Islandia* 22 Dec 1990, consecrated 6 Jan 1991, formerly Secretary of the Congregation for Religious Life and Societies of Apostolic Life, formerly Archbishop-Bishop of Valparaíso 24 Sept 1996, translated to the Metropolitan See of Santiago 24 April 1998, Archbishop of that same See.

[Simón Bolívar 2845, Santiago, Chile]

133. Julio *Terrazas Sandoval,* a member of the Congregation of the Most Holy Redeemer [Redemptorists], Priest of the Title of *Saint John Baptist de'Rossi*, created by His Holiness Pope John Paul II 21 Feb 2001, b at Vallegrande, Archdiocese of Santa Cruz de la Sierra (Bolivia) 7 March 1936, ordained 29 July 1962, formerly Titular Bishop of Apisa Major in Proconsulari 15 April 1978, consecrated 8 June 1978, formerly Bishop of Oruru 9 Jan 1982, promoted to the Metropolitan See of Santa Cruz de la Sierra 6 Feb 1991, Archbishop

of that same See.

[Calle Paquio esquina Achachairu, Santa Cruz, Bolivia]

134. Wilfrid Fox *Napier*, a member of the Order of Friars Minor of Saint Francis [Franciscans], Priest of the Title of *Saint Francis of Assisi in Acilia*, created by His Holiness Pope John Paul II, *b* at Swartberg, Diocese of Kokstad (South Africa) 8 March 1941, ordained 25 July 1970, formerly Bishop of Kokstad 29 Nov 1980, consecrated 28 Feb 1981, promoted to the Metropolitan See of Durban 29 May 1992, Archbishop of that same See.

[154 Gordon Road, Durban 4001, Kwazulu-Natal, South Africa]

135. Óscar Andrés *Rodríguez Maradiaga*, a member of the Salesian Society of Saint John Bosco [Salesians], Priest of the Title of *Our Lady of Hope*, created by His Holiness Pope John Paul II 21 Feb 2001, *b* at Tegucigalpa, same Archdiocese (Honduras) 29 Dec 1942, ordained 28 June 1970, formerly Titular Bishop of Pudentiana *in Numidia* 28 Oct 1978, consecrated 8 Dec 1978, promoted to the Metropolitan See of Tegucigalpa 8 Jan 1993, Archbishop of that same See.

[Apartado 106, Tegucigalpa, Honduras].

136. Bernard *Agré*, Priest of the Title of *Saint John Chrysostomus in Monte Sacro Alto*, created by His Holiness Pope John Paul II 21 Feb 2001, *b* at Monga, now Archdiocese of Abidjan (Ivory Coast) 2 March 1926, ordained 20 July 1953, formerly Bishop of Man 8 June 1968, consecrated 3 Oct 1968, translated to the residential See of Yamoussoukro 6 March 1992, promoted to the Metropolitan See of Abidjan 19 Dec 1994, Archbishop of that same See.

[01 B.P. 1287, Abidjan 01, Ivory Coast]

137. Ignacio Antonio *Velasco García*, a member of the Salesian Society of Saint John Bosco [Salesians], Priest of the Title of *Saint Mary Domenica Mazzarello*, created by His Holiness Pope John Paul II 21 Feb 2001, *b* at Acarigua, now Diocese of Guanare (Venezuela) 17 Jan 1929, ordained 17 Dec 1955, formerly Titular Bishop of Utimmira *in Proconsulari* 23 Oct 1989, consecrated 6 Jan 1990, promoted to the Primatial and Metropolitan See of Caracas 27 May 1995, Archbishop of that same See and Primate of Venezuela.

[Apartado 954, Caracas 1010, Venezuela]

138. Juan Luis *Cipriani Thorne*, a member of the Clergy of the personal Prelature of Opus Dei, Priest of the Title of *Saint Camillus de Lellis in Hortis Sallustianis*, created by His Holiness Pope John Paul II 21 Feb 2001, *b* at Lima, same Archdiocese (Peru) 28 Dec 1943, ordained 21 Aug 1977, formerly Titular Bishop of Turuzi in

Proconsulari 23 May 1988, consecrated 3 July 1988, promoted to the Metropolitan See of Ayacucho 13 May 1995 and further translated to the Primatial and Metropolitan See of Lima 9 Jan 1999, Archbishop of that same See and Primate of Peru.

[Calle Los Nogales 249, San Isidro, Lima 27, Peru]

139. Francisco *Álvarez Martínez,* Priest of the Title of *Saint Mary Queen of Peace in Monte Viridi,* created by His Holiness Pope John Paul II 21 Feb 2001, *b* at Santa Eulalia de Ferroñes Llanera, Archdiocese of Oviedo (Spain) 14 July 1925, ordained 11 June 1950, formerly Bishop of Tarrazona 13 April 1973, consecrated 3 June 1973, formerly Bishop of Calahorra y La Calzada-Logroño 20 Dec 1976, formerly Bishop of Orihuela-Alicante 12 May 1989, promoted to the Metropolitan and Primatial See of Toledo 23 June 1995, Archbishop Emeritus of that See and former Primate of all the Spains 29 Oct 2002.

[Arco de Palacio 3, 45002 Toledo, Spain]

140. Cláudio *Hummes,* a member of the Order of the Minor Friars of Saint Francis [Franciscans], Priest of the Title of *Saint Anthony of Padua in Via Merulana,* created by His Holiness Pope John Paul II 21 Feb 2001, *b* at Montenegro, Archdiocese of Porto Alegre (Brazil) 8 Aug 1934, ordained 3 Aug 1958, formerly Titular Bishop of Arcadia *in Crete* 22 March 1975, consecrated 25 May 1975, succeeded to the residential See of Santo André 29 Dec 1975, promoted to the Metropolitan See of Fortaleza 29 May 1996, further translated to the Metropolitan See of São Paulo 13 April 1998, Archbishop of that same See.

[C.P. 1674, Luz, 01106-010 São Paulo, Brazil]

141. Varkey *Vithayathil,* a member of the Congregation of the Most Holy Redeemer *[Redemptorists],* Priest of the Title of *Saint Bernard ad Thermas,* created by His Holiness Pope John Paul II 21 Feb 2001, *b* at Parur, now Archeparchy of Ernakulam-Angamaly of the Syro-Malabarians 29 May 1927, ordained 12 June 1954, formerly Titular Archbishop of Achrida *in New Epyrus* 11 Nov 1996, consecrated 6 Jan 1997, translated to the Titular Archiepiscopal See of Antinoe *in Thebaide* 19 April 1997, promoted to the Major Metropolitan See of Ernakulam-Angamaly of the Syro-Malabarians 18 Dec 1999, Major Archbishop of that same See.

[Major Archbishop's House, Kochi 682031, Ernakulam, Kerala, India]

142. Jorge Mario *Bergoglio,* a member of the Society of Jesus [Jesuits], Priest of the Title of *Saint Robert Bellarmine,* created by His Holiness Pope John Paul II 21 Feb 2001, *b* at Buenos Aires, same

Archdiocese (Argentina) 17 Dec 1936, ordained 13 Dec 1969, formerly Titular Bishop of Auca *in Hispania* 20 May 1922, consecrated 27 June 1992, promoted to the Archiepiscopal Coadjutorship of Buenos Aires 3 June 1997, succeeded to that Metropolitan See 28 Feb 1998, Archbishop of that same See and Primate of Argentina.
[Avenida Rivadavia 415, C1002AAC, Buenos Aires, Argentina]

143. José da Cruz *Policarpo*, Priest of the Title of *Saint Anthony in Campo Martio*, created by His Holiness Pope John Paul II 21 Feb 2001, *b* at Alvorninha, Patriarchate of Lisbon 26 Feb 1936, ordained 15 Aug 1961, formerly Titular Bishop of Caliabria *in Lusitania* 26 May 1978, consecrated 29 June 1978, promoted to the Patriarchal Coadjutorship of Lisbon 5 March 1997, succeeded to that Patriarchal See 24 March 1998, Patriarch of Lisbon.
[Casa Patriarcal, Quinta do Cabeço, Rua do Seminário 1885-076 Moscavide, Portugal]

144. Severino *Poletto*, Priest of the Title of *Saint Joseph in Via Triumphali*, created by His Holiness Pope John Paul II 21 Feb 2001, *b* at Salgaredo, Diocese of Treviso (Veneto, Italy) 18 March 1933, ordained 29 June 1957, formerly Coadjutor Bishop of Fossano 3 April 1980, consecrated 17 May 1980, succeeded to that See [and Countship] 29 Oct 1980, translated to the [Princely] residential See of Asti 16 March 1989, promoted to the Metropolitan See of Turin 19 June 1999, Archbishop of that same See.
[Via Arcivescovado 12, 10121 Torino, Italy].

145. Cormac *Murphy-O'Connor*, Priest of the Title of *Saint Mary supra Minervam*, created by His Holiness Pope John Paul II 21 Feb 2001, *b* at Reading, Diocese of Portsmouth (England) 24 Aug 1934, ordained 28 Oct 1956, formerly Bishop of Arundel and Brighton 17 Nov 1977, consecrated 21 Dec 1977, promoted to the Metropolitan See of Westminster 15 Feb 2001, Archbishop of that same See and *Præses Perpetuus totius Cœtus Episcopalis Angliæ et Cambriæ.*
[Archbishop's House, Westminster, London SW1P 1QJ].

146. Edward Michael *Egan*, Priest of the Title of *Saints John and Paul*, created by His Holiness Pope John Paul II 21 Feb 2001, *b* at Oak Park, Archdiocese of Chicago (United States of America) 2 April 1932, ordained 15 Dec 1957, formerly Titular Bishop of Allegheny *in Pennsylvania* 1 April 1985, consecrated 22 May 1985, translated to the residential See of Bridgeport 5 Nov 1988, promoted to the Metropolitan See of New York 11 May 2000, Archbishop of that same See.

[1011 First Avenue, NewYork, NY 10022, United States of America].
147. Lybomir *Husar,* a member of the Order of Ukrainian Studite Monks, Priest of the Title of *Saint Sophie in Via Boccea,* created by His Holiness Pope John Paul II 21 Feb 2001, *b* at Lemberg, same Archdiocese (now Ukraine) 26 Feb 1933, ordained 30 March 1958, formerly Titular Bishop *absolute* and consecrated 2 April 1977, confirmed in the Titular See of Nisa in Lycia 22 Feb 1996, promoted to the Major Metropolitan See of Lemberg of the Ukrainians 25 Jan 2001, Major Archbishop of that same See.
[P. Sviatoho Jura 5, 79000 Lviv, Ukraine].
148. Karl *Lehmann,* Priest of the Title of *Pope Saint Leo I called the Great,* created by His Holiness Pope John Paul II 21 Feb 2001, *b* at Sigmaringen, Archdiocese of Freiburg im Breisgau (Baden-Württenberg, Germany) 16 May 1936, ordained 10 Oct 1963, Bishop of Mainz 21 June 1983, consecrated 2 Oct 1983, Bishop of that See.
149. Jean *Honoré,* Priest of the Title of *Saint Mary of Health in Primavalle,* created by His Holiness Pope John Paul II 21 Feb 2001, *b* at Saint-Brice-en-Coglès, Archdiocese of Rennes (Brittany, France) 13 Aug 1920, ordained 29 June 1943, formerly Bishop of Évreux 24 Oct 1972, consecrated 17 Dec 1972, promoted to the Metropolitan See of Tours 13 Aug 1981, resigned that See 22 July 1997, Archbishop Emeritus of that same See
[1 Allée de la Rocaille, F-37390 La Membrolle-sur-Choisille, France].

Order of Cardinal Deacons

Into this Order are created Titular Archbishops and Bishops, who relinquish their (archi)episcopal Title upon cardinalitial creation and assume that of creation, as well as Priests who, by command of Blessed Pope John XXIII, normally first receive episcopal consecration upon a titular Archiepiscopal See, relinquished on the day of creation. Normally resident in Rome, those belonging to this Order may after ten years be advanced by option to the Order of Cardinal Priests if at least ordained Priests. In 1858 Blessed Pope Pius IX created the last Deacon a Cardinal Deacon, Teodolfo Mertel (1806-1899) who was never ordained to the Priesthood and who died as Protodeacon. The public proclamation of a new Pope is the duty of the Cardinal Protodeacon according to the traditional formula: *Annuntio vobis gaudium magnum: habemus Papam.*

150. Luigi *Poggi,* **Protodeacon** of *Saint Mary in Domnica ad Navicellam* since 26 Feb 2002 with Sovereign Papal consent given in

Consistory of the same day, created by His Holiness Pope John Paul II with that Deaconry 26 Nov 1994, *b* at Piacenza, now Diocese of Piacenza-Bobbio (Emilia, Italy) 25 Nov 1917, ordained 28 July 1940, formerly Titular Archbishop of Forontoniana *in Byzacene* 3 April 1965, former Apostolic Nuncio, consecrated 9 May 1965, Emeritus Librarian and Archivist Emeritus of the Holy Roman Church.
[*Vatican City*].

151. Carlo *Furno*, Deacon of *The Sacred Heart of Christ The King*, created by His Holiness Pope John Paul II 26 Nov 1994, *b* at Bairo Canavese, Diocese of Ivrea (Piedmont, Italy) 2 Dec 1921, ordained 25 June 1944, formerly Titular Archbishop of Abari *in Byzacene* 1 Aug 1973, former Apostolic Nuncio, consecrated 16 Sept 1973, Archpriest of the Patriarchal Liberian Basilica of Saint Mary Major's on the Esquiline, Grand Master of the Equestrian Order of the Holy Sepulchre of Jerusalem, Pontifical Delegate to the Patriarchal Basilica of Saint Francis of Assisi.
[*Vatican City*].

152. Jan Pieter *Schotte*, a member of the Congregation of the Immaculate Heart of Mary called Missionaries of Scheut, Deacon of *Saint Julian of the Flemish* at that Royal Belgian Church, created by His Holiness Pope John Paul II 26 Nov 1994, *b* at Beveren-Leie, Diocese of Bruges or Brugge (Belgium) 29 April 1928, ordained 3 Aug 1952, formerly Titular Bishop of Silli *in Numidia* 20 Dec 1983, consecrated 6 Jan 1984, formerly promoted Titular Archbishop of the same See 24 April 1985, Secretary General of the Synod of Bishops, President of the Labour Office of The Apostolic See.
[*Vatican City*].

153. Gilberto *Agustoni*, Deacon of *Saints Urban and Lawrence ad Primam Portam*, created by His Holiness Pope John Paul II 26 Nov 1994, *b* at Schaffhausen, [formerly Princely] Diocese of Basle (Switzerland), ordained 20 April 1946, formerly Titular Archbishop of Caprulæ *in Veneto* 18 Dec 1986, consecrated 6 Jan 1987, Prefect Emeritus of the Supreme Tribunal of the Apostolic Signature.
[*Vatican City*].

154. Jorge Arturo *Medina Estévez*, Deacon of *Saint Sabbas on the Aventine*, created by His Holiness Pope John Paul II 21 Feb 1998, *b* at Santiago de Chile, same Archdiocese, 23 Dec 1926, ordained 12 June 1954, formerly Titular Bishop of Thibilis *in Numidia* 18 Dec 1984, consecrated 6 Jan 1985, translated to the residential Episcopal See of Rancagua (Chile) 25 Nov 1987 and further to that of Valparaíso 16 April 1993, resigned that See 21 June 1996, promoted

Archbishop-Emeritus Bishop of Valparaíso 19 Sept 1996, surrendering that title upon cardinalitial creation, Prefect of the Congregation for Divine Cult and the Discipline of the Sacraments. [*Vatican City*].

155. Darío *Castrillón Hoyos*, Deacon of *The Most Holy Name of Mary at the Trajan Forum*, created by His Holiness Pope John Paul II 21 Feb 1998, *b* at Medellín, same Archdiocese (Colombia) 4 July 1929, ordained 26 Oct 1952, formerly Titular Bishop of Villa Regis *in Numidia* 2 June 1971, consecrated 18 July 1971, succeeded by right of Coadjutorship to the residential Episcopal See of Pereira 1 July 1976, promoted to the Metropolitan See of Bucaramanga 16 Dec 1992, resigned that See 15 June 1996, Prefect of the Congregation for the Clergy and President of the Pontifical Commission *Ecclesia Dei*. [*Vatican City*].

156. Lorenzo *Antonetti*, Deacon of *Saint Agnes in Agone*, created by His Holiness Pope John Paul II 21 Feb 1998, *b* at Romagnano Sesia, Diocese of Novara (Piedmont, Italy) 31 July 1922, ordained 26 May 1945, formerly Titular Archbishop of Rusellæ *in Ætruria* 23 Feb 1968, former Apostolic Nuncio, consecrated 12 May 1968, President Emeritus of the Administration of the Patrimony of The Holy See. [*Vatican City*].

157. James Francis *Stafford*, Deacon of *Jesus the Good Shepherd in Montagnola*, created by His Holiness Pope John Paul II 21 Feb 1998, *b* at Baltimore, same Archdiocese (United States of America) 26 July 1932, ordained 15 Dec 1957, formerly Titular Bishop of Respecta *in Numidia* 19 Jan 1976, consecrated 29 Feb 1976, translated to the residential See of Memphis 17 Nov 1982, promoted to the Metropolitan See of Denver 30 May 1986, resigned that See 20 Aug 1996, President of the Pontifical Council for the Laity [*Vatican City*].

158. Giovanni *Cheli*, Deacon of *Saints Cosmas and Damian on the Roman Forum*, created by His Holiness Pope John Paul II 21 Feb 1998, *b* at Turin (Piedmont, Italy) 4 Oct 1918, ordained 21 June 1942, formerly Titular Archbishop of Santa Iusta *in Sardinia* 8 Sept 1978, former Apostolic Nuncio, consecrated 16 Sept 1978, President Emeritus of the Pontifical Council for Pastoral care of Migrants and Itinerants. [*Vatican City*].

159. Francesco *Colasuonno*, Deacon of *Saint Eugene I Pope*, created by His Holiness Pope John Paul II 21 Feb 1987, *b* at Grumo-Appula, now Archdiocese of Bari-Bitonto (Apulia, Italy) 2

Jan 1925, ordained 28 Sept 1947, formerly Titular Archbishop of
Truentum *in the Marches* 6 Dec 1974, consecrated 9 Feb 1975,
former Apostolic Nuncio.
[*Vatican City*].
160. Dino *Monduzzi*, Deacon of *Saint Sebastian on the Palatine*,
created by His Holiness Pope John Paul II 21 Feb 1998, *b* at
Brisighella, now Diocese of Faenza-Modigliana (Romagna, Italy) 2
April 1922, ordained 22 July 1945, formerly Titular Bishop of Capri
18 Dec 1986, consecrated 6 Jan 1987, Prefect Emeritus of the Papal
Household.
[*Vatican City*].
161. Agostino *Cacciavillan*, Deacon of *The Holy Guardian Angels in
regione Civitatis Horti*, created by His Holiness Pope John Paul II
21 Feb 2001, *b* at Novale, Diocese of Vicenza (Veneto, Italy) 14 Aug
1926, ordained 26 June 1949, formerly Titular Archbishop of
Amiternum *in Aprutio* 17 Jan 1976, consecrated 28 Feb 1976, former
Apostolic Nuncio, President of the Administration of the Patrimony
of the Holy See 5 Nov 1998.
[*Vatican City*].
162. Sergio *Sebastiani*, Deacon of *Saint Eustace*, created by His
Holiness Pope John Paul II 21 Feb 2001, of the Diocesan Clergy of
the [Princely] Diocese of Ascoli Piceno, *b* at Montemonaco, now
Diocese of San Benedetto del Tronto-Ripatransone-Montalto
(Marches, Italy) 11 April 1931, ordained 15 July 1956, formerly
Titular Archbishop of Cæsarea in Mauretania 27 Sept 1976,
consecrated 30 Oct 1976, former Apostolic Nuncio, President of the
Prefecture of Economic Affairs of the Holy See 3 Nov 1997.
[*Vatican City*].
163. Zenon *Grocholewski*, Deacon of *Saint Nicholas in Carcere*,
created by His Holiness Pope John Paul II 21 Feb 2001, *b* at Bródki,
[Princely] Archdiocese of Poznan (Poland) 11 Oct 1939, ordained 27
May 1963, formerly Titular Bishop of Acropolis *in Salernitano* 21
Dec 1982, consecrated 6 Jan 1983, formerly Titular Archbishop of
the said See 16 Dec 1991, Prefect of the Congregation for Catholic
Education, Seminaries and Institutes of Studies 15 Nov 1999.
[*Vatican City*].
164. José *Saraiva Martins*, a member of the Congregation the
Missionaries Sons of the Immaculate Heart of Mary [*Claretians*],
Deacon of *Our Lady of the Sacred Heart*, created by His Holiness
Pope John Paul II 21 Feb 2001, *b* at Gagos, Diocese of Guarda
(Portugal) 6 Jan 1932, ordained 16 March 1957, formerly Titular

Archbishop of Thuburnica *in Proconsulari* 26 May 1988, consecrated
2 July 1988, Prefect of the Congregation for Causes of Saints 30 May
1998.
[*Vatican City*].

165. Crescenzio *Sepe,* Deacon of *God the Merciful Father*, created by
His Holiness Pope John Paul II 21 Feb 2001, *b* at Carinaro, Diocese
of Aversa (Campania, Italy) 2 June 1943, ordained 12 March 1967,
formerly Titular Archbishop of Gradum *in Veneto* 2 April 1992,
consecrated 26 April 1992, Prefect of the Congregation for
Evangelisation of Peoples and Grand Chancellor of the Pontifical
Urbanian University 9 April 2001.
[*Vatican City*].

166. Jorge María *Mejía*, Deacon of *Saint Jerome a Caritate in Via
Iulia*, created by His Holiness Pope John Paul II 21 Feb 2001, *b* at
Buenos Aires, same Archdiocese (Argentina) 31 Jan 1923, ordained
22 Sept 1945, formerly Titular Bishop of Apollonia *in New Epyrus* 8
March 1986, consecrated 12 April 1986, formerly Titular Archbishop
of that same See 5 March 1994, Archivist and Librarian of the Holy
Roman Church 7 March 1998.
[*Vatican City*].

167. Mario Francesco *Pompedda*, Deacon of *The Annunciation of
the Blessed Virgin Mary in Via Ardeatina*, created by His Holiness
Pope John Paul II 21 Feb 2001, *b* at Ozieri, same Diocese (Sardinia,
Italy) 18 April 1929, ordained 23 Dec 1951, formerly Titular
Archbishop of Bisarchium *in Sardinia* 29 Nov 1997, consecrated 6
Jan 1998, Prefect of the Supreme Tribunal of the Apostolic
Signature 16 Nov 1999.
[*Vatican City*].

168. Walter *Kasper*, Deacon of *All Saints in Via Appia Nova*, created
by His Holiness Pope John Paul II 21 Feb 2001, b at Heidenheim-
Brenz (Württenberg, Germany), now Diocese of Rottenburg-
Stuttgart 5 March 1933, ordained 6 April 1957, formerly Bishop of
Rottenburg-Stuttgart 17 April 1989, consecrated 17 June 1989,
resigned that See 31 May 1999, President of the Pontifical Council
for Promoting Unity of Christians 3 March 2001.
[*Vatican City*].

169. Roberto *Tucci*, a member of the Society of Jesus *[Jesuits]*, Deacon
of *Saint Ignatius of Loyola in Campo Martio*, created by His
Holiness Pope John Paul II, *b* at Naples, same Archdiocese (Italy) 19
April 1921, ordained 24 Aug 1950.

170. Leo *Scheffczyk*, Deacon of *Saint Francis Xavier in Garbatella*,

created by His Holiness Pope John Paul II 21 Feb 2001, *b* in [then] Beuthen [then] [Princely] Diocese of Breslau [then Germany] now Archdiocese of Wroc aw (Poland) 21 Feb 1920, ordained 29 June 1947.
[*Dall'Armistrasse 3a, 80638 München, Germany*].

171. Avery *Dulles*, a member of the Society of Jesus *[Jesuits]*,   Deacon of *The Most Holy Names of Jesus and Mary in Via Lata*, created by His Holiness Pope John Paul II 21 Feb 2001, *b* at Auburn, Diocese of Rochester (New York, United States) 24 Aug 1918, ordained 16 June 1956.
[*Fordham University, Bronx, NY 10458, U.S.A.*].

(Status 1 November 2002: 171 Cardinals of whom now 114 Electors in Conclave)

<hr>

ITALY
(House of Savoy)

Catholic: Founded by Umbertus I Biancamano "of the White Hands", Count of Sabaudia (Savoy) 1032; inherited Piedmont through the marriage of Count Othon (✝ 1060) to Adelaide, Margravine of Segusium (Suse, Prov of Turin, Italy) 1091; Duke of Caputlacensis (Chablais, Savoie, France) and Augusta Praetoria (Aosta, Prov of Turin) 1238; Prince of the Holy Empire 11 June 1313; Duke of Savoy 19 Feb 1417; King of Cyprus 1485 - 1490; the Duchy of Savoy was conquered by France from 1535 to 1559; Count of Asti 1538; King of Sicily 1713 - 1718; King of Sardinia 9 May 1720; King of Italy 17 March 1861; incorporation of the Papal States 9 Oct 1870. The last King of Italy was Umberto II (*b* 15 Sept 1904; ✝ 18 March 1983) who left the country following a referendum on 2 June 1946 which showed that the majority of Italians were in favour of a republic.
Arms:- Gu, a cross arg: ensigned with the Royal Helmet, and thereon, issuant of the Crown Royal, is set the Crest. Surrounding the shield the Collar of the Order of the Annunciation. *Crest:*- a lion's face, winged or. *Supporters:*- Two lions reguardant ppr. The achievement is borne on a mantle gu, semée of roses or, and crosses bottonée (for Saint Maurice) arg, and surmounted by the Royal Crown of Italy. Members of the Royal family bear the title of Prince or Princess of Savoy with the qualification of Royal Highness.

VITTORIO EMANUELE (IV) Alberto Carlo Teodoro Umberto Bonifacio Amedeo Damiano Bernardino Gennaro Maria, **PRINCE**

OF NAPLES, *b* at Naples 12 Feb 1937, Grand Master Supreme Order of the Annunziata, Grand Master Order of Saints Maurice and Lazarus, the Civil Order of Savoy, and the Order of Merit of Savoy, Bailiff Gd Cross Hon & Dev of Sov Mil Order of Malta, Bailiff Gd Cross of Justice Constantinian Order of St George, Kt Order of Saint Andrew, Gd Cross Orders of Saint Alexander Nevsky, the White Eagle, Saint Anne, Saint Stanislas, the Redeemer of Greece, the Immaculate Conception of Vila Viçosa, & of Karageorge, son of Umberto II, King of Italy, etc (*b* 15 Sept 1904; ✠ 18 March 1983; *succ* on his father's abdication 9 May 1946, left the country 13 June 1946 following a referendum (2 June) on the form of government which showed a majority in favour of a republic) and Princess Marie José of Belgium (*b* at Ostende 4 Aug 1906; ✠ at Geneva 27 Jan 2001); *m* at Teheran 7 Oct 1971, Marina (*b* at Geneva 12 Feb 1935), Dame Gd Cross Order of Sts Maurice and Lazarus, Dame Gd Cross Hon and Dev Sovereign Military Order of Malta, Dame Star Cross Order, dau of René Ricolfi Doria and Iris Benvenuti.

[*23 route d'Hermance, 1222 Vésenaz, nr Geneva, Switzerland*].

Son

1. *Emanuele Filiberto* Umberto Reza Rene Maria, Prince of Venice, *b* at Geneva 22 June 1972, Kt Order of the Annunziata, Gd Cross Order of Saints Maurice and Lazarus.

Sisters

1. Princess *Maria Pia* Elena Elisabetta Margherita Milena Mafalda Ludovica Tecla Gennara, *b* at Naples 24 Sept 1934, Dame of Hon Sovereign Military Order of Malta; *m* at Cascais, Portugal 12 Feb 1955 (*m* diss by div 1967), Prince Alexander of Yugoslavia (*b* at White Lodge, Richmond, Surrey 13 Aug 1924; *m* 2ndly at Paris 2 Nov 1973, Princess Barbara of Liechtenstein), Lt British Air Force.

[*61 boulevard St. Antoine, 78000 Versailles, France*].

2. Princess *Maria Gabriella* Giuseppa Aldegonda Adelaide Margherita Ludovica Felicita Gennara, *b* at Naples 24 Feb 1940, Gd Cross Order of Saints Maurice and Lazarus; *m* at Eze, France 21 June 1969 (*m* diss by div at Nov 1990), as his 2nd wife, Robert Zellinger de Balkány (*b* at Ichlód, Romania 4 Aug 1931).

[*62 rue de Varenne, 75007 Paris, France; Rue Florissant 135, 1200 Geneva, Switzerland*].

3. Princess *Maria Beatrice* Elena Margherita Ludovica Caterina Francesca Romana, Gd Cross Order of Saints Maurice and Lazarus;

b at Quirinal Palace, Rome 2 Feb 1943; *m* at Cuidad Juarez, Mexico 1 April 1970 (civ) and at Cordóba, Agentina 9 Jan 1971 (relig), Luis Rafael Reyna-Corvalán y Dillon (*b* at Cordóba 18 April 1939; ✠ at Cuernavaca, Mexico 18 Feb 1999).
[*Morelo 164, Acapantzingo Cuernavaca, Mexico*].

Brothers of Great-Grandfather

Issue of Vittorio Emanuele II, King of Sardinia, later (from 1861) King of Italy (*b* 14 March 1820; ✠ 9 Jan 1878) and Archduchess Adelaide of Austria (*b* 3 June 1822; *m* 12 April 1842; ✠ 20 Jan 1855), having had issue, among whom,

Son

Prince *Amedeo* Ferdinando Maria, *b* at Turin 30 May 1845; ✠ at Turin 18 Jan 1890, *cr* **Duke of Aosta** 1845, accepted the crown of Spain and was proclaimed as Amadeo I, King of Spain and the Indies 16 Nov 1870, abdicated 11 Feb 1873; *m* 1stly at Turin 30 May 1867, Princess Maria Vittoria (*b* at Paris 9 Aug 1847; ✠ at San Remo 8 Nov 1876), dau of Carlo Emanuele, Prince della Cisterna e di Belriguardo and Countess Louise de Mérode. He *m* 2ndly at Turin 11 Sept 1888, his niece, Princess Maria Letizia (*b* at Paris 20 Nov 1866; ✠ at Moncalieri 25 Oct 1926), only dau of Prince Napoleon (Bonaparte), Head of the Imperial House of France and Princess Clotilde of Savoy, and had issue by his first wife, among whom,

Son

Prince *Emanuele Filiberto* Vittorio Eugenio Alberto Genova Giuseppe Maria, 2nd **Duke of Aosta**, *b* at Genoa 13 Jan 1869; ✠ at Turin 4 July 1931, Marshal of Italy, Senator of the Kingdom, etc; *m* at Kingston-on-Thames, Surrey 25 June 1895, Princess Hélène (*b* at York House, Twickenham, Middlesex 13 June 1871; ✠ at Castellamare di Stabia 21 Jan 1951; *m* 2ndly 1936 Col Otto Campini), dau of Prince Philippe of Bourbón-Orléans, Count of Paris, Head of the Royal House of France and Infanta Maria Isabel of Spain, and had issue,

> 1. Prince *Amedeo* Umberto Isabella Luigi Filippo Maria Giuseppe Giovanni, 3rd **Duke of Aosta**, *b* at Turin 21 Oct 1898; ✠ in a POW Camp in Nairobi, Kenya 3 March 1942, Viceroy of Ethiopia, Gov-Gen East Africa, Gen Italian Air Force, Senator of the Kingdom, etc; *m* at Naples 5 Nov 1927, his 1st cousin, Princess Anne (*b* at Nouvion-en-Thierache 5 Aug 1906; ✠ at Sorrento 19 March 1986), Dame Star Cross

Order, Dame Gd Cross Hon and Dev Sovereign Military Order of Malta, dau of Prince Jean of Bourbon-Orleans, Prince of France, Duke de Guise and Princess Isabelle of Bourbon-Orleans, and had issue,

    1. Princess *Margherita* Isabella Maria Vittoria Emanuela Elena Gennara, *b* at Bourg-en-Bresse 7 April 1930, Dame Star Cross Order, Dame of Hon and Dev Sovereign Military Order of Malta; *m* at Bourg-en-Bress 28 Dec (civ) and at Brou 29 Dec (relig) 1953, Archduke Robert of Austria (*b* at Schönbrunn 8 Feb 1915; ✠ at Basel 7 Feb 1966), Dr rer pol, Bank Director, son of Karl I, Emperor of Austria and Princess Doña Zita of Bourbon-Parma.
    [*Obere Turmatt 4, 6370 Stans, Switzerland*].
    2. Princess *Maria Cristina* Giusta Elena Giovanna, *b* at Miramar, nr Trieste 12 Sept 1933, Dame of Justice Gd Cross Constantinian Order of St George; *m* at Jacarézinho, Brazil 29 Jan 1967, Prince Dom Casimiro of Bourbon-Two Sicilies (*b* at Warsaw 8 Nov 1938), Economist; MBA at I.N.S.E.A.D
    [*Rua Atlantica 256 - CEP 0144-000 , São Paulo (SP), Brazil*].

2. Prince *Aimone* Roberto Margherita Maria Giuseppe Torino, 4th **Duke of Aosta**, *b* at Turin 9 March 1900; ✠ at Buenos Aires, Argentina 29 Jan 1948, *cr* Duke of Spoleto (ad personam) 22 Sept 1904, proclaimed as Tomislav II, King of Croatia, Prince of Bosnia and Herzegovina, Voivode of Dalmatia, Tuzla and Temun 18 May 1941, finally abandoned all claim to that crown 1943, Vic-Adm Italian Navy, Kt Order of St Annunziata, Bailiff Gd Cross Hon and Dev Sovereign Military Order of Malta; *m* at Florence 1 July 1939, Princess Irene (*b* at Athens 13 Feb 1904, ✠ at Fiesole, nr Florence 14 April 1974), Dame Star Cross Order, dau of Constantine I, King of the Hellenes and Princess Sophie of Prussia, and had issue,

    1. Prince *Amedeo* Umberto Costantino Giorgio Paolo Elena Maria Fiorenzo Zvonimir, 5th **Duke of Aosta**, Prince della Cisterna e di Belriguardo, Marquess di Voghera, Count di Ponderano, *b* at Florence 27 Sept 1943, Kt Order of the Annunziata, Gd Cross Order of Saints Maurice and Lazarus, Kt Hon & Dev of Sov Mil

Order of Malta, Bailiff Gd Cross Constantinian Order
of Saint George; *m* 1stly at Sintra, Portugal 22 July
1964 (*m* diss by div 26 April 1982 and annulled 1986),
Princess Claude (*b* at Larache, Morocco 11 Dec 1943;
m 2ndly at Port au Prince 27 April 1982, Arnaldo R La
Cagnina), Dame Gd Cross Constantinian Order of St
George, dau of Prince Henri of Bourbón-Orleans, Count
de Paris, Head of the Royal House of France and
Princess Isabella of Orléans-Bragança. He *m* 2ndly at
Villa Spedalotto, Bagheria, nr Palermo 30 March 1987,
Donna Silvia (*b* at Palermo 30 Dec 1953), Gd Cross
Order of Saints Maurice & Lazarus, Gd Cross
Constantinian Order of St George, Dame Hon & Dev
of Sov Mil Order of Malta, dau of Don Vincenzo
Paternò, Marquess di Regiovanni, Count di Prades,
Baron di Spedalotto and Rosanna Bellardo Ferraris di
Celle, and has issue from his first wife,
[*San Rocco, 52029 Castiglion Fibocchi, Prov. Arezzo,
Italy*].

> 1. Princess *Bianca* Irene Olga Elena Isabella
> Fiorenza Maria, *b* at Florence 2 April 1966; *m*
> at Il Borro 11 Sept 1988, Count Giberto
> Arrivabene Valenti Gonzaga (*b* at Rome 5 July
> 1961).
> [*Palazzo Papadopoli, Venice, Italy*].
> 2. Prince *Aimone* Umberto Emanuele Filiberto
> Luigi Amedeo Elena Maria Fiorenzo, Duke of
> Apulia, *b* at Florence 13 Oct 1967, Kt Order of
> Annunziata, Kt of Hon and Dev Sovereign
> Military Order of Malta.
> [*Il Borro, 52040 San Giustino Valdarno, Prov.
> Arezzo, Italy*].
> 3. Princess *Mafalda* Giovanna Shams Maria
> Fiorenza Isabella, *b* at Florence 20 Sept 1969;
> *m* at Il Borro 18 Sept 1994 (*m* diss by div 1999),
> Don Alessandro Ruffo di Calabria of the Princes
> di Palazzolo (*b* at Turin 4 Nov 1964); She *m*
> 2ndly .at London 27 April (civ) 2001, *Francesco*
> Lombardo di San Chirico (*b* at Milan 31 Jan
> 1968).
> [*Via Marsala 11, Milan, Italy*].

Brother of Great-Great-Grandfather

Issue of King Carlo Alberto who *succ* as King of Sardinia 27 April 1831, Regent of the Kingdom of Sardinia for one week after the abdication of King Vittorio Emanuele I 1821, Viceroy of Sardinia 1829, abdicated in favour of his elder son 23 March 1849 (*b* 29 Oct 1798; ✝ 28 July 1849) and Princess Maria Teresa of Tuscany, Archduchess of Austria (*b* 21 March 1801; *m* 30 Sept 1817 ✝ 12 Jan 1855), having had issue, among whom,

Son

Prince *Ferdinando* Maria Alberto Amedeo Filiberto Vincenzo, *b* at Florence 15 Nov 1822; ✝ at Turin 10 Feb 1855, *cr* Duke of Genoa 1831, Adm Sardinian Navy; *m* at Dresden 22 April 1850, Princess Elisabetta (*b* at Dresden 4 Feb 1830; *m* 2ndly at Aglié Oct 1856, Niccolo, Marquess Rapallo; ✝ at Stresa 14 Aug 1912), dau of Johann I, King of Saxony, and had issue, among whom,

Son

Prince *Tomaso* Alberto Vittorio, 2nd Duke of Genoa, *b* at Turin 6 Feb 1854; ✝ at Turin 15 April 1931, Adm Italian Navy, Senator, Regent of Italy 1915-18; *m* at Nymphenburg 14 April 1883, Princess Isabella (*b* at Nymphenburg 31 Aug 1863; ✝ at Rome 26 Feb 1924), dau of Prince Adalbert of Bavaria and Infanta Amalia of Spain, and had issue, among whom,

1. Prince *Eugenio* Alfonso Carlo Maria Giuseppe, *b* at Turin 13 March 1906; ✝ at São Paulo 12 Aug 1996, 5th Duke of Genoa, *cr* Duke of Ancona *ad personam* 31 March 1906, Col Italian Army, Kt of Dev Sovereign Military Order of Malta, Bailiff Gd Cross Constantian Order of St George; *m* at Schloß Nymphenburg 29 Oct 1938, Princess *Lucia* Maria Raniera (*b* at Schloß Nymphenburg 9 July 1908*b* at Schloß Nymphenburg 9 July 1908; ✝ at São Paulo 3 Nov 2001), Dame Star Cross Order, Dame Gd Cross Constantinian Order of St George, Dame of Hon Sovereign Military Order of Malta, dau of Prince Don Ferdinando of Bourbon-Two Sicilies, Duke of Calabria and Princess Maria of Bavaria, and had issue,

1. Princess Maria *Isabella* Elena Immacolata Barbara Anna Pace, *b* at Rome 23 June 1943, *m* at Rome 19 Feb and at Lausanne 29 April 1971, Count Alberto Frioli (*b* at Rimini 7 April 1943), Shipowner. [*Rua General Mena Barreto 145, Jardim Paulista,*

01433-010, São Paulo, Brazil.

———◆———

LIECHTENSTEIN

Catholic: The Founder of this Seigneural House of Lower Austria was Hugo of Lichtenstein 1133 - 1156, named after the fortified castle of Liechtenstein, near Mödling, Lower Austria. Heinrich I of Liechtenstein, Lord of Nikolsburg 1249 (sold in 1560); acquired Feldsberg (see below) *ca* 1395; granted Palatine rights (primogeniture), Prague 30 March 1607; Prince of the Holy Roman Empire and of Liechtenstein (primogeniture), Vienna 20 Dec 1608; Duke of Troppau (primogeniture), Linz 28 Dec 1613; the dignity of Prince was confirmed and extended to the cadet Line, Vienna 23 June 1620; Prince and Duke of Jägerndorf, Prague 13 May 1623; the title of Prince was confirmed for both of the cadet lines (of Maximilian and Gundaker) and all of their descendants, Vienna 12 Sept 1623; Palatine rights were granted (primogeniture) for the cadet Line of Gundaker, Vienna 14 Nov 1633; creation of the Lordships of Kromau, Ostrau, etc in Moravia into the Principality of Liechtenstein, Vienna 20 Dec 1633; acquired the Lordships of Schellenberg 18 Jan 1699 and of Vaduz 22 Feb 1712; creation of these Lordships into the Principality of Liechtenstein, Vienna 23 Jan 1719.

Arms:- Quarterly: 1st, or, an eagle displayed sa, beaked and membered of the first, charged with a crescent trefoiled at the extremities, and crowned or (Silesia); 2nd, barry of eight or and sa a crown of rue arched in bend vert (Kuenring); 3rd, per pale, gu and arg (Troppau); 4th, or, a harpy sa, crowned or, visage arg and armed of the field (Schellenberg); enté en pointe: azure, a bugle-horn stringed or (Jägendorf); over all an escutcheon of pretence: per fesse or and gu (Liechtenstein). The achievement is born on a mantle purp, fringed and tasselled or, doubled erm and surmounted by the Princely Crown.

Members of the Princely Family bear the title of Prince or Princess of Liechtenstein with the qualification of Serene Highness.

Johannes **(HANS)-ADAM II** Ferdinand Alois Josef Maria Marko d'Aviano Pius, *b* at Zurich 14 Feb 1945 (godson of HH Pope Pius XII), **PRINCE OF LIECHTENSTEIN**, Duke of Troppau and Jägerndorf, Count of Rietberg, son of Franz Joseph II, Prince of Liechtenstein, etc (*b* 16 Aug 1906, appointed Regent of the Principality 30 March and *succ* his great-uncle 25 July 1938; ✝ 13 Nov 1989) and Countess Georgine (Gina) von Wilczek (*b* 24 Oct 1921; *m* 7 March 1943, ✝ 18 Oct 1989); *m* at Vaduz 30 July 1967, Countess Marie Aglaë (*b* at Prague 14 April 1940), dau of Ferdinand, Count Kinsky von Wchinitz and Tettau and Countess Henriette von

Ledebur-Wicheln.
[*Schloß Vaduz, 9490 Vaduz, Liechtenstein*].

Sons and Daughter

1. *Alois* Philipp Maria, Hereditary Prince of Liechtenstein, *b* at Zurich 11 June 1968; *m* at Vaduz 3 July 1993, Princess and Duchess Sophie (*b* at Munich 28 Oct 1967), dau of Max Emanuel, Duke in and Prince of Bavaria and Countess Elizabeth Christina Douglas, and has issue,
[*Schloß Vaduz, 9490 Vaduz, Liechtenstein*].

　　1. Prince *Joseph* Wenzel Maximilian Maria, *b* at London 24 May 1995.

　　2. Princess *Marie Caroline* Elizabeth Immaculata, *b* at Grabs, Switzerland 17 Oct 1996.

　　3. Prince *Georg* Antonius Constantin Maria, *b* Grabs, Switzerland 20 April 1999.

　　4. Prince *Nikolaus* Sebastian Alexander Maria, *b* at Grabs, Switzerland 6 Dec 2000.

2. Prince *Maximilian* Nikolaus Maria, *b* at St Gall, Switzerland 16 May 1969; *m* at Vaduz 21 Jan (civ) and at Manhatten, New York 29 Jan (relig) 2000, Angela (*b* Bocas del Toro, Panama 3 Feb 1958), dau of Javier Francisco Brown and Silvia Maritza Burke.
[*Schloß Vaduz, 9490 Vaduz, Liechtenstein*].

　　1. Prince *Alfons* Constantin Maria, *b* at London 18 May 2001.

3. Prince *Constantin* Ferdinand Maria, *b* at St Gall 15 March 1972; *m* at Cicov 17 July 1999, Countess Marie (*b* at Graz 16 July 1975), dau of Count Alois Kálnoky de Köröspatak and Baroness Sieglinde von Oer.
[*Schloß Vaduz, 9490 Vaduz, Liechtenstein*].

4. Princess *Tatjana* Nora Maria, *b* at St Gall 10 April 1973, *m* at Vaduz 5 June 1999, Philipp von Lattorff (*b* at Graz 25 March 1968).
[*Goldgeben 30, 3464 Hausleiten, Austria*].

Brothers and Sister

1. Prince *Philipp Erasmus* Alois Ferdinand Maria Sebaldus, *b* at Zurich 19 Aug 1946, Kt of Justice St John of Jerusalem, Banker; *m* at Brussels 11 Sept 1971, Isabelle (*b* at Renaix 24 Nov 1949), goddau of HM Queen Elisabeth of the Belgians, dau of Jean de l'Arbre de Malander and Guillemette Grassal, and has issue,
[*Pavillon Colombe, 3 Rue Edith Wharton, 95350 St. Brice sous Forêt, France*].

1. Prince *Alexander*, *b* at Basel 19 May 1972.
[*84 Rue du Faubourg Saint Honore, 75008 Paris, France*]
2. Prince *Wenzeslaus*, *b* at Uccle 12 May 1974.
[*Pavillon Colombe, 3 Rue Edith Wharton, 95350 St. Brice sous Forêt, France*]
3. Prince *Rudolf* Ferdinand, *b* at Uccle 7 Sept 1975.
[*Pavillon Colombe, 3 Rue Edith Wharton, 95350 St. Brice sous Forêt, France*]

2. Prince *Nikolaus* Ferdinand Maria Josef Raphael, *b* at Zurich 24 Oct 1947, Ambassador for Liechtenstein to the Kingdom of Belgium and to the European Union; Ambassador to the Holy See, resident in Brussels, Kt of Hon and Dev Sovereign Military Order of Malta, Kt of Justice St John of Jerusalem; *m* at Luxemburg 20 March 1982, Princess Margaretha (*b* at Schloß Betzdorf 15 May 1957), dau of Jean, Grand Duke of Luxembourg, Duke of Nassau, Prince of Bourbon-Parma and Princess Joséphine Charlotte of Belgium, and has issue,
[*Liechtensteinische Mission, 1 Palace du Congrès, 1000 Brussels, Belgium; Schloß Vaduz, 9490 Vaduz, Liechtenstein*].

    1. Prince Leopold Emanuel, *b* at Brussels 1984; ✝ at Brussels 1984.
    1. Princess *Maria Anunciata* Astrid Joséphine Veronica, *b* at Brussels 12 May 1985.
    2. Princess *Marie-Astrid* Nora Margarita Veronica, *b* at Brussels 26 June 1987.
    3. Prince *Josef-Emanuel* Leopold Marie, *b* at Brussels 7 May 1989.

3. Princess Norberta (*Nora*) Elisabeth Maria Assunta Josefine Georgine et omnes sancti, *b* at Zurich 31 Oct 1950; *m* at Vaduz 11 June 1988, Don Vicente Sartorius y Cabeza de Vaca, 4th Marquess de Mariño (*b* at Madrid 30 Nov 1931; ✝ at Ibiza 22 July 2002), Lawyer.
[*Calle Eduardo Dato 19/6D, 28010 Madrid, Spain*].

4. Prince Franz Josef *Wenzel* Georg Maria, *b* at Zurich 19 Nov 1962; ✝ at Vaduz 28 Feb 1991.

Brothers and Sisters of Father

Issue of Prince Aloys of Liechtenstein (*b* 17 June 1869; renounced his rights of succession to the Throne of Liechtenstein in favour of his eldest son 26 Feb 1923; ✝ 16 March 1955) and Archduchess Elisabeth Amalia of Austria (*b* 7 July 1878; *m* 20 April 1903; ✝ 13

March 1960), among whom,

1. Prince *Karl Alfred* Maria Johannes Baptista Heinrich Aloys Georg Hartmann Ignatius Benediktus Franz Joseph Rochus, *b* at Schloß Frauenthal, Steiermark, 16 Aug 1910; ✝ at Hainburg 17 Nov 1985, Dipl Forestry; *m* at Schloß Persenbeug 17 Feb 1949, Archduchess Agnes (*b* at Schloß Persenberg 14 Dec 1928), Dame Star Cross Order, dau of Archduke Hubert Salvator of Austria, Prince of Tuscany and Princess Rosemary zu Salm-Salm, and has issue, among whom, [*Porzellangasse 48/D/23, 1090 Vienna, Austria*].

    1. Prince *Dominik* Volkmar Hubert Alois Maria Josef Thaddaus Thomas Paulus Karl Ignatius Severius, *b* at Vienna 20 June 1950, Mag rer soc et oec; *m* at Spitz an der Donau, Upper Austria 9 Oct 1980, Eva Maria (*b* at Vienna 4 July 1943; ✝ 24 Feb 1998), dau of Otto Lösch and Baroness Hildegard von Felder.
    [*Rudolfsplatz 6, 1010 Vienna, Austria*].

    2. Prince *Andreas* Duarte Emanuel Ulrich Benedikt Josef Maria Karl Rafael Ignatius Mathias Paulus, *b* at Vienna 25 Feb 1952; *m* at Madrid 29 Sept 1978, Silvia (*b* at Madrid 2 May 1952), dau of Don Luis Prieto y Calle and Doña Olimpia Figueroa.
    [*Puerto de Hierro, Fuente de Milanos 2, 28035 Madrid, Spain*].

    3. Prince *Gregor* Heinrich Augustiunus Judas Thaddaus Josef Maria Pius Paulus Antonius Stefan Salvator, *b* at Vienna 18 April 1954.
    [*Dorfstraße 7A, 9495 Triesen, Liechtenstein*].

    4. Princess *Maria Pia* Ludovika Ulrika Elisabeth Paschaline Katharina Ignatia Luola Johanna Josela, *b* at Vienna 6 Aug 1960, MA, M Pol Sc.; Ambassador for Liechtenstein to the Republic of Austria and to the Organisation for Security and Co-operation in Europe; *m* at Vienna 4 Aug 1995, *Max* Alexander Kothbauer (*b* at Vienna 30 March 1950), Mag rer soc et oec.
    [*Tunnelstraße 8/8, 1010 Vienna, Austria*].

    5. Princess *Katharina* Maria Christina Henriette Valerie Agnes, *b* at Vienna 27 Jan 1964, mag rer soc et oec; *m* at Kensington, London (civ) and at Chelsea London 16 Nov (relig) 1991, Jeremy St Goar Kelton (*b* at London 21 Oct 1960).

[*6 Admiral Square, Chelsea Harbour, London, SW10 0UU*].

6. Princess *Birgitta* Ulrike Rosa Marie Elisabeth Aloisia Hermenegilde, *b* at Vienna 13 April 1967, stud rer soc et oec; *m* at Vaduz 18 Dec (civ) and at Persenbeug 30 Dec (relig) 2000, Count Otto Jankovich-Bésán de Pribér, Vuchin et Duna-Szekcsö (*b* at Bad Homburg 11 Jan 1967), Actor.
[*Karmeliterplatz 1, 1020 Vienna, Austria*].

2. Prince *Georg* Hartmann Maria Josef Franz de Paula Aloys Ignatius Benediktus Martin, *b* at Gross-Ullersdorf 11 Nov 1911; ✠ at Vienna 18 Jan 1998, Dr rer agr, Dipl Engineer; *m* at Schloß Althausen, Württemberg 23 Sept 1948, Duchess Marie Christine (*b* at Tübingen 2 Sept 1924), Dame Star Cross Order, dau of Philipp Albrecht, Duke of Württemberg, Head of the Royal House of Württemberg and Archduchess Helene of Austria, and has issue,
[*Franziskaner Platz 1, 1010 Vienna, Austria*].

　　1. Princess *Margarita* Maria Helene Rosa Aloisia Phillipine Elisabeth Georgine Josefa Konrada Pia Ignatia, *b* at Vienna 1 May 1950, Dipl Interior Archictecture; *m* at Einsiedeln Switzerland 20 Sept 1974, Peter Klien (*b* at Wolfurt 6 Sept 1946), Architect.
　　[*Hofi 501, 9497 Triesenberg, Liechtenstein*].
　　2. Princess *Maria Assunta* Elisabetha Philippine Rosa Helene Aloisia Georgine Josefa Benedikta Pia Ignatia, *b* at Vienna 28 April 1952, Dipl Biology; *m* at Vaduz 24 April (civ) and at Vienna 9 May (relig) 1981, Harald Link (*b* at Basel 12 Jan 1955), lic oec.
　　[*135 Soi Polo of Wireless Road, Bangkok 10330, Thailand*].
　　3. Princess *Isabelle* Maria Helene Carolina Alfreda Josefa Monika Pia Georgina Hemma Henriette Ignatia, *b* at Vienna 17 May 1954, Dr of Med; *m* at Munich 23 Feb (civ) and at Vienna 28 Feb (relig) 1976, Raimund, Count zu Erbach-Fürstenau (*b* at Heidelberg 2 April 1951), Forester.
　　[*Schloß Fürstenau, 64720 Michelstadt-Steinbach, Odenwald, Germany*].
　　4. Prince *Christoph* Alois Maria Ferdinand Josef Philipp Pius Konrad Thaddaus Ruppert Paulus Ignatius, *b* at Vienna 15 Jan 1958, Dr of Law.
　　[*Matschilsstraße 291, 9495 Triesen, Liechtenstein*].
　　5. Princess *Marie Helene* Diane Rosa Elisabeth Aloysia Phillipine Josefa Gabriella Pia Antonia Ignatia, *b* at Vienna 8 Sept 1960, Med Assistant, Stud Social Paediatrics.

[Franziskaner Platz 1, 1010 Vienna, Austria].

6. Princess *Georgina* Maria Agnes Philippine Elisabeth Ignatia, *b* at Vienna 13 Nov 1962, cand med; *m* at Vaduz 11 Oct (civ) and at Friedrichshafen 23 Nov (relig) 1985, Clemens, Count von Waldburg zu Zeil and Trauchburg (*b* at Munich 13 April 1960), Dipl Business, Finance Director Archbishopric of Berlin, Lt-Col (Res).

[Kleinaustraße 16, 14169 Berlin-Zehlendorf, Germany].

7. Princess *Michaela* Maria Henriette Ulrike Aloisia, *b* at Vienna 5 July 1969, Student History and Politics.

[Franziskaner Platz 1, 1010 Vienna, Austria].

3. Princess Marie *Henriette* Theresia Aloisia Franziska Sophie Josepha Michaela Adelheid Annunziata Elisabeth Ignatia Benedikta et omnes sancti, *b* at Vienna 6 Nov 1914, Dame Star Cross Order; *m* at Vienna 24 Aug 1943, Peter, Count and Noble Lord von and zu Eltz genannt Faust von Stromberg (*b* at Vienna 28 Oct 1909; ✝ at Vienna 28 Feb 1992), Dr of Law.

[Löwelstraße 12/7, 1010 Vienna, Austria].

4. Prince *Heinrich* Hartneid Maria Franz de Paula Johann Alois Joseph Ignatius Benediktus Hilarion, *b* at Gross-Ullersdorf 21 Oct 1920; ✝ at Grabs Switzerland 29 Nov 1993, appointed Chargé d'affaires of the Principality in Switzerland 1944, Ambassador of Liechtenstein at Berne; *m* at Vienna 23 April 1968, Countess Amalie (*Ali*) (*b* at Olmutz 22 May 1935), dau of Leopold, Count Podstatzky-Lichtenstein and Countess Marie (Minki) Kinsky von Wchinitz and Tettau, and has issue,

[Bangarten 4, 9490 Vaduz, Liechtenstein].

    1. Princess *Maria Elisabeth*, *b* at Berne 30 June 1969.

    [Neufeldstraße 129, 3012 Bern, Switzerland].

    2. Prince *Hubertus* Alois, *b* at Berne 24 May 1971.

    [Sonneggstraße 42, 8006 Zurich, Switzerland].

    3. Princess *Marie Therese* Eleonore, *b* at Berne 29 Jan 1974.

    [Bangarten 4, 9490 Vaduz, Liechtenstein].

Brothers of Grandfather

Issue of Alfred, Prince of Liechtenstein (*b* 11 June 1842, ✝ 8 Oct 1907) and Princess Henriette of Liechtenstein (*b* 6 June 1843; *m* 26 April 1865; ✝ 24 Dec 1931), having had issue, among whom,

Sons

1. Prince *Johannes*, *b* at Vienna 6 Jan 1873; ✝ at Hollenegg 3 Sept

1959, Austrian Navy, sometime Naval Attaché at Rome, Kt Order of the Golden Fleece; *m* at Budapest 6 Sept 1906, Countess Marie Gabrielle (*b* at Budapest 7 Dec 1886; ✠ at Vienna 14 Dec 1961), Dame Star Cross Order, Dame of Hon Sovereign Military Order of Malta, dau of Géza, Count Andrássy von Czik-Szent-Király and Krasna-Horka and Countess Eleonore von Kaunitz, and had issue, among whom,

    1. Prince *Alfred* Géza Johann Dionys Maria Josef, *b* at Bétler, Hungary 27 June 1907; ✠ at Frauental 28 Dec 1991; *m* at Schloß Horin, nr Melník 16 April 1932, Princess Ludmila (*b* at Rozdalovice, Bohemia 13 Aug 1908; ✠ at Graz 11 Jan 1974), dau of Friedrich, Prince of Lobkowicz and Countess Josephine von Thun and Hohenstein, and had issue,

        1. Princess *Maria Christa* Anna Eleonore Henriette, *b* at Graz 2 Feb 1933; *m* at Hollenegg 2 July 1960 (*m* diss by div at Paris 6 March 1973), Roland, Marquess de Roys de Lédignan Saint-Michel (*b* at St Jean, Cap Ferrat 1 Oct 1934).

        [*7 Rue Henner, 75009 Paris, France*].

        2. Prince *Franz Géza* Johannes Konrad Thaddaus, *b* at Graz 19 Jan 1935; *m* at La Palazzina, Bologna 14 June 1969, Laura (*b* at Bologna 12 Jan 1941), dau of Paolo Malvezzi-Campeggi, Marquess di Dozza and Margherita Cosulich, and has issue,

        [*Schloß Frauenthal, Ulrichsberg 1, 8530 Deutschlandsberg, Steiermark, Austria*].

           1. Prince *Alfred* Paolo, *b* at Graz 16 Nov 1972.

           [*Schloß Hollenegg, 8530 Deutschlandsberg, Steiermark, Austria*].

           2. Prince *Lukas* Wolfgang, *b* at Graz 18 Nov 1974.

           3. Princess *Livia* Margherita, *b* at Graz 7 April 1977.

        3. Prince *Friedrich* Emanuel Maria Thaddäus Konrad, *b* at Graz 30 Sept 1937; *m* at Hollenegg 8 Jan 1972, Anne Marie (*b* at Gams, nr Frauenthal 3 May 1948), dau of Hans Ortner and Maria Waldherr, and has issue,

        [*Burg, 8333 Riegersburg, Steiermark, Austria*].

           1. Prince *Emanuel* Friedrich Eugen Nikolaus, *b* at Graz 29 Nov 1978.

[8333 Riegersburg 21, Steiermark, Austria].
2. Prince *Ulrich* Constantin Wladimir Peter, *b* at Graz 12 Aug 1983.

4. Prince *Anton Florian* Johannes Constantin Konrad Thaddaus, *b* at Graz 21 April 1940, Dipl Engineer Forestry; *m* at St Stefan im Gailtal, Carinthia 29 June 1968, Baroness Rosemarie (*b* at Klagenfurt 15 Dec 1943), dau of Günther, Baron Dreihann-Holenia von Sulzberg am Steinhof and Baroness Marie Elisabeth von and zu Aichelburg-Zossenegg, and has issue,
[Haldenstraße 21, 9495 Triesen, Liechtenstein].

    1. Princess *Ludmila* Stefanie, *b* at Geneva 14 Jan 1974; *m* at Vaduz 7 April (civ) and at St Stefan, Austria 15 July (relig) 1995, Count Christoph von Calice (*b* at Vienna 30 May 1964).
    [Boerhaevegasse 7, 1030 Vienna, Austria; Schloß Greiffenstein, 9623 St. Stefan, Kärnten, Austria].
    2. Prince *Georg* Clemens, *b* at Männedorf 17 Oct 1977.

2. Prince *Johannes* Franz de Paula Gabriel Ildefons Felix Klemens Maria Josef, *b* at Vienna 18 May 1910; ✝ at St Gallen 22 Jan 1975, Kt Sovereign Military Order of Malta; *m* at Maria-Schein, Bohemia 16 Nov 1936, Countess Karoline (*b* at Krzemusch 23 March 1912; ✝ at Grabs 29 Nov 1996), dau of Eugen, Count von Ledebur-Wicheln and Countess Eleonore Larisch von Moennich, and had issue,

    1. Prince *Eugen* Hartmann Johannes Franz, *b* at Mahr-Sternberg 20 March 1939, Dipl Engineer Forestry; *m* at Ebenthal, Carinthia 27 July 1968, Countess Maria Theresia (*b* at Ebenthal 24 May 1945), dau of Leopold Zeno, Count von Goëss and Countess Theodora Kottulinsky, Baroness von Kottulin, Krzizkowitz and Dobrzenicz, and has issue,
    [Haus Oopennig, 9062 Moosburg, Kärnten, Austria].

        1. Prince *Johannes* Leopold Petrus Maria, *b* at St Gallen 28 Jan 1969, Lic oec HSG, Dr nat; *m* atVienna 12 May 2001, Countess *Kinga* (*b* at Vienna 1 Oct 1973), Mag. phil., dau of Count Eduard (Ede) Károlyi de Nagy-Károlyi and Countess Ilona Kendeffy de Malomviz.

2. Princess *Anna* Theodora Maria, *b* at St Gallen 28 Nov 1970, stud jur; *m* at Moosburg 12 June 1993, Alexander, Count Kottulinsky, Baron von Kottulin, Krzizkowitz and Dobrezenicz (*b* at Graz 30 July 1967).
[*Hardtgasse 6/15, 1190 Vienna, Austria*].

3. Princess *Marie Ileana* Josefa, *b* at Klagenfurt 20 July 1974; *m* at Vaduz 2 June (civ) and at Moosburg 10 June (relig) 2000, Ferdinand, Count von Trauttmansdorff-Weinsberg (*b* at Vienna 24 Sept 1970).
[*Gut Dornau, 2544 Leobersdorf, Austria*].

4. Princess *Sophie* Barbara Maria, *b* at St Veit an der Glan 16 April 1984.

2. Prince *Albrecht Johannes* Géza Augustinus Wilhelm Maria, *b* at Mähr-Sternberg 28 May 1940, *cr* Baron von Landskron 28 Jan 1971; *m* 1stly (morganatically) at Vaduz 3 Sept 1966 (*m* diss by div at Vaduz 1971), Tamara (*b* at Suojärvi, Finland 17 June 1939), *cr* Baroness von Landskron by Franz Joseph II, Prince of Liechtenstein 8 Aug 1966, dau of Walter Johannes Nyman and Elsa Mildred Berttel, and has issue (*cr* Baron and Baronesses von Landskron),

1. Baroness *Tatiana* von Landskron, *b* at Paris 2 March 1965; *m* at St Gallen ...., Bruno Thurnherr (*b* at ...).

2. Baron *Albrecht Géza* von Landskron, *b* at Paris 2 April 1967.

Prince Albrecht Johannes *m* 2ndly at Paris, 23 July 1974, Mylena, dau of Joseph Tullio and Clelia Giordano, and has further issue,
[*7 rue Bixio, 75007 Paris, France*].

3. Baroness *Lorenza* von Landskron, *b* at Neuilly sur Seine 16 April 1975; *m* at Paris 2 March 1996, Don Antonio de Balzo di Presenzano (*b* at Naples 21 April 1962).

3. Princess *Barbara* Eleonora Marie, *b* at Mährisch-Sternberg 9 July 1942; *m* at Paris 2 Nov 1973, Prince Alexander of Yugoslavia (*b* at Richmond Park, England 13 Aug 1924; *m* 1stly at Cascais, Portugal 12 Feb 1955, Princess Maria Pia of Savoy; that *m* diss by div 1967),

Lt RAF.
[*53 Avenue Montaigne, 75008 Paris, France*].

3. Prince *Constantin* Franz Nikolaus Karl Heinrich Dagobert
Anton von Padua Idlefons Maria, *b* at Vienna 23 Dec 1911; ✠
at Grabs 28 March 2001; *m* 1stly at Vienna 19 March 1941,
Maria Elisabeth (*b* at Branek 23 May 1921; ✠ in an air raid on
Vienna 10 Sept 1944), dau of Lt-Col Albert von Leutzendorff
and Baroness Elisabeth von Diller. He *m* 2ndly at Vaduz 21
Dec 1976 (civ) and 10 Jan 1977 (relig), Countess Helene
(Ilona) (*b* at Sárosd 17 May 1921; *m* 1stly 23 Aug 1943, Nikolaus
(Miklós), Count Cziráky de Czirák et Dénesfalva who was *ka*
at Battonya, Kom Csandád 13 Sept 1944), dau of Ladislaus
(László), Count Esterházy de Galántha, Proprietor of Sárosd
and Countess Charlotte (Sarolta) (Sári) Széchenyi de Sárvár-
Felsóvidék, and had issue by his first wife,

　　　1. Princess *Monica* Maria Theresia Elisabeth, *b* at
　　　Vienna 8 April 1942; *m* at Rio de Janeiro 25 Nov 1960
　　　(*m* diss by div at Bravos, Mexico 21 June 1969 and
　　　annulled by Sacred Rota at Rome 15 Sept 1972), André
　　　Franz Jordan (*b* at Lemberg, Poland 10 Sept 1933).
　　　She has since reverted to her maiden name and bears
　　　the name title of Princess von and zu Liechtenstein
　　　by permission of the Head of the Princely House.

2. Prince *Alfred* Roman, *b* at Vienna 6 April 1875; ✠ at Schloß
Waldstein, nr Peggau, Steiermark 25 Oct 1930, Kt of Hon and Dev
Sovereign Military Order of Malta; *m* at Munich 19 Feb 1912,
Princess Theresia Maria (*b* at Munich 1 June 1887; ✠ at Schloß
Waldstein 29 March 1971), Dame Star Cross Order, dau of Prince
Moritz zu Oettingen-Oettingen and Oettingen-Wallerstein and
Countess Maria Waldbott von Bassenheim, and had issue,

　　　1. Princess *Maria Benedikta* Henriette Therese Gabriele
　　　Angela Ildefonsa, *b* at Munich 21 March 1913; ✠ at Graz 10
　　　Jan 1992, Dr of Phil.

　　　2. Prince Johann (*Hans*) Baptist Moritz Heinrich Alfred
　　　Idlefons Benedikt Maria Josef, *b* at Schloß Waldstein 6 Aug
　　　1914, Dr of Law, Dipl Engineer Forestry; *m* at Burgweinting,
　　　nr Regensburg 1 Nov (civ) and at Regensburg 7 Nov (relig)
　　　1944, Princess Clothilde (*b* at Regensburg 30 Nov 1922), Dame
　　　Star Cross Order, dau of Karl August, 10th Prince (Fürst)
　　　von Thurn and Taxis and Princess Maria Anna of Bragança,
　　　Infanta of Portugal, and has issue,

[*Dietersdorf 7, 3441 Judenau, NÖsterr., Austria*].

    1. Prince *Gundakar* Albert Alfred Petrus, *b* at Vienna 1 April 1949, Mag rer soc et oec; *m* at Dreux, Dept Eure et Loire 22 July (civ) and at Friedrichshafen 29 July (relig) 1989, Princess Marie (*b* at Boulogne-sur-Seine 3 Jan 1959), dau of Henri VII, Count of Paris, Duke of France and Duchess Marie Therese of Württemberg, Duchess de Montpensier, and has issue, [*Herrenhub 1, 3051 St. Christophen, Lower Austria; Caixa Postal 117, 78400-000 Diamantino, Mato Grosso, Brazil*].

        1. Princess *Leopoldine* Eleonore Therese Marie, *b* at Vienna 27 June 1990.

        2. Princess *Marie Immaculata* Elisabeth Rose Adelgunde, *b* at Vienna 15 Dec 1991.

        3. Prince *Johann Wenzel* Karl Emmernan Bonifatius Maria, *b* at Vienna 16 March 1993.

        4. Princess *Margarete* Franciska Daria Wilhelmine Marie, *b* at Vienna 10 Jan 1995.

        5. Prince *Gabriel* Karl Bonaventura Alfred Valerian Maria, *b* at Vienna 6 May 1998.

    2. Princess *Diemut* Margarete Maria Benedicta Anna, *b* at Vienna 1 April 1949 (twin with Prince Gundakar); *m* at Vaduz 29 June (civ) and Heiligenkreuz, Lower Austria 17 July (relig) 1982, Ulrich Köstlin (*b* at Stuttgart 31 Dec 1951), Dr of Law.
[*Ahrenshooperzeile 5, 14129 Berlin, Germany*].

    3. Prince *Alfred* Heinrich Michael Benedikt Maria, *b* at Vienna 17 Sept 1951; *m* at Vaduz 22 March (civ) and at Schloß Waldstein 6 April (relig) 2002, Raffaella Ida (*b* at Tlemcen, Algeria 12 Dec 1966), dau of Tino Sangiorgi and Bruna Ferrari.
[*Richtergasse 4/8, 1070, Vienna, Austria*].

    4. Princess A*delgunde* Maria Anna Therese Mafalda Eleonore, *b* at Vienna 10 Aug 1953.
[*Schellingstraße 59, 80799, Austria*].

    5. Prince Karl *Emmeran* Duarte Johannes Theobald Benedikt, *b* at Regensburg 1 July 1955.
[*Schloß Altenberg, 89428 Syrgenstein, Germany*].

    6. Princess Maria *Eleonore* Bernadette Hildegarde, *b* at Vienna 14 Nov 1958.

[*Straning 77, 3722, Lower Austria*].

7. Prince *Hugo* Karl August, *b* at Vienna 20 Feb 1964; *m* at Vaduz 11 July (civ) and at Nershiem, Germany 11 July (rel) 1998, Arabella (*b* at Hamburg 9 June 1971), dau of Wolfgang Ohlmeier and Angela Maria Sendker, and has issue,

[*Schloß Altenberg, 89428 Syrgenstein, Germany*].

    1. Princess *Maria* Aurelia Margarete Antonia Angela Clotilde, *b* at Munich 7 Oct 1998.

3. Prince *Heinrich* Karl Vincenz Maria Benediktus Justinus, *b* at Graz 5 Aug 1916; ✠ at Graz 17 April 1991, Dr of Phil, Kt Order of the Golden Fleece; *m* at Lignières, France 12 Sept 1949, Archduchess Elisabeth (*b* at El Pardo, Madrid 31 May 1922; ✠ at Graz 6 Jan 1993), Dr rer pol, Dame Star Cross Order, dau of Karl I, Emperor of Austria, King of Hungary, etc and Princess Doña Zita of Bourbon-Parma, and has issue,

    1. Prince *Vincenz* Karl Alfred Maria Michael et omnes sancti, *b* at Graz 30 July 1950, Dr of Law, Kt Order of the Golden Fleece; *m* at Paris 5 March (civ) and 7 March (relig) 1981 (diss by div at Vienna 19 Nov 1991; annulled at Vienna 18 Oct 1994), Hélène (*b* at Neuilly-sur-Seine 26 Sept 1960), Dame Star Cross Order, dau of Count Maurice de Cossé-Brissac of the Dukes de Brissac and Béatrice Millin de Grandmaison. He *m* 2ndly at Venice 19 Jun 1999 Roberta (*b* at Milan 12 Feb 1953), dau of Mario Valeri Manera and Maria Gaggia and has issue,

    [*Schloß Waldstein, 8122 Waldstein, Steiermark, Austria*].

        1. Princess *Adelheid* Marie Beatrice Zita, *b* at Vienna 25 Nov 1981.

        2. Princess *Hedwig* Maria Beatrice Hermine, *b* at Vienna 28 Nov 1982.

2. Prince *Michael* Karl Alfred Maria Felix Moritz et omnes sancti, *b* at Graz 10 Oct 1951, adopted by his aunt, Princess Eleonore of Liechtenstein (see below), Mag rer soc et oec; *m* at Vaduz 31 Jan (civ) and at Baden-Baden 8 Feb (relig) 1986, Hildegard (*b* at Mannheim 12 Feb 1948), Dr Engineer, Pharmacist, dau of Robert Max Josef Peters and Berta Elisabeth Beeck, and has issue,

[*Sonnblickstraße 4, 9490 Vaduz, Liechtenstein*].

      1. Princess *Therese* Maria, *b* at Munich 22 Feb 1987.

      2. Princess *Gisela* Maria, *b* at Feldkirch, Vorarlberg, Austria 26 June 1990.

      3. Princess *Charlotte* Maria Benedikta Eleonore Adelheid et omnes sancti, *b* at Graz 3 July 1953, Dipl Translator; *m* at Waldstein 31 Aug 1979, Pieter van der Byl (*b* at Cape Town, South Africa 11 Nov 1923 ✝ Fairfield, South Africa 15 Nov 1999), former Foreign Minister and Minister of Defence in Rhodesia.
[*Fairfield, Napier, Cape Province 7270, South Africa*].

      4. Prince *Christof* Karl Alfred Maria Michael Hugo Ignatius et omnes sancti, *b* at Graz 11 April 1956, Dr of Law.
[*Los Naranjos 37, 38360 El Sauzal, Tenerife, Spain*].

      5. Prince *Karl* Maria Alfred Michael Georg et omnes sancti, *b* at Graz 31 Aug 1957, adopted by his aunt, Princess Maria Benedikta of Liechtenstein (see above).
[*8122 Schloß Waldstein bei Peggau, Steiermark, Austria*].

    4. Princess *Eleonore* Henriette Maria Josefa Germana Idlefonsa, *b* at Schloß Waldstein 28 May 1920, adopted her nephew, Michael, Prince of Liechtenstein (*b* at Graz 10 Oct 1951) at Vaduz 28 June 1977 (see above).

3. Prince *Karl* Aloys, *b* at Frauenthal 16 Sept 1878; ✝ at Frauenthal 20 June 1955, Regent of the Principality of Liechtenstein 1920, Kt of Hon and Dev Sovereign Military Order of Malta; *m* at Stuttgart 31 March (civ) and at Tegernsee 5 April (relig) 1921, Princess Elisabeth (*b* at Schloß Lichtenstein, Reutlingen, Württemberg 23 Aug 1894; ✝ at Frauenthal 13 Oct 1962), dau of Wilhelm, 2nd Duke of Urach, Count of Württemberg, and had issue,

      1. Prince *Wilhelm* Alfred Heinrich Karl Theodor Otto Gero Maria Josef, *b* at Frauenthal 29 May 1922, Bailiff Gd Cross Hon and Dev Sovereign Military Order of Malta, renounced his titles and rights as a Prince of Liechtenstein and was *cr* Count von Hohenau by Franz Josef II, Prince of Liechtenstein 11 July 1950. He was re-established in the name and title of Prince von and zu Liechtenstein by permission of the Head of the Princely House 28 Oct 1980; *m* at Kitzbühel 21 Aug 1950, Emma (*b* at Klagenfurt 14 May 1926; ✝ at Vienna 31 Aug

1984), dau of Felix Georg von Guthmannsthal-Benvenuti and Hermine Krum, and has issue (who have borne the title of Prince or Princess of Liechtenstein from 28 Oct 1980).
[*Hintzerstraße 11, 1030 Vienna, Austria*].

    1. Prince *Felix Karl* Wilhelm Otto Leopold Maria, *b* at Graz 22 May 1951, Psychotherapist.
    [*Sternwartestraße 40, 1180 Vienna, Austria*].
    2. Prince *Benedikt Ulrich* Edmund Vincenz Josef Maria, *b* at Vienna 22 Jan 1953, Painter; *m* at Vienna 22 Sept 1988, Maria (*b* at St Pölten 23 Nov 1958), dau of Friedrich Schoisswohl and Stefanie Jud.
    [*Newald Gasse 3/26, 1090 Vienna, Austria*].
    3. Princess *Maria-Theresia* Emma Elisabeth Felicia Josefa Regina, *b* at Graz 30 Dec 1953; *m* at London 25 July (civ) and at Vienna 23 Sept (relig) 1978, Aurel Edward, Count Dessewffy de Csernek et Tarkeö (*b* at Greta, Australia 8 April 1950), Merchant Banker.
    [*10 The Boulevard, Hawthorn, Victoria 3122, Australia*].
    4. Prince *Stefan Alois* Rupert Wilhelm Barnabas Maria, *b* at Graz 11 June 1957, Master Carpenter, has born the name of Heildborgh from 16 Jan 1989; *m* at Spitz, Austria 25 Aug 1988 (*m* diss by div at Vienna 12 April 1991), *Andrea* Rixta Eva Eleonore (*b* at Vienna 24 Dec 1958), dau of Ernst von Kloss and Rixta Hartig.
    [*Neuling Gasse 48, 1030 Vienna, Austria*].
    5. Prince *Heinrich*, *b* at Graz 20 Nov 1964, Kt of Hon and Dev Sovereign Military Order of Malta.
    [*Hintzerstraße 11, 1030 Vienna, Austria*].

2. Princess *Maria Josepha* Henriette Amelie Florestine Zita Franziska Therese Carola Valerie Elisabeth Ludovika, *b* at Hollenegg 6 July 1923, Dr of Phil, Sister Maria Adelheid.
[*Zisterzienserinnenkloster Marienfeld, 2041 Maria Roggendorf, NÖsterreich, Austria*].

3. Princess *Franziska de Paula* Henriette Marie Amelie Mechtildis Benedikta Petra de Alcantara, *b* at Hollenegg 14 June 1930; *m* there 29 May 1965, Rochus, Count von Spee (*b* at Borken 25 Oct 1925; ✝ at Cologne 30 Aug 1981).
[*Grunerstraße 3, 51067 Cologne, Germany*].

4. Prince *Wolfgang* Johannes Baptist Johannes Evangelist Idlefons Franz de Paula Josef Maria, *b* at Graz 25 Dec 1934,

Mag jur, Ambassador for Liechtenstein to Switzerland; *m* at
Wang 12 July (civ) and at Isareck 18 July (relig) 1970, Countess
Gabrielle (*b* at Isareck 11 March 1949), dau of Franz Xavier,
Count Basselet de La Rosée, Proprietor of Isarek and Inkoben
and Princess Eleonore of Lobkowicz, and has issue,
[*Kleiner-Haus, Kruckenberg 14, 8530 Deutschlandsberg,
Austria*].

    1. Princess *Stephanie* Elisabeth Eleonore Maria, *b* at
    Salzburg 12 April 1976.
    [*Lackierer Gasse 4/14, 1090 Vienna, Austria*].
    2. Prince *Leopold* Franz Karl Maria, *b* at Salzburg 21
    May 1978.
    [*Lackierer Gasse 4/14, 1090 Vienna, Austria*].

Brother of Great-Great-Grandfather

Issue of Johann I, Prince of Liechtenstein (*b* 27 June 1760; ✠ 20
April 1836) and Landgravine Josephine of Fürstenberg-Weitra (*b* 21
June 1776; *m* 12 April 1792; ✠ 23 Feb 1848), having had issue,
among whom,

Son

Prince *Eduard* Franz Ludwig, *b* at Vienna 22 Feb 1809; ✠ at Karlsbad
27 June 1864, Lt-Field Marshal Austrian Army; *m* at Chorostków,
Galicia 16 Oct 1836, Countess Honoria (*b* at Ochlopo 1 Aug 1813; ✠
at Brünn 1 Sept 1869), Dame Star Cross Order, widow of Thaddäus
Kownacki, and dau of Count Johann Choloniów-Choloniewski,
Marshal of the Nobility in Galicia and Josefa Rzyszczewska (w Pobog),
and had issue,

Son

Prince Maria Johann *Aloys, b* at Lemberg 25 June 1840; ✠ at Güns
29 March 1885, Austrian Army; *m* at Pressburg 26 Nov 1870,
Countess Anna (*b* at Ramholz 13 May 1849; ✠ at Schwarzach im
Pongau 17 Sept 1933; *m* 2ndly at Salzburg 6 Nov 1892, Andreas,
Count Plater Syberg who ✠ at Bozen 18 June 1928), Dame Star
Cross Order, dau of Adolph, Count von Degenfeld-Schonburg and
Countess Sidonie Berényi von Karáncs-Berény, and had issue, among
whom,

Sons

1. Prince *Friedrich* Aloys Johannes Maria, *b* at Arad 12 Sept 1871; ✠
at Rosegg 10 Oct 1959, Proprietor of Rosegg and Viktring, Kärnten

and Liechtenstein, nr Judenburg, Steiermark, Major-Gen Austrian Army; *m* at Vienna 14 Oct 1897, Countess Maria (Irma) (*b* at Vienna 24 May 1877; ✠ at Rosegg 24 Nov 1956), Dame Star Cross Order, dau of Géza, Count Apponyi de Nagy-Appony and Countess Paula Széchenyi de Sárvár-Felsövidék, and had issue,

1. Prince *Aloys* Géza Georg Hubert Maria, *b* at Vienna 18 June 1896; *ka* at Buzowka, Russia 19 Feb 1943, Major; *m* at Villach 6 Oct (civ) and at Würzburg 20 Oct (relig) 1938, Countess Hertha-Maria (*b* at Würzburg 31 Aug 1919; *m* 2ndly at Maria-Buch, nr Judenburg, Steiermark 8 May 1958, Erwin Janik who was *b* at Marburg an der Drau 20 March 1906, ✠ at Judenburg 7 Jan 1996, Dipl Engineer Forestry), dau of Luitpold, Count Wolffskeel von Reichenberg and Baroness Sophie von Guttenberg of the Steinenhausen, and had issue, [*Weißkirchnerstraße 25, 8750 Judenburg, Steiermark, Austria*].

1. Prince *Luitpold* Rudolf Georg Hubertus, *b* at Würzburg 11 April 1940, Dipl Eng Forestry; *m* at Salzburg 22 Nov 1969, (*m* diss by div at Judenburg 20 Aug 1997) Countess Ulrike Margarethe (*b* at Salzburg 29 Dec 1945), dau of Ottmar, Count von Habsburg-Lothringen and Helene Moser, and has issue, among whom,
[*Khunn Gasse 6-8/4/9, 1030 Vienna, Austria*].

1. Prince *Carl Georg* Alois Maria, *b* at Graz 19 Sept 1978.
[*Weißkirchner Straße 21, 8750 Judenburg, Austria*].

2. Princess *Maria-Gabrielle*, *b* at Würzburg 7 Sept 1942, Dr of Med, Radiologist; *m* at Baden, nr Vienna 2 Aug 1968, Alfons Matthias Brandis (*b* at Baden, nr Vienna 19 July 1922).
[*Andreas Hoferstraße 24, 5020 Salzburg, Austria*].

2. Prince *Alfred* Joseph Karl Maria, *b* at Pressburg 6 June 1900, ✠ at Klagenfurt 29 March 1972; *m* at Ungarschitz 24 June 1928, Countess Polixena Therese (*b* at Teschendorf, Mecklenburg 16 Oct 1905; ✠ at Conegliano, Prov Treviso 11 Aug 1984), Dame Star Cross Order, dau of Manfred Eduard, 5th Prince (Fürst) von Collalto and San Salvatore and Princess Thekla zu Isenburg and Büdingen in Büdingen, and had issue, among whom,

1. Prince *Alexander* Friedrich Manfred Maria, *b* at
Vienna 14 May 1929; *m* at Bronnbach an der Tauber
7 Jan 1961, Princess Josephine (*b* at Bronnbach 17
May 1937), Dame Star Cross Order, dau of Karl, 8th
Prince (Fürst) zu Löwenstein-Wertheim-Rosenberg
and Carolina Rignon of the Counts Rignon, and has
issue,
[*Haus Nr. 2, Schloß Rosegg, 9232 Rosegg, Kärnten,
Austria; Loch Gasse 5, 9490 Vaduz, Liechtenstein*].

    1. Prince *Christian* Alfred Carl Manfred
Alexander Joseph Maria, *b* at Klagenfurt 14
Nov 1961, Dr of Med; *m* at Vaduz 10 March
(civ) and at Maria-Thann 20 May (relig) 1989,
Countess Marie-Christine (*b* at Ravensburg 2
July 1962), Stud of Phil, dau of Josef, Count
von Waldburg-Zeil-Hohenems and Baroness
Maria Benedikta von Redwitz, and has issue,
[*Moosburgerstraße 21, 9210 Pörtschach,
Austria*].

        1. Princess *Carolina* Maria Josepha
Florentine, *b* at Villach 3 June 1990.
        2. Prince *Augustinus* Maria Alfons
Emanuel, *b* at Basel, Switzerland 20 May
1992.
        3. Princess *Johannes* Maria Nikolaus
Antonius, *b* at Bern, Switzerland 3 July
1995.
2. Prince *Stefan* Carl Manfred Alfred Alexander
Joseph Maria, *b* at Klagenfurt 14 Nov 1961 (twin
with Prince Christian), Mag rer soc oec; *m* at
Vienna 18 June 1988, Countess Florentine (*b*
at Vienna 1 Jan 1963), dau of Romedio, Count
von Thun and Hohenstein and Countess Sophia
von Cassis-Faraone, and has issue,
[*Haus Nr. 1, Schloß Rosegg, 9232 Rosegg,
Kärnten, Austria*].

    1. Prince *Lukas* Romedio Alexander
Alfred Antonius Stephan Maria, *b* at
Zurich 27 April 1990.
    2. Prince *Konrad* Emanuel Josef Michael
Franziskus Stephan Maria, *b* at

Frankfurt-am-Main 15 Feb 1992.

3. Princess *Anna* Maria Carolina Christine Sophia Florentine Clara, *b* at Frankfurt-am-Main 24 Aug 1994.

4. Princess *Rita* Maria Thérèse Alexandra Bettina Marguerite Florentine, *b* at Klagenfurt 27 March 1999.

3. Prince *Emanuel* Alexander Pius Friedrich Joseph Franz Maria, *b* at Klagenfurt 5 May 1964; *m* at Csiscò, Slovakia 27 May 1995, Countess Alexandra (*b* at Bruck 9 June 1966), dau of Alois, Count Kálnoky von Köröspatak and Baroness Sieglinde von Oer, and has issue, [*Haus Nr. 2, Schloß Rosegg, 9232 Rosegg, Kärnten, Austria*].

1. Princess *Polixena* Marie Benedikta Florentine Alexandra Emanuel, *b* at Klagenfurt 12 Oct 1996.

2. Prince *Josef* Maria Alexander Edoardo Ferdinand Emanuel, *b* at Klagenfurt 15 December 1998.

2. Princess *Elisabeth* Franziska Anna Thekla Maria Therese Manfreda Leopoldine Juliane Antonia, *b* at Vienna 17 Jan 1932; *m* at Rosegg 31 Oct 1964, Ricardo, Baron Winspeare Guicciardi (*b* at Naples 17 Oct 1912; ✠ 15 Jan 2002), Dr sc pol.

[*Piazza di Castello, 73030 Depressa, Prov. Lecce, Italy*].

3. Princess *Aloysia* Emanuela Maria, *b* at Vienna 23 Jan 1904; ✠ at Viktring 18 July 1992; *m* at Rosegg 17 Aug 1929, Joseph, Reichsritter von Miller zu Aichholz (*b* at Triest 28 May 1897; ✠ at Klagenfurt 30 Dec 1976), Economist, President Prudential Investment Trust Inc.

2. Prince *Eduard* Viktor Maria, *b* at Laibach 2 Sept 1872; ✠ at Monte Carlo 8 March 1951, Dr of Law; *m* at Wischenau, nr Misslitz 31 Aug 1898, Countess Olga (*b* at Stuttgart 11 April 1873; ✠ at Salzburg 14 Feb 1966), dau of Friedrich, Count von Pückler, Count and Lord zu Limpurg-Sontheim-Gaildorf and Countess Karoline von Spiegel zum Diesenberg-Hanxleden, and had issue, among whom,

1. Prince *Johannes* Baptist Alois Ferdinand Lucas Anton Josef Maria, *b* at Salzburg 18 Oct 1899; ✠ at Honolulu,

Hawaii 5 Nov 1979; *m* 1stly at London 29 July 1931 (*m* diss by div 1943), Aleene (*b* at Parker, Texas 25 Jan 1902; ....), dau of Charles McFarland. He *m* 2ndly at St Johns, Arizona, USA 27 Aug 1945, Jean Ann French (*b* at Des Moines, Iowa, USA 12 Oct 1917).

[*999 Wilder Avenue, Apt. 1001, Honolulu, Hawaii 96822, U.S.A.*].

2. Prince *Ferdinand* Alois Andreas Josef Anton Maria, *b* at Salzburg 18 Jan 1901; ✠ at Neuilly-sur-Seine 7 July 1981; *m* 1stly at London 14 Jan 1925 (*m* diss by div 1934 and ecclesiastically annulled 1939), Shelagh (*b* at Winnington, Cheshire, England 6 Feb 1902; ✠ at Cambridge 6 Nov 1983; *m* 2ndly 1934, Georg Otto Suppancic; that *m* diss by div 1952), granted the title of Countess von Rietberg 5 Dec 1951, dau of Roscoe Brunner of the Baronets Brunner and Ethel Houston, and had issue (who bear the title of Count or Countess von Reitberg), among whom,

    1. Count *Christopher*, *b* at ... 8 May 1926, late 15th/19th Hussars; *m* at ... 17 Sept 1955, Kathleen (*b* at .....; ✠ at London 6 Nov 1982), dau of Alfred Thayer Mahan of Orangeburg, New York, USA, and has issue,

    [*20 Verney House, Jerome Crescent, London, NW8 8SG*].

        1. Countess Gabrielle Catherine, *b* at ... 13 Jan 1957.

        2. Count Mark Andreas, *b* at ... 30 June 1959.

    2. Countess Ethel *Elisabeth* Olga Mary, *b* at Schloß Soss, St Pölten 11 Sept 1928; ✠ at ....14 Nov 1999; *m* 1stly at Cambridge 1953 (*m* diss by div at 1961), Klaus Bruno von Brehm. She resumed her maiden name by Deed Poll 1962, and *m* 2ndly at Johannesberg 16 April 1968, Richard Douglas Loftus Onslow, of the Earls of Onslow (*b* at Nakuru, Kenya 11 Jan 1928).

    [*4 Castlestead, Pateley Bridge, Harrogate, North Yorkshire HG3 5QF*].

Prince Ferdinand *m* 2ndly at Stockholm 7 Sept 1940 (*m* diss by div .... and ecclesiastically annulled 26 Nov 1959), Brita (*b* at Stockholm 8 Oct 1919; ✠ at Kristianstad, Sweden 9 June 1971; *m* 2ndly 20 Nov 1948, Carl Lohmand; that *m* diss by div; *m* 3rdly 5 Feb 1955, Ulf Björkman), dau of Gen Bengt Nordenskiöld (Royal Swedish Airforce) and Dagmar Werner.

He *m* 3rdly at Long Island, New York, USA 21 Aug 1950 (*m* diss by div), Dorothy Haidel (*b* at St Louis, USA 29 May 1895; ✝ at Kitzbühel 11 April 1961), widow of .... Oelrichs. He *m* 4thly at Sucy-en-Brie, nr Paris 19 Dec 1968, Georgette Maria [*51 Boulevard d'Auteuil, 92100 Boulogne, France*] (*b* at Lille 8 Sept 1916; *m* 1stly, Pierre Alexandre; that *m* diss by div), granted the name and title of Princess von and zu Liechtenstein by the Head of the Princely House 31 June 1975, dau of Hubert Ansay and Lucienne Legrand, and had further issue by his second wife,

3. Prince Johannes (*Hanno*) Eduard Bengt Henrik Andreas Maria, *b* at Helsingborg 3 Nov 1941, Dipl Engineer, BA, Kt of Hon and Dev Sovereign Military Order of Malta; *m* at Danderyd, Sweden 11 May 1968 (civ) and at Stockholm 11 May 1974 (relig), Kerstin (*b* at Stockholm 16 June 1939), BA, Industrial Nurse, granted the name and title of Princess von and zu Liechtenstein by the Head of the Princely House 11 May 1974, dau of Carl Gustav Lennart Lundberg and Tyra Elisabet Felldin, and has issue,
[*Karlbergsvägen 22, 11327 Stockholm, Sweden*].

1. Prince *Jan Andreas*, *b* at Danderyd 21 Aug 1968, M.B.A., Kt of Hon and Dev Sovereign Military Order of Malta; *m* at Vaduz 4 Aug (civ) and at Stockholm 12 Aug (relig) 2000, Lena (*b* at Borg 19 May 1969), dau of Gösta Johansson and Viola Ivarsson-Svakko.
[*Kungstensgatan 28, 2 uppg. 4tr., 11357 Stockholm, Sweden*].

2. Prince *Max Peder*, *b* at Solna, Sweden 21 Feb 1972, M.Sc., Kt of Hon and Dev Sovereign Military Order of Malta.
[*Karlbergsvägen 22, 11327 Stockholm, Sweden*].

LIPPE

Reformist:- Founded by Bernhard, Lord of Lippe (a castle in Lippstadt) living in 1123; acquired Detmold, etc *ca* 1150; acquired Schwalenberg *ca* 1322; the order of primogeniture was established 1368; acquired Sternberg 1405; took the title of Count 1528; confirmation of the title of Count of the Holy Empire 1529; partition of lands between the sons of Count Simon VI (*b* 6 April 1555; ✝ 17 Dec 1613), Simon VII (✝ 26 March 1627) received Detmold; Otto (✝ 18 Nov 1657) received Brake (line extinct 21 Feb 1709); Hermann (✝ 23 Aug 1620) received Schwalenberg, but left no descendants; and Philipp (✝ 10 April 1681) received Alverdissen and was ancestor of the Princes of Schaumburg-Lippe (see that family). Another partition took place between the sons of Count Simon VII: Hermann Adolf (✝ 10 Oct 1666) continued the line of Detmold and Idocus (or Jobst) Hermann (✝ 6 July 1678) was ancestor of the lines of Biesterfeld and Weissenfeld.

A: LIPPE

Founded by Simon VII, Count of Lippe-Detmold (*b* 30 Dec 1587; ✝ 26 March 1627).

I: PRINCELY LINE

Founded by **Friedrich Carl August**, Count and Noble Lord of Lippe-Biesterfeld, etc (*b* 20 Jan 1706; ✝ 31 July 1781), grandson of Count Jobst Hermann (see above). This line attained Sovereign status on the extinction of the Detmold line when Count Leopold *succ* Prince Alexander, as Leopold IV, Prince of Lippe (*b* 30 May 1871; ✝ 30 Dec 1949) in 1905. This line ceased to reign in 1918.

Arms:- Quarterly of nine: 1st and 9th, arg, five millrings in saltire sa (Vianen); 2nd and 8th, gu, a swallow close ppr perched upon a star of eight points or (Schwalenberg); 3rd and 7th, vair and barry gu (Goye or Lordship of Ameyde); 4th and 6th, or, a star of eight points gu (Sternberg); 5th, on an escutcheon of pretence, arg, a rose gu barbed and seeded ppr (Lippe). The shield is ensigned by the Princely Crown. *Supporters:-* Two angels vested of a dalmatic, that of the dexter charged with the arms of Lippe, and holding a banner with the arms of Lippe, and that of the sinister charged with the arms of Schwalenberg and holding a banner with the arms of Schwalenberg. Members of the I Princely Line bear the title of Prince or Princess zur Lippe with the qualification of Serene Highness.

ARMIN Leopold Ernst Bruno Heinrich Willa August, **PRINCE OF LIPPE,** Noble Lord and Count of Biesterfeld, Count of Schwalenberg and Sternberg, Hereditary Burggrave of Utrecht, etc, *b* at Detmold 18 Aug 1924, Dr rer nat, Biologist, *succ* his father as Head of the Princely House of Lippe, son of Leopold IV, Prince of Lippe (*b* 30 May 1871; ✝ 30 Dec 1949) and Princess Anna zu Isenburg and Büdingen in Büdingen (*b* 10 Feb 1886; *m* 26 April 1922; *m* 1stly at Büdingen 21 Nov 1911, Ernst, Count and Noble Lord of Lippe-Weissenfeld who was *ka* 11 Sept 1914; ✝ 8 Feb 1980) ; *m* at Göttingen 27 March (civ) and at Celle 29 March (relig) 1953, Traute

(*b* at Hänigsen, Burgdorf, 16 Feb 1925), Dr rer nat, dau of Gustav Becker and Charlotte Meyer, and has issue,
[*Schloß, 32756 Detmold, Germany*].

Son

Prince *Stephan* Leopold Justus Richard, *b* at Detmold 24 May 1959, LL.M (U.S.A.), Lawyer and Tax Consultant, Capt (Res); *m* at Detmold 13 Oct (civ) and 15 Oct (relig) 1994, Countess Maria (*b* at Frankfurt-am-Main 12 Aug 1968), dau of Otto, Count zu Solms-Laubach and Princess Madaleine zu Sayn-Wittgenstein-Berleburg, and has issue,
[*Friedrich-Ebertstraße 5, 32756 Detmold, Germany*]

    1. Prince *Bernhard* Leopold Baptist Ernst Georg Ludwig, *b* at Detmold 9 Sept 1995.

    2. Prince *Heinrich Otto* Gustav-Adolf Michael Wico, *b* at Detmold 8 April 1997.

    3. Prince *Wilhelm* Benjamin Hans Karl Maximilian Paul, *b* at Detmold 12 Oct 1999.

    4. Princess *Luise* Anna Astrid Christiane Viktoria, *b* at Detmold 16 April 2001.

Half-Brothers and Sister

Issue of Leopold IV, Prince of Lippe (*b* at 30 May 1871; ✢ 30 Dec 1949); *succ* his father as Regent of the Principality of Lippe 26 Sept 1904, and Prince Alexander as reigning Prince 25 Oct 1905; renounced the throne 12 Nov 1918, and his 1st wife, Princess Bertha of Hesse-Philippsthal-Barchfeld (*b* 25 Oct 1874; *m* 16 Aug 1901; ✢ at Detmold 19 Feb 1919).

1. *Ernst* Leopold Chlodwig Julius Alexis Wilhelm Heinrich, Hereditary Prince (Erbprinz) of Lippe, Senior Male Member until his death, *b* at Detmold 12 June 1902; ✢ at Detmold 24 May 1987, Lt (ret); *m* 1stly at Berlin 16 July 1924 (*m* diss by div at Berlin 1935), Charlotte (*b* at Dresden 23 May 1900; ✢ at Neustadt an der Weinstrasse 24 June 1974; *m* 2ndly at Berlin 28 Dec 1938, Richard Busolt), dau of Clemens Friedrich Illeken and Mathilde Therese Wilhelmine Heinisch. He *m* 2ndly at Berlin 5 June 1937, Horta-Elise (*Helga*) (*b* at Berlin 13 April 1911; ✢ at Detmold 6 May 1970), dau of Ernst Friedrich Wilhelm Weiland and Wilhelmine Anne Agnes Favre, and by her had issue,

    1. Prince *Ernst-Leopold* Bernhard Chlodwig Wilhelm Ottokar, *b* at Berlin 14 March 1940, Dr of Med; *m* at Datteln 12 June

(civ) and at Burg Kriegshofen 2 Aug (relig) 1969, Katrin (*b* at
Wernigerode 5 Oct 1941), dau of Lt-Col Karl Reinhard Hein
and Charlotte Schlichting, and has issue,
[*Residenzstraße 27, Cappel, 32825 Blomberg-Cappel,
Germany*].

    1. Princess *Nikola* Helga, *b* at Datteln 10 April 1971;
m at Cappel 1 Aug 1996, Olaf Christian Grünberg (*b*
at Wilhelmshaven 19 May 1969).
[*Am Kollhahn 2, 58791 Werdohl, Germany*].

    2. Princess *Julia,* *b* at Datteln 3 Oct 1972; *m* at Cappel
25 June 1999, Joachim Tiedau (*b* at Dorsten 11 May
1970).
[*Schloßplatz 2a, 32756 Detmold, Germany*].

2. Princess *Victoria* Christine Agnes Berta, *b* at Berlin 7 May
1943; ✠ at Bonn 25 Aug 1988; *m* 1stly at Detmold 19 Sept
1968 (*m* diss by div at Bonn 26 April 1977), Wolfram Wickert
(*b* at Shanhai 30 May 1941). She *m* 2ndly at Bonn 7 Dec 1984,
Christoph Pudelko (*b* at Florence 23 Feb 1932), Art Dealer.
[*Heinrich von Kleiststraße 11, 53113 Bonn, Germany*].

2. Leopold Bernhard Wilhelm Friedrich Heinrich Alexis Otto, Prince
of Lippe, *b* at Detmold 19 May 1904; ✠ at Detmold 5 July 1965.

3. Princess Karoline (*Lilli*) August Adelheid Mathilde Marie Luise
Pauline, *b* at Detmold 4 Aug 1905, *m* at Detmold 29 Sept 1932, Hans,
Count von Kanitz (*b* at Podangen 17 Nov 1893; ✠ at Bückeburg 25
Aug 1968), Major-Gen (ret).
[*Thomas Mannstraße 54, 31707 Bad Eilsen, Germany*].

4. Prince *Chlodwig* Luitpold Friedrich August Georg Rudolf
Christian Maximilian, *b* at Detmold 27 Sept 1909; ✠ at Starnberg 13
Feb 2000; *m* at Munich 27 March 1940, Veronika (*b* at Worms 31 Dec
1915), dau of Georg Holl and Josephine Giggenbach, and has issue,
[*Riedener Weg 34, 82319 Starnberg, Germany*].

    1. Prince *Winfried-Chlodwig* Leopold Ernst Georg, *b* at Munich
21 April 1941, Banker, Art Dealer; *m* at Munich 6 July 1967,
Katharine (*b* at Vienna 13 Feb 1942), dau of George Henry
Rochman, Col US Army (ret) and Maria Reuser.
[*Riedener Weg 34, 82319 Starnberg Germany*].

5. Princess *Sieglinde* Bertha Elisabeth Adelheid Juliane Calma
Bathildis Marie Anna, *b* at Detmold 4 March 1915; *m* at Detmold 6
Dec 1942, Friedrich-Carl Heldman (*b* at Schötmar, Lippe 21 May
1904; ✠ at Detmold 26 April 1977), Businessman.
[*Hornschestraße 37, 32756 Detmold, Germany*].

Brothers of Father

Issue of of Count Ernst of Lippe (*b* 9 June 1842; ✝ 26 Sept 1904; Regent of Principality of Lippe from 22 June 1897) and Countess Karoline von Wartensleben (*b* 6 April 1844; *m* 16 Sept 1869; ✝ 10 July 1905).

1. Prince *Bernhard* Kasimir Friedrich Gustav Heinrich Wilhelm Eduard, *b* at Oberkassel 26 Aug 1872; ✝ at Munich 19 June 1934, Proprietor of Woynowo, Kr Bomst, Major Prussian Army; *m* at Ölber, Kr Wolfenbüttel 4 March 1909, Armgard (*b* at Driburg 18 Dec 1883; ✝ at Warmelo, Gmde Diepenheim, The Netherlands 27 April 1971; *m* 1stly at Hanover 24 Oct 1905, Bodo, Count von Oeynhausen who ✝ at Hanover 29 Nov 1909; that *m* diss by div at Paderborn 1908), *cr* Countess of Biesterfeld 8 Feb 1909 and Princess of Lippe-Biesterfeld with the qualification of Serene Highness 24 Feb 1916, dau of Baron Aschwin von Sierstorpff-Cramm, Counts of Driburg, etc and Baroness Hedwig von Sierstorpff of the Counts Driburg, and had issue, among whom (from 24 Feb 1916 Princes of Lippe-Biesterfeld with the qualification of Serene Highness),

    1. Prince *Bernhard* Leopold Friedrich Eberhard Julius Kurt Karl Gottfried Peter, *b* at Jena 29 June 1911, *cr* Prince of the Netherlands with the qualification of Royal Highness 7 Jan 1937, Land Commander of the Netherlands Order of St John of Jerusalem; *m* at The Hague 7 Jan 1937, Juliana, Queen of the Netherlands (*b* at The Hague 30 April 1909; *succ* on her mother's abdication 4 Sept 1948; abdicated in favour of her dau 30 April 1980 since when she has been known as a Princess of the Netherlands, Duchess of Mecklenburg), dau of Wilhelmina, Queen of the Netherlands and Heinrich, Duke of Mecklenburg, Prince of the Netherlands, and has issue (see that family).

    [*Palace Soestdijk, 3744 AA Baarn, Prov. Utrecht, Netherlands*].

2. Prince *Julius Ernst* Rudolf Friedrich Franz Viktor, *b* at Oberkassel 2 Sept 1870, ✝ there 15 Sept 1952, Dr of Law, Kt of St John of Jerusalem; *m* at Neustrelitz 11 Aug 1914, Duchess Marie (*b* at Neustrelitz 8 May 1878; ✝ at Oberkassel 14 Oct 1948; *m* 1stly at Richmond, Kew, London 22 June 1899, Georges Jametel, comes romanus since 8 May 1886; that *m* diss by div 31 Dec 1908), dau of Adolf Friedrich, Grand Duke of Mecklenburg-Strelitz and Princess Elisabeth of Anhalt, and had issue,

1. Princess *Elisabeth Caroline* Adelheid Friederike Leopoldine Armgard, *b* at Dresden-Blasewitz 23 Jan 1916; *m* at Dresden 15 Feb 1939, Ernst-August, Prince zu Solms-Braunfels (*b* at Darmstadt 10 March 1892; ✝ at Karlsruhe 24 July 1968), Dr of Law, Lawyer, Major (ret).
[*Lichtentaler Allee 100, 76530 Baden-Baden, Germany*].

2. Prince *Ernst August* Bernhard Alexander Eduard Friedrich Wilhelm, *b* at Dresden-Blasewitz 1 April 1917; ✝ at Ansbach 13 June 1990, Proprietor of Hohenzieritz and Zippelow with Forst Rosenholz, Mecklenburg, Kt of Honour of St John of Jerusalem; *m* at Oberkassel, nr Bonn 3 March 1948, Christa Irene (*b* at Leipzig 2 July 1923), Dame Bavarian Order of St Theresia, dau of Curt von Arnim, Proprietor of Kitzscher and Otterwisch and Stephanie von Stechow, and has issue,
[*Fünfbronn 22, 91174 Spalt, Germany*].

    1. Prince *Friedrich Wilhelm* Ernst Victor Alexander, *b* at Neuwied 7 Sept 1947, Business Manager; *m* at Munich 18 Sept 1991 (civ), Andrea (*b* at Rio de Janeiro, Brazil 9 Feb 1966), dau of Günther Messner and Lieselotte Trzoska, and has issue,
    [*Deisenhofenerstraße 51, 81539 Munich, Germany*].

        1. Princess *Catharina* Celeste Andrea Frieda, *b* at Munich 20 Sept 1991.
        2. Princess *Marie Christine* Adelheid Dominique Natascha Ursula, *b* at Starnberg, nr Munich 25 Aug 1996.

    2. Princess *Marie Stephanie* Elisabeth Caroline Gloria, *b* at Beuel, nr Bonn 26 Aug 1949; *m* 1stly at Bonn 30 April (civ) and at Schloß Syburg, nr Treuchtlingen, MFranken 8 May (relig) 1971 (*m* diss by div at Bonn 14 Nov 1985), Nikolaus von Itzenplitz (*b* at Grieben, nr Stendal 7 Feb 1943). She *m* 2ndly at Bad Homburg 12 Oct 1989 (*m* diss by div at Bad Homburg 12 April 1995), Wulf, Baron von Schimmelmann (*b* at Steinhöring, Kr Ebersberg, Bavaria 19 Feb 1947), Prof, Dr.
    [*In der Steingasse 24, 61440 Oberursel, Germany*].

    3. Prince *Ernst August* Friedrich Carl Georg Wilhelm, *b* at Bonn 24 Dec 1952, Dipl Economics; *m* at Heidelberg 22 May (civ) and at Bodman am Bodensee

14 June (relig) 1981 (*m* diss by div at Essen 4 Oct 1990), Countess Maria Benedicta (*b* at Stuttgart 18 Oct 1959), dau of Johannes (Hans), Count von Magnis and Baroness Bernhardine von Salmuth, and has issue, [*Funfbronn 22, 91174 Spalt, Germany*].

> 1. Princess *Maria Donata* Bernhardine Margarethe Stephanie Millona Annunziata, *b* at Bonn 7 Feb 1982.

4. Princess Regina *Marie Christine* Emanuela Anna Charlotte Friederike Juliane, *b* at Bonn 13 Dec 1959; *m* at Spalt, MFranken 11 Nov (civ) and at Fünfbronn, nr Spalt 12 Nov (relig) 1983, Peter Clemens Jacubowsky (*b* at Rio de Janeiro 14 July 1953), lic oec, HSG, Ind Financial Consultant.
[*Herzbachweg 6, 63571 Gelnhausen, Germany*].

Brothers of Grandfather

Issue of Count Julius (*b* 2 April 1812; ✝ 17 May 1884) and Countess Adelheid zu Castell-Castell (*b* 18 June 1818; *m* 30 April 1839; ✝ 11 July 1900), having had issue, among whom,

Sons

1. Prince *Rudolf* Wolfgang Ludwig Ernst Leopold, *b* at Neudorf, nr Bentschen, Posen 27 April 1856; ✝ at Drogelwitz, nr Weissholz, Glogau 21 June 1931, Major Prussian Army, Kt of St John of Jerusalem; *m* at Dresden 2 Nov 1889, Princess Luise (*b* at Langenselbold, nr Hanau 12 Dec 1868; ✝ at Meerholz, Gelnhausen 21 Nov 1959), *cr* Princess of Ardeck 28 July 1876, dau of Wilhelm, Prince of Hesse-Philippsthal-Barchfeld and Princess Marie of Hanau, Countess of Schaumburg, since 28 July 1876 Princess of Ardeck, and had issue,

> 1. Prince August *Friedrich Wilhelm*, *b* at Berlin 27 Nov 1890, ✝ there 24 Oct 1938, Major; *m* at Breslau 1 July 1932, Godela (*b* at Glogau 17 Dec 1906; ✝ at Lemgo 2 Nov 1989), dau of Eberhard von Oven and Maria Wittkop, and had issue,
>
>> 1. Prince *Rudolf* Ludwig Eberhard Bernhard, *b* at Berlin 8 Jan 1937, Dr of Phil, Dipl Economics, Prof of Social Philosophy and Aesthetics University of Oldenburg, Prof for the Philosophy of Lifeforms, University of Witten; *m* at Paris 4 April 1979, Béatrice (*b* at Nice 9 July 1943; *m* 1stly at Paris

30 April 1970, Bernard, Marquess de Grammont; that
m diss by div at Paris 18 March 1977/22 Nov 1978),
dau of Jean Colonna de Giovellina and Yvonne
Amoretti, and has issue,
[*Kloster, 27798 Hude bei Oldenburg, Germany*].

    1. Prince Jean *Friedrich* Christian Wladimir
    Hermann Simon Henrich, *b* at Berlin 11 Jan
    1982.

2. Princess *Marie Adelheid* Mathilde Karoline Elise Alexe
Auguste Albertine, *b* at Drogelwitz 30 Aug 1895; ✠ at
Tangstedt, Kr Stormarn 25 Dec 1993, since 22 Oct 1936 she
bore the name Princess Reuss zur Lippe; *m* 1stly at Drogelwitz
19 May 1920 (*m* diss by div at Guben 18 Feb 1921), Heinrich
XXXII, Prince Reuss (*b* at Constantinople 4 March 1878; ✠
at Bad Tölz 6 May 1935); *m* 2ndly at Bremen 12 April 1921 (*m*
diss by div at Berlin 23 June 1923), Heinrich XXXV, Prince
Reuss (*b* at Mauer, nr Vienna 1 Aug 1887; ✠ at Dresden-
Loschwitz 17 Jan 1936); *m* 3rdly at Berlin 24 Feb 1927 (*m* diss
by div at Berlin 2 Oct 1936), Friedrich Kurt (Hanno)
Konopath (*b* at Berlin 24 Feb 1882; ✠ at Hamburg 22 Sept
1962).

2. Prince *Friedrich Wilhelm* Franz Julius Ludwig Calixt, *b* at Neudorf,
nr Bentschen 16 July 1858; *ka* at Liège 6 Aug 1914, Col and Cmdr Inf
Rgts 74; *m* at Meerholz 10 Jan 1895, Countess Gisela (*b* at Meerholz
27 May 1871; ✠ at Gelnhausen 22 June 1964), dau of Carl, Count zu
Isenburg and Büdingen in Meerholz and Princess Agnes zu Isenburg
and Büdingen in Büdingen, and had issue, among whom,

    1. Prince *Simon Casimir* Rudolf Gustav Wolfgang Otto
    Friedrich, *b* at Potsdam 24 Sept 1900; ✠ at Gauting-Stockdorf
    9 Dec 1980, Lt-Col, Kt of St John of Jerusalem; *m* at Stettin
    17 Oct 1935, Ilse (*b* at Lindenfeld, nr Labes, Pommern 1 May
    1909), dau of Paul Splittgerber, Proprietor of Lindenfelde
    and Elisabeth Afheldt.
    [*Wohnstift Augustinum, Römerweg 9, 32756 Detmold,
    Germany*].

II: LINE OF LIPPE-WEISSENFELD

Reformist and Catholic: Founded by Ferdinand Johann Ludwig,
Count and Noble Lord of Lippe-Weissenfeld (*b* 22 Aug 1709; ✠ 18
June 1781); ceded Weissenfeld to the reigning Line of Lippe-Detmold
24 May 1762; the Branches below descend from two sons of the

Founder.

Arms:- Quarterly of four 1st and 4th arg, a rose gu barbed and seeded ppr (Lippe); 2nd and 3rd gu, a swallow close ppr perched upon a star of eight points or (Schwalenberg). The shield is ensigned ba the Princely Crown. Supporters:- Two Angels vested of a dalmatic, that of the dexter charged within the arms of Lippe, and that of the sinister charged with the arms of Schwalenberg and holding a banner with the arms of Schwalenberg.

Members of Line II of Lippe-Weissenfeld bear the title of Prince or Princess zur Lippe-Weissenfeld with the qualification of Serene Highness.

1st Branch

Founded by Count Friedrich Ludwig (*b* 2 Sept 1737; ✝ 14 May 1791); his sons founded the two Sub-Branches below:

✝ 1st Sub-Branch ✝

Founded by Count Ferdinand (*b* 20 Nov 1772; ✝ 21 June 1846). This Sub-Branch is now extinct.

2nd Sub-Branch

Founded by Count Christian (*b* 21 Feb 1777; ✝ 21 Oct 1859).
Members of this Branch bear the title of Prince or Princess with the qualification of Serene Highness.

CLEMENS, PRINCE OF LIPPE-WEISSENFELD, *b* at Dresden 15 July 1860; ✝ at Proschnitz 29 April 1920, granted the title of Prince zur Lippe-Weissenfeld and the qualification of Serene Highness for himself, his wife and their descendants at Detmold 28 Feb 1916, Cmdr St John of Jerusalem, son of Count Franz (*b* 17 Sept 1820; ✝ 26 July 1880) and Baroness Marie von Beschwitz (*b* 20 Aug 1836; *m* 11 May 1859; ✝ 30 Aug 1921); *m* at Proschwitz 7 Jan 1901, Friederike (Frieda) (*b* at Proschwitz 24 Aug 1878; ✝ at Meissen 25 Jan 1942), *cr* Baroness at Dresden 21 Dec 1900, Proprietor of Proschwitz, in Meissen and Gersdorf, nr Rosswein, dau of Dietrich von Carolowitz, Proprietor of Proschwitz and Johanne von Arnim, Proprietor of Oberau, nr Meissen and Gersdorf.

Sons

1 **Prince Carl Franz Ferdinand,** *b* at Dresden 16 July 1903; *ka* nr Lublin, Poland 26 Sept 1939, Proprietor of Baruth with Buchwalde and Rackel, etc, Lt; *m* at Guteborn, nr Ruhland 5 Sept 1928, Princess Dorothea (*b* at Guteborn 3 Oct 1905; ✝ 17 Dec 2000), dau of Ulrich, Prince von Schönburg-Waldenburg, Proprietor of Guteborn, Silesia and Gusow, Mark and Princess Pauline zu Löwenstein-Wertheim-Freudenberg, and had issue,

1. Prince *Franz* Clemens Ulrich, *b* at Dresden 14 Oct 1929; ✠ at Aurich 1 July 1995, Dipl Land Management; *m* at Düsseldorf 28 Oct 1969 (*m* diss by div Dec 1980), Lucia (*b* at Düsseldorf 4 Aug 1922; *m* 1stly at Düsseldorf 31 Dec 1948, Josef Rudolf Ditgens; that *m* diss by div at Düsseldorf 16 Oct 1964), dau of Matthias Stassen and Maria Peters.
[*Duisbergerstraße 34, 40477 Düsseldorf, Germany*].

2. Princess *Margarete* Friederike Pauline, *b* at Dresden 28 April 1932, Teacher Secondary School; *m* at Minden, Westfalen 27 June 1969, Heyo Hamer (*b* at Mettmann, Bez Düsseldorf 12 Oct 1931), Dipl Ed, Dr Ed Prof hc.
[*Hindenburgstraße 19, 26789 Leer, Germany*].

2. Prince Theodor Georg Ludwig *Christian*, *b* at Döberkitz 12 Aug 1907; ✠ at Bischofsheim, Rhön 24 Oct 1996, Proprietor of Teichnitz, nr Bautzen, Lubachau, nr Kleinwelka, Proschwitz, nr Meissen, Gersdorf, nr Rosswein, and Sornitz, Dipl Land Management; *m* at Bayerhof, UFranken 17 Oct 1935, Countess Pauline (*b* at Bayerhof 3 Dec 1913; ✠ at Bischofsheim 5 March 2002), dau of Friedrich, Count zu Ortenburg and Princess Ilka zu Löwenstein-Wertheim-Freudenberg, and had issue,

    1. Prince *Clemens* Friedrich-Ludwig Bernhard Simon-Ferdinand, *b* at Dresden 16 Sept 1937, Dipl Engineer; *m* at Schweinfurt 11 Jan 1964 (*m* diss by div 1988), Heidi [*Pemperion Oaks, 3006 Montfort Loop, Richmond 2, VA 23294, U.S.A.*] (*b* at Schweinfurt 23 Feb 1940), dau of Julius Fery and Elisabetha Maienberger, and has issue,
    [*Lynwood Drive, Rte. 3, Box 499, Madison Heights, VA. 24572, U.S.A.*].

        1. Prince *Jan Hendrik* Christian, *b* at Bridgeport, Connecticut, USA 26 Aug 1970; *m* at Naruna, Virginia 17 July 1993 (*m* diss by div 1996), Tara Ninette Jones (*b* at ....).
        [*Lynwood Drive, Rte. 3, Box 499, Madison Heights, VA. 24572, U.S.A.*].

        2. Princess *Christine-Elisabeth*, *b* at Shelton, Connecticut 19 July 1973.
        [*Lynwood Drive, Rte. 3, Box 499, Madison Heights, VA. 24572, U.S.A.*].

2. Prince *Friedrich* Christian Hermann Georg Heinrich, *b* at Dresden 18 March 1939, Management Consultant.
[*Cronstettenstraße 32, 60322 Frankfurt-am-Main, Germany*].

3. Princess *Elisabeth* Ilka Friederike Anna-Luise, *b* at Bautzen 8 Dec 1940; *m* at Bischofsheim, Rhön 8 July (civ) and 4 Aug (relig) 1961, Prosper, Count zu Castell-Castell (*b* at Köstritz 4 Sept 1922; ✠ at Frankfurt-am-Main 3 Jan 1989), Cmmdr in Bavaria St John of Jerusalem.
[*La Rosa di Pietra Latera, 05017 Monteleone d'Orvieto, Prov. Terni, Italy*].

4. Prince *Ferdinand* Jobst Hermann Carl Ernst Joachim, *b* at Bautzen 14 Nov 1942, Management Consultant, Businessman, Kt of Justice St John of Jerusalem; *m* at Munich 18 June (civ) and 19 June (relig) 1970, Baroness Karoline (*b* at Plauen, Vogtland 30 Nov 1939), Music Teacher, dau of Joachim, Baron von Feilitzsch, Proprietor of Kürbitz, Vogtland and Ilse von Feilitzsch, and has issue,
[*Mozartstraße 9, 32756 Detmold, Germany*].

    1. Princess *Felizitas*, *b* at Höxter, Westfalen 20 March 1971.
    [*Mozartstraße 9, 32756 Detmold, Germany*].
    2. Princess *Ilka*, *b* at Munich 20 Jan 1973.
    [*Mozartstraße 9, 32756 Detmold, Germany*].
    3. Prince *Ferdinand*, *b* at Detmold 5 Sept 1976.
    [*Mozartstraße 9, 32756 Detmold, Germany*].

5. Prince *Christian* Franz Georg, *b* at Teichnitz 18 Oct 1945, Dr of Med, Dipl Business Studies, Kt of Hon St John of Jerusalem.
[*Cronstettenstraße 32, 60322 Frankfurt-am-Main, Germany; Johanniter Krankenhaus, Sedlitzerstraße 2, 1809 Heidenau, Germany*].

6. Prince *Georg* Christian Heinrich Herbert Bernhard, *b* at Schweinfurt 25 June 1957, Dr of Economics, Dipl. Ing. Agriculture, Hon. Consul of the Kingdom of the Netherlands, Proprietor of Proschwitz; *m* at Meissen-Proschwitz 1 Oct 1995, Alexandra (*b* at Kassel 18 Dec 1963),Mag.pol., TV-Journalist , dau of Dietrich Gerlach (Colonel) and Agnes von Rumohr.
[*Wilsdrufferstraße 12, 01662 Meissen, Germany*].

2nd Branch

Founded by Count Karl Christian (*b* 15 Aug 1740; ✠ 5 April 1808); the Sub-Branches below were founded by his sons.

1st Sub-Branch
Founded by Count Bernhard (*b* 22 Feb 1779; ✠ 7 Aug 1857).

Armin Hugo Bernhard Frithjof Hermann **KURT, PRINCE OF LIPPE-WEISSENFELD,** *b* at Jena 5 March 1855; ✠ at Schliersee, Bavaria 10 Oct 1934, granted the title of Prince zur Lippe-Weissenfeld and the qualification of Serene Highness for himself, his wife and their descendants at Detmold 9 Nov 1918, Proprietor of See, nr Niesky, OLausitz; *m* 1stly at Dresden 10 Oct 1885 (*m* diss by div at Niesky 18 Jan 1924), Sophie (*b* at Dresden 9 April 1857; ✠ at Niesky, OLausitz 18 Feb 1945), dau of Ernst von Klengel and Countess Pauline zur Lippe-Weissenfeld. He *m* 2ndly at Schliersee 3 Feb 1924, Johanna (*b* at Haynau, Silesia 16 June 1894; missing from 1945 ✠ at Stuttgart 28 March 1987), dau of Rudolf Krischke and Alice Nay, and has issue by his first wife, among whom,

Sons and Daughters

1. Prince *Karl Christian,* *b* at Martinswaldau, nr Kaiserswaldau, Silesia 21 Oct 1889; ✠ at Jauer, Silesia 18 Sept 1942, Proprietor of See, nr Niesky, Dr of Phil; *m* at Dessau 26 July 1928, Hedwig-Maria (*b* at Stefanswalde, Bez Bremberg 29 Dec 1903; ✠ at Hamburg 29 Nov 1988), dau of Hans von Trotha of the House of Hecklingen and Countess Hedwig von der Schulenburg, Proprietor of Kruge, nr Eberswalde, and had issue,

    1. Prince *Karl-Christian* Jobst Hans Armin, *b* at Dessau 2 Sept 1930.

    [*Haus Steinburg, Martiniweg 6, 33617 Bielefeld - Bethel, Germany*].

2. Prince *Kurt Bernhard* Gottfried Andreas, *b* at See 4 July 1901; ✠ at Niesky 6 April 1961; *m* at Berlin 8 July 1941, Lilli (*b* at Berlin 15 Sept 1904 ✠ at Niesky 29 Oct 1997), dau of Friedrich Zetzsche and Elisabeth Rübner, and had issue,

    1. Prince *Frithjof-Ludwig* Bernd Gottfried Karl Jürgen, *b* at Oberschreiberhau, Riesengebirge 24 Nov 1943; *m* at Leuthen, nr Cottbus 7 Dec 1968, Regina (*b* at Leuthen 27 March 1949), dau of Arthur Rheinhold Endermann and Ursula Krause, and has issue,

    [*Hauptstraße 1, 03058 Schorbus bei Cottbus, Germany*].

        1. Prince *Torsten* Frithjof, *b* at Cottbus 7 March 1969.

        2. Prince *Sven,* *b* at Cottbus 18 Nov 1974.

2nd Sub-Branch

Catholic: Founded by Count Hermann (*b* 20 March 1783; ✝ 21 Feb 1841).

ALFRED Karl Friedrich Georg Franz, **PRINCE OF LIPPE-WEISSENFELD**, *b* at Vienna 22 Aug 1922, Dr of Phil, Kt of Hon Sovereign Military Order of Malta, son of Prince Alfred, (*b* at Scheibbs, Lower Austria 6 Feb 1896; ✝ at Baden, nr Vienna 4 Jan 1970; granted the title of Prince with the qualification of Serene Highness at Detmold 9 Nov 1918);and Countess Franziska (*b* at Schönborn 14 Dec 1902; *m* 3 Aug 1921; *m* diss by div at 27 July 1932; ✝ at Zurich 12 Sept 1987); *m* at Innsbruck 26 March (civ) and 11 June (relig) 1955, Baroness Irmgard (*b* at Dornbirn, Vorarlberg 22 Jan 1929), dau of Gustav, Baron Wagner von Wehrborn and Elisabeth Hämmerle, and has issue,

[*Berg, 4880 St. Georgen am Attersee, Austria*].

Son and Daughters

1. Princess *Teresa*, *b* at Innsbruck 19 March 1956, Interior Decorator.

[*Weikl-Villa, 5020 Salzburg, Austria*].

2. Princess *Elisabeth*, *b* at Munich 28 July 1957; *m* at Glücksburg 23 Sept (civ) and 3 Oct (relig) 1981, Prince Christoph of Schleswig-Holstein-Sonderburg-Glücksburg (*b* at Schloß Louisenlund, nr Schleswig 22 Aug 1949), Dipl Engineer Agriculture.

[*Gut Grünholz, 24351 Damp, Ostholstein, Germany*].

3. Prince *Bernhard* Friedrich Karl Georg Heinrich, *b* at Geneva 8 Feb 1960, Mag oec; *m* at Grünwald 17 Nov 1994 (civ) and at Munich 13 May 1995 (relig), Nina Alexandra (*b* at Frankfurt-am-Main 20 May 1968), Mag oec, dau of Jochen Mackenrodt and Sibylle Fahr.

[*Via Giovanni Lanza 146, 00184 Rome, Italy; Goldgasse13, 5020 Salzburg, Austria*].

Sister

1. Princess *Teresa* Amalia Franziska Elisabeth Maria, *b* at Vienna 21 July 1925, *m* 1stly at Lugano 1 Aug 1948 (*m* diss by div at Lugano 14 May 1954), Heinrich, Baron Thyssen-Bornemisza (*b* at The Hague 2 April 1921; ✝ at Spain 26 April 2002), Industrialist; *m* 2ndly at Kloten, nr Zurich 9 April 1960, Friedrich Maximilian, Prince zu Fürstenberg (*b* at Schloß Wechselburg, Saxony 26 July 1926; ✝ at

Vienna 2 Nov 1969), Businessman.
[*Schloß Werenwag, 88631 Beuron-Hausen, Germany*].

Brother of Grandfather

Issue of Oktavio, Count and Noble Lord of Lippe-Weissenfeld (*b* 6
Nov 1808; ✠ 13 Feb 1885) and his first wife, Countess Maria von
Mengersen (*b* at Rheder, Westfalen 4 Aug 1809; *m* 24 Oct 1833; ✠ at
Teplitz 26 Feb 1863), having had issue, among whom,

Son

1. Count Egmont (*b* 10 May 1841; ✠ 22 July 1896) and Baroness
Karola von Stillfried and Rathenitz (*b* 22 May 1847; *m* 16 April 1879;
✠ 7 Sept 1925), granted the title of Prince with the qualification of
Serene Highness at Detmold 9 Nov 1918) and had issue among whom,

    1. Prince *Alfred* Rudolf Maria Egmont, *b* at Prerau 26 May
    1881; ✠ at Goldegg, nr St Pölten 14 March 1960, granted the
    title of Prince with the qualification of Serene Highness for
    himself, his wife and their descendants at Detmold 9 Nov
    1918; *m* at Ebenthal, Carinthia 30 July 1917, Countess Anna
    (*b* at Ebenthal 28 July 1895; ✠ at Goldegg 27 July 1972),
    Dame Star Cross Order, dau of Leopold, Count von Goëss,
    Proprietor of Ebenthal, etc, and Countess Marianne von Thurn
    and Valsassina-Como-Vercelli, and had issue, among whom,

        1. Princess *Sophie* Marianne Theresa Josephine Petra
        Paula Hippolyta, *b* at Alt-Wartenburg 29 June 1922;
        m at Walcher, nr Vöcklamarkt, Upper Austria 15
        March 1950, Sergio Figueroa Tagle (*b* at Santiago de
        Chile 21 July 1923).
        [*Manoir de Mongareaux, 77320 La Ferté Gaucher,*
        France].
        2. Princess *Theodora* Maria Helene Leopoldine Georgine
        Ricarda Pascala, *b* at Alt-Wartenburg 4 April 1924,
        Dame Star Cross Order; *m* at Salzburg 17 Aug 1946,
        Franz Weikhard, Prince von Auersperg (*b* at Goldegg,
        nr St Pölten 19 Feb 1923), Proprietor of Goldegg.
        [*Schloß Goldegg, 3100 St. Pölten, NÖsterr., Austria*].

B. SCHAUMBURG-LIPPE
(See that Family)

LUXEMBOURG
(HOUSE OF NASSAU)

Founded by Rutbert, Count of Zutphen 1059, who married Ermentrud of Hammerstein, dau of Conradin, Count Otto of Hammerstein (✠ 1036), who inherited possessions situated between the Lahn and the Sieg; Counts of Nassau (an der Lahn) in the eleventh century; partition of possessions 12 Dec 1255 between two sons of Count Heinrich (✠ 1254), Walram (see below) and Otto (see The Netherlands).

Line of Walram

Catholic and Evangelical: Founded by Walram, Count of Nassau, Idstein, Wiesbaden and Weilburg (✠ 1289); King of the Romans 6 Jan 1292 - July 1298; Princely Count of Nassau, Würzburg 1366; the dignity of Prince of the Holy Empire was confirmed and renewed, Vienna 4 Aug 1688 and Vienna 5 Sept 1737; Imperial confirmation of the order of primogeniture 6 Oct 1755 and 10 Dec 1766; a Treaty of Succession was concluded with the cadet Line of Otto (The Netherlands), 30 June 1783; qualification of "Durchlauchtigst Hochgeboren" (primogeniture), Vienna 3 Dec 1784; Duke of Nassau-Usingen 30 Aug 1806; Duke of Nassau, Count of Katzenelnbogen and Diet, etc 24 March 1816; the Duchy of Nassau was united with the Kingdom of Prussia by Prussian Decree 20 Sept 1866; Treaty concluded between the Duke and the Kingdom of Prussia at the end of Sept 1867; Grand Duke of Luxembourg at the extinction in the male line of the cadet Line of Otto (see The Netherlands) 23 Nov 1890; Family Statute of 16 April 1907 allowed for the eventual succession through the female line.

Arms:- Quarterly: 1st, and 4th, az, semée of billetes or, a lion rampant and crowned or, armed and langued gu (Nassau); 2nd and 3rd, barry of ten arg and az, a lion queue fourchée gu, armed, langued and crowned or (Luxembourg). The shield is ensigned with the Royal Crown, without a cap. *Supporters:-* Two lions reguardant or, armed and langued gu. *Motto:-* Ich dien. The achievement is borne on a mantle gu, fringed and tasselled or, doubled erm and surmounted by the Royal Crown, without a cap.

Members of the Grand Ducal family bore the title of Prince or Princess of Luxembourg, Bourbon-Parma and Nassau with the qualification of Royal Highness until 1986, since when they have been styled "Nassau", Prince or Princess of Luxembourg with the qualification of Royal Highness.

HENRI Albert Gabriel Felix Marie Guillaume, **GRAND DUKE OF LUXEMBOURG,** Duke of Nassau, Prince of Bourbon-Parma, Count Palatine of the Rhine, Count of Sayn, Königstein, Katzenelnbogen and Dietz, Burggrave of Hammerstein, Lord of

Mahlberg, Wiesbaden, Idstein, Merenberg, Limburg and Eppstein, following the abdication of his father on 18 Dec 2000, *b* at Schloß Betzdorf 16 April 1955, son of Grand Duke Jean, Grand Duke of Luxembourg, former Head of the Grand Ducal House of Luxembourg (*b* 5 Jan 1921; abdicated as Sovereign and as Head of the Grand Ducal House on 7 Oct 2000 - see below) and Princess Joséphine-Charlotte of Belgium (*b* 11 Oct 1927); *m* at Luxembourg 14 Feb 1981, María Teresa (*b* at Marianao, Havana, Cuba 22 March 1956), dau of Don José Antonio Mestre y Alvarez-Tabio and María Teresa Batista y Falla.
[*Schloß Fischbach, 2013 Luxembourg*].

Sons and Daughters

1. Crown Prince *Guillaume* Jean Joseph Marie, Hereditary Grand Duke of Luxembourg, Prince of Nassau, etc, from 18 Dec 2000, *b* at Luxembourg 11 Nov 1981, Kt of the Golden Lion of the House of Nassau.
2. Prince *Félix* Léopold Marie Guillaume, *b* at Luxembourg 3 June 1984.
3. Prince *Louis* Xavier Marie Guillaume, *b* at Luxembourg 3 Aug 1986.
4. Princess *Alexandra* Joséphine Teresa Charlotte Marie Wilhelmine, *b* at Luxembourg 16 Feb 1991.
5. Prince *Sébastien* Henri Marie Guillaume, *b* at Luxembourg 16 April 1992.

Father and Mother

Jean Benoit Guillaume Marie Robert Louis Antoine Adolphe Marc d'Aviano, **Grand Duke of Luxembourg,** Duke of Nassau, Prince of Bourbon-Parma, Count Palatine of the Rhine, Count of Sayn, Königstein, Katzenelnbogen and Dietz, Burggrave of Hammerstein, Lord of Mahlberg, Wiesbaden, Idstein, Merenberg, Limburg and Eppstein, abdicated as Sovereign Grand Duke of Luxembourg on 7 Oct 2000, in favour of eldest his son and heir, Crown Prince Henri Albert Gabriel Felix Marie Guillaume, Hereditary Grand Duke of Luxembourg, *b* at Colmar-Berg 5 Jan 1921, Lieut-Rep Grand Duchy 4 May 1961 - 12 Nov 1964, Kt Gd Cross Order of the Golden Lion of Nassau, Order of the Oaken Crown, and of Civ and Mil Order of Merit of Adolphe of Nassau, KG 1973, Kt Gd Cross Order of Malta, Order of Holy Sepulchre, and of the Constantinian Order of St George, Gd Collar Order of the Golden Spur (Holy See), Kt Gd

Cross Order of the Seraphim (Sweden), Order of Pius IX (Holy See), Order of Leopold I (Belgium), Order of the Lion (The Netherlands), and Gd Cross Legion d'Honneur (France); *m* at Luxembourg 9 April 1953, Princess Joséphine-Charlotte (*b* at Brussels 11 Oct 1927), dau of Léopold III, King of the Belgians and Princess Astrid of Sweden. [*Schloß Berg, 7710 Colmar-Berg, Luxembourg*].

Brothers and Sisters

1. Princess *Marie Astrid* Charlotte Léopoldine Wilhelmine Ingeborg Antonia Elisabeth Anne Alberte, *b* at Betzdorf 17 Feb 1954; *m* at Luxemburg 6 Feb 1982, Archduke Karl Christian of Austria (*b* at Château de Beloeil 26 Aug 1954), Bank Director.
[*30 Route de Covéry, 1252 Meinier, Kt. Genf, Switzerland*].

2. Prince *Jean* Felix Marie Guillaume, *b* at Betzdorf 15 May 1957, renounced his rights to the Throne 26 Sept 1986 and assumed the name of Jean Nassau; *m* at Paris 27 May (civ) and 28 May (relig) 1987, Hélene Suzanne (*b* at St Germain-en-Laye 31 May 1958), *cr.* Countess of Nassau by Royal Decree 21 Sept 1995, dau of François Vestur and Cécile Ernestine Buisson, and has issue,
[*2 avenue Ingres, 75116 Paris, France*].

> 1. Countess *Marie-Gabrielle* Cécile Charlotte Sophie of Nassau, *b* at Paris 8 Sept 1986.
> 2. Count *Constantin* Jean Philippe Maric Albert Marc d'Aviano of Nassau, *b* at Paris 22 July 1988.
> 3. Count *Wenceslas* François Baudouin Léopold Juraj Marie Marc d'Aviano of Nassau, *b* at Paris 17 Nov 1990.
> 4. Count *Carl-Johan* Felix Juien Marc d'Aviano of Nassau, *b* at Paris 15 Aug 1992.

3. Princess *Marguerite* Antonia Marie Félicité, *b* at Betzdorf 15 May 1957 (twin with Prince Jean); *m* at Luxemburg 20 March 1982, Prince Nikolaus von und zu Liechtenstein (*b* at Zurich 24 Oct 1947), Ambassador for Liechtenstein to the Kingdom of Belgium and to the European Union; Ambassador to the Holy See, resident in Brussels, Kt of Hon and Dev Sovereign Military Order of Malta, Kt of Justice St John of Jerusalem.
[*Liechtensteinische Mission, 1 Place du Congrès 1000 Brussels, Belgium*]

4. Prince *Guillaume* Marie Louis Christian, *b* at Betzdorf 1 May 1963; *m* at Sélestat, Bas Rhin, France 8 Sept (civ) and at Versailles 24 Sept (relig) 1994, Sibilla (*b* at Paris 12 June 1968), dau of Paul-Annik Weiller and Donna Olimpia Torlonia of Princes di

Civitella-Cesi.
[*Palais grand-ducal, 2013 Luxembourg*].

    1. Prince *Paul-Louis* Jean Marie Guillaume, *b* at Luxembourg 4 March 1998.

    2. Prince *Leopold* Guillaume Marie Joseph, *b* at Luxembourg 2 May 2000.

    3. Princess *Charlotte* Wilhelmina Maria da Gloria, *b* at Luxembourg 2 May 2000 (twin with Prince Leopold).

Brothers and Sisters of Father

1. Princess *Elisabeth* Hilda Zita Marie Anne Antonia Frederique Wilhelmine Louise, *b* at Colmar-Berg 22 Dec 1922; *m* at Luxembourg 9 May 1956, Franz Ferdinand, Duke (Herzog) von Hohenberg (*b* at Artstetten 13 Sept 1927; ✠ at Ried in der Riedmark, Austria 15 Aug 1977).
[*Wasserhof, 2 rue du Moulin, 7430 Fischbach-Mersch, Luxembourg*].

2. Princess *Marie Adélaïde* Louise Thérèse Wilhelmine, *b* at Colmar-Berg 21 May 1924, Dame of Hon Sovereign Military Order of Malta; *m* at Luxembourg 10 April 1958, Carl Josef, Count Henckel von Donnersmarck (*b* at Romolkwitz, Neumarkt 7 Nov 1928), Lic rer oec.
[*Diethelmstraße, Fürigen, 6362 Obbürgen, NW, Switzerland*].

3. Princess *Marie Gabrielle* Adelgunde Wilhelmine Louise, *b* at Colmar-Berg 2 Aug 1925; *m* there 5 Nov (civ) and 6 Nov (relig) 1951, Knud, Count von Holstein-Ledreborg (*b* at Ledreborg 2 Oct 1919; ✠ there 25 June 2001).
[*Ledreborg, 4320 Lejre, Denmark*].

4. Prince *Charles* Frederic Louis Guillaume Marie, *b* at Colmar-Berg 7 Aug 1927; ✠ at Imbarcati, Prov Pistoia, Italy 26 July 1977; *m* at Guildford, Surrey, England 1 March 1967, Joan Douglas (*b* at New York USA 31 Jan 1935; *m* 1stly, James B Moseley; that *m* diss by div at Washoe, Nevada USA 12 Dec 1955 and ecclesiastically annulled at Rome 22 June 1963; *m* 3rdly at Isleboro, Maine, USA 3 Aug 1978, Philippe de Noailles, 8th Duke de Mouchy, Prince-Duke de Poix), dau of Clarence Douglas Dillon and Phyllis C Ellsworth, and has issue,
[*Château de Mouchy, Mouchy-le-Chatel, 60250 Jouy, Oise, France*].

    1. Princess *Charlotte* Phyllis Anne Joel, *b* at New York 15 Sept 1967; *m* at Mouchy-le-Chatel, Oise, France 26 June (civ) and at St Rémy-de-Provence 18 Sept (relig) 1993, Mark Victor Cunningham (*b* at Harrogate 24 Sept 1965).

2. Prince *Robert* Louis Francois Marie, *b* at Fischbach 14 Aug 1968; *m* at Boston, Mass, USA 29 Jan 1994, June Elizabeth Houston (*b* at Louisville, Kentucky 9 June 1966), *cr.* Countess of Nassau by Royal Decree, dau of Dr Theodore Ongaro and Katherine Houston.

    1. Countess *Charlotte* of Nassau, *b* at Boston U.S.A. 20 March 1995.

    2. Count *Alexander* of Nassau, *b* at Aix-en-Provence 19 April 1997.

5. Princess *Alix* Marie Anne Antonia Charlotte Gabrielle, *b* at Colmar-Berg 24 Aug 1929; *m* at Luxembourg 17 Aug 1950, Antoine, 14th Prince de Ligne (*b* at Brussels 8 March 1925).
[*Château de Beloeil, 7979 Beloeil, Hainaut, Belgium*].

MECKLENBURG

Lutheran and Catholic: Founded by Niklot, the heathen Prince of the Obotrites, the Chizzini and the Circipani (1131), Lord of Schwerin (✝ 1160); Prince of the Holy Empire 1170; Prince of Mecklenburg 1166; Lord of Stargard 15 Jan 1304; Lord of Rostock 21 May 1323; Duke of Mecklenburg 8 July 1348; Count of Schwerin 31 Mar 1359; Prince of Wenden 1436; Prince of Schwerin and Ratzeburg 21 Oct 1648; The two lines below descend from a grandson and a son of Duke Adolph Fridrich I (✝ 27 Feb 1658).

Arms:- Quarterly of six: 1st, or, a buffalo's head cabossed sa, armed and ringed arg, crowned or and langued gu (Duchy of Mecklenburg); 2nd, az, a griffin segreant (Lordship of Rostock) or (Principality of Wenden); 3rd, per fess, in chief az, a griffin segreant or, and in base vert, a bordure arg (Principality of Schwerin); 4th, gu, a cross patée arg crowned or (Principality of Ratzeburg); 5th, gu, a dexter arm arg issuant from clouds arg in sinister flank and holding a finger ring or (County of Schwerin); 6th, or, a buffalo's head oblique sa, armed arg, crowned or and langued gu (Principality of Wenden); over all, an escutcheon of pretence, per fess gu and or (County of Schwerin). The shield is ensigned by the Royal Crown without a cap. *Supporters:-* Dexter, a buffalo rampant reguardant sa (Mecklenburg); sinister, a griffin or. The achievement is borne on a mantle gu, fringed and tasselled or, doubled erm and surmounted by a Grand Ducal Crown. *Mottoes:-* Avito viret honore (Mecklenburg-Strelitz); Per aspera ad astra (Mecklenburg-Schwerin).

I: ✝ MECKLENBURG-SCHWERIN ✝
(✝ Extinct ✝)
Founded by Duke Christian Ludwig II (*b* 25 May 1683; ✝ 30 May

1756), grandson of Adolf Friedrich I (see above); inherited Schwerin 11/21 June 1692, Güstrow 1695; the order of primogeniture was established 8 March 1701; Grand Duke 14 June 1815; abdication of the dynasty 14 Nov 1918. The House of Mecklenburg-Schwerin became on 31 July 2001.

Grand Dukes and Hereditary Grand Dukes and their wives bore the qualification of Royal Highness. Other members of the family bear the title of Duke or Duchess of Mecklenburg with the qualification of Highness.

✝ **FRIEDRICH FRANZ (V)** ✝ Michael Wilhelm Nikolaus Franz-Joseph Ernst August Hans, **HEREDITARY GRAND DUKE OF MECKLENBURG-SCHWERIN,** *b* at Schwerin 22 April 1910; ✝ at Blankensee 31 July 2001 son of Friedrich Franz IV, Grand Duke of Mecklenburg-Schwerin (*b* 9 April 1882; ✝ 17 Nov 1945) and Princess Alexandra of Hanover (*b* 29 Sept 1882; *m* 7 June 1904; ✝ 30 Aug 1963); *m* at Wiligrad 11 June 1941 (*m* diss by div 22 Sept 1967; remarried at Glücksburg 22 April 1977), Karin-Elisabeth (*b* at Breslau 31 Jan 1920), dau of Col Dr Walther von Schaper and Baroness Elisabeth-Luise von Münchhausen.

[*Oesterleystraße 49, 22587 Hamburg - Blankenese, Germany*].

Brother

1. Duke *Christian Ludwig* Ernst August Maximilian Johann Albrecht Adolf Friedrich, *b* at Ludwigslust 29 Sept 1912; ✝ at Eckernförde 18 July 1996, granted the qualification of Royal Highness by his father 1 Feb 1943; *m* at Glücksburg 5 July (civ) and 11 July (relig) 1954, Princess Barbara (*b* at Hemmelmark 2 Aug 1920; ✝ there 31 May 1994), dau of Prince Sigismund of Prussia and Princess Charlotte Agnes of Saxe-Altenburg, and adopted dau of her grandmother Irene, Princess Heinrich of Prussia, née Princess of Hesse and by Rhine, and has issue,

      1. Duchess *Donata*, *b* at Kiel 11 March 1956, Librarian; *m* at London 14 Aug (civ) and at Eckernförde, Holstein 19 Sept (relig) 1987, Alexander von Solodkoff (*b* at Cologne 20 Jan 1951).

      [*Hemmelmark, 24360 Schnepfenhaus, Germany; 21 Clonmel Road, London, S.W.6.*].

      2. Duchess *Edwina*, *b* at Kiel 25 Sept 1960; *m* at Eckernförde 20 Sept (civ) and 14 Oct (relig) 1995, Konrad von Posern (*b* at Innsbruck 24 July 1974)

      [*Hemmelmark, 24360 Schnepfenhaus, Germany; Schloß,*

09634 Hirschfeld/Sachsen, Germany].

Half-Brother of Grandfather

Issue of Friedrich Franz II, Grand Duke of Mecklenburg-Schwerin, etc (*b* 28 Feb 1823; ✠ 15 April 1883) and his third wife, Princess Marie of Schwarzburg-Rudolstadt (*b* 29 Jan 1850; *m* 4 July 1868; ✠ 22 April 1922) having had issue, among whom,

Son

Duke *Adolf Friedrich* Albrecht Heinrich, *b* at Schwerin 10 Oct 1873; ✠ at Eutin 5 Aug 1969, Dr hc Univ Rostock, Col Prussian Army, former Gov of Togo, Hon Pres of German Olympic Committee, Kt Order of Black Eagle, of the Seraphim, of the Elephant, of the Order of St Hubert and of the Order of the Crancelin, Kt of Hon Johaniter Order, etc; *m* 1stly at Gera 24 April 1917, Princess Victoria Feodora (*b* at Potsdam 21 April 1889; ✠ at Rostock 18 Dec 1918), dau of Henrich XXVII, Prince (Fürst) Reuss and Princess Elise zu Hohenlohe-Langenburg. He *m* 2ndly at Ludwigslust 15 Oct 1924, Princess Elisabeth (*b* at Rossla 23 June 1885; ✠ at Eutin 16 Oct 1969; *m* 1stly 15 Dec 1909, Duke Johann Albrecht of Mecklenburg who ✠ 16 Feb 1920), dau of Botho, Prince (Fürst) zu Stolberg-Rossla and Princess Hedwig zu Isenburg and Büdingen in Büdingen, and had issue by his first wife,

    1. Duchess *Woizlawa Feodora* Elise Marie Elisabeth, *b* at Rostock 17 Dec 1918; *m* at Bad Doberan, Mecklenburg 15 Sept 1939, Prince Heinrich I Reuss (*b* at Krietern, Kr Breslau 8 Oct 1910; ✠ at Büdingen, 10 March 1982).
    [*Am Pfaffenwald 12, 63654 Büdingen, Hesse, Germany; Otto Dix Straße 20, 07548 Gera, Germany].*

II: MECKLENBURG-STRELITZ

Founded by Duke Adolf Friedrich II (*b* 19 Oct 1658; ✠ 12 May 1708), son of Duke Adolf Friedrich I (see above); the order of primogeniture was established 8 March 1701; Grand Duke 28 June 1815; The throne became vacant 23 Feb 1918 on the death by suicide of Grand Duke Adolf Friedrich VI (*b* 17 June 1882). His heir, and first cousin once removed was Duke Carl Michael of Mecklenburg-Strelitz, who never assumed the title of Grand Duke, having renounced the succession privately by letter (received 1919 after the revolution), and become a naturalised Russian subject 7 Aug 1914, Lt-Gen Russian Army, Kt Order of St Andrew. He adopted his nephew (who was the son of his elder brother by a morganatic marriage to Natalia Feodorovna Wonlarskaja who was created Countess von Carlow by Friedrich

Wilhelm, Grand Duke of Mecklenburg-Strelitz 18 March 1890), Georg, Count von Carlow (*b* 5 Oct 1899; ✝ 6 July 1963) who assumed the title of Duke of Mecklenburg, which was confirmed and approved with the qualification of Serene Highness by Grand Duke Kyrill of Russia 18 July 1929, and recognized by the Grand Ducal House of Mecklenburg-Schwerin 23 Dec 1929, assumed the qualification of Highness 18 Dec 1950. The present Head of the family is his grandson. The Grand Dukes and their wives bore the qualification of Royal Highness. Other members of the family bear the title of Duke or Duchess of Mecklenburg with the qualification of Highness.

Georg-**BORWIN** Friedrich Franz Carl Stephan Konrad Hubertus Maria, **DUKE OF MECKLENBURG**, *b* at Freiburg-im-Breisgau 10 June 1956, son of Georg Alexander, Duke of Mecklenburg (*b* 27 Aug 1921; ✝ 26 Jan 1996) and Archduchess Helene (Ilona) of Austria (*b* 20 April 1927; *m* 20 Feb/30 April 1946; *m* diss by div 17 Dec 1974); *m* at Hinterzarten 24 Dec 1985 (civ) and at Hinterzarten, Schwarzwald 19 July 1986 (relig), Alice (*b* at Hinterzarten 2 Aug 1959), dau of Dr Jürgen-Detlev Wagner and Marianne Biehl, and has issue,

[*79856 Hinterzarten, Schwarzwald am Kesslerberg 1, Germany*].

Sons and Daughter

1. Duchess Helene *Olga* Feodora Donata Maria Katharina Theresia, *b* at Freiburg im Breisgau 13 Oct 1988.
2. Duke Georg *Alexander* Michael Heinrich Ernst Franz Ferdinand Maria, *b* at Freiburg im Breisgau 17 July 1991.
3. Duke Carl *Michael* Borwin Alexander Georg Friedrich Franz Hubertus Maria, *b* at Freiburg im Breisgau 30 Jan 1994.

Mother

Archduchess Helene (*Ilona*), Duchess of Mecklenburg, *b* at Budapest 20 April 1927, Dame Gd Cross Hon and Dev Sovereign Military Order of Malta, dau of Archduke Joseph Franz of Austria and Princess Anna of Saxony; *m* at Sigmaringen 20 Feb (civ) and 30 April (relig) 1946 (*m* diss by div at Freiburg im Breisgau 17 Dec 1974), *Georg Alexander* Andreas Carl Michael Peter Philipp Ignatius Maria, Duke of Meckenburg, *b* at Nice 27 Aug 1921; ✝ at Mirow 26 Jan 1996).

[*Fasanenstraße 9, 79110 Freiburg-Lehen, Germany*].

Sisters

1. Duchess *Elisabeth Christine* Auguste Louise Irene Anna Cecilie

Margarethe Maria Immaculata Scholastika Katharina Gabriele et omnes sancti, b at Sigmaringen 22 March 1947; m at Ludenscheid 15 Nov 1974 (civ) and at Burg Hohenzollern 3 May 1975 (relig) (m diss by div at Bonn 15 Dec 1997), Alhard, Baron von dem Bussche-Ippenburg, genannt von Kessell (b at Ippenburg 30 June 1947).

[*Viktoriastraße 15, 53173 Bonn, Germany*].

2. Duchess *Marie Katharina* Elisabeth Henriette Friederike Sophie Josephine et omnes sancti, b at Stuttgart 14 Nov 1949; m at Bonn 17 March (civ) and at Biengen 15 July (relig) 1978, Wolfgang Thaddäus von Wasiliewski (b at Bonn 15 Dec 1951).

[*Valhallastraße 8, 80639 Munich, Germany*].

3. Duchess Caroline Louise *Irene* Margarethe Helene Margarita Albertine Konrada, b at Frieburg-im-Breisgau 18 April 1952; m at Mexico City 22 Sept 1979 (civ) and at Biengen 26 July 1980, Constantin Harold Harmsen (b at Hamburg 28 April 1954), Banker.

[*Am Weigelsgarten 6, 60433 Frankfurt-am-Main, Germany*].

Brother of Father

Issue of of Georg, Duke of Mecklenburg, formerly Count von Carlow (see above) (b 5 Oct 1899; ✠ 6 July 1963; m 2ndly 25 July 1956, Archduchess Charlotte of Austria - b 1 March 1921; ✠ 23 July 1989) and his first wife, Irina Mikhailovna Raievskaja (b 18 Aug 1892; m 7 Oct 1920; ✠ 22 Jan 1955), having had issue among whom,

1. Duke *Carl Gregor* Georg Friedrich Franz Heinrich Norbert Wenceslaus Johann Nepomuk Lazarus Clemens Maria de Mercede et omnes sancti, b at Remplin 14 March 1933, Dr of Phil, MA, Art Historian, m at Hechlingen 18 Dec 1965 (civ) and at Burg Hohenzollern 23 April 1966 (relig), Princess Maria Margarete (b at Sigmaringen 2 Jan 1928), dau of Prince Franz Joseph Hohenzollern-Emden and Princess Maria Alix of Saxony.

[*Villa Silberburg, 72379 Hechingen , Germany*].

MONACO
(House of Grimaldi)

The Genoese family of Grimaldi can be traced authentically to Otto Canella (*ca* 1070 - 1143), Consul of Genoa in 1133, and derives its name from his son Grimaldo, Consul of Genoa in 1162, 1170 and 1184. His great-great-grandson Rainier I (✠ 1314) was Admiral of

France, Baron of San Demetrio in the kingdom of Naples and Seigneur of Cagnes in Provence. Rainier's son Charles I, also Admiral of France, acquired the Lordship of Monaco in 1331 and that of Menton in 1346 and ✝ 1357. His descendants reigned as Seigneurs of Monaco until 1457 when Catalan Grimaldi was succeeded by his daughter Claudine (1451 - 1514), who on her marriage in 1465 conveyed her rights to her husband Lambert Grimaldi (1425 - 94) of the Antibes branch of the family. France recognized the independence of the Seigneurie in 1512 and in 1524 Monaco was placed under Spanish protection. In 1612 Honoré II assumed the title of Prince and, after concluding a treaty with France in 1641, received the duché-pairie of Valentinois and the marquisate of Baux in 1642. Prince Antoine I was succeeded in 1731 by his daughter Louise-Hippolyte, whose husband Jacques Goyon de Matignon assumed the name and arms of Grimaldi. The Goyon family traces its descent from Etienne de Gouyon who *m* Luce de Matignon *ca* 1200. The male line again failed on the death of Prince Louis II on 9 May 1949, when he was succeeded by his grandson the present Sovereign Prince whose mother was Louis II's natural daughter, Charlotte, Hereditary Princess of Monaco, Duchess of Valentinois, styled Mlle de Valentinois from *ca* 1906, legitimated and granted the title of Duchess of Valentinois by ordinance of Prince Albert I 16 May 1919 (*b* 30 Sept 1898; ✝ 15 Nov 1977). She married Count Pierre de Polignac (see Polignac), who assumed the name and arms of Grimaldi and renounced her rights of succession in favour of her only son 30 May 1944.

Arms:- Arg, three bars composed of five fusils each gu. The shield is encircled by the Collar of the Order of St Charles. *Supporters:-* Two minor friars, each carrying a raised sword. *Motto:-* Deo juvante. The achievement is borne on a mantle gu, fringed and tasselled or, doubled ermine and surmounted by a Princely Crown.

Members of the Princely family bear the title of Prince or Princess of Monaco with the qualification of Serene Highness.

RAINIER III Louis Henri Maxence Bertrand, **SOVEREIGN PRINCE OF MONACO**, Duke of Valentinois, Marquis des Baux, Comte de Carladès, Baron du Buis, Seigneur de Saint-Remy, Sire de Matignon, Comte de Torigni, Baron de Saint-Lô, Baron de la Luthumière, Baron de Hambye, Duc d'Estouteville, de Mazarin et de Mayenne, Prince de Château-Porcien, Comte de Ferrette, de Belfort, de Thann et de Rosemont, Seigneur d'Isenheim, Marquis de Chilly, Comte de Longjumeau, Baron de Massy, Marquis de Guiscard, *b* at Monaco 31 May 1923, founded Order of Cultural Merit 1952, Order of the Grimaldi 1954, and Order of the Crown of Monaco 1960, son of Charlotte, Hereditary Princess of Monaco (*b* 30 Sept 1898; ✝ 15 Nov 1977) and Pierre, Comte de Polignac (*b* 24 Oct 1895; *m* 19

March 1920; separated 20 March 1930; div by ordinance of Prince Louis II 18 Feb 1933; ✠ 10 Nov 1964); *m* at Monaco 18 April (civ) and 19 April (relig) 1956, Grace (*b* at Philadelphia, Pennsylvania, USA 12 Nov 1929; ✠ at Monaco 14 Sept 1982), dau of John Brendan Kelly and Margaret Maier.

[*Palace Princier, Monaco*].

Son and Daughters

1. Princess *Caroline* Louise Marguerite, *b* at Monaco 23 Jan 1957; *m* 1stly at Monaco 28 June (civ) and 29 June (relig) 1978 (*m* diss at Monaco 9 Oct 1980 and annulled at Rome 26 Feb 1992, confirmed 20 June 1992), Philippe Junot (*b* at Paris 19 April 1940), Financier. She *m* 2ndly at Monaco 29 Dec 1983 (civ), Stefano Casiraghi (*b* at Milan 8 Sept 1960; ✠ at Monaco 3 Oct 1990), Industrialist. She *m* 3rdly at Monaco 23 Jan 1999 (civ) Prince *Ernst August* Albert Paul Otto Rupprecht Oskar Berthold Friedrich-Ferdinand Christian-Ludwig; Prince of Hanover; Prince of Great Britain and Ireland Duke of Brunswick and Lüneburg; removed from the line of succession to the British Throne on 23 Jan 1999 upon marriage to a Catholic, (*b* at Hanover 26 Feb 1954); he *m* 1stly at Pattensen 28 Aug (civ) and at Schloß Marienburg 30 Aug (relig) 1981 (*m* diss by div at London 23 Oct 1997), Chantal Hochuli (*b* at Zurich 2 June 1955).

[*Villa Le Clos Saint-Pierre, Monaco; Hurlingham Lodge, Hurlingham Road, London SW6 3RD; Calenberg, 30978 Schulenburg an der Leine, Germany*].

2. *Albert* Alexandre Louis Pierre, Hereditary Prince of Monaco, Marquis des Baux, *b* at Monaco 14 March 1958, Grand Officer of the Lion of Senegal National Order, Grand Cross of the Order of St. Charles, Grand Officer of the Legion of Honor of France, Kt Sovereign Military Order of Malta.

[*Palace Princier, Monaco*].

3. Princess *Stéphanie* Marie Elisabeth, *b* at Monaco 1 Feb 1965; *m* at Monaco 1 July (relig) 1995 (*m* diss by div at Monaco 4 Sept 1996), Daniel Ducruet (*b* at Beausoleil, Alpes-Maritimes, France 27 Nov 1964)

[*Palace Princier, Monaco*].

Sister

Princess *Antoinette* Louise Alberte Suzanne, *b* at Paris XVI 28 Dec 1920, *cr* Baroness de Massy by her brother Prince Rainier III 15 Nov 1951; *m* 1stly at the Monegasque Consulate, Genoa 21 Oct 1951 (*m*

diss by div at Monaco 10 May 1954), Alexandre-Athanase (Aleco) Noghès (b at Monaco 15 June 1916). She m 2ndly at the Monegasque Consulate General, The Hague 2 Dec 1961 (m diss by div at Monaco 17 July 1973), as his 2nd wife, Mâitre Jean Rey (b at Monaco 22 Oct 1914; ✚ there 17 Sept 1994). She m 3rdly at Monaco 28 July 1983 (civ), John Gilpin (b at Southsea, Hampshire 10 Feb 1930; ✚ at London 5 Sept 1983), Ballet Dancer.
[Villa Le Bout du Monde, 06360 Eze, Alpes-Maritimes, France].

MONTENEGRO
(HOUSE OF PETROVIC-NJEGOŠ)

Orthodox: Founded by Danilo Petrovic-Njegoš who obtained the hereditary Dignity of Vladika (Bishop) of Montenegro 1711 (Theocracy); Danilo I Petrovic-Njegoš was recognized as Sovereign Prince and heir of Montenegro by Russia 21 March 1852 and established sucession by male primogeniture; Prince Nicholas I (Nikola) assumed the qualification of Royal Highness 6/19 Dec 1900 and the title of King 15/28 Aug 1910; the annexation of Montenegro to the Kingdom of the Serbs, Croats and Slovenes was proclaimed 13 Nov 1918, but was not recognized by King Nicholas I (Nikola I) (Grandfather of the new King, Alexander I, King of the Serbs, Croats and Slovenes; later Alexander I, King of Yugoslavia) and a Government-in-Exile was maintained by him and his successors under the Premiership of King Nicholas's former ADC and Ambassador to Washington (1918), General Antoine (Anto) Gvozdenovic (Imperial Russian Privy Counsellor, General Imperial Russian, French, Montenegrin and Yugoslav Armies) until the Conference of Ambassadors at Paris gave international recognition to the union 13 July 1922. King Nikola I was succeeded on his death by his son, Danilo II, who abdicated after one week, and then by his grandson, King Michael I (father of the present heir) who remained in exile until his death in 1986. King Michael I became prisoner in a Nazi concentration camp during World War II after refusing to return to the throne as a puppet King. Also descended from the House of Obrenovic (See Serbia/ Yugoslavia), through Prince Yephrem, brother of Milos Obrenovic I, Prince of Serbia (elected Hereditary Prince of Serbia by the National Assembly 1827 and recognised by Sultan Mahmud II, 15 Aug 1830).
Arms:- Gu, an eagle displayed arg armed and crowned or, holding in its dexter claw a sceptre and in the sinister an orb all ppr; charged on the breast with an escutcheon of pretence, az a lion passant or armed and or, armed and langued gu, on a terrace vert. The shield

is ensigned by the Royal Crown.

Members of the Royal Family bear the title of Prince or Princess Petrovic-Njegoš of Montenegro with the qualification of Royal Highness for the children of Kings, or titular heads of the dynasty and Highness for other members. From 21 January 2001 The Hereditary Prince is styled Grand Duke of Grahavo and Zeta.

NICHOLAS (NIKOLA II) Michael Francis, **CROWN PRINCE OF MONTENEGRO**, *b* at Paris 24 July 1944, Architect, Founder and President of the Cetinje Biennale of Contemporary Art, son of Michael I, King of Montenegro, Grand Duke of Grahavo and Zeta (*b* 14 Sept 1908; *succ* 7 March 1921 and reigned initially under the regency of his Grandmother, Queen Milena of Montenegro, *née* Vukotic, and his ministers; ✠ 24 March 1986) and Geneviève Prigent (*b* 4 Dec 1919; ✠ 27 Jan 1991; *m* 27 Jan 1941; *m* diss by div 11 April 1949); *m* at Trebeurden, Côtes-du-Nord 27 Nov 1976, *Francine* (*b* at Casablanca, Morocco 27 Jan 1950), Fashion Designer, dau of *Antoine Navarro* and Rachel Wazana.

[*c/o John Kennedy, 9 Cork Street, Mayfair, London W1S 3LL*].

Son and Daughter

1. Princess *Altinaï*, *b* at Les Lilas, Seine-Saint-Denis 27 Oct 1977.
[*c/o John Kennedy, 9 Cork Street, Mayfair, London W1S 3LL*].
2. Grand Duke *Boris*, Hereditary Prince (Petrovic-Njegoš) of Montenegro, Grand Duke of Grahavo and Zeta, *b* at Les Lilas 21 Jan 1980.
[*c/o John Kennedy, 9 Cork Street, Mayfair, London W1S 3LL*].

THE NETHERLANDS
(HOUSE OF ORANGE-NASSAU)

Dutch Reformed Church (Calvinist): Founded by Otto, Count of Nassau-Siegen, Dillenburg and Beilstein (✠ *ca* 1290); Count of Diet (in Nassau) 1384; Count of Vianden 1417; inherited the Dutch Lordships of Leck, Breda, etc through the marriage (1403) of Count Engelbert to Jeanne, dau and heiress of the House of Polanen, etc; Burggrave of Antwerp 13 May 1487; inherited the principality of Orange (Vaucluse, France) with 32 Lordships in Burgundy, through the marriage of Count Henri (*b* 1483; ✠ 1538) to Claude of Chalon (✠ 1521), sister and heiress of the last Prince of Orange from the House of Chalon, 3 Aug 1530; Count of Katzelnelnbogen 30 June 1557; Stadhouder of the provinces of the Netherlands (Utrecht 23 Jan

1579) 1559 to 6 Nov 1650 and 1672 to 19 March 1702; Hereditary
Stadhouder of Holland and Zealand 1674, of Gueldre, Utrecht and
Over-Yssel 1675; King of Great Britain 21 April 1689 to 19 March
1702 (William III); Prince of the Holy Roman Empire and of Nassau,
Prague 25 Nov 1652; Hereditary Stadhouder of Frisia 1675; the
principality of Orange was ceded to France 11 April 1713; the title of
Prince of Orange was confirmed by a treaty concluded with the King
of Prussia 16 June 1732; Hereditary Stadhouder of all the provinces
of the Netherlands 22 Nov 1747 to 1795; qualification of "Durchlauchtig
Hochgeboren", Vienna 3 July 1750; a Treaty of Succession was
concluded with the Senior Line of the House of Nassau 30 June 1783
(see Luxembourg); Hereditary Sovereign Prince of the Netherlands
6 Dec 1813; succession in the female line was introduced 29 March
1814 (confirmed 2 Aug 1884); King of the Netherlands and Duke of
Luxembourg 16 March 1815; Grand Duke of Luxembourg 9 June
1815 to 23 Nov 1890 when that Grand Duchy was separated from this
Line because of the operation of the Salic Law. For the early history
of the House of Nassau - see LUXEMBOURG
Arms:- Az, billety a lion rampant crowned or, armed and langued
gu, holding in the dexter forepaw a sword and in the sinister, a shief
of arrows ppr. The shield is ensigned with the Royal Crown of the
Netherlands. *Supporters:-* Two lions guardant or, armed and langued
gua. *Motto:-* Je maintiendrai. The achievement is borne on a mantle
gu, fringed and tasselled or, doubled erm and surmounted by the
Royal Crown of the Netherlands.
The sons of the Queen bear the titles of Prince of the Netherlands,
Prince of Orange-Nassau, Jonkheer van Amsberg with the qualification
of Royal Highness. The sisters of the Queen bear the titles of Princess
of the Netherlands, Princess of Orange-Nassau, Princess of
Lippe-Biesterfeld with the qualification of Royal Highness. By a
Royal Decree of 2 Jan 1967, the children of Princess Margriet bear
the titles of Prince or Princess of Orange-Nassau, van Vollenhoven
with the qualification of Highness.

BEATRIX Wilhelmina Armgard, **QUEEN OF THE
NETHERLANDS,** *b* Baarn, Utrecht 31 Jan 1938, Gd Mistress Mil
Willems Order, Order of the The Netherlands Lion, Order of
Orange-Nassau, of the House of Orange, and House Order Golden
Lion of Nassau, Lady of the Order of the Garter (1989), Royal
Victorian Chain (1982), GCVO) (1958), etc, dau of Juliana, Queen
of the Netherlands (*b* at The Hague 30 April 1909; abdicated 30
April 1980) and Prince Bernhard of Lippe-Biesterfeld, *cr* Prince of
the Netherlands with the qualification of Royal Highness 7 Jan 1937
(*b* at Jena 29 June 1911; *m* at The Hague 7 Jan 1937); *m* at
Amsterdam 10 March 1966, Claus von Amsberg (*b* at Dotzingen, nr
Hitzacker an der Elbe 6 Sept 1926; ✠ at Amsterdam 6 Oct 2002),

naturalised in the Netherlands and *cr* Prince of the Netherlands, Jonkheer van Amsberg 16 Feb 1966, and has issue,
[*Paleis Huis ten Bosch, Bezuidenhoutseweg 10, 2594 AV, The Hague, The Netherlands*].

Sons

1. *Willem-Alexander* Claus Georg Ferdinand, Crown Prince of The Netherlands, Prince of Orange, Prince of Orange-Nassau, Jonkheer van Amsberg, *b* at Baarn, Utrecht 27 April 1967; *m* at Amsterdam 2 Feb 2002, *Maxima* (*b* at Buenos Aires 17 May 1971), dau of Jorge Horacio Zorreguieta Stefanini and Maria del Carmen Cerruti Carricart.
2. Prince Johan *Friso* Berhard Christian David, *b* at Baarn, Utrecht 25 Sept 1968.
3. Prince *Constantijn* Christof Frederik Aschwin, *b* at Baarn, Utrecht 11 Oct 1969; *m* at The Hague 17 May (civ) and at The Hague 19 May (relig) 2001, *Petra* Laurentien (*b* at Leiden 25 May 1966), dau of Laurens Jan Brinkhorst, Agriculture Minister of The Netherlands and Jantien Heringa.

    1. Princess *Eloise* Sophie Beatrix Laurence, Countess van Oranje-Nassau, jonkvrouwe van Amsberg, *b* at The Hague 8 June 2002.

Sisters

1. Princess *Irene* Emma Elisabeth, *b* at Baarn, Utrecht 5 Aug 1939, *m* at Rome 29 April 1964 (*m* diss by div at Utrecht 26 May 1981), Prince Don Carlos Hugo of Bourbon-Parma (*b* at Paris 8 April 1930).
[*Vredehofstraat 31, 3761 HA Soest, The Netherlands*].
2. Princess *Margriet* Francisca, *b* at Ottawa, Canada 19 Jan 1943, *m* at The Hague 10 Jan 1967, Pieter van Vollenhoven (*b* at Schiedam 30 April 1939), (*cr* Princes of Orange-Nassau, van Vollenhoven, with the qualification of Highness),
[*Huis "Het Loo", Apeldoorn, Prov. Gelderland, The Netherlands*].

    1. Prince *Maurits* Willem Pieter Hendrik, *b* at Baarn, Utrecht 17 April 1968; *m* at Apeldoorn 30 May 1998, Marie Hélène *Marilène* (*b* at Dieren 4 Feb 1970), dau of Hans van den Broek, European Commissioner and sometime Foreign Minister of the Netherlands, and José van Schendel.
    [*Huis "Het Loo", Apeldoorn, Prov. Gelderland, The Netherlands*].

        1. Princess Anastasia (*Anna*) Margriet Joséphine van Lippe-Biesterfeld van Vollenhoven, *b* Amsterdam 15

April 2001.

2. Prince *Lucas* Maurits Peter Henri van Lippe-Biesterfeld van Vollenhoven, *b* Amsterdam 26 Oct 2002.

2. Prince *Bernhard* Lucas Emmanuel, *b* at Nijmegen 25 Dec 1969; *m* at Utrecht (civ) 6 Jul 2000 (relig) 8 Jul 2000, Annette (*b* The Hague 18 Apr 1972), dau of Ulrich Sekrève and Jolanda de Haan.

[*Huis "Het Loo", Apeldoorn, Prov. Gelderland, The Netherlands*].

1. Princess *Isabella* Lily Juliana van Vollenhoven, *b* at Amsterdam 14 May 2002.

3. Prince *Pieter*- Christiaan Michiel, *b* at Nijmegen 22 March 1972.

[*Huis "Het Loo", Apeldoorn, Prov. Gelderland, The Netherlands*].

4. Prince *Floris* Frederik Martijn, *b* at Nijmegen 10 April 1975.

[*Huis "Het Loo", Apeldoorn, Prov. Gelderland, The Netherlands*].

3. Princess Maria *Christina*, *b* at Baarn, Utrecht 18 Feb 1947; *m* at Baarn (civ) and at Baarn, Utrecht (relig) 28 June 1975 (*m* diss by div at The Hague 25 April 1996), *Jorge* Pérez Guillermo (*b* at Havana, Cuba 1 Aug 1946), Hotelier.

[*Postbus 30412, 2500 GK The Hague, The Netherlands*].

Mother and Father

JULIANA Louise Emma Marie Wilhelmina, **Queen of the Netherlands** (since her abdication known as **Princess Juliana of Orange-Nassau**, by her own request), Duchess of Mecklenburg, former Gd Mistress Mil Willems Order, Order of the The Netherlands Lion, Order of Orange-Nassau, of the House of Orange, and House Order Golden Lion of Nassau, *b* at The Hague 30 April 1909, acted as Princess-Regent of the Netherlands 14 Oct-1 Dec 1947 and 14 May-30 Aug 1948, *succ* her mother on her abdication and was inaugurated at Amsterdam 6 Sept 1948, Lady of the Order of the Garter 1958, Royal Victorian Chain 1950, abdicated in favour of her eldest dau 30 April 1980; *m* at The Hague 7 Jan 1937, Prince *Bernhard* Leopold Friedrich Eberhard Julius Curt Karl Gottfried Peter of Lippe-Biesterfeld (*b* at Jena 29 June 1911), naturalised in The Netherlands 24 Nov 1936 and *cr* Prince of the Netherlands with the

qualification of Royal Highness 7 Jan 1937, GCB, GCVO, GBE, etc.
[*Palace Soestdijk, Baarn, Prov. Utrecht, The Netherlands*].

NORWAY
(SCHLESWIG-HOLSTEIN-SONDERBURG-GLÜCKSBURG)

Lutheran: Independent Monarchy since 1905. Carl, Prince of
Denmark (see that family) was elected King of Norway 18 Nov 1905,
accepted the crown on the same day and reigned as Haakon VII,
King of Norway.
Arms:- Gu, a lion rampant crowned or, holding in his paws the long
handled axe of St Olav blade arg, handle or. The shield is encircled
by the Collar of the Order of St Olav. *Motto:-* Alt for Norge. The
achievement is borne on a mantle gu, fringed and tasselled or,
doubled erm and surmounted by the Royal Crown of Norway.
Members of the Royal Family bear the title of Prince or Princess of
Norway with the qualification of Royal Highness.

HARALD V, KING OF NORWAY, *b* at Skaugum 21 Feb 1937,
Gen Norwegian Army and Airforce, Admiral Norwegian Navy, Hon
Col Royal Marines (GB), Hon Col Green Howards, Gd Master of the
Royal Norwegian Order of St Olav, Gd Master Royal Norwegian
Order of Merit, St Olav's Medal, Kt Gd Cross Order of Leopold
(Belgium), Kt Gd Cross Order of the Southern Cross (Brazil), Kt
Order of the Elephant (Denmark), Gd Cmdr "with diamonds" Order
of the Dannebrog (Denmark), Kt Gd Cross with Collar Order of the
White Rose (Finland), Olympic Cross of Merit 1st Class (Finland),
Kt Gd Cross Legion of Honour (France), Kt Gd Cross Order of the
Saviour (Greece), The Hundredth Anniversary Memorial Medal of
the Greek Royal House, Golden Olympic Order, Kt Gd Cross with
Collar Icelandic Order of the Falcon, Kt Gd Cross Italian Order of
Merit, Kt Gd Cross Order of Chrysanthemum (Japan), Yugoslavian
Grand Star, Kt Gd Cross Civ and Mil Order of Merit of Adolph of
Nassau (Luxembourg), Commemoration Medal - Wedding
(Luxembourg), Kt Gd Cross Crown Order of the Family Order of
Orange (Netherlands), Cmdr Order of the Golden Ark
(Netherlands), Queen Beatrix' Coronation Medal 1980 (Netherlands),
Kt Gd Cross Order of the White Eagle (Poland), Kt Gd Cross Order
of Aviz (Portugal), Kt Gd Cross Order of Carlos III (Spain), Order
del Loison de Oro - Chain (Spain), Kt Gd Cross Royal Victorian
Order, The Royal Victorian Chain, Kt Most Noble Order of the

Seraphim with Collar (Sweden), King Gustav V's 90th Anniversary
Medal (Sweden), Kt Most Noble Family Order with Collar
(Thailand), Kt Gd Cross 1st Class Order of Merit of the Federal
Republic of Germany, The   Decoration of Honour for Merit - Grand
Star (Austria), son of Olav V, King of Norway (b 2 July 1903; succ 21
Sept 1957; ✠ 17 Jan 1991) and Princess Märtha of Sweden (b 28
March 1901; m 21 March 1929; ✠ 5 April 1954); m at Oslo 29 Aug
1968, Sonja (b at Oslo 4 July 1937), Dame Gd Cross with Collar Order
of St Olav, Dame Gd Cross the Royal Norwegian Order of Merit, St
Olavs Medal, Dame Order of the Elephant (Denmark), Dame Gd
Cross Order of the White Rose   (Finland), Dame Gd Cross National
Order of Merit (France), Golden Olympic Order, Dame Gd Cross
Icelandic Order of the Falcon, Dame Gd Cross Civ and Mil Order of
Merit of Adolph of Nassau (Luxembourg), Dame Gd Cross Crown
Order of the Family Order of Orange (Netherlands), Queen Beatrix'
Coronation Medal 1980 (Netherlands), Cmndr Order of the Instruçao
Publica
(Portugal), Dame Order of Isabella the Catholic (Spain), Dame Gd
Cross Order of Carlos III (Spain), Dame Most Noble Order of the
Seraphim (Sweden), Dame Gd Cross 1st Class Order of Merit of the
Federal Republic of Germany, The Decoration of Honour for Merit -
Grand Star (Austria), dau of Carl August Haraldsen and Dagny
Ulrichsen.
[Royal Palace, 0010 Oslo, Norway; Skaugum, 1370 Asker, Norway].

Son and Daughter

1. Princess *Märtha Louise*, b at Oslo 22 Sept 1971, Dame Gd Cross
with Collar Order of St Olav, Dame Order of the Elephant
(Denmark), Dame Gd Cross Order of the White Rose (Finland),
Dame Gd Cross Icelandic Order of the Falcon, Cmdr Gd Cross Royal
Order of the Northern Star (Sweden); *from Feb 2002 no longer
styled Royal Highness or in line of succession*; m at Trondheim 24
May 2002, *Ari* Mikael Behn (b at Århus 30 Sep 1972).
[Royal Palace, 0010 Oslo, Norway].
2. *Haakon Magnus*, Crown Prince of Norway, b at Oslo 20 July 1973,
Lt Norwegian Navy, Kt Gd Cross with Collar Order of St Olav, Kt Gd
Cross Royal Norwegian Order of Merit, Kt Order of the Elephant
(Denmark), Kt Most Noble Order of the Seraphim (Sweden); m at
Oslo 25 Aug 2001, Mette-Marit (b at Kristiansand 19 Aug 1973).(to
be styled Crown Princess Mette-Marit of Norway), dau of Sven Olaf
Bjarte Hoiby and Marit Tjessem.

[*Ullevaalveien 7, 0010 Oslo, Norway*].

Sisters

1. Princess *Ragnhild* Alexandra (bears the name of Princess Ragnhild, Mrs Lorentzen with the qualification of Highness), *b* at Oslo 9 June 1930, Dame Gd Cross with Chain of Order of St Olav; *m* at Asker, nr Oslo 15 May 1953, Erling Sven Lorentzen (*b* at Ullern (Oslo) 28 Jan 1923), Businessman.

[*Husebyveien 6, 0379 Oslo, Norway*].

2. Princess *Astrid* Maud Ingeborg (bears the name of Princess Astrid, Mrs Ferner with the qualification of Highness), *b* at Oslo 12 Feb 1932, Dame Gd Cross with Chain of Order of St Olav; *m* at Asker 12 Jan 1961, Johan Martin Ferner (*b* at Oslo 22 July 1927), Businessman.

[*Vinderen in Oslo, Norway*].

OLDENBURG

Lutheran: Founded by Egilmar I, Count of Aldenburg, living in 1088; Lord of Wildeshausen 1143; subjugated the Stedinger 1234; constructed Schloß Delmenhorst 1247; inherited Jever 1575 and 1818, Kniphausen 1624; the county of Oldenburg passed to the collateral line of Holstein-Denmark 19 June 1667 and was ceded to Russia in exchange for Holstein 1 July 1773; Russia in turn ceded it to Friedrich August, Duke of Holstein-Gottorp (✝ 1785) 14 Dec 1773; elevation of the county into a Duchy, Vienna 29 Dec 1774 (announced publicly 22 March 1777); Friedrich August's son and successor Duke Wilhelm was the last (Protestant) Prince-Bishop of Lübeck, and when the bishopric was secularised in 1803 its territory was acquired by Oldenburg, Grand Duke of Oldenburg 9 June 1815; acquired the Duchy of Birkenfeld (residence of the Counts Palatine 1584, Principality of Baden 1776) 1817; abdication of the dynasty 11 Nov 1918.

Arms:- Quarterly and enté pointe: 1st, or, two bars gu; 2nd, az a cross patée and fitchée or; 3rd, az, a cross patée or, ensigned with a mitre or, charged with a cross patée arg; 4th, checky, arg and gu, and enté en pointe, az, a lion rampant or. The shield is ensigned with the Royal Crown.

Members of the Grand Ducal family bear the title of Duke or Duchess of Oldenburg with the qualification of Highness. The Grand Dukes and Hereditary Grand Dukes and their wives had the qualification of Royal Highness, which is also used by the present Head of the family and his son.

ANTON GÜNTHER Friedrich August Josias, **DUKE OF OLDENBURG,** *b* at Lensahn 16 Jan 1923, Dipl Forestry, son of Nikolaus, Hereditary Grand Duke of Oldenburg (*b* 10 Aug 1897; ✠ 3 April 1970) and Princess Helene zu Waldeck and Pyrmont (*b* 22 Dec 1899; *m* 26 Oct 1921; ✠ 18 Feb 1948); *m* at Kreuzwertheim am Main 7 Aug 1951, Princess Ameli (*b* at Frankfurt-am-Main 4 March 1923), eldest dau of Udo, 6th Prince (Fürst) and Herr (Lord) zu Löwenstein-Wertheim-Freudenberg and Countess Margarete zu Castell-Castell. [*Güldenstein, 23738 Lensahn, Ostholstein, Germany*].

Son and Daughter

1. Duchess *Helene* Elisabeth Bathildis Margarete, *b* at Rastede 3 Aug 1953, Dr of Agriculture, Media & Performing Arts.
[*Oldenburgerstraße 202, 26180 Rastede, Germany*].
2. Duke *Christian* Nikolaus Udo Peter, *b* at Rastede 1 Feb 1955, Dipl Business; *m* at Bad Segeberg 22 Sept (civ) and at Pronstorf, Holstein 26 Sept 1987, Countess Caroline (*b* at Kiel 10 April 1962), dau of Christian, Count zu Rantzau, Proprietor of Pronstorf and Héloise von Lettow-Vorbeck, and has issue,
[*Güldenstein, 23738 Lensahn, Ostholstein, Germany*].

    1. Duke *Alexander* Paul Hans-Caspar Andreas Daniel Carl Philippe, *b* at Lübeck 17 March 1990.
    2. Duke *Philipp* Konstantin Wittekind Raimund Clemens Hans-Heinrich, *b* at Lübeck 28 Dec 1991.
    3. Duke *Anton* Friedrich Ludwig Jan Vincent, *b* at Lübeck 9 Jan 1993.
    4. Duchess *Katharina* Bibiane Edwina Isabell, *b* at Lübeck 20 Feb 1997.

Brothers and Sisters

1. Duchess *Rixa* Elisabeth Bathildis Emma Cecilie, *b* at Lensahn 28 March 1924; ✠ near Lensahn 1 April 1939.
2. Duke *Peter* Friedrich August Max, *b* at Lensahn 7 Aug 1926; *m* at Kreuzwertheim 7 Aug 1951, Princess Gertrud (*b* at Langenzell, nr Bammental, Kreis Heidelberg 24 Jan 1926), dau of Udo, 6th Prince and Lord (Fürst and Herr) zu Löwenstein-Wertheim-Freudenberg and Countess Margarete zu Castell-Castell, and has issue,
[*Lensahner Hof, 23738 Lensahn, Ostholstein, Germany*].

    1. Duke *Friedrich August* Nikolaus Udo Peter Philipp, *b* at Lensahnerhof 26 Sept 1952, Dipl Agriculture; *m* at Lensahn 22 Dec 1981 (civ) and at Nanyuki, Kenya 9 Jan 1982 (relig)

Belinda Rose (*b* at Nairobi, Kenya 10 Nov 1954), Pilot, dau of Major Digby Tatham Warter and Jane Boyd, and has issue, [*Lensahnerhof, 23738 Lensahn, Germany*].

    1. Duchess *Anastasia* Caroline Margarete Adelheid, *b* at Cambridge 10 Oct 1982.

    2. Duchess *Alice* Joanna Helene Susannah, *b* at Cambridge 15 April 1986.

    3. Duchess *Cara* Emma Amanda Bettina, *b* at Cambridge 14 June 1993.

2. Duchess *Margarete* Elisabeth Bathildis Ameli Eilika Barbara Marie-Alix Altburg, *b* at Lübeck 16 May 1954, Kindergarten Teacher; *m* at Lensahn 27 June 1985, Philippe, Prince von Croÿ (*b* at Mühlheim 8 Sept 1957), Director of Accountant Society.

[*Aussenschlag 3, 21521 Wohltorf, Germany*].

3. Duke *Nikolaus* Anton-Gunther Max Johann Alfred Ernst, *b* at Lübeck 21 May 1955, Lawyer; *m* at Lensahn 19 June 1982, Anna Klara Maria (*b* at Mühlheim 7 May 1958), Lawyer, dau of Karl Byron Dyckerhoff and Ellen Rhodius, and has issue, [*Baron Voghtstraße 129, 22607 Hamburg, Germany*].

    1. Duke *Christoph* Christian Ludwig Friedrich Wilhelm, *b* at Hamburg 31 Dec 1985.

    2. Duke *Georg* Friedrich August Carl Constantin Hubertus Klaus, *b* at Hamburg 29 Jan 1990.

    3. Duke *Oscar* Philippe Raimund Thomas Jan, *b* at Hamburg 31 Jan 1991.

    4. Duke *Georg-Moritz* Friedrich Ferdinand Egilmar Huno, *b* at Lübeck 25 June 1957.

    [*Lensahnerhof, 23738 Lensahn, Germany*].

3. Duchess *Eilika* Stephanie Elisabeth Thekla Juliana, *b* at Lensahn 2 Feb 1928; *m* at Rastede 10 Aug 1950, Emich, 7th Prince (Fürst) zu Leiningen (*b* at Coburg 18 Oct 1926; ✝ at Amorbach 30 Oct 1991). [*83916 Amorbach, Odenwald, Germany*].

4. Duke *Egilmar* Friedrich Franz Stephan Wilhelm, *b* at Lensahn 14 Oct 1934.

[*Karl Theodorstraße 44, 80803 Munich, Germany*].

5. Duke *Friedrich August* Wilhelm Christian Ernst, *b* at Rastede 11 Jan 1936; *m* 1stly at Berlin 3 Dec (civ) and 4 Dec (relig) 1965 (*m* diss by div at Munich 23 Nov 1989), Princess Marie Cécile (*b* at Cadinen, Kreis Elbing 28 May 1942), eldest dau of Louis Ferdinand, Prince of

Prussia, Head of the Royal House and Grand Duchess Kira of Russia. He *m* 2ndly at Rüdenhausen 9 Feb 1991, Countess Donata (*b* at Rüdenhausen 20 June 1950; *m* 1stly 24 May 1975, Prince Louis Ferdinand of Prussia who was ✠*k* in army manoeuvres 11 July 1977), dau of Siegfried, 4th Prince (Fürst) zu Castell-Rüdenhausen and Countess Irene zu Solms-Laubach, and has issue by his first wife,

[*Sievershagen, 23738 Lensahn, Ostholstein, Germany*].

    1. Duke *Paul-Wladimir* Nikolaus Louis-Ferdinand Peter Max Karl-Emich, *b* at Lübeck 16 Aug 1969, Dipl In agr, Lt (Res); *m* at Bronnbach an der Tauber 20 Jan 2001, *Maria* del Pilar (*b* at Madrid 20 Oct 1970), dau of Jaime Méndez de Vigo y del Arco and Princess Monika of Löwenstein-Wertheim-Rosenberg.

[*Sievershagen, 23738 Lensahn, Ostholstein, Germany*].

    2. Duchess *Rixa* Marie-Alix Kira Altburg, *b* at Lübeck 17 Sept 1970, Dress Designer.

[*9 rue des Grands Augustins, 75006 Paris, France*].

    3. Duchess *Bibiane* Maria Alexandra Gertrud, *b* at Oldenburg 24 June 1974.

[*Sievershagen, 23738 Lensahn, Ostholstein, Germany*].

6. Duchess *Altburg* Elisabeth Hilda Ingeborg Marie Luise Mathilde, *b* at Lensahn 14 Oct 1938; *m* at Rastede 8 July 1966, Rüdiger, Baron von Erffa (*b* at Regensburg 19 April 1936), Proprietor of Ahorn and Finkenau, Dipl Agriculture Eng.

[*Hirsch Gasse18, 63654 Büdingen-Eckartshausen, Germany*].

7. Duke *Huno* Friedrich Peter Max, *b* at Lensahn 3 Jan 1940, Dipl Eng, Capt (res); *m* at Rastede 6 June 1970, Countess Felicitas-Anita (Fenita) (*b* at Berlin 5 July 1941), yst dau of Johann Ludwig, Count Schwerin von Krosigk, Proprietor of Lemmersdorf, Kr Prenzlau, Uckermark and Baroness Ehrengard von Plettenberg of the Counts Heeren, and has issue,

[*Segebergerstraße 37, 24629 Kisdorf-Wohld, Germany*].

    1. Duchess *Beatrix* Amelie Ehrengard Eilika, *b* at Lübeck 27 May 1971, cand jur, Banker.

[*Segebergerstraße 37, 24629 Kisdorf-Wohld, Germany*].

    2. Duchess *Sophie* Altburg Marie Cécile Margarete, *b* at Lübeck 6 Nov 1972.

[*Segebergerstraße 37, 24629 Kisdorf-Wohld, Germany*].

8. Duke *Johann* Friedrich Adolf, *b* at Lensahn 3 Jan 1940 (twin with Duke Huno), Businessman, Capt (Res); *m* at Waldsachsen (civ) and at Schonungen am Main (relig) 9 Oct 1971, Countess Ilka (*b* at Würzburg 29 June 1942), elder dau of Alfred-Friedrich, Count zu

Ortenburg and Jutta von Lücken, and has issue,
[*Güldenstein, 23738 Lensahn, Ostholstein, Germany*].

    1. Duchess *Eilika* Helene Jutta Clementine, *b* at Bad Segeberg
23 Aug 1972; *m* at St Stephen's Basilica, Budapest 18 Oct
1997 (relig), Archduke Georg of Austria (*b* at Starnberg 16
Dec 1964), Kt Order of the Golden Fleece.
[*Szent István Park 17/7, 1137 Budapest, Hungary*].

    2. Duchess *Tatjana* Ingeborg Altburg Elisabeth Marita, *b* at
Bad Segeberg 11 Nov 1974.

    3. Duke *Konstantin* Nikolaus Alram Heinrich Hubertus, *b* at
Bad Segeberg 13 Dec 1975.

PORTUGAL
(House of Bragança)

Catholic: Founded by Alphonso I (✝ 1461), natural son of João I,
King of Portugal (*b* 1357; ✝ 14 Aug 1433), created Duke of Bragança
1442; King of Portugal and of Brazil since 1 Dec 1640; the sons of
King João VI (*b* 13 May 1767; ✝ 10 March 1826) and Infanta Doña
Carlotta Joaquina of Spain (*b* 25 April 1775; *m* 9 Jan 1790; ✝ 7 Jan
1830), founded the two lines of this family (see also Brazil); the
elder, Dom Pedro IV, King of Portugal (*b* 11 Oct 1798; ✝ 24 Sept
1834) proclaimed himself Emperor of Brazil with the name of Dom
Pedro I 12 Oct 1822 (his son, Emperor Dom Pedro II (*b* 2 Dec 1825;
✝ 5 Dec 1891) was deposed of the throne of Brazil 15 Nov 1889 - see
that family), and renounced the throne of Portugal 2 May 1826 in
favour of his daughter Dona Maria II da Gloria (*b* 4 April 1819; ✝ 15
Nov 1853) who reigned from 1826-8 and 1834-53. Her great-grandson,
King Manoel II (*b* 15 Nov 1889; ✝ 2 July 1932) lost the throne
through revolution 5 Oct 1910 and died without issue. The younger
son of King Joao VI, Infante DonMiguel, Duke of Bragança (*b* 26 Oct
1802; ✝ 14 Nov 1866) was King of Portugal from 30 June 1828 to 26
May 1834 and the line below descends from him.

Arms:- Arg, five escutcheons in cross az, each charged with as many
plates in saltire, all within a bordure gu, charged with seven castles
or. The achievement is borne on a mantle gu, fringed and tasselled
or, doubled erm and surmounted by the Royal Crown.

The children of the King or Queen and of the heir or heiress to the
Throne bear the title of Infante Don or Infanta Doña of Portugal.
The heir or heiress to the Throne and his or her eldest son or
daughter have the qualification of Royal Highness (HRH); the other
members of the Royal Family have the qualification of Highness
(HH) only. All members of the Royal Family use the prefix of Dom

or Dona before their Christian names.

Dom **DUARTE** Pio Nuno João Miguel Gabriel Rafael, **DUKE OF BRAGANCA,** of Guimarães and of Barcelos, Marquis of Vila Viçosa, Count of Arraiolos, of Ourém, of Barcelos, of Faria and of Neiva, of Guimaraes, etc, *b* at Berne, Switzerland 15 May 1945, Grand Master of the Order of the Immaculate Conception of Vila Viçosa, Grand Master of the Order of Santa Isabel, Bailiff Gd Cross Hon and Dev Sovereign Military Order of Malta, Kt Order of the Golden Fleece (Austria), Kt Order of St Januarius, Bailiff Gd Cross Constantinian Order of St George, Kt Order of Annunziata, Gd Cross White Eagle of Yugoslavia, Kt Order of Calatrava, son of Dom Duarte (II), Duke of Bragança, declared Head of the Royal House by all Portuguese Monarchists (*b* 23 at Seebenstein 23 Sept 1907; ✠ at Ferragudo 24 Dec 1976) and Princess Maria Francisca of Orléans and Bragança (*b* at Château d'Eu, France 8 Sept 1914; *m* at Rio de Janeiro 13 Oct (civ) and at Petropólis 15 Oct 1942; (relig), ✠ at Lisbon 15 Jan 1968); *m* at Lisbon at the Church of Jeronimos, 13 May 1995, Dona Isabel Ines (*b* at Lisbon 22 Nov 1966), Dame Grand Cross of the Order of the Immaculate Conception of Vila Viçosa, dau of Don Jorje de Herédia of the counts of Ribeira Brava and Doña Raquel Leonor de Castro Pinheiro Curvello.

[*Rua dos Duques de Bragança 10-1, 1200 Lisbon, Portugal*].

Son and Daughter

1. Infante Dom *Afonso* de Santa Maria Miguel Gabriel Rafael, Prince of Beira, *b* at Lisbon 25 March 1996.
2. Infanta Doña Dona *Maria Francisca* Isabel Micaela Gabriela Rafaela Paula, *b* at Lisbon 3 March 1997.
3. Infante Dom *Diniz* de Santa Maria Francisco João Miguel Gabriel Rafael, *b* at Lisbon 25 Nov 1999.

Brothers

1. Infante Dom *Miguel* Rafael Gabriel Xavier Teresia Maria Felix, Duke of Vizeu, *b* at Berne 3 Dec 1946, Grand Cross of the Order of the Immaculate Conception of Vila Viçosa.
[*Quinta das Fidalgas, Santar, P-3520 Nelas*].
2. Infante Dom *Henrique* Nuno João Miguel, Duke of Coimbra, *b* at Berne 6 Nov 1949, Grand Cross of the Order of the Immaculate Conception of Vila Viçosa,
[*Rua do Campo 2, São Pedro, P-2710 Sintra*].

Half-Brother of Father

Issue of Infante Don *Miguel* (II) Maria Carlos Egidio Constantino Gabriel Rafael Gonzaga, Francisco de Paula e de Assis Januário, Duke of Bragança, by his first wife; Pretender to the Throne of Portugal, abdicated his rights in favour of his son (Dom Duarte II) by his second wife 31 July 1920, *b* at Kleinheubach 19 Sept 1853, ✣ at Seebenstein 11 Oct 1927; *m* at Ragensburg 17 Oct 1877, *Elisabeth* Maria Maximiliane (*b* at Dresden 28 May 1860; ✣ at Öldenburg 7 Feb 1881), dau of Prince *Maximilian* Anton Lamoral, Hereditary Prince Thurn and Taxis and Princess Therese Hélène of Bavaria, having had issue among whom,

Son

1. Infante Dom *Miguel* Maximiliano Sebastao Maria, Duke of Vizeu, *b* at Reichenau 22 Sept 1878; ✣ at New York 21 Feb 1923, renounced his rights to the Throne of Portugal for himself and his descendants 21 July 1920; *m* at Tulloch Castle, nr Dingwall, Scotland 15 Sept 1909, Anita (*b* at Elberon, New Jersey USA 17 Aug 1886; ✣ at Newport Rhode Island 1977; she *m* 2ndly, 2 April 1946, Lewis Gouverneur Morris, of Newport, Rhode Island, USA), created Princess of Bragança by Emperor Franz Josef (1909), dau of William Rhinelander Stewart and Annie M Armstrong, and issue, among whom,

> 1. Dom *John* Miguel Guilherme Aloisio Maria Jose Rafael Gabriel Francisco de Assis Carlos Henrique Antonio Sebastiao Huberto de Braganca, *b* at Pippingford, Sussex, England 7 Sept 1912; ✣ at West Palm Beach, Florida 12 March 1991, American Citizen; *m* 1stly at New York 21 May 1948 (*m* diss by div April 1955), Winifred Dodge Seyburn (*b* at Detroit 12 June 1917, *m* 1stly 10 Sept 1938, Edward M McIlvain, *m* 3rdly 3 May 1955, George Morris Cheston *b* at Philadelphia, 7 Aug 1917), dau of Wesson Seyburn and Winifred Dodge [*229 Spruce Street, Philadelphia, PA 19106 USA*]. He *m* 2ndly 15 May 1971, Katherine King Bahnson (*b* at Winston Salem, North Carolina 28 March 1921; *m* 1stly Agnew H Bahnson ✣ 3 June 1964; *m* 3rdly at Roaring Gap, North Carolina, Sept 1994, John Griffith Johnson *b* at Winston-Salem, North Carolina, 16 Oct 1915), dau of James Frank King and Sarah Katherine Millner, and has issue from his first wife,
> [*P.O. Box 1203, Rancho Sante Fe CA 92067 USA*]

>> 1. Dom *Miguel* William, *b* at Glenn Cove, New York 25

Sept 1951; *m* at Boston 27 Sept 1980, Barbara (*b* at
Miami, Florida 20 Sept 1954), dau of Samuel Fales
and Barbara Foote, and has issue,

[*301 Berkley Street, Boston MA 02116, USA*]

    1. Dom *Miguel* Samuel, *b* at Boston 3 Feb 1986.
    2. Doña *Annabel* Barbara, *b* at Boston 6 May
    1989.
    3. Doña *Camilla,* Fales *b* at Boston 21 Oct
    1990.

2. Dom Miguel (*Michael*) Luis Guilherme Maria, *b* at Berlin
7 Sept 1915; ✠ at Palm Beach, Florida 19 Feb 1996, American
Citizen, Civil Airlines Pilot; *m* at Miami, Florida, USA 18
Nov 1946, Barbara Ann (*b* at Roanoke, Virginia, USA 16 Sept
1921, *m* 1stly Henry Scholz Jr *b* May 1922 *d.*.), dau of Albert
Hughson and Margaret Apperson, and has issue,

[*596 North County Road, Palm Beach, Florida, FL33480,
USA*]

    1. Doña *Anita* Stewart, *b* at Stanford, Connecticut
    USA 24 Oct 1947; *m* 1stly at Bedford, New York 28
    March 1968 (*m* diss by div 1982), George Alfred
    Wardman (*b* at New York 30 Jan 1946). She *m* 2ndly
    at Bedford New York 16 Sept1982, John James
    Stockbridge (*b* at Kingston, New York 28 Feb 1943, *m*
    1stly 24 Feb 1968, *m* dis by div 1982, Karen Weiler).
    [*191 Sarlet Street, Mt Kisco, New York 10549, USA*]
    2. Doña *Michele, b* at Stanford, Connecticut USA 5
    Oct 1949.
    [*2434 22nd Street, San Francisco, CA94114, USA*]

Sister of Father

Issue of Infante Dom *Miguel* (II) Maria, Carlos, Egidio, Constantino,
Gabriel, Rafael, Gonzaga, Francisco de Paula e de Assis Januário,
Duke of Bragança, Pretender to the Throne of Portugal, *b* at
Kleinheubach 19 Sept 1853, ✠ at Seebenstein 11 Oct 1927; and his
second wife *Maria Therese* Sophie Pia Anna Melchiora (*b* at Rome 4
Jan 1870; ✠ at Vienna 17 Jan 1935), dau of Karl Heinrich Franz 6th
Prince of Löwenstein-Wertheim-Rosenberg by his second wife
Princess Sophie of Liechtenstein, having had issue among whom,

Daughter

1.Infanta Doña *Maria Adelaide* Emmanuela Amalia Michaela

Raphaela, *b* at St Jean de Luz, Dept Basses-Pyrénées 31 Jan 1912; *m* at Vienna 7 July (relig) and 13 Oct (civ) 1945, Nicolaas van Uden (*b* at Venlo, Prov Limburg, Netherlands 5 March 1921; ✠ at Lisbon 5 Feb 1991), Dr of Med, Dr of Phil, Prof.
[*Rua de Vasco da Gama 9, São João da Caparica, Trafaria, Portugal*].

PRUSSIA
(HOUSE OF HOHENZOLLERN)

Evangelical :- Founded by Burchardus of Zolorin (Hohenzollern, Sigmaringen) who ✠ *ca* 1061; invested with the Burggraviate of Nuremberg by the Holy Roman Emperor through the marriage of Count Friedrich of Zollern (✠ 1125) to Sophie, daughter of the last Burggrave of the House of the Counts of Raabs *ca* 1191; it is probable that the two lines of this family descend from two sons of this marriage - see also HOHENZOLLERN.

The Royal Line below descends from Konrad, Count of Zollern, Burggrave of Nuremberg 1208 - 1261 who inherited the Burggraviate of Nuremberg with the counties of Raabs and Abensberg *ca* 1227; Burggrave Friedrich V obtained recognition as a Prince of the Empire 17 March 1363; his son Friedrich VI was invested at the Council of Konstanz as Friedrich I, Elector and Margrave of Brandenburg 18 April 1417; Elector Georg Wilhelm (✠ 1640) obtained the Duchy of Prussia from the King of Poland 28 Aug 1618 and his son Friedrich Wilhelm, known as The Great Elector, freed Prussia from feudal subjection to Poland in 1657, conquered Pomerania, and suceeded in defeating the Swedish invasion of Prussia in 1674; two of his sons by his second marriage founded the lines of Brandenburg-Schwedt (extinct 12 Dec 1788 and 22 June 1762 respectively), while the eldest surviving son and successor Friedrich III assumed the title of King in Prussia with Imperial sanction in 1701; the title was amended to King of Prussia 13 Sept 1742. King Wilhelm I was proclaimed German Emperor 18 Jan 1871. His grandson, Emperor Wilhelm II, abdicated 28 Nov 1918. Questions relating to the Headship of the Imperial House are currently before the German Courts whom it has been ruled that House Law, and renunciation of claims and rights have no effect under the German Constitution. The matter of a head of a dynasty nominating an heir, other than his successor by primogeniture is the subject of litigation, the result of which is awaited in a dispute surrounding the pre-eminence of Prince Georg Friedrich or his uncle, Prince Friedrich Wilhelm.

Arms:- Arg, an eagle displayed sa, langued gu, armed, membered, treflé on the wings and crowned or, holding in the dexter claw a

sceptre also or, surmounted by an eagle displayed sa, and in sinister claw an orb az, banded and surmounted with a cross or, charged on the breast with the cypher FR or. The shield is ensigned by the Royal Crown of Prussia and encircled by the Collar of the Order of the Black Eagle.
Members of the Family bear the title of Prince or Princess of Prussia with the qualification of Royal Highness. The Head of the Family bears the qualification of Imperial and Royal Highness.

GEORG FRIEDRICH Ferdinand, **PRINCE OF PRUSSIA,** *b* at Bremen 10 June 1976, Grand Master Order of the Black Eagle, Co-Grand Master Hohenzollern House Order, Grand Master Luise Order, *succ* his grandfather as Head of the Imperial and Royal House of Prussia 25 Sept 1994, son of Prince Louis Ferdinand (*b* 25 Aug 1944; ✠*k* 11 July 1977) and Countess Donata zu Castell-Rüdenhausen (*b* 21 June 1950; *m* 24 May 1975; *m* 2ndly 9 Feb 1991, Duke Friedrich August of Oldenburg).
[*Sievershagen, 23738 Lensahn, Ostholstein, Germany*].

Sister
Princess *Cornelie-Cécile* Viktoria Irene, *b* posthumously at Bremen 30 Jan 1978.

Mother
Donata Emma, Duchess Friedrich August of Oldenburg, *b* at Rüdenhausen 20 June 1950, dau of Siegfried, 4th Prince (Fürst) zu Castell-Rüdenhausen and Countess Irene zu Solms-Laubach; *m* 1stly at Rüdenhausen 24 May 1975, Prince Louis Ferdinand Prince of Prussia (*b* at Golzow, Neumark 25 Aug 1944; ✠*k* in army manoeuvres at Bremen 11 July 1977), Lt (Res), Banker. She *m* 2ndly at Rüdenhausen 9 Feb 1991, Duke Friedrich August of Oldenburg (*b* at Rastede 11 June 1936; *m* 1stly, Princess Marie Cécile of Prussia - see below),
[*Sievershagen, 23738 Lensahn, Ostholstein, Germany*].

Brothers and Sisters of Father
Issue of Louis Ferdinand, Prince of Prussia, Head of the Royal House of Prussia (*b* 9 Nov 1907; ✠ 25 Sept 1994 and Grand Duchess Kira Kirillovna of Russia (*b* 9 May 1909; *m* 2 May (civ and relig orth) and 4 May (relig ev) 1938; ✠ 8 Sept 1967).

1. Prince Louis Ferdinand *Friedrich Wilhelm* Hubertus Michael

Kirill, *b* at Berlin-Grünewald 9 Feb 1939, renounced his rights to the Throne for himself and his descendants at Bremen 18 Sept 1967 - upon legal interpretation (1998) renunciations and acts goverened by House Laws were ruled by the German Courts to be unenforceable in proper law, recognition of House Law in any form was ruled in breach of the Federal Constitution, Dr of Phil, Historian; *m* 1stly at Plön, Holstein 22 Aug 1967 (*m* diss by div 1976), Waltraud (*b* at Kiel 14 April 1940), [*Kieler Kamp 11, 24306 Plön, Germany*], dau of Alois Freydag and Annemarie Rolfs, and has issue,

> 1. Prince *Philip* Kirill Friedrich Wilhelm Moritz Boris Tanko, *b* at Eutin 23 April 1968; *m* at Kiel-Kronshagen 28 June (civ) and at Koppelsberg, Plön-Dörnick 2 July (relig) 1994, *Anna* Christine (*b* at Preetz, Schleswig-Holstein 2 April 1968), dau of Eggert Soltau and Annegret Graupner, and has issue, [*Kieler Kamp 11, 24306 Plön, Germany*].
>
> > 1. Prince *Paul Wilhelm* Philipp Friedrich Aloysius Johannes Mose, *b* at Eutin, Schleswig-Holstein 4 Oct 1995.
> >
> > 2. Princess *Maria Luise* Anna Helene Julie Margarethe Elisabeth, *b* at Eutin 12 March 1997.

Prince Friedrich Wilhelm *m* 2ndly at Hechingen 24 April 1976, Ehrengard (*b* at Berlin 7 June 1943), dau of Lt-Col Günter von Reden and Ehrengard von Hülsen, and has further issue, [*Koenigsallee 9, 14193 Berlin, Germany; Deliusweg 20, 28359 Bremen, Germany*].

> 2. Prince *Friedrich Wilhelm* Louis Ferdinand Kyrill, *b* at Berlin 16 Aug 1979.
>
> 3. Princess *Viktoria Luise* Kira Ehrengard, *b* at Berlin 2 May 1982.
>
> 4. Prince *Joachim Albrecht* Bernhard, *b* at Berlin 26 June 1984.

2. Prince Wilhelm Heinrich *Michael* Louis Ferdinand Friedrich Franz Wladimir, *b* at Berlin 22 March 1940, renounced his rights to the Throne for himself and his descendants at Bremen 29 Aug 1966 - upon legal interpretation (1998) renunciations and acts goverened by House Laws were ruled by the German Courts to be unenforceable in proper law, recognition of House Law in any form was ruled in breach of the Federal Constitution, Businessman, Director; *m* 1stly at Düsseldorf-Kaiserswerth 23 Sept (civ) and at Bremen-Borgfeld 25 Sept (relig) 1966 (*m* diss by div at Königstein, Taunus 18 March 1982), Jutta (*b* at Fiessen 27 Jan 1943), dau of Otto Jorn and Ernestine

Prübenau. He *m* 2ndly at Bad Soden, Taunus 23 June 1982, Brigitte (*b* at Kitzbühel 17 Sept 1939), dau of Hans Viktor von Dallwitz-Wegner and Elisabeth Heimann, and has issue by his first wife, [*Im Altenspohl 14, 72406 Bisingen-Thanheim, Germany*].

    1. Princess *Micaela* Maria, *b* at Berlin 5 March 1967.
    [*Fleischergasse 3, 60487 Frankfurt-am-Main, Germany*].
    2. Princess *Natalie* Alexandra Caroline, *b* at Frankfurt-am-Main 13 Jan 1970.
    [*Heinrichstraße 223, 64287 Darmstadt, Germany*].

3. Princess *Marie Cécile* Kira Viktoria Louise, *b* at Cadinen 28 May 1942; *m* at Berlin 3 Dec (civ) and 4 Dec (relig) 1965 (*m* diss by div at Munich 23 Nov 1989), Duke Friedrich August of Oldenburg (*b* at Rastede 11 June 1936; *m* 2ndly at Rüdenhausen 9 Feb 1991, Countess Donata of Castell-Rüdenhausen, widow of Prince Louis Ferdinand of Prussia - see above), Dipl Land Management.
[*Sonnenbichlstraße 21, 83071 Stephanskirchen-Eitzing, Germany*].
4. Princess *Kira* Auguste Viktoria Friederike, *b* at Cadinen 27 June 1943; *m* at Munich 10 Sept 1973 (*m* diss by div at Mühldorf am Inn Jan 1984), Thomas Liepsner (*b* at St Louis, Missouri, USA 20 Jan 1945), Archeologist.
[*Frassbach 13, Neumarkt - St. Veit, Austria*].
5. Prince *Christian Sigismund* Louis Ferdinand Kilian, *b* at Bad Kissingen 14 March 1946, Manager; *m* at Damp, Holstein 29 Sept 1984, Countess Nina (*b* at Kiel 13 March 1954), dau of Ludwig, Count zu Reventlow and Nina Pryadkin, and has issue,
[*Wümmehof, Bremen - Borgfeld, Germany*].

    1. Prince *Christian Ludwig* Michael Friedrich Ferdinand, *b* at Bremen 16 May 1986.
    2. Princess *Irina* Maria Nina Kira, *b* at Bremen 4 July 1988.
6. Princess *Xenia* Sophie Charlotte Cecilie, *b* at Bremen-Oberneuland 9 Dec 1949; ✝ at Selendorf, nr Lütjenburg, East Holstein 18 Jan 1992; *m* at Bremen 26 (civ) and 27 (relig) Jan 1973 (*m* diss by div at Munich 6 March 1978), Per-Edvard Lithander (*b* at Wasa nr Göteborg, Sweden 10 Sept 1944), Businessman.
[*Sehlendorfer Hof, 54424 Sehlendorf bei Lütjenburg, Germany*].

Brothers and Sisters of Grandfather

Issue of Crown Prince Wilhelm of the German Empire and of Prussia (*b* 6 May 1882; ✝ 20 July 1951) and Duchess Cecilie of Mecklenburg-Schwerin (*b* 20 Sept 1886; *m* 6 June 1905; ✝ 6 May 1954), among whom,

1. Prince *Wilhelm* Friedrich Franz Joseph Christian Olaf, *b* at Marmopalace, nr Potsdam 4 July 1906; ✠ at Nivelles of wounds received in battle 26 May 1940, renounced his rights as first born son 1933; *m* at Bonn 3 June 1933, Dorothea (*b* at Bonn 10 Sept 1907; ✠ at Bonn-Bad Godesberg 7 May 1972), only dau of Alexander von Salviati and Helene (Ella) Crasemann, and had issue,

> 1. Princess *Felicitas* Cecilie Alexandring Helene Dorothea, *b* at Bonn 7 June 1934; *m* 1stly at Bonn 12 Sept 1958 (*m* diss by div at Hamburg 5 May 1972), Dinnies von der Osten (*b* at Köslin 21 May 1929), Dipl Econ. She *m* 2ndly 27 Oct 1972, Jörg von Nostitz-Wallwitz (*b* at Verden am der Aller 26 Sept 1937), Banker.
>
> [*Am Sachsenwald 3, 21521 Wohltorf, Lauenburg, Germany*].
>
> 2. Princess *Christa* Friederike Alexandrine Viktoria, *b* at Schloß Klein-Obisch 31 Oct 1936, Art Dealer; *m* at Wahlscheid, Siegkreis (civ) and at Auel, Siegkrei (relig) 24 March 1960, Peter Liebes (*b* at Munich 18 Jan 1926; ✠ at Bonn 5 May 1967). She has since reverted to her maiden name.
>
> [*Bürkleinstraße 14, 80538 Munich, Germany*].

2. Prince *Hubertus* Karl Wilhelm, *b* at Marmorpalace 30 Sept 1909; ✠ at Windhoek, SW Africa 8 April, 1950, Capt German Airforce; *m* 1stly at Oels, Silesia 29 Dec 1941 (*m* diss by div at Berlin 4 Jan 1943), Baroness *Maria-Anna* Sybilla Margaretha (*b* at Bromberg 9 July 1916; *m* 2ndly at Joachimsthal 19 March 1945, Constantin Hahm; that *m* diss by div at Bückeburg 12 Dec 1947), dau of Alexander, Baron von Humboldt-Dachroeden and Katharina Daum [*Volksdorfer Weg 20, 22391 Hamburg, Germany*]. He *m* 2ndly at Schloß Prillwitz, nr Hohenzierlitz, Mecklenburg 5 June 1943, Princess Magdalene (*b* at Leipzig 20 Aug 1920), dau of Prince Heinrich XXXVI Reuss and Princess Hermine von Schönburg-Waldenburg, and by her had issue, among whom,

[*Gartenhaus, Am Hain 11, 63654 Büdingen, OHesse, Germany*].

> 1. Princess *Anastasia* Viktoria Cecilie Hermine, *b* at Brieg 14 Feb 1944 (Catholic since 13 Oct 1965); *m* at Bronnbach an der Tauber 8 Oct (civ) and at Erbach, Rheingau 8 Nov (relig) 1965, Aloys-Konstantin, 9th Prince (Fürst) zu Löwenstein-Wertheim-Rosenberg (*b* at Würzburg 16 Dec 1941), Lt Col (Res).
>
> [*63924 Schloß Kleinheubach bei Miltenberg, Germany*].

3. Prince *Friedrich* Georg Wilhelm Christoph, *b* at Berlin 19 Dec

1911; ✝ at Reinhartshausen 20 April 1966, lived in England as "George Mansfield"; *m* (non-dynastic) at Little Hadham, Herts, England 30 July 1945, Lady Brigid (*b* in London 30 July 1920; ✝ at Patmore Hall 8 March 1995; *m* 2ndly at Old Windsor, Berkshire 3 June 1967, Major Anthony Patrick Ness), dau of Sir Rupert Edward Cecil Lee Guiness, 2nd Earl of Iveagh and Lady Gwendolen Onslow of the Earls of Onslow, and had issue,

    1. Prince Frederick *Nicholas, b* at London 3 May 1946; *m* at The Temple Church, City of London 27 Feb 1980, Hon Victoria (*b* at London 7 March 1952), dau of Stormont Mancroft Samuel Mancroft, 2nd Baron Mancroft and Diana Elizabeth Lloyd, and has issue,

    [*Maperton House, Maperton, nr Wincanton, Somerset*].

        1. Princess *Beatrice* Victoria, *b* at London 10 Feb 1981.
        2. Princess *Florence* Jessica, *b* at London 29 July 1983.
        3. Princess *Augusta* Lily, *b* at London 15 Dec 1986.
        4. Prince *Frederick* Nicholas Stormont, *b* at London 11 June 1990.

    2. Prince William *Andrew, b* at London 14 Nov 1947; *m* at London 2 Jan 1979, Alexandra (*b* at Brünn 28 Dec 1947; *m* 1stly at London 17 Dec 1972, Tom Aisbeth; that *m* diss by div), dau of Frantisek Blahová and Vlasta Dokupilová, and has issue,

        1. Princess *Tatiana* Brigid Honor, *b* at London 16 Oct 1980.
        2. Prince *Friedrich* Alexander, *b* at London 15 Nov 1984.

    3. Princess *Victoria* Marina Cecilia, *b* at London 22 Feb 1952; *m* at Albury, Herts 3 May 1976, Philippe Alphonse Achache (*b* at Toulouse, France 25 March 1948).

    [*50 Tite Street, London SW3 4JA*].

    4. Prince *Rupert* Alexander Frederick, *b* at London 28 April 1955, cand jur; *m* at London 8 Jan 1982, Ziba (*b* at Teheran 12 Dec 1954), dau of Mortéza Rastegar-Javaheri and Rabeéh Baghaii Kermani, and has issue,

    [*53 Redington Road, London, N.W.3.*].

        1. Princess *Brigid* Elisabeth Soraya, *b* at London 24 Dec 1983.
        2. Princess *Astrid* Katherine Rabeéh, *b* at London 16 April 1985.

5. Princess *Antonia* Brigid Elizabeth Louise, *b* at London 28 April 1955 (twin with Prince Rupert); *m* London 3 Feb 1977, Charles, Marquess Douro of the Dukes of Wellington (*b* at Windsor, Berks 19 Aug 1945).

[*Apsley House, 1 Piccadilly, London W1V 9FA*].

Brothers of Great-Grandfather

Issue of Wilhelm II, Emperor of Germany, King of Prussia etc (*b* 27 Jan 1859; *succ* as Emperor 15 June 1888; abdicated 28 Nov 1918; ✝ 4 June 1941) and his first wife, Princess Auguste Viktoria of Schleswig-Holstein-Sonderburg-Augustenburg (*b* 22 Oct 1858; *m* 27 Feb 1881; ✝ 11 April 1921), having had issue, among whom,

Sons

1. Prince *Adalbert* Ferdinand Berengar Viktor, *b* at Marmorpalace, nr Potsdam 14 July 1884; ✝ at La Tour-de-Peilz, nr Montreux, Switzerland 22 Sept 1948; *m* at Wilhelmshaven 3 Aug 1914, Princess Adelheid (*b* at Cassel 16 Aug 1891; ✝ at La Tour-de-Peilz 25 April 1971), dau of Prince Friedrich of Saxe-Meiningen, Duke of Saxony and Princess Adelheid of Lippe, and had issue, among whom,

    1. Prince *Wilhelm Victor* Freund Ernst Friedrich Georg Adalbert, *b* at Kiel 15 Feb 1919; ✝ at Munich 7 Feb 1989, Businessman; *m* at Donaueschingen 20 July 1944, Countess Marie-Antoinette (*b* at Hohenthurm 27 June 1920), dau of Friedrich, Count Hoyos-Sprinzenstein, Baron zu Stichsenstein and Wilhelmine von Wuthenau of the Counts Hohenthurm, and had issue,

        1. Princess *Marie-Louise* Marina Franziska, *b* at Konstanz 18 Sept 1945, Paediatric Nurse, Dame Star Cross Order; *m* at Hechingen 19 May (civ) and at Donaueschingen 22 May (relig) 1971, Rudolf, Count von Schönburg-Glauchau and Waldenburg (*b* at Wechselburg 25 Sept 1932).

        [*Quinta Maria Louisa, 29600 Marbella, Prov. Malaga, Spain*].

        2. Prince *Adalbert-Adelhart* Alexander Friedrich Joachim Christian, *b* at Konstanz 4 March 1948, Businessman; Kt of St John of Jerusalem, *m* at Glentorf, nr Brunswick 14 June 1981, Eva Maria (*b* at Shahi, Iran 30 June 1951), dau of Dr Gunter Kudicke and Barbara Ziegler, and has issue,

[*Kirschäckerweg 10, 81247 Munich, Germany*].

    1. Prince *Alexander* Friedrich Wilhelm Victor Marcus, *b* at Munich 3 Oct 1984.

    2. Prince *Christian* Friedrich Wilhelm Johannes, *b* at Munich 3 July 1986.

    3. Prince *Phillip* Heinrich Adalbert Gunter, *b* at Munich 2 July 1986 (twin with Prince Christian).

2. Prince *August Wilhelm* ("Auwi") Heinrich Gunther Viktor, *b* at StadtSchloß, Potsdam 29 Jan 1887; ✝ at Stuttgart 25 March 1949, MP; *m* at Berlin 22 Oct 1908 (*m* diss by div at Potsdam 16 March 1920), Princess Alexandra Viktoria (*b* at Grunholz 21 April 1887; ✝ at Lyons 15 April 1957; *m* 2ndly at Grünholz 7 Jan 1922, Arnold Rümann who ✝ 6 Dec 1951; that *m* diss by div at Berlin 3 July 1933), dau of Friedrich Ferdinand, Duke zu Schleswig-Holstein-Sonderburg-Glücksburg and Princess Karoline Mathilde zu Schleswig-Holstein, and had issue,

    1. Prince *Alexander Ferdinand* Albrecht Achilles Wilhelm Joseph Viktor Karl Feodor, Major Luftwaffe (ret), *b* at Berlin 26 Dec 1912; ✝ at Wiesbaden 12 June 1985; *m* at Dresden 19 Dec 1938, Irmgard (*b* at Mainz 22 Aug 1912; *m* 1stly, Werner Rosendorff; that *m* diss by div 10 Aug 1933), dau of Friedrich Weygand and Karla Franziska Oheim, and had issue,

    [*Schuppstraße 49, Wiesbaden-Sonnenberg, Germany*].

        1. Prince *Stephan Alexander* Dieter Friedrich, *b* at Dresden 30 Sept 1939; ✝ at Erlangen 12 Feb 1993, Businessman; *m* 1stly at Wiesbaden 28 Feb 1964 (*m* diss by div 1976), Heide (*b* at Frankfurt-am-Main 6 Feb 1939), dau of Dr Ernst Schmidt and Gertrud Gundlach. He *m* 2ndly at Kochel am See 19 June 1981, Hannelore Maria (*b* at Passau 26 Oct 1952), dau of Leo Kerscher and Martha Sufcak, and has issue from his first wife,

        [*Trabelshof, 89250 Senden, Germany*].

            1. Princess *Stephanie* Viktoria Luise Irmgard Gertrud, *b* at Mannheim-Neckarau 21 Sept 1966; *m* at Pondicherry, India 19 April 1991, Amadi Mbaraka Bao (*b* at Lindi, Tanzania 4 June 1958).

            [*Aufheim, 89250 Senden, Germany*].

3. Prince *Oskar* Karl Gustav Adolf, (35th Master of the Knights

1926-1958) Kt of St John of Jerusalem (Bailiwick of Brandenburg), *b* at Marmorpalace 27 July 1888; ✠ at Munich 27 Jan 1958; *m* at Berlin 31 July 1914, Countess Ina Marie, *cr* Countess von Ruppin 27 July 1914, took the name of Princess of Prussia in conformity with   German Civil Law 3 Nov 1919, recognized as Princess of Prussia with the qualification of Royal Highness 26 Aug 1940 (*b* at Bristow 27 Jan 1888; ✠ at Munich 17 Sept 1973), dau of Karl, Count von Bassewitz-Levetzow and Countess Margarethe von der Schulenburg, and had issue, among whom,

>   1. Prince *Wilhelm-Karl* Adalbert Erich Detloff (36th Master of the Knights 1958-1999) Kt of St John of Jerusalem (Bailiwick of Brandenburg), *b* at Potsdam 30 Jan 1922; *m* at Destedt, nr Brunswick 1 March 1952, Armgard (*b* at Destedt 17 Feb 1926), dau of Friedrich (Fritz) von Veltheim, Proprietor of Destedt and Cremlingen and Ottonie von Alvensleben, and has issue,
>   [*Einbeckerstraße 21, 37603 Holzminden, Germany*].

>   >   1. Princess *Donata-Victoria* Ina-Marie Ottonie, *b* at Bonn 24 Dec 1952.
>   >   [*Heimhuderstraße 53, 20148 Hamburg, Germany*].
>   >   2. Prince *Wilhelm-Karl* Oskar Friedrich, *b* at Bonn 26 Aug 1955, MA, Businessman, Kt of Justice St John of Jerusalem.
>   >   [*Kanalstraße 9, 80538 Munich, Germany*].
>   >   3. Prince *Oskar* Hans Karl Michael, *b* at Bonn 6 May 1959, (37th Master of Knights 1999-)Kt of St John of Jerusalem; *m* at Berlin 17 July (civ) and at Ahlden 3 Oct (relig) 1992, Auguste (*b* at Amsterdam 16 May 1962), dau of Ralf Zimmermann von Siefart and Maria von Frankenberg and Proschlitz, and has issue,
>   >   [*Lietzenseeufer 7, 14057 Berlin, Germany*].

>   >   >   1. Prince *Oskar* Julius Alvo Carlos, *b* at Hanover 29 Nov 1993.
>   >   >   2. Princess *Wilhelmine* Auguste Donata Maria Armgard, *b* at Munich 7 July 1995.
>   >   >   3. Prince *Albert* Burchard Karl Markus Nikolaus, *b* at Munich 13 July 1998.

4. Prince *Joachim* Franz Humbert, *b* at Berlin 17 Dec 1890; ✠ at Potsdam 18 July 1920; *m* at Schloß Bellevue, nr Berlin 11 March 1916, Princess Marie Auguste (*b* at Schloß Ballenstedt 10 June 1898; ✠ at Essen 22 May 1983; *m* 2ndly at Berlin-Schoneberg 27 Sept 1926,

Johannes Michael, Baron von Loën; that *m* diss by div at Berlin 18
April 1935 since when she resumed her maiden name), dau of Eduard,
Duke of Anhalt and Princess Luise of Saxe-Altenburg, and had
issue,

1. Prince Karl *Franz Joseph* Wilhelm Friedrich Eduard Paul,
b at Potsdam 15 Dec 1916; ✠ at Arica, Chile 23 Jan 1975,
Capt (ret); *m* 1stly at Doorn 1 Oct (civ) and at Berlin 5 Oct
(relig) 1940 (*m* diss by div 5 Sept 1946), Princess Henriette (*b*
at Berlin 25 Nov 1918; ✠ at Neuendettelsau 16 March 1972),
dau of Prince Johann Georg von Schoenaich-Carolath and
Princess Hermine Reuss (later 2nd wife of Emperor Wilhelm
II), and had issue, among whom,

1. Prince *Franz Wilhelm* Victor Christoph Stephan, *b*
at Grünberg, Silesia 3 Sept 1943, Businessman; *m* at
Dinard 4 Sept (civ) and at Madrid 22 Sept (relig) 1976
(*m* diss by div at Madrid 15 Dec 1986), Grand Duchess
Maria [*Ker Agonid, 35800 St. Briac-sur-Mer, France*]
(*b* at Madrid 23 Dec 1953), dau of Grand Duke Vladimir
Kirillovitch of Russia and Princess Leonida Bagration-
Mukhransky , and has issue,
[*Apartado 6097, 28080 Madrid, Spain*].

1. Prince *Georg, b* at Madrid 13 March 1981.
2. Prince *Franz Friedrich* Christian, *b* at Grünberg 17
Oct 1944, Businessman; *m* at Neuwied 23 Oct 1970 (*m*
diss by div 1996), Gudrun (*b* at Ischenrode 29 Jan
1949), dau of Horst Winkler and Edith Salz, and has
issue,
[*P.O. Box 1211, 21707 Himmelpforten, Germany*].

1. Princess *Christine, b* at Koblenz 22 Feb
1968; *m* at Hamburg 6 Aug (civ) and 6 Aug
(relig Russian Orthodox) 1993, Milos Kovacevi*f*
(*b* at Belgrade 21 Feb 1964), Dr of Med.
Prince Franz Joseph *m* 2ndly at Hamburg 9 Nov 1946 (*m* diss
by div 1959), Luise Dora (*b* at Hamburg 5 Sept 1909; ✠ there
23 April 1961; *m* 1stly, Fritz Simon; that *m* diss by div 1940),
dau of Max Emil Theodor Hartmann and Dora Wandel. He *m*
3rdly at Lima, Peru, Eva Maria (*b* at Pisco, Peru 10 June
1922; ✠ at Lima 1 March 1987), dau of Norberto Herrera
Carraczco and Juana Valdeavellano Otero, and by her had
further issue,

1. Princess *Alexandra* Marie Auguste Juana Consuelo

Eva, *b* at Lima, Peru 29 April 1960; *m* at Lima 28 April 1989 (*m* diss by div 1992), Juan Diego Martinez Lercari (*b* at Lima 10 Jan 1953). She *m* 2ndly at Lima 21 June (civ) and Burg Hohenzollern, Hechingen 7 Oct (relig) 1995, Alberto Reboa Devoto (*b* at Lima 19 May 1952). [*Apartado 4096, Lima, Peru*].

2. Princess *Desirée* Anastasia Maria Benedicta, *b* at Lima, Peru 13 July 1961; *m* at Lima 25 May 1983, Juan Carlos Gamarra Skeels (*b* at Lima 15 Nov 1954), Peruvian Diplomat.

[*Peruvian Embassy, Bucharest, Romania*].

Brother of Great-Great-Grandfather

Issue of Friedrich III, German Emperor and King of Prussia (*b* 18 Oct 1831; *succ* 9 March 1888; ✝ 15 June 1888) and Victoria, Princess Royal of Great Britain and Ireland (*b* 21 Nov 1840; *m* 25 Jan 1858; ✝ 5 Aug 1901), having had issue, among whom,

Son

Prince Albert Wilhelm *Heinrich*, *b* at Neues Palace, Potsdam 14 Aug 1862; ✝ at Herrenhaus Hemmelmark, nr Eckerforde, Schleswig-Holstein 20 April 1929, Grand Adm Imp Navy, Kt Order of Merit (with Oak Leaves), Kt Order of the Garter (1889-1915), etc; *m* at Charlottenburg 24 May 1888, Princess Irene (*b* at Darmstadt 11 July 1866; ✝ at Herrenhaus Hemmelmark 11 Nov 1953), dau of Ludwig IV, Grand Duke of Hesse-Darmstadt and Princess Alice of Great Britain and Ireland, and had issue, among whom,

    1. Prince Wilhelm Viktor Karl August Heinrich *Sigismund*, *b* at Kiel 27 Nov 1896; ✝ at Puntarenas, Costa Rica 14 Nov 1978, Lt German Army (ret), Plantation Owner, Costa Rica; *m* at Hemmelmark 11 July 1919, Princess Charlotte Agnes (*b* at Potsdam 4 March 1899; ✝ at Hemmelmark 16 Feb 1989), dau of Ernst II, Duke of Saxe-Altenburg, and had issue,

        1. Prince *Alfred* Friedrich Ernst Heinrich Conrad, *b* at Finca Santa Sofia Guatemala 17 Aug 1924; *m* at Southampton, Long Island, New York 15 Dec 1984, Maritza (*b* at Gombaszög, Bez Rosenau am Sajo 6 Aug 1929; ✝ at Rochester, Minnesota 1 Nov 1996; *m* 1stly, Dirk van Wilpe; that *m* diss by div 1963), dau of Julius Zaladörgicse et Kiskapornok and Ilona Literáti (of Hungarian nobility).

[*Apartado 856 Centro Colón, 1007 José de Costa Rica, A.C.*]

Brothers of Great-Great-Great-Great-Grandfather

Issue of King Friedrich-Wilhelm III (*b* 3 Aug 1770; ✝ 7 June 1840) and Princess Louise of Meckenburg-Strelitz (*b* 10 March 1776; *m* 24 Dec 1793; ✝ 19 July 1810), having had issue, among whom,

Sons

1. Prince Friedrich *Karl* Alexander, *b* at Charlottenburg 29 June 1801; ✝ at Berlin 21 Jan 1883, Gen Field Marshal Prussian Army, 32nd Herrenmeister (Master of the Knights 1852-1883) Kt of St John of Jerusalem; *m* at Charlottenburg 26 May 1827, Princess Marie (*b* at Weimar 3 Feb 1808; ✝ at Berlin 18 Jan 1877), dau of Karl Friedrich, Grand Duke of Saxe-Weimar-Eisenach and Grand Duchess Maria Pavlovna of Russia, and had issue, among whom,

Son

Prince *Friedrich Karl* Nikolaus, *b* at Berlin 20 March 1828; ✝ at JagdSchloß Klein-Glienicke, nr Potsdam 15 June 1885, Gen Field Marshal Royal Prussian Army; Field Marshal Imp Russian Army; *m* at Berlin 29 Nov 1854, Princess Maria Anna (*b* at Dessau 14 Sept 1837; ✝ at Friedrichroda, Thüringen 12 May 1906), dau of Leopold, Duke of Anhalt and Princess Friederike of Prussia, and had issue, among whom,

Son

Prince Joachim Karl Wilhelm *Friedrich Leopold*, *b* at Berlin 14 Nov 1865; ✝ at Flatow, Westpreussen 13 Sept 1931, Lt-Col Royal Prussian Army (ret); *m* at Berlin 24 June 1889, Princess Luise Sophie (*b* at Kiel 8 April 1866; ✝ at Bad Nauheim 28 April 1952), dau of Friedrich, Duke of Schleswig-Holstein and Princess Adelheid zu Hohenlohe-Langenburg, and had issue, among whom,

Son

Prince Joachim Viktor Wilhelm Leopold *Friedrich Sigismund*, *b* at JagdSchloß Klein-Glienicke 17 Dec 1891; ✝ in a riding accident at Lucerne 6 July 1927; *m* at JagdSchloß Klein-Glienicke, nr Potsdam 27 April 1916, Princess Marie Luise (*b* at Ödenburg, Hungary 10 Feb 1897; ✝ at Neu-Fahrland, nr Potsdam 1 Oct

1938), dau of Friedrich, Prince of Schaumburg-Lippe and Princess Louise of Denmark, and had issue,

1. Princess *Luise* Viktoria Margarete Antoinette Sieglinde Alexandrine Thyra Stephanie, *b* at Klein-Glienicke 23 Aug 1917; *m* at Potsdam 12 Sept 1942 (*m* diss by div at Hamm 2 June 1949), Hans Reinhold (*b* at Berlin-Charlottenburg 20 Nov 1917), Lt-Col (ret). Princess Luise has reverted to her maiden name. [*Schloß, Westfügel, 31675 Bückeburg, Germany*].

2. Prince *Friedrich Karl* Viktor Stephan Christian, *b* at Klein-Glienicke 13 March 1919, Dipl Land Man, Kt of St John of Jerusalem; *m* 1stly at Nikolskoe in Berlin-Wannsee 13 Dec 1961, Lady Hermoine (*b* at Johannesburg, S Africa 2 March 1925; ✠ at Findhorn Bridge, Moray, Scotland 2 Sept 1969; *m* 1stly, John Oliver Roberts; that *m* diss by div at London 26 Oct 1960), dau of Archibald John Morton Stuart, Earl of Moray and Mabel (May) Wilson. He *m* 2ndly at Rottach-Egern 11 Feb 1974 (*m* diss by div at Munich 7 March 1978), Adelheid (Heidi) (*b* at Soest 16 Setp 1943), dau of Florens von Bockum genannt Dolffs, Proprietor of Völlinghausen and Ahse, Kr Soest and Ursula von Krause. [*Finca son Peña, Puig Vista, 07430 Llubl, Majorca, Spain*].

2. Prince Friedrich Heinrich *Albrecht*, *b* at Königsberg im Preussen 4 Oct 1809; ✠ at Berlin 14 Oct 1872, Lt-Gen Royal Prussian Cav; *m* 1stly at The Hague 14 Sept 1830 (*m* diss by div at Berlin 28 March 1849), Princess Marianne (*b* at Berlin 9 May 1810; ✠ at Schloß Reinhatshause, Rheingau 29 May 1883), dau of Wilhelm I, King of the Netherlands, Grand Duke of Luxemburg and Princess Wilhelmine of Prussia. He *m* 2ndly at Berlin 13 June 1953, Rosalie (*b* at Berlin 29

Aug 1820; ✠ at Schloß Albrechtsberg, nr Dresden 5 March 1879), *cr* Countess von Hohenau 28 May 1853, dau of Gustav von Rauch and Rosalie von Holtzendorff, and had issue, among whom, from his first marriage,

> **Son**
>
> Prince Friedrich Wilhelm Nikolaus *Albrecht,* *b* at Berlin 8 May 1837; ✠ at Kamenz, Silesia 13 Sept 1906, Gen Field Marshal Royal Prussian Army, Rector Univ of Göttingen, Pres of the Royal Academy of the Sciences in Erfurt, Regent of the Duchy of Brunswick (since 21 Oct 1885), 33rd Herrenmeister (Master of the Knights 1883-1906) Kt of St John of Jerusalem; *m* at Berlin 19 April 1873, Princess Marie (*b* at Eisenberg 2 Aug 1854; ✠ at Kamenz 8 Oct 1898), dau of Ernst I, Duke of Saxe-Altenburg and Princess Agnes of Anhalt-Dessau, and had issue, among whom,
>
> > **Son**
> >
> > Prince *Friedrich Wilhelm* Viktor Karl Ernst Alexander Heinrich, *b* at Kamenz 12 July 1880; ✠ at Weisser Hirsch, nr Dresden 8 March 1925, Dr phil hc, Maj.-Gen. Royal Prussian Army (ret); *m* at Potsdam 8 June 1910, Princess Agathe (*b* at Rauden 24 July 1888; ✠ at Wiesbaden 12 Dec 1960), dau of Viktor, Duke von Ratibor, Fürst von Corvey, Prince zu Hohenlohe-Schillingsfürst and Countess Maria Breunner-Enkevoirth, Proprietor of Grafenegg-Neuaigen, and had issue, among whom,
> >
> > > 1. Princess *Marie Therese* Auguste Viktoria Friederike Henriette Charlotte Agathe, *b* at Berlin 2 May 1911; *m* at Freiburg im Breisgau 13 May 1932, Rudolph Hug (*b* at Hammerschmiede, nr Aalen 21 Oct 1885; ✠ at Lützelsachsen an der Bergstrasse 17 Nov 1972), Col (ret).
> > > [*Weinheimerstraße 72, 69469 Weinheim-Lützelsachsen, Germany*].

REUSS

Lutheran: Founded by Erkenbert, Lord of Weida, who was living in 1122. His descendants were appointed Vogts (Imperial Stewards) at Weida, Gera and Plauen by the Emperor Heinrich VI, in whose honour every male of the family has been named Heinrich ever since; acquired Lobenstein 1278 and Schleiz between 1289 and 1317. Heinrich the Young, Vogt of Plauen 1276-92, m Countess Jutta of Schwarzburg-Blankenburg, and from 1289 bore the surname "der Russe" (the Russian) as son-in-law of Sophie, dau of Daniel, King of Galicia (✝ 1264). From 1426 to 1572 the family held the Burgraviate of Meissen with the right to vote in the College of Princes of the Empire. Kranichfeld was acquired in 1451, but sold to Saxony in 1615. Heinrich III Reuss "der Friedsame" (the Mild), Edler Herr von Plauen zu GreizandKranichfeld (✝ 1535) was the common ancestor of the several branches of the family, all of which are extinct with the exception of the second branch of the Younger Line.

Elder Line: ✝ Reuss-Greiz ✝
(✝ Extinct ✝)

Founded by Heinrich Reuss the Elder, Noble Lord of Plauen at Untergreiz (b 1506; ✝ 22 March 1572); the right of succession was established 1668 and 1681; Count of the Holy Empire, Eger 26 Aug 1673; commenced the enumeration of all the male members of the family in a continuing sequence at Greiz 1693; Prince of the Holy Empire, Brandeis 12 May 1778; abdication of the dynasty 11 Nov 1918. This line became extinct in the male line 13 Oct 1927.

The members of the family bore the title of Prince or Princess Reuss Elder Line with the qualification of Serene Highness.

Younger Line.

Founded by Heinrich Reuss the Younger, Lord of Plauen of Gera (b 29 Dec 1530; ✝ 6 April 1572); inherited Lobenstein and Schleiz at the extinction of the Elder Line of Plauen (formerly the Line of the Burggraves of Meissen) 1572 and of the Middle Line of Reuss 1616; separation of the Line of Gera (extinct 1802) by the elder son of Heinrich Posthumus and last son of Heinrich the Young, 1635; Count of the Holy Empire, Eger 26 Aug 1673; establishment of the order of primogeniture and the foundation of the Line of Köstritz in 1690; the lines below descend from two sons of Count Heinrich I Reuss Younger Line of Schleiz (b 26 March 1639; ✝ 18 March 1692); abdication of the dynasty 11 Nov 1918. A resolution of the Family Council decided that the designation of "Younger Line" added to the family name of Reuss should be discontinued 5 June 1930.

✚ I: Reuss-Schleiz ✚
(✚ Extinct ✚)

Founded by Count Heinrich XI Reuss Younger Line of Schleiz (*b* 12
April 1669; ✚ 28 July 1726); inherited Gera 1802; Prince of the Holy
Empire 9 April 1806. This Line became extinct in the male line in
autumn 1945.
Members of the family bore the title of Prince or Princess Reuss
with the qualification of Serene Highness.

II: Reuss-Schleiz-Köstritz

Founded by Heinrich XXIV Younger Line of Reuss-Schleiz Köstritz
(*b* 26 July 1681; ✚ 24 July 1748); his sons founded the two Houses
below.
Members of the family bear the title of Prince or Princess Reuss
with the qualification of Serene Highness.

First House

Founded by Count Heinrich IX of the cadet branch of Reuss-Köstritz
(*b* 15 Sept 1711; ✚ 16 Sept 1780); assumed the title of Prince 6 Oct
1817; inherited Köstritz at the extinction of the line of Reuss-Schleiz
(Princes since 1806)

HEINRICH IV, PRINCE (FÜRST) REUSS-KÖSTRITZ,

Count and Lord of Plauen, Lord of Greiz, Kranichfeld, Gera, Schleiz
and Lobenstein, *b* at Ernstbrunn 26 Oct 1919, Cmdr Austrian Branch
Kt of St John of Jerusalem, son of Heinrich XXXIX (*b* 23 June 1891;
✚ 24 Feb 1946) and Countess Antonie zu Castell-Castell (*b* 18 April
1896; *m* 7 Aug 1918; ✚ 4 May 1971); *m* at Varlar 10 June 1954,
Princess Marie Luise (*b* at Varlar 18 Aug 1918), dau of Otto, Prince
(Fürst) zu Salm-Horstmar and Countess Rosa zu Solms-Baruth, and
has issue,
[*2115 Schloß Ernstbrunn, Lower Austria, Austria*].

Son and Daughters

1. Prince *Heinrich XIV, b* at Vienna 14 July 1955, Dipl Eng,
Forester, Lt (res), Kt of St John of Jerusalem; *m* at Munich 25 April
(civ) and at Regensburg 30 April (relig) 1995, Baroness Johanna
(*b* at Ehrang, nr Trèves 12 Sept 1971), dau of Jan, Baron Raitz von
Frentz and Baroness Kunigunde von Hoenning O'Carroll, and has
issue,
[*2115 Schloß Ernstbrunn, Lower Austria, Austria*].

    1. Prince *Heinrich XXIX, b* at Mistelbach, Lower Austria 2
    March 1997.

2. Princess Anna Elisabeth *Johanetta, b* at Vienna 29 June 1957,

mag theology, Minister; *m* at ... 1991, Phillip, Baron von Hohenbühl Ansitz Gleifheim.

[*39057 St. Michael-Eppan, Italy*].

3. Princess *Caroline* Adelma Henriette Anna Elisabeth, *b* at Vienna 21 June 1959, Mag oec; *m* at Ernstbrunn 28 Sept 1991, Carl Philipp, Baron von Hohenbühel gt Heufler zu Rasen (*b* at Bozen 25 July 1957).

[*Ansitz Gleifheim, 39507 St. Michael, Eppan, Italy*].

4. Princess *Espérance* Anna Elisabeth Eleonore, *b* at Vienna 22 July 1962, Decorator; *m* at Ernstbrunn 20 Aug 1989, Johannes, Count Kinsky von Wchinitz and Tettau (*b* at Regensburg 7 Aug 1964), Banker.

[*Repská 10 Bílá Hora, 16000 Prague, Czech Republic*].

Brothers and Sisters

1. Prince *Heinrich VI*, *b* at Vienna 27 June 1922; ✝*k* near Stalingrad 5 Dec 1942, Lt.

2. Princess *Amadea* Caroline Anna Elisabeth Gertrud Viola Eleonore, *b* at Vienna 23 July 1923; *m* at Ernstbrunn 2 Jan 1959, Reinhold Sachs (*b* at Osseningken 26 July 1922; ✝ at Berlin 22 Sept 1989), Dr of Agr, Dipl Land Management, Dipl Psychology, Prof of Agriculture University of Berlin.

[*Sedanstraße 28A, 12167 Berlin, Germany*].

3. Princess *Gertrud Renata* Anna Elisabeth Jutta Gasparine, *b* at Vienna 5 Nov 1924; *m* at Versailles 30 Sept (civ) and at Castell 14 Oct (relig) 1950, Henri, Baron Grand d'Esnon (*b* at Paris 24 Jan 1918), Col (ret).

[*Château d'Esnon, 89210 Brienon sur Armancon, Dept. Yonne, France*]

4. Prince *Heinrich VII*, *b* at Gera 14 May 1927; ✝ 8 Feb 2002; *m* at Utrecht 14 Aug 1971, Baroness Brigitte Barbara Renée (*b* at Soerabaja, Java 22 March 1940), dau of Alexander Frederik, Baron van Tuyll van Serooskerken and Countess Angelika von Lüttichau, and has issue,

[*Pfarrer Socherstraße 52, 82041 Oberhaching, Germany*].

    1. Princess *Cucile* Angelika Lucile Amadea, *b* at Munich 23 July 1972.

    2. Prince *Heinrich XIX*, *b* at Munich 17 May 1974.

    3. Prince *Heinrich XXII*, *b* at Munich 8 Aug 1976.

5. Princess *Elisabeth Donata* Regina Emma Clementine, *b* at Vienna 8 June 1932; *m* at Vienna 14 May 1960, Right Rev Peter Coleman

LLB, MLitt, former Bishop of Crediton, (*b* at London 28 Aug 1928; ✠
at Salisbury 27 Dec 2001), .
[*Boxenwood Cottage, West Bagborough, nr. Taunton, Somerset,
TA4 3HQ*].

Brother of Great-Grandfather

Issue of Prince Heinrich LXIII (*b* 18 June 1786; ✠ 27 Sept 1841) and
his first wife Countess Éléonore zu Stolberg-Wernigerode (*b* 26 Sept
1801; *m* 21 Feb 1819; ✠ 14 March 1827), having had issue, among
whom,

Son

Prince *Heinrich VII*, *b* at Klipphausen 14 July 1825; ✠ at Trebschen
2 May 1906, Gen Cavalry, Adj-Gen German Ambassador in Vienna,
Kt Swedish Adler Order; *m* at Weimar 6 Feb 1876, Princess Marie
Alexandrine (*b* at Weimar 20 Jan 1849; ✠ at Trebschen 6 May 1922),
dau of Karl Alexander, Grand Duke of Saxe-Weimar-Eisenach, Duke
of Saxony and Princess Sophie of the Netherlands, and had issue,
among whom,

Sons

1. Prince *Heinrich XXXV*, *b* at Mauer, nr Vienna 1 Aug 1887; ✠ at
Dresden-Loschwitz 17 Jan 1936; *m* 1stly at Altenburg 20 April 1911
(*m* diss by div 4 March 1921), Princess Maria (*b* at Schloß
Albrechtsberg, nr Dresden 6 June 1888; ✠ at Hamburg 12 Nov 1947;
she reverted to her maiden name in 1932), dau of Prince Albert of
Saxe-Altenburg, Duke of Saxony and Princess Maria of Prussia. He
m 2ndly at Bremen 12 April 1921, Princess Marie Adelheid (*b* at
Drogelwitz 30 Aug 1895; ✠ at Tangstedt, Kr Stormarn 25 Dec 1993,
known since 22 Oct 1936 as "Princess Reuss zur Lippe"; *m* 1stly at
Drogelwitz, nr Weissholz, Kr Glogau 19 May 1920, Heinrich XXXII,
Prince Reuss, that *m* diss by div at Guben 18 Feb 1921; she *m* 3rdly
at Berlin 24 Feb 1927, Friedrich Kurt (Hanno) Konopath; that *m*
diss by div at Berlin 2 Oct 1936), dau of Prince Rudolf of Lippe and
Princess Luise von Ardeck, and by her had issue,

 1. Prince *Heinrich V*, *b* at Erpen, Kr Iburg 26 May 1921; ✠
 at Hamburg 28 Oct 1980, Dr of Law, Lawyer; *m* at Hamburg-
 Blankenese 22 June 1961, Ingrid (*b* at Hamburg 9 March
 1936; ✠ there 15 Feb 1991), dau of Ernst Eugen Jobst and
 Gertrud Neumann, and had issue,

  1. Princess *Maria Alexandra* Luise Hermine Dora
  Helene, *b* at Hamburg 1 Sept 1963; *m* at Erbach 11

July (civ) and 13 July (relig) 1985, *Eberhard*, Hereditary Count (Erbgraf) zu Erbach-Erbach (*b* at Erbach 2 June 1958).

[*Hofgut Habrich, 64720 Highelstadt, Germany*].

2. Prince *Heinrich Ico*, *b* at Hamburg 18 Oct 1964, stud jur; *m* at Lechenich 8 May (civ) and 17 July (relig) 1999, Baroness Corinna (*b* at ... 12 Nov 1967), dau of Harald, Baron von Elmendorff and Renate Kurig, and has issue,

[*Forsthaus Fuhrenkamp, 21379 Lüdersburg, Germany*].

    1. Princess *Henriette* Josephine Viktoria-Lise, *b* at Hamburg 16 Nov 2000.

3. Princess *Caroline* Marie Adelheid Greia Gabriele Elisabeth, *b* at Hamburg 30 Dec 1968; *m* at Hamburg 25 Feb 1995, Sebastian Papst (*b* at ... 20 Aug 1971).

[*Frauenthal 16, 20149 Hamburg, Germany*].

Half-Brother of Great-Grandfather

Issue of Prince Heinrich LXIII (*b* 18 June 1786; ✧ 27 Sept 1841) and his second wife, Countess Caroline zu Stolberg-Wernigerode (*b* 16 Dec 1806; *m* 11 May 1928; ✧ 26 Aug 1896), having had issue, among whom,

Son

Prince *Heinrich XII, b* at Dresden 8 March 1829; ✧ at Bad Liebenstein 15 Aug 1866; *m* at Pless 6 June 1858, Countess Anna (*b* at Fürstenstein 23 July 1839; ✧ at Dresden 14 March 1916; *m* 2ndly at Fürstenstein 25 Sept 1869, Heinrich XIII, Prince Reuss who ✧ at Baschkow, Posanie 3 Jan 1897), dau of Johann Heinrich X, Fürst von Pless and Ida de Stechow des Kotzen, and had issue, among whom,

    1. Prince *Heinrich XXVIII, b* at Stonsdorf, Riesengebirge 3 June 1859; ✧ at Berlin 8 March 1924; renounced his name and title at Ebersdorf 15 July 1908 and assumed the name "Count von Dürrenberg", Kt of Hon Kt of St John of Jerusalem; *m* 1stly at Laubach 18 Sept 1884 (*m* diss by div 4 June 1907), Countess Magdalene (*b* at Jannowitz 11 Dec 1863; ✧ at Oberstdorf, Allgäu 21 April 1925), dau of Friedrich, Count zu Solms-Laubach and Countess Marianne zu Stolberg-Wernigerode. He *m* 2ndly at London 12 Oct 1908, Grace Sawyer (*b* at Belgaum, India 15 March 1874; ✧ .at London 17

Feb 1958), dau of Col. George Westrenen Sawyer and Mary Elizabeth Allen, and had issue, among whom from his first wife,

Sons

1. Prince *Heinrich XXXIV, b* at Stonsdorf 4 June 1887; ✠ at Frankfurt-am-Main 30 April 1956, Dr of Law; *m* at Trebschen 12 Dec 1909, Princess Sophie Renata (*b* at Mauer, nr Vienna 27 June 1884; ✠ at Giessen 19 Jan 1968), dau of Heinrich VII, Prince Reuss and Princess Marie Alexandrine of Saxe-Weimar-Eisenach, and had issue,

    1. Prince *Heinrich I, b* at Krietern 8 Oct 1910; ✠ at Büdingen OberHesse 10 March 1982, adopted 19 Jan 1935 by Heinrich XLV, Hereditary Prince Reuss Younger Line (*b* 1895; ✠*k* 1945), Farmer, Lt-Col (ret), Kt of Hon Kt of St John of Jerusalem; *m* at Bad Doberan, Mecklenburg 15 Sept 1939, Duchess Woizlawa Feodora (*b* at Rostock 17 Dec 1918), dau of Duke Adolf-Friedrich of Mecklenburg and Princess Victoria Feodora Reuss Younger Line, and had issue,
    [*Am Pfaffenwald 12, 63654 Büdingen, OHesse, Germany; Otto Dix Straße 20, 07548 Gera, Germany*].

        1. Princess *Feodora* Elisabeth Sophie, *b* at Gera 5 Feb 1942, Kindergarden Teacher; *m* at Schlitz 28 Aug (civ) and at Herrnhaag, nr Büdingen 10 Sept (relig) 1967, Gisbert, Count zu Stolberg-Wernigerode (*b* at Radenz, Kr Krotoschin 2 May 1942), Banker.
        [*Am Wildenstein 7, 63654 Büdingen, OHesse, Germany*].

        2. Prince *Heinrich VIII, b* at Gera 30 Aug 1944, Banker, Lt (res); *m* at Schwarzenbeck 14 June (civ) and at Basthorst, Kr Hzgt Lauenburg 16 June (relig) 1973, Baroness Dorit (*b* at Hamburg 8 Jan 1948), dau of Franz, Baron von Ruffin, Proprietor of

Basthorst and Carla Busson, and has issue,
[*Kaiser Sigmundstraße 59, 60329 Frankfurt-am-Main, Germany*].

    1. Prince *Heinrich XX, b* at Hamburg 24 Nov 1975.

    2. Prince *Heinrich XXIII, b* at Hamburg 1 March 1979.

3. Prince *Heinrich IX, b* at Büdingen 30 June 1947, Businessman; *m* at Rimsting am Chiemsee 5 Oct (civ) and 6 Oct (relig) 1984, Baroness Amélie (*b* at Munich-Pasing 20 Feb 1959), Paediatric Nurse, dau of Albrecht, Baron Besserer von Thalfingen and Countess Marie Rose Grundemann von Falkenberg, and has issue,
[*Franfurter LandStraße 44, 61440 Oberusrsel/Ts, Germany*].

    1. Princess *Johanna* Woizlawa Maria Anna Gaudete, *b* at Frankfurt-am-Main 15 Dec 1985.

    2. Prince *Heinrich XXVI, b* at Frankfurt-am-Main 30 Nov 1988.

4. Prince *Heinrich X, b* at Büdingen 28 July 1948; *m* at Büdingen (civ) and at Herrnhaag (relig) 11 Sept 1976 (separated Dec 1985; *m* diss by div at Frankfurt-am-Main 30 April 1990), Baroness Elisabeth [*Nesenstraße 9, 60322 Frankfurt-am-Main, Germany*] (*b* at Stockholm 7 April 1946; *m* 1stly at Stockholm 28 June 1969, Klaus-Peter, Baron von der Borch, *b* at Potsdam 14 March 1943; that *m* diss by div at Hamburg 4 Oct 1972; Annuled at Augsburg 18 Dec 1991), dau of Erik Samuel, Baron Akerhielm af Margrethelund and Astrid Ekenberg. He *m* 2ndly at Wiesbaden 7 May (civ) and 11 May (relig) 1991, Countess

Antoinette (*b* at Hebenshausen 15 Aug 1949; *m* 1stly at Lausanne 7 Sept 1972, André Régné, that *m* diss by div at Vevey Switzerland 17 Dec 1975), dau of Adolf-Heinrich, Count von Arnim-Boitzenburg and Maria Henschel, and has issue from his first wife, [*Carl Schurichtstraße 8, 65187 Wiesbaden, Germany*].

> 1. Princess *Benigna* Cecilia Anastasia Elisabeth Sophie, *b* at Frankfurt-am-Main 29 Dec 1980. [*Nesenstraße 9, 60322 Frankfurt-am-Main, Germany*].
>
> 2. Prince *Heinrich XXIV*, *b* at Frankfurt-am-Main 23 May 1984. [*Nesenstraße 9, 60322 Frankfurt-am-Main, Germany*].

5. Prince *Heinrich XIII*, *b* at Büdingen 4 Dec 1951, Dipl Eng; *m* at Büdingen 1 Aug 1989 (civ), Susan Doukht (*b* at Teheran 14 April 1956), dau of Ali Akbar Jalali and Fateme Nayer Sarmadi, and has issue,

[*Rossertstraße 14, 60323 Frankfurt-am-Main, Germany*].

> 1. Princess *Elena* Paria Marie Cicil, *b* at Frankfurt-am-Main 9 Dec 1989.
>
> 2. Prince *Heinrich XXVIII*, *b* at Frankfurt-am-Main 22 May 1991.

6. Prince *Heinrich XV*, *b* at Büdingen 9 Oct 1956, Furniture Restorer; *m* at Büdingen 15 April 1999, Anija Charlotte (*b* at Canterbury 22 Jan 1965), dau of George Brain Nooth-Cooper and Heike Gesche, and has issue,

[*Hauptstraße 54, 63654 Büdingen-Orleshausen, Germany*].

> 1. Prince *Heinrich XXX*, *b* at Hanau 21 June 1999.

2. Prince *Heinrich III*, *b* at Breslau 27 July 1919; ✥ at Vienna 7 July 1993, Dr of Law, Dr of Biology, Lt-Col (ret); *m* 1stly at Frohnleiten, Steiermark 13 March 1944 (*m* diss by div at Leoben 13 May 1955), Baroness Franziska (*b* at Vienna 12 Dec 1919; ✥ at Munich 11 April 1964; *m* 2ndly at Bruck an der Mur 21 Sept 1955, Percy Lippitt; that *m* diss by div at Innsbruck 21 Oct 1960), dau of Franz, Baron Mayr von Melnhof, Proprietor of Kaiserberg, Steiermark, and Princess Maria zu Hohenlohe-Waldenburg-Schillingsfürst, von Ratibor and Corvey, and has issue,

> 1. Princess *Antoinette* Maria Anna Magdalena Cecilie Georgine, *b* at Feldkirch 11 Jan 1945; *m* 1stly at Kitzbühel 21 May 1976 (*m* diss by div 1984), Otto Vogl (*b* at Halle 22 March 1932). She *m* 2ndly at New York Nov 1984, Peter Michael De Scheel (*b* ...), Businessman.
> [*Haus Gerber, 3778 Schönried, Switzerland*].
>
> 2. Princess *Felizitas* Maria Gertrude Katharina, *b* at Mauritzen, Bez Frohnleiten, Steiermark 26 Oct 1946; *m* 1stly at Rabertshausen, Kr Giessen 1 July (civ) and at Graz 9 July (relig) 1967 (*m* diss by div at Munich 3 July 1974), Peter, Prince zu Sayn-Wittgenstein-Berleburg (*b* at Hamburg 5 Feb 1940), Businessman. She *m* 2ndly at Munich 25 Oct 1974, that *m* diss by div 10 March 1992, Franz Clemens, Count von Schönborn-Wiesentheid (*b* at Breslau 3 Oct 1939), Bank Director.
> [*La Renardière, 7 chemin de Mapraz, 1225 Chene-Bourg, Kt Genf, Switzerland*].
>
> 3. Prince *Heinrich XII*, *b* at Mautern, Steiermark 13 Oct 1950; *m* 1stly at

Mautern 30 May (civ) and at Bad Ausee 3 June (relig) 1973 (*m* diss by div at Leoben 10 Sept 1980), Countess Henriette (*b* at Pöchlarn, Lower Austria 3 March 1951; *m* 2ndly at Washington DC 11 March 1981, Bruce Tompson, *b* at Orange NJ 7 Dec 1946), dau of Alois, Count von Meran and Baroness Elisabeth von Tinti, and has issue,

1. Princess *Anna* Franziska Irina, *b* at Munich 20 Jan 1975.
[*Danklerhube, 8774 Mautern, Austria*].

2. Prince *Heinrich XXI*, *b* at Leoben 27 July 1976.
[*Danklerhube, 8774 Mautern, Austria*].

3. Princess *Maximiliana* Maria Paula, *b* at Leoben 30 June 1977.
[*Danklerhube, 8774 Mautern, Austria*].

Prince Heinrich XII *m* 2ndly at Saalfelden 18 Sept 1983 (civ) and at Schloß Wald 26 Sept (relig) 1983 (*m* diss by div at Vienna 27 March 2000), Countess Henriette (*b* at Vienna 9 Jan 1961), dau of Karl Josef, Count von Seilern and Aspang and Countess Henriette von Seilern and Aspang, Proprietor of Hörmanns, and has further issue,
[*Stallburggasse 2, 1010 Vienna, Austria*].

4. Prince *Heinrich XXV*, *b* at Leoben 7 Oct 1984.

5. Princess *Maria* Concetta Sieglinde Alexandra Marina, *b* at Leoben 15 Dec 1988.

6. Princess *Viktoria* Alexandra Wolfgang, *b* at Leoben 20 May 1993.

Prince Heinrich III *m* 2ndly at Utrecht 5 Sept 1964, Countess Odylia (*b* at Armhein, Gelderland 26 Oct 1939), dau of Constantin, Count zu Castell-Castell and Countess Luitgardis von Rechteren-Limpurg, and has further issue,

[*Landgoed Beverweerd, Herenstraat 25, 3985 RP Werkhoven, Netherlands*].

    4. Prince *Heinrich XVII*, *b* at Salzburg 9 Nov 1968.; *m* at Vienna 22 Sept 2001, Letizia (*b* at Geneva 31 Aug 1969), dau of Alexander Hoffman and Noelle Scaler Walser.

    [*Salesianergasse 8/2, 1030 Vienna, Austria*].

2. Prince *Heinrich XXXVI*, *b* at Stonsdorf 10 Aug 1888; ✞ at Oberstdorf 10 April 1956, Dr of Phil; *m* at Droyssig 5 Oct 1919, Princess Hermine (*b* at Langenzell 18 Sept 1899; ✞ at Rheda, Westfalen 2 Sept 1982), dau of Heinrich, Prince von Schönburg-Waldenburg, Proprietor of Droyssig and Quesnitz, Kr Weissenfels and Princess Olga zu Löwenstein-Wertheim-Freudenberg, and had issue,

    1. Princess *Magdalene* Pauline, *b* at Leipzig 20 Aug 1920; *m* at Schloß Prillwitz, nr Hohenzieritz, Mecklenburg 5 June 1943, Prince Hubertus of Prussia (*b* at Marmorpalace, nr Potsdam 30 Sept 1909; ✞ at Windhoek, Southwest Africa 8 April 1950), Capt German Airforce.

    [*Gartenhaus, Am Hain 1, 63654 Büdingen, OHesse, Germany*].

    2. Princess *Caroline*, *b* at Leipzig 7 May 1923; *m* at Frankfurt-am-Main (civ) and at Wiesbaden 4 Oct (relig) 1950, Alfred, Count von Wedel, Baron Wedel-Jarlsberg (*b* at Berlin 22 Feb 1895; ✞ at Cologne 18 Oct 1973), Major (res), Businessman.

    [*Bettinaplatz 6, 60325 Frankfurt-am-Main, Germany*].

Half-Brother of Great-Great-Great-Grandfather

Issue of Prince Heinrich XLIV (*b* 20 April 1753; ✠ 3 July 1832) and his second wife, Baroness Augustine zu Eisenbach (*b* 9 Aug 1771; *m* 12 May 1792; ✠ 21 Nov 1805).

Son

Prince *Heinrich LXXIV, b* at Brunswick 1 Nov 1798; ✠ at Jänkendorf, Haute-Lusace 22 Feb 1886; *m* 1stly at Weissstein 14 March 1825, Countess Clementine (*b* at Kuchendorf 20 Feb 1805; ✠ at Jänkendorf 10 June 1849), dau of Leopold, Count von Reichenbach-Goschütz and Ernestine von Czettritz and Neuhaus. He *m* 2ndly at Ilsenburg 13 Sept 1855, Countess Éléonore (*b* at Gedern 20 Feb 1835; ✠ at Ilsenburg, Saxony 18 Sept 1903), dau of Hermann, Hereditary Count (Erbgraf) zu Stolberg-Wernigerode and Countess Emma zu Erbach-Fürstenau, and had issue, among whom, from his first wife,

Son

Prince *Heinrich IX, b* at Neuhoff 3 March 1827; ✠ at Neuhoff, nr Schmiedeberg 1 Aug 1898, Major-Gen Prussian Army; *m* at Zülzendorf 12 May 1852, Baroness Anna (*b* at Zülzendorf 15 Aug 1829; ✠ at Niesky 1 March 1907), dau of August, Baron von Zedlitz and Leipe, Proprietor of Zülzendorf and Countess Jenny von Roedern, having had issue, among whom,

Son

Prince *Heinrich XXVI, b* at Neuhoff 15 Dec 1857; ✠ at Jena 10 June 1913; *m* at Ullersdorf 19 Nov 1885, Countess Viktoria (*b* at Ullersdorf 11 Sept 1863; ✠ at Djurscholm, Sweden 10 July 1949), dau of Adolf, Count von Fürstenstein, Proprietor of Ullersdorf and Elisabeth von Watzdorf, Proprietor of Wiesenburg, and had issue, among whom,

(In 1887 at a family conference, the sons were recognised as members of the sovereign house eligible to succeed bearing the arms of Reuss and the name Counts of Plauen with the qualification of Illustrious Highness: - *Reference Almanach de Gotha 1939*)

> **Sons**
>
> 1. Prince *Heinrich Harry (Prince Reuss (Count) von Plauen),* *b* at Görlitz 28 March 1890; ✠ at Meggen, nr Lucerne 29 July 1951, Proprietor of Jänkendorf, Kr Rothenburg, OLausitz, Lt-Col (ret), adopted 1 May 1927 by Prince Heinrich XXX Reuss (*b* 1864; ✠ 1939) when he received the right to the qualification of Serene Highness for himself and his

descendants; *m* at Moschen 21 April 1921, Baroness Huberta (*b* at Neustadt, OSilesia 14 April 1889; ✝ at Meggen, Kt Lucerne 19 June 1974), dau of Franz-Hubert, Count von Tiele-Winckler, Proprietor of Moschen and Jelka von Lepel, and had issue,

    1. Prince *Heinrich Enzio, b* at Lucerne 21 Feb 1922, ✝ at Hamburg 27 March 2000, Dipl Forestry, Advertising Executive; *m* 1stly at Malmö, Sweden 31 Aug 1949 (*m* diss by div 8 Feb 1954), Louise (*b* at Malmö 1 Nov 1918; ✝ 22 Feb 1989; she *m* 2ndly Theodor Ankarcrona, ✝ at Boserup 4 Feb 1984), dau of Gustav, Baron Peyron and Emma Kockum, and had issue,

        1. Prince *Heinrich Ruzzo, b* at Lucerne 24 May 1950, ✝ at Landskrona 29 Oct 1999; *m* at Sandelfjord, Norway 31 Aug 1974 (*m* diss by div at Oslo 15 June 1986), Metta (*b* at Oslo 17 May 1948), dau of Sigurd Rinde and Bess Freng, and has issue,

            1. Princess *Henriette* Anna-Bess Helle Mette, *b* at Oslo 2 June 1977.
            [*Boston, U.S.A.*].
            2. Princess *Pauline* Margaretha Emma-Louise Mette, *b* at Oslo 2 June 1977 (twin with Princess Henriette).
            [*London*].

Prince Heinrich Ruzzo *m* 2ndly at Hörsholm, Denmark 26 Aug 1992, Anni-Frid Lyngstad (*b* at Ballangen, Norway 15 Nov 1945; *m* 1stly at 1978, Benny Andersson, *m* diss by div 1981), dau of Alfred H and Synni Lyngstad.

Prince Heinrich Enzio *m* 2ndly at Offenbach am Main 24 Oct 1954, Countess Feodora (*b* at Burkersdorf 26 Nov 1931; ✝ at Unterstedt 8 April 1999), dau of Sylvius, Count von Pückler, Baron von Groditz and Baroness Alice von Richthofen of the Counts Seichau, and had further issue,

    1. Prince *Heinrich* Achaz, *b* at Düsseldorf 5 April 1956; *m* at Hamburg 28 July 1989, Johanna (*b* at Hamburg 9 Jan 1965), dau of Dieter Guthmann and Friederieke Gutschov, and has issue,

[*Jürgensallee 7a, 22609 Hamburg, Germany*].
  1. Prince Heinrich *Caspar*, *b* at
  Hamburg 1 April 1993.
  2. Prince Heinrich *Jacob*, *b* at Hamburg
  31 Jan 1999.

2. Princess Marina Carolina, *b* at Hamburg 27
Oct 1964.
[*Sierichstraße 50, 22301 Hamburg, Germany*]
3. Prince Heinrich Patrick, *b* at Hamburg 21
June 1966.
[*Grovestraße 15, 22083 Hamburg, Germany*].
2. Princess *Edina* Huberta, *b* at Lucerne 25 June 1923;
m 1stly at Jänkendorf 6 Feb 1944 (*m* diss by div at
Darmstadt 5 June 1950), Max-Erdmann, Count von
Roedern, Baron zu Krappitz and Herr zu Bergck (*b* at
Berlin 21 Feb 1918), Businessman. She *m* 2ndly at
Darmstadt 29 Jan 1952 (*m* diss by div at Darmstadt 11
Nov 1966), Franz Frey (*b* at Michelstadt 23 Sept 1923),
Dipl Eng.
[*Staudach 100, 9546 Bad Kleinkirchheim, Austria*].
2. Count *Enzio* Heinrich, *b* at Kiel 13 July 1897; ✣ at Freiburg
20 Dec 1973, Proprietor of Wiesenburg, Kr Zauch-Belzig,
Major (ret); *m* 1stly at Dresden 14 Sept 1922 (*m* diss by div at
Berlin 11 July 1928), Nina (*b* at Worms 11 April 1898; ✣ at
Silesia .. Nov 1944), dau of Hermann Cotta and Nina Fütschow.
He *m* 2ndly at Broby, Södermanland, Sweden 5 Jan 1935, Maj
(*b* at Stockholm 2 Feb 1911; ✣ at Bühler Höhe 26 Sept 1969),
dau of Carl William Nisser, Proprietor of Broby and Anna
Wising, and by her had issue,
  1. Count *Rigo* Heinrich, *b* 7 Nov 1935; *m* at Stockholm
  5 Sept (civ) and at Djurholm (relig) 5 Oct 1963 (*m* diss
  by div), *Marianne* (*b* at Porjus 17 Sept 1942), dau of
  Bengt Alexson and Gunvor Wagner; he *m* 2ndly, at
  Lidingo 26 Aug 1967, Agneta (*b* at Stockholm 21 April
  1942; ✣ in an air accident at Athens 7 Oct 1979), dau
  of Fritz, Count von Rosen and Countess Viveka af
  Björnö, and has issue,
    1. Count *Richard-Heinrich*, *b* at Vienna 4 March
    1964.
    2. Countess *Anna* Henrietta Victoria, *b* at
    Freiburg im Breisgau, Germany 2 May 1969; *m*

at Eckenförde, Germany 31 Aug 1991, Vinzenz,
Count von Kageneck (*b* at Freiburg am
Breisgau 7 Jan 1972).

3. Count *Enzio* Victor Heinrich, *b* at Freiburg
am Breisgau 7 Jan 1972.

4. Count *Friedrich* Rigo Heinrich, *b* at Freiburg
am Breisgau 7 Jan 1972 (twin with Count Enzio).

2. Countess *Henriette, b* at Berlin 10 May 1938; *m* at
Bettna, Sweden 18 May 1963 (*m* diss by div 1971),
Friedrich-Carl, Count von Schweinitz and Krain, Baron
von Kauder (*b* at Breslau 11 June 1937).

Second House
**Founded by Count Heinrich XXIII of the cadet branch of
Reuss-Köstritz (*b* 9 Dec 1722; ✠ 3 Sept 1787); assumed the title of
Prince 30 June 1851.**

HEINRICH XI Licco, **PRINCE REUSS,** *b* at Berlin 28 Aug
1934, Businessman, son of Heinrich XXXVII, Prince Reuss (*b* 1 Nov
1888; ✠ 9 Feb 1964) and Stephanie Clemm von Hohenberg (*b* 25 Dec
1900; *m* 7 Aug 1933; ✠ 10 Feb 1990); *m* at Breitenbach am Herzberg,
Kr Ziegenhain 20 July (civ) and at Burg Herzberg 21 July (relig)
1961, Baroness Ulfa (*b* at Berlin 17 April 1935), dau of Siegried,
Baron von Dörnberg and Marie-Elisabeth Lorenz.
[*Leiblstraße 25, 14467 Potsdam, Germany*].

Sons and Daughters
1. Princess *Henriette* Charlotte Sophie Stefanie Marie Elisabeth, *b*
at Hamburg 24 April 1964; *m* at Mainz 24 July (civ) and at Breitenbach
am Herzberg 29 July (relig) 1989, Rupprecht, Count zu Solms Baruth
(*b* at Munich 5 Aug 1963), Banker.
[*Hochweg 4a, 85250 Altomünster, Germany*].

2. Prince Heinrich XVI (*Henry*), *b* at Wiesbaden 8 Dec 1965, Banker,
Lt (res); *m* at Schweinsberg OHesse 17 Sept 1994, Baroness Julia (*b*
at Bonn 22 Sept 1968), dau of Baron Kraft Schenck zu Schweinsberg
and Jutta Müller.
[*Gluckstraße 23, 60318 Frankfurt-am-Main, Germany*].

3. Prince Heinrich XVIII (*Henrik*), *b* at Wiesbaden 10 Aug 1969; *m*
at Berlin 16 Feb (civ) and at Wettenhausen, Schwaben 28 April
(relig) 2001, Diana (*b* at Augsburg 6 May 1972), dau of Georg von
Hagen and Antonia, Countess Zichy de Zich et Vásonkeö.
[*Gartenstraße 111, 10115 Berlin, Germany*].

4. Princess Friederike Alexandrine, *b* at Bonn 5 April 1976.
[*Peterstraße 35-37, 20355 Hamburg, Germany*].

Sister

Princess *Marianne* Charlotte Katharina Stefanie, *b* at Berlin 29 July 1936, Translator; *m* 1stly at Garmisch-Partenkirchen 18 June (civ) and at Grainau 28 July (relig) 1973, Avery Brundage (*b* at Detroit 28 Sept 1887; ✚ at Garmisch-Partenkirchen 8 May 1975), Engineer, President International Olympic Committee. She *m* 2ndly at Minden, Nevada 23 Feb 1987, Friedrich Karl Feldmann (*b* at Zurich 15 Dec 1915), Dr of Eng.
[*1106 Dulzura Drive, Montecito, Santa Barbara, CA 93108, U.S.A.*].

Brother of Father

Prince *Heinrich XLII*, *b* at Ludwigslust 22 Sept 1892; ✚ at Garmisch-Partenkirchen 10 March 1949, Col (ret); *m* 1stly at Berlin 28 Dec 1923, Charlotte (*b* at Berlin 30 Nov 1892; ✚ at Garmisch-Partenkirchen 16 Sept 1944; *m* 1stly at Berlin 3 Feb 1914, Werner Alfred Eduard Lent; that *m* diss by div at Berlin 3 March 1920), dau of Franz Hugo Nawrath and Emma Löser. He *m* 2ndly at Garmisch-Partenkirchen 3 Nov 1947, Anneliese (*b* at Halle an der Saale 11 July 1915; ✚ at Garmisch-Partenkirchen 17 Feb 1997; *m* 1stly at Halle 26 Sept 1936, Harald Weberstaedt; that *m* diss by div at Berlin 15 June 1946), dau of Karl Taube and Klara Margarethe Dabelow, and by her had issue,
[*Zoepritzstraße 16, 82467 Garmisch-Partenkirchen, Germany*].

> 1. Princess *Alexandrine*, *b* at Garmisch-Partenkirchen 27 April 1948; *m* at Munich 27 March (civ) and at Garmisch-Partenkirchen 28 March (relig) 1975, Uwe Schulze (*b* at Hindenburg 10 Jan 1940), who assumed the name "Prince Reuss" Nov 1979 according to German law.
> [*Ortlindestraße 2, 81927 Munich, Germany*].

ROMANIA
(HOUSE OF HOHENZOLLERN)

Romanian Orthodox: Prince Karl of Hohenzollern-Sigmaringen (*b* **20 April 1839;** ✚ **27 Sept/10 Oct 1914) was elected as reigning Prince of Romania with hereditary rights by a plebiscite on 8/20 April 1866 - 12/24 Oct 1866; received the qualification of "Royal Highness" 13/ 25 Oct 1878; proclaimed King of Romania 14 March 1881; having no**

descendants, his nephew Prince Ferdinand of Hohenzollern-Sigmaringen was designated heir-apparent and bore the title of Crown Prince of Romania from 18 March 1889 until he became King in 1914; his son, Carol II, King of Romania, as Crown Prince renounced his rights of succession to the Throne at Milan 28 Dec 1925 (made Law 4 Jan 1926), returned to Romania three years later and was reinstated in his rights 6 June 1930, being proclaimed King at Bucharest 8 June 1930, he again abdicated in favour of his son Michael 6 Sept 1940; the dynasty was exiled when Michael I, King of Romania was forced to sign an act of abdication on 30 Dec 1947 and to leave the country on 2 Jan 1948; Michael I, King of Romania maintained his claim to the Throne of Romania rejecting the validity of the so-called abdication which as King, had not been signed with his assent and was implemented as an act of force contrary to law. Members of the Royal Family bear the title of Prince or Princess of Romania with the qualification of Royal Highness. A new Dynastic Law allowing for the succession of females to the Throne (but recognizing male primogeniture amongst siblings) was announced by Michael I, King of Romania on 30 Dec 1997, on the 50th Anniversary of his forced Abdication, in Bucharest, where he also announced the appointment of his eldest daughter, Princess Margarita, as Crown Princess of Romania and Heir Apparent.

Arms:- Quarterly: 1st, az an eagle wings displayed and inverted, crowned or, armed and langued gu, holding a sceptre and sword and in its beak a cross patée, and in dexter chief a sun in splendour, also or (Wallachia); 2nd, gu, an auroch's (or bull's) head cabossed with a mullet between the horns and a crescent or in sinister chief (Moldavia); 3rd, gu, a demi-lion crowned issuant from a coronet, holding in the fore-paws a star of five points or (Banat); 4th, az, two dolphins respectant, heads in base and tails in chief, arg (Dobrudja); over all an escutcheon of pretence, quarterly, arg and sa (Hohenzollern). *Supporters:-* Two lions rampant or, armed and langued gu. *Motto:-* Nihil sine Deo. The achievement is born on a mantle purp, fringed and tasselled or, doubled erm and surmounted by the Royal Crown.

MICHAEL (MIHAI) I, KING OF ROMANIA, reigned firstly from 1927 to 1930, then bore the title of Crown Prince of Romania, Grand Voivode of Alba Julia during his father's reign, reigned secondly from 1940 until he was forced to abdicate on 30 Dec 1947 and leave the country on 2 Jan 1948, renewed his claim to the throne at London 4 March 1948, *b* at Foisor 25 Oct 1921, son of King Carol II (*b* 16 Oct 1893; ✠ 4 April 1953) and Princess Helen of Greece and Denmark (*b* 3 May 1896; *m* 10 March 1921; *m* diss by div 21 June 1928; ✠ 28 Nov 1982); Collar and Grand Master of the Order of Carol I of Romania; Order of Faithful Service; Order of The Crown of

Romania and the Star of Romania; Grand Cross of the Royal
Victorian Order; Grand Cross of the Legion of Honour of France;
Grand Cross of the Order of Leopold of Belgium; Collar of the Order
of the Annunciata; Grand Cross, Order of St Saviour of Greece;
Chief Commander, Legion of Merit of the United States of America;
Order of Victory of the USSR; Bailiff Grand Cross Honour and
Devotion, Sovereign Military Order of Malta, etc, etc; Marshal of the
Romanian Armed Forces, *m* at Athens 10 June 1948, Princess Anne
(*b* at Paris 18 Sept 1923), Grand Cross of the Order of Carol I of
Romania; Grand Cross of the Order of St Sophia and Olga of Greece;
Dame Grand Cross Honour and Devotion, Sovereign Military Order
of Malta; Croix de Guerre of France, only dau of Prince Don René of
Bourbon Parma and Princess Margrethe of Denmark, and has issue,
[*The Elisabeta Palace, Bucharest, Romania; Villa Serena, 77 chemin
Louis Dégallier, 1290 Versoix-Geneva, Switzerland*].

Daughters

1. *Margarita*, Crown Princess of Romania (1997), Princess of
Hohenzollern (1983), *b* at Lausanne 26 March 1949; Grand Cross of
the Order of Carol I of Romania; *m* at Lausanne 21 Sept 1996, *Radu*
Duda (*b* at Iasi 7 June 1960); created Prince of Hohenzollern-Veringen
(*ad personam*) with the qualification of Serene Highness by order of
Friedrich Wilhelm, Prince (Fürst) von Hohenzollern, at Sigmaringen
1 January 1999.
[*The Elisabeta Palace, Bucharest, Romania*].

2. Princess *Elena*, *b* at Lausanne 15 Nov 1950, Art Restorer; *m* 1stly
at Durham, England 20 July (civ) and at Lausanne 24 Sept (relig)
1983 (*m* diss by div at Sunderland, 28 Nov 1991), Dr (Leslie) Robin
Medforth-Mills (*b* at Sproatley, Yorkshire 8 Dec 1942; ✝ at Geneva
3 Feb 2002). She *m* 2ndly at Peterlee, Co. Durham, 14 Aug 1998,
Alexander Philips Nixon McAteer (*b* at Easington Co. Durham 22
Oct 1964).
[*Villa Serena, 77 chemin Louis Dégallier, 1290 Versoix-Geneva,
Switzerland*].

3. Princess *Irina*, *b* at Lausanne 28 Feb 1953; *m* at Lausanne 10 Dec
1983 (civ) and at Phoenix, Arizona 11 Feb 1984 (relig), *John* Kreuger
(*b* at Solna, Sweden 3 Aug 1945), Horse Breeder, Businessman.
[*Villa Serena, 77 chemin Louis Dégallier, 1290 Versoix-Geneva,
Switzerland*].

4. Princess *Sophie*, *b* at Tatoi, Athens 29 Oct 1957; ceased to bear
her rank and title on 29 Aug 1998 by Order of the King; and is

consequently known as Mrs Biarneix; *m* at Paris 29 Aug 1998, *Alain* Michael Leonce Biarneix (*b* at Nancy 10 July 1957; now known as Alain "de Laufenbourg").

[*Villa Serena, 77 chemin Louis Dégallier, 1290 Versoix-Geneva, Switzerland*].

5. Princess *Maria, b* at Hellerup, Denmark 13 July 1964; *m* at New York 16 Sept 1995 (Officially Seperated 2000), Kazimierz (*Casimir*) Wieslaw Mystkowski (*b* at Las-Poczylowo, Lonza, Poland 13 Sept 1958), Financial Analyst.

[*Villa Serena, 77 chemin Louis Dégallier, 1290 Versoix-Geneva, Switzerland*].

RUSSIA
(House of Romanov/ Romanoff)

Orthodox: The Russian State was founded by Rurik, a Norse adventurer ruling at Novgorod 862 - 1114, at Kiev 913 - 1240 with sovereign dignities; Grand Duke of Vladimir 1157, of Smolensk 1170, of Moscow 1328, Grand Duke of Novgorod and Seigneur of Pskow 1478, Tsar of Moscow, Vladimir and Novgorod 16 Jan 1547, of Astrakhan 1554, of Siberia 1581. When this Line failed in the direct male line in 1598 the Throne was occupied by a number of usurpers and pretenders until finally, Mikhail Feodorovitch Romanov (*b* 12 July 1596; *d* 12 July 1645) was elected Tsar of Russia with hereditary rights 21 Feb 1613. He was descended from André Kobyla, a Boyar living in the 8th century who emigrated from Prussia. Prince of Estonia 1710, of Livonia 1721, Tsar and Autocrat of all the Russias 2 Nov 1721. Peter, Duke of Holstein-Gottorp (*b* 21 Feb 1728; *d* 17 July 1762), grandson of Duke Friedrich IV (Holstein, Line II, Branch I), son of Duke Karl-Friedrich of Holstein-Gottorp (*b* 00 April 1700; *d* 18 June 1739) and Anna (*b* 27 Jan/7 Feb 1708; *m* 21 May/1 June 1725; *d* 4/15 May 1728), daughter of Peter the Great of the House of Romanov (*b* 30 May/9 June 1672; *d* 28 Jan/8 Feb 1725) and his second wife, Catherine-Alexandrovna, née Skavronska (*d* 6/17 May 1737), was nominated Grand Duke of Russia and successor to the throne, under the name of Peter Feodorovitch, by his mother's sister, Empress Elisabeth (*b* 18/29 Dec 1709; *d* 25 Dec 1761/5 Jan 1762, 18 Nov 1742 and succeeded as Emperor Peter III, 5 Jan 1762. Emperor of the Chersonnese Taurica 1778, Emperor of Kiev 4 Jan 1793, Grand Duke of Lithuania, Volhynie and Podolie, Prince of Courland 24 Oct 1795, Grand Duke of Finland 17 Sept 1809, Emperor of Poland 26 Feb 1832. Emperor Nicholas II was the last Emperor to rule (abdicated in favour of his brother 15 March 1917) and was assassinated with his family at Ekaterinburg 16/17 July 1918.

Arms:- Or, a double-headed eagle displayed sa, beaked, langued and membered gu, each head crowned with a Royal Crown, holding in the dexter claw a sceptre and in the sinister claw an orb all or, the mounted figure of St George slaying the dragon all ppr, charged on the dexter wing with the arms of the Kingdoms of Kazan, Astrakhan, Siberia and Novgorod and on the sinister wing with the arms of the Grand Duchies of Kiev, Taurica and Finland and the Kingdom of Poland. The Collar of the Order of St Andrew is placed around the shield of the arms of Moscow on the breast of the eagle. The whole is ensigned with the Imperial Crown of Russia.

N.B. Although the Julian Calendar was in use in Russia, all dates herein are according to the Gregorian Calendar.

The Romanov Family Association elected Nicholas Romanovitch as Senior Male Representative at Paris 31 Dec 1992 and again by re-election of confirmation on Russian soil at Peterhof, St Petersburg (at the Private residence of the Emperors' of Russia) on 18 July 1998 at the conclusion of ceremonies following the burial of the mortal remains of Emperor Nicholas II and other members of the Imperial Family assassinated at Ekaterinburg on 17 July 1918. A claim to the headship of the Imperial House of Russia is made by Maria Vladimirovna, issue of the last Head of the Imperial House of Russia, Grand Duke Vladimir Kirillovitch (*See below Line II*); based on the interpretation of male primogeniture succeeding only among the issue of marriages of equal rank, following which, after the total extinction of the male line, female succession is permitted; and on the basis of the mandated wish of Grand Duke Vladimir to alter the rules of succession in his daughter's favour. Both Maria Vladimirovna and Nicholas Romanovitch (*Lines I and II - See below*) are the issue of mothers of equal rank (Part V, tables of Russian Nobility) and previously by dynasts of equal rank.

The titles of the Imperial Family were regulated by an Imperial Decree (Ukase) 14 July 1886, whereby the children, grandchildren and siblings of Emperors were accorded the title of Grand Duke or Grand Duchess of Russia with the qualification of Imperial Highness. All other descendants were accorded the title of Prince or Princess of Russia with the qualification of Serene Highness, except the eldest son of each great-grandson who was to have the qualification of Highness. There is a tendency for members of the family born since the Revolution to drop the designation "of Russia" and use the surname Romanov, while retaining the title of Prince or Princess with the appropriate qualification. Since the Revolution the Head of the Imperial Family of Russia in Exile granted various titles to Family Members. While these titles are not in accordance with the Family Statutes, they are generally recognized as a courtesy and therefore are listed.

LINE I - Descent from Emperor Nicholas I

The line descends directly from **EMPEROR NICHOLAS I,
EMPEROR and AUTOCRAT OF ALL THE RUSSIAS**,
(*b* at Gatshina 25 Jul 1796; ✚ at St Petersburg 18 Feb 1855); and
Empress Alexandra Feodorovna, born Princess Charlotte of Prussia
(*b* at Charlottenberg 13 Jul 1798; *m* at St Petersburg 1 Jul 1817; ✚ at
St Petersburg 18 Feb 1855); through their third son Grand Duke
Nicholas, (*b* at Tsarskoe Selo 8 Aug 1831; ✚ at Kiev 25 April 1891)
and Duchess Alexandra of Oldenburg, (*b* at St Petersburg 2 June
1838; *m* at St Petersburg 6 Feb 1856; ✚ at Kiev 25 April 1900);
through their second son, Grand Duke Peter, (*b* at St Petersburg 22
Jan 1866; ✚ at Cap d'Antibes 17 June 1931) and Princess Militza of
Montenegro (*b* at Cetinje 26 July 1866; *m* at Peterhof 7 Aug 1889; ✚
at Alexandria, Egypt 5 Sept 1951); through their only son, Prince
Roman, (*b* at Peterhof 17 Oct 1896; ✚ at Rome 23 Oct 1978) and
Countess Prascovia Dimitrievna Cheremetev (*b* Poltava 15 Oct 1901;
m at Cap d'Antibes16 Nov 1921; ✚ Rome 21 Dec 1980); and had
issue,

NICHOLAS ROMANOV, PRINCE OF RUSSIA, *b* at Cap
d'Antibes 26 Sept 1922, *m* at Cannes 21 Jan 1952, Sveva (*b* at
Florence 15 July 1930), dau of Walfredo, Count della Gherardesca
and Nicoletta of the Marquesses de Piccolellis, and has issue,
[*Châlet A Le Daguay, 1838 Rougemont, Switzerland*].

Daughters

1. Princess *Natalia, b* at Rome 4 Dec 1952; *m* at San Vincenzo 30
April 1973, Giuseppe Consolo (*b* at Naples 6 Sept 1948).
[*Via Sebastiano Conca 13, 00197 Rome, Italy*].

2. Princess *Elisaveta, b* at Rome 7 Aug 1956; *m* at San Vincenzo 14
May 1983, Mauro Bonacini (*b* at Salsomaggiore Terme 13 May 1950).
[*Via Agostino Bassi 13, 00191 Rome, Italy*].

3. Princess *Tatiana, b* at Rome 12 April 1961; *m* 1stly at San Vincenzo
2 July 1983 (*m* diss by div 1990), Giambattista Allessandri (*b* at Oslo
31 Dec 1958).She *m* 2ndly at San Giovanni di Marignano 29 Aug
1998 Giancarlo Tirotti (*b* at Rome 1 Nov 1947).
[*Strada per Gradara 13/15, 61010 Tavullia, Italy*].

Brother

Prince *Dimitri, b* at Cap d'Antibes 17 May 1926, Historian Author of "The Orders, Medals and History of the Kingdom of Bulgaria" (1982), "The Orders, Medals and History of Greece" (1987), "The Orders, Medals and History of Montenegro" (1988), "The Orders, Medals and History of the Kingdoms of Serbia and Yugoslavia" (1996), The Orders, Medals and History of Imperial Russia (1999); *m* 1stly at Copenhagen 21 Jan 1959, Jeanne (*b* at Copenhagen 1 June 1936; ✠ at Copenhagen 12 May 1989), dau of Axel von Kauffmann and Inge Kier. He *m* 2ndly at Kostroma, Russia 28 July 1993, Dorrit (*b* at Olinda, Brazil 22 April 1942), MA, dau of Erik Reventlow and Nina Bente.

[*Engvej 5, 2960 Rungsted Kyst, Denmark*].

LINE I - Descent from Emperor Alexander II

The Line descends directly from **ALEXANDER II, EMPEROR AND AUTOCRAT OF ALL THE RUSSIAS,** *b* at Moscow 29 April 1818; ✠ *assasinated* at St Petersburg 13 March 1881, crowned at Moscow 7 Sept 1856, KG 1867; *m* 1stly at St Petersburg 28 April 1841, Maria Alexandrovna, formerly Princess Marie (*b* at Darmstadt 8 Aug 1824; ✠ at St Petersburg 9 June 1880), dau of Ludwig II, Grand Duke of Hesse-and-by-Rhine and Princess Wilhelmine of Baden, through their third son Grand Duke *Vladimir,* *b* at St Petersburg 22 April 1847; ✠ at St Petersburg 17 Feb 1909, Gen of Inf Russian Army and Adjt-Gen; *m* at St Petersburg 28 Aug 1874, Maria Pavlovna, formerly Duchess Marie (*b* at Ludwigslust 14 May 1854; ✠ at Contrexéville, France 6 Sept 1920), dau of Friedrich Franz II, Grand Duke of Mecklenburg-Schwerin and Princess Auguste Reuss-Schleiz-Köstritz, through their second son **Grand Duke Kirill,** *b* at Tsarskoie-Selo 12 Oct 1876; ✠ at Neuilly-sur-Seine 13 Oct 1938, proclaimed himself Curator of the Throne at St Briac, Brittany 8 Aug 1922 and later as the Emperor and Autocrat of all the Russias 31 Aug 1924, formerly Rear-Adm Imp Russian Navy; *m* at Tegernsee 8 Oct 1905, Victoria Feodorovna, formerly Princess Victoria Melita (*b* at Malta 25 Nov 1876; ✠ at Amorbach 2 March 1936; *m* 1stly, Ernst Ludwig, Grand Duke of Hesse-and-by-Rhine; that *m* diss by div at Darmstadt 21 Dec 1901), dau of Alfred, Duke of Saxe-Coburg-Gotha, Duke of Edinburgh, Prince of Great Britain and Ireland and Grand Duchess Maria Alexandrovna of Russia, through their eldest son **Grand Duke Vladimir,** *Prince with the qualification of Highness; assumed the titles of Grand Duke of Russia with the qualification of Imperial Highness on his father's recommendation,* became Head of the Imperial House of Romanov on the death of his father, (*b* at

Borga, Finland 30 Aug 1917; ✠ at Miami 21 April 1992); *m* at Lausanne, Switzerland 12 Aug (civ) and 13 Aug (relig) 1948, Princess Leonida (*b* at Tiflis 6 Oct 1914; *m* 1stly, Sumner Moore Kirby; that *m* diss by div at Nice 18 Nov 1937), dau of Georgi Alexandrovitch, Prince Bagration-Mukhransky and Elena Zlotnicka, and had issue,

Daughter

1. Princess *Maria,* *b* at Madrid 23 Dec 1953, (*assumed the style of Grand Duchess of Russia with the qualification of Imperial Highness on her father's recommendation); m* at Madrid 22 Sept (relig) 1976 (*m* diss by div at Madrid 15 Dec 1986), Prince *Franz Wilhelm* of Prussia (*b* at Grünberg, Silesia 3 Sept 1943) by whom she has issue (*See that family*) .

[*Guisando 17, Ciudad Puerto de Hierro, 28035 Madrid, Spain; Ker Argonid, 35800 Saint Briac-sur-Mer, France*].

LINE II - Descent from Emperor Alexander II

The Line descends directly from **ALEXANDER II, EMPEROR AND AUTOCRAT OF ALL THE RUSSIAS,** and Empress Maria Alexandrovna (*See above*); through their sixth son Grand Duke Paul, (*b* at Tsarskoie-Selo 3 Oct 1860; ✠ *assassinated* at St Petersburg 30 Jan 1919), Gen of Cav and Adjt-Gen Russian Army; *m* 1stly at St Petersburg 17 June 1889, Princess Alexandra (*b* at Corfu 30 Aug 1870; ✠ at Ilinskoie, nr Moscow 24 Sept 1891), dau of George I, King of the Hellenes and Grand Duchess Olga Constantinovna of Russia, through their second son Grand Duke Dimitri, (*b* at Ilyinskoie 18 Sept 1891; ✠ at Davos, Switzerland 5 March 1942), capt Russian Cavalry, Aide-de-Camp; *m* at Biarritz 21 Nov 1926 (*m* diss by div at Bayonne, France 6 Dec 1937) Ann-Audrey (*b* at New York 4 Jan 1904; ✠ at Palm Beach Florida, 25 Nov 1971), known as Princess Romanovsky-Ilyinsky, dau of John Josiah Emory and Leila Alexander and had issue,

Son

1. Prince *Paul,* *b* in London 27 Jan 1928, naturalised an American citizen under the name "Ilyinsky" by which he is known, and by which his issue are similarly known, former Mayor of Palm Beach (1991-2001), Florida; *m* 1stly at Honolulu, Hawaii 29 July 1949 (*m* diss by div 1952), *Mary* Evelyn (*b* at Memphis, Tennessee April 1925), dau of William Prince. He *m* 2ndly at Palm Beach, Florida 1

Oct 1952, *Angelika* (*b* at Paris 22 March 1932), dau of Philip Kauffmann and Floria Kneidecker, and by her has issue,
[*270 Algoma Road, Palm Beach, FL 33480, U.S.A.*].

    1. Prince *Dimitri,* "Ilyinsky" *b* at Palm Beach 1 May 1954; *m* at New Haven, Connecticut 22 Sept 1979, Martha (*b* at New Haven 15 June 1952), dau of Ted Irvine McDowell and Phyllis Murray, and has issue,
    [*195 South Street, Litchfield Connecticut 06759 U.S.A.*]

        1. Princess *Catherine* Adair, "Ilyinsky" *b* at Cincinatti 4 Aug 1981.
        [*195 South Street, Litchfield Connecticut 06759 U.S.A.*]
        2. Princess *Victoria* Bayard, "Ilyinsky" *b* at Cincinnati 23 Nov 1984.
        [*195 South Street, Litchfield Connecticut 06759 U.S.A.*]
        3. Princess *Lela* McDowell, "Ilyinsky" *b* at Cincinnati 26 Aug 1986.
        [*195 South Street, Litchfield Connecticut 06759 U.S.A.*]

2. Princess *Paula-Marie,* "Ilyinsky" *b* at Palm Beach 18 May 1956; *m* at Cincinatti, Ohio 30 May 1980, *Marc* Allen Comisar (*b* at Cincinnati 17 June 1953).
[*3663 Brandon Road Cincinatti, 45226 Ohio, U.S.A.*].

3. Princess *Anna,* "Ilyinsky" *b* at Palm Beach 4 Sept 1959; *m* 1stly at Henniker, New Hampshire 9 May 1981 (*m* diss by div 27 April 1990), Robin Dale de Young (*b* at Cambridge, Massachussets 25 Dec 1952). She *m* 2ndly at Cincinnati, Ohio 18 Dec 1992, *David* Wise Glosinger (*b* at Dayton, Ohio 11 July 1953).
[*6635 Wyman Lane, Cincinnati, 45243 Ohio*].

4. Prince *Michael,* "Ilyinsky" *b* at Palm Beach 3 Nov 1959; *m* 1stly at Cincinnati 1 May 1986 (*m* diss by div 1987), Marcia Lowe (*b* at Minnisota 6 Nov 1966), dau of Douglas Lowe and Katherine. He *m* 2ndly at Cincinnati 4 Nov 1989, Paula (*b* at Cincinnati 1 Sept 1965), dau of Jack Craig Maier and Blanche Frisch. He *m* 3rdly at Cincinnati 21 May 1999 Lisa Marie (*b* at Fort Wright, Kentucky 17 May 1973), dau of James Schiesler and Charlene Adam (*m* diss by div June 2001).
[*7705 Ahwenasa Lane, Indian Hill, Cincinnati, 45243 Ohio, United States of America*].

1. Princess *Alexis* Taylor "Ilyinsky", *b* at Cincinati 1 March 1994.

Emperor Alexander II, *m* 2ndly (morganatically) at St Petersburg 18 July 1880, Princess Ekaterina (*b* at Moscow 3 Nov 1847; ✠ at Nice 15 Feb 1922), *cr* Princess Yourievsky with the qualification of Serene Highness 17 Dec 1880, dau of Mikhail Mikhailovitch, Prince Dolgorouky and Vera Gavrilovna Vichnevsky, and had further issue (*cr* Princes and Princess Yourievsky) (*See Part III*)

LINE II - Descent from Emperor Nicholas I

The line descends directly from **EMPEROR NICHOLAS I, EMPEROR and AUTOCRAT OF ALL THE RUSSIAS**, and Empress Alexandra Feodorovna (*See above*), through their second son Grand Duke Constantine, (*b* at St Petersburg 21 Sept 1827; ✠ at Pavlovsk 25 Jan 1892), Gen-Adm Russian Navy; *m* at Pavlovsk 11 Sept 1848, *Alexandra* Iossifovna, formerly Duchess Alexandra (*b* at Altenburg 8 July 1830; ✠ at St Petersburg 6 July 1922), dau of Joseph, Duke of Saxe-Altenburg and Duchess Amelia of Württemberg, through their second son, Grand Duke Constantin, *b* at Strelna 22 Aug 1858; ✠ at Pavlovsk 15 June 1915, Gen Russian Army; *m* at St Petersburg 27 April 1884, Elisaveta Mavrikievna, formerly Princess Elisabeth (*b* at Meiningen 25 Jan 1865; ✠ at Leipzig 24 March 1927), 2nd dau of Prince Moritz of Saxe-Altenburg, Duke of Saxony (Princes and Princesses of Russia with the qualification of Highness),and has issue amongst whom,

Sons

1. Prince *Ioann*, *b* at Pavlovsk 5 July 1886; ✠ *assassinated* by the Bolsheviks at Alapaievsk 17/18 July 1918, Staff Capt of Horse Russian Army, later a sub-deacon Orthodox Church; *m* at Peterhof 3 Sept 1911, Princess Elena Petrovna (*b* at Rijeka, Montenegro 4 Nov 1884; ✠ at Nice 16 Oct 1962), dau of Peter I, King of Serbia, and Princess Zorka of Montenegro, and had issue amongst whom,

1 Princess *Ekaterina*, *b* at Pavlovsk 25 July 1915, styled Serene Highness; *m* at Rome 15 Sept 1937 (judicially separated 1945), Nobile Ruggero, Marquess Farace di Villaforesta (*b* in London 4 Aug 1909; ✠ at Rome 14 Sept 1970).

[*P.O. Box 481, 11000 Montevideo, Uruguay*].

LINE III - Descent from Emperor Nicholas I

The line descends directly from **EMPEROR NICHOLAS I, EMPEROR and AUTOCRAT OF ALL THE RUSSIAS**, and Empress Alexandra Feodorovna (*See above*), through their fourth son Grand Duke *Michael*, (*b* at Peterhof 25 Oct 1832; ✠ at Cannes, France 26 Feb 1933); Field Marshal Imp Russian Army, Pres Council of the Empire; *m* at St Petersburg 28 Aug 1857, Olga Feodorovna, formerly Princess *Cäcilie* (*b* at Karlsruhre 20 Sept 1839; ✠ at Kharkoff 12 April 1891), dau of Leopold, Grand Duke of Baden, through their fourth son Grand Duke *Alexander*, *b* at Tiflis 13 April 1866; ✠ at Roquebrune, Alpes-Maritimes, France 26 Feb 1933; *m* at Peterhof 6 Aug 1894, Grand Duchess Xenia (*b* at St Petersburg 6 April 1875; ✠ at Wilderness House, Hampton Court, Middx 20 April 1960), elder dau of Alexander III, Emperor of Russia and Princess Dagmar of Denmark, and had issue (*Princes and Princess of Russia with the qualification of Highness*), amongst whom,

Sons

1. Prince Andrei (*Andrew*), *b* at St Petersburg 24 Jan 1897; ✠ at Provender, Kent 8 May 1981; *m* 1stly at Yalta 12 June 1918, Elisaveta Fabrizievna (*b* at Snamenskoie 8 Jan 1887; ✠ at Wilderness House, Hampton Court, Middx 29 Oct 1940; *m* 1stly Alexander Alexandrovitch de Friderici), dau of Don Fabrizio Ruffo, Duke di Sasso-Ruffo and Princess Natalia Alexandrovna Mestchersky, and had issue, among whom,

> 1. Prince *Michael*, *b* at Versailles 15 July 1920; *m* 1stly at Sydney, NSW, Australia 24 Feb 1953 (*m* diss by div Sept 1953), Jill Murphy (*b* at Horsham, Victoria, Australia 21 Oct 1921). He *m* 2ndly at Sydney 23 July 1954, Shirley (*b* at Brisbane 4 March 1916; ✠ at Sydney 20 June 1983), dau of Gordon Rowe Cramond and Dorothée-Elisabeth Chapman. He *m* 3rdly at Sydney 14 July 1993, Giulia (*b* at Milan 7 March 1930), dau of Giuseppe-Maria Crespi and Beatrice Martinengo.
> [*6 Wallaroy Crescent, Double Bay 2028, Sydney, Australia*].
> 2. Prince *Andrew*, *b* at London 21 Jan 1923, naturalised a US citizen 20 Dec 1954; *m* 1stly at San Francisco, California, USA 9 Sept 1951 (*m* diss by div 1959), Helen (*b* at Tokyo, Japan 7 March 1927), dau of Constantin Afanasievitch Dournev and Felixa Stanislavna Zapalski, and has issue,
> [*P.O. Box 508 Inverness, California 94937, USA*].

1. Prince *Alexis*, *b* at San Francisco 27 April 1953; *m* at Oakland 19 Sept 1987, *Zoetta* (*b* at Memphis, Tennessee 25 Nov 1956), dau of Robert Leisy and Ellen Teller.

[*1004 Harvard Road, Oakland, California 94610, U.S.A.*].

Prince Andrew *m* 2ndly at San Francisco 21 March 1961, Kathleen (*b* at San Francisco 1 March 1935; ✠ there 8 Dec 1967), formerly wife of Gilbert Roberts Jr, dau of Dr Frank Norris and Alice McCreevy. He *m* 3rdly, Inez (*b* at Santa Monica, California 11 Oct 1933), dau of Franz von Bachelin and Anita Hirtfeld, and has further issue by his second wife,

2. Prince *Peter*, *b* at San Francisco 21 Nov 1961.

[*P.O. Box 281, 12758 Sir Francis Drake Blvd., Inverness, California 94937, U.S.A.*].

3. Prince *Andrew*, *b* at San Francisco 20 Feb 1963; ✠ at Bombay 24 Jan 2001; *m* at Point Reyes Station, California 12 June 1989, Elizabeth (*b* at San Francisco 25 April 1964), dau of Armand Fernando Flores and Cecil Virginia Sherod, and has issue,

1. Princess *Natasha* Kathleen, *b* at San Rafael, California 2 Feb 1993.

Prince Andrei (*Andrew*) *m* 2ndly at Norton, nr Faversham, Kent 21 Sept 1942, *Nadine* Sylvia Ada (*b* at Lynsted, Kent 5 June 1908; ✠ at Faversham, 6 Jun 2000), eldest dau of Lt-Col Herbert McDougall and Sylvia Borgström, and had further issue,

3. Princess *Olga*, *b* at London 8 April 1950; *m* at London 1 Oct 1975 (seperated 1989), Thomas Mathew (*b* at London 8 July 1945)

[*Provender, Provender Lane, Faversham, Kent, ME13 0ST*].

2. Prince *Feodor*, *b* at St Petersburg 23 Dec 1898; ✠ at Ascain, France 30 Nov 1968; *m* at Paris 31 May 1923 (*m* diss by div at Paris 22 July 1936), Princess Irina (*b* at Paris 21 Dec 1903; ✠ at Biarritz 15 Nov 1990), dau of Grand Duke Paul Alexandrovitch of Russia and his 2nd (morganatic) wife, *Olga* Valerianovna Karnovitch, Countess Hohenfelsen, Princess Paley, and had issue,

1. Prince *Mikhail*, *b* at Paris 4 May 1923; *m* 1stly there 15 Oct 1958, Helga (*b* at Vienna 22 Aug 1926), dau of Ludwig Staufenberger and Fréderika Schmoll. He *m* 2ndly at Josse, France 14 Jan 1994, Maria de las Mercedes (*b* at Hospitalet, Prov of Barcelona, Spain 26 Aug 1960), dau of Ramón Ustrell

and Carmen Cabani, and has issue by his first wife,
[*Carrer Poca Farina, 2417130 L'Escala (Girona) Spain*].

    1. Prince *Mikhail* Paul, *b* at Paris 31 July 1959; ✙ at Mumbai, India 24 Jan 2001, and had issue,

        1. Princess *Tatiana,* *b* at Bayonne 21 Oct 1986, adopted by her grandfather, Prince Mikhail Feodorovich by the Tribunal de Grande Instance de Bayonne 20 March 1995.
        [*Carrer Poca Farina, 2417130 L'Escala (Girona) Spain*].

    2. Princess *Irina,* *b* at Fontenay-sous-Bois, France 7 May 1934; *m* 1stly at Biarritz 23 Dec 1955 (*m* diss by div at Pau 11 March 1959), André-Jean Pelle (*b* at Biarritz 29 Nov 1923). She *m* 2ndly at Le Pin, France 26 Dec 1962, Victor Marcel Soulas (*b* at St Méen le Grand, France 26 Aug 1939).

3. Prince *Nikita,* *b* at St Petersburg 16 Jan 1900; ✙ at Cannes 12 Sept 1974; *m* at Paris 19 Feb 1922, Countess Maria (*b* at Tsarskoie-Selo 13 Feb 1903 ✙ at Cannes 15 June 1997), dau of Ilarion Ilarionovitch, Count Woronzov-Daschkov and Irina Vassilievna Narishkine, and had issue,

    1. Prince *Nikita,* *b* at London 13 May 1923, Historian, co-author of "Ivan the Terrible", BA, MA, PhD cand; *m* at London 14 July 1961, Janet Anne (*b* at Oklahoma City, Oklahoma, USA 24 April 1933), dau of Michael Schonwald and Ethel Dimond, and has issue,
    [*200 East 66th Street, New York, NY 10021, U.S.A.*].

        1. Prince *Féodor, b* at New York 30 Nov 1974.

    2. Prince *Alexander, b* at Paris 4 Nov 1929; ✙ at London 22 Sept 2002; *m* at New York 23 Feb (civ) and at Cannes 18 July (relig) 1971, Donna Maria (*b* at Palermo 29 Nov 1931), dau of Don Corrado Valguarnera, Prince di Niscemi and Margaret Hirsch.
    [*1136 Fifth Avenue, New York, NY 10028, U.S.A.*].

4. Prince *Dimitri, b* at Gatshina 15 Aug 1901; ✙ at London 7 July 1980, served in WWII as Lt-Cmdr RNVR, Hon Pres Russian Benevolent Soc 1917; *m* 1stly at Paris 25 Nov 1931 (*m* diss by div 1947), Countess Marina (*b* at St Petersburg 20 Nov 1912; ✙ 1969), dau of Sergei Alexandrovitch, Count Golenistchev-Kutuzov and Maria Alexandrovna Besobrasov. He *m* 2ndly at London 29 Oct 1954, Sheila (*b* at Sydney, NSW, Australia 9 Sept 1898; ✙ at London 13 Oct 1969), widow of W/Cmdr Sir John Charles Penistone Milbanke,

12th Bt, RAF, previously wife of Hon Francis Edward Scudamore St Clair-Erskine, styled Lord Loughborough, and dau of Harry Chisholm of Sydney, NSW, Australia and Margaret McKellar, and has issue by his first wife,

    1. Princess *Nadejda*, *b* at Boulogne-sur-Seine 4 July 1933; ✝ at Vancouver 17 Sept 2002; *m* 1stly at London 20 Dec 1952 (*m* diss by div 1976), Anthony *Brian* Allen, MB, BS (*b* at Connah's Quay, N Wales 6 May 1931) [*935 Terrace Avenue, Victoria BC V8S 3V2, Canada*]. She *m* 2ndly at San Francisco May 1977, *William* Thomas Hall Clark (*b* at Montreal 17 March 1924; ✝ at Victoria, BC 16 Feb 1995).

5. Prince *Rostislav*, *b* at Todor, Crimea 24 Nov 1902; ✝ at Cannes 31 July 1978; *m* 1stly at Chicago 14 Sept 1928 (*m* diss by div at Chicago 9 Nov 1944), Princess Alexandra (*b* at Marijno, Novgorod 20 May 1905; *m* 2ndly, Lester Armour II who ✝ at Lake Forest, Illinois 26 Dec 1970), dau of Prince Paul Pavlovitch Galitzine and Princess Alexandra Nikolaievna Mestchersky, and had issue,

    1. Prince *Rostislav*, *b* at Chicago 3 Dec 1938; ✝ London 7 Jan 1999; *m* 1stly at Winnetka, Illinois 9 Sept 1960 (*m* diss by div Waukegan, Illinois 28 Nov 1978), Stephena Verdel (*b* at Maracaibo, Venezuela 15 Dec 1938), dau of Edgar Joseph Cook and Sidney Hunt, and has issue,

        1. Princess *Stephena* Alexandra, *b* at Chicago 21 Jan 1963; *m* at Lake Bluff, Illinois 23 Dec 1988, William Porter Boggess III (*b* at Lake Forest, Illinois 31 March 1960).

        [*253 West Sheridan Place, Lake Bluff, IL 60044, U.S.A.*].

Prince Rostislav *m* 2ndly at Lake Forest, Illinois 12 Aug 1980, Christia (*b* at Rockford, Illinois 3 April 1949; she *m* 2ndly 6 July 2002 at Rye, East Sussex, Hon David Russell, *b* at London 27 May 1947; *m* 1stly April Arbon 15 Nov 1980, *m* diss by div 1998), dau of Harold Noregaard Ipsen and Lorraine Wrobel, and has further issue,

[*Mounts Field, Rye Hill, Rye, East Sussex TN31 7NH*].

    2. Princess *Alexandra*, *b* at Lake Forest, Illinois 9 June 1983.

    [*Mounts Field, Rye Hill, Rye, East Sussex TN31 7NH*].

    3. Prince *Rostislav*, *b* at Lake Forest, Illinois 21 May 1985.

    4. Prince *Nikita*, *b* at London 24 March 1987.

Prince Rostislav *m* 2ndly at Chicago 7 Nov 1945 (*m* diss by div at
Chicago 11 April 1951), *Alice* (*b* at Chicago 30 May 1923; ✚ at Skokie,
Illinois 21 Oct 1996 *m* 2ndly *William* Stueber), dau of *Alvin* Eilken
and *Rose* Schultz. He *m* 3rdly at London 19 Nov 1954, Hedwig (*b* at
Habelschwerdt 6 Dec 1905; ✚ at Grasse 9 Jan 1997), formerly wife of
Berkeley Everard Foley Gage, CMG (later Sir Berkeley Gage, KCMG),
dau of *Carl* von Chappuis, Proprietor of Liegnitz, Silesia and
Baroness *Gertrud* von Richthofen, and had further issue by his
second wife,

    2. Prince *Nicholas*, *b* at Chicago 8 Sept 1945; *m* at Wheaton,
Illinois, USA 24 Aug 1966 (*m* diss by div), *Pamela* (*b* at
Chicago 7 July 1944), dau of *Matthew* Kuzinkowski and *Estelle*
Slowik, and has issue,

        1. Prince *Nicholas* Christopher, *b* at Oak Park, Illinois
30 July 1968; *m* at Rolling Meadows, Illinois 13 May
1995, Lisa Marie (*b* at Chicago 28 March 1971), dau of
Thomas Baron Glowa and *Linda* Mary Lesiewicz, and
has issue,

            1. Prince *Cory* Christopher, *b* at Arlington
Heights, Illinois 5 Dec 1994.

            2. Prince *Daniel-Joseph*, *b* at Chicago, Illinois 19 March
1972.

            3. Princess *Heather* Noel, *b* at Park Ridge, Illinois 6
Nov 1976.

6. Prince *Vassili,* *b* at Gatshina 7 July 1907; ✚ at Woodside,
California 23 June 1989; *m* at New York 31 July 1931, Princess
Natalia (*b* at Moscow 26 Oct 1907; ✚ at Woodside, California 28
March 1989), dau of Prince *Alexei* Vladimirovitch Galitzine and
Lubov Glebov, and had issue,

    1. Princess *Marina,* *b* at San Francisco 22 May 1940; *m* at
Woodside, California 8 Jan 1967 (m diss by div), *William*
Lawrence Beadleston (*b* at Long Branch, New Jersey USA 31
July 1938).

    [*P.O. Box 88, Woody Creek, Aspen, CO 81656, U.S.A.*].

———◆———

SAXONY
(HOUSE OF WETTIN)

Founded by Burkhard, Count in the Grabfeld (✝ 908). His great-great-grandson Count Dedi I (✝ 1009) received the northern County of Hassegau from Emperor Otto III in 997. His son Dietrich II (✝ 1034) inherited Eilenburg and acquired lower Lusatia. The Castle of Wettin which gave its name to the dynasty, was acquired in the 11th century, but sold to the Archbishop of Magdeburg in 1288. Dietrich II's grandson, Heinrich I, Count of Eilenburg (✝ 1103), was invested with the Margraviate of Meissen in 1088. His son Heinrich II (✝ 1123) was succeeded by his cousin once removed, Conrad, Count of Wettin (✝ 5 Feb 1157), who was invested as Margrave of Meissen by Emperor Lothar in 1127 and also became Margrave of Lusatia in 1136. Margrave Heinrich "the Illustrious" (✝ 1288) obtained Voigtland from Emperor Friedrich II in 1243 and the eventual investiture of the Landgraviate of Thuringia and Palatinate of Saxony; Friedrich "the Warlike" obtained the Duchy of Saxe-Wittenberg and the Electoral dignity from Emperor Sigismund 6 Jan 1423 and was solemnly invested at Buda 1 Aug 1425. The two lines below descend from his grandsons who partitioned their territories in 1485.

I: ERNESTINE LINE

Lutheran and Catholic: Founded by the Elector Ernst, Duke of Saxony, Landgrave of Thuringia, Lord of Coburg, etc (b 24 March 1441; ✝ 26 Aug 1486); Johann Friedrich "the Magnanimous", Elector of Saxony was forced in 1547, following his participation of the war of the Schmalkalden League and his capture by Emperor Karl V, to sign the Capitulation of Wittenberg, whereby the Electoral dignity was transferred to the Junior, or Albertine Line of the House (see below). He retained the title of Duke of Saxony and the scattered territories of Weimar, Jena, Eisenach, Gotha, Henneberg and Saalfeld, to which Altenburg and some other districts were added by the Treaty of Schaumburg in 1554. Johann Friedrich forbade his sons to divide their possessions, but his wishes were disregarded after the death of his youngest son in 1565, the two survivors founding the lines of Saxe-Coburg-Eisenach and Saxe-Weimar with an arrangement to exchange territories every three years. Many divisions and sub-divisions followed. The common ancestor of the existing branches was Johann, Duke of Saxe-Weimar (✝ 1605), one of his sons, Wilhelm founded the branch of Saxe-Weimar-Eisenach; another son, Ernst "the Pious" being the common ancestor of the other four existing branches of this line.

I: Weimar Branch
SAXE-WEIMAR-EISENACH

Founded by Wilhelm, Duke of Saxe-Weimar (✝ 17 May 1662), who also inherited Eisenach on the death of his younger brother Albert in 1644 and the County of Henneberg 9 Aug 1660. His sons inherited a quarter of the Duchy of Altenburg 16 May 1672, and founded the lines of Saxe-Eisenach, Saxe-Marksuhl and Saxe-Jena which were all reunited in 1741, when the principle of primogeniture was adopted to secure the territories from further divisions. Duke Carl August was granted some 660 square miles in additional territory at the Congress of Vienna and received the title of Grand Duke 21 April 1814. The dynasty ceased to reign 9 Nov 1918.

Arms:- Quarterly: 1st, az, a lion contournée barry arg and gu; 2nd, or, a lion rampant sa; 3rd, tierced per pale, dexter, or, on a mount vert, a cock sa, wattled gu; sinister, gu, in fess, a bend or; 4th, per pale, dexter arg a lion contournée sa, and over all in fesse a bend or; sinister, bendy arg and az. Over all an escutcheon of pretence, barry of ten, az and sa a wreath of rue in bend vert (Saxony), surmounted by a Royal Crown. The shield is ensigned with the Royal Crown. *Supporters:-* Two lions rampant guardant crowned or. *Motto:-* Vigilando ascendimus.

Members of the Grand Ducal Family bear the titles of Prince or Princess of Saxe-Weimar-Eisenach, Duke or Duchess of Saxony with the qualification of Highness. The Head of the Grand Ducal Family and his wife have the qualification of Royal Highness.

MICHAEL-Benedict Georg Jobst Carl Alexander Bernhard Claus, **PRINCE OF SAXE-WEIMAR-EISENACH,** Duke of Saxony, Duke of Jülich, Kleve and Berg, also Engern and Westfalen, Landgrave (Landgraf) in Thüringen, Margrave (Markgraf) zu Meissen, Princely Count zu Henneberg, Count zu der Mark and Ravensberg, Lord (Herr) zu Ravenstein and Tonna, Count (Graf) zu Wettin, *b* at Bergellern, nr Bamberg 15 Nov 1946, Trustee Wartburgstiftung, Eisenach, Chairman of Supervisory Board Reum AG, Hardheim, Corporate Advisor and Bank Manager, son of Carl-August, Hereditary Grand Duke of Saxe-Weimar-Eisenach (*b* 28 July 1912; ✝ 14 Oct 1988) and Baroness Elisabeth von Wangenheim (*b* 16 Jan 1912; *m* 4 Oct 1944; ✝ 1984); *m* 1stly at Hamburg-Eimsbüttel 9 June (civ) and at Linnep, nr Breitscheid 4 July (relig) 1970 (*m* diss by div at Düsseldorf 9 March 1974), Renate (*b* at Heidelberg 17 Sept 1947; *m* 2ndly at Düsseldorf 4 Dec 1976, Andreas, Baron Freytag von Loringhoven), dau of Konrad Henkel and Jutta von Hülsen. He *m* 2ndly at London 15 Nov 1980, Dagmar (*b* at Niederpöcking 24 June 1948; *m* 1stly ...; that *m* diss by div ......), dau of Heinrich Hennings and Margarethe Schacht, and has issue by his second wife, [*Spinozastraße 12a, 68165 Mannheim, Germany*].

Daughter

Princess *Leonie* Mercedes Augusta Silva Elisabeth Margarethe, *b* at Frankfurt-am-Main 30 Oct 1986.

Sisters

1. Princess *Elisabeth* Sophie Feodora Mathilde Dorothea Louise Adelaide Vera Renate, *b* at Burgellern, nr Bamberg 22 July 1945, Businesswoman; *m* at Munich 10 July 1981 (*m* diss by div 5 July 1983), Mindert Diderick de Kant (*b* at Leeuwarden, Netherlands 6 Aug 1934). She has since reverted to her maiden name.
[*Thomas Mann Allee 2, 81679 Munich 80, Germany*].

2. Princess *Beatrice-Maria* Margareta Dorothea Felicitas Virginie, *b* at Bamberg 11 March 1948, took the name Princess of Saxe-Weimar and Eisenach-Davidson; *m* at London 9 Dec 1977, Martin Charles Davidson (*b* at London 23 Sept 1940), Businessman, and has a dau who bears the name of Saxe-Weimar-Eisenach,
[*36 Paddenswick Road, London W.6.*].

    1. *Bettina* Maude Elisabeth Anna Amalia, *b* at London 11 March 1979.

Brothers and Sister of Father

Issue of Wilhelm Ernst, Grand Duke of Saxe-Weimar-Eisenach (*b* 10 June 1876; ✝ 24 April 1923) and Princess Feodora of Saxe-Meiningen (*b* 29 May 1890; *m* 4 Jan 1910; ✝ 12 March 1972), among whom,

1. Prince *Bernhard Friedrich* Viktor Rupprecht Adalbert Ernst Ludwig Hermann Heinrich, *b* at Weimar 3 March 1917; ✝ at Wiesbaden 23 March 1986; *m* at Heinrichau 12 March 1943 (*m* diss by div at Munich 24 Sept 1956), Princess Felicitas (*b* at Potsdam 31 March 1920), dau of Emich, Prince zu Salm Horstmar and Princess Sabine von Schoenaich-Carolath, and had issue, among whom
[*Pfingstrosenstraße 83, 81377 Munich, Germany*].

    1. Princess *Katharina* Feodora Adelheid Sabine Sophie Felicitas Sieglinde, *b* at Breslau 30 Nov 1943; *m* at Hechingen (civ) and at Burg Hohenzollern (relig) 25 May 1968 (*m* diss by div at Hechingen 1 July 1985), Prince Emanuel of Hohenzollern (*b* at Munich 23 Feb 1929; ✝ at Hechingen 8 Feb 1999).
    [*Germeringer Straße 2, 81677 Munich, Germany*].

    2. Prince *Wilhelm* Ernst Emich Georg Rudolf, *b* at Höxter, Westphalia 10 Aug 1946, Self-Employed; *m* at Munich 30

May (civ) and 1 June (relig) 1973 (*m* diss by div at Munich 18
April 1985), Éva Katalin (Katharina) (*b* at Obervellach,
Kärnten 10 Nov 1945) [*Schloß Sandsee, 91785 Pleinfeld,
Germany*]; *m* 2ndly 9 Sept 1991, Carl Friedrich, Prince von
Wrede), dau of Dezsö Tibor László Kovarcz de Kovarczfalva
and Éva-Maria Fiala, and has issue,
[*Gleimstraße 2, 81677 Munich, Germany*].

    1. Princess *Désirée* Elisabeth Katharina Felicitas
Sophie, *b* at Munich 19 July 1974; *m* at Pleinfeld 6
July (civ) and at Ellingen, Germany 8 July (relig)
2000, Florian, Count von and zu Hoensbroech (*b* at
Kellenberg Castle, nr Jülich 1 March 1969), Business
Management.
[*Schützenhüttenweg 28, 60598 Frankfurt-am-Main,
Germany*].

    2. Prince *Georg Constantin* Friedrich Wilhelm
Johannes, *b* at Munich 13 April 1977, Bank Manager.
[*Schloß Sandsee, 91785 Pleinfeld, Germany*].

2. Prince *Georg* Wilhelm Albert Bernhard, *b* at Heinrichau 24 Nov
1921, renounced his rights as a member of the Grand Ducal House of
Saxe-Weimar-Eisenach and assumed the name of Jörg Brena, 22 Jan
1953, High School Teacher, Concert Singer; *m* at Freiburg-im-Breisgau
5 Feb (civ) and at Calascino, nr Brissago, Switzerland 8 March
(relig) 1953, Gisela (*b* at Hamburg 5 May 1930 ✠ at Freiburg-im-
Breisgau 26 July 1989), dau of Wilhelm Erich Jänisch and
Marie-Heloïse Donner, and has issue,
[*Am Römerbrunnen 9, 79189 Bad Krozingen, Germany*].

    1. Luise *Ariane*, *b* at Freiburg-im-Breisgau 17 Jan 1954.

    2. Adelheid *Cornelie*, *b* at Freiburg-im-Breisgau 22 June
1955; *m* at Freiburg-im-Breisgau 14 Dec 1976, (*m* diss by div
at at Freiburg-im-Breisgau), Thomas-August Landsberg (*b* at
Gottingen 17 May 1945); *m* 2ndly at Freiburg-im-Breisgau 19
April 1984 Dietmar Berron-Brena, (*b* at Stuttgart 6 March
1956).

    3. *Isabel* Magdalene, *b* at Freiburg-im-Breisgau 14 Oct 1959.

II: Gotha Branch

**Founded by Ernest I "the Pious", Duke of Saxe-Gotha (*b* 25 Dec
1601; ✠ 26 March 1675), Princely Count of Henneberg 9 Aug 1660;
Lord of Kranichfeld 1663; inherited three quarters of the Duchy of
Altenburg, Coburg (the lands of Henneberg) 16 May 1672. This
Branch was divided into seven sub-branches (1680 and 1681), the
four remaining are treated below. By virtue of a family pact the**

reigning Dukes and their direct descendants in the first generation as well as heirs presumptive of the Ernestine Lines were granted the qualification of Highness 3 April 1844.

A. SAXE-MEININGEN

Founded in 1681 by Bernhard I, Duke of Saxe-Meiningen (✠ 27 April 1706), 6th son of Ernst "the Pious", Duke of Saxe-Gotha. On the extinction of the sub-branch of Saxe-Gotha-Altenburg in 1825, the Duchy of Saxe-Meiningen gained much additional territory, more than doubling its area. The dynasty ceased to reign 10 Nov 1918.

Arms:- Quarterly: 1st, az, a lion contournée barry arg and gu crowned or; 2nd, or, on a mount vert, a cock az, wattled gu; 3rd, gu, a column arg crowned or; and 4th, or, a lion rampant, per fess, sa and arg; over all an escutcheon of pretence, barry of ten, or and sa, a wreath of rue in bend vert (Saxony), surmounted by a Royal Crown. The shield is ensigned with the Royal Crown.

Members of the Ducal House bear the title of Prince or Princess of Saxe-Meiningen, Duke or Duchess of Saxony. A convention of the Ernestine Line of the House of Saxony held 3 April 1844 decided that the qualification of Highness should be borne by all the children of a reigning Duke and of an heir presumptive with other members of the Ducal House retaining the qualification of Serene Highness.

Johann **FRIEDRICH-KONRAD** Carl Eduard Horst Arnold Matthias, **DUKE OF SAXE-MEININGEN,** Duke of Saxony, Head of the Ducal House, *b* at Ziegenberg 14 April 1952, Banker, Dipl rer pol, son of Bernhard (IV), Duke of Saxe-Meiningen, Head of the Ducal House, etc (*b* 30 June 1901; ✠ 4 Oct 1984) and his second wife, Baroness Wera Schaffer von Bernstein (*b* at Frankfurt-am-Main 10 Aug 1914; *m* 11 Aug 1948; *m* diss by div 29 Sept 1975; ✠ 24 Oct 1994).

[*61030 Ober Mörlen/Ziegenberg, bei Bad Nauheim, Germany*].

Sisters

1. Princess Marie *Eleonore Adelheid* Feodora Sophie Helene Gisela Edelgarde, *b* at Ziegenberg 9 Nov 1950; *m* at Virginia, USA 22 Oct 1982, Peter E Rosden (*b* at Washington 10 Jan 1947), Lawyer.
[*5024 Wissioming Road, Bethesda, Md 20816 USA*]

2. Princess *Almut Huberta Anna Victoria, b* at Butzbach, Ober Hesse 25 Sept 1959; *m* at Vorsfelde 14 Oct (civ) and at Nordsteimke, Wolfsburg 16 Oct (relig) 1993, Eberhard von Brunswick (*b* 5 March 1954), Farmer.
[*Gut Wettin, Könnernsche Straße 37, 06198 Wettin, Germany*].

Half-Brother and Sister

Issue of Bernhard (IV), Duke of Saxe-Meiningen, Duke of Saxony,
Head of the Ducal House (*b* 30 June 1901; ✠ 4 Oct 1984) and his first
wife, Margot Grossler (*b* 22 Jan 1911; *m* 25 April 1931; *m* diss by div
10 June 1947). Issue of this marriage do not have dynastic rights or
bear the qualification of Highness.

1. Princess *Feodora* Adelheid May Luise, *b* at Schloß Pitzelstetten,
nr Klagenfurt 27 May 1932, Dr of Phil; *m* at Söcking 8 April 1967,
Burkhard Kippenberg (*b* at Starnberg 8 April 1927).
[*Oberdorf 19, 78337 Öhningen am Bodensee, Germany*].
2. Prince *Friedrich-Ernst* Georg Bernhard, *b* at Meiningen 21 Jan
1935, Industrialist, Antique Dealer; *m* 1stly at Schwieberdingen,
Württemberg 3 March 1962 (*m* diss by div 12 April 1973), Ehrengard
(*b* at Stralsund 25 Oct 1933), yr dau of Helmut von Massow and
Ursula von Buch-Tornow. He *m* 2ndly at Coburg 11 June (civ) 12
June (relig) 1977, Princess Beatrice (*b* at Bern 15 July 1951), dau of
Friedrich Josias, Prince of Saxe-Coburg and Gotha and Denyse von
Muralt, and has issue from his second wife,
[*Sonnen Weg 5, 4313 Möhlin, Switzerland*].
    1. Princess *Marie* Alexandra Elisabeth Beatrice, *b* at Heilbronn
    5 July 1978.
    2. Prince Friedrich *Constantin,* *b* at Heilbronn 3 June 1980

Brothers and Sisters of Father

Issue of Prince Friedrich of Saxe-Meiningen (*b* 12 Oct 1861; *ka* 23
Aug 1914) and Countess Adelheid of Lippe-Biesterfeld (*b* 22 June
1870; *m* 25 April 1889; ✠ 3 Sept 1948), among whom,

1. **Georg (III), Duke of Saxe-Meiningen,** assumed the title of
Duke on his accession, *b* at Cassel 11 Oct 1892; ✠ in a Russian POW
Camp at Chernopovetz, Siberia 6 Jan 1946; *m* at Freiburg-im-Breisgau
22 Feb 1919, Countess Klara-Marie (*b* at Darmstadt 31 May 1895; ✠
nr Tumitz, Austria 10 Feb 1992), eldest dau of Alfred, Count von
Korff genannt Schmissing-Kerssenbrock and Baroness Helene von
Hilgers, and had issue, among whom,
    1. Prince *Friedrich-Alfred* Carl Ludwig Vincenz Maria, *b* at
    Jena 4 April 1921, since 1953 a Carthusian monk.
    [*Charterhouse of the Transfiguration, nr Arlington, Vermont
    05250, U.S.A.*].
    2. Princess *Regina* Helene Elisabeth Margarete, *b* at Würzburg

6 Jan 1925, Supreme Lady Protectress Star Cross Order, Dame
Gd Cross Hon and Dev Sovereign Military Order of Malta; *m*
at Nancy 10 May 1951, Archduke Otto of Austria, formerly
Crown Prince of Austria and Hungary, Head of the Imperial
House of Austria (*b* at Villa Wartholz, nr Reichenau 20 Nov
1912), Dr of Pol and Soc Sciences, Mem Acad of Moral and
Pol Sciences Institut de France in Paris, Head and Sovereign
Order of the Golden Fleece, Kt of Hon Teutonic Order,
German Bundesverdienstkreuz, Bavarian Verdienstorden,
Carlos III and Order of Africa (Spain), Papal Gregorius Order,
etc, Bailiff Gd Cross Hon and Dev Sovereign Military Order
of Malta, Member of the European Parliament, uses the style
of Dr Otto von Habsburg.
[*Hindenburgstraße 15, 82343 Pöcking, nr Starnberg, Upper
Bavaria, Germany*].

B. ✠SAXE-ALTENBURG
formerly HILDBURGHAUSEN
(✠ Extinct ✠)

Founded in 1680 by Ernst, Duke of Saxe-Hildburghausen (✠ 17 Oct
1715), 9th son of Ernst "the Pious", Duke of Saxe-Gotha. He was the
first of the Saxon Dukes to establish the right of primogeniture in his
Duchy. Duke Friedrich (*b* 29 April 1763; ✠ 29 Sept 1834) ceded the
Duchy of Saxe-Hildburghausen to Saxe-Meiningen 12 Nov 1826,
receiving in exchange the Duchy of Saxe-Altenburg. The dynasty
ceased to reign 13 Nov 1918.

Arms:- Quarterly: 1st, arg, a rose gu (Altenburg); 2nd, arg, three
bars az (Eisenberg); 3rd, or, semée of hearts gu, a lion contournée sa,
crowned gu (Orlamünde); 4th, az, a lion rampant, per pale, or and
arg (Pleissen); over all, an escutcheon of pretence, barry of ten, or
and sa, a wreath of rue in bend vert (Saxony), surmounted by a
Royal Crown. *Supporters:-* Two lions crowned or, each holding a
banner, per fess vert and or. The shield is ensigned with the Royal
Crown.

Members of the Ducal Family bore the title of Prince or Princess of
Saxe-Altenburg, Duke or Duchess of Saxony with the qualification of
Highness.

✠ Wilhelm **GEORG-MORITZ** Ernst Albert Friedrich Carl
Constantin Eduard Max, **HEREDITARY PRINCE OF
SAXE-ALTENBURG,** Duke of Saxony, etc, *b* at Potsdam 13 May
1900; ✠ at Rendsburg 13 Feb 1991, Lt Prussian Army, son of Ernst
II, Duke of Saxe-Altenburg (*b* 31 Aug 1871; ✠ 22 March 1955) and

Princess Adelheid of Schaumburg-Lippe (*b* 22 Sept 1875; *m* 17 Feb 1898; *m* diss by div 1920; ✠ 27 Jan 1971).

C. SAXE-COBURG AND GOTHA
formerly COBURG-SAALFELD

Founded in 1680 by Johann Ernst, Duke of Saxe-Saalfeld (✠ 17 Dec 1729), 11th son of Ernst "the Pious", Duke of Saxe-Gotha. He inherited the Duchy of Saxe-Coburg on the death of his brother Albrecht in 1699. The right of primogeniture was introduced in 1733, and in 1735 the title of Duke of Saxe-Coburg-Saalfeld was adopted. On the re-arrangement of the Saxon Duchies following the extinction of the line of Gotha in 1825, Duke Ernst I received Gotha and ceded Saalfeld to Saxe-Meiningen 12 Nov 1826, assuming the title of Saxe-Coburg and Gotha 16 Nov 1826. This Duchy later passed to Prince Alfred, Duke of Edinburgh, second son of Prince Albert of Saxe-Coburg and Gotha (heir presumptive 1844-1861) and his wife Queen Victoria of Great Britain and Ireland; then to the only son of their youngest son Prince Leopold, Duke of Albany (see below). The dynasty ceased to reign 14 Nov 1918.

Arms:- Quarterly: 1st, az, a lion contournée barry arg and gu crowned of the second (Landgraviate of Thuringia); 2nd, or, a lion rampant sa (Julich); 3rd, or, on a mount vert a cock contournée sa wattled gu (Henneberg); 4th, sa, a lion rampant or (Coburg); over all, an escutcheon of pretence, barry of ten or and sa, a wreath of rue in bend vert (Saxony). *Supporters:-* Two lions reguardant crowned or. *Motto:-* Treu and fest. The achievement is borne on a mantle gu, fringed and tasselled or, doubled erm and surmounted by the Royal Crown.

Members of the Ducal family bear the title of Prince or Princess of Saxe-Coburg and Gotha, Duke or Duchess of Saxony with the qualification of Highness.

ANDREAS Michael Armin Siegfried Friedrich Hans Hubertus, **PRINCE OF SAXE-COBURG and GOTHA** *b* at Casel 21 March 1943, son of Friedrich Josias, Prince of Saxe-Coburg and Gotha (*b* at Schloß Callenberg 29 Nov 1918; ✠ 24 January 1998 at Grein an der Donau) and Countess Victoria-Louise zu Solms-Baruth (*b* at Cassel 13 March 1921); *m* at Hamburg 18 June (civ) and 31 July (Relig) 1971, Carin (*b* at Hamburg 16 July 1946), dau of Adolf Wilhelm Martin Dabelstein and *Irma* Maria Marguerite Cellsen, and has issue,
[*Elsässerstraße 8, 96450 Coburg, Germany. Greinburg 3, 4360 Grein an der Donau, Upper Austria, Austria*].

Sons and Daughter

1. Princess *Stephanie* Sibylla, *b* at Hamburg 31 Jan 1972.
2. Hereditary Prince *Hubertus* Michael, *b* at Hamburg 16 Sept 1975.
3. Prince *Alexander* Philipp, *b* at Coburg 4 May 1977.

Mother

CountessVictoria-Louise (*b* at Cassel 13 March 1921; *m* at Casel, Nieder Lusatia 25 Jan 1942; *m* diss by div at Coburg 19 Sept 1946; *m* 2ndly at Steinwänd, nr Werfen, Ld Salzburg 6 Nov 1947, Richard CB Whitten, Major US Army), only dau of Hans, Count zu Solms-Baruth and Princess Caroline-Mathilde of Schleswig-Holstein-Sonderburg-Glücksburg.

[*74210 Military Road, Covington, LA 70433, U.S.A.*]

Half Brother and Sister

Issue of **Friedrich Josias** Carl Eduard Ernst Kyrill Harald, **Prince of Saxe-Coburg and Gotha** (*b* at Schloß Callenberg 29 Nov 1918; ✛ 24 Jan 1998 at Grein an der Donau) and his second wife, Denyse Henriette (*b* at Basel 14 Dec 1923; *m* at San Francisco, 14 Feb 1948; *m* diss by div at Hamburg 17 sept 1964; *m* 2ndly at Flims, Kt Graubünden 8 Dec 1983, Werner Leuch who ✛ 20 March 1984), dau of Gaston Robert von Muralt and Pierette Gabrielle Maurice. Prince Friedrich Josias *m* 3rdly at Hamburg 30 Oct 1964, Katherine (*b* at Berlin 22 April 1940), dau of Dietrich Karl Bremme and Margarethe Spottke, and had issue by his second wife among whom,

[*Schloß Grein, Greinburg 3, 4360 Grein, Austria*]

1. Princess Maria *Claudia* Sibylla, *b* at San Francisco 22 May 1949; *m* at Berne 17 March 1971 (*m* diss by div at Graubünden 6 July 1998), Gion Schäfer (*b* at Chur, Kt Graubünden 20 July 1945).

[*Sulé, 7017 Flims, Kt. Graubunden, Switzerland*].

2. Princess *Beatrice* Charlotte, *b* at Berne 15 July 1951; m at Coburg 11 June (civ) and 12 June (relig) 1077, Prince *Friedrich-Ernst* Georg Bernhard of Saxe-Meiningen (*b* at Meiningen 21 Jan 1935).

[*Sonnenweg 4, 4313 Möhlin, Kt Aargau, Switzerland*].

3. Prince *Adrian* Vincenz Edward, *b* at Coburg 18 Oct 1955, Musician, known as "*Adrian Ooburg*"; *m* 1stly at **Born** 10 Oct (civ) 1984 (*m* diss by div at Bern 8 Jan 1993), Lea (*b* at Marthalen, nr Zürich 5 Jan 1960), dau of Marcel Rinderknecht and Elsbeth Ulrich. He *m* 2ndly at Bern 11 July 1997, Getrud (*b* at Olten, Solothurn 18 March 1958), dau of Georges Krieg and Johanna Sacher, and has issue with his 1st wife,

[*Wildermettweg 52, 3006 Bern, Switzerland*].
    1. Prince *Simon*, *b* at Bern 10 March 1985.
    2. Prince *Daniel*, *b* at Bern 26 Jan 1988.

Brother and Sisters of Father

Issue of (Leopold) **Karl Eduard** George Albert, **Duke of Saxe-Coburg and Gotha**; 2nd **Duke of Albany, Earl of Clarence, Baron Arklow** (*b* 19 July 1884; ✠ 6 March 1954), struck off the Roll of Peers of the United Kingdom of Great Britain and Ireland, 28 March 1919, by the Order of the King in Council in pursuance of the Enemy Peers and Princes Forfeiture of British Titles, Order in Council 1919 (SR & O 1919/475) under the Titles Deprivation Act 1917 (7 & 8, Geo V c 47); and in 1915 struck off the Roll of the Order of the Knights of the Garter; *m* Princess Victoria-Adelheid (*b* 31 Dec 1885; *m* 11 Oct 1905 ✠ 3 Oct 1970), dau of Friedrich-Ferdinand, Duke of Schleswig-Holstein-Sonderburg-Glücksburg and Princess Caroline Mathilde of Schleswig-Holstein, and had issue among whom,

1. *Johann Leopold* Wilhelm Albert Ferdinand Viktor, Hereditary Prince of Saxe-Coburg and Gotha, *b* at Callenberg, nr Coburg 2 Aug 1906; ✠ at Grein 4 May 1972 (renounced his Membership to the Princely House at Berlin 27 Feb 1932); *m* 1stly at Niedersedlitz, Dresden 9 March (civ) and at Dresden (relig) 14 March 1932 (*m* diss by div at 27 Feb 1962), Baroness Feodora (*b* at Wolka 7 July 1905; ✠ at Schrobenhausen 23 Oct 1991; *m* 1stly 8 Nov 1924, Wolf, Baron Pergler von Perglas; that *m* diss by div 9 May 1931), dau of Bernhard, Baron von der Horst and Elsa Gürtler. He *m* 2ndly at Bad Reichenhall 3 May (civ) and 5th May (relig) 1963, Maria-Theresia (*b* at Bad Reichenhall 13 March 1908; ✠ at Grein 7 April 1996; *m* 1stly 7 March 1934, Werner Müller; that *m* diss by div 21 March 1962), dau of Max Reindl and Elisabeth Ortner, and had issue by his first wife, among whom,

    1. Princess Caroline Mathilde Adelheid Sibylla *Marianne Erika*, *b* at Hirschberg 5 April 1933; *m* at Muhlacker,Württemberg 5 Dec 1953, Michael Adelbert Wilfred Neilsen (*b* at Frankfurt-am-Main 12 Aug 1923;✠ at Vienna 20 Sept 1975).
    [*Tannenstraße 8, 66129 Saarbrücken-Bübingen, Germany*].
    2. Prince *Ernst-Leopold* Eduard Wilhelm Josias, *b* at Hirschberg 14 Jan 1935; ✠ at Kreuth 27 June 1996; *m* 1stly at Herrenberg, Württemberg 3 Feb (civ) and 4 Feb (relig) 1961

(*m* diss by div 23 May 1963), Ingeborg (*b* at Nordhausen Harz 16 Aug 1937), dau of Richard Henig and Emmy Duckwitz, and has issue,

    1. Prince *Hubertus* Richard Ernst Eduard, *b* at Herrenberg 8 Dec 1961, in whom is vested the right to claim the suspended Dukedom of Albany, Earldom of Clarence and Barony of Arklow of the United Kingdom of Great Britain and Ireland, and who takes precedence over the head of the family in the line of sucession to the Throne of Great Britain and Northern Ireland; *m* at Garmisch-Partenkirchen 9 Mar 1993, Barbara (*b* at Kaiserslautern 21 May 1959), dau of Eugen Weissman and Renate Spettel, and has issue,

    [Scheckersgraben 30, 67735 Mehlbach, Germany].

        1. Prince *Sebastian* Hubertus, *b* at Kaiserslautern.16 Jan 1994

Prince Ernst-Leopold *m* 2ndly at Regensburg 29 May 1963 (*m* diss by div 20 Sept 1985), Gertraude *Monika* (*b* at Strobitz, Kreis Cottbus 1 July 1938; *m* 2ndly 10 July 1996, Reinhold Hochgesang), dau of Hermann Horst Pfeiffer and Gertrud Marianne Jardin, *[Weinbergstraße 4, 97509 Stammheim, Germany]*. He *m* 3rdly at Grünwald 20 Jan 1986, *Sabine* Margarete (*b* at Königsberg 25 June 1941; ✠ at Bad Wiessee 27 June 1996), dau of Alfred Karl Biller and *Marie* Margarete Elise Pieper, and had further issue by his second wife,

    2. Princess *Victoria* Feodora Monika, Dr. Agr., *b* at Regensburg 7 Sept 1963; *m* 1stly at Rheda-Wiedenbrück 28 Nov 1986 (*m* diss by div at Rotenburg 30 September 1999), *Peter* Jakob Schmitt (*b* at Bingen Büdesheim 15 June 1954); she m 2ndly at Visselhövede 24 Dec (civ) 1999 and at St Johannis-Kirche, Visselhövede 29 April (relig) 2000, Gerd Armbrust, MBA University of Wales (*b* at Visselhövede 16 Dec 1954)

    [Worthstraße 8, 27374 Visselhövede, Germany]

    3. Prince Ernst-*Josias* Carl Eduard Hermann Leopold, *b* at Landshut 13 May 1965; *m* at Münich 5 July (civ) and at Eurasburg 13 July (relig) 1996, Birgit Michaela Marion (*b* at Munich 22 Feb 1965), dau of Elmar Bodo Archibald Meissner and Berta Katharina Fischer, and has issue,

[Adelheidstraße 25c, 80798 Munich, Germany]

    1. Princess *Sophie* Alexandra Maria Katharina, *b* at Munich 22 Aug 2000.

4. Prince *Carl-Eduard,* Wilhelm Josias, *b* at Regensburg 27 July 1966; *m* at Carloforte, Italy 31 July (civ) and at Munich 25 Sept (relig) 1998, Stephanie (*b* at Munich 7 Feb 1968), dau of Hans Kolo and Waldtrand Detsch.

[Oberlanderstraße 10, 81373, Munich, Germany].

    1. Princess *Emilia* Lucia Josephine *b* at Munich 24 March 1999.

5. Prince Friedrich-*Ferdinand* Georg Ernst Albert, *b* at Regensburg 13 Dec 1968; *m* at Garmisch 14 May 1999, Erika (*b* at Garmisch-Partenkirchen 5 April 1956), dau of Sattlers Johann Ostheimer and Katharina Grät, and has issue,

[Loisacherstraße 10, 82467 Garmisch-Partenkirchen, Germany].

    1. Prince *Nicolas* Ferdinand-Christian Ernst Albert-Lothar Prüssing, *b* at Garmisch-Partenkirchen 12 Oct 1987.

6. Princess *Alice-Sibylla* Calma Beatrice,*b* at Regensburg 6 Aug 1974.

[Prof Carl Raeyserstraße 2, 82467, Garmisch-Partenkirchen, Germany].

3. Prince *Peter* Albert Friedrich Josias, *b* at Dresden 12 June 1939; *m* at Tegernsee 11 May (civ) and 12 May (relig) 1964, Roswitha (*b* at Wolnzach, Kreis Pfaffenhofen an der Ilm 1 Sept 1945), dau of Robert Breuer and Hedwig Harraschein, and has issue,

[Stiftunglouiselund, 24357 Güby, Germany].

    1. Prince *Peter,* Karl Eduard Alexander, *b* at Münich 4 Oct 1964; *m* at Kiel 28 June (civ) and at Posel/Louisenlund 30 June (relig) 1991 (*m* diss by div), Katherin (*b* at Oldenburg 13 Sept 1962), dau of *Jan* Hermann Kempin and *Sigmarie* Gisela Pfitzner, and has issue,

[Sorthum 14, 27632 Midlum, Nr Bremerhaven, Germany].

    1. Prince *Malte* Alexander Maximilian, *b* at Eutin, OHolstein 20 Dec 1990.

2. Prince *Malte* Georg Albert, *b* at Ingolstadt 6 Oct 1966; *m* at Hanover 11 July (civ) and at Louisenlund l 19 July (relig) 1997, *Nicola* Freiderike (*b* at Hanover 25 Nov 1967), dau of *Klaüs-Jurgen* Friedrich Wilhelm von Seydlitz-Kurzbach and *Michaela* Katharine Metzner.

[*Stormstraße 15, 30177 Hanover, Germany*]

Brother of Great-Great-Great-Grandfather

Issue of **Franz, Duke of Saxe-Coburg-Saalfeld** (*b* 15 July 1750; ✝ 9 Dec 1806) and his second wife, Countess Augusta Reuss-Lobenstein and Ebersdorf (*b* 19 Jan 1757; *m* 13 June 1777; ✝ 16 Nov 1831), having had issue, among whom,

Son

Prince *Ferdinand* Georg August, *b* at Coburg 28 March 1785; ✝ at Vienna 27 Aug 1851; *m* at Vienna 2 Jan 1816, Princess Antoinette von Koháry (*b* at Vienna 2 July 1797; ✝ there 25 Sept 1862), having had issue, among whom,

Son

Prince *August* Louis Viktor, *b* at Vienna 13 June 1818; ✝ at Schloß Ebenthal 26 July 1881 (granted the qualification of Highness for himself and his descendants 2 May 1881); *m* at St Cloud 20 April 1843, Princess Marie-Clémentine (*b* at Neuilly 3 June 1817; ✝ at Vienna 16 Feb 1907), dau of Louis Philippe I, King of the French, and had issue, among whom,

Son

Prince Ludwig *August* Maria Eudes, *b* at Eu 9 Aug 1845; ✝ at Karlsbad 14 Sept 1907, Brazilian Admiral; *m* at Rio de Janeiro 15 Dec 1864, Princess Leopoldina (*b* at Rio de Janeiro 13 July 1847; ✝ at Vienna 7 Feb 1871), dau of Dom Pedro II, Emperor of Brazil and Princess Therese of Bourbón-Two Sicilies, and had issue, among whom,

Sons

1. Prince *August Leopold* Philipp Maria Michael Gabriel Raphael Gonzaga, *b* at Rio de Janeiro 6 Dec 1867; ✝ at Schladming 11 Oct 1922; *m* at Vienna 30 May 1894, Archduchess Karoline (*b* at Alt-Münster 5 Sept 1869; ✝ at Budapest 12 May 1945), Dame Star Cross Order, dau of Karl Salvator, Archduke of Austria and Princess

Maria Immakulata of Bourbón-Two Sicilies, and had issue, among whom,

1. Prince *Rainer* Maria Joseph Ignaz Florian Michael Gabriel Raphael Gonzaga, *b* at Pola 4 May 1900; ✠*k* at Gyömrö, nr Budapest 25 March 1945 (officially declared deceased at Munich 19 May 1961 with effect from 31 Dec 1945); *m* 1stly at Munich 15 Dec 1930 (*m* diss by div at Munich 9 May 1935), Johanna (*b* at Salzburg 17 Sept 1906; ✠ at Innsbruck 17 Nov 1992), dau of Heinrich Károlyi (Carl) de Károly-Patty and Vasvár and Paula Gamon. He *m* 2ndly at Budapest 13 Feb 1940, Edith (*b* at Budapest 31 May 1913 ✠ at Munich 14 Aug 1997), dau of Alexander Kózol (of Hungarian nobility) and Aloisia Heissler, and had issue by his first wife,

    1. Prince *Johannes Heinrich* Friedrich Werner Konrad Rainer Maria, *b* at Innsbruck 28 March 1931, Banker; *m* 1stly at München 24 Oct 1957 (*m* annulled at München 26 May 1965 and diss by div at Innsbruck 4 July 1968), Baroness Gabriele (*b* at Tinz, nr Breslau 22 June 1921), Portrait Painter and Restorer, dau of Franziskus, Baron von Fürstenberg, Proprietor of Eresburg and Maria Emma von Ruffer, Proprietor of Kokoschütz, and had issue,
    [*Lerchenauerstraße 2, 80809 München, Germany*].

        1. Princess *Felicitas* Franziska Johanna Maria Gabriela Elisabeth Pauline Helene Stephanie Leopoldine Alexandra Sophie Mathilde Josepha Anna Karoline Immaculata Emanuela, *b* at Sorengo 6 April 1958, adopted by her great-uncle Ernst, Prince of Saxe-Coburg and Gotha; *m* at München 15 Nov 1987, Sergei Sergeievitsch Trotzky (*b* at Salzburg 22 June 1948).
        [*Villa Coburg, 8962 Gröming, Austria*].

    Prince Johannes Heinrich *m* 2ndly at München 15 Oct (civ) and at Kloster Andechs 12 Nov (relig) 1968 (*m* diss by div at Innsbruck 27 Aug 1993), Princess Mathilde (*b* at Bamberg 17 Jan 1936), Dr of Med, dau of Friedrich Christian, Margrave of Meissen, Prince and Duke of Saxony, Head of the Royal House of Saxony and Princess Elisabeth Helene von Thurn and Taxis.
    [*Hörwarthstraße 42, 80804 Munich, Germany*].

2. Prince *Philipp* Josias Maria Joseph Ignatius Michael Gabriel Raphael Gonzaga, *b* at Walterskirchen, Lower Austria 18 Aug 1901, ✠ at Vienna 18 Oct 1985, Kt of Hon Sovereign Military Order of Malta; *m* at Budapest 23 Sept 1944, Sárah Aurelia (*b* at Orsova 8 Feb 1914; ✠ 31 Dec 1994), dau of Imre Hálasz and Aurelia Xenia Maximovna Saladuchin, and had issue,

    1. Prince *Philipp August* Ferdinand, *b* at Budapest 3 Jan 1944, Forester; *m* 1stly at Innsbruck 23 Sept 1968, Bettina (*b* at Vienna 11 Feb 1944; ✠ 30 Jan 1989), dau of Paul Pfretschner and Johanna Swrtnik, and has issue,

        1. Princess *Isabelle, b* at Vienna 12 April 1969.

        2. Prince *Maximilian, b* at Vienna 20 July 1972.

        3. Prince *Alexander, b* at Vienna 30 June 1978.

    Prince Philipp August *m* 2ndly at Salzburg 1 March 1991, Rosemarie (*b* at Salzburg 22 Oct 1952), dau of Dr. Paul Jäger and Rosina Haase, and has further issue,

    [*Schloßgasse 1, 2170 Walterskirchen, Austria*].

        4. Princess *Christina* Janine Roseanne, *b* at Salzburg 30 Sept 1995.

3. Prince *Ernst* Franz Maria Joseph Ignatius Thaddeus Felix Michael Gabriel Rafel Gonzaga, *b* at Gerasdorf 25 Feb 1907; ✠ at Gröbming, Steiermark 9 June 1978; *m* at Dürnkrut (civ) and at Ebenthal (relig) 4 Sept 1939, Irmgard (*b* at Aue, Saxony 22 Jan 1912; ✠ at Rottenmann 1 Jan 1976), dau of Wilhelm Röll and Augusta Woydt, and adopted his great-niece,

    1. Princess Felicitas of Saxe-Coburg and Gotha, *b* at Sorengo 6 April 1958 (see above).

II: ALBERTINE LINE
ROYAL HOUSE OF SAXONY

Catholic: Founded by Albert "the Courageous", Duke of Saxony etc (*b* 27 July 1443; ✠ 12 Sept 1500) - Acquired the remaining fiefs of the Duchy of Cleves and County of Mark 1483; Elector of Saxony 4 June 1547; Princely Count of Henneberg (see 1st Line) 1583 (until 10 June 1815); acquired Voigtland 1569; confirmation of the titles of Duke of Jülich, of Cleves and of Berg, Count of Mark and of Ravensberg and Lord of Ravenstein 19 Sept 1666; Hereditary Margrave of Upper and Lower Lusatia 30 May 1635 (until 10 June 1815); King of Poland 27

June 1697 - 5 Oct 1763; King of Saxony 11 Dec 1806. The dynasty ceased to reign 13 Nov 1918.

Arms:- Barry of ten, or and sa, over all a wreath of rue in bend, vert. The shield is ensigned with the Royal Crown of Saxony and surrounded by the Riband of the Order of the Crown of Rue. *Supporters:-* Two lions reguardant or, armed and langued gu. *Motto:-* Providentiae memor.

Members of the Royal House of Saxony bear the titles of Prince or Princess of Saxony, Duke or Duchess of Saxony with the qualification of Royal Highness. The Head of the Royal House bears the title of Margrave of Meissen.

MARIA EMANUEL, MARGRAVE OF MEISSEN, Prince

of Saxony, Duke of Saxony, *b* at Prüfening, nr Regensburg 31 Jan 1926, Bailiff Gd Cross Hon and Dev Sovereign Military Order of Malta, Kt Order of the Golden Fleece, son of Friedrich Christian, Margrave of Meissen (*b* 31 Dec 1893; ✠ 9 Aug 1968) and Princess Elisabeth Helene von Thurn and Taxis (*b* 15 Dec 1903; *m* 16 June 1923; ✠ 22 Oct 1976); *m* at Vevey, Switzerland 23 June 1962, Princess Anastasia-Luise (*b* at Regensburg 22 Dec 1940), Dame Gd Cross Hon and Dev Sovereign Military Order of Malta, dau of Prince Eugen of Anhalt and Anastasia Jungmeier.

[*Ascania Nova, Avenue de Sully 102, 1814 La-Tour-de-Peilz, Kt. Vaud, Switzerland*].

Brother and Sisters

1. Princess *Maria Josepha, b* at Bad Wörishofen 20 Sept 1928, Journalist.

[*Agnesstraße 16, 80798 Munich, Germany*].

2. Princess *Maria Anna* Josepha, *b* at Bad Wörishofen 13 Dec 1929; *m* at Paris 1 May 1952, Roberto Afif, (*b* at Mexico City 30 Nov 1916; ✠ there 13 Dec 1978), lic jur.

[*Knöbelstraße 28, 80538 Munich, Germany*].

3. Prince *Albert* Joseph Maria Franz-Xaver, *b* at Bamberg 30 Nov 1934, Dr of Phil, Historian; *m* at Munich 10 April (civ) and 12 April (relig) 1980, Elmira (*b* at Lodz 25 Dec 1930), dau of Emil Henke and Lydia Müller.

[*Grünwalderstraße 225d, 81545 Munich, Germany; Osterseestraße 22, 82194 Gröbenzell, Germany*].

4. Princess *Mathilde* Maria Josepha Anna Xaveria, *b* at Bamberg 17 Jan 1936, Dr of Med; *m* at Munich 15 Oct (civ) and at Kloster Andechs 12 Nov (relig) 1968 (*m* diss by div at Innsbruck 27 Aug 1993), Prince Johannes Heinrich of Saxe-Coburg and Gotha (*b* at

Innsbruck 28 March 1931), Banker.
[*Reithmannstraße 2, 6020 Innsbruck, Austria*].

Brothers and Sisters of Father

Issue of Friedrich August III, King of Saxony who renounced the
Throne 13 Nov 1918 (*b* 25 May 1865; ✝ 18 Feb 1932) and Princess
Louise of Tuscany, Archduchess of Austria, *cr* "Countess of
Montignoso" 13 July 1903 (*b* 2 Sept 1870 ✝ 23 March 1947; *m* 21 Nov
1891; *m* diss by div 11 Feb 1903; *m* 2ndly 25 Sept 1907, Enrico
Toselli; legally separated 12 June 1912), among whom,

1. Prince *Ernst Heinrich* Ferdinand Franz Joseph Otto Maria
Melchiades, *b* at Dresden 9 Dec 1896; ✝ at Neckarhausen,
Hohenzollern 14 June 1971, Capt Saxon Army (ret), Bailiff Gd Cross
Hon and Dev Sovereign Military Order of Malta; *m* 1stly at Schloß
Hohenburg, nr Lenggries, Bavaria 12 April 1921, Princess Sophie (*b*
at Colmar-Berg 14 Feb 1902; ✝ at Munich 24 May 1941), yst dau of
William IV, Grand Duke of Luxembourg and Infanta Doña Maria
Anna of Portugal. He *m* 2ndly at Paris 28 June 1947, Virginia (*b* at
Frankfurt-am-Main 17 Dec 1910; ✝ at Co Meath 5 Feb 2002), dau of
Lt-Col Karl Ferdinand Dulon and Virginie Ringeisen, and has issue
by his first wife,

    1. Prince Albrecht Friedrich August Johannes Gregor *Dedo*,
    b at Munich 30 May 1922.

    2. Prince Georg *Timo* Michael Nikolaus Maria, *b* at Munich
    22 Dec 1923; ✝ at Emden 21 April 1982; *m* 1stly at Mülheim
    an der Ruhr 7 Aug 1952, Margrit (*b* at Mülheim 9 May 1932;
    ✝ there 6 June 1957), dau of Curl Lucas and Hildegard Stube.
    He *m* 2ndly at Marburg an der Lahn 3 Feb (civ) and 5 Feb
    (relig) 1966 (*m* diss by div at Marburg 6 Feb 1973), Charlotte
    (*b* at Dresden 11 March 1919) [*Freiherr vom Steinstraße 71,
    35041 Marburg - Wehrda, Germany*], dau of Peter Gottfried
    Schwindack and Elsa Katharina Brod. Prince Timo *m* 3rdly
    at Emden 26 March (civ) 1974, Erina Emilie (*b* at Emden 23
    July 1921; *m* 1stly 24 Dec 1946, Georg Dinkla; that *m* diss by
    div 1 April 1948; *m* 2ndly 2 July 1949, Arthur Hardisty, that
    m diss by div 14 Feb 1962; *m* 4thly June 1985, Paul Spinat
    who ✝ 23 Feb 1989, when she reverted to the name of her
    third husband) [*Hansastraße 23, 26723 Emden, Germany*],
    Businesswoman, dau of Heinrich Robert Eilts and Emilie
    Gallikowski, and has issue by his first wife,

1. *Rüdiger* Karl Ernst Timo Aldi, *b* at Mulheim 23 Dec 1953, Psychologist; *m* at Willich 14 June 1974, Astrid (*b* at Halle an der Saale 5 June 1949; ✠ at Steiningert Nov 1989), dau of Heinz Linke and Elvira Wandke, and has issue,

[*Hestert 19, 47826 Kevalaer, Germany*].

    1. *Daniel* Timo, *b* at Duisburg 23 June 1975.

    2. *Arne* Benjamin, *b* at Duisburg 7 March 1977.

    3. *Nils*, *b* at Duisburg 6 Nov 1978

2. *Iris* Hildegard Sophie Margrit Gisela, *b* at Mulheim 21 Sept 1955; *m* 1stly at Mülheim 21 March 1975, *Hans*-Jürgen Hadam (*b* at Mülheim 18 Oct 1950; ✠ at Mülheim 10 Jan 1977). She *m* 2ndly at Essen-Borbeck 20 May (civ) and at Mülheim 22 July (relig) 1977 (*m* diss by div 1983), Wolfgang König, adopted Count Deym von Stritez (*b* at Agram 10 Jan 1943), Businessman. She *m* 3rdly 1990, Ulrich Schumacher (*b* at..). She *m* 4thly at Sonsbeck 11 Nov 1996, Wolfgang Döhring (*b* at Salphia 6 March 1941).

3. Prince Rupprecht Hubertus *Gero* Maria, *b* at Munich 12 Sept 1925.

SCHAUMBURG-LIPPE
(HOUSE OF LIPPE)

Reformation: For the early history of the House of Lippe, see that family. This branch was founded by Philipp, Count and Noble Lord of Lippe (*b* 18 July 1601; ✠ 10 April 1681), Seigneur of Alverdissen, Lipperode and Uhlenburg who inherited, through his sister Elisabeth (✠ 1646), mother of Otto V (✠ 1640), last Count of Schaumburg and of Holstein-Pinneberg, the sovereignty of some parts of the ancient county of Schaumburg on the Weser and assumed the title of Count of Schaumburg, Lippe and Sternberg, which later evolved to Schaumburg-Lippe; attained sovereign status in 1806 and was recognised as Prince of Schaumburg-Lippe 18 April 1807. The dynasty ceased to reign 16 Nov 1918.

Arms:- Quarterly: 1st and 4th, arg, a rose gu, barbed and seeded ppr (Lippe); 2nd and 4th, gu, a swallow close ppr perched upon a star of eight points or (Schwalenberg); over all, an escutcheon gu, per fess arg and of the field between three demi-nettle leaves and as many passion nails in pairle of the second (Schaumburg). *Supporters:*- Two angels vested arg, each holding in his exterior hand a palm erect

vert. The achievement is borne on a mantle gu, fringed and tasselled
or, doubled ermine and surmounted by the Royal Crown.
Members of the Princely Family bear the title of Prince or Princess
of Schaumburg-Lippe with the qualification of Serene Highness.
Admission as a family member depends on the consent of the Head
of the Princely Family.

Friedrich August **PHILIPP-ERNST** Wolrad, **PRINCE (FÜRST)
OF SCHAUMBURG-LIPPE,** Noble Lord of Lippe, Count of
Schwalenberg and Sternberg, b at Hagenburg 26 July 1928, Dipl rer
pol, Kt of Justice St John of Jerusalem, son of Wolrad, Prince (Fürst)
of Schaumburg-Lippe (b 19 April 1887, ✠ 15 June 1962) and
Princess Bathildis of Schaumburg-Lippe (b 11 Nov 1903; m 15 April
1925; ✠ 29 June 1983); m at Bückeburg 3 Oct 1955, Baroness
Eva-Benita (b at Vollrathsruhe 18 Nov 1927), Dr rer nat, elder dau of
Hans-Werner, Count von Tiele-Winckler and Countess Elisabeth
von Bassewitz.
[*Schloß, 31675 Bückeburg, Germany; 4571 Steyrling, Upper
Austria, Austria*].

Sons

1. Adolf Friedrich *Georg-Wilhelm* Wolrad Hans-Werner, Hereditary
Prince (Erbprinz) of Schaumburg-Lippe, b at Freiburg-im-Breisgau
14 July 1956; ✠ nr Steinbergen, Kr Schaumburg 31 July 1983.
2. Ernst August *Alexander* Christian Victor Hubert, Hereditary
Prince (Erbprinz) of Schaumburg-Lippe, b at Dusseldorf 25 Dec
1958; m at Bückeburg 29 Aug 1993 (m diss by div 2002), Princess
Marie Louise (b at Stuttgart 25 Sept 1972), [*Ungererstraße 44, 80802
Munich, Germany*], dau of Otto, Prince zu Sayn-Wittgenstein-
Berleburg and Baroness Annette von Cramm, and has issue,
[*Schloßplatz 1, 31675 Bückeburg, Germany*].

   1. Prince Ernst-August Alexander Wilhelm Bernhard Krafft
   Heinrich-Donatus, b at Hanover 13 May 1994.

Brothers and Sister

1. Albrecht *Georg-Wilhelm* Eugen, Hereditary Prince (Erbprinz) of
Schaumburg-Lippe, b at Hagenburg 26 Jan 1926; kg at Nossige, nr
Meissen 20 April 1945.
2. Prince *Konstantin* Karl-Eduard Ernst-August Stephan
Alexander, b at Hagenburg 22 Dec 1930, Eng agr, Businessman; m
1stly at Hanover 28 Dec 1956, Sigrid (b at Hirschberg, Silesia 2 Sept
1929; ✠ at Bielefeld 30 Aug 1997), dau of Gerhard Knape and

Lieselotte Hennig, and has issue,

    1. Prince *York* Karl-Albrecht Konstantin, *b* at Bielefeld 4 June 1960, Businessman; *m* at Bielefeld 5 Sept (civ) and 12 Sept (relig) 1986, Susanne (*b* at Bielefeld 10 Sept 1961; ✠ there 19 Dec 1992), dau of Gerhard Seidensticker and Gisela Weiner, and has issue,

    [*Am Südhang 19, 33739 Bielefeld, Germany*].

        1. Prince *Nicolai*-York Gerhard Konstantin, *b* at San Diego, California 23 April 1989.

    2. Princess *Tatjana* Sibylle Viktoria Juliane, *b* at Bielefeld 12 Nov 1962.

    [*Ravenna Straße 9a, 81545, Munich, Germany*].

Prince Konstantin *m* 2ndly at Bielefeld 6 Nov (civ) 1998, *Petra* (*b* at Salzkoten 18 Feb 1951), dau of Werna Maass and Ruth Laugwitz and has further issue by her.

[*Holbeinstraße 2, 33615 Bielefeld, Germany*].

    3. *Oliver* Konstantin Mortimer, *b* at Bielfeld 27 March 1988.

3. Princess Elsa *Viktoria-Luise* Marie Barbara Elisabeth Bathildis Wera, *b* at Hagenburg 31 July 1940, *m* 1stly at Willing, nr Bad Aibling, Bavaria 16 Dec 1966 (civ) and at Bückeburg 30 Jan 1967 (relig), as his 3rd wife, Karl-Georg Kurt Gustav, Count von Stackelberg (*b* at Arensburg, Insel Oesel 1 Aug 1913; ✠ at Rosenheim 28 Aug 1980), Dr of Law. She *m* 2ndly at Bückeburg 27 June (civ) and 28 June (relig) 1983, Jürgen von Goerne (*b* at Allenstein 12 Feb 1908; ✠ at Munich 3 March 2001), Col (ret), Ritterkreuz. Princess Viktoria-Luise bears the name of Countess (Gräfin) von Stackelberg-von Goerne.

[*Mauerkircherstraße 163, 81925 Munich, Germany*].

Brothers of Father

Issue of Georg II, Prince of Schaumburg-Lippe (*b* 10 Oct 1846; ✠ 29 April 1911) and Princess Marie Anna of Saxe-Altenburg (*b* 14 March 1864; *m* 16 April 1882; ✠ 3 May 1918), having had issue, among whom,

Sons

1. Prince *Stephan* Alexander Viktor, *b* at Stadthagen 21 June 1891; ✠ at Kempfenhausen 10 Feb 1965, Capt of Horse Prussian Army, Embassy Counsellor; *m* at Rastede 4 June 1921, Duchess Ingeborg-Alix (*b* at Oldenburg 20 July 1901; ✠ at Bienebek 10 Jan 1996), dau of Friedrich August, Grand Duke of Oldenburg and

Duchess Elisabeth of Mecklenburg, and had issue, among whom,

1. Princess *Marie-Alix*, *b* at Bückeburg 2 April 1923; *m* at Glücksburg 9 Oct 1947, Peter, Duke of Schleswig-Holstein-Sonderburg-Glücksburg (*b* at Schloß Louisenlund, nr Schleswig 30 April 1922; ✝ at Gut Bienebek 30 Sept 1980).

[*Gut Bienebek, 24351 Thumby-Schwansen, Germany*].

2. Prince *Heinrich* Konstantin Friedrich Ernst, *b* at Bückeburg 25 Sept 1894; ✝ at Minden 11 Nov 1952, Capt (ret); *m* at Berlin 30 May (civ) and at Sophineureuth, nr Schonwald, Franconia 10 June (relig) 1933, Countess Marie-Erika (*b* at Hofgeismar 10 Feb 1903; ✝ at Bad Oeynhausen 15 July 1964; *m* 1stly at Berlin 19 Dec 1924, Walter Bronsart von Schellendorff who ✝ 12 Sept 1958; that *m* diss by div at Berlin 30 Nov 1927), dau of Albert, Count von Hardenberg and Waldtraut von Arnim, and had issue,

1. Princess *Dagmar* Marie Elisabeth, *b* at Berlin-Wilmersdorf 18 Feb 1934; *m* 1stly at Kronberg, Taunus 7 May 1956, Christoph Kalau vom Hofe (*b* at Schwierse, Kreis Oels 16 Sept 1931; ✝ at Caracas, Venezuela 8 Oct 1981), Businessman. She *m* 2ndly at Celle 27 Jan 1989, Heinz Heine (*b* at Grosslichterfelde, nr Berlin 8 Jan 1907; ✝ at Celle 26 Feb 1991), Col (ret).

[*Hodenbergstraße 3, 29223 Celle, Germany*].

3. Prince *Friedrich Christian* Wilhelm Alexander, *b* at Bückeburg 5 Jan 1906; ✝ at Wasserburg am Inn 20 Sept 1983; *m* 1stly at Seelasgen, Mark 25 Sept 1927, Countess Alexandra (*b* at Stein, nr Nuremberg 29 June 1904; ✝ between Wels and Linz an der Donau 9 Sept 1961), only dau of Wolfgang, Count zu Castell-Rudenhausen and Baroness Hedwig von Faber. He *m* 2ndly at Glücksburg 8 Oct (civ) and 15 Oct (relig) 1962, Princess Marie Luise (*b* at Berlin 8 Dec 1908; ✝ at Wiesbaden 29 Dec 1969; *m* 1stly at Primkenau, Kr Sprottau 19 April 1934, Rudolf Carl, Baron von Stengel; that *m* diss by div at Munich 10 Aug 1955), eldest dau of Prince Albert of Schleswig-Holstein-Sonderburg-Glücksburg and Countess Ortrud zu Isenburg and Büdingen in Meerholz, adopted dau of Ernst Günther, Duke of Schleswig-Holstein. He *m* 3rdly at Schlangenbad 6 March 1971, Helene (*b* 12 March 1913), dau of Maximilian Mayr and Antonie von Bartolf (née Barth), and had issue by his first wife, among whom,

[*Maximilianstraße 4, 83435 Bad Reichenhall, Germany*].

1. Prince *Albrecht Wolfgang*, *b* at Berlin 5 Aug 1934; *m* 1stly at Salzburg 7 Jan 1961 (*m* diss by div 9 March 1962), Catherine (*b* at Wilmington, Delaware, USA 13 Dec 1941), dau of Irving

Whitenack-Hurt and Virginia Catlin. He *m* 2ndly at Linz an
der Donau 6 May (civ) and 8 May (relig) 1964 (*m* diss by div
at Linz 25 April 1974), Heidemarie (*b* at Grundlsee, Austria
31 Aug 1945) [*Roseggerstraße 32, 4020 Linz an der Donau,
Austria*], dau of Herbert Günther and Hilda Gasperl. He *m*
3rdly at Linz an der Donau 16 July 1983, Gertrude (*b* at Linz
5 Nov 1951), dau of Johann Friedhuber and Rosa
Blauensteiner, and had issue by his second wife,
[*Hauserstraße 19, 4020 Linz an der Donau, Austria*].

> 1. Prince *Stephan* Wilhelm Ernst, *b* at Linz an der
> Donau 10 Sept 1965; *m* at Gallneukirchen 24 Sept
> 1988, Andrea Maria (*b* at Pasching 9 July 1966),
> Kindergarten Teacher, dau of Florian Reichl and
> Annemarie Dallinger, and has issue,
> [*4204 Reichenau 73, Austria*].
>
>> 1. Prince *Raphael* Elias, *b* at Reichenau 5 April
>> 1989.
>
> 2. Princess *Alexandra* Maria Christina, *b* at Linz an
> der Donau 15 Jan 1967.
> [*Roseggerstraße 32, 4020 Linz an der Donau, Austria*].

2. Princess *Christine* Marie-Louise Auguste Friederike, *b* at
Berlin 16 Oct 1936; *m* at Lehenleiten, nr Scharnstein, Austria
21 Sept 1958, Albrecht, Baron von Susskind-Schwendi (*b* at
Schweinfurt 20 Feb 1937), Forester and Land Owner.
[*Schloßstraße 15, 89431 Bächingen an der Brenz, Germany*].

Brother of Great-Grandfather

Issue of Georg I Wilhelm, Prince of Schaumburg-Lippe (*b* 20 Dec
1784; ✠ 21 Nov 1860) and Princess Ida of Waldeck and Pyrmont (*b*
26 Sept 1796; *m* 23 June 1816; ✠ 12 April 1869), having had issue,
among whom,

Son

Prince *Wilhelm* Karl August, *b* at Bückeburg 12 Dec 1834; ✠ at
Ratiboritz 4 April 1906, Proprietor of the Lordship of Nachod in
Bohemia, Gen of Cav Austrian Army, Hereditary Member Council of
the Austrian Empire; *m* at Dessau 30 May 1862, Princess Bathildis
(*b* at Dessau 29 Dec 1837; ✠ at Nachod 10 Feb 1902), dau of Prince
Friedrich of Anhalt and Princess Marie of Hesse-Cassel, and had
issue, among whom,

Sons

1. Prince *Friedrich* Georg Wilhelm Bruno, *b* at Ratiboritz 30 Jan 1868; ✠ at Kudowa, Silesia 12 Dec 1945, Major-Gen Austrian Army; *m* 1stly at Copenhagen 5 May 1896, Princess Louise (*b* at Copenhagen 17 Feb 1875; ✠ at Ratiboritz 4 April 1906), dau of Frederik VIII, King of Denmark and Princess Louise of Sweden and Norway, and had issue, among whom,

    1. Prince *Christian* Nikolaus Wilhelm Friedrich Albert Ernst Stephan, *b* at Ödenburg, Hungary 20 Feb 1898; ✠ at Bückeburg 13 July 1974, Lt-Col (ret); *m* at Fredensborg, Denmark 9 Sept 1937, Princess Feodora (*b* at Jaegersborghus 3 July 1910; ✠ at Bückeburg 17 March 1975), eldest dau of Prince Harald of Denmark and Princess Helena of Schleswig-Holstein-Sonderburg-Glücksburg, and had issue,

        1. Prince *Wilhelm* Friedrich Harald Christian Ernst-August Carl Gustav, *b* at Glienicke, nr Potsdam 19 Aug 1939, Banker; *m* at Munich 14 Dec (civ) 1970 and 7 Jan (relig) 1971, Ilona (*b* at Breslau 17 Oct 1940), dau of Georg-Alfred, Ritter Hentschel von Gilgenheimb and Rosemarie von Wietzlow, and has issue,

        [*Jyllingevej 59, 2720 Copenhagen, Denmark*].

            1. Prince *Christian* Hubertus Clemens-August Friedrich-Sigismund Louis-Ferdinand Harald, *b* at Munich 4 Sept 1971.

            [*Winterhuder Marktplatz 2, 22299 Hamburg, Germany*].

            2. Princess *Désirée* Alexandra Felicitas Rosemarie Feodora, *b* at Copenhagen 27 June 1974; *m* at Glesborg, Denmark 1 Sept 2001, *Michael* Frederik Luel (*b* at Arhus, Denmark 7 Oct 1969).

            [*Meilgaard Castle, Meilgaard, Denmark*].

        2. Prince *Waldemar* Stephan Ferdinand Wolrad Friedrich Karl, *b* at Glienicke 19 Dec 1940, Banker; *m* at Karlebo 10 Sept 1977 (*m* diss by div 1991), Anne-Lise (*b* at Copenhagen 8 Aug 1946; ✠ 27 Aug 1994), dau of Aage Poul Johansen and Grethe Inge Fetzlaff, and has issue,

        [*Postfach 2419, 26389 Wilhelmschaften, Germany*].

            1. Princess *Eleonore-Christine* Eugenie Benita

Feodora Maria, *b* at Hørsholm, Denmark 22
Dec 1978.
[*Nygårdsvej 6 I, 2100 Copenhagen, Denmark*].
3. Princess *Marie-Louise* Friederike Cecilie
Alexandrine Helena Bathildis Stephanie, *b* at
Hagenburg 27 Dec 1945, Nurse.
[*c/o Matz, Hinüberstraße 4, 31675 Bückeburg,
Germany*].
4. Prince *Harald* Christian Leopold Gustav, *b* at
Hagenburg 27 March 1948; *m* 1stly at Bückeburg 22
July 1976 (*m* diss by div at Bückeburg 1980), Petra
Wera (*b* at Heessen 24 Sept 1956; *m* 1stly at Bad
Eilsen 7 Feb 1974, Heino Busch; that *m* diss by div at
Bückeburg 8 July 1975), dau of Heinz Herwin Kirstein
and Edith Leske. He *m* 2ndly at Bückeburg 23 Sept
1988, Gabriele (*b* at Coesfeld 26 July 1962), dau of
Ludwig Hagemann and Edeltraut Pasierbsky.
[*Graf-Wilhelm-Straße 4, 31707 Bad Eilsen, Germany*].
Prince Friedrich *m* 2ndly at Dessau 26 May 1909, Princess
Antoinette Anna (*b* at Schloß Georgium, nr Dessau 3 March 1885; ✠
at Dessau 3 April 1963), only dau of Leopold, Hereditary Prince of
Anhalt and Princess Elisabeth of Hesse, and had further issue,
among whom,
4. Prince *Leopold* Friedrich Alexander Wilhelm Eduard, *b* at
Nachod 21 Feb 1910.
[*Westermühlstraße 25, 80469 Munich, Germany*].
2. Prince Christian *Albrecht* Gaetano Karl Wilhelm, *b* at Ratiboritz
24 Oct 1869; ✠ at Linz an der Donau 25 Dec 1942, Col Austrian
Army; *m* 1stly at Stuttgart 6 May 1897, Duchess Elsa (*b* at Stuttgart
1 March 1876; ✠ at Pfaffstätt, nr Munderfing, Upper Austria 27 May
1936), dau of Eugen, Duke of Württemberg and Grand Duchess
Vera Constantinovna of Russia. He *m* 2ndly at Braunau am Inn 24
June 1939, Maria (*b* at Prague 26 July 1897; ✠ at Linz 25 Dec 1942),
dau of Anton Josef Wilhelm Herget and Sophia Anna Bamberger,
and had issue by his first wife, among whom,
1. Prince Wilhelm Eugen Georg Constantin *Max, b* at Wels,
Upper Austria 28 March 1898; ✠ at Salzburg 4 Feb 1974,
Major (ret); *m* at Bad Homburg vor der Höhe 9 May 1933,
Helga Claire Lee (*b* at Cologne 24 Feb 1911), Colonial Dame
of America (descended from Edward Winslow, one of the
Founding Fathers of the British Colonies in North America -

21 Nov 1620), dau of Carl Hermann Joseph Roderbourg and Claude Lennox Miller.
[*Schloß Pfaffstätt, 5222 Munderfing, OÖsterr., Austria; Le Columbia Palace, 11 ave. Princesse Grace, 98000 Monte Carlo, Monaco*].

2. Prince *Franz Josef* Adolf Ernst, *b* at Wels 1 Sept 1899; ✠ at Kassel 7 July 1963; *m* at Munich 29 Jan 1959, Maria Theresia (*b* at Neutitschein, Mähren 29 July 1912; *m* 1stly at Schönau, nr Neutitschein 20 Aug 1932, Erich, Ritter Hörmann von Wüllerstorf and Urbair who ✠ 19 April 1962; that *m* diss by div; she *m* 2ndly at Kaltwassertal, Kr Strehlen 24 July 1943, Hans Heinrich von Tschirschky and Boegendorff (*b* at ...; ✠ at Überlingen 3 Dec 1995); that *m* diss by div at Munich 24 June 1957), dau of Anton Peschel and Josefine Rossmanith. [*Klachau, 8982 Tauplitz, Steiermark, Austria*].

SERBIA
(HOUSE OF OBRENOVIC)

(✠ Extinct In The Male Line ✠)

Orthodox: The dynasty was founded by Visna, a Serbian peasant woman who married firstly Obren Martinovic. Her first issue, Milan, was said to have been murdered by Kara George, the peasant leader and founder of the Karadjordjevi*f* dynasty (*see below*). Milan was succeeded by his half brother Milos Obrenovic who was elected Prince of Serbia by the Nation on 6 Nov 1817 and Duke of Rudnik; in 1827 the National Assembly recognised Prince Milos as a Hereditary Prince; he was succeeded in turn by four successors, the last of whom (*below*) was murdered, with his wife, in the Royal Palace in Belgrade on 10 June 1903, by agents of the Karadjordjevi dynasty (*see below*) - the mutilated bodies of King Alexander I Obrenovic and Queen Draga were tossed into the street from the Palace balcony, whereupon the dynasty became extinct. King Alexander I had an illegitimate half-brother, the natural son of King Milan IV, by Madam Artemisia Christi (his Secretary); Obren Christi made an unsuccessful attempt to claim the Throne in 1906.

✠ **ALEXANDER I**, Obrenovic **KING OF SERBIA,** *b* Belgrade 15 Aug 1876; ✠*assasinated* at Belgrade 10 June 1903; died without issue, reigned under a Regency until he arrested his own regents and proclaimed himself of age on 13 April 1893; *m* at Belgrade 5 Aug

1900, Draga (*b* at Gorni Milanovac 23 Sept 1876; *m* 1stly Colonel Mashin; ✝*assassinated* at Belgrade 10 June 1903) dau of Andrej Lunjevic.

———◆———

SERBIA
(SOMETIME YUGOSLAVIA)
(HOUSE OF KARADJORDJEVIC)

Orthodox: Originally founded by George Petrovic, a Serbian peasant and pig merchant, who became named Kara-George (*Black George*) (*b* 3 Sept 1752; assassinated 13 July 1817) and who led an uprising of Serbs at the beginning of the 19th century. Supreme Leader (*Gospodar*) of the Serbs 24 Jan/5 Feb 1804 to 21 Sept 1813. His son Alexander I Kara-Georgevic (*b* 29 Sept/11 Oct 1806; ✝ 21 April/3 May 1885) was proclaimed Prince Regent (non-Hereditary) of Serbia by the Assembly of Toptchidere after the expulsion of the Obrenovic Dynasty 15 Sept 1842, recognised by Turkey 27 June 1848, forced to leave Belgrade 12 Dec 1858, abdicated 3 Jan 1859. His son, Peter I Kara-Georgevic (*b* 29 June 1844; ✝ 16 April 1921) was proclaimed King of Serbia 2/15 June 1903; his son Alexander, King of the Serbs, Croats and Slovenes since Nov 1918; named the Kingdom of Yugoslavia since 3 Oct 1929. The dynasty ceased to reign when the Constituent Communist Assembly abolished the Monarchy without Referendum on 29 Nov 1945. Of the five members of the dynasty to rule, two were assassinated, and four of the five were forced to abdicate or seek exile - the penultimate monarch, King Aexander I was assasinated while on a State visit to France.

Arms: (of the Kingdom of Yugoslavia) - Gu, an eagle displayed arg, beaked and membered or, charged with an escutcheon parted per fess and the chief per pale: 1st, gu, a cross arg, between four beagles or back to back (Serbia); 2nd, checky gu and arg (Croatia); 3rd, az, a crescent arg surmounted by three stars or, one and two (Slovenia). The shield is ensigned with the Royal Crown of Yugoslavia. The achievement is borne on a mantle purp, fringed and tasselled or, doubled erm and surmounted by the Royal Crown of Yugoslavia.

The sons of kings bear the title of princes royal (kraljevic) and with all other members of the Royal Family bear the title of Prince or Princess Karadjordjevic, (but have previously assumed the style "*of Yugoslavia*" - outside that Country only). Princesses following marriage, only by permission of the Head of the Dynasty, children and grandchildren of reigning sovereigns only with the automatic qualification of Royal Highness, thereafter Highness. The Dynasty became hereditary in 1903, by male primogeniture, with no female rights of secession.

The state of Yugoslavia was created on 3 Oct 1929 as the Kingdom of Yugoslavia, and later the component parts of Bosnia and Hercegovina, Croatia, Macedonia, Montenegro, Serbia and Slovinia became part of a Federal Republic. The Karadjordjevic Dynasty reigned briefly as Kings of Yugoslavia for sixteen years. The State of Yugoslavia was dismantled during the 1990's leaving only a rump of Serbia and Montenegro, retaining the style of Yugoslavia. With the final negotiations to abolish of the name Yugoslavia this year, that State will be replaced by a new loose federation of Serbia and Montenegro, each almost entirely autonomous. Historically both Serbia and Montenegro have their own dynasties and thrones (Karadjordjevic of Serbia *established 1804*; Petrovic-Njegos of Montenegro - *established 1697* - *See MONTENEGRO*).

ALEXANDER, CROWN PRINCE ALEXANDER

KARADJORDJEVIC, *b* at London 17 July 1945, Order of Saint Lazarus, Gd. Master Orders of Star of Karageorge; White Eagle; the Yugoslavian Crown, and Saint Sava, Kt of Saint Januarius, Gd Cross Orders of Immaculate Conception of Villa Viçosa, Saints Maurice and Lazarus, Pedro I and the Rose of Brazil, Bailiff Gd Cross Hon & Dev and Gd Cross of Merito Melitense of Sov Mil Order of Malta, Bailiff Gd Cross Constantinian Order of St George, 1ˢᵗ class Order of Saint Sava, Capt British Army (retd.), son of Peter II Karadjordjevic, King of Yugoslavia (*b* 6 Sept 1923; ✚ 3 Nov 1970) and Princess Alexandra of Greece and Denmark (*b* 25 March 1921; *m* 20 March 1944; ✚ 30 Jan 1993); *m* 1stly at Villamanrique de la Condesa, Prov Sevilla, Spain 1 July 1972 (*m* diss by div at Virginia, USA 19 Feb 1985), Princess Maria da Gloria (*b* at Petrópolis, Brazil 13 Dec 1946; *m* 2ndly at Seville 24 Oct 1985, Don Ignacio de Medina y Fernández de Córdoba, Duque de Segorbe, Conde de Moriana del Río, Grandee of Spain), dau of Dom Pedro Gastão, Prince of Orléans and Bragança and Princess Doña María de la Esperanza of Bourbon-Two Sicilies. He *m* 2ndly at London 20 Sept (civ) and 21 Sept (relig) 1985, (*Clairy*) Katherine (*b* at Athens 13 Nov 1943; *m* 1stly at Athens 25 Nov 1962, Jack W Andrews; that *m* diss by div at Washington, DC 7 April 1984), dau of Robert Batis and Anna Dosti, and has issue by his first wife,

[c/o Bieli Dvor, Belgrade, Republic of Serbia and Montenegro].

Sons

1. *Peter,* Hereditary Prince of Yugoslavia, *b* at Chicago, Illinois, USA 5 Feb 1980, Kt Order of Saint Prince Lazarus, Gd Cross Orders of Star of Karageorge, the White Eagle, the Yugoslavian Crown, and

Saint Sava.
[*c/o Bjeli Dvor, Belgrade, Republic of Serbia and Montenegro*].
2. Prince *Philip, b* at Falls Church, Virginia, USA 15 Jan 1982, Gd
Cross Order of Star of Karageorge.
[*c/o Bjeli Dvor, Belgrade, Republic of Serbia and Montenegro*].
3. Prince *Alexander, b* at Falls Church, Virginia, USA 15 Jan 1982
(*fraternal twin with Prince Philip*), Gd Cross Order of Star of
Karageorge.
[*c/o Bjeli Dvor, Belgrade, Republic of Serbia and Montenegro*]

Brothers of Father

Issue of Alexander I Karadjordjevic, King of Yugoslavia (*b* at Cetinje,
Montenegro 4 Dec 1888; ✞ *assassinated* at Marseilles 9 Oct 1934) and
Princess Marie of Romania (*b* at Gotha 8 Jan 1900; *m* at Belgrade 8
June 1922; ✞ at London 22 June 1961).

1. Prince *Tomislav, b* at Belgrade 19 Jan 1928; ✞ at Oplenac 12 July
2000; (*Heir Presumptive to the Throne of Yugoslavia from 10 Oct
1934 - 17 July 1945*), Gd Cross Orders of the Star of Karageorge, the
White Eagle, the Yugoslavian Crown, Saint Sava, Fidelity of Baden,
Cmdr Ven Order of Saint John of Jerusalem; *m* 1stly at Salem,
Baden 6 June 1957 (*m* diss by div at London 14 Dec 1981), Princess
Margarita [*4 Pencombe Mews, Denbigh Road, London, W11*], (*b* at
Salem 14 July 1932), dau of Berthold, Margrave of Baden and
Princess Theodora of Greece and Denmark, and has issue,
    1. Prince *Nikolas, b* at London 15 March 1958, Gd Cross
    Order of Star of Karageorge; *m* at Faarburg, Denmark 30 Aug
    (civ) and at Düsseldorf 22 Nov (relig) 1992, Ljiljana (*b* at
    Zemun, Belgrade 27 Dec 1959; *m* 1stly Ivan Coric; that *m* diss
    by div 1992), dau of Lazar Licanin and Maria Militca Sasic,
    and has issue,
    [*Leibnitz 12, 63071 Offenbach, Germany*].
        1. Princess *Maria, b* at Belgrade 4 Aug 1993.
    2. Princess *Katarina, b* at London 28 Nov 1959; *m* at London
    5 Dec 1987, George *Desmond* de Silva (*b* at Ceylon 13 Dec
    1939), QC, Kt of Justice, Order of St John.
    [*Marlands House, Itchingfield, Nr Horsham, West Sussex;
    16 Berry Walk, London, S.W.3.*].
Prince Tomislav *m* 2ndly at Bournville, nr Birmingham 16 Oct 1982,
Linda (*b* at London 22 June 1949), dau of Holbrook van Dyke Bonney
and Joan Evans, [*Orchard Cottage, Redlands Farm, Kirdford, West*

*Sussex RH14 OLD; Oplenac, ul Kraljica Maria, 31340 Topola, Serbia,
Republic of Serbia and Montenegro]* and has further issue,

    3. Prince *George*, Gd Cross Order of Star of Karageorge; *b* at
London 25 May 1984.

    [*Orchard Cottage, Redlands Farm, Kirdford, West Sussex
RH14 OLD*].

    4. Prince *Michael*, Gd Cross Order of Star of Karageorge; *b* at
London 15 Dec 1985.

    [*Orchard Cottage, Redlands Farm, Kirdford, West Sussex
RH14 OLD*].

2. Prince *Andrej*, *b* at Bled, Slovenia 28 June ✠ at Irvine, California,
USA 7 May 1990; Gd Cross Orders of the Star of Karageorge, the
White Eagle, Yugoslavian Crown, and Saint Sava; *m* 1stly at
Kronberg, Taunus 2 Aug 1956 (*m* diss by div at London 31 May
1962), Princess Christina (*b* at Kronberg 10 Jan 1933; *m* 2ndly at
London 3 Dec 1962, Robert van Eyck; that *m* diss by div at London
15 Dec 1985), dau of Prince Christoph of Hesse and Princess Sophie
of Greece and Denmark, and has issue, among whom,

    1. Princess Maria *Tatiana*, *b* at London 18 July 1957; *m* at St
    Paul de Vence, France 30 June 1990, *Gregory* Per Edward
    Anthony Michael Thune-Larsen *b* at London 11 Aug 1953.

Prince Andrej *m* 2ndly at Langton Green, nr Tunbridge Wells, Kent
18 Sept (civ) and at Amorbach 12 Oct (relig) 1963 (*m* diss by div at
Frankfurt-am-Main 10 July 1972), Princess Kira (*b* at Coburg 18 July
1930), dau of Karl, Prince (Fürst) zu Leiningen and Grand Duchess
Maria Kyrillovna of Russia, [*Flat 4, 6 Frognal, Hampstead, London
NW3.*]. He *m* 3rdly at Palm Springs, California 30 March 1974, Eva
Maria (*b* at Vrnjacka Banja 26 Aug 1926; *m* 1stly Frank Lowe; that *m*
diss by div 1973), dau of Milan Andjelkovic and Eva Jovanovic, [*355
Valmont Sur Palm Springs 92262 California U.S.A.*], and has
further issue by his second wife,

    3. Princess *Lavinia* Marie, *b* at London 18 Oct 1961; *m* at
    London 20 May 1989 (*m* diss by div at London 14 June 1993),
    Erastos Dimirios Sideropoulos (*b* at Alexandria Egypt 31 Mar
    1943); she *m* 2ndly at London 4 Oct 1998 Austin
    Prichard-Levy (*b* at Roma, Queensland 20 Jan 1953).
    [*Flat 6 St Saviour's Court, Alexandra Park Road, Haringey,
    London N22 7AZ*].

    4. Prince Karl *Wladimir* Kirill Andrej, Gd Cross Order of
    Star of Karageorge; *b* at London 21 March 1964; *m* at London
    18 April 2000, Brigitte (*b* at Schottmar [Bad Salzuflen] 7 July

1956; *m* 1stly Woldgang Staudte; *m* diss by div), dau of *Helmut* Georg Muller and *Gerda* Auguste Klara Martha Freida Sander. [*Lehnkuhlstraße 34, 32108 Bad Saltufen, Germany*].

    1. Prince *Kyrill* Andrej Alexander; *b* at London 18 June 2001; ✢ at London 18 June 2001.

5. Prince *Dimitri* Ivan Mihailo, Gd Cross Order of Star of Karageorge, *b* at London 12 April 1965.
[*224e Walm Lane, Cricklewood, London, NW2 3BS*].

Brother of Great-Grandfather

Issue of Alexander I Karadjordjevic, Prince of Serbia (*b* 29 Sept 1806; ✢ 3 May 1865) and Persida Nenadovic (*b* 3 1813; ✢ 29 March 1873), having had issue, among whom,

Son

Prince *Arsen, b* at Temesvár 4 April 1859; ✢ at Paris 19 Oct 1938, Gen Russian Army; Cmdr-Gen Yugoslavian Army; *m* at St Petersburg 19 April 1892 (*m* diss by div 14 Dec 1896), Princess Aurora (*b* at Kiev 3 Nov 1873; ✢ at Turin 28 June 1904; *m* 2ndly at Genoa 4 Nov 1897, Nicola, Count Noghera), dau of Paul Pavlovitch Demidoff, Prince di San Donato and Princess Helena Petrovna Trubetzkoy, and had issue,

Son

Prince *Paul, b* at St Petersburg 15 April 1893; ✢ at Paris 14 Sept 1976, Gd Cross Orders of Star of Karageorge, the White Eagle, Yugoslavian Crown and Saint Sava, Kt Orders of the Garter, the Annunziata, the Elephant, the Saint-Esprit, Gd Cross Royal Victorian Order, Gd Cross with Collar Order of Carol I of Roumania, Gd Cross Orders of the Redeemer, the Phoenix, Kt Gd Cross Légion d'Honneur, etc, Gen Yugoslavian Army, BA, MA, Hon DCL, Prince Regent of Yugoslavia 9 Oct 1934 - 27 March 1941; *m* at Belgrade 22 Oct 1923, Princess Olga (*b* at Tatoi, nr Athens 29 May 1903; ✢ at Paris 16 Oct 1997), Gd Cross Orders of Saints Olga and Sophia; dau of Prince Nicholas of Greece and Denmark and Grand Duchess Helena Vladimirovna of Russia, and had issue, among whom,

    1. Prince *Alexander, b* at White Lodge, Richmond, Surrey 13 Aug 1924, Gd Cross Orders of Star of Karageorge, the White Eagle, Yugoslavian Crown and Saint Sava, Kt Order of the Annunziata, etc, Lt (British) Royal Air Force (ret); *m* 1stly at Cascais, Portugal 12 Feb 1955 (*m* diss by div at Paris 1967), Princess Maria Pia (*b* at Naples 24 Sept 1934), Dame of Hon

Sovereign Military Order of Malta, dau of Umberto II, King of
Italy and Princess Marie José of Belgium, and has issue,
[*4 Majka Jevrocime, Belgrade, Republic of Serbia and
Montenegr].*

 1. Prince *Dimitri* Nicolas Paul Georg Maria, *b* at
 Boulogne-sur Seine 18 June 1958.
 [*5 boulevard Richad Wallace, 922000 Neuilly sur Seine
 France*].

 2. Prince *Michael* Umberto Anton Peter Maria, *b* at
 Boulogne-sur-Seine 18 June 1958 (*fraternal twin with
 Prince Dimitri*).
 [*5 boulevard Richad Wallace, 922000 Neuilly sur Seine
 France*].

 3. Prince Sergius (*Serge*) Vladimir Emanuel Maria, *b*
 at Boulogne-sur-Seine 11 March 1963, Photographer;
 m at Saint-Nom-la-Breteche, Yvelines 6 Nov (civ) and
 at Merlinge, nr Geneva 30 Nov (relig) 1985 (*m* diss by
 div at Paris 29 October 1986), Sophie (*b* at Boulogne-
 sur-Seine 1 April 1962), dau of Betrand de Toledo and
 Françoise Gallier.
 [*Via Gaudenzio Ferraris, 10184 Torino, Italy*].

 4. Princess *Helene* Olga Lydia Tamara Maria, *b* at
 Boulogne-sur-Seine 11 March 1963 (twin with Prince
 Serge); *m* at Neuilly-sur-Seine 12 Jan 1988, Thierry
 Gaubert (*b* at Paris 16ème 14 May 1951)
 [*5 boulevard Richad Wallace, 922000 Neuilly sur Seine
 France*].

Prince Alexander *m* 2ndly at Paris 2 Nov 1973, Princess
Barbara (*b* at Mährisch-Sternberg 9 July 1942), dau of Prince
Johannes von and zu Liechtenstein and Countess Karoline
von Ledebur-Wicheln, and has further issue,

 5. Prince *Dušan* (Duchan) Paul, *b* at St Gallen 25
 Sept 1977.
 [*4 Majka Jevrocime, Belgrade, Republic of Serbia
 and Montenegro*]

2. Princess *Elisabeth, b* at Belgrade 7 April 1936; *m* 1stly at
Maryland, USA 21 Jan 1961 (*m* diss by div 7 March 1969),
Howard Oxenberg (*b* at New York 27 July 1919). She *m* 2ndly
at London 23 Sept 1969 (*m* diss by div 25 Jan 1978), Neil
Balfour (*b* at Lima, Peru 12 Aug 1944), Banker. She *m* 3rdly
at Lima, Peru 28 Feb 1987, Senator Manuel Ulloa (*b* at Lima

12 Nov 1922; ✠ at Spain 6 Aug 1992).
[*180 West 58th Street, Penthouse D, New York, N.Y. 10019,
U.S.A.*].

SPAIN
(HOUSE OF BORBÓN)

Catholic: For the early history of the Bourbón Family see
BOURBÓN-ORLEANS (France). This Branch was founded
by Philippe, Duke d'Anjou (*b* 19 Dec 1683; ✠ 9 July 1746)
who reigned as King Felipe V of Spain from 24 Nov 1700;
King of Naples and Sicily 1700 - 1713; Semisalic Law was
introduced 1713; King Carlos III (*b* 20 Jan 1716; ✠ 13/14
Dec 1788) established his third son Ferdinando as King of
the Two Sicilies, with reciprocal rights of all his sons to both
thrones in the Pragmatic Decree of 6 Oct 1759. King Carlos
IV (*b* 12 Nov 1748; ✠ 19 Jan 1819) abdicated 6 May 1808;
his son Fernando, Prince of the Asturias (*b* 14 Oct 1784; ✠
29 Sept 1833) became King Fernando VII after 19 March
1808; abdicated 19 March/6 May 1808, restored in March
1814; Semisalic Law was abolished and the succession to the
throne established 29 March 1830 (The Carlists never
recognised this abolition and continued to claim the Crown
until its extinction in the male line in 1936); His daughter,
Queen Isabel II was forced to leave the country 30 Sept 1868
and abdicated in favour of her son, Alfonso 25 June 1870, he
was proclaimed King Alfonso XII 20 Dec 1874. King Alfonso
XIII left the country 14 April 1931 and a republic was
proclaimed. A military dictatorship ensued from 1936 until
1975. King Alfonso XIII's grandson, King Juan Carlos I, was
proclaimed King 22 Nov 1975.

The King of Spain bears the qualification of His Majesty the
King of Spain but has not relinquished the ancient titles of
the Spanish Crown, including that of Catholic Majesty. By
Decree of 1987 regulating the titles of the Royal Family, the
children of the Sovereign and of the eldest son or heir of the
Sovereign bear the title of Infante or Infanta of Spain with
the qualification of Royal Highness and the style Serenísimo
Señor or Serenísima Señora. The Heir Apparent bears the

title of Prince of the Asturias, and the ancient titles pertaining to that position. The children of Infants and Infantas of Spain are entitled to the qualification of Excellency *ad personam*. The Ducal titles conferred on several Infantas, are lifetime titles *ad personam* although frequently extended by courtesy to their spouses. Other Members of the Royal family bear no title as of right unless conceded to them by the reigning Sovereign or by virtue of descent from another Royal House. Members of the Royal Family may be raised to the rank of Infantes "Infantes de Gracia" by the Sovereign's designation.

JUAN CARLOS I, KING OF SPAIN, designated heir to the throne with the title of the Prince of Spain by General Francisco Franco, Chief of State 22 July 1969, proclaimed King 22 Nov 1975, Capt-Gen Armed Forces, etc, *b* at Rome 5 Jan 1938, Sov of the Order of the Golden Fleece, Gd Master of the Orders of Carlos III, Isabella the Catholic, St Hermengildo, etc, and of the Mil Orders of Santiago, Calatrava, Alcántara and Montesa, Kt Order of the Garter, Kt Order of the Seraphim, Kt Order of the Elephant, Kt Order of the Annunziata, Kt Order of St Januarius, Bailiff Gd Cross Hon and Dev Sovereign Military Order of Malta, Bailiff Gd Cross Constantinian Order of St George, Gd Cross Order of Pius IX, Gd Cross Order of the Saviour of Greece Cd Cross Order of Leopold (Belgium), etc, titled Prince of the Asturias 1941 - 1969, son of Don Juan, Count of Barcelona, Prince of the Asturias (from 21 June 1933), Head of the Royal House of Spain who renounced his dynastic rights in favour of his son King Don Juan Carlos I on 14 May 1977 (*b* 20 June 1913; ✝ 1 April 1993) and Princess Maria de las Mercedes of Bourbón-Two Sicilies (*b* at Madrid 23 Feb 1910; *m* at Rome 12 Oct 1935, ✝ 1 Jan 2000); *m* at Athens 14 May 1962, Princess Sofia (*b* at Psychiko, nr Athens 2 Nov 1938), dau of Paul I, King of the Hellenes and Princess Friederike of Hanover, Princess of Great Britain and Northern Ireland.
[*Palacio de la Zarzuela, 28048 El Pardo, Madrid, Spain*].

Son and Daughters

1. Infanta Doña *Elena* Maria Isabel Dominga de Borbón y Grecia, *b* at Madrid 20 Dec 1963, *cr* Duchess of Lugo March 1995, Gd Cross Order of Carlos III; *m* at Seville 18 March 1995, Don Jaime de Marichalar y Sáenz de Tejada (*b* at Pamplona 7 April 1963).
[*José Ortega y Gasset 30, 28006, Madrid, Spain*].

2. Infanta Doña *Cristina* Federica Victoria Antonia de Borbón y Grecia, *b* at Madrid 13 June 1965, *cr* Duchess of Palma de Mallorca 9 Oct 1997, Gd Cross Order of Carlos III; *m* at Barcelona 4 Oct 1997, Don Iñaki Urdangarin Liebaert (*b* at Zumárraga, Guipúzcoa 15 Jan 1968).

[*Avenida Diagonal 676 bis, 08034 Barcelona, Spain*].

3. Infante Don *Felipe* Juan Pablo Alfonso y Todos los Santos de Borbón y Grecia, Prince of the Asturias, Prince of Viana and Prince of Gerona, *b* at Madrid 30 Jan 1968, Kt Order of the Golden Fleece, Gd Cross Order of Carlos III, Kt Order of Santiago, Gd Cross Royal Victorian Order (1988) etc.

[*Palacio de la Zarzuela, 28048 El Pardo, Madrid, Spain*].

Brother and Sisters

1. Infanta Doña *Maria del Pilar* Alfonsa Juana Victoria Luisa Ignacia y Todos los Santos, *b* at Cannes 30 July 1936, *cr* Duchess of Badajoz by her father 13 April 1967 and recognised in Decree by Gen Franco (Official Bulletin 17 April 1967), Dame Gd Cross Order of Maria Luisa, Dame Gd Cross Constantinian Order of St George; *m* (non-dynastic and placed her voluntary renunciation of her rights for herself and her descendants at the disposal of her father 13 Feb 1967) at the Jeronimos de Belem, Lisbon 5 May 1967, Don Luís Goméz-Acebo y Duke de Estrada, Viscount de la Torre (Official Bulletin 29 Sept 1971), Duke of Badajoz *jure uxoris* (until the Royal Decree of Nov 1987)(*b* at Madrid 23 Dec 1934; ✠ there 9 March 1991), Lawyer.

[*Mirlo 12, Somosaguas, Madrid, Spain*].

2. Infanta Doña *Margarita* Maria de la Victoria Esperanza Jaime Felicidad Perpetua y Todos los Santos, *b* at Rome 6 March 1939, *cr* Duchess of Soria (Official Bulletin 23 June 1981) and *succ* her kinsman Don Manfredo de Borbón y Bernaldo de Quirós as 2nd Duchess of Hernani and Grandee of Spain (letter of succession 20 April 1981, Official Bulletin 27 May 1981, confirmed by Royal Decree 27 Oct 1981), Dame Gd Cross Order of Maria Luisa, Dame Gd Cross Constantinian Order of St George; *m* (non-dynastic and placed her voluntary renunciation of her rights for herself and her descendants at the disposal of her father) at Estoril 12 Oct 1972, Don Carlos Zurita y Delgado (*b* at Antequera, Prov Malaga 9 Oct 1943), MD.

[*Jorge Juan 9, 28001, Madrid, Spain*].

3. Infante Don *Alfonso* Cristino Teresa Angel Francisco de Asís y Todos los Santos, *b* at Rome 3 Oct 1941; ✠ at Estoril 29 March 1956.

Brothers and Sisters of Father

Issue of Alfonso XIII, King of Spain and The Indies (*b* 17 May 1886; ✝ 28 Feb 1941; *succ* at birth under the Regency of his mother, Queen Maria Cristina until 17 May 1902; left the country without abdicating 14 April 1931; abdicated at Rome in favour of his third son on 15 Jan 1941, Juan, Prince of the Asturias, Count of Barcelona (*b* 20 June 1913; ✝ 1 April 1993) , and Princess Victoria Eugenia of Battenberg (*b* 24 Oct 1887; *m* 31 May 1906; ✝ 15 April 1969) among whom,

Dukes d'Anjou

*(Primogeniture claimant - Bourbón; Throne of France;
see Appendix V)*

1. Infante Don *Jaime* Luitpoldo Isabelino Enrique Alejandro Alberto Alfonso Victor Acacio Pedro Pablo Maria, **Duke d'Anjou**, *b* at San Ildefonso 23 June 1908; ✝ at St Gallen, Switzerland 20 March 1975, Duke of Segovia, renounced all rights of succession to the Throne of Spain for himself and his descendants (under the Constitution of 1876) 21 June 1933 (and confirmed this renuciation 23 July 1945 and 17 June 1947) following the death of his father he assumed the title of Duke d'Anjou as primogeniture representative of the House of Bourbón 28 March 1946, *cr* Duke of Segovia by his father 4 March 1935, Kt Order of the Golden Fleece, Gd Cross Carlos III, Gd Cross Order of Isabel the Catholic, Gr Com Order of Calatrava, Kt Order of St Januarius, Kt Order of the Elephant of Denmark, Bailiff Gd Cross Constantinian Order of St George; *m* (non-dynastic in Spain) 1stly at Rome 4 March 1935 (*m* diss by div at Bucharest 6 May 1947; confirmed at Turin 3 June 1949), Donna Emanuela (*b* at Rome 8 Nov 1913; *m* 2ndly at Vienna 21 Nov 1949, Antonio Sozzani who was *b* at Milan 19 July 1918, Banker) [*Piazza di Campitelli 3, 00186 Rome, Italy*], dau of Roger, Viscount de Dampierre, 2nd Duke of San Lorenzo and Donna Vittoria Ruspoli of the Princes di Poggio-Suasa. He *m* 2ndly (non-dynastic in Spain) at Innsbruck 3 Aug 1949, Charlotte (*b* at Konigsberg, Prussia 2 Jan 1919; ✝ at Berlin 3 July 1979 *m* 1stly N. Büchler and 2ndly at Königsberg im Preussen Jan 1939, .N Hippler; that *m* diss by div 1940), Opera Singer, dau of Otto Eugen Tiedemann and Luise Klein, and had issue by his first wife among whom,

    1. Don *Alfonso* Jaime Marcelino Manuel Victor Maria de Borbón y Dampierre, **Duke d'Anjou**, *b* at Rome 20 April 1936; ✝ at Beaver Creek, Colorado 30 Jan 1989, *cr* Duke of Bourbón by father 25 Nov 1950, and Duke of Burgundy, *succ*

his father as primogeniture representative of the House of
France 20 March 1975 and assumed the title of Duke d'Anjou
3 Aug 1975, *cr* Duke of Cádiz with the qualification of Royal
Highness, Spain 22 Nov 1972 (title limited *ad personam* Nov
1987), Spanish Ambassador to Sweden 1970-73, President
Spanish Institute of Culture 1973, Gd Cross Order of Isabel
the Catholic, Bailiff Gd Cross Constantinian Order of St
George, Gd Cross Sts Maurice and Lazarus, Gd Cross Order
of the Polar Star of Sweden, Kt of Hon and Dev Sovereign
Military Order of Malta; *m* at El Pardo 8 March 1972 (legally
separated 16 Nov 1979; *m* diss by div at Madrid 14 May 1982
and religiously annulled at Madrid 16 Dec 1986), Maria del
Carmen (*b* at Madrid 26 Feb 1951; *m* 2ndly at Rueil-Malmaison,
Dept Hauts-de-Seine 11 Dec 1984, Jean Baptiste Mario Rossi,
Antiquarian; that *m* diss by div 20 June 1995), dau of Don
Cristóbal Martinez y Bordiú, 10th Marquess de Villaverde
and Doña Maria del Carmen Franco y Polo, Duchess de Franco
(Daughter of General Franco), and has issue among whom,

> 1.Don *Lúis Alfonso* Gonzalo Victor Manuel Marco de
> Borbón y Martínez-Bordiu, **Duke d'Anjou**, *b* at Madrid
> 25 April 1974, *cr* Royal Highness, without dynastic
> rights, at birth by General Franco; retained this rank
> until the Royal Decree of Nov 1987, at which time the
> right of succession to the Dukedom of Cádiz was also
> lost and the title became *ad personam* to his father, *cr*
> Duke of Touraine by his father 19 Sept 1981, and
> Duke of Bourbón 27 Sept 1984, *succ* his father as
> primogeniture representative of the House of France,
> and assumed the title of Duke d'Anjou 2 Feb 1989.
> [*Hermanos Becquer 7, 28006 Madrid, Spain*].

2. Don *Gonzalo* Victor Alfonso José Bonifacio Antonio Maria
y Todos los Santos de Borbón y Dampierre, *b* at Rome 5 June
1937, *cr* Duke of Aquitaine by his father 21 Sept 1972; *m* 1stly
at Puerto Vallarta, Mexico 28 Jan 1983 (*m* diss by div 18
April 1983), Carmen (*b* at Madrid 23 April 1947; *m* 1stly at
Madrid 28 Dec 1970, Juan Antonio de La Mora; that *m* diss
by div 1978), dau of Rafael Harto and CarmenMontealegre.
He *m* 2ndly at Madrid 25 June (civ) and Olmedo, nr Valladolid
30 June (relig) 1984 (separated at Madrid 7 March 1986/5
May 1987); *m* diss by div at Madrid 31 Jan 1989; *m* annulled
at Florence May 1995), Maria de las Mercedes (*b* at Valencia

15 Oct 1963), dau of Luis Licer and María de las Mercedes
García y Estrada. He *m* 3rdly at Genoa, Italy 12 Dec 1992
(civ) and at Rome 17 Sept 1995 (relig), Emanuela (*b* at Genoa
22 March 1960), dau of Vincenzo Protalongo and Sofia
Hardouin of the Dukes de Gallese. He has recognised a natural
dau by Sandra Lee (*b* at Jacksonville, Forida 25 Aug 1936)
Landry (now Mrs Alfred Worden),
[*Chermin Praz Buchilly 103, 1000 Lausanne 25, Switzerland*].
    1. *Estafania* Michelle de Borbón, *b* at Coral Gables,
    Florida 19 June 1968; *m* at Palm Beach, Florida 27
    July 1995, Richard Carl McMasters II (*b* at West Palm
    Beach, Florida 25 March 1972).

Sisters of Grandfather

Issue of Alfonso XII, King of Spain (*b* 28 Nov 1857; ✠ 25 Nov 1885;
succ his mother 29 Dec 1874) and his second wife, Archduchess
Maria Christina of Austria (*b* 21 July 1858; *m* 29 Nov 1879; ✠ 6 Feb
1929), Regent for her son, Alfonso XIII, King of Spain, from his birth
until 17 May 1902 among whom

1. Doña *Maria* de las *Mercedes* Isabella Theresia Christina Alfonsia
Hyazintha, Princess of the Asturias, *b* at Madrid 11 Sept 1880; ✠
there 17 Oct 1904, Dame Star Cross Order; *m* at Madrid 14 Feb 1901,
Prince Carlos of Bourbón-Two Sicilies, Infante of Spain (*b* at Gries,
nr Bolzano 10 Nov 1870; ✠ at Seville 11 Nov 1949; *m* 2ndly at
Woodnorton, Evesham, Worcester 16 Nov 1907, Princess Louise of
Bourbón-Orleans), renounced for himself and descendants the throne
of Two-Sicilies in the event of succeeding at Cannes 14 Dec 1900 and
was naturalised a Spanish subject and granted the title of Infante of
Spain 7 Feb 1901, and had issue (granted the title of Infants of Spain
by Royal Decrees of King Alfonso XIII 29 Jan 1903 and 15 Oct 1904
(- see **BOURBÓN-TWO SICILIES**)

2. Infanta Doña Maria Theresia (*Teresa*) Isabel Eugenia Patrocinio
Diego, *b* at Madrid 12 Nov 1882, ✠ there 23 Sept 1912, Dame Star
Cross Order, Dame Order of Maria Luisa, Dame of Hon Bavarian
Orders of St Theresia and St Elisabeth; *m* at Madrid 12 Jan 1906,
Prince Ferdinand Maria of Bavaria (*b* at Madrid 10 May 1884; ✠
there 5 April 1958; *m* 2ndly at Fuenterrabia 1 Oct 1914, Maria Luisa
de Silva y Fernández de Henestrosa who was *cr* Duchess de Talavera
de la Reina and a Grandee of Spain by King Alfonso XIII 25 June/

2 Sept 1914, and Infanta of Spain with the qualification of Royal
Highness 17 May 1927; dau of Luis de Silva y Fernández de Córdova,
10th Count de Pié de Concha, 17th Marquess de Zahara, etc and
Maria de los Dolores Fernández de Henestrosa y Fernández de
Córdoba); Infante of Spain, naturalised in Spain 20 Oct 1905;
renounced his rights as a member of the Royal House of Bavaria 29
June 1914 following his second marriage but received *ad personam*
the right, title, rank and arms of a Prince of Bavaria 3 Aug 1914, Kt
Spanish Order of the Golden Fleece, etc, and had issue (Infants of
Spain).

    1. Infante Don *José Eugenio* Alfonso Fernando Mariano Teresa
    Antonio Jesús Santiago Isidro Ramón Braulio y Todos los
    Santos, *b* at Madrid 26 March 1909; ✠ at Nice 16 Aug 1966, Kt
    Spanish Order of the Golden Fleece; *m* (non-dynastic in
    Bavaria & Spain) at Urrugne, nr St Jean de Luz,
    Basses-Pyrénées, France 25 July 1933, María de la Asuncion
    Solange (Marisol) (*b* at London 30 Sept 1913, *cr* Countess de
    Odiel by King Alfonso XIII of Spain July 1933, dau of Don
    Fernando de Mesia y Fitz-James-Stuart, Count of Mora, Duke
    de Tamames (nephew of the Empress Eugénie of France) and
    Marie Solange de Lesseps of the Vicomtes de Lesseps, and
    had issue,

        1. Doña María *Cristina* Paz Teresa Alfonsa Eugenia
        Rita y Todos los Santos, *b* at Paris 6 Feb 1935, Condesa
        de Odiel by maternal cession; *m* at Madrid 12 July
        1967, Juan Manuel de Urquijo y Novales (*b* at San
        Sebastian 8 Dec 1937; ✠ at Madrid 9 Oct 2002).
        [*Darro 22, Madrid 2, Spain*].
        2. Don *Fernando* Juan Luis José María Santiago y
        Todos los Santos, *b* at San Remo, Italy 3 April 1937; *m*
        at Biarritz, France 14 May 1966, (officially separated
        1974), Sofía (*b* at Barcelona 13 Oct 1941), dau of José
        de Fugarolas de Arquer and Sofía de Aris y Moysi and
        has issue,
        [*Henares 8, Madrid 2, Spain*].
            1. *Cristina*, *b* at Geneva 7 Feb 1974.
        3. Doña María *Teresa* Luisa Fernanda y Todos los
        Santos, *b* at Madrid 11 Jan 1941; *m* there 23 Nov 1963,
        (*m* diss by div at Monaco 19 Nov 1983), Alfonso
        Marquez y Patiño Castillejo y Losada, Marquis de Castro
        (*cr.* by Prince Rainier of Monaco) (*b* at San Sebastian

7 Aug 1936; ✠ at Marbella 24 March 1994).

Sister of Great-Grandmother

Issue of Ferdinand VII, King of Spain (*b* 13 Oct 1784; ✠ 29 Sept 1833) and his fourth wife, Princess Cristina of Bourbón-Two Sicilies (*b* 27 April 1806; *m* 11 Dec 1829; ✠ 22 Aug 1878; *m* 2ndly at Madrid 28 Dec 1833, Don Fernando Muñoz y Sánchez, Duke de Riansares).

Daughter

Dona Maria *Luisa Fernanda, b* at Madrid 30 Jan 1832; ✠ at Seville 2 Feb 1897; *m* at Madrid 10 Oct 1846, Prince Antoine of Orléans, Duke de Montpensier, (*b* at Neuilly 31 July 1824; ✠ at Sanlucar de Barrameda 4 Feb 1890), *cr* Infante of Spain 10 Oct 1859, son of Louis Philippe I, King of the French, and had issue (Infants of Spain), among whom,

Son

Infante Don *Antonio* Maria Luís Felipe Juan Florencio, *b* at Seville 23 Feb 1866; ✠ at Paris 24 Dec 1930, 4th Duke of Galliera; *m* at Madrid 6 March 1886, his first cousin, Infanta Doña Eulalia (*b* at Madrid 12 Feb 1864; ✠ at Irun 8 March 1958), dau of Isabel II, Queen of Spain and Infant Don Francisco de Asis of Spain, and had issue,

    1. Prince Don *Alfonso* Maria Francisco Antonio Diego, *b* at Madrid 12 Nov 1886; ✠ at Sanlucar de Barrameda 10 Aug 1975, 5th Duke de Galliera, Gen Spainish Air Force, resigned the Dukedom of Galliera to his eldest son 1937; *m* at Schloß Rosenau, nr Coburg 15 July 1909, Princess Beatrice (*b* at Eastwell Park, Ken 20 April 1884; ✠ at El Botanico, Sanlucar de Barrameda 13 July 1966), dau of Alfred, Duke of Saxe-Coburg and Gotha, Prince of Great Britain and Ireland, Duke of Edinburgh, etc and Grand Duchess Maria of Russia, and had issue among whom,

        1. Prince Don *Alvaro* Antonio Carlos Felipe Fernando, 6th Duke of Galliera on his father's resignation of the Dukedom 14 July 1937, *cr* Royal Highness and Prince of Orleans y Sajonia-Coburgo-Gotha by Royal Decree of King Alfonson XIII, 21 May 1912, *b* at Coburg 20 April 1910; ✠ at Monte Carlo 22 Aug 1997; *m* at Rome 10 July 1937 (non-dynastic in Spain), Carla (*b* at Milan 13 Dec 1909; ✠ at Monte Carlo .. July 1999), dau of Leopoldo Girolamo Parodi Delfino, Senator of the

Kingdom of Italy and Lucia Henny, and has issue,

1. Doña *Gerarda* de Orleans-Bourbón y Parodi
Delfino, *b* at Rome 25 Aug 1939; *m* at New
York 26 July 1963 (*m* diss by div 1977 and
annulled 18 July 1990), Harry Freeman Saint
(*b* at New York 13 Feb 1941). She *m* 2ndly at
Monaco 17 Nov 1990 (Officially Seperated 1998),
Ignacio Romero y de Solis, 6th Marquess de
Marchelina (*b* at Seville 20 Oct 1937).
[*Levies 9, 41004 Sevilla, Spain*].

2. Don *Alonso* de Orleans-Bourbón y Parodi
Delfino, *b* at Rome 23 Aug 1941; ✝ at Houston,
USA 7 Sept 1975, Diplomat, Consul of Spain at
Houston USA; *m* at Naples 12 Jan 1966, Emilia
(*b* at Naples 6 April 1940), dau of Don Vincenzo
Ferrara-Pignatelli, Prince di Strongoli, Count
di Melissa, Baron di Silvi e Castiglione and
Noble Francesca Pulci-Doria, and had issue,

1. Don *Alfonso* , 7th Duke de Galliera,
b at Santa Cruz de Teneriffe, Canary
Islands 2 Jan 1968; *m* at Paris 28 Feb
1994 (civ), Véronique (*b* at Verviers,
Belgium 16 Nov 1970), dau of Jean Marie
Goeders and Anne Marie Grosjean, and
has issue,

1. Don *Alfonso, b* at Paris 15 July
1994.

2. Don *Alvaro, b* at Santa Cruz de
Teneriffe, Canary Islands 4 Oct 1969.

3. Doña *Beatriz* de Orleans-Bourbón y Parodi
Delfino, *b* at Seville 27 April 1943; *m* at Rome
25 April 1964 (*m* diss by div 4 Aug 1989),
Tomasso of the Counts Farini, Patrician of
Ravenna (*b* at Turin 16 Sept 1938).

4. Don *Alvaro* Jaime de Orleans-Bourbón y
Parodi Delfino, *b* at Rome 1 March 1947; *m* at
Campiglione 22 May 1974, Giovanna (*b* at
Campiglione 10 April 1945), dau of Casimiro
San Martino di San Germano d'Aglie, Marquess
di San Germano and Donna Maria Cristina
Ruffo di Calabria of the Dukes de Guardia

Lombarda (sister of Queen Paola of the Belgians), and has issue,
[*Botanico, 11540 Sanlucar de Barrameda, Cadiz, Spain*]

    1. Doña *Pilar, b* at Rome 27 May 1975.
    2. Don *Andrès, b* at Rome 9 July 1976.
    3. Doña *Alois, b* at Rome 24 March 1979.

Brother of Great-Great-Grandfather

Issue of Carlos IV, King of Spain and the Indies (*b* 11 Nov 1748; ✠ 19 Jan 1819) and Princess Maria Luisa of Bourbón-Parma (*b* 9 Dec 1751; *m* 4 Sept 1766; ✠ 2 Jan 1819), having had issue, among whom,

Son

Infante Don *Francisco de Paula* Antonio Maria, *b* at Madrid 10 March 1794; ✠ at Madrid 13 Aug 1865; *m* 1stly by proxy at Naples 15 April and in person at Madrid 12 June 1819, his niece, Princess Luisa Carlota (*b* at Portici 24 Oct 1804; ✠ at Madrid 29 Jan 1844), dau of Francesco I, King of the Two Sicilies and Infanta Doña Maria Isabel of Spain. He *m* 2ndly (morganatically) at ... 1851, Teresa (*b* at ...; ✠ at .. 29 Dec 1863), dau of Don Arredondo, having had issue, among whom, from his first wife,

Sons

Dukes of Seville

1. Infante Don (with the Rank of Royal Highness) *Francisco de Asis* Maria Fernando, declared King of Spain and the Indies by R Decree 10 Oct 1846, *b* at Aranjuez 13 May 1822; ✠ at Épinay-sur-Seine 16 April 1902, Capt-Gen Spanish Army; *m* at Madrid 10 Oct 1846, Isabel II, Queen of Spain and the Indies (*b* at Madrid 10 Oct 1830; ✠ at Paris 9 April 1904), having had issue (see above).

2. Infante Don (with the Rank of Royal Highness) *Enrique* Maria Fernando Carlos Francisco Luis, **1st Duke of Seville**, Grandee of Spain (18 April 1823), *b* at Alcazar Real de Sevilla 17 April 1823; ✠ in a duel with his cousin the Duke of Monpensier at Alarcón, nr Madrid 12 March 1870; *m* at Rome (non dynastic marriage in Spain) 6 May 1847, Elena María de la Asunción (*b* at Valencia 16 Oct 1821; ✠ at Madrid 29 Dec 1863), dau of Antonio de Castelvi y Fernández de Córdoba, 9th Count of Castellá and Margarita Shelly, and had issue, among whom,

Sons

1. Don (with the Rank of Excellency) *Francisco de Paula* Maria de la Trinidad Enrique Gabriel Rafael Edmundo Buenaventura, *b* at Toulouse 29 March 1853; ✠ at Madrid 28 March 1942, General; *m* 1stly at Havana, Cuba 15 Sept 1877, Maria Luisa (*b* at Guamutas, Cuba 14 May 1856; ✠ at Madrid 7 June 1887), dau of Don José María de la Torre y Armenteros and Doña María de los Dolores de Bassave y Ziburu, having had issue, among whom,

　　Son

　　1. HE Don *Francisco de Paula* María Enrique Alfonso José Rafael Miguel Gabriel, *b* at Madrid 16 Jan 1882; ✠ at Madrid 6 Dec 1952, Lt-Gen, Mil Gov of Madrid, Member of Cortés; *m* at Madrid 21 Aug 1907, Enriqueta (*b* at Madrid 18 June 1885; ✠ at Valencia 5 Nov 1968), **4th Duchess de Seville** and Grandee of Spain, dau of Don Enrique Pio de Borbón, 2nd Duke de Seville and Joséphine Parade, and had issue,

　　　　1. HE Don *Francisco* de Paula Enrique María Luis, *b* at Santander 16 Nov 1912; ✠ at Madrid 18 Nov 1995, Army Officer, renounced succession the title of Duke de Seville and Grandee of Spain in favour of his son 1968; *m* 1stly at Madrid 4 Oct 1942 or 4 Nov 1941 (*m* annulled ...), Enriqueta (*b* at Malaga 13 Oct 1925; ✠ at Madrid 16 May 1962), dau of Ignacio Escasany y Auzeill and Enriqueta de Miquel y Mas, 2nd Marchioness de la Pobla de Claramunt, and had issue,

　　　　　　1. HE Don *Francisco* de Paula Enrique, **5th Duke of Seville** and Grandee of Spain (Official Bulletin 10 Dec 1974), *b* at Madrid 16 Nov 1943, Banker; *m* at Baden-Baden 5 July (civ) and 7 July (relig) 1973 (*m* diss by div at Madrid 30 June 1989), Countess Beatrix (*b* at Schloß Donaueschingen, Baden-Württemberg 28 June 1947), dau of Günther, Count von Hardenberg and Princess Maria Josepha zu Fürstenberg, [*Urbanización de Golf, Cabo la Nao, 28290 Las Matas, Madrid*]; He *m* 2ndly at Vienna 19 Oct 1991 (officially separated at Madrid 17 June 1993), Isabel Eugenia (*b* at Vienna 23 June 1959), dau of Franz M Karanitsch and Tatjana Cimlov Karacevcev, and has issue by his first wife,

[*Modesto Lafuente 32, 28003 Madrid, Spain*].

   1. Doña *Olivia* Enricheta María Joséfa, *b* at London 6 April 1974.

   2. Doña *Cristina* Elena, *b* at Madrid 2 Sept 1975.

   3. Don *Francisco* de Paula Joaquín, *b* at Madrid 21 Jan 1979.

  2. Don *Alfonso* Carlos, *b* at Madrid 10 Feb 1945; *m* at Madrid 2 July 1971, María Luisa (*b* at Madrid 15 April 1949), dau of Lucian Yordi and María Luisa Villacampa, and has issue,

    1.Don *Alfonso* Nicolas Enrique, *b* at Madrid 16 Nov 1973.

    2. Doña *Alexandrina* María Luisa, *b* at Madrid 24 May 1976.

Don Francisco *m* 2ndly at Madrid 15 March 1967, María Josefa (*b* at Madrid 11 Dec 1928), dau of Nicolas García de Lobez and Dolores Salvador, and had further issue,

[*Roncal 5, El Viso, 28002 Madrid, Spain*].

   3. Don *Enrique* Ignacio, *b* at Madrid 18 March 1970.

  [*Las Lomas del Bosque, 28670 Villaviciosa de Odón, Madrid, Spain*].

2. Don *José* Maria Enrique Alberto, *b* at Madrid 16 Dec 1883; ✠ at Madrid 28 Oct 1962, Col Infantry; *m* at Madrid 21 July 1909, María Luisa (*b* at Madrid 22 Feb 1890; ✠ at Madrid 5 Feb 1926), dau of Narciso Rich y Martínez and Estrella Carbajo y Gómez de Terán, and had issue among whom,

  1. Don *Carlos* Luís José Francisco de Borbón y Rich, *b* at Madrid 22 March 1915; ✠ at Madrid 12 Nov 1978; *m* at Madrid 15 Feb 1939, María de los Milagros (*b* at Ciempzuelos, Madrid 12 May 1916; ✠ at Madrid 20 April 1993), dau of Pascual de Oro y Sanchín and Carolina Fernández de Cevallos y Fernández de Devallos, and had issue,

   1. Don *Carlos* José Maria de los Dolores, *b* at Madrid 26 June 1940.

   [*Goya 117, 28009, Madrid, Spain*]

   2. Doña *María de los Milagros*, *b* at Madrid 27 Nov 1941; *m* at Madrid 20 Dec 1965, Juan

Ignacio Lopez Pérez (*b* at Bilbao 24 May 1931).
[*Pez Austral 12, Colonia La Estrella, 28007 Madrid, Spain*]

2. Don *Alberto* José Luis Fernando de Borbón y Rich, *b* at Madrid 2 Nov 1916; ✝ at Madrid 24 Aug 1998, (naturalised French as Albert de Bourbón 24 March 1970); *m* at Madrid 30 Jan 1950, (officially separated) Maria de los Dolores (*b* at Cuntis Piñeiro, Pontevedra 4 June 1920), [*9 rue de l'abbé Rousselot, 75017 Paris, France*], dau of José Campos y Garcia and Manuela Guerra Puente, and has issue among whom,

1. Don *Enrique* José Borbón y Campos, *b* at Madrid 11 Jan 1948, legitimised by his parent's marriage.
[*9 rue de l'abbé Rousselot, 75017 Paris*]

2. Doña *Beatriz* Eugenia Borbón y Campos, *b* at Madrid 6 Dec 1949, legitimised by her parent's marriage; *m* 1stly at Paris 27 April (civ) and 28 April (relig) 1972 (*m* diss by div 19 Nov 1979), Jean Baptiste Bernard Venturini (*b* at Vichy 3 Nov 1944). She *m* 2ndly at Copenhagen 28 Dec 1979, Anders Jefferts (*b* at Copenhagen 17 Dec 1947).
[*Ronda Manuel Grancro 69, 28043, Madrid, Spain*]

3. Doña *María Luisa* Borbón y Campos, *b* at Madrid 19 Dec 1951; *m* 1stly at Cancun, Mexico .. Jan 1979 (*m* diss by div 1981), Diego San Juan. She *m* 2ndly at Madrid 12 Dec 1989, Luis Zuloega Gallejo (*b* at San Sebastian 10 Aug 1941).
[*Lagasca 51, 28001, Madrid, Spain*]

Don Alberto de Bourbón recognised a natural son 7 Oct 1985 (Judgement rendered at Paris 14 Jan 1987), [*Don Ramón de la Cruz 68, 28001 Madrid, Spain*].

4. *François-Richard* Joubert, *b* at Paris 21 Feb 1933, known as François-Richard de Bourbón-Joubert, adopted by Marie-Henri Joubert and Paule-Annonciade (Février) Joubert; *m* at Villedommage, Marne 30 Oct 1964, Christine-Jacqueline Letixerant (*b* at ...).

3. Doña *Beatriz* Josefa Luisa de Borbón y Rich, *b* at Madrid 13 June 1918; *m* at Madrid 6 May 1935, Juan Ricoy y de Pereira (*b* at Cambados, Pontevedra 16 May 1908; ✠ at Luga, nr Madrid 19 Jan 1964).
[*Padilla 22, 28006 Madrid, Spain*].

4. Don *Alvaro* José Luis Francisco Narcisio de Borbón y Rich, *b* at Tetouan, Morocco 2 Jan 1922; *m* at Rute, Córdoba 19 June 1961, María del Carmen (*b* at Rute 26 Feb 1930), dau Augustin Cruz Pérez and Carmen Villen Seija, and has issue,
[*Pedro Antonio de Alarcón 37, 18004, Granada, Spain*]

    1. Doña Maria de los *Milagros*, *b* at Rute 9 May 1962; *m* at Granada 28 Nov 1987, Manuel Molina y Muñoz (*b* at Granada 6 Dec 1959).
    [*Paseo de la Pampa 1, 28940 Fuenlabrada, Madrid, Spain*]

    2. Doña *Maria* del Carmen Borbón y Cruz; *b* at Rute 9 May 1962 (twin with Doña Maria de los Milagros); *m*, at Granada 6 Dec 1988, Gustavo Adolfo Porras Chavarino (*b* at Granada 13 Feb 1965).
    [*Calle Ancha 73, 14700 Palma del Rio*]

Don Francisco de Paula *m* 2ndly at Madrid 15 Feb 1890, Felisa Carolina Rafaela Maria (*b* at Havana, Cuba 14 June 1861; ✠ at Madrid 25 Sept 1943), dau of Carlos de Léon y Navarrete and Felisa Navarro de Balboa y Sánchez-Yebra, 2nd Marchioness of Balboa, and had further issue, among whom,

3. Don *Enrique* María Francisco de Paula, 3rd Marquess of Balboa (Royal Decree 24 May 1917), *b* at Madrid 0 July 1891; *erec* by Republican forces at Aravaca, nr Madrid 29 Oct 1936 with his son and brother; *m* at Madrid 15 June 1917, Isabel de Esteban y Iranzo, 3rd Countess of Esteban (*b* at Madrid 6 June 1894; ✠ at Madrid 14 Nov 1964), dau of Rafael de Esteban y La Torre, 2nd Count of Esteban and Luisa de Iranzo y Daguerre, and had issue among whom,

    1, Doña (with the Rank of Excellency) *Isabel* Maria de las Mercedes, *b* at Madrid 23 Sept 1918; *succ* her father as 4th Marquess of Balboa (Official Bulletin 6 April 1956) and her mother as 4th Marchioness of Balboa (Official Bulletin 4 Jan 1966) and is 4th Countess of Esteban.

[*Velazquez 23, 28001, Madrid, Spain*]

4. HE Don *Alfonso* María Francisco Martin Felix Joaquín Rafael Miguel, 2nd Marquess of Squillache and Grandee of Spain (Official Bulletin 14 Aug 1915), *b* at Madrid 24 Oct 1893; *exec* by Republican forces at Aravaca, nr Madrid 29 Oct 1936, Gentleman of the Chamber to Alfonso XIII; *m* at Barcelona 3 July 1925, *Maria* Luisa (*b* at Barcelona 23 May 1898; ✠ at Madrid 11 Oct 1981), dau of Baldomero de Caralt y Sala and María de Mas y Martí, and had issue among whom,

   1. HE Don *Alfonso* Luis, 3rd Marquess of Squillache, Grandee of Spain (Official Bulletin 2 March 1951), *b* at Madrid 5 May 1929, Diplomat, Order of Isabel the Catholic, Kt Order of Christ (Portugal), Cmdr Order of St Olav (Norway), Gd Officer Order of Phoenix (Greece) Gd Officer Order of Orange-Nassau, Officer Civ Merit (Spain); *m* at Alicante 6 Jan 1958, Maria Teresa Rojas y Roca de Togores, Countess of Casa Rojas (Official Bulletin 16 Aug 1974) (*b* at Madrid 7 Feb 1929), renounced succession to titles of Marchioness de las Bosch de Ares and Grandee of Spain, and of Beniel, and Countess of Torrellan in favour of her children, dau of Carlos de Rojas y Moreno, 8th Marquess de los Bosch de Ares and Grandee of Spain, etc and Maria Teresa Roca de Togores y Pérez de Pulgar, and has issue,

[*Factor 14, 28013 Madrid, Spain*].

     1. HE Doña *María* José de Borbón y Rojas, 10th Marchioness de los Bosch de Ares and Grandee of Spain (Official Bulletin 7 Oct 1994), *b* at Madrid 27 Dec 1958; *m* at Berne, Switzerland 11 April 1987, Ramón de la Cierva y García Bermudez (*b* at Madrid 28 March 1956).

[*Tamayo y Baus 6, 28004 Madrid, Spain*]

     2. HE Doña *Ana* Isabel de Borbón y Rojas, 13th Marchioness de Beniel (Official Bulletin 27 Nov 1997), *b* at Madrid 18 Feb 1960; *m* at San Lorenzo de Escorial, nr Madrid 7 Jan 1989, Daniel Tobár y Rojas (*b* at Santiago de Chile 28 Sept 1950).

[*Juliana 18, El Escorial, 28280 Madrid, Spain*]

     3. HE Doña *Maria* Leticia de Borbón y Rojas,

8th Countess of Torellano (Official Bulletin 5 Oct 1994), *b* at Madrid 4 Jan 1962.

2. HE Don *Alberto* Enrique María Vicente Ferrer Francisco de Paula Antonio, *b* at Madrid 22 Feb 1854; ✠ at Madrid 21 Jan 1939, *cr* 1st Duke of Santa Elena and Grandee of Spain (Royal Decree 31 July 1917), 1st Marquess of Santa Elena and Grandee of Spain (Royal Decree 24 Oct 1878), Capt-Gen of Valladolid and the Canary Islands, Lt-Gen; *m* 1stly at Beaumont de Lomagne, Tarn-et-Garonne 26 Nov (civ) and 27 Nov (relig) 1878, Marguerite Joséphine (*b* at Beaumont de Lomagne 27 June 1855; ✠ at Château de Bonneville, Sérignac 12 Aug 1915; widow of José María de la Viesca, 2nd Marquess de Viesca de la Serra), dau of Louis Hélène Oscar d'Ast, Baron de Novelé and Francisca de Paula de Castellvi y Shelly Fernández de Córdoba. He *m* 2ndly at Madrid 30 Jan 1918, Clotilde (*b* at Madrid 3 June 1869; *exec* by the Republican forces at Madrid 18 Dec 1936), dau of Miguel Gallo y Ruíz and Manuela Diez de Bustamante. He *m* 3rdly at Madrid 5 June 1937, Isabel Rodríguez de Castro y Bueno, of the Marquesses de Bueno Mena (*b* at Seville 19 April 1888; ✠ at Madrid 7 May 1947), and had issue, among whom, from his first wife,

   1. HE Don *Alberto* María Francisco de Paula Enrique Vicente Ferrer Luis Isidoro Benigno Oscar, 2nd Duke and Marquess de Santa Elena and Grandee of Spain (14 April 1956), *b* at Madrid 12 Feb 1883; ✠ at Valladolid 1 Dec 1959; *m* at Valladolid 10 July 1908, María Luisa (*b* at Valladolid 30 April 1887; ✠ at Madrid 13 Dec 1976), dau of José Antonio Pintó y Lara of the Counts de Añorga and María de Lecanda y Toca, and had issue,

      1. HE Don *Alfonso* María Alberto Luis José de Calasanz Antonio de Padua Javier Pedro Regalado, *b* at Valladolid 27 Aug 1909; ✠ from wounds at Lerida 25 Dec 1938; *m* at Madrid 19 March 1933, Doña María de las Angustias, 10th Marchioness de Santa Fé de Guardiola (1925) (*b* at Valladolid 17 Oct 1907; ✠ at Valladolid 8 June 1939), dau of Cristóbal Pérez del Pulgar y Ramírez de Arellano, 1st Marquess of Abaicon, and Felisa Alba y Bonifaz, and had issue,

        1. HE Don *Alberto* Enrique Alfonso María Cristóbal Luis Fernando, 3rd Duke and Marquess de Santa Elena and Grandee of Spain (2 April 1960), 11th Marquess de Santa Fé de

Guardiola (2 May 1958), *b* at Seville 23 Nov 1933; ✠ at Madrid 28 June 1995; *m* at Valladolid 27 June 1959, Eugenia (*b* at Madrid 10 Oct 1934), dau of Gonzalo María Sánchiz y Calatayud, 3rd Marquess de Montemira and María de la Concepción Mendaro y Romero, and had issue among whom,

[*General Martínez Campos 39, 28010 Madrid, Spain*].

    1. HE Don *Alfonso* Gonzalo, 4th Duke and Marquess de Santa Elena and Grandee of Spain (24 Nov 1995), 12th Marquess de Santa Fé de Guardiola (24 Sept 1981), *b* at Madrid 31 March 1961; *m* 1stly at The Hague 20 July (civ) 1981 (*m* annulled ...), Patricia (*b* at The Hague 23 Feb 1958), dau of Johannes.Doornkamp and Liselotte Wearech; He *m* 2ndly at Madrid 11 Feb 1993, María (*b* at Madrid 29 Dec 1956), dau of Luis Escriva de Romani, Count de Glimes de Brabante and Grandee of Spain and María Soto y Colón de Carvajal, and has issue,

[*Paseo de la Castellana 98, 28046 Madrid, Spain*].

        1. Doña *Maria*, *b* at Madrid 10 Jan 1994.

        2. Doña *Eugenia*, *b* at Madrid 10 Jan 1994 (twin with Maria).

        3. Don *Alfonso*, *b* at Madrid 2 Feb 1995.

    2. Doña *Maria Luisa*, *b* at Madrid 22 April 1962.

[*General Martínez Campos 39, 28010 Madrid, Spain*].

    3. Doña *Eugenia*, *b* at Madrid 22 April 1962 (twin with Doña *Maria Luisa)*.

2. Doña *María* de las Angustias Margarita Immacolada, *b* at Seville 19 Aug 1935, entered Dominican Order May 1956.

[*Colegio de Santo Domingo, Valladolid, Spain*]
3. Don *Alfonso* María José Cristobal Alberto, *b*
at Valladolid 4 June 1937, Army Officer; *m* at
Seville 4 Oct 1961; (officially separated), Inés
(*b* at Seville 17 Dec 1939), [*Avenida de Portugal
17, Seville, Spain*], dau of Lt-Col Fernando de
Medina y Garbey, 6th Count de Campo Rey
and Mariana Atienza y Benjumea, and has
issue,
[*Cortijo Rompezapatos, Ctra. de Sevilla a
Mérida, Seville, Spain*]
   1. Don *Alfonso*, *b* at Seville 27 April
   1963.
   2. Don *Fernando*, *b* at Seville 15 June
   1966; *m* at Sevile 17 Sept 1999, Maria (*b*
   at....), dau of Jose Vallejo Osorno and
   Angeles Miras y Vilches
   3. Don *Jaime*, *b* at Seville 19 July 1971.
2. Doña *María Luisa*, *b* at San Sebastian 6 Sept 1918;
m at Valladolid 26 Sept 1941, Nicolas Gereda y de
Bustamante (*b* at Valladolid 11 April 1916).
[*Muro 4, 47004 Valladolid, Spain*]

Brother of Great-Great-Grandfather

Issue of Carlos III, King of Spain and the Indies (*b* 20 Jan 1716; ✠ 14
Dec 1788, *succ* his great-uncle Antonio as Carlo I, Duke of Parma
and Piacenza 29 Dec 1731, conquered Naples and became Carlo VII,
King of Naples and Sicily 15 May 1735, resigning the Duchy of Parma
to his brother Felipe, invested as King of Naples and Sicily and
titular King of Jerusalem by the Pope 12 May 1738, *succ* his
half-brother, King Fernando VI as King of Spain and the Indies 10
Aug 1759, ceded the Kingdom of Naples and Sicily to his third son
Fernando 6 Oct 1759) and Duchess Maria Amalia of Saxony (*b* 24
Nov 1724; *m* 9 May/19 June 1738; ✠ 27 Sept 1760), having had issue,
among whom,

Son

Infante Don *Gabriel* Antonio Francisco Javier Juan Nepomuceno
José Serafin Pascual Salvador, *b* at Portici 11 May 1752; ✠ at the
Escurial 23 Nov 1788, Gd Prior Order of the Hosp of St John of
Jerusalem for Castile and Leon; *m* by Proxy as Lisbon 12 April and in

person at Aranjuez 23 May 1785, Infanta Doña Maria Ana Vitória (*b* at Lisbon 15 Dec 1768; ✠ at the Escurial 2 Nov 1788), dau of Maria I, Queen of Portugal and the Algarves and Pedro III, Titular King of Portugal and the Algarves, and had issue (recognised as Infants and Infanta Doñas of Portugal by their maternal grandmother Queen Maria I 18 Feb 1785), among whom,

Son - Borbón y Bragança
Infante Don *Pedro Carlos* Antonio Rafael José Javier Francisco Juan Nepomuceno Tomas de Villanueva Marcos Marcelino Vicente Ferrer Raymundo Nanato Pedro de Alcantara Fernando, *b* at Aranjuez 18 June 1786; ✠ at Rio de Janeiro 4 July 1812, Adm-Gen Royal Portuguese Marines 1810, Gd Prior Order of the Hosp of St John of Jerusalem for Castile and Leon, etc; *m* at Rio de Janeiro 13 May 1810, Infanta Doña Maria Teresa of Portugal, Princess of Beira (*b* at Queluz 29 April 1793; ✠ at Trieste 17 Jan 1874; *m* 2ndly 20 Oct 1838, Don Carlos de Borbón, Count de Molina), dau of João VI, King of the United Kingdom of Portugal, Brazil and the Algarves and Infanta Doña Carlota Joaquina of Spain, and had issue,

Son
Infante Don *Sebastián* Gabriel Maria Carlos Juan José Francisco Javier de Paula Miguel Bartolome de San Geminiano Rafael Gonzaga, Infant of Portugal (9 Nov 1811) and Infant of Spain (8 April 1924), *b* at Rio de Janeiro 4 Nov 1811; ✠ at Pau 13 Feb 1875, Gd Prior Order of the Hosp of St John of Jerusalem for Castil and Leon, Capt.-Gen. Spanish Army, etc; *m* 1st by proxy at Naples 7 April and in person at Madrid 26 May 1832, Princess Maria Amelia (*b* at Pozzuoli, nr Naples 25 Feb 1818; ✠ at Madrid 6 Nov 1857), dau of Francesco I, King of the Two Sicilies and Infanta Doña Maria Isabella of Spain. He *m* 2ndly at Madrid 19 Nov 1860, Infanta Maria Cristina (*b* at Madrid 5 June 1833; ✠ at Madrid 19 Jan 1902), dau of Infant Don Francisco de Paula of Spain, Duke de Cadiz and Princess Luisa Carlota of Bourbón-Two Sicilies, and had issue from his second wife, among whom,

Sons
1. HE Don *Pedro* de Alcántara María de Guadelupe Teresa Isabel Francisco de Asis Gabriel Sebastián Cristino, *b* at Madrid 12 Dec 1862; ✠ at Paris 5 Jan 1892, cr Duke de Durcal and Grandee of Spain (Royal Decree 4 April and 25 Nov 1885); *m* at Madrid (non-dynastic in Spain) 6 April 1885, María de la Caridad (*b* at

Guantanamo, Cuba 19 Sept 1867; ✠ at Berlin 10 Feb 1912; *m* 2ndly 2 Nov 1904, Louis Ferdinand Bessières who ✠ 4 Sept 1951), dau of Gen Juan Antonio de Madan y Uriondo and Francisca de Uriondo y de Saavedra Dugi, and had issue among whom,

    1. HE Don *Fernando* Sebastían, 2nd Duke de Durcal and Grandee of Spain (24 June 1908), *b* at Paris 4 Feb 1891; ✠ at Madrid 28/29 March 1944, Chamberlain to King Alfonso XIII; *m* at Barcelona 19 Oct 1912, María Leticia (*b* at Barcelona 14 March 1890; ✠ at Madrid 29 Nov 1981), dau of Pedro Bosch-Labrús, 1st Viscount de Bosch-Labrús and Josefa Blat y Caparols, and had issue,

        1. HE Doña *María Christina,* 3rd Duchess de Durcal and Grandee of Spain (31 Oct 1950), *b* at Madrid 15 May 1913; *m* at Madrid 8 April 1931 (*m* diss by div 10 Dec 1959), Antenor Patiño y Rodríguez (*b* at Oturo, Bolivia 12 Oct 1896; ✠ at New York 2/3 Feb 1982; *m* 2ndly at London 8 Jan 1960, Béatrice de Rivera). [*Place des Vosges, 75004 Paris, France*].

        2. Doña *Leticia* Fernanda, *b* at Madrid 22 June 1915; *m* 1stly at Rome 27 Nov 1940 (*m* annulled by the Holy See 1956), Paolo Venturi Ginori Lisci, Marquess of Riparbella, Patrician of Florence [*Via Ghibellina 73, Firenze, Italy*] (*b* at Florence 22 April 1915; he *m* 2ndly 10 Oct 1957, Amalia Borgnino). She *m* 2ndly at Zurich 10 July 1958, Stefano Franceschi (*b* at Florence 16 June 1903; ✠ at Geneva 1 Feb 1981).

2. HE Don *Luis* Jesus María Isabel José Francisco de Asís Sebastían Cristino, or 1st Duke Ansola and Grandee of Spain (30 May 1886 and by Royal Decree 15 March 1887), *b* at Madrid 17 Jan 1864; ✠ at Algiers 24 Jan 1889; *m* at Madrid 31 May 1886, *Ana* (1st Marchioness of Atarfe) Germana Pia María (*b* at Valencia, Spain 19 March 1866; ✠ at Vitoria, Spain 11 Sept 1934; she *m* 2ndly 30 Nov 1890, Manuel Mendez de Vigo), dau of José María Bernaldo de Quiros y Gonzalez de Cienfuegos, 8th Marquess de Campo Sagrado, Señor of the Casa de Quiro and María Cristina Muñoz y Borbon-Dos Sicilias, 1st Marchioness de la Isabella and Viscountess de la Dehesilla, and had issue among whom,

    1. Don Luis Alfonso Francisco José María, 2nd Duke de Ansola and Grandee of Spain (Royal Decree 30 Oct 1896), 2nd Marquess of Atarfe, *b* at Paris 9 May 1887; ✠ at Biarritz 19 May 1942, granted the qualification of Serene Highness by

Carlos I, King of Portugal; *m* at London 16 July 1914
(separated), Beatrice Mary (*b* at Maidstone, Kent 28 Aug
1891; ✝ at Madrid 6 Jan 1979), dau of James Harcourt
Harrington and Elizabeth Susannah Hipkins; having had issue
(a natural son by Blanche Georgette Pages), whom he
recognised in an Act dated 27 Aug 1934,

    1. *Louis* Georges de Bourbón, *b* at Paris 31 May 1922;
    m at Paris 27 March 1951, Madeleine Marie (*b* at
    Charmant, Charente 23 Dec 1926), dau of Francis
    Priestnall and Blanche Duverdier.

SWEDEN
(HOUSE OF BERNADOTTE)

Lutheran: Founded by Jean Baptiste Jules Bernadotte (*b* at Pau,
Basses-Pyrénées, France 26 Jan 1763; ✝ at Stockholm 8 March 1844);
joined French Army 1780; Sgt-Major 1788; Lieut 1791; Gen 1794;
French Ambassador to Vienna 1798; C-in-C Army of Observation of
the Lower Rhine and Min of War 1799; Counsellor of State and
C-in-C Army of the West 1800; Gov Hanover 1804; Marshal of the
Empire 1804; Prince and Duc de Pontecovo (town in the Province of
Caserta, Italy) 5 June 1806; Gov Hanseatic Towns 1807; elected
Crown Prince of Sweden by the Swedish State 21 Aug 1810, and
adopted by King Carl XIII of the House of Holstein-Gottorp (*b* 7 Oct
1748; ✝ 5 Feb 1818, also King of Norway from 4 Nov 1814); took the
name of Carl Johan 5 Nov 1810; *succ* King Carl XIII in 1818 as Carl
XIV Johan, King of Sweden and Norway; King Oscar II renounced
the crown of Norway 26 Oct 1905.
The Greater National Arms: Azure a cross formy throughout or, in the
first and fourth quarter three open crowns two and one or, in the
second and third quarter three streams bendwise sinister argent
surmounted by a lion rampant crowned with an open crown all or
armed and langued gules; an inescutcheon overall party per pale,
dexter tierced in bend azure, argent and gules, a garb or (House of
Vasa), sinister azure issuant from water in base a bridge of three
arches and two crenellated towers all argent, beneath an eagle wings
inverted head turned to sinister grasping a lightning-bolt and in
chief the constellation of Charles's Wain all or (House of Bernadotte).
The shield is royally crowned and encircled with the insignia of the
Order of the Seraphim. *Supporters:* Two lions reguardant queue fourché
royally crowned or, armed and langued gules, standing upon a plinth
or. The Shield and Supporters are surrounded by an armorial mantle
purpure lined ermine, fringed, tied and tufted cords and royally
crowned or. *The Lesser National Coat of Arms:* Azure three open

crowns two and one or. The shield is royally crowned and may be encircled with the insignia of the Order of the Seraphim. Three open crowns arranged two above and one below are to be regarded as the Lesser National Coat of Arms also when the shield and the royal crown are not shown. *Motto* (of His Majesty the King): For Sweden - in keeping with the times.

Members of the Royal House of Sweden bear the title of Prince or Princess of Sweden with the qualification of Royal Highness.

CARL XVI GUSTAF Folke Hubertus, **KING OF SWEDEN,** *b* at Haga 30 April 1946, *succ* his grandfather 1973, Kt Orders of the Seraphim, of the Elephant, of the Garter, Royal Victorian Chain, Gd Cross French Order of the Legion of Honour, Hon Adm British Navy from 1975, son of Gustaf Adolf, Prince of Sweden, Duke of Västerbotten (*b* 22 April 1906, ✝*k* in a flying accident 26 Jan 1947) and Princess Sibylla of Saxe-Coburg and Gotha (*b* 18 Jan 1908; *m* 19 Oct/20 Oct 1932; ✝ at Stockholm 28 Nov 1972); *m* at Stockholm 19 June 1976, Silvia Renate (*b* at Heidelberg 23 Dec 1943), Dame Order of the Seraphim, etc, dau of Walther Sommerlath and Alice Soares de Toledo.

[*Royal Palace, 11130 Stockholm, Sweden*].

Son and Daughters

1. *Victoria* Ingrid Alice Désirée, Crown Princess of Sweden, Duchess of Västergötland, *b* at Stockholm 14 July 1977.
2. Prince *Carl Philip* Edmund Bertil, Duke of Värmland, *b* at Stockholm 13 May 1979.
3. Princess *Madeleine* Thérèse Amelie Josephine, Duchess of Hälsingland and Gästrikland, *b* at Drottningholm 10 June 1982.

Sisters

1. Princess *Margaretha* Désirée Victoria, *b* at Haga 31 Oct 1934; *m* at Gärdslösa, Isle of Öland 30 June 1964 (diss by div 1996), John Ambler (*b* at Horsham, Sussex 6 June 1924).
[*Tulip Cottage, Church Enstone, Chipping Norton, Oxfordshire OX7 4NL, United Kingdom*]
2. Princess *Birgitta* Ingeborg Alice, *b* at Haga 19 Jan 1937; *m* at Stockholm 25 May (civ) and at Sigmaringen 30 May (relig) 1961, Prince Johann Georg of Hohenzollern (*b* at Sigmaringen 31 July 1932), Dr of Phil.
[*Geschwister Hirschstraße 2, 82031 Grünwald, Germany*].
3. Princess *Désirée* Elisabeth Sibylla, *b* at Haga 2 June 1938; *m* at Stockholm 5 June 1964, Niclas, Baron Silfverschiöld (*b* at Koberg 31

May 1934).
[*Koberg, 46691 Sollebrunn, Sweden*].
4. Princess *Christina* Louise Helena, *b* at Haga 3 Aug 1943; *m* at
Stockholm 15 June 1974, Tord Magnuson (*b* at Stockholm 7 April
1941).
[*Villa Beylon, Ulriksdal, 17079 Solna, Sweden*].

Brothers and Sister of Father

Issue of Gustaf VI Adolf, King of Sweden (*b* 11 Nov 1882; ✠ 15 Sept
1973; *succ* 29 Oct 1950) and his first wife, Princess Margaret of Great
Britain and Ireland (*b* 15 Jan 1882; *m* 15 June 1905; ✠ 1 May 1920),
among whom,

1. Prince *Sigvard* Oscar Fredrik, Duke of Uppland, *b* at Drottningholm
7 June 1907; ✠ at Stockholm 4 February 2002; renounced his rights
of succession and style and titles as a Prince of Sweden and assumed
the surname of BERNADOTTE 7 March 1934, *cr* Count Bernadotte
af Wisborg by Grand Duchess Charlotte of Luxembourg 2 July 1951;
m 1stly in London 8 March 1934 (*m* diss by div 14 Oct 1943), Erika (*b*
at Wilmersdorf, Berlin 12 July 1911), dau of Anton Patzek and Marie
Anna Lala. He *m* 2ndly at Copenhagen 26 Oct 1943 (*m* diss by div 6
June 1961) Sonia (*b* at Copenhagen 12 Oct 1909), dau of Robert
Alexander Christensen Robbert and Ebba Elisabeth Suenson. He *m*
3rdly at Stockholm 30 July 1961, Marianne (*b* at Helsingborg 15 July
1924; *m* 1stly, Gabriel Tchang; that *m* diss by div), dau of Helge
Lindberg and Thyra Dahlman, and has issue by his second wife,

    1. Count *Michael* Alexander Sigvard, *b* at Copenhagen 21
    Aug 1944; *m* at Stuttgart 6 Feb 1976, *Christine* Diotima (*b* at
    Stuttgart 26 April 1947), dau of Ernst Wellhöfer and Erna
    Kromer, and has issue,
    [*Trollingerstr 48, 71364 Winnenden, Germany*].

        1. Countess *Kajsa* Michaela Sophia, *b* at Stuttgart 12
        Oct 1980.
        [*Trollingerstr 48, 71364 Winnenden, Germany*].

2. *Bertil* Gustaf Oscar Carl Eugen, Duke of Halland, *b* at Stockholm
28 Feb 1912; ✠ at Stockholm 5 Jan 1997, Gen and Adm Swedish
Forces, Kt Order of the Elephant, GCB, etc; *m* at Drottningholm 7
Dec 1976, Lilian (*b* at Swansea 30 Aug 1915; *m* 1stly 27 Sept 1940,
Ivan Sackville Craig; that *m* diss by div at London 7 Nov 1947), dau
of William John Davies and Gladys Curran.
[*Villa Solbacken, Djurgardsbrunn, 11525, Stockholm, Sweden*].

3. Prince *Carl Johan* Arthur, Duke of Dalecarlia, *b* at Stockholm 31 Oct 1916, renounced his rights of succession and style and titles as a Prince of Sweden and assumed the surname of BERNADOTTE 19 Feb 1946, *cr* Count Bernadotte af Wisborg by Grand Duchess Charlotte of Luxembourg 2 July 1951; *m* 1stly at New York 19 Feb 1946, Kerstin (*b* at Stockholm 4 March 1910; ✠ at Båstad 11 Sept 1987; *m* 1stly 29 June 1935, Dr Axel Johnson; that *m* diss by div 22 Dec 1936), dau of Dr Henning Wijkmark and Elin Larsson. He *m* 2ndly at Copenhagen 29 Sept 1988, Countess Gunnila (*b* at Stockholm/Engelbrekt 12 May 1923), dau of Nils, Count Wachtmeister af Johannishus and Baroness Märta De Geer af Leufsta and, with his first wife, adopted two children,

[*Kungsberga, Båstad, Sweden*]

    1. *Monica* Kristina Margaretha, *b* at Salzburg 5 March 1948 (adopted 1951); *m* at Stockholm 16 Jan 1976 (*m* diss by div), Johan Peder, Count Bonde af Björnö (*b* at Göteborg 5 May 1950).

    [*Rosendalsterrassen 9, 11521 Stockholm, Sweden*]

    2. Carl Henning *Christian*, *b* at Stockholm 3 Dec 1949 (adopted 1950); *m* at Zurich 13 Sept 1980, Marianne (*b* at Zurich 3 Jan 1958), dau of Jacques Walter Jenny and Caroline Yvonne Wenter, [and has issue, two sons and one dau].

    [*2513 Marlborough Road, 44118 Cleaveland Ohio USA*]

Brother of Grandfather

Issue of Gustaf V, King of Sweden (*b* 16 June 1858; ✠ 29 Oct 1950; *succ* his father 8 Dec 1907) and Princess Victoria of Baden (*b* 7 Aug 1862; *m* 20 Sept 1881; ✠ 4 April 1930), having had issue, among whom,

Son

Prince Carl *Wilhelm* Ludwig, Duke of Södermanland, *b* at Tullgarn 17 June 1884; ✠ at Stenhammar, nr Flen 5 June 1965, Dr of Phil, Major-Gen and Rear-Admiral Swedish Orders, Kt Order of the Black Eagle, Kt Order of the Annunziata, Kt Order of the Elephant; *m* at St Petersburg 20 April/3 May 1908 (*m* diss by div 13 March 1914), Grand Duchess Maria Pavlovna (*b* at St Petersburg 6/18 April 1890; ✠ at Konstanz 13 Dec 1958; *m* 2ndly at Pavlosk 6/19 Sept 1917, Sergei Michaeilovitch, Prince Putjatin), dau of Grand Duke Paul Alexandrovitch of Russia and Princess Alexandra of Greece, and had issue,

Prince Gustaf *Lennart* **Nicolaus Paul, Duke of Småland**, *b* at Stockholm 8 May 1909, renounced his rights of succession and style and titles as a Prince of Sweden and assumed the surname of BERNADOTTE 20 Feb 1932, *cr* Count Bernadotte af Wisborg by Grand Duchess Charlotte of Luxembourg 2 July 1951; *m* 1stly at London 20 Feb 1932 (*m* diss by div at Constance 27 Jan 1972), Karin (*b* at Nora, nr Örebrö 7 July 1911; ✠ at Eskilstuna 9 Sept 1991), dau of Sven Nissvandt and Anna-Lisa Lindberg, and has issue,

[*Schloß Mainau, 78465 Isle of Mainau, Germany*].

     1. Countess *Birgitta,* *b* at Stockholm 3 May 1933; *m* at Kreuzlingen, Switzerland 10 June (civ) and at Mainau 11 (relig) June 1955, Fritz Straehl (*b* at Constance 20 Nov 1922).

     [*Schloß Mainau, 78465 Isle of Mainau, Germany*].

     2. Countess *Marie Louise,* *b* at Stockholm 6 Nov 1935; ✠ at Constance 24 May 1988; *m* at Litzelstetten 10 Sept (civ) and at Mainau 11 Sept (relig) 1956, Rudolf Kautz (*b* at Engen 24 Aug 1930).

     3. Count Carl-Johan (*Jan*) Gustaf Wilhelm, *b* at Stockholm 9 Jan 1941; *m* 1stly at Torö, Sweden 3 May 1965 (*m* diss by div 13 April 1967), Gunnilla (*b* at Stockholm 3 Sept 1941), dau of Erik Stampe and Elsa Malmgren. He *m* 2ndly at Mainau 26 June 1967 (*m* diss by div 30 Oct 1970), Anna (*b* at Stockholm 18 April 1944; *m* 2ndly 29 Aug 1978, Robert Looft), dau of Allan Skarne and Birgitta Ströman, and by her has issue,

     [*Im Reutersfeld 85, 54294 Trier, Germany*].

         1. Countess *Sophia* Magdalena Maria Birgitta, *b* at Stockholm 3 May 1968.

Count Jan *m* 3rdly at Constance 23 June 1972 (*m* diss by div 28 June 1997), Annegret (*b* at Bremen 15 Nov 1938, *m* 1stly 14 May 1959, Dr Hans Drenckhahn; that *m* diss by div), dau of Hans Thomssen and Alice Bleeck, and has further issue,

         2. Countess Cia *Rosemarie,* *b* at Constance 30 Sept 1972.

Count Jan *m* 4thly at Diepolz 6 Sept 1974 (*m* diss by div 1987), Marita-Else (*b* at Diepolz 7 Dec 1953; ✠ at Tübingen 30 Sept 2001), dau of Albert Berg and Gisela

Grossman, and has further issue,

   3. Count *Alexander-Wilhelm*, *b* at Constance 25 March 1977.

   4. Count *Stefan* Albert, *b* at Constance 4 Nov 1980.

   [*Ringelberghohl 20A, 76229 Karlsruhe, Germany*].

Count Jan *m* 5thly at .. (*m* diss by div ..) .. (*b* at ..), dau of ..; Count Jan *m* 6thly at ..., *Silke* (*b* at ..), dau of ..Braun.

   4. Countess Karin Cecilia (*Cia*), *b* at Stockholm 9 April 1944; *m* at Litzelstetten 28 March (civ) and at Constance 31 March (relig) 1967 (*m* diss by div 30 Aug 1974), Hansjörg Baenkler (*b* at Constance 24 Sept 1939).

   [*Jälund, 64051 Stärnhov, Sweden*].

Count Lennart *m* 2ndly at Mainau 29 April 1972, Sonja (*b* at Litzelstetten 7 May 1944), dau of Wolfgang Haunz and Anita Mayr, and has further issue,

   5. Countess *Bettina*, *b* at Scherzingen, Switzerland 12 March 1974.

   [*Schloß Mainau, 78465 Isle of Mainau, Germany*].

   6. Count *Björn*, *b* at Scherzingen 13 June 1975.

   [*Schloß Mainau, 78465 Isle of Mainau, Germany*].

   7. Countess *Cathcrina*, *b* at Scherzingen 11 April 1977.

   [*Schloß Mainau, 78465 Isle of Mainau, Germany*].

   8. Count *Christian*, *b* at Schwezingen 25 April 1979.

   [*Schloß Mainau, 78465 Isle of Mainau, Germany*].

   9. Countess *Diana*, *b* at Scherzingen 18 April 1982.

   [*Schloß Mainau, 78465 Isle of Mainau, Germany*].

Brothers of Great-Grandfather

Issue of Oscar II, King of Sweden and Norway (*b* 21 Jan 1829; *succ* his brother 19 Aug 1872; ✠ 8 Dec 1907) and Princess Sophie of Nassau (*b* 9 July 1836, *m* 6 June 1857; ✠ 30 Dec 1913), having had issue, among whom,

Sons

1. Prince *Oscar* Carl August, Duke of Gotland, *b* at Drottningholm 15 Nov 1859; ✠ at Stockholm 4 Oct 1953, renounced his rights of succession and style and titles as a Prince of Sweden and assumed

with Royal authorization the title of Prince Bernadotte with the
qualification of Highness 15 March 1888, *cr* Count af Wisborg by
Grand Duke Adolphe of Luxembourg 2 April 1892; *m* at Christchurch
Register Office (civ) and at a St Stephen's Church, Bournemouth,
Hampshire (relig) 15 March 1888, Ebba Henrietta (*b* at Jönköping 24
Oct 1858; ✛ at Stockholm 16 Oct 1946), dau of Carl Munck af Fulkila
and Baroness Henrietta Cederström, and had issue (Counts and
Countesses Bernadotte af Wisborg), among whom,

    1. Count *Carl* Oscar, *b* at Karlskrona 27 May 1890; ✛ at
Malmsjö 23 April 1977; *m* 1stly at Stockholm 15 March 1915
(*m* diss by div 20 March 1935), Marianne (*b* at Frötuna,
Uppsala 6 Oct 1893; ✛ at Stockholm 31 July 1978), dau of
Louis, Baron de Geer af Leufsta and Märtha Johanna Fredrika
Cederström, and had issue, among whom,

        1. Countess *Dagmar* Ebba Märtha Marianne, *b* at
Stockholm 10 April 1916; *m* at Frötuna, Uppsala, 16
Oct 1936, Col Nils-Magnus von Arbin (*b* at Skörtinge
17 Aug 1910; ✛ at Kimstad 4 March 1985).
        [*Tångestad, 610 20 Kimstad, Sweden*].
        2. Count *Oscar* Carl Emanuel, *b* at Stockholm 12 July
1921; *m* 1stly at Björnstorp 18 March 1944 (*m* diss by
div 14 Sept 1949), Ebba (*b* at Stockholm 26 July 1918),
dau of Nils, Baron Gyllenkrok and Countess Charlotte
Wachtmeister af Johannishus, and has issue,
        [*Klostergatan 21, 75321 Uppsala, Sweden*].
            1. Countess *Ebba* Marianne Charlotte, *b* at
Stockholm 2 March 1945; *m* at Rasbo, Uppsala
14 March 1970 (officially separated 2002),
Pontus Reuterswürd (*b* at Kristianstad 28 May
1943).
            [*Bergsjoeholm, 271 91 Ystad, Sweden*].
        Count *Oscar m* 2ndly at New York 18 Oct 1950,
Gertrud (*b* at Stockholm 10 May 1916; ✛ Frötuna,
Uppsala, 18 Feb 1999), dau of Johannes Ollén and
Lydia Lindgren, and has further issue,
            2. Countess *Christina*, *b* at Stockholm 21 Dec
1951; *m* 1stly at Rasbo, Uppsala 18 Jun 1977
(*m* diss by div at Rasbo, Uppsala 1980) Baron
Peder Langenskiöld (*b* Göteborg 13 Mar 1950);
m 2ndly at Paris 31 Mar 1982 (*m* diss by div
1998) *Lars* Hedström (*b* Göteborg 21 Aug 1947).

[*215 Ave Tour Gandolphe, 06160 Cap d'Antibes, France*].

3. Countess *Birgitta, b* at Witullsberg 21 Dec 1953; *m* Rasbo 31 May 1980 (*m* diss by div 28 Aug 1990) Richard van Helleputte (*b* Montreuil-sous-Bois 5 Feb 1955).

[*Vittulsbergs Gård, 755 94 Uppsala, Sweden*].

4. Count *Carl* Louis, *b* at Witullsberg 1 June 1955; *m* at Stockholm 23 May 1981 Charlotte (*b* at Stockholm 24 Dec 1954) dau of Rey Urban and Eva Ericsson.

[*Frötuna Gård, Rasbo 75596 Uppsala, Seden; Villagatan 16, 114 32 Stockholm, Sweden*].

    1. Countess *Josephine* Eva, *b* at Stockholm 5 Jan 1984.

    2. Countess *Fredrika* Charlotte, *b* at Stockholm 8 Aug 1985.

    3. Countess *Elsa* Marianne, *b at* Stockholm 22 Nov 1988.

3. Countess Märtha Elsa *Catharina, b* at Stockholm 14 April 1926; *m* at Stockholm 9 Oct 1948, Tore Henrik Nilert (*b* at Stockholm 9 Feb 1915).

Count Carl *m* 2ndly at Grödinge 20 April 1937, Gerty (*b* at Södertälje 30 Oct 1910), dau of Fritz Börjesson and Gertrud Palm, and had further issue,

4. Count *Claës* Carl, *b* at Frotuna 17 July 1942; *m* at Lund 22 Nov 1969, Birgitta (*b* at Veberöd 30 May 1943), dau of Truls Magnusson and Sigrid Christofferson, and has issue,

[*Viresjö Säteri, 570 21 Malmbäck, Sweden*].

    1. Count *Carl Johan* Edward, *b* at Stockholm 7 Dec 1970; *m* at Strängnäs 9 June 2001 Anna (*b* at Uppsala 10 January 1971) dau of Per Olsson and Anne-Sofie Jarenius.

    [*Skär Säteri, 645 93 Strängnäs, Sweden*].

        1. Count *Carl* Wilhelm Olof, *b* at Stockholm 26 April 2002.

    2. Countess *Louise* Maria Ingrid, *b* at Malmbäck 29 Nov 1973.

    [*Baumeistergasse 76, 2/4, 1160 Vienna, Austria*].

2. Count *Folke, b* at Stockholm 2 Jan 1895; assassinated in Jerusalem 17 Sept 1948, Hon KBE (1947), Hon MD University of Copenhagen, Oslo and Uppsala, President Swedish Red Cross and Swedish Boy Scouts, UN Mediator in Israel 1948, Kt Gd Cross Orders of the North Star, Dannebrog, Crown of Belgium, Leopold II, Orange-Nassau, White Rose, St Olav and Polonia Restituta, Grand Officer Légion d'Honneur, author of "The Fall of the Curtain", "Instead of Arms" and "To Jerusalem"; *m* at New York 1 Dec 1928, Estelle (*b* at Pleasantville, New York, USA 26 Sept 1904; W at St Paul de Vence 28 May 1984; *m* 2ndly at Stockholm 3 March 1973, Carl-Eric Ekstrand), dau of Edward Manville and Estelle Romaine, and had issue, among whom,

    1. Count *Folke, b* at Pleasantville, New York 8 Feb 1931, MD, practising Ortologist; *m* at Grangärde, Sweden 2 July 1955, Christine Maria (*b* at Örebro 9 Jan 1932), dau of Gunnar Glahns and Anna Öhström, and has issue,

    [*Sysslomansgatan 16, 753 13 Uppsala, Sweden*].

        1. Countess *Anna* Christine, *b* at Uppsala 22 Nov 1956; *m* at Stockholm 26 May 1989, Per Larsén (*b* at Lidingö 19 June 1953).

        [*Toftvägen 15, 181 42 Lidingö, Sweden*].

        2. Count Carl *Folke, b* at Uppsala 2 Dec 1958; *m* at Uppsala 12 Aug 2000, *Birgitta* Elisabeth (*b* at Borås 23 Feb 1959), dau of Lennart Larsson and Anna Klasson.

        [*Zälghagsweg 46, 4457 Diegten, Switzerland*].

            1. Count *Carl* Folke, *b* at Uppsala 22 March 1998.

            2. Count *William* Eric, *b* Uppsala 4 Feb 2002.

        3. Countess *Maria* Estelle, *b* at Uppsala 27 April 1962; *m* at Uppsala 14 May 1983, Umberto Ganfini (*b* at Sienna, Italy 11 Nov 1955).

        [*Via Campania 9, 531 00 Sienna, Italy*].

        4. Count *Gunnar* Fredrik, *b* at Uppsala 24 Nov 1963; *m* at Uppsala 2 June 1990, Karin (*b* at Uppsala 15 May 1963), dau of Klas Emil Lindsten and Ruth Barbro Margareta Stein.

        [*Kärrvägen 3, 756 46 Uppsala, Sweden*].

1. Count *Ockie* Klas Vilhelm, *b*.at Uppsala 5 Aug 1996.

2. Countess *Astrid* Rut Estelle, *b*.at Uppsala 10 Feb 1999.

2. Count *Bertil* Oscar, *b* at Stockholm 6 Oct 1935, Cmdr Order of St Alexandre (Bulgaria); *m* at Copenhagen 28 Sept 1966, Rosemarie (*b* at Copenhagen 7 June 1942; ✠ at Stockholm 1 Nov 1967), dau of Peter Heering and Lissen Ibsen. He *m* 2ndly at Chelsea 27 May 1981, Jill (*b* at Brighton, Sussex 2 May 1947), dau of George Burn Rhodes and Dorothy Ethel Maddox (Lincoln), and has issue,

[*57 Bedford Gardens, London, W8 7EF*].

1. Count *Oscar* Alexander, *b* at Merton, London 1 March 1982.

2. Count *Edward* Gustav, *b* at Merton, London 18 April 1983.

3. Countess *Astrid* Désirée Estelle, *b* at London 9 Feb 1987.

2. Prince Oscar *Carl* Vilhelm, Duke of Västergötland, *b* at Stockholm 27 Feb 1861; W there 25 Oct 1951, Gen Swedish Army, Hon MD, etc; *m* at Copenhagen 27 Aug 1897, Princess Ingeborg (*b* at Charlottenlund 2 Aug 1878; W at Stockholm 11 March 1958), dau of Frederik VIII, King of Denmark, and had issue, among whom.

1. Prince *Carl* Gustaf Oscar Fredrik Christian, Duke of Östergötland, *b* at Stockholm 10 Jan 1911, renounced for himself and his descendants his rights of succession to the Throne and style and titles as a Prince of Sweden and was *cr* Prince Bernadotte (*ad personam*) by his brother-in-law, King Léopold of the Belgians 6 July 1937; *m* 1stly at Friedhem 6 July 1937 (*m* diss by div 11 Jan 1951), Countess Elsa (*b* at Stockholm 7 Feb 1904; W at Stockholm 15 April 1991, *m* 1stly Adolf, Count von Rosen; that *m* diss by div), dau of Eugène, Count von Rosen, Gd Master of Ceremonies at the Swedish Court and Eleonore Wijk. He *m* 2ndly at Danderyd 10 Nov 1954 (*m* diss by div 3 April 1962), Ann Margareta (*b* at Danderyd 22 March 1921; W at Churriana, Malaga, Spain 3 Sept 1975), dau of Carl Frithiof Willgott Larsson. He *m* 3rdly at Rabat, Algeria 8 June 1978, Kristine (*b* at Eidsfos, Norway 22 April 1932), dau of Johan Riverlsrud and Elna .... and has issue by his first wife,

1. Countess *Madeleine* Astrid Ingeborg Ella Elsa (Bernadotte), *b* at Stockholm 8 Oct 1938; *m* 1stly at Stockholm 6 Oct 1962 (*m* diss by div 1980), Charles-Albert, Count Ullens de Schooten-Whettnall (*b* at Cairo, Egypt 16 Nov 1927) [*Eikestraat 96, 3080 Tervuern, Belgium*]. She *m* 2ndly at Corfu, Greece 2 Nov 1980, Nicos Kogevinas (*b* at Corfu 6 Sept 1918). [*La Ferme de l'Ours, 01220 Divonne-les-Bains, France*].

TURKEY
(HOUSE OF OSMAN)

Islamic -The House of Osman traces its origin to Oghuz, grandson of Noah, who gave his name to the Oghuz tribe, situated around the Transoxiana in the Altai mountains. The tribe was divided into twenty four branches, the most influential of which was the Kayi; founding both the Seljuk and Ottoman Dynasties. Oghuz warriors entered the Middle East about the tenth century, giving rise to the Seljuk Dynasty in 1055. The Oghuz had become defenders of Islam, with the title Gazi and Tugrul Bey, protector of Islam, and of the Caliphate, was recognized by the Abbassid Caliph, as temporal Ruler. Tugrul Bey, became the Founder of the Seljuk Dynasty, with northern Iran under Seljuk control and Iraq submissive to its rule. As Sultan, the Seljuk ruler assumed much of the Caliph authority, except spiritual.

Suleyman Shah (Gunduz Alp), leader of the Oghuz Kayi tribe, ruled an area of Mahan in the northeastern Iran in the late 12th century. While fleeing Mongol invaders he drowned in the Euphrates while attempting to enter Syria. At this point the family divided and of the three sons, two turned back to Horasan to serve under the Mongols, while the third, Ertugrul continued westward into Anatolia. Ertugrul Gazi offered the services of his army to the Seljuk Sultan, and in return for this service, was accorded in the year 1250, the small districts of Sogut and Domanic in western Anatolia. From here the Ottoman Empire was born. Upon the death of Ertugrul Gazi (1281), his son Othman, or Osman, (born in Sogut in 1258), became Osman I Gazi and established in 1299 the independent Ottoman Dynasty, in his own name. The Ottoman Empire survived for 641 years in the direct line.

Since the reign of Sultan Ahmed I, in the eighteenth century, the Crown is passed to the eldest male dynast. The present head is the grandson of Sultan Abdul Hamid II and succeeded his first cousin. Members of the Imperial Family bear the titles of Prince and Princess

of Turkey, with the qualification on Imperial Highness. A Crown
Prince is known as Veliahd and Sehzade and Efendi Hazretleri,
while princes are also known as Sehzade and Efendi Hazretleri. The
Mother of a Ruling Sultan took the style Valide Sultan (Queen
Mother) while official wives bore the style, Kadin and Efendi
Hazretleri. The first wife of the Sultan was Bas Kadin Efendi or
Imperial Majesty.For a list of the living dynasts, as of 17th
March 2000, see :-*Appendix VI.*

CROWN PRINCE Ertugrul **OSMAN** of **TURKEY**, Sehzade
and Efendi Hazretleri, and 43rd Head of the Imperial House, known
in exile as Ertogroul Osman, Sehzade and Efendi Hazretleri, *b* at
Constantinople 18 Aug l912; son of Mehmed *BurhanEddin* (*b* at
Yildiz Palace, Constantinople 19 Dec 1885; ✠ at New York 15 June
1949; *m* 2ndly at Paris 29 April 1925, Georgina Leonora Mosselmans,
b at The Hague 23 Aug 1900; ✠ 1969; *m* diss by div at Vienna 8 Nov
1925, 1st wife of Lord Sholto George Douglas of the Marquesses of
Queensbury; he *m* 3rdly at London 3 July 1933, Elsie Deming
Jackson, *b* at New York 6 Sept 1879; ✠ at New York 12 May 1952) and
Aliye Nazliar Hanim Huseyin (*b* at Adarpazari 13 Oct 1892; *m* at
Nishntashi 7 June 1909; *m* diss by div at Montreux, Switzerland 10
Nov 1919; ✠ at Ankara 31 Aug 1976; she *m* 2ndly at Paris 2 April
1920, Mehmed Cavit Bey, Ottoman Min of Finance; *+executed* at
Ankara 12 Aug 1926)*; m* 1stly at New York 20 Jan 1947, Gulda
Twerskoy (*b* at at Johannesburg 20 March 1915; ✠ at New York 16
Sept 1985). He *m* 2ndly at New York 27 Sept 1991, Zeyneb, (*b* at
Istanbul 16 Dec 1940) dau of Abdul Fettah Tarzi and Dr Pakize
Izzct Saltik (and niece of King Amanullah and Queen Soraya of
Afghanistan).
[*c/o Almanach de Gotha, 9 Cork Street, Mayfair, London. W1S
3LL*]

Brother

1. Prince Mehmed *Fahreddin* Sehzade and Efendi Hazretleri, *b* at
Constantinople 26 Nov 1911; ✠ at New York 13 July 1968; *m* at Paris
(not recognisd by the Imperial Court) 31 Aug 1933, Catherine
Pappadopoulos (*b* at Paris 30 May 1011 ✠ at Paris 1944).

TUSCANY
(HOUSE OF HABSBURG-LORRAINE)

See entry for- AUSTRIA *See pg. 37*

WALDECK
(HOUSE OF WALDECK)

Evangelical: Founded by Widukind III, Count of Schwalenberg (Principality of Lippe) 1116 - 1137; acquired the castle of Waldeck *ca* 1150, the castle of Wildungen and its dependencies *ca* 1290; Count of the Holy Roman Empire and of Waldeck, Cologne 14 Feb 1349, confirmed 22 June 1548; inherited the county of Pyrmont 1631; the title of High and Wellborn "Hoch and Wohlgeboren" was conferred at Vienna 25 Feb 1627; laid claim to the County of Rappolstein (Ribeaupierre, Haute-Alsace) and of the Lordships of Hoheneck and of Geroldseck (through the marriage 2 July 1658 of Count Christian Ludwig (*b* 29 July 1635; ✝ 12 Dec 1706) to Anne-Elisabeth of Rappolstein (*b* 7 March 1644; ✝ 6 Dec 1676) after the death of her uncle, last Count of Rappolstein 28 July 1673. The lines below descend from two sons (half-brothers) of Christian-Ludwig, Count zu Waldeck-Eisenberg, Pyrmont and Rappolstein, etc.
Arms:- Quarterly of nine: 1st and 9th, argent, a cross moline gu (Pyrmont); 2nd and 8th, arg, three inescutcheons gu (Rappolstein); 3rd and 7th, arg, three crows' heads, sa, langued gu and crowned or (Hoheneck); 4th and 6th, arg, billetty (in fess) az and a lion rampant gu, crowned or (Geroldseck); 5th eight points sa (Waldeck). The achievement is borne on a mantle purp, fringed and tasselled or, doubled erm and surmounted by the Princely Crown.

I: PRINCES OF WALDECK AND PYRMONT

Founded by Count Friedrich Anton Ulrich (*b* 27 Nov 1676; ✝ 1 Jan 1728); Prince of the Holy Empire and of Waldeck and Pyrmont, Count of Rappolstein, etc. with the qualification "Hochgeboren" (Highborn), Vienna 6 Jan 1712; received the right to vote with the Princes of the Holy Empire 1719; qualification of Serene Highness 8 June 1815. The dynasty ceased to reign 13 Nov 1918.
Members of the Princely Family bear the title of Prince or Princess of Waldeck and Pyrmont with the qualification of Serene Highness.

WITTEKIND Adolf Heinrich Georg-Wilhelm, **PRINCE (FÜRST) OF WALDECK AND PYRMONT,** Count (Graf) zu Rappolstein, Lord (Herr) zu Hohenack and Geroldseck am Wasigen, etc, *b* at Arolsen 9 March 1936, son of Josias, Prince (Fürst) zu

Waldeck and Pyrmont, etc (*b* 13 May 1896; ✠ 30 Nov 1967) and Duchess Altburg of Oldenburg (*b* 19 May 1903; *m* 25 Aug 1922); *m* at Frohnleiten, Steiermark 1 April (civ) and at Arolsen 19 May (relig) 1988, Countess Cäcilia (*b* at Frohnleiten 23 Aug 1956), dau of Carl-Anton, Count von Goëss-Saurau and Baroness Marie Mayr von Melnhof.

[*Schloß, 34454 Arolsen, Waldeck, Germany*].

Sons

1. *Carl-Anton* Christian Gustav Clemens Alexander, Hereditary Prince of Waldeck and Pyrmont, *b* at Arolsen 25 Dec 1991.
2. Prince *Josias* Christian Alexander, *b* at Arolsen 7 July 1993.
3. Prince *Johannes* Eberhard Wittekind, *b* at Arolsen 7 July 1993 (twin with Prince Josias).

Sisters

1. Princess *Margarethe* Sophie Charlotte, *b* at Munich 22 May 1923; *m* at Arolsen 27 March 1952 (*m* diss by div at Michelstadt 10 July 1979), Franz August, Count zu Erbach-Erbach (*b* at Erbach 5 Feb 1925).

[*Nees von Esenbeckstraße 10, 64711 Erbach, Odenwald, Germany*] .

2. Princess *Alexandra* Bathildis Elisabeth Luise Helene Emma, *b* at Rastede 25 Sept 1924; *m* at Arolsen 28 June 1949, Botho, Prince zu Bentheim and Steinfurt (*b* at Ilsenburg 29 June 1924; ✠ at Arolsen 9 June 2001), Lt-Col (ret).

[*Rauchstraße 25, 34454 Arolsen, Germany*].

3. Princess *Ingrid*, *b* at Munich 2 Sept 1931.

[*Schloß, 34454 Arolsen, Waldeck, Germany*].

4. Princess *Guda*, *b* at Arolsen 22 Aug 1939; *m* 1stly at Arolsen 31 Aug (civ) and 9 Sept (relig) 1958 (*m* diss by div at Koblenz 3 Jan 1967), Friedrich Wilhelm, 7th Prince (Fürst) zu Wied (*b* at Stuttgart 2 June 1931; ✠ at Salmon Arm, Canada, 28 Aug 2000) She *m* 2ndly at Schaumburg, nr Diez 4 March (civ) and 9 March (relig) 1968, Horst Dierkes (*b* at Hanover 21 Feb 1939), Dr of Med.

[*Am Carmen-Sylva-Garten 3, 56564 Neuwied - Feldkirchen, Germany*].

Brothers and Sister of Father

Issue of Friedrich, Prince (Fürst) of Waldeck and Pyrmont, etc (*b* 20 Jan 1865; ✠ 26 May 1946) and Princess Bathildis of Schaumburg-Lippe (*b* 21 May 1873; *m* 9 Aug 1895; ✠ 6 April 1962), among whom,

1. Prince *Max* Wilhelm Gustav Hermann, *b* at Arolsen 13 Sept 1898; ✠ there 23 Feb 1981, Lt-Col (ret); *m* at Kiel 12 Sept 1929, Countess Gustava (*b* at Segeberg 7 Dec 1899; ✠ at Arolsen 27 Oct 1986), dau of Karl, Count von Platen Hallermund and Elfriede von Köppen, and had issue,

    1. Princess *Marie-Louise* Bathildis Elfriede Olga, *b* at Kiel 3 Nov 1930; *m* at Arolsen 22 Mar (civ) and 23 May (relig) 1951, Albrecht, Prince (Fürst) zu Castell-Castell (*b* at Castell 13 Aug 1925).

    (97355 Castell, UFranken, Germany).

    2. Prince *Friedrich-Carl* Georg Viktor, *b* at Kiel 21 Aug 1933, Dipl Eng; *m* at Arolsen 24 Jan (civ) and at Berlin 26 Jan (relig) 1959, Ingeborg (*b* at Halle an der Saale 2 July 1932), dau of Wolf von Biela and Adelheid Schneider, and has issue, [*Helisosteig 31, 34454 Arolsen, Germany*].

        1. Princess *Caroline* Gustava Adelheid, *b* at Hanover 8 Jan 1960; *m* at Hamburg 29 Aug (civ) and 27 Oct (relig) 1985, Cord-Georg Hasselmann (*b* at Hamburg 4 July 1956), Dr of Law, Lawyer.
        [*Kirchweg 57, 14129 Berlin, Germany*].

        2. Princess *Donata* Altburg Helene-Sophie, *b* at Hanover 2 Feb 1961, MA, Dipl Inform; *m* at Munich 10 Aug (civ) and at Arolsen 6 Sept (relig) 1987, Markus Conrad (*b* at Hamburg 24 Oct 1959), Dr rer pol.
        [*Kösterbergstraße 4, 22587 Hamburg, Germany*].

        3. Princess *Juliane Bathildis*, *b* at Hanover 25 June 1962; *m* at Lübesk 13 Dec (civ) 1991 and at Arolsen 11 April (relig) 1992 (*m* diss by div at Lübeck 3 May 1996), Gerhard Kappe (b at Stadhagen 7 May 1956); she m 2ndly at Bad Schwartan 14 May (civ and relig) 1999, Stephan Hobe (*b* at Bremen 11 Dec 1957), Dr of law and prof.
        [*Heideweg 40, 53229 Bonn, Germany*].

    3. Prince *Georg-Viktor* Ludwig Adolf, *b* at Schwerin 11 July 1936; *m* at Arolsen 25 Jan (civ) and at Hanover 6 Feb (relig) 1963, Margarete (*b* at Fürstenwalde 7 Feb 1938), Vetenarian, dau of Kurt von Klitzing and Barbara Euen, and has issue, [*Diemel Weg 14, 59494 Soest, Germany*].

        1. Princess *Friederike*, *b* at Arolsen 28 Dec 1963, Dr. vet.med.; *m* at Hanover 21 May (civ) and at Arolsen 10 June (relig) 1989, Michael Paar (*b* at Mühlheim,

Ruhr 10 Sept 1963), Dr of Vet Med.
[*Upp'Hoff 16, 27367 Sottrum, Germany*].
2. Princess *Barbara* Ingemarie Helene-Sophie, *b* at
Kassel 15 March 1965, Dipl Inform; *m* at Bad Aibling
18 March (civ) and at Soest 4 May (relig) 1991,
Christian Düsel (*b* at Rome 28 July 1962), Dipl Eng.
[*Spirknerstraße 27, 84137 Vilsbiburg, Germany*].
3. Prince *Christian-Ludwig* Friedrich-Carl Albrecht
Hubertus Claus, *b* at Arnsberg 16 May 1967, Lt; *m* at
Oldenburg 27 Jan (civ) 1994 and at Hohenstein 20
may (relig) 1995, Countess Camilla (at Eutin 27 Dec
1970) dau of Count Christian von Holck and Barbara
von Gottberg, and has issue,
[*Schloß, 23758 Farve, Germany*].
>1. Prince *Christian* Wolrad Johannes Welf Max,
>*b* at Oldenburg 6 March 1998.
>2. Prince *Victor* Paul Nikolaus Ferdinand
>Joachim, *b* at Oldenburg 23 June 2000.
>3. Prince *Casimir*, *b* at ... 5 Feb 2002.
4. Prince *Wolrad* Friedrich August Wittekind Florenz
Michael, *b* at Soest 28 May 1974.
[*Arcisstraße 64, 80799 Munich, Germany*].
4. Princess *Helene-Sophie* Ingeborg Margarethe Elisabeth
Gustava, *b* at Schwerin 27 Oct 1943; *m* at Arolsen 11 May
1974 (*m* annulled at Kassel 2 Sept 1975), Michael, Baron von
Forstner (*b* at Halle an der Saale 24 March 1946), Dipl Eng.
[*Hattroper Weg 66a, 59494 Soest, Germany*].
2. Prince *Georg Wilhelm* Karl Viktor, *b* at Arolsen 10 March 1902; ✝
there 14 Nov 1971, Lt-Col (ret); *m* at Kiel 20 Jan 1932, Countess
Ingeborg (*b* at Schleswig 27 Feb 1902; ✝ at Arolsen 30 Aug 1991),
dau of Karl, Count von Platen Hallermund and Elfriede von Köppen,
and had issue,
1. Prince *Josias* Friedrich Wilhelm, *b* at Hanover 23 Nov
1935; *m* at Karlsruhe 25 April (civ) and 29 April (relig) 1972,
Vita (*b* at Vienna 4 Dec 1939), dau of Wilhelm Schwenkreis
and Luise Kurz, and has issue,
[*Habichts Weg 15, 60437 Frankfurt-am-Main, Germany*].
>1. Prince *Alexander* Georg-Wilhelm Thomas, *b* at
>Frankfurt-am-Main 24 Nov 1972.
>2. Prince *Clemens* Georg Heinrich, *b* at
>Frankfurt-am-Main 30 Aug 1975.

2. Prince *Georg-Friedrich* Nikolaus, *b* at Hanover 22 Nov 1936, Lt-Col; *m* at Arolsen 29 Aug (civ) and 30 Aug (relig) 1961, Princess Sixtina (*b* at Stolberg 4 Nov 1933), dau of Wolff-Heinrich, Prince and Count (Fürst and Graf) zu Stolberg-Stolberg and Irma Erfert, and has issue,
[*An der Bullungsburg 14, 34454 Arolsen, Germany*].

    1. Princess Christine *Henriette* Bathildis, *b* at Ludwigsburg 6 April 1963, Dipl Geography; *m* at Arolsen 18 Aug (civ) and 19 Aug (relig) 1989, Hermann, Count zu Castell-Rüdenhausen (*b* at Würzburg 26 June 1963), Advertising Executive.
    [*Goethestraße 8, 93152 Nittendorf, Germany*].
    2. Princess Marie *Isabelle, b* at Arolsen 28 Aug 1965, Career Counsellor.
    [*Leinfeldenserstraße 62, 70597 Stuttgart, Germany*].
    3. Prince *Philipp*- Heinrich Wittekind, *b* at Flensburg 12 April 1967.
    [*An der Bullungsburg 14, 34454 Bad Arolsen, Germany*].

3. Princess *Rixa* Bathildis Elfriede, *b* at Brunswick 14 July 1939; *m* at Arolsen 31 May 1975, Hansjoachim von Wartenberg (*b* at Dresden 9 June 1935), Businessman.
[*Esseggerstraße 18, 71067 Sindelfingen, Germany*].

4. Prince *Volkwin* Georg Ludwig, *b* at Brunswick 20 Sept 1940, Major; *m* 1stly at Bad Pyrmont 1 Dec 1967 (civ) and at Bad Driburg 2 March 1968 (relig) (*m* diss by div at Rheinbach 22 April 1980), Baroness Orlinda (*b* at Bielefeld 11 Aug 1938; *m* 2ndly 22 May 1980, Ruprecht Rauch; diss by div 4 Feb 1992), dau of Eccard, Baron von Gablenz and Orlinda von Caprivi, and has issue,

    1. Prince Friedrich *Anton-Ulrich* Peter, *b* at Arolsen 4 July 1969; *m* at Hammerstein.17 Sept 1994, Baroness Elizabeth (*b* at Celle 6 Feb 1972), dau of Baron Egbert von Hammerstein-Equord and Astrid von Meien.
    [*Theodor-Storm-Straße 9, 60431 Frankfurt, Germany*].
    2. Prince *Nikolaus* Carl Ferdinand, *b* at Limburg an der Lahn 2 Nov 1970; *m* at … 29 Sept 2002, Princess Katharina (*b* at Munich 21 Nov 1972), dau of Prince Andreas zu Hohenlohe-Langenburg and Princess Luise von Schönburg-Waldenburg.
    [*Viktoriaplatz 4 80803 Munich, Germany*].

Prince Volkwin *m* 2ndly at Osterberg 6 Dec 1980, Baroness Friederike (*b* at Mindelheim, Schwaben 18 Sept 1955), [*Leifstraße 13, 81549 Munich, Germany*], dau of Bernhard, Baron von Gablenz and Felicitas von Willich, and has further issue,

[*Heerstraße 40a, 53340 Meckenheim, Germany*].

3. Prince *Ludwig* Wilhelm Heinrich Sigmund, *b* at Bonn 1 Feb 1983.

[*Leifstraße 13, 81549 Munich, Germany*].

4. Princess Johanna Helene Ingeborg *Felicitas*, *b* at Bonn 12 March 1984.

[*Leifstraße 13, 81549 Munich, Germany*].

5. Prince *Christian-Peter* Carl, *b* at Arolsen 9 Jan 1945, Lt.-Col.; *m* at Hanover 25 March (civ) and at Bad Pyrmont 5 June (relig) 1971, Sybille (*b* at Lauenstein, Niedersachsen 8 Nov 1948), dau of Karl Pieper and Rosemarie Schmidt von Knobelsdorf, and has issue,

[*Im Hagen 42, 14532 Kleinmachnow, Germany*].

    1. Prince *Georg-Wilhelm* Karl, *b* at Lüneburg 18 Oct 1972; *m* at Arolsen 14 April (civ) and at Alsfeld-Altenburg 19 April (relig) 1997 Baroness Freda (*b* at Kassel 23 April 1973), dau of Berthold Riedesel, Baron zu Eisenbach and Beatrix von Winterfeldt, and has issue,

    [*Holebyweg 5, 23714 Bad Malente, Germany*]

        1. Prince *Friedrich-Carl* Ulrich Alexander Johannes , *b* at Munich 15 Feb 1999.

        2. Prince *Max* Georg Ludwig Wolrad, *b* at Berlin 25 Dec 2000.

        3. Princess *Sophie* Charlotte Helene Constanze, *b* at Lüneburg 15 Aug 2002.

    2. Princess *Katharina-Sophie* Ingeborg Rosemarie, *b* at Lüneburg 30 March 1974; *m* at Hamburg 20 May (civ) 1999 and at Kleinmachnow 13 May (relig) 2000, Matthias Hoyer (*b* at Hamburg 2 Nov 1970).

    [*Sierichstraße 59, 01300 Hamburg, Germany*].

II: COUNTS OF WALDECK AND PYRMONT
(✠ Extinct ✠)

Founded by Josias (*b* 20 Aug 1696; ✠ 2 Feb 1763); inherited Bergheim after the death of his elder brother Heinrich Georg 3 Aug 1736;

inherited part of the county of Waldeck-Gaildorf in Württemberg 1774 (passed to the Counts of Bentinck 1888); qualification of Illustrious Highness 1 Aug 1844.
Members of this branch bear the title of Count or Countess of Waldeck and Pyrmont with the qualification of Illustrious Highness.

✠ **GEORG** Wilhelm Heinrich Karl, **COUNT OF WALDECK AND PYRMONT**, also Limpurg-Gaildorf, *b* at Bergheim 8 June 1876; ✠ at Laasphe 8 June 1966, Col (ret), son of Adalbert, Count of Waldeck and Pyrmont (*b* 19 Feb 1833; ✠ 24 July 1893) and Princess Agnes zu Sayn-Wittgenstein-Hohenstein (*b* 18 April 1834; *m* 3 Aug 1858; ✠ 18 Feb 1886); *m* 1stly at Berlin-Charlottenburg 8 March 1921, Alwine Dransfeld (formerly wife of his brother) (*b* at Münster 17 Dec 1876; ✠ at Emmaburg, nr Laasphe 1 June 1938; *m* 1stly at London 23 Nov 1906, Alexander, Count of Waldeck and Pyrmont; that *m* diss by div 2 Feb 1921), created "Frau von Gellen" by Friedrich, Prince (Fürst) of Waldeck and Pyrmont 5 Dec 1909. He *m* 2ndly at Frankfurt-am-Main 24 July 1939, Katharina (Kitty) Beitsch (*b* at Bingen am Rhein 1 Dec 1903; ✠ 1990), and had issue among whom,

Daughter - 2nd Marriage
1. Countess *Ilse* Marie Anna Margareta, *b* at Marburg 20 Aug 1941; *m* at Laasphe 14 May 1966, Manfred Schuster (*b* at Laasphe 1934), Eng.
[*Memelstraße 13, 34537 Bad Wildungen, Germany*].

———◆———

WÜRTTEMBERG
(HOUSE OF WÜRTTEMBERG)

Catholic: Founded by Conrad of Wirtemberg (1081 - 1092) living at Castle Wirtemberg, on the Rotenberg, near Stuttgart; Ludwig, comes de Wirtemberg 1137; acquired the county of Urach 1260, the county of Calw *ca* 1308 (1345), the seigneural land of the ancient Dukes of Teck 1325 (1381); inherited the county of Mömpelgard (Montbéliard, Doubs, France) 1444; Eberhard the Bearded became Duke of Wirtemberg 31 July 1495; the county of Mömpelgard was ceded to France in 1801 and was compensated with Eilwangen in 1803. Friedrich II, Duke of Württemberg was proclaimed Elector 27 April 1803, and King 1 Jan 1806.
Arms:- Quarterly: 1st or, three lions passant in pale sa (Swabia); 2nd paly bendy sinister sa and or (Teck); 3rd az, a flag-staff ppr headed

arg in bend, flotant therefrom to the sinister and returned round the staff a pennon or, charged in the hoist with an eagle sa (being the Standard of the Holy Roman Empire); 4th gu, two barbels hauriant addorsed or (Montbeliard); over all an escutcheon of pretence, or, three stag's attires fessways in pale points to the sinister sa. The shield is ensigned by the Royal Crown of Württemberg. *Supporters:-* Dexter, a lion rampant sa crowned or (Swabia) and sinister, a stag ppr (Württemberg). *Motto:-* Furchtlos and Treu.

Members of the Royal Line bore the title of Prince or Princess of Württemberg with the qualification of Royal Highness. On the establishment of the Kingdom in 1806, the brothers of King Friedrich I with their wives and children assumed the title of Duke or Duchess of Württemberg and were granted the qualification of Royal Highness by Royal Decree 11 Sept 1865.

CARL Maria Peter Ferdinand Philipp Albrecht Joseph Michael Pius Konrad Robert Ulrich, **DUKE OF WÜRTTEMBERG,** *b* at Friedrichshafen 1 Aug 1936, Kt Order of the Golden Fleece, etc, Senator of the University of Tübingen and Hohenheim, son of Philipp-Albrecht, Duke of Württemberg (*b* 14 Nov 1893; ✝ 15 April 1975) and Archduchess Rosa of Austria (*b* 22 Sept 1906; *m* 1 Aug 1928; ✝ 17 Sept 1983); *m* at Altshausen 18 July (civ) and 21 July (relig) 1960, Princess Diane (*b* at Petropolis, Brazil 24 March 1940), Dame of Justice Grand Cross Constantinian Order of St George, Dame Sovereign Military Order of Malta, dau of Henri, Count de Paris, Head of the Royal House of France and Princess Isabelle of Orléans and Bragança.

[*Schloß Altshausen, 88361 Kr. Ravensburg, Germany; Schloß Friedrichshafen, 88045 Württemberg, Germany*].

Sons and Daughters

1. Duke *Friedrich* Philipp Carl Franz Maria, *b* at Friedrichshafen 1 June 1961; *m* at Altshausen 11 Nov (civ) and 13 Nov (relig) 1993, Princess Marie (*b* at Munich 27 Dec 1973), dau of Ulrich, Prince zu Wied and Ilke Fischer, and has issue,
[*Schloß Friedrichshafen, 88045 Württemberg, Germany*].

    1. Duke *Wilhelm* Friedrich Carl Philipp Albrecht Nikolaus Erich Maria, *b* at Ravensburg 13 Aug 1994.

    2. Duchess *Marie-Amelie* Diane Katharina Beatrix Philippa Sophie, *b* at Ravensburg 12 March 1996.

    3. Duchess *Sophie-Dorothée* Martina Johanna Henriette Charitas Maria, *b* at Ravensburg 19 Aug 1997.

2. Duchess *Mathilde* Marie-Antoinette Rosa Isabelle, *b* at

Friedrichshafen 11 July 1962; *m* at Altshausen 17 Nov (civ) and 19 Nov (relig) 1988, Erich, Hereditary Count (Erbgraf) von Waldburg zu Zeil and Trauchburg (*b* at Ravensburg 21 Nov 1962).
[*Schloß Rimpach, 88299 Leutkirch 3, Germany*].

3. Duke *Eberhard* Alois Nikolaus Heinrich Johannes Maria, *b* at Friedrichshafen 20 June 1963, M.B.A., Banker.
[*88361 Schloß Altshausen, Germany*].

4. Duke *Philipp* Albrecht Christoph Ulrich Maria, *b* at Friedrichshafen 1 Nov 1964, Dr phil., M.A., Art Historian; *m* at Altshausen 28 June (civ) and at Tegernsee 27 July (relig) 1991, Princess and Duchess Marie (*b* at Munich 26 June 1969), dau of Prince Max Emanuel of Bavaria, Duke in Bavaria and Countess Elizabeth Christina Douglas, and has issue,
[*Ditmarstraße 33, 60487, Frankfurt-am-Main Germany, Germany*].

     1. Duchess *Sophie* Anastasia Assunta Marie Pauline, *b* at Munich 15 Jan 1994.

     2. Duchess *Pauline* Philippa Adelheid Helena Marie, *b* at London 15 April 1996.

     3. Duke *Carl Theodor* Philipp Maria Max Emanuel, *b* at London 15 June 1999.

5. Duke *Michael* Heinrich Albert Alexander Maria, *b* at Friedrichshafen 1 Dec 1965.
[*Schloß Altshausen, 88361 Kr. Ravensburg, Germany*].

6. Duchess Eleonore *Fleur* Juanita Charlotte Eudoxia Marie-Ange, *b* at Friedrichshafen 4 Nov 1977.
[*Schloß Altshausen, 88361 Kr. Ravensburg, Germany*].

Half-Sister

Issue of Philipp-Albrecht, Duke of Württemberg (see above) and his first wife, Archduchess Helene of Austria (sister of his second wife) (*b* 30 Oct 1903; *m* 24 Oct 1923; ✠ 8 Sept 1924).

Duchess *Marie Christine* Helene Philippine Albertine Margarethe Amélie Elisabeth Therese Rosa Josepha Antonia Hedwig Aloysia, *b* at Tübingen 2 Sept 1924, Dame Star Cross Order; *m* at Schloß Altshausen 23 Sept 1948, Georg, Prince von and zu Liechtenstein (*b* at Gross-Ullersdorf, Mähren 11 Nov 1911; ✠ at Vienna 18 Jan 1998), Dr rer agr, Dipl Eng.
[*Franziskaner Platz 1, 1010 Vienna, Austria; Schennastraße 3, 39012 Meran-Obermais, Italy*].

Brother and Sisters

1. Duchess *Helene* Maria Christine Rosa Margarethe Albertine Philippine Amélie Therese Josepha Antonia Alix Petrine Paula Pia, *b* at Stuttgart 29 June 1929, Dame of Justice Grand Cross Constantinian Order of St George; *m* at Altshausen 22 Aug (civ) and at Friedrichshafen am Bodensee 23 Aug (relig) 1961, Friedrich, Marquess Pallavicini (*b* at Budapest 23 Dec 1924), Businessman.
[*Schloßstraße 16, 88361 Altshausen, Kr. Ravensburg, Germany*].

2. Duke *Ludwig* Albrecht Maria Philipp Peter Ferdinand Karl Gottfried Georg Alfons, *b* at Stuttgart 23 Oct 1930, renounced his rights of succession and membership of the Royal House of Württemberg for himself and his descendants at Altshausen 29 June 1959 and 19 Jan 1960; *m* 1stly at Stuttgart 16 Feb 1960 (*m* diss by div at Stuttgart 12 Dec 1970), Baroness Adelheid (*b* at Sigmaringen 3 Aug 1938), [*Im Zehen 25, 73732 Esslingen, Germany*], dau of Johann Franz, Baron von and zu Bodman of the Counts Bodman and Maria Anna Otto, and has issue,
[*Faulhaberstraße 8, 82515 Wolfratshausen, Germany*].

    1. *Christoph* Albrecht Philipp Maria Bernhard Rudolf Andreas, *b* at Stuttgart 30 Nov 1960; *m* at Esslingen 29 Dec 2000, Iris Caren (*b* at Pforzheim 19 Nov 1963), dau of Herbert Hertzger and Gertrud Bregler.
    [*Hellerweg 51, 73728 Esslingen, Germany*].

    2. *Isabelle* Helene Maria Rositta Christina Alix Andrea, *b* at Stuttgart 30 Nov 1960 (twin with Christoph).
    [*Bereiteranger 2, 81541 Munich, Germany*].

    3. *Sybilla* Rositta Maria-Christina Maria-Magdalena, *b* at Stuttgart 29 May 1963.
    [*Mörikestraße 11, 73728 Esslingen, Germany*].

Duke *Ludwig* *m* 2ndly at Munich 14 Aug 1972 (*m* diss by div at Munich 14 Oct 1988), Angelika (*b* at Kiel 17 Jan 1942), [*Hartstraße 28b, 82346 Andechs-Frieding, Germany*], dau of Hans Joachim Kicssig and Theda Haake, and has further issue,

    4. *Christiane* Beate Alexandra, *b* at Munich 16 Sept 1973.
    [*Schönbuchstraße 10/1, 71093 Weil im Schönbuch, Germany*].

3. Duchess *Elisabeth* Maria Margarethe Alix Helene Rosa Philippine Christine Josepha Therese vom Kinde Jesu, *b* at Stuttgart 2 Feb 1933, Dame of Justice Grand Cross Constantinian Order of St George; *m* at Altshausen 18 July (civ) and 19 July (relig) 1958, Prince Don Antoine of Bourbon-Two Sicilies (*b* at Cannes 20 Jan 1929), Dipl Eng.

[*70 Chaussée de Louvain, 1410 Waterloo, Belgium*].

4. Duchess *Marie Therese* Nadejda Albertine Rosa Philippine Margarethe Christine Helene Josepha Martina Leopoldine, *b* at Altshausen 12 Nov 1934, granted the title "Duchess of Montpensier" by the Head of the Royal House of France, Dame of Justice Grand Cross Constantinian Order of St George; *m* at Dreux, Eure-et-Loire 5 July 1957 (legally separated at Paris 23 Feb 1977; *m* diss by div there 3 Feb 1984), Prince Henri d' Orléans, Count of Clermont [later Prince Henri VII Count of Paris and Duke of France] (*b* at Woluwé-Saint-Pierre, nr Brussels 14 June 1933).

[*18 Rue Rousselet, 75007 Paris, France*].

5. Duchess *Marie-Antoinette* Conrada Rosa Helene Michaele Josepha Christine Margarethe Pia, *b* at Altshausen 31 Aug 1937.

[*Schloß Altshausen, 88361 Kr. Ravensburg, Germany*].

Brother of Father

Issue of Albrecht, Duke of Württemberg (*b* 23 Dec 1865; ✠ 29 Oct 1939) and Archduchess Margarete Sophie of Austria (*b* 13 May 1870; *m* 24 Jan 1893; ✠ 24 Aug 1902), having had issue, among whom,

Son

Duke *Albrecht Eugen* Maria Philipp Carl Joseph Fortunatus, *b* at Stuttgart 8 Jan 1895; ✠ at Schwäbisch Gmünd 24 June 1954, Capt (ret), last owner of the Seigneural property of Carlsruhe, Silesia; *m* at Bad Margenthheim 24 Jan 1924, Princess Nadejda (*b* at Sofia 30 Jan 1899; ✠ at Stuttgart 15 Feb 1958), Dame Star Cross Order, Dame of Hon Bavarian Order of St Theresa, dau of Ferdinand I, King of Bulgaria and Princess Doña Marie Louise of Bourbon-Parma, and had issue,

> 1. Duke *Ferdinand Eugen* Albrecht Maria Joseph Ivan Rilsky Philipp August Clemens Karl Robert Ludwig Boris Cyrill Franz de Paula, *b* at Carlsruhe, Upper Silesia 3 April 1925, Forest Director, Kt of Hon Sovereign Military Order of Malta.
> [*Hölderlinstraße 32, 70174 Stuttgart, Germany; Albrechtstraße 29, 88045 Friedrichshafen, Württemberg, Germany*].

> 2. Duchess *Margarethe Louise* Eudoxie Nadejda Maria Josepha Albertine Therese Amélie Elisabeth Benedicta Rosa Catharina Elisabetha-Bona, *b* at Carlsruhe, Upper Silesia 25 Nov 1928; *m* at Altshausen 7 Aug (civ) and 8 Aug (relig) 1970 François, Luce-Bailly Viscount de Chevigny (*b* at Paris 15 June 1923).

[*25 Rue Rennequin, 75017 Paris, France*].

3. Duke *Eugen Eberhard* Albrecht Maria Joseph Ivan Rilsky Robert Ulrich Philipp Odo Carl Hubert, *b* at Carlsruhe, Upper Silesia 2 Nov 1930, MBA, Banker; *m* at Mondsee, Austria 31 Aug (civ) and at Salzburg 3 Sept (relig) 1962 (*m* diss by div at Frankfurt-am-Main 6 April 1972; ecclesiastically annulled at Rome 7 Nov 1973), Archduchess Alexandra (*b* at Sonnberg, Austria 21 May 1935; *m* 2ndly 22 Aug (civ) and 29 Dec (relig) 1973, Victor, Baron von Baillou), dau of Archduke Anton of Austria and Princess Ileana of Roumania.

[*Kohlbrandstraße 22, 60385 Frankfurt-am-Main, Germany*].

4. Duke *Alexander Eugen* Philipp Albrecht Ferdinand Maria Joseph Ivan Rilsky Johannes-Joseph vom Kreuz, *b* at Stuttgart 5 March 1933,

Dr of Phil, Art Historian.

[*Prinzregentenstraße 87, 81675 Munich, Germany*].

5. Duchess *Sophie* Eudoxie Louise Josepha Margarethe Theresia vom Kinde Jesu Konrada Donata, *b* at Stuttgart 16 Feb 1937; *m* at Altshausen 17 Feb (civ) and 18 Feb (relig) 1969 (*m* diss by div at Munich 11 Feb 1974; ecclesiastically annulled at Freiburg im Breisgau 18 Oct 1976), Antonio Manuel Roxo de Ramos-Bandeira (*b* at Santa Isabel, nr Lisbon 2 Aug 1937; ✝ at Rio de Janeiro 23 Feb 1987), Portuguese Consul.

[*25 Avenue Pierre I de Serbie, 75016 Paris, France; Prinzregentenstraße 87, 81675 Munich, Germany*].

———◆———

(YUGOSLAVIA)

See entry for - **SERBIA** *pg.349*

———◆———

ALMANACH

DE

GOTHA

2003
MMIII

186th Edition

(Volume I)

PART TWO
(Deuxième Partie)

Genealogies of the Mediatized Princes

and Princely Counts of Europe

& The Holy Roman Empire

ARENBERG

Catholic: This family from Hainaut, traces its descent from Fastre de Ligne (Charter of Gérard, Bishop of Cambray), living in 1047; then Thierry de Ligne near Leuze, in the Belgian province of Hainaut, 1142 - 1176; earlier references to Arenberg are to be found as far back as the 5th century at Villebois - Ain; Duke Arenberg, Supreme Commander, (under Kings Clotharie II and Dagobert I) was killed in action by Basquish guerrillas in 635. Various members of the family appear, attested, during the 8th and 9th century, including Hartmann, a military leader, killed at the battle of Unstrut river. After the battle of Unstrut river, King Henry (the first elected Germanic King, 919-936) fought the Huns shortly after the family had taken possession of domain in the Eifel, thereafter known as Arenberg. The Count Consort, Jean de Ligne (b 1523; killed in the Battle of Heiligerlée 24 May 1568) married Marguerite de La Marck (b 1527; m 18 Oct 1547; ✝ 1596) , ruler of Arenberg (sister and heiress of Count Robert III de La Marck and Arenberg - see below) she became Princess of the Holy Roman Empire, the Count Consort, Jean de Ligne inherited Barbançon (possession of the House of Abbeville) circa 1480; Count of Arenberg (Regency of Koblenz) through his marriage to Marguerite de la Marck. Count Robert III, (last Count of Arenberg of the House of the Counts de la Marck); Count of Arenberg and of the Holy Empire 1549 (by Charles V for Jean - see above); Princes of the Holy Empire and erection of the county of Arenberg into a Princely County of the Holy Empire, Vienna 5 March 1576; right to sit and vote in the College of Princes of the Empire 17 Oct 1576; inherited Aarschot and Chimay, Ducal titles of Aarschot and of Croÿ, with the dignity of Spanish Grandee First Class through the marriage of Charles, Prince of Arenberg (b 1550; ✝ 1616) to Anne de Croÿ-Chimay, 13 Jan 1612; Duke of Arenberg (for all descendants) and erection of their lands into the Duchy of Arenberg, Vienna 9 June 1644; recompensed (in the Peace of Lunéville 9 Feb 1801) for the loss of territories on the left bank of the Rhine with a new sovereign duchy on the right bank and with the bailliage of Meppen (region of Osnabrück), which was part of the Bishopric of Münster, 20 Nov 1802, and the County of Recklinghausen (heartland of the Ruhr) which was part of the Archbishopric of Cologne, 1 Feb 1803; these two territories with the bailliage of Dülmen (since 1803 the Sovereign Duchy of the House of Croÿ) formed the Duchy of Arenberg, reigning until 13 Dec 1810 (at that date Meppen and Dülmen were incorporated into France following the occupation of 26 Dec 1810 and 22 Jan 1811; and the County of Vest-Recklinghausen was annexed to the Grand Duchy of Berg). Following the wars of liberation, whereupon the entire duchy was occupied by Prussian troops, bilateral negotiations between Great Britain (House of Hanover) and Prussia resulted in the 1815 Treaty of Vienna retrospectively regarding the dispossessed Duke of Arenberg among the Mediatized Houses and accepting the annexation. The elevation of Meppen into the Duchy of Arenberg-Meppen by Hanover on 9 May 1826 also confirmed the qualification of "Durchlaucht" (primogeniture) by the German Diet 18 Aug 1825; confirmed in Prussia 21 Feb 1832 and 3 March 1833; Hereditary Member of the former Prussian House of Lords 12 Oct 1854, previously Duke Prosper-Louis had been appointed to the hereditary House of Lords of the Kingdom of Hanover, in the first rank, prior to the incorporation of Hanover into Prussia following the battle of Langensalza (1866).

(Founder of the First House of Arenberg was Ulrich of Arenberg (1032); Hereditary Burggrave and Protector of Cologne.)

Members of the family bear the title of Prince or Princess and Duke or Duchess of Arenberg with the qualification Serene Highness. It is the custom that the Head of the House alone is referred to as "The Duke of Arenberg".

JEAN-ENGELBERT, 12TH DUKE OF ARENBERG, 18th 18th Duke of Aarschot, 7th Duke of Meppen, 7th Prince of Recklinghausen, Count de la Marck, *etc, b* at The Hague 14 July 1921, MA, Dr of Law, Dr honoris causa; honorary citizen of Enghien (Belgium) and of Aarschot (Belgium),Officer of the Order of Leopold (Belgium), Officer of the Order of the Crown (Belgium), Commander (Grosskreuz des Verdienstordens) of the Federal Republic of Germany, Kt of Hon Sovereign Military Order of Malta, Commander Order of the Holy Sepulchre, Kt Bavarian Order of St George; *succ* his kinsman, Eric Engelbert, 11th Duke of Arenberg, etc (see below), son of Prince and Duke Evrard (*b* 18 Feb 1892; ✠ 12 Aug 1969) and Countess Anne-Louise de Merode (*b* 13 Sept 1894; *m* 25 Aug 1920; ✠ 18 Nov 1969); *m* at Berchtesgaden 18 Jan (civ) and 20 Jan (relig) 1955, Princess Sophie (*b* at Starnberg 20 June 1935), Dame of Hon Sovereign Military Order of Malta, Dame of Hon Bavarian Orders of St Theresia and St Elisabeth, dau of Rupprecht, Crown Prince of Bavaria and Princess Antonia of Luxemburg-Nassau.

[*10 Avenue des Acacias, 1006 Lausanne, Switzerland*].

Sons and Daughter

1. Prince and Duke *Léopold-Engelbert* Evrard Ruprecht Gaspard, *b* at Tervuren 20 Feb 1956, Lic jur, MBA, Kt Sovereign Military Order of Malta; *m* at Funchal, Madeira 9 Sept (relig) 1995, Countess Isabel (*b* at Aachen 7 June 1963), dau of Wilhelm, Count zu Stolberg-Stolberg and Princess Irena-Frederika von Isenburg, and has issue, [*19 Ave. l'Avenir, 1009 Pully, Switzerland*].

    1. Princess and Duchess *Natasha* Sophie Gaspara Maria
Annunziata, *b* at Brussels 21 Dec 1996.
    2. Prince and Duke *Philip-Leopold* Jean Engelbert Wilhelm
Melchior, *b* at Lausanne 20 May 1999.

2. Prince and Duke *Charles-Louis* Felix Melchior, *b* at Tervuren 13
March 1957, Banker, Lt Belgian Army (Res), Kt of Hon Sovereign
Military Order of Malta, Kt. Order of the Crown (Belgium) Lic jur,
m at Florence 7 Nov (civ) and at the Church of Santo Spirito,
Florence 26 Nov (relig) 1988, Fiammetta (*b* at Florence 22 May
1959), Dr Agronomy,of dau of Vittorio de Frescobaldi of the
Marquesses di Montecastello della Pineta, Patrician of Florence and
Bona Marchi, and has issue,
[*Maison Royale, 46 Quai Gustave Ador, 1207 Geneva, Switzerland*].
    1. Princess and Duchess *Anne-Hélène* Sophie Vittoria Laura
Gaspara, *b* at London 7 Nov 1989.
    2. Prince and Duke *Evrard-Guillaume* Engelbert Jean
Melchior, *b* at Lausanne 18 Jan 1996.

3. Princess and Duchess *Marie-Gabrielle* Elisabeth, *b* at Tervuren
2 June 1958; *m* at Lausanne-Ouchy 28 Jan 1984, Gilles, Morel de
Boncourt-Humeroeuille (*b* at Humeroeuille, Pas-de-Calais 10 May
1955), who has the courtesy rank and title of Count, Forester, son of
Gérard, de Boncourt-Humeroeuille and Nicole de Hautecloque.
[*Pierre Brune, Chateau de Bort, 87480 St. Priest Taurion, France*].

4. Prince and Duke *Henri* Antoine Marie, *b* at Tervuren 20 May
1961, Hotel Manager; *m* at Brussels 12 Jan (civ) and at La Bastide
dan Gras, nr Nimes 28 April(relig) 2001, Vicomtesse Dainé Marie
Thérèse (*b* at ...... 1972), dau of Vicomte André de Spoelberch and
of Claude de Clermont-Tonnerre.
[*38 ave. Mont-Repos, 1005 Lausanne, Switzerland*]

5. Prince and Duke *Etienne* Albert Charles Marie Melchior, *b* at
Brussels-Uccle 11 Dec 1967; Bank Director, Dipl. EHL, MSc (Boston
Univ), Hon Citizen City of Minneapolis (USA), Kt of Hon and Dev
Sovereign Military Order of Malta, *m* at Abbaye de Bonmont,
Switzerland 17 Sept 1994, Adrienne (*b* at Geneva 21 Dec 1970),BSc
(London School of Economics) dau of Dr Pierre Keller and
Claire-Jeanne de Senarclens.
[*rue Charles Bonnet 6, 1206 Geneva, Switzerland*].

Brothers and Sister
1. Prince and Duke *Antoine-Guillaume* Louis, *b* at The Hague 14
Sept 1923, Kt of Hon Sovereign Military Order of Malta, Commander

Order of the Holy Sepulchre, Kt Constantinian Order of St George; *m* at Madrid 29 Nov 1967, Doña Maria Carvajal y Xifré (*b* at Madrid 9 March 1917; ✠ there 8 Nov 1968), dau of Don Francisco Carvajal y Hurtado de Mendoza, Count de Fontanar and Doña Maria Xifré y Chacón, Marchioness de Isasi, Countess de Campo Alegre.
[*Maraia, Pollensa, Mallorca, Spain*].

2. Prince and Duke *Etienne-Evrard* Marie Joseph Balthasar, *b* at The Hague 18 Feb 1925; ✠ at Ouchy 25 June 1985, Dr of Med, Kt of Hon Sovereign Military Order of Malta.

3. Princess and Duchess *Marie-Elisabeth* Jeanne Melchiorre Sophie Pauline, *b* at Munich 21 Jan 1929; ✠ at San Remo, Italy 7 Nov 1996, Dame of Hon Sovereign Military Order of Malta; *m* at Brussels 8 Oct (civ) and 9 Oct (relig) 1958, Don Guido Orazio, Duke Borea d'Olmo (*b* at San Remo 25 April 1925), Hon Danish Consul at San Remo, Kt of Hon Sovereign Military Order of Malta, Grand Officer Order Pro Merito Melitense, Commander Order of Saints Maurice and Lazarus, Kt (1st Class) Order of the Dannebrog.
[*Palazzo Borea, 18038, San Remo, Italy*].

Brother of Father

Issue of Prince and Duke Jean d'Arenberg (*b* 18 Oct 1850; ✠ 2 April 1914) and Princess and Duchess Sophie of Arenberg (*b* 26 July 1871; *m* 24 Sept 1889; ✠ 29 May 1961).

Prince and Duke *Robert-Prosper* Paul Jean Antoine Engelbert Eugene Marie Ernest Joseph Gaspard Etienne, *b* at Pesch am Rhein 10 Aug 1895; ✠ at Munich 24 Feb 1972, Kt of Hon Sovereign Military Order of Malta; *m* at Munich 20 March (civ) and 21 March (relig) 1922, Princess Gabrielle (*b* at Ellingen 26 June 1895; ✠ at Munich 14 Nov 1971), dau of Philipp, Prince (Fürst) von Wrede and Princess Anna of Lobkowicz, and had issue,

1. Princess and Duchess *Rose-Sophie* Caroline Gabrielle Robertine Anne Jeanne Marie Josephine Caspara, *b* at Pesch 23 Dec 1922; *m* at Munich 6 July 1943, Karl Theodor, Baron von and zu Guttenberg (*b* at Weisendorf 23 May 1921; ✠ at Guttenberg 4 Oct 1972), Proprietor of Guttenberg, etc, 1st Lt (retd.) 1957 member of the West German Parliament; Parliamentary Secretary of State
[*Schloßallee 1, 95358 Guttenberg, Germany*].

2. Princess and Duchess *Anna-Eugenia* Pauline Gabrielle Robertine Marie de Mercedes Melchiore, *b* at Ellingen 5 July

1925; ✠ at San Angel, Mexico DF 9 June 1997, Veterinary
Surgeon, Dame Star Cross Order; *m* at Beaulieu,
France 18 Nov (civ) and 19 Nov (relig) 1952, Archduke Felix
of Austria (*b* at Schönbrunn 31 May 1916), Banker.
[*Reyna 193, San Angel, Mexico 20, D.F., Mexico*].

Brother of Great-Grandfather

Issue of Prosper-Louis, 7th Duke of Arenberg (*b* 28 April 1785; ✠ 27
Feb 1861) and Princess Ludmilla of Lobkowitz (*b* 15 March 1798; *m*
26 Jan 1819; ✠ 10 Jan 1868), having had issue, among whom,

Son

Engelbert-August Anton, **8th Duke of Arenberg,** *b* at Brussels
11 May 1824; ✠ at Héverlé, Leuven, Belgium 28 March 1875, Kt
Order of the Golden Fleece; *m* at Vienna 27 May 1868, Princess and
Duchess Eleonore (*b* at Vienna 19 Feb 1845; ✠ at Montreux 28 Nov
1919), dau of Ernst, Prince and Duke of Arenberg and Princess
Sophie von Auersperg, and had issue, among whom,

Son

Engelbert Prosper Ernest **Marie** Joseph Jules Balthasar Bénoit
Antoine Eléonore Laurent, **9th Duke of Arenberg,** *b* at Salzburg
10 Aug 1872; ✠ at Lausanne 15 Jan 1949, Hon citizen of the City of
Meppen and of the City of Recklinghausen, Bailiff Gd Cross Hon and
Dev Sovereign Military Order of Malta; *m* at Brussels 14 Oct 1897,
Princess Hedwige (*b* at Paris 4 May 1877; ✠ at Neuilly-sur-Seine 22
Sept 1938), Dame Star Cross Order, dau of Charles, Prince of Ligne
and Charlotte de Gontaut Biron of the Counts de Gontaut Biron,
and had issue, among whom,

    1. **Eric** Charles Auguste Hedwige **Engelbert** Antoine
Balthasar, **11th Duke of Arenberg,** etc, *b* at Héverlé 17
Oct 1901; ✠ at Punta del Este, Uruguay 13 Sept 1992; *m* at
Lausanne 20 Aug 1940, Marie Thérèse (*b* at Dijon 3 June
1911; *m* 1stly at Dijon 16 Jan 1934, Guillaume Le Verdier who
✠ at Rio de Janeiro Aug 1934; *m* 2ndly 31 March 1940, Henri
de Belsunce who was ✠*k* in action Ibarrogat, Italy 13 May
1944), dau of Jean, Marquis de la Poëze d'Harambure and
Madeleine Le Gouz de Sainte-Seine, and adopted the children
of his wife by her second marriage,
[*Villa d'Arenberg, Lido Punta del Este, Uruguay*].

1. *Laetitia* Marie Madeleine Suzanne Valentine de Belsunce, *b* at Broumana, Lebanon 2 Sept 1941, adopted at Paris 15 Feb 1956, bears the name "de Belsunce d'Arenberg"; *m* at St Gilgen am Wolfgangsee 19 June (civ) and at Menetou-Salon, Cher 28 July (relig) 1965, Leopold Franz, Archduke of Austria, Prince of Tuscany, Head of the Grand Ducal House of Tuscany (*b* at Leutstetten 25 Oct 1942), Engineer. [*Gabelsbergerstraße 15, 80333 Munich, Germany; Carrasco, Montevideo, Uruguay*].

2. *Rodrigue* Henri Jean Louis Marie de Belsunce, *b* at Yzeures sur Creuse 8 Aug 1942, adopted at Paris 15 Feb 1956, bears the name "de Belsunce d'Arenberg". [*Villa d'Arenberg, Lido Punta del Este, Uruguay; 44 Avenue Général Guison, 1009 Pully, Switzerland*].

Brother of Great-Great-Grandfather

Issue of Louis-Engelbert, 6th Duke d'Arenberg (*b* 3 Aug 1750; ✝ 7 March 1820) and Louise-Pauline de Brancas of the Dukes de Brancas (*b* 23 Nov 1755; *m* 19 Jan 1773; ✝ 10 Aug 1812), having had issue, among whom,

Son

Prince and Duke *Pierre* d'Alcantara Charles, *b* 2 Oct 1790; ✝ 27 Sept 1877, created duc-pair de France 1828; *m* 1stly 27 Jan 1829, Alix-Marie-Charlotte de Talleyrand of the Dukes de Perigord (*b* 4 Nov 1808; ✝ 12 Sept 1842); *m* 2ndly 19 June 1860, Countess Caroline (*b* 27 Nov 1801; ✝ 18 June 1875), dau of Alois Wenzel, Prince of Kaunitz-Ritberg, and widow of Anton Gundakar, Count von Starhemberg, and had issue, among whom, by his first wife,

Son

Prince and Duke *Auguste* Louis Alberic, *b* at Paris 15 Sept 1837; ✝ at Paris 24 Jan 1924; *m* at Paris 18 June 1868, Jeanne (*b* at Paris 20 March 1850; ✝ Paris 24 March 1891), dau of Louis Charles, Count de Greffulhe and Félicité de La Rochefoucauld of the Dukes d'Estissac, and had issue, among whom,

Son

Prince and Duke Charles-Louis *Pierre, b* at Menetou-Salon, Cher, France 14 Aug 1871; ✠ at Paris 3 Aug 1919; *m* at Paris 11 June 1904, Emma Louise (*b* at Baillon, nr Asniere-sur-Oise 3 Oct 1883; ✠ at Hay-les-Roses, Val de Marne 1 Oct 1958), dau of Armand, Count de Gramont, Duke de Lesparre and Hélène Duchesne of the Dukes de

Gillevoisin Conegliano, and had issue,

 1. Prince and Duke *Charles* -August Armand, *b* at Paris 27 May 1905; ✠ at Paris 11 June 1967; *m* at Paris 29 Dec 1960, Margaret (Peggy) (*b* at New York 18 Oct 1932; ✠ nr Paris 16 Oct 1977; *m* 1stly at New York 14 April 1951, Thomas Moore Bancroft; that *m* diss by div at Alabama 10 May 1960, she *m* 3rdly at Marrakesh, Morocco 5 July 1968, Emmanuel de Crussol, Duke d'Uzés), dau of Frederick Henry Bedford and Margaret Wright Stewart, and had issue,

  1. Prince and Duke *Pierre* Frédéric Henri Charles, *b* at Bern 19 Aug 1961, Kt Sovereign Military Order of Malta; Member of the Sacred Military Constantinian Order of St George; *m* 1stly in the Philippines 1995 (*m* diss by div) Marie Christine Kraff de Laubarède, and has issue,

   1. Princess and Duchess *Aliénor* (*b* at …).

  Prince and Duke Pierre *m* 2ndly at Philadelphia, Pennsylvania 19 Sept (civ) and at Bourges 11 Oct (relig) 1997, Silvia (*b* at Neuilly-sur-Seine, Paris 13 June 1963), dau of Count *Henri-Jean* de Castellane, and Countess Isabella di Rovasenda, and has further issue,

  [*7 The Vale, London SW3 6AG; Chateau de Menetou Salon, 18510 Menetou Salon, Cher, France*].

   1. Princess and Duchess *Lydia* Athenaïs Margaret Alix Isabelle Emma Marie Beatrix, *b* at Geneva 26 Oct 1998.

   2. Princess and Duchess *Dorothée-Anastasia*, *b* at Saanen, Switzerland 27 July 2000.

 2. Prince and Duke *Armand* -Louis Hélie, *b* at Paris 14 April 1906; ✠ at Paris 29 Jan 1985, Kt Sovereign Military Order of Malta; *m* at Paris 7 Aug (civ) and 9 Aug (relig) 1941, Gabrielle (*b* at Biarritz 8 Sept 1920), dau of Charles (Carlos) de Lambertye, Marquess de Gerbeviller and Lina Sancho-Mata y

Contreras, and had issue,
[*20 rue Oudinot, 75007 Paris, France*].

    1. Princess and Duchess *Marie-Virtudes* Loraine,
b at Paris 9 June 1947; *m* 1stly at Paris 21 April 1967
(*m* diss by div Paris 27 June 1983), Louis-Jean Loppin,
Count de Montmort (*b* at Paris 11 Oct 1943). She *m*
2ndly at Neuilly-sur-Seine 14 Oct 1983, Georges Hervet
(*b* at Bourges 5 June 1924), Banker.
[*74 Boulevard Maurice Barrès, 92200
Neuilly-sur-Seine, France*].

    2. Prince and Duke *Charles* Louis Pierre Armand
Engelbert Roland, *b* at Paris 20 Feb 1949; *m* at St Cirq
la Popie, Lot 25 Oct 1975 (*m* diss by div at Paris on 17
Nov 1986), Philomène (*b* at St Cirq lapoqie, Lot 9 Jan
1939), dau of Pierre Toulouse and Denise Delvert,
and has issue,
[*21 Rue du Cirque,75008, Paris, France*].

        1. Princess and Duchess *Marie*, Gabrielle
Charlotte, *b* at Paris 2 Aug 1977.

◆━◆━◆

AUERSPERG

**Catholic: This feudal family traces its descent from Adolf I (von
Ursperg), Lord of Auersberg (*b* 990; ✝ 1060) taking their name from
the castle of "Unter Auerperg" in Carniola, authenticated dominus
Errandus (or Herrandus) de Owersperch living, 7 April 1220;
investiture as Hereditary Grand Chamberlain and Hereditary Grand
Marshal of Carniola and of the Marche Wende, Neustadt 5 Jan 1463
for the brothers Johann, Georg and Wilhelm of Auersperg; renewed
at Graz 7 Dec 1594 (for the extant line); Baron of the Holy Empire 14
March 1550 (for Herward of Auersberg); Count of the Holy Empire
with the qualification of "Wohlgeboren", Regensburg 11 Sept 1630
(for the cousins Dietrich and Hans Andreas von Auersperg); acquired
the Lordship of Gottschee from Georg Bartholomä Khisel, Count zu
Gottschee, Laibach 9 July 1641; Prince of the Holy Empire
(primogeniture) with the qualification of "Hochgeboren" and "Unser
Oheim", Palatine of Regensburg 17/18 Sept 1653 (for Johann
Weikhard, Count of Auersperg; investiture of the Duchy of
Münsterberg and of Frankenstein (Silesia), Ebersdorf 30 July 1654;
acquired Thengen and Nellenburg in Swabia, Innsbruck 24 Oct
1663; erected into a Princely County, Regensburg 14 March 1664
(sold to the Grand Duchy of Baden in 1811); investiture as Hereditary
Grand Marshal of the Tyrol 7 Sept 1780; the title "Duke of**

Münsterberg and of Frankenstein" lost after the sale of that Duchy to Prussia in 1791; Duke of Gottschee, Vienna 11 Nov 1791; the title of Prince of the Holy Empire was extended to all descendants with the qualification of "Hochgeboren", Vienna 21 Dec 1791; received the qualification of "Durchlaucht" (primogeniture) 10 Aug 1825 by the German Diet; confirmed in Austria 7 Oct 1825; qualification extended to all descendants 27 April 1869; Hereditary Member of the former Austrian House of Lords 18 April 1861. The two Lines below descend from two sons of Wilhelm, 6th Prince of Auersperg (b 9 April 1749; ✝ 16 March 1822).

Members of the family bear the title of Prince or Princess von Auersperg with the qualification of Serene Highness.

LINE I

This line descends from Prince Wilhelm (b 5 Oct 1782; ✝ 25 Jan 1827).

KARL-ADOLF Franz Joseph Maria Alois Ferdinand Gobertus, **10TH PRINCE (FÜRST) VON AUERSPERG,** Duke of Gottschee, Princely Count of Wels, b at Goldegg 13 March 1915, Kt Sovereign Military Order of Malta, son of Hereditary Prince (Erbprinz) Adolf von Auersperg (b 9 Aug 1886; ✝ 7 Nov 1923) and Countess Gabrielle von Clam and Gallas (b 29 Oct 1890; m 28 April 1914; ✝ 31 Aug 1979); succ his grandfather, Karl, 9th Prince (Fürst) von Auersperg, etc (b 26 Feb 1859; ✝ 19 Oct 1927); m 1stly at Vienna 3 Feb 1937, Countess Margit (b at Kupcseny 18 April 1914; ✝k in a motor accident nr Paysandú, Uruguay 22 Jan 1959), Dame Star Cross Order, dau of Ladislaus, Prince of Batthyány-Strattmann von Német-Ujvár and Countess Marie-Therese von Coreth zu Coredo and Starkenberg. He m 2ndly at Vienna 6 Oct 1961, Countess Feodora (b at Baruth 5 April 1920; m 1stly at Glienicke, nr Potsdam 28 Nov 1942, Gert Schenk who ✝ at Vienna 23 Aug 1957), dau of Friedrich, 3rd Prince (Fürst) zu Solms-Baruth and Princess Adelheid of Schleswig-Holstein-Sonderburg-Glücksburg.
[Spiegelberg 6, 6372 Oberndorf, Tirol, Austria]

Sons and Daughters - 1st Marriage

1. *Adolf* Karl Gobertus, Hereditary Prince (Erbprinz) von Auersperg, b at Vienna 30 Oct 1937; m at Montevideo, Uruguay 17 Aug 1961, Maria de las Mercedes (b at Carrasco, nr Montevideo 22 April 1941), dau of Alberto Tournier and Maria Angelica Da Camara Canta, and has issue,

[*Casilla de Correo 69, Leandro Gómez 1288, Paysandú, Uruguay*].

    1. Prince *Carl Adolf* , *b* at Montevideo 9 May 1962; *m* at Paysandú, Uruguay 12 May 1990, Anabella Lina (*b* at Rio Negro, Uruguay 1 Oct 1961), dau of Juan Chimaylov and Aquilina Maciel.

    [*Calle Montevideo 761, Paysandú, Uruguay*].

    2. Prince *Alexander, b* at Montevideo 8 Sept 1963; *m* at Paysandú, Uruguay 13 Dec 1986, Maria Graciela (*b* at Paysandú 10 Dec 1964), dau of Nicolas Leyba and Ana Maria Buschiazzo, and has issue,

    [*Calle Colon 1055, Paysandú, Uruguay*].

        1. Princess Maria *Ximena, b* at Paysandú 19 May 1987.

        2. Princess *Maria Magdalena, b* at Paysandú 17 Sept 1990.

        3. Prince *Alejandro* Maria, *b* at Paysandú 16 July 1993.

    3. Princess *Margarita, b* at Montevideo 2 Feb 1966; *m* at Paysandú 2 March 1991, Victor Alvarez (*b* at Montevideo 17 June 1965), Veterinary Surgeon.

    4. Princess *Mercedes, b* at Montevideo 10 Aug 1968, Dr of Med; *m* at Montevideo 24 March 1995, Ricardo A Ercoli (*b* at Montevideo 9 May 1964), Engineer.

    [*Calle 26 de Marzo 1006, Ap. 501, Montevideo, Uruguay*].

    5. Prince *Andreas, b* at Montevideo 10 Jan 1980.

2. Prince *Ferdinand* Sigismund Gobertus, *b* at Steinamanger 22 Nov 1939; *m* at Montevideo 23 Dec 1971 (*m* diss by div at Montevideo 30 March 1984), Liliana (*b* at Montevideo 17 Nov 1943), dau of Juan Jacobo Faget and Maria Sara Llovet, and has issue,

[*Av. Brasil 2446, 7.p., Montevideo, Uruguay*].

    1. Princess *Maria Fernanda, b* at Montevideo 7 Aug 1971.

    [*Calle Leyenda Patria 3064, p.2., Montevideo, Uruguay*].

    2. Princess *Johanna, b* at Vienna 8 June 1974.

    [*Calle Leyenda Patria 3064, p.2., Montevideo, Uruguay*].

    3. Prince *Ferdinand, b* at Montevideo 20 March 1976.

    [*Calle Leyenda Patria 3064, p.2., Montevideo, Uruguay*].

    4. Princess *Isabel, b* at Montevideo 26 April 1977.

    [*Calle Leyenda Patria 3064, p.2., Montevideo, Uruguay*].

    5. Princess *Carolina, b* at Montevideo 17 April 1979.

    [*Calle Leyenda Patria 3064, p.2., Montevideo, Uruguay*].

3. Princess *Gabrielle, b* at Steinamanger 14 Jan 1941; *m* at Montevideo 4 May 1970 (*m* diss by div at Montevideo 7 July 1989), José

Enrique Faget Llovet (*b* at Montevideo 1946), Businessman.
[*Calle 21 de Septiembre 2869, Ap. 902, Montevideo, Uruguay*].
4. Princess *Johanna*, *b* at Vienna 22 Oct 1942; *m* at St Pölten 8 Sept
1962 (*m* diss by div at Montevideo 11 Oct 1991), German Mailhos
(*b* at Montevideo 24 Feb 1933).
[*Calle Peabody 2001 esqu. Gioia, Colon, Montevideo, Uruguay*].

Daughter - Second Marriage

5. Princess *Caroline* Mathilde Adelheid Gobertina, *b* at Vienna 24
May 1962; *m* at Vienna 19 May 1985, Christoph Preiser (*b* at Vienna
23 March 1959), Dr of Law.
[*Grinzingerstraße 5, 1190 Vienna, Austria*].

Brother and Sisters

1. Princess *Agathe* Eleonore Marie Gobertine, *b* at Goldegg 25 Sept
1916; ✛ at Cascais, Portugal 13 Jan 1983; *m* at Goldegg 14 April
1943, Johann Georg von Radey (*b* at Pardubitz 24 Jan 1908; ✛*k* in
action in Russia 12 Jan 1944).
2. Princess *Marie-Immakulata* Eleonore Josefa Gobertina Sephanie,
b at Goldegg 26 Dec 1917; *m* at Goldegg 18 April 1959, Engelbert
Kainz (*b* at Waidhofen an der Thaya 10 Oct 1905; ✛ there 4 June
1993), Dipl Engineer.
[*Jägerhaus, 3830 Waidhofen a.d. Thaya, Austria*].
3. Princess *Eleonore* Maria Josefa Ernestine Gobertina, *b* at
Grafenstein 22 Sept 1919, Dame Star Cross Order, Professor; *m* at
Goldegg 25 June 1971, Wolfgang, Count von Stillfried-Mettich (*b* at
Schönwald 1 July 1905; ✛ at Bogotá, Columbia 3 Feb 1983).
[*Franz-Schulk-Straße 3/7, 5020 Salzburg, Austria*].
4. Princess *Christiane* Johanna Ernestine Marie Gobertina, *b* at
Goldegg 10 Sept 1920, Dame Star Cross Order; *m* at Buenos-Aires 15
Nov 1952, Anton, Count Széchenyi de Sárvár-Felsövidék (*b* at
Vienna 31 March 1924), Forester
[*Schloß, 4973 St. Martin im Innkreis, Austria*].
5. Prince *Franz Weikhard* Rudolf Marie Gobertus Konrad, *b* at
Goldegg 19 Feb 1923; *m* at Salzburg 17 Aug 1946, Princess Theodora
(*b* at Alt-Wartenburg, nr Vöcklabruck 1 April 1924), Dame Star
Cross Order, dau of Alfred, Prince zur Lippe-Weissenfeld and
Countess Anna von Goëss, and has issue,
[*Schloß Goldegg, 3100 St. Pölten, Austria*].

     1. Prince *Egmont* Alfred Franz von Assisi Adolf Maria
Engelbert Weikhard, *b* at Goldegg 7 June 1947; *m* at

Weinburg, nr Brunnsee, Styria 24 May (civ) and 7 June (relig) 1980, Donna Maria Beatrice (*b* at Brunnsee 24 April 1947), Dame Star Cross Order, dau of Don Adinolfo, Count Lucchesi Palli and Countess Sarolta Teleki de Szék, and has issue, [*Schloß Goldegg, 3100 St. Pölten, Austria*].

    1. Princess *Teresa* Maria Michaela Theodora Charlotte Gobertina, *b* at St Pölten 25 March 1981.

    2. Princess *Valerie* Maria Agnes Bernadette Paula Anna Gobertina, *b* at St Pölten 29 Jan 1983.

    3. Prince *Georg* Maria Maximilian Adinolfo Franz Paul Gobertus, *b* at St Pölten 25 Jan 1985.

    4. Princess *Bernadette* Maria Francisca Benedikta Gabriele Beatrice Gobertina, *b* at St Pölten 11 July 1987.

2. Prince *Andreas* Karl Egmont Leopold Franz Callistus, *b* at Goldegg 14 Oct 1949; *m* at Winchester 21 April 1979, Julia Rosemary (*b* at Newbury, Berkshire 29 April 1955), dau of Brigadier David Llewelyn Griffith and Naomi Gardiner, and has issue, [*Schloß Goldegg, 3100 St. Pölten, Austria*].

    1. Prince *Lukas* Christoph Maria Gobertus, *b* at St Pölten 27 Aug 1981.

    2. Princess *Stephanie* Theodora Maria Gobertina, *b* at St Pölten 29 Oct 1982.

    3. Princess *Katharina* Sophie Maria Gobertina, *b* at St Pölten 25 Jan 1988.

    4. Princess *Nicola* Rosemarie Maria Gobertina, *b* at St Pölten 4 May 1991.

3. Princess *Christiane* Gobertina, *b* at Goldegg 13 Jan 1953; *m* 1stly at Goldegg 20 Sept 1975 (*m* diss by div at Vienna 7 March 1993), Alexander, Baron von Tinti (*b* at Vienna 3 July 1950). She m 2ndly at Castelldefels, nr Barcelona 3 April 1993, José Enrique Faget Llovet (*b* at Montevideo 4 Feb 1946), Businessman. [*Avenida del Poal 54, 08860 Castelldefels, nr Barcelona, Spain*].

4. Princess *Aglaë* Carola, *b* at Goldegg 22 Jan 1956; *m* at Heiligenkreuz, Lower Austria 31 Oct 1975, Robert Ratzenböck (*b* at Vienna 30 March 1941), Engineer. [*Schloß Goldegg, 3100 St. Pölten, Austria*].

5. Prince *Philipp* Constantin Maria Gobertus, *b* at Vienna 22

May 1969; *m* at Salzburg 24 Sept 1994, Countess Henriette (*b* at Salzburg 15 March 1968), dau of Maximilian, Count Kielmansegg and Marlies Adomat, and has issue,
[*Schloß Goldegg, 3100 St Pölten, Austria*].

    1. Prince *Ferdinand* Oderich Gobertus Maria Heinrich, *b* at St Pölten 3 Jan 1995.

    2. Prince *Leopold* Parkratius Maria Govertus Stephan, *b* at St Pölten 14 April 1996.

    3. Princess *Camila* Josefa Maria Goberta, *b* at St Pölten 14 Dec 1997

Brothers of Father

Issue of Karl, 9th Prince von Auersperg (*b* 26 Feb 1859; ✝ 19 Oct 1927) and Countess Eleonore von Breunner-Enckevoirth (*b* 28 July 1864; *m* 10 Nov 1885; ✝ 20 Jan 1920), having had issue, among whom,

Sons

1. Prince *Karl* Alain August Maria Gobertus, *b* at Goldegg 16 Jan 1895; ✝ at Wald, Lower Austria 30 April 1980, adopted by his aunt Ernestine, Countess Coudenhove (née Countess von Breunner) 6 Dec 1928; authorised by the Hungarian Minister of Justice at Budapest 10 Jan 1929 to bear the name "Auersperg-Breunner", Proprietor of Ainödt, Wlasim, Wald, etc, Kt Sovereign Military Order of Malta; *m* at Graz 30 Aug 1927, Countess Henriette (*b* at Graz 25 June 1904; ✝ at Schloß Wald 8 Oct 2000), Dame Star Cross Order, dau of Franz, Count von Meran and Princess Marie von and zu Liechtenstein, and had issue,
[*Schloß Wald, 3144 Wald, Austria*].

    1. Princess *Eleonore* Marie Gobertine Henriette, *b* at Goldegg 12 Sept 1928, Dame Star Cross Order; *m* at Vienna 4 July (civ) and at Wald 8 Sept (relig) 1960, Georg, 3rd Duke (Herzog) von Hohenberg (*b* at Artstetten, Austria 25 April 1929), Dr of Law, Ambassador (ret).
[*Salesianer Gasse(, 1030 Vienna, Austria*].

    2. Prince *Karl* Marie Franz Gobertus, *b* at Goldegg 26 April 1930; *m* at Eisenkappel, Carinthia 8 June 1955, Countess Friederike (*b* at Reichwaldau 20 Aug 1936), dau of Georg Adam, Count von Starhemberg and Princess Anna Agnes von Isenburg, and has issue,

[*Estancia Los Leones, 6614 Rivas FCNGSSM, Argentina;
Schloß Wald, 3144 Wald, Austria*].

    1. Prince *Franz-Joseph* Karl Georg Heinrich Maria
Gobertus, *b* at Buenos Aires 20 July 1956; *m* at Zell
am See 30 Jan 1982, Marietta (*b* at Graz 22 March
1956), dau of Hermann Kastner-Lanjus-Wellenburg
and Elfriede Tausch, and has issue,
[*3144 Wald-Auern, Austria*].

        1. Prince *Camilo* Johannes Gobertus Maria,
b at Buenos Aires 22 Jan 1984.

        2. Princess *Sophie* Caroline *Quirine* Maria,
b at Buenos Aires 15 Sept 1985.

        3. Prince *Douglas* Nicolas *Gobertus* Maria, *b* at
Buenos Aires 23 May 1987.

        4. Princess *Nicoleta* Maria, *b* at Buenos Aires
29 Jan 1991.

    2. Princess *Sophie* Irene Henriette Marie Gobertina,
b at Buenos Aires 17 April 1958; *m* at Buenos Aires 18
April (civ) and at Wald, Lower Austria 31 May (relig)
1997, Ricardo Francisco Bisso (*b* at Buenos Aires 30
Jan 1959), Lic, MA, Business Consultant.
[*Alicia Moreau de Justo 1848, 1107 Cap.Fed.,
Argentina*].

    3. Prince *Karl* Georg Adolf Maria Gobertus, *b* at
Vienna 17 Feb 1960, Banker, Mag rer soc oec; *m* at
Pyhra 2 April (civ) and at Athens 16 June (relig)
1994, Demetra (*b* at Athens 23 Feb 1963), dau of Ilias
Lalaounis and Lila Altzitzoglou, and has issue,
[*19 Coleherne Court, The Boltons, London SW5
0DL*].

        1. Prince *Karl Ilias* Nikolaus Gobertus Maria,
b at London 27 July 1995.

        2. Princess *Alexia* Theodora Gobertina Maria,
b at London 28 Nov 1996.

        3. Prince *Dimitri*, *b* at ... 2000.

    4. Princess *Stephanie* Maria Anna Georgine Rudolfine
Friederike Gobertina, *b* at Buenos Aires 17 April 1964;
m at Wald 1 July 1990, Nikolaus, Count Szápáry von
Muraszombath Széckisziget and Szápár (*b* at Vienna
30 May 1959), Mag phil, MBA, Forester.
[*Hautznerstraße 12, 3843 Dobersberg a.d. Thaya,*

Austria].

5. Prince Wilhelm *Alexander* Friedrich Maria Gobertus, *b* at Vienna 23 April 1968; *m* 1996 Maddalena degli Albertini, and has issue,

    1. Prince *Carlo* (*b* at ...)

3. Prince *Heinrich* Weikhard Rudolf Gobertus Felix Maria, *b* at Ainödt 21 May 1931, Kt of Hon and Dev Sovereign Military Order of Malta; *m* at Schloß Persenbeug 6 July 1959, Archduchess Elisabeth (*Sissy*) (*b* at Schloß Persenbeug 18 March 1935 ✠✠ in a motor accident at Ybbs 9 Oct 1998), Dame Star Cross Order, dau of Archduke Hubert Salvator of Austria and Princess Rosemary zu Salm-Salm, and has issue, [*Schloß Wald, 3144 Wald, Austria; Estancia "Los Leones", RA-6614 Rivas FCNGSM, Argentina*].

    1. Prince Johann *Weikhard* Karl Thaddäus Severin Gobertus Maria, *b* at Buenos Aires 23 Oct 1961; *m* at Vienna 7 June 2002, Countess Maria Philippa (*b* at Brussels 1 Oct 1974), dau of Andreas, Count Calice and Maria Fernanda, Noble Lady (Edle) von Steinhart. [*Schloß Wald, 3144 Wald, Austria*].

    2. Princess *Isabel* Maria Ernestine Silvester Thaddäa Leopoldina Gobertina, *b* at Vienna 31 Dec 1962; *m* at Schloß Wald 12 Sept 1987, Hugues, Baron Stier, Viscount de Saint-Jean (*b* at Paris 13 Feb 1960). [*Calle Olazábal 1993, RA-1428 Buenos Aires, PB D Argentina*].

    3. Prince *Maximilian* Andreas Karl Blasius Thaddäus Gobertus Maria, *b* at Vienna 3 Feb 1964; ✠ at Innsbruck 12 Oct 1990.

    4. Princess Maria *Dominica* Valerie Romana Eleonora Thaddäa Gobertina, *b* at Buenos Aires 28 Feb 1970; *m* at St. Pölten 23 Nov 1991, Thomas, Baron von Schenk, Dr of Med (*b* at Vienna 24 March 1963). [*Weinheberstraße 47, 3040 Neulengbach, Austria*].

4. Princess *Ernestine* Johanna Maria Gobertina Laurentia, *b* at Ainödt 5 Sept 1930. [*Auenbrugger Gasse 2/24a, 1030 Vienna, Austria*].

5. Princess *Johanna* Agathe Maria Gobertina, *b* at Ainödt 4 May 1934; *m* at Wald 2 Sept 1959, Johannes, Count von and zu Trauttmansdorff-Weinsberg (*b* at Vienna 20 Feb 1929), Businessman.

[Taubstummen Gasse2, 1040, Vienna, Austria].

6. Princess *Aglaë* Marie Eleonore Gobertina, *b* at Wald 27
July 1937; *m* at Wald 12 Jan 1961, Stephan Salomon von
Friedberg (*b* at Vienna 14 Feb 1932).

*[Esteplatz 6, 1030 Vienna, Austria; 3034 Maria Anzbach,
Austria]*.

7. Princess Anna Maria (*Marianne*) Henrietta Eleonora
Gobertina, *b* at Zseliz, Bars, Hungary 15 Dec 1943; *m* at
Salem 21 Sept (civ) and at Wald 21 Oct (relig) 1967, Prince
Ludwig of Baden (*b* at Karlsruhe 16 March 1937), Forester.

*[Schloß Zwingenberg, 69412 Eberbach, Bad. Neckertal,
Germany]*.

LINE II

This line descends from Prince Vinzenz (*b* 9 June 1790; ✚ 16 Feb
1812) who succeeded his kinsman, Count Johann Adam (*b* 27 Aug
1721; ✚ without direct heirs 1795) by virtue of a Diploma 21 Dec
1791; Prince of the Holy Empire (this dignity transferrable through
the order of primogeniture or, by default, through the male line of
Line I), Count of Gottschee and of Wels, Lord of Schönberg and
Seissenberg with the qualification of "Hochgeboren", Vienna 15
July 1746; Hereditary Grand Marshal in Tyrol.

FRANZ JOSEF Gobert Eduard Maria, **PRINCE (FÜRST) VON
AUERSPERG-TRAUTSON**, *b* at Salzburg 11 Dec 1954,
Proprietor of Weitwörth, Farmer and Forester, Kt of Hon Sovereign
Military Order of Malta, son of Prince Eduard Karl (*b* 9 Nov 1917; ✚
11 June 2000) and Countess Isabelle d'Aspremont Lynden (*b* 29
April 1923; *m* 19 Feb 1954; ✚ 9 April 2001); *m* at Brussels 10 Sept
1994, Archduchess Constanza (*b* at Château de Beloeil, Belgium 19
Oct 1957), Dame Star Cross Order, dau of Archduke Carl Ludwig of
Austria and Princess Yolande de Ligne.

[Weitwörth 21, 5110 Oberndorf, nr Salzburg, Austria].

Daughters

1. Princess *Alexandra*, *b* at Brussels 9 Feb 1998; ✚ there 9 Feb 1998.
2. Princess *Anna* Maria, *b* at ... Sept 24 1997, adopted.
3. Princess Ladislaja (*Laya*), *b* at ... 26 Feb 1999.

Brother and Sister

1. Prince *Gobert* Johannes Erasmus Maria Josef, *b* at Salzburg 8
March 1956, Dipl Agr Engineer, Lt (Res); *m* at Gutenstein 30 Aug
1980, Countess Ladislaja (*b* at Petropolis, Brazil 26 June 1957),
Physiotherapist, dau of Heinrich, Count Hoyos, Baron zu

Stichsenstein, Proprietor of Gutenstein, Lower Austria and Baroness Maria Theresia Mayr von Melnhof, and has issue, [*Weyr Gasse9/2/5, 1030 Vienna, Austria*].

    1. Princess *Isabelle*, *b* at Vienna 14 Jan 1982.

    2. Princess *Aglae*, *b* at Vienna 31 May 1984.

    3. Prince *Johannes* Nepomuk, *b* at Vienna 8 Sept 1985.

    4. Prince *Albrecht*, *b* at Vienna 25 June 1989.

2. Princess *Maria* Beatrice, *b* at Salzburg 11 Sept 1957,   Physiotherapist; *m* at Oberndorf 30 Aug 1981, Paul Lovrek (*b* at Salzburg 11 Jan 1954), Dipl Engineer, Vice-President Arbeiter Kammer, Salzburg, son of August Lovrek and Countess Aloisia Czernin von Chudenitz.
[*Ziegelstadelstraße 7b, 5026 Salzburg, Austria*].

Brothers and Sisters of Father

1. Princess *Anna* -Berta Zita Maria, *b* at Salzburg 4 Jan 1919; *m* at Maria Plain, nr Salzburg 8 Oct 1945, Hans Suchner (*b* at Ottmachau, Silisia 29 May 1917), Dr of Med, Med Director.
[*Stifsbogen 74, Apt 2084, 81375 Munich, Germany*].

2. Prince *Karl* Borromaus Ferdinand Zdenko Maria Josef Julius, *b* at Salzburg 10 April 1920, Manufacturer; ✝ at Starnberg 18 Jan 1998; *m* 1stly at Vienna 3 Nov 1944 (*m* diss by div at Salzburg 6 March 1952), Elisabeth (*b* at Rain, nr Klagenfurt 20 Sept 1924; ✝ at Cascais, Portugal 3 Oct 1995; *m* 2ndly at Munich 4 Sept 1956, Wilhelm, Count von Magnis), Interpreter, dau of Felix, Ritter von Gutmannsthal-Benvenuti, Proprietor of Rain and Hermine Krum, and has issue,

    1. Princess *Elisabeth*, *b* at Haidenburg, Bavaria 9 Aug 1945; *m* at Maria Bühel, Oberndorf 29 Dec 1979, Wolfgang von Schmieder (*b* at Munich 23 Nov 1939), Land Owner, Businessman.
    [*19 route de la Capite, 1223 Cologny, Switzerland*].

    2. Princess *Hedwig*, *b* at Seekirchen, nr Salzburg 9 Aug 1946; *m* at Forsbach, Cologne 31 Aug 1966, Alfred Neven Du Mont (*b* at Cologne 29 March 1927; ✝ at Keulen 28 Oct 1995).
    [*Am Kurtenwald 6, 51503 Forsbach, Bez. Cologne, Germany*].

    3. Prince *Franz* -Erasmus, *b* at Salzburg 22 June 1949, Television and Music Producer; *m* at Schlitz, Upper Hessen 1 July 1977, Christine (*b* at Fulda 23 March 1946), dau of Walter Zöller and Dorothea Becker, and has issue,
    [*Hauptstraße 98, 82327 Tutzing, Germany*].

      1. Princess *Anna, b* at Frankfurt-am-Main 25 July 1978.

      2. Prince Carl *Ferdinand, b* at Lauterbach 12 Aug 1982.

Prince Karl *m* 2ndly at London 8 April 1953, Penelope (*b* at Welham Hall 12 Aug 1925), dau of Captain Thomas George Gibson of Welham Hall and Mary Helen Craigh, and has further issue,

[*10 Carrer de La Pau, Palma de Mallorca, 07012 Spain*].

    4. Princes *Charles* Eduard Benedictus Maria, *b* at Colchester 22 Dec 1953, Businessman; *m* at Rösrath, Bez Cologne 3 Jan 1986, Denise Michaela (*b* at Heidenheim an der Brenz 26 June 1959), dau of Hans-Dieter and Ingeborg Lupp, and has issue,

[*Bergische Landstraße 57, 51503 Rösrath, Bez Cologne, Germany*].

      1. Princess *Vivienne* Katharina Leonessa Denise, *b* at Cologne 6 May 1987.

      2. Prince *Jérôme* Dominik Maurice Kai Charles, *b* at Cologne 13 July 1988.

    5. Prince *Georg* Alexander, *b* at Cologne 24 Aug 1955, Film and Television Producer; *m* at Grafing, nr Munich 26 July 1978, Neonila (Nora) (*b* at Munich 2 April 1951), dau of Wasilij Bazmanov and Irene Lapszhowa, and has issue,

[*Bensbergerstraße 134, 51503 Rösrath, Bez. Cologne, Germany*].

      1. Princess *Yolanda, b* at Munich 13 Oct 1977.

      2. Princess *Larissa, b* at Munich 25 Jan 1979.

      3. Prince *Andrey* Benedikt, *b* at Munich 1 Jan 1982.

      4. Prince *Nikolas, b* at Munich 16 Dec 1983.

3. Prince *Franz* -Josef Adam Vincenz Ludwig Maria, *b* at Salzburg 8 Aug 1921, Kt of Hon and Dev Sovereign Military Order of Malta, Dipl Engineer, Architect.

[*Dompfarre, Kapitalplatz, 5020 Salzburg, Austria*].

4. Prince *Georg-Christian* Karl Maria Joseph, *b* at Salzburg 11 Sept 1922, Kt of Hon and Dev Sovereign Military Order of Malta; *m* at Vienna 26 June 1955, Countess Eliane (*b* at Brussels 19 Jan 1927), dau of Ferdinand, Count du Chastel de la Howarderie and Blanche de Coëtnempren de Kersaint of the Counts de Coëtnempren de Kersaint, and has issue,

[*Gußhaußtraße 8, 1040 Vienna, Austria*].

      1. Princess *Zdenka* Maria Bianca Hedwig Franziska Ferdinada,

b at Vienna 7 Oct 1956; *m* at Vienna 25 April 1981, Ferdinand, Count von Orsini and Rosenberg (*b* at Klagenfurt 28 May 1953), Hotelier.

[*9131 Grafenstein, Carinthia, Austria*].

2. Princess *Elisabeth,* Maria Josefa Ghisliane, *b* at Vienna 27 Feb 1960; *m* at Vienna 27 Oct 1990, Andreas Lovrek (*b* at Salzburg 6 March 1958), Dr of Law.

[*Dr. Friedrich Oedl Weg 4, 5083 Gartenau-St. Leonhard, Austria*].

5. Princess *Maria* Perpetua Euphemia, *b* at Weitwörth 5 June 1929, Dame Star Cross Order; *m* at Weitwörth 16 July 1950, Heriprand (Ariprand), Count von Thurn and Valsassina-Como-Vercelli (*b* at Bleiburg 1 June 1925; ✠ at Klagenfurt 31 July 1996), Proprietor of Eisenkappel and Proprietor of Bleiburg, Dr rer pol.

[*Ziegelstadelstraße 1, 5026 Salzburg-Aigen, Austria*].

6. Prince *Johannes* von Nepomuk Alfred Josef Maria Franziskus Stefanus Rembertus, *b* at Weitwörth 29 Jan 1934, Prof of Music; *m* 1stly at Eisenkappen, Carinthia 16 July 1959 (*m* diss by div at Korneuburg 11 Aug 1971), Countess Irene [*Goldeg Gasse2, Atelier, 1040 Vienna, Austria*] (*b* at Birstein 7 March 1940; *m* 2ndly at Vienna 1 Sept 1972, Johann Heinrich, Baron von Tinti who ✠ at Pochlarn an der Donau 23 Dec 1986; that *m* diss by div 12 April 1985), dau of Georg, Count von Starhemberg and Princess Anna Agnes von Isenburg, and has issue,

    1. Prince *Vincenz,* *b* at Klagenfurt 17 July 1960, Dr of Med; *m* at Vienna 19 May 1990, Catherine (*b* at Vienna 4 March 1962), dau of Peter Feldscher and Countess Maria Theresia von Hartig, and has issue,

    [*Tillysburg, 4490 St. Florian, Austria*].

        1. Prince *Clemens* Ferdinand Johannes Peter Maria, *b* at Vienna 5 May 1991.

        2. Princess *Paula* Michaela Marie Therese Irene, *b* at Vienna 26 Sept 1992.

        3. Prince *Constantin* Georg Franz Josef Peter Anton Maria, *b* at Linz, Upper Austria 24 Nov 1993.

        4. Princess *Clara* Patricia Anna Carla Maria, *b* at Linz 2 Oct 1995.

    2. Princess *Marie Gabriele* Sophie Emanuela Margarita, *b* at Lisbon 7 June 1962; *m* at Würflach, Lower Austria 18 Sept 1983, Ludwig Soukup (*b* at Vienna 5 June 1960), Finance Manager.

[*Sternwartestraße 13-39, 1180 Vienna, Austria*].

3. Prince *Ferdinand* Eduard, *b* at Klagenfurt 21 Nov 1964, Hotelier; *m* at Vienna (civ) and at Perchtoldsdorf, Lower Austria 1 June (relig) 1991, Pia (*b* at Vienna 20 May 1968), dau of Gottfried Merckens and Monika Held, and has issue, [*Schirgenwald Allee 2, 2380 Perchtoldsdorf, Austria*].

    1. Princess *Philippa* Valerie Vera Maria, *b* at Vienna 15 Nov 1994.

    2. Princess *Cecilie* Maria Diletta Marietta, *b* at Vienna 27 May 1997.

4. Prince Wilhelm *Maximilian*, *b* at Klagenfurt 11 Oct 1968, Mag jur; *m* at Albisano, nr Garda, Verona 21 Sept 1996, Maddalena (*b* at Bussolengo, Prov Verona 31 Dec 1971), dau of Count Pieralberto degli Albertini da Prato and Countess Anna von Thun and Hohenstein.

[*Villa Albertini, 6 Via San Carlo, Garda, Prov. Verona, Italy*].

Prince Johannes *m* 2ndly at Salzburg 23 May 1972 (*m* diss by div Vienna 15 Nov 1976), Urdar [*Gregor Mendel-Straße 11-2-14, 2514 Traiskirchen, Austria*] (*b* at Berlin 30 Dec 1934; *m* 1stly at Lambach Austria 13 Aug (civ) and at Degerndorf, Bavaria 27 Aug (relig) 1960, Ulrich von Pott; that *m* diss by div at Wels 8 Sept 1970), dau of Jürgen von Bonin and Liess von Zerboni di Sposetti. He *m* 3rdly at Vienna 17 Feb (civ) 1976, Adelheid (*b* at Vienna 18 Nov 1941), dau of Erich Wellert and Marie Leopoldine Himmer, and by her has further issue,

[*Pötzleinsdorferstraße 77, 1180 Vienna, Austria*].

    5. Princess Agnes Berta, *b* at Vienna 19 March 1977.

    [*Esterházy Gasse10/6, 1060 Vienna, Austria*].

Brothers and Sister of Grandfather

Issue of Eduard, Prince von Auersperg (*b* 8 Jan 1863; ✚ 18 March 1956) and Princess Maria von Schönburg-Hartenstein (*b* 17 Dec 1861; *m* 6 June 1885; ✚ 25 Aug 1945), having had issue, among whom,

1. Prince *Eduard*, *b* at Weitwörth 7 April 1893; ✚ at Stainz, Styria 3 April 1948; *m* at Grafenstein, nr Grottau 4 Aug 1921, Countess Sophie (*b* at Horn, Lower Austria 9 June 1900; ✚ at Rekawinkel, nr Pressbaum 28 June 1980), Dame Star Cross Order, dau of Franz, Count von Clam and Gallas and Countess Maria Hoyos, Baroness zu

Stichsenstein, and had issue, among whom,

1. Princess *Marie Sophie* Leopoldine Elisabeth Clothilde, *b* at Friedland 15 Nov 1922; *m* at Vienna 26 May (relig) and Maria Plain, nr Salzburg 22 July (reig) 1951, *Hubert* Richard Johann, Baron von Doblhoff (*b* at Ctenice, nr Prague 30 July 1926), Dipl Engineer.
[*Marchettstraße 56, 2500 Baden, nr Vienna, Austria*].

2. Princess *Eleonore*, *b* at Friedland 29 Jan 1924, Nurse; *m* at Regina, Saskatchewan, Canada 28 Nov 1953, Forest Ernest Barber (*b* at Renssalaer, Indiana, USA 31 Dec 1922; ✝ at Florida 3 April 1992).
[*Dampfshiffstraße 12/1/1, 1030 Vienna, Austria*].

3. Prince *Herward* Franz, *b* at Friedland 11 Sept 1926; *m* 1stly at Salzburg 18 Sept 1948 (*m* diss by div 14 Jan 1970), Maria (*b* at Steinamanger 6 Jan 1930), dau of Koloman Tákach de Duka and Anna Marie Baly (of Hungarian nobility). He *m* 2ndly at Vienna 21 Nov 1970, Elke (*b* at Vienna 27 Dec 1943), dau of Eduard Langer and Ferdinanda Niedermoser, and has issue by his first wife,
[*Bräumühl Weg 37/6, 5101 Bergheim, nr Salzburg, Austria*].

1. Princess *Christiane* Maria Sophie, *b* at Weitwörth 2 Aug 1949; *m* at Vienna 11 Sept 1972, Christoph Ringler (*b* at Bozen 18 Feb 1945), Dipl Engineer.
[*Engerthstraße 221, 1020 Vienna, Austria*].

2. Prince *Herward* Eduard, *b* at Salzburg 18 June 1952; *m* at Vienna 7 Oct 1972 (*m* diss by div at Vienna 21 Jan 1982), Barbara (*b* at Vienna 18 April 1951), dau of Wilhelm Serenscy and Leonore Niedermeyer. He *m* 2ndly at Baden 10 June 1997, Gabriele Beatrix (*b* at Vienna 16 Nov 1953; *m* 1stly 14 Oct 1976, Hermann Singer; that *m* diss by div 30 April 1984, dau of Wolfgang Stieglitz and Margarete Teuschl, and has issue from his first wife,
[*Mommsen Gasse6, 1040 Vienna, Austria; Felsenstraße 24, 2761 Waidmannsfeld, Austria*].

1. Princess *Feodora* Aglaë, *b* at Vienna 30 June 1973; *m* at Carinthia 19 May 1997, Thomas Rebernig, who has taken the name "Rebernig-Auersperg" (*b* at Klagenfurt 1 Feb 1973).
[*Anton Störck Gasse84/1, 1210 Vienna,*

Austria].

2. Princess *Manora* Estella, *b* at Pernach, Carinthia 6 Feb 1977.

3. Princess Marie-*Alexandra*, *b* at Salzburg 11 Nov 1954; *m* at Dürnstein 9 July 1983, Ernst Gollner (*b* at Linz 15 Sept 1953).

[*4170 Haslach am Bach 1, Upper Austria, Austria*].

4. Princess Maria *Kinga* Aglaë, *b* at Vienna 31 Jan 1959; *m* at Dürnstein 12 July 1976 (*m* diss by div at Vienna 10 Dec 1983), Alexius Göschl (*b* at Vienna 16 Feb 1951), Dr rer soc oec. She *m* 2ndly at Vienna 20 Jan 1984, Otto Walter (*b* at Vienna 14 Jan 1923), Dr rer soc oec, Dipl Business.

[*Opernring 9, 1010 Vienna, Austria*].

5. Princess Marie *Charlotte* Andrea, *b* at Vienna 27 Sept 1960.

[*Mommsen Gasse 6, 1040 Vienna, Austria*].

4. Prince *Johannes* Weikardt, *b* at Friedland 30 Jan 1930, Kt of Hon and Dev Sovereign Military Order of Malta; *m* at Vancouver, Canada 30 May 1955, Baroness Nelly (*b* at Vienna 13 Dec 1928), Dr of Med and Phil, University Professor, dau of Viktor, Baron Gutmann de Gelse et Belisce and Luise Bloch-Bauer, and has issue,

[*3519 Point Grey Road, Vancouver, B.C., V6R 1A7, Canada*].

1. Princess *Maria* Elisabeth, *b* at Vancouver, Canada 27 Nov 1956; *m* at Vancouver 15 Aug 1981, David Harris (*b* at Newport, Wales 4 Nov 1954), Lawyer.

[*3212 W. 36th Avenue, Vancouver, B.C., V6N 2R6, Canada*].

2. Prince *Eduard* Viktor, *b* at Vancouver 29 July 1958, Dr of Med; *m* at Maple Ridge, British Columbia, Canada 14 Sept 1991, Nancy (*b* at Salmon Arm, British Columbia 16 Nov 1963), dau of Gordon Andrews and Jean Altmeyer, and has issue,

[*23970-130th Avenue, Maple Ridge, B.C. V2X 7E7, Canada*].

1. Prince *John* Gordon, *b* at Maple Ridge 4 May 1993.

2. Prince *Steven* Victor, *b* at Maple Ridge 20 June 1995.

3. Princess *Natalie* Christine, *b* at Maple Ridge

10 Jan 1997.

5. Princess *Clotilde* Maria Formosa, *b* at Friedland 4 Aug 1931, Dame Star Cross Order.
[*Via Santa Margherita a Montici 52, 50125 Florence, Italy*].

6. Prince *Franz* Karl Maria Formosa, *b* at Haindorf 26 July 1935, Kt Sovereign Military Order of Malta.
[*Rainer Gasse24/1/7, 1040 Vienna, Austria*].

7. Prince *Anton* Franz Pankraz, *b* at Haindorf 12 Jan 1938, ✠ 17 Dec 2000; *m* at Vienna 5 Sept (civ) and 24 Sept (relig) 1966 (*m* diss by div at Munich 9 Dec 1968), Erika (*b* at Northeim, Hanover 22 Aug 1946; *m* 2ndly at Fürstenfeldbruck, Bavaria 28 Feb/7 March 1970, Arved von Oettingen; that *m* diss by div at Passau 20 Feb 1975; she has since reverted to her maiden name), dau of Otto von Scheven and Margarete Merlin de Douai, and has issue,
[*Rainer Gasse24/1/7, 1040 Vienna, Austria; Burgerspital Gasse1, 1060 Vienna, Austria*].

    1. Princess *Stephanie* Eva-Maria Margarete Sophie, *b* at Munich 3 Aug 1967; *m* at Ingolstad 22 Aug (civ) and at Neuburg an der Donau 3 Sept (relig) 1994, Philipp, Count von Waldstein-Wartenberg (*b* at Munich 13 July 1965), Dr of Med.
    [*Ismanigerstraße 82, 81675 Munich, Germany*].

2. Prince *Alois* Maria Joseph Alexander, *b* at Weitworth 26 Oct 1897; ✠ at Salzburg 6 Sept 1984, Dr of Law, Major; *m* at Salzburg 25 Feb 1933, Countess Henriette (*b* at Bucharest 1 Jan 1903; ✠ at Glanegg 20 Nov 1994; *m* 1stly at Vienna 17 Oct 1922, Johannes, 5th Prince (Fürst) von Orsini and Rosenberg who ✠ at Vienna 7 Feb 1932), dau of Friedrich, Count Larisch von Moennich, Proprietor of Schönhof, Near Mährisch-Ostrau and Countess Marie von Beroldingen, and had issue,

    1. Princess *Henriette, b* at St Johann im Pongau 2 Sept 1933; *m* at Werfen, nr Salzburg 1 Feb (civ) and at Blühnbach, nr Salzburg 14 Feb (relig) 1969, Arndt von Bohlen and Halbach (*b* at Berlin-Charlottenburg 24 Jan 1938; ✠ at Munich 8 May 1986), Businessman.
    [*Haus Nagele, Im Jodelfeld 5, 6370 Kitzbühel, Austria*].

2. Prince *Alfred* Eduard Friedrich Vincenz Martin Maria, *b* at Salzburg 20 July 1936; ✠ at Salzburg 19 June 1992; *m* 1stly at Gotham, USA 20 July 1957 (*m* diss by div), Martha (*b* at Menassis, Virginia, USA 1 Sept 1931; *m* 2ndly at New

York 6 June 1966, Claus Borberg, adopted von Bülow), dau of
George W Crawford and Annie Laurie Warmack, and has
issue,
[*1215 Fifty Avenue, New York, N.Y. 10029 U.S.A.*].

> 1. Princess *Annie-Laurie* Henriette, *b* at Munich 11
> March 1958; *m* 1stly at Salzburg 31 May 1980 (*m* diss
> by div 1988), Franz Kneissl (*b* at Kufstein 2 May
> 1956), Industrialist; *m* 2ndly at New York 9 June 1989,
> Ralph Heyward Isham (*b* at Moscow 17 April 1956),
> Banker.
> [*1215 Fifty Avenue, New York, N.Y. 10029 U.S.A.*].
> 2. Prince *Alexander* Anton Johannes Georg Maria,
> *b* at New York 13 June 1959; *m* at New York 9 June
> 1995, Nancy Louise (*b* at New York 11 June 1959), dau
> of Jerrold G and Marcia Weinberg, and has issue,
> > [*829 Park Avenue, New York, N.Y. 10021, U.S.A.*].
> > 1. Princess *Anna* Sharp, *b* at New York 17 Nov
> > 1995.

Prince Alfred *m* 2ndly at Vienna 3 Oct 1968 (*m* diss by div
1979), Hannelore Auer (*b* East Prussia; *m* 2ndly at Bad
Münstereifel 3 April 1979, Heinz-Georg Kramm, the singer
"Heino"), Actress, Model. He *m* 3rdly at Nairobi, Kenya 23
March 1979, (Noble) Beatrice Kyd (*b* at Graz 4 Aug 1950),
dau of Ludwig Eugen Kyd, Edler von Rebenburg and Edle
Isolde von Mack, and by her has further issue,
[*Casa Watatu, Marbella Hill Club, Marbella, Prov. Malaga,
Spain*].

> 3. Princess *Cécile, b* at Graz 3 May 1980.

3. Prince *Luitpold* Aloisius Eduard Friedrich Heinrich Maria,
b at Salzburg 6 Nov 1937; ✠ at Asunción, Paraguay 2 June
1985; *m* at Osorno, Chile June 1961, Lilian Susy (*b* at Osorno,
Chile 25 March 1938; ✠ at Conception, Chile 19 Oct 1986),
dau of Wilhelm Feltes and Frida Amalie Schmidt, and has
issue,

> 1. Prince *Andreas* Alois Wilhelm, *b* at Osorno, Chile 2
> Jan 1962; *m* at Osorno, Chile 10 Oct 1987, Marlene
> Beatrix Ruiz (*b* at Osorno, Chile ...), dau of Carlos
> Ruiz and Gloria Binder, and has issue,
> [*Manuel Rodriguez 815, Dept 203, Osorno, Chile*].
> > 1. Princess *Stephanie* Marlene, *b* at Osorno,
> > Chile 19 Sept 1988.

2. Prince *Christopher* Andreas, *b* at Osorno, Chile 10 Feb 1990.

3. Prince *Alfred* Johann Maria Anton Rupert, *b* at Weitworth 26 Sept 1899; ✠ at Hamburg 10 Sept 1968, Dr of Med, Prof of Psychiatry Univ of Concepción, Chile; *m* 1stly at Vienna 2 July 1927 (*m* diss by div Mexico 16 April 1947), Countess Martha (*b* at Kitzbühel 1 Dec 1889; ✠ at Innsbruck 21 Aug 1970; *m* 1stly at Bruneck 9 June 1917, Anton, Count von Thurn-Valsassina and Taxis; that *m* diss by div 26 May 1922 and annulled at Rome 25 Feb 1927), dau of Marcus Matz, Count von Spiegelfeld, Baron von Spiegelfeld and Baroness Albertine Tschiderer von Gleifheim. He *m* 2ndly at Mexico 17 Aug 1947, Ingeborg (*b* at Wandsbek 18 March 1913; ✠ at Mainz 28 June 1996; *m* 1stly at Vienna 26 Aug 1937, Rudolf (Raoul) Käuffler; that *m* diss by div 6 May 1940 and annulled at Munich 1958), Dr of Med, dau of Richard von Hardt, Proprietor of Wonsowo in Posen and Else von Bülow, and had issue by his second wife,

1. Princess *Andrea* Isabel Franziska, *b* at Vienna 23 Oct 1943; ✠ at Montevideo, Uruguay 26 Dec 1991; *m* 1stly at Trysa, Kassel 23 Aug (civ) and at Willingshausen, nr Treysa 28 Aug (relig) 1965 (*m* diss by div at Marburg 1976), Alexander von Schwertzell zu Willingshausen, Proprietor of Rommershausen (*b* at Rommershausen, nr Treysa 26 June 1938). She *m* 2ndly at Asunción, Paraguay 26 Oct 1977, Walter Restuccia Aramberi (*b* at Paso del Toro, Uruguay 23 April 1923), Architect.

[*Casilla 53-0-23, Punta del Este, Uruguay*].

2. Prince *Alfred* Reimar Eduard, *b* at São Paulo, Brazil 7 April 1948; *m* at Weil im Schönbuch 9 July 1982, Jutta (*b* at Mannheim 22 November 1942; *m* 1stly at Mannheim 16 October 1964, Eberhard Winkler; that *m* diss by div at Mannheim 1976), dau of Hermann-Otto Ahrend and Irmgard Johanna Schöntaube.

[*Schopfheimerstraße 22, 68239 Mannheim, Germany*].

3. Prince *Johannes* Alexander Aloys, *b* at São Paulo 18 July 1949; *m* at London 8 Jan 1979, Claudia (*b* at Paris 2 April 1952), dau of Nils Nilson and Alexandra Moskalenko (Moissy), and has issue,

[*27 Rivercourt Road, London W6 9FT*].

1. Prince *Alexander* Felix Nils Alfred, *b* at London 11 Sept 1980.

2. Prince *Maximilian* Anthony, *b* at London 8 Nov

1983.

Brother of the Prince's Great-Grandfather

Issue of Vincenz, Prince von Auersperg (*b* 15 July 1812; ✝ 7 July 1867) and Countess Wilhelmine von Colloredo-Mannsfeld (*b* 16 July 1826; *m* 29 April 1845; ✝ 19 Dec 1898), having had issue, among whom,

Son

Prince *Engelbert-Ferdinand* Maria, *b* at Vienna 21 Feb 1859; ✝ at Schloß Luhsa, nr Pystian 18 July 1942; *m* at Prague 27 Aug 1883, Princess Gabriele (*b* at Vienna 21 Oct 1862; ✝ at Prague 2 Sept 1948), dau of Prince Ludwig zu Hohenlohe-Langenburg, and had issue,

Son

Prince Karl *Hieronymus* Vincenz Maria, *b* at Grunberg, Lower Austria 30 Sept 1892; ✝*k* in an air raid over Nuremberg 20 Oct 1944); *m* at Budapest 4 May 1918, Countess Klementine (*b* at Zabola 30 Jan 1897; ✝ at Stein, nr Fehring 5 Sept 1984), dau of Armin, Count Mikes von Zabola and Countess Klementine Bethlen de Bethlen, and had issue, among whom,

> 1. Princess *Wilhelmine* Maria Sieglinde, *b* at Vienna 29 June 1921; *m* at Vienna 6 Nov 1950, Arnold, Count von Keyserling (*b* at Schloß Friedrichsruh 9 Feb 1922), Prof of Philosophy Vienna School of the Applied Arts.
> [*Heumarkt 7/11, 1030 Vienna, Austria*].
> 2. Princess *Margarethe* Maria Sigune, *b* at Vienna 26 Jan 1926; *m* at Sprechenstein Tyrol, 22 Sept 1955, Piero Luigi Brandini (*b* at Castelfiorentini 24 June 1919 ✝ at Castelfiorentini 7 Feb 1990).
> [*Via Alessandro Scarlatti 8, 50144 Florence, Italy*].

------◆------

BENTHEIM
(HOUSE OF GÖTTERSWICK)

Reformist: Otto (yr son of Hermann, 1st Count of Salm, King of Germany 1081 - 88; ✝ 1088), was 1st Count of Bentheim. His dau and eventual heiress, Sophia (✝ 1176) *m* Dirk VI, Count of Holland (✝

1157) and their second son, Otto III (I), Viscount of Utrecht, *succ* as 4th Count of Bentheim. Hedwig, dau of John, 8th Count, *m* Eberwin de Güterswyk (✠ circa 1370) from a Rhineland family tracing its descent from Évervinus de Gotterswich (Gotterswich), living in 1191; Evervinus nobilis vir de Gotirsvich 22 April 1256; Lord of Steinfurt (see Line II) 1421 and 1432; family pact between Bentheim and Steinfurt 19 March 1487; Lord of Wevelinghoven 1492 and 1513 through the marriage of Count Arnould of Bentheim-Steinfurt to Catherine of Gemen; Count of Steinfurt, Worms 26 April 1495 (for Everwyn II, Count of Bentheim and Lord of Steinfurt); acquired the County of Tecklenburg (Münster, County of Tekeneburg 1129), and of Rhéda (see below) through the marriage (13 Feb 1553) of Éverwyn III, Count of Bentheim (*b* 1536; ✠ 19 Feb 1562) to Anne, Countess of Tecklenburg of the House of Schwerin (*b* 5 July 1532; ✠ 23 Aug 1582); acquired the bailliages of Hoya (see below), Ucht and Freudenberg 1583 through a family pact between Tecklenburg and Hesse-Cassel 20 April 1575; succeeded to the lands of Neuenahr (Count of Hohen-Limburg, Lordships of Helpenstein, Lennep, Alpen, bailliage of Cologne) 1589 and 1602 through the marriage (1573) of Arnould II, Count of Bentheim (*b* 11 Oct 1554; ✠ 11 Jan 1606) to Magdalena, Countess of Neuenahr (*b* 1548; ✠ 23 Dec 1626); partition of lands 27 Oct 1609 between the sons of Arnold II, Count of Bentheim-Tecklenburg, Steinfurt and Limburg, Lord of Rheda, two of whom founded the lines below.

LINE I: BENTHEIM-TECKLENBURG

Founded by Adolf, Count of Tecklenburg-Rhéda (*b* 17 July 1577; ✠ 5 Nov 1623); Hereditary Bailiff of Cologne 1602; the county of Tecklenburg was ceded to Prussia in 1729; received the Prussian title of Prince of Bentheim with the qualfication of "Durchlaucht" for all descendants, Berlin 20 June 1817; Hereditary Member of the former Prussian House of Lords 12 Oct 1854.
Members of this Line bear the title of Prince or Princess zu Bentheim-Tecklenburg with the qualification of Serene Highness.

MORITZ-CASIMIR Widukind Gumprecht, **6TH PRINCE (FÜRST) ZU BENTHEIM-TECKLENBURG,** Count of Tecklenburg and Limburg, Lord of Rheda, Wevelinghofen, Hoya, Alpen and Helpenstein, Hereditary Bailiff of Cologne, *b* at Rheda 19 Oct 1923, son of Adolf, 5th Prince (Fürst) zu Bentheim-Tecklenburg (*b* 29 June 1889; ✠ 4 Jan 1967) and Princess Amélie von Schönburg-Waldenburg (*b* 27 April 1902; *m* 26 July 1922; ✠ 19 March 1995); *m* at Rheda 26 July 1958, Countess Huberta (*b* at Duivelskloof 28 Feb 1932), dau of Dietrich-Werner, Count von Hardenberg and Baroness Ingeborg Rüdt von Collenberg, adopted dau of Heinrich, Count von Hardenberg and Alice-Louise du Pasquier.

[*Schloß Rheda, 33378 Rheda-Wiedenbrück, Germany*].

Sons

1. *Carl-Gustav* Moritz-Casimir, Hereditary Prince (Erbprinz) zu
Bentheim-Tecklenburg, *b* at Herford 2 June 1960.
[*Warendorferstraße 152b, 48145 Münster, Germany*].

2. Prince *Philipp* Adolf Moritz-Casimir, *b* at Rheda 15 June 1964.
[*Carlmeyerstraße 9, 33613 Bielefeld-Braunheide*].

3. Prince *Christoph* Heinrich Moritz-Casimir, *b* at Rheda 29 May
1966; ✠ at Plön 1 July 1987.

4. Prince *Maximilian* Nicolaus Moritz-Casimir, *b* at Rheda 6 Aug
1969; *m* at Rheda-Wiedenbrück 12 Sept (civ) and at Schloß Rehda
30 Sept (relig) 2000, Marissa Clare (*b* 20 Oct 1973), dau of the Hon
Seymour Fortescue, of the earls Fortescue, and Julia Pilcher.
[*Otto Nagelstraße 4, 14467 Potsdam, Germany*].

Brothers and Sister

1. Prince *Nikolaus* Moritz Casimir, *b* at Rheda 12 March 1925, Painter,
Graphic Artist; *m* at Werenwag, Baden 15 Sept 1951, Countess
Franziska (*b* at Hohenthurm 28 Sept 1921), dau of Friedrich, Count
Hoyos, Baron von Stichsenstein and Wilhelmine von Wuthenau.
[*Kloster Herzebrock, 33442 Herzebrock-Clarholz, Germany*].

2. Princess *Gustava*, *b* at Rheda 21 Oct 1929; *m* at Rheda 14 Oct
1952, Botho, Count von Hohenthal (*b* at Wurzen 9 July 1926),
Businessman, Kt of St John of Jerusalem.
[*Ulrich von Hassellstraße 21, 82067 Ebenhausen, Isartal, Germany*].

3. Prince *Heinrich* Karl Moritz Casimir, *b* at Rheda 1 Feb 1940; *m* at
Düsseldorf 3 April 1979 (*m* diss by div 1 June 1990), Annick Suzanne
(*b* at Boulogne 5 March 1945), dau of Jean Julien Louis Gagnaire and
Colette Vouaux, and has issue,
[*Hüttenstraße 32, 40215 Düsseldorf, Germany; Pixelerstraße 4,
33378 Rheda-Wiedenbrück, Germany*].

 1. Prince *Cédric* Karl Moritz Casimir, *b* at Antibes 26 Nov
 1978.

 2. Princess *Amélie* Aline Tatjana Yveline, *b* at Rheda 10 Dec
 1982.

LINE II: BENTHEIM and STEINFURT

Founded by Arnold-Jobst, Count of Bentheim-Bentheim (*b* 4 April
1580; ✠ 10 Feb 1643); Hereditary Bailiff of Cologne 28 Nov 1778;
Prussian title of Prince of Bentheim with the qualification of
"Durchlaucht" for all descendants, Berlin 21 Jan 1817; Hereditary
Member of the former Prussian House of Lords 12 Oct 1854;

Hereditary Member of the former House of Lords of Württemberg 11 Feb 1875; Prussian title of Prince of Bentheim and Steinfurt for Alexis, 4th Prince Hubertusstock 6 Oct 1895.
Members of this Line bear the title of Prince or Princess zu Bentheim and Steinfurt with the qualification of Serene Highness.

CHRISTIAN Max Gustav Albrecht, **6TH PRINCE (FÜRST) ZU BENTHEIM** and **3RD PRINCE ZU BENTHEIM AND STEINFURT,** Count zu Tecklenburg and Limburg, Lord of Rheda, Wevelinghofen, Hoya, Alpen and Helpenstein, Hereditary Bailiff of Cologne, *b* at Burgsteinfurt 9 Dec 1923, Major German Airforce (Res), Kt of Justice St John of Jerusalem, son of Viktor Adolf, 5th Prince (Fürst) zu Bentheim and 2nd Prince zu Bentheim and Steinfurt (*b* 18 July 1883; ✠ 4 June 1961) and Princess Stephanie zu Schaumburg-Lippe (*b* 19 Dec 1899, *m* 9 Sept 1921; ✠ 2 May 1925); *m* at Burgsteinfurt 7 Aug 1950, Sylvia (*b* at Burkersdorf 16 May 1930), dau of Sylvius, Count von Pückler, Baron von Groditz, Proprietor of Oberweistritz and Burkersdorf in Schweidnitz, Silesia, and Baroness Alix von Richthofen, and has two adopted daughters and his nephew,
[*Schloß Burgsteinfurt, 48565 Steinfurt, Westphalia, Germany*].

Son and Daughters

1. Princess *Caroline* Marie-Louise Charlotte, *b* at Langenfeld 29 Jan 1966, adopted at Scheinfeld 10 Oct 1967 and at Burgsteinfurt 10 Jan 1968, bears the name and title of "Princess zu Bentheim and Steinfurt"; *m* at Steinfurt 7 June (civ) and 8 June (relig) 1996, Baron Friedrich von Weichs zur Wenne (*b* at Eslohe 10 Sept 1966).
2. Princess *Alexa* Rose-Marie Theda Pya, *b* at Munich 19 Aug 1968, adopted at Burgsteinfurt 22 March/19 Aug 1971, bears the name and title of "Princess zu Bentheim and Steinfurt"; *m* at ... 1992, Bernd Engels.
3. Prince Carl *Ferdinand,* *b* at Rheine 5 Oct 1977, son of Prince Reinhard zu Bentheim and Steinfurt and his wife, Angelica Emmermann (see below), adopted at Münster 11 April 1989, and at Nordhorn 13 March 1992,

Brother

1. *Alexis* Friedrich Carl Christian, Hereditary Prince (Erbprinz) zu Bentheim and Steinfurt, *b* at Burgsteinfurt 30 July 1922; ✠*k* in action over the Mediterranean 2 Dec 1943, Kt Expect Teutonic Order.

Half-Brothers and Sisters

Issue of Victor Adolf, 5th Prince zu Bentheim and Steinfurt and his second wife, Princess Rosa-Helene zu Solms-Hohensolms-Lich (*b* 14 Aug 1901; *m* 30 June 1931; ✠ 14 April 1963).

1. Princess *Juliane* Henriette Eleonore, *b* at Münster, Westphalia 22 Dec 1932, Kindergarten Principal.
[*Schloß Burgsteinfurt, 48565 Steinfurt, Westphalia, Germany*].

2. Prince *Reinhard* Georg, *b* at Münster 27 March 1934, Kt of Honour of St John of Jerusalem; *m* at Hamburg-Altona 22 Aug (civ) and at Steinfurt 30 Aug (relig) 1975, Angelica (*b* at Perleberg 31 Aug 1944), dau of Heinz Emmermann and Johanna Ermlich, and has issue,
[*Schloß Bentheim, 48455 Bad Bentheim, Germany*].

     1. Prince Carl *Ferdinand*, *b* at Rheine 5 Oct 1977, adopted by his uncle (see above).

     2. Princess *Johanna* Charlotte, *b* at Rheine 5 Oct 1977 (twin with Prince Ferdinand).

     3. Prince *Christoph* Peter, *b* at Rheine 17 Nov 1978.

     4. Princess *Aleida* Elisabeth, *b* at Rheine 24 Oct 1980.

3. Princess *Marie-Adelheid*, *b* at Münster 14 April 1935; *m* at Burgsteinfurt 30 Dec 1965, István (Stefan) von Beliczey de Baicza (*b* at Budapest 10 Nov 1936), Dipl Engineer.
[*Mörikestraße 2, 51429 Bergisch-Gladbach - Herkenrath, Germany*].

4. Princess *Charlotte* Elisabeth, *b* at Münster 3 July 1936; *m* at Burgsteinfurt 23 May 1964, Wolfgang Winkhaus (*b* at Münster 11 May 1929), Manufacturer.
[*Bockhorner Heide 46, 48291 Telgte, Kr. Warendorf, Germany*].

5. Prince *Ferdinand* Ludwig Franz, *b* at Münster 13 Aug 1938, Dr rer nat; *m* at Burgsteinfurt 29 Dec 1970 (civ) and at Mons, Belgium 10 Jan (relig) 1971, Leonie (*b* at Esslingen 24 Oct 1946), dau of Wolfgang Keller and Christa Corvinus, and has issue,
[*Hennesenbergstraße 32, 53332 Bornheim, Germany*].

     1. Princess *Christiane* Margarete, *b* at Bonn 25 April 1974; *m* at Burgsteinfurt 19 May 2001, Christian Bolz (*b* at ......).

     2. Prince Alexis Matthias, *b* at Bonn 31 July 1971; ✠ at Vejle, Denmark 10 Aug 1975.

     3. Princess *Friederike* Charlotte, *b* at Bonn 23 Aug 1976.

6. Prince *Otto-Victor,* *b* at Münster 24 July 1940, Lawyer, Kt of Hon St John of Jerusalem.
[*Preusserstraße 20, 06217 Merseburg, Germany*].

7. Prince *Oskar* Arnold, *b* at Burgsteinfurt 8 March 1946, Archivist,

Museum Director; *m* at Linz am Rhein 16 July (civ) and at
Burgsteinfurt 16 Aug (relig) 1980, Margot (*b* at Bonn 29 Aug 1938),
dau of Alfred Lücke and Ria Eilfgang.
[*Kommende 51a, 48565 Steinfurt, Westphalia, Germany*].

Brothers of Father

Issue of Alexis, 4th Prince zu Bentheim and Steinfurt (*b* 17 Nov
1845; ✠ 21 Jan 1919) and Princess Pauline zu Waldeck and Pyrmont
(*b* 19 Oct 1855; *m* 7 May 1881; ✠ 3 July 1925), having had issue,
among whom,

Son

Prince *Karl* Georg, *b* at Bentheim 10 Dec 1884; ✠ at Münster 14
Feb 1951, Col German Airforce; *m* at Haseldorf, Holstein 24 July
1914, Princess Margarete (*b* at Davos-Dorf 5 June 1888; ✠ at
Burgsteinfurt 18 April 1980), dau of Emil, Prince von Schoenaich-
Carolath-Schilden, Proprietor of Haseldorf and Katharina von
Knorring, and had issue, among whom,

    1. Prince *Manfred* Alexander Josias Ludwig Friedrich
Sieghard, *b* at Burgsteinfurt 31 July 1918; ✠ at Jesteburg 18
Dec 1985, Banker, First Lt German Army; *m* 1stly at
Stockholm 1 Sept 1953 (*m* diss by div at Hamburg 10 Feb
1956), Karin [*Kararinenstraße 7, 81479 Munich, Germany*]
(*b* at Cologne 6 July 1929), dau of Wilhelm von   Grumme-
Douglas and Annabel von Arnim. He *m* 2udly at Hamburg 22
Oct 1957, Irene [*Lüllau 10, 21266 Jesteburg, Nordheide,
Germany*] (*b* at Hamburg 2 June 1931), dau of Kurt-Victor
von Sydow and Irmgard Christoph.

    2. Prince *Hubertus* Friedrich Gustav Leopold Johann Georg
Christian-Ernst, *b* at Ilsenburg 26 Oct 1919, Lt.-Col. German
Airforce; *m* at Haseldorf 6 Aug 1957, Eva Luise (*b* at Jena 20
Oct 1925), dau of Artur Wagner and Elise Hühn, and has
issue,
[*Schloß Bentheim, 48455 Bad Bentheim, Germany*].

        1. Prince *Rudolf* Alexander Botho Georg Manfred
Christian, *b* at Oldenburg 28 April 1959, Dipl Pedag.
[*Schloß Bentheim, 48455 Bad Bentheim, Germany*].
        2. Princess *Huberta* Sylvia Juliane Maria Irene
Dorothea Gerda Luise, *b* at Oldenburg 19 June 1961;
m at Berlin 29 June (civ) and at Bad Bentheim 7 Oct

(relig) 1995, Ulrich Deuse (*b* at Korbach 15 Dec 1961), Dr.

[*Kösterstraße 2, 14165, Berlin, Germany*].

3. Prince *Nikolaus* Friedrich-Christian Karl Reinhard Peter, *b* at Oldenburg 3 Oct 1962, Dr of Medicine; *m* at Burg Bentheim 31 Aug 2001, N Taufighi-Chirazi (*b* at …), dau of …

[*Feurigstraße 56, 10827 Berlin, Germany*].

4. Prince *Botho* Alexander Adolf, *b* at Ilsenburg 29 June 1924; ✝ at Arolsen 9 Jun 2001, Lt-Col German Army; *m* at Arolsen 28 June 1949, Princess Alexandra (*b* at Rastede 25 Sept 1924), dau of Josias, Prince (Fürst) zu Waldeck and Pyrmont and Duchess Altburg of Oldenburg, and had issue,

[*Rauchstraße 25, 34454 Arolsen, Germany*].

1. Prince *Georg-Victor* Karl Josias, *b* at Münster 30 March 1950, Banker, Stockbroker; *m* at Kreuth am Tegernsee 23 Nov 1984 (civ) and 16 March 1985 (relig), Madeleine-Rose (*b* at Skien, Norway 10 Oct 1945), dau of Bernd Arnold Gerdes and Elisabeth Schmidt, and has issue,

[*Jagdhaus Schmerbachgrund 8, 83707 Bad Wiessee, Germany*].

1. Prince *Maximilian* Bernd Botho Wolfgang Reiner Paul Enrique Antony, *b* at Munich 1 May 1986.

2. Prince *Wolfgang* Manfred Friedrich Christian, *b* at Arolsen 17 Feb 1952; *m* at Vienna 28 Nov 1994, Karin (*b* at Vienna 10 Sept 1962), dau of .. and Elfriede Moser, and has issue,

[*Mittermayer Gasse6/1, 1130 Vienna, Austria*].

1. Prince *Benedikt* Botho Georg-Viktor Ferdinand Sandor, *b* at Vienna 12 May 1995.

BENTINCK

Reformist: This feudal family originated in Gelderland, documented since 1304 in the person of Wennemer Bentinck (the Seigneurial Manor near Gorssel, Gelderland bears the same name); this branch descends from Henric Benthinck who was invested with the fiefdom of Arensberg, near Heerde in 1400; admitted to the Knights of

Gelderland 1377. The Hon William Bentinck (*b* 6 Nov 1704; ✣ 13 Oct 1774), second son of the Earl of Portland and brother of the 1st Duke of Portland (see Part III) was created a Count of the Holy Empire, Vienna 29 Dec 1732; acquired the Lordships of Knyphausen and Varel through his marriage to Charlotte-Sophie, Countess of Aldenburg (*b* 4 Aug 1715; *m* 1 June 1733; ✣ 5 Feb 1800); received the qualification of "Erlaucht" (primogeniture) by the German Diet 12 Aug 1845; the above-mentioned Lordships were reunited with the Crown of Oldenburg 1854; British recognition of the title of Count 22 March 1886 (ends with Henry, 10th Count Bentinck, etc., 11th Earl of Portland); inherited the Lordship of Waldeck-Limpurg in Württemberg; Hereditary Member of the former House of Lords of Württemberg, 18 Dec 1888; authorised by the Prince of Waldeck to join the name and arms of Waldeck 18 Sept 1889.

Members of the family bear the title of Count or Countess of Bentinck with the qualification of Illustrious Highness. The validity of the Royal Licence to use the title of Count or Countess in England ended with the 10th Count of Bentinck and Waldeck-Limpurg.

TIMOTHY Charles Robert Noel, **11TH COUNT BENTINCK and WALDECK-LIMPURG,** Count of Aldenburg, *b* at Barton, Campbellstown, Tasmania 1 June 1953, Actor, son of Henry, 10th Count of Bentinck and Waldeck-Limpurg, 12th Earl of Portland, Viscount Woodstock, Baron Cirencester, (*b* 2 Oct 1919; ✣ Jan 1997) and Pauline Mellowes (*b* 15 Oct 1921; ✣ 10 Jan 1967); *m* at London 8 Sept 1979, Judith Ann (*b* at Newcastle-under-Lyme 10 Oct 1952), dau of John Robert Emerson and Mary Elizabeth Graham.
[*3 Stock Orchard Crescent, Islington, London N7 9SL*].

Sons

1. The Hon *William Jack* Henry, Viscount Woodstock *b* at London 19 May 1984.
2. The Hon *Jasper* James Mellowes, *b* at London 12 June 1988.

Step Mother

Jenifer Countess of Bentinck and Waldeck-Limpurg, Countess of Portland, *b* at London 13 May 1936, dau of Reginald Hopkins and Nancy Paige; *m* at Nettleden 23 Feb 1974, as his 2nd wife, Henry, 10th Count of Bentinck and Waldeck-Limpurg, 11th Earl of Portland, Viscount Woodstock, Baron Cirencester, (*b* at London 2 Oct 1919; ✣ at London Jan 1997); The last of the line entitled to use, under Royal Licence, the title of Count or Countess of Bentinck and

Waldeck-Limpurg in England; Lt Coldstream Guards (Ret),wounded twice in action (WWII - and prisoner-of-war); former cowboy in California; Producer BBC (Ret), jackaroo sheep station Tasmania (1952-55); author: *Anyone Can Understand the Atom* (1965); *The Avenue of Flutes* (1966); *Iswong* (1971); *Countdown at Woomera* (1961); advertising executive.

Sisters

1. Lady *Sorrel* Deirdre, *b* at Selbourne, Hants 22 Feb 1942, Businesswoman; *m* at Nettleden 24 June 1972 (*m* diss by div 1988), Sir John Philip Lister-Kaye, 8th Baronet (*b* at Wakefield, Yorks 8 May 1946).
[*18 Rankeillor Street, Edinburgh EH8 9HZ, Scotland*].

2. Lady *Anna* Cecilia, *b* at Selbourne 18 May 1947, Actress; *m* 1stly at Berkhamstead 24 July 1965 (*m* diss by div 1974), Jasper Hamilton Holmes (*b* at Hartford, nr Northwich, Cheshire 14 Nov 1943). She *m* 2ndly at Islington 19 July 1975 (*m* diss by div 1977), Nicholas George Spafford Vester (*b* at Cambridge 30 March 1944).
[*64 Croftdown Road, London NW5*].

Sister of Father

Countess *Brydgitte* Blanche, *b* at Bristol 11 Nov 1916; *m* at London 2 Feb 1937, Jonkheer Adriaan van der Wyck (*b* at The Hague 22 June 1906; ✠ at Haren 4 Nov 1973).
[*Rijksstraatweg 242, Haren, Prov. Groningen, The Netherlands*].

Brothers of Great-Grandfather

Issue of Charles Aldenburg-Bentinck, 4th Count of Bentinck (*b* 4 March 1792; ✠ 28 Oct 1864) and Countess Mechtilde of Waldeck-Pyrmont (*b* 23 June 1826; *m* 30 Jan 1846; ✠ 28 Feb 1899), having had issue, among whom,

Son

1. **William** Charles Philipp Otto, **6th Count van Bentinck and Waldeck-Limpurg-Gaildorf,** Count von Aldenburg, Lord of Gaildorf, *succ* his brother, Henry, 5th Count (Grandfather of the present Head - *b* 30 Oct 1846; ✠ 18 March 1903; ceded the Headship of the Family to his brother 30 Nov 1874), *succ* his mother as Lord of Middachten, Obdam and Weldam, *b* at Frankfurt-am-Main 28 Nov 1848; ✠ at Middachten 2 Nov 1912, Kt Commander Teutonic Order, Kt of Justice St John of Jerusalem, Kt Gd Cross Order of the Red Eagle; *m* at Kasteel Twickel, Overijssel 8 March 1877, Baroness

Maria Cornelia (*b* at The Hague 13 Jan 1855; ✠ there 13 Sept 1912), Lady of Twickel, Weldam, Obdam, Olidam, Wegdam, Spierdijk, Hensbroek, Zipe, Wogmeer and Kernheim, dau of Jakob Derek Carel, Baron von Heeckeren van Wassanaer, Lord of Twickel and Baroness Isabella Antoinetta Sloet van Toutenborg, and had issue, among whom,

> 1. **Willem** Frederik Carel Hendrik, **7th Count van Bentinck and Waldeck-Limpurg-Gaildorf**, etc, *b* at London 22 June 1880, ✠ at Stuttgart 29 Dec 1958, Capt Prussian Army, sometime Imperial German Attaché in London, Kt and Land Commander of the Teutonic Order, Kt of St John of Jerusalem; *m* at Salzburg 27 Aug 1923, Baroness Adrienne (*b* at Wassanaer 12 April 1891; ✠ at Gaildorf 9 Oct 1982; *m* 1stly, René Labouchere; that *m* diss by div), dau of Baron Philips Ernst Vegelin van Claerbergen and Baroness Albertine Marie van Hangest d'Yvoy, and had issue,

>> 1. Countess *Sophie* Mechtild Marie, *b* at Middachten 10 June 1924; *m* at Schloß Pommersfelden 29 Nov 1950 (*m* diss by div 23 June 1978), Don Enrico Gaetani, Count dell'Aquila d'Aragona of the Dukes di Laurenzana (*b* at Naples 14 April 1926), Dr of Phil. [*Piazza della Trinita dei Pellegrini 91, 00186 Rome, Italy*].

>> 2. Countess *Isabelle* Adrienne, *b* at Middachten 3 July 1925, auf Middachten and Gaildorf; *m* there 20 Dec 1951, Aurel, Count zu Ortenburg (*b* at Budapest 30 August 1927), Farmer. [*Schloß Birkenfeld, 8617 Maroldsweisach*].

2. Count *Godard* John George Charles, *b* at Middachten 3 Aug 1857; ✠ at Casteel Amerongen 4 Jan 1940, matriculated into the Dutch nobility as Count van Aldenburg Bentinck 24 June 1920, Lord of Amerongen, Ginkel, Elst, Zuylenstein, Leersum, Lievendael, Wayestein and Eckenweil, Kt of St John of Jerusalem; *m* at The Hague 11 June 1884, Countess Louise (*b* at Brussels 28 Jan 1861; ✠ at Amerongen 27 Jan 1910), dau of Jules August, Count van Bylandt and Baroness Frédérique Julie van der Duyn, and had issue, among whom,

> 1. Godard **Adriaan** Henry Jules, **9th Count van Bentinck and Waldeck-Limpurg-Gaildorf**, Lord of Middachten, Amerongen, Ginkel and Elst, Lord of Gaildorf, etc, *b* at Middachten 21 Feb 1887; ✠ at Amsterdam 4 Aug 1968,

Electro-technical Engineer, Entomologist, Kt Cmdr Teutonic Order; *m* 1stly at Overseen 11 Jan 1921, Jacoba (*b* at The Hague 22 April 1888; ✣ at Leersum 12 July 1949), dau of Jacobus Johannes van den Heuvel and Evertje Kuil. He *m* 2ndly at Amsterdam 16 Feb 1961, Alieda (*b* at Amsterdam 16 Feb 1909), dau of Frits Vlieger and Janna van der Weg. [*Saxen-Weimar-Laan 22, Amsterdam-Z., The Netherlands*].

CASTELL

Seigneural family from Franconia, authenticated from Rubbrath de Castele 3 March 1057 et comes liber 1097; Rubertus comes de Castelo 1205; the two existing Lines below descend from two sons of Count Christian Friedrich Carl (*b* 26 Feb 1730; ✣ 15 Oct 1773); Family Law instituted 6 Dec 1794; confirmed 1796 and 1807; a Family Treaty was concluded 6 July 1827; modified by a new Family Law 14 June 1861.

LINE I: CASTELL-CASTELL

Evangelical: Founded by Count Albrecht Friedrich Karl (*b* 2 May 1766; ✣ 11 April 1810); Hereditary Member of the Bavarian "Reichsräte" 26 May 1818; received the qualification of "Erlaucht" (primogeniture) by the German Diet 13 Feb 1829; recognized in Bavaria 22 April 1829; extended to all descendants 7 March 1901; Bavarian title of "Fürst" (Prince) with the qualification of "Durchlaucht" (primogeniture), Munich 7 March 1901.

The Head of this Line and his wife bear the title of Prince and Princess zu Castell-Castell with the qualification of Serene Highness and cadet members bear the title of Count or Countess zu Castell-Castell with the qualification of Illustrious Highness.

ALBRECHT Friedrich Carl, **3RD PRINCE (FÜRST) ZU CASTELL-CASTELL,** *b* at Castell 13 Aug 1925, Kt of Hon St John of Jerusalem, son of Carl, 2nd Prince (Fürst) zu Castell-Castell (*b* 8 May 1897; ✣*k* in action 10 May 1945) and Princess Anna-Agnes zu Solms-Hohensolms-Lich (*b* 11 Jan 1899; *m* 12 Sept 1923; ✣ 8 Sept 1987); *m* at Arolsen 22 May (civ) and 23 May (relig) 1951, Princess Marie-Louise (*b* at Kiel 3 Nov 1930), dau of Max, Prince (Fürst) zu Waldeck and Pyrmont and Countess Gustava von Platen Hallermund. [*Bergstraße 3, 97355 Castell, Ufranken, Germany*].

Sons and Daughters

1. Countess *Philippa* Emma, *b* at Castell 23 Jan 1952; *m* at Castell 27 May (civ) and 28 May (relig) 1977, Michael, Prince zu Salm and

Salm-Salm (*b* at Heimerzheim 16 Jan 1953).
[*Schloß Wallhaüsen, 55595 Kr. Bad Kreuznach, Germany*].
2. Countess *Johanna* Bathildis, *b* at Castell 23 Jan 1952 (twin with Countess Philippa); *m* at Castell 2 Sept (civ) and 3 Sept (relig) 1977, Johannes, Prince of Lobkowicz (*b* at Munich 22 Aug 1954).
[*Jinonická 61, 15600 Prague 5, Czech Republic; Zámek, 26285 Drahenice, Czech Republic*].
3. *Maximilian* Friedrich Carl, Hereditary Count (Erbgraf) zu Castell-Castell, *b* at Castell 23 May 1953; ✠ at Würzburg 21 Dec 1974.
4. *Alexander* Friedrich Carl, Hereditary Count (Erbgraf) zu Castell-Castell, *b* at Castell 26 Nov 1954, Merchant Banker; *m* at Castell 27 Jan (civ) and 29 Jan (relig) 1983 (*m* diss by div at Munich April 1991), Marion (*b* at Düsseldorf 1 Oct 1957), dau of Walter Stepp and Sigrid Christiani, and has issue,
[*Blücherstraße 1, 80634 Munich, Germany*].
    1. Count *Conradin* Albrecht Walther Friedrich Carl, *b* at Deggendorf 23 Feb 1984.
    2. Countess Dorothea *Richiza* Louise, *b* at Deggendorf 31 May 1985.
5. Count *Georg* Friedrich Carl, *b* at Castell 26 Nov 1956; *m* at Bonn 21 June (civ) and at Ahlden an der Aller 5 Aug (relig) 1983, Franziska (*b* at Düsseldorf 20 June 1961), dau of Dr Albrecht Greuner and Baroness Beatrix von Oldershausen, and has issue,
[*Spanische Allee 79, 14129 Berlin, Germany*].
    1. Count *Jacob* Albrecht Friedrich Carl, *b* at Bonn 30 Jan 1984.
    2. Countess *Johanna* -Franziska Beatrix Marie, *b* at Bonn 20 March 1985.
    3. Count *Anton* Georg Friedrich Carl, *b* at Berlin 16 Sept 1988.
    4. Count *Franz* Georg Friedrich Carl, *b* at Berlin 17 April 1991.
    5. Countess *Emilie* Gustava Inge Louise, *b* at Berlin 20 Aug 1995.
6. Count *Ferdinand* Friedrich Carl, *b* at Castell 20 May 1965; *m* at Schwabisch-Gmund 31 July (relig) 1999, Countess Marie-Gabrielle (*b* at Geislingen an der Steige 7 May 1971) dau of Count Gottfried von Degenfeld-Schonburg and Princess Wilhelmine of Windisch-Graetz, and has issue,
[*Schloßplatz 1, 97355 Castell, UFranken, Germany*].

1. Count *Carl*, *b* at ... May 2001.

7. Countess *Stephanie*, *b* at Castell 26 Sept 1966; *m* at Castell 20 Aug (civ) and 22 Aug (relig) 1993, Georg, Count von Khevenhüller-Metsch (*b* at Madrid 24 Sept 1960).

[*Mittlerer Reisberg 13b, 61350 Bad Homburg, Germany*].

Brother and Sisters

1. *Philipp* Friedrich Carl, Hereditary Count (Erbgraf) zu Castell-Castell, *b* at Castell 11 July 1924; ✠*k* in action nr Wojciechowska, Poland 21 Oct 1944.

2. Countess *Jutta* Gertrud Emma, *b* at Castell 26 April 1927; ✠ at Wiesbaden 13 Nov 1993; *m* at Castell 12 Sept 1952, Hans Wolfram (Hans-Wolf), Baron von Werthern (*b* at Munich 3 March 1925).

[*Klenze-Straße 70, 80469 Munich, Germany*].

3. Countess *Elisabeth* Margarete, *b* at Castell 23 Dec 1928; ✠ at Castell 5 Jan 2001, Dr of Med; *m* at Castell 3 Jan 1958, Hans Wolf (*b* at Wesermunde 3 July 1928), Dr of Med, Prof.

[*Im Oberdorf 6, 97355 Castell, UFranken, Germany*].

4. Countess *Angelika* Marie, *b* at Castell 3 Aug 1933; *m* at Castell 12 June 1959, Hans-Hubertus, Burgrave and Count zu Dohna-Schlobitten (*b* at Waldburg, Königsberg 21 May 1925), Kt of Jusice of St John of Jerusalem.

[*Uhlandstraße 10, 14482 Potsdam-Babelsberg, Germany*].

5. Countess *Christiana* Dorothea Renata, *b* at Castel 29 Oct 1934; *m* at Castell 12 Aug 1954, Maximilian, Baron von Lerchenfeld (*b* at Bamberg 17 Jan 1926), Dipl Forestry, Kt of St John of Jerusalem.

[*Schloß Heinersreuth, 95355 Presseck, UFranken, Germany*].

Brothers and Sisters of Father

Issue of Friedrich Carl, 1st Prince zu Castell-Castell (*b* 22 July 1864; ✠ 3 Jan 1923) to Countess Gertrud zu Stolberg- Wernigerode (*b* 5 Jan 1872; *m* 26 June 1895; ✠ 29 Aug 1924), having had issue, among whom,

1. Count *Constantin* Friedrich, *b* at Castell 27 Oct 1898; ✠ at Würzburg 2 Nov 1966, Col German Army; *m* at Castell 1 July (civ) and at Hummelo, Gelderland 8 July (relig) 1933 (*m* diss by div at Utrecht 27 Oct 1956), Countess Luitgardis (*b* at Rechteren, Dalfsen 4 March 1908; ✠ at Werkhoven, Utrecht 3 April 1989), Proprietor of Beverweerd, dau of Adolph, Count von Rechteren-Limpurg, Proprietor of Rechteren and Baroness Marguerite van Heeckeren

van Enghuizen, Proprietor of Enghuizen, Beverweerd and Odijk, and had issue,

    1. Countess *Renata*, b at Pähl, Bavaria 27 April 1934.

    [*Meerkout 40, 3972 Dribergen-Kleinstommern, The Netherlands*].

    2. Countess *Odylia*, b at Arnheim, Gelderland 26 Oct 1939; m at Utrecht 5 Sept 1964, as his 2nd wife, Prince Heinrich III Reuss (b at Breslau 27 July 1919; ✠ at Vienna 7 July 1993), Dr of Law, Dr of Biology.

    [*Salesianergasse 8, 1030 Vienna, Austria*].

2. Count *Wilhelm* Friedrich, b at Castell 12 Dec 1901; ✠ at Wertheim 11 Nov 1968, naturalised in the USA as William F Castell 11 April 1940; m at Indianapolis, Indiana, USA 5 April 1930, Ella Hutt (b at Monroe City, Missouri, USA 25 Sept 1905; ✠ at San Pedro, CA, USA 30 May 1980), dau of Joseph William Hutt and Anna Mary Williams, and had issue,

    1. *Angela* Agnes, b at Anderson, Indiana, USA 28 July 1931; m at Hollywood, California 16 July 1955, Edward Schlag (b at Los Angeles 12 Jan 1932), Dr of Chemistry, Prof.

    [*Osterwaldstraße 91, 80805 Munich, Germany*].

    2. *Maria* Gertrud, b at Anderson, Indiana 15 April 1936, BS, Nurse; m 1stly at Los Angeles 15 April 1954 (m diss by div at Los Angeles 26 May 1966), Paul Eugene Gilette (b at Los Angeles 23 Dec 1929). She m 2ndly at Palo Alto, CA, USA 26 Dec 1968, Abner Malcolm Greene (b at Elisabeth, New Jersey 31 Oct 1938), BA, Teacher.

    [*741 Paul Avenue, Palo Alto, Ca. 94306, U.S.A*]

    3. *Margaret* Anna, b at Anderson, Indiana 15 April 1936 (twin with Maria), BA, MA; m 1stly at Los Angeles 15 April 1954 (m diss by div at Los Angeles 2 July 1975), David Gilette (b at Los Angeles 14 Dec 1928). She m 2ndly at Los Angeles 10 June 1976, Howard Applegate (b at Meriden, Conn, USA 9 Sept 1926), BSEE, MBA, Electrical Engineer.

    [*1649 Old Arcata Road, Bayside, Ca. 95524, U.S.A.*].

    4. *James* William, b at Royal Oak, Michigan 10 Sept 1945; m at New York City 11 Oct 1985, Susan Linda Molnar (b at Bronx, New York 27 Dec 1947).

    [*Pinecrest Retreats, 15 Conscience Bay Road, Setauket, NY 11733, U.S.A.*].

4. Count *Georg* Friedrich, b at Castell 12 Nov 1904; ✠ there 6 Sept 1956, Lt-Col German Army, Sculptor; m at Nohra nr Weimar (civ)

and at Isseroda nr Weimar (relig) 2 May 1938, Gudrun (*b* at Isseroda 12 Aug 1919; ✠ at Castell 22 May 1997), dau of Heinrich von Eichel genannt Streiber and Baroness Hildegard von der Leyen zu Bloemersheim, and had issue,

1. Countess *Maria*, *b* at Isseroda 31 Aug 1941; *m* at Castell 30 July (civ) and 31 July (relig) 1965, Reiner Schmidt (*b* at Hof an der Saale 13 Nov 1936), Prof of Law.
[*Bachwiesenstraße 75, 86459 Gessertshausen, Germany*].

2. Countess *Monika* Renata, *b* at Isseroda 20 Dec 1943; *m* at Munich 26 Feb (civ) and at Heldritt 18 May (relig) 1973, Carl-Joachim von Butler (*b* at Eisenach 21 Oct 1941), Kt of St John of Jerulsalem.
[*Seestraße 11, 16818 Binenwalde, Germany*].

3. Count *Wolfgang-Georg* Carl Friedrich, *b* at Würzburg 5 Jan 1949, Dipl Agricultural Engineer; *m* at Hindelang, Allgäu 5 April (civ) and 17 July (relig) 1983, Verena (*b* at Bad Kissingen 9 March 1952), dau of Helmut Alt and Eva-Maria Kappler, and has issue,
[*Bergstraße 5, 97355 Castell, Germany*].

    1. Countess *Cilly* Freya, *b* at Frankfurt-Höchst 22 May 1987.

    2. Count *Heinrich* Georg, *b* at Kitzingen 29 Dec 1988.

Count Wolfgang-Georg also adopted two sons,

    1. *Matthias* Marc, *b* at Frankfurt-am-Main 3 Aug 1984, bears the name, "Count zu Castell-Castell".

    2. *Clemens* Benedikt, *b* at Friedberg 15 Jan 1986, bears the name "Count zu Castell-Castell".

4. Count *Friedrich* Rupert Heinrich, *b* at Würzburg 18 Dec 1950.
[*Abtsleitenweg 10, 97074 Würzburg, Germany*].

5. Countess *Gabriele* Louise, *b* at Würzburg 3 Jan 1955; *m* 1stly at Munich 2 Dec 1977 (*m* diss by div at Munich 13 May 1982), Nikolaus Thouret (*b* at Nordhausen 27 Aug 1941). She *m* 2ndly at Munich 30 Dec 1983 (civ) and at Castell 30 June (relig) 1984 (*m* diss by div March 1993), Eduard Weig (*b* at Munich 18 July 1952), Doctor.
[*Graßlweg 4, 85049 Ingolstadt, Germany*]

5. Countess *Emma* Klothilde, *b* at Castell 8 June 1907; *m* at Castell 21 July 1934, Eugen, Baron von Lotzbeck (*b* at Munich 24 Feb 1882; ✠ at Assenhausen 22 May 1942), Col.
[*Stift Brunneck, Cramer Klettstraße 1, Apt 556, 85521 Ottobrunn,*

Germany].

Brother of Grandfather

Issue of Carl, 1st Count zu Castell-Castell (*b* 23 May 1826; ✠ 2 Jan 1886) and Countess Emma zu Solms-Rödelheim and Assenheim (*b* 19 Aug 1831; *m* 23 Sept 1856; ✠ 2 June 1904), having had issue, among whom,

Son

Count *Otto* Friedrich, *b* at Castell 123 May 1868; ✠ at Hochburg, Austria 8 July 1939, Major-Gen Bavarian Army, Kt of St John of Jerusalem; *m* at Langenzell 5 Oct 1903 Princess Amelie (*b* at Langenzell 24 June 1883; ✠ at Hochburg, Austria 23 Sept 1978), dau of Alfred, Prince zu Löwenstein-Wertheim-Freudenberg and Countess Pauline von Reichenbach-Lessonitz, and had issue, among whom,

  1. Count *Luitpold* Alfred Friedrich Karl, *b* at Langenzell 14 Nov 1904; ✠*k* in a flying accident, Bankta, nr Sofia 6 Nov 1941, Dr of Law, Lt, Kt of St John of Jerusalem; *m* at Copenhagen 22 Jan 1937, Princess Alexandrine-Louise (*b* at Jaegersborghus 12 Dec 1914; ✠ at Copenhagen 26 April 1962), dau of Prince Harald of Denmark and Princess Helena of Schleswig-Holstein-Sonderburg Glücksburg, and had issue,

    1. Countess *Amelie*- Alexandrine Helena Caroline Mathilde Pauline, *b* at Berlin 25 May 1938; *m* at Hochburg 3 Sept (civ) and 5 September (relig) 1965, Oscar, Ritter von Miller zu Aichholz (*b* at Vienna 7 July 1934), Industrialist

    [*Am Heumarkt 13, 1030 Vienna, Austria*].

    2. Countess *Thyra* Antonie Marie-Therese Feodora Agnes, *b* at Berlin 14 Sept 1939; *m* at Copenhagen 3 Nov 1961, Karl Moes (*b* at Copenhagen 17 Oct 1937), Antique Dealer.

    [*Parkvaenqet 11, 2920 Charlottenlund, Copenhagen, Denmark*].

  2. Count *Gustav* Friedrich Wilhelm Ernst Franz Ulrich Richard Udo Hermann, *b* at Munich 9 Dec 1911; ✠*k* in action over Steyning, Sussex, England 19 Jan 1941, Capt German Airforce; *m* at Braaby, Denmark 14 July 1937, Baroness Vibeke (*b* at Copenhagen 9 April 1915; ✠ Copenhagen 14 Jan 2000;

m 2ndly at Skellerup 23 Oct 1958, Erik, Baron Juel-Brockdorff
b 26 Nov 1906 ✠ 6 Feb 1995), dau of Christian, Baron von
Lotzbeck, Proprietor of Astrup and Fanny Evers, and had
issue,
[*Hindemae Molle 5540, Denmark*].

    1. Countess *Christa* Fanny Amelie Friederike, *b* at
Kolberg 19 May 1938; *m* at Copenhagen 18 Aug 1962
(*m* diss by div at Munich 8 Aug 1973), Franz, Count
von Walderdorff (*b* at Hauzenstein 20 Nov 1930). She
has since reverted to her maiden name.
[*Tivolistraße 1, 80538, Munich 22, Germany*].

    2. Count Friedrich *Carl* Otto Luitpold, *b* at Kolberg
5 July 1940, Dipl Forestry, Kt of Justice of St John of
Jerusalem; *m* at Ach, Austria 2 May (civ) and 24 May
(relig) 1967, Baroness Adelheid (Heidi) (*b* at Graz 22
April 1939), dau of Johannes (Hans), Baron Jordis von
Lohausen and Baroness Margarethe von Eiselsberg,
and has issue,
[*Hochburg, 5122 Ach, Austria*].

        1. Countess *Amelie* Margarethe Clementine,
b at Salzburg 18 Feb 1968; *m* at Ach 19 July
(civ) and 22 July (relig) 1990, Christian Wagner
(*b* at Santiago de Chile 13 Nov 1963).
[*Casilla 110a, Villarrica, Flor del Lago, Chile*].
        2. Countess *Marie-Therese* Verene Johanna
Vibeke, *b* at Salzburg 3 Aug 1972, Graphic
Designer; *m* at Kronwinkl 10 Aug (civ) and at
Schloß Hochburg, Upper Austria 3 Sep (rel)
1995, Count Casper von Preysing-Lichtenegg-
Moos, M.A., Ec. and pol., lt.-res., Kt Bavarian
Order of St George, *b* at Munich 26 April 1970.
[*Schloß Kronwinkl, 84174 Eching 5, Austria;
5 Chesson Road, London W14 9QR*]

    3. Countess *Christiana* Alexandrine Clarissa Helvig,
b at Salzburg 25 May 1974; *m* at Hochberg 13 Sept
1997, Count Georg von Thurn und Valsassina-Como-
Vercelli (by adoption Vrints zu Falkenstein, *b* at
Klagenfurt 18 Oct 1956.
[*2161 Poysbrunn, Austria*]

    4. Count Friedrich-*August* Johann Gustav Erik, *b* at
Salzburg 27 Jan 1979.

[Franz-Josef-Straße 28, 80801 Munich, Germany]
3. Countess *Marie-Therese* Pauline Mechtild Ludmilla Antonie, *b* at Munich 20 Dec 1917; *m* at Burghausen, Altötting 2 July (civ) and at Hochburg 3 July (relig) 1937 (*m* diss by div at Coesfeld 26 March 1979), Philipp Franz, Prince (Fürst) and Rheingrave zu Salm-Horstmar (*b* at Várlar 31 March 1909), Dipl Forestry, Lt.-Col.
[Oberförsterei Varlar, 48720 Rosendahl, Germany; Forsthaus Hörndl 52, Tarsdorf, Austria].

Brother of Great-Grandfather
Issue of Count Freidrich-Ludwig (*b* 2 Nov 1791; ✠ 21 April 1875) and Princess Emilie zu Hohenlohe-Langenburg (*b* 27 Jan 1793; *m* 25 June 1816; ✠ 20 July 1859), having had issue, among whom,

Son
Count *Gustav* Friedrich Ludwig Eugen Emil, *b* at Castell 17 Jan 1829; ✠ at Berchtesgaden 7 July 1910, Lt-Gen Bavarian Army, Kt Order of St Hubertus, Kt of St John of Jerusalem; *m* at Augsburg 11 Sept 1869, Countess Elisabeth (*b* at Dresden 8 Dec 1851; ✠ at Oberstdorf, Allgäu 10 Feb 1929), Dame of Hon Bavarian Order of St Theresia, dau of Karl, Count von Brühl, Proprietor of Seifersdorf and Countess Ludmilla von Renard, and had issue, among whom,

Son
Count *Wolfgang* Friedrich Julius Magnus, *b* at Munich 27 May 1877; ✠ at Breslau 8 Feb 1940, Lt-Col Saxon Army, Kt of Hon St John of Jerusalem; *m* at Ernstbrunn 5 Oct 1920, Princess Sibylle (*b* at Köstritz 26 Sept 1888; ✠ at Castell 21 March 1977), dau of Heinrich XXIV, Prince (Fürst) Reuss-Köstritz and Princess Elisabeth Reuss, and had issue,

    1. Count *Prosper* Friedrich Karl Gustav Heinrich, *b* at Köstritz 4 Sept 1922; ✠ at Frankfurt-am-Main 3 Jan 1989, Cmdr St John of Jerusalem; *m* at Bischofsheim, Rhön 8 July (civ) 4 Aug (relig) 1961, Princess Elisabeth (*b* at Bautzen 8 Dec 1940), dau of Christian, Prince zur Lippe-Weissenfeld, Proprietor of Teichnitz bei Bautzen and Countess Pauline zu Ortenburg, and had issue,
    [Elvirastraße 1, 80636 Munich, Germany; La Rosa di Pietra Latera, 05017 Monteleone d'Orvieto, Prov. Terni., Italy].

        1. Count *Johannes* Friedrich, *b* at Munich 17 Aug

1962, Photographer; *m* at Isernhagen 5 Jun (rel) and
at Hamburg 7 Jun (relig) 1997, Stefanie (*b* at Kiel 28
Apr 1966), Dentist, dau of Dr Geter Hinz and
Marianne Mayer, and has issue,
[*Glashüttenstraße 31, 20357 Hamburg, Germany*].

>> 1. Count *Victor* Alexander, *b* at Hamburg 1
>> Feb 2000.

2. Count *Heinrich* Friedrich, *b* at Munich 3 June
1966; *m* at Munich 11 Sep (rel) and at Ebenau nr
Salzburg 13 Sep (relig) 1997, Countess Huberta (*b* at
Gräfelfing 13 Mar 1970), dau of Clemens, Count Hahn
von Burgsdorff and Victoria von Arnim, and has issue,
[*Dinardstraße 7, 82319 Starnberg, Germany*].

>> 1. Count *Prosper* Friedrich Carl Clemens, *b* at
>> Starnberg 5 Sep 1998.
>> 2. Count *Moritz* Friedrich Anton Johannes,
>> *b* at Starnberg 13 Apr 2000.

2. Count *Friedrich Ludwig* Hubertus Anton, *b* at Schloß
Ernstbrunn, Lower Austria 5 Oct 1927; ✝ at Würzburg 29
Jan 1968; *m* at Karlsruhe 8 Apr (civ) and 16 May (relig) 1958,
Countess Amélie (*b* at Hermsdorf 26 May 1930), dau of Otto,
Count von Pfeil and Klein Ellguth and Elise von Zitzewitz;
and had issue,
[*Rathausplatz 1, 97355 Castell, UFranken, Germany*].

> 1. Count *Andreas* Wolfgang Otto Prosper Heinrich
> Friedrich, *b* at Würzburg 15 May 1959; *m* 1stly at
> Karlsruhe 13 Sept (civ) and 14 Sept (relig) 1985 (*m*
> diss by div 5 July 1994), Beate (*b* at Karlsruhe 21 July
> 1958), dau of Walter Staudt and Ingrid Jösel; *m* 2ndly
> at Castell 12 April (civ) and at Sugenheim 31 May
> (relig) 1997, Maren (*b* at Hamburg 29 Jan 1969), dau of
> Hans Goebel and Ingrid Arpe, and has issue, from his
> second wife,
> [*Äussere Bahnhofstraße 60, 91593 Burgbernheim,
> Germany*].

>> 1. Countess *Johanna* Maria Amélie Ingrid, *b* at
>> Kitzingen 21 Jan 1999.
>> 2. Count *Kilian* Friedrich-Ludwig Hans, *b* at
>> Neustadt 28 Oct 2000.

> 2. Count *Johann-Philipp* Carl Alexander Ulrich
> Friedrich, *b* at Veitshöchheim 14 Sept 1960; ✝ at

Karlsruhe 5 Oct 1985; *m* 1stly at Karlsruhe 27 May
(civ) and 5 July (relig) 1980 (*m* diss by div 1994),
Elvira (*b* at Karlsruhe 23 Dec 1960; *m* 2ndly at
Karlsruhe 28 Dec 1993, Christian Müller, *b* at 19 Oct
1962), dau of Kurt Adolf Dambach and Maria Geldner.
[*Karlstraße 121, 76137 Karlsruhe, Germany*].

3. Countess *Désirée* Sibylle Elise Barbara Margarethe
Isa, *b* at Veitshöchheim 14 Sept 1960 (twin with Count
Johann-Philipp); *m* 1stly at Herzberg am Harz 8 Oct
(civ) and 9 Oct (relig) 1982 (*m* diss by 9 Sept 1987),
Klaus Steffanowski (*b* at Herzberg am Harz 28 Jan
1956). She *m* 2ndly at Schönwalde 9 Aug (civ) and 10
Aug (relig) 1990, Peter Grage (*b* at Neustadt, Holstein
1 Jan 1970), Farmer.
[*Alte Abstswinder Straße 28, 97353 Wiesentheid,
Germany*].

4. Count *Hubertus* Friedrich Aurel Georg-Michael, *b*
at Veitshöchheim 16 Sept 1961; *m* at Karlsruhe 27
May (civ) and 28 May (relig) 1988, Waldtraut (*b* at
Karlsruhe 21 July 1960), dau of Heinz Möloth and Ilse
von Bergen, and has issue,
[*Bahnhof Schaidt 3, 76744 Wörth-Schaidt, Germany*].

    1. Count *Constantin* Friedrich Heinz Ludwig,
    b at Karlsruhe 3 Feb 1990.

    2. Countess *Antonia* Jessica Amélie Espérance,
    b at Karlsruhe 17 Sept 1994.

5. Countess *Friederike-Christiane* Amélie
Marie-Louise, *b* at Wertheim 18 April 1964; *m* at Castell
18 Sept (civ) and 19 Sept (relig) 1987, Andreas
Wassmann (*b* at Herzberg 11 April 1963).
[*Kiefernweg 4, 37412 Herzberg am Harz, Germany*].

LINE II: CASTELL-RÜDENHAUSEN

Evangelical. Founded by Count Christian Friedrich (*b* 21 April 1772;
✝ 28 March 1850); Hereditary Member of the Bavarian "Reichsräte"
26 May 1818; received the qualification of "Erlaucht" (primogeniture)
by the German Diet 13 Feb 1829; recognized in Bavaria 22 April
1829, extended to all descendants 7 March 1901; Bavarian title of
"Fürst" (Prince) (primogeniture) with the qualification of
"Durchlaucht", Munich 7 March 1901.
The Head of this Line and his wife bear the title of Prince and
Princess zu Castell-Rüdenhausen with the qualification of Serene

Highness and cadet members bear the title of Count or Countess zu
Castell-Rüdenhausen with the qualification of Illustrious Highness.

SIEGFRIED Casimir Friedrich, **4TH PRINCE (FÜRST) ZU
CASTELL-RÜDENHAUSEN,** *b* at Rüdenhausen 16 Feb 1916;
succ his brother Rupert, 3rd Prince (Fürst) zu Castell-Rüdenhausen
(*b* 1 June 1910; missing in action 28 Aug 1944; declared officially
deceased 19 May 1951), Co-Proprietor of Fürstlich Castell'schen
Bank, son of Casimir, 2nd Prince (Fürst) zu Castell-Rüdenhausen
(*b* 10 March 1861; ✝ 25 April 1933) and Countess Mechtilde von
Bentinck (*b* 20 Dec 1877; *m* 1 Sept 1905; ✝ 13 Dec 1940); *m* at
Laubach 17 Oct 1946, Countess Irene (*b* at Laubach 25 June 1925),
dau of Georg Friedrich, Count zu Solms-Laubach and Princess
Johanna zu Solms-Hohensolms-Lich.
[*97355 Rüdenhausen, UFranken, Germany*].

Sons and Daughter

1. *Johann-Friedrich* Hereditary Count (Erbgraf) zu
Castell-Rüdenhausen, *b* at Rüdenhausen 27 Jan 1948; *m* at Quinta
da Bela Vista, nr Sintra, Portugal 11 June 1983, Countess Maria (*b*
at Würzburg 28 July 1958), dau of Karl, Count von Schönborn-
Wiesentheid and Donna Graziela Alvares Pereira de Melo of the
Dukes of Cadaval, and has issue,
[*Schloßstraße 3, 97355 Rüdenhausen, UFranken, Germany*].

  1. Count *Otto* Friedrich, *b* at Würzburg 31 May 1985.
  2. Countess *Olga* Graziella, *b* at Würzburg 31 Jan 1987.
  3. Countess Anna *Magdalena,* *b* at Würzburg 8 March 1989.
  4. Count *Anton* George Friedrich, *b* at Würzburg 4 March
     1992.

2. Count *Manto* Friedrich, *b* at Rüdenhausen 31 Jan 1949, Police
Commissioner; *m* at Rüdenhausen 28 July 1984, Eva (*b* at Werfen,
Salzburg 26 March 1964), dau of Roman Lorenz and Eva Grünewald,
and has issue,
[*Parkstraße 11, 97355 Rüdenhausen, UFranken, Germany*].

  1. Countess *Marie* Karoline Johanna Mechtild, *b* at Kitzingen
     17 Jan 1985.

3. Countess *Donata* Emma, *b* at Rüdenhausen 20 June 1950; *m* 1stly
at Rüdenhausen 24 May 1975, Prince Louis Ferdinand of Prussia (*b*
at Golzow, Neumark 25 Aug 1944; ✝*k* in army manoeuvres at Bremen
11 July 1977). She *m* 2ndly at Rüdenhausen 9 Feb 1991, Duke
Friedrich August of Oldenburg (*b* at Rastede 11 Jan 1936; *m* 1stly at

Berlin 3/4 Dec 1965, Princess Marie Cécile of Prussia; that *m* diss by div at Munich 23 Nov 1989).
[*Gut Sievershagen, 23738 Manhagen, Ostholstein, Germany*].

4. Count *Christian* Friedrich Casimir, *b* at Rüdenhausen 8 Aug 1952, Banker; *m* at St Michielsgestel, Nordbrabant 16 Sept (civ) and at Vught 17 Sept (relig) 1977, Carolina (*b* at Rotterdam 7 Dec 1952), dau of Georg Hintzen and Agneta Krantz, and has issue,
[*Schloß Twickel, 7495 SE Delden, The Netherlands*].

    1. Count *Jurriaan* George Frederik, *b* at Amsterdam 19 June 1978.
    [*Achterharingvliet 246, 3011 DC Rotterdam, The Netherlands*].

    2. Count *Roderik* Frederik, *b* at Amsterdam 19 June 1980.
    [*Schloß Twickel, 7495 SE Delden, The Netherlands*].

    3. Countess *Clara* Marie, *b* at Hengelo, Netherlands 30 Dec 1983.

5. Count *Rupert* Friedrich, *b* at Rüdenhausen 25 Sept 1954; *m* at Rüdenhausen 2 Feb (civ) and 3 Feb (relig) 1979 Baroness and Lady Alexandra (*b* at Budingen 6 Nov 1952), dau of Thilo, Count and Lord von Werthern-Beichlingen and Princess Walpurgis zu Stolberg-Wernigerode, and has issue,
[*Ringstraße 29, 97355 Abtswind, UFranken, Germany*].

    1. Count *Philipp* Rupert Fridrich Franz, *b* at Dettelbach 24 July 1979.
    [*Ringstraße 29, 97355 Abtswind, UFranken, Germany*].

    2. Count *Leopold* Rupert Friedrich, *b* at Dettelbach 25 April 1981.

    3. Countess *Sophia* Marie Walpurgis Irene, *b* at Dettelbach 18 July 1983; ✝ at Abtswind 23 March 1987,

    4. Countess *Gloria* Donata, *b* at Kitzingen 31 Jan 1987.

6. Count *Karl* Friedrich, *b* at Rüdenhausen 21 Oct 1957, Photographer.
[*Schloßstraße 10, 97355 Rüdenhausen, Ufranken, Germany*].

7. Count *Hermann* Friedrich, *b* at Wurzburg 20 June 1963; *m* at Arolsen 18 Aug (civ) and 19 Aug (relig) 1989, Princess Henriette (*b* at Ludwigsburg 6 April 1963), dau of Georg-Friedrich, Prince zu Waldeck and Pyrmont and Princess Sixtina zu Stolberg-Stolberg, and has issue,
[*Goethestraße 8, 93152 Nittendorf, Germany*].

    1. Countess *Annabell* Florentina, *b* at Heilbron 4 Feb 1991.

    2. Countess *Cecilie* Victoria, *b* at Heilbron 6 Sept 1991.

3. Count Casimir Friedrich Wilhelm, *b* at Heilbronn 6 July 1994.

8. Count *Matthias* Georg Friedrich, *b* at Würzburg 13 April 1966; *m* at Hamburg 12 Jul (civ) and at Rüdenhausen 20 July (relig) 1996, Cristine (*b* at Hamburg 10 Dec 1974), dau of Mathias Blau and Sabine Stobbe, and has issue, [*Brombeerweg 51, 22339 Hamburg, Germany*].

1. Countess *Victoria* Sophie Christiane Donata, *b* at Hamburg 13 Nov 1998.

2. Count *Louis* Friedrich Casimir Matthias, *b* at Hamburg 13 Jan 2001.

Brothers and Sisters

1. Countess *Marie* Emma Agnes Victoria Elisabeth Caroline Mechtilde, *b* at Düsseldorf 8 March 1907; ✝ at Oberstaufen 11 Feb 1980.

2. **Rupert** Wolfgang Wilhem Friedrich Casimir, **3rd Prince (Fürst) zu Castell-Rüdenhausen**, *b* at Düsseldorf 1 June 1910; missing in action 28 Aug 1944; ✝*k* declared dead 19 May 1951, Capt Germany Army; *succ* his father 25 April 1933.

2. Countess *Marthe* Luitgardis Berthe Agnes Thekla Luise Ida, *b* at Rudenhausen 19 Jan 1912; ✝ at Rüdenhausen 10 Aug 1924.

3. Countess *Elisabeth* Clea Freda Amelie Irmgard Marie Hedwige, *b* at Rüdenhausen 24 Aug 1914; *m* 1stly at Rüdenhausen 26 April 1939, Friedrich-Wolfgang , Count zu Castell-Rüdenhausen (*b* at Berlin 27 June 1906; ✝*k* in action over Portland 11 June 1940). She *m* 2ndly at Rüdenhausen 11 Jan 1947, Theodor Duvelius (*b* at Wilhelmshaven 16 May 1916).

4. Count *Unico* Friedrich Heinrich Erwein Casimir, *b* at Rüdenhausen 5 Aug 1923; ✝*k* in action near Riga 20 Sept 1944.

Brothers of Father

Issue of Wolfgang, 1st Prince zu Castell-Rüdenhausen (*b* 21 April 1830; ✝ 13 Jan 1913) and Princess Emma zu Isenburg and Büdingen in Büdingen (*b* 23 Feb 1841; *m* 17 May 1859; ✝ 22 April 1926), having had issue, among whom,

Sons

1. Count *Alexander* Friedrich Lothar, *b* at Rüdenhausen 6 July 1866; ✝ at Oberstdorf, Allgäu 11 April 1928, Proprietor of Schwanberg, UFranken, Manufacturer, Major Bavarian Army, declared for

himself and the descendants of his first marriage the name and title of "Counts and Countesses von Faber-Castell", Munich 2 Feb 1898 (see that family); *m* at Stein, nr Nuremberg 28 Feb 1898 (*m* diss by div at Munich 26 Feb 1918), Baroness Ottilie (*b* at Stein 6 Sept 1877; ✠ at Nuremberg 28 Sept 1944; *m* 2ndly at Dresden 5 My 1918, Philipp, Baron von Brand zu Neidstein), dau of Wilhelm, Baron von Faber and Bertha Faber. He *m* 2ndly at Stein, nr Nuremberg 15 July 1920, Countess Margit (*b* at Duppau, North Bohemia 30 Sept 1886; ✠ at Schloß Schwanberg, nr Kitzingen 25 Oct 1973; *m* 2ndly at Munich 14 Sept 1933, Rüdiger, Prince zu Lippe-Weissenfeld), dau of Curt, Count Zedtwitz von Moraván and Duppau, Proprietor of Duppau mit Sachsengrün and Countess Margarete of Lippe-Weissenfeld, and had issue, among whom, from his second wife,

    1. Count *Radulf* Friedrich Kurt Casimir Adolf Sigmund Ferdinand Roland, *b* at Stein 22 Aug 1922.

    [*Schloß Schwanberg, 8711 Rödelsee, nr Kitzingen, Germany; Haus Castell, Fuggerstraße 12, 8980 Oberstdorf, Germany*].

2. Count *Hugo* Friedrich Alfred, *b* at Rüdenhausen 4 April 1871; ✠ at Golssen 30 Sept 1936, Major Prussian Army; *m* at Klitschdorf 14 Nov 1900, Countess Clementine (*b* at Potsdam 13 April 1881; ✠ at Lich, Upper Hessen 3 May 1971), dau of Otto, Count zu Solms-Sonnenwalde and Countess Helene zu Solms-Baruth, and had issue, among whom,

    1. Count *Friedrich-Wolfgang* Otto, *b* at Berlin 27 June 1906; missing in action over Portland 11 July 1940; ✠*k* declared dead at Berlin 28 Nov 1946, Capt German Airforce and Lufthansa Pilot; *m* 1stly at Coburg 14 Dec 1931 (*m* annulled at Berlin 2 May 1938), Princess Caroline Mathilde (*b* Coburg 22 June 1912; ✠ at Erlangen 5 Sept 1983; *m* 2ndly at Berlin 22 June 1938, Max Schnirring who was ✠*k* at Stralsund 7 July 1944; *m* 3rdly at Coburg 21 Dec 1946, Karl Otto Andéee; that *m* diss by div at Coburg 27 Dec 1947), dau of Karl Eduard, Duke of Saxe-Coburg and Gotha and Princess Viktoria Adelheid of Schleswig-Holstein-Sonderburg-Glücksburg, and had issue,

        1. Count *Bertram* Friedrich, *b* at Berlin 12 July 1932, Painter and Graphic Artist; *m* at Vienna 10 Oct 1964, Countess Felizitas (Fee) (*b* at Vienna 20 Sept 1944), dau of Hanno, Count von Auersperg and Klothilde Ryndziak, and has issue,

[*Nibelungen Gasse3/16, 1010 Vienna, Austria*].

    1. Count *Dominik* Dimitrij Johannes Friedrich, *b* at Vienna 20 July 1965, Actor.

[*Webgasse 3, 1060 Vienna, Austria*]

    2. Count *Michael* Alexej Friedrich Wolfgang, *b* at Vienna 4 Nov 1967.

[*Rüdigergasse 5, 1060 Vienna, Austria*]

2. Count *Conradin* Friedrich, *b* at Berlin 10 Oct 1933; *m* at Helsingfors 6 July 1961, Märta Catharina (*b* at Helsingfors 17 April 1939), dau of Bjarne Lönegren and Göta Ingeborg Isaksson, and has issue,

[*Hagalandet, 10230 Ingå Station, Finland*].

    1. Countess *Anne-Charlotte* Catharina Victoria, *b* at Helsingfors 7 April 1962; *m* at Ekenäs 4 July 1986, Martti Rappu (*b* at St Karins, Finland 26 Oct 1963).

    [*Hagalandet, 10230 Ingå Station, Finland*].

    2. Count *Carl-Eduard* Friedrich Hubertus, *b* at Helsingfors 15 March 1964; *m* at Kapernaumskirchen, Copenhagen 6 March 1999, Lisbeth Marie (*b* at Soborg 24 March 1969), dau of Leif Rauning and Kirsten Inge Rasmussen, and has issue,

    [*Theklavej 9, 2400 Copenhagen, Denmark*]

        1. Countess *Sarah* Caroline Victoria, *b* at Copenhagen 19 Sept 1999.

3. Countess *Victoria Adelheid* Clementine Louise, *b* at Coburg 26 Feb 1935, Dame Sovereign Military Order of Malta; *m* at London 20 June 1960, Miles Huntington-Whiteley, of the Baronets Huntington-Whiteley, Stockbroker (*b* at Fareham, Hampshire 18 July 1929).

[*6 Matheson Road, West Kensington, London, W14 8SW*].

Count Friedrich-Wolfgang *m* 2ndly at Rüdenhausen 26 April 1939, Countess Elisabeth (*b* at Rüdenhausen 24 Aug 1914; *m* 2ndly at Rüdenhausen 11 Jan 1947, Theodor Düvelius), dau of Casimir, Prince (Fürst) zu Castell-Rüdenhausen and Countess Mechtild von Bentinck, and had further issue,

[*Heimgartenstraße 3, 82449 Uffing am Staffelsee, Germany*].

    4. Count *Hesso* Fridrich, *b* at Würzburg 17 April

1940, Kt of Hon St John of Jerusalem; *m* at Hamburg 9 May (civ) and 10 May (relig) 1975, Adelheid (*b* at Hamburg 24 Feb 1938), dau of Ansgar von Nell and Barbara Steinle.

[*Henkenbergstraße 91, 44797 Bochum-Stiepel, Germany*].

3. Count *Hermann* Friedrich Julius, *b* at Rüdenhausen 27 Aug 1872; ✣ at Würzburg 16 Feb 1941, Lt-Col Bavarian Army; *m* at Klitcshdorf 18 July 1903, Countess Freda (*b* at Potsdam 18 July 1882; ✣ at Holzkirchen, Bavaria 4 Aug 1980), dau of Otto, Count zu Solms-Sonnenwalde and Countess Helene zu Solms-Baruth, and had issue, among whom,

1. Count *Hubertus* Friedrich Wolfgang Otto Peter Eberhard Hugo Wilhelm, *b* at Munich 12 Feb 1909; ✣ at Kitzingen 2 Sep 1995, Member South African Government, Kt of Hon St John of Jerusalem; *m* 1stly at Swakopmund, SW Africa 16 June 1939 (*m* diss by div 3 Dec 1948), Margarethe (*b* at Vogelsang, Wismar 26 June 1909; ✣ at Johannesburg 26 Jul 1997; *m* 2ndly at Windhoek 18 Jan 1949, Ralph, Count von Lüttichau), dau of Richard Schröder and Margarethe Wrede. He *m* 2ndly at Mariental, SW Africa 24 Oct 1951, Herta (*b* at Berlin 28 Aug 1911; ✣ at Windhoek 13 March 1995), dau of Julius Edlich and Martha Hepke, and has issue by his first wife,

1. Count *Ferdinand* Otto Friedrich Richard, *b* at Windhoek 25 March 1940, Architect, Kt of Honour of St John of Jerusalem; *m* at Brunswick-Mascherode 24 Aug (civ) and 7 Sept (relig) 1968, Dagmar (*b* at Potsdam 28 Nov 1944), dau of Alexander Wrede and Adelheid von Doering, and has issue,

[*Am Kohlikamp 28, 38126 Braunschweig, Germany*].

1. Countess *Alexandra* Elza Friederike, *b* at Brunswick 20 Jan 1969.

[*St Benedikt Straße 14, 97072 Würzburg, Germany*]

2. Countess *Victoria* Eleonore Adelheid Freda Margarethe, *b* at Johannesburg, South Africa 23 Jan 1972.

[*Lychener Straße 19, 10437 Berlin, Germany*]

3. Countess *Donata* Marie Elisabeth, *b* at Johannesburg 13 Aug 1976, Flight Attendant.

[*Röderbergweg 108, 60385 Frankfurt, Germany*]

2. Count *Hubertus-Hermann* Friedrich Richard, *b* at Windhoek 30 Aug 1941, Dipl Commercial Artist; *m* at Frankfurt-am-Main 8 July 1974, Christine (*b* at Klagenfurt 21 Dec 1945), dau of Rudolf Offner and Christina Kollman, and has issue,

[*Osterbekstraße 112, 22083 Hamburg, Germany*].

    1. Count *Constantin* Philipp Manto Tassilo Rudolf Hubertus, *b* at Frankfurt-am-Main 31 May 1976.

3. Countess *Freda* -Margarethe, *b* at Windhoek 11 Feb 1943.

[*P.O. Box 9145, Windhoek, Namibia*].

2. Countess *Clementine* Erika Hedwig Mechtilde Ottilie Marka Martina Helene, *b* at Munich 30 Jan 1912; *m* 1stly at Berlin 26 Oct 1939 (*m* diss by div 27 Oct 1954), Wilhelm Utermann (*b* at Annen, nr Witten, Westphalia 3 Oct 1912; ✝ at Roggersdorf 11 Aug 1991); she remarried 2ndly, her first husband at Hartpenning, nr Holzkirchen 24 Jan 1967.

[*Holzhäuslerweg 5, Roggersdorf, 83607 Holzkirchen, Bavaria, Germany*].

4. Count *Wolfgang* Friedrich Heinrich Philipp, *b* at Rüdenhausen 22 June 1875; ✝ at Munich 19 Dec 1930, Proprietor of Seeläsgen, Brandenburg, etc, Major Prussian Army, Kt of Hon St John of Jerusalem; *m* at Stein 27 Sept 1903, Baroness Hedwig (*b* at Stein 17 Nov 1882; ✝ at Frankfurt an der Oder 17 Feb 1937), Dame of Hon Bavarian Order of St Theresia, dau of Wilhelm, Baron von Faber and Bertha Faber, and had issue,

    1. Countess *Alexandra* Hedwig Johanna Bertha Marie, *b* at Stein 29 June 1904; ✝ at Linz an der Donau 9 Sept 1961; *m* at Seeläsgen 25 Sept 1927, Friedrich Christian, Prince of Schaumburg-Lippe (*b* at Bückeburg 5 Jan 1906; ✝ at Wasserburg am Inn 20 Sept 1983; *m* 2ndly at Glücksburg 8/ 15 Oct 1962, Princess Marie Luise of Schleswig-Holstein-Sonderburg-Glücksburg who ✝ at Wiesbaden 29 Dec 1969; *m* 3rdly at Schlangenbad 6 March 1971, Hélène Mayr).

    2. Count *Wulf Diether* Wolfgang Christian Ernst Otto Paul Karl, *b* at Berlin 20 Nov 1905; ✝ at Grünwald, nr Munich 1 July 1980, former Lufthansa Pilot, Dir of Munich Airport; *m* 1stly at Munich 22 June 1928 (*m* diss by div at Berlin 15 Dec 1941), Princess Hildegard (*b* at Söcking, nr Starnberg 12

April 1903; ✠ at Munich 12 April 1990; *m* 1stly at Salzburg 10 Jan 1922, Carl-Max, Count von and zu Sandizell; that *m* diss by div at Munich 5 March 1928 and annulled 16 Feb 1929), dau of Friedrich, Prince von Hanau, Count of Schaumburg and Countess Hildegard Almásy de Zsadány et Török-Szent-Miklós. He *m* 2ndly at Berlin 16 Feb 1942, Luise (*b* at Vienna 31 Oct 1910; ✠ at Munich 23 Jan 1985), Actress, dau of Major Richard Ullrich and Aloysia Bernert, and by her had issue,

> 1. Countess *Gabriele* Alexandra Gertrude Editha Luise, *b* at Dresden 30 Jan 1943; *m* at Munich 11 March 1963 (*m* diss by div at Munich 14 Nov 1985), Rolf Kröning (*b* at Berlin 19 June 1940), Lufthansa Pilot.
> [*Hugo Junkersstraße 6a, 82031 Grünald, nr Munich, Germany*].
> 2. Countess *Michaela* Nina Dorothea, *b* at Munich 4 Oct 1945; *m* at Kempten, Allgäu 5 Jan 1968, Bernd Rosemeyer (*b* at Berlin 12 Nov 1937), Dr of Med, Prof of Orthopaedics University of Munich.
> [*Kaiser Ludwigstraße 38a, 82031+ Grünwald, nr Munich, Germany*].

Brother of Grandfather

Issue of Adolf, Hereditary Count zu Castell-Rüdenhausen (*b* 15 March 1805; ✠ 11 June 1849) and his first wife, Countess Clara von Rantzau-Breitenburg (*b* 29 May 1807; *m* 21 Sept 1827; ✠ 30 June 1838), having had issue, among whom,

Son

Count *Kuno Friedrich* Franz Albrecht Ernst Christian, *b* at Rüdenhausen 12 Feb 1832; ✠ at Tübingen 3 April 1897, Royal Bavarian Chamberlain, *m* at Sutten 4/16 May 1857, Countess Emma (*b* at Kabillen, Curland 20 Nov/2 Dec 1834; ✠ at Winnental, nr Winnenden, Württemberg 21 Oct 1912), dau of Johann, Count von Keyserling, Proprietor of Sutten and Countess Louise von Keyserling, Proprietor of Kabillen, and had issue, among whom,

Sons

1. Count Friedrich *Paul* Adolf, *b* at Sutten 18 Nov 1862; ✠ at

Baden-Baden 1 Feb 1938, Col Prussian Army; *m* at Graz 29 Oct 1896, Baroness Marie (*b* at Graz 29 June 1875; ✚ at Hamburg 17 May 1961), dau of Karl Albert, Baron von Hayn and Maria Englhofer, and had issue,

> 1. Count *Hermann-Albrecht* Kuno Franz Karl-Maria, *b* in Berlin 4 Aug 1897; ✚ at Hamburg 30 Oct 1975, Lawyer; *m* 1stly at Berlin 28 Sept 1937, Ulrike (*b* at Hanover 14 May 1913; ✚ at Berlin 12 Sept 1938), dau of Elard von Seeler and Ulrike Bourjau, and had issue,
>
>> 1. Countess *Ulrike, b* at Berlin 12 Sept 1938, Film Editor.
>>
>> [*Prof.-Brix-Weg 2, 22767 Hamburg, Germany*].

Count Hermann-Albrecht *m* 2ndly at Berlin-Charlottenburg 29 June 1940, Ruth (*b* at Hamburg 2 Sept 1915; ✚ at Hamburg 16 Jul 2000), dau of Albert von Enckevort and Hingulda Reitzner von Heidelberg, and had further issue,

> 2. Count *Friedrich, b* at Berlin-Schmargendorf 27 July 1942, Banker, Kt of Hon St John of Jerusalem; *m* 1stly at Hamburg 14 Oct 1966 (*m* diss by div at Hamburg 22 Jan 1974 since when she reverted to her maiden name), Barbara (*b* at Bad Polzin 23 Oct 1943), dau of Arthur Martin Hans Nörenberg and Lieselotte Gertrud Schütz, and has issue,
>
> [*Vörn Barkholt 47, 22359 Hamburg-Volksdorf, Germany*].

>> 1. Count *Philip* Friedrich Casimir, *b* at Hamburg 9 Feb 1970; *m* at Hamburg 6 Sept 1996, Ulrike (*b* at Hannover 10 Aug 1970), dau of Jürgen Buhr and Maria Luise Waterbeck.
>>
>> [*Eppendorfer Baum 12, 20249 Hamburg, Germany*].

Count Friedrich *m* 2ndly at Ossiach 2 Oct 1977, Isnelda (*b* at Waiern-Feldkirchen 13 Aug 1955), dau of Alois Pribernig and Elisabeth Winkler, and has further issue,

[*Buchenallee 14, 22529 Hamburg, Germany*].

>> 2. Countess *Solveig* Ruth Elisabeth, *b* at Hamburg 30 Oct 1980.
>>
>> [*Buchenallee 14, 22529 Hamburg-Lokstedt, Germany*].

>> 3. Count *Manto* Friedrich Philip, *b* at Hamburg

24 March 1982.

3. Countess *Eveline, b* at Marktheidenfeld 12 Oct 1948; *m* 1stly at Hamburg 3 July 1970 (*m* diss by div at Hamburg 22 May 1980), Georg Gerhard von Drateln (*b* at Hamburg 1 Sept 1947). She *m* 2ndly at Hamburg 5 May 1983, Manfred Wolf (*b* at Hamburg 23 Aug 1949).

[*Kortenland 41, 22395 Hamburg-Bergstedt, Germany*].

4. Countess *Sybille, b* at Marktheidenfeld 23 Aug 1950; *m* at Hamburg 28 May 1970 (*m* diss by div 15 Dec 1977), Erwin Gunther Heinz Ziemer (*b* at New York 26 Jan 1947), Businessman.

[*Hellkamp 74, 20255 Hamburg-Eimsbüttel, Germany*].

2. Count *Oskar* Friedrich Hermann, *b* at Luby, Govt of Kowno 19 Nov/1 Dec 1869; ✝ at Wismar 18 Oct 1919; *m* at Pussen 17/29 July 1899, Baroness Adelheid (Ada) (*b* at Windau, Kurland 3/15 May 1872; ✝ at Lubeck 17 Nov 1948), dau of Wilhelm, Baron von Seefeld and Lucie von Wolski, and had issue, among whom,

1. Count *Manfred* Friedrich Paul, *b* at Pussen 21 July 1902; ✝*k* in action 5 Feb 1945; *m* at Bockstadt, nr Eisfeld, Thüringen 30 Aug 1933, Elisabeth (*b* at Bockstadt 25 June 1911; ✝ at Kaufering 10 Jun 1998), dau of Hermann Stettmund von Brodorotti, auf Bockstadt and Baroness Ilse von Münchhausen, Proprietor of Bockstadt, and had issue,

1. Count *Rüdiger* Friedrich Paul, *b* at Coburg 25 June 1934, Notary; *m* at Coburg 29 Aug 1964, Waltraud (*b* at Coburg 16 May 1941), dau of Dr Werner Diezel and Johanna Diesel, and has issue,

[*Herterichstraße 91b, 01477 Munich, Germany*]

1. Countess *Uta* Elisabeth, *b* at Coburg 24 July 1967; *m* at Ottobrunn, nr Munich 16 Oct 1996, Jan Reichel (*b* at Hamburg 11 Mar 1964), Dip. Ing.

[*Hirtenstraße 28, 85521 Ottobrunn, Germany*]

2. Countess *Margarethe* Johanna, *b* at Coburg 28 Feb 1972.

[*Sohnckestraße 3, 81479 Munich, Germany*].

2. Count *Ruprecht* Friedrich Siegfried Wolfgang Paul, *b* at Berlinchen, Neumark 30 Dec 1940, Pastor, Military Deacon, Kt of Justice and Chaplain of the Order of St John of Jerusalem; *m* at Erlangen 23 (civ) and 24

(relig) Feb 1968, Dorothea (*b* at Erlangen 20 Feb 1943), dau of Walther von Loewenich and Elisabeth Thielicke, and has issue,
[*Kaskadenweg 24, 81247 Munich, Germany*].

    1. Countess *Annette* Karoline, *b* at Erlangen 5 Sept 1969, Musician; *m* at Wiesbaden 9 April 1999, Hristo Kouzmanov (*b* at Sofia, Bulgaria 19 Oct 1974), Musician.
    [*Taunusstraße 18, 65183 Wiesbaden, Germany*]
    2. Count *Bernhard* Friedrich Volker, *b* at Erlangen 18 March 1972.
    [*Görresstraße 8, 80798 Munich, Germany*]
    3. Countess *Adelheid* Dorothea, *b* at Munich 1 July 1982.

3. Count *Börries* Friedrich Frommhold Hans Gotthard Oskar, *b* posthumously at Lüneburg 13 July 1945, Dr of Med, Pediatrician; *m* at Coburg 27 Dec 1969, Barbara (*b* at Coburg 25 March 1944), dau of Otfried Engel and Gudrun Hammerschmidt, and has issue,
[*86916 Kaufering, Germany*].

    1. Count *Christian* Friedrich, *b* at Erlangen 23 June 1970, ✝ at Munich 4 Jan 2002.
    2. Count *Wolfgang* Manfred, *b* at Erlangen 30 Nov 1971, Ph.D.
    [*Hartmannstraße 47, 91052 Erlangen, Germany*].
    3. Countess *Ines* Alexandra, *b* at Erlangen 19 June 1974; *m* at Kaufering 3 Aug 2002, Gerhard Munk (*b* at Ottingen, Bavaria 5 Dec 1976).
    [*Domprobststraße 68, 91056 Erlangen, Germany*].
    4. Countess *Amelie* Elisabeth, *b* at Erlangen 11 Dec 1975.
    [*Nördliche Stadtmauerstraße 22, 91054 Erlangen, Germany*].

COLLOREDO-MANNSFELD

Catholic: This feudal Swabian family traditionally originates from Waldsee; Leiabordo de Waldsee was invested with the Castle of Mels in Italy by Poppo d'Aquileja in 1031; Glizoio de Mels appears authentically with his brothers 25 Oct 1247; Glizoio founded the line of Colloredo and Henri the line of Mels-Colloredo; Permission to attack the Castle of Colloredo (near Udine, Friaul) 4 Dec 1302; Barons authorised in Prague 19 March 1588 and Barons of the Holy Empire with "de Waldsee" and confirmation of descent by Emperor Rudolf II 31 July 1591 (for the whole family); Hereditary Grand Huntsman of the Kingdom of Bohemia, Prague 13 Sept 1723; qualification of "Hoch and Wohlgeboren", Vienna 11 Dec 1724 and Count of the Holy Empire, Vienna 11 Dec 1724; received (ad personam) into the Swabian College of Counts of the Holy Empire 17 Aug 1737; Lord of Lower Austria 22 June 1743; Bohemian Prince (primogeniture), Vienna 24 Dec 1763; Hungarian Indigenat 1765; joined the name and arms of Mannsfeld (region of Merseburg) through the marriage of Prince Franz Gundaccar (b 28 May 1731; ✝ 27 Oct 1807) to Marie-Isabelle (b 29 Aug 1749; m 6 Jan 1771; ✝ 21 Oct 1794), heiress of the last Count of Mannsfeld, Vienna 26 Feb 1789; received the qualification of "Durchlaucht" (primogeniture) by the German Diet 18 Aug 1825; confirmed in Austria 9 Oct 1829.

The Head of the family and his wife bear the title of Prince and Princess von Colloredo-Mannsfeld with the qualification of Serene Highness and other members of the family bear the title of Count or Countess von Colloredo-Mannsfeld. The eldest son of the Head of the Family bears the title of Count of Mannsfeld.

HIERONYMUS (*Jerome*) Weikhard Maria, **9TH PRINCE (FÜRST) VON COLLOREDO-MANNSFELD,** Count von Waldsee, Vicegraf von Mels, Marchese di Santa Sofia, b at Monmouth, Illinois, USA 16 March 1949, son of Count *Friedrich* Hieronymus Heinrich Richard Maria (b at Berlin 3 April 1917 ✝ at Öblarn 29 July 1991) and Christa von Kries(b at Hamburg 4 June 1922; m 4 June 1946; diss by div 7 May 1955; ✝ at Dubrovnik 12 Sept 1972); *succ his uncle,* Hieronymus 8th Prince (Fürst) von Colloredo-Mannsfeld (b 9 June 1912; ✝ 2 Dec 1998), having been adopted by his uncle, Josef 7th Prince (Fürst) von Colloredo-Mannsfeld, (b 4 June 1910; ✝ 30 Jan 1990), at Gröbming, Styria 15 Feb 1965 and at Vienna 5 May 1966; m 1stly at Öblarn 14 June (civ) and 15 June (relig) 1975 (m diss by div at Vienna 4 Oct 1977 and religiously annulled at Graz 27 Feb 1982), Alexandra [*Lenau Gasse19, 1080 Vienna, Austria*] (b at Munich 26 Feb 1955), Dr of Med, dau of Igor von Glasenapp and

Antonia Raumer. He *m* 2ndly at Vienna 26 July 1979 (civ) and Kleinsölk, Styria 28 Sept (relig) 1982, Livia Anna (*b* at Prague 3 May 1956), dau of Paul Fuchs and Jirina Sladka, and has issue by his second wife.

[*Schloß Gstatt, 8960 Öblarn, OSteiermark, Austria; 8960 Öblarn 34, OSteiermark, Austria*]

Sons

1. Count *Paul-Josef* Hieronymus Maria, Count of Mannsfeld, *b* at Vienna 8 June 1981.
2. Count *Lelio* Friedrich Georg, *b* at Vienna 24 Jan 1985.

Step Mother

Martine, Countess *Friedrich* von Colloredo-Mannsfeld (*b* at Saigon 8 May 1937; *m* 1stly ....), dau of Louis Andrieux and Germaine Parkosch; *m* at at Vienna 20 Oct 1975 as his 2nd wife, Count *Friedrich* Hieronymus Heinrich Richard Maria (*b* at Berlin 3 April 1917; ✠ at Öblarn 29 July 1991).

[*Auhofstraße 21/c/1, 1130 Vienna, Austria*]

Sister

Countess *Isabella* Josefa Maria, *b* at Geneva 29 Feb 1952, Mag med vet.

[*Aschberg, 3051 St. Christophen, Austria*].

Brothers of Father

1. **Josef** Leopold Hieronymus Alexander Maria, **7th Prince (Fürst) von Colloredo-Mannsfeld,** Count von Waldsee, Vicegraf von Mels, Marchese di Santa Sofia, *b* at Pola 4 June 1910; ✠ at Salzburg 30 Jan 1990, Dr rer pol; *m* 1stly at Reith 25 March 1939, Anna Maria (*b* at Innsbruck 1 June 1908; ✠ at Beamsville, Ontario, Canada 25 June 1953; *m* 1stly, Roderich Menzel; that *m* annulled at Leitmeritz 1 Jan 1937), dau of Dr Hans Rabl and Josefine Riszdörfer-Izdenczy. He *m* 2ndly at Munich 1 March 1988, Antonia [*Schloß Gstatt, 8960 Öblarn, OSteiermark*] (*b* at Munich 20 May 1922; *m* 1stly at Munich 18 Jan 1943, Helmut Berger; that *m* diss by div at Munich 14 July 1948; *m* 2ndly at Munich 20 Sept 1948, Igor von Glasenapp; that *m* diss by div at Wolfratshausen 9 Feb 1988), dau of Wilhelm Raumer and Josefine Fischer. The Prince adopted his grandsons and nephew (see below), and had issue by his first wife,

     1. Countess *Kristina* Josefine Nadine Maria, *b* at Prague 19 Dec 1940; *m* 1stly at Öblarn 10 Sept (civ) and 11 Sept 1960

(*m* diss by div at Vienna 18 May 1965), Georg, Prince zu
Fürstenberg (*b* at Strobl 13 Aug 1923), Dr of Law. She *m*
2ndly 1965 (*m* diss by div at Toronto 29 Aug 1973), Jan van
Hamel (*b* at .....) and 3rdly at Wadi Firan, Egypt 22 May 1975
(*m* diss by div at Athens 16 Nov 1983), Michael Begert (*b* at
Berne, Switzerland ...). She has since reverted to her maiden
name, and has issue who were adopted by her father, Josef,
7th Prince (Fürst) von Colloredo-Mannsfeld Sept 1988, *inter
alias,*

[*Schloß Gstatt, 8960 Öblarn, Upper Steiermark*].

> 1. *Leonhard* Josef Colloredo-Mannsfeld, *b* at ... 10 Feb
> 1964.
> 2. *Derek* Josef Colloredo-Mannsfeld, *b* at ... 25 June
> 1966.
> 3. *Stephan* Cyrill, *b* at ... 12 Nov 1976.

2. **Hieronymus** Medardus Alexander Felicianus Maria, **8th Prince
(Fürst) von Colloredo-Mannsfeld,** Count von Waldsee, Vicegraf
von Mels, Marchese di Santa Sofia, *b* at Berlin 9 June 1912, *succ* his
brother, Joseph, 7th Prince (see below), son of Hieronymus, Count
von Colloredo-Mannsfeld (*b* 3 Nov 1870; ✝ 29 Aug 1942) and
Countess Berthe von Kolowrat-Krakowsky (*b* 21 June 1890; *m* 10 Aug
1909; *m* diss by div 8 Jan 1926; ✝ 29 Jan 1982).

Brother of Great Grandfather

Issue of Joseph, 5th Prince von Colloredo-Mannsfeld (*b* 26 Feb 1813;
✝ 22 April 1895) and Theresia von Lebzeltern (*b* 27 April 1818; *m* 27
May 1841; ✝ 19 Jan 1900), having had issue, among whom,

Son

Count *Franz de Paula* Ferdinand Gundaccar, *b* at Vienna 1 Aug
1847; ✝ at Sierndorf 22 Oct 1925; *m* 1stly at Prague 23 Jan 1874,
Baroness Maria (*b* at Doxan 26 May 1850; ✝ at Volosca, nr Fiume 5
May 1881), dau of Johann, Baron Lexa von Aehrenthal, Proprietor of
Doxan, Gross-Skal, etc and Countess Maria von Thun and Hohenstein.
He *m* 2ndly at Gross-Skal 6 Sept 1884, Baroness Elisabeth (*b* at
Prague 2 March 1858; ✝ at Sierndorf 29 July 1890), sister of his first
wife, and had issue, among whom, from his first wife,

Sons

1. Count *Rudolf* Josef Ferdinand Maria, *b* at Sierndorf 16 Aug 1876;
✝ there 21 March 1948; *m* at Schloß Sichrow 20 Sept 1922, Princess
Johanna (*b* at Sichrow 16 July 1890; ✝ at Vienna 15 March 1961),

Dame Star Cross Order, dau of Alain, Prince (Fürst) Rohan, 12th Duke of Montbazon and Bouillon and Princess Johanna von Auersperg, and had issue, amongst whom,

    1. Countess Maria *Johanna* Ernestine Bertha Sylvia, *b* at Vienna 25 July 1923, Dame Star Cross Order, Dame of Hon Sovereign Military Order of Malta; *m* at Sierndorf, nr Stockerau, Lower Austria 19 April 1969, Anton, Baron von Aretin (*b* at Munich 15 Aug 1918; ✝ at Aldersbach, nr Vilshofen, Bavaria 12 June 1981), Brewer.

    [*94501 Aldersbach bei Vilshofen, Lower Bavaria, Germany*].

2. Count *Ferdinand* Johannes Hieronymus Maria, *b* at Sierndorf 5 June 1878; ✝ at Vienna 18 Dec 1967, Kt Order of the Golden Fleece; *m* at New York 10 May 1909, Eleonore (Nora) (*b* at New York 27 Dec 1881; ✝ at New York 25 Feb 1939), dau of Charles Oliver Iselin and Frances Garner, and had issue, among whom,

    1. Count *Franz Ferdinand* Romanus, *b* at Rome 1 March 1910; ✝*k* in action nr Berck-sur-Mer, Pas-de- Calais 10 Jan 1944; *m* at Boston, Massachusetts, USA 3 Oct 1933, Mabel (*b* at Boston 4 March 1912; ✝ at Needham, Massachusetts, USA 26 March 1965; she *m* 2ndly 7 Oct 1944, Thomas Hunter Lines; that *m* diss by div 1951), dau of Joseph Gardener Bradley and Mabel Warren, and had issue,

        1. Countess Mabel Bayard *Elizabeth*, *b* at New York 28 Aug 1936; *m* at New York 27 Aug 1959 (*m* diss by div at New York May 1972), Frederick Romley (*b* at Boston, Massachusetts 1936). She *m* 2ndly at Upper Marlboro, Maryland 1972, Peter Eugene Vladimirovitch Silitch of the Marquesses de Techernigoff (*b* at New York 26 Sept 1935).

        [*Route 1, Box 27, Strange Creek, W.V. 26639, U.S.A.*].

    2. Count Franz *Rudolf* Maria, *b* at Paris 10 Aug 1938, Forester, Farmer; *m* at Munich 20 Sept 1962, Princess Maria Alexandra (Almerie) (*b* at Prague 21 Oct 1939), dau of Johann (Hans), Prince von Thurn and Taxis and Princess Maria Julia of Lobkowicz, and has issue,

    [*Schloßpark 1, 2011 Sierndorf, Lower Austria*].

        1. Count *Antony* Georg Ferdinand Maria, *b* at Vienna 25 April 1964; *m* at Vienna 3 Sept 1988, Claudia Dorothea (*b* at Vienna 5 Sept 1965), dau of Ernst Walter Pless and Dorothea Emilie Maria Rabe, and has issue,

[*Reith 103, 3553 Schiltern, Lower Austria*].

    1. Count Jacob Ernst Rudolf, *b* at Vienna 23 Feb 1995.

    2. Countess *Laura* Dorothea Maria, *b* at Tulle 22 Aug 1997.

2. Countess *Theresita*, *b* at Vienna 27 Dec 1965, stud oec soc; *m* at Salzburg 22 July 1996 (civ) and at Sierndorf 28 June 1997 (relig), *Christoph* Oliver Herbert Lieben-Seutter (*b* at Vienna 3 June 1964).

[*Wohltebeeigasse, 7/12, 1040 Vienna, Austria*].

3. Count *Nikodemus* Ferdinand Christian Bruno, *b* at Vienna 10 Nov 1969, stud agriculture.

[*Schloßpark 1, 2011 Sierndorf, Lower Austria*].

4. Countess *Mabel* Marie Frederike Johanna, *b* at Vienna 8 Dec 1978.

3. Count *Ferdinand* Peter Ernst, *b* at London 19 Sept 1939; *m* at Boston 26 May 1962, Suzanna (*b* at Boston 4 Nov 1940), dau of John Endicott Lawrence and Anne Tuckermann, and has issue,

[*Winthrop Street, South Hamilton, MA 01982, U.S.A.*].

    1. Count *Franz Ferdinand*, *b* at Boston 28 Jan 1963; *m* at Boston 30 July 1988, Anne (*b* at New York 1 April 1963), dau of Donald Smith Dowden and Anne Feeney, and has issue,

    [*635 Highland Street, South Hamilton, MA 01982, U.S.A.*].

        1. Count *Franz Josef*, *b* at Boston 25 April 1990.

        2. Count *Johann Ferdinand*, *b* at Boston 6 January 1994.

        3. Count *Simon Rudolf*, *b* at ... 12 July 1995.

        4. Countess *Anne* Peabody, *b* at ... 00 July 1999.

2. Count *Rudolf Josef*, *b* at Boston 11 April 1965, Ph.D, Prof of Anthropology; *m* at Jackson Hole, Wyoming 11 July 1992, Franchesca (*b* at Swaziland 29 March 1964), dau of Jeremy

Varcoe and Wendy Moss, and has issue,
[*227 Ferson Avenue, Iowa City, IA 52246, U.S.A.*].

1. Count *Schulyer John*, *b* at Santa Monica, California 11 Jan 1996.
2. Countess *Mia Wendy*, *b* at Santa Monica California, 30 Sept 1997.
3. Countess *Zoe Liesl*, *b* at Iowa City, Iowa 27 Sept 2002.

3. Countess *Anne* Elizabeth, *b* at Boston 3 Nov 1967; *m* at Hamilton, Massachusetts 28 Nov 1992, Donald Kent Penfield (*b* at Middleton, Connecticut 30 April 1962).
[*RR1, 75D Sharon, VT 05065, U.S.A.*].

CROŸ

Catholic: This feudal family originated in the County of Ponthieu (Picardy) and can be authentically traced from Guermond and Robert of Croÿ living in the early part of the 12th century (Archives of the Somme at Amiens); Jacques, Sire de Croÿ married Marguerite d'Airaines in 1287 and founded the branch of Solre, the only surviving branch of the family and was the third son of Philippe de Croÿ, Comte de Chimay; Antoine de Croÿ, Lord of Sempy (✝ 1546) married Louise of Luxembourg; Comte de Chimay 1470; Comte de Solre (Northern France) 3 Nov 1590; the Lordship of Croÿ was raised to a Duchy June 1598 by King Henri IV of France with a clause giving the Head of the Family the right to bear the title of "Duke of Croÿ"; this right was confirmed by King Louis XV in 1768; Spanish Grandee 1st Class 1598; Duc d'Havré 1627; Prince de Solre 14 Nov 1677; acquired Dülmen 1803; accorded the qualification of "Durchlaucht" (primogeniture) by the German Diet 18 Aug 1825, confirmed in Prussia 21 Feb 1832 and extended to all members of the family 3 March 1833; Hereditary Member of the former Prussian House of Lords 12 Oct 1854. The family is divided into three lines descending from the sons of August, 9th Duke of Croÿ (*b* 3 Nov 1765; ✝ 19 Oct 1822).

The Head of the family and his wife bear the title of Duke and Duchess von Croÿ and cadet members bear the title of Prince or Princess of Croÿ with the qualification of Serene Highness.

CROŸ-DÜLMEN
(WESTPHALIAN BRANCH)

CARL Emanuel Ludwig Petrus Eleonore Alexander Rudolf Engelbert Benno, **14TH DUKE (HERZOG) VON CROŸ**, *b* at Düsseldorf 11 Oct 1914, Lic jur, Kt Sovereign Military Order of Malta, son of Karl, 13th Duke of Croÿ (*b* 11 April 1889; ✝ 2 Aug 1974) and Nancy Leishman (*b* 2 Oct 1894; *m* 27 Oct 1913; ✝ 22 Feb 1983); *m* at Leutstetten 17 June (civ) and at Nymphenburg 18 June (relig) 1953, Princess Gabriele (*b* at Berchtesgaden 10 May 1927), Dame of Hon Bavarian Orders of St Theresia and St Elisabeth, dau of Crown Prince Rupprecht of Bavaria and Princess Antonia of Luxemburg and Nassau.

[*Schloß Merfeld, 48249 Dülmen, Westphalia, Germany*].

Sons and Daughter

1. Princess *Marie-Theresia* Antonia Nancy Charlotte, *b* at Dülmen 29 March 1954.

[*Hartwickstraße 21 40547 Düsseldorf, Germany*].

2. *Rudolf* Carl Rupprecht, Hereditary Prince (Erbprinz) von Croÿ, *b* at Dülmen 8 July 1955, Kt Sovereign Military Order of Malta; *m* at Schloß Sünching, nr Regensburg 24 Oct (civ) and 24 Oct (relig) 1987, Alexandra Serafimovna (*b* at Sünching 7 July 1960), dau of Serafim Nikolaievif Miloradovif and Baroness Agnes von Hoenning-O'Carroll, and has issue,

[*Schloßpark 1, 48249 Dülmen, Westphalia, Germany*].

   1. Prince *Carl-Philipp-Emanuel* Rudolph Zdenko Seraphim Maria, *b* at Münster 18 Aug 1989.

   2. Princess *Xenia-Maria-Alexandra* Antonia Agnes Gabrielle Camilla, *b* at Münster 26 Dec 1990.

   3. Prince *Marc-Emmanuel* Carl Rudolph Zdenko Seraphim Maria, *b* at Münster 6 April 1992.

   4. Prince *Heinrich-Carl-Rupprecht* Rudolph Zdenko Seraphim Maria, *b* at Münster 9 Dec 1993.

   5. Prince *Alexander-Carl* Rudolph Zdenko Seraphim Maria, *b* at Münster 9 March 1995.

   6. Princess *Anastasia* Maria Irina Adelgunde Gabrielle Agnes Sophie, *b* at Münster 12 Jan 1998.

3. Prince *Stefan* Clemens Philipp, *b* at Merfeld 17 May 1959; *m* at Wezembeek-Oppem, Belgium 25 Aug (civ) and at Bonquetôt 15 Sept (relig) 1990, Comtesse Béatrice (*b* at Brussels 8 Sept 1964), dau of François, Count du Chastel de la Howarderie and Countess Regine

de Liedekerke-Paihle, and has issue,
[*Charée de la Sarte 14, 1390 Grez Ocean, Belgian*].

> 1. Princess *Charlotte* Régine Gabrielle Sophie, *b* at Münster 22 Dec 1992.
> 2. Prince *Lionel* Carl François Eric, *b* at Münster 3 Jan 1996.
> 3. Princess *Camille* Regine Gabrielle Nancy, *b* at Münster 6 Feb 1998

Sisters

1. Princess *Antoinette* Emma Laurenzia Charlotte Ludmille Juliette Marthe Helene Sabina, *b* at Berlin 27 Oct 1915; *m* 1stly at Nordkirchen 14 June 1944 (*m* diss by div 24 Aug 1947 and annulled at Münster 3 Dec 1952/Cologne 18 Dec 1953), Jürgen von Goerne (*b* at Allenstein 12 Feb 1908; ✣ 3 March 2001), Col (ret). She *m* 2ndly at Hamburg 18 Feb 1948 (*m* diss by div at London 27 July 1956), Frederick Nelson Tucker (*b* at London 3 Dec 1919). She *m* 3rdly at Münich 4 March 1981 (civ) and 14 Jan 1982 (relig), Douglas Auffmordt (*b* at Lausanne 7 April 1917).
[*22 Blvd. Jean Mermoz, 92200 Neuill s/S, France; Vorpark 31, 48249 Dülmen, Westphalia, Germany; Ca'n Punxa, 07460 Pollensa, Mallorca, Spain*].

2. Princess *Marie-Luise* Natalie Engelberta Ludmilla Nancy Julie, *b* at Dülmen 18 Dec 1919; *m* 1stly at New York 11 March 1941 (*m* iss by div in Nevada 1949), Richard Metz (*b* at New York 19 June 1912). She *m* 2ndly at New York 27 Nov 1952, Nelson Slater (*b* at Webster, Mass, USA 7 July 1893; ✣ 22 April 1968). She *m* 3rdly 23 July 1969, Frederick B Adams (*b* at Greenwich, Connecticut, USA 28 March 1910; ✣ January 2001), Chevalier Légion d'Honneur, Cmdr Order of the Crown (Belgium).
[*208 rue de Rivoli, 75001 Paris, France*].

Half-Brother

Issue of the 13th Duke and his third wife, Marie Louise Wiesner (*b* at Wandsbek 22 June 1904; *m* at Berlin 28 Jan 1933; ✣ at Nordkirchen 13 Feb 1945; *m* 1stly 23 Dec 1924, Werner Koch von Hernhaussen; that *m* diss by div 10 July 1930).

1. Prince *Clemens* Franz Carl Anselm, *b* at Berlin 5 July 1934, Forester; *m* at Neudau, Styria 9 June 1962, Countess Madeleine (*b* at Graz 11 Nov 1941; ✣ at Graz 16 Jan 1999), dau of Johann (Hans) Adalbert, Count Kottulinsky, Proprietor of Nedau and

Baroness Cécile-Maria von Ottenfels genannt von Gschwind, and has issue,

[*8553 St. Oswald ob Eibiswald, Steiermark, Austria*].

    1. Prince *Carl* Clemens, *b* at Graz 5 March 1963; *m* at St Oswald, Styria 25 Aug 1990, Michaela (*b* at Vienna 8 May 1962), dau of Peter Reuschel and Liselotte Reidingen, and has issue,

    [*8553 St Oswald ob Eibiswald, Steiermark, Austria*].

        1. Prince *Vinzenz* Hans Carl Clemens, *b* at Vienna 14 Aug 1993.

        2. Prince *Sebastian* Josef Alexander Carl Peter, *b* at Vienna 19 Feb 1995.

        3. Princess *Katharina* Stefanie Ebba Madeleine Liselotte, *b* at Vienna 1 Nov 1996.

        4. Princess *Veronika* Antoinette Madeleine Michaela, *b* at Vienna 14 Nov 1998.

    2. Princess *Cécile* Marie-Louise Charlotte Brigitte, *b* at Graz 21 Feb 1964; *m* at München 19 Oct (civ)1994 and St Oswalds 29 July (relig) 1995, ✠ at Ali-Reza Esmaeili (*b* at Kangavar, Persia 20 Sept 1963); retained her maiden name following marriage, passed on *inter alias* to her issue.

    [*8553 St Oswald ob Eibiswald, Steiermark, Austria*].

    3. Prince *Constantine* Andreas Reginald Hans, *b* at Graz 20 Sept 1968; *m* at Las Vegas, Nevada 26 June 1994 (*m* diss by div), Kiraiki (Sandy) (*b* at Athens 28 April 1969), dau of Athanasse and Haido Triantopoulos, and has issue,

    [*8553 St Oswald ob Eibiswald, Steiermark, Austria*].

Brothers and Sister of Father

Issue of the Karl 12th Duke von Croÿ (*b* 29 Jan 1859; ✠ 28 Sept 1906) and Princess and Duchess Ludmilla d'Arenberg (*b* 29 June 1870; *m* 25 April 1888; ✠ 9 Sept 1953), having had issue, among whom,

Son

Prince *Anton* Prosper Clemens, *b* at Brussels 6 Jan 1893; ✠ at Gams am Kamp, Lower Austria 29 Oct 1973, Kt of Hon Sovereign Military Order of Malta; *m* 1stly at Marienloh, Paderborn 23 May 1922, Rosalie (*b* at Fürstenberg 5 Aug 1894; ✠ at Münster, Westphalia 28 March 1942), dau of Bogislav von Heyden-Linden and Countess Elisabeth von Westphalen zu Fürstenberg, and had issue, among whom,

1. Princess *Maria Elisabeth* Ludmilla Josepha, *b* at Paderborn 10 March 1923; *m* at Grumsmühlen, Lingen 23 June 1944, Matthias, Count von Schmettau (*b* at Potsdam 22 June 1918; ✠ at Bonn 21 Aug 1986).
[*Schloß Ehreshoven, 51766 Engelskirchen, Germany*].

2. Prince Carl *Alfred* Friedrich Bogislaus Joseph, *b* at Marienloh 4 March 1924, Farmer, Forester; *m* at Haus Seelen, nr Xanten 7 May 1952, Baroness Huberta (*b* at Haus Seelen 2 Feb 1928), dau of Karl-Reinhard, Baron von Wolff-Metternich, Proprietor of Seelen and Elisabeth von Boch, and has adopted his nephew,
[*Grumsmühlen, 49838 Langen, Emsland, Germany*].

    1. *Nikolaus* Engelbert Albert Johannes, Count von Schmettau, *b* at Bochum 21 July 1953, son of Matthias, Count von Schmettau and Princess Maria Elisabeth of Croÿ (see above); *m* 1stly at Adelebsen 3 July (civ) and Vinsebeck 8 July (relig) 1989, Countess Maria del Pilar (*b* at Bonn 21 Dec 1959), dau of Peter Wolff Metternich zur Gracht and Marie Christine, Altgräfin zu Salm-Reifferscheidt-Krautheim und Dyck; He *m* 2ndly at Wulfshagen 11 May 2001, Countess Anna Sophia (*b* at Eckernförde 15 April 1970), dau of Count Friedrich zu Reventlow and Jutta Lage.

3. Prince *Clemens* Anton Philipp Joseph, *b* at Grumsmühlen 7 Sept 1926, Kt of Hon Sovereign Military Order of Malta; *m* at Engelskirchen 27 July 1955, Countess Marie Therese (*b* at Berlin 11 Dec 1927), dau of Walter, Count von Schaesberg, Proprietor of Woltersdorf and Lübsee, Pommern and Countess Hermine von Redern, and has issue,
[*Holunderweg 18, 51519 Odenthal-Erberich, Germany*].

    1. Prince *Eugen-* Alexander Clemens Josef, *b* at Mülheim an der Ruhr 22 April 1956; *m* at Wehrden, Höxter 29 Sept 1984, Carolyn-Huberta (*b* at Bonn-Dottendorf 12 March 1953), dau of Joachim Christopher von Hennigs, Proprietor of Buggow in Greifswald and Baroness Gisela Ostman von der Leye.
[*Brühlmeerweg 55, 40667 Meerbusch, Germany*].

    2. Prince *Philippe* Alexander Alfred Josef, *b* at Mülheim 8 Sept 1957; *m* at Lensahn 27 June 1985, Duchess Margarete (*b* at Lübeck 16 May 1954), dau of Peter, Duke of Oldenburg and Princess Gertrud zu

Löwenstein-Wertheim-Freudenberg, and has issue,
[*Postaerstraße 16b, 01796 Pirna, Germany*].

    1. Prince *Alexander* Friedrich-August Albrecht Ernst, *b* at Düsseldorf 6 March 1987.

    2. Prince *Maximilian* Johannes Alexander Engelbert, *b* at Düsseldorf 31 May 1988.

    3. Princess *Rosalie* Franziska Carolyn Marie-Eugenie, *b* at Düsseldorf 23 Oct 1990.

3. Prince *Albrecht-Alexander* Walter Josef, *b* at Mülheim 8 May 1959, Journalist.
[*Robert Blumstraße 9, 60385 Frankfurt-am-Main, Germany*].

4. Prince *Engelbert Alexander* Maximilian Josef, *b* at Mülheim 8 May 1962; *m* at Schloß Zeil 16 April (civ) and 7 July (relig) 1990, Princess Elisabeth (*b* at Ravensburg 30 July 1966), dau of Georg, 7th Prince (Fürst) von Waldburg zu Zeil and Trauchburg and Princess Marie Gabrielle of Bavaria, and has issue,
[*Zur Amtsschlade 43, 58802 Balvel, Germany*].

    1. Princess *Marie* Isabelle Sophie Hermine, *b* at Hadamar 6 May 1991.

    2. Prince *Constantin* Maria Walter Erich, *b* at Menden 19 July 1992.

    3. Prince *Carl* Georg Clemens Nicodemus, *b* at Menden 13 Sept 1994.

    4. Princess *Philippa*, *b* at Menden 21 Feb 1999.

4. Princess *Margarethe* Maria Christina Emanuela Henriette Anna Katharina, Dame of Hon Sovereign Military Order of Malta, *b* at Grumsmühlen 11 Oct 1930; *m* at Grumsmühlen 7 June 1956, Heinrich, Count von Schaesberg (*b* at Berlin 12 Feb 1922; ✝ at Tannheim, Kr Biberach an der Riss 22 Jan 1996), Farmer, Forester.
[*88459 Tannheim, Kr. Biberach an der Riss, Germany*].

Prince Anton *m* 2ndly at Buchberg 15 May 1944, Princess Wilhelmine (*b* at Vienna 18 May 1906; ✝ at Authal 7 April 1990), dau of Klemens, Prince von Croÿ (see below) and Princess Christiane von Auersperg, and had further issue,

5. Prince *Anton* Egon Clemens, *b* at Grumsmühlen 27 Aug 1945, Farmer, Forester; *m* 1stly at Maria Dreieichen, Lower Austria 29 Sept 1970 (*m* diss by div at Leoben 18 May 1988), Maria Antonia [*Schlögl Gasse16a, 1120 Vienna, Austria*]

(*b* at Vienna 25 Oct 1950), dau of Herbert Fundulus and Countess Eva Marie von Schönfeldt and had issue,
[*Schloß Authal, 8740 Zeltweg, Steiermark, Austria*].

> 1. Princess *Sophie* Margarethe, *b* at Vienna 3 April 1971; *m* at Zeltweg 22 April (civ) and at Weißkirchen, Styria 30 Sept (relig) 2000, Baron Hermann von Rotenhan (*b* at Bamberg 16 Aug 1968).
> [*Schloß Eyrichshof, 96106 Ebern, Germany*].
> 2. Princess *Valerie* Christiane, *b* at Vienna 18 April 1972.
> [*Herren Gasse6-8/4/4/15, 1010 Vienna, Austria*].
> 3. Prince *Anton Clemens, b* at Vienna 19 July 1974.
> [*Schloß Authal, 8740 Zeltweg, Austria*].
> 4. Princess *Isabelle* Maria Benedikta, *b* at Vienna 20 Jan 1976.
> [*Schloß Authal, 8740 Zeltweg, Austria*].
> 5. Princess *Franziska* Barbara, *b* at Vienna 14 July 1977.
> [*Schlögl Gasse16a, 1120 Vienna, Austria*].
> 6. Princess *Stefanie* Maria Manuela, *b* at Vienna 6 Jan 1980.
> [*Schlögl Gasse16a, 1120 Vienna, Austria*].

Prince *Anton* Egon Clemens *m* 2ndly at Gars am Kamp 13 June 1989, Antoinette (*b* at Graz 12 Feb 1959), dau of Friedrich von Leutzendorff and Lady and Countess Wilhelmine zu Stubenberg, and has issue further issue,
[*Schloß Authal, 8740 Zeltweg, Steiermark, Austria*].

> 7. *Marie* Therese, *b* at Leoben 5 May 1991.
> 8. Anton Ferdinand, b at Leoben 20 Jan 1994.

Brothers of Great-Grandfather

Issue of Alfred, 10th Duke von Croÿ (*b* 22 Dec 1789; ✠ 14 July 1861) and Princess Éléonore zu Salm-Salm (*b* 6 Dec 1794; *m* 21 June 1819; ✠ 6 Jan 1871), having had issue, among whom,

Sons

(BOHEMIAN BRANCH)

1. Prince Alexis Wilhelm Zephyrius Viktor, *b* at Prague 13 Jan 1825; ✠ at Nauheim 20 Aug 1898; *m* at Prague 18 June 1853, Princess Franziska (*b* at Pahorelic, Moravia 4 Aug 1833; ✠ at Gries 3 March 1908), dau of Prince Maximilian zu Salm-Salm and Countess Rosine

von Sternberg, and had issue, among whom,

Sons

1. Prince *Maximilian* Rudolf Karl Dietrich Anna, *b* at Schweckhausen, Westphalia 16 Jan 1864; ✝ at Slabetz, nr Rakonitz, Bohemia 20 May 1920, Proprietor of Slabetz; *m* at Krimitz, Bohemia 6 Oct 1908, Princess Caroline (*b* at Konopischt, Bohemia 4 Oct 1873; ✝ at Isareck, Bavaria 11 Feb 1951), dau of Prince Franz of Lobkowicz and Countess Kunigunde von Sternberg, and had issue, among whom,

    1. Prince *Alexis* Franz Antonius Maximilian Carolus Benediktus Mathias Maria, *b* at Slabetz 24 Feb 1910, Proprietor of Slabetz, Kt of Hon Sovereign Military Order of Malta; *m* 1stly at Petschau, Bohemia 7 Oct 1931, Countess Elisabeth (*b* at Vienna 15 Nov 1911; ✝ at Aicha vorm Wald, nr Vilshofen, Bavaria 21 March 1995), Dame Star Cross Order, dau of Heinrich, 6th Duke of Beaufort-Spontin, Proprietor of Petschau, Bohemia and Countess Marie-Adelheid von Silva-Tarouca. He *m* 2ndly at Prague 12 Oct 1996, Jana (*b* at Pilsen 16 Nov 1959), dau of Miloslav Belohávková and Danuse Vodáková, and has issue from his first wife,

    [94529 Schloß Aicha, nr Vilshofen, Bavaria, Germany].

        1. Prince *Maximilian* Heinrich Karl Maria, *b* at Slabetz 9 Sept 1932; *m* at Münich (civ) and at Altötting 29 Nov (relig) 1958 (*m* diss by div 1973), Asja [*Landshuter Allee 49, 80637 Münich, Germany*] (*b* at Dalmatia 10 July 1932), dau of Dragomir and Ivana Lukiſ, and has issue,

        (*Schraudolphstraße 9 80538 Münich*)

            1. Prince *Alexis*, *b* at Münich 24 Sept 1959.

            [*Kammerhof 5, 85354 Freising, Germany*].

            2. Princess *Anna*, *b* at Landshut 11 Feb 1965.

        2. Prince *Albrecht* Maria Johann Gerhard Michael, *b* at Slabetz 24 June 1938, Engineer, Lawyer, Kt Bav Order of St George; *m* at Münich 6 July 1965, Baroness Dagmar (*b* at Würzburg 25 Sept 1936), dau of Johann, Baron von Peckenzell and Herta Hechler, and has issue,

        [94529 Schloß Aicha vorm Wald; Residenzplatz, 96032 Passau, Germany].

            1. Princess *Isabelle* Maria Gabriele Johanna Franziska Cypriana, *b* at Passau 16 Sept 1971.

    2. Prince *Albrecht* Maria Alexis Engelbert Georg, *b* at Passau 9 July 1973.

3. Princess *Maria* Anna Eleonore Antonia Mathaea, *b* at Slabetz 20 Sept 1939; *m* at Aicha 4 April 1964, Tamás Vass de Bihar (*b* at Penc, Hungary 15 May 1936), Dipl Engineer.

[*Seestraße 234, 86938 Schondorf am Ammersee, Germany*].

4. Princess *Anna* Maria Friederike Alberta, *b* at Slabetz 24 Feb 1943, Dame Star Cross Order; *m* at Aicha vorm Wald, Lower Bavaria 10 Aug (civ) and 6 Oct (relig) 1962, Wolfram, Baron von Strachwitz and Gross-Zauche (*b* at Maserwitz, Neumarkt, Silesia 10 Aug 1933), Lt-Col.

[*Weiherstraße 19, 53913 Swissttal-Miel, Germany; Pruszowice, Ul. Lozinska 26, 51231 Wroclaw, Poland*].

2. Prince *Max* Ignaz Anton Gerhard Benedikt Karl Maria, *b* at Slabetz 12 June 1912; ✠ at Stadtbergen 2 Sept 1992; *m* at Prague 23 May 1938, Countess Caroline (*b* at Subotica 8 May 1918; ✠ at Augsburg 3 March 1981), dau of Raoul, Count von Busseul and Princess Marie-Therese of Lobkowicz, and has issue, among whom,

    1. Prince *Josef* Maria, *b* at Petschau 8 July 1941, Dipl Engineer; *m* at Bergheim 25 March (civ) and at Waldenburg 20 April (relig) 1968, Princess Hilda (*b* at Waldenburg 31 Dec 1943), dau of Friedrich Karl, Prince (Fürst) zu Hohenlohe-Waldenburg-Schillingsfürst and Princess (Fürstin) Mechthilde of Urach, Countess of Württemberg, and has issue,

[*Sonnenblumenstraße 47, 81377 Münich, Germany*].

        1. Princess *Marie-Therese* Caroline Mechtilde, *b* at Augsburg-Göggingen 3 Sept 1969.

        2. Prince *Maximilian* Hubertus Maria, *b* at Münich 1 March 1971.

        3. Prince *Benedikt* Karl-Josef Maria, *b* at Münich 30 Nov 1977.

    3. Prince *Alfred* Maria, *b* at Petschau 4 Jan 1945.

(FRENCH BRANCH)

2. Prince *Georges* Viktor, *b* at L'Hermitage 30 June 1828; ✠ at Paris 15 April 1879; *m* at Paris 22 Jan 1862, Marie de Durfort-Civrac de Lorge of the Dukes de Lorge (*b* at Paris 15 Jan 1841; ✠ at Chambray, Eure 28 Dec 1910), having had issue, among whom,

Son

1. Prince *François* Marie Emmanuel Joseph, *b* at Paris 18 March 1873; ✠ at Lascours, Dept Gard 3 Feb 1950, Capt French Army; *m* at Paris 9 Oct 1908, Simone (*b* at Lascours 28 April 1885; ✠ 20 Sept 1974), dau of Jean Humbert de Chaponay and Mathilde Duplat de Monticourt, and had issue, among whom,

    1. Prince *François Emmanuel* Georges Marie Pierre, *b* at Juigné-sur-Mayenne, Dept Maine-et-Loire 15 Aug 1913; ✠ at Magagnosc, France 13 Jan 1993; *m* at Indochina 1 Dec 1941, Cécile Dumont (*b* at ...), and has issue, among whom,
    [*81 rue de Grenelle, Petit Hôtel d'Estrées, 75007, Paris, France*].

        1. Princess *Isabelle,* *b* at Saigon, Vietnam 7 Feb 1943; *m* at Juigné-Béné, Maine et Loire 7 July 1967 (*m* diss by div), Antoine, Duke de Lévis-Mirepoix, Duke of San Fernando Luis (*b* at New York 18 May 1942).
        [*Château de Léran, 096000 Laroque d'Olmes, France; La Revelle, Teulat, 81500 Lavaur, France*].

    2. Princess Simone Marie Mathilde *Armande,* *b* at Château Lascours 6 Nov 1917; *m* there 20 Oct 1942, Joachim de Pierre de Bernis (*b* at Quincandon, Dept Gard 18 Dec 1912; ✠ there 4 Dec 1965).
[*Château de Salgas, Vebron, 48400 Florac, Dept de Lozère, France*].

    3. Prince Robert Marie *François Georges,* *b* at Paris 4 June 1920.
[*30140 Anduze, France*].

Brother of the Great-Great-Grandfather

Issue of Auguste, 9th Duke (*b* 3 Nov 1765; ✠ 19 Oct 1822) and his first wife, Anne-Victurnienne Henriette de Rochechouart of the Dukes de Mortemart (*b* 7 May 1773; *m* 10 Jan 1789; ✠ 10 July 1806), having had issue, among whom,

Sons
(BELGIAN BRANCHES)
1. Prince *Ferdinand* Victurnien Philippe, *b* at Paris 31 Oct 1791; ✠
at Château du Roeulx 4 Sept 1865, Major-Gen Dutch Army; *m* at
Roeulx 3 Sept 1810, Princess Constance Anne Louise de Croÿ-Solré
(*b* at Condé sur Escaut 9 Aug 1789; ✠ at Château du Roeulx 2 Dec
1869), having had issue, among whom,

Sons
1st Line - ROEULX
1. Prince *Emmanuel, b* at Brussels 13 Dec 1811; ✠ at le Roeulx 16
July 1865; *m* at Dülmen 14 July 1841, Princess Léopoldine of Croÿ (*b*
at Dülmen 9 Aug 1821; ✠ at Florence 26 May 1907), and had issue,
among whom,

> **Sons**
> 1. Prince Alfred *Emmanuel, b* at Dülmen 18 March 1842; ✠
> at Bruges 21 May 1888; *m* at London 12 Jan 1875, Elizabeth
> Mary (*b* at Landhearn, England 29 Dec 1855; ✠ at Bellignies,
> Dept Nord 7 Sept 1912), dau of Charles Samuel Parnall and
> Elizabeth Simmonds, and had issue, among whom,

>> **Sons**
>> 1. *Léopold* Marie Charles Edouard Emmanuel, Prince
>> of Croÿ-Solre, *b* at San Remo 20 Feb 1877; ✠ at St
>> Benin d'Azy, Nievre, France 22 Dec 1965 (title of
>> Prince of Croÿ-Solré with the qualification of Serene
>> Highness confirmed in Belgium 2 Jan 1933); *m* at Paris
>> 23 Oct 1918, Jacqueline (*b* at Chantonnay, Dept
>> Vendée 9 March 1889; ✠ at St Benin d'Azy 13 Sept
>> 1977), dau of Zénobe de Lespinay and Marie-Thérèse
>> Benoist d'Azy, and had issue,

>>> 1. Princess *Elisabeth* Marie Claire Léopoldine
>>> Jacqueline, *b* at St Benin d'Azy 13 Dec 1921.
>>> [*4 rue Florence Blumenthal, 75016 Paris,
>>> France*].
>>> 2. Princess *Marie-Dorothée* Constance Marie,
>>> *b* at St Benin d'Azy 19 Aug 1924; *m* at St
>>> Benin d'Azy 19 Oct 1967 (*m* diss by div at
>>> Nevers, Dept Nievre, France 18 Oct 1979),
>>> Helmut Häferer (*b* at Gotha 11 April 1945).
>>> [*Manoir de Valotte, 58270 St. Benin d'Azy,
>>> Nievre, France*].

3. Princess Emmanuelle *Claire* Constance Marie, *b* at St Benin d'Azy 22 Sept 1925, ✠ at London 14 Apr 2000; *m* at St Benin d'Azy 22 July (civ) and 23 July (relig) 1955 (*m* diss by div at London 27 Jan 1967), Richard Tyser (*b* at London 16 Jan 1930).

[*31 Limerston Street, London S.W.10*].

4. Prince *Léopold* Emmanuel Marie Réginald Jean Elie, Prince de Croÿ-Solre, *b* at St Benin d'Azy 17 Nov 1926; ✠ at Brussels 7 July 1997; *m* at St Gilles 23 Nov 1956, Monique (*b* at Brussels 25 April 1923; ✠ there 12 Dec 1979), dau of Marc Minette d'Oulhaye and Countess Elisabeth d'Aspremont Lyden, and has issue,

> 1. Prince *Emmanuel* Léopold Jean Marc Réginald Marie Gobert, *b* at Uccle 28 Aug 1957; *m* at Paris 23 May (civ) and 25 May (relig) 1985, Maria-Luisa (*b* at Bogotá, Colombia 20 Sept 1964), dau of Diego Uribe Vargas and Emma Gaviria Lievano, and has issue,
>
> [*Rathkenney House, Rathkenny, Navan, Co. Meath, Ireland*]
>
> > 1. Prince *Leopold* Emmanuel Jean Diego Gustavo, *b* at Salamanca, Spain 14 June 1988.
> > 2. Prince *Jean* Diego Patrick Antoine Francis, *b* at Mullingar, Ireland 18 Dec 1994.
>
> 2. Prince *Henri* Jean Humbert Marie Gobert, *b* at Nevers, Dept Nièvre 28 Sept 1958; *m* at Solre, Dept Nord 25 June 1994, Maria del Solario (*b* at Popayan, Colombia 6 Feb 1961), dau of Luciano Patiño Álvarez and Maria del Socorro Fernández de Córdoba, and has issue,
>
> [*c/o Rathkenney House, Rathkenny, Navan, Co. Meath, Ireland*]
>
> > 1. Princess *Anne* Monique Yolande Maria del Socorro

Goberta, *b* at Luxemburg 15 Aug 1995.

2. Princess *Anita,* *b* at Luxemburg 1 Sept 1996.

3. Princess *Jacqueline* Constance Marie Elisabeth Gobertine, *b* at Uccle 10 May 1960.

4. Princess *Eléonore* Diane Gobertine, *b* at Uccle 13 Aug 1964.

5. Princess *Florence* Paule Thérese Marie Léopoldine, *b* at St Benin d'Azy 14 Dec 1927; *m* at St Benin d'Azy 22 July (civ) and 23 July (relig) 1955, Léopold, Count de Lannoy (*b* at Woluwe-St Pierre 10 Nov 1926), Electrical Engineer.

[*38 avenue Emile Duray, 1050 Brussels, Belgium*].

6. Princess *Catherine* Hélene Isabelle Marie Léopoldine, *b* at St Benin d'Azy 1 April 1929; ✠ at Paris 10 May 1992.

7. Princess Jacqueline *Rose* Marie Denyse Léopoldine, *b* at St Benin d'Azy 8 Aug 1930; *m* at St Benin d'Azy 23 June 1962, Silvano de Freitas Branco, Viscount do Porto da Cruz (*b* at Funchal, Madeira 29 Sept 1925).

[*La Vieille Régie, 58270 St. Benin d'Azy, Dept Nièvre, France; Quinta de Abuxarda, Mato Penedos, 2750 Cascais, Portugal*].

8. Princess *Emmanuelle* Thérese Marie Anna Léopoldine, *b* at St Benin d'Azy 22 Feb 1932; *m* at St Benin d'Azy 7 Jan 1971, Oliver Charbonneaux (*b* at Saint Dizier, Dept Haute Marne 12 Dec 1942), Farmer.

[*58270 St. Benin d'Azy, Dept Nièvre, France*].

2. Prince *Réginald* Charles Alfred, *b* at London 26 Sept 1878; ✠ at Woluwe-St Pierre 13 April 1961, Belgian Minister in Stockholm (the title of Prince with the qualification of Serene Highness was confirmed in Belgium 8 Jan 1934), Order of the Polar Star, Order of the Legion of Honour, Order of the British Empire, Order of Pius IX; *m* at Brussels 25 Oct 1920, Princess

Isabelle (*b* at Brussels 23 Sept 1889; ✠ there 11 Dec 1968), dau of Ernest, 10th Prince de Ligne and Diane de Cossé-Brissac of the Dukes de Brissac, and had issue, among whom,

> 1. Princess *Diane-Marie* Léopoldine Jacqueline Ernestine Emmanuelle, *b* at Brussels 25 Jan 1927.
> [*Château de Bellignies, 59570 Bavay, Dept Nord, France*].

2. Prince *Gustave* Ferdinand Guillaume Alfred, *b* at Dülmen 19 May 1845; ✠ at Le Roeulx 3 Sept 1889; *m* at Paris 15 June 1868, Louise (*b* at Paris 28 March 1842; ✠ at Drée, Dept Saone-et-Loire 5 May 1916), dau of Charles, Count de Croix and Amélie de Tournon Simiane, and had issue, among whom,

Sons

1. Prince August Marie Gustave *Etienne* Charles Emmanuel, *b* at Le Roeulx 18 Oct 1872; ✠ at Paris 4 June 1932 (the title of Prince with the qualification of Serene Highness was confirmed in Belgium 17 Feb 1927), Kt Spanish Order of the Golden Fleece, Bailiff Gd Cross Sovereign Military Order of Malta; *m* at Héverlé 2 Dec 1896, Princess and Duchess Marie-Salvatrix (*b* at Héverlé 26 April 1874; ✠ at Le Roeulx 9 May 1956), dau of Englebert-August, Duke d'Arenberg and Princess and Duchess Eleonore d'Arenberg, and had issue, among whom,

> 1. *Etienne-Gustave* Emmanuel Antoine Engelbert Marie, Prince de Croÿ du Roeulx, *b* at Brussels 9 Sept 1898; ✠ at Brussels 8 Jan 1990, Ambassador, Kt Gd Cross Sovereign Military Order of Malta, name confirmed at Belgium 27 Oct 1947; *m* at Paris 12 July 1922, Alyette (*b* at Paris 4 March 1903; ✠ at Andresy 17 July 1990), dau of Michel Marie Robert de Pomereu and Alexandrine Marie Isabelle de Mun of the Marquesses de Mun, and has issue, among whom,
>
> > 1. Prince *Rodolphe* Etienne Alexandre Antoine Marie, *b* at Paris 8 April 1924; *m* 1stly at Angerville-Bailleul, Seine-Maritime 30 Nov (civ) and 15 Dec (relig)

1945 (*m* diss by div at Paris 23 June
1954), Odile (*b* at Paris 5 Aug 1926;
m 2ndly at Neac, Gironde 27 March
1965, Kim Moltzer who was *b* at Berlin
10 March 1938), dau of Raymond de
Bailleul and Isabelle Buccica, and has
issue,
[*Château du Roeulx, 7078 Roeulx,
Henegau, Belgium*].

1. Prince *Olivier* Etienne Joseph
Rodolphe Antoine Marie, *b* at
Neuilly-sur-Seine 1 June 1948;
m at Biereek 6 July (civ) and at
Korbeek-Lo 11 July (relig) 1981,
Isabelle (*b* at Orp le Grand,
Belgium 25 May 1954), dau of
Georges   Bochkoltz   and
Jacqueline Franck, and has
issue,
[*Château de Roeulx, 7078 Roeulx,
Hennegau, Belgium*].

1. Princess *Marguerite*
Jacqueline   Marie
Désirée, *b* at Uccle 10
Jan 1982.
2. Prince *Hadrien*
Etienne Georges André
Hélène Aldo, *b* at Uccle
9 Sept 1983.
3. Princess *Alexandra*,
b at Uccle 9 July 1988.
2. Princess *Alyette* Isabelle
Odile Marie, *b* at Neuilly-sur-
Seine 13 July 1951; *m* at Neuilly-
sur-Seine 23 Jan 1976, Charles
Antoine, Prince de Ligne de La
Trémoïlle (*b* at Boulogne-
Billancourt, nr Paris 30 Sept
1946).
[*Château d'Antoing, 7640
Antoing, Hennegau, Belgium*].

Prince Rodolphe *m* 2ndly at Paris 26 Jan 1967, Hélène (*b* at Paris 27 Dec 1937; ✠ at Brussels 31 Aug 1995; *m* 1stly at Paris 3 July 1958, Charles-Arthur de Rochechouart, Marquess de Mortemart of the Dukes de Mortemart who was *b* at Paris 20 March 1934 and ✠ at Amenas, Sahara 10 May 1961), dau of Adolphe de Pierre de Bernis-Calvière and Louise de Dorlodot, and has further issue, [*Château de Roeulx, 7078 Roeulx, Hennegau, Belgium*].

> 3. Prince *Maximilien* Marc Antoine Ghislain Jacques Etienne, *b* at Brussels 9 May 1971.

2. Prince *Philippe* Robert Etienne, *b* at Paris 13 May 1928; *m* at New York 25 Sept 1967, Denise-Melina (*b* at Nantes, France 12 Aug 1926), dau of Ernest Lannegrace and Marthe Mangin. [*2 Square Boileau, 78150 Le Chesnay, France*].

2nd Line - RUMILLIES

2. Prince *Juste* Marie Fernand Victurien, *b* at Paris 19 Feb 1824; ✠ at Brussels 7 Dec 1908; *m* at Brussels 28 Sept 1854, Countess Marie-Magdelaine (*b* at Brussels 17 Sept 1833; ✠ there 18 April 1885), dau of Léon, 5th Duke d'Ursel and Sophie d'Harcourt of the Dukes d'Harcourt, and had issue, among whom,

Sons

1. Prince *Charles* Joseph Henri Marie, *b* at Le Roeulx 19 May 1869; ✠ at Rumillies 29 May 1943 (title of Prince with the qualification of Serene Highness confirmed Belgium 26 Jan 1892); *m* at Rumillies 15 April 1896, Countess Mathilde (*b* at Rumillies 6 Feb 1868; ✠ there 19 Sept 1946), dau of Albert, Count de Robiano of Rumillies and Countess Berthe van der Straten Ponthoz, and had issue, among whom,

1. Princess *Marie-Immaculée* Claire Elisabeth Gérardine
Marguerite, *b* at Rumillies 16 Oct 1905, Dame Star Cross
Order, Order of the Holy Sepulchre and Constantinian Order
of St George; *m* at Rumillies 7 Sept (civ) and 8 Sept (relig)
1926, Thierry, Count van Limburg Stirum (*b* at Brussels 28
Dec 1904; ✠ at Huldenberg 13 Dec 1968), Mayor of
Huldenberg.
[*Château de Huldenberg, 3040 Huldenberg, Belgium*].
2. Prince *Emmanuel* Marie Joseph Pierre Gérard, *b* at
Rumillies 24 April 1908, ✠ at Brussels 6 Nov 1997, Civil
Engineer; *m* at Rumillies 7 Aug (civ) and at Overijse 12 Aug
(relig) 1944, Countess Nicole (*b* at Overijse 25 June 1919),
dau of John, Count de Marnix de Sainte-Aldegonde and
Countess Thérèse d'Oultremont, and have issue,
[*8 avenue des Dominicaines, 1950 Kraainem, Belgium*].

> 1. Princess *Isabelle* Gabrielle Marie Emmanuelle
> Mathilde Jeanne Gaétane Ghislaine, *b* at Etterbek 4
> July 1945; *m* at Kraainem 1 March (civ) and at Rumillies
> 14 March (relig) 1968, Wolfgang, Count d'Ursel of the
> Dukes d'Ursel (*b* at Grez-Doiceau 1 March 1936), Dr
> of Law.
> [*Château du Bercuit, 1390 Grez-Doiceau, Belgium*].
> 2. Princess *Marie* Gabrielle Gaétane Thérèse Nicole
> Ghislaine, *b* at Rumillies 4 Dec 1946; *m* at Kraainem
> 25 Aug (civ) and 3 Sept (relig) 1971, Prince Adrien de
> Merode (*b* at Woking, Surrey 16 April 1946), Dr of
> Law.
> [*Avenue de Tervueren 382 bte 7, 1150 Brussels,
> Belgium*].
> 3. Prince *Guillaume* Gabriel Joseph Juste Pierre
> Gaétan Marie Ghislain, *b* at Rumillies 10 April 1950;
> *m* at Venice 16 Dec 1989, Countess Isabella (*b* at
> Frankfurt-am-Main 26 April 1960), dau Manfredo,
> Prince di Collalto e San Salvatore and Trinidad Castillo
> of the Marquesses di Jura Real, and has issue,
> [*7540 Rumillies, Hennegau, Belgium*].

>> 1. Prince *Emmanuel* Manfredo Juste Marie, *b*
>> at Uccle 9 Dec 1990; authorized at Rome 27
>> July 1994 to add the name of "Collalto" to his
>> own.
>> 2. Princess *Violette* Maria Trinidad Giuliana,

b at Tournai 12 Feb 1995.
>> 4. Prince *Charles* Louis Gabriel Joseph Gaétan Marie Ghislain, *b* at Rumillies 17 June 1951.
>> [*8 avenue des Dominicaines, 1950 Kraainem, Belgium*].

2. Prince *Joseph* Emmanuel Marie Sophie Ignace, *b* at Brussels 20 Feb 1873; ✠ at Verviers 25 Oct 1968; *m* at Paris 9 Feb 1904, Genevieve (*b* at Tarbes, Pyrenées 22 Nov 1882; ✠ at Spa 18 Oct 1937), dau of Adolphe Collinet de la Salle and Marguerite Antoinette Perier, and had issue, among whom,

>> 1. Princess *Marguerite* Genevieve Marie Françoise Ghislaine, *b* at Spa 11 July 1912.
>> [*Mont-Avry, 4880 Spa, Belgium*].

(AUSTRIAN BRANCH)

2. Prince Philipp, *b* 26 Nov 1801; ✠ at Ems 2 Aug 1871, Lt.-Gen. Austrian Army; *m* at Anholt 28 July 1824, Princess Johanna zu Salm-Salm (*b* at Anholt5 Aug 1796; ✠ at Dusseldorf 22 Nov 1868), and had issue, among whom,

Son

Prince *Alexander* Gustav August, *b* at Berlin 21 Aug 1828; ✠ at Buchberg am Kamp, Lower Austria 5 Dec 1887; *m* at Laer, Wesphalia 4 Aug 1863, Countess Elisabeth (*b* at Münster, Wesphalia 14 June 1834; ✠ at Buchberg 30 Oct 1910), dau of Klemens, Count von Westphalen zu Fürstenberg and Countess Kunigunde von Aicholt, and had issue, among whom,

Sons

1. Prince *Wilhelm* Hubert Ernst, *b* at Buchberg 6 Oct 1869; ✠ at Tulln, Lower Austria 18 April 1918; *m* at Arad 15 Sept 1898, Desideria (Dezsi) (*b* at Kis-Zombor 11 May 1874; ✠ at Graz 6 Sept 1935), dau of Istvan Rónay de Zombor and Ilona Rónay de Zombor, and had issue,

>> 1. Prince *Stephan* Alexander Maria Wilhelm, *b* at Paulis, Hungary 7 Aug 1899; ✠ at Tulsa, Oklahoma, USA 3 Sept 1066; *m* at Houston, Texas 21 June 1928, Beatrix (*b* at Beaumont Texas 2 Jan 1904), dau of Oskar Homer Taylor.

2. Prince *Klemens* Maria Hubertus Joseph Alexander, *b* at Buchberg am Kamp 31 March 1873; ✠ at Vienna 23 Nov 1926, Proprietor of Buchberg and Gars; *m* at Vienna 31 Jan 1903, Princess Christiane (*b* at Slatinan, Bohemia 24 Nov 1878; ✠ at Carlslust, nr Nieder-Fladnitz,

Lower Austria 16 May 1945), Lady-in-Waiting, Dame Star Cross Order, dau of Franz-Josef, Prince von Auersperg and Countess Wilhelmine Kinsky von Wchinitz and Tettau, and had issue, among whom,

> 1. Princess Marie *Gabrielle* Wilhelmine Caroline Christiane Antonia, *b* at Vienna 11 April 1908; ✚ at Vienna 27 Nov 1958.
>
> 4. Prince *Karl* Franz Antonius Klemens Alexander Kaspar Melchior Balthasar, *b* at Vienna 7 Jan 1912; ✚ there 10 March 1983; *m* 1stly at Graz 7 Sept 1939, Baroness Barbara (*b* at Graz 24 Jan 1906; ✚k in a motor accident at Spillern, nr Stockerau 27 Nov 1958), dau of Ferdinand, Baron Söll von and zu Teissenegg, Proprietor of Stainburg and Elvira Ceconi, Noble von Moncecon. He *m* 2ndly at Vienna 4 May 1977, Eva Maria (*b* at Budapest 21 July 1909; ✚ at Vienna 14 April 1985), dau of Stephan Winckhler von Winckelstein and Maria Rausch, and had issue by his first wife, among whom,
>
>> 1. Prince *Ferdinand* Maria Carl Clemens Franz Judas Thadäus, *b* at Buchberg 23 June 1940, Major; *m* at Ladendorf, Lower Austria 4 April 1972, Marie Antoinette (*b* at Göttingen 8 Feb 1948), dau of Max Huck and Countess Leopoldine von Khevenhüller-Metsch, and has issue,
>> [*Stadl-Paura, 4650 Lambach, Austria*].
>>
>>> 1. Prince *Clemens, b* at Vienna 13 Aug 1974.
>>
>> 2. Princess *Elisabeth* Maria Brigitte Christiane Barbara, *b* at Buchberg 21 Dec 1941; *m* at Vienna 4 June 1966 (*m* diss by div at Vienna 20 June 1980), Albrecht, Baron von dem Bongart (*b* at Vienna 9 Jan 1940), Dipl Engineer, Forester.
>> [*Belvedere Gasse8/17, 1040 Vienna, Austria*].
>>
>> 3. Princess *Christiane* Maria Elvira Antonia Thaddäa, *b* at Buchberg 11 Feb 1945; *m* at Salzburg 25 Nov 1978, Johann Andreas, Ritter von Miller zu Aichholz (*b* at New York 27 Oct 1940), Farmer.
>> [*Bräuhof 46, 8993 Grundlsee, Austria*].

3. Prince *Alexander* Marie August Stephan Klemens, *b* at Buchberg 31 March 1873 (twin with Prince Klemens); ✚ at Bad Ischl 10 July 1937, Major Austrian Cavalry, Kt of Hon Sovereign Military Order of Malta; *m* at Vienna 19 Nov 1908, Countess Mathilde (*b* at Vienna 27 April 1881; ✚ at Bad Ischl 20 April 1949), dau of Georg, Count von

Stockau and Eveline Baltazzi, and had issue, among whom,

> 1. Prince *Anton* Philipp Maria Josef Ignatius Georg
> Alexander, *b* at Königsfeld 1 Sept 1909; ✠ at Kitzbühel 3
> March 1976; *m* 1stly at Rauden 11 Nov 1940 (*m* diss by div 22
> Oct 1948), Princess Klementine (*b* at Rauden, nr Ratibor,
> Silesia 24 Apil 1918), dau of Viktor, Duke von Ratibor and
> Prince von Corvey, Prince zu Hohenlohe-Schillingsfürst-
> Breunner-Enkevoirth, Proprietor of Grafenegg-Aeuaigen, etc
> and Princess Elisabeth zu Oettingen-Oettingen and
> Oettingen-Spielberg, and had issue,

>> 1. Princess Alexandra (*Sandra*) Marie Sybille Sofie,
>> *b* at Rauden 31 Dec 1941; *m* at Corvey 15 Sept 1963
>> (*m* diss by div 21 June 1984), Alexander, Count von
>> Bismarck-Schönhausen (*b* at London 20 Feb 1935).

>> 2. Prince Franz *Clemens* Viktor Maria, *b* at Corvey 25
>> Sept 1946, Bank Clerk.

>> [*Staufenstraße 39, 60323 Frankfurt-am-Main,
>> Germany*].

Prince Anton *m* 2ndly at The Hague 8 June 1964, Margriet
(*b* at The Hague 5 Jan 1932), dau of Guillaume Pierre Charles
Krayenbrink and Everdina Jurriana deHoog, and has further
issue,

>> 3. Princess *Patricia* (*Pita*), *b* at St Johann, Tirol 22
>> Dec 1964, Journalist; *m* at Brooklyn, New York 28
>> Sept 1999, Franz-Martin, Count von Trauttmansdorff-
>> Weinsberg (*b* at London 16 Feb 1964).

>> [*340 East 5th Street, Spt D3, New York, NY 10003,
>> U.S.A.*].

> 2. Prince *Alexander* Georg Maria Ignatius, *b* at Königsfeld 27
> Nov 1912, ✠ 3 May 2002; *m* 1stly at London 17 Feb 1938
> (*m* diss by div at London March 1968), Anne (*b* at London 16
> Aug 1917; ✠ at Münich 27 May 1986), dau of William
> Campbell and Dorothy Lang. He *m* 2ndly at London 25 July
> 1970, Ethel Evelyn Primrose (*b* at London 22 March 1928),
> dau of Aubrey Brooke Winch and Marie Elspeth Agnes
> Makgill, and had issue by his first wife,

> [*5 Eland Road, London SW11 5JX*].

>> 1. Princess *Charlotte* Alexandra Maria Clotilde, *b* at
>> London 31 Dec 1938; *m* 1stly at Langenburg 5 June
>> 1965 (*m* diss by div at Crailsheim 26 May 1990), Kraft,
>> Prince zu Hohenlohe-Langenburg (*b* at Schwäbisch

Hall 25 June 1935). She *m* 2ndly at Frankfurt-am-Main 23 June 1993, Johannes, Baron von Twickel (*b* at Berlin 25 July 1940), Bank Director.
[*Scheffelstraße 11, 60318, Frankfurt-am-Main, Germany*].

2. Princess *Emma* Rosanne, *b* at Sutton, Surrey 30 Dec 1943; *m* at Münich 20 May (civ) and at Aurach, nr Kitzbühel 8 June 1964 (*m* diss by div), Ferdinand, Count von Waldburg zu Wolfegg and Waldsee (*b* at Waldsee 17 Dec 1933).
[*Waldtrude Ringerstraße 60, 81827 Münich, Germany*].

3. Prince *Maximilian Richard* Alexander, *b* at London 2 June 1946, Banker; *m* at Salzburg ......, Christine (*b* 1 June 1948), dau of Wilhelm Krutschnik and Jutta Golibersuch, and has issue,
[*Mooswiese, Oberleiten Weg 9, 6370 Kitzbühel, Tirol, Austria*].

> 1. Prince *Oliver* Jan, *b* at Kitzbühel 29 Aug 1970.
> 2. Prince *Alexander* Christian, *b* at Kitzbühel 22 Dec 1974.

ERBACH

Lutheran: This Rhenish family can be traced authentically to Eberhard of Erbach, living in 1148; ministeriales imperii circa 1200, later "Dienstmannen" of the Palatinate; erection of Erbach (comprising 523 square kilometers in Starkenburg) into a County of the Holy Empire 15 Aug 1532, ratification of arms, Vienna 9 July 1755; the Lines below descend from three sons of Georg Albrecht II, Count of Erbach-Fürstenau (✠ 1717).

LINE I: ERBACH-FÜRSTENAU

Founded by Count Philipp Karl (*b* 1677; ✠ 1736) - Right of primogeniture was confirmed 17 Nov 1768; Hereditary Member of the First Chamber of the Grand Duchy of Hesse 17 Jan 1820; received the qualification of "Erlaucht" (primogeniture) by the German Diet 13 Feb 1829; extended to all family members, Hesse 7 March 1914. Members of this Line bear the title of Count or Countess zu Erbach-Fürstenau with the qualification of Illustrious Highness.

RAIMUND Adalbert Alfred Josef Hans Ulrich Franz Kraft Friedrich, **COUNT (GRAF) ZU ERBACH-FÜRSTENAU,** Herr zu Breuberg, Wildenstein and Rothenberg, *b* at Heidelberg 2 April 1951; *m* at Munich 23 Feb (civ) and at Vienna 28 Feb (relig) 1976, Princess Isabella (*b* at Vienna 17 May 1954), Dr of Med, dau of Georg, Prince of Liechtenstein and Duchess Marie Christine of Württemberg.

[*Schloß Fürstenau, 64720 Michelstadt - Steinbach, Odenwald, Germany*].

Sons and Daughter

1. *Louis* Christian Albrecht Kraft Nis, Hereditary Count (Erbgraf) zu Erbach-Fürstenau, *b* at Freiburg im Breisgau 13 Sept 1976.
2. Count *Philipp* Christoph Eberhard Karl Emich Christian, *b* at Freiburg 27 Jan 1979.
3. Count *Nikolaus* Georg Andreas Gabriel, *b* at Erbach 6 Aug 1984.
4. Countess *Margarita* Marie-Helene Eleonora Eilika Andrea, *b* at Erbach 12 June 1986.

Mother

Countess Elisabeth (*b* at Berlin 17 June 1929), dau of Alfred, Count zu Erbach-Fürstenau (see below) and Maria-Domina von Maltitz; *m* at Fürstenau 17 June 1950, *Eugen*, Count zu Erbach-Fürstenau (*b* at Fürstenau 13 May 1923; ✠ at Fürstenau 26 Dec 1987).

[*Schloß Fürstenau, 64720 Michelstadt - Steinbach, Odenwald, Germany; Hofgut Etzean, 64743 Beerfelden, Germany*].

Sister and Brother

1. Countess *Lukardis* Elisabeth Helene Maria Domina Angelika, *b* at Darmstadt 2 April 1953, Nurse.

[*Falltorstraße 5, 60395 Frankfurt-am-Main, Germany*].

2. Count *Kraft* Ulrich Alfred Friedrich-Karl Ludolf Walterius, *b* at Darmstadt 9 March 1962; ✠ at Etzean, nr Beerfelden 3 Aug 1980.

Sister of Father

Issue of Raimund, Count zu Erbach-Fürstenau (*b* 21 Feb 1868; ✠ 2 Jan 1920) and Princess Helen zu Solms-Braunfels (*b* 15 Feb 1890; *m* 21 April 1921; ✠ 22 Oct 1969).

Countess *Jutta* Luise Elisabeth Therese Friederike Marie-Agnes, *b* at Fürstenau 3 April 1922; ✠ at Darmstadt 13 Nov 1968; *m* at Jugenheim (civ) and at Darmstadt (relig) 28 June 1952, Peter Heilbig (*b* at Berlin 26 Aug 1922).

Brother of Grandfather

Issue of Alfred, Count zu Erbach-Fürstenau (*b* 6 Oct 1813; ✝ 25
Oct 1874) and Princess Louise zu Hohenlohe-Ingelfingen (*b* 25 March
1835; *m* 28 March 1859; ✝ 15 July 1913), having had issue, among
whom,

Son
Adalbert Adolf Ludwig Edgar Hugo Eberhard, **Count (Graf) zu
Erbach-Fürstenau**, etc, *b* at Fürstenau 2 Feb 1861; ✝ at
Krähenberg, Odenwald 28 Sept 1944, renounced his rights as Head
of the Family in favour of his son 9 Dec 1928; *m* at Varlar, Westphalia
19 April 1900, Princess Elisabeth (*b* at Varlar 18 Dec 1870; ✝ at
Michelstadt, Odenwald 4 July 1953), dau of Otto, Prince (Fürst) zu
Salm-Horstmar and Countess Emilie zur Lippe-Biesterfeld, and had
issue,

 1. Ludwig Gustav Otto Hermann Arthur Elias Raimund
 Alfred, Count zu Erbach-Fürstenau, etc, *b* at Fürstenau
 11 April 1905, *succ* his father 9 Dec 1928 on his father's
 renunciation; *m* 1stly at Berlin 13 Sept 1926 (*m* diss by div at
 Michelstadt 28 July 1977), Maria-Domina (*b* at Cologne 23
 Oct 1904), dau of Hans-Ulrich von Maltitz and Elsa Kempner.
 He *m* 2ndly at Michelstadt 26 Aug (civ) and 17 Sept (relig)
 1977, Maria-Esther (*b* at Nipkau 26 Dec 1903; ✝ at Fürstenau
 11 June 1983; she *m* 1stly at Lipsa 27 July 1924, Manfred von
 Schumann; that *m* diss by div at Leipzig 3 April 1939; she *m*
 2ndly at Saarbrucken 14 Jan 1947, René Leboucq; that *m* diss
 by div at Paris 13 Jan 1954), dau of Otto von Puttkamer and
 Marie von Blücher, and had issue by his first wife,
 [*Schloß Fürstenau, 64720 Michelstadt-Steinbach, Odenwald,
 Germany*].

  1. Countess *Eleonore* Maria-Magdalena Emmy Elisabeth
  Alexandra Luise, *b* at Berlin 10 June 1927; *m* at São
  Paulo, Brazil 16 Nov 1949, Nicolaas Gerardus van de
  Roemer (*b* at Modjokerto, Java 20 April 1922; ✝ at
  Darmstadt 12 April 1961).
  [*Walther-Rathenau-Allee 2, 64720 Michelstadt-
  Steinbach, Odenwald, Germany*].

  2. Countess *Elisabeth* Marie-Margarethe Else, *b* at
  Berlin 17 June 1929; *m* at Fürstenau 17 June 1950,

Eugen, Count zu Erbach-Fürstenau (*b* at Fürstenau 13 May 1923; ✝ at Fürstenau 26 Dec 1987).

[*Schloß Fürstenau, 64720 Michelstadt-Steinbach, Odenwald, Germany; Hofgut Etzean, 64743 Beerfelden, Germany*].

3. Countess *Maria-Angelica* Elisabeth, *b* at São Paulo 17 Oct 1941; *m* at Munich 12 Feb (civ) and at Fürstenau 24 Feb (relig) 1968 (*m* diss by div at Munich 19 June 1972), Kurt-Joachim (Jockel) Riedesel, Baron zu Eisenbach (*b* at Lauterbach 29 Dec 1943). She has since reverted to her maiden name.

[*Possartstraße 6, 81679 Munich, Germany*].

2. Countess *Luise* Matilde Elise Sophie Gertrud, *b* at Fürstenau 10 July 1901; ✝ at Erbach 11 Jan 1985.

LINE II: ERBACH-ERBACH

Founded by Count Georg Wilhelm (*b* 1686; ✝ 1757); the right of primogeniture was confirmed 25 June 1783; added the name and arms of the Counts of Wartenberg, Vienna 20 Jan 1806; inherited the Holy Roman Empire county of Wartenberg-Roth 10 March 1818; Hereditary Member of the First Chamber of the Grand Duchy of Hesse 17 Jan 1820; received the qualification of "Erlaucht" (primogeniture), Hesse 17 Feb 1820, and in Bavaria 22 April 1829; extended to all family members, Hesse 7 March 1914, Hereditary Member of the Bavarian "Reichsräte" 9 Dec 1842.

Members of this Line bear the title of Count or Countess zu Erbach-Erbach with the qualification of Illustrious Highness.

FRANZ August Gustav Adam Hubertus Friedrich Wilhelm Hans Karl, **COUNT ZU (GRAF) ERBACH-ERBACH** and von Wartenberg-Roth, Lord (Herr) zu Breuberg, Wildenstein, Steinbach, Curl and Ostermannshofen, *b* at Erbach 5 Feb 1925, son of Alexander, Count of Erbach-Erbach (*b* 16 Sept 1891; ✝ 21 Jan 1952) and Christa von Zülow (*b* 21 June 1894; *m* 26 July 1920; ✝ 15 Aug 1962); *m* 1stly at Arolsen 27 March 1952 (*m* diss by div at Michelstadt 10 July 1979), Princess Margarethe [*Nees von Esenbeckstraße 10, 64711 Erbach, Odenwald, Germany*] (*b* at Munich 22 May 1923), dau of Josias, Prince (Fürst) of Waldeck and Pyrmont and Duchess Altburg of Oldenburg. He *m* 2ndly at Schloß Eulbach 17 Aug 1979 Christa (*b* at Frankfurt-am-Main 14 Aug 1947), dau of Helmut Blösinger and Anna Elisabeth Riegel.

[*64711 Schloß Erbach, Germany; JagdSchloß Eulbach, 64720*

Michelstadt-Würzberg, Germany].

Son and Daughter - 1st Marriage

1. Countess *Alexandra* Polyxene Elisabeth Bathildis Ingrid Amélie, *b* at Frankfurt-am-Main 2 Aug 1955; *m* at Erbach 2 July 1983, Ulrich Bugiel (*b* at Hemer 11 Nov 1946).
[*Studenten Weg 9, 61381 Friedrichsdorf-Köppern, Germany*].
2. Franz *Eberhard* Wittekind Botho Heinrich Nikolaus Georg Wilhelm, Hereditary Count (Erbgraf) zu Erbach-Erbach, *b* at Erbach 2 June 1958, Banker; *m* at Erbach 11 July (civ) and 13 July (relig) 1985, Princess Alexandra (*b* at Hamburg 1 Sept 1963), dau of Heinrich V, Prince Reuss and Ingrid Jobst.
[*JagdSchloß Eulbach, 64720 Michelstadt-Würzberg, Germany*].

> 1. Countess *Felicitas* Alexandra Magita Elena, *b* at Erbach 27 June 1987.
> 2. Count Franz *Georg-Albrecht* Wittekind Karl-Emich Raimund Kraft Carl, *b* at Erbach 6 June 1989.
> 3. Count Franz *Konrad* Ludwig Heinrich Gustav, *b* at Erbach 12 Dec 1991.

Son - Second Marriage

3. Count Franz *Magnus-Alexander* Eginhard Andreas Philipp, *b* at Erbach 13 April 1982.

Line III ERBACH-SCHÖNBERG

Founded by Count Georg August (*b* 1691; ✝ 1758); the right of primogeniture was confirmed 28 Dec 1748; Hereditary Members of the First Chamber of the Grand Duchy of Hesse 17 Jan 1820; received the qualification of "Erlaucht" (primogeniture) by the German Diet 13 Feb 1829; received the Hessian title of Prince with the qualification of "Durchlaucht", Wolfsgarten 18 Aug 1903.

Members of this Line bear the title of Prince or Princess zu Erbach-Schönberg with the qualification of Serene Highness.

DIETRICH Wilhelm, **5TH PRINCE and COUNT (FÜRST and GRAF) ZU ERBACH-SCHÖNBERG,** Herr zu Breuberg and Wildenstein, *b* at Gross-Gerau 27 March 1954, Lawyer, Barrister, son of Ludwig, 4th Prince and Count (Fürst and Graf) zu Erbach-Schönberg (*b* 17 Oct 1926; ✝ 23 Nov 1998) and Rosemarie Moshage (*b* at Schlewecke, Wolfenbüttel 22 Sept 1927; m (civ) 9 March and (relig) 10 March 1950); *m* at Gross-Gerau 18 May (civ) and at Schönberg 19 May (relig) 1984, Monika (*b* at Karlsruhe 10 July 1955), Dr of Phil,.dau of Martin Recknagel and Martha Zita

Springer, and has issue,
[*Kurfürstenplatz 40, 60486 Frankfurt-am-Main, Germany*].

Daughter

1. Princess *Elisabeth* Diana Patricia Mona Annabel Ulrike
Andrea, *b* at Frankfurt-am-Main 22 June 1985.

Mother

Rosemarie, Dowager Princess and Countess zu Erbach-Schönberg
(*b* at Schlewecke, Wolfenbüttel 22 Sept 1927), dau of Karl Moshage
and Ottilie Rasche.
[*Robert-Bosch-Straße 5, 65428 Rüsselsheim, Germany*].

Brother and Sisters

1. *Burckhard* Alexander Maynolf Wittekind, Hereditary Prince
(Erbprinz) zu Erbach-Schönberg, *b* at Gross-Gerau 7 April 1951;
✝ at Frankfurt-am-Main 30 June 1998, Dipl Econ.
2. Princess *Uta* Edda Marie Jutta Annemarie, *b* at Gross-Gerau
1 Aug 1955.
[*Mühlfeld 19, 64521 Gross-Gerau, Germany*].
3. Princess *Patricia* Jutta Anja Ilse, *b* at Kronberg, Taunus 15 Dec
1967.
[*Am Flurgraben 4, 65428 Rüsselsheim, Germany*].

Brother and Sister of Father

Issue of Georg-Ludwig, 3rd Prince and Count (Fürst and Graf) zu
Erbach-Schönberg (*b* 1 Jan 1903; ✝ 27 Jan 1971) and Marie
Margarethe Deringer (of Russian nobility) (*b* 12/25 Dec 1903; *m* 2
July 1925; ✝ 22 Dec 1967), having had issue, among whom,

1. Prince *Maynolf* Wilhelm Victor Richard Josias Ludwig-Christian
Waldemar, *b* at Darmstadt 13 May 1936, Car Mechanic; *m* 1stly at
Darmstadt 14 May 1959 (*m* diss by div at Darmstadt 11 Feb 1970),
Marie Katharine (*b* at Damstadt 16 Jan 1921; ✝ at..1992 ; *m* 1stly 6
April 1959, August Roger, that *m* diss by div), dau of Anton Adam
August Markert and Theresia Grimm. He *m* 2ndly at Erbach 16
March 1970 (*m* diss by div at Wiesbaden 10 Oct 1972), Erika (*b* at
Lahr, Schwarzwald 1 June 1938), dau of Friedrich List and Marka
Volk. He *m* 3rdly at Darmstadt 21 April 1976, Solveig (*b* at Gera 25
May 1949), dau of Horst Schlegel and Gertrud Abele, and by her has
issue,
[*Im Neuroth 43, 64732 Bad König - Zell, Germany*].

1. Princess *Isabelle, b* at Erbach 24 Aug 1977; *m* at Horb Neckar 17 July (civ) and at Mühringen/Schwarzwald 18 July (relig) 1998, Andreas Ellinger (*b* at... 4 Aug 1977) (*Schelmenwasen 28/1, 72160 Horb-Mühlen/Schwarzwald*).
2. Prince *Peter, b* at Erbach 11 Aug 1981.

ESTERHÁZY DE GALÁNTHA

Catholic: This Hungarian family can be traced from Benedict Esterhas (✣ circa 1552), who *m* circa 1526, Helene Bessenyey de Galantha, 1539 - 65, authenticated since 1549 under the name of "Esterhas de Galántha"; their grandson Nikolaus Esterházy de Galántha (*b* 1583; ✣ 1645) was created Baron Pozsony (Hungary) 10 April 1613; Count of Forchtenstein (Hungary - Frakno), Sopron 24 June 1626; Paul, Baron Esterházy de Galántha, Count of Forchtenstein (Frakno, County of Sopron) (*b* 1635; ✣ 1713) was created a Prince of the Holy Empire (ad personam) 7 Dec 1687, and (primogeniture) with the qualification of "Hochgeboren", Pozsony 23 March 1712; the title of Prince was extended to all descendants, Vienna 21 July 1783; acquired the Abbey of Edelstetten in Bavaria 22 May 1804, erected into a Princely County, Vienna 17 Dec 1804; received the qualification of "Durchlaucht" (primogeniture) by the German Diet 18 Aug 1825; confirmed in Austria 7 Oct 1825; extended to all family members 27 April 1869 (with effect from 5 May 1869).
Members of the family bear the title of Prince or Princess Esterházy de Galántha with the qualification of Serene Highness.

ANTON Rudolf Marie Georg Christoph Hubertus Johannes Karl Aglaë, **13TH PRINCE ESTERHÁZY DE GALÁNTHA,** Princely Count of Edelstetten, Count of Forchtenstein, *b* at Vienna 27 Dec 1936, Ing. comm. University of Louvain, Belgium; *succ* his uncle, Paul, 12th Prince Esterházy de Galántha (*b* 23 March 1901; ✣ 25 May 1989), son of Prince Anton Esterházy de Galántha (*b* 22 July 1903; ✣*k* in action 31 Dec 1944) and Countess Gabrielle Apponyi von Nagy-Appony (*b* 25 April 1910; ✣ 16 Feb 1986; *m* 22 Oct 1935; *m* 2ndly 8 Jan 1948, Peter, Count Draskovich von Trakostjan; that *m* annulled 30 March 1951; *m* 3rdly 15 Nov 1948 Wladimir, Count Mittrowsky von Mitrowitz; that *m* annulled 7 March 1950); *m* at Munich 24 Jan 1986, Ursula (*b* at Nuremberg 2 Oct 1941), dau of Maximilian Koenig (Lt. Col.) and Anna Magdalena Schönborn. [*Liebigstraße 37, 80538 Munich, Germany*].

Son

1. Prince *Pál-Antal* Nikolaus Maximilian, *b* at Munich 18 Feb 1986.

Brothers and Sisters of Father

Issue of Nikolaus, 11th Prince Esterházy de Galántha (*b* 5 July 1869; ✝ 6 April 1920) and Countess Margit Cziraky von Czirak and Denesfalva (*b* 11 Aug 1874; *m* 16 Nov 1898; ✝ 18 Aug 1910), among whom,

1. **Paul** Maria Alois Anton Nikolaus Viktor, **12th Prince Esterházy de Galántha,** etc, *b* at Eisenstadt 23 March 1901; ✝ at Zurich 25 May 1989, Dr jur and pol; *m* at Budapest 3 Aug 1946, Melinda (*b* at Budapest 24 May 1920), dau of Dr of Law, Dezsö Ottrubay and Rose von Schmidt.
[*Schloß, 7000 Eisenstadt, Burgenland, Austria*].
2. Prince *Ladislas* (*László*) Anton Nikolaus Marie Paul Quirinus, *b* at Leka 4 June 1905, ✝ at Schloß Lockenhaus, Austria 5 Jan 2000, Dr rer pol; *m* at Budapest 17 Nov 1929, Countess Maria (Marietta) (*b* at Weppendorf, Eisenburg 26 Feb 1905), Dame Star Cross Order, dau of Alexander, Count Erdödy von Monyórokerék and Monoszló and Countess Elisabeth Draskovich von Trakostjan, and has issue, among whom,
[*Schloße, 7442 Léka Austria*].

    1. Princess *Elisabeth* Margit Bernadette Alexandra Maria Agathe, *b* at Budapest 5 Feb 1931, Dame Star Cross Order; *m* at Vienna 4 April 1956, Georg, Count von Enzenberg zum Freyen and Jöchelsthurn (*b* at Tratzberg, Tyrol 28 July 1926).
    [*Castel Campan, 33052 Caldaro-Kaltern, Italy; Schloß Tratzberg, 6200 Jenbach, Tirol, Austria*]

    2. Princess *Margit* Maria Bernadette Elisabeth Ilona, *b* at Budapest 11 April 1936, Dame Star Cross Order; *m* at Munich 28 Jan (civ) and at Vienna 19 Feb (relig) 1966, Manfred, Count von Schönborn-Wiesentheid (*b* at Munich 19 May 1935; ✝ at Munich 4 June 1989), Banker.
    [*Hauptplatz 8, 7442 Lockenhaus, Austria*].

    3. Princess *Ilona* Maria Elisabeth Margit Bernadette Therese, *b* at Budapest 30 Sept 1939; *m* at Vienna 31 Aug 1968, Georg, Ritter von Hennig (*b* at Vienna 3 Sept 1937), Dr of Law, Austrian Ambassador; New Dehli, Tokyo and London.
    [*Akademiestraße 2, 1010 Vienna, Austria*].

    4. Princess *Katalin* Maria Therese Antonia, *b* at Budapest 7

June 1943; *m* 1stly at Vienna 29 July 1967 (*m* annulled at London 1978), Nicholas David Pilbrow (*b* 20 Sept 1943). She *m* 2ndly at London 4 Feb 1977 (civ) and 3 March 1977 (relig), Timothy Landon (*b* at Victoria, BC, Canada 20 Aug 1942), Brigadier.

[*Faccombe Manor, Faccombe, nr Andover, Hampshire*].

4. Princess *Bernadette* Marie Alexia Angelique, *b* at Esterhazá 17 July 1910; ✥ at Berne 18 April 1974; *m* at Budapest 26 June 1937 Julius, Count Szechényi von Sárvár-Felsövidék (*b* at Achau, Lower Austria 11 Oct 1910; *m* 2ndly at...Harriet Bodmer, *b* at Zurich 21 March 1922), Architect.

[*Petit route des Jarins, 13210 St remy de Provence, France; Wittelikerstraße 40, Zöllikon, Switzerland; 900 Spyglass Lane, Naples, FL 33940, U.S.A.*].

———◆———

FUGGER

Catholic: This Swabian family originate from Graben, Lechfeld and can be traced authentically to Johann Fugger who emigrated to Augsburg 1367, received Freedom of the City in 1370; Letter of concession to bear Arms 1473 (by Emperor Frederick III for the sons of Jacob Fugger, founder of the important commercial company of Fugger); the younger of his sons, called Jacob "den Reichen" (the rich) (✥ 1525 without descendants); Imperial Chancellor, Banker and Industrialist (Noble of the Holy Empire 3 May 1511; Count of the Holy Empire 17 July 1514); acquired the County of Kirchberg and the Lordship of Weissenhorn (Swabia, Bavaria) 1507 by Counts of the Holy Empire (for the sons of his brother Georg Fugger, Raimund and Anton - founders of the two Lines below - and their cousin, Hieronymus Fugger), Augsburg 14 Dec 1530; Hungarian Noble 1535.

LINE I: FUGGER VON KIRCHBERG
(✥ Extinct ✥)

Founded by Raimund, Count of Kirchberg and Weissenhorn (*b* at Augsburg 24 Oct 1489; ✥ 3 Dec 1535); Hereditary Member of the Bavarian "Reichsräte" 26 May 1818; received the qualification of "Erlaucht" (primogeniture), in Württemberg 27 July 1829, and in Bavaria 18 Nov 1842 and previously by the German Diet 13 Feb 1829; extended to all descendants 7 March 1911.

Members of this Line bear the title Count or Countess Fugger von Kirchberg and zu Weissenhorn with the qualifcation Illustrious Highness.

✝ **CLEMENS** Joseph Raymund Ludwig Maria, **15th COUNT (GRAF) FUGGER VON KIRCHBERG AND ZU WEISSENHORN,** Lord of Kirchberg, Weissenhorn, Pfaffenhofer, Marstetten, Wullenstetten and Bach, *b* at Munich 22 Nov 1905; ✝ at Oberkirchberg 31 Dec 1968, Dr of Law; *succ* his brother Johannes, Count Fugger von Kirchberg, etc, who renounced his rights at Munich 1 July 1935, son of Georg Raymund, Count Fugger von Kirchberg, etc (*b* 2 Jan 1850; ✝ 6 Jan 1909) and Countess Amelie von Montgelas (*b* 4 March 1867; *m* 18 Jan 1896; ✝ 22 March 1936); *m* at Niederstotzingen 11 June 1929, Countess Elisabeth (*b* at Igling, Bavaria 1 June 1907), dau of Count Ludwig von Maldeghem, Proprietor of the Lordship of Igling, Proprietor of Niederstotzingen, etc and Countess Blanka Dezasse de Petit-Verneuille.
[*Oberkirchberg, 7901 Illerkirchberg, Württ.*].

Daughter

1. Countess *Maria-Elisabeth* Gudila, *b* at Augsburg 13 Oct 1948; known from 15 Sept 1969 as "Thun-Hohenstein - Countess Fugger von Kirchberg and zu Weissenhorn"; *m* at Oberkirchberg, nr Ulm 18 Oct 1969, Jaroslav, Count von Thun and Hohenstein (*b* at Kwassitz, Mähren 23 March 1935), Industrialist.
[*Oberkirchberg, 7901 Illerkirchberg, Württemberg, Germany*].

Brother

JOHANNES Hartmann Antonius von Padua Gabriel Raymund Joseph Maria, **14th COUNT (GRAF) FUGGER VON KIRCHBERG AND ZU WEISSENHORN,** *b* at Gries, nr Bozen 9 April 1897; ✝ at Paris 22 Feb 1985; (renounced his rights of succession on behalf of his brother Clemens at Munich 1 July/20 Aug 1935 and at Stuttgart 12 Oct 1935); *m* at Munich 22 July 1926 (*m* annulled at Munich 27 Jan 1937), Maria (*b* at Munich 11 July 1896; ✝ there 23 Aug 1941), Actress, dau of Karl Dillard and Maria Hoffmann. He *m* 2ndly at Grünwald, nr Munich 14 April 1967, Edith (*b* at Hamburg-Barmbek-Uhlenhorst 6 Sept 1906), widow of Johannes Julser, dau of Max Radsack and Clara Maria Moritz.
[*Sperberstraße 8, 8201 Rohrdorf Thansau, Kr. Rosenheim, Bavaria*].

LINE II

Founded by Anton, Count Fugger von Kirchberg and zu Weissenhorn (*b* 10 June 1493; ✝ 14 Sept 1560); the two branches below descend from his sons; acquired the Lordship of Glött (Swabia) 1536, and of Babenhausen 1538.

First Branch: FUGGER VON GLÖTT
(✠ Extinct ✠)

Founded by Count Hans (*b* 1531; ✠ 1598); Hereditary Member of the Bavarian "Reichsräte" 26 May 1818; received the qualification of "Erlaucht" (primogeniture) by the German Diet 13 Feb 1829; confirmed in Bavaria 22 April 1829; extended to all members of the family 7 March 1911; Bavarian title (primogeniture) of Fürst (Prince) with the qualification of "Durchlaucht", Munich 30 Dec 1913 (for Carl-Ernst, Count Fugger von Glött).

The Head of this Branch and his wife bore the title of Prince or Princess Fugger von Glött with the qualification of Serene Highness and cadet members bear the title of Count or Countess Fugger von Glött with the qualification of Illustrious Highness.

✠ **JOSEPH ERNST** Hermann Theodor Karl Maria, **2ND PRINCE (FÜRST) FUGGER VON GLÖTT**, Lord of Glött, etc, *b* at Kirchheim 26 Oct 1895; ✠ at Miesbach, Bavaria 13 May 1981, Cmdr Order of St George, Kt Teutonic Order, son of Carl Ernst, 1st Prince (Fürst) Fugger von Glött (*b* 2 July 1859; ✠ 25 April 1940) and Countess Elisabeth von Quadt zu Wykradt and Isny (*b* 11 Sept 1862; *m* 1 Nov 1891; ✠ 16 Aug 1940); *m* 1stly at Namedy 18 May 1920 (*m* diss by div at Berlin 15 May 1943 since when she reverted to her maiden name), Princess Stephanie (*b* at Potsdam 8 April 1895; ✠ at Diessen am Ammersee 7 Aug 1975), dau of Karl Anton, Prince of Hohenzollern and Princess Josephine of Belgium. He *m* 2ndly at Maria-Steinbach 8 Dec 1975, Angela (*b* at Pähl, Bavaria 4 Dec 1935), dau of Johannes von Kienlin, Proprietor Proprietor of Erolzheim and Kirchberg and Countess Irmgard von Moy, and adopted his nephew,

Son

Count *Albert* Magnus Maria Robert Karl Ludwig Ferdinand Antonius von Padua Konrad von Parzham Melchior Martin Marinus, Count Fugger von Glött, formerly Count von and zu Arco-Zinneberg, *b* at Munich 12 Nov 1932, adopted by Joseph Ernst, 2nd Prince (Fürst) Fugger von Glött9 May 1961 (Name legally changed 16 Jan 1961 and acknowledged by the Family Elders 24 Sept 1962 with equal status to the other Heads of the Family granted), son of Ferdinand, Count von and zu Arco-Zinneberg and Countess Maria Fugger von Glött; *m* at Kirchheim, Swaben 29 April (civ) and 10 May (relig) 1961, Baroness Elisabeth (*b* at Munich 4 June 1932), dau of Georg, Baron von Hertling and Countess Clara von Walterskirchen, Baroness zu Wolfsthal, and has issue,

[Hauptstraße 2, 8949 Kirchheim, Schwaben].

    1. Count *Ulrich* Maria Joseph-Ernst Georg Ferdinand Albertus Magnus Rupertus, *b* at Krumbach, Schwaben 8 Dec 1963; *m* at Kloster Linna nr Jüterbog on 18 Sept 1999, Donata (*b* at Hamburg-Bergedorf 20 Jan 1965), dau of Alexander von Arnim and Marie Agnes Hausendorff.

    2. Countess *Maria-Theresia* Elisabeth Klara Anna Andrea Pia, *b* at Krumbach 16 Aug 1967.

    3. Countess *Katharina* Maria Elisabeth Hildegard Karolina Ida, *b* at Krumbach 22 Jan 1970.

Brother of Grandfather

Issue of Fidelis, Count Fugger von Glött (*b* 7 March 1795; ✢ 8 Jan 1876) and Baroness Maria Theresia von Pelkhoven (*b* 6 Jan 1799; *m* 14 Oct 1820; ✢ 26 June 1862), having had issue, among whom,

Son

Count *Alfred*, *b* at Glött 25 June 1822; ✢ at Banjaluka, Bosnia-Hercegovina 23 April 1900; *m* at Ober-Langenstadt 16 Nov 1867, Baroness Franziska (*b* at Brückenau 28 July 1835; ✢ at Banjaluka 20 April 1919, Dame of Hon Bavarian Order of St Theresia, dau of Karl, Baron von Künsberg, Proprietor of Langenstadt and Baroness Theresia von Cunibert, and had issue, among whom,

Son

Count *Josef* Karl Augustin Maria Alfred Franziskus Eduard Ignatius, *b* at St Margarethen, nr Linz 19 March 1874; ✢ at Holzhausen am Ammersee 25 April 1944, Major; *m* at Kappeln 21 Oct 1915, Baroness Maria-Kristine (*b* at Muffendorf am Rhein 15 Sept 1889; ✢ at Haunstetten, nr Augsburg 29 May 1958), dau of Kaspar, Baron von Loë and Countess Antonia Korff genannt Schmising-Kerssenbrock, and had issue, among whom,

    1. Countess *Maria-Karla* Josepha Eugenia Franziska Antonia, *b* at Kappeln 2 May 1918, *m* at Salonika 28 Aug 1943 (*m diss* by div at Stuttgart 25 March 1948 since when she has reverted to her maiden name), Richard Rixrath (*b* at St Germain 14 May 1912), Businessman.

Second Branch: FUGGER VON BABENHAUSEN
Founded by Count Jakob (*b* 1542; ✢ 1598); Prince of the Holy Empire

(primogeniture) with the qualification of "Hochgeboren" and elevation of Babenhausen into a Principality of the Holy Empire, Vienna 1 Aug 1803; Hereditary Member of the Bavarian "Reichsräte" 26 May 1818; received the qualification of "Durchlaucht" (primogeniture) by the German Diet 18 Aug 1825.

The Head of this Branch and his wife bear the title of Prince or Princess Fugger von Babenhausen with the qualification of Serene Highness and cadet members bear the title of Count or Countess Fugger von Babenhausen with the qualification of Illustrious Highness.

HUBERTUS Viktor, **8TH PRINCE (FÜRST) FUGGER VON BABENHAUSEN,** Count von Kirchberg and Weissenhorn, Lord of Boos, Heimertingen, Wald, Wellenburg, Burgwalden and Markt, *b* at Augsburg 23 Nov 1946, son of Friedrich Carl, 7th Prince (Fürst) Fugger von Babenhausen (*b* 26 Nov 1914; ✚ 22 Dec 1979) and Countess Gunilla Bielke (*b* 8 July 1919; *m* 10 Oct 1942); *m* at Oettingen 10 Oct (civ) and 22 Oct (relig) 1977, Princess Alexandra (*b* at Oettingen 9 Oct 1948), dau of Alois, Prince (Fürst) zu Oettingen-Oettingen and Oettingen-Spielberg and Countess Elisabeth Gabriele zu Lynar.

[*Schloß Wellenburg, 86199 Augsburg - Bergheim, Germany; Schloß Babenhausen, 87727 Babenhausen, Schwaben, Germany*].

Sons and Daughter

1. Countess *Franziska* Victoria Elisabeth Maria, *b* at Memmingen 12 April 1979.
2. Count *Leopold* Sebastian Ferdinand Alois Maria, *b* at Augsburg 14 May 1980.
3. Count *Alexander* Emanuel Josef Ernst Markus Maria, *b* at Augsburg 21 Nov 1981.
4. Countess *Anastasia* Jasmin Katharina Maria, *b* at Palm Beach, Florida 2 July 1986.
5. Count *Nikolaus* Franz Anselm Dominikus Maria, *b* at ... 28 Feb 1993.

Brothers and Sister

1. *Carl-Anton* Maria, *b* at Babenhausen 10 Dec 1944 (renounced his rights of succession on behalf of his brother Hubertus at Augsburg 23 Dec 1970, since 27 March/3Aug 1979 known as "Count Fugger-Babenhausen de Polignac" and since ... as "Fürst Fugger-Babenhausen de Polignac"; *m* at Biberach, nr Augsburg 18 Aug (civ) and at Paris 20 Sept (relig) 1975 (*m* diss by div at Paris 28 Nov 1988), Princess Hélène (*b* at Mouchamps, Dept Vendée 1 Oct 1944),

dau of Armand Louis, Prince de Polignac and Jeanne de Chabot of the Counts de Chabot, and has issue,

[*Villa Lillefors, Jahn Strasse 23, 86485 Biberbach, Germany*].

      1. Countess Marie-*Yolande* Jeanne Elisabeth, *b* at Boulogne-Billancourt, France 9 Aug 1978 (has taken the name "de Polignac").

      2. Count *Pierre-Edmond* Hector Gabriel, *b* at Boulogne-Billancourt 12 Feb 1981 (has taken the name "de Polignac").

2. Count *Markus* Albrecht Maria, *b* at Augsburg 15 March 1950.

[*Schloß Babenhausen 87727 Babenhausen, Schwaben, Germany*].

3. Count *Johannes* Albrecht Maria, *b* at Augsburg 20 Dec 1957; *m* at Babenhausen 10 Dec 1982 (civ) and at Neutrauchburg 15 Jan 1983 (relig), Princess Maria (Miriam) (*b* at South Bend, Indiana, USA 2 Jan 1961), dau of Nikolaus, Prince of Lobkowicz and Countess Josefine von Waldburg zu Zeil and Trauchburg, and has issue,

[*Heinrich-von-Kleiststraße 35, 6380 Bad Homburg, Germany*].

      1. Count *Constantin* Franziskus Anselm Maria, *b* at Munich 23 July 1986.

      2. Count *Philipp* Georg Rudolf Maria, *b* at Berlin 14 Nov 1988.

4. Countess *Tatiana* Elisabeth Sibylle Maria, *b* at Augsburg 20 Nov 1959; *m* at Babenhausen 20 Sept (civ) and 13 Dec (relig) 1986, Hubertus, Baron Rukavina von Vidovgrad (*b* at Buenos Aires 17 Dec 1949).

[*Schloßbergstraße 37, 8702 Zollikon, Zurich, Switzerland*].

Brother and Sisters of Grandfather

Issue of Karl, 5th Prince Fugger von Babenhausen (*b* 15 March 1861; ✝ 5 July 1925) and Princess Eleonora (Nora) zu Hohenlohe-Bartenstein (*b* 4 Oct 1864; *m* 8 Jan 1887; ✝ 1 March 1945), among whom,

1. Countess *Sylvia* Rose Eleonore Leopoldine Caroline Marie, *b* at Maria Enzersdorf 8 May 1892; *m* at Schloß Wellenburg 7 Jan 1926 (*m* diss by div at Berlin 22 Dec 1928), Friederich, Count Münster, Baron von Grothaus (*b* at Hamburg 20 June 1891; ✝ at Berlin 6 Jan 1942).

2. Count *Leopold* Heinrich Carl Friedrich Maria, *b* at Ödenburg 18 July 1893; ✝ at Hamburg 8 July 1966, Maj-Gen, Kt Hohenzollern House Order, Cmdr Bavarian Order of St George, Kt of Hon Sovereign Military Order of Malta; *m* at Vienna 23 Feb 1924 (*m* diss by div at Munich 28 Oct 1936; annulled 29 Dec 1936), Countess Vera (*b* at Munich 4 June 1904; ✝ at Kirkwood, Missouri 18 Sept 1959;

m 2ndly at Vienna 1 June 1938, Kurt, Edler von Schuschnigg), dau of Rudolf, Count Czernin von and zu Chudenitz and Princess Vera zu Hohenlohe-Waldenburg-Schillingsfürst-Kaunitz, and had issue, among whom,

     1. Count *Rudolf* Karl Maria, *b* at Babenhausen 1 Jan 1927; ✠ at Bombay, India 8 March 1984; *m* 1stly at Milan 8 Aug 1949 (*m* diss by div at Augsburg 24 Jan 1956), Maria Teresa (*b* at Premeno, Novara 20 July 1922; *m* 2ndly at Lenno, Como 27 June 1975, Josef, Count von Thun and Hohenstein), dau of Benigno Crespi and Fanny Gandolfi, and had issue,

         1. Countess *Maria* Isabella, *b* at Milan 15 June 1950; ✠ at Chamonix 8 Dec 1980; *m* at Munich 25 Sept 1971, Vittorio Fracassi Ratti Mentone of the Marquesses di Torre Rossano (*b* at Turin 20 Dec 1940).

         [*Via Donato 20, 13100 Vercelli, Italy*].

Count Rudolf *m* 2ndly at Geneva 16 Nov 1959 (*m* diss by div at Darmstadt 15 Nov 1965), Maria Leila (*b* at Karachi, Pakistan 8 Sept 1929), dau of Prof Adrian Duarte and Milicent Mitch-Gan, and had further issue,

[*8 Avenue Fraisse, 1006 Lausanne, Switzerland*].

     2. Countess *Christiane* Vera Rani, *b* at Geneva 18 Jan 1960.

     [*Les Pres de Chavannes, 1261 Chavannes-de-Bogis, Switzerland*].

     3. Countess *Patricia* Elisabeth Sylvia Munira, *b* at Geneva 3 Aug 1962.

     [*8 Avenue Fraisse, 1006 Lausanne, Switzerland*].

     4. Countess *Alexandra* Maria Sophie, *b* at St Gallen 1 Dec 1964.

     [*4 rue des Lombards, 75004 Paris, France*].

FÜRSTENBERG

Catholic: This Swabian feudal family can be traced authentically to Egino comes de Urahe (Urach, a fortress and town in Württemberg) circa 1070; inherited the lands of the House of Zähringen in the Baar, etc, 18 Feb 1218; Count of Vurstenberc (Fürstenberg), near Villingen, Donaueschingen, Baden-Württemberg 1250; Landgrave of Baar 18 Jan 1283; acquired (through an alliance) the County of Heiligenberg and the Lordships of Jungnau and Trochtelfingen

(Hohenzollern) 1534, the Lordships of Mösskirch and Gundelfingen 1637, the Landgraviate of Stühlingen and the Lordship of Hohenhöven 1639; Treaty of Heredity 1576, 1699 and 1803; Grand Palatinate, Vienna 13 March 1627 and 10 Nov 1642; Prince of the Holy Empire in favour of the line of Heiligenberg Straubin, extinct 10 Oct 1716; partition of lands between the sons of Prosper Ferdinand, Landgrave of Fürstenberg-Stühlingen (b 12 Sept 1662; ✝ 21 Nov 1704), who were the founders of two Lines, 29 July 1755, of which only the Princely Line is still extant. The Princely Line was founded by Landgrave Joseph Wilhelm Ernst (b 12 April 1699; ✝ 29 April 1762); Prince of the Holy Empire (primogeniture) with the qualification of "Hochgeboren", Vienna 10 Dec 1716; institution of the fideicommis of Pürglitz in Bohemia for the wife of the founder, Marie-Anne, née Countess of Waldstein, 1756; the title of Prince was extended to all descendants, Vienna 19 Jan 1762; received the qualification of "Durchlaucht" by the German Diet 18 Aug 1825; the branches below descend from two sons of Prince Carl Egon (b 28 Oct 1796; ✝ 22 Oct 1854) who suceeded to Pürglitz 13 Dec 1799 and to the Principality of Fürstenberg 17 May 1804.

Members of the family bear the title of Prince or Princess zu Fürstenberg with the qualification of Serene Highness.

Principal Branch: SWABIAN

Founded by Prince Maximilian Egon (b 29 March 1822; ✝ 27 July 1873); Hereditary Member of the First Chamber of the Grand Duchy of Baden 22 Aug 1818; Hereditary Member of the former House of Lords of Württemberg 25 Sept 1819; Hereditary Member of the former Prussian House of Lords 12 Oct 1854; Hereditary Member of the former Austrian House of Lords 1861; Rejoined with the branch of Pürglitz after the death of Prince Carl Egon, 27 Nov 1896. This Branch was sub-divided into three branches, two of which are still extant.

HEINRICH Maximilian Egon Karl Joachim Paul Felix Konrad Hubertus Eusebius Leo Maria Wilhelm Friedrich Alexius Martin, **11TH PRINCE (FÜRST) ZU FÜRSTENBERG**, Landgraf in der Baar und zu Stühlingen, Graf zu Heiligenberg and Werdenberg, Freiherr zu Gundelfingen, Herr zu Hause im Kinzigtal, Mösskirch, Hohenhöwen, Wildenstein, Waldspert, Werenwag, Immendingen, Pürglitz, etc, b at Schloß Heilingonborg 17 July 1050, ouoo his father, son of Joachim Egon, 10th Prince (Fürst) zu Fürstenberg (b 28 June 1923; ✝ 9 July 2002); m at Rome 11 Nov 1976, Princess Maximiliane (b at Trieste 16 Nov 1952), dau of Maximilian, Prince (Fürst) zu Windisch-Graetz and Maria Luisa Serra.
[78166 Schloß Donaueschingen, Germany].

Sons

1. *Christian* Joachim Maximilian Egon Hugo Eusebius Maria Hubertus, Hereditary Prince (Erbprinz) zu Fürstenberg, *b* at Donaueschingen 22 Nov 1977.
2. Prince *Antonius* Hugo Egon, *b* at Starnberg 14 June 1985.

Mother

Countess *Paula*, *b* at Aulendorf 22 May 1926, dau of Joseph Erwin, Count zu Königsegg-Aulendorf and Countess Lucia von Wilczek; *m* at Königseggwald 25 June 1947, Joachim Egon, 10th Prince (Fürst) zu Fürstenberg (*b* at Schloß Grund, Pürglitz, Bohemia 28 June 1923; ✠ at Donaueschingen 9 Jul 2002), Kt Order of the Golden Fleece, Bailiff Gd Cross Hon and Dev Sovereign Military Order of Malta, Cmdr Papal Order of St Gregorius, Kt Order of Black Eagle, Kt Order of Fidelity (Baden), Cmdr Bav Order of St George, Hon Citizen of Donaueschingen, Heiligenberg and Friedenweitz.
[*78166 Schloß Donaueschingen, Germany*].

Brothers and Sisters

1. Princess *Amélie-Egona* Maria Huberta Maximiliane Georgine Ricarda Joachima Pauline Eusebia, *b* at Donaueschingen 3 April 1948.
[*78166 Schloß Donaueschingen, Germany*].
2. Princess *Marie-Antoinette* Egona Maximiliane Wilhelmine Huberta Sophie Eusebia Joachime Pauline Elisabeth, *b* at Donaueschingen 15 May 1949; *m* 1stly at Donaueschingen 16 April 1977 (*m* diss by div at Munich 7 March 1980), Johannes, Count von Schönborn-Wiesentheid (*b* at Würzburg 3 July 1949). She *m* 2ndly at Pöcking 15 Dec 1980, Thomas Bagusat (*b* at Berlin 12 July 1941).
[*Ziegelstadel 9, 86911 Diessen-St Georgen am Ammersee, Germany*].
3. Prince *Karl-Egon* Friedrich Maximilian Wilhelm Eusebius Maria Hubertus Leo, *b* at Donaueschingen 3 April 1953.
[*78166 Schloß Donaueschingen, Germany*].
4. Prince and Landgrave *Johannes* Joseph Wilhelm Ernst Eduard Egon Eusebius Hubertus Maria Maximilian Bernhard, *b* at Villingen 15 April 1958; adopted by Karl Egon, Prince (Fürst) and Landgrave of Fürstenberg-Weitken (*b* 1891; ✠ 1973); *m* 1stly at Freilassing 28 Feb (civ) and at Vienna 11 Dec (relig) 1985 (*m* diss by div Krems 19 Oct 1994), Veronika Paul (*b* at Kettwig 15 Sept 1948), and has issue,
   1. Prince *Vincenz* Heinrich Egon Joachim Gottfried Hubertus

Maria Erwein, *b* at Vienna 16 March 1985.
[*Meierhof 74, 3970 Weitra, Austria*].
Prince and Landgrave Johannes *m* 2ndly at Gmund am Tegernsee 30 May 1996, Stephanie (*b* at Munich 31 May 1961), dau of Albrecht Theodor Heiden and Christel Daleiden, and has further issue,
[*Schwarzau 1, 3971 St Martin, Austria*].
    2. Prince *Ludwig* Maximilian Anton Egon Albrecht Joachim Hubertus Maria, *b* at Munich 28 Dec 1997.
    3. Prince *Johann-Christian* Egon Theodor Gerhard Hubertus Maria, *b* at Munich 30 April 1999.
5. Princess *Anna Lucia* Egona Eusebia Huberta Ines Paula Joachima Wilhelmine Maximiliane, *b* at Villingen 3 Nov 1965; *m* at Donaueschingen 18 Feb (civ) and at Stühlingen 19 Feb (relig) 1994, James Giraldo (*b* at New York 4 Oct 1964), Banker.
[*44 Quai Gustave Ador, 1207 Genf, Switzerland*].

Brother and Sisters of Father

1. Princess *Maria Josepha* Egona Sofia Wilhelmine Joachima Maximiliane Friederike, *b* at Werenwag 23 April 1922; *m* at Donaueschingen 27 Feb 1943, Günther, Count von Hardenberg (*b* at Schwedt an der Oder 14 Feb 1918; ✝ at Baden-Baden 19 Jan 1985), Capt.
[*Hermann-Sielcken-Straße 47, 76530 Baden-Baden, Germany*].
2. Prince *Friedrich Maximilian* Egon Hubertus Joseph Maria Karl Anna, *b* at Schloß Wechselburg 26 July 1926; ✝ at Vienna 2 Nov 1969, Kt Bavarian Order of St George, Kt Sovereign Military Order of Malta; *m* at Kloten, nr Zurich 9 April 1960, Princess Teresa (*b* at Vienna 21 July 1925; *m* 1stly at Lugano 1 Aug 1946, Heinrich, Baron Thyssen Bornomisza; that *m* diss by div at Lugano 14 May 1954), dau of Alfred, Prince of Lippe-Weissenfeld and Countess Franziska von Schönborn-Buchheim, and had issue,
[*Schloß Werenwag, 88631 Beuron, Germany*].
    1. Princess *Teresa* Sophie Antoinette, *b* at Vienna 18 Nov 1960; *m* at St Moritz 4 March (civ) and at Schloß Werenwag 14 May (relig) 1989, Angelo Giuseppe Bucarelli (*b* at Rome 9 April 1952), Architect.
    [*Via Garibaldi 88, 00153 Rome, Italy*].
    2. Prince *Maximilian* Joachim Alfred Egon Karl Hubertus Maria Leo, *b* at Vienna 27 May 1962; *m* at Jagtshausen 16 Dec (civ) and at Schöntal 2 May (relig) 1992, Baroness Diana (*b* at Coblenz 9 Oct 1965), dau of Götz, Baron von Berlichingen

and Alexandra von Vultejus, and has issue,
[*Schloß Werenwag, 88631 Beuron-Hausen, Germany*].

    1. Princess *Clarissa* Anna Lucia Katherina Teresa Alexandra Maria, *b* at Freiburg 18 Feb 1993.

    2. Prince *Friedrich* Götz Constantin Christian Maximilian Hubertus Maria, *b* at Freiburg 8 April 1995.

    3. Princess *Alina* Louisa Mafalda Virginia Astrid Birgit Maria, *b* at Zürich Feb 2001.

3. Princess *Katarina* Maria Josepha Egona Elisabeth, *b* at Zurich 19 Nov 1966; ✝ at London 16 Jan 1992.

3. Princess Sophie *Antoinette* Oktavia Benedikta Wilhelmine Maria Egona Huberta, *b* at Tübingen 10 Feb 1934; ✝ at Munich 14 Jan 1991; *m* at Donaueschingen 28 June (civ) and 1 July (relig) 1954 (*m* diss by div at Munich 1963), Philipp-Constantin, Count von Berckheim (*b* at Mannheim 20 Sept 1924; ✝ at Weinheim an der Bergstrasse 6 Oct 1984).

Brother of Great-Grandfather

Issue of Maximilian Egon I, Prince zu Fürstenberg (*b* 29 March 1822; ✝ 27 July 1873) and Countess Leontine von Khevenhüller-Metsch (*b* 25 Feb 1843; ✝ 9 Aug 1914; *m* 23 May 1860; *m* 2ndly 31 May 1875, Prince Emil Egon zu Fürstenberg).

Son

Prince Karl *Emil* Egon Anton Maximilian Leo Wratislaw, *b* at Prague 16 Feb 1867; ✝ at Strobl am Wolfgangsee 21 Feb 1945, Ambassador to Madrid, Kt Order of the Golden Fleece, Bailiff Gd Cross Hon and Dev Sovereign Military Order of Malta; *m* at Keszthely 23 July 1902, Countess Maria (*b* at Baden-Baden 24 May 1881; ✝ at Strobl 2 March 1953), Lady-in-Waiting, Dame Star Cross Order, Dame of Hon Sovereign Military Order of Malta, dau of Tassilo, Prince Festetics de Tolna and Lady Mary Douglas-Hamilton of the Dukes of Hamilton, and had issue, among whom,

    1. Prince *Tassilo* Egon Maria Karl Georg Leo, *b* at Brussels 10 June 1903; ✝ at Strobl am Wolfgangsee 15 July 1989, Kt of Hon Sovereign Military Order of Malta; *m* 1stly at Turin 19 Nov 1938 (*m* diss by div), Clara (*b* at Turin 7 April 1920; *m* 2ndly 30 March 1974, Giovanni Nuvoletti), dau of Eduardo Agnelli and Donna Virginia Bourbón del Monte of the Princes di San Faustino. He *m* 2ndly at Paris 17 Oct 1975, Cecilie

Blaffer (*b* at ...; *m* 1stly, Edward J Hudson; that *m* diss by div at Houston, Texas 1963), and has issue by his first wife, [*5350 Strobl am Wolfgangsee, Austria; 31021 Marocco, nr Venice, Italy; Villa Bella, 32043 Cortina d'Ampezzo, Italy; 29 rue Delaborderie, 92200 Neuilly-sur-Seine, France*].

    1. Princess Virginia (*Ira*) Carolina Theresa Pancrazia Galdina, *b* at Rome 18 April 1940; *m* 1stly at Venice 17 Sept (civ) and 21 Sept (relig) 1955 (*m* diss by div at Mexico City 14 Dec 1960 and annulled at Madrid 18 Dec 1969), Alfonso, Prince zu Hohenlohe-Langenburg (*b* at Madrid 28 May 1924; *m* 2ndly at Las Vegas 3 May 1973, Jacqueline Lane; that *m* diss by div at Stanfield, Conn, USA 18 March 1985). She *m* 2ndly at Reno, Nevada, USA 12 Jan 1961 (*m* diss by div at Las Vegas, Nevada Jan 1964), Francisco Pignatari (*b* 1916; ✝ at São Paulo Oct 1977), Industrialist.
[*7 Chesterfield Hill, London W1*].

    2. Prince *Eduard* Egon Peter Paul Giovanni, *b* at Lausanne 29 June 1946; *m* 1stly at Montfort-l'Amaury, Dept Seine-et-Oise 16 July 1969 (*m* diss by div at), Diane (*b* at Brussels 31 Dec 1946; *m* 2ndly at City Hall, New York 2 Feb 2001, Barry Diller), dau of Léon Halfin and Liliane Nahmias. He *m* 2ndly 1983, Lynn Marshall (*b* at .....), and has issue by his first wife, [*745 5th Avenue, New York, NY 10151, U.S.A.; Via Spartaco 6, 20100 Milan, Italy*].

        1. Prince *Alexandre* Egon, *b* at New York 25 Jan 1970; *m* at New York 28 Oct 1995, Alexandra (*b* at New York 8 Oct 1972), dau of Robert Miller and Marie Chantal Pesantes, and has issue,

            1. Princess *Talita*, *b* at New York 7 May 1999.

            2. Prince *Tassilo*, *b* at New York 20 Aug 2001.

        2. Princess *Tatiana* Desirée, *b* at New York 16 Feb 1971.

    3. Prince *Sebastian* Egon Rainer Maria Timotheus, *b* at Laussanne 24 Jan 1950; *m* at Hof, nr Salzburg 28 Sept 1972, Elisabetta Guarnati (*b* at Riva am Gardasee 19 June 1951), and has issue,

[*Via Padana 234, 30030 Malcontenta, Prov. Venedig, Italy*].

    1. Princess *Virginia* Maria Clara, *b* at Genoa 5 Oct 1974; *m* at ... 1992, Baron Alexandre Csillaghy de Pacsér (**b** at ...).

2. Prince *Georg* Egon Hubertus Karl Wolfgang, *b* at Strobl 13 Aug 1923, Dr of Law, Kt of Justice Sovereign Military Order of Malta; *m* 1stly at Oblarn, Styria 10 Sept (civ) and 11 Dept (relig) 1960 (*m* diss by div at Vienna 18 May 1965), Countess Christina (*b* at Prague 19 Dec 1940; *m* 2ndly 1965, Jan van Hamel; that *m* diss by div; *m* 3rdly May 1975, Michael Begert, that *m* diss by div), [*Schloß Gstatt, 8960 Öblarn, OSteiermk, Austria*], dau of Joseph, 7th Prince (Fürst) von Colloredo-Mannsfeld and Anna Maria Rabl. He *m* 2ndly at Korneuburg, Austria 1 Aug 1978 (*m* diss by div at Korneuburg 26 Feb 1997), Victoria Taves (*b* at Rio de Janeiro 7 March 1957; *m* 2ndly at Sant Appiano, nr Florence 11 Oct 1997, Prince Michael von Schönburg-Hartenstein, *b* at Vienna 22 Feb 1960), dau of Guy Hunter Pullen and Margarete Pullen, and had issue by his first wife,

    [*Myliusstraße 31, 60323 Frankfurt-am-Main, Germany*].

    1. Princess *Diega* Katharina Berta Anna Marie, *b* at Vienna 12 Dec 1961; ✠ at Danzig 2 Jan 1975.

Second Branch: KÖNIGSHOF
(✠ Extinct ✠)

Founded by Prince Emil Egon (*b* 25 Sept 1825; ✠ 15 May 1899), brother of Maximilian Egon I (see above); Institution of the fideicommis of Königshof 1 June 1866 (confirmed 21 April 1867).

✠ **EMIL EGON** Karl Leo Max, **PRINCE ZU FÜRSTENBERG**, *b* at Laná, Bohemia 13 Jan 1876; ✠ at Vienna 3 Sept 1964, Dr of Law; *m* at Vienna 28 Feb 1922, Baroness Margarethe (Daisy) (*b* at Prague 19 July 1904; ✠ at Vienna 1 Dec 1988), dau of Vincenz, Baron von Gecmen-Waldek and Baroness Margarete von Waldek.

Daughters

1. Princess *Leontine* Elisabeth Maria Emilie Vincenzia, *b* at Klafterbrunn, Austria 23 April 1924; *m* at St Gilgen, nr Salzburg (civ) and at Strobl (relig) 16 Sept 1945 (*m* diss by div at Munich 20 Nov 1958), Donat Oswald, Baron von Richthofen (*b* at Berlin 8

March 1920; at ✝ Wartenberg 14 Jan 1999).
[*Singerstraße 12, 1010 Vienna, Austria*].
2. Princess *Amelie* Maria Margarethe Emilie Vinzenzia Josefa, *b* at
Bad Ischl, Austria 12 Nov 1945; *m* at Vienna 19 April 1969, Augustin
d'Aboville of the Counts d'Aboville (*b* at Brouay, Calvados 8 June
1937).
[*134 avenue Victor Hugo, 75116 Paris, France*].

HARRACH

Catholic and Evangelical: This feudal Bohemian/Austrian family
most likely took their name from Harruck (Harrouche) near Freystadt,
Upper Austria and can be traced authentically to Bohonik (Wohunk)
of Harrach, a Knight living 28 Nov 1309; acquired the Lordship of
Rohrau (Lower Austria) 7 Sept 1524; Baron of Rohrau in the
Hereditary States of Austria, Vienna 12 April 1550; Baron of the
Holy Empire 4 Jan 1552; "Erbstallmeister" (Hereditary Master of
the Horse) in Austria unter der Enns, Augsburg 29 May 1559;
Hungarian Indigenat 1563; Grand Palatinate, Vienna 12 April 1550;
Bohemian Lord 21 Feb 1577; "Oberst-Erblandstallmeister"
(Hereditary Grand Master of the Horse) in Austria ober der Enns 3
March 1627; Count of the Holy Empire and elevation of Rohrau into
a County with the title of Count of Rohrau, Vienna 20 July 1627;
joined the names and arms of Thannhausen through the marriage of
Count Alois Thomas Raimund (*b* 8 March 1669; ✝ 7 Nov 1742) to
Anne-Cecile (*b* at Graz 24 March 1674; *m* 22 Aug 1695; ✝ at Vienna
7 Feb 1721), widow of Count Michel Oswald Thun (✝ at Prague 31
Jan 1694) and heiress of the last Count of Thannhausen, Vienna 26
Aug 1708; received into the College of Swabian Counts of the Holy
Empire 6 July 1752 (for Ferdinand Bonaventura Anton, Count of
Harrach who ✝ 28 Jan 1778) with the right of succession for his
nephew Ernst Guidon (*b* 8 Sept 1723; ✝ 23 March 1783) and his
heirs; received the qualification of "Erlaucht" (primogeniture) by
the German Diet 13 Feb 1829; inherited Rohrau at the extinction of
the Younger Line, 22 Sept 1886.
Members of the family bear the title of Count or Countess von
Harrach and the Head of the family bears the qualification of
Illustrious Highness.

LINE II:

Founded by Count Ernst Christoph Joseph (*b* 29 May 1757; ✝ 14 Dec
1838).

ERNST LEONHARD Otto Georg Johann Konrad Maria Schnee Hubertus, **COUNT (GRAF) VON HARRACH ZU ROHRAU AND THANNHAUSEN,** Noble Lord, Lord of the County of Rohrau, Baron zu Prugg and Pürrhenstein, Lord of Starkenbach, Jilenice, Sadowa and Storckow, Kt Sovereign Military Order of Malta, *b* at Munich 5 Aug 1920, son of Ernst, Count von Harrach zu Rohrau and Thannhausen (*b* 26 Oct 1879; ✠ 12 Aug 1971) and Countess Elisabeth von Preysing-Lichtenegg-Moos (*b* 15 Nov 1883; *m* 22 Nov 1905; ✠ 27 Feb 1932); *m* at Klagenfurt 7 Oct 1948, Hermine (*b* at Kindberg 2 Oct 1922), dau of Franz Neukirchner and Anna Pusch.
[*Schloßmühl Gasse 11, 2460 Bruck an der Leitha, Austria*].

Son and Daughter

1. Countess *Christiane* Anna Elisabeth, *b* at Santiago de Chile 27 Dec 1949.
[*Willer Gasse 27, 1236 Vienna, Austria*].
2. *Ernst* Georg Franz Christian, Hereditary Count (Erbgraf) von Harrach, *b* at Santiago de Chile 22 June 1951; *m* at Vienna 19 Sept 1977, Angela (*b* at Vienna 7 Feb 1954), dau of Rudolf Rojahn and Baroness Johanna Possanner von Ehrenthal, and has issue,
[*Schillerstraße 8, 2460 Bruck an der Leitha, Austria*].

    1. Count *Ernst* Heinrich Rudolf Gyri, *b* at Vienna 11 Feb 1979.

Sister

1. Countess *Christiane* Marie Therese Elisabeth Leopoldine Ernestine Maximiliane, *b* at Vienna 12 Oct 1916; *m* at London 4 June 1952 (*m* diss by div at London 20 Feb 1967), Arthur T Battagel (*b* at Watford 30 June 1908; ✠ at Sittleworth, West Sussex 7 Nov 1991), Major (Res).
[*Grödigerstraße 293/I, 5081 Anif, Austria*].

Half-Brother of Father

Issue of Johann, Count von Harrach, etc (*b* 2 Nov 1828; ✠ 12 Dec 1909; *m* 2ndly 15 Oct 1878, Princess Maria Theresia von Thurn and Taxis) and his first wife, Princess Maria Margareta of Lobkowicz (*b* 13 July 1837; *m* 2 Aug 1856; ✠ 2 Sept 1870), having had issue, among whom,

Son
Otto Johann Nepomuk, **Count von Harrach**, etc, *b* at Prague 10
Feb 1863; ✢ at Schloß Hradek, near Königgrätz, Bohemia 10 Sept
1935, Kt Sovereign Military Order of Malta; *m* at Vienna 14 Jan
1902, Princess Karoline (*b* at Prague 22 Feb 1873; ✢ at Vienna 15
March 1959), Lady-in-Waiting, Dame Star Cross Order, Dame of Hon
Sovereign Military Order of Malta, dau of Karl, Prince (Fürst) zu
Oettingen-Oettingen and Oettingen-Wallerstein and Countess
Ernestine Czernin von and zu Chudenitz, and had issue,

    1. **Johann** Nepomuk Anton Karl Leonhard Otto Bonaventura
    Maria Kleophas, **Count von Harrach** etc, *b* at Prugg 25
    Sept 1904; ✢ at Bad Kreuznach 12 May 1945, Proprietor of
    Prugg and Rohrau, Lower Austria; *m* at Altaussee 16 Oct
    1940, Countess and Noble Lady Stephanie (*b* at Altaussee 30
    Sept 1917), Dame Star Cross Order, dau of Erwein, Count
    and Noble Lord von and zu Eltz genannt Faust von Stromberg
    and Countess Johanna von Schönborn-Wiesentheid, and had
    issue, among whom,
    [*2471 Schloß Rohrau, Lower Austria*].

        1. Countess *Johanna* Alexandra Georgine Amalie, *b* at
        Königgrätz 10 July 1944; *m* at Vienna 10 Sept 1966,
        Eberhard, Count von Waldburg zu Zeil and
        Trauchburg (*b* at Zeil 30 April 1940).
        [*2471 Schloß Rohrau, Lower Austria*].

Brother of Great-Grandfather
Issue of Franz Ernst, Count von Harrach, etc (*b* 13 Dec 1799; ✢ 26
Feb 1884) and Princess Anne of Lobkowicz (*b* 23 Jan 1809; *m* 29 May
1827; ✢ 25 Oct 1881), having had issue, among whom,

Son
Count *Alfred-Karl*, *b* at Prague 9 Oct 1831; ✢ at Abbazia 5 Jan
1914; *m* at Vienna 26 July 1869, Princess Anna of Lobkowicz (*b* at
Vienna 5 April 1847; ✢ at Aschach an der Donau 25 Nov 1934),
having had issue, among whom,

Son
Count *Franz* Marie Alfred, *b* at Traunkirchen 26 July 1870; ✢ at
Iglau, Moravia 14 May 1937, Proprietor of Aschach and Stauff, Upper
Austria, Janowitz and Gross-Meseritsch and Zhorz in Moravia, Bailiff

Sovereign Military Order of Malta, Kt Teutonic Order, Imp and
Royal Chamberlain and Privy Councillor; *m* 1stly at Vienna 29 May
1895, Countess Gabrielle (*b* at Frohnsburg, Lower Austria 15 Nov
1874; ✠ at Baden, near Vienna 12 Sept 1896), dau of Siegmund,
Count von Khevenhüller-Metsch and Countess Marianne zu
Herberstein. He *m* 2ndly at Vienna 30 June 1902, Princess Sarah
(*b* at Sagh 4 Dec 1880; ✠ at Gross-Meseritsch 10 June 1908), Dame
Star Cross Order, dau of Chlodwig, Prince zu Hohenlohe-Waldenburg-
Schillingsfürst and Countess Franziska Esterházy von Galántha,
and by her had issue, among whom,

    1. Countess Anne Marie (*Nany*) Nicolette, *b* at Schloß
    Aschach 6 Dec 1906, Proprietor of Janowitz and Rabenstein;
    m at Prague 1 Aug 1928, Franz (*Fery*) de Rosty-Forgách de
    Barkócz (*b* at Gács, Hungary 31 Oct 1892; ✠ at Santiago de
    Chile 27 Sept 1957), Co-Proprietor of Vilke, Hungary, Dr of
    Law, adopted son of his maternal uncle, Anton, Count Forgach
    von Ghymes and Gács.
    [*Hallerstraße 75, 20146 Hamburg, Germany*].

Count Franz *m* 3rdly at Seefeld 1 Feb 1910, Countess Alice (*b* at
Gross-Harras 10 July 1879; ✠ at Aschach an der Donau 10 Feb
1962), Lady-in-Waiting, Dame Star Cross Order, dau of Maximilian,
Count zu Hardegg, Proprietor of Glatz and im Machland and
Countess Alice de la Fontaine d'Harnoncourt-Unverzagt, and by
her had further issue,

    2. Countess *Alice* Louise Marie, *b* at Vienna 23 Sept 1916,
    Proprietor of Aschach and Stauff; *m* at Aschach 29 July 1940,
    Karl, Baron Dreihann-Holenia von Sulzberg am Steinhof (*b*
    at Morawetz, Mähren 15 July 1906; ✠ at Aschach 2 July
    1978), Dr of Law.
    [*Harrachstraße 3, 4082 Aschach an der Donau, Austria*].

Line II Harrach zu Rohrau and Thannhausen

Founded by Count Ferdinand Joseph (*b* 17 March 1763; ✠ 5 Dec
1841).
Members of this Line bare the title of Count or Countess von Harrach
zu Rohrau and Thannhausen.

Son

Count *Karl* Philipp, *b* at Prague 16 Nov 1795; ✠ at Breslau 25 Nov
1878, proprietor of Gross-Sägewitz in Silesia; *m* 1stly at Stremplowitz
10 July 1828, Countess Theresia Sedlnitzky (*b* at Troppau 26 Aug

1810; ✠ at Rosnoschau 23 Sept 1834). He *m* 2ndly at Dresden 5 July 1838, Baroness Isabella von Pfister (*b* at Vienna 14 Nov 1812; ✠ at Dresden 5 April 1896), and had issue, among whom,

Son - 2nd Marriage

2. Count *Ernst*, *b* at Krolkwitz, near Breslau 20 June 1845; ✠ at Klein-Krichen 10 June 1896; *m* at Halle 5 April 1872, Adele, Baroness von Jenna (*b* at Köthen 16 March 1852; ✠ at Klein-Krichen 3 July 1905), having had issue, among whom,

> ### Son
> Count *Manfred* Karl Theodor Viktor Ernst, *b* at Klein-Krichen, 10 May 1878; ✠ at Bad Nauheim 11 Sept 1924, Proprietor of Klein-Krichen, Kt of Hon St John of Jerusalem; *m* at Meyenburg, Ostprignitz 24 May 1906, Magdalene (*b* at Demmin 26 July 1881; ✠ at Deuna 13 Oct 1945), Proprietor of Meyenburg, dau of Theodor von Rohr genannt von Wahlen-Jürgass, Proprietor of Ganzer I, and of Meyenburg and Anna von Heyden, and had issue, among whom,
>
> > 1. Count *Günther* Karl Theodor Ernst Manfred, *b* at Klein-Krichen 13 Aug 1908; ✠ at Köhn near Kiel 12 Oct 1969, Proprietor of Gross-Sägewitz, (later Segen), nr Breslau; *m* 1stly at Dresden 17 March 1932, Countess Hertha-Louise (*b* at Dresden 26 Dec 1907; ✠ at Segen 4 Nov 1939), dau of Traugott, Count von Pfeil and Klein-Ellguth and Johanna von Krauss, and by her had issue, among whom,
> >
> > > 1. Count *Albrecht* Leopold Günther, *b* at Breslau 1 July 1936, Programmer; *m* at Giekau, Plön, East Holstein 22 July 1966, Anna (*b* at Düsseldorf 17 Nov 1936), dau of Carlo Giuseppe Massa and Maria Margareta Bleith, and had issue,
> > >
> > > [*Rembrandtstraße 21, 40237 Düsseldorf, Germany*].
> > >
> > > > 1. Countess *Isabel* Claudia Vera, *b* at Düsseldorf 27 Jan 1967, Financial Advisor; *m* at Krefeld-Nordingen 16 June 1995, Marek Gehrmann (*b* at Düsseldorf 2 Aug 1966), Estate Manager. [*Lakronstraße 52, 40625 Düsseldorf*,

Germany].

Count Günther *m* 2ndly at Sommerfeld, near Stralsund 9 June 1941, Brigitte (Brita) (*b* at Stralsund 4 April 1912), dau of Konrad von Schaevenbach, Proprietor of Sommerfeld and Baroness Elisabeth von Esebeck, and had further issue, among whom,
[*Wilhelmshöhe, 23701 Eutin, Germany*].

> 2. Countess *Herta Elisabeth* Magdalene Brigitte, *b* at Breslau 5 June 1942, Florist; *m* at Giekau, Plön 14 Aug 1964, Manfred Hoins (*b* at Lehrte 10 Aug 1943; ✠ at Hanover 17 Nov 1971).
> [*Südring 11, 31275 Lehrte, Hanover, Germany*].

> 3. Countess *Vera* Magdalene Brigitte, *b* at Schönberg, Holstein 23 Dec 1949, Art Historian; *m* at Stuttgart-Untertürkheim 16 Dec 1983, Johannes Wahle (*b* at Meschede 12 Aug 1951), Research Engineer.
> [*Schulerstraße 16, 73666 Hohengehren, bei Stuttgart, Germany*].

> 4. Countess *Agnes* Henriette Magdalene Brigitte, *b* at Lütjenburg, Holstein 28 June 1954, Psychologist.
> [*Frohnhoferstraße 9, 12165 Berlin, Germany*].

2. Count *Leonhard* Ferdinand Theodor Ernst Leopold Manfred, *b* at Klein-Krichen 8 April 1912; ✠ at Neu-Schönberg near Kiel 13 Sept 1985, Proprietor of Klein-Krichen; *m* at Berlin 18 July 1939, Maria Cecilie (*b* at Berlin 26 Aug 1914), dau of Hermann Johannes and Elise Thiele, and had issue,
[*Strandstraße 225, 24217 Schönberg bei Kiel, Germany*].

> 1. Count Johannes Leonhard *Bonaventura* Hermann Manfred, *b* at Klein-Krichen 2 Sept 1940, Haulage Contractor; *m* 1stly at Cologne 23 Dec 1964 (*m* diss by div at Hanau 18 Feb 1971), Rita [*Röntgenstraße 14, 63454 Hanau, Germany*] (*b* at Breslau 9 Oct 1939), dau of Horst Schirdewahn and Ruth Lotze. He *m* 2ndly at Bruchköbel near Hanau 2 Dec 1971, Waltraud (*b* at Bruchköbel 3 July 1942), dau of Wilhelm

King and Wilhelmine Simon, and has issue by his first wife,

[*Rob. Kochstraße 13, 63486 Bruchköbel, Germany*].

    1. Countess *Stephanie, b* at Cologne 23 Jan 1967.

    [*Musikantenweg 16, 60316 Frankfurt-am-Main, Germany*].

    2. Count *Maximilian, b* at Hanau 16 May 1969.

    [*Röntgenstraße 14, 63454 Hanau, Germany*].

2. Count Christoph Leonhard *Manfred* Hartmann Leopold, *b* at Klein-Krichen 18 Jan 1943, Dr of Med; *m* at Kiel 11 Feb 1971, Ursula (*b* at Berlin 11 Dec 1937), dau of Hermann Vorsatz and Gisela Gohlke, and has issue,

[*Heidbergstraße 15, 24582 Bordesholm, Germany*].

    1. Countess Sofia *Nike, b* at Kiel 18 June 1971.

    2. Count *Vigo* Hartmann, *b* at Kiel 7 April 1973.

3. Count Joachim Leonhard *Dietrich* Ernst Wilhelm, *b* at Burgundenau near Görlitz 4 Feb 1945, Prof, Dr rer nat habil, Dipl Phys; *m* at Munich 19 April 1973, Evelyn (*b* at Neisse an der Oder 23 Jan 1944), dau of Fritz Lobe and Elisabeth Gertrud Hentschel, and has issue,

[*Immenhof 2, 55128, Mainz, Germany*].

    1. Countess *Daphne* Louise Rosa Isabella Cecilie, *b* at Heidelberg 19 Jan 1976.

    2. Countess *Xenia* Sophie Anna Eleonore Gwendolyn, *b* at Heidelberg 18 July 1980.

    3. Countess *Berenike* Claire Marie Lavinia Elisabeth, *b* at Heidelberg 20 Feb 1983.

3. Count *Wichard* Karl Ferdinand Ernst Theodor Manfred, *b* at Klein-Krichen 6 March 1916; Dr of Agriculture; Dipl Eng Agr, Agricultural Attaché (Ret),

Kt of Justice St John of Jerusalem, Proprietor of Meyenburg (Brandenburg); *m* at Deuna, Eichsfeld 19 Nov (civ) and 20 Nov (relig) 1944, Countess Jutta (*b* at Bad Grund, Harz 27 Oct 1923), dau of Eberhardt, Count vom Hagen, Proprietor of Rüdigershagen, Deuna, etc and Noble (Edle) and Baroness Edelgarde von Plotho, and has issue,

[*Rüdigerstraße 79, 53179 Bonn, Germany*].

    1. Count *Jobst-Babo* Manfred Eberhard Ernst-Theodor Wichard, *b* at Göttingen 19 Aug 1946, Banker; *m* at Wolbeck, Münster 23 Oct 1968, Baroness Eva-Marie (*b* at Worms 31 Dec 1946), Prof, Dr of Pol Science, dau of Ludwig, Baron von Heyl zu Herrnsheim and Gisela Greiser, and has issue,

    [*Lersnerstraße 34, 60322 Frankfurt-am-Main, Germany*].

        1. Count *Wichard-Babo* Ludwig Hanno Manfred, *b* at Münster 13 May 1969.

        [*Kolonaden 47, 20354 Hamburg, Germany*].

        2. Count *Leonhard* Carl Johannes, *b* at Düsseldorf 20 Feb 1975; *m* at ... 2002, Melissa (*b* at ...), dau of Robert Rieder and Judy-Anne Stone.

        3. Countess *Verena* Caroline Marie, *b* at Düsseldorf 16 April 1976.

    2. Count *Hanno* Günther Siegbert Wichard, *b* at Göttingen 19 Feb 1948, MA, PhD; *m* at Northiam, Sussex 3 Dec 1970, Viola (*b* at London 22 Jan 1948), dau of Frederic Marsh and Elisabeth Baxter, and has issue,

    [*29 Queens Road, Tunbridge Wells, TN4 9LZ*].

        1. Count *Istvan* Matthew Johannes, *b* at Filderstadt, Württemberg 4 Nov 1976.

        2. Countess *Amelie* Ruth Johanna, *b* at Oxford 27 Jan 1979.

        3. Count *Georg* Alexander Frederick, *b* at Edinburgh 7 March 1983.

HOHENLOHE

This Seigneural Franconian family (1096 "de baronibus", see Hohenloh. Urk-Buch I, 9; 1182 "liberae conditionis", ibidem I, 17) can be traced authentically to Cuonradus et frater ejus de Wichartesheim (Weikersheim, Württemberg) and Heinricus living 1153 who bore the name of the ancient castle of Hohenloch (in the village of Hohlach) near Uffenheim in Franconia, Bavaria; and his sons Konrad, Heinrich and Albert in 1178; acquired Langenburg 1232/34, the Regensburg fief of Oehringen with Neuenstein and Waldenburg (Württemberg) 1250; Count of Hohenlohe and of Ziegenhain 1450; Union of Heredity 1511; partition of lands between two sons of Count Georg I (b 17 Jan 1488; ✝ 16 March 1551) who founded the Lines below, 1555; qualification of "Durchlaucht" in Württemberg for Members all Lines of the House of Hohenlohe, Stuttgart 3 Feb 1902.

LINE I: NEUENSTEIN

Founded by Ludwig Kasimir, Count of Hohenlohe (b 12 Jan 1517; ✝ 24 Aug 1568); Joined the name and arms of the extinct House of Langenburg 1558; separation of the premier line of Langenburg (extinct 1590) 1586; separation of the Line of Langenburg by Count Philipp-Ernst (b 11 Aug 1584; ✝ 29 June 1628); Count of Gleichen 15 Jan 1631; the Branches below descend from two sons of Count Heinrich Friedrich (b 5 Sept 1625; ✝ 5 June 1699).

1ST BRANCH
HOHENLOHE-LANGENBURG

Lutheran and Catholic: Founded by Albrecht Wolfgang, Count of Hohenlohe-Langenburg (b 6 July 1659; ✝ 17 April 1715); Prince of the Holy Empire and ratification of Arms 7 Jan 1764; the title of Prince of Hohenlohe-Langenburg was confirmed with the qualification of "Hochgeboren" granted, Vienna 29 May 1772; Hereditary Member of the First Chamber in the Kingdom of Württemberg 25 Sept 1819. Members of this Branch bear the title of Prince or Princess zu Hohenlohe-Langenburg with the qualification of Serene Highness.

KRAFT Alexander Ernst Ludwig Georg Emich, **9TH PRINCE (FÜRST) ZU HOHENLOHE-LANGENBURG**, Count von Gleichen, b at Schwäbisch Hall 25 June 1935, son of Gottfried, 8th Prince (Fürst) zu Hohenlohe-Langenburg (b 24 March 1897; ✝ 11 May 1960) and Princess Margarita of Greece and Denmark (b 18 April 1905; m 20 April 1931; ✝ 24 April 1981); m 1stly at Zwingenberg 5 June 1965 (m diss by div at Crailsheim 26 May 1990), Princess Charlotte (b in London 31 Dec 1938; she m 2ndly at Frankfurt-am-

Main 23 June 1993, Johannes, Baron von Twickel), dau of
Alexander, Prince von Croÿ and Anne Campbell. He *m* 2ndly at
Graz, Austria 22 May 1992, Irma Gisela Christine (*b* at Graz 29 June
1946), dau of Eugen Pospesch and Gisela Spanring.
[*74595 Schloß Langenburg, Württemberg, Germany*].

Son and Daughters - 1st Marriage

1. Princess *Cécilie* Marita Dorothea, *b* at Crailsheim 16 Dec 1967;
m at Cadouin 6 June 1998, Count Cyril Amédéo de Commarque (*b* at
Périgeux 12 Aug 1970).
2. *Philipp* Gottfried Alexander, Hereditary Prince (Erbprinz) zu
Hohenlohe-Langenburg, *b* at Crailsheim 20 January 1970.
3. Princess *Xenia* Margarita Anne, *b* at Crailsheim 8 July 1972.

Brothers and Sister

1. Princess *Beatrix* Alice Marie Melita Margarita, *b* at Schwabisch
Hall 10 July 1936; ✠ at Langenburg 15 Nov 1997.
2. Prince Georg *Andreas* Heinrich, *b* at Schwabish Hall 24 Nov 1938;
m at Burghausen-an-der-Inn 9 Sept 1968, Princess Luise (*b* at
Frankfurt-an-der-Oder 12 Oct 1943), yst dau of Georg, Prince von
Schönburg-Waldenburg and Countess Pauline zu Castell-Castell,
and has issue,
[*Tristanstraße 18a, 80804 Munich, Germany*].
     1. Princess *Katharina*, *b* at Munich 21 Nov 1972.
     2. Princess *Tatjana*, *b* at Munich 10 Feb 1975.
3. Prince *Ruprecht* Sigismund Philipp Ernst, *b* at Langenburg 7
April 1944; ✠ at Munich 8 April 1978.
4. Prince *Albrecht* Wolfgang Christof, *b* at Langenburg 7 April 1944
(twin with Prince Ruprecht); ✠ at Berlin 23 April 1992; *m* at
Berlin-Zehlendorf 23 Jan 1976, Maria (*b* at Freiberg, Saxony 30 Nov
1933), dau of Willy Fischer and Marie Fiedler, and has issue,
[*Altensteinstraße 38a, 14195 Berlin, Germany*].
     1. Prince *Ludwig*, *b* at Berlin 21 April 1976.

Brother of Great-Great-Great-Great-Grandfather

Issue of Ludwig, 1st Prince zu Hohenlohe-Langenburg (*b* 20 Oct
1696; ✠ 16 Jan 1765) and Countess Eleonore of Nassau-Saarbrücken
(*b* 30 July 1707; *m* 25 Jan 1723; ✠ 15 Oct 1769) and had issue, among
whom,

Son

Prince *Friedrich Ernst,* *b* at Langenburg 16 May 1750; ✝ as a POW at Villers-Cotterêtes, France 24 Oct 1794, Lt-Gen Dutch Army; *m* at Wolwega, Friesland 7 Feb 1773, Baroness Madeleine Adrienne (*b* at The Hague 23 April 1746; ✝ at Minneresbergen 28 Sept 1822), dau of Onno, Baron Zwier van Haren and Sara-Adèle van Huls, and had issue, among whom,

Son

Prince Karl *Gustav* Wilhelm, *b* at Leuwarden 29 Aug 1777; ✝ at Brünn (Brno) 26 June 1866, Field Marshal Austrian Army; *m* at Brünn 16 Jan 1816, Landgravine Frederika Ladislava (*b* at Wels 27 June 1781; ✝ at Brünn 11 July 1858), dau of Friedrich Joseph Maximilian, Landgrave of Fürstenberg-Weitra and Countess Josepha Theckla von Schellenberg, and had issue, among whom,

Son

Prince *Ludwig* Karl Gustav, *b* at Graz 11 Jan 1823; *dka* at Königgrätz 3 July 1866, Col. Austrian Army; *m* at Prague 20 Sept 1857, Countess Gabriele (*b* at Prague 30 Sept 1840; ✝ at Rothenhaus, Bohemia 29 June 1923), *m* 2ndly at Prague 7 Sept 1867, Ladislaus, Count von Thurn and Hohenstein), dau of Johann Nepomuk, Count von and zu Trauttmansdorff-Weinsberg and Gabriele Isabella de Longueval, Countess von Buquoy, and had issue, among whom,

Sons

1. Prince *Gottfried* Karl Joseph, *b* at Czegled, Hungary 15 Jan 1860; ✝ at Rothenhaus 19 Nov 1933, Member Austrian House of Lords; *m* at Vienna 31 Aug 1890, Countess Anna (*b* at Vienna 4 March 1865; ✝ at Weikersheim, nr Mergentheim, Württemberg 25 July 1954), Imperial and Royal Lady-in-Waiting, Dame Star Cross Order, dau of Erwin, Count von Schönborn-Buchheim and Countess Franziska von und zu Trauttmansdorff-Weinsberg, and had issue, among whom,

    1. Prince *Ludwig* Erwin Gottfried Karl Eduard Maria, *b* at Rothenhaus 13 Oct 1892; ✝ at Ödenburg (Sopron), Hungary 26 May 1945, First Lt Austrian Army, Kt of Hon Sovereign Military Order of Malta; *m* at Seregélyes, Stuhlweissenburg 5 Nov 1921, Countess Irma (*b* at Tornanádaska, Abauj-Torna 5 July 1894; ✝ at Dorfen, Bavaria 9 Dec 1967), dau of János,

Count Hadik de Futak, Proprietor of Seregélyes and Countess Alexandra Zichy von Zich and Vásonykeö, and had issue, among whom,

  1. Prince *Alexander* Gottfried Ludwig Johann Maria, *b* at Seregélyes 3 Sept 1922; ✚ at Hohenpolding 27 Feb 1993; *m* 1stlyat Budapest 11 Oct 1946 (*m* diss by div at Frankfurt-am-Main 27 Feb 1968), Ilona (*b* at Budapest 29 March 1914), former wife of Miklos Tóth. He *m* 2ndly at Munich 16 June 1970, Rosa Theresia (Rosemarie) (*b* at Tostberg, Bavaria 4 Feb 1927), dau of August Bitterman and Rosalia Rinder, and had issue, by his first wife, among whom,
  [*Grossstockach 69, 8251 Hohenpolding*].

    1. Prince *Albrecht* Ladislaus Alfred, *b* at Bisce, Hungary 15 May 1948.

  2. Prince Max Egon *Gottfried, b* at Seregélyes 27 Nov 1924; *m* 1stly at Hintersee, nr Berchtesgaden 6 May 1961 (*m* diss by div at Munich 2 Dec 1976), Uta (*b* at Freiburg im Breisgau 13 June 1936), dau of Rudolf von Freyhold and Wera Scheff, and has issue,

    1. Princess *Andrea* Christina Maria, *b* at Munich 2 Sept 1961.

    2. Prince *Hubertus* Konstantin Ludwig Franz Maria, *b* at Prien am Chiemsee 11 Dec 1967; *m* at ...1999, Karina Therese Marie (*b* at ...1968), dau of Jan-Ernst Frowein and Marie-Thérèse von Malaisé, and has issue,

      1. Prince *Conrad* Alfred Felix Philipp Max Ernst Maria, *b* at ...10 Jan 2001.

Prince Gottfried *m* 2ndly at Unterwössen 17 Dec 1979, Ursula (*b* at Diepholz 8 June 1951), dau of Ludwig Roll and Wilma Evers, and has further issue,
  [*Point 1, 8218 Unterwössen*].

    3. Prince *Christian, b* at Prien 14 Jan 1980.

  3. Princess *Johanna* Amalie Susanne Maria Henriette, *b* at Seregélyes 20 Sept 1926.
  [*Rankestraße 2, 80538 Munich 40*].

  4. Prince *Louis* Johann Karl Anton Maria, *b* at Seregélyes 16 Sept 1930.
  [*Calle Amenabar, Buenos Aires, Argentina*].

 3. Prince Max *Egon* Maria Erwin Paul, *b* at Rothenhaus 19

Nov 1897; ✠ at Marbella, Spain 13 Aug 1968, Dr rer pol, Lt, Kt Bavarian Order of St George, Kt of Hon Sovereign Military Order of Malta, Gd Cross Order of Carlos III; *m* at Madrid 12 Oct 1921, Doña Maria de la Piedad Iturbe y Scholtz, Marquesa de Belvis de las Navas (*b* at Paris 31 Aug 1892; ✠ at Madrid 26 Nov 1990), Dame Gd Cross Order of Maria Luisa, dau of Manuel Iturbe y del Villar and Doña Maria de la Trinidad von Scholtz and Hermensdorff, Marchioness de Belvis de las Navas, and had issue, among whom,

1. Princess *Maria* de la Piedad y de la Consolacion Francisca de Asis Maximiliana Manuela Godofreda Anna Mathilde Jesus de Lexo Guadelupe de la Santísima Trinidad y todos los Santos, Marchioness de Belvis de las Navas (transferred by her mother 1960), *b* at San Sebastian, Spain 26 Aug 1922; *m* at Madrid 13 June 1945, Claudio Gamazo y Arnús, Marquess de Soto Aller (*b* at Madrid 3 Feb 1916; ✠ at Madrid 4 Dec 1984).

[*Padilla 32, Madrid*].

2. Prince *Alfonso* Maximiliano Victorio Eugenio Alexandro Maria Pablo de la Santísima Trinidad y todos los Santos, *b* at Madrid 28 May 1924; *m* 1stly at Venice 17 Sept (civ) and 21 Sept (relig) 1955 (*m* diss by div Mexico City 14 Dec 1960 and annulled at Madrid 18 Dec 1968), Princess Virginia (Ira) (*b* at Rome 18 April 1940; she *m* 2ndly at Reno, Nevada, USA 12 Jan 1961, Francisco Pignatari; that *m* diss by div Las Vegas, Nevada Jan 1964), dau of Prince Tassilo zu Fürstenberg and Claire Agnelli, and has issue,

1. Prince *Christoph* Victorio Egon Umberto, *b* at Lausanne 8 Nov 1956.

[*Marbella Club, 29600 Marbella, Prov. Malaga, Spain*],

2. Prince *Hubertus*, *b* at Mexico City 31 May 1959.

[*Marbella Club, 29600 Marbella, Prov. Malaga, Spain*].

Prince Alfonso *m* 2ndly at Las Vegas 3 May 1973 (*m* diss by div at Stanfield, Conn, USA 18 March 1985), Jaqueline (Jackie) Lane (*b* 16 May 1943), Actress. He *m* 3rdly at Vaduz 15 Feb 1991, Maria Luisa (*Marilys*)

Haynes (*b* at York 16 Feb 1941; *m* 1stly, ..Gaggero;
that *m* diss by div; ✠ at Ronda, Spain 31 Oct 2000),
and has further issue by his second wife,
[*Marbella Club, 29600 Marbella, Prov. Malaga, Spain*].

    3. Princess *Arriana* Theresa Mara, *b* at London
    15 Oct 1975; *m* at Marbella 30 June 2001, Dixon
    Boardman (*b* at ... 7 Nov 1945; *m* 1stly Pauline
    Munn Baker, *b* at New York 16 Feb 1948;
    m diss by div), Banker.

3. Prince *Christian Kraft* Ferdinand Viktor Maria de
la Santísima Trinidad y todos los Santos, *b* at
Eisenberg, Bohemia 28 July 1925; ✠ at Marbella 11
Nov 1980; *m* at El Quexigal, Spain 4 May 1955, Carmen
de la Cuadra y de Medina (*b* at Madrid 6 June 1933),
dau of Don Ildefonso de la Cuadra y Escriva and Doña
Carmen de Medina ya Lopez Quesada, and has issue,
[*Calle Principe de Vergara 136, 28016 Madrid, Spain*].

    1. Prince Fernando *Alfonso* Maximiliano
    Federico Sanson Timoteo de la Santísima
    Trinidad y todos los Santos, *b* at Madrid 24 Jan
    1956; *m* at ..., Francesca Garrigues y Aldrich
    (*b* at ...).

    2. Princess *Maria* de la Santísima Trinidad,
    b at Madrid 8 April 1957; *m* at Marbella, Spain
    4 July 1977 (*m* diss by div), Alfonso Martínez
    de Irujo y Fitzjames Stuart, 16th Duque de
    Aliaga (*b* at Madrid 22 Oct 1950).
    [*Genil 7, Madrid, Spain*].

    3. Princess *Christine Eugenie* Maria de la
    Santísima Trinidad y todos los Santos, *b* at
    Madrid 1 Nov 1958; *m* at Madrid 19 June 1982,
    José Maria Juncadella y Salisachs (*b* 20 April
    1935).
    [*Paseo Pintos Rosales 8, 28008, Madrid, Spain*].

4. Princess *Elisabeth Christine* de la Santísima Trinidad
Luise Maria de la O Natividad y todos los Santos, *b* at
Madrid 25 Dec 1927; ✠ 23 April 1975; *m* at El Quexigal
11 June 1952, Joaquin Bertran y Caralt (*b* at Barcelona
3 Feb 1928; ✠ at Barcelona 22 May 1975).

5. Prince *Max Emanuel* Maria Alexander Vicot Bruno
de la Santísima Trinidad y todos los Santos, *b* at Vienna

6 Oct 1931; ✠ at Marbella 1 Dec 1994; *m* at Seville 3
June 1961 (*m* diss by div May 1985), Ana Luisa de
Medina y Fernández de Córdoba, Marchioness de
Navahermosa, Countess de Ofalia [*Soto de Viñuelas,
Peña Excaurre 82, 28770 Colmenar Vieljo, Prov.
Madrid, Spain*] (*b* 2 May 1940; ✠ at Marbella 1 Dec
1994; *m* 2ndly 14 Oct 1985, Jaime Urzaiz), dau of Don
Rafael de Medina y Villalonga and Victoria Eugenia
Fernández de Córdoba y Fernández de Henestrosa,
16th Duchess de Medinaceli. He *m* 2ndly at Madrid 7
Jan 1989, Magdalena (Magda) [*Calle Doctor Arce 28,
28002 Madrid, Spain*] (*b* at Barcelona 10 July 1939; *m*
1stly 30 July 1960, Vicente Olmedilla y Maguiro, Count
de Cerragería; that *m* diss by div), dau of Trino
Foncuberte y Rog and Adelaïda Alonsoo-Martínez y
Huelin, Marchioness de Bellamar and has issue by his
first wife,

    1. Prince *Marco, b* at Madrid 8 March 1962;
    m at Ronda, Spain 1 June 1996, Sandra (*b* at
    ...), dau of Hans Carl Schmidt-Polex and Karin
    Goepfer, and has issue,

        1. Princess Victoria, *b* at ... 1997.
        2. Prince Alex, *b* at ...

    2. Prince *Pablo, b* at Madrid 5 March 1963;
    m at Toledo 8 June 2002, Maria (*b* at ...), dau of
    Carlos del Prado y Ruspoli, Marquis de Caicedo,
    and Teresa Muguiro y Pidal.

    3. Princess *Flavia, b* at Madrid 9 March 1964;
    m at Seville 17 Dec 1990, José Luis Villalonga
    Suarez.

    [*11 Chipstead Street, London SW6*].

6. Princess *Beatriz* Maria Christina Johanna Margarita
Alexandra Feodora Charlotte Taddea Dagoberta Pia
de la Piedad Heilige Dreifaltigkeit and aller Heiligen,
b at Rothenhaus 5 May 1935; *m* at El Quexigal 7 May
1959 (*m* diss by div at Madrid 1990 and religiously
annulled 1988), Don Gonzalo Fernández de Córdoba
y Larios, 9th Duke de Arión [*Malpica de Tajo, Prov.
Toledo, Spain*] (*b* at Malaga 14 Feb 1934; *m* 2ndly 10
Nov 1990, Reyes Mitjans Verea, Marchioness de
Ardales).

[Bidasoa 6, 28002 Madrid, Spain].

5. Prince *Karl Erwin* Leopold Gottfried Franziskus Maria, *b* at Rothenhaus 1 Dec 1903; ✠ at Hosskirch, nr Aulendorf 4 May 1983; *m* at Grundlsee 21 Aug 1934, Countess Victoria (*b* at Vienna 21 Oct 1914; ✠ at Ravensburg .. April 1978), dau of Ottokar, Count Czerninvon and zu Chudenitz and Countess Maria Kinsky von Wchinitz and Tettau, and has issue, among whom,

    1. Princess *Alexandra* Anna Maria Viktoria Karoline Elisabeth Vincenzia, *b* at Dresden 19 July 1935, Dipl Psych; *m* at Hosskirch, nr Aulendorf 18 July 1959, Thilo von Trotha (*b* at Skopau 4 Oct 1926; ✠ at Pfaffenhofen 29 June 1966).

    [Tettnangerstraße 78, 88214 Ravensburg, Germany].

    2. Princess *Isabella* Maria Anna Karoline Viktoria Walburga, *b* at Komotau 19 Feb 1941; *m* 1stly at Hosskirch, Württemberg 26 July 1969 (*m* diss by div), Malte Frantz (*b* 20 JulY 1939). She *m* 2ndly 7 Sept 1979, Josef von Garzuly (*b* at Budapest 3 Aug 1933).

    [Dossenweg 19, A-5034 Salzburg-Morzg., Austria].

    3. Princess *Maria*, *b* at Gorkau, Bohemia 3 July 1944.

    [Neuhäuserstraße 68, 79199 Kirchzarten, Germany].

    4. Prince *Ottokar* Johannes Gottfried Marie, *b* at Hosskirch 18 Feb 1953.

    [7961 Hosskirch, Württemberg, Germany].

2ND BRANCH

Lutheran: Founded by Cristian Kraft, Count of Hohenlohe-Ingelfingen (*b* 15 July 1668; ✠ 2 Oct 1743); Prince of the Holy Empire and ratification of Arms 7 Jan 1764; the title of Prince of Hohenlohe-Ingelfingen was confirmed with the qualification of "Hochgeboren" granted, Vienna 29 May 1772; this branch was divided into two sub-branches by the sons of Prince Friedrich Ludwig (*b* 31 Jan 1746; ✠ 15 Feb 1818), of which only the elder sub-branch is still extant.

HOHENLOHE-OEHRINGEN

Founded by August, Prince of Hohenlohe-Oehringen (*b* 27 Nov 1784; abdicated 1 Jan 1849; ✠ 15 Feb 1853); Hereditary Member of the First Chamber of the Kingdom of Württemberg 25 Sept 1819; Hereditary Member of the former Prussian House of Lords 12 Oct 1854; granted the Prussian title of Duke of Ujest with lands in Upper Silesia erected into a Duchy, Königsberg 18 Oct 1861. Members of this sub-branch bear the title of Prince or Princess zu

Hohenlohe-Oehringen with the qualification of Serene Highness.

KRAFT Hans Konrad, **8TH PRINCE (FÜRST) ZU HOHENLOHE-OEHRINGEN,** 5th Duke of Ujest, Count von Gleichen, *b* at Breslau 11 Jan 1933, son of August, 7th Prince (Fürst) zu Hohenlohe-Oehringen (*b* 28 April 1890; ✠ 2 Aug 1962) and Valerie von Carstanjen (*b* 3 April 1908; ✠ 4 Dec 1979; *m* 11 Nov 1930; *m* diss by div 16 Aug 1946); *m* at Geiselgasteig, nr Munich 24 June 1959, Katharina (*b* at Berlin 24 Dec 1938), dau of Dr Peter von Siemens and Julia Lienau.
[*Karlsvorstadt 19, 76413 Öhringen, Germany*].

Son and Daughters

1. Princess *Margarita* Katharina Elisabeth, *b* at Munich 28 April 1960; ✠✠ in a motor accident nr Allershausen, Kr Freising 27 Feb 1989; *m* at Amorbach 8 June (civ) and at Neuenstein, Württemberg 16 June (relig) 1984, Karl-Emich, Prince (Fürst) zu Leiningen (*b* at Amorbach 12 June 1952; *m* 2ndly at Munich 24 May (civ) and at Venice 15 June (relig) 1991 (diss by div at Munich 3 March 1998), Gabriele Renate Thyssen, who *m* 2ndly Prince Karim (IV) Aga Khan).

2. Princess *Christina* Valerie Julia, *b* at Munich 27 Nov 1961; *m* at Neuenstein 18 May (civ) and 20 May (relig) 1995, Jan-Gisbert Schultze (*b* 12 Feb 1961).
[*Kommandant-Trufanowstraße 35, 04105 Leipzig, Germany*].

3. *Kraft,* Hereditary Prince (Erbprinz) zu Hohenlohe-Oehringen, *b* at Munich 31 Oct 1966.

Sisters

1. Princess *Alexandra* Olga Elsa, *b* at Berlin 11 March 1931; *m* at Munich 24 May 1960, Egid Hilz (*b* at Landau, Pfalz 24 June 1932), Dr Eng.
[*Hegenigstraße 58, 91056 Erlangen-Kosbach*].

2. Princess *Dorothea* Elisabeth, *b* at Slawentzitz 27 July 1935; *m* at Lawrence, Long Island, USA 13 Dec 1970, Janos Farkas (*b* at Budapest 8 July 1942).
[*1301-D Potomac Drive, Houston, TX 77057, U.S.A.*].

Half-Sister

Issue of August, 7th Prince zu Hohenlohe-Oehringen and his third wife, Erika Himmelein (*b* 2 Dec 1916; *m* 6 April 1948).

Princess *Dagmar* Maria Victoria, *b* at Schwäbisch Hall 14 Sept 1948; *m* at Munich 13 Sept 1988, Rainer Hykes (*b* at Düsseldorf 4 Jan 1959).
[*Herzogstraße 132, 80797 Munich, Germany*].

Step-Mother

Erica, Dowager Princess zu Hohenlohe-Oehringen, *b* at Langenburg, Crailsheim 2 Dec 1916, ✠ 24 Aug 2000, dau of Friedrich Konrad Himmelein and Marie Karoline Urban; *m* at Esslingen am Neckar 6 April 1948, as his third wife, August, 7th Prince (Fürst) zu Hohenlohe-Oehringen (*b* at Madrid 28 April 1890; ✠ at Stuttgart 2 Aug 1962; *m* 1stly at Berlin-Grunewald 16 Jan 1928, Ursula von Zedlitz; that *m* diss by div 8 Feb 1930; *m* 2ndly at Bonn 11 Nov 1930, Valerie von Carstanjen; that m diss by div 16 Aug 1946).

Brother of Grandfather

Issue of Hugo, 4th Prince zu Hohenlohe-Oehringen, 1st Duke von Ujest (*b* 27 May 1816; ✠ 23 Aug 1897) and Princess Pauline zu Fürstenberg (*b* 11 June 1829; *m* 15 April 1847; ✠ 3 Aug 1900), having had issue, among whom,

Son

Prince *Max* Anton Karl, *b* at Slawentzitz 2 March 1860; ✠ at Berlin 14 Jan 1922, Maj-Gen (Prussian Army), Kt of St John of Jerusalem; *m* at Wiesbaden 11 Feb 1890, Countess Helene (*b* at Paris 3 March 1865; ✠ at Berlin 21 May 1901), dau of Paul, Count von Hatzfeldt and Helene Moulton, and had issue,

    1. Prince *Waldemar* Hugo Hermann Maximilian, *b* at Berlin 2 Dec 1890; ✠ at Crailsheim 25 Oct 1965, First Lt Prussian Cavalry; *m* at Berlin 6 Oct 1923 (*m* diss by div 1936), Nina (*b* at Moscow 7/19 Nov 1898; ✠ at Rome 27 Aug 1965; *m* 2ndly at Florence 31 Jan 1948, Prince Kraft zu Hohenlohe-Oehringen), dau of Ilja Chischine and Zinaida Ashkenazy, and had issue,

        1. Prince *Wolfgang* Maxmilian Leonce Hans Clemens August Rüdiger, *b* at Berlin 22 Feb 1925, adopted 22 June 1953 by his step-father, Prince Kraft zu Hohenlohe-Oehringen (*b* 16 March 1892; ✠ 2 Sept 1985); *m* at Teheran, Iran 15 May 1959, Jaqueline (*b* at Wellington, New Zealand 4 May 1933), dau of Cecil Graham Tonge and Wainoni Rayward, and had issue,

[Chemin des Mollies 134, 1293 Bellevue, Kt. Geneva, Switzerland; Borgo San Jacopo 9, 50123 Firenze, Italy].

      1. Princess *Margaret* Helene Alexandra, *b* at Swansea, Wales 11 Dec 1961; *m* at Chelsea 1 Feb 1992, Stuart L Bentham (*b* at London 28 May 1948).

      [Flat 2, 19 Eaton Place, London SW1X 8BN].

      2. Prince *Heinrich* Maximilian Waldemar Alexander, *b* at Rio de Janeiro 21 Sept 1968.

      [6 Ladbroke Square, Flat 2, London W11 3LX].

2. Prince *Max Hugo* Paul Friedrich Karl Egon, *b* at Berlin 25 March 1893; ✣ at Schrozberg, Württemberg 17 Oct 1951; *m* 1stly at Stein, nr Nuremberg 17 May 1920 (*m* diss by div at Munich 17 June 1931), Countess Maria-Gabrielle (Mariella) (*b* at Stein 31 Aug 1900; ✣ at Schloß Appelhof, nr Nuremberg 26 Nov 1985; *m* 2ndly at Berlin 24 April 1935, Lüder Lahmann who ✣ at Frankfurt-am-Main 18 July 1959), dau of Alexander, Count von Faber-Castell and Baroness Ottilie von Faber. He *m* 2ndly at Radewitz, nr Wartin, Randow .... 1941 (*m* diss by div at Radewitz 1942), Hella (*b* at Verden an der Aller 25 Feb 1883; ✣ at Radewitz 7 Jan 1943; *m* 1stly 26 Oct 1906, Rudolf von Prittwitz and Gaffron; that *m* diss by div 1919; *m* 2ndly *m* 27 Feb 1920, Otto von Ziethern who ✣ 17 Nov 1928), dau of Paul von Ramin and Gunhild von Ramin. He *m* 3rdly at Garmisch-Partenkirchen 12 Aug 1950, Marianne Lieselotte, since 30 Aug 1955, Alexandra Charlotte Elisabeth Juanita Diefenthal (*b* at Cologne-Lindenthal 18 Feb 1925; ✣ at Oberstaufen, Allgäu 21 Oct 1977), dau of Peter Diefenthal and Elisabeth Blum, and had issue, by his first wife,

      1. Prince *Rupprecht* Max Christian Kraft Roland Hermann, *b* at Bad Kissingen 5 July 1921, Dr of Med, *m* 1stly at Freiburg im Breisgau 25 July 1944, Gabriele (*b* at Dortmund 23 Oct 1925; ✣ at Karlsruhe 11 May 1969), dau of Theodor Wiemer and Hedwig Pahlen. He *m* 2ndly at Konstanz 26 March 1970 (*m* diss by div at Berlin 15 March 1973), Sibylle (*b* at Stuttgart 12 Oct 1932; *m* 1stly at Munich 2 Nov 1925, Prince Kraft Alexander zu Hohenlohe-Oehringen; that *m* diss by div at Konstanz March 1970), dau of Erwin Dochtermann and Johanna Hausner. He *m* 3rdly at Grünwald, nr Munich 19 April 1973, Dietlind-Birgit

(*b* at Wiener Neustadt 6 Oct 1944), dau of ... Koch and ...., and has issue by his first wife,
[*Hauptstraße 15, 86825 Bad Wörishofen, Germany*].

    1. Prince *Christian-Krafft* Max Theodor Alexander, *b* at Hohenlimburg, Westphalia 5 Jan 1945, Businessman; *m* 1stly at Porz 15 June 1967 (*m* diss by div at Siegburg 10 June 1985), Karin (*b* at Cologne 5 Aug 1941), dau of Detlef von Witzleben and Felicitas Beckmann. He *m* 2ndly at Hürth 19 Oct 1986, Helga (*b* at Metz 6 Sept 1942), dau of Wilhelm Müller and Irma Mechler, and has issue from his first marriage,
[*Lohgraben 16, 96272 Hochstadt am Main, Germany*].

        1. Prince *Stephan* Christian-Krafft Theodor Detlev Albert Oktavio, *b* at Porz 31 Oct 1967, Telecommunications Electrician.
[*Aachenerstraße 392, 50933 Cologne, Germany*].

        2. Princess *Michaela* Gabriele Monica, *b* at Porz 10 April 1972; *m* at Cologne 25 July 1996, Ralph Richter (*b* at Berlin 15 Nov 1967).
[*Niehlerstraße 184, 50733 Cologne, Germany*].

    2. Princess *Katharina*, *b* at Neidstein, Pfalz 7 Feb 1947; *m* 1stly at Munich 15 May 1973 (*m* diss by div Munich 27 April 1979), Peter, Ritter Ahsbahs von der Lanze (*b* at Budapest 19 Dec 1940, ✝ at Budapest 10 Feb 1997); *m* 2ndly at Munich 14 July 1983 (*m* diss by div), Karl-Heinz Sassen, assumed the name of Hohenlohe-Oehringen with the qualification of Prince (*b* at Gleiwitz 3 Jun 1940), Lawyer. She *m* 3rdly at ... 5 May 1989 Frank Michael Stede, assumed the name of Hohenlohe-Oehringen with the qualification of Prince (*b* Salzkotten, Paderborn 24 Oct 1956.
[*Sommerstraße 19, 85757 Karlsfeld nr Munich, Germany*]

2. Prince *Kraft Alexander* Waldemar August Christian-Ernst Gottfried, *b* at Munich 2 Nov 1925, Director of Municipal Theatre at Fürth; *m* 1stly at Heidelberg 5 Nov 1949 (*m* diss by div at Memmingen, Allgäu 21 March 1955), Dagmar (*b* at Berlin-Charlottenburg 24 Sept 1926; *m* 1stly at Schwaben 2 July 1948, Friedrich-Carl, Count von Gessler; that *m* diss by div 29 Aug 1949), dau of Gustav Engelbrecht and Sidonie von Knoblauch, and has issue,

> 1. Prince *Alexander* Gottfried Kraft Max Rupprecht Nikolaus Philipp-Ernst Heinrich, *b* at Wiesbaden 31 Jan 1951, Gov Minister Saxon Landesregierung; *m* at Möglingen 4 June 1981, Gabriele (*b* at Reutlingen 16 Aug 1952), dau of ...... Gramer and ...., and has issue,
> [*Liliensteinstraße 3a, 01277 Dresden, Germany*].

> > 1. Princess *Nina* Mariella Sophie, *b* at Stuttgart 27 March 1990.
> > 2. Prince *Philipp* Frederik Kraft, *b* at ... 27 April 1992.

> 2. Princess *Feodora* Dorothee Mariella Sidonie Wilhelmine Nina Irmgard Felicitas, *b* at Osterberg 23 April 1952, Still-Life and Portrait Painter.
> [*Gaiglstraße 14, 80335 Munich, Germany*].

Prince Kraft Alexander *m* 2ndly at Hamburg 2 Nov 1957 (*m* diss by div March 1970), Sibylle (*b* at Stuttgart 12 Oct 1932; *m* 2ndly, Prince Rupprecht zu Hohenlohe-Oehringen; that *m* diss by div at Berlin 15 March 1973), dau of Erwin Dochtermann and Johanna Hausner. He *m* 3rdly at Ulm 25 July 1970 (*m* diss by div at Fürth 11 Aug 1978), Ursula (*b* at Nuremberg 27 Jan 1938), dau of Heinz Rieck und Mathilde von Müller. He *m* 4thly at Fürth 20 June 1988, Renata (*b* at ...), dau of Dr Erhard Müller and Ruth Jeschur, and has further issue, by his second wife,
[*Königstraße 103, 90762 Fürth, Germany*].

> 3. Princess *Stephanie* Maria Johanna Gesche Angela, *b* at Hamburg 16 Jan 1959; ✝ at Konstanz 19 June 1989.

Prince Kraft also adopted the son of his first wife,
inter alias,

> 4. Johann Gustav *Peter Engelbrecht, b* at
> Altenstadt an der Iller 1 Oct 1945, Lawyer, has
> born the name "Prince zu Hohenlohe-
> Oehringen since 18 May 1951; *m* 1stly at
> Krefeld 27 July 1968 (*m* diss by div at Munich
> 26 June 1990), Diemuth (*b* at Tegernsee), dau
> of Ulrich Janssen and Gunhild Esters He *m*
> 2ndly at Munich 26 March 1993, Burggräfin
> and Countess Ursula (*b* at Munich 13 may 1951),
> dau of Alfred Burgrave and Count zu Dohna-
> Schlobitten and Gertrud Sigel, and has issue
> by his first wife,
> [*Rudliebstraße 25, 81925 Munich, Germany*].
>> 1. Cosima, *b* at Munich 14 Jan 1973.
>> 2. Antonia Dagmar, *b* at Munich-Pasing
>> 10 July 1975.

Brother of Great-Grandfather

Issue of August, 3rd Prince (*b* 27 Nov 1784; ✠ 15 Feb 1853) and
Duchess Louise of Württemberg (*b* 4 June 1789; *m* 28 Sept 1811;
✠ 26 June 1851), having had issue, among whom,

Son

Prince *Felix* Eugen Wilhelm Ludwig Albrecht Karl, *b* at Oehringen
1 March 1818; ✠ at Asnieres, nr Paris 8 Sept 1900, Col; *m* at Cassel
12 June 1851, Princess Alexandrine (*b* at Fulda 22 Dec 1830; ✠ at
Aeschach, nr Lindau 20 Dec 1871), dau of Friedrich Wilhelm I,
Elector of Hesse Cassel and Gertrude Falkenstein, Princess von
Hanau, Countess von Schaumburg, and had issue, among whom,

Sons

1. Prince Victor Hugo *Kraft* Friedrich Wilhelm Moritz, *b* at Mainz
19 Jan 1861; ✠ at Enns, Upper Austria 11 Sept 1939; *m* at Paris 10
Oct 1885 (*m* diss by div at Laon 11 Feb 1901), Marie (*b* at Paris 25
Dec 1863; ✠ at Brunswick 5 Jan 1924; *m* 2ndly at Coburg 5 Nov 1901,
Julius, Baron von Wangenheim who was killed at Brunswick 10 Feb
1944), dau of Charles de Vassinhac, Marquis d'Imécourt and
Marguerite de Galliffet, and adopted his nephew (see below),

> 1. Prince *Kraft* Alexander Ulpiano, Baron von Gabelstein,

b at Zippendorf, Mecklenburg 9 March 1896; ✠ at Enns, Upper Austria 3 Jan 1994, Lt-Col German Army; *m* at Piesing, nr Burghausen 15 Sept 1924, Baroness Margarete (*b* at Regensburg 6 Feb 1905; ✠ at Maiming 17 July 1935), dau of Anton, Baron von Ow and Baroness Margarete von Malsen, and had issue (Princes and Princesses zu Hohenlohe-Oehringen and Barons and Baronesses of Gabelstein),

> 1. Prince *Kraft* Leo Ulrich, *b* at Neuhaus 4 July 1925; *m* at Seefeld 30 March 1957, Margit (*b* at Innsbruck 10 March 1930), dau of Wilhelm Profanter and Maria Sesessmeier, and has issue,
>
>> 1. Princess *Monika, b* at Innsbruck 28 Dec 1957.
>> 2. Princess *Christa, b* at Innsbruck 19 Feb 1960; *m* at Innsbruck 9 May 1987, Andreas, Count of Ségur-Cabanac, Dr of Laws (*b* at Neutenstein 2 March 1958).
>> [*Alter Schmidberg 2, 4470 Enns, Austria*]
>> 3. Prince *Stephan, b* at Munich 30 Oct 1961.
>
> 2. Princess *Elisabeth* Maria Anna, *b* at Neuhaus 25 July 1926.
> 3. Princess *Marie Therese* Antoinette Margarete Auguste, *b* at Neuhaus 5 Nov 1928.

LINE II: WALDENBURG (-SCHILLINGSFÜRST)

Catholic and Lutheran: Founded by Count Everard (*b* 11 Oct 1535; ✠ 9 March 1570); joined the name and arms of the extinct House of Langenburg 1558; separation of the House of Schillingsfürst by the third son of Count Georg Friedrich I; Georg Friedrich II, Count of Hohenlohe-Waldenburg (*b* 16 June 1595; ✠ 20 Sept 1635); two of his sons founded the lines below,

A. HOHENLOHE-BARTENSTEIN
1st Branch: BARTENSTEIN

Founded by **Christian, Count of Hohenlohe-Waldenburg-Schillingsfürst-Bartenstein** (*b* 31 Aug 1627; ✠ 15 June 1675); Prince of the Holy Empire with ratification of Arms and the qualification of "Hochgeboren", Frankfurt-am-Main 21 May 1744; elevation of Bartenstein into a Principality of the Holy Empire, Vienna 1 Aug 1757; Hereditary Member of the First Chamber of the Kingdom of Württemberg 25 Sept 1819; Hereditary Member of the Bavarian "Reichsräte" 1 Sept 1887.

Members of this Branch bear the title of Prince or Princess zu Hohenlohe-Bartenstein (after 9 Sept 1906 with the addition of "and

Jagstberg") with the qualification of Serene Highness.

FERDINAND Michael Carl Emich Peter Philipp Johannes, **9TH PRINCE (FÜRST) ZU HOHENLOHE-BARTENSTEIN,** *b* at Bartenstein 6 March 1942, Cmdr Bavarian Order of St George, Kt Sovereign Military Order of Malta, 1st-Lt (Res), son of Karl, 8th Prince (Fürst) zu Hohenlohe-Bartenstein (*b* 20 Oct 1905; ✠ 7 May 1950) and Baroness Clara von Meyern-Hohenberg (*b* 7 Nov 1912; *m* 20 Aug 1936); *m* at Oettingen 8 Jan (civ) and 19 Jan (relig) 1971, Princess Franziska (*b* 14 Oct 1947), eldest dau of Alois, 10th Prince (Fürst) zu Oettingen-Oettingen and Oettingen-Spielberg and Countess Elisabeth Gabriele zu Lynar.
[*Schloß Bartenstein, 74575 Schrozberg-Bartenstein, Germany*].

Sons and Daughters

1. *Maximilian* Leopold Carl Alois, Hereditary Prince (Erbprinz) zu Hohenlohe-Bartenstein, *b* at Munich 29 March 1972.
[*Schloß Bartenstein, 74575 Schrozberg-Bartenstein, Germany*].
2. Prince *Felix* Michael Otto Johannes, *b* at Munich 27 Dec 1973.
3. Princess *Alice* Henriette Alexandra Elisabeth, *b* at Bad Mergentheim 28 Sept 1978.
4. Princess *Margherita* Lucia Gabriele Maria, *b* at Bad Mergentheim 7 Sept 1979.
5. Princess Georgina (*Gina*) Franziska Michaela Maria, *b* at Bad Mergentheim 30 Sept 1982.

Sisters

1. Princess *Franziska* Maria Elisabeth Germana Hildegard Anna, *b* at Bartenstein 22 May 1937; *m* 1stly at Bartenstein 4 June 1959 (*m* dis by div at Hertford Connecticut 19 July 1966), Alexander Frowein (*b* at Oosterbeek, nr Arnheim Gelderland 9 Nov 1934, ✠ at Fort Myers, Florida, USA 13 Oct 1999), Businessman. She *m* 2ndly at Schenectady, New York 10 Dec 1966, Maximilien, Baron de Watteville-Berckheim (*b* at Evreux, Dept Eure, France 2 Jan 1940).
[*27 Rue Chanelz, 75016 Paris, France*].
2. Princess *Henriette* Maria Margarete Magdalena Therese, *b* at Bartenstein 23 Aug 1938; *m* at Bartenstein 22 March (civ) and 20 April (relig) 1964, Hans Veit, Count zu Toerring-Jettenbach (*b* at Munich 11 Jan 1935).
[*Steubstraße 12, 81925 Munich, Germany*].

Brother of Father

Issue of Johannes, 7th Prince zu Hohenlohe-Bartenstein and Jagstberg (*b* 20 Aug 1863; ✠ 19 Aug 1921) and Archduchess Anna of Austria, Princess of Tuscany (*b* 17 Oct 1879; *m* 12 Feb 1901; ✠ 30 May 1961), having had issue, among whom,

1. Prince *Friedrich* August Hermann Maria Peter Rasso, *b* at Aeschach, nr Lindau 3 Sept 1910; ✠ at Bonn-Bad Godesberg 16 May 1985, Industrialist; *m* at Lindau 19 Jan (civ) and at Birnau 20 Jan (relig) 1959, Marie Claire (*b* at Aubenas, Dept Ardeche, France 2 Aug 1916; *m* 1stly, Ulrich Pernice; that *m* diss by div Berlin 17 July 1941), dau of Ferdinand Henri Buet, Marquess de Villars and Georgette Giraud, and had issue,
[*Kapellenstraße 19, 65193 Wiesbaden, Germany*].
    1. Princess *Helena* Maria Margarethe Francesca Anna Alix Rosa Elisabeth Katharina, *b* at Heidelberg 22 March 1960; *m* at Bonn 12 Oct 1985 (*m* diss by div..), Carl-Friedrich, Count Schaffgotsch genannt Semperfrei von and zu Kynast and Greifenstein, Baron zu Trachenberg (*b* at Rio de Janeiro 4 July 1951), Journalist.
    [*Wilhelminenstraße 19, 65193 Wiesbaden, Germany*].

2nd Branch: JAGSTBERG
Hereditary Member of the First Chamber of the Kingdom of Württemberg.

ALEXANDER Maria Ladislaus Johannes Carl Ludwig, **6TH PRINCE (FÜRST) ZU HOHENLOHE-JAGSTBERG,** *b* at Haltenbergstetten 25 Aug 1937, son of Albrecht, 5th Prince (Fürst) zu Hohenlohe-Jagstberg (*b* 9 Sept 1906; ✠ 23 Jan 1996) and Countess Therese (Sissy) von Mirbach-Geldern-Egmont (*b* 11 Aug 1911; *m* 22 Oct 1936); *m* 1stly at Fuschl 7 June 1963 (*m* diss by div 12 Nov 1974), Princess Michaela [*Avenida Libertador 1559 7 21, RA-1016 Buenos Aires C.F., Argentina*] (*b* at Berlin 9 March 1940; *m* 2ndly 14 Feb 1975, Wolfgang, Prince zu Oettingen-Oettingen and Oettingen-Wallerstein; that *m* diss by div 23 Jan 1985; she *m* 3rdly 20 Sept 1985, Alfonso Siegfriedo von der Becke-Klüchtzner), dau of Hugo, Prince von Schönburg-Waldenburg and Waltraut Benedicta von Klüchtzner, and has issue,
[*Schloß Haltenbergstetten, 97996 Niederstetten, Württemberg, Germany*].

Son and Daughter

1. Princess *Antoinette* Maria Therese Benedicta Olga, *b* at Munich 24 Feb 1964; *m* at Frankfurt-am-Main 24 Oct 1992 (*m* diss by div at Frankfurt-am-Main 27 Oct 1996), Mark Meier-Preschany (*b* at Basel 16 June 1963).
[*Städelstraße 3, 60596 Frankfurt-am-Main, Germany*].

2. Prince Karl (*Carlo*) Alexander Maria Hugo Albrecht Johannes, Hereditary Prince (Erbprinz) zu Hohenlohe-Jagstberg, *b* at Munich 15 Aug 1967; *m* at Gibraltar 27 Dec 1995, Sabine Elisabeth Fritz (*b* at Koblenz 14 Feb 1965).
[*Landweidenstraße 6, 60488 Frankfurt-am-Main, Germany*].

Mother

Therese (Sissy), Dowager Princess zu Hohenlohe-Jagstberg (*b* at Munich 11 Aug 1911), dau of Alfons, Count von Mirbach-Geldern-Egmont and Countess Maria Hoyos, Baroness zu Stichsenstein; *m* at Munich 22 Oct 1936, Albrecht, 5th Prince (Fürst) zu Hohenlohe-Jagstberg (*b* at Munich 9 Sept 1906; ✟ at Niederstetten, Württemberg 23 Jan 1996), Senior Member of the Princely House of Hohenlohe.
[*Schloß Haltenbergstetten, 97996 Niederstetten, Württemberg, Germany*].

Brother and Sister

1. Prince *Johannes* Maria Carl Alfons Friedrich Leopold, *b* at Haltenbergstetten 2 Dec 1939, adopted by his uncle, Ladislaus, Count von Mirbach-Geldern-Egmont, Proprietor of Roggenburg, nr Neu-Ulm 24 June 1980 and bears the name, "Count von Mirbach-Geldern-Egmont, Prince zu Hohenlohe-Jagstberg"; *m* at Haltenbergstetten 22 Dec 1969, Andrea (*b* at Ulm 18 Oct 1944), dau of Karl Vogel and Ingeborg Schreiber, and has issue,
[*89297 Roggenburg, nr Neu-Ulm, Germany; Schloß Haltenbergstetten, 97996 Niederstetten, Germany*].

   1. Princess *Isabella* Michaela Maria Therese Ingeborg Andrea, *b* at Heilbronn 2 April 1972.

   2. Prince *Lamoral* Maria Karl Albrecht Constantin, *b* at Heilbronn 27 Dec 1973.

2. Princess *Eleanore* Maria Irene Anna Elisabeth Margarethe, *b* at Haltenberstetten 17 Oct 1940; *m* there 6 June 1970, Peter, Baron von Kap-herr (*b* at Gleiwitz 22 Aug 1934), Bank Director.
[*Haus Sunderberg, Forstweg 45, 21218 Seevetal-Hittfeld, Germany*].

B. HOHENLOHE-WALDENBURG-SCHILLINGSFÜRST

Founded by **Ludwig Gustav, Count of Hohenlohe-Waldenburg-Schillingsfürst** (*b* 8 June 1634; ✝ 21 Feb 1697); Prince of the Holy Empire with ratification of Arms and the qualification of "Hochgeboren", Frankfurt-am-Main 21 May 1744; title confirmed in Prussia 29 Dec 1744; confirmed by the Elector of Saxony 2 Feb 1745; elevation of the County of Waldenburg into a Principality of the Holy Empire and ratification of Arms, Vienna 14 Aug 1757; foundation of the House (of Hohenlohe) Order of the Phoenix 1758; partition of lands between two sons of Prince Carl Albrecht II (*b* 21 Feb 1742; ✝ 14 June 1796), founders of the branches below, 5 April 1807.

1st Branch: WALDENBURG

Founded by **Carl Albrecht III, Prince of Hohenlohe-Waldenburg-Schillingsfürst** (*b* 29 Feb 1776; ✝ 15 June 1843) who granted the Lordship of Schillingsfürst to his younger brother, 5 April 1807 (see 2nd Branch below); Hereditary Member of the First Chamber of the Kingdom of Württemberg 25 Sept 1819.

Members of this Branch bear the title of Prince or Princess zu Hohenlohe-Waldenburg-Schillingsfürst with the qualification of Serene Highness.

FRIEDRICH KARL Josef Gero Michael Maria Aloisius, **9TH PRINCE (FÜRST) ZU HOHENLOHE - WALDENBURG - SCHILLINGSFÜRST,** *b* at Waldenburg 19 June 1933, Forester, Kt of Hon Sovereign Military Order of Malta, son of Friedrich Karl, 8th Prince (Fürst) zu Hohenlohe-Waldenburg-Schillingsfürst (*b* 31 July 1908; ✝ 24 Oct 1982) and Princess Mechthilde of Urach, Countess of Württemberg (*b* 4 May 1912; *m* 24 May 1932); *m* at Munich 16 April 1966, Marie-Gabrielle (*b* at Berlin 29 Aug 1942), dau of Josias von Rantzau and Countess Ludovica von Quadt zu Wykradt and Isny.

[*74638 Schloß Waldenburg, Württemberg, Germany*].

Brother and Sisters

1. Prince *Hubertus* Ludwig Wilhelm Michael Maria, *b* at Waldenburg 11 March 1935, Dipl Eng; *m* at Piesing, Bavaria 21 July 1959, Baroness Adelheid (*b* at Schönau 11 Dec 1937), dau of Johann-Anton, Baron von Ow, Proprietor of Piesing, and Baroness Helene Riederer von Paar zu Schönau, and has issue,

[*Waldhof, 74182 Obersulm 3 - Echenau, Kr. Heilbronn, Germany*].

    1. Princess *Antonia* Maria Therese, *b* at Heilbronn 26 Aug 1961, Journalist; *m* at Waldenburg 1 Aug 1987, Eberhard von Alten (*b* at Rehoboth, S W Africa 10 April 1954), Bank

Director.
[*Mainstraße 38, 63263, Neu-Isenburg, Germany*].

2. Prince *Felix* Friedrich Karl Michael Maria, *b* at Heilbronn 12 March 1963, Dipl Eng, *m* at Lynchburg, Va, USA 16 April 1994, Barbara Ross (*b* at Easton, Maryland, USA 29 Oct 1966), dau of Prof Dr Ross Hutcheson Dabney and Charlotte Gmelin, and has issue,
[*Langestraße 76, 74638, Waldenburg-Sailach, Germany*].

>   1. Prince *Konrad, b* at Lohr 29 Oct 1995.
>   2. Princess *Francis, b* at Künzelsau 16 July 1997.
>   3. Princess *Maria, b* at Germany 7 Aug 1999.

3. Prince *Franz* Nikolaus Michael Maria, *b* at Heilbronn 12 Aug 1965, Dipl Business Studies; *m* at Lima, Peru 25 Nov 1995, Vera (*b* at Salzgitter 30 June 1969), MBA, Dipl Business Studies, dau of Armin Bülow and Elvira Tong, and has issue,
[*Oettingenstraße 66, 80538 Munich, Germany*].

>   1. Princess *Alice* Antonia Maria, *b* at Munich 28 March 1998.
>   2. Princess *Elena, b* at ...1999)

4. Prince *Maximillian* Michael Maria, *b* at Heilbronn 12 Feb 1967, Dipl Business Studies, 1st Lt (Res); *m* at Munich 12 Sept 1996, Jutta (*b* at Heilbronn am Neckar 29 Dec 1967), dau of Ulrich Mössner and Heide Kühlmann.
[*Sternwartstraße 1, 81679 Munich, Germany*].

2. Princess *Amélie* Elisabeth Therese Maria, *b* at Waldenburg 11 Dec 1936; ✝ at Moone Abbey, Ireland 19 March 1985; *m* at Waldenburg 16 Oct 1956, Clemens, Count von Matuschka, Baron von Toppolczan and Spaetgen (*b* at Pitschen, Nieder Silesia 26 July 1928).
[*Moone Abbey, Athy, Co. Kildare, Ireland*].

3. Princess *Therese* Maria Gabriele Carola Hilda, *b* at Waldenburg 8 Sept 1938; *m* at Schwaigern, Württemberg 23 Aug (civ) and at Waldenburg 25 Sept (relig) 1986, Josef Hubert, Count and Lord von Neipperg (*b* at Schwaigern 22 July 1918), Capt (Ret).
[*74193 Schwaigern, Württemberg, Germany*].

4. Princess *Hilda* Carola Marie Gabrielle Franziska, *b* at Waldenburg 21 Dec 1943; *m* at Bergheim 25 March (civ) and at Waldenburg 20 April (relig) 1968, Prince Josef of Croÿ (*b* at Petschau 8 July 1941), Dipl Eng.
[*Sonnenblumenstraße 47, 81377 Munich, Germany*].

Mother

Mechthilde Maria Gabriele Florestine-Sophie Devota, Dowager Princess zu Hohenlohe-Waldenburg-Schillingsfürst, *b* at Stuttgart 4 May 1912, dau of Wilhelm, 2nd Duke of Urach, Count of Württemberg and Duchess Amélie in Bavaria; *m* at Stuttgart 15 May (civ) and at Lichtenstein 24 May (relig) 1932, Friedrich Karl, 8th Prince (Fürst) zu Hohenlohe-Waldenburg-Schillingsfürst (*b* at Waldenburg 31 July 1908; ✠ there 24 Oct 1982).

[*Laurach, 74638 Waldenburg, Württemberg, Germany*].

Brother of Grandfather

Issue of Friedrich Karl, 5th Prince zu Hohenlohe-Waldenburg-Schillingsfürst (*b* 5 May 1814; ✠ 26 Dec 1884) and Princess Therese zu Hohenlohe-Schillingsfürst (*b* 19 April 1816; *m* 26 Nov 1840; ✠ 7 Jan 1891), having had issue, among whom,

Son

Prince *Chlodwig* Karl Joseph Maria, *b* at Kupferzell 1 Jan 1848; ✠ at Budapest 8 Jan 1929; *m* 1stly at Vienna 15 Jan 1877, Countess Franziska (*b* at Vienna 24 Sept 1856; ✠ at Abbazia 10 Jan 1884), Dame Star Cross Order, dau of Moritz, Count Esterházy, Baron zu Galántha and Princess Polyxena of Lobkowicz. He *m* 2ndly at Budapest 2 March 1890, Countess Sárolta (*b* at Fünfkirchen 16 Oct 1856; ✠ at Budapest 15 June 1928), Lady-in-Waiting, Dame Star Cross Order, dau of Georg, Count Mailáth von Székhely, Proprietor of Láca, Kom Zemplin and Baroness Stephanie Hildeprand von Prandau, and had issue, among whom by his first wife,

Sons

1. Prince *Friedrich Franz Augustin Maria*, *b* at Budapest 15 Feb 1879; ✠ at Curitibá, Brazil 24 May 1958; *m* 1stly in London 12 May 1914 (*m* diss by div Budapest 29 July 1920), Stéphanie (*b* at Vienna 16 Sept 1898; ✠ at Geneva 13 June 1972), dau of Johann (Hans) Richter and Baroness Ludmilla Kuranda. He *m* 2ndly at Budapest 6 Dec 1920, Countess Emanuela (Ella) (*b* at Ikervár 11 April 1883; ✠ at Curitibá 12 Dec 1964; *m* 14 June 1902, Emil, Count Dessewffy; that *m* diss by div 1920), dau of Ludwig, Count Batthyány von Német-Újvár and Countess Helene Andrássy von Csik-Szent-Király and Kraszna-Horka, and had issue, by his first wife,

1. Prince *Franz* Josef Rudolf Hans Weriand Max Stefan Anton, *b* at Vienna 5 Dec 1914, Writer.

[43 Boulevard Exelmans, 75016 Paris, France].

2. Prince *Karl-Egon* Johann Nepomuk Joseph Maria, *b* at
Ságh 4 May 1882; ✠ at Buenos Aires 24 July 1971; *m* (not in
accordance with Family Law) at Budapest 20 Jan 1923, Edith
(*b* at Stuhlweissenburg 31 July 1895; ✠ at Buenos Aires 9
Aug 1964), dau of Károly Gáspár de Néver et Verebély and
Mária Deák de Kis-Jóka et Kehida, and had issue,

    1. Prince *Siegfried* Walter Carl Egon Zoltan Franziska,
    b at Budapest 12 Nov 1923, Industrialist; *m* at
    Montevideo 23 April 1962, Baroness Maria (Mary) (*b*
    at Alttitschein, Moravia 14 Nov 1929; *m* 1stly at Buenos
    Aires 18 Aug 1953, Tibor, Count Teleki von Czék; that
    m diss by div at Montevideo Nov 1960), dau of Karl,
    Baron Kast von Ebelsberg and Countess Gabrielle
    Deym von Stritez.

    [Av. 11 de Septiembre 1735, RA-1426 Buenos Aires
    C.F., Argentina].

    2. Princess *Senta-Maria* Edith Franziska, *b* at
    Budapest 15 April 1926; *m* at Buenos Aires 16 March
    1971, Ivan, Baron Rubido-Zichy de Zagorje et Zich (*b*
    at Modern, Pressburg 9 Sept 1908; ✠ at Buenos Aires
    19 Aug 1995).

    [Tagle 2782, Buenos Aires, Argentina].

2nd Branch: SCHILLINGSFÜRST

Founded by Franz Joseph, Prince of Hohenlohe-Waldenburg-
Schillingsfürst (*b* 26 Nov 1787; ✠ 14 Jan 1841); Prince of Hohenlohe-
Schillingsfürst **through the acquisition of the Lordship of**
Schillingsfürst, granted by his elder brother 5 April 1807 (see 1st
Branch above); Hereditary Member of the Bavarian "Reichsräte" 26
May 1818; inherited the Duchy of Ratibor etc in Prussian Silesia
and the Principality of Corvey in Westphalia (succeeding the
Landgrave Victor Amedeus of Hesse-Rothenburg who ✠ 12 Nov
1834) for Prince Viktor, the elder son (see 1st House) and also the
Lordship of Treffurt in Erfurt for Prince Chlodwig, the second son
(see 2nd House) of Prince Franz Josef (see above); the two brothers
renounced the Principality of Schillingsfürst 14 Jan 1841 in favour of
their younger brother Prince Philipp Ernst (*b* 24 May 1820; ✠ 3 May
1845). On Philipp's death Chlodwig was reassigned Schillingsfürst
(see 2nd House below).

1st House: RATIBOR and CORVEY

Founded by Viktor, Prince of Hohenlohe-Schillingsfürst (*b* 10 Feb

1818; ✠ 30 Jan 1893); Duke of Ratibor and Prince of Corvey (Prussian titles; primogeniture), Berlin 15 Oct 1840 (Diploma, Breslau 11 Sept 1890); Hereditary Member of the former Prussian House of Lords 12 Oct 1854.

The Head of this House and his wife bear the title of Duke and Duchess of Ratibor, Prince and Princess of Corvey, Prince and Princess of Hohenlohe-Schillingsfürst and cadet members bear the title of Prince or Princess von Ratibor and von Corvey, Prince or Princess zu Hohenlohe-Schillingsfürst, all with the qualification of Serene Highness.

FRANZ ALBRECHT Maximilian Wolfgang Josef Thaddaus Maria Metternich-Sándor, **4TH DUKE (HERZOG) VON RATIBOR and 4TH PRINCE (FÜRST) VON CORVEY,** Prince zu Hohenlohe-Schillingsfürst-Breunner-Enkevoirth, *b* at Rauden 23 Oct 1920, adopted at Budapest 6 July 1926 by Princess Klementine von Metternich-Sándor (*b* 1870; ✠ 1963), son of Viktor, 3rd Duke of Ratibor, etc (*b* 2 Feb 1879; ✠ 11 Nov 1945) and Princess Elisabeth zu Oettingen-Oettingen and Oettingen-Spielberg (*b* 31 Oct 1886; *m* 19 Nov 1910; ✠ 2 Oct 1976); *m* at Dyck 2 Oct 1962, Altgräfin Isabella (*b* at Alfter 19 Feb 1939), dau of Franz Joseph, 6th Prince (Fürst) and Altgraf zu Salm-Reifferscheidt-Krautheim and Dyck and Princess Cecilie zu Salm and Salm-Salm, Wild and Rheingräfin. [*Schloß Neuaigen, 3430 Tulln, Austria; Schloß Corvey, 37671 Höxter, Westphalia, Germany*].

Sons

1. *Victor,* Hereditary Prince (Erbprinz), *b* at Vienna 28 March 1964; *m* at Heiligenkreuz 16 May 1998, Alexandra (*b* at Vienna 24 April 1969), dau of Kurt von Wohlgeruth and Renate ...., and has issue,
  1. Princess *Cecilia, b* at Vienna 14 Aug 2000.
2. Prince *Tassilo* Ferdinand, *b* at Vienna 23 Oct 1965; *m* at Winhöring 4 July 1999, Countess *Clarissa* (*b* at Munich 31 March 1965), day of Hans Veit Count zu Toerring-Jettenbach and Princess Henriette zu Hohenlohe-Bartenstein, and has issue,
  1. Princess *Charlotte* Margita Elisabeth Marie, *b* at Vienna 20 Nov 2000.
3. Prince *Stephan* Aloysius, *b* at Vienna 2 July 1968.
4. Prince *Benedikt* Christian, *b* at Vienna 25 Jan 1971.
5. Prince *Philipp Stanislaus, b* at Vienna 14 May 1976.

Sister

5. Princess *Klementine* Gabrielle Georgine Benoite Marie, *b* at

Rauden 24 April 1918; *m* at Rauden 11 Nov 1940 (*m* diss by div at Paderborn 22 Oct 1948), Prince Anton von Croÿ (*b* at Konigsfeld 1 Sept 1909; ✠ at Kitzbühel 3 March 1976).
[*Barerstraße 50a, 80799 Munich, Germany*].

Brother of Father

Issue of Viktor, 2nd Duke von Ratibor and 2nd Prince von Corvey, Prince zu Hohenlohe-Schillingsfürst (*b* 6 Sept 1847; ✠ 9 Aug 1923) and Countess Maria von Breunner-Enkevoirth (*b* 23 Aug 1856; *m* 19 June 1877; ✠ 25 June 1929).

Brothers of Grandfather

Issue of Viktor, 1st Duke von Ratibor and 1st Prince von Corvey, Prince zu Hohenlohe-Schillingsfürst (*b* 10 Feb 1818; ✠ 30 Jan 1893) and Princess Amelie zu Fürstenberg (*b* 12 Feb 1821; *m* 19 April 1845; ✠ 17 Jan 1899), having had issue, among whom,

Sons

1. Prince *Egon* Moritz, *b* at Rauden 4 Jan 1853; ✠ at Gotha 10 Feb 1896, Proprietor of Herbsleben, nr Gotha, ADC to Alfred, Duke of Saxe-Coburg, Kt Sovereign Military Order of Malta; *m* at Raudnitz, Bohemia 16 Nov 1885, Princess Leopoldine (*b* at Kosten 9 March 1867; ✠ at Jauer, Silesia 7 March 1936), dau of Moritz, 9th Prince (Fürst) of Lobkowicz and Princess Maria Anna zu Oettingen-Oettingen and Oettingen-Wallerstein, and had issue,

    1. Prince *Moritz* Franz Max Viktor Rudolf Leopold Egon Maria, *b* at Ratibor 17 March 1890; ✠ at Hochdorf, Vaihingen an der Enz 22 Oct 1972, Lt Col (ret); *m* at Budapest (civ) and at Breslau (relig) 1921, Elisabeth (*b* at Dresden 14 Aug 1898; ✠ at Steinebach, Upper Bavaria 21 Jan 1968), dau of Anton Puschner and Emma Maria Bauer, and had issue,

        1. Princess *Elisabeth, b* Breslau 12 Feb 1922; *m* at Berlin 14 Sept 1942, Ernst Zobel (*b* at Strassburg 1 May 1917; ✠ ... 3 April 1972), Major Luftwaffe, Engineer.
        [*Hohenlohestraße 35, 80637 Munich, Germany*].

    2. Prince *Ernst* Paul Zdenko Viktor Karl Egon Maria, *b* at Ratibor 5 Aug 1891; ✠ at Estoril, Portugal 17 June 1947, Lt Imp German Navy; *m* 1stly at Wilkendorf, Oberbarnim 14 Aug 1922 (*m* diss by div Berlin 23 Sept 1925 and annulled Berlin 20 Dec 1940), Adele von Curo; enobled 2 July 1910, in Prussia (*b* at Cologne 8 April 1899; ✠ at Davos 15 Feb 1974;

m 1stly Berlin 23 Feb 1918, Adriaan Willem Mosselmans; that *m* diss by div The Hague 5 Oct 1920), dau of Joseph May and Caroline Esser; adopted dau of Georg von Caro. He *m* 2ndly at Estoril Portugal 25 Aug 1942 (civ) and 6 March 1942 (relig), Consuelo Regina Maria (*b* at London 7 Sept 1909; ✝ at Lausanne 28 Dec 1985; *m* 2ndly at Paris 23 Dec 1964, Jacques Roux, Ambassador), dau of William Stephan Eyre and Eva Angelina Valdeavellano Canaval, and had issue, by his first wife,

1. Prince Egon Maria *Alexander* Karl Borromäus Leopold Moritz, *b* at Berlin 14 Nov 1923; ✝ at Stuttgart 11 Aug 1989, Agricultural Engineer, Veterinary Surgeon; *m* at Hochdorf, Vaihingen an der Enz 3 Sept (civ) and at Ludwigsburg 10 Sept (relig) 1959, Countess Irmela (*b* at Stuttgart 9 Oct 1937), dau of Hubertus, Count Leutrum von Ertingen, Proprietor of Nippenburg, and Marie-Luise Steiner, adopted dau of Alice, Baroness von Tessin, née Krause, and has issue,

[*Schloß Unterriexingen, 71706 Markgröningen, Germany*].

    1. Princess *Andrea* Huberta Maria Felicitas Alexandra Natascha, *b* at Stuttgart 7 Aug 1960; *m* at Unterriexingen 16 Oct 1993, Fernando José Kreis-Gana (*b* at Santiago de Chile 2 April 1954).

    [*Auf der Körnerwiese 14, 60322 Frankfurt-am-Main, Germany*].

    2. Prince *Nikolaus* Alexander Maria Norwin Ernst Hubertus, *b* at Stuttgart 30 Nov 1962, Dipl Business Studies, 1st Lt (Res); *m* at Hamburg 9 Aug (civ) and at Markgröningen 18 Sept (relig) 1999, Jeanette (*b* at Duisburg 24 Aug 1966) dau of Ralph-Wolfgang Kraehe and Ingrid Blauel.

    3. Prince *Alexander* Maria Johannes Clemens Michael Carol, *b* at Stuttgart 26 Feb 1965, Banker.

2nd House: HOHENLOHE-SCHILLINGSFÜRST

Founded by Prince Chlodwig (*b* 31 March 1819; ✝ 6 July 1901);

Prussian title of Prince of Ratibor and of Corvey, Berlin 15 Oct 1840 (Diploma Breslau 11 Sept 1890); Prince of Hohenlohe-Schillingsfürst by virtue of the treaty concluded with his elder brother, Victor (founder of the First House) 15 Oct 1845.

Members of this House bear the title of Prince or Princess zu Hohenlohe-Waldenburg-Schillingsfürst, of Ratibor and of Corvey, with the qualification of Serene Highness.

KARL-ALBRECHT Moritz Hieronymus Franz Josef Aloys Michael Alexander Maria, **11TH PRINCE (FÜRST) ZU HOHENLOHE-SCHILLINGSFÜRST, PRINCE VON RATIBOR AND CORVEY,** *b* at Vienna 30 April 1926, Kt Bav Order of St George, son of Franz Josef, 10th Prince (Fürst) zu Hohenlohe-Schillingsfürst, etc (*b* 6 June 1894; ✝ 3 Jan 1970) and Princess Aglaë von Schönburg-Hartenstein (*b* 16 Jan 1891; *m* 17 Nov 1924; ✝ 20 Feb 1965); *m* at Seewiesen 24 Oct 1965, Countess Ladislaja (*b* at Graz 3 Jan 1926; *m* 1stly at Stainz 22 Feb 1957, Johannes, Baron Economo von San Serff; that *m* diss by div and annulled 12 June 1962), Dame Star Cross Order, dau of Franz, Count von Meran, Proprietor of Stainz and Brandhof and Princess Wilhelmine von Auersperg.

[*91583 Schillingsfürst, MFranken, Germany*].

Son and Daughter

1. Princess Marie-*Aglaë* Wilhelmine Rosa Johanna Ladislaja Gabriele Agathe, *b* at Schillingsfürst 22 April 1966; *m* at Tannheim 12 Feb 1994, Georg, Count von Schaesberg (*b* at Munich 21 June 1962), Forester.

[*R.R.2 Waltersdorf Farm, Chapeau JOX 1MO, Quebec, Canada*].

2. *Philipp-Ernst* Moritz Franz-Joseph Karl-Albrecht Michael, Hereditary Prince (Erbprinz) zu Hohenlohe-Schillingsfürst, *b* at Schillingsfürst 14 May 1967; ✝ at Cologne 3 Aug 1993.

Sister

1. Princess *Johanna* Elisabeth Isabella Christine Erika Rosa, *b* at Vienna 18 May 1930; *m* 1stly at Dombühl 16 March 1956 (*m* diss by div Rothenburg ob der Tauber 9 Sept 1958), Volkart Heim (*b* at Teplitz-Schönau 23 Feb 1928), Painter. She *m* 2ndly at Velden, nr Hersbruck, M Frankonia 22 March 1961, Dr Thomas Rehner (*b* at Jaad, Siebenbürgen 30 Aug 1918), Head Chemist and Manager of Eckart-Bronze-Farbwerke in Fürth.

[*Effnerstraße 58, 90480 Nürnberg - Mögeldorf, Germany*].

Brother of Father

Issue of Moritz, 9th Prince zu Hohenlohe-Schillingsfürst, etc (*b* 6 Aug 1862; ✠ 27 Feb 1940) and Princess and Altgräfin Rosa zu Salm-Reifferscheidt-Krautheim and Dyck (*b* 12 April 1868; *m* 19 Aug 1893; ✠ 1 Dec 1942), having had issue, among whom,

Son

Prince *Chlodwig* Alfred Peter Ferdinand Jokob Joseph Nikolaus Anton Maria, *b* at Alt Ausee, 30 July 1897; ✠ at Munich 3 May 1968; *m* 1stly at Olmütz 21 Sept 1927 (*m* diss by div at Palm Beach, Florida 7 March 1943 and annulled at Augsburg 1 Feb 1943), Mabel (*b* at Philadelphia 9 Nov 1886; ✠ ...; she *m* 1stly, Gifford Cochran; that *m* diss by div; she 3rdly at Labelle 11 May 1950, Kai James Cameron Clark), dau of Madison Taylor and Emily Drayton. He *m* 2ndly at Bad Aussee 24 April 1946, Mercedes (*b* at Kassel 2 April 1909; *m* 1stly 9 Jan 1931, Helmut von Riddler; that *m* diss by div; ✠ at Alt-Aussee 9 Oct 1996), dau of Alfred von Krüger and Felicitas von Pawel-Rammingen, and by her had issue,

> 1. Princess *Manon* Christiane Rosa Felicitas Maria Elisabeth Mercedes, *b* at Alt-Aussee 1 Feb 1948; *m* at Alt-Aussee 9 Sept 1973 (*m* diss by div 7 Dec 1987), Balint Béry (of Hungarian nobility) (*b* at Vienna 11 Jan 1944).
>
> [*8992 Alt-Aussee, Steiermark, Austria; Clemensstraße 122, 80796 Munich, Germany*].

Brother of Great-Grandfather

Issue of Franz-Joseph, 1st Prince zu Hohenlohe-Waldenburg-Schillingsfürst, etc (*b* 26 Nov 1787; ✠ 14 Jan 1841) and Princess Constance zu Hohenlohe-Langenburg (*b* 23 Feb 1792; *m* 29 March 1815; ✠ 25 July 1847), having had issue, among whom,

Son

Prince *Konstantin* Viktor Ernst Emil, *b* at Wildegg 8 Sept 1828; ✠ at Vienna 14 Feb 1896, Bailiff Gd Cross Hon and Dev Sovereign Military Order of Malta, Kt Order of the Golden Fleece; *m* at Weimar 15 Oct 1859, Princess Marie (*b* at Woronince 18 Feb 1837; ✠ at Schloß Friedstein 21 Jan 1920), dau of Nicolas, Prince zu Sayn-Wittgenstein-Berleburg and Caroline Elisabeth Ivanovska (of Polish nobility), and had issue, among whom,

Sons

1. Prince *Konrad* Maria Eusebius, *b* at Vienna 16 Dec 1863; ✠ at

Leoben, Styria 21 Dec 1918, Imp and Royal Minister of the Interior 1916-18, Kt Order of the Golden Fleece; *m* at Vienna 10 June 1888, Countess Franziska (*b* at Vienna 23 March 1866; ✝ at Bad Reichenhall 16 Sept 1937), Dame Star Cross Order, dau of Erwin, Count von Schönborn-Buchheim and Countess Franziska von and zu Trauttmansdorff-Weinsberg, and had issue,

1. Prince *Alfred* Konstantin Chlodwig Peter Maria, *b* at Salzburg 31 March 1889; ✝ at Prestwick, Scotland 21 Oct 1948; *m* 1stly at Washington DC, USA 14 Dec 1916, Catherine (*b* at Washington DC 27 March 1892; ✝ at Vienna 21 June 1929), dau of Alexander Britton and Louise Reed. He *m* 2ndly at Vienna 29 Jan 1934, Felicitas (Fee) (*b* at Hirschwang *nr* Reichenau, Austria 1 Sept 1900; ✝ at Vienna 9 June 1975; *m* 1stly at Hirschwang 30 Nov 1921, James Wendell Southard who ✝ at Hirschwang 22 Aug 1927), dau of Richard, Ritter von Schoeller and Emmi Siedenburg, and had issue, by his first wife, among whom,

    1. Prince *Alexander* Konrad Maria, *b* at Bern 16 Feb 1918, ✝ at Delray Beach, Florida, USA 9 Jan 1984; *m* 1stly at Paris 14 Oct 1939 (*m* diss by div at New York ...), Peggy (*b* at New York 11 June 1921; ✝ there 21 May 1964), dau of Theodor Schulze and Margaret Thompson. He *m* 2ndly at Greenwich, Connecticut, USA May 1951, and at Salzburg 10 Oct 1961, Patricia Wilder (*b* at Macon, Georgia, USA 8 Sept 1918; ✝ at New York 8 Feb 1995; *m* 1stly ...; that *m* diss by div), and had issue by his first wife,

        1. Princess *Catherine,* *b* at Washington 30 May 1943; *m* 1stly at New York 5 June 1964 (*m* diss by div at ...), William Edward Cook (*b* at ... 27 Oct 1940). She 2ndly George Jacobus (*b* at .... 5 Jan 1931).
        [*921 SO Ocean Boulevard, Delray Beach, Florida 33444, U.S.A.*].
        2. Prince *Christian* -Conrad *b* at Washington 2 Jan 1945, Dr of Law; *m* at Washington 23 Nov 1965, Nora (*b* at Washington 26 Feb 1945), dau of Andreas Gotthard Ronhovde and Virginia Sedman, and has issue,
        [*2710 Foxhall Road, Washington, D.C. 20007, USA*].

1. Prince *Philip* Alder, *b* at Washington 28 Oct 1967, Dr of Law; *m* at Wolf Creek, Montana 5 Aug 1995, Andrea (*b* at Washington 16 Sept 1967), dau of Douglas Whiting Rankin and Marie Louise Backus.

[*14D, 410 Central Park West, New York, NY 10025, U.S.A.*].

2. Prince *Konrad* Boyce, *b* at Washington 28 Oct 1967 (twin with Prince Philip); *m* at New York 13 Dec 1991, Zulfia (*b* at Kazan, Russia 31 Aug 1967), dau of Kharras Akhmetshin and Kadria Mukhlisova.

[*5C, 205 3rd Avenue, New York, NY 10003, U.S.A.*].

3. Prince *Paul* Alexander, *b* at Washington 17 Jan 1973.

2. Prince *Konrad* Maximilian Alfred Maria, *b* at Bern 16 Aug 1919; ✝ at Nikolskoje 16 May 1943 from wounds received in battle, adopted by Prince Karl Gottfried zu Hohenlohe-Ingelfingen (*b* 1879 - ✝ 1960); *m* at Glanegg, nr Salzburg 29 Sept 1942, Baroness Ladislaja (*b* at Salzburg 23 Dec 1920; *m* 2ndly at Salzburg 25 July 1946, Jakob, Count and Lord von and zu Eltz genannt Faust von Stromberg), Dame Star Cross Order, dau of Friedrich, Baron Mayr von Melnhof, Proprietor of Glanegg, and Countess Maria-Anne von Meran.

3. Prince *Viktor* Constantin Maria, *b* at Friedstein 20 April 1922, Dr of Med; *m* at Toronto, Ontario, Canada 5 June 1948, Countess Viktoria-Margarita (Vita) (*b* at Munich 25 Sept 1926), dau of Wilhelm Viktor, Count von Lüttichau and Margarita Pennington.

[*Schloß Friedstein, 8950 Stainach, Steiermark, Austria*]

2. Prince *Erwin* Franz Maria, *b* at Prague 27 July 1890; ✝ at Graz 25 May 1950, Dr of Law; *m* at Vienna 20 Oct 1917, Countess Alexandra (*b* at Baden-Baden 1 March 1884; ✝ at Vienna 23 April 1963; *m* 1stly at Keszthely 26 Oct 1905, Karl, Prince zu Windisch-Graetz who ✝ at Vienna 15 Sept 1915), Dame Star Cross Order, dau of Tassilo, Prince Festetics de

Tolna, and had issue,

    1. Prince *Tassilo* Erwin Benediktus Eustatius Maria,
b at Vienna 4 July 1918; ✠ at Vienna 10 April 1979; *m*
at Vienna 18 Dec 1947, Countess Antoinette (*b* at
Vienna 26 Oct 1925), dau of Carl Hugo, Count von
Seilern and Aspang, Proprietor of Wasserburg, and
Countess Marie Johanna Larisch von Moennich, and
had issue,

[*Boulevard des Suisses 17, Monte Carlo, Monaco*].

      1. Prince *Constantin* Friedrich Hubertus, *b* at
Vienna 19 April 1949, Dipl Engineer.

[*Stroh Gasse21, 1030 Vienna, Austria*].

      2. Princess *Alexandra* Maria Huberta Dorothea,
b at Stechen, nr Rottenmann, Styria 6 Aug
1950; *m* at Vienna 29 Nov 1979 (*m* diss by div
at Vienna 11 Sept 1987), Walter Mauritz (*b* at
Vienna 3 June 1947).

[*Stroh Gasse21, 1030 Vienna, Austria*].

      3. Prince *Philipp* Oswald Friedrich Erwin
Hubert Maria, *b* at Vienna 23 Jan 1952, Interior
Decorator.

[*165 Perry Street, New York, NY 10014,
U.S.A.*].

      4. Princess *Carola* Lucrezia Maria, *b* at Vienna
7 June 1953, Dr of Med.

[*Cumberlandstraße 13, 1140 Vienna, Austria*].

      5. Princess *Maria Johanna*, *b* at Vienna 1
March 1959, Psychologist.

[*Linzer Gasse55, 5020 Salzburg, Austria*].

      5. Prince *Karl-Albrecht* Hubertus Maria, *b* at
Vienna 27 Aug 1960; *m* at Ulrichskirchen 16
April 1988, Countess Maria Teresa (*b* at Milan
19 June 1964), dau of Aleco, Count von
Bulgarini, Count d'Elci and Countess Maria
zu Hardegg, Proprietor of Glatz and im
Machlande, and has issue,

[*Stroh Gasse21a, 1030 Vienna, Austria*].

        1. Princess *Alice* Antoinette Maria
Theresia Filippa Alexander, *b* at
Vienna 31 May 1990.

3. Prince *Hubert* Philipp Maria, *b* at Vienna 13 April 1893; ✠

at Salzburg 30 Nov 1969; *m* at Vienna 22 April 1919, Countess Eleonore (Hella) (*b* at Tavarna 26 Oct 1895; ✠ at Vienna 15 Nov 1923), dau of Andreas, Count von Hadik de Futak and Countess Klara Zichy.

ISENBURG/YSENBURG

This seigneural Rhenish family can be traced authentically to Raginbold, living circa 963 who took his name from the ancient fortress of Isenburch in the Engersgau (actually Isenburg, near Neuwied), Reginboldus comes et advocatus ecclesiae Trevirensis 1075; and Count Reimbold I of Isemburg living in 1093; Counts im gau Einrich (links der unteren Lahn bis an den Rhein); acquired parts of the County of Arnstein 1137; Lords of Covern (until 1266); Lords and Counts of Nieder Isenburg (1179 - 1664); Lords and Counts of Limburg an der Lahn (1232 - 1414); Counts of Wied (1326 - 1462); acquired the County of Cleeberg and the Lordship of Büdingen circa 1213; acquired the fortress of Birstein in Fulda 8 Sept 1438; County of the Holy Empire Argentinae 30 Aug 1442; erection of the Lordship of Büdingen into a Count of the Holy Empire, Brisac 1 Sept 1442; acquired half of Offenbach (see below) 24 May 1419 (28 May 1420) and the other half 11 March 1486; the lines below descend from two sons of Wolfgang Ernst I, Count of Isenburg-Birstein (*b* 29 Dec 1560; ✠ 21 May 1633).

LINE I: BIRSTEIN

Founded by Count Wolfgang Heinrich (*b* 20 Oct 1588; ✠ 27 Feb 1635); divided into two Lines - Offenbach which became extinct 21 Sept 1718 and Birstein which was founded by the younger son of Johann Ludwig, Count of Isenburg-Birstein, Count Wilhelm Moritz I (*b* 3 Aug 1657; ✠ 8 March 1711). Two of his sons founded the Branches below, of which only the first Branch is still extant.

1st Branch: ISENBURG (-BIRSTEIN)

Catholic: Founded by Count Wolfgang-Ernst III (Prince Wolfgang-Ernst I) (*b* 5 April 1686; ✠ 15 April 1754); inherited the possessions of the elder line of Offenbach (extinct 21 Sept 1718) with the exception of Philippseich (see below); Prince of the Holy Empire with the qualification of "Hochgeboren", Frankfurt-am-Main 23 March 1744; titles recognised in Prussia 28 July 1744; and recognised by the Elector of Saxony 31 Aug 1744; received a Vote in the Council of Princes of the Holy Empire 25 Feb 1803; lands were reunited with parts of the county of Schönborn-Heussenstamm and parts of the Lordship of Grosschlag and erected into the Sovereign Principality

of Isenburg in the Confederation of the Rhine and received the
qualification of Serene Highness (for the Prince and his descendants),
19 July 1806; the Principality was Mediatized and placed under the
sovereignty of Austria at the Congress of Vienna 9 June 1815, ceded
to the Grand Duchy of Hesse 3 Nov 1815; divided between
Hesse-Darmstadt and Hesse-Cassel 10 July 1816; Hereditary Member
of the First Chamber of the Grand Duchy of Hesse 17 Dec 1820;
Hereditary Member of the former Prussian House of Lords 4 Nov
1868; confirmation in Hesse of the rights of all members of the
Princely House to bear the qualification of Serene Highness,
Darmstadt 28 April 1913.
Members of this Branch bear the title of Prince or Princess von
Isenburg with the qualification of Serene Highness.

FRANZ ALEXANDER Karl Friedrich Christian Hubert Georg
Gabriel Maria, **8TH PRINCE (FÜRST) VON ISENBURG,**
b at Birstein 22 July 1943, son of Franz Ferdinand, 7th Prince
(Fürst) von Isenburg (*b* 17 July 1901; ✠ 9 Dec 1956) and Countess
Irina Alexandrovna Tolstoy (*b* 13/26 Jan 1917; *m* 22 July 1939; ✠ 20
June 1998); *m* at Donaueschingen 3 Jan (civ) and at Rottach-Egern,
Bavaria 15 Jan (relig) 1968, Countess Christiane (*b* at Munich 2 Oct
1941), dau of Achatius, Count von Saurma, Baron von and zu der
Jeltsch and Countess Maria Blanca von Maldeghem.
[*63633 Schloß Birstein, über Wächtersbach, Hesse, Germany*].

Sons and Daughters

1. *Alexander* Wolfgang Georg Paul Maria, Hereditary Prince
(Erbprinz) von Isenburg, *b* at Frankfurt-am-Main 16 June 1969.
2. Princess *Katharina* Elisabeth Helene Maria, *b* at Basel 21 Oct
1971.
3. Princess *Isabelle* Sophie Gabrielle, *b* at Frankfurt-am-Main 26
April 1973; *m* at Birstein 25 April 1998, Prince Friederich August
Maximilian Wilhelm *Carl* zu Wied (*b* at Neuwied 27 Oct 1961).
4. Princess *Sophie* Johanna Maria, *b* at Frankfurt-am-Main 7 April
1978.
5. Prince *Viktor* Carl Johannes, *b* at Frankfurt-am-Main 11 April
1979.

Sisters

1. Princess Irene (*Irina*) Friederike Cecilie Theresia Antoinette
Helene Alexandra Sophie Anna Maria Luise, *b* at Birstein 30 Sept
1940; *m* at Birstein 20 Aug (civ) and 28 Aug (relig) 1961 (*m* diss by
div at Berlin-Charlottenburg 28 May 1970), Wilhelm, Count zu

Stolberg-Stolberg (*b* at Ascherode, Hohenstein 2 June 1927). She *m* 2ndly at Munich 1 Sept 1980 (*m* diss by div at Munich 7 July 1986 since when she has reverted to her maiden name), Jan ter Meer (*b* at Ruhlben, nr Plön 19 March 1946).

[*63633 Schloß Birstein, über Wächtersbach, Hesse, Germany*].

2. Princess *Maria* Annunciata Franziska Felizitas Caroline Sophie Gabrielle Imagina, *b* at Birstein 14 Sept 1941.

[*63633 Schloß Birstein, über Wächtersbach, Hesse, Germany*].

3. Princess *Elisabeth Christiane* Helene Huberta Margarethe Madeleine Maria Fatima, *b* at Birstein 5 April 1945; *m* at Birstein 15 June (civ) and 16 July (relig) 1974, Franz Josef von Halem (*b* at Grabs, Switzerland 11 June 1941), Businessman.

[*Schloßstraße 2, 63633 Birstein, über Wächtersbach, Hesse, Germany*].

Brothers of Grandfather

Issue of Karl, 5th Prince (Fürst) von Isenburg (*b* 29 July 1838; ✠ 4 April 1899) and Marie Louise, Archduchess of Austria and Princess of Tuscany (*b* 31 Oct 1845; *m* 31 May 1865; ✠ 27 Aug 1917), having had issue, among whom,

Sons

1. Prince *Viktor Salvator* Karl Maria Leopold Anton Aloys Josef Rainer Johannes Kasimir, *b* at Offenbach 29 Feb 1872; ✠ at Berlin 4 Feb 1946, Lt-Col Prussian Army; *m* morganatically at Nuremberg 11 April 1908, Leontine (*b* at Schlackenwerth 27 Jan 1886; ✠ at Berlin-Charlottenburg 7 Nov 1950, *cr* Baroness of Rombach by the Grand Duke of Hesse-Darmstadt 31 March 1908), dau of Dr Anton Rohrer and Antonia Hartmann, and had issue, a son.

3. Prince *Alfons* Maria Leopold Anton Karl Alois Josef Franz Pius Johannes Michael Heinrich, *b* at Offenbach 6 Feb 1875; ✠ at Langenselbold 22 April 1951; *m* at Petschau Bohemia 1 Dec 1900, Countess Pauline (*b* at Puris 8 Nov 1876; ✠ at Langenselbold 11 Dec 1955), dau of Frederic, 5th Duke and Prince de Beaufort-Spontin and Princess Marie Melanie von Ligne, and had issue,

    1. Princess *Margarete* Marie Alfonsa Luise Melanie Antoinette Paula Frederike, *b* at Langenselbold 16 Oct 1901.

    [*63505 Schloßpark, Langenselbold bei Hanau, Germany*].

    2. Princess *Marie* Imagina Aloyusia Friederike Thusnelda Wunibalde Lucia Bertha, *b* at Langenselbold 13 Dec 1902;

✣ at Langenselbold 6 Feb 1997.

3. Princess *Elisabeth* Franziska Marie Melanie Norberta, *b* Langenselbold 6 June 1904; ✣ at Munich 31 Jan 1982; *m* at St Truijen, Limburg, Belgium 12 May (civ) and at Langenselbold 19 May (relig) 1934, Johannes Eggen van Terlan (*b* at Gent 23 June 1883; ✣ at Bonn 28 Dec 1952) Dr of Law, Univ Prof.

4. Prince Maria *Ernst* Hubertus Alfons Karl Friedrich Stephan Thomas, *b* at Langenselbold 26 Dec 1906; ✣ at Langenselbold 17 Dec 1991; *m* at Nairobi, Kenya 8 Feb 1937, Fiona (*b* at Pretoria, South Africa 17 Feb 1917), dau of William Davidson and Elizabeth Agnes McIntyre, and had issue,
[*Schloßpark 1, 63505 Langenselbold bei Hanau, Germany*].

    1. Princess Maria *Pauline* Elisabeth Margarethe Stephanie Fiona Antoinette, *b* at Moshi, Tanganyika 23 Nov 1937; *m* at Nairobi 3 Aug 1962, Francis Cain (*b* at Southsea, nr Plymouth 27 May 1934; ✣ at Nairobi 28 Nov 1982).
    [*Schloßpark 1, 63505 Langenselbold bei Hanau, Germany*].

    2. Prince Maria *Carl* Alfons Wilhelm Ernst Heinrich Johannes David Nikolaus, *b* at Moshi 6 Dec 1939; *m* at Princeton, New Jersey, USA 5 June 1965, Valerie (*b* at Washington, DC 12 Nov 1942), dau of John O'Dea and Valerie Luise Chuhran, and has issue,
    [*1109 Glade Street, Winston-Salem, North Carolina 27101, USA*].

        1. Princess Maria *Stephanie* Elizabeth, *b* at Englewood, New Jersey 4 Jan 1969.
        2. Prince *Charles* Matthew, *b* at Vlaardingen, The Netherlands 9 March 1971.
        3. Princess *Megan* Anne, *b* at Westfield, New Jersey 20 Feb 1976.

    3. Prince Maria Franz Wilhelm (*William*) Eugen Wolfgang Ernst Walter Ludwig, *b* at Moshi 4 June 1941; *m* 1stly at Nairobi 23 Sept 1967, Gillian (*b* at Kisumu, Kenya 11 Feb 1943; ✣ at Cambridge 16 March 1985), dau of Bertram Bowers and Cecily Walker. He *m* 2ndly at Bournemouth 15th April 1989, Judith (*b* at London 20 Nov 1943; *m* 1stly 27 July 1963, Alistair Ramsay who ✣ at Mozambique 6 Nov 1987),

dau of Albert Saunders and Annie Gentry, and has issue from his first wife,
[*10 Dover Road, Branksome Park, Poole, BH13 6DZ, Dorset*].

> 1. Princess Marie *Louise*, *b* at Nairobi 16 Jan 1970; *m* at Bournemouth 5 September 1998. *Stephen* Charles Drew (*b* at Ickenham, Middlesex 17 Jan 1966).
> [*222 North Road, Wimbledon, London SW19 1T2*].
>
> 2. Princess *Catherine* Gillian, *b* at Nairobi 22 March 1976.

4. Prince Maria Victor Alexander Alfons Richard Heinrich Robert Casimir Michael *John*, *b* at Karatu, Tanganyika 2 June 1944; *m* at Nairobi 15 Aug 1975, Sigrid (*b* at Sagan, Lower Silesia 23 Oct 1944), dau of Walter Maas and Hilda Bruckauf, and has issue,
[*Schloßpark 1, 63505 Langenselbold, Germany*].

> 1. Prince Maria *John Philipp* Ernst William Friedrich Alfons Heinrich Georg, *b* at Hanau 3 March 1977.
>
> 2. Prince Maria *Richard Ludwig* Friedrich Wilhelm Paul Frank Albert Johann, *b* at Hanau 5 May 1979.
>
> 3. Princess *Marie Christine* Katharina Margarete Pauline, *b* at Hanau 1 Aug 1981.

5. Prince Maria *Richard* Leonard Benedict Anton James Quentin Friedrich Ernest, *b* at Oldeani, Tanganyika 3 Feb 1946; *m* at Mbabane, Swaziland 4 July 1970, Joy (*b* at Nairobi 25 April 1948), dau of Hubert Watkins and Ella Silvorthorne, and has issue,
[*20 Hawthorne Gardens, Hockley, Essex SS5 4SW, England*].

> 1. Prince *Kevin* Antony Barry, *b* at Nairobi 31 Oct 1972.
>
> 2. Prince *Carl* James Quentin, *b* at Nairobi 26 Aug 1975.

5. Prince Maria *Heinrich* Leon Alfons Friedrich Karl Maximilian, *b* at Langenselbold 16 Sept 1913; ✝ as a POW at Tiflis 12/13 Jan 1946.

2nd Branch: ISENBURG-PHILIPPSEICH
(✝ Extinct ✝)

Reformist: Founded by Wilhelm Moritz II zu Isenburg and Büdingen
in Birstein, later Count Wilhelm Moritz zu Isenburg and Büdingen
in Philippseich (*b* 23 July 1688; ✝ 7 March 1772); succeeded on the
extinction of the Offenbach Line 21 Scpt 1718; qualification of
"Erlaucht" (primogeniture) by the German Diet 13 Feb 1829;
extended to all members of the family 7 March 1914; devolved to the
1st Branch 5 Jan 1920 when this Branch became extinct in the male
(legitimate) Line. However, through the morganatic marriage of a
first cousin once removed of the last reigning Prince, it continues as
"Counts and Countesses zu Büdingen".
Members of this Branch bore the title of Count or Countess zu
Isenberg and Büdingen in Philippseich with the qualification of
Serene Highness.

Line II: BÜDINGEN

Evangelical: Founded by Count Johann Ernst (*b* 21 June 1625; ✝ 8
Oct 1673); partition of lands and creation of the Branches below 23
July 1687.

1st Branch: ISENBURG AND BÜDINGEN IN BÜDINGEN
(✝ Extinct ✝)

Founded by Count Johann Casimir (*b* 10 July 1660; ✝ 23 Sept 1693);
Hereditary Member of the First Chamber of the Grand Duchy of
Hesse 17 Dec 1820; Prince in the Grand Duchy of Hesse with the
qualification of "Durchlaucht", Darmstadt 9 April 1840 (for Ernst
Casimir, Count of Isenburg and Büdingen in Büdingen).
Members of this Branch bear the title of Prince or Princess zu
Isenburg and Büdingen in Büdingen with the qualification of Serene
Highness.

✝ **CARL** Gustav **6TH PRINCE (FÜRST) ZU ISENBURG
AND BÜDINGEN,** *b* at Frankfurt-am-Main 11 Sept 1875; ✝ at
Büdingen 15 May 1941, Capt Imp German Navy, Kt of Honour of St
John of Jerusalem, son of Alfred, Prince (Fürst) zu Isenburg and
Büdingen (*b* 31 Dec 1841; ✝ 3 May 1922) and Countess Luitgard zu
Castell-Rüdenhausen (*b* 23 Aug 1843; *m* 17 July 1870; ✝ 4 June
1927); *m* at Burg Schwalenberg 16 Sept 1920, Princess Marie (*b* at
Oberkassel nr Beuel 21 June 1890; ✝ at Büdingen 27 Nov 1973), dau
of Friedrich, Count zur Lippe-Biesterfeld and Princess Marie zu
Löwenstein-Wertheim-Freudenberg, having adopted his kinsman
(Contract at Wächtersbach 17 Sept 1936, confirmed at Giessen 27

May 1937 and at Munich 13 Oct 1937).

Adopted Son

Otto Friedrich, Fürst zu Isenburg and Büdingen in Wächtersbach, *b* at Halberstadt 16 Sept 1904; ✠ 25 Sept 1990 (see Isenburg and Büdingen in Wächtersbach).

Brother

Prince Ernst *Diether, b* at Frankfurt-am-Main 30 March 1881; ✠ at Büdingen 21 April 1965, Major Prussian Army, Kt Hohenzollern House Order, Kt of Hon St John of Jerusalem; *m* at Neustrelitz 21 Jan 1930, Countess Sigrid (*b* at Potsdam 13 Jan 1909; ✠ at Büdingen 1 May 1964), dau of Hans, Count von Blumenthal and Countess Melanie von der Schulenburg, Proprietor of Bodendorf, and had issue,

1. Princess *Luitgard* Sigrid Melanie Anna Marie, *b* at Giessen 30 Oct 1930; *m* at Frankfurt-am-Main (civ) and at Kranichstein, nr Darmstadt 12 Dec 1959, Friedrich Karl Bunn (*b* at Frankfurt-am-Main 22 Sept 1933), Lawyer, Notary.
[*Castellerstraße 48, 65719 Hofheim-Diedenbergen, Germany*].

2. Princess *Heilwig* Helene Lonny Carola, *b* at Büdingen 15 Sept 1933; *m* at Colchester, Essex 15 Sept 1959, Udo Janssen (*b* at Esens, East Friesland 21 Sept 1931).
[*Oldenburgerstraße 8, 23883 Lehmrade, Holstein, Germany*].

3. Princess *Jutta* Thekla Felizitas Marie Luise Sophie, *b* at Büdingen 28 Feb 1936; *m* at Frankfurt-am-Main 10 Nov 1962 (*m* diss by div at Büdingen .. 1986), Herwart Neuhaus (*b* at Herne, Westphalia, Germany 13 Jan 1935), Dipl Eng.
[*Am Hain 8, 63654 Büdingen, Upper Hessen, Germany*].

2nd Branch: ISENBURG AND BÜDINGEN IN WÄCHTERSBACH

Founded by Count Ferdinand Maximilian (*b* 24 Dec 1661; ✠ 14 March 1703); Hereditary Member of the First Chamber of the Grand Duchy of Hesse 17 Dec 1820; title of Prince in the Electorate of Hesse with the qualification of "Durchlaucht", Cassel 17 Aug 1865 (for Ferdinand Maximilian, Count zu Isenburg and Büdingen in Wächtersbach); Hereditary Member of the former Prussian House of Lords 16 Nov 1867; Kt of the Prussian Order of St John.
Members of this Branch bear the title of Prince or Princess zu Isenburg and Büdingen in Wächtersbach with the qualification of Serene Highness.

WOLFGANG-ERNST Ferdinand Heinrich Franz Karl Georg Wilhelm, **4TH PRINCE (FÜRST) ZU ISENBURG AND BÜDINGEN IN WÄCHTERSBACH,** *b* at Frankfurt-am-Main 20 June 1936, *succ* his father, son of Otto Friedrich, 3rd Prince (Fürst) zu Isenburg and Büdingen in Wächtersbach (*b* 16 Sept 1904; ✝ 25 Sept 1990) and Princess Felizitas Reuss (*b* 5 July 1914; *m* 3 Sept 1935; ✝ 25 June 1989); *m* at Haubenmühle, Upper Hessen 27 Jan (civ) and at Rodheim 28 Jan (relig) 1967, Princess Leonille (*b* at Hamburg 6 July 1941), dau of Casimir Johannes, Prince zu Sayn-Wittgenstein-Berleburg and Ingrid Alsen.
[*Schloß, 63654 Büdingen, Upper Hessen, Germany*].

Sons and Daughter

1. *Casimir Alexander* Lucian Friedrich Peter Franz Ferdinand Benedikt Wittekind, Hereditary Prince (Erbprinz) zu Isenburg and Büdingen *b* at Frankfurt-am-Main 30 Dec 1967, Banker.
2. Prince *Ferdinand-Maximilian* Philipp Heinrich Richard Thomas, *b* at Frankfurt-am-Main 28 July 1969.
3. Princess *Felizitas-Magdalena* Anita Ida Elisabeth, *b* at Basel 22 Feb 1980.

Brothers and Sister

1. Princess Sophie *Alexandra* Cecilie Anna Maria Friederike Benigna Dorothea, *b* at Frankfurt-am-Main 23 Oct 1937; *m* at Büdingen 20 Sept (civ) and 21 Sept (relig) 1960, Welf Heinrich, Prince of Hanover, Prince of Great Britain and Ireland, Duke of Brunswick and Lüneburg (*b* at Gmunden, Austria 11 March 1923; ✝ at Frankfurt-am-Main 12 July 1997), Dr of Law.
[*Neuwiesenstraße 22, 60528 Frankfurt-am-Main - Niederrad, Germany*].
2. Prince *Ferdinand Heinrich* Karl August Hermann Gotthard, *b* at Frankfurt- am-Main 19 Oct 1940; ✝ at Büdingen 8 March 1989; *m* at Glücksburg an der Ostsee 2 Jan (civ) and 5 Jan (relig) 1975, Princess Elisabeth (*b* at Schleswig 10 Sept 1945), dau of Friedrich Ferdinand, Prince of Schleswig-Holstein-Sonderburg-Glücksburg and Duchess Anastasia of Mecklenburg, and had issue,
[*Christinenhof, 63654 Büdingen, Upper Hessen, Germany*].

    1. Prince J*ohann-Georg* Gerd Max Alexander Sylvester Gisbert, *b* at Frankfurt-am-Main 8 July 1976.
    2. Prince *Ludwig-Ferdinand* Wittekind Heinrich Friedrich-August Joachim, *b* at Frankfurt-am-Main 6 Feb

1979.

4. Prince *Christian Albrecht* Franz Nikolaus Heinrich Wolfgang, *b* at Frankfurt-am-Main 3 Jan 1943; *m* at Büdingen 17 Feb 1966, Monika (*b* at Rome 29 Jan 1940), dau of Johann Ludwig, Baron von Plessen, Proprietor of Marutendorf, Holstein of the Counts von Plessen-Cronstern, and Maria Immaculata von Wuthenau of the Counts von Wuthenau-Hohenthurm, and has issue,
[*Mittelgründauer Hof, 63584 Gründau, Germany*].

 1. Princess *Margita Octavia* Alexandra Silvia Felizitas Irmgard Madeleine, *b* at Frankfurt-am-Main 7 Nov 1966; m at ... May 1999, Archduke Maximilien of Austria (*b* at Boulogne-Billancourt 8 Feb 1961).

 2. Prince Johann *Albrecht* Philipp Alexander Stefan Axel Wittekind Leonille, *b* at Frankfurt-am-Main 10 July 1968; *m* at Büdingen 5 Sept (civ) and 6 Sept (relig) 1997, Alexandra (*b* at Heidelberg 14 Aug 1967), dau of Prof Dr Klaus Pohle and Maria Carmen Mendez Alvarado.

 3. Princess *Donata Elisabeth* Verena Franziska, *b* at Basel 22 Feb 1970.

 [*Weiherhof, 63607 Wächtersbach, Germany*].

5. Prince *Johann-Ernst* Friedrich Karl Diether Franz Alexander Heinrich *Sylvester*, *b* at Gelnhausen 31 Dec 1949; *m* at Ebenthal, Carinthia 3 June 1983, Countess Hemma-Christiane (*b* at Ebenthal 12 March 1957), dau of Leopold-Zeno, Count von Goëss and Countess Theodora Kottulinsky, Baroness von Kottulin, and has issue,
[*Haus Preiserle, 63654 Büdingen-Rinderbügen, Germany*].

 1. Prince *Friedrich-Leopold* Christian Ulrich Pierot, *b* at Frankfurt-am-Main 6 Nov 1983.

 2. Princess *Dorothea* Cecilie Henriette, *b* at Frankfurt-am-Main 23 May 1986.

Sister of Father

Issue of Ferdinand Maximilian, Hereditary Prince zu Isenburg and Büdingen (*b* 25 June 1880; ✠ 11 March 1927) and Countess Margarethe (Margita) von Dönhoff (*b* 19 April 1876; *m* 19 Dec 1903; ✠ 22 Sept 1954).

1. Princess *Gabriele* Georgine Gustava Resita Klausine Karoline Imagina Marion (Catholic from 1957), *b* at Berlin 23 Nov 1911, ✠ at Munich 13 Jan 2000; *m* at Berlin 21 Feb 1942, Franz, Prince zu

Sayn-Wittgenstein-Berleburg (*b* at Frankfurt-am-Main 24 Aug 1910), Dr of Phil.
[*Holbeinstraße 14, 81679 Munich, Germany*].

<hr>

KHEVENHÜLLER-METSCH

Catholic: This family originated and appear (authenticated) in Villach, Carinthia, 1396 (Vienna State Archives); confirmation of Arms by King Wenzel 10 Jan 1425 (for Johann Chefenhüler); acquired the fortress of Aichelberg 1427; "Erblandstallmeister" in Carinthia, Vienna 13 March 1565; Baron of the Holy Empire by Letters Patent dated 16 Oct 1566; Austrian Count, Vienna 23 July 1673; Count of the Holy Empire, Vienna 6 Jan 1725; Bohemian Incolat with the qualification of "Hoch and Wohlgeboren" 23 Jan 1725; received into the Swabian College of Counts of the Holy Empire 24 Oct 1737; permission to join the name and arms of Metsch through the marriage of Count and Prince Johann Joseph to Caroline Marie Augustine, elder daughter of Johann Adolf, Count of Metsch, 11 March 1751 (for the Empire) and 24 April 1751 (for the Hereditary States); Bohemian Prince (primogeniture) with the qualification of "Hochgeboren", Vienna 20 Dec 1763; Prince of the Holy Empire (primogeniture), Ratisbonan 30 Dec 1763; "Obersthofmeister" in Austria under der Enns, Vienna 3 Dec 1775; Hereditary Member of the former Austrian House of Lords; qualification of "Durchlaucht" (primogeniture) by the German Diet 18 Aug 1825; recognised in Austria 7 Oct 1825.
The Head of the family and his wife bear the title of Prince and Princess von Khevenhüller-Metsch with the qualification of Serene Highness and cadet members bear the title of Count or Countess von Khevenhüller-Metsch.

MAX Alfred Bartholomäus Friedrich Anton Franz Eduad Joachim Anna Maria Schnee Oswald Hubertus, **9TH PRINCE (FÜRST) VON KHEVENHÜLLER-METSCH** and zu Aichelberg, Count (Graf) zu Hohenosterwitz and Annabichl, Baron zu Landskron and Wernberg, Erbherr auf Carlsberg, Riegersburg and Ladendorf, *b* at Heiligenberg 5 Aug 1919, Kt Order of the Golden Fleece, Kt Sovereign Military Order of Malta, Kt Order of St George, son of Franz Eduard, 8th Prince (Fürst) von Khevenhüller-Metsch (*b* 3 Dec 1889; ✠ 31 Jan 1977) and Princess Anna zu Fürstenberg (*b* 19 April 1894; *m* 16 Aug 1913; ✠ 19 Aug 1928); *m* at Munich 19 Jan 1956, Countess Wilhelmine (*b* at Naklo, Tarnowitz 16 March 1932), Dame Star Cross Order, Dame of Hon Sovereign Military Order of

Malta, dau of Lazarus, Count Henckel von Donnersmarck and Countess Franziska von and zu Eltz genannt Faust von Stromberg. [*Schloß Osterwitz, 9314 Launsdorf, Kärnten, Austria; Schloß Pellendorf 1, 2191 Gaweinstal, Austria*].

Sons and Daughters

1. Maria *Johannes* Franz Xaver Lazarus Maximilian Felix, Hereditary Count (Erbgraf) von Khevenhüller-Metsch, *b* at Lugano-Sorengo 20 Nov 1956, Mag rer oec; *m* at Rome 3 July 1986, Donna Camilla (*b* at Rome 1 Jan 1962), dau of Don Giovanni Angelo Borghese, Prince di Nettuno and Lydia Cremisini of the Counts Cremisini, and has issue,
[*Via Vivaio 4, 20122 Milan, Italy*].

    1. Countess *Franzisca Lydia* Maria, *b* at Rome 22 April 1988.

    2. Countess *Helena* Flavia *Lauretana*, *b* at Rome 10 Dec 1990.

    3. Countess *Sophie Maria* Gabriela, *b* at Rome 28 Feb 1992.

    4. Countess Cecilie Maria Caterina, *b* at Rome 29 March 1997.

2. Count Maria *Bartholomäus* Lazarus Maximilian Hubertus, *b* at Lugano-Sorengo 1 Jan 1958, Dr of Law, Lt Col (Res), Kt of Hon Sovereign Military Order of Malta; *m* at Comillas, Spain 2 July 1988, Cristina (*b* at San Sebastian 22 Aug 1962), dau of Don Manuel Sanchez de Movellán, Marquess de Movellán and Mary Garcia Ogara, and has issue,
[*Donoso Montesinos 18, 28036 Madrid, Spain*].

    1. Count *Ludwig Andreas*, *b* at Las Palmas, Spain 5 Nov 1988.

    2. Countess *Clara*, *b* at Madrid 26 Oct 1990.

    3. Countess *Gabriela*, *b* at Madrid 2 Jan 1993.

    4. Count *Philipp*, *b* at Hong Kong 6 July 1998.

3. Count Maria *Karl* Maximilian Georg Hubertus, *b* at Lugano-Sorengo 11 March 1959, Engineer, Lt (Res), Kt of Hon Sovereign Military Order of Malta; *m* at Ossaich 5 Sept 1992, Laura (*b* at Neuilly 28 Aug 1968), dau of Alain Gailly de Taurines and Lora Toppan Ives, and has issue,
[*Schloß Pellendorf, 2191 Gaweinstal, Austria*].

    1. Count Maria *Maximilian* Eduard Johannes Christoph Alain, *b* at Klagenfurt 24 Sept 1993.

    2. Count Maria *Franz* Christoph Karl, *b* at Mistelbach 26 March 1995.

    3. Count Maria *Sigmund* Friedrich Georg Rudolf, *b* at Mistelbach 30 Dec 1997.

4. Countess Maria *Victoria*, *b* at Klagenfurt 7 July 2000.
4. Count *Georg* Christoph Heinrich Hubertus, *b* at Madrid 24 Sept 1960, Mag rer oec, Lt (Res); *m* at Castell 22 Aug 1993, Countess Stephanie (*b* at Castell 26 Sept 1966), dau of Albrecht, 3rd Prince (Fürst) zu Castell-Castell and Princess Marie-Louise zu Waldeck and Pyrmont, and has issue,
[*Landwehrweg 11, 61350 Bad Homburg, Germany*].

    1. Countess *Hemma* Marie Louise Franziska *b* at Vienna 17 July 1994.

    2. Countess *Teresa* Marie Johanna Sophie Leopoldine, *b* at Frankfurt-am-Main 16 Jan 1996.

    3. Countess *Marie* Elisabeth Gustava Pillar, *b* at Frankfurt-am-Main 27 Aug 1998.

5. Countess Maria *Melanie* Anna Teresa, *b* at Madrid 22 April 1967; *m* at Möckmühl 7 June (civ) 1993 and at Hochosterwitz 19 June (relig) 1993, Hubertus, Count von Waldburg zu Wolfegg and Waldsee (*b* at Möckmühl 15 May 1964), Forester.
[*Schloß Assumstadt, 74219 Möckmühl - Züttlingen, Germany*].
6. Countess Maria *Isabel* Francisca Caroline, *b* at Madrid 30 March 1972.
[*Schloß Osterwitz, 9314 Launsdorf, Kärnten, Austria*].

Sisters

1. Countess *Irma* Maximillienne Franziska Melanie Anne Eduardine Stephanie, *b* at Donaueschingen 3 Aug 1914; ✠ at Schloß Niederosterwitz 17 June 1954; *m* at Madrid 26 Feb 1941, Silvio Scherz (*b* at Villach 3 Aug 1908; ✠ at ... 28 March 1973).
2. Countess *Melanie,* *b* at Schönborn 18 Oct 1915; ✠ at Vienna 24 Oct 1991; *m* at Osterwitz 12 June 1951, Peter, Count Draskovich von Trakostjan (*b* at Sellye, Baranya, Hungary 2 April 1916; ✠ at Vienna 9 Dec 1993).
3. Countess *Helene* (*Hella*) Marie Anne Franziska, *b* at Vienna 4 April 1921, Dame of Hon Bav Orders of St Theresia and St Elisabeth, Dame Star Cross Order; *m* 1stly 15 Aug 1953, Prince Konstantin of Bavaria (*b* at Munich 15 Aug 1920; ✠*k* in a flying accident at Hechingen 30 July 1969). She *m* 2ndly at Munich 16 Nov (civ) and at Innsbruck 21 Nov (relig) 1970, Prince Eugen of Bavaria (*b* at Munich 16 July 1925; ✠ at Grasse, Dept Alpes-Maritimes, France 1 Jan 1997).
[*87541 Hinterstein, Germany*].

Brother of Great-Grandfather

Issue of Franz, 4th Prince von Khevenhüller-Metsch (*b* 7 April 1762; ✝ 2 July 1837) and his third wife, Countess Christine Zichy zu Zich and Vásonykëo (*b* 30 April 1792; *m* 15 June 1912; ✝ 20 July 1830), having had issue, among whom,

Son

Richard Maria Johannes Basilius, **5th Prince (Fürst) von Khevenhüller-Metsch**, etc, *b* at Talheim, Lower Austria 23 May 1813; ✝ at Ladendorf 29 Nov 1877, Kt Order of Leopold, Kt Order of St Stephen of Hungary; *m* at Vienna 8 Dec 1836, Countess Antonia (*b* at Vienna 18 April 1818; ✝ at Vienna 10 Jan 1870), Dame Star Cross Order, dau of Eduard, Prince (Fürst) Lichnowsky and Countess Eleonore Zichy zu Zich and Vásonykeö, having had issue, among whom,

Son

Count *Sigismund* Maria, *b* at Vienna 31 May 1841; ✝ at Graz 10 July 1879, Lt-Col Austrian Army; *m* at Vienna 5 Oct 1872, Countess Maria Anna (*b* at Graz 8 Dec 1851; ✝ at Baden nr Vienna 2 Aug 1921; *m* 2ndly at Prague 24 Sept 1890, Maximilian, Count von Orsini and Rosenberg), Dame Star Cross Order, dau of Friedrich, Count zu Herberstein and Countess Therese von Dietrichstein, and had issue, among whom,

Son

Anton Sigismund Joseph Maria **7th Prince (Fürst) von Khevenhüller-Metsch**, etc, *b* at Vienna 26 July 1873; ✝ at   Salzburg 8 Nov 1945, Kt of Hon Sovereign Military Order of Malta, Kt Bavarian Order of St George; *m* at Vienna 4 June 1910, Countess Gabrielle (*b* at Vienna 12 Feb 1893; ✝ there 4 April 1972), Lady-in-Waiting, Dame Star Cross Order, dau of Alfons, Count von Mensdorff-Pouilly, Proprietor of Preitenstein, Boskowitz with Klein-Hradisko in Moravia and Countess Ida Paar, and had issue, among whom,

> 1. Countess *Leopoldine* Gabrielle Maria, *b* at Vienna 23 Feb 1913; *m* at Berlin 11 Feb 1941, Max Huck (*b* at Jästersheim, Guhrau 22 Aug 1910; ✝ at Graz 19 Feb 1978), Col (Ret).
> [*2126 Ladendorf, Bez. Mistelbach, NÖsterreich, Austria*].

KÖNIGSEGG-AULENDORF

Catholic: This Swabian feudal family can be traced authentically to
Mengoz de Fronhove (Fronhofen, Württemberg) living 1171;
ministeriales of the Guelfs, then of Hohenstaufen 1191; Eberhardus
de Kunigsegge, frater domini Bertholdi de Fronhoven is the first to
be named after Königsegg (a bailiwick in Saulgau) 1251; acquired
Aulendorf (see below) after 1381; Baron von Königsegg zu Aulendorf
of the Holy Empire, 1470; Qualification of "Wohlgeboren", Linz 20
Nov 1613; Count of the Holy Empire (elevation of Königsegg into a
County of the Holy Empire) with the qualification of "Hoch and
Wohlgeboren", Vienna 29 July 1629; Registered as a Nobleman in
Lower Austria 1750; Hungarian Indigenat 1751; qualification of
"Erlaucht" (primogeniture) by the German Diet 13 Feb 1829.
Hereditary member of the First Chamber of Württemberg.
Members of the family bear the title of Count or Countess zu
Königsegg-Aulendorf with the qualification of Illustrious Highness
for the Head of the Family.

JOHANNES von Nepmuk Maria Eusebius Pius, **COUNT (GRAF)
ZU KÖNIGSEGG-AULENDORF,** *b* at Königseggwald 13 April
1925, Hon Cmdr Bavarian Order of St George, son of Joseph Erwin,
Count zu Königsegg-Aulendorf (*b* 19 March 1891; ✠ 14 March 1951)
and Countess Lucia von Wilczek (*b* 9 June 1895; *m* 15 Oct 1918; ✠ 6
Dec 1977); *m* at Munich 27 Sept 1955, Baroness Stefanie (*b* at
Sátoralja-Ujhely, Hungary 19 Nov 1929), dau of Friedrich, Baron
Waldbott von Bassenheim and Archduchess Maria-Alice of Austria.
[*88376 Königseggwald über Aulendorf, Württemberg, Germany*].

Sons and Daughter

1. Countess *Isabelle* Gabrielle Maria Appolonia Eusebia, *b* at   Munich
23 July 1956; *m* at Königseggwald 28 June 1987, Adam-Petrus, Count
Schall-Riacour (*b* at Kirchhellen, Westfalen 17 Sept 1949), Designer.
[*Schloßstraße 8, 50226 Frechen-Bachem, Germany*].
2. *Maximilian* Ulrich Philipp Eusebius Benno, Hereditary Count
(Erbgraf) zu Königsegg-Aulendorf, *b* at Munich 16 June 1958; *m* at
Villefranche-sur-Mer 26 Sept 1987, Countess Marie Valerie (*b* at
Nice 2 March 1966), dau of Ferdinand, Count Kinsky von Wchinitz
and Tettau and Countess Hedwig von Ballestrem, and has issue,
[*Kirchplatz 3, 88376 Königseggwald über Aulendorf, Württemberg,
Germany*].

    1. Count *Philipp* Maria Markus Wenzel Eusebius, *b* at
    Ravensburg 10 Aug 1988.

2. Count *Nikolaus* Maria Franziskus Eusebius Kajetan, *b* at Ravensburg 7 Aug 1990.

3. Countess *Marie-Alice* Eleonore Henriette Eusebia, *b* at Ravensburg 1 Aug 1992.

4. Countess *Marie-Gabrielle* Theresa Anna Eusebia, *b* at Ravensburg 29 Aug 1995.

3. Count *Markus* Maximilian Eusebius Johannes, *b* at Munich 16 May 1963; *m* at Königseggwald 23 May (civ) and at Hohenems 14 July (relig) 1990, Countess Philippa (*b* at St Gallen 2 Dec 1968), dau of Franz Josef, Count von Waldburg zu Zeil and Hohenems and Countess Priscilla von Schönborn-Wiesentheid, and has issue, [*Parkstraße 4, 7131 Halbturn, Burgenland, Germany*].

    1. Countess *Nathalie* Isabelle Cäcile Eusebia, *b* at Ravensburg 22 Nov 1991.

    2. Count *Constantin* Maximilian Imre Eusebius, *b* at Vienna 5 Nov 1993.

    3. Count *Géza* Paul Stefan Eusebius, *b* at Vienna 29 Jan 1998)

Brothers and Sisters

1. *Karl Seyfried* Franz Xavier Marie Eusebius Dominikus, Hereditary Count (Erbgraf) zu Königsegg-Aulendorf, *b* at Königseggwald 4 Aug 1919; ✠*k* in action in the Soviet Union 6 Oct 1942.

2. Countess *Elisabeth* Hedwig Maria Eusebia, *b* at Königseggwald 2 May 1921; ✠ at Ulm 21 April 1929.

3. Countess *Monika* Elisabeth Johanna Maria Eusebia, *b* at Königseggwald 24 June 1923, Dame Star Cross Order; *m* at Königseggwald 3 Dec 1951, Albert Germanus, Count von Rechberg und Rothenlöwen zu Hohenrechberg (*b* at Herrlinghausen 29 Nov 1912), Proprietor of Donzdorf.

[*In der Breite 2, 73072 Donzdorf, Württemberg, Germany*].

4. Countess *Paula* Maria Eusebia Julia, *b* at Aulendorf 22 May 1926; *m* at Königseggwald 25 June 1947, Joachim Egon, 10th Prince (Fürst) zu Fürstenberg (*b* at Schloß Grund, Purglitz, Bohemia 20 June 1923, ✠ at Donaueschingen 9 July 2002).

[*Salzmannhaus, 78166 Schloß Donaueschingen, Germany*].

4. Count *Maximilian* Gregor Eusebius, *b* at Vienna 13 Sept 1932; *m* at Hamburg 3 June 1967, Nessrin (*b* at Bad Harzburg 30 Aug 1943), dau of Khalil Touba and Mahsultan Tebatebai, and has issue, [*Tesdorpfstraße 22, 20148 Hamburg, Germany*].

    1. Count *Frédéric* Ali Eusebius, *b* at Hamburg 20 Feb 1969.

5. Countess *Veronika* Franz de Paula Lucia Eusebia, *b* at Munich 7
June 1938; *m* at Königseggwald 3 Sept 1968, Helmut Brand (*b* at
Düsseldorf 10 July 1932), Dr of Law, Lawyer.
[*Terrassenstraße 7, 36041 Fulda-Gläserzell, Germany*].

Brother of Father

Issue of Franz Xaver, Count zu Königsegg-Aulendorf (*b* 29 Dec 1858;
✝ 26 April 1927) and Countess Hedwig von Neipperg (*b* 22 July 1859;
m 12 June 1881; ✝ 23 Oct 1916), having had issue, among whom,

Son

Count Maria *Hermann Albrecht*, *b* at Königseggwald 27 April 1896;
✝ at Stuttgart 11 Aug 1963, Lt Württemberg Army; *m* at Stuttgart
19 Oct 1940, Eva (*b* at Stuttgart-Degerloch 15 May 1915), dau of Emil
Belz and Agnes Ellinger, and had issue,
[*Agnesstraße 17, 70597 Stuttgart - Degerloch, Germany*].

   1. Count *Harald* Hermann Erwin Eusebius, *b* at Stuttgart 31
   Jan 1942; *m* at Hilversum, Netherlands 12 April 1969,
   Margaritha Maria (*b* at Hilversum 31 Aug 1940), dau of Willem
   Hendrik Pieters and Maria Josefa Nunnemann, and has issue,
   [*Alemannenstraße 87, 71272 Renningen, Württemberg,
   Germany*].

      1. Count *Gregor* Harald Johannes Gerard Eusebius,
      b at Stuttgart 24 Feb 1970, Banker.
      2. Count *Daniel* Alexander, *b* at Munich 9 May 1973.
      3. Count *Patrick* Sascha, *b* at Munich 25 April 1975.
   2. Countess *Marina* Lucia Agnes Antoinette Esebia, *b* at
   Sigmaringen 28 March 1944; *m* at Stuttgart 5 July 1972, Bruce
   Guthier (*b* at Oak Park, Illinois, USA 20 May 1927),
   Businessman.
   [*868 Leonard Road, Los Angeles, CA 90040, U.S.A.*].

———◆———

KUEFSTEIN

**Catholic: This Family originated in Lower Austria and traditionally
take their name from Küfstein, Tyrol and are probably of the same
stock as the family of Kuofstein who can be traced authentically to
Sigihart of Kuofstein, living in 1180. This branch appear authenticated
in 18 Oct 1407; acquired Feinfeld 1414, Greillenstein 1534; Baron of
the Holy Empire with the name of "Kuefstainer, Baron zu Gailnstein
and Lord of Spitz", Prague 2 Feb 1602; Lord in Lower Austria 1602**

(both for Johann Georg Kueffstainer who ✝ 1603, since 1587 Lord of Spitz an der Donau); authorised "Herr von Kuefstain, Baron auf Greyllenstain and Herr zu Spitz", Vienna 18 Sept 1622; qualification of "Wohlgeboren", Vienna 24 June 1624; Hereditary Grand Master of the Silver in Austria an der Enns 25 June 1624 (all for Johann Jakob who ✝ 1633); Count of the Holy Empire with the qualification of "Hoch and Wohlgeboren" and ratification of Arms 13 Feb 1637 (not expedited because of the death of King Ferdinand II 15 Feb 1637); Hungarian Indigenat 1647; renewed Ebersdorf 7 Sept 1654 and Vienna 18 Feb 1709; Bohemian Incolat 1645; Grand Palatine, Vienna 8 Sept 1737; "Landmann" in Styria 1658 and 22 May 1737; foundation of the fideicommis 4 April 1699; Lord in Moravia 1725; "Landmann" in Carinthia 1736; received (ad personam) into the Swabian College of Counts of the Holy Empire 1737; "Landmann" in Carniola 14 June 1737, Goritz 3 July 1737 and in Tyrol 1739; received the qualification of "Erlaucht" (primogeniture) by the German Diet 13 Feb 1829; recognised in Austria 9 Oct 1829; Hereditary Member of the former Austrian House of Lords 18 April 1861.

Members of the family bear the title Count or Countess von Kuefstein with the qualification of Illustrious Highness for the Head of the family only.

KARL FERDINAND Franz Ernst Maria, **COUNT (GRAF) VON KUEFSTEIN**, Baron auf Greillenstein and Lord of Spitz, auf Greillenstein, Burgschleinitz, Viehofen and Zagging, *b* at Viehofen 6 March 1923, son of Ferdinand, Count von Kuefstein (*b* 1 Feb 1885; ✝ 25 March 1958) and Countess Stephanie von Marschall (*b* 18 Nov 1886; *m* 16 Sept 1920; ✝ 21 June 1974); *m* at Loosdorf 8 May 1949, Countess Gabriele (*b* at Boskowitz 7 Feb 1926), Dame Star Cross Order, dau of Eduard, Count von Mensdorff-Pouilly and Countess Giselda von Collalto und San Salvatore.

[*Schloß Greillenstein, 3592 Röhrenbach, Bez. Horn, Lower Austria*].

Sons and Daughter

1. Countess *Alexandra* Stephanie Thekla Maria, *b* at Vienna 11 April 1950, Dame Star Cross Order; *m* at Greillenstein 7 Sept 1974, Georg Friedrich, Count Kinsky von Wchinitz und Tettau (*b* at Mährisch-Kromau 27 March 1941).

[*Resselweg 13, 4222 Luftenberg, Ober Österreich, Austria*].

2. Count *Johann Georg* Ferdinand Alfons Andreas Maria, Hereditary Count (Erbgraf) von Kuefstein, *b* at Vienna 9 Aug 1951, Dr of Law; *m* at Salzburg 24 April 1977, Baroness Anna (*b* at Salzburg 16 Nov 1952), Dame Star Cross Order, dau of Christoph,

Baron von Thienen-Alderflycht and Countess Isabella Serényi von Kis-Serény, and has issue,

[*Schloßbergstraße 1, 3107 St. Pölten - Viehofen, Austria; Salmgasse 25, 1030 Vienna, Austria*].

　　　1. Count Johann-*Ferdinand* Karl Christoph Wolfgang Ignatius Maria, *b* at Salzburg 31 July 1979.

　　　[*Salmgasse 25, 1030 Vienna, Austria*].

　　　2. Countess *Catharina* Margarethe Mechtildis Maria, *b* at Salzburg 6 Nov 1980.

　　　[*Salmgasse 25, 1030 Vienna, Austria*].

　　　3. Countess *Theresa* Alexandra Gabriele Isabella Maria, *b* at Horn 11 Aug 1982; ✠ at Vienna 11 March 1987.

　　　4. Countess *Clara* Theresa Angelika Magdalena Maria, *b* at Vienna 25 July 1989.

　　　[*Salmgasse 25, 1030 Vienna, Austria*].

3. Count *Andreas* Ferdinand Alfons Eduard Maria, *b* at Vienna 9 Aug 1954; Forester; *m* at 9 May (civ) and at Eberau, Burgenland 24 May (relig) 1986, Princess Elisabeth (*b* at Leutstetten 22 Jan 1959), dau of Prince Rasso of Bavaria and Archduchess Theresa of Austria, and has issue,

[*Schloß Greillenstein, 3592 Röhrenbach, Austria*].

　　　1. Countess *Marie-Isabell,* *b* at Horn 26 Feb 1987.

　　　2. Countess *Marie-Carolin,* *b* at Horn 14 Aug 1988.

　　　3. Countess *Marie-Eleonor,* *b* at Horn 6 July 1990.

　　　4. Count *Hans-Ludwig* Maria, *b* at Horn 22 April 1996, ✠ there 22 April 1996.

　　　5. Countess Marie-Amelie, *b* at Horn 2 April 1997.

　　　6. Count *Karl* Antonius Gabriel, *b* at Horn 16 Dec 2000.

4. Count *Heinrich* Hans Manfred Maria, *b* at Vienna 18 Feb 1958; *m* at Allaud 27 Aug (civ) 1992, Andrea (*b* at Vienna 29 Dec 1960), dau of Erich Linzpichler and Irmingard Maier.

[*Björnsongasse 29, 1130 Vienna, Austria*].

　　　1. Count *Felix* Eduard Maximilian Maria, *b* at Vienna 6 Nov 1998.

Sisters

1. Countess Maria della *Pace* Karoline Anna Adelheid Theresia vom Kinde Jesu, *b* at Viehofen 2 April 1924.

[*7432 Schloß Bernstein, Burgenland, Austria*].

2. Countess *Vittoria* Gabrielle Guidobaldine, *b* at Vienna 8 Oct 1929, Dame Star Cross Order; *m* at Greillenstein 30 June 1951,

Johannes, Count von Blanckenstein (*b* at Battelau, Moravia 23 May 1923).
[*Weidern 1, 3107 St. Pölten, Austria*].

LEININGEN
(COUNTS OF SAREBRUCK)

This Seigneural family from Saargau can be traced authentically to Siegbert, Count of Sarebrugka (Sarrebruck, Treves) living in 1080; inherited the County of Liningen through the marriage of Count Simon II (✝ 1211) to Lukarde, sister and heiress of Friedrich, last Count of Liningen (✝ 1220) and took the name and arms of Liningen for their second son Friedrich 1220; acquired the County of Dagsburg (near Sarreburg, Lorraine) circa 1240; partition of lands between the sons of Count Friedrich IV in 1317 and 1318; Count Friedrich V, founder of the Line of Leiningen-Dagsburg or Alt-Leiningen. Landgrave of Leiningen 1328; Princely Landgrave 1444 (title extinct 1467, a part of their lands passed to the House of Westerburg - now also extinct); Jofried, younger brother of Friedrich V founded the line of Leiningen-Hartenburg; inherited Aspremont (Apremont, Meuse, France) through the marriage of Count Emich VII (✝ 30 March 1495) to Anne of Autel 1466; partition of lands 27 June 1560 between two sons of Count Emich IX of Leiningen-Dagsburg (*b* 1498; ✝ 10 Jan 1541), the younger son founded the Line of the Counts of Leiningen-Dagsburg-Falkenburg which is now extinct and the elder son, Johann-Philipp, 1st Count of Leiningen-Dagsburg-Hartenburg (*b* 25 Dec 1539; ✝ 8 Sept 1562) founded the Princely Line, the only line still extant; received the right of primogeniture 26 Feb 1725; confirmed 22 Feb 1753; Prince of the Holy Empire with ratification of Arms and the qualification of "Hochgeboren", Vienna 3 July 1779; compensated, with title indemnified, for the loss of possessions on the left bank of the Rhine in 1801, with Mosbach, Amorbach, Miltenberg 25 Feb 1803; Hereditary Member of the Bavarian "Reichsräte" 26 May 1818; Hereditary Member of the First Chamber of the Grand Duchy of Hesse 17 May 1820; qualification of "Durchlaucht" (primogeniture) by the German Diet 18 Aug 1825; Hereditary Member of the First Chamber of the Grand Duchy of Baden 22 May 1833.
Members of the family bear the title of Prince or Princess zu Leiningen with the qualification of Serene Highness.

There is currently a dispute, through litigation, to the succession to the Head of the Family. Prince Andreas has challenged his brother's right to the succession on the basis of a marriage which it is claimed is not in accordance with the Family Statutes.

KARL-EMICH Nikolaus Friedrich Hermann, **8TH PRINCE (FÜRST) ZU LEININGEN,** Pfalzgraf zu Mosbach, Graf zu Dürn, Herr zu Amorbach, Miltenberg, Bischofsheim, Boxberg, Hardheim, Schüfp and Lauda, *b* at Amorbach 12 June 1952, son of Emich, 7th Prince (Fürst) zu Leiningen, etc (*b* 18 Oct 1926; ✠ 30 Oct 1991) and Duchess Eilika of Oldenburg (*b* 2 Feb 1928; *m* 10 Aug 1950); *m* 1stly at Amorbach 8 June (civ) and at Neuenstein, Württemberg 16 June (relig) 1984, Princess Margarita (*b* at Munich 28 April 1960; ✠*k* in a car accident nr Freising 27 Feb 1989), dau of Kraft, Prince (Fürst) zu Hohenlohe-Oehringen and Katharina von Siemens. He *m* 2ndly at Munich 24 May (civ) and at Venice 15 June (relig) 1991 (*m* diss by div at Munich 3 March 1998), *Gabriele* Renate Thyssen.(*b* at Frankfurt-am-Main 1 April 1963, dau of Helmut Friedhelm Homey and Renate Kerkhoff, assumed the family name of her step-father, Bodo Thyssen; She *m* 2ndly at Aiglemont, France 30 May 1998; Prince Karim (IV) Aga Khan (*b* 13 Dec 1936), and is styled HH Begum Juaara Aga Khan, [*Aiglemont, 60270 Gouviex, France*]. [*63916 Amorbach, Odenwald, Germany*].

Daughter - 1st Marriage
1. Princess *Cecilia* Maria Stephanie, *b* at Frankfurt-am-Main 10 June 1988.

Daughter - 2nd Marriage
2. Princess *Theresa* Anna Elisabeth, *b* at Frankfurt-am-Main 26 April 1992.

Brother and Sisters
1. Princess *Melita* Elisabeth Bathildis Helene Margarita, *b* at Amorbach 10 June 1951.
[*63916 Amorbach, Odenwald, Germany*].
2. Prince *Andreas,* *b* at Frankfurt-am-Main 27 Nov 1955, Banker; *m* at Amorbach 5 Oct (civ) and Gmunden, Austria 11 Oct (relig) 1981, Princess Alexandra (*b* at Hanover 18 Feb 1959), dau of Ernst August, Prince of Hanover, of Great Britain and Ireland, Duke of Brunswick and Princess Ortrud of Schleswig-Holstein-Sonderburg-Glücksburg, and has issue,
[*60596 Frankfurt-am-Main, Germany*].

    1. Prince *Ferdinand* Heinrich Emich Christian Karl, *b* at Frankfurt-am-Main 12 Aug 1982.
    2. Princess *Olga* Margarita Valerie Elisabeth Stephanie Alexandra, *b* at Frankfurt-am-Main 24 Oct 1984.

3. Prince *Hermann* Ernst Johann Albrecht Paul, *b* at
Frankfurt-am-Main 13 Sept 1987.

3. Princess *Stephanie* Margarita, *b* at Frankfurt-am-Main 1 Oct 1958.
[*63916 Amorbach, Odenwald, Germany*].

Mother

Eilika, Dowager Princess zu Leiningen, *b* at Lensahn 2 Feb 1928,
dau of Nikolaus, Hereditary Grand Duke of Oldenburg and Princess
Helene of Waldeck and Pyrmont; *m* at Rastede 10 Aug 1950, Emich,
7th Prince (Fürst) zu Leiningen, etc (*b* at Coburg 18 Oct 1926; ✠ at
Amorbach 30 Oct 1991).

[*63916 Amorbach, Odenwald, Germany*].

Brothers and Sisters of Father

Issue of Karl, 6th Prince zu Leiningen (*b* 13 Feb 1898; ✠ 2 Aug 1946)
and Grand Duchess Maria Kirillovna of Russia (*b* 2 Feb 1907; *m* 24
Nov 1924; ✠ 27 Oct 1951), among whom,

1. Prince *Karl* Wladimir Ernst Heinich, *b* at Coburg 2 Jan 1928; ✠
at Vered Hagalil, MP Korazim Israel 28 Sept 1990; *m* 1stly at
Amorbach 14 Feb (civ) and at Cannes 20 Feb (relig) 1957 (*m* diss by
div at Frankfurt-am-Main 4 Dec 1968), Princess Marie Louise
[*236 Woodland Road, Madison, N.J. 07940, U.S.A.*] (*b* at Sofia 13 Jan
1933; *m* 2ndly at Toronto, Ontario, Canada 16 Nov 1969, Bronislaw
Chrobok who was *b* at Kattowitz 27 Aug 1933, Investment Banker),
dau of King Boris III, King of Bulgaria, Duke of Saxony and Princess
Giovanna (Joanna) of Savoy, and has issue,

[*8762 Amorbach, Odenwald, Germany*].

    1. Prince Karl *Boris* Frank Markwart, *b* at Toronto, Ontario,
Canada 17 April 1960; *m* 1stly at West Field, New Jersey 14
Feb 1987 (*m* diss by div 9 July 1996), *Millena* Eileen (*b* at
Sofia 22 Aug 1962), dau of Wladimir Manov and Elly Nedeva,
and has issue,

        1. Prince *Nicolas* Alexander Karel Friedrich, *b* at
Philadelphia 25 Oct 1991.

Prince Karl *m* 2ndly at Neptune New Jersey 11 Sept 1998,
Cheryl Anne (*b* at Jersey City, New Jersey 9 Aug 1962), dau
of Henry Francis Riegler and Janice Rankin and has further
issue,

[*518 Central Avenue, Union Beach, N.J. 07735, USA*].

    2. Prince *Karl* Heinrich, *b* at Long Branch, New Jersey

17 Feb 2001.

2. Prince *Hermann* Friedrich Roland Fernando, *b* at Toronto 16 April 1963; *m* at Oakville 11 March (civ) and 16 May (relig) 1987, Deborah (*b* at Belfast 2 Dec 1961), dau of Robert Cully and Myrna Ruth, and has issue,

[*84 Raymar Place, Oakville, Ontario, Canada, L6J 6M1*].

> 1. Princess *Tatjana* Victoria Maureen, *b* at Toronto 27 Aug 1989.
> 2. Princess *Nadia* Christianne Ruth, *b* at Toronto 16 Dec 1991.
> 3. Princess *Alexandra*, Sophia Marie *b* at Oakville 18 Dec 1997.

2. Princess *Kira* Melita Feodora Marie Victoria Alexandra, *b* 18 July 1930; *m* at Langton Green, nr Tunbridge Wells 28 Sept (civ) and at Amorbach 12 Oct (relig) 1963 (*m* diss by div at Frankfurt-am-Main 10 July 1972), Prince Andrej of Yugoslavia (*b* at Bled, Slovinia 28 June 1929; ✠ at Irvine, California, USA 7 May 1990). He *m* 1stly Princess *Christina* Margarethe, *b* at Kronberg 10 Jan 1933; *m* at Kronberg 1 Aug (civ) and at Kronberg-im-Taunus 2 Aug (relig) 1956; that *m* diss by div at London 31 May 1962; she *m* 2ndly in London 3 Dec 1962 (*m* diss by div at London 3 Feb 1986), Robert Floris van Eyck (*b* at The Hague, 3 May 1916; ✠ at Ashford 19 Dec 1991), dau of Prince Christoph of Hesse and Princess Sophie of Greece and Denmark. Prince Andrej *m* 3rdly at Palm Springs, California 30 March 1974, Eva Maria (*b* at Vrnjacka Banja 26 Aug 1926; *m* 1stly F Lowe; that *m* diss by div 1973), dau of Milan Andjelkovi*f* and Eva Jovanovi*f*.

[*Flat 4, 6 Frognal, Hampstead, London N.W.3.*].

3. Princess *Mechtilde* Alexandra, *b* at Würzburg 2 Jan 1936; *m* at Amorbach 25 Nov 1961, Karl-Anton Bauscher (*b* at Grafenwöhr, OPfalz 26 Aug 1931, Engineer.

[*Ohmstraße 6, 96050 Bamberg, Germany*].

4. Prince *Friedrich* Wilhelm Berthold, *b* at Würzburg 18 June 1938, ✠ at Miesbach nr Tegernsee, Bavaria, 31 Aug 1998, *m* 1stly at Würzburg 9 July 1960 (*m* diss by div at Würzburg 4 July 1962), Karin Evelyne Göss (*b* at Nuremberg 27 May 1942). He *m* 2ndly at Gemünden 23 Aug 1971, Helga (*b* at Gemünden 5 Jan 1940), dau of Hans Eschenbacher and Sophie Theobald.

[*Torhaus 168, 69427 Schloßau, Germany*].

Brother of Grandfather

Issue of Emich, 5th Prince zu Leiningen (*b* 18 Jan 1866; ✝ 18 July 1939) and Princess Feodora zu Hohenlohe-Langenburg (*b* 23 July 1866; *m* 12 July 1894; ✝ 1 Nov 1932), having had issue, among whom,

Son

Prince *Hesso* Leopold Heinrich, *b* at Amorbach, 29 July 1903; ✝ at Pförn, nr Rottach-Egern, Bavaria 19 June 1967; *m* at Amorbach 11 July (civ) and at Schweiklberg 12 July (relig) 1933, Countess Marie Louise (*b* at Honnef am Rhein 31 July 1905), dau of Franz, Count von Nesselrode, Proprietor of Burg Vilszelt near Unkel am Rhein, etc and Maria-Rita von Weise, and adopted a son,

[*Hessosruh, Pförn 83700 Rottach-Egern, Germany; Artur Kutscher Platz 1, 80802 Munich, Germany*].

> 1. Prince Franz *Hesso* Hubertus Maria Siegbert Viktor Philipp Maximilian Karl, *b* at Pernitz, Austria 10 March 1944 as Wolfgang Karl von Renteln; adopted 19 May / 29 Aug 1950; officially became a Prince of Leiningen 13 Feb 1953, Director Deutsche Bank AG, Paris.
>
> [*c/o Deutsche Bank, 10 Place Vendome, 75001 Paris, France*].

LEYEN

(✝ Extinct ✝)

Catholic: This feudal family from Trier have been recognised since 1158 are documented in 1272 with Werner von der Leyen, under the name of Guntreve (Gondorf-sur-Mosel, near Mayen) who resided in the fortified castle of Leyen (or Gondorf); Baron of the Holy Empire with the qualification of "Wohlgeboren", Ratisbon 20 Sept 1653; invested with Hohengeroldseck (near Offenburg, Baden) 1705, Count of the Holy Empire with the qualification of "Hoch and Wohlgeboren", Frankfurt-am-Main 22 Nov 1711; received into the Swabian College of Counts of the Holy Empire 1711, Count of the Austrian Hereditary States 5 Feb 1716; assumed the title of Prince on joining the Confederation of the Rhine 12 July 1806, Hereditary Member of the First Chamber of the Grand Duchy of Baden 1819; received the title of "Durchlaucht" (primogeniture) by the German Diet 18 Aug 1825. Members of the family bear the title of Prince or Princess von der Leyen and Hohengeroldseck with the qualification of Serene Highness.

✠ **FERDINAND** Maria Erwein Harthard Antonius Michael Joseph, **6TH PRINCE VON DER LEYEN and HOHENGEROLDSECK,** Lord of Waal and Unterdiessen, *b* at Waal 5 May 1898; ✠ at Munich 9 Sept 1971, Kt Order of St George, son of Erwein, 4th Prince von der Leyen and Hohengeroldseck (*b* 31 March 1863; ✠ 18 Sept 1938) and Altgravine Marie Charlotte zu Salm-Reifferscheidt-Krautheim and Dyck (*b* 14 April 1867; *m* 22 May 1890; ✠ 4 April 1944).

Brother

Erwein Otto Phillip Leopold Franz Joseph Ignatius, **5th Prince von der Leyen and Hohengeroldseck,** Herr zu Waal and Unterdiessen, *b* at Waal 31 Aug 1894; ✠ at Rome 13 Feb 1970; *m* at Rome 10 Jan 1924, Donna Maria Nives (*b* at Rome 16 Aug 1898; ✠ there 6 Aug 1971), Dame Star Cross Order, dau of Antonio, Prince Ruffo, Prince della Scaletta, etc and Donna Ludovica of the Princes Borghese, and had issue, among whom,

1. Princess *Maria Antonia* Ernestina Johanna Josefa Michaela Gabriele, *b* at Munich 22 Dec 1927, Lady of Justice Constantinian Order of St George.
[*Schloß, 8939 Waal, Schwaben; SchellingStraße 138, 80797 Munich, Germany*].

4. Princess *Marie-Adelheid* Fernanda Helene, *b* at Rome 17 May 1929, Dame Star Cross Order; *m* at Rome 27 April 1957, Georg, Baron von Freyberg-Eisenberg (*b* at Nictheroy, Brazil 10 March 1926), Proprietor of Haldenwang and Unter-Knöringen, Dipl Forestry, and has issue, (*Inter Alius*)
[*v.-Freyberg-Straße 4, Schloß, 8871 Haldenwang, nr. Günzburg*].

    1. *Philipp* Erwein Konrad Alfred Eugen Bonifatius Melchoir Georg Arbogast, *b* at Krumbach Swabia 14 May 1967, adopted by his grandfather Erwein, 5th Prince von der Leyen 1969 and has borne the name and style of **Prince von der Leyen and Hohengeroldseck** since his adoption, and subsequent issue have also borne the style prince or princess from Christening, Proprietor of Schloß Waal; *m* at Salzburg 1 Oct 1989, Baroness Elisabeth (*b* at Salzburg 17 Sept 1969), dau of Claus, Baron von Gagern and Erica Swoboda, and has issue,
[*Fürst-von-der-Leyen-Platz 1, 86875 Waal, Germany*].

1. Prince *Wolfram* Georg Erwein Carl Friedrich Lorenz Eugen Arbogast, *b* at Oxford 22 Nov 1990.

2. Prince *Georg* Erwein Maximilian Nikolaus Vittorio Hubertus Eugen Arbogast, *b* at Schwabmünchen 27 Jan 1992.

3. Princess Maria *Cecilia* Elisabeth Maurizia Ludovica Alice Ernestine, *b* at Landsberg am Lech 12 Jan 1999.

4. Princess Maria *Nives* Alexandra Nicola Eugenie Adelheid Gisela, *b* at Landsberg am Lech 13 Feb 2001.

LOBKOWICZ

Catholics: Feudal family from Bohemia; Nicolaus de Ujezd, Lord of Milcoves, took the name of the Castle of Lobkovic, acquired by his father, Mares d'Ujezd in 1408 and took the name of "Nicolaus de Ujezd alias de Lobkowicz"; Lord in Bohemia since 1479; Prince of the Holy Empire, Vienna 17 Aug 1624; erection of the Lordship of Neustadt an der Waldnaab into the Princely County of Sternstein, Ravensburg 23 Aug 1641 (the County was sold to Bavaria in 1807; with the title reserved); acquired the Duchy of Sagan (in Silesia, which was sold 1785) 9 July 1646; received into the College of Princes of the Holy Empire (for the Head of Sternstein) 30 June 1653; Hungarian Indigenat 20 Nov 1663; foundation of a fideicommis under the principle of primogeniture in the Will of Wenzel Eusebius, Duke of Sagan 10 Feb 1677; transferred to free property of the last usufruct by family contract 4 May 1925. The branches below descend from the two sons (half-brothers) of Prince Ferdinand August (*b* 7 Sept 1655; ✝ 3 Oct 1715); a family convention agreed the spelling of the name as "Lobkowicz" 9 Jan 1919.

Members of the family bear the title of Prince or Princess of Lobkowicz with the qualification of Serene Highness

LINE I

Founded by Prince Philipp-Hyacinth (*b* 26 Feb 1680; ✝ 21 Dec 1734). The Ducal title of Sagan (see below) was transferred to Raudnitz, Vienna 3 May 1786; received the qualification of "Durchlaucht" (primogeniture) by the German Diet 7 Oct 1825; confirmed in Austria 7 Oct 1825; extended to all members of the family 27 April 1869; "Landmann" in Styria 30 May 1836; Hereditary Member of the former Austrian House of Lords 18 April 1861.

JAROSLAV Franz von Assisi Klemens Gabriel Eleonora Josef Anton Johann Bosco Joachim Felix Maria, **14TH PRINCE OF LOBKOWICZ,** Duke von and zu Raudnitz, Princely Count of Sternstein, *b* at Pilsen 16 Aug 1942, Dipl Engineer, Kt of Hon Sovereign Military Order of Malta, Kt Bavarian Order of St George, son of Jaroslav, 13th Prince of Lobkowicz (*b* 18 June 1910; ✠ 7 May 1985) and Countess Gabrielle von Korff gennant Schmising-Kerssenbrock (*b* 29 Nov 1917; *m* 11 July 1940); *m* at Chévry-en-Sereine 29 July 1971, Elisabeth (*b* at Paris 25 Aug 1947), dau of Guy de Vienne and Geneviéve Mouchet de Battefort de Laubespin.
[*Plzenská 401, 32200 Plzen-Krimice, Czech Republic; Snemovní 11, 11800 Prague 1, Czech Republic*].

Sons and Daughters

1. Prince *Vladimir* Jaroslav Johann Jerome Guy Clemens Franz, Hereditary Prince of Lobkowicz, *b* at Paris 15 Dec 1972.
[*Plzenská 401, 32200 Plzen-Krimice, Czech Republic*].
2. Prince *Jaroslav* Nikolaus Johann Geoffrey Friedrich Guy Franz, *b* at Paris 15 July 1974, member of the Congregation of the Legion of Christ.
[*Legionari di Christo, Via degli Aldobrandeschi 190, 00163 Rome, Italy*].
3. Prince *Philippe* Louis Jean-Paul Wenzelas Marie Guy Jaroslav, *b* at Boulogne-sur-Seine 26 Aug 1981.
[*Snemovní 11, 11800 Prague 1, Czech Republic*].

Mother

Gabrielle, Dowager Princess of Lobkowicz, dau of Clemens, Count von Korff gennant Schmising-Kerssenbrock and Countess Marianne von Waldstein, Herrin von Wartenberg, *b* at Klattau, Bohemia 29 Nov 1917, Dame Star Cross Order; *m* at Prague 11 July 1940, Jaroslav Claude Friedrich Aloys, 13th Prince of Lobkowicz, etc (*b* at Zámacek-Pilsen 18 June 1910; ✠ at Krimitz 7 May 1985; *succ* his brother, Friedrich Franz, 12th Prince of Lobkowicz, 1954).
[*Plzenská 401, CS-32200 Plzen-Krimice, Czech Republic*].

Brothers and Sisters

1. Princess Marie Lapidata *Polyxena* Anna Clementine Jaroslava Aloisia Gabrielle Theresia Cunigonde Melanie Paula de Cruce Walburga Eleonora Leopoldina Antonia Odilia Johanna Bosco Josefa, *b* at Prague 28 April 1941; *m* at Vejprnice, nr Pilsen 22 April 1961, Theobald, Count Czernin von and zu Chudinitz (*b* at Prague 7 July

1936).

[*28901 Dimokury 1, Czech Republic*].

2. Princess Marie Immaculata *Leopoldine* Clementina Aloisia Theresia Jaroslava Gabriella Antonia Eleonora Anna Odilia Marta, *b* at Pilsen 8 Dec 1943, Dame Star Cross Order; *m* at Vejprnice 4 July 1964, Bosco, Count von Sternberg (*b* at Prague 25 Nov 1936).

[*Riegerova ul. 244, 33900 Klatovy, Czech Republic*].

3. Prince *Franz* von Assisi Karl Friedrich Klemens Jaroslav Alois Leopold Gerhard Telesporus Odilius Johann Bosco Paul Marie, *b* at Pilsen 5 Jan 1948, Ordained as a Priest at Prague 15 Aug 1972, Bishop of Prague (consecrated at Prague 7 April 1990).

[*Biskupstvi Ostravské Opavé, Namesti Msgra Sramka 4, 71000 Ostrava, Czech Republic*].

4. Prince *Zdenko* Adalbert Clemens Jaroslav Alois Franz von Assisi Gerhart Albert Pius Maria, *b* at Pilsen 8 April 1954, Librarian, Ordained as a Priest at Prague 13 Jan 1990 in the Praemonstratenser Order.

[*Farni urad, 35007 Cheb[Eger] Czech Republic*].

Brothers and Sisters of Father

Issue of Jaroslav, 11th Prince of Lobkowicz (*b* 26 March 1877; ✠ 24 Oct 1953) and Countess Marie de Beaufort Spontin (*b* 6 Aug 1885; *m* 11 May 1905; ✠ 22 Feb 1942), having had issue, among whom,

1. Princess Marie *Kunigonde* Melanie Margarete Franziska Friederike Antonia, *b* at Krimitz, Pilsen 11 Sept 1906, Dame Star Cross Order; *m* at Krimitz 13 June 1932, Charles, Count van Limburg-Stirum (*b* at Huldenberg 15 Sept 1906; ✠ at Brussels 14 June 1989), Belgian Senator, Master of the Court of Leopold III.

[*Val des Seigneurs 32/66, 1150 Brussels, Belgium*].

2. Princess *Gabrielle* Therese Caroline Frederika Pia Jeanne Marie, *b* at Krimitz 8 Jan 1919, Dr of Law.

[*Jhulverského 9, 37000 Ceské Budéjovice [Budweis] Czech Republic*].

3. Prince *Johann* Nepomuk Emanuel Maria Joseph, *b* at Krimitz 25 Dec 1920, ✠ at Breuilpont 10 Feb 2000, Dr of Law, Kt of Hon Sovereign Military Order of Malta; *m* 1stly at Breuilpont 25 June (civ) and at Paris 29 June (relig) 1945, Countess Marie Therese (*b* at Lösch, nr Brünn 23 April 1922; ✠ at Breuilpont 3 June 1978), Dame Star Cross Order, dau of Karl, Count of Belcredi, Proprietor of Lösch and Countess Therese Kálnoky von Köröspatak. He *m* 2ndly at Breuilpont 19 Dec 1981, Countess Pauline (*b* at Berlin 7 April 1926),

dau of Louis, Count von Ursel and Genevieve le Peletier de Rosanbo, and had issue by his first wife,

[*27640 Château Breuilpont, Dept Eure, France; 1 rue Auguste Vacquerie, 75116 Paris, France*].

    1. Prince *Wenzel* Eusebius Karl Jaroslav Friedrich Johann Ludwig Maria et omnes Sancti Patroni Bohemiae, *b* at Paris 14 March 1953, Mag jur, Kt Bavarian Order of St George; *m* at Salperwick, Pas de Calais 4 April 1981, Armelle (*b* at Lille 23 Dec 1955), dau of Phillipe de Guillebon and Soizik Didelot of the Barons Didelot, and has issue,

    [*33 Rue Jules Lejeune, 1050 Brussels, Belgium; 27640 Château de Breuilpont, Dept Eure, France*].

        1. Prince *Jan* Philippe Louis Jaroslave Marie Joseph Cheron et omnes Sancti Patroni Bohemiae, *b* at Paris 12 Dec 1987.

        2. Prince *Aloys* Richard Jean Marie Joseph et omnes Sancti Patroni Bohemiae, *b* at Paris 14 June 1992.

        3. Prince *Karl* Wenceslas Marie Joseph et omnes Sancti Patroni Bohemiae, *b* at Brussels 18 Oct 1993.

        4. Prince *Nicolas* Cyrille Marie Joseph et omnes Sancti Patroni Bohemiae, *b* at Brussels 18 Oct 1993 (twin with Karl).

    2. Princess *Therese* Eleonore Marie Kunigonde Melanie et omnes Snacti Patroni Bohemiae, *b* at Paris 20 Oct 1954, Lic jur; *m* at Breuilpont 21 April 1979, Claude de Langle of the Marquesses de Langle (*b* at Neuilly-sur-Seine 18 Nov 1947), Engineer, Lic sc ec.

    [*160 rue de l'Université, 75007 Paris, France; Château St Elier, St Jouan-des-Guérets, 35430 Chateauneuf-Ille-Vilaine, France*].

    3. Princess *Marguerite* (*Margit*) Melanie Therese Marie Jaroslava Anna Richarda Zdenka et omnes Sancti Bohemiae, *b* at Paris 9 September 1957, Dame Star Cross Order; *m* at Brieulpont 23 May 1981, Thierry de La Rochefoucauld of the Dukes d'Estissac (*b* at Paris 19 June 1949), Dipl sc commerce.

    [*51 Rue de Passy, 75016 Paris, France*].

4. Prince *Christian* Friedrich Karl Jaroslav Aloys Anton Johann Pius Maria, *b* at Krimitz 12 June 1924, ✠ 2 Sept 2001, Agricultural Engineer, Kt of Hon Sovereign Military Order of Malta; *m* at Kremsmünster 26 June 1954, Countess Maria-Theresia (*b* at Prague 1 Aug 1922), Dame Star Cross Order, dau of Ferdinand, Count zu

Trauttmansdorff-Weinsberg and Princess Marie zu Schwarzenberg, and has issue,

[*70 chaussée de Charleroi, 1060 Brussels, Belgium*].

    1. Prince *Ferdinand* Johannes Jaroslav Eleonore Karl Anton Pius Maria, *b* at Ipamu, Belgian Congo 17 Dec 1955, Kt of Hon Sovereign Military Order of Malta, Kt Bavarian Order of St George.

    [*70 chaussée de Charleroi, 1060 Brussels, Belgium*].

    2. Prince *Ladislav* Friedrich Joseph Karl Camille Christian Pius Maria, *b* at Ipamu 11 June 1957, Kt of Hon Sovereign Military Order of Malta; *m* at Tongres, Limburg, Belgium 20 July 1985, Anne (*b* at Tongres 18 March 1964), dau of Xavier, Count de Briey and Béatrice de Schaetzen of the Barons de Schaetzen, and has issue,

    [*Grand Lambroux 2, 1440 Braine-le-Château, Belgium*].

        1. Princess *Ludmilla* Francine Béatrice Marie-Thérèse Isabelle, *b* at Brussels 4 Nov 1986.

        2. Princess *Ysaline* Béatrice Ladislav Ferdinand, *b* at Brussels 26 Aug 1988.

        3. Prince *Christian* Ladislas Patrick Xavier, *b* at Brussels 17 Dec 1991.

        4. Prince *Maximilian* Xavier Ludmilla, *b* at Brussels 24 Aug 1994.

    3. Princess Marie *Isabelle* Christine Wilhelmine Jaroslava Andrea Pia Bartolemia, *b* at Knokke-sur-Mer, Belgium 24 Aug 1960.

    [*70 chaussée de Charleroi, 1060 Brussels, Belgium*].

6. Prince *Ladislav* Otto Karl Friedrich Rafael Alois Johann Nepomuk Pius Maria, *b* at Krimitz 24 Oct 1925, ✠ at Uccle 28 Jan 1986, (reg into the Belgium Nobility 31 Aug 1957 by Diploma 12 Feb 1958 as "Prince de Lobkowicz" with the qualification Serene Highness), Lic sc hist, Cmdr Bavarian Order of St George, Kt of Obedience Sovereign Military Order of Malta, Kt Gd Cross Constantinian Order of St George; *m* at Maleves, Brabant 28 Aug 1954, Countess Thérèse (*b* at Brussel 23 Jan 1932), dau of Etienne, Count d'Elzius du Chenoy and Countess Nathalie d'Oultremont, and has issue,

[*50 avenue Winston Churchill, 1180 Brussels; Sternstein, 1360 Thorembais-les-Béguines, Belgium*].

    1. Prince *Stepán Ladislav* Pie Marie Ghislain, *b* at Louvain 29 July 1957, lic jur, Lawyer, Member of City Government of Brussels, Kt of Hon Sovereign Military Order of Malta, Kt of

Justice Constantinian Order of St George; *m* at Moulbaix, Hennegau 15 Sept 1984, Countess Barbara (*b* at Ath 30 May 1957), lic jur, dau of Aymard, Count von Ursel and Viscountess Nadine de Spoelberch, and has issue,
[*466 A, Avenue Dolez, 1180 Brussels, Belgium; Château de Moulbaix, 7812 Moulbaix, Belgium*].

> 1. Prince *Léopold* Ladislas Aymard Claude Pie Marie, *b* at Uccle 9 Sept 1989.
>
> 2. Prince *Frederic* Aymard Ladislas Jean Népomucène Pie Marie, *b* at Uccle 6 May 1991.
>
> 3. Prince *Ariane* Thérèse Nathalie Colienne Ludovic Marie, *b* at Uccle 30 Jan 1996.

2. Princess *Nathalie* Pie Charlotte Marie de Lorette Ghislaine *b* at Louvain 17 Dec 1958, lic sc oec, Radio Officer Belgian Merchant Navy; *m* at Brussels July 1997 Count Jan (*Yannick*) Antoine Henri Marie Robert d'Ursel (*b* at Uccle 8 June 1950).
[*Avenue Maurice 31, bte 14, 1050 Brussels, Belgium*].

3. Prince *Bernard Ladislav* Philipe Pie Marie, *b* at Louvain 14 May 1960, lic sc pol, Kt of Hon Sovereign Military Order of Malta; *m* at Brussels 30 Sept 1995, Sophie-Aimée (*b* at Paris 31 Oct 1966), dau of Dominique Lefebvre and Claudie Rayroux Le Juge de Segrais, and has issue,
[*Teniersdreef 10, 3090 Overijse, Belgium*].

> 1. Princess *Cordélia* Marguerite Gaëtanne Colombe Sophie Marie Polyxène et tous les Saints Patrons de Bohême, *b* at Uccle, Belgium 20 Nov 1996.
>
> 2. Prince *Rodolphe* Ladislas Dominique Bruno Bernard Jean-Népomucène Marie Popel et tous les Saints-Patrons de Bohême, b at Uccle, Belgium 3 Jan 2001.

6. Princess Marie *Melanie* Johanna Therese vom Kinde Jesu Frederika Anna-Agnes Pia, *b* at Krimitz 28 Jan 1928; *m* at Breuilpont, Eure, France 4 Nov 1961, Pierre Bazinet (*b* at Angouleme 13 Dec 1925).
[*La Malignerie, 25 Route de la Croix, 28520 Sorel-Moussel, France*].

Elder Brother of Great-Grandfather

Issue of Franz Joseph Maximilian, 7th Prince of Lobkowicz (*b* 8 Dec 1772; ✠ 15 Dec 1816) and Princess Marie-Caroline von Schwarzenberg (*b* 7 Sept 1775; *m* 2 Aug 1792; ✠ 24 Jan 1816), having had issue, among whom,

Son

Ferdinand Joseph, 8th Prince of Lobkowicz, *b* at Oberhellerbrunn 13 April 1797; ✝ at Vienna 18 Dec 1868; *m* there 9 Sept 1826, Princess Marie (*b* 31 Dec 1808; ✝ 24 May 1871), dau of Maurice Joseph, Prince von and zu Liechtenstein and Princess Leopoldine Esterházy von Galántha, and had issue, among whom,

Son

Moritz Aloyse Joseph Marcellin, **9th Prince of Lobkowitz,** Duke of Raudnitz, Princely Count of Sternstein, etc, Kt Order of the Golden Fleece, Kt Sovereign Military Order of Malta, Imperial and Royal Chamberlain and Privy Councillor, *b* at Inzersdorf, nr Vienna 2 June 1831; ✝ at Roudnice 4 Feb 1903, renounced the possession of his properties 21 Oct 1920, without the rights as Head of the House, to his son Maximilian by declaration certified at Bilin 23 Aug 1933; *m* at Prague 21 April 1857, Princess Marie-Anna (*b* at Wallerstein 1 Feb 1839; ✝ at Koswig 23 Dec 1912), dau of Friedrich, Prince and Lord (Fürst and Herr) zu Oettingen-Wallerstein and Landgravine Sophie von Fürstenburg, having had issue, among whom,

Son

Ferdinand Zdenko Maria, **10th Prince of Lobkowicz,** etc, Kt Order of the Golden Fleece, Kt Sov Order of Malta, *b* at Prague 23 Jan 1858; ✝ at Nelahozeves 22 Dec 1938, resigned 21 Oct 1920 when he was succeeded by his second cousin, Jaroslav, 11th Prince of Lobkowicz; *m* at Vienna 4 Sept 1884, Countess Maria Anna Bertha (*b* at Prague 7 Aug 1857; ✝ at Komotau, Bohemia 9 April 1932), dau of Karl Erwin, Count and Lord von Neipperg and Princess Rosa of Lobkowicz, and had issue, among whom,

Sons

1. Prince *Ferdinand Joseph* Maria Moritz Johannes der Evangelist, *b* at Bilin 27 Dec 1885; ✝ at Prague 10 Jan 1953, renounced his rights of succession as Head of the Princely House 20 Oct 1920, Dr of Law, Imperial and Royal Chamberlain; *m* at Prague 5 Feb 1921, Clotilde Leopoldine (Ilka) Volkov (*b* at Vienna 6 Dec 1888; ✝ at Munich 23 Jan 1970), and had issue,

    1. Princess *Ludmilla* Maria Rosario Anna-Bertha Angela Magdalena Leopoldine, *b* at Prague 1 Oct 1922; ✝ there 1 Dec 1952; *m* at Geneva 30 Aug 1947, Albert de Ridder (*b* at

Biarritz 13 May 1918).

[*Les Troubadours, 1883 Arveys-Villars, Vaud, Switzerland*].

2. Prince *Maximilian Erwin* Maria Joseph Antonius von Padua Heinrich Thomas, *b* at Bilin 29 Dec 1888; ✠ at Dover, Mass USA 1 April 1967, Dr of Law, Czechoslovakian Ambassador; *m* at London 1 Dec 1924, Gillian Margaret Hope (*b* at London 16 Oct 1890; ✠ at Dover, Mass 2 March 1982; *m* 1stly 30 June 1911, Francis Hugh Bonham-Carter; that *m* diss by div at London 1923), dau of Aylmer Coghill Somerville and Emmeline Sophie Sykes, and had issue,

    1. Prince *Martin* Maximilian Georg, *b* at London 21 Dec 1928; *m* at Lexington, Kentucky, USA 12 Sept 1952, Margaret Juett (*b* at Lexington 27 Aug 1930), and has issue,

[*270 Dedham Street, Dover, MA 02030, U.S.A.*].

        1. Prince *Martin* Maximilian, *b* at Lexington 23 Aug 1954; *m* at Webster 25 Sept 1983, Diana (*b* at Webster 24 April 1958), dau of Richard Woznicki and Virginia Grzych, and has issue,

            1. Princess *Elisabeth* Amalie, *b* at Boston 3 April 1988.

            2. Prince *Richard* Martin, *b* at Newton 5 April 1990.

        2. Prince *John* Brooks, *b* at Boston, Mass. 31 Dec 1956.

        3. Princess *Margaret* Somerville, *b* at Boston 25 Sept 1959.

        4. Prince *William* Easton, *b* at Boston, Massachusetts 7 April 1961; *m* at Cohasset, Massachusetts, 14 Sept 1992, Alexandra (*b* at Boston 28 Aug 1963) dau of Radu Florescu and Nicole Michel, and has issue.

            1. Prince *William* Rudolf *b* at Boston 5 Sept 1994.

            2. Princess *Ileana* Yvonne, *b* at Boston 15 May 1997.

            3. Princess *Sophia*, *b* at Prague, 19 Oct 2001.

2. Prince *Dominik* Nikolaus Patrik, *b* at London 6 Dec 1930; *m* 1stly at Concord, Mass 8 June 1955 (*m* diss by div 23 April 1971), Louise Brooks(*b* at Boston 18 Oct 1931). He *m* 2ndly at Falmouth, Mass 11 Aug 1972, Sarah Elisabeth Stafanoni (*b* at Boston 18 April 1938), and has issue by his first wife,

[*Gross Street, Dover, Mass 02030, USA*].

        1. Prince *Nicholas* Henry, *b* at Boston 3 Feb 1957; *m* at Reno, Nevada, USA 28 May 1977, Sally (*b* at Reno 27

Oct 1956), dau of Jack Shaw and Zeldy ..., and has issue,

> > 1. Princess *Nicole* Anne, *b* at Rockport, Maine 14 July 1981.
> > 2. Princess *Hope* Sandra, *b* at Key West, Florida 16 May 1983.
> > 3. Prince *Dominik*, *b* at Rockport, Maine 22 March 1985.

> 2. Princess *Louisa* Brooks, *b* at Boston 1 Oct 1958; *m* at ......, Steven Parady (*b* at ......).
> 3. Prince *Thomas* Brooks, *b* at Boston 29 Nov 1960, *m* at Wilmington, Delaware 1988, Amanda Ann (*b* at Wilmington 1 Aug 1965), dau of John McGrath and Margaret ......, and has issue,

> > 1. Prince *Henry* Brooks, *b* at Stomybrook, New York 17 Oct 1990.
> > 2. Prince *John* Ryan, *b* at Longbranch, New York 28 July 1992.

> 4. Princess *Gillian* Somerville, *b* at Boston 24 July 1963.

3. Prince *Oliver* Carl Jan, *b* at London 15 April 1934; ✠ at Greenwich, Conn USA 25 May 1972; *m* at Perickley, Pennsylvania 19 Sept 1960, Marjorie G (*b* at Pittsburgh, Penn 30 April 1935), dau of Alex Hunter and Marjorie ..., and has issue,

> 1. Prince *Mark* Oliver, *b* at New York 20 March 1962; *m* at Dedham, Mass 6 June 1981, Anita (*b* at Boston 29 Dec 1960), dau of Dominic Torraco and Mary Leticia McGhee, and has issue,

> > 1. Prince *Joshua* Paul, *b* at Dedham 26 Nov 1981.

> 2. Princess *Andrea* Stuart, *b* at Greenwich 5 Feb 1965; *m* at ... Green, ... (*m* diss by div ...)

Brother of Great-Grandfather

Issue of Franz Josef Maximilian, 7th Prince of Lobkowicz (*b* 8 Dec 1772; ✠ 15 Dec 1816) and Princess Marie-Caroline zu Schwarzenberg (*b* 7 Sept 1775; *m* 2 Aug 1792; ✠ 24 Jan 1816), having had issue, among whom,

Son

Prince *Josef* Franz Karl, *b* at Vienna 17 Feb 1803; ✠ at Prague 18 March 1875, Major-Gen Austrian Army; *m* 1stly at Prague 20 Aug 1835, Countess Antoinette (*b* at Prague 7 May 1815; ✠ at Pardubitz 31 Dec 1835), younger dau of Karl, Court Kinsky von Wchnitz and Tettau and Countess Elisabeth von Thun and Hohenstein. He *m* 2ndly at Vienna 11 May 1848, Princess Sidonie (*b* at Lemberg 4 Oct 1828; ✠ at Unterberkovic 25 Feb 1917), dau of August Longin, Prince of Lobkowicz and Countess Marie-Sidonie Kinsky von Wchnitz and Tettau, having had issue from his second wife, among whom,

Sons

1. Prince Maria *Ferdinand* Georg August Melchior, *b* at Unterberkovic 26 June 1850; ✠ at Milan 22 April 1920, Kt Order of the Golden Fleece, Kt Sovereign Military Order of Malta, Kt Bavarian Order of St George, Kt Order of St Stephen of Hungary, Chief Marshal in the Kingdom of Bohemia; *m* at Vienna 11 Nov 1883, Countess Ida Maria (*b* at Vienna 23 Oct 1865; ✠ at Unterberkovic 4 April 1919), Lady-in-Waiting, Dame Star Cross Order, Dame of Hon Sovereign Military Order of Malta, dau of Leopold, Count Podstatzky-Lichtenstein, Proprietor of Weselicko, and Countess Franziska Paar, and had issue,

    1. Prince Maria *Joseph Ferdinand* Zdenko Kaspar Viktor, *b* at Unterberkovic 4 Sept 1885; ✠*k* nr Jaroslau, Galicia 25 Oct 1914, Dr of Law, Lt; *m* at Pruhonice 21 Oct 1913, Countess Gisela Helene (*b* at Trmice 14 June 1887; ✠ at Prague 21 Feb 1958; *m* 2ndly at Unterberkovic 27 Jan 1917, Moritz, Prince of Lobkowicz who ✠ at Telc 7 Aug 1944), Dame Star Cross Order, dau of Ernst; Count von Silva-Tarouca and Countess Maria von Nostitz-Rieneck, and had issue,

        1. Princess *Maria Antonia* Josefa Ignatia Kaspara, *b* at Pruhonice 8 Aug 1914, Dame Star Cross Order; *m* at Prague 26 Jan 1937, Friedrich, Count Strachwitz von Camminetz and Gross-Zauche (*b* at Zdounek, Moravia 2 June 1904; ✠ at Vienna 22 Jan 1985), Dr of Law.

        [*Malteser-Hospiz, Bürgerspitalgasse 1, 1060 Vienna, Austria*].

    2. Prince Maria *Leopold* Willibald Bernhard Balthasar, *b* at Unterberkovic 7 July 1888; ✠ at Prague 15 May 1933,

Proprietor of Unterberkovic, Vintírov, Bohemia, Lt Col (Res);
Kt of Hon Sovereign Military Order of Malta; *m* at Vienna 11
April 1918, Franziska (Fanny) (*b* at Margarethen am Moos,
Lower Austria 22 Aug 1893; ✠ at Wels 3 Nov 1972), Dame
Star Cross Order, dau of Alfred, 2nd Prince (Fürst) von
Montenuovo and Countess Franziska Kinsky von Wchinitz
and Tettau, and had issue, among whom,

> 1. Princess *Maria Julia* Franziska Ida Kaspara
> Walpurga, *b* at Prague 25 Feb 1919, Dame Star Cross
> Order; *m* at Prague 26 Jan 1939, Johann (Hans), Prince
> von Thurn and Taxis, Proprietor of Lissa (*b* at Schloß
> Mzell, Bohemia 28 June 1908; ✠ at Freiburg im
> Breisgau 3 April 1959).
> [*Mauerkircher Straße 181, 81925 Munich, Germany*].
> 2. Princess *Amalie* Franziska Ida Melchiora Pauline
> Leonhardine, *b* at Unterberkovic 25 Jan 1921, Dame of
> Hon Sovereign Military Order of Malta; *m* at
> Unterberkovic 23 May 1944, Franz, Prince zu
> Schwarzenberg (*b* at Prague 24 March 1913; ✠ at
> Unzmarkt 9 March 1992), Dr of Law, Prof of Political
> Science Loyola University Chicago, Kt Gd Cross
> Sovereign Military Order of Malta, Bailiff Gd Cross of
> Justice Constantinian Order of St George. Princess
> Amalie adopted 24 Jan 1993 her kinswoman, Princess
> Elisabeth zu Schwarzenberg (*b* 1 Oct 1947 - see that
> family)
> [*Rennweg 2, 1030 Vienna, Austria; 26293 Nalzovice
> nr Sedlcany, Czech Republic*].
> 3. Princess *Leopoldine* Bertha Marie Franziska Ida
> Balthasar Leonhardine, *b* at Unterberkovic 14 Nov
> 1926, Dame of Hon and Dev Sovereign Military Order
> of Malta; *m* at Unterberkovic 22 Aug 1945, Johann,
> Count Dobrzensky von Dobrzenicz (*b* at Chotebor,
> Bohemia 19 June 1911; ✠ at Havlickuv Brod 7 Feb
> 1996).
> [*Zámek, 58301 Chotebor, Czech Republic*].

3. Prince Maria *Moritz* Alexander Florian Kaspar, *b* at
Unterberkovic 3 May 1890; ✠ at Telc 7 Aug 1944; Lt.-Col.;
m at Unterberkovic 27 Jan 1917, Countess Gisela Helene
(*b* at Trmice 14 June 1887; ✠ at Prague 21 Feb 1958; *m* 1stly
at Pruhonice 21 Oct 1913, Joseph Ferdinand, Prince of

Lobkowicz who was ✠k nr Jaroslau, Galicia 25 Oct 1914),
Dame Star Cross Order, dau of Ernst, Count von Silva-Tarouca
and Countess Maria von Nostitz-Rieneck, and had issue,

1. Princess Maria *Ida* Josefa Murizia Melchiora, *b* at
Unterberkovic 15 Oct 1917; *m* 1stly at Prague 3 May
1939, Humprecht, Count Czernin von Chudenitz,
Proprietor of Hlusice in Bohemia (*b* at Dymokury 9
Feb 1909; ✠ at Ples, nr Prague 19 Sept 1944). She *m*
2ndly at Prague 27 Dec 1946, Fabrizio, Count Franco
(*b* at Verona 3 Jan 1903; ✠ at Vicenza 29 Oct 1983),
Dr of Law, Italian Ambassador.
[*Pila di Arcugnano, 36100 Vicenza, Italy*].

2. Prince *Josef* Ferdinand Maria Mauritius Leonhard
Christianus Petrus Canisius Balthasar, *b* at Dolní
Berkovice 20 Dec 1918; ✠ at Melník 24 April 1946,
Proprietor of Cítov and Damineves, Bohemia; *m* at
Prague 29 Aug 1940, Countess Gabriele (*b* at Dymokury
18 Jan 1913; *m* 2ndly at Prague 30 Aug 1952, Stanislav
Staffa who was *b* at Pustimer 10 May 1924; ✠ at
Wetaskiwin, Canada 28 Sept 1995), dau of Theobald,
Count Czernin von and zu Chudenitz, Proprietor of
Dymokury and Countess Marie Kinsky von Wchinitz
and Tettau, and had issue,

1. Prince Maria *Ferdinand* Josef Leopold Judas
Thaddäus Wenzl Melchior Linhart, *b* at Prague
3 Nov 1942; *m* at Vancouver, British Columbia
6 Nov 1976, Lenka (*b* at Pribram 11 Aug 1952),
dau of Oldrich Svatek and Alena Cimrova, and
has issue,
[*112, Cedarille Green SW, Calgary, Alberta
T2W 2H4, Canada*].

1. Prince Maria *Christopher* Prokop,
b at Vancouver 5 June 1977.

2. Prince Maria *Nicholas* Josef, *b* at
Calgary, Alberta, Canada 24 July 1979.

2. Prince *Prokop* Wenzl Joseph Linhart Judas
Thaddäus Humprecht Rimigius Theresia Jesu
Balthasar Maria, *b* at Cítov 1 Oct 1944, System
Analyst; *m* at Edmonton, Alberta, Canada 8
Nov 1975, Susan (*b* at Edmonton 22 Oct 1948),
dau of Dr John Albert Marty Shields and Helen

Lee Anderson, and has issue,
[*10641-69 Street, Edmonton, Alberta T6A 2S9, Canada*].

    1. Princess *Michelle* Catherine Gabriela, *b* at Edmonton, Alberta 28 Sept 1978.

    2. Prince Maria *Stephan* Prokop Vaclav, *b* at Edmonton 7 Feb 1981.

    3. Prince Maria *Mark* David Josef, *b* at Edmonton 22 Nov 1982.

3. Prince Maria *Franz* de Paula Moritz Josef Leonhard Wolfgang Franz von Assisi Romanus Laurentius Pius Caspar, *b* at Prague 9 Aug 1927, ✝ there 15 April 1998, Dr of Med; *m* at Prague 1 July 1952, Hanna (*b* at Prague 17 Jan 1928), Dr of Med, dau of Bohumil Novák and Maria Seifert, and has issue,
[*U Malvazinky 26, 15000 Prague 5 - Smichov, Czech Republic*].

    1. Princess *Jeanne* d'Arc Zdenka Gisela Kaspare, *b* at Prague 20 Oct 1953; ✝ at Rokyany 19 Dec 1969.

    2. Princess *Maria* Leopoldine Gabriele Melchiora, *b* at Prague 26 April 1959, Dr of Med; *m* at Prague 23 June 1984, Ludvig Hlaváč (*b* at Prague 20 June 1956), Dr of Med.
[*Gottwaldova ul. 685/II, 37704 Jindrichuv Hradec, Czech Republic*].

    3. Prince *Michael* Amadeo Ferdinand Balthasar, *b* at Prague 20 July 1964, Dr rer nat, Dipl Geology; *m* at Prague 1 July 1989, Lucie (*b* at Prague 26 Sept 1963), Teacher, dau of Vladimir Navratilov and Emma Maconauer, and has issue,
[*Zapova 20, 15000 Praque 5 - Smichov, Czech Republic*].

        1. Prince Maria *Tobias* Georg Gabriel Christoph Johannes Nepomuk Balthasar, *b* at Prague 23 May 1992.

        2. Prince Maria *Christoph* Johann Tobias Franz de Paula Melchior, *b* at Prague 9 Aug 1997.

2. Prince Maria *Zdenko* Vincenz Pius Kaspar, *b* at Vienna 5 May

1858; ✠ at Harrachsdorf, Bohemia 13 Aug 1933, Kt Order of the Golden Fleece, Field Marshal; *m* at Prague 6 May 1883, Countess Paula (*b* at Prague 22 Jan 1861; ✠ there 9 Feb 1922), Lady-in-Waiting, Dame Star Cross Order, dau of Erwein, Count von Schönborn and Countess Christine von Brühl, and had issue,

    1. Prince Maria *Erwein* Karl Petrus von Alcantara Romanus Damianus Balthasar, *b* at Prague 28 Feb 1887; ✠ at Stepperg, nr Neuburg an der Donau 28 Sept 1965, Bailiff Gd Cross Sovereign Military Order of Malta; *m* at Vukovár 24 May 1923, Countess and Noble Lady Antoinette (*b* at Vukovar, Croatia 17 May 1899; ✠ at Eltville 16 April 1989), dau of Jakob, Count and Noble Lord von and zu Eltz genannt Faust von Stromberg and Princess Marie of Lobkowicz, and had issue,

        1. Princess Maria Paula *Barbara* Kaspara Petra von Alcantara Friederika Thoma von Aquin Walpurga Thekla Karolina, *b* at Vukovar, Yugoslavia 6 March 1924.
        [*Englschalkinger Straße 10, 81925 Munich, Germany*].
        2. Princess Maria *Sidonia* (Sonia) Sophie Melchiora Petra von Alcantara Valentina Faustina, *b* at Vukovar, Yugoslavia 14 Feb 1925.
        [*Schloß Ehreshoven, 51766 Engelskirchen, Germany*].
        3. Princess Maria Anna *Lidwina* (Nina) Balthasara Petra von Alcantara Gratiana Vladimira Liberata, *b* at Vukovar, Yugoslavia 18 Dec 1928.
        [*Nymphenburgerstraße 172, 80634 Munich, Germany*].

3. Prince Maria *August* Georg Ferdinand, *b* at Dolní Berkovice 2 Feb 1862; ✠ at Vienna 10 Aug 1921, Kt of Hon Teutonic Order, Marshal of the Court in Vienna; *m* at Prague 3 Oct 1897, Countess Marie (Irma) (*b* at Retzhof, nr Leibnitz, Styria 29 Oct 1866; ✠ at Vienna 14 July 1950), Lady-in-Waiting, Dame Star Cross Order, dau of Eduard, Count Pálffy d'Erdöd, Baron von Ujezd and Marie von Walterskirchen, Baroness zu Wolfsthal, and had issue,

    1. Prince Maria *Eduard* Joseph August Sidonius Johann Nepomuk Anton Aloys Kaspar, *b* at Schloß Hradiste, nr Blovic, Bohemia 20 June 1899; ✠ at Freiburg im Breisgau 2 Jan 1959, Kt of Hon Sovereign Military Order of Malta; *m* at Watch-Hill, Rhode Island, USA 29 Aug 1925, Anita (*b* at Pern, Illinois 4 Nov 1903; ✠ at New York 14 May 1976; *m* 2ndly at … Erwin Hoy Watts; *m* 3rdly at …. John Caroll Griswold),

dau of Christian Bai Lihme and Olga Hegeler, and had issue, among whom,

 1. Prince Maria *Eduard* August Joseph Wilhelm Ignatius Patricius Hubertus Kaspar, *b* at New York 12 June 1926, Kt of Hon and Dev Sovereign Military Order of Malta; *m* at Besson, Allier 11 Dec 1959 (civ) and at Paris 7 Jan 1960 (relig), Princess Françoise (*b* at Paris 19 Aug 1928), dau of Don Xavier, Duke of Bourbon-Parma and Marie Madeleine de Bourbon-Busset of the Counts de Bourbon-Busset, and has issue, [*30 avenue de New York, 75116 Paris; Manoir d'Ujezd, Grainville Ymauvill, 76110 Goderville, Seine-Maritime, France*].

  1. Prince Marie *Edouard-Xaver* Ferdinand August Gaspard, *b* at Paris 18 Dec 1960; ✠ at Paris 24 May 1984.

  2. Prince Marie *Charles-Henri* Hugues Xavier Bénoit Michel Edouard Joseph Bathazar, *b* at Paris 17 May 1964, Kt of Dev Sovereign Military Order of Malta. [*30 avenue Marceau, 75008 Paris, France*].

  3. Princess Marie *Gabrielle* Anita Olga Thérèse de Lisieux Gaspara, *b* at Paris 11 June 1967. [*30 avenue Marceau, 75008 Paris, France*].

 2. Princess *Anita* Maria Olga Thérèse de Lisieux Camilla Balthasara, *b* at Neuilly-sur-Seine 13 Dec 1937, Journalist; *m* 1stly at St Luperce, Eure-et-Loire 20 Sept 1958 (*m* diss by div at Paris 10 Nov 1982), Charles Louis, Count de Cossé-Brissac of the Dukes de Brissac (*b* at Lyon 23 May 1931). She *m* 2ndly at ... 29 May 1999, Jean Charles (*b* at ...). [*1 bis, rue de Buenos Aires, 75007 Paris, France; Château de Flonville, St Luperce, 28190 Courville-sur-Eure, France*].

LINE II

Founded by Prince Georg Christian (*b* 10 Aug 1686; ✠ 9 Oct 1753); Galician Indigenat 19 Oct 1825; "Landmann" in Styria 16 Oct 1833; Hereditary Member of the former Austrian House of Lords 15 Dec 1883.

ANTONIUS Otakar Maria Kaspar, **PRINCE OF LOBKOWICZ,**
b at Zurich 23 April 1956, Art Dealer, *succ* his father, son of Otakar,
Prince of Lobkowicz (*b* 28 Jan 1922; ✞ 1 June 1995) and Countess
Susanna Széchényi von Sárvár Felsövidék (*b* 10 Dec 1932; *m* 7 Oct
1954).
[*Park Avenue 30, Apt 9 N, New York, NY 10016, U.S.A.*].

Brother

1. Prince *Georg* Johannes Maria Melchior, *b* at Zurich 23 April 1956
(twin with Prince Anton), lic oec; *m* at Morcote, Tessin 3 Dec 1988,
Bettina (*b* at Zurich 18 July 1958), dau of Henri Egli and Hedwig
Naef.
[*Vlasská 17, Malá Strana, 10000 Prague 1, Czech Republic*].

Mother

Susanna, Princess of Lobkowicz (*b* at Vienna 10 Dec 1932), dau of
János, Count Széchényi von Sárvár Felsövidék and Juliana,
Countess Széchényi von Sárvár Felsövidék; *m* at Grundlsee 7 Oct
1954 (*m* diss by div at Zurich 1 Nov 1966, Annulled at Sitten 19 Dec
1979), Otakar, Prince of Lobkowicz (*b* at Prague 28 Jan 1922; ✞ at
Vienna 1 June 1995).
[*Sternenstraße 27, 8002 Zurich, Switzerland*].

Brothers and Sisters of Father

Issue of Johann, Prince of Lobkowicz (*b* 6 Nov 1885; ✞ 11 Jan 1952)
and Countess Marie Czernin von and zu Chudenitz (*b* 2 Dec 1899;
m 13 Jan 1921; ✞ 28 Aug 1965).

1. Princess *Anna* Maria Henrica Frederica Johanna Hyacintha
Melchiora, *b* at Drahenice 6 March 1923.
[*Schloß Kahlsperg, 5411 Oberalm, Austria*].
2. Princess *Maria Theresia* Clothilde Klementine Josefa Johanna
von Nepomuk Balthasara, *b* at Vienna 16 March 1925; *m* at Mariazell
10 Oct 1957, Carl, Baron von Kellersperg (*b* at Brunn 31 Jan 1908; ✞
at Graz 12 April 1973).
[*Nernst Gasse5, 8010 Graz, Austria*].
3. Prince *Nikolaus* (*Mikulás*) Maria Georg Johannes von Nepomuk
Ottokar Agilulf Felix Kaspar, *b* at Prague 9 July 1931, Dr of Phil, Dr
Helmult, Dr of, Prof of Political Theory and Phil Univ of Munich,
Pres Cath Univ of Eichstätt, Kt Order of the Golden Fleece; *m* 1stly
at Reichenhofen 11 July (civ) and at Schloß Zeil 28 Aug (relig) 1953,

Countess Josefine (*b* at Munich 13 Dec 1929, ✠ there 12 March 1999), dau of Erich August, 6th Prince (Fürst) von Waldburg zu Zeil and Trauchburg and Princess Monika zu Löwenstein-Wertheim-Rosenberg. He *m* 2ndly at Mörnsheim 27 Sept (civ) and at Rome 15 Oct (rel) 1999, Aleksandra (*b* at Danzig 23 March 1953), dau of Zbigniew Cieslinska and Helena Finkelstein, and has issue by his first wife,

[*Am Kirchberg 6, 91804 Mörnsheim, Germany; Madalinskiego 15/9, 02513 Warsar, Poland*].

> 1. Prince Maria *Johannes* (*Jan*) Erich Christophorus Melchior Augustinus Franziskus, *b* at Munich 22 Aug 1954; *m* at Castell 2 Sept (civ) and 2 Sept (relig) 1977, Countess Johanna (*b* at Castell 23 Jan 1952), dau of Albrecht, Prince (Fürst) zu Castell-Castell and Princess Marie-Louise zu Waldeck and Pyrmont, and has issue,
>
> [*Jinonicka 61, 15600 Prague 5, Czech Republic; Zamek, 26285 Drahenice, Czech Republic*].
>
>> 1. Prince Maria *Nikolaus* Franziskus Balthasar, *b* at Munich 15 Sept 1978.
>> 2. Princess *Marie-Sophie* Anna Kaspara, *b* at Munich 6 Jan 1980.
>> 3. Prince Maria *Maximilian* Karl Melchior, *b* at Munich 4 Jan 1982.
>> 4. Princess Maria *Lioba* Theresa Kaspara, *b* at Munich 23 Sept 1985.
>> 5. Prince Maria *Wenzel* Gustin Melchior, *b* at Munich 4 Dec 1986.
>> 6. Princess *Agnes* Christina Sixtina Caspara, *b* at Memmingen, Bavaria 11 Nov 1992.
>> 7. Princess *Ida* Maria Clara Caspara, *b* at Drahenice, Czech Republic 9 Oct 1996.
>
> 2. Prince Maria *Erich-Georg* Gabriel, *b* at Munich 31 Oct 1955, Dr of Phil, *m* at Tuntenhausen, Bavaria 17 Aug (civ) and at Beyharting 11 September (relig) 1982, Countess Christina (*b* at Munich 7 April 1961), dau of Peter, Count von Hohenthal and Bergen and Baroness Irmgard von Herman, and has issue,
>
> [*Schloß Maxlrain, 83104 Tuntenhausen, Upper Bavaria, Germany*].
>
>> 1. Prince Maria *Peter* Nikolaus Ferdinand Melchior Alfons, *b* at Munich 1 Aug 1983.

2. Prince *Felix* Maria Johannes Levin Caspar Eusebius, *b* at Munich 3 Aug 1985.

3. Princess Anna *Elisabeth* Maria Christina Balthasara Margaretha, *b* at Munich 20 July 1987.

4. Princess Maria *Ludmila* Franziska Monika Bettina Irmgard, *b* at Munich 20 March 1991.

5. Princess Maria *Louisa* Beatrice Viviana Isabelle Caspara Elisabeth, *b* at Munich 4 July 1995.

3. Prince Maria *Franz* Gabriel Josef Kaspar Cyrillus, *b* at Munich 25 March 1957, Dr of Med, Dermatologist; *m* at Oettingen 2 Oct (civ) and 10 Oct (relig) 1981, Princess Margarita (*b* at Munich 31 July 1957, ✝ at Bad Aibling, Upper Bavaria 23 Feb 2000), dau of Alois, Prince (Fürst) zu Oettingen-Oettingen and Oettingen-Spielberg and Countess Elisabeth zu Lynar, and has issue,
[*Bahnhofstraße 11, 83646 Bad Tölz, Germany*].

1. Princess Maria *Polyxena* Elisabeth Cyrilla Teresa, *b* at Munich 10 Feb 1983.

2. Prince *Joseph* Maria Alois Franz Melchior, *b* at Munich 27 Nov 1984.

3. Prince *Alois* Maria Xaver Cyrillus, *b* at Munich 6 April 1987.

4. Princess *Teresa* Maria Anna Cyrilla, *b* at Bad Tölz 28 Feb 1994.

4. Princess Maria *Monika* Josepha Theresia, *b* at Munich 11 Aug 1958; *m* at Munich 26 July 1985, Michael, Baron von Gagern (*b* at Hovestadt, Westphalia 18 Sept 1942), Dr of Phil.
[*Teufelsbergstraße 12, 81249 Munich, Germany*].

5. Princess Maria (*Miriam*) Elisabeth Lioba Walburga Monika, *b* at South Bend, Indiana, USA 2 Jan 1961; *m* at Babenhausen, Swabia 11 Dec 1982 (civ) and at Neutrauchburg 15 Jan 1983 (relig), Johannes, Count Fugger von Babenhausen (*b* at Augsburg 20 Dec 1957).
[*Heinrich v. Kleiststraße 35, 61350 Bad Homburg, Hessen, Germany*].

4. Prince Maria *Friedrich* Leopold Georg Christian Johannes von Nepomuk Gregor Pontianus Melchior, *b* at Prague 17 Nov 1932, ✝ at USA 2 Feb 1998, Dr of rer nat, Prof Univ of Rochester, New York, USA; *m* at Ober-Aegeri 6 July 1960 (*m* diss by div at Rochester, NY … 1982), Désirée [*608 Hellendale Road, Rochester 9, NY 14609,*

USA] (*b* at Topolcany 25 Oct 1939), dau of Tibor Mérey de Kasposmérö et Kisdovorán and Margarethe Spiess von Braccioforte, *m* 2ndly at Rochester 22 Aug 1992, Carolyn (*b* at Trenton, Florida 26 Jan 1940), dau of ....Dey and .... and has issue by his first wife.

[*2633 Glenwood Road, Royal Dake, MI 48673, U.S.A.*].

    1. Prince *Philip* Peter Maria Wenzel Stephan Friedrich Hyazinth Barnabas Kaspar, *b* at Rochester, New York, USA 22 May 1961, BA; *m* at New York 23 Sept 1989, Gail (*b* at New York 5 July 1960), dau of ....MacDonald and ....

    [*17 East 89th Street, New York, NY 10123, U.S.A.*].

    2. Princess *Marie Christine* Elisabeth Margaretha Désirée Melchiora, *b* at Rochester 3 April 1963.

    [*608 Hellendale Road, Rochester 9, NY 14609, U.S.A.*].

LOOZ AND CORSWAREM

Catholic: Feudal family originating in Limburg, Belgium, from the Manor of Borgworm (Warem) who can be traced authentically to Robert de Corswarem, a Knight living in 1213; Lord of Nielle circa 1300; of Hierges circa 1500; of Longchamps (Prov of Namur, Belgium) through the marriage of Franz I of Looz-Corswarem to Antoinette von Gülpen circa 1600; title of Duke of Looz-Corswarem and of Corswarem-Looz of the Netherlands and of the Hereditary States, with the right of transfer, 24 Dec 1734 for the brothers Ludwig and Joseph, Counts of Corswarem; transfer of titles to Wilhelm Joseph, Count of Looz-Corswarem (✝ 1803) and the elder son of last Karl (*b* 1769; ✝ 1822 - see below) and the title of Duke of Corswarem-Looz to the son of Arnould, later Prince of Rheina-Wolbeck by virtue of the Will (25 Aug 1785) of Duke Carl Alexander (✝ 28 Feb 1792); confirmation of that transfer 16 Feb 1816; received qualification of "Durchlaucht" (primogeniture) by the German Diet 18 Aug 1825. The Principality of Rheina-Wolbeck was received as compensation for lands lost in Belgium 26 March 1800 and passed to the House of Laumay Clerveaux 7 Sept 1839; readjusted after the extinction of that House by the Head of the House of Looz and Corswarem 17 Sept 1931.

Members of the family bear the title of Prince or Princess de Looz et Corswarem with the qualification of Serene Highness.

THIERRY Robert Henri Camille, **11TH DUKE OF LOOZ and CORSWAREM,** *b* at Tübingen 10 Sept 1948, Banker, son of Robert, 10th Duke of Looz and Corswarem (*b* 5 May 1914; ✠ 16 Aug 1997) and his second wife, Christiane La Carrière (*b* 11 Feb 1920; *m* 6 Aug 1946); *m* at Lacanau, Gironde 29 June 1973, Alix (*b* at Lacanau 13 Aug 1949), dau of Jean de Bertier and Marie-Josiphe Faugère de Biensan, and has issue,

[*93 Allée du Lac Inférieur, 78110 Le Vésinet, France*].

Son and Daughters

1. Princess *Laurence* Marie Anne, *b* at Paris 18 Dec 1977.
2. Princess *Agnès* Christine Marie, *b* at Paris 27 July 1979.
3. Prince *Guillaume* Joseph Arnaud, *b* at Monaco 18 Feb 1993.

Mother

Christiane, Duchess of Looz and Corswarem, *b* at Baccarat, Meurthe-et-Moselle 11 Feb 1920, dau of Henri La Carrière and Ernestine Collin; *m* at Nancy 6 Aug 1946, Robert Camille, 10th Duke of Looz and Corswarem (*b* at St Laurent 5 May 1914; ✠ at Lourdes 16 Aug 1997; *m* 1stly at Pont-à-Mousson, Meurthe-et-Moselle 22 July 1939, Huguette La Carrière who ✠ at St Laurent 11 Feb 1945, sister of his second wife), French Croix de Guerre 1940-45.

[*6 Rue du Maréchal Lyautey, 65100 Lourdes, France*].

Brother and Sister

1. Princess *Anne* Huguette Marie, *b* at Tübingen 11 Aug 1947; *m* 1stly at Heers, Limburg 24 Oct 1970 (*m* diss by div Liège 6 June 1978), Michel, Viscount Desmaisières (*b* at Seville 4 March 1929). She *m* 2ndly at Brussels 27 July 1978, Gianni Jannuzzi (*b* at Rome 6 Nov 1935), Italian Ambassador to Buenos-Aires.

[*Av. del LiGertador, General San Martin, Buenos-Aires, Argentina*].

3. Prince *Gilles* Louis Thierry, *b* at Metz 3 Aug 1955; *m* at Lac-Masson, Quebec, Canada 26 July 1994, Lise (*b* at Montreal 5 Oct 1965), dau of Antoine Michel and Raymonde Poirier.

[*5151 rue McDonald, Montreal, Quebec H3X 2VG, Canada*].

Brother of Father

Issue of Camille, 9th Duke de Looz et Corswarem (*b* 21 Jan 1887; ✠ 12 June 1968) and Céline Foulon (*b* 18 March 1887; *m* 18 April 1910; ✠ 7 March 1952).

1. Prince *René, b* at St Laurent 22 Jan 1921; ✠ at Rhein, Westfalen 16 Jan 1988; *m* at Koekelberg 23 Feb 1952, Marie-Louise (*b* at Anderlecht 29 May 1921; *m* 1stly at ... Alphonse Flore; that *m* diss by div ....), dau of Jean Vanloo and Trinette Van Roy, adopted dau of Guillaume, Baron van den Bogaerde de Terbrugge and Baroness Albertine van Heeckeren van Kell.

[*Hertaweg 11, 48431 Rheine, Westfalen, Germany*].

Brothers of Grandfather

Issue of Camille, Prince of Looz and Corswarem (*b* 3 March 1853; ✠ 19 Jan 1929) and his second wife, Marie Féron (*b* 21 Nov 1864; *m* 2 June 1906; ✠ 29 June 1908), having had issue, among whom (legitimated by their parent's marriage),

Sons

1. Prince *Louis* Guillaume Eugene Frederic, *b* at St Laurent 3 May 1891; ✠ at Athus 28 May 1940; *m* at Paris 13 July 1915, Madeleine (*b* at Mouzon, Ardennes 6 April 1896), dau of Louis Francois Tissière and Adèle Alexandre, and had issue,

[*26 Rue du Centre, 6790 Athus, Belgium*].

> 1. Prince *Gilbert* Camille Louis François, *b* at Paris 14 April 1916; ✠ at Arlon 6 Aug 1974; *m* at Arlon 17 Jan 1939 (*m* diss by div Athus 21 Dec 1946), Simone (*b* at Arlon 4 April 1922; *m* 2ndly at Herstal 23 Nov 1949, Albert Lepiemme), dau of Henri Camille Bertrand and Stéphanie Jeannette Simon. He *m* 2ndly at Paris 15 March 1949, Renée (*b* at Paris 7 Dec 1916), dau of René Salvert and Berthe Estelle Laurençaut, and had issue from his first wife,
>
> [*11 Rue des Acacias, 6792 Halanzy, Belgium*].
>
> > 1. Princess *Madeleine* Suzanne Jeanne, *b* at Athus 31 May 1939; *m* at Halanzy 15 June 1963, Yvon-Albert Hans (*b* at Halanzy 16 July 1939).
> >
> > [*13 Rue Jules Bary, 6792 Halanzy, Belgium*].
>
> 2. Prince *Gaston* Louis Gilbert, *b* at Ixelles 16 Nov 1922; *m* at Pettingen, Luxemburg 12 Feb 1948, Catherine (*b* at Differdingen, Luxemburg 24 Dec 1923), dau of Jean Spleles and Catherine Pleimling, and has issue, among whom,
>
> [*13 Rue des Acacias, 6788 Halanzy, Belgium*].
>
> > 1. Prince *Gilbert* Louis, *b* at Pettingen 8 Nov 1948; *m* at Heinsch 5 July 1974, Liliane (*b* at Heinsch 20 July 1953), dau of Alphonse Colles and Marcelle Léonie

Lescrenier.

2. Princess *Marie-Astrid* Arnauld, *b* at Pettingen 14 Feb 1952; *m* at Halanzy 30 June 1973, Christian Roger (*b* at Mont-Saint-Martin 3 May 1949).
[*41c, Rue Adrien Victor, 6778 Musson, Belgium*].

3. Prince *Jean-Marie* René, *b* at Pettingen 30 Jan 1955; *m* at Aubange 16 April 1977, Marina (*b* at Rulles 16 March 1961), dau of Roger Edouard Keser and Marcelle Paul.
[*55 Habergy, 6780 Messancy, Belgium*].

4. Princess *Léone* Alexandria, *b* at Pettingen 13 July 1956; *m* at Halanzy 10 July 1976, Christian Dewaey (*b* at Houdeng-Goegnies 22 July 1955).
[*36 Rue Adrien Victor, 6778 Musson, Belgium*].

3. Princess *Ghislaine* Marie Louise, *b* at Ixelles 7 April 1927; *m* at Charleroi 18 Dec 1954, Alexandre Vandeville (*b* at Seneffe 18 May 1932).
[*13 Rue du Belvédere, 6090 Couillet, Belgium*].

5. Princess *Fernande* Maxime, *b* at Pettingen, Luxemburg 12 Nov 1931; *m* at Charleroi 26 Dec 1953, Michel Stiepen (*b* at Jumet 17 Sept 1930).
[*193 Rue Hodister, 5490 Bomal-sur-Ourthe, Belgium*].

2. Prince Charles Arnould *Georges*, *b* at St Laurent 30 Oct 1897; ✝ at Récicourt, Meuse 16 Jan 1968; *m* 1stly at St Laurent 14 Feb (civ) and at Villecloye, Meuse 16 Feb (relig) 1920, Gabrielle (*b* at Saulmory-et-Villefranche, Meuse, 30 March 1890; ✝ at Verdun 7 Dec 1956), dau of Louis, Baron de Bonnay de Malberg and Pauline Lafalise. He *m* 2ndly at Antibes 28 Jan 1959, Odette (*b* at Récicourt 2 Dec 1903), dau of Chéri René Chevallier and Marie-Françoise Octavie Liénard, and had issue by his second wife,
[*Récicourt, 55120 Clermont-en-Argonne, France*].

1. Prince *Alain*, *b* at Arrancy-sur-Crusne, Meuse 7 Feb 1921; ✝ at Nancy 23 Dec 1974; *m* at Verdun 12 Nov 1945, Jacqueline (*b* at Chalons-sur-Marne 29 Oct 1924), dau of Major Louis Grandemange, and Marguerite Miraucourt, and had issue,
[*86 Rue de la République, 54220 Malzéville, France*].

1. Prince *Bernard* Michel Jean, *b* at Nancy 16 Jan 1947; *m* at Nancy 3 Aug 1970, Françoise (*b* at Nancy 25 Jan 1948; ✝ at Nancy 2 Oct 1992), dau of Pierre Esprit and Suzanne Simon, and has issue,
[*2 Rue de la Gare, 54760 Moizons-Leyr, France*].

1. Princess *Alexandra* Christiane Annick, *b* at Essey-les-Nancy, Meurthe-et-Moselle 31 Oct 1972.
2. Princess *Aurélie* Elisabeth Aline, *b* at Essey-Les-Nancy 24 Aug 1975.
3. Prince *Julien* Alain Jean Noël, *b* at Essey-les-Nancy 1 March 1978.

LÖWENSTEIN-WERTHEIM

This family descends from the morganatic marriage of the Elector Palatine Friedrich I (*b* 1 Aug 1425; ✝ 12 Dec 1476) to Klara Tott of Augsburg in 1471. Their son Ludwig (*b* 29 Sept 1463; ✝ 28 March 1524) received the county of Löwenstein (near Heilbronn, Württemberg) 28 Dec 1476; Count of the Holy Empire 27 Feb 1494; inherited the County of Wertheim (near Mosbach, Baden), Rochefort (Prov of Namur, Belgium) etc, through the marriage (1567) of Count Ludwig (*b* 17 Feb 1530; ✝ 13 Feb 1611) to Anne, daughter and heiress of Ludwig, Count of Stolberg-Königstein-Wertheim, and took the name of Löwenstein-Wertheim circa 1600; partition of lands between two sons of this marriage, from whom the Lines below descend.

LINE I: LÖWENSTEIN-WERTHEIM-FREUDENBERG

Evangelical; Founded by Count Christoph Ludwig (*b* 3 May 1568; ✝ 17 Feb 1618) who married 1592, Elisabeth, Countess of Manderscheid (*b* 1569; ✝ 1626) heiress of the County of Virneburg; the right of primogeniture was established at a family convention 14 April 1767; received the Bailiwick of Freudenberg (near Mosbach, Baden) with title indemnified for the County of Virneburg in the Eifel (acquired in 1620 and sold in 1801) and took the name of that Bailiwick, as *Fürst* 1803; Bavarian title of Prince conferred at Munich 19 Nov 1812; confirmed in the Grand Duchy of Hesse 17 Dec 1812; Prince in Württemberg 27 Feb 1813; Hereditary Member of the Bavarian "Reichsräte"; Hereditary Member of the First Chambers of the Kingdom of Württemberg and of the Grand Duchy of Baden; qualification of "Durchlaucht" (primogeniture) by the German Diet 18 Aug 1825.

Members bear of this Line bear the title of Prince or Princess zu Löwenstein-Wertheim-Freudenberg with the qualification of Serene Highness.

ALFRED-ERNST Friedrich Karl Richard Otto Konstantin Kasimir Bernhard, **7TH FÜRST (PRINCE) and HERR (LORD) ZU**

LÖWENSTEIN-WERTHEIM-FREUDENBERG, Count zu Limpurg, Princely Count zu Umpfenbach, Lord zu Breuberg and Mondfeld, *b* at Schloß Triefenstein 19 Sept 1924, son of Udo, 6th Fürst (Prince) zu Löwenstein-Wertheim-Freudenberg (*b* 8 Sept 1896; ✝ 28 Dec 1980) and Countess Margarete zu Castell-Castell (*b* 27 Oct 1899; *m* 3 May 1922; ✝ 24 Dec 1969); *m* at Kreuzwertheim 9 Sept 1950, Ruth-Erika (*b* at Buggenhagen 25 June 1922), dau of Hans Detlef von Buggenhagen and Baroness Ruth von Rosenberg.
[Hauptstraße 37, 97892 Kreuzwertheim am Main, Germany].

Sons and Daughters

1. *Ludwig* Udo Hans Peter Alfred, Erbprinz (Hereditary Prince) zu Lowenstein-Wertheim-Freudenberg, *b* at Kreuzwertheim 24 May 1951, Lt-Col (Res), Dipl Business; *m* 1stly at Kreuzwertheim 28 May (civ) and at Behringersdor, nr Nuremberg 29 May (relig) 1976, Verena (*b* at Sigmaringen 31 Jan 1952; ✝ at Kreuzwertheim 26 Oct 1985), dau of Claus von Stülpnagel-Dargitz, Proprietor of Lübbenow, and Rita von Lekow. He *m* 2ndly at Kreuzwertheim 4 Aug (civ) and at Schöntal an der Jagst 12 Sept (relig) 1987, Countess Elisabeth (*b* at Möckmühl 7 June 1962), dau of Ludwig, Count von Waldburg zu Wolfegg and Waldsee and Princess Stephanie von Schönburg-Waldenburg, and has issue by his second wife,
[Hauptstraße 37, 97892 Kreuzwertheim am Main, Germany].

    1. Princess *Sophie* Amelie Margarita Alexandra Monika Isabel, *b* at Wertheim 1 Sept 1988.

    2. Princess *Amelie* Anastasia Sylvia Alexandra Ruth Elisabeth, *b* at Wertheim 15 Aug 1990.

    3. Prince Ludwig Hubertus Alfred-Ernst Sebastian Carl Roman, *b* at Wertheim 30 June 1994.

2. Princess *Ameli* Margarete Marielies Ingeborg, *b* at Kreuzwertheim 20 Feb 1953, Dipl Geology; *m* at Kreuzwertheim 5 May (civ) and at Wertheim 6 May (relig) 1978, Constantin von Brandenstein-Zeppelin of the Counts von Brandenstein-Zeppelin (*b* at Biberach an der Riss 22 June 1953) Dipl Business.
[Burg Brandenstein, 36381 Schlüchtern 3 - Elm, Germany].

3. Princess *Dorothee* Antonie Brigitte Pauline, *b* at Kreuzwertheim 30 Oct 1955, Teacher; *m* at Kreuzwertheim 12 Oct (civ) and 13 Oct (relig) 1984, Chrisoph Schücking (*b* at Kassel 5 Nov 1951), Dr of Law.
[Herzbergstraße 11, 60439 Frankfurt am Main, Germany].

4. Prince *Udo* Alexander Richard Albrecht, *b* at Kreuzwertheim 17 June 1957, Dip Agr Eng, Land Manager, Kt of St John of Jerusalem;

m at Bad Homburg-Gonzenheim 25 Aug 1984, Isabel (*b* at Bad Homburg 30 Sept 1957), dau of Willwerner von Bergen and Elisabeth von Oertzen, and has issue,

[*Remlerstraße 1, 69120 Heidelberg, Germany*].

    1. Princess *Viktoria* Elisabeth Georgia Susanne Dorothee, *b* at Heidelberg 12 Feb 1990.

    2. Prince *Georg* Ludwig Bernd Markus Ulrich, *b* at Heidelberg 16 May 1993.

    3. Prince *Philipp* Constantin Gisbert Falk André, *b* at Heidelberg 11 June 1998.

5. Princess *Ruth* Marie-Luise Orlinda Heideline, *b* at Kreuzwertheim 30 Dec 1959, Doctor of Med; *m* at Freiburg 13 Sept (civ) Kreuzwertheim 14 Sept (relig) 1991, Herbert Köppl (*b* at Freising 9 May 1950), Doctor of Med.

[*Muttenzer Straße 39, 76639 Grenzach-Wyhlen, Germany*].

Sisters

1. Princess *Ameli* Gertrud Pauline Antoinie Madeleine Wanda Elisabeth *b* 4 Mar 1923; *m* at Kreuzwertheim 7 Aug 1951, Anton Günther, Duke of Oldenburg (*b* at Lensahn 16 Jan 1923), Dipl Land Management.

[*Güldenstein, 23738 Lensahn, Holstein, Germany*].

2. Princess *Gertrud* Olga Ilka Emma Agnes Magdalena Mechtild, *b* at Langenzell, nr Bammental, Kreis Heidelberg 24 Jan 1926; *m* at Kreuzwertheim 7 Aug 1951, Peter, Duke of Oldenburg (*b* at Lensahn 7 Aug 1926).

[*Lensahner Hof, 23738 Lensahn, Holstein, Germany*].

3. Princess *Pauline* Elisabeth Renata Luitgard, *b* at Heidelberg 9 June 1928, Dr of Med; *m* at Tegernsee 29 Dec 1956, Dr Hans Günther Horst (*b* at Oldenburg 23 Oct 1913; ✝ at Tegernsee 7 March 1989), Doctor of Med.

[*Burgstallerstraße 11, 83703 Gmund am Tegernsee, Germany*].

Brothers of Grandfather

Issue of Wilhelm, 4th Prince zu Lowenstein-Wertheim-Freudenberg (*b* 19 March 1817; ✝ 10 March 1887) and his first wife, Countess Olga Clara von Schönburg-Forderglauchau (*b* 28 Jan 1831; *m* 20 April 1852; ✝ 16 March 1868), having had issue, among whom,

Sons

1. Prince *Wilhelm* Gustav Ludwig, *b* at Kreuzwertheim 25 Jan 1863; ✠ at Tilsit 17 Aug 1915, Major Prussian Army, Member Prussian Chamber of Deputies, Kt of St John of Jerusalem; *m* at Baden-Baden 26 Nov 1887, Baroness Luise (*b* at Heidelberg 16 April 1859; ✠ at Munich 19 May 1927), dau of Bernhard, Baron von Fabrice and Countess Ida von Schönburg-Forderglauchau, and had issue, among whom,

Son

Prince *Wolfgang* Wilhelm Gustav Karl Ludwig, *b* at Drehnow 25 Nov 1890; ✠ at Pulawy, Poland 8/9 July 1945, Major; *m* 1stly at Frankfurt-am-Main 22 Oct 1920 (*m* diss by div at Berlin 8 Feb 1938), Princess Olga (*b* at Bonn 25 Oct 1880; ✠ at Heidelberg 1 July 1961; she *m* 1stly at Langenzell 5 Oct 1898, Heinrich, Prince von Schönburg-Waldenburg who ✠ at Rheda 28 Dec 1945; that *m* diss by div at Leipzig 20 Aug 1920), dau of Prince Alfred zu Löwenstein-Wertheim-Freudenberg and Countess Pauline von Reichenbach-Lessonitz. He *m* 2ndly at Lindau im Bodensee 17 Nov 1938, Eugenie (*b* at Würzburg 14 Aug 1900; ✠ at Vilsbiburg 6 Sept 1982), dau of Jakob von Fortenbach and Eugenie Schmidt, and had issue,

1. Prince *Wolfram* Hubertus Wilhelm Heinrich, *b* at Berlin 21 Oct 1941, Writer as "Wolfram zu Mondfeld"; *m* at Grünwald 10 April 1974 (*m* diss by div at Landshut 8 Dec 1984), Elisa Christiane (*b* at Berlin 19 June 1941), dau of Fritz Ernst Werner Schwennicke and Auguste Marie Wachsmuth, and has issue, [*Hofhegenberg, 82297 Steindorf-Paar, Germany*].

1. Prince *Wolfram* Michael Nikolaus Friedrich Jakob, *b* at Munich 12 Dec 1980.

Brother of Great-Grandfather

Issue of Wilhelm, Prince zu Löwenstein-Wertheim-Freudenberg (*b* 27 April 1783; ✠ 15 Aug 1847) and Baroness Dorothea-Christina von Kahlden-Malzin (*b* 8 Nov 1791; *m* 26 July 1812; ✠ 16 Dec 1860), having had issue, among whom,

Son

Prince *Leopold* Emil Ludwig Konrad, *b* at Geneva 26 Nov 1827; ✠ at Munich 13 March 1893 (Catholic), Kt Hon and Dev Sovereign Military Order of Malta; *m* at Hamburg 4 Aug 1861, Amalia Augusta

Henriette (*b* at Detmold 3 March 1836; ✠ at Munich 14 March 1909), *cr* "Baroness Wollrabe von Wallrab" *ad personam,* Bavaria 1 Dec 1869 and "Countess von Löwenstein-Scharffeneck" by the King of Bavaria 15 Jan 1875 (matriculated 8 May 1875), dau of Ludwig Wollrabe and Emilie Wagner, and had issue, among whom,

Son

Prince *Maximilian* Karl Friedrich, *b* at Schloß Patzau, Bohemia 13 July 1871; ✠ at Vienna 11 April 1952, Bavarian Chamberlain, Capt. Bavarian Cavalry; *m* 1stly Munich 4 Nov 1895 (*m* diss by div at München 8 May 1912), Hon *Constance* Valerie Sophie (*b* at London 28 April 1875; ✠ at London 10 Oct 1963; *m* 2ndly at London 6 June 1912, Volrath von Alvensleben), dau of Henry, 1st Baron Pirbright (UK Peerage), of Pirbright, Baron von Worms and Baroness Françoise von Todesco. He *m* 2ndly at Ansbach 20 Dec 1915, Baroness Adelaide (*b* at Guttenstein 13 Aug 1883; ✠ at Vienna 9 June 1970), dau of Reinhard, Baron von Berlichingen and Ada Müller and had issue, among whom from his first wife,

Sons

1. Prince Felicien *Leopold* Maximilian Friedrich Ludwig Hubertus, *b* at Salzburg 13 March 1903; ✠ at Ventimiglia 6 Sept 1974; *m* 1stly at Munich 6 July 1932 (*m* diss by div at London 23 July 1947), Countess *Bianca* Henrietta Maria Fischler von Treuberg (*b* at Munich 29 Sept 1913; ✠ at Paris 19 May 1984; *m* 2ndly 24 Aug 1948, Peter Rosoff who ✠ at London 14 March 1979). He *m* 2ndly at London 6 Aug 1947, Diana (*b* at London 18 Dec 1921; ✠ at London 1 April 1967), dau of Sir Victor Gollancz and Ruth Lowy, and had issue by his first wife,

    1. Prince *Rupert* Ludwig Ferdinand Friedrich Constantin Lolfredo Leopold Herbert Maximilian Hubert Johannes Heinrich, *b* at Palma de Mallorca 24 Aug 1933, Kt Gd Cross Hon and Dev and Vice-Pres British Association of Sovereign Military Order of Malta, Bailiff Gd Cross with Collar and Pres British Association of Constantinian Order of St George, Kt Order of St Januarius, Kt Order of St Stephen of Tuscany, Cmdr Venerable Order of St John, Cmdr Merito Melitense of Malta, Banker; *m* at London 18 July 1957, Josephine Clare (*b* at London 26 Jan 1931), Dame of Hon and Dev Sovereign Military Order of Malta, Dame Gd Cross Constantinian Order of St George, dau of Capt Montague Lowry-Corry of the Earls

Belmore and Hon Mary Biddulph of the Barons Biddulph, and has issue,
[*Petersham Lodge, River Lane, Richmond TW10 7AG*].

    1. Rev Br (Prince) *Rudolph* Amadeus Johannes, *b* at London 17 Nov 1957, Order of Preachers.
[*St Dominic's Priory, London, NW5 4LB*].

    2. Prince *Konrad* Friedrich Ottocar, *b* at London 26 Nov 1958.
[*Brudershaft St Petrus, 088145 Witgratsbau, Germany*].

    3. Princess *Marie-Theodora* Marjorie, *b* at London 11 July 1966, *m* at London 26 Sept 1998, Count Manfredi della Gherardesca (*b* at Florence 5 Aug 1961).
[*43 Palace Garden Terrace London W8*].

2. Prince *Hubertus* Friedrich Maria Maximilian Leopold Ludwig, *b* at Schloß Schönworth 14 Oct 1906; ✠ at Bonn 28 Nov 1984, Member German Bundestag; Prof of History Univ. of Heidelberg; Editor *"Die Zeit"*; *m* at Palermo 4 April 1929, Helga (*b* at Loftus, Norway 27 Aug 1910), dau of Wilhelm-Franz Schuylenburg and Hermine Cornelia Barendine, née Schuylenburg, and had issue,
[*Lahnstraße 50, 53175 Bonn-Bad Godesberg, Germany*].

    1. Princess *Marie-Elizabeth* Katharina Gabriela Dorothea Konstanza Edwarda, *b* at New York 26 Nov 1939; *m* at... Gernot Renauer (*b* at....).

    2. Princess *Konstanza-Maria* Isabella Michaela Franziska Helga Richarda, *b* at Franklin, New Jersey, USA 4 July 1942; *m* at Bonn-Bad Godesberg 12 Aug 1969 (civ) (*m* diss by div 13 July 1978), Manfred Schmidt-Werthern (*b* at Traunstein 12 Aug 1944).
[*Holsteinstraße 31, Berlin, Germany*].

    3. Princess *Margareta-Maria* Michaela Thérèsa Mauritia Carclina Huberta, *b* at Wertheim 3 Oct 1948; *m* at Bonn 10 Aug 1974, Botho von Schwarzkopf (*b* at Poggenmühlen, nr Bremen 17 Feb 1948).
[*Poggenmühlen, nr Bremen, Germany*].

LINE II: LÖWENSTEIN-WERTHEIM-ROSENBERG

Catholic: Founded by Count Johann Dietrich, Count of Löwenstein-Wertheim-Rochefort (*b* 1584; ✠ 1644); Confirmation of the title of Count of Wertheim 4 June 1613; Prince of the Holy Empire (primogeniture) with the qualification of "Hochgeboren", Vienna 3

April 1711; the title was extended to all descendants, Frankfurt-am-Main 8 Jan 1712; confirmed by the Elector of Bavaria 23 March 1712; Bohemian Incolat, Vienna 6 May 1712; the right of succession by primogeniture was agreed at a family convention 1768; received the villages of Wörth and Trennfurt in Mainz, the Württemberg Bailiwicks of Rothenfels (Lower Franconia, Bavaria), the Abbeys of Bronnbach and Neustadt, the Württembergoise Administrations of Widdern and Thalheim; perpetual rent of 12000 florins for the right of navigation of the Rhine and a second perpetual rent of 28000 florins with title indemnified of the County of Püttlingen and the Lordships of Scharfeneck, Cugnon, Herbimont, Agimont, Chasse-pierre and the Tiers of Neufchateau, lost in 1801, and adopted the name of Rosenberg 25 Feb 1803; Hereditary Member of the First Chambers of Bavaria, Württemberg, Baden and Hesse; received the qualification of "Durchlaucht" (primogeniture) by the German Diet 18 Aug 1825.

Members bear the title of Prince or Princess zu Löwenstein-Wertheim and Rosenberg with the qualification of Serene Highness.

ALOIS-KONSTANTIN Karl Eduard Joseph Johann Konrad Antonius Gerhard Georg Benediktus Pius Eusebius Maria, **9TH FÜRST (PRINCE) ZU LÖWENSTEIN-WERTHEIM AND ROSENBERG,** Lord of Löwenstein, Wertheim, Bronnbach, Breuberg and Rosenberg, *b* at Würzburg 16 Dec 1941, *succ* his father, Lawyer, Lt-Col (Res), Kt Gd Cross Order of St Sepulchre of Jerusalem, Kt Bavarian Order of St George, son of Karl, 8th Fürst (Prince) zu Löwenstein-Wertheim-Rosenberg (*b* 8 Feb 1904; ✠ 23 Aug 1990) and Carolina of the Counts Rignon (*b* 17 Feb 1904; *m* 7 Jan 1935; ✠ 20 Sept 1975); *m* at Bronnbach an der Tauber 8 Oct (civ) and at Erbach, Rheingau 8 Nov (relig) 1965, Princess Anastasia Victoria (*b* at Brieg 14 Feb 1944), Dame Order of Queen Luise, dau of Prince Hubertus of Prussia and Princess Magdalene Reuss. [*63924 Schloß Kleinheubach bei Miltenberg, Germany*].

Sons and Daughter

1. Prince *Carl-Friedrich* Hubertus Georg Eduardo Paolo Nickolo Franz Alois Ignatius Heironymus Maria, Hereditary Prince (Erbprinz) zu Löwenstein-Wertheim-Rosenberg, *b* at Frankfurt-am-Main 30 Sept 1966; *m* at Brenken 16 May (civ) Schloß Erpernburg 8 Aug (relig) 1998, Baroness Stephanie Sophie Maria Coletta (*b* at Paderborn 21 April 1970), Doctor of Med, dau of Count Georg Droste zu Vischering, Baron von und zu Brenken auf Erpernburg and Countess Rosa von Nostitz-Rieneck, and has issue, [*Box 1130, Majorstuveien 17, 0367 Oslo, Norway*].

  1. Princess *Augustina* Sophia Carolina Dominique Anastasia Rosa Magdalene Kiliana Margarethe Maria, *b* at Oslo 8 July 1999.

  2. Prince *Nicodemus*, *b* at Oslo 2 Aug 2001.

2. Prince *Hubertus* Maximilian Gabriel Franz Louis Konstantin Dominik Wunibald Maria, *b* 18 Dec 1968.
[*Auf der Körnerwiese 13, 60322 Frankfurt-am-Main, Germany*].

3. Princess *Christina* Maria Johanna Caroline Madalene Osy Cecilie Hermine Isidora Anastasia Victoria, *b* at Frankfurt-am-Main 4 April 1974; *m* at Kleinheubach 5 Oct 2002, Guido von Rohr (*b* at Hannover 27 Sept 1969).
[*63924 Schloßkleinheubach, Germany*].

4. Prince *Dominik* Wilhelm Christian Nikolaus Sturmius Antonius Charles Benedikt Felix Maria, *b* at Frankfurt-am-Main 7 March 1983.

Sisters

1. Princess *Maria* Aloisia Josephine Consolata Immaculata Benedikta Theresia Antonia Johanna Carla Conrada Leonharda, *b* at Munich 6 Nov 1935, Dame Star Cross Order; *m* at Bronnbach 25 Aug (civ) and 12 Sept (relig) 1956, Archduke Joseph Arpád of Austria (*b* at Budapest 8 Feb 1933).
[*Knöbelstraße 28, 80538 Munich, Germany; Avenida General Carmona 3, 2765 Estoril, Portugal*].

2. Princess *Josephine* Aloisia Edoarda Maria Immaculata Consolata Theresia Antonia Johanna Benedicta Carla Conrada, *b* at Bronnbach 17 May 1937, Dame Star Cross Order; *m* at Bronnbach 27 Dec (civ) and 7 Jan (relig) 1961, Prince Alexander of Liechtenstein (*b* at Vienna 14 May 1929).
[*9232 Rosegg, Kärnten, Austria; Lochgasse 5, 9420 Vaduz, Liechtenstein*].

3. Princess *Monika* Maria Immaculata Consolata Benedikta Aloisia Josephone Theresia Antonia Johanna Carla Conrada Vitalis, *b* at Bronnbach 28 April 1939, Dame Star Cross Order; *m* at Bronnbach 11 Sept (civ) and 22 Sept (relig) 1968, Don Jaime Méndez de Vigo y del Arco (*b* at Madrid 23 Nov 1933), Lawyer.
[*Calle Cortuny 14, 28010 Madrid, Spain*].

4. Princess *Christiana* Maria Josephine Aloisia Consolt Immaculata Theresia Antonia Johanna Carla Conrada Rita, *b* at Würzburg 18 Sept 1940, Dame Star Cross Order, Dame of Hon Sovereign Military Order of Malta; *m* at Bronnbach an der Tauber 4 March (civ) and 12 April (relig) 1966, Michael, Archduke of Austria (*b* at Budapest 5

May 1942), Businessman.
[*Hintzerstraße 9, 1030 Vienna, Austria*].

6. Princess *Elizabeth-Alexandra* Ninfa Paula Nicoletta Franziska Anastasia Carla Johanna Benedicta Conrada Rita Consolata Maria, *b* at Würzburg 2 May 1944; *m* at Reicholzheim 9 July (civ) and at Bronnbach 25 July (relig) 1973, Don José Maria Trénor y Suárez de Lezo, heir of the Marquess de Serdañola (*b* at Valencia 25 July 1939).
[*Pedralbes 16, 08034 Barcelona, Spain*].

7. Princess *Lioba* Ernestine Paola Aloisia Josephine Edoarda Benedicta Consolata Immaculata Rita Conrada Maria, *b* at Bonnbach 2 Oct 1946, Dame Star Cross Order; *m* at Richolzheim 28 May (civ) and at Bronnbach 22 July (relig) 1969, Moritz, Prince zu Oettingen-Oettingen and Oettingen-Wallerstein (*b* at Munich 20 May 1946).
[*86745 Hohenaltheim bei Nördlingen, Germany*].

Brother of Father

Issue of Aloys, 7th Prince zu Lowenstein-Wertheim-Rosenberg (*b* 15 Sept 1871; ✠ 25 Jan 1952) and Countess Josephine Kinsky von Wchinitz and Tettau (*b* at Alderkosteletz 23 Aug 1874; *m* 27 Sept 1898; ✠ 23 April 1946).

1. Prince Maria *Johannes* Paul Kilian Joseph Alois Anton Michael, *b* at Kleinheubach 8 July 1919, ✠ at Habitzheim 1 Dec 2000, Dr of Agriculture, Dipl Land Management, Kt Gd Cross Sovereign Military Order of Malta; *m* at Wissen 30 Aug 1949, Baroness Christine (*b* at Wissen 31 July 1927), Dame Sovereign Military Order of Malta, dau of Felix, Count von Loë, Proprietor of Wissen and Princess Isabella zu Salm-Salm, and has issue,
[*Semderstraße 11, 04853 Olzberg - Habitzheim, Germany*].

    1. Prince Maria *Michael* Alois Felix Thomas Cyriacus Bernward Johannes, *b* at Wissen 20 Dec 1950, Lawyer, Kt of Hon and Dev Sovereign Military Order of Malta; *m* at Ahrensburg, Holstein 26 May (civ) and at Hamburg-Harvestehude 27 May (relig) 1989, Andrea (*b* at Hamburg 27 April 1961), dau of Jürgen Reuter and Christina Heinze.
[*Kronberger Straße 42, 60323 Frankfurt-am-Main, Germany*].

        1. Princess Maria *Clara* Elisabeth Katharina Justina Christiane Josephine, *b* at Hamburg 1 July 1990.

        2. Princess Maria *Elisabeth* Carolina Ignatia Benedikta, *b* at Frankfurt-am-Main 31 Oct 1991.

        3. Princess Maria *Carolina* Johanna Paula, *b* at

Frankfurt-am-Main 7 April 1993.

    4. Princess Maria *Konstantin* Franziskus Michael Johannes Georg Bruno Bartholomaus *b* at Frankfurt-am-Main 9 March 1995

2. Prince Maria *Karl* Emanuel Ludger Petrus, *b* at Hees, nr Weeze 18 Jan 1952, Kt of Hon and Dev Sovereign Military Order of Malta; *m* at Borlinghausen 30 July 1978, Baroness Maria-Assunta (*b* at Borlinghausen 12 Aug 1952), dau of Franz, Baron von Weichs zur Wenne and Baroness Marie-Leonie von Wolff-Metternich, and has issue,
[*Borner Feld 8b, 41379 Brüggen, Germany*].

    1. Prince *Philipp* Bernhard Franz Konstantin Maria, *b* at Bonn 20 Aug 1979.

    2. Princess *Katharina* Marie Leonie Martina, *b* at Bonn 10 June 1981.

    3. Prince *Felix* Johannes Clemens Martin, *b* at Frankfurt-am-Main 14 Dec 1984.

    4. Princess Marie *Amelie* Susanna Stefanie Mathilde Laurentia, *b* at Viersen 14 March 1988.

3. Prince Maria *Felix* Friedrich Johannes Pius Faustinus, *b* at Hees 15 Feb 1954, Dr of Agriculture, Kt of Hon Sovereign Military Order of Malta; *m* at Bad Aussee, Styria 12 June 1977, Countess Elisabeth (*b* at Pöchlarn 25 July 1955), dau of Alois, Count von Meran and Baroness Elsa (Elisabeth) von Tinti, and has issue,
[*Hofgut Habitzheim, 64853 Otzberg-Habitzheim, Germany*].

    1. Princess Maria *Sophie* Johanna Paula Roberta Antonia, *b* at Munich 13 June 1979.

    2. Princess Maria *Johanna* Josephine Franziska, *b* at Freising 9 March 1981.

    3. Princess Maria *Louisa* Barbara Isabella Elisabeth Christine, *b* at Port-au-Prince, Haiti 23 June 1984.

    4. Princess Maria *Theresa* Michaela Yolanda, *b* at Darmstadt 29 Nov 1985.

    5. Princess *Marie* Assunta Alexandra Theresa, *b* at Darmstadt 9 May 1988.

    6. Princess Maria *Alexandra* Beatrix Felicia Ignatia, *b* at Darmstadt 31 July 1993.

4. Princess Maria *Isabella* Josefine Ulrike Ludmilla Christine, *b* at Schluifeld, nr Wessling, Bavaria 2 Nov 1956, Journalist; *m* at Bonn 18 March 1995, Manfred Lutz (*b* at Bonn 18 March

1954).

[*Wasserburgstraße 2, 53919 Weilerswst-Metternich, Germany*].

5. Princess Maria *Josefine* Sophie Konrada Monika Afra, *b* at Schluifeld 23 April 1958, Dipl Biology; *m* at Habitzheim 6 June 1998, *Heribert* Rustiger (*b* at Dieburg 18 Sept 1959).

[*Sydower Feld 4, 16359 Biesenthal, Germany*].

6. Prince Maria *Martin* Carl Wolfgang Franz Rasso, *b* at Schluifeld 15 April 1961, became Jesuit Priest as Father Löwenstein.

[*Offenbacher Landstrasse 224, 60599 Frankfurt-am-Main, Germany*].

7. Prince *Stephan* Wenzeslaus Erwein Korbinian Rosario, *b* at Munich 7 Oct 1968, Stud Phil, Lt (Res), Journalist; *m* at Wallfahrtskerk 6 July 1996, Andrea Elisabeth (*b* at Beckum 12 Dec 1966), dau of.Klaus Pilatus and Irmgard Bücker, and has issue.

[*Waldstraße 108/110, 63623 Neu-Isenburg, Germany*].

    1. Princess *Clara* Maria Claudia Huberta Forentina, *b* at Munich 17 May 1999.

Brother of Grandfather

Issue of Karl, 6th Prince zu Löwenstein-Wertheim-Rosenberg who later became a Dominican Monk (*b* 21 May 1934; ✠ 8 Nov 1921) and his second wife, Princess Sophie von and zu Liechtenstein (*b* 11 July 1837; *m* 4 May 1863; ✠ 25 Sept 1899), having had issue, among whom,

Son

Prince *Johannes* Baptista Maria Angelus Joseph Konstantin Michael Leopold Karl, *b* at Kleinheubach 29 Aug 1880; ✠ at Newport, Rhode Island, USA 18 May 1956, Capt Prussian Cavalry; *m* at Berlin 19 Feb 1917, Countess Alexandra (*b* at Berlin 3 Nov 1888; ✠ at Geneva 5 March 1971; *m* 1stly at Washington 27 March 1911, Raimund, Count de Pourtalès who ✠ at Yvoire, Haute-Savoie 25 July 1914), dau of Johann-Heinrich, Count von Bernstorff and Jeanne Luckemeyer, and had issue, among whom,

    1. Princess Marie *Sophie* Cäcilie, *b* at Munich 13 Feb 1922, Sister Order of the Sacred Heart.

    [*Via Belzoni 82, 35100 Padua, Italy*].

METTERNICH-WINNEBURG

(✠ Extinct ✠)

Catholic: The feudal Rhenish family originates from a branch of the
Hemmerich (Hemberg) and adopted the name of Metternich at the
end of the 13th century after a village situated in the Schwarzbach
near Euskirchen; Arnold von Metternich, ancient "Zehntgrave"
appeared authentically since 27 March 1297; Carl von Metternich
1350; acquired Winneburg (near Cochem) and Beilstein (near Zell)
by Lothar von Metternich (*b* 31 Aug 1551; ✠ 7 Sept 1623, Elector of
Treves since 1599), 1616; Baron of the Holy Empire, Vienna 28 Aug
1635; recognised by the Elector Palatinate 10 June 1638; recognised
in Bohemia and Bohemian Incolat, Linz 20 March 1646; name of
"von Winneberg zu Beylstein" and ratification of Arms 24 Nov 1655;
qualification of "Wohlgeboren" 28 May 1654; Count of the Holy
Empire with the qualification of "Hoch and Wohlgeboren" and
elevation of the Lordships of Winneberg and of Beylstein into a
County of the Holy Empire, Vienna 20 March 1679; the title of
Count was confirmed in Bohemia 16 Feb 1682; Bohemian Incolat 15
Oct 1716; loss of the County of Winneburg-Beylstein 1801; and
donation, with title indemnified of Ochsenhausen, Abbey of the
Holy Empire (near the Danube, sold to Württemberg 8 March
1825), 1803; title of Prince of the Holy Empire (primogeniture) with
the qualification of "Hochgeboren" and elevation of Ochsenhausen
into a Principality of the Holy Empire, Vienna 30 June 1803;
"Landmann" in Styria 19 Nov 1812; Prince authorised (title extended
to all descendants), Vienna 20 Oct 1813; Member of the State of
Lords of Lower Austria 13 Nov 1813; "Landmann" in Carinthia 13
Jan 1814; Duca di Portella (Sicilian title) 14 Feb 1816; Spanish
Grandee First Class 1 Oct 1818, qualification of "Durchlaucht"
(primogeniture) by the German Diet 18 Aug 1825, confirmed in
Austria 7 Oct 1825; extended to all members of the family 27 April
1869 (with effect from 9 May 1869); Hungarian Indigenat 26 Sept
1825; "Landmann" in Tyrol 2 Aug 1836; Hereditary Member of the
former Austrian House of Lords 18 April 1871.
Members of the family bear the title of Prince or Princess von
Metternich-Winneburg with the qualification of Serene Highness.

✠ **PAUL** Alfons Maria Clemens Lothar Philippus Neri Felix
Nikomedes, **6TH PRINCE (FÜRST) VON METTERNICH-
WINNEBURG,** 5th Duke di Portella, Count of Königswart, *b* at
Vienna 26 May 1917; ✠ at Rolle, Switzerland 21 Sept 1992; son of
Klemens-Wenzel, 5th Prince (Fürst) von Metternich-Winneburg
(*b* 9 Feb 1869; ✠ 13 May 1930) and Doña Isabel de Silva y Carvajal,
9th Countess de Castillejo (*b* 3 May 1880; *m* at 4 Oct 1905; ✠ 8 Feb
1980); *m* at Berlin 6 Sept 1941, Princess Tatiana (*b* at St Petersburg

1 Jan 1915), dau of Ilarion Sergeievich, Prince Wassiltchikoff and Lydia Leonidovna, Princess Wjasemsky.
[*65366 Schloß Johannisberg, Geisenheim, Rheingau, Germany*].

NEIPPERG

Catholic: This Franconian family are descended from Birtilo von Schwaigern living in 1120 and can be authenticated to Reingebodus von Niberch (Neipperg, near Schwaigern) 1 Aug 1241; Baron of the Holy Empire between 1658 and 1672; Count of the Holy Empire with the qualification of "Hoch and Wohlgeboren", Vienna 5 Feb 1726; Lord of Upper Austria, Vienna 20 July 1748; received into the Swabian College of Counts of the Holy Empire 1766; Lord in Lower Austria, Vienna 9 Jan 1771; Hereditary Member of the former Württemberg House of Lords 25 Sept 1819; received the qualification of "Erlaucht" (primogeniture) by the German Diet 13 Feb 1829.
Members of the family bear the title of Count or Countess von Neipperg.

Maria **JOSEF HUBERT** Ernst Vincenz Amadeus Anton Benediktus Konrad Apollinarius, **COUNT and LORD (GRAF AND HERR) VON NEIPPERG**, *b* at Schwaigern 22 July 1918, *succ* his father, Capt (Ret), Kt Order of the Golden Fleece, Kt of Hon Sovereign Military Order of Malta, Gd Cross Bavarian Order of St George, Kt Order of the Golden Fleece, son of Anton-Ernst (Attila), Count and Lord (Graf and Herr) von Neipperg (*b* 18 Dec 1883; ✠ 28 Dec 1947) and Countess Anna von Silva-Tarouca (*b* 28 Sept 1888; *m* 19 Oct 1911; ✠ 17 July 1971); *m* 1stly at Munich 21 Dec 1950 (civ) and 3 Feb (relig) 1951, Countess Marie Franziska (*b* at Krzemusch 5 Nov 1920; ✠ at Heidelberg 14 June 1984), Dame Star Cross Order, dau of Eugen, Count von Ledebur-Wicheln and Countess Eleonore Larisch von Moennich. He *m* 2ndly at Schwaigern 23 Aug (civ) and at Waldenburg 25 Sept (relig) 1986, Princess Therese (*b* at Waldenburg 8 Sept 1938), dau of Friedrich Karl, 8th Prince (Fürst) zu Hohenlohe Waldenburg-Schillingsfürst and Princess (Fürstin) Mechtilde von Urach, Countess von Württemberg.
[*74193 Schwaigern, Württemberg, Germany*].

Sons and Daughters - 1st Marriage

1. *Karl-Eugen* Johannes Nepomuk Erwin Michael, Hereditary Count (Erbgraf) zu Neipperg, *b* at Schwaigern 20 Oct 1951, Dipl Agr Eng;

m at Pöcking, Bavaria 9 July (civ) and 30 July (relig) 1977, Archduchess Andrea (*b* at Würzburg 30 May 1953), Dame Star Cross Order, dau of Otto, Archduke of Austria, former Crown Prince of Austria and Hungary and Princess Regina of Saxe-Meiningen, and has issue,

[*74193 Schwaigern, Württemberg, Germany*].

    1. Count Maria *Philipp* Karl Friedrich Hubert Magnus, *b* at Heilbronn-Neckargartach 6 Sept 1978.

    2. Count Maria *Benedikt* Reinhard Michael Alois Leo, *b* at Heilbronn-Neckargartach 11 April 1980.

    3. Count Maria *Dominik* Georg Christoph Johannes Pantaleon, *b* at Warendorf 27 July 1981.

    4. Countess Maria *Hemma* Nathalie Sophie Franziska Georgine, *b* at Oelde, Warendorf 11 Oct 1983.

    5. Countess Maria *Katharina* Franziska Monika Elisabeth Georgina, *b* at Rheda-Wiedenbrück 23 April 1986.

2. Count *Reinhard Franz* von Assisi Ferdinand Benedikt, *b* at Schwaigern 5 Feb 1953, Dr of Phil, Homeopath; *m* 1stly at Eberstadt 22 March (civ) and at Wimpfen im Tal 19 April (relig) 1979 (*m* diss by div at Heilbronn 20 Sept 1989 and religiously annulled at Rothenburg 10 Dec 1990), Johanna (Hanne) (*b* at Eberstadt 4 Feb 1956), dau of Hans Märker and Anneliese Weissgerber. He *m* 2ndly at Weilheim 12 Oct (civ) and at Waldkirch 13 Oct (relig) 1992, Baroness Stephanie (*b* at Geilenkirchen 24 May 1965), dau of Franz-Ludwig, Baron von Eynatten, Proprietor of Trips and Franziska von Zehmen, and has issue,

[*Steinatstraße 12, 78052 Villingen-Schwenningen-Obereschach, Germany*].

    1. Countess *Maria Regina, b* at Rottweil 3 Sept 1993.

    2. Countess Maria *Helena, b* at Rottweil 29 March 1996.

3. Countess *Maria Anna* Gabrielle Eleonore, *b* at Schwaigern 14 Feb 1955, known as Sister Marianna in the Order of the Little Sisters of Jesus.

[*Gothaerstraße 10, 99958 Gräfentonna, Germany*].

4. Countess Maria *Franziska* Eleonore Katharina, *b* at Schwaigern 7 April 1956; *m* at Schwaigern 21 Oct (civ) and 22 Oct (relig) 1977, Friedrich, Count von and zu Westerholt and Gysenberg (*b* at Freckenhorst 8 June 1949), Dipl Agr Eng.

[*48231 Freckenhorst über Münster, Westfalen, Germany*].

5. Count Maria *Stephan* Christoph Heinrich Alfred Emmeran, *b* at Schwaigern 28 June 1957, Dipl Agr Eng; *m* at Schwaigern 13 Aug

(civ) and at Steisslingen, nr Singen am Hohentwiel 29 Aug (relig) 1982, Baroness Sigweis (*b* at Singen 26 Feb 1959), dau of Fidelis, Baron von Stotzingen and Countess Margerita (Gita) von Bullion, and had issue,

[*Château Canon La Gaffelière, 33330 St. Emilion, Gironde, France*].

    1. Countess *Marie-Beatrice* Barbara Bernadette, *b* at Libourne, Gironde, France 13 July 1984; ✠ at Arendonk, Belgium 20 Aug 1994.

    2. Countess Maria *Caroline* Marita Therese, *b* at Libourne 10 Oct 1986.

    3. Countess Maria *Diane* Andrea Manuela-Franziska Gabrielle, *b* at Talence, Bordeaux, France 19 Jan 1990.

    4. Countess Maria *Philippa* Franziska Nathalie Stephanie, *b* at Talence 23 Feb 1991.

    5. Count Maria *Ludovic* Bernhard Niklas Karl Joseph, *b* at Talence 19 April 1994.

6. Count Maria *Christoph* Bernhard Amadeo Antonius, *b* at Schwaigern 30 July 1958 (known as Pater Christoph Maria CRV).

[*Domplatz 1, 9063 Maria-Saal, Austria*].

7. Countess Maria *Barbara* Sofie Michaela Elisabeth Eleonore, *b* at Schwaigern 4 Jan 1960; *m* at Donzdorf 20 Aug (civ) and at Schwaigern 30 Aug (relig) 1986, Bernhard, Hereditary Count (Erbgraf) von Rechberg and Rothenlöwen zu Hohenrechberg, (*b* at Göppingen 10 Jan 1956), Dipl Agr Eng.

[*In der Breite 1, 73072 Donzdorf, Germany*].

8. Count Maria *Johannes* Alfred Josef Adalbert, *b* at Schwaigern 30 April 1964, Banker.

[*74193 Schwaigern, Germany*].

Brother and Sisters

1. Countess *Eleonore* Marie Antonia Anna Ernestine Huberta Beatrix Gabrielle Benedikta Josefine Felicitas, *b* at Schwaigern 26 Aug 1912; ✠ at Vollrads 9 Jan 1989; *m* at Schwaigern 27 Aug 1936, Richard, Count von Matuschka, Baron von Greiffenclau zu Vollrads, Baron von Toppolczan and Spaetgen (*b* at Wiesbaden 11 May 1893; ✠ at Vollrads 4 Jan 1975).

2. Maria *Karl Reinhard* Antonius Ernst Amadeus Georg Benediktus Hubertus Franziskus Christopherus Josef Erwin Faustinus, Hereditary Count (Erbgraf) von Neipperg, *b* at Schwaigern 15 Feb 1915; ✠*k* in action, nr Proposk, Russia 28 July 1941, Lt.

3. Countess *Marie Gabrielle* Anna Antonia Beatrix Pia Benedicta

Felicitas Huberta Hedwig Wilhelmine Walburga, *b* at Schwaigern 25
Feb 1920, Health Teacher (ret).
[*St. Vinzenz, Baumannstraße 72/23, 88239 Wangen, Germany*].

Brothers of Father

Issue of Reinhard, Count and Lord von Neipperg (*b* 30 July 1856; ✠
15 Nov 1919) and Countess Gabrielle von Waldstein-Wartenberg (*b*
19 Aug 1857; *m* 30 July 1880; ✠ 28 Oct 1948), having had issue,
among whom,

Sons

1. Count Maria *Alfred* Karl Benediktus Ignatius Friedrich Hubertus
Reinhard Felix Franz von Sales Joseph Aloysius, *b* at Schwaigern 21
June 1888; ✠ at Grünwald 11 Sept 1941, Lt-Col German Airforce, Kt
Bavarian Order of St George; *m* at Teaschen, Bohemia 8 Jan 1920,
Countess Marie (*b* at Prague 15 March 1897; ✠ at Regensburg 18
Feb 1971), Dame Star Cross Order, dau of Jaroslav, 2nd Prince
(Fürst) von Thun and Hohenstein and Countess Marie Chotek von
Chotkowa and Wognin, and had issue, among whom,

  1. Countess Marie *Elisabeth* Cäcilia Thaddaa Benedicta, *b* at
  Grünwald 21 Nov 1921, Dame Star Cross Order; *m* at Bedford,
  New York, USA 17 July 1954, Emmerich (Imre), Count
  Hunyady von Kéthely (*b* at Ürmény, Neutra, Hungary 9 Nov
  1900; ✠ at Newark, New Jersey, USA 4 May 1956).
  [*Uhlandstraße 16, 74821 Mosbach-Neckarelz, Germany*].

  2. Countess Maria *Gabrielle* Wilhelmine Benedikta, *b* at
  Grünwald 27 April 1928; ✠ at Münstertal 14 Dec 1976; *m* at
  Köfering, nr Regensburg 31 Aug (civ) and 27 Sept (relig)
  1956, Hubertus, Baron von Landenberg (*b* at Freiburg im
  Breisgau 29 Aug 1922), Dr of Law, Banker.
  [*Johannis, 79219 Stauffen, Germany; Blauenstraße 5, 79189
  Bad Krotzingen, Germany*].

  3. Countess Maria *Anna-Bertha* Benedikta Thaddäa Konrade
  von Parzheim, *b* at Grünwald 21 July 1934.
  [*93096 Köfering bei Regensburg, OPfalz, Germany*].

2. Count Maria *Erwin* Josef Sidonius Benediktus Franziskus von
Sales Petrus Friedrich Ignatcius Hubertus Johannes von Nepumuk
Felix Maurus, *b* at Schwaigern 15 Jan 1897; ✠ at Stuttgart-Vaihingen
5 Dec 1957, Dr of Med, Kt of Hon Sovereign Military Order of Malta;
m at Munich 28 April 1927, Countess Hissa (*b* at Pommerswitz,
Leobschütz 26 Feb 1906; ✠ at Salzburg 4 June 1985), dau of

Alexander, Count von Hatzfeldt zu Trachenberg and Hanna Aoki of the Viscounts Aoki, and had issue, among whom,

1. Countess Maria *Immakulata* Hanna Elisabeth Benedicta Euphrasia, *b* at Munich 13 March 1928; *m* at Johannesburg, South Africa 14 July 1956, Klaus-Werner Meilchen (*b* at Kaiserslautern 30 March 1920; ✠ at Curitiba, Brazil 24 Feb 1985).
[*Im Eichbäumle 51a, 76139 Karlruhe, Germany*].

2. Countess Maria *Hedwig* Gabrielle Nathalie Benedicta Lioba Laurentia, *b* at Seeshaupt 10 Aug 1929; *m* at Cairo 19 Feb (civ) and 11 April (relig) 1955, Sir Anthony James Williams (*b* at London 28 May 1923; ✠ at Danzig 23 May 1990), British Ambassador (Ret).
[*Jollys Farmhouse, Salehurst, Robertsbridge, East Sussex TN32 5PS England*].

3. Countess Maria *Nathalie* Gabrielle Benedikta Bernhardine, *b* at Stuttgart 20 May 1948, Dame Star Cross Order, Dame Sovereign Military Order of Malta; *m* at Schwaigern 24 July 1970, Niklas, Altgraf zu Salm-Reifferscheidt-Raitz (*b* at Vienna 20 Sept 1942), Forestry Engineer.
[*Weissenwolffstraße 12-14, 4221 Steyregg, Upper Austria*].

OETTINGEN

Catholic: Seigneural family from Riesgau, who originate from Fredericus comes 987 or his son Sigehardus comes in pago Riezzin 1007, and Chuno comes de Otingen (Oettingen) 1150 and his brother comes Ludevicus de Othingen 4 June 1147; Confirmation of all priviledges etc, Basel St Antony's day 1434; the branches below descend from two sons of Count Wilhelm II (*b* 1544; ✠ 14 Oct 1602).

LINE I
OETTINGEN-SPIELBERG

Founded by Count Wilhelm III (*b* 10 Sept 1570; ✠ 3 Jan 1600); Prince of Holy Empire (primogeniture) with the qualification of "Hochgeboren" Vienna 18 July 1734; Bohemian Incolat 21 March 1745; the title of Prince was extended to all descendants at Vienna 19 Dec 1765; Prince of Oettingen-Oettingen and of Oettingen-Spielberg by virtue of an accord with the branch of Oettingen-Wallerstein 2 Jan 1781; Hereditary Member of the "Reichsräte" in Bavaria 5 Dec 1818; received the qualification of "Durchlaucht"

(primogeniture) by the German Diet 18 Aug 1825; Grand Master of
the Crown of Bavaria 1855.
Members of this Line bear the title of Prince or Princess zu Oettingen-
Oettingen and Oettingen-Spielberg, with the qualification of Serene
Highness.

ALBRECHT Ernst Otto Joseph Maria Notger, **11TH PRINCE
(FÜRST) ZU OETTINGEN-OETTINGEN AND
OETTINGEN-SPIELBERG,** b at Munich 7 Feb 1951, Kt of
Bavarian Order of St George; Kt of Hon Sovereign Military Order of
Malta, *succ* his father, son of Alois, 10th (Fürst) Prince zu Oettingen-
Oettingen and Oettingen-Spielberg (b 3 Sept 1920; ✠ 30 Nov 1975)
and Countess Elisabeth Gabriele zu Lynar (b at Görlsdorf 17 May
1922; m at Oettingen 10 Oct 1946); m at Oettingen 26 June (civ) and
at Bartenstein 2 July (relig) 1980, Angela (b at Neuhaus, nr Schliersee
20 Oct 1951), dau of Hans Jank and Märta Larsson.
[*86732 Oettingen, Bavaria, Germany*].

Son and Daughters

1. *Franz-Albrecht* Alois Christian Ferdinand Maria Notger,
Hereditary Prince (Erbprinz) zu Oettingen-Oettingen and Oettingen-
Spielberg, b at Munich 16 Sept 1982.
2. Princess *Theresa* Elisabeth Märta Alexandra Maria Notgera, b at
Augsburg 5 Jan 1984.
3. Princess *Antonia* Carolina Johanna Edda Maria Notgera, b at
Augsburg 26 Feb 1987.
4. Princess *Nora* Amelie Claudia Christiana Maria Notgera, b at
West Palm Beach, Florida 10 June 1990.

Mother

Elisabeth Gabrielle, Dowager Princess zu Oettingen-Oettingen and
Oettingen-Spielberg, b at Görlsdorf, Uckermark 17 May 1922, dau of
Ernst, Prince zu Lynar, Count von Redern and Countess Viktoria
von Redern; m at Oettingen 10 Oct 1946, Alois, 10th Prince (Fürst)
zu Oettingen-Oettingen and Oettingen-Spielberg (b at Kreuth 3
Sept 1920; ✠ at Zurich 30 Nov 1975; *succ* his father 16 Feb 1952),
Lt.-Col., Kt of Hon Sovereign Military Order of Malta.
[*Parkhaus Wildpark, 86732 Oettingen, Bavaria, Germany*].

Sisters

1. Princess *Franziska* Romana Theresia Notgera, b at Munich 14 Oct

1947; *m* at Oettingen 8 Jan (civ) and 19 Jan (relig) 1971, Ferdinand, Prince (Fürst) zu Hohenlohe-Bartenstein (*b* at Bartenstein, Crailsheim, Württemberg 6 March 1942), Lt-Col (Res).
[*Schloß Bartenstein, 74575 Schrozberg, Germany*].

2. Princess *Alexandra* Pia Notgera, *b* at Oettingen 9 Oct 1948; *m* at Oettingen 10 Oct (civ) and 22 Oct (relig) 1977, Hubertus, Prince (Fürst) Fugger von Babenhausen (*b* at Augsburg 23 Nov 1946).
[*Schloß Wellenburg, 86183 Augsburg - Bergheim, Germany; Schloß 87727 Babenhausen, Germany*].

3. Princess *Gabriele* Elisabeth Aloisia Notgera, *b* at Munich 22 July 1953, PD, Dr rer nat; *m* at Grünwald 10 Aug 1990 (civ) and at Berlin 22 Jan 1994 (relig), Peter Gollwitzer (*b* at Nabburg 29 June 1950), Prof of Phil.
[*Krampasplatz 1, 14199 Berlin, Germany*].

4. Princess *Margarita* Agnes Maria Notgera, *b* at Munich 31 July 1957, ✠ at Munich 23 Feb 2000; *m* at Oettingen (civ) 2 Oct and 10 Oct (relig) 1981, Franz, Prince of Lobkowicz (*b* at Munich 25 March 1957), Dr of Med.
[*Barnhofstraße 11, 83646 Bad Tölz, Germany*].

LINE II
OETTINGEN-WALLERSTEIN

Founded by Count Wolfgang III (*b* 26 March 1573; ✠ 5/7 Sept 1598); Lord of Lower Austria 4 April 1672; Prince of Holy Empire with the qualification of "Hochgeboren", Vienna 5 March 1774; Prince of Oettingen-Oettingen and of Oettingen-Wallerstein by virtue of an accord with the branch of Oettingen-Spielberg 2 Jan 1781; Hereditary Member of the Bavarian "Reichsräte" 26 May 1818; Hereditary Member of the First Chamber of the Kingdom of Württemberg 25 Sept 1819; received the qualification of "Durchlaucht" (primogeniture) by the German Diet 18 Aug 1825.
Members of this Line bear the title of Prince or Princess zu Oettingen-Oettingen and Oettingen-Wallerstein, Count or Countess zu Oettingen-Baldern and Lord or Lady (Herr or Herrin) von Soetern, with the qualification of Serene Highness.

MORITZ, Eugen Carl Friedrich Anton Kraft Notger Maria, **8TH PRINCE AND LORD (FÜRST AND HERR) ZU OETTINGEN-OETTINGEN AND OETTINGEN-WALLERSTEIN,** Count zu Oettingen and Baldern, Lord von Soetern, auf Wallerstein, *b* at Munich 20 May 1946, Kt Sovereign Military Order of Malta, Kt Bavarian Order of St George, *succ* his father, son of Karl Friedrich, 7th Prince and Lord (Fürst and Herr) zu Oettingen-Oettingen and Oettingen-Wallerstein, etc (*b* 23 May 1917; ✠ 30 March 1991) and Countess Delia Schenk von Stauffenberg (*b* 4 March 1919; *m* 24 July (civ) and 26 July (relig) 1942); *m* at Reicholzheim 28 May (civ) and Bronnbach 22 July (relig) 1969, Princess Lioba (*b* at Bronnbach 2 Oct 1946), Dame Star Cross Order, dau of Karl, Prince (Fürst) zu Löwenstein-Wertheim-Rosenberg and Carolina Rignon of the Counts Rignon.

[*86745 Hohenaltheim bei Nördlingen, Germany*].

Sons

1. *Carl-Eugen* Moritz Markwart Kraft Friedrich Petrus Notger Maria, Hereditary Prince (Erbprinz) zu Oettingen-Oettingen and Oettingen-Wallerstein, *b* at Munich 29 April 1970, Kt Bavarian Order of St George; *m* at Sayn 24 June (civ) and 6 June (relig) 1994 (*m* diss by div 2002), Princess Alexandra (*b* at Munich 20 Aug 1973), dau of Alexander, 7th Prince (Fürst) zu Sayn-Wittgenstein-Sayn and Countess Gabriela von Schönborn-Wiesentheid, and has issue,

[*Neues Schloß, Herrenstraße 78, 86757 Wallerstein, Germany*].

    1. Princess *Helena* Maria Johanna Gabriela Lioba Notgera, *b* at London 10 Dec 1995.

    2. Prince *Johannes*, Carl Moritz Alexander Rudolf Notger Maria, *b* at Augsbourg 12 June 1998.

2. Prince Ludwig-*Maximilian* Constantin Moritz Nikolaus Notger Maria, *b* at Munich 1 Dec 1972; *m* at Wallerstein 14 June (relig) and at Maria Taferi 30 Aug (civ) 1997, *Stephanie* Nathalie (*b* at Vienna 12 Dec 1971), dau of Andreas von Lederer and Countess Henriette zu Salm-Raifferschedt-Raiz, and has issue,

[*Elias-Holl-Weg 3c, 85072 Eichstätt, Germany*]

    1. Princess *Claire* Therese Maria Lioba Henriette Notgera, *b* at Vienna 30 Sept 1998.

3. Prince *Friedrich-Alexander* Albrecht Johannes Christian Moritz Stephan Notger Maria, *b* at Munich 2 Aug 1978.

[*Calle Castello 122/2C, E-28006 Madrid, Spain*]

Mother

Delia Marie Gabriele, Dowager Princess and Lady (Fürstin and Herrin) zu Oettingen-Oettingen and Oettingen-Wallerstein, *b* at Stuttgart 4 March 1919, dau of Markwart, Count Schenk von Stauffenberg, Proprietor of Amerdingen, and Olga Böhl de Liagre; *m* at Bamberg 24 July (civ) and at Greifenstein 26 July (relig) 1942,

Karl Friedrich, 7th Prince and Lord (Fürst and Herr) zu Oettingen-Oettingen and Oettingen-Wallerstein, etc (*b* at Munich 23 May 1917; ✠ at Ebersberg 30 March 1991), Grand Commander and Chancellor Bavarian Order of St George.

[*Moritzschlössle, 86757 Wallerstein, Schwaben, Germany*].

Brothers and Sister

1. Princess *Ernestine* Konstanze Olga Alexandra Maria Notgera, *b* at Wallerstein 18 Oct 1943; *m* at Rome 29 Nov 1967, Raffaello Massini (*b* at Macerata 4 Aug 1928, ✠ at Rome Jan 19 2001), Dr of Med.

[*La Gufotta, Via Cassia 1415, Casale 8, 00123 La Storta, Rome, Italy*].

3. Prince *Krafft Ernst* Markwart Carl Friedrich Notger Maria, *b* at Munich 9 April 1951; *m* at Wallerstein 26 April (civ) and at Inning am Ammersee 12 Sept (relig) 1981, Helen (*b* at Munich 15 Aug 1956), dau of Germanus Theo Lins and Eleonore Sophie Woerner, and has issue,

[*Uttenstetten 1, 86742 Fremdingen, Germany*].

    1. Prince *Philipp-Carl* Anton Eugen Markwart Notger Maria, *b* at Munich 11 Sept 1983.

    2. Prince *Leopold-Ludwig* Wolfgang Moritz Carl Notger Maria, *b* at London 5 June 1987.

Brothers and Sister of Father

Issue of Eugen, 6th Prince and Lord zu Oettingen-Oettingen and Oettingen-Wallerstein (*b* 22 March 1885; ✠ 3 Oct 1969) and Princess Marianne zu Hohenlohe-Waldenburg-Schillingsfürst (*b* 19 Aug 1895; *m* 3 Aug 1916; ✠ 23 March 1978).

1. Princess *Rose-Marie* Ernestine Elisabeth Notgera, *b* at Munich 12 March 1923; *m* at Wallerstein 9 Aug (civ) and 10 Aug (relig) 1949, Franz, Count Strassoldo, Baron von Graffemberg, (*b* at Munich 22 Feb 1917; ✠ at Bonn 11 June 1994), Col (Ret).

[*Puchon 86, 8992 Altaussee, Steiermark, Austria*].

2. Prince *Wolfgang* Kraft Notger Franz Joseph Alexander Maria, *b* at Munich 1 Aug 1924, ✠ at Seyfriedsberg 4 April 2001, Possessor of the Lordship of Seyfriedsberg (Secundogeniture), Lt (Ret); *m* 1stly at Wallerstein 18 June 1950, Countess Henriette (*b* at Gratzen 4 Aug 1917; ✠ at Krumbach, Swabia 3 March 1967; *m* 1stly at Gratzen 28 April 1941, Johann, Count von Ledebur-Wicheln who

was killed at Korsør, Denmark 21 May 1945), dau of Carl de Longueval, Count von Buquoy and Countess Valerie Kinsky von Wchinitz and Tettau. He *m* 2ndly at Wachtberg-Berkum 14 Feb 1975, Princess Michaela (*b* at Berlin 9 March 1940; *m* 1stly at Fuschl 7 June 1963, Alexander, Hereditary Prince (Erbprinz) zu Hohenlohe-Jagstberg; that *m* diss by div 12 Nov 1974; *m* 3rdly at ..., .. von der Becke-Klüchtzner), dau of Hugo, Prince von Schönburg-Waldenburg and Waltraut Benedicta von Klüchtzner. He *m* 3rdly at Ziemetshausen 16 Jan 1986, Countess Angela (*b* at Oberstadion, nr Ehingen, Württemberg 24 Aug 1942; *m* 1stly at South San Gabriel, California, USA 6 Nov 1965, Andrzej Jan Ruttié; that *m* diss by div at Santa Barbara, California ... 1971; she *m* 2ndly at Oberstadion 19 Sept 1975, Gerwin Franzen; that *m* diss by div at Munich 13 Oct 1985), dau of Zdenko, Count von Schönborn, Proprietor of Oberstadion, and Ingeborg (Inge) von Bomhard, and has issue by his first wife, among whom,

[*Schloß Seyfriedsberg, 86473 Ziemetshausen, Germany*].

    1. Princess *Isabelle* Marie-Valerie Notgera, *b* at Munich 8 June 1952, Couturier; *m* at Ziemetshausen 6 April (civ) and at Seyfriedsberg 15 April (relig) 1978 (*m* diss by div at Munich 21 Oct 1980), Claus Police (*b* at Kressbronn am Bodensee 20 March 1944), Advertising Executive. She *m* 2ndly at Ziemetshausen 7 June 1985, Gert Sielaff (*b* at Munich 8 Oct 1951), Dipl Business.

[*Hugo-Vogelstraße 16, 14109 Berlin, Germany*].

    2. Princess *Elisabeth* - Marie Henriette Notgera, *b* at Munich 12 June 1953; *m* 1stly at Brussels 8 Sept (civ) and at Uccle 10 Sept (relig Orthodox) 1978, Nicolas Nikolaievich Zoubov (of Russian nobility) (*b* at Brussels 14 May 1941, ✝ at Bombay 24 March 1996), Engineer. She *m* 2ndly at Brussels 6 Feb 2000, Kolia Constantinowitsch van Ginneken (*b* at Antwerp 26 May 1959).

[*27 avenue des Etangs, 1420 Braine l'Alleud, Belgium*].

    3. Princess *Rose-Marie* Sophie Notgera, *b* at Munich 26 Oct 1955; *m* at Ziemetshausen 2 May (civ) and 6 May (relig) 1978, Wilhelm-Emanuel von Halem (*b* at Gleiwitz 20 Feb 1941), Lawyer.

[*Forst Allee 31, 26524 Hage, Germany*].

ORSINI AND ROSENBERG

Catholic: A feudal family originating in Rosenberg in Styria that can be authenticated since 1289; "Landmann", Carinthia 30 Jan 1621; Baron of Lerchenau and of the Holy Empire, Lord of Magereckh and Grafenstein, Vienna 2 Aug 1633; Count with the qualification of "Wohlgeboren" 8 Oct 1648; Chief Burgrave in Carinthia 29 July 1652; Hereditary Grand Master of the Court in Carinthia, Laxenburg 1 June 1660; "Landmann" in Styria 5 July 1660; received the qualification of "Hoch and Wohlgeboren" (primogeniture), Vienna 4 Sept 1661; Count of the Holy Empire with the qualification of "Hoch and Wohlgeboren", Ödenburg 29 May 1681; Lord in Lower Austria 1687; Bohemian Incolat, Vienna 7 Jan 1695; "Landmann" in Goritz 30 Oct 1781; Prince of the Holy Empire (primogeniture) with the qualification of "Hochgeboren", Frankfurt-am-Main 9 Oct 1790; received the qualification of "Durchlaucht" (primogeniture) by the German Diet 18 Aug 1825; recognised in Austria 7 Oct 1825; Hereditary Member of the former Austrian House of Lords 18 April 1861.

The Head of the family bears the title of Prince von Orsini and Rosenberg with the qualification of Serene Highness. Cadet Members of the family bear the title of Count or Countess von Orsini and Rosenberg.

HEINRICH Johannes Friedrich Maria, **6TH PRINCE (FÜRST) VON ORSINI AND ROSENBERG,** Baron auf Lerchenau and Grafenstein, *b* at Welzenegg 29 Jan 1925, Kt of Hon Sovereign Military Order of Malta, *succ* his father, son of Johannes, 5th Prince (Fürst) von Orsini and Rosenberg (*b* 8 May 1893; ✝ 7 Feb 1932) and Countess Henriette Larisch von Moennich (*b* 1 Jan 1903; ✝ 20 Nov 1994, *m* 2ndly 25 Feb 1933, Alois, Prince von Auersperg who ✝ 6 Sept 1984); *m* at Gradisch 20 July 1947, Countess Eleonore (*b* at Ebenthal 16 May 1928), Dame Star Cross Order, dau of Johann Anton, Count von Goëss and Countess Marie Valerie von Meran. [*9131 Grafenstein, Kärnten, Austria*].

Sons and Daughters

1. Countess *Ludislaja* Maria Anna Henriette Hippolitta Josefa, *b* at Klagenfurt 26 July 1948, Dame Star Cross Order; *m* at Grafenstein 20 Aug (civ) and 30 Aug (relig) 1969, Christian, Baron Nádherny von Borutin (*b* at Nieder-Adersbach, Bohemia 22 July 1939), Insurance Agent.

[*St. Georgenerstraße 91, 9020 Klagenfurt, Austria*].

2. *Johannes* Andreas Alois Heinrich Anton Josef Maria, Hereditary

Count (Erbgraf) von Orsini and Rosenberg, *b* at Klagenfurt 26 Aug 1949; *m* at Altenburg, nr Horn, Austria 23 Sept 1978, Countess Marie Eleonore (*b* at Vienna 23 March 1956), dau of Matthias, Count von Thun and Hohenstein and Countess Eleonore Hoyos, Baroness zu Stichsenstein, and has issue,

[*Hans Weigelstraße 7, 5082 Grödig, Salzburg, Austria*].

    1. Count *Heinrich* Johannes Matthias Josef Maria, *b* at Salzburg 3 Sept 1979.

    2. Countess *Johanna* Maria Andrea, *b* at Salzburg 6 March 1981.

    3. Count *Paul* Markus Lukas, *b* at Salzburg 14 Oct 1982.

3. Count *Ferdinand* Friedrich Andreas Heinrich Josef Maria, *b* at Klagenfurt 28 May 1953, Hotelier; *m* at Vienna 25 April 1981, Princess Zdenka (*b* at Vienna 7 Oct 1956), dau of Georg-Christian, Prince von Auersperg and Countess Eliane du Chastel de la Howarderie, and has issue,

[*9131 Grafenstein, Kärnten, Austria*].

    1. Count *Konrad* Maria Leopold Georg Heinrich, *b* at Vienna 15 Nov 1982.

    2. Countess *Theresia* Maria Elisabeth Eleonore Eliane, *b* at Vienna 28 May 1984.

    3. Count *Ludwig* Gabriel Sylvester Wenzel Maria, *b* at Klagenfurt 28 Sept 1989.

4. Count *Markus* Antonius Andreas Heinrich Josef Maria, *b* at Klagenfurt 8 Aug 1955, Banker; *m* at Klagenfurt 3 June 1984, Gabriele (*b* at Klagenfurt 3 Oct 1959), Dr of Law, dau of Gerhard Lukan and Gisela Singer, and has issue,

[*9131 Grafenstein, Kärnten, Austria*].

    1. Countess *Valerie* Susanne Henriette, *b* at Graz 6 July 1986.

    2. Count *Maximilian* Christian Maria, *b* at Klagenfurt 8 Dec 1988.

5. Count *Matthias* Johannes Andreas Heinrich Josef Maria, *b* at Klagenfurt 8 Aug 1955 (twin with Count Markus), Forester; *m* 1stly at Liebenfels 9 June 1985 (*m* diss by div at .. 1987 and annulled 1992), Brigitte (*b* at Klagenfurt 13 July 1957), Dr of Med, dau of Josef Kogler and Marlies Nagele. He *m* 2ndly at Schloß Stein, Carinthia 26 July 1992, Michaela (*b* at Andau 28 June 1958; ✝ at Höhenbergen, Carinthia 19 June 1993), dau of Michael Lang and Clara Lidy. He *m* 3rdly at Maria Loretto 6 May 1995, Countess Huberta (*b* at Vienna 13 April 1966), dau of Johannes, Count von and zu Trauttmansdorff-Weinsberg and Princess Johanna von Auersperg-Breunner, and has

issue by his third wife,

[*Gut Höhenbergen, 9121 Tainach, Kärnten, Austria*].

    1. Countess *Antonia* Gabriele Maria, *b* at Klagenfurt 23 Oct 1995.

    2. Count *Philipp* Thomas Mathias Maria, *b* at Klagenfurt 26 March 1998.

6. Countess *Henriette* Josefine Sophia Maria, *b* at Klagenfurt 15 May 1957; *m* at Grafenstein 16 June 1979, Eberhard Crain (*b* at Salzburg 13 April 1948), Dr of Law.

[*Schloß Stefling, 93149 Nittenau, Germany*].

7. Countess *Andrea* Franziska Joseph Maria, *b* at Klagenfurt 21 May 1958; *m* at Grafenstein 18 Sept 1983, Guy Littlejohn (*b* at New Plymouth, New Zealand 26 Aug 1958), Designer.

[*9 Cronulla Ave., Mermaid Beach, 4218 Goldcoast City, Queensland, Australia*].

Brother and Sisters

1. Count *Johann* Andreas Heinrich Maria Hubertus, *b* at Welzenegg 3 July 1926, Kt of Hon Sovereign Military Order of Malta; *m* at Sturefors, nr Linköping, Sweden 22 Oct 1953, Countess *Catharina* Maria Alexandra (*b* at Linköping 12 Nov 1930), Dame Sovereign Military Order of Malta, dau of Thure-Gabriel, Count Bielke and Countess Birgitta Sparre af Söfdeborg, and has issue,

[*Sonnegg, 9141 Eberndorf, Kärnten, Austria*].

    1. Count *Andreas* Heinrich Hubertus Seraphin Maria, *b* at Klagenfurt 3 Sept 1954, Graphic Artist; *m* at Maria Trost, nr Graz 20 May 1983, Eleonore (*b* at Graz 22 Sept 1955), dau of Rudolf Wallner and Countess Maria Hoyos, Baroness zu Stichsenstein, and has issue,

    [*Wasser Gasse 27, 1030 Vienna, Austria*].

        1. Count *Raphael* Johannes Gobertus Serafin Maria, *b* at Graz 3 March 1984.

        2. Count *Luca* Alexander Gobertus Serafin Maria, *b* at Graz 20 March 1986.

        3. Count *Luis* Paul Seraphin Gobertus Maria, *b* at Graz 16 Feb 1989.

    2. Countess *Birgitta* Gunilla Gabriella Maria, *b* at Klagenfurt 2 Oct 1955, ✝ 17 July 2000; *m* at Völkermarkt 14 Nov 1981, Peter Treppo (*b* at Völkermarkt 19 Oct 1952).

    [*Schwantalerstraße 45, 5026 Salzburg, Austria*].

    3. Countess *Cäcilia* Mariora, *b* at Klagenfurt 4 Aug 1961;

m at Eberndorf 1 Oct 1988, Christian, Count von Seilern and Aspang (*b* at Vienna 3 Dec 1958).
[*Alt Prerau, 2164 Wildendürnbach, Austria*].

4. Count *Hubertus* Nikolaus Maria, *b* at Klagenfurt 15 Oct 1962; *m* at Stainz 16 July 1997, Monika (*b* at Graz 23 Nov 1967), dau of Johann *Hans* Keil and Countess Charlotte von Meran, Baroness von Brandhofen, and has issue,
[*Sonnegg, 9141 Eberndorf, Kärnten, Austria*].

   1. Count *Paul*, *b* 12 Aug 1999.

   2. Countess *Clara*, *b* at Klagenfurt 1 Sept 2001.

2. Countess *Maria Anna*, *b* at Klagenfurt 20 Aug 1927; *m* at Kitzbühel 16 Dec 1948, Friedrich, Baron Mayr von Melnhof (*b* at Schloß Glanegg 5 July 1924), Proprietor of Glanegg, Dipl Forestry.
[*Schloß Glanegg, 5082 Grödig, Ld Salzburg, Austria*].

3. Countess *Franziska* Johanna Maria Helen, *b* at Welzenegg 28 April 1930; *m* at Schwaz, Tirol 21 Oct 1994, Franz Illing (*b* at Vienna 25 Oct 1909; ✠ at Schwaz 29 Jan 1997).
[*Umlberg 17, 6123 Terfens, Tirol, Austria*].

Brother of Great-Grandfather

Issue of Franz Seraphim, 2nd Prince von Orsini and Rosenberg (*b* 18 Oct 1762; ✠ 4 Aug 1832) and Countess Marie-Caroline von Khevenhüller-Metsch (*b* 14 March 1767; *m* 27 Dec 1786; ✠ 24 Aug 1811), having had issue, among whom,

Son

Count *Friedrich* Sigismund Adam Ferdinand Johann Nepomuk Carl Borromäus Erasmus, *b* at Vienna 3 June 1801; ✠ at Klagenfurt 13 April 1887, Imperial Chamberlain and Grand Master of the Court in Carinthia, Major; *m* at Damtsach 3 Nov 1839, Baroness Johanna (*b* at Damtschach, Carinthia 1 Nov 1815; ✠ at Klagenfurt 5 Jan 1892), Proprietor of Damtschach, Dame Star Cross Order, dau of Felix, Baron Jöchlinger von Jochenstein, Proprietor of Pfannberg and Hartenstein, and Countess Maria Battyány von Német-Ujvár, and had issue, among whom,

Sons

1. Count *Felix* von Valois, *b* at Schloß Loretto, nr Klagenfurt 22 June 1846; ✠ at Csakathurn 15 July 1905, Proprietor of Damtschach, Kt Order of the Iron Crown, Lt-Field Marshal; *m* at Vienna 5 May 1875,

Baroness Franziska (*b* at Prague 3 March 1853; ✣ at Salzburg 6 Nov 1932), Dame Star Cross Order, dau of Leopold, Baron Henniger von Seeberg and Baroness Josepha Dobrzensky von Dobrzenicz, and had issue,

1. Count *Felix* Maria Johanna, *b* at Theresienstadt 9 Aug 1886; ✣ at Damtschach, Carinthia 21 July 1962, Proprietor of Damtschach, Dr of Law, Kt of Hon Sovereign Military Order of Malta; *m* at Salzburg 23 Oct 1928, Countess Marianne (*b* at Krakau 30 Jan 1902, ✣ at Damtschach 17 Jan 1999), Dame Star Cross Order, dau of Heinrich, Count von Fünfkirchen and Countess Mathilde von Collato and San Salvatore, and had issue,

[*Damtschacherstraße 18, 9241 Wernberg, Kärnten, Austria*].

1. Count *Felix* Heinrich Oktavian Maria, *b* at Salzburg 16 Aug 1929, Dipl Eng, Architect; *m* at Damtschach 22 Sept 1960, Brigitte (*b* at Linz 10 Oct 1937), dau of Johannes Theodore Würtz and Elvira Brucker, and has issue,

[*Schloß Damtschach, 9241 Föderlach, Kärnten, Austria*].

1. Count *Markus* Felix Maria, *b* at Vienna 30 Oct 1961.
[*Schubertring 8, 1010 Vienna, Austria*].
2. Countess *Anna* Cäcilia Maria, *b* at Klagenfurt 30 April 1965; *m* at ... 21 July 1990, Alexander Krasser (*b* at ... 8 Jan 1960).
3. Countess *Maria* Felicitas Michaela, *b* at Klagenfurt 29 Sept 1966; *m* at ... 29 March 1994, Christian Gürtner (*b* at Gainberg 13 July 1962).
4. Countess *Johanna* Sofia Maria, *b* at Klagenfurt 21 May 1968, Actress.
[*Schubertring 8, 1010 Vienna, Austria*].

2. Count *Lothar*, *b* at Schloß Loretto, nr Klagenfurt 8 Oct 1853; ✣ there 9 June 1932, Kt of Hon Teutonic Order, *m* at Klagenfurt 26 April 1883, Countess Angelika (*b* at Pressburg 31 Dec 1855; ✣ at Unterach am Attersee 25 Oct 1939), Dame Star Cross Order, dau of Julius, Count von Hoditz and Wolframitz and Countess and Lady (Herrin) Johanna zu Stubenberg, and had issue,

1. Count *Wolfgang* Felix, *b* at Damtschach 13 July 1887; ✣ at Vienna 11 Jan 1965, Dr of Law; *m* at Vienna 17 July 1916,

Anna (*b* at Vienna 14 July 1892; ✛ at Klagenfurt 23 Sept 1961), dau of Josef Genser and Anna Floder, and had issue,

1. Count Wolfgang (*Wolf*) Andrä Josef, *b* at Klagenfurt 27 April 1917; ✛ at Vienna 10 Dec 1991, Dr of Phil; *m* at Vienna 27 May 1950, Dietgard (*b* at Vienna 27 Oct 1924), dau of Oswald von Heinrich and Elisabeth von Kirchmayr, and has issue,
[*Billrothstraße 40, 1190 Vienna, Austria*].

1. Count Wolfgang *Gerrit* Oswald Siegfried, *b* at Klagenfurt 29 July 1951, Businessman; *m* at Klagenfurt 25 June 1975, Rosemarie (*b* at St Veit an der Glan 27 Aug 1952), dau of Cyrill Wasle and Theodora Isop, and has issue,
[*Liebharths Gasse34, 1160 Vienna, Austria*].

1. Count Wolf *Andrä*, *b* at Vienna 24 Nov 1984.

2. Count *Helge* Christian Lothar Wilhelm, *b* at Vienna 12 April 1954; *m* at Klagenfurt 29 Aug 1994, Barbara (*b* at Graz 2 March 1963), Graphic Designer, dau of Erich Lazar and Maria Mauser, and has issue,
[*Bacherweg 20a, 8010 Graz, Austria*].

1. Countess *Isabelle* Marie Sophie, *b* at Vienna 4 April 1997.

ORTENBURG
(COUNTS OF SPANHEIM)

Evangelical and Catholic: This family is descended from comes Siegfridus in pago Bustrissa (Pustertal), who ✛ 1065, of the Seigneural Franco-Rhenish family of Spanheim 25 Jan 1048; Margrave in the Margraviate against Hungary 7 March 1045 to 1046; his grandson, Henri IV (✛ 1123) received the right of the Duchy of Carinthia after his godfather, Henri III, last Duke of Carinthia of the House of Eppenstein; Duke of Carinthia 1122 - 1269 and 1275 - 1279; Count of Ortenburg (Lower Bavaria) since Rapoto I, comes de Ortenberch (✛ 1190); Count Palatine of Bavaria 1209 - 1248; the County of Ortenburg was recognised as an immediate State of the Holy Empire by the Imperial Chamber 4 March 1573; publication in Bavaria of the qualification of "Hoch and Wohlgeboren" 5 May 1684; the county of Ortenburg was surrendered to Bavaria in 1805; received into the

College of Bavarian Counts 23 Oct 1812; Hereditary Member of the Bavarian "Reichsräte" 5 Dec 1818; received the qualification of "Erlaucht" (primogeniture) 22 April 1829 in Bavaria; and by the German Diet 13 Feb 1829; extended to all members of the family 7 March 1911.
Members of the family bear the title of Count or Countess zu Ortenburg with the qualifcation of Illustrious Highness.

ALRAM Karl Gottfried Hans Ladislaus, **COUNT (GRAF) ZU ORTENBURG,** Count and Lord zu Tambach, Lord zu Birkenfeld, *b* at Budapest 23 Oct 1925, Forester, son of Franz, Count (Graf) zu Ortenburg (*b* 16 Aug 1875; ✠ 3 Dec 1936) and Countess Ily (Helene) Semsey de Semse (*b* 16 May 1895; *m* 30 Dec 1924; ✠ 16 Oct 1978); *m* at Tannheim, Württemberg 21 Oct 1954, Countess Agathe (*b* at Mainz 14 May 1925), dau of Joseph, Count von Schaesberg and Countess Ghislaine de Berlaymont, and has issue,
[*Am Wildpark, 96479 Tambach, OFranken, Germany*].

Sons and Daughters

1. Countess *Marie-Isabell* Ily Ghislaine, *b* at Bamberg 1 Sept 1955; *m* at Weitramsdorf 17 April (civ) and at Tambach 17 April (relig) 1978, Antonius (Tonio), Baron von Salis-Soglio, Proprietor of Gemünden, Hunsrück and Mandel, Kreuznach, Dipl Business, Forester (*b* at Wimborn 12 Sept 1948).
[*Schloß, 55490 Gemünden, Hunsrück, Germany*].
2. *Heinrich* Franz Josef Georg Maria, Hereditary Count (Erbgraf) zu Ortenburg, *b* at Bamberg 11 Oct 1956, Forester; *m* at Weitramsdorf 21 Sept (civ) and at Hechingen 6 Oct (relig) 1990, Princess Désirée (*b* at Munich 27 Nov 1963), dau of Prince Johann Georg of Hohenzollern and Princess Birgitta of Swuden, and has issue,
[*Schloß Allee 1, 96479 Tambach, OFranken, Germany*].
    1. Count *Carl-Theodor* Georg Philipp Maria, *b* at Lichtenfels 21 Feb 1992.
    2. Count *Frederik* Hubertus Ferdinand Maria, *b* at Lichtenfels 7 Feb 1995.
    3. Countess *Caroline* Maria Franzika Christina Stephanie, *b* at Lichtenfels 22 March 1997.
3. Countess *Stephanie* Hildegard Philippa Maria, *b* at Bamberg 12 April 1958, Florist.
[*Querqualto, 06062 Citta della Pieve, Italy*].
4. Count *Karl* Johannes Ghislain Maria, *b* at Bamberg 17 July 1960, Lic phil.

[Cresswell Gardens, London, SW5 0PJ].

Brother

1. Count *Aurel* Ladislaus Franz Heinrich Ernst, *b* at Budapest 30
Aug 1927, ✝ at Middachten 13 Oct 2001, Proprietor of Birkenfeld,
Land Manager, Kt of St John of Jerusalem; *m* at Middachten,
Gelderland 20 Dec 1951, Countess Isabelle (*b* at Middachten 3 July
1925), Proprietor of Middachten, Gelderland, and Gaildorf,
Württemberg, dau of Wilhelm, Count von Aldenburg-Bentinck and
Waldeck-Limpurg and Baroness Adrienne Vegelin van Claerbergen,
and has issue,
*[Kasteel Middachten, 6994 JC De Steeg, The Netherlands; Schloß
Birkenfeld, 96126 Maroldsweisach, Germany]*.

    1. Count *Franz* Wilhelm Friedrich Ladislaus, *b* at Coburg 12
    June 1953, Lic econ; *m* at Wrestedt 3 June (civ) and at
    Nettelkamp, nr Uelzen 5 June (relig) 1993, Countess Gustava
    (*b* at Bevensen 18 Oct 1955), dau of Adolf, Count Grote and
    Baroness Mechtilde von Uslar Gleichen.
    *[Liebfrauenstraße 27, 61440 Oberursel, Germany; Kasteel
    Middachten, 6994 JC De Steeg, The Netherlands]*.

        1. Count *Vincent* Carl Wilhelm, *b* at Frankfurt-am-
        Main 7 Aug 1995.
        2. Count Cecil *Alexander* Carl Wilhelm, *b* at Frankfurt-
        am-Main 16 Oct 1997.
        3. Count *Caspar* Franz Maximilian, *b* at Frankfurt-am-
        Main 16 Jan 2001.

    2. Count *Philipp* Wilhelm, *b* at Bamberg 9 April 1955, Dipl
    Eng; *m* at Maroldsweisach 17 Aug (civ) and at Ellecom 1 Oct
    (relig) 1988, Mirjam (*b* at Haarlem, Holland 16 March 1958),
    Dr of Law, dau of Hendrik Kalf and Ina Kruyer, and has issue,
    [Schloß Birkenfeld, 96126 Maroldsweisach, Germany].

        1. Countess Julia *Sophie* Rebecca, *b* at Münster 11
        Feb 1991.
        2. Count *Felix* Christian David, *b* at Münster 1 April
        1992.
        3. Countess *Marie* Thérèse Serah, *b* at Lichtenfels 22
        Aug 1994.
        4. Count *Johannes* Casper Daniel, *b* at Lichtenfels 4
        May 1997.

3. Countess *Nadine* Marie Elisabeth, *b* at Bamberg 1 May
1957; *m* at Birkenfeld 27 June 1981, Albrecht, Count von

Brandenstein-Zeppelin (b at Biberach an der Riss 5 Aug 1950), Proprietor of Mittelbiberach, Lawyer.
[*Schloß, 88441 Mittelbiberach, Germany*].

Brother of Great-Grandfather

Issue of Count Josef-Carl (b 30 Aug 1780; ✠ 28 March 1831) and Countess Caroline of Erbach-Erbach (b 21 Nov 1779; m 6 Oct 1799; ✠ 6 Dec 1825), among whom,

Son

Count *Friedrich* Carl Ludwig, b at Erbach 14 Jan 1805; ✠ at Tambach 10 Nov 1860, Kt Teutonic Order; m at Mühlhausen 10 Sept 1830, Ernestine von Rentz (b at Mühlhausen 9 Dec 1807; ✠ at Coburg 23 Jan 1891), having had issue, among whom,

Son

Count *Friedrich* Albrecht Ludwig Franz, b at Mühlhausen 3 Oct 1831; ✠ at Sonneberg 28 Aug 1904; m at Graz 30 May 1870, Princess Anastasia (b at Cerlenkow 12 Aug 1840; ✠ at Wiener-Neustadt 28 Dec 1912), dau of Joseph, Prince (Fürst) von Wrede and Anastasia Feodorovna Petrova-Solovova, having had issue, among whom,

Son

Count *Friedrich* Joseph Franz Emanuel, b at Coburg 23 July 1871; ✠ at Bayerhof 4 March 1940, Royal Bavarian Ambassador, Major Bavarian Army; m at Langenzell 26 July 1905, Princess Ilka (b at Langenzell 9 Jan 1887; ✠ at Schweinfurt 31 March 1971), dau of Alfred, Prince zu Löwenstein-Wertheim-Freudenberg and Countess Pauline von Reichenbach-Lessonitz, and had issue, among whom,

    1. Count *Alfred-Friedrich* Franz Otto Hugo Amelung, b at Berlin 12 May 1906; ✠ at Schweinfurt 3 Sept 1973; m at Berlin 28 May 1930, Jutta (b at Danzig 21 June 1906; ✠ at Schweinfurt 23 Dec 1991), dau of Leopold von Lücken and Irmgard von Brünneck, and had issue,

        1. Count *Botho* Friedrich Leopold Harald Manfred Otto Wolf, b at Würzburg 21 April 1937, Land Manager; m at Bevensen 23 Oct 1970 (civ) and at Molzen 9 Jan 1971 (relig), Baroness Ilse (b at Bevensen 16 April 1943), dau of Hilmar, Baron von dem Bussche-Haddenhausen and Osterhold von Lüneburg, and has issue,

        [*Bayerhof, Gädhaimerstraße 1, 97453 Schonungen,*

Germany; Klostergut Wülfinghausen, 31832 Springe, Germany].

    1. Countess *Anna-Madeleine*, *b* at Lübeck 28 Oct 1971, Assistant Manager; *m* at Berlin 13 Dec 1999 (civ) and at Wülfingshausen 6 May (relig) 2000, Hervé -Alexander Perrin de Nelle (*b* at Munich 1 July 1971).
    [*Château de Cuq-Larriveau, 47430 Le Mas D'Agenais, France*].

    2. Count *Friedrich*, *b* at Oldenburg, Holstein 11 Jan 1974, Lt. (Res).

    3. Countess *Christiane*, *b* at Oldenburg, Holstein 10 April 1975.
    [*Klostergut Wulfinghausen, 31832 Springe, Germany*].

2. Count *Engelbert* Wilhelm Udo Heinrich, *b* at Würzburg 11 March 1939, Businessman; *m* at Montreal, Quebec, Canada 6 March 1965, Margot   (*b* at Berlin 5 Aug 1942), dau of Georg Pöllmann and Theodora Pavity, and have issue,
[*2367 Ventura Drive, Oakville, Ontario LGL 2H5, Canada*].

    1. Count *Peter*, *b* at Montreal 1 March 1970, Businessman.

3. Countess *Ilka* Irmgard Pauline Hanna Lili Harriet, *b* at Würzburg 29 June 1942; *m* at Waldsachsen (civ) and at Schonungen am Main (relig) 9 Oct 1971, Johann, Duke of Oldenburg (*b* at Lensahn 3 Jan 1940), Businessman, Capt (Res).
[*Bäderstraße 37a, 23738 Lensahn, Ostholst, Germany*].

4. Count *Joachim* Christian Manfred Gustav-Albrecht, *b* at Würzburg 26 May 1944, Lawyer, Tax Consultant, Capt (Res); *m* at Bodenwerder 28 Aug (civ) and 10 Oct (relig) 1970, Ilsabe (*b* at Hamburg 8 Sept 1945), dau of Wilhelm von Brünneck and Waldtraut von Stülpnagel, and have issue,
[*Ruffini Allee 8, 82166 Gräfelfing, Germany*].

    1. Count *Moritz* Friedrich Carl, *b* at Bonn 25 May 1975.
    [*Gentzstraße 1, 80796 Munich, Germany*].

    2. Count *Christian* Joachim, *b* at Bonn 28 May

1977, Banker.

    3. Count *Rupprecht* Georg Botho Aurel, *b* at Bonn 23 Nov 1979.

    5. Countess *Yvonne* Elisabeth Amélie Marie-Luise, *b* at Würzburg 2 Jan 1948; *m* at Parensen, Hanover 27 June (civ) and at Schonungen am Main 18 July (relig) 1970, Ludwig von Breitenbuch (*b* at Ranis, Thüringen 23 Sept 1935), Land Manager, Proprietor of Parensen. [*Hauptstraße 1, 37176 Nörten-Hardenberg - Parensen, Germany*].

2. Countess *Amélie* Anastasia Pauline Madeleine Elisabeth, *b* at Langenzell 19 Dec 1909; *m* at Bayerhof 10 April 1934, Heinrich, Burggraf and Count zu Dohna-Schlobitten (*b* at Potsdam 24 April 1907; ✞*k* at Maubeuge, France 22 May 1940). [*Ehrwalderstraße 10, 82467 Garmisch-Partenkirchen, Germany*].

PAPPENHEIM

Evangelical and Catholic: Feudal Franco-Swabian family which takes its name from a castle on the Altmühl in Bavaria and probably descend from Henricus Caput or cum capite 1111 and can be traced authentically from Heinricus de Pappenheim 1138 - 47, 1141; Hereditary Marshal of the Holy Empire probably since 1100; authenticated since 1141; Count of the Holy Empire (for Count Gottfried Heinrich and his cousin) with the qualification of "Hoch and Wohlgeboren", confirmed at Prague 19 Jan 1628, Vienna 1 Oct 1740, Frankfurt-am-Main 12 July 1742 and recognised by the Elector of Saxony 11 March 1745; Hereditary Member of the "Reichsräte" in Bavaria 25 Feb 1825; Bavarian qualification of "Erlaucht" (primogeniture) 25 Aug 1831 and by the German Diet 13 Feb 1829; extended to all family members 7 March 1911; Family Law established 16 April 1864.

Members of the family bear the title of Count or Countess zu Pappenheim with the qualification of Illustrious Highness.

ALBERT Julius Joseph Alexander Siefried, **COUNT and LORD (GRAF and HERR) ZU PAPPENHEIM,** *b* at Budapest 21 Jan 1943, BA Econ, Businessman, Director, son of Alexander, Count and Lord (Graf and Herr) zu Pappenheim (*b* 3 March 1905; ✞ 6

April 1995) and his first wife, Maria Zeyk de Zeykfalva (*b* 10 April 1912; *m* 8 Feb 1941; *m* diss by div 1957; ✠ 10 Oct 1974).
[*52 rue des Chavannes, 2016 Cortaillod, Kt. Neuchâtel, Switzerland*].

Sister

1. Countess *Nicolette* Ilona Erzsébet Georgine Cecile Maria, *b* at Budapest 6 Dec 1941; *m* at Salzburg 29 Sept 1964, Michael Pössenbacher (*b* at Munich 11 March 1941), Businessman.
[*Casa Caymán, Careyes, Jalisco, Mexico*].

Step-Mother

Princess Eduarda (*Edina*), Countess zu Pappenheim, *b* at Salzburg 16 Oct 1903, dau of Prince Eduard of Liechtenstein and Countess Olga von Pückler and Limpurg; *m* 1stly at Vienna 12 July 1922, Viktor, Count zu Trauttmansdorff-Weinsberg (*b* at St Jean, France 16 May 1895; ✠ at Salzburg 3 Aug 1969), Capt Austrian Cavalry. She *m* 2ndly at Maria-Kirchenthal, nr Lofer 20 Aug 1975, Alexander, Count (Graf) and Lord zu Pappenheim (*b* at Iszka Szent-György, Hungary 3 March 1905; ✠ at Salzburg 6 April 1995; *succ* his kinsman, Ludwig Friedrich, Count and Lord zu Pappenheim who ✠ 23 Nov 1960 - see below), Proprietor of Iszka Szent-György, Kt of Hon Sovereign Military Order of Malta.
[*Aignerstraße 19, 5026 Salzburg-Aigen, Austria*].

Brother and Sisters of Father

Issue of Siegfried Alexander, Count zu Pappenheim (*b* 12 Jan 1868; ✠ 26 May 1936) and Countess Elisabeth Károlyi von Nagy-Károly (*b* 17 May 1871; *m* 15 Jan 1903; ✠ 21 March 1954) and had issue, among whom,

1. Count *Georg* Eduard Paul Viktor Haupt, *b* at Schloß Parád, Heves 28 July 1909; ✠ at Munich 15 Oct 1986, Diplomat; *m* 1stly at Jettingen, Swabia 24 Sept 1947 (*m* annulled at Munich-Freising 24 April 1969; *m* diss by div Bonn 17 Dec 1970), Karin (*b* at Kloster Neuendorf, Gardelegen 10 July 1913), dau of Fritz von Veltheim and Brita von Lindequist [*Parzivalstraße 10, 80804 Munich, Germany*]. He *m* 2ndly at Munich 30 Dec 1970, Elisabeth (*b* at Potsdam 18 April 1924; *m* 1stly at Tiefenbach, nr Oberstdorf 9 April (civ) and 14 July (relig) 1960, Walter Kopp, who ✠ at Quito, Ecuador 12 Sept 1965), dau of Lothar Blankenburg and Henriette Rathjen, and has issue by his first wife,

[*Giselherstraße 16, 80804 Munich, Germany*].

    1. Count *Alexander* Maria Haupt, *b* at Schliersee 27 Aug 1948, Kt of Hon Sovereign Military Order of Malta, Judge Bavarian Administrative Court; *m* at Vienna 19 Sept (civ) and 23 Oct (relig) 1977, Countess Marie Christine (*b* at Vienna 11 Nov 1950), Dame Star Cross Order, dau of Heinrich, Count von Hartig and Altgräfin Elisabeth zu Salm-Reifferscheidt-Raitz, and has issue,

[*Josef Sammerstraße 3, 82031 Grünwald, nr Munich, Germany*].

    1. Countess *Caroline* Maria Gabriele Dorothea Elisabeth Catharina, *b* at Vienna 4 Aug 1978.

    2. Countess *Maria Elisabeth*, *b* at Vienna 6 Feb 1980; ✛ at Pappenheim 15 March 1980.

    3. Count *Georg* Heinrich Maria Otto Gotthard Haupt, *b* at Vienna 26 June 1981.

    4. Countess *Maria Theresia* Gabriele Katharina Elisabeth, *b* at Vienna 15 Sept 1982.

Brother of Grandfather

Issue of Count Friedrich Albert (*b* 18 July 1777; ✛ 1 July 1860) and Baroness Marie Antonie Taenzl de Trazberg (*b* 6 April 1793; *m* 14 Dec 1814; ✛ 6 April 1861), having had issue, among whom,

Sons

1. **Ludwig, Count and Lord (Graf and Herr) zu Pappenheim,** *b* 5 Dec 1815; ✛ 2 Aug 1883; *m* at Sans Souci 11 July 1854, Countess Anastasia von Schlieffen (*b* 9 Jan 1827; ✛ 22 April 1898), and had issue, among whom,

    1. **Ludwig** Magnus Heinrich Carl Haupt, **Count and Lord (Graf and Herr zu Pappenheim,** *b* at Pappenheim 10 March 1862; ✛ 5 June 1905, Lt (Res); *m* at Baden-Baden 24 April 1896, Countess Julie Rüdiger (*b* at Lublin 25 June 1868; ✛ 17 Jan 1950), dau of Friedrich, Count Rüdiger and Sophie von Krusenstern and had issue, among whom,

        1. **Ludwig Friedrich** Karl Marlie Franz Haupt, **Count and Lord (Graf and Herr) zu Pappenheim,** *b* at Berlin 8 June 1898; ✛ at Pappenheim 23 Nov 1960, Capt, Kt of Justice of St John of Jerusalem; *m* 1stly at Marquartstein, Bavaria 1 June 1922, Baroness Liutta (*b* at Munich 19 Dec 1900; ✛ at Erlangen 14 March

1959), dau of Joseph, Baron von Ribeaupierre and Mathilde Mutzenbecher. He *m* 2ndly at Munich 7 Oct 1959 (civ) and at Bayreuth 21 March 1960 (relig), Elisabeth (*b* 26 Jan 1903; ✠ Kreut, nr Munich 16 July 1919), dau of Joseph Popp and Johanna Wölfel, and had issue by his first wife, among whom,

    1. Countess *Beatrix* Julie Theodora Marie Mathilde, *b* at Pappenheim 12 Oct 1924; *m* at Pappenheim 7 Sept 1952, Kurt, Baron von Süsskind (*b* at St Gallen, Switzerland 13 March 1904; ✠ at Dennenlohe 22 Aug 1980), Proprietor of Dennenlohe, Forester and Farmer. She has since reverted to her maiden name. [*Schloß Dennenlohe, 91743 Unterschwaningen bei Gunzenhausen, MFranken, Germany*].

    2. Countess *Ursula* Rüdiger Antonie Nacka Sophie, *b* at Pappenheim 9 April 1926, Proprietor of Pappenheim (since 1959), Dipl Land Management; *m* at Pappenheim 16 April (civ) and 18 April (relig) 1949, Gert, Count von der Recke von Volmerstein (*b* at Kiel 22 Feb 1921; ✠ at Pappenheim 17 March 1991), Dr of Agriculture, Dipl Land Management; from 27 March 1979 to 20 July 1979 bore the name "Count von der Recke-Volmerstein-Count zu Pappenheim" following a legal name change; She reverted to her maiden name 10 July 1979. [*Neues Schloß, 91788 Pappenheim, MFranken, Germany*].

2. Count *Maximilian* Joseph Karl Friedrich, *b* at Dennenlohe 5 Sept 1824; ✠ at Möhren 10 July 1906, Lord of Möhren-Gundelsheim, Gd Marshal of the Court of the Queen Mother of Bavaria, Kt Bav Order of St George, Cmdr Bavarian Commandery of St John of Jerusalem; *m* at Pappenheim 23 Oct 1860, Countess Luise von Schlieffen (*b* at Berlin 23 Aug 1838; ✠ at Pappenheim 12 April 1924), Order of St Theresa; dau of Karl Count von Schlieffen and Countess Petrovna Shuvalov, having had issue, among whom,

    1. Count *Friedrich* Ferdinand Heinrich Wilhelm Haupt, *b* at Pappenheim 11 Dec 1863; ✠ at Munich 26 Aug 1926, Kt of Honour of St John of Jerusalem, Master of the Household of Crown Prince Rupprecht; *m* at Berlin 26 Feb 1907, Countess

Irma (*b* at Berlin 12 May 1877; ✠ at Treuchtlingen 6 July 1968), dau of Georg, Count von Kanitz and Countess Helene von Hatzfeldt zu Trachenberg, and had issue, among whom,

    1. Count *Maximilian* Georg Albrecht Haupt, *b* at Munich 9 Jan 1908; ✠ at Chailly-sur-Montreux 30 April 1995, Proprietor of Möhren-Gundelsheim, Kt of Honour of St John of Jerusalem (1948-1964); *m* 1stly at Potsdam 14 Sept 1940, Hildegard (*b* at Diesdort, Altmark 8 Jan 1914; ✠ at Baden-Baden 7 Feb 1973), dau of Georg Schulz and Eleonore Leskür. He *m* 2ndly at Munich 21 Sept (civ) and at Baden-Baden 12 Oct (relig) 1973, Renate (*b* at Bremen 4 Oct 1930), dau of Friedrich Carl Rung and Elfriede Lameyer, and has issue from his first wife,

    [*La Corduire, 1816 Chailly-sur-Clarens, Switzerland*].

        1. Countess *Michaela* Irma, *b* at Munich 5 Jan 1942; *m* at Munich 3 April 1965 (*m* diss by div at Rosenheim 11 March 1983), Otto Kurzendorfer (*b* at Munich 27 July 1937), Dipl rer pol, Engineer.

        [*83075 Bad Feilnbach, Upper Bavaria, Germany*].

        2. Count *Stephan* Friedrich Georg Haupt, *b* at Würzburg 15 March 1944.

        [*255 Massachusetts Avenue, Boston, MA 02115, U.S.A.*].

    2. Count *Rudolf* Heinrich Klemens Haupt, *b* at Munich 25 Dec 1910; ✠ at Pappenheim 14 Feb 1999, Kt of Justice of St John of Jerusalem; *m* at Zurich 5 Aug (civ) and at Pappenheim 11 Aug (relig) 1955, Helen Elisabeth (*b* at Zurich 4 Aug 1927), dau of Rudolf Bodmer and Helene Alice Stadler, and has issue,

    [*Weidstraße 1, 8808 Pfäffikon, Kt. Schwyz, Switzerland*]

        1. Countess *Isabella* Dorothea Beatrice Alice Luisa, *b* at Washington 8 Dec 1956, Lic oec; *m* 1stly at Aarau 12 June (civ) and at Zurich 18 June (relig) 1981 (*m* diss by div at Zurich 31 Aug 1990), Henry Erik Benteler (*b* at Göttingen 21 Oct 1952), Lic oec, Businessman. She *m* 2ndly at Zurich 1 Sept 1995, Josef Wolfgang

Kogler (*b* at Klagenfurt 13 Oct 1958), Mag oec.
[*Lederer Gasse17, 1080 Vienna, Austria;
Weidstraße 1, 8808 Pfäffikon, Kt. Schwyz,
Switzerland*].
2. Countess *Alexandra* Charlotte Brigitte
Dorothea Ursula, *b* at Washington 29 July 1958,
Lic jur.
[*Steulistraße 29, 8032 Zurich, Switzerland*].
3. Countess *Stephanie* Constance Beatrice
Valerie Lucie, *b* at Washington 14 July 1960;
m at Frankfurt 7 July 1999, Andreas Grunwald
(*b* at Frankfurt 30 March 1965).
[*Paradiesstraße 12a, 8802 Kilchberg,
Switzerland*].
4. Count *Christian* Rudolf Kield Gottfried
Heinrich Haupt, *b* at Washington 28 June 1963,
Lic jur; *m* at Pfaeffikon/Sz 4 Sept (civ) 1991
and at Zurich 7 Sept (relig) 1991 (*m* diss by div
at Zurich 14 Jan 1993), Sophie
[*Hafnerwaldstraße 20c, 9012 St. Gallen,
Switzerland*] (*b* at Baden-Baden 8 July 1966;
m 2ndly 5 April 1993, Manfred Gutsman),
adopted dau of Ladislaus von Hoffmann de
Nagysötétág and Beatrix Nottmeyer.
[*Merkurstraße 35, 8032 Zurich, Switzerland*].
3. Countess *Iphigenie* Luise Irma Editha Alice, *b* at
Munich 3 June 1912.
[*3725 Mayette Ave., Santa Rosa, California 95405,
U.S.A.*].

PLATEN HALLERMUND

**Lutheran and Catholic: This feudal family originated in Pomerania
under the name of "mit der Plate, cum plata, cum thorace" since
Otto cum plata, miles 1255; and Hennig de Platen living circa 1396;
Baron of the Holy Empire 1630; title was confirmed at Vienna 28 Jan
1670; Count of the Holy Empire and Noble Lord with the qualification
of "Hoch-Wohlgeboren", Vienna 20 July 1689; publication in Salzburg
6 March 1690; title recognised by the Elector of Saxony 9 May 1693;
and by the Elector of Brandenburg 30 May 1693; the investiture of**

the County of Hallermund was received from the Elector of Hanover 1704; received into the College of the Counts of Westphalia 7 Aug 1709; Hereditary Member of the former House of Lords of Hanover 1819; qualification of "Erlaucht" (primogeniture) by the German Diet 13 Feb 1829; Prussian confirmation of the right to bear the title of Count for all descendants in the male line, of Georg Wilhelm Friedrich, Count of Platen-Hallermund (✠ 13 Jan 1873 - Hereditary Postmaster General, Hanover); Reichsgrafen.

Members of the family bear the title of Count or Countess von Platen Hallermund with the qualification of Illustrious Highness for the Head of the family only.

ERIK Peter Georg Erasmus, **COUNT and NOBLE LORD (GRAF AND EDLER HERR) VON PLATEN HALLERMUND,** Proprietor of Weissenhaus and Futterkamp, Bachelor of Commerce, *b* at Kiel 21 April 1939, Hereditary Postmaster General of Hanover, Kt of Justice of St John of Jerusalem, son of Clemens, Count and Noble Lord (Graf and Edler Herr) von Platen Hallermund (*b* 18 July 1902; ✠ 20 June 1983) and Eleonore de Weerth (*b* 26 May 1907; *m* 15 May 1935; ✠ 17 Oct 1993); *m* at Schönberg, nr Kiel 23 Sept 1967, Henriette (*b* at Ottwitz, Strehlen 4 Jan 1939), dau of Werner von Gellhorn, Proprietor of Ottwitz and Barbara von Perbandt.

[*Friederikenhof, 23758 Wangels, Schleswig-Holstein, Germany*].

Son and Daughter

1. *Erasmus-Bent* Werner Clemens Cornel, Hereditary Count (Erbgraf) von Platen Hallermund, *b* at Göttingen 10 Feb 1971.
2. Countess *Amely-Hedwig* Barbara Eleonore, *b* at Kiel 1 April 1973.
3. Count *Clemens* Erik Paul Georg Sklode, *b* at Kiel 3 Sept 1974.
4. Count *Sebastian* Felix Albrecht George Peter, *b* at Kiel 27 March 1976.

Sister

1. Countess *Sabine* Margarethe Ilse Cornelia, *b* at Kiel 26 June 1946, Proprietor of Sondermühlen, Laer and Königsbrück, Hanover; *m* at Weissenhaus 3 July 1971, Karl-Friedrich, Baron von Richthofen (*b* at Breslau 19 Feb 1940), Dr of Pol Science.

[*Gut Sondermühlen, Nordenfelder Weg 45, 49324 Melle, Germany*].

Brother of Father

Issue of Erasmus, Count and Noble Lord von Platen Hallermund (*b* 26 Sept 1877; ✠ 11 July 1930) and Ilse von der Marwitz (*b* 22 March 1881; *m* 1 Oct 1901; ✠ 25 Aug 1939), having had issue, among whom,

Son

Count *Georg* Wilhelm Wolf, *b* at Ludwigslust 2 Nov 1910; ✠ at Kiel 29 Oct 1963, Proprietor of Sehlendorf, Kr Plön, Airforce Major, Kt of Justice of St John of Jerusalem; *m* at Wesermünde 16 May 1941, Beatrice (*b* at Wesermünde 6 Sept 1918), dau of Christian Brüggemann and Beatrice Droge, and had issue,
[*Sehlendorf, 24327 Blekendorf, Schleswig-Holstein, Germany*].

    1. Count *Jörg* Christian, *b* at Spieka-Altendeich 1 June 1945, Proprietor of Sehlendorf; *m* at Thelendhof, nr Uedem, Kr Kleve 15 Oct 1970 (*m* diss by div 1990), Countess Annabel (*b* at Düsseldorf 12 June 1947), dau of Count Hans-Georg von Arnim, Proprietor of Thelenhof, and Anne-Marie Fink, and has issue,
    [*Sehlendorf, 24327 Blekendorf, Holstein, Germany*].

        1. Countess *Adelheid,* *b* at Uedem 1 April 1971; *m* at Blickendorf 24 July 1999), Eduard Bauer (*b* at Uedem 19 Dec 1959).

        2. Countess *Elisabeth,* *b* at Oldenburg 21 Nov 1974.

        3. Count *Georg-Dietlof,* *b* at Oldenburg 27 Aug 1978.

    2. Countess *Annette* Ilse Christine, *b* at Oldenburg, Holstein 24 Dec 1946; *m* at Blekendorf, Holstein 25 May 1974, Jürgen Hartig (*b* at Dresden 8 Nov 1939), Architect.
    [*Lindenberg 197, 82343 Pöcking, Germany*].

    3. Countess *Regine* Beatrice, *b* at Oldenburg 13 June 1952; *m* at Altrip 14 Dec 1979, Wolfgang Schade (*b* at Bad Wiessee 14 July 1945), Engineer.
    [*Sauerbruchstraße 29, 67122 Altrip, Germany*].

Brother of Grandfather

Issue of Georg, Hereditary Count and Noble Lord von Platen-Hallermund (*b* 2 Oct 1837; ✠ 19 Sept 1881) and Marie von der Schulenburg (*b* 18 March 1841; *m* 1 Oct 1864; ✠ 11 June 1886), having had issue, among whom,

Son

Carl Julius Erasmus, **Count and Noble Lord (Graf and Edler Herr) von Platen Hallermund,** *b* at Lübeck 18 Sept 1870, Proprietor of Weissenhaus, Futterkamp, etc, Hereditary Postmaster of Hanover; *succ* his grandfather, Carl, Count and Noble Lord (Graf and Edler Herr) von Platen Hallermund (*b* 3 Sept 1810; ✝ 9 Nov 1887); *m* at The Hague 17 Sept 1895, Elisabeth (*b* at Huis den Donck, nr Rotterdam 1 Aug 1875; ✝ at Altaussee, Styria 4 April 1970), dau of Karl, Count von Alten and Baroness Caroline Groeninx van Zoelen, and had issue, among whom,

    1. Countess *Alice, b* at Wiessenhaus 28 April 1910, Dr of Med; *m* at Altaussee, Styria 29 Dec 1956, Augusto, Baron Ricciardi (*b* at Naples 7 Oct 1915; ✝ at ...).
    [*Piazza Margana 19, 00186 Rome, Italy*].

Brother and Half-Brothers of Great-Grandfather
Issue of Carl, Count and Noble Lord von Platen Hallermund (*b* 3 Sept 1810; ✝ 9 Nov 1887) and:

A) his first wife, Countess Mathilde de Pace (*b* 11 Oct 1815; *m* 7 Nov 1836; ✝ 3 Sept 1850), having had issue, among whom,

Son
1. Count *Magnus* Karl Christian Bernhard, *b* at Sehlendorf 26 March 1849; ✝ at Berlin 19 Nov 1900, Capt Austrian Cavalry; *m* at Trieste 1 July 1876, Baroness Friederike (*b* at Venice 19 April 1855; ✝ at Vienna 11 Jan 1924), dau of Ferdinand, Baron von Bianchi, Duke di Casalanza and Countess Anna Kinsky von Wchinitz and Tettau, and had issue, among whom

    1. Count Zdenko *Magnus* Karl Friedrich, *b* at Vienna 7 June 1880; ✝ at Hamburg 21 July 1943, Capt; *m* 1stly at Hamburg 21 Nov 1919 (*m* diss by div at Hamburg 22 April 1927), Maria Kugelmann (*b* at Hamburg 22 Nov 1886; ✝) He *m* 2ndly at Hamburg 27 May 1927, Baroness Marie Nathalja (Aja) (*b* at Helsingfors, Finland 5 July 1893; ✝ there 5 July 1978), dau of Gösta August, Baron Sackleen and Catharina Chestakov (of Russian nobility), and had issue by his second wife,

        1. Count *Carl* Gustav Magnus (Gösta), *b* at Hamburg 31 Oct 1932, Dr of Econ; *m* at Stockholm 15 March 1958, Clary Margareta (*b* at Helsingfors 9 Jan 1936), dau of Birger August Stark and Elsie Margareta Ekholm, and has issue,
        [*Hermannstraße 5, 60318 Frankfurt-am-Main, Germany*].

            1. Countess Anne *Marina* Margareta, *b* at

Helsingfors 9 Aug 1958.
[*Hermannstraße 5, 60318 Frankfurt-am-Main, Germany*].
2. Countess *Eva* Maria Cecilia, *b* at Frankfurt-am-Main 18 Sept 1965.
[*Hermannstraße 5, 60318 Frankfurt-am-Main, Germany*].

B) his second wife, Baroness Louise von Hollen (*b* 19 Dec 1833; *m* 15 March 1857; ✠ 29 April 1895), having had issue, among whom,

Sons

1. Count *Ernst* Karl Ludwig Kaspar, *b* at Sehlendorf 25 Jan 1859; ✠ at Redden, nr Domnau 19 Jan 1916, Proprietor of Galben and Redden in Prussia; *m* at Hohenwalde 19 Aug 1887, Baroness Maria (*b* at Hohenwalde 14 July 1868; ✠ at Charlottenau, nr Rheinsberg 13 Feb 1932), dau of Albrecht, Baron von Hollen, Proprietor of Hohenwalde and Marie von Restorff, and had issue, among whom,

1. Count *Herbert* Karl Ludwig Albrecht Nathango Georg, *b* at Galben, Kr Friedland 17 Aug 1888; ✠ at Heuershof, nr Stettin 3 July 1945; *m* 1stly at Königsberg 29 Dec 1919 (*m* diss by div 15 May 1922), Hedwig (*b* at Königsberg 28 April 1889; she *m* 2ndly at Merseburg 1 May 1924 Eberhard Roscher) [*Kaiserplatz 19, Halle an der Saale, Germany*], dau of Eugen von Hegener and Anna von Gottberg. He *m* 2ndly at Königsberg 8 Aug 1922, Charlotte Elisabeth (*b* at Königsberg 3 Nov 1903; *m* diss by div Züllchow, nr Stettin 13 Oct 1941; she *m* 2ndly at Leeskow, Nieder Lausitz 22 Jan 1942, Otto Schnack who ✠ 15 Feb 1945), dau of Hans Schultz, Proprietor of Syballen, and Marie Werner, and by her had issue, among whom,
[*Im Lämpchen 12, 30459 Hanover, Germany*].

1. Countess *Luise* Marie Ella Freda Elisabeth, *b* at Neukuhren 26 June 1923; *m* 1stly at Krakow 26 June 1944 (*m* diss by div 7 June 1955), Heinz Lietz (*b* at Berlin 23 March 1908). She *m* 2ndly at Düsseldorf 3 Nov 1956, Kurt Eberhard Poppe (*b* at Breslau 2 Aug 1897; ✠ at Düsseldorf 30 Aug 1965). She *m* 3rdly at Düsseldorf 5 July 1968, Günther Kautzky (*b* at Reischenberg 9 July 1913; ✠ 21 April 1979), Dipl Eng.
[*Homburgerstraße 18, 40474 Düsseldorf, Germany*].

2. Count *Ernst Friedrich* Wilhelm Ludwig Theodor, *b* at Neukuhren 14 Nov 1924; *m* at Glückstadt 31 Jan 1947, Jutta (*b* at Glückstadt 13 June 1925), dau of Gustav Hahn and Paula Witt, and has issue,
[*Esingerstraße 59, 25436 Tornesch, Holstein, Germany*].

> 1. Count *Ernst-Günther* Herbert Gustav Rudolf, *b* at Glückstadt 24 Jan 1948, Bank Director, Capt (Res); *m* at Tornesch 9 Sept 1982, Bärbel (*b* at Hamburg 18 Jan 1957), dau of Franz and Liselotte Kropidlowski, and has issue,
> [*Am Steinberg 65, 25436 Uetersen, Germany*].
>
>> 1. Countess *Sandra* Marina Charlotte, *b* at Pinneberg 27 Aug 1986.

3. Countess *Elisabeth* Sophie Olga Henriette Ottilie Marie, *b* at Neukuhren 23 April 1926; *m* at Hanover 10 Aug 1956, Horst Hartwich (*b* at Schwerin 6 Feb 1927), Businessman.
[*Friedrich Ebert Platz 11, 30459 Hanover, Germany*].
4. Countess *Annemarie* Friederike Karola, *b* at Neukuhren 13 Oct 1929.
[*99759 Wülfingerode über Nordhausen, Thüringen, Germany*].
5. Count *Hans-Georg* Alexander Eugen, *b* at Charlottenau, nr Rheinsberg, Mark 18 Sept 1931, Land Manager; *m* at Hanover-Davenstedt 23 April 1962, Inge (*b* at Hanover 24 Jan 1939; *m* diss by div 20 Nov 1984), dau of August Jotzo and Johanna Stolte, and has issue,
[*Am Davenstedter Holz 4, 30455 Hanover - Davenstedt, Germany*].

> 1. Count *Frank* Heinz Ernst Friedrich Max, *b* at Hanover 2 Nov 1962, Businessman; *m* at Hanover 24 March 1983, Doris Kafka (*b* at Nienburg an der Weser 9 Nov 1959), and has issue,
> [*Bassenbrink 26, Rodenberg, Germany*].
>
>> 1. Count *Philipp*, *b* at Hanover 20 July 1983.
>
> 2. Count *Dirk*, *b* at Hanover 18 April 1970.

[*Am Davenstedter Holz 4, 30455 Hanover - Davenstedt, Germany*].

  6. Countess *Christa* Ostava Olga Ruth, *b* at Charlottenau, nr Rheinsberg, Mark 24 Dec 1932; *m* at Redderse über Hanover 28 April 1959, Heinz Rogge (*b* at ... 2 Oct 1931), Land Manager.
[*Redderse, 39264 Gehrden, Germany*].

2. Count *Friedrich* Christian Julius, *b* at Sehlendorf 18 Feb 1860; ✠ at Kassel 4 July 1930; *m* at Schwerin 12 Nov 1901, Baroness Leontine (Lilli) (*b* at Parchim 2 Sept 1876; ✠ at Hofgeismar 6 Oct 1954), dau of Detlev, Baron von Stenglin and Antonie von Cleve, and had issue, among whom,

  1. Count *Friedrich* Wilhelm Anton Maximilian Karl, *b* at Langensalza 18 Nov 1902; ✠ at Düsseldorf 26 Feb 1978, Businessman; *m* at Kassel 3 May 1939, Ilse (*b* at Schleswig 14 Feb 1904; ✠ at Düsseldorf 15 Feb 1987; *m* 1stly Adolf Friedrich Krüger-Haye who ✠ at Berlin 30 June 1935), dau of Albert Müller-Klug and Frieda Stenz, and had issue,

    1. Countess *Karin* Ilse Ellen, *b* at Kassel 17 Nov 1941; *m* at Düsseldorf 16 Jan 1965, Gerd von Coelln (*b* at Berlin 21 June 1940), Banker.

3. Count *Oscar* Rudolf Karl Marius, *b* at Sehlendorf 18 March 1865; ✠ at Weissenhaus, Holstein 14 April 1957, Marshal of The Prussian Court, Vice-Admiral German Navy, Kt of St John of Jerusalem; *m* 1stly at Kreppelhof 11 Jan 1904, Countess Armgard (*b* at Kreppelhof 1 June 1877; ✠ at Berlin 18 Feb 1912), dau of Udo, Count zu Stolberg-Wernigerode and Countess Elisabeth von Armin. He *m* 2ndly at Wildenfels 9 Feb 1915 (*m* diss by div 15 Nov 1922), Countess Sophie (*b* at Wildenfels 9 Feb 1877; ✠ at Lübbenau, Spreewald 4 Dec 1956; she *m* 2ndly at Wildenfels 6 Sept 1924, Otto, Count zu Solms-Wildenfels), dau of Friedrich, Count zu Solms-Wildenfels and Countess Anne von Bentinck, and had issue by his first wife, among whom,

  1. Count *Wilhelm* Karl Udo Viktor Oskar, *b* at Kiel 1 June 1906; ✠ at Lucipa, Angola, West Africa 11 March 1949, Farmer in Angola; *m* 1stly at Grotau, Bohemia 16 Dec 1933 (*m* diss by div at 4 April 1941), Gerda (*b* at Grottau 23 March 1908) [*Gutenbergstraße 51, 70176 Stuttgart, Germany*], dau of Ernst Jaschke and Anna Kirschner, and had issue,

    1. Count *Ernst-Wilhelm*, *b* at Reichenberg, Bohemia 20 Oct 1933, Technician; *m* at Benguela, Angola 9

Nov 1957, Carlotta Teresa (*b* at Benguela 29 Feb 1936),
dau of Georg Sautter and Terese Auguste Riedel, and
has issue,

[*9 Flangkop, Privatbag 9364, Verwoerdpark, 1453
Johannesburg, South Africa*].

    1. Countess *Elisabeth*, *b* at Benguela 28 Feb
1959; *m* at Alberton, South Africa 6 Oct 1984,
Richard Haith, Businessman.

    [*188 Flamingo Street, Halfway Garden, Midrand
1686, TVL, South Africa*].

    2. Count *Bernhard* Wilhelm, *b* at Mariano
Machado, Angola 16 Aug 1961, Instrument
Technician; *m* at Alberton, South Africa 18
March 1989, Zita (*b* at Lourenço Marques,
Maputo, Mozambique 26 Feb 1961), BA, dau
of Emilio Vieira and Olinda da Silva Nunes,
and has issue,

    [*12 Dassen Road, P.O. Box 8617, Verwoerdpark,
1453 Alberton-Johannesburg, South Africa*].

        1. Countess *Nicole*, *b* at Johannesburg
25 Sept 1989.

        2. Count *Oscar Wilhelm*, *b* at
Johannesburg 2 July 1991.

    3. Count *Rudolf-Christian*, *b* at Mariano
Machado, Angola 27 Dec 1962; *m* at Cape
Town, South Africa 2 July 1988, Debbi Kim
(*b* at Johannesburg 9 Aug 1966), dau of Peter
Thornton Korck and Patricia Vera West, and
has issue,

    [*9 Slangkop Road, P.O. Box 9364, Verwoerdpark,
1453 Alberton-Johannesburg, South Africa*].

        1. Countess *Victoria* Vera, *b* at
Johannesburg 16 Dec 1988.

        2. Count *Christian* Karl, *b* at
Johannesburg 2 Aug 1990.

        3. Countess *Stephanie* Teresa, *b* at Cape
Town 20 July 1994.

2. Count *Oscar*, *b* at Lucipa 14 July 1935; ✝ at Hameln
11 June 1984; *m* at Mariano Machado, Angola 9 Aug
1958, Helga (*b* at Potsdam 13 Dec 1937), dau of Alfred
Konen and Margarete Zabel, and had issue,

[*Meierbreite 10, 37688 Beverungen, Germany*].

　　　　1. Countess *Anna-Christine, b* at Caluquembe,
　　　　nr Mariano Machado, Angola 25 Feb 1961.
　　　　2. Count *Alfred-Wilhelm, b* at Caluquembe 18
　　　　Feb 1963.

Count Wilhelm *m* 2ndly at Ganda, Angola 19 Jan 1944,
Ingeburg Gudrun Gisela (*b* at Helbra, Eisleben 15 May 1906),
dau of Friedrich Wilhelm Martin and Anna Ida Buch, and
had further issue,

[*Haslacher Weg 40, 89075 Ulm-Böfingen, Germany*].

　　　　3. Count *Rudolf* Oskar Tuure Friedrich, *b* at Mariano
　　　　Machado, Angola 29 May 1944; *m* at Baienfurt,
　　　　Ravensburg 31 May 1980, Baroness Viktoria (*b* at
　　　　Baienfurt 13 Jan 1956), dau of Ludolf, Baron von König
　　　　and Erika von Platen, and has issue,

　　　　[*Soconoki, BF 138 Bunja, Haute Zaire*].

　　　　　　　　1. Countess *Anne, b* at Weingarten 3 Oct 1982.
　　　　　　　　2. Count *Felix, b* at Weingarten 31 March 1984.

4. Count *Wilhelm* Ludwig Karl Ernst Friedrich, *b* at Weissenhaus 29
July 1878; ✣ at Mummendorf, Mecklenburg 10 Jan 1914, Proprietor
of Mummendorf, Capt German Army; *m* at Schwerin 16 Nov 1904,
Elisabeth (*b* at Brandenburg an der Havel 3 July 1880; ✣ at
Mummendorf 8 Jan 1938), dau of Oskar von Boddien and Marie von
Keller, and had issue, among whom,

　　　　1. Count *Carl-Oskar* Wilhelm Friedrich Max Alfons Hans,
　　　　b at Mummendorf 22 May 1907; ✣ at Moorhausen, nr Jever
　　　　28 April 1963, Proprietor of Mummendorf; *m* 1stly at
　　　　Mummendorf 25 June 1938, Lise-Lotte (*b* at Brunow, Mark 18
　　　　July 1909; ✣ at Lübeck 9 Sept 1945), dau of Johann Veit and
　　　　Emma Liesbeth Mohs. He *m* 2ndly at Moorhausen 8 Oct 1950,
　　　　Marie-Luise (*b* at Bremen 22 April 1915; ✣ at Moorhausen 21
　　　　May 1984; *m* 1stly at Jever 24 April 1937, Hermann Allmers;
　　　　that *m* diss by div at Oldenburg 1939; *m* 3rdly at Sillenstede,
　　　　Oldenburg 30 Oct 1971, Hans Joachim von Winterfeld), dau
　　　　of Enno Mettcker and Maria Berlage, and had issue by his
　　　　first wife,

　　　　　　　　1. Count *Wilhelm* Ludwig Oskar, *b* at Lübeck 11 May
　　　　　　　　1939, Businessman; *m* at Lübeck 25 July (civ) and at
　　　　　　　　Blekendorf 27 July (relig) 1995, Karin (*b* at Gleiwitz,
　　　　　　　　Upper Selisia 5 Dec 1940; *m* 1stlt Dr Günter Blum,
　　　　　　　　diss by div 1983), dau of Kurt Kusse and Anna Gülland..

[*Bahnhofstraße 20, 23611 Bad Schwartau, Germany*].

2. Countess *Ilka-Maria* Elisabeth, *b* at Lübeck 14 July 1940; *m* at Altenkrempe, nr Neustadt, East Holstein 7 July 1973, Hans-Burkhard Herrmann (*b* at Schashagen, East Holstein 19 July 1944), Businessman.

[*P.O.B. 1472, 1620 Kempton Park, Transvaal, South Africa*].

3. Count *Henning* August Alexander, *b* at Lübeck 24 Feb 1943, Businessman; *m* 1stly at Wienhausen, Celle 22 March 1969 (*m* diss by div at Lüneburg 8 Jan 1974), Sabine [*Schlagsdorferstraße 17, 19217 Schlagbruegge, Germany*] (*b* at Dresden 11 March 1942; *m* 2ndly at Hamburg 8 July 1977, Dr Ferdinand von Wedel MD), dau of Rüdiger, Count von der Osten, Proprietor of Gross-Jannewitz, in Pommerania, and Anneliese von Besser, and has issue,

      1. Countess *Julia* Liselotte, *b* at Vancouver, BC, Canada 11 June 1971.

Count Henning *m* 2ndly at Hamburg 10 Aug 1976, Baroness Tina (*b* at Salzburg 11 July 1949), dau of Wolfgang, Baron von Dürfeld and Countess Christiane von Thun and Hohenstein, and by her has further issue,

[*Arcona House, Box 678, 108 Mile Ranch, British Columbia, VOK 2ZO Canada*].

      2. Countess *Donata* Amelia, *b* at Vancouver 25 June 1983.

      3. Countess *Ilka* Isabelle, b at Vancouver 19 Nov 1987.

Brother of Great-Great-Grandfather

Issue of Georg, Count von Platen Hallermund (*b* 8 Nov 1785; ✠ 13 Jan 1873) and Countess Juliane von Hardenberg (*b* 22 Oct 1788; *m* 7 Nov 1809; ✠ 18 Aug 1833), among whom,

Son

Count *Georg* Adolf Hans August, *b* at Weissenhaus 16 Sept 1827; ✠ at Kaden, nr Alveslohe, Holstein 28 Aug 1881, Proprietor of Kaden; *m* at Rantzau, Plön 22 Aug 1857, Elise (*b* at Plön 9 Sept 1827; ✠ at Preetz, Holstein 4 Jan 1909), dau of Hans Adolf von Warnstedt and Countess Susanne von Baudissin, and had issue, among whom,

Sons

1. Count *Georg* Hans Julius, *b* at Friederikenhof 7 Nov 1858; ✠ at Kaden 9 Dec 1927, Proprietor of Kaden, Hon Provost of the Convent of Preetz, Commander St John of Jerusalem; *m* at Espe 20 Oct 1887, Countess Rosalie (*b* at Espe, Seeland 6 June 1866; ✠ at Preetz, Holstein 9 Oct 1924), dau of Otto, Count von Moltke, Proprietor of Espe and Bonderup, and Lilie Sehested-Juul (of Danish nobility), and had issue, among whom,

> **Sons**
>
> 1. Count *George* Otto Carl Gustav, *b* at Kaden 9 Nov 1888; ✠ 9 Oct 1961, Proprietor of Kaden, Capt Saxon Army, Kt of St John of Jerusalem; *m* at Stuttgart 14 Oct 1919, Gabriele (*b* at Luxembourg 13 March 1894; ✠ at Kaden 19 July 1963), dau of Alfred von Bülow and Countess Marie von Dillen-Spiering, and had issue,
>
> > 1. Countess *Marie-Agnes* Rosa Thyra Albinia Gabriele, *b* at Kaden 27 Aug 1920; *m* at Hamburg 19 Sept (civ) and at Kaden 21 Sept (relig) 1944, Wolfgang von Erlach (*b* at Bern 17 Nov 1918), Lawyer.
> > [*Rüti-Wassbergholzweg 2, 8126 Zumikon bei Zürich, Switzerland*].
> >
> > 2. Countess *Elisabeth* Marie Louise Gabriele Margarethe, *b* at Kaden 2 Jan 1922, entered the Convent of Preetz.
> > [*Klosterhof 14, 24211 Preetz, Holstein, Germany*].
> >
> > 3. Count *Georg* Alfred Adam Martin, *b* at Kaden 26 Feb 1927; ✠ at Camrose, Alberta 25 April 1991, Proprietor of Kaden; *m* 18 Jan 1956, Ingrid (*b* 18 Jan 1935), dau of Alfred Wiegels and Käthe Kauffmann, and has issue,
> > [*P.O. Box 1288, Camrose, Alberta T4V 1X2, Canada*].
> >
> > > 1. Count *Georg* Arthur, *b* at Bad Segeberg 6 Nov 1956; *m* at 5 March 1983, Glenys (*b* Edmonton, Alberta 24 July 1957), dau of William Drake and Dulcie Pike, and has issue,
> > >
> > > > 1. Count *George* Matthew, *b* at Alberta 8 June1986.
> > > >
> > > > 2. Count *Erik*, *b* at Alberta 29 Oct 1987.
> > > >
> > > > 3. Count *Christian*, *b* at Alberta 31 July 1992.
> > >
> > > 2. Countess *Gabriela* Elisabeth, *b* at Bad

Segeberg 23 April 1960.

3. Count *Bernhard* Christian, *b* at Bad Segeberg 14 May 1961, *m* 3 Aug 1984, Valerie (*b* at Camrose, Alberta 9 May 1961), dau of Lloyd Thompson and Marlen Lawes and has issue,

> 1. Countess *Christina* Elizabeth, *b* at Alberta 25 March 1986.
>
> 2. Count *Adam* Christian, *b* at Alberta 6 January 1988
>
> 3. Countess *Kertisha*, *b* at Alberta 20 March 1991.

4. Countess *Jacqueline* Annette, *b* at Bad Segeberg 22 Jan 1964.

2. Count *Gustav* Julius Christian, *b* at Kaden 22 June 1894; ✠ at the Military Hospital nr Graudenz June 1945, Lt.-Col.; *m* at Haseldorf 10 Sept 1920 (*m* diss by div 2 Nov 1934), Princess Gabriele (*b* at Haseldorf 23 Sept 1897; ✠ at Hamburg 17 May 1964; she *m* 2ndly at Hamburg-Blankenese 30 March 1937, Joachim (Jochen) von Schinckel who ✠ at Hamburg 3 May 1976), dau of Emil, Prince von Schönaich-Carolath and Catharina von Knorring, and had issue, among whom,

> 1. Count *Hans-Osman* Otto Georg Botho Christian, *b* at Hellerholz 28 Aug 1921, Insurance Executive; *m* 1stly at Hamburg 2 Oct 1944 (*m* diss by div .. Aug 1950), Irmgard (Virginia) (*b* at Hamburg 15 May 1924), dau of Gottlieb Siemers and Hedwig (Hedi) Danielsen, adopted dau of Walter Siemers, and has issue,
>
> > 1. Countess *Béatrice* Catharina Gabriele, *b* at Hamburg 25 Sept 1945, Journalist; *m* at Hamburg-Eimsbüttel 1 Dec 1966 (*m* diss by div at Hamburg 19 Jan 1970), Eric von Witzleben (*b* at Rostock 25 May 1932), Architect.
> >
> > [*Rathausufer 21, 40213 Düsseldorf, Germany*].

Count Hans-Osman *m* 2ndly at Hamburg Blankenese ✝ June 1952 (*m* diss by div 17 Sept 1970), Wendula (*b* at Merkendorf, nr Neustadt, Holstein 18 Nov 1930), dau of Rudolf Riekken and Helga Oswald. He *m* 3rdly at Hamburg-Blankenese 1 April 1971 (*m* diss by div 29 March 1973), Bettina (*b* at Hamburg 14 Jan 1943), dau of Hans Reinhold Schmidt and Katharina Meisch. He

m 4thly at Hamburg 1 Nov 1974, Roswita (*b* at Warsaw 2 Jan 1942), dau of Paul Kostrzewa and Halina Koszelik, and had further issue by his second wife,
[*Feldbrunnenstraße 6, 20148 Hamburg, Germany*].

    2. Countess *Nicola, b* at Hamburg 15 May 1955. [*Richard Dehmelstraße 4, 22587 Hamburg-Blankenese, Germany*].

    3. Count *Thimo, b* at Hamburg 18 June 1956. [*Richard Dehmelstraße 4, 22587 Hamburg-Blankenese, Germany*].

2. Count *Wilke* Carl Alexander Hans Heinrich, *b* at Haseldorf 15 March 1927; ✝ 15 Feb 1949.

3. Count *Hans* Georg Carl Joseph, *b* at Kaden 24 Sept 1896; ✝ at Andernach 28 April 1968, Proprietor of Hellerholz in Holstein, Lt, Land Manager; *m* at Hanover 9 Feb 1938 (*m* diss by div at Flensburg 18 May 1956), Baroness Elisabeth (*b* at Frankfurt an der Oder 25 April 1913; ✝ at Munich 8 Feb 1983), dau of Nikolaus, Baron von Lyncker and Hertha von Wolff, and had issue,

    1. Count *Hans-Detlev* Karl Georg Christian, *b* at Berlin-Charlottenburg 14 Nov 1938, Capt Marines; *m* 1stly at Düsseldorf-Kaiserswerth 7 Oct 1960 (*m* diss by div), Adelheid (Heide) [*Steinenkamp 36, 47137 Duisburg, Germany*] (*b* at Berlin 26 May 1938), dau of Wilhelm Fischer and Elisabeth Schuster. He *m* 2ndly at Elmshorn 20 Dec 1985, Marianne (*b* at Uetersen 3 Sept 1941), dau of Johannes Hormann and Annemarie Münster, and has issue by his first wife,
[*Parkstraße 17, 25436 Uetersen, Holstein, Germany*].

        1. Countess *Nicole* Dinah Patricia Christiana Elisabeth, *b* at Duisburg-Meiderich 12 Jan 1963.

        2. Count *Markus* Hennige, *b* at Duisburg 8 June 1967; ✝ there 10 Aug 1970.

    2. Countess Eleonore-Christine (*Lori*) Agnes Gabriele Elisabeth, *b* at Hamburg 14 Nov 1939; *m* at Andernach 23 Aug (civ) and at Maria Laach 26 Oct (relig) 1963, Heribert Freusberg (*b* at Andernach 21 July 1915), Dr of Med.
[*Waldstraße 18, 82166 Gräfelfing, Germany*].

    3. Countess *Christiana*- Elisabeth Margarethe Renata Hildegard, *b* at Hamburg 11 Dec 1941; *m* at Keitum,

Sylt 2 Oct 1964, Günther Hausmann (*b* at Krefeld 30 June 1926), Painter and Graphic Artist.
[*Ollnsstraße 6, 25336 Elmshorn, Germany*].

4. Count *Hans-Henninge* Georg Heinrich-Bolko, *b* at Hamburg 7 April 1943, Insurance Agent; *m* at Munich 28 April 1972, Renate (*b* at Stuttgart 4 March 1949), dau of Josef Küsgens and Hildegard Kinting.
[*Hochstraße 9, 8021 Deining, Germany*].

4. Count *Christian-* Gottlob, *b* at Kaden 10 Jan 1900; ✠ at Uetersen, Holstein 13 Nov 1976, Land Manager; Hon Provost of Uetersen Monastery; *m* at Krakow, nr Güstrow 18 Sept 1943, Ilse-Maria (*b* at Krakow 4 Sept 1920), dau of Cuno Kelling and Minna Subbert, and had issue,
[*Kloster 4, 25436 Uetersen, Holstein, Germany*].

    1. Countess *Agnes-Isabell,* *b* at Malchow, Mecklenburg 10 Dec 1944; *m* 1stly at Uetersen, Holstein 29 April 1967 (*m* diss by div 13 May 1971), Klaus Peter Supthut (*b* at ...). She *m* 2ndly at Uetersen 12 Sept (civ) and at Hohenstein, East Holstein 13 Sept (relig) 1975, Erich, Count von Holck (*b* at Lübeck 6 Feb 1929), Land Manager, Businessman.

2. Count *Julius* Christian Karl, *b* at Friederikenhof 14 Jan 1861; ✠ at Berlin 10 Dec 1941, Major Saxon Army; *m* at London 3 June 1907, Hedwig von Erlin (*b* at Gommern, Magdeburg 18 April 1878; ✠ at Berlin 11 March 1950; declared a member of the Saxon nobility from the date of marriage at Dresden 27 Sept 1909 with Diploma 2 Dec 1909), dau of ... Schmeckebier, and had issue,

    1. Countess *Ilsa Liane* Helga Daniela, *b* at at Wilmersdorf, nr Berlin 26 March 1908; ✠ at Innsbruck 5 Feb 1955; *m* 1stly at Berlin 13 May 1930, Eberhard Mohnike (*b* at ... ; killed accidentally 14 Oct 1930), Lt-Col. She *m* 2ndly at Gries, nr Bozen 10 Dec 1931, Carl Künigl, Count zu Ehrenburg (*b* at Ehrenburg 17 April 1905), Proprietor of Ehrenburg.
    [*Schloß Ehrenburg (Casteldarne), 39030 Kiens (Chienes), Pustertal, Germany*].

2. Countess *Edela Geraldine* Gustave Elisabeth, *b* at Berlin-Wilmersdorf 2 May 1910; *m* at Berlin 3 July 1935 (*m* diss by div), Karl Sydow (*b* at Kiel 7 Nov 1901), Bank Director.
[*Godeffroystraße 44, 22587 Hamburg-Blankenese, Germany*].

    —◆—

PÜCKLER AND LIMPURG
(✠ Extinct ✠)

Lutheran and Catholic: Feudal family from Silesia who can be
authenticated to dominus Nicolaus Pincerna 1306; acquired
Blumenthal, Principality of Neisse 1365; Henricus dictus Pokeler
alias Pincerna appears authentically 22 May 1365; this branch is
descended from Nicolaus Poekeler, Lord of Blumenthal who in 1486
acquired the Lordship of Groditz, Principality of Oppeln; Bohemian
Baron Pückler von Gröditz, PresSburg 5 March 1655; inherited the
seigneural lands of Burg-Farrnbach, Brunn and Tanzenhaidt (in
Franconia) through the marriage of Baron Karl-Franz (b 23 March
1648; ✠ 5 Jan 1708), eldest son of Baron Georg Josef (✠ 1679), to
Anna Cordula Kresser, Baroness von Burgfarrnbach (✠ 1683), and
separation of the Franconian Line from the Silesian Line circa 1690
(issue of the younger son of Baron Georg Josef who ✠ 1679; Count of
the Holy Empire with the qualification of "Hoch and Wohlgeboren",
Laxenberg 10 March 1690; Bohemian Count, Vienna 22 Nov 1691;
received (ad personam) into the Franconian College of Counts of the
Holy Empire with the qualification of "Hoch and Wohlgeboren" 7
April 1740; inherited a sixth of the Bailiwick of Ober-Sontheim
(exchanged in 1839) in the County of Limpurg (near Jagst,
Württemberg) through the marriage of Count Christian (b 6 Dec
1705; ✠ 17 Feb 1786) to Caroline-Christine, Countess of Löwenstein-
Wertheim (b 7 Aug 1719; ✠ 6 April 1793); the fideicommis of Burg-
Farrnbach was founded in the Last Will and Testament of Count
Christian Wilhelm Karl 16 July 1784; inherited the Bailiwick of
Sontheim-Galldorf in the same County through the marriage of
Count Friedrich Philipp Karl (b 1740; ✠ 3 Oct 1811) to Marie
Friederike Amöne, Countess von Welz and Limpurg 1764; the two
Lines below descend from two sons of Count Friedrich Philipp Karl
and his second wife, Luise, Baroness von Gaisberg-Helfenberg (b 4
Nov 1759; m 18 Oct 1780; ✠ 14 March 1835).

Line I
(✠ Extinct ✠)

Founded by Count Friedrich (b 12 Feb 1788; ✠ 1 July 1867); Bavarian
Collation of the qualification of "Erlaucht" 31 July 1834 by virtue of
a resolution of the German Diet 13 Feb 1829.

Line II
(✠ Extinct ✠)

Founded by Count Ludwig Friedrich Karl Maximilian (b 11 April
1790; ✠ 16 Aug 1854); Hereditary Member of the former House of

Lords of Württemberg 1879 and 30 July 1893; Bavarian Confirmation
of the qualification of "Erlaucht" 22 July 1835 by virtue of a resolution
of the German Diet 13 Feb 1829.
Members of this branch bear or bore the title of Count or Countess
von Pückler and Limpurg, Baron or Baroness von Groditz with the
qualification of Illustrious Highness.

✠ SIEGFRIED Ludwig Johannes, **10th COUNT (GRAF) VON
PÜCKLER, COUNT and LORD (GRAF AND HERR) ZU
LIMPURG-GAILDORF,** Baron von Groditz, *b* at Oberaudorf,
Upper Bavaria 25 Feb 1871; ✠ there 27 Feb 1963, son of Count
(Graf) Eduard von Pückler, Baron von Groditz (*b* 18 Sept 1832; ✠ 24
June 1907) and Marguerite (Etha) Schönlein (*b* 27 Sept 1828; ✠ 8
July 1906), *succ* his cousin, Gottfried, Count (Graf) von Pückler,
Count and Lord (Graf and Herr) zu Limpurg-Gaildorf (*b* 20 April
1871; ✠ 26 Nov 1957); *m* at Munich 7 Nov 1905, Countess
Marie-Louise (*b* at Munich 15 June 1879; ✠ at Oberaudorf 25 March
1962), dau of Moritz, Count von Bothmer and Sophie, Edle von
Taeuffenbach.

Daughter
Countess *Waltraut* Margarete Sophie Cäcilie, *b* at Oberaudorf 31
Oct 1913; *m* there 20 March 1953, Joseph Kiendl (*b* at Oberaudorf 5
Dec 1910; ✠ 21 Jan 1975).
[*Schützenstraße 6, 83080 Oberaudorf, Upper Bavaria, Germany*].

Brother of Father
Issue of Count Ludwig (*b* 1790 - see above) and Countess Luise von
Bothmer (*b* 19 March 1803; *m* 9 May 1824; ✠ 16 Jan 1876).

Ludwig, August Friedrich Ernst Georg, **Count (Graf) von
Pückler, Count and Lord (Graf and Herr) zu Limpurg-Gaildorf,**
etc, *b* at Burgfarrnbach 29 April 1825; ✠ there 12 July 1906, Kt of St
John of Jerusalem, renounced in favour of his eldest son 30 July 1893;
m at Mannheim 23 May 1861, Baroness Auguste (*b* at Mannheim 25
July 1829; ✠ at Burgfarrnbach 29 Sept 1910), dau of Wilhelm, Baron
von Wöllwarth-Lauterburg and Baroness Henriette von Saint-André,
and had issue, among whom,

Sons
1. Count *Richard* Franz Georg, *b* at Burgfarrnbach 21 Nov 1872; ✠
at Schwiebus, nr Frankfurt an der Oder 20 April 1942, Lt-Col, Kt of
St John of Jerusalem ; *m* at Lagow, nr Frankfurt an der Oder 9 Oct

1908, Wanda (*b* at Leuthen 30 Dec 1889; ✠ at Frankfurt-am-Main 15 Aug 1968), Proprietor of Lagow, Neumark, dau of Hans Wurmb von Zinck, Proprietor of Witzschersdorf and Countess Margarete von Wylich and Lottum of the Princes Putbus, and had issue, among whom,

> 1. Countess *Margot* Mirjam Marie Alma Eleonore Erika, *b* at Ludwigsburg 3 July 1916; *m* 1stly at Berlin 4 Feb 1942, Heinrich Manfred von Zitzewitz (*b* at Berlin 4 April 1909; ✠*k* in action 26 Feb 1942). She *m* 2ndly at Nüremberg 7 Feb 1952, her brother-in-law, Gerd, Baron Schäffer von Bernstein (*b* at Frankfurt-am-Main 12 Aug 1917), Proprietor of Schutzforst Ziegenberg, Farmer.
> [*Usingerstraße 116, 61239 Ober-Mörlen - Ziegenberg, Germany*].

———◆———

QUADT

Catholic: This feudal family originated in Jülich and Gerderland and can be authenticated to Johann Quade, Member of the Nobility of Berg 1313, filiation proved to Peter the Quade, a knight living 1256; inherited the Lordship of Wykradt (Wickrath, near Grevenboich, North Rhine-Westphalia, succeeded the House of von Hompesch) 1498; Imperial Investiture and received into the Westphalian College of Counts of the Holy Empire 15 July 1502; Grand Master of the Court of the Duchy of Gelderland and "Erbdrost" of the County of Zütphen through the marriage (1568) of Dietrich II Quadt zu Wykradt (✠ 1590) to Marie von Flodrop zu Leuth (✠ 1626); title of Baron of the Holy Empire confirmed with the qualification of "Wohlgeboren", Regensburg 14 Feb 1664; foundation of fideicommis 2 Nov 1669; Count of the Holy Empire with the qualification of "Hoch and Wohlgeboren", Vienna 17 April 1752; loss of possessions on the left bank of the Rhine 1801; compensated with the county of Isny (Württemberg) with title indemnified 25 Feb 1803; Mediatized and placed under the sovereignty of Bavaria and Württemberg; Hereditary Member of the former House of Lords of Württemberg 25 Sept 1819; received the title of "Erlaucht" (primogeniture) by the German Diet 13 Feb 1829; Family Law established 28 Oct 1838; Hereditary Member of Bavarian "Reichsräte" 16 May 1851; Bavarian title of Fürst (Prince - primogeniture) with the qualification of "Durchlaucht", Munich 12 March 1901; authorisation to use the title in Württemberg 2 April 1901; Bavarian authorisation to the qualification of "Illustrious Highness" 7 March 1911; authorised in Württemberg 4 May 1912.

The Head of the family and his wife bear the title of Prince and Princess von Quadt zu Wykradt and Isny with the qualification of Serene Highness and cadet members bear the title of Count or Countess with the qualification of Illustrious Highness.

PAUL Franz von Assisi Georg Ghislain Edmund Maria Alexander, **4TH PRINCE (FÜRST) VON QUADT ZU WYKRADT AND ISNY**, *b* at Isny 28 Nov 1930, Kt Bavarian Order of St George, *succ* his brother, Alban, 3rd Prince (Fürst) von Quadt zu Wykradt and Isny 24 Sept 1942; son of Alexander, 2nd Prince (Fürst) von Quadt zu Wykradt and Isny (*b* 1 May 1885; ✠ 11 July 1936) and Countess Maria-Anna Esterházy de Galántha, Countess von Forchenstein (*b* 5 Oct 1898; *m* 25 Nov 1920; ✠ 21 Jan 1952); *m* at Berg (civ) 1 Sept and at Nymphenburg (relig) 3 Sept 1955, Princess Marie Charlotte (*b* at Munich 30 May 1931), Dame of Hon Bavarian Orders of St Theresia and St Elisabeth, dau of Albrecht, Duke of Bavaria and Countess Marita Draskovich von Trakostjan.

[*88316 Isny im Allgäu, Germany*].

Sons and Daughters

1. *Alexander* Albrecht Maria Ghislain Peter Paul Georg Mauritius, Hereditary Count (Erbgraf) von Quadt zu Wykradt and Isny, *b* at Munich 18 Jan 1958; *m* at Isny 14 Sept (civ) and at Stainz, Austria 11 Oct (relig) 1992, Martina (*b* at Graz 7 Dec 1960), dau of Johann Keil and Countess Charlotte Meran, and has issue,

[*88316 Isny im Allgäu, Germany*].

    1. Countess *Philippa* Johanna Charlotte Stephanie Maria Wilhelmine Ghislaine, *b* at Ravensburg 25 Dec 1994.

    2. Countess *Charlotte* Sophie Monika Marianne Ghislain Marie, *b* at Ravensburg 21 Oct 1996.

    3. Countess *Anna*, *b* at Ravensburg 23 Oct 2001.

2. Countess *Maria-Anna* Gabriolle Ghislaine, *b* at Friedrichshafen 8 April 1960; *m* at Isny 7 Sept (civ) and 8 Sept (relig) 1991, Alexander Schenk, Count von Stauffenberg (*b* at Bamberg 10 March 1954), Dr of Med.

[*Haldenbergerstraße 10, 86956 Schongau, Germany*].

3. Countess Maria *Georgina* Ghislaine Caroline, *b* at Munich 28 Dec 1962; *m* at Isny 5 Sept (civ) and 7 Sept (relig) 1985, Peter, Count and Noble Lord von and zu Eltz genannt Faust von Stromberg (*b* at Zurich 7 Nov 1948).

[*Am Riedfeld 6, 82229 Seefeld, Germany*].

4. Count *Bertram* Ernst Maria Ghislain Paul Ingbert, *b* at Ravensburg

22 Oct 1966, Journalist.
[*Gaisbach 93, 76534 Baden-Baden, Germany*].

Brothers and Sister

1. **Alban** Paul Eugen Bertram Franz von Assisi Thaddäus Maria Alexander, **3rd Prince (Fürst) von Quadt zu Wykradt and Isny**, *b* at Isny 14 Sept 1921; *succ* his father Alexander, 2nd Prince (Fürst) von Quadt zu Wykradt and Isny (*b* 1 May 1885; ✠ 11 July 1936); killed at Gaburewo, nr Woronesh, Russia 24 Sept 1942.

2. Count *Peter* Eugen Gottfried Franz von Assisi Bertram Ghislain Maria Alexander, *b* at Isny 7 Jan 1923; ✠ at Munich 26 Jan 1979, Dr of Med, Pediatrician, Kt of Hon and Dev Sovereign Military Order of Malta; renounced his rights of succession on the death of his older brother, Alban, 3rd Prince, in favour of his younger brother, Paul; *m* at Dortmund (civ) and at Münster, Westphalia (relig) 11 Feb 1953, Sibylle (*b* at Stettin 11 Feb 1923; ✠ at Ravensburg 26 Dec 1992), Dr of Med, dau of Ferdinand Klems and Hedwig Nierhoff.

3. Countess *Maria* Thomas Ludovica Ehrentraut Benedikta Ghislaine Rupperta Bertha Alexander, *b* at Isny 17 Nov 1925; ✠ at Maryland, USA 25 Nov 1991; *m* at Isny 6 Nov 1950, Peter, Count Praschma, Baron von Bilkau (*b* at Herischdorf 31 July 1925; ✠ at Maryland, USA 13 Nov 1991), Lawyer.

Brothers of Father

Issue of Bertram, 1st Prince (Fürst) von Quadt zu Wykradt and Isny (*b* 11 Jan 1849; ✠ 14 May 1927) and Princess Ludovika von Schönburg-Hartenstein (*b* 3 July 1856; *m* 27 Nov 1879; ✠ 5 July 1932), having had issue, among whom,

1. Count *Eugen* Franziskus de Paula Joseph Maria Alban Kaspar, *b* at Isny 6 Jan 1887, Sometime Bavarian Minister of Finance, Major (Res), Kt of Hon Sovereign Military Order of Malta, Chapter Commander Bavarian Order of St George; ✠ 19 Oct 1940; *m* at Munich 21 Sept 1909, Countess Pauline (*b* at Königseggwald 1 March 1885; ✠ at Tuttlingen 9 June 1961), dau of Franz Xaver, Count zu Königsegg-Aulendorf and Countess Hedwig von Neipperg, and had issue, among whom,

    1. Count *Karl* Erwin Maria Bertram Eusebius Angelius Konrad Benediktus Stafanus, *b* at Munich 2 Sept 1916; ✠ at Burtenbach 27 May 1975; *m* at Troppau 21 March 1943, Dorothea (*b* at Mährisch-Ostrau 1 July 1921; *m* 1stly at

Troppau 16 March 1940, Günther Latter; that *m* diss by div at Troppau 17 Dec 1942), dau of Karl Kuntze and Luise Neumann, and had issue,
[*Pfänderstraße 33, 80636 Munich, Germany*].

    1. Count *Karl-Franz*, *b* at Munich 29 June 1946, Publisher; *m* 1stly at Munich 29 Sept 1967 (*m* diss by div 3 Sept 1973), Christa (*b* at Munich 21 Feb 1944), dau of Georg Walcher and Rosa Fruth, and had issue,

        1. Count *Oliver* Karl Eurgen Gerd, *b* at Munich 9 April 1968.

        [*Klugstraße 11, 80638 Munich, Germany*].

Count Karl-Franz *m* 2ndly at Munich 3 Feb 1978, Jutta (*b* at Giessen 29 Aug 1949), dau of Werner Rittel and Hildegard Koller, and had further issue,
[*Watzmannstraße 46, 85598 Baldham, Germany*].

    2. Countess *Alexandra* Christiane Liselotte, *b* at Munich 18 Jan 1980.

    3. Countess *Katharina* Antonie Sophie, *b* at Munich 14 Oct 1981.

2. Countess *Ruth* Ricarda Maria Paula, *b* at Buch am Ammersee 25 Sept 1950; *m* at Munich 18 Jan 1974, Franz Xaver Riedhammer (*b* at Nitzlbuch, nr Auerbach 6 June1952).
[*Nitzlbuch, 8352 Auerbach, Germany*].

3 Count *Peter* Alexander Maria Eugen, *b* at Buch 22 Jan 1954; *m* at Munich 1 Oct 1980, Hannelore (*b* at Nuremberg 6 Nov 1955), dau of Michael Konrad and Ruth Schwarz, and has issue,
[*Josef Fischhuberstraße 42, 82319 Starnberg, Germany*].

    1. Count *Simon-Michael* Ferry Maria Rupert, *b* at Munich 16 April 1985.

4. Countess *Isabelle* Charlotte Maria Antoinette, *b* at Munich 31 Jan 1961.
[*Pfänderstraße 33, 80636 Munich, Germany*].

Count Karl also adopted a daughter,

5. *Monika* Latter, *b* at Troppau 27 Jan 1941, known from 1 Dec 1964 as "Countess von Quadt zu Wykradt and Isny"; *m* at Munich 26 June 1969, Gerhard Klotz (*b* at Kiessen 23 Dec 1945).
[*Adolf Pineggerstraße 24, 8000 Munich - Blunenau,*

Germany].

———◆◆◆———

RECHBERG

Catholic: Feudal family originating in Swabia authenticated to Ulricus de Rehpec living 22 Jan 1179; Minister of the Hohenstaufen 1189 and 1226; marscalci of the Duchy of Swabia 1194 - 1226; Lord of Donzdorf 1397, of Weissenstein at the end of the 14th century; Baron of the Holy Empire 4 Dec 1601; received into the Swabian College of Counts of the Holy Empire (ad personam) 22 April 1613; received the title of Count (Bavaria) 25 Oct 1810; (Württemberg) 6 Nov 1810; received the qualification of "Erlaucht" (primogeniture) by the German Diet 13 Feb 1829, confirmed in Württemberg 3 May 1829.

Members of the family bear the title of Count or Countess von Rechberg and Rothenlöwen zu Hohenrechberg with the qualification of Illustrious Highness.

ALBERT Germanus Friedrich Otto Aloysius Johannes, **COUNT (GRAF) VON RECHBERG AND ROTHENLÖWEN ZU HOHENRECHBERG,** *b* at Herringhausen 29 Nov 1912, Kt of Hon Sovereign Military Order of Malta, son of Albert Adolf, Count (Graf) von Rechberg and Rothenlöwen zu Hohenrechberg (*b* 3 April 1887; ✚ 28 Oct 1983) and Baroness Theresia von Schorlemer (*b* 22 Sept 1887; *m* 12 July 1910; ✚ 17 Feb 1955); adopted by his uncle, Joseph, Count (Graf) von Rechberg and Rothenlöwen zu Hohenrechberg whom he succeeded (*b* 1885; ✚ 1967); *m* at Königseggwald 3 Dec 1951, Countess Monika (*b* at Königseggwald 24 June 1923), Dame Star Cross Order, dau of Joseph Erwin, Count zu Königsegg-Aulendorf and Countess Lucia von Wilczek.
[*In der Breite 2,73072 Donzdorf, Württemberg, Germany*].

Sons and Daughters

1. Countess *Dorothee* Maria Monika Wilhelmine Clementine, *b* at Donzdorf 27 Sept 1952.
[*73072 Donzdorf, Württemberg, Germany*].
2. Countess *Andrea* Maria Philippine Henriette, *b* at Göppingen 25 May 1954, Dipl Eng.
[*Von-Eisenberg-Straße 13, 89356 Haldenwang, Germany*].
3. *Bernhard* Alfred Josef Johannes, Hereditary Count (Erbgraf) von Rechberg and Rothenlöwen zu Hohenrechberg, *b* at Göppingen 10

Jan 1956, Banker, Dipl Agr Eng; *m* at Donzdorf 20 Aug (civ) and at Schwaigern 30 Aug (relig) 1986, Countess Barbara (*b* at Schwaigern 4 Jan 1960), dau of Josef Hubert, Count and Lord von Neipperg, Proprietor of Schwaigern, and Countess Maria von Ledebur-Wicheln, and has issue,

[*In der Breite 1, 73072 Donzdorf, Württemberg, Germany*].

> 1. Countess Maria *Elisabeth* Franziska Dorothee, *b* at Schwäbisch Gmünd 4 Nov 1989.
>
> 2. Countess Maria *Johanna* Sigweis Andrea, *b* at Schwäbisch Gmünd 7 Feb 1991.
>
> 3. Countess Maria *Antonia* Stephanie Elisabeth, *b* at Schwäbisch Gmünd 4 July 1993.
>
> 4. Count Maria *Konrad* Karl-Eugen Stephan, *b* at Schwäbisch Gmünd 12 Nov 1994.
>
> 5. Count Maria *Gaudenz* Johannes Ferdinand Bernhard, *b* at Schwäbisch Gmünd 15 Jan 1996.
>
> 6. Countess Maria *Monika* Nadine Marianne, *b* at Schwäbisch Gmünd 22 March 2000.

4. Count *Nikolaus* Josef Erwin, *b* at Göppingen 20 March 1958; *m* at Berlin 4 Dec 1997, Ariane (*b* at Munich 19 May 1968), dau of Frank Röhl and Angelika Wägner, and has issue,

[*Starnbergstraße 6, 10781 Berlin, Germany*].

> 1. Count *Leon* Lukas, *b* at Berlin 1 Jan 1996.

5. Count *Ernst Michael* Hubertus *b* at Krumbach 20 Dec 1961; ✞ at Freiburg im Briesgau 8 May 1982.

Brother of Great-Great-Grandfather

Issue of Maximilian-Emmanuel, Count von Rechberg and Rothenlöwen (*b* 9 Aug 1736; ✞ 19 March 1819) and Baroness Maria Walpurga von Sandizell (*b* 3 Jan 1744; *m* 17 Oct 1764; ✞ 4 Sept 1818), among whom,

Son

Count *Johann Nepomuk* Joseph Maria Karl Johann von Kreuz, *b* at Donzdorf 24 Nov 1773; ✞ at Munich 8 May 1817; *m* at Munich 1 Feb 1808, Countess Julie Barbier von Schroffenberg (*b* at Hegenheim 30 July 1778; ✞ at Munich 8 June 1853), having had issue,

Son

Count *Ludwig* Hermann Gaudenz, *b* at Munich 15 Jan 1814; ✞ 30 July 1887, Lt-Gen Bavarian Army, Aide-de-Camp to Ludwig II, King of Bavaria, Kt Order of St Hubertus; *m* at Irlbach 18 July 1839,

Countess Gabrielle de Bray (*b* at Dorpat 9 March 1818; ✝ at Munich 6 May 1900), having had issue, among whom,

Son

Count *Ernst* Bero Franz Xaver Johann Nepomuk Gabriel, *b* at Munich 3 June 1840; ✝ there 6 Dec 1913, Proprietor of Elkofen, Kt Sovereign Military Order of Malta; *m* at Munich 17 July 1873, Catherine Mary Howard (*b* at London 3 April 1846; ✝ at Munich 15 Feb 1905), having had issue, among whom,

Son

Count *Wolfgang* Franz Gaudenz Aloys Joseph Maria, *b* at Elkofen 7 Dec 1883; ✝ at Bersberg 25 Dec 1971, Proprietor of Elkofen, Bailiff Gd Cross Hon and Dev Sovereign Military Order of Malta; *m* at Schräbsdorf, Frankenstein, Lower Schleswig 1 May 1918, Countess Maria Franziska (*b* at Schräbsdorf 22 Sept 1896; ✝ at Munich 16 Oct 1974), dau of Friedrich, Count Strachwitz von Gross-Zauche and Camminetz and Countess Frida von Soden-Fraunhofen, and had issue,

> 1. Count *Friedrich-Ernst* Bernhard Bero Maximilian Joseph Maria, *b* at Schräbsdorf 3 Aug 1919; ✝ at Regensburg 30 April 1965, Director of Deutsche Bank at Regensburg, Dr of Law, Major (Res), Kt of Hon Sovereign Military Order of Malta, Kt Bav Order of St George; *m* at Herdringen 10 Sept 1956, Baroness Rose-Marie (*b* at Lorzendorf 4 Dec 1931; *m* 2ndly at Elkofen 19 Aug (civ) and 26 Aug (relig) 1967, Anton, Count von Wengersky, Baron von Ungershütz), dau of Karl-Anton, Count Saurma von der Jeltsch-Lorzendorf and Countess Maria Lory von Matuschka, Baroness von Toppolczan and Spaetgen, and had issue,
> [*Schloß Elkofen 1, 85567 Grafing bei München, Germany*].
>> 1. Countess *Fiona*- Pia Franziska-Maria Lory, *b* at Munich 8 March 1958; *m* at Vienna 25 April (civ) and at Grafing, near Munich 6 July 1985, Karl Eugen, Count Czernin von Chudenitz (*b* at Vienna 25 July 1956), Proprietor of Enzesfeld, Dipl Eng, Underwriter, Lt (Res).
>> [*Forsthaus, 2551 Enzesfeld, Austria*].
>> 2. Count *Max Emanuel* Wolfgang Karl Anton Laurentius Maria, *b* at Munich 25 Sept 1959, Proprietor of Elkofen, Capt (Res), Kt Bav Order of St George;

m at Schloß Zeil 30 Dec 1988 (civ) and 8 April 1989 (relig), Countess Adelheid (*b* at Ravensburg 28 Nov 1964), dau of Georg, Prince (Fürst) von Waldburg zu Zeil and Trauchburg and Princess Marie Gabrielle of Bavaria, and has issue,
[*Schloß Elkofen, 85567 Grafing bei München, Germany*].

> 1. Count *Friedrich* Carl Albrecht Valentinian Max Emanuel Maria, *b* at Munich 12 Jan 1990.
> 2. Count *Max-Emanuel* Secundus Karl Caspar Felix Maria, *b* at Munich 12 July 1991.
> 3. Countess *Sophie* Maria Caroline Martha, *b* at Munich 17 July 1994.

2. Count *Albrecht* Ludwig Adam Gaudenz Joseph Maria, *b* at Schräbsdorf 23 Sept 1920, Dr of Law, Capt (ret), Kt of Hon Sovereign Military Order of Malta, Chapter Cmdr Bav Order of St George; *m* at Prien 5 Feb 1962, Baroness Freude (*b* at Dresden 31 March 1931), dau of Max, Baron Varnbüler von and zu Hemmingen and Ellen Hoesch, and has issue, among whom,
[*Maria Eichstraße 54a, 85567 Gräfelfing bei München, Germany*].

> 1. Count *Ulrich* Alexander Wolfgang Max Joseph Maria, *b* at Munich 30 Dec 1962.
> [*Lerchenfeldstraße 11, 80538 Munich, Germany*].
> 2. Count *Thomas* Albrecht Johannes Antonius Anzio Maria, *b* at Munich 16 Nov 1967.
> [*Priesterseminar, Georgenstraße 14, 80799 Munich, Germany*].

3. Countess *Agnes* Frida Katharina Maria Gabriele Josepha, *b* at Schräbsdorf 10 Oct 1921; *m* at Elkofen 22 May 1947, Ole Risom (*b* at Copenhagen 3 Oct 1919, ✠ at New York 18 Aug 2000).
[*Harbor Lane, Roslyn Harbor, Long Island, N.Y. 11576, USA*].

4. Countess *Margarethe* Maria Gabriele Elisabeth Josepha, *b* at Elkofen 28 May 1926; *m* at Elkofen 26 Jun 1948, Ignaz Wessel, Baron von Landsberg-Velen (*b* at Alsbach, nr Engelskirchen 29 Sept 1921), Proprietor of Steinfurt, Lt.-Col. (Res).
[*Haus Steinfurt, 48317 Drensteinfurt, Westfalen, Germany*].

5. Countess *Elisabeth* Therese Hedwig Maria Josefa, *b* at Elofen 15 Oct 1930, ✠ at Rio de Janeiro 30 March 1999; *m* at Santa Cruz, Bolivia 16 July 1957, David Monteiro de Barros Lins (*b* at Belo Horizonte 4 Aug 1915), Diplomat.
[*Praia de Botafogo 280/401, Rio de Janeiro, Brazil*].

RECHTEREN LIMPURG
(HOUSE OF VAN HEECKEREN)

This feudal family descends from the family of van Heeckeren in the Duchy of Gelderland, authenticated in Éverardus miles de Hekere living in 1236 descending from Frederic de Hekeren, a knight living in 1295 (✠ 1320); took the name of Rechteren through the marriage of Frederic de Hekeren (✠ 2 Nov 1386) to Luitgard, daughter and heiress of the last Lord of Rechteren (a Castle situated in the province of Overyssel) circa 1350; Baron 5 June 1350; inherited part of the county of Limpurg-Speckfeld (a ruin near Markt Einersheim), adopted the name of Limpurg and received the right to sit and vote in the Franconian College of the Counts of the Empire through the marriage of Joachim, Count of Rechteren Rechteren, Schulenburg and Ehse (*b* 28 Dec 1687; ✠ 15 March 1719) to Amelie (*b* 5 June 1689; ✠ 2 April 1754), one of the three daughters and heiresses of Georg Everard, last Count of Limpurg-Speckfeld (✠ 1705); the lines below descend from two sons of Count Johann Everard Adolph (*b* 1714; ✠ 1754); acquired the Lordships of Almelo in the Netherlands, through the marriage (second) of the above-mentioned Count Johann Everard Adolph to Sophie Carolina Florentina, daughter and heiress of Adolph Philip, Count of Rechteren Almelo (✠ 1805).

ELDER LINE

Reformist: Founded by Count Friedrich Ludwig Christian (*b* 29 Feb 1748; ✠ 8 Sept 1814); Received into the Nobility of Overyssel and of Gelderland in 1814 and 1816 respectively.
Members of the family bear the title of Count or Countess van Rechteren Limpurg with the qualification of Illustrious Highness.

ADOLPH Frederik Lodewijk, **COUNT VAN RECHTEREN LIMPURG,** *b* at Berlin 10 July 1931, Lord of Almelo and Vriezenveen, Mag jur, Estate Manager, son of Willem, Count van Rechteren Limpurg (*b* 9 Jan 1898 ✠ 21 Feb 1992) and Baroness Fay van Heemstra (*b* 3 Dec 1908; *m* 12 Aug 1930; ✠ 2 July 1968); *m* at The Hague 8 Oct 1966, Elisabeth Catharina (*b* at Pasoeroean, Java 30 June 1936), dau of Cornelis Buis and Agnes Knegtmans, and has

issue,

[*Huize Almelo, 7607 Almelo, The Netherlands*].

Sons

1. Count *Max* Willem Arthur, Hereditary Count van Rechteren Limpurg, *b* at Almelo 25 Feb 1967; *m* at Zimbabwe 3 Aug 1996, *Philippa* Louise Dione (*b* at Zimbabwe 11 June 1966), dau of George Stanger and Dione Phillips, and has issue,

    1. Countess *Elisabeth* Fay Sophia, *b* at Harare, Zimbabwe 6 December 1997.

    2. Countess *Catherine* Dione Mary, *b* at Harare, Zimbabwe 6 December 1997 (twin with Countess Elisabeth).

2. Count *Christiaan* Adolph, *b* at Almelo 7 Jan 1971.

Brother of Great-Grandfather

Issue of Count Adolph (*b* 13 Oct 1793; ✠ 31 March 1851) and Baroness Elisabeth-Wilhelmine van Massow (*b* 4 Oct 1793; *m* 4 April 1824; ✠ 18 Dec 1882), among whom,

Son

Count *Jacob* Hendrik, Lord of Rechteren and Berborg, *b* at Almelo 6 Dec 1831; ✠ at Zwolle 13 Jan 1878; *m* at Rechteren 9 June 1859, Countess Jacqueline van Rechteren, dau of Jakob Hendrik and Gertrud Agnes, Baroness van Vos van Steenwijk (*b* at Zwolle 28 Aug 1837; ✠ at Kasteel de Leemcule 19 June 1901), having had issue, among whom,

Son

1. Count *Adolph Reinhard* Zeyger, *b* at Rechteren 12 May 1909; ✠ there 13 March 1962, Kt Teutonic Order, Lord of Rechteren, de Leemcule and Verborg; *m* at London 4 June 1937, Baroness Carola (*b* at Villa Beukenhorst in Wassenaar 21 March 1900; *m* 1stly at Paris 31 Aug 1928, Philippe Koechline Schwartz; that *m* diss by div at Paris 12 Feb 1936), dau of Carel, Baron van Lynden and Countess Adolphine van Limburg Stirum, and had issue,

[*Kasteel Rechteren, 7721 Dalfsen, The Netherlands*].

    1. Countess *Elisabeth* Marguérite Carola, *b* at The Hague 5 June 1938, Lady of Rechteren, Leemcule and Verborg.

    [*Kasteel Rechteren, 7721 Dalfsen, The Netherlands*].

2. Count Adolph *Sweder* Hubertus, *b* at Rechteren 3 Nov 1910; ✠ at Utrecht 19 Dec 1972, Kt Teutonic Order, Lord of Enghuizen; *m* 1stly at at Berlin 16 May (civ) and at Detmold 19 May (relig) 1935

(*m* diss by div at Arnheim 15 June 1944), Princess Eleonore (*b* at Dresden 11 Aug 1913; ✠ at The Hague 19 Oct 1964), dau of Ernst, Count and Noble Lord zu Lippe-Weissenfeld and Princess Anna zu Isenburg and Büdingen in Büdingen. He *m* 2ndly at Laren, Gelderland 16 Dec 1953, Ruby Ellen (*b* at Clinton, British Columbia 20 Nov 1902; ✠ at Doetinchem 30 Jan 1973; *m* 1stly at Vancouver 17 May 1926, Adolph, Count van Rechteren Limpurg who ✠ at Deventer 19 Feb 1952), dau of George Alexander Mitchell and Charlotte Caroline Mundorff, and had issue by his first wife,

1. Count Adolph *Roderik* Ernst Leopold, *b* at Berlin 25 Nov 1938, Kt Teutonic Order, Lord of Enghuizen; *m* at Hummelo 14 Dec 1973, Ingrid (*b* at Amsterdam 30 Dec 1935; *m* 1stly at The Hague .. Klynstra; that *m* diss by div 1970), dau of Dirk Pieksma and Nikola Evers, and has issue,

[*Huize Enghuizen, Kasteellaan 1, 6999 DA Hummelo, Gelderland, The Netherlands*].

1. Count Adolph *Patrick* Alexander, *b* at Doetinchen 9 July 1976.

2. Countess *Anna* Pia Amalaswintha, *b* at Arnheim 27 Sept 1940; ✠ at Essen 12 May 1994; *m* at Essen 30 Aug (civ) and at Hummelo 31 Aug (relig) 1968, Hans Günter, Count zu Solms-Laubach (*b* at Munich 26 June 1927), Lawyer.

[*Hunsrückstraße 19, 45133 Essen - Bredeney, Germany*].

YOUNGER LINE
(✠ Extinct ✠)

Lutheran: Founded by Count Friedrich Reinhard Burkhard Rudolf (*b* 22 Sept 1751; ✠ 20 June 1842); Hereditary Member of the Bavarian "Reichsräte" 26 May 1818; received the Bavarian qualification of "Erlaucht" (primogeniture) 11 Feb 1823, 22 April 1829 and 3 March 1911; confirmed by the German Diet 13 Feb 1829.

✠ **FRIEDRICH** Ludwig Botho Alfred Conrad, **COUNT (GRAF) VON RECHTEREN-LIMPURG-SPECKFELD,** *b* at Markt Einersheim 26 Nov 1875; ✠ at Fürth, Breisgau 9 June 1955, Forester, Kt of St John of Jerusalem, *succ* 23 April 1907, son of Friedrich Reinhard, Hereditary Count (Erbgraf) von Rechteren-Limpurg-Speckfeld (*b* 3 July 1841; ✠ 29 July 1893) and Countess Christine zu Stolberg-Wernigerode (*b* 13 Sept 1853; *m* 22 Sept 1874; ✠ 20 March 1933); *m* at The Hague 17 Oct 1907, Countess Adolphina (*b* at Dordrecht 3 Sept 1888; ✠ at Eefde 16 Sept 1974) dau of

Willem, Count van Rechteren-Limpurg and Baroness Constance van den Santheuvel.

SALM

Seigneural family descending from Sigrid, Count in the Moselgau (✝ 15 Aug 998); Count of Lucilinburch (Lützelburg, Luxemburg) 963; Count of Salmis in the Oisling (Osning, Ardennes, a ruin near Old Salm, Luxemburg) 1035; Hermann I opposing King to Henri IV 1081 - 1084; Henri II (1171 - 1244); Count Henri I de Blamont, 1125 - 66, Prevost of Senones, who built the Castle of Salme on the Wasichen (Salm in the Vosges, now a ruin near Schirmeck, Lower Alsace), founded the Line of Salm-Superior 1204; the main branch (extinct in the male line 1475) succeeded as Wildgraves and Rhinegraves by the House of Salm-Inferior, extinct in the male line 1415/6 and inherited by the Reifferscheidt, who originate from the Counts of Vianden; Friedrich, Count of Salm, is documented for the first time in 1171 as the brother of Count Sifrid of Vianden.

A: SALM-SUPERIOR

Authenticated since Sifridus de Lapide 1170, and his son Wolfram who appears circa 1200 as "comes Reni" or "de lapide comes" (Rheingrafenstein, near Dreuznach); Rhinegrave of Stein 1223; inherited the Wildgraviate of Dhaun (fortified castle, today a ruin, near Kirn) 1350, the Wildgraviate of Kyrburg and the Lordship of Limburg on the Lahn 1409; inherited the County of Salm and the Lordships of Morchingen, Puttlingen, Warsberg and Rotzlar through the marriage (14 Nov 1459) of Johann V, Rhinegrave of Stein, Wildgrave of Dhaun-Kyrburg (b 17 Nov 1436; ✝ after 2 Sept 1495) to Johanetta, daughter and heiress of Simon, Count of Salm-Superior, in 1475; inherited the Lordships of Diemeringen, Vinstingen and Rigenweiler circa 1500; partition of possessions and the creations of the Houses of Dhaun and Kyrburg (extinct in 1688) 6 Jan 1520; three sons of Philipp-Franz, Wild and Rhinegrave of Dhaun, Count of Salm (b 4 Aug 1518; ✝ 28 Jan 1561) founded the branches of Salm, of Grumbach (see below) and of Dhaun (extinct 10 June 1750).

I: Line of SALM

Catholic: Founded by Friedrich, Wildgraf and Rhinegraf of Salm (b 3 Feb 1547; ✝ 26 Oct 1608), Lord of the County of Salm and the Lordships of Vinstingen, Augweiler, Bayon and Neufviller (Neuviller, Meurthe-et-Moselle, France); partition (20 Feb 1634) between the sons of Philipp-Otto (b 22 May 1575; ✝ 23 Nov 1634) and Friedrich II Magnus (b 29 June 1606; ✝ 27 Jan 1673); the title of Prince of Salm and of the Holy Empire for Philipp-Otto and his male descendants (extinct 23 Nov 1738) with transmission to the heirs in possession of the Princely County of Salm, Ravensburg 8 Jan 1623 (primogeniture); acquired the Lordship of Anholt (see below) through the marriage (22 Oct 1641) of Prince Leopold-Philipp-Carl to Marianne, daughter and heiress of Thierry, last Count of Bronkhorst-Anholt, 5 Dec 1645; received the qualification of Serene Highness 25 Nov 1697; inherited (with the Ducal Houses of Bourbon-Condé and Ursel) the sovereign principality of Arches and of Charleville (in the Ardennes) and the Duchy of Montferrat (Allesandria, Italy), after the extinction (5 July 1708) of the male line of the Ducal House of Mantua Montferrat; the branches below descend from two sons of Carl-Florentin, Wildgrave and Rhinegrave of Salm (✝ 4 Sept 1676) and Marie-Gabrielle (m 14 Dec 1659; ✝ 8 Feb 1709), sister and heiress of François-Paul de Lalaing, Comte de Hoogstraeten (Anvers, Belgium), 21 June 1691.

1st Branch: SALM-SALM

Founded by Wilhelm-Florentin, Wildgraf and Rhinegraf of Salm (b 12 May 1670; ✝ 6 June 1707), succeeded to part of the Rhine and Wildgraviate at the extinction (16 Nov 1688) of the line of the Rhinegraves and Wildgrafs of Kyrburg; his son Nicolas-Leopold, Wildgraf and Rhinegraf of Salm and of Hoogstraeten (succeeded 1709 - inherited from his grandmother - see above) (b 25 Jan 1701; ✝ 4 Feb 1770), succeeded to the Princely County of Salm (primogeniture) and the title of Prince of the Holy Empire and to the Lordship of Anholt 23 Nov 1738; the title of Prince of the Holy Empire and the inheritance of the Lordship was confirmed 23 Nov 1738; confirmation of the title of Prince of the Holy Empire conferred 3 Jan 1623, Vienna 14 Jan 1739; Dutch title of Duke of Hoogstraeten 6 Jan 1740; title of Prince of Salm-Salm through an accord with the second branch 16 Oct 1743; loss of possessions on the left bank of the Rhine (the principality of Salm in the German territory of Lorraine and the French territories of Meurthe-et-Moselle, and parts of the Wild and Rhinegraviate near Kreuznach and Simmern, and the Lordship of Ogéviller, in Meurthe-et-Moselle) through the Peace of Lunéville of 9 Feb 1801; compensated, with title indemnified, by two parts of the Bailiwicks of Ahaus and Bocholt which were formed into the Principality of Salm 22 Oct 1802; reigned until 28 Feb 1811; Duke of the French Empire 31 Dec 1811; placed under the sovereignty of Prussia 1815; acquired the third part of the above Bailiwicks from the second branch 1825; qualification of "Durchlaucht" (conferred 25 Nov 1697) confirmed by the German Diet 18 Aug 1825; Hereditary Member of the former Prussian House of Lords 12 Oct 1854.

Members of this branch bear the title of Prince or Princess zu Salm and Salm-Salm with the qualification of Serene Highness.

CARL PHILIPP Josef Petrus Coelestinus Balthasar, **14TH PRINCE (FÜRST) ZU SALM, 9TH PRINCE (FÜRST) ZU SALM-SALM AND 9TH PRINCE (FÜRST) ZU SALM-KYRBURG,** Wild-und-Rheingraf, Fürst zu Ahaus and Bocholt, Duke von Hoogstraeten, Count zu Anholt, Lord of Vinstingen and Werth, *b* at Anholt 19 May 1933, son of Nikolaus Leopold, 13th Prince (Fürst) zu Salm-Salm, etc (*b* 14 Feb 1906; ✠ 15 Jan 1988) and his first wife, Princess Ida von Wrede (*b* 26 Feb 1909; *m* 19 July 1928; *m* diss by div 1948; ✠ 25 Oct 1998); *m* 1stly at Munich 4 Feb (civ) and 8 Feb (relig) 1961 (*m* diss by div at Munich 16 Aug 1979), Erika (*b* at Berlin 19 March 1935), dau of Ernst von Morgen and Countess Margarethe Schlitz genannt Görtz. He *m* 2ndly at Rhede 19 July 1993, Elisabeth (*b* at Lindau 12 Feb 1951), dau of Albert Frisch and Irmgard Zapp.

[*Haus Rhede, 46414 Rhede, Germany*].

Sons and Daughters

1. *Emanuel* Philipp Nikolaus Johann Felix, Hereditary Prince (Erbprinz) zu Salm-Salm, *b* at Münster, Westfalia 6 Dec 1961; *m* at Isselburg 11 Sept (civ) and at Köln 19 Dec (relig) 1992, Zita (*b* at Münster 26 Nov 1970), dau of Burchard von Klot-Heydenfeldt and Countess Rixa von Westphalen zu Fürstenberg.

[*Haus Rhede, 46414 Rhede, Germany*].

2. Prince *Philipp* Petrus Andreas Antonius Joachim, *b* at Münster 5 July 1963; *m* at Paris 6 Oct (civ) and at Notre-Dame-des-Victoires, Paris 17 Oct (relig) 2000, Hermine (*b* at Paris 29 April 1975), dau of Michel de Cassan-Floyrac and Isabelle de Mengin.

[*Tenstraße 11, 80798 Munich, Germany*].

3. Princess *Felicitas* Marcellina Josepha Flaminia Maria, *b* at Düsseldorf 2 June 1965; *m* at Anholt 17 Aug (civ) and 22 Sept (relig) 1990, Christoph von Grolman (*b* at Hanover 6 March 1959).

[*7 Anderson Road, Greenwich, CT 06830, U.S.A.*].

4. Prince *Clemens* Angelus Paul Ferdinand Moritz, *b* at Düsseldorf 10 Nov 1966, *m* at Kühtai, Tyrol 9 Apr 1994, Countess *Johanna* Paula Irene Adelheid Maria (*b* at Hamburg 13 Aug 1969), dau of Count *Ferdinand* Maria Immaculata Josef Martin Hubert zu Stolberg-Stolberg and Baroness Jutta von Cramm

[*Mühlbaurstraße 5, 81677 Munich, Germany*].

Brother and Sisters

1. Princess *Konstanze* Maria Theresia Jakobea Kaspara, *b* at Anholt

25 July 1929; ✣ at Düsseldorf 13 April 1980; *m* at Düsseldorf 22 Jan 1975, Joseph Zdenko, Count von Thun and Hohenstein (*b* at Prague 31 Dec 1907; ✣ at Düsseldorf 22 Feb 1976).

2. *Alfred* Franz Emanuel Christophorus Bruno Melchior, Hereditary Prince (Erbprinz) zu Salm-Salm, *b* at Anholt 6 Oct 1930; ✣ in a air raid at Anholt, Westphalia 21 March 1945.

3. Princess *Anna* Huberta Maria Alfonsa Kaspara, *b* at Anholt 2 Aug 1935; *m* at Salzburg 19 Dec 1995, Count Paul von Degenfeld-Schönburg (*b* at Klausenburg 23 May 1924).
[*Pienzenauerstraße 127, 81925 Munich, Germany*].

4. Princess *Margarethe* Cecilie Johanna Alfonsa Melchiora, *b* at Anholt 2 Aug 1935 (twin with Princess Anna); *m* Petersberg, nr Bonn 23 Sept 1957, György Scheftsik de Szolnok (*b* at Törökszentmiklos, Hungary 11 July 1926; ✣ at Paris 30 April 1965).
[*"Pontac", Salleboeuf, 33370 Tresses, France*].

Half-Brothers
Issue of Nicolaus Leopold, 13th Prince zu Salm, etc, and:

A) his second wife, Eleonore (*b* at Prebendow 24 Nov 1919; *m* at Hamburg-Eimsbüttel 19 Oct 1950; *m* diss by div 1961), widow of Harras Ursus Cammineci (*m* 28 Oct 1940) who was killed in Russia 23 July 1944, dau of Wilhelm-Siegfried von Zitzewitz and Eleonore Heyn; issue among whom,

5. Prince *Ludwig-Wilhelm* Carl Emanuel Jörg Nikolaus, *b* at Hamburg 15 April 1953; *m* at Anmühle 9 Dec (civ) 1994 and (relig) 6 May 1995 (*m* diss by div 2001), Christiane (*b* at Mainz 2 Oct 1966), Chairman of television network, dau of Volker Hansen and Jutta Wagner.
[*Mauerkircher Straße 12, 81679 Munich, Germany*].

B) his third wife, Maria (*b* at Grolley, nr Fribourg 23 June 1930; ✣ at Geneva 9 Jan 1982; *m* at Bern 23 March 1962; *m* diss by div at Geneva 6 June 1972), dau of Léon Moret and Angela Diagostini; issue among whom,

6. Prince *Christian-Nikolaus* Lucius Piero Angelus, *b* at Geneva 25 Aug 1964.
[*26 Avenue de Miremont, 1206 Geneva, Switzerland*].

Step-Mothers

1. *Eleonore* Sophie Wilhelmine, Princess zu Salm, Salm-Salm and Salm-Kyrburg, *b* at Prebendow 24th Nov 1919, dau of Wilhelm-Siegfried von Zitzewitz and Eleonore Heyn; *m* 1stly at ... 28 Oct 1940, Harras Ursus Cammineci who was killed in Russia 23 July 1944. She *m* 2ndly at Hamburg-Eimsbüttel 19 Oct 1950 (*m* diss by div 1961), Nikolaus Leopold, 13th Fürst zu Salm and 8th Fürst zu Salm-Salm and Salm-Kyrburg, etc.

[*Börnsenerstraße 7, 21521 Aumühle, Bez. Hamburg, Germany*].

2. *Maria,* Princess zu Salm, Salm-Salm and Salm-Kyrburg, *b* at Grolley, nr Fribourg 23 June 1930; ✠ at Gevenva 1982, dau of Josef León Moret and Angela Diagostini; *m* at Bern 23 March 1962 (*m* diss by div at Geneva 6 June 1972), Nikolaus Leopold, 13th Fürst zu Salm and 8th Fürst zu Salm-Salm and Salm-Kyrburg, etc.

3. *Christiane,* Princess zu Salm, Salm-Salm and Salm-Kyrburg, *b* at Herford 8 May 1958, dau of Kurt Kostecki and Edith Ortmann; *m* at Preussisch Oldendorf 19 April 1984, Nikolaus Leopold, 13th Fürst zu Salm and 8th Fürst zu Salm-Salm and Salm-Kyrburg, etc.

[*Heckengang 3, 31812 Bad Pyrmont, Germany*].

Sister of Father

Issue of Emanuel, Hereditary Prince zu Salm Salm (*b* 30 Nov 1871; killed 19 Aug 1916) and Archduchess Maria Christina of Austria (*b* 17 Nov 1879; *m* 10 May 1902; ✠ 6 Aug 1962), having had issue, among whom,

1. Princess *Isabelle* Maria Rosa Katharina Antonia, *b* at Potsdam 13 Feb 1903, Dame of Hon Sovereign Military Order of Malta; *m* at Schloß Anholt 8 Sept 1925, Felix, Count von Loë (*b* at Wissen 1 Sept 1896; ✠ at Schwaneburg from wounds received in battle 25 July 1944), Proprietor of Wissen, etc, Dr rer pol, Major.

[*Friedenstraße 53, 47623 Kevalaer, NRhein, Germany*].

Brother of Grandfather

Issue of Alfred, 12th Fürst zu Salm (1623), 7th Fürst zu Salm-Salm (1743) and 7th Fürst zu Salm-Kyrburg (*b* 13 March 1946; ✠ 20 April 1923) and Countess Rosa von Lützow (*b* 31 March 1850; *m* 18 Oct 1869; ✠ 5 Feb 1927), having had issue, among whom,

Son

Prince *Franz* Emanuel Konstantin, *b* at Anholt 30 Aug 1876; ✠ at Loburg, nr Coesfeld 10 Jan 1964, Capt Prussian Army; *m* at Prague

16 Nov 1912, Baroness Maria Anna (*b* at Datschitz, Moravia 11 March 1891; ✝ at Loburg 22 Feb 1979), Proprietor of Maleschau with Sukdol, Bez Kuttenberg, Bohemia and Wallhausen, nr Kreuznach, Dame Star Cross Order, dau of Karl, Baron von and zu Dalberg and Countess Gabriele von Spiegel zum Diesenberg-Hanzleden, and had issue, among whom,

    1. Princess Maria *Christine* Rosa, *b* at Charlottenburg 21 Nov 1914.

[*Haus Loburg, 48653 Coesfeld, Westfalen, Germany*].

    2. Princess *Auguste* Franziska Karoline, *b* at Charlottenburg 14 Jan 1916; *m* at Oggersheim, Pfalz 20 Dec 1953, Kurt Brubach (*b* at Nothweiler 24 Sept 1921).

[*Unterer Felsenberg 1, 76887 Böllenborn, Germany*].

    3. Prince *Franz* Karl Alfred Emanuel Aloysius Josef Maria, *b* at Münster, Westphalia 22 Feb 1917, Proprietor of Wallhausen; *m* at Heimerzheim 30 Oct 1951, Baroness Maria (*b* at Heimerzheim 3 Dec 1923), dau of Albert, Baron von Boeselager and Baroness Maria Theresia von Salis-Soglio, and has issue,

[*Schloß Wallhausen, 55595 Kr. Bad Kreuznach, Germany*].

        1. Prince *Michael* Alfred Wolfgang Dietrich Hendrik Antonius Maria, *b* at Heimerzheim 16 Jan 1953, Dipl Business, President VDP; *m* at Castell 27 May (civ) and 28 May (relig) 1977, Countess Philippa (*b* at Castell 23 Jan 1952), dau of Albrecht, Prince (Fürst) zu Castell-Castell and Princess Marie-Louise zu Waldeck and Pyrmont, and has issue,

        [*Schloß Wallhausen, 55595 Kr. Bad Kreuznach, Germany*].

            1. Princess Christina *Marie* Anna Florentina, *b* at Dettelbach 9 June 1978.

            2. Prince *Constantin* Carl Maria, *b* at Dettelbach 22 April 1980.

            3. Prince *Felix* Franz Georg Maria, *b* at Dettelbach 5 Nov 1981.

            4. Princess Marie-Anna Franziska, *b* at Kitzingen 22 Feb 1986.

            5. Princess *Antonia* Cecilie Theresa Gustava, *b* at Kitzingen 5 Dec 1987.

            6. Princess *Cecily* Henriette Philippa Maria, *b* at Bad Kreuznach 4 Dec 1989.

2. Princess *Maria* Katharina Anna Antonia Gabriele Huberta, *b* at Heimerzheim 2 April 1954; *m* at Wallhausen 31 May 1980, Christoph Rechberg (*b* at Bad Hersfeld 19 May 1950), Assessor.
[*Burgstraße 15, 61476 Kronberg, Germany*].

3. Princess *Jeanne* Marie-Theresia Eleonore Antoinette, *b* at Heimerzheim 18 Aug 1955.
[*Winzererstraße 30a, 80797 Munich, Germany*].

4. Princess *Adelheid* Christiane Johanna Albertine Antonia Maria, *b* at Heimerzheim 21 June 1958; *m* 1stly at Altenberg 29 Dec 1981 (*m* diss by div 1994), Ekkehart Panek (*b* 20 April 1962), Builder. She *m* 2ndly at Witten 13 Sept 1997, Martin Geck (*b* at Witten 19 March 1936), Professor of Music.
[*Stockumer Bruch 66, 58454 Witten, Germany*].

5. Princess *Antoinette* Sophie Flaminia Alexandra Maria, *b* at Heimerzheim 28 July 1959.
[*Niebuhrstraße 19, 53113 Bonn, Germany*].

6. Princess *Christiane* Flaminia Nathalie Elisabeth Huberta Maria, *b* at Wallhausen 6 March 1962, Actress; *m* at Krefeld 27 Nov 1989, Daniel Werner (*b* at Wiesbaden 29 July 1957), Actor.
[*Kütterweg 9, 47807 Krefeld, Germany*].

7. Prince *Franziskus*- Hendrick Philipp Alfred Hermann Wolfgang Heribert Stephan Joseph Maria, *b* at Wallhausen 23 Dec 1963, stud jur.
[*Haus Löburg, Birksfeld 1, 48653 Coesfeld, Germany*].

8. Prince *Georg*- Alfred Winfried, *b* at Bad Kreuznach 29 May 1969.
[*Schloß Wallhausen, 55595 Kr. Bad Kreuznach, Germany*].

4. Princess *Elisabeth* Henriette Maria Felizitas Pia, *b* at Loburg 8 Feb 1922, Dr of Med, Eye Specialist.
[*Gleuelerstraße 22, 50823 Cologne, Germany*].

2nd Branch: SALM-KYRBURG
(✠ Extinct ✠) - see the Barons of Rennenberg

II: Line of GRUMBACH, actually SALM-HORSTMAR

Lutheran: Founded by Johann Christoph (b 22 Oct 1555; ✝ 3 Aug 1585), Wild and Rhinegrave of Grumbach (in the region of Treves) and Rhingrafenstein, Count of Salm, Lord of Vinstingen, Diemeringen and Puttlingen; inherited the Bailiwicks of Thronecken, Wildenburg and Wörrstadt after the extinction (16 Nov 1688) of the ancient House of Kyrburg, 21 Nov 1701; introduction of the order of primogeniture 18 Dec 1700; inherited half of the lands of Dhaun and the Castle of Dhaun (see below) 20 Dec 1764 after the extinction of the branch of Dhaun 10 June 1750; loss of possessions situated on the left bank of the Rhine 1801; compensated, with title indemnified, with the County of Horstmar (near Münster) 12 Nov 1802; received the Prussian title of Prince of Salm-Horstmar with the qualification of "Durchlaucht", Berlin 22 Nov 1816 (for Wilhelm Friedrich, Rhinegrave of Salm-Horstmar; Hereditary Member of the former Prussian House of Lords 12 Oct 1854; Family Law established 9 Oct 1899.

Members of this line bear the title of Prince or Princess zu Salm-Horstmar with the qualification of Serene Highness.

PHILIPP-OTTO Luitpold Karl Christoph Hans Ruppert, 5TH PRINCE (FÜRST) and RHEINGRAF ZU SALM-HORSTMAR, Wildgraf zu Dhaun and Kyrburg, Rheingraf zum Stein, Lord of Vinstingen, Diemeringen and Püttlingen, Hereditary Marshal of the Palatinate, b at Münster 2 June 1938, Dipl Forestry, Kt of Honour of St John of Jerusalem; son of Philipp Franz, 4th Prince (Fürst) and Rheingraf zu Salm-Horstmar (b 31 March 1909; ✝ 8 Nov 1996) and Countess Marie Therese zu Castell-Castell (b at Munich 30 Dec 1917; m 3 July 1937; m diss by div 26 March 1979; ✝ 11 July 2002), m at Stuttgart 30 Sept 1971, Katrin Christine (b at Strasbourg 24 Feb 1942), Dipl Psychology, dau of Heinrich Sauter and Doris Beutelspacher, and has issue,
[Varlar 70, 48720 Rosendahl, Germany].

1. Prince Philipp Gustav Thomas Carl, Hereditary Prince zu Salm-Horstmar, b at Münster 11 March 1973.
[Ewaldistraße 38, 48155, Münster, Germany].

2. Prince Christian Christof Alexander, b at Münster 20 May 1975.
[Hauptstraße 16-18, 65347 Eltville-Hattenheim, Germany]

Brothers

1. Prince Gustav-Friedrich Georg Heinrich Ludwig Ferdinand Philipp Franz, b at Munich 22 Oct 1942, MA (Oxon), Banker; m at Hamburg-Altona 10 June (civ) and at Hamburg-Nienstedten 12 June (relig) 1976 (m diss by div at London 20 Sept 1985), Beatrice [83 Stoddridge Street, London, SW6 3TD] (b at Hamburg 24 Sept

1952; she *m* 2ndly at London 13 Sept 1986, Baron Erik Hugo Loudon, *b* 5 Aug 1938), dau of Ruthard von Frankenberg and Ludwigsdorf and Elisabeth von Oswald, and has issue,
[*Flat B, 54 Lennox Gardens, London, SW1X ODJ*].

    1. Prince *Maximilian* Philipp Albrecht, *b* at Hamburg 12 May 1979.
    [*83 Stoddridge Street, London, SW6 3TD*]
    2. Prince *Leopold* Christof Constantin, *b* at Hamburg 27 Nov 1982.
    [*83 Stoddridge Street, London, SW6 3TD*].

2. Prince Johann *Christof* Udo Albrecht Karl Adolf, *b* at Münster 27 July 1949, Insurance Broker; *m* at Hanover 11 Feb 1978, Sigrid (*b* at Hanover 15 Oct 1950), dau of Otto Schreyer and Sigrid von Waltersdorff, and has issue,
[*Dörpfeldstraße 17, 22609 Hamburg, Germany*].

    1. Princess Sophie Eleonore, *b* at Hamburg 20 Jan 1980.
    2. Princess Marie Christine, *b* at Hamburg 1 Oct 1981.

Step-Brother

Issue of Philipp Franz, 4th Prince (Fürst) and Rheingraf zu Salm-Horstmar (*b* 31 March 1909; ✠ 8 Nov 1996) and Barbara Christa Pohl (*b* at Waldenburg, Schles 10 March 1939; *m* 1 June 1979).
[*Sitterstiege 14, 48653 Coesfeld, Germany*].

1. Prince *Carlos Federico*, *b* at Concordia, Prov Entre Rios, Argentina 11 Feb 1965; *m* at Reasfeld 10 June 1994 Margret (*b* at Rosendahl 14 Sept 1965), dau of Hubert Feldman and Hildegard Altenau, and has issue,
[*Sitterstiege 14, 48653 Coesfeld, Germany*].

    1. Prince *Constantin* Louis, *b* at Coesfeld 16 Nov 1994.
    2. Prince *Adrian* Nikolaus, *b* at Coesfeld 20 Oct 1996.

Brothers and Sisters of Father

Issue of of Otto II, 3rd Prince (Fürst) and Rheingraf zu Salm-Horstmar (*b* 23 Sept 1867; ✠ 2 March 1941) and Countess Rosa zu Solms-Baruth (*b* 8 June 1884; *m* 10 Sept 1903; ✠ 12 June 1945), among whom,

1. Prince *Karl Walrad* Emich Hermann Bolko Friedrich, *b* at Varlar 8 Jan 1911; ✠ at Düsseldorf 2 July 1991; *m* at Bielefeld 3 Sept 1952, Susanne (*b* at Reichenberg 21 July 1922; *m* 1stly Rudolf Oetker; that *m* diss by div), dau of Ferdinand Jantsch and N Karrer, and has

issue,

[*Am Fischerbreuel 4, 40489 Düsseldorf - Angermund, Germany*].

    1. Princess *Alexandra* Marie-Luise Brigitte Ingeborg, *b* at Düsseldorf 29 May 1953, Dipl Cosmetology; *m* at Düsseldorf 7 Sept 1979, Richard, Baron von Herman (*b* at Ulm 16 Nov 1947), Proprietor of Dieshof, Upper Bavaria, Banker.

    [*Dieshof, 86554 Pöttmes, Upper Bavaria, Germany; An der Rennbahn 3, 76473 Iffezheim, Germany*].

2. Princess *Marie Luise* Eleonore Adelma Rosa, *b* at Varlar 18 Aug 1918; *m* at Varlar 10 June 1954, Heinrich IV, Prince Reuss, Prince (Fürst) Reuss-Köstritz (*b* at Ernstbrunn 26 Oct 1919).

[*2115 Schloß Ernstbrunn, Upper Austria*].

Brother of Grandfather

Issue of Otto I, 2nd Fürst and Rheingraf zu Salm-Horstmar (*b* 8 Feb 1833; ✞ 15 Feb 1892) and Countess Emilie zur Lippe-Biesterfeld (*b* 1 Feb 1841; *m* 18 June 1864; ✞ 11 Feb 1892), among whom,

Son

Prince *Emich* Karl Rudolf Friedrich Wilhelm Otto, *b* at Varlar 5 Feb 1883; ✞ at Bremen 10 May 1959, Major Prussian Army, Kt of St John of Jerusalem; *m* at Potsdam 2 Aug 1914, Princess Sabine (*b* at Carolath 12 Oct 1893; ✞ at Bremen 14 Aug 1965), dau of Karl, Prince (Fürst) zu Carolath-Beuthen and Countess Katharina von Reichenbach-Goschütz, and had issue,

    1. Princess *Sieglinde* Emmy Katharina Elisabeth Erika Rosy Friederike Carola, *b* at Carolath 27 Aug 1915; *m* at Wickede, Ruhr 29 Dec 1964, Franz Bussmann (*b* ...).

    [*Kurzentrum, 27305 Bruchhansen-Vilsen, Germany*].

    2. Princess *Rosemarie* Sabine Adelheid Anna Luise Wanda Henriette, *b* at Carolath 24 Feb 1918; *m* at Höxter 24 Sept 1948, Conrad Kirchmeyer (*b* at Bremen 25 May 1908), Dr of Law.

    3. Princess *Felicitas* Sophie Katharine Margarethe Hermine Irene, *b* at Potsdam 31 March 1920; *m* at Heinrichau, Silesia 12 March 1943 (*m* diss by div at Munich 24 Sept 1956), Prince Bernhard Friedrich von Saxe-Weimar-Eisenach, Duke of Saxony (*b* at Weimar 3 March 1917; ✞ at Wiesbaden 23 March 1986).

    [*Pfingstrosenstraße 83, 81377 Munich, Germany*].

B: SALM-INFERIOR
(House of Reifferscheidt)

Catholic: Founded by Gerhard of Limburg, Lord of Reifferscheidt (Regent of Aix-la-Chapelle), son of Walram, Count of Arlon (Luxemburg), Lord of Limburg (Liège, Belgium, after 1130, Lord of Reifferscheidt) who appears authentically 1153 - 66; acquired the Lordship of Bedburg (Regency of Cologne; this Lordship was bequeathed circa 1550) circa 1226; inherited the Lordship of Dyck (see below) 1357; acquired the County of Salm through the marriage of Johan III of Reifferscheidt-Bedburg (✣ after 1417) to Richarda, daughter of Count Wilhelm of Salm-Inferior of the Counts of Vianden, 1416; this dignity was confirmed in the Court of the Nobility, Luxemburg 6 Feb 1455; inherited the Lordship of Alfter (Regency of Cologne) 1445; re-acquired the Lordships of Bedburg and Hackenbroich 1600; received the qualification of "Hochgeboren" and recognition of the ancient title of Count 28 Jan 1628; the first line (see below) descend from Eric Adolph, Count of Salm-Reifferscheidt-Bedburg (1619 - 1678); his grandson, Count Anton, founded the second line (see below).

LINE I: SALM-REIFFERSCHEIDT-KRAUTHEIM AND DYCK
(✣ Extinct ✣)

Founded by Count Carl (b 1697; ✣ 1755); loss of the Lordship of Reifferscheidt-Bedburg 1801 and donation, with title indemnified of the Bailiwick of Krautheim (near Mosbach, Baden); Prince of the Holy Empire (primogeniture) and elevation of the Lordships of Krautheim and Gerlachsheim into a Principality of the Holy Empire, Vienna 7 Jan 1804 (for the following line); received the qualification of "Durchlaucht" by the German Diet 18 Aug 1825; sold these lands to the Grand Duchy of Baden 1839; Grand Ducal decree to guarantee the personal rights as Mediatized Lords to the Princely House, 27 March 1839; inherited the majorat of Dyck (see below) and the hereditary right to a Seat in the former Prussian House of Lords, received the Prussian title of Prince (non hereditary) in favour of the children of Prince Leopold who immigrated to Prussia; Alfred (the 5th Prince), Marie and Rose, 21 Sept 1891.
The Head of this line and his wife bore the title of Prince or Princess zu Salm-Reifferscheidt-Krautheim and Dyck and with the qualification of Serene Highness while cadet Members bear the title of Altgraf or Altgräfin zu Salm-Reifferscheidt-Krautheim and Dyck.

✣ FRANZ JOSEF Alfred Leopold Hermann Maria, 6TH PRINCE (FÜRST) AND ALTGRAF ZU SALM-REIFFERSCHEIDT-

KRAUTHEIM AND DYCK, Lord of Krautheim, Gerlachsheim, Dyck, Alfter and Hackenbroich, *b* at Vienna 7 April 1899; ✣ at Bonn 13 June 1958, Kt Bav Order of St George, Bailiff Sovereign Military Order of Malta, etc; son of Alfred, 5th Prince (Fürst) and Altgraf zu Salm-Reifferscheidt-Krautheim and Dyck (*b* 23 June 1863; ✣ 6 July 1924) and Countess Marie-Dorothea von Bellegarde (*b* 27 June 1873; *m* 28 April 1896; ✣ 1 Feb 1945); *m* at Anholt 27 May 1930, Princess Cäcilie (*b* at Potsdam 8 March 1911; ✣ at Dyck 11 March 1991), Dame Star Cross Order, Dame of Hon Sovereign Military Order of Malta, dau of Emanuel, Hereditary Prince zu Salm and Salm-Salm and Archduchess Maria-Christina of Austria, and had issue among whom,

Daughters

1. Altgräfin *Marie-Christine* Erwine Isabelle Innocentia Thaddäa, *b* at Alfter, nr Bonn 4 Jan 1932, Dame Star Cross Order; *m* at Alfter 18 July (civ) and 27 July (relig) 1955, Peter, Count Wolff-Metternich zur Gracht (*b* at Göttingen 5 March 1929).
[*37137 Schloß Adelebsen, Germany; Schloß Dyck, 41363 Jüchen, Germany*].

2. Altgräfin *Marie-Anne* Friederike Christine Leopoldine Emanuela Helena, *b* at Alfter 18 Aug 1933; *m* 1stly at London 27 July 1964, Hon Alexander Campbell Geddes of the Barons Geddes (*b* at Dublin 24 Sept 1910; ✣ at London 22 Sept 1972), Engineer, Lt-Col. She *m* 2ndly at Dyck 27 Nov 1978, Otto von Simson (*b* at Berlin-Dahlem 17 June 1912; ✣ at Berlin 23 May 1993; *m* 1stly Princess Louise von Schönburg-Hartenstein who ✣ at Berlin 11 April 1976), Art Historian.
[*55 Chelsea Square, London SW3 6LH*].

3. Altgräfin *Rosemary* Ferdinande Dorothea Mathea Michaela Josepha Thaddäa, *b* at Alfter 24 Feb 1937, Dame Star Cross Order; *m* at Alfter 11 Sept 1959, Johannes, Count Huyn (*b* at Warsaw 3 July 1930).
[*Grabenfeldstraße 19, 83083 Neukirchen am Simssee, Germany*].

4. Altgräfin *Isabella* Marie Franziska Gabrielle Pia, *b* at Alfter 19 Feb 1939; *m* at Dyck 2 Oct 1962, Franz Albrecht Metternich-Sándor, Duke von Ratibor and Fürst von Corvey, Prince zu Hohenlohe-Schillingsfürst (*b* at Rauden 23 Oct 1920).
[*Schloß Neuaigen, 3430 Tulln, Austria; Schloß Corvey, 37671 Höxter, Westfalen, Germany*].

5. Altgräfin *Cecilie* Christine Caroline Maria Immaculata Michaela

Thaddäa, *b* at Bonn 14 Dec 1943.
[*Singerstraße 11, 1010 Vienna, Austria*].

LINE II: SALM-REIFFERSCHEIDT-RAITZ

Founded by Count Anton (*b* 1720; ✝ 1769); Hungarian Indigénat 10 April 1765; acquired the Lordships of Blansko 12 Jan 1763 and 1766, of Raitz and Jedownitz 24 March 1763, all in Moravia; Prince of the Holy Empire (primogeniture) with the qualification of "Hochgeboren", Frankfurt-am-Main 12 Oct 1790; received the qualification of "Durchlaucht" (primogeniture) by the German Diet 18 Aug 1825, recognised in Austria 4 Feb 1845; Hereditary Member of the former Austrian House of Lords.
The Head of this Line and his wife bear the title of Prince or Princess and Altgraf and Altgräfin of Salm-Reifferscheidt-Raitz with the qualification of Serene Highness while cadet members bear the title of Altgraf and Altgräfin zu Salm-Reifferscheidt-Raitz.

HUGO Christian Karl Maria Markus, **7TH PRINCE (FÜRST) AND ALTGRAF ZU SALM-REIFFERSCHEIDT-RAITZ,** *b* at Vienna 18 June 1973, son of Hugo, 6th Prince and Altgraf zu Salm-Reifferscheidt-Raitz (*b* 12 Dec 1933; ✝ 4 Oct 1974) and Silvia-Gabrielle Scheid (*b* 25 May 1944; *m* 2ndly at Kitzbühel 4 Feb 1976, Henry Milles-Lade, 5th Earl Sondes; that *m* diss by div 15 Jan 1982; she *m* 3rdly at Vienna 27 Aug 1985, Wolfgang, Baron von Stillfried and Rattonitz).
[*Prinz Eugenstraße 18, 1040 Vienna, Austria*].

Mother

Silvia-Gabrielle, Baroness Wolfgang von Stillfried and Rattonitz, *b* at Vienna 25 May 1944, dau of Hans Otto Scheid and Elsie Werner; *m* 1stly at Gmunden, Austria 26 Sept 1970, Hugo, 6th Prince (Fürst) and Altgraf zu Salm-Reifferscheidt-Raitz (*b* at Brünn 12 Dec 1933; ✝ at Vienna 4 Oct 1971). She *m* 2ndly at Kitzbühel 4 Feb 1976 (*m* diss by div at London 15 Jan 1982), Henry Milles-Lade, 5th Earl Sondes (*b* at London 1 May 1940). She *m* 3rdly at Vienna 27 Aug 1985, Wolfgang, Baron von Stillfried and Rattonitz (*b* at Munich 3 April 1943), Lawyer.
[*Prinz Eugenstraße 18, 1040 Vienna, Austria*].

Sisters of Father

Issue of Hugo, 5th Prince and Altgraf zu Salm-Reifferscheidt-Raitz (*b* 14 Oct 1893; ✝ 2 March 1946) and Countess Leopoldine von

Mensdorff-Pouilly (b 6 Sept 1895; m 23 Nov 1920; ✠ 30 March 1980), among whom,

1. Altgräfin *Ida* Leopoldine Eleonore Elisabeth Maria, b at Raitz 17 Oct 1921; m at Raitz 12 Sept 1944 (m diss by div at Vienna 28 June 1968), Philipp, Ritter von Schoeller (b at Vienna 23 Aug 1921), Industrialist.
[*Neuling Gasse8, 1030 Vienna, Austria*].
2. Altgräfin *Maria Elisabeth* Leopoldine Hippolyta, b at Raitz 17 Aug 1931; adopted dau of Altgräfin Marie Elisabeth zu Salm-Reifferscheidt-Raitz (b 1908; ✠ 1984); m at Brünn 14 April 1956 (m diss by div at Vienna 29 June 1971), Georg Cubuk (b at Brünn 1 Sept 1928; ✠ at Düsseldorf 9 Dec 1984), Dipl Eng. She has since reverted to her maiden name.
[*Prinz Eugenstraße 36, 1040 Vienna, Austria*].

Brother of Great-Great-Grandfather
Issue of Hugo, 2nd Fürst and Altgraf zu Salm-Reifferscheidt-Raitz (b 15 Sept 1803; ✠ 18 April 1888) and Altgräfin Leopoldine zu Salm-Reifferscheidt-Krautheim (b 24 June 1805; m 6 Sept 1830; ✠ 4 July 1878), having had issue, among whom,

Son
Altgraf *Erich* Adolf, b at Raitz 2 Oct 1836; ✠ there 29 Aug 1884; m at Irun, Spain 6 Nov 1865, Doña Maria del Pilar (b at Naples 24 Jan 1843; ✠ at Vienna 5 April 1893), Dame Star Cross Order, dau of Don Ignacio Alvarez de Toledo y Palafox Portocarrero, Count de Sclafani of the Dukes de Medina-Sidonia and Doña Teresa Alvarez de Toledo y Silva, and had issue,

    1. Altgraf *August* Hugo Leopold Ignaz Maria Pamfilio, b at Madrid 7 Sept 1866; ✠ at Vienna 25 March 1942, Gd Cross Swedish Order of the Northern Star; m at Vienna 25 May 1895, Baronesse Gabrielle (b at Nagy-Szöllös 6 Oct 1868; ✠ at Vienna 17 Aug 1942), Proprietor of Tarna, Lady-in-Waiting, Dame Star Cross Order, dau of Sigmund, Baron Perényi de Perény and Baroness Petronella Perényi de Perény, Proprietor of Tarna, and had issue, among whom,

        1 *Niklas* Maria Joseph Franz Erich Sigmund August Ignatius, Algraf zu Salm-Reifferscheidt-Ungnad-Weissenwolff, b at Vienna 25 Dec 1904; ✠ at Linz an der Donau 12 April 1970, Proprietor of Steyregg, Kt of

Hon and Dev Sovereign Military Order of Malta,
adopted son (at Vienna 18 Dec 1944/2 Sept 1946) of
Irene, Countess Szápáry, born Ungnad, Countess von
Weissenwolff; *m* 1stly at Vienna 23 July 1940, Princess
Irene (*b* at Göding 3 June 1911; ✠ at Vienna 15 May
1960), Dame Star Cross Order, dau of Hugo, Prince
von Thurn and Taxis and Henriette Ungnad, Countess
von Weissenwolff. He *m* 2ndly at Salzburg 1 July 1961,
Princess Antonie (*b* at Schloß Steyregg 24 June 1908;
✠ at Alkoven 5 Jan 1962; she *m* 1stly at Maria Plain,
near Salzburg 6 July 1941, Herbert Humer who ✠ 2
Feb 1951), sister of his first wife, and had issue by his
first wife,

> 1. Altgräfin *Henriette* Maria Irene Gabrielle
> Antonie Theresia Monika, *b* at Vienna 4 May
> 1941, Dipl Nursing; *m* at Steyregg 7 Feb 1970,
> Andreas, Baron von Lederer (*b* at Malang, Java
> 29 Sept 1933), Engineer.
> [*Barmherzigen Gasse 19, 1030 Vienna,
> Austria*].
> 2. Altgraf *Niklas* Hugo August Leopold
> Bonifatius Franz Eustachius Maria, *b* at Vienna
> 20 Sept 1942, Forester, Engineer, Kt of Hon
> and Dev Sovereign Military Order of Malta; *m*
> at Schwaigern, Württemberg 24 July 1970,
> Countess Nathalie (*b* at Stuttgart 20 May 1948),
> Dame Star Cross Order, Dame of Hon Sovereign
> Military Order of Malta, dau of Erwin, Count
> von Neipperg and Countess Hissa von Hatzfeldt
> zu Trachenberg, and has issue,
> [*Weissenwolffstraße 12, 4221 Steyregg, Upper
> Austria*].
>
>> 1. Altgräfin *Irene* Maria Hissa Henriette
>> Katharina Gabrielle, *b* at Linz 24 March
>> 1971; *m* at Steyregg 17 Aug (civ) and
>> there 31 Aug (relig) 1996, Klaus
>> Gollhofer-Berger (*b* at Salzburg 1 June
>> 1971).
>> [*Lokstedter Steindamm 88, 22529
>> Hamburg, Germany*].
>> 2. Altgraf *Niklas* Maria Franz Karl

Erwin Vinzenz, *b* at Linz 19 July 1972,
Kt of Hon and Dev Sovereign Military
Order of Malta; *m* at Steyregg 24 Apr
(civ) and at Benediktbeuren, Bavaria
15 July (relig) 2000, Countess Nathalie
(*b* at Munich 20 Dec 1974), dau of Franz,
Count von Ballestrem and Baroness
Andrea von Stotzingen.
[*Weißenwolffstraße 14, 4221 Steyregg,
Austria*].
3. Altgräfin *Sophie* Marietta Anna
Katharina, *b* at Linz 30 April 1975.
4. Altgraf *Paul* Maria Karl Christoph
Ulrich, *b* at Linz 4 July 1979.
5. Altgräfin *Gabrielle* Maria
Immakulata, b at Linz an der Donau 27
Sept 1981; ✠ at Steyregg 1 Jan 1982.
6. Altgraf *Conrad* Maria Stephan
Norbert Benedikt, *b* at Steyregg 10 Feb
1985.

3. Altgraf *Franz* Anton Benedikt Paul Matthias
Maria, *b* at Vienna 24 Feb 1944, Dr of Law, Kt
of Hon and Dev Sovereign Military Order of
Malta; *m* at Mareit, near Sterzing, Prov Bozen
9 Aug 1970, Baroness Barbara (*b* at Nahoschitz,
Bohemia 12 Sept 1944), dau of Gobert Wenzl,
Baron von Sternbach, Proprietor of Wolfsthurn
in Mareit and Maria Antonia, Edle von
Edelmann, and has issue,
[*Buchen Weg 17, 4810 Gmunden, Upper
Austria*].

1. Altgraf *Philipp* Hieronymus Maria,
b at Innsbruck 1 June 1971.
[*Buchenweg 17, 4810 Gmunden, Upper
Austria*].
2. Altgräfin *Johanna* Andrea Maria,
b at Salzburg 7 Feb 1974; *m* at Gmunden
30 May (civ) and at Oberaurach nr
Kitzbühel 13 June (relig) 1998, Don José
Manuel de la Infiesta y Rollán (*b* at
Madrid 26 March 1969), Stockbroker.

[*10a Yeomans Row, London, SW3 2AH*].

3. Altgräfin *Marie* Elisabeth Antonia, *b* at Salzburg 3 June 1976.

[*Buchenweg 17, 4810 Gmunden, Upper Austria*].

4. Altgravine *Franziska* Barbara Maria, *b* at Vöcklabruck 10 Dec 1981.

4. Altgräfin *Gabrielle* Maria Henriette Kunigunde Franziska Johanna, *b* at Steyregg, Upper Austria 29 Aug 1946; *m* at Steyregg 17 Oct 1970, Maximilian (Max) Lobmeyr von Hohenleiten (*b* at Klagenfurt 12 Sept 1944), Dr of Law.

[*Weissenwolffstraße 14, 4221 Steyregg, Upper Austria*].

5. Altgräfin *Elisabeth* Maria Antonia Benedikta Bernadette, *b* at Steyregg 11 Oct 1948, Dame Star Cross Order; *m* at Steyregg 1 July 1972, Heinrich, Edler von Schuschnigg (*b* at Schwanberg 25 Oct 1944), Dipl Eng, Architect.

[*Wasser Gasse29, 1030 Vienna III, Austria*].

6. Altgraf *Karl* Maria Niklas Benedikt Augustinus Johannes, *b* at Linz an der Donau 31 Jan 1951, Banker, Kt of Hon and Dev Sovereign Military Order of Malta; *m* at Salzburg 23 April 1995, Countess Eva Maria (*b* at Porto Alegre, Brazil 3 Feb 1958), dau of Gábor, Count Keglevich de Buzin and Countess Klara Madarassy de Mezö-Madaras, and has issue,

[*Weissenbachstraße 5, 5026 Salzburg-Aigen, Austria*].

1. Altgraf *Johannes* Maria Stephan Ezechiel, *b* at Salzburg 10 Apr 1997.

2. Altgrafin *Gabriel* Maria Niklas, *b* at Salzburg 31 May 1998.

3. Altgrafin *Maria* Assunta Constanza Irene, *b* at Salzburg 5 May 2000.

SAYN-WITTGENSTEIN
(COUNTS OF SPANHEIM)

This family traces its descent from Stephan I and his son Stephan II, Count of Spanheim (Sponheim) of the Franco-Rhenish Lords of Spanheim 1052; his son Meginhart, Count of Spanheim (Sponheim) (a fortified castle west of Bad Kreuznach, today a ruin) authenticated living in 1128; Counts of Seyne (today Sayn, near Koblenz) through the marriage of Gottfried III, Count of Sponheim (✝ 1223) to Adelaide, sister and heiress of Heinrich III, last Count of Sayn (✝ 1247), acquired the county of Wittgenstein with the Bailiwicks of Berleburg, Laasphe, etc (Westphalia) through the marriage of Salentin, Count of Sayn to Adelheid, daughter and heiress of Siegfried III, last Count of Wittgenstein (✝ 1357) and joined the name and arms of Wittgenstein 1361; the Lines below descend from two sons of Count Ludwig (✝ 2 July 1605).

LINE I:
SAYN-WITTGENSTEIN-BERLEBURG
Founded by Georg, Count zu Sayn-Wittgenstein-Berleburg (b 1565; ✝ 1631); the branches below descend from two sons of Count Ludwig Franz (b 17 April 1660; ✝ 25 Nov 1694).

First Branch - BERLEBURG
Evangelical: Founded by Count Casimir (b 31 Jan 1687; ✝ 5 June 1741); Prince of the Holy Empire with the qualification of "Hochgeboren", Vienna 4 Sept 1792; publication in the Bavarian Electorate 15 Jan 1793; received the qualification of "Durchlaucht" (primogeniture) by the German Diet 18 Aug 1825; Hereditary Member of the former Prussian House of Lords 12 Oct 1854. Members of this Branch bear the title of Prince or Princess zu Sayn-Wittgenstein-Berleburg.

RICHARD-Casimir Karl August Robert Konstantin, **PRINCE (FÜRST) ZU SAYN-WITTGENSTEIN-BERLEBURG,** Count zu Sayn, Lord zu Homburg, Neumagen, Vallendar and Neuenhemsbach, b at Giessen 29 Oct 1934; son of Gustav Albrecht, 5th Prince (Fürst) zu Sayn-Wittgenstein-Berleburg (b 28 Feb 1907; ✝k Summer 1944) and Margareta Fouché d'Otrante (b 28 March 1909; m 26 Jan 1934); m at Schloß Fredensborg, Denmark 3 Feb 1968, Princess Benedikte (b at Copenhagen 29 April 1944), dau of Frederick IX, King of Denmark and Princess Ingrid of Sweden. [Schloß Berleburg, 57319 Bad Berleburg, Westfalen, Germany].

Son and Daughters

1. *Gustav* Frederik Philip Richard, Hereditary Prince (Erbprinz) zu Sayn-Wittgenstein-Berleburg, *b* at Frankfurt-am-Main 12 Jan 1969. [*Schloß Berleburg, 57319 Bad Berleburg, Westfalen, Germany*].

2. Princess *Alexandra* Rosemarie Ingrid Benedikte, *b* at Copenhagen 20 Nov 1970; BA University College, London employed at UNESCO; *m* at Graasten Slotskirke 6 June 1998, *Jefferson*-Friedrich Volker Benjamin, Count von Pfeil and Klein-Ellguth (*b* at Mainz 12 July 1967), BA European Business School, London, financier. [*Schloß Berleburg, 57319 Bad Berleburg, Westfalen, Germany*].

3. Princess *Nathalie* Xenia Margareta Benedikte, *b* at Copenhagen 2 May 1975. [*Schloß Berleburg, 57319 Bad Berleburg, Westfalen, Germany*].

Mother

Margareta, Dowager Princess zu Sayn-Wittgenstein-Berleburg, *b* at Elghammer, nr Björnlunda 28 Feb 1909, dau of Charles, Duke Fouché d'Otrante and Countess Madeleine Douglas; *m* at Björnlunda 26 Jan 1934, Gustav Albrecht, 5th Prince (Fürst) zu Sayn-Wittgenstein-Berleburg, etc (*b* at Berleburg 28 Feb 1907; missing in Russia Summer 1944; declared legally deceased 29 Nov 1969). [*Schloß Berleburg, 57319 Bad Berleburg, Westfalen, Germany*].

Brother and Sisters

1. Princess *Madeleine* Olga Dora Edle Benedicte, *b* at Giessen 22 April 1936; *m* at Berleburg 29 July 1958, Otto, Count zu Solms-Laubach (*b* at Laubach 26 Aug 1926; ✝ there 1 March 1973). [*Schloß, 35321 Laubach, Germany*].

2. Prince *Robin* Alexander Wolfgang Udo Eugen Wilhelm Gottfried, *b* at Giessen 29 Jan 1938; *m* 1stly at New York 29 Jan 1970, Birgitta (*b* in Sweden 1 April 1942; *m* diss by div 4 Oct 1979; she *m* 2ndly 22 March 1980, Olivier Fouret), dau of Fredrik af Klercker and Birgitta Zätterström, and has issue,

    1, Prince *Sebastian*, *b* at New York 30 Jan 1971, *m* at Château Villebardin 6 July 2002, Julie Toussaint (*b* at ....), dau of Philippe Toussaint and ......

    2. Princess *Natascha*, *b* at New York 24 Nov 1973.

Prince Robin *m* 2ndly at Paris 29 Nov 1979, Marie Christine Agnes (*b* 20 Feb 1938; *m* 1stly at ..., Jean Francois Malle; that *m* diss by div 29 Jan 1979), dau of Serge Heftler-Louiche and Jeanine Rosambert, and has further issue,

[*7 rue Amyot, 75005 Paris, France*].
    3. Princess *Marie, b* at Paris 11 July 1980.
3. Princess *Tatjana* Louise Ursula Therese Elsa, *b* at Giessen 31 July 1940; *m* at Kronberg, Taunus 1 June (civ) and 3 June (relig) 1964 (*m* diss by div at Kiel 16 Oct 1974), Moritz, Prince of Hesse (*b* at Racconigi, Piedmont 6 Aug 1926), Dipl Land Management.
[*Maria Louisenstraße 56, 22301 Hamburg, Germany*].
4. Princess *Pia* Margareta, *b* at Giessen 8 Dec 1942.
[*Schloß Berleburg, 57319 Berleburg, Westfalen, Germany*].

Brothers of Father
Issue of Richard, 4th Prince (Fürst) zu Sayn-Wittgenstein-Berleburg (*b* 27 May 1882; ✠ 25 April 1925) and Princess Madeleine zu Löwenstein-Wertheim-Freudenberg (*b* 8 March 1885; *m* 21 Nov 1905; ✠ 30 Jan 1976).

1. **Christian Heinrich** Wolfgang Amelung Karl Friedrich Beno, **5th Fürst zu Sayn-Wittgenstein-Hohenstein**, *b* at Berleburg 20 Sept 1908; ✠ Schwarzenau, nr Bad Berleburg 17 Aug 1983, adopted 3 May/7June 1927 by his kinsman August, Prince (Fürst) zu Sayn-Wittgenstein-Hohenstein, whom he succeeded;
[*see-Sayn-Wittgenstein-Hohenstein below for the subsequent issue of this line*].
2. Prince *Ludwig Ferdinand* Paul Franz Stanislaus Ulrich Otto Ludolf, *b* at Berleburg 4 April 1910; ✠*k* nr Shitomir, Russia 22 Nov 1943, Lt.-Col. German Army; *m* at Varlar, Westphalia 5 Aug 1935, Princess Friederike Juliane (*b* at Varlar 5 Oct 1912, ✠ at Horstmar 3 July 2000), dau of Otto II, Prince (Fürst) and Rheingraf zu Salm-Horstmar and Countess Rosa zu Solms-Baruth, and had issue,
    1. Princess *Marita* Rosy Luise Olympia, *b* at Osterwick, Westfalen 15 Aug 1936, ✠ at Göddenstedt 7 July 2000, Dipl Land Management; *m* at Berleburg 9 Jan 1971, Ulrich, Count Grote (*b* at Bevensen 12 Jan 1940), Banker.
    [*Forsthaus, 61194 Niddatal-Wickstadt, Germany*].
    2. Prince *Otto-Ludwig* Richard Hermann Franz Christian Adolf Erwin, *b* at Osterwick 25 Feb 1938, Kt of Honour of St John of Jerusalem; *m* at Stuttgart 28 Jan 1965, Baroness Annette (*b* at Nahrstedt, Altmark 15 April 1944), Art Dealer, dau of Burghard, Baron von Cramm, Proprietor of Nahrstedt and Gisela von Conrad, and has issue,
    (*Am Fuchsrain, 57339 Erndtebrück, Germany;*

Frankfurterstraße, 61476 Kronberg, Taunus, Germany).

    1. Prince *Stanislaus* Otto Ludwig Burghard, *b* at Stuttgart 15 Sept 1965; *m* at Kochel am See 22 May 1993, Elisabeth Winterstein (*b* at Munich 25 Oct 1967), and has issue,

    [*Parkstraße 2, 60322 Frankfurt-am-Main, Germany*].

        1. Prince *Friedrich* Karl Konstantin Burghard, *b* at Frankfurt-am-Main 20 Oct 1996.

    2. Princess *Stefanie* - Christina Gisela, *b* at Stuttgart 25 Dec 1966; *m* at Erndtebrück 11 May 1991, Maximilian, Baron von Loë (*b* at Ludwigshafen am Rhein 1 June 1965; adopted by his great-aunt Franziska (who ✠ 1991) at Brühl 30 Aug and at Bonn 26 Nov 1984 and bears the name "Count Berghe von Trips").
[*Siegesstraße 12, 90902 Munich, Germany*].

    3. Princess *Marie-Louise* Ulrike Olympia, *b* at Stuttgart 25 Sept 1972; *m* at Bückeburg 27 Aug (civ) and at Schloss Bückeburg 29 Aug (relig) 1993 (*m* diss by div at Munich 14 Feb 2002), Alexander, Hereditary Prince (Erbprinz) zu Schaumburg-Lippe (*b* at Dusseldorf 25 Dec 1958).

    4. Princess *Vanessa-Irina* Caroline Else, *b* at Siegen 29 Aug 1978.

    5. Prince *Maximilian-Alexander* Louis-Ferdinand Georg Philipp Ulrich, *b* at Siegen 31 July 1980.

3. Prince *Johann-Stanislaus* Karl Friedrich Ludwig Sebastian, *b* at Osterwick 9 Aug 1939, Dr of Law, Lawyer, Kt of Honour of St John of Jerusalem; *m* at Marburg an der Lahn 29 April 1971, Almut Leonhards (*b* at Alt-Temmen, Templin 6 Dec 1943), and has issue,

[*Speestraße 92, 4032 Linlorf, Germany*].

    1. Prince *Otto-Ludwig* Christian Alexander, *b* at Düsseldorf-Kaiserswerth 12 April 1972.

    2. Princess *Isabelle* Ulrike Tatjana Leonie, *b* at Düsseldorf-Kaiserswerth 15 July 1974.

    3. Prince *Constantin* Ferdinand Rudolf Stanislaus, *b* at Düsseldorf-Kaiserswerth 27 Nov 1978.

4. Prince *Ludwig-Ferdinand* Fridrich Hans Rudolf Winrich Klaus, *b* at Osterwick 25 Jan 1942, Dipl Business, Dipl Forestry; *m* at Bärbo, Län Södermanland 6 Sept 1975, Countess Yvonne (*b* at Bärbo 4 April 1951), Physiotherapist,

dau of Bengt, Count Wachtmeister af Johannishus, Proprietor of Nääs, Ksp Bärbo, and Anna Wennerholm, and has issue, [*Schloß Wittgenstein, 57334 Bad Laasphe, Germany*].

    1. Prince *Carl* -Albrecht Schering Stanislaus Maximilian, *b* at Munich 2 Nov 1976.

    2. Princess *Anna* -Natascha Monique Marita Thérèse, *b* at Munich 15 March 1978.

    3. Prince *August-Frederik* Wendelin Otto Henrik, *b* at Siegen 22 Jan 1981.

    4. Princess *Theodora-Louise* Victoria Juliana Yvonne, *b* 29 Dec 1986.

5. Princess *Ulrike-Christine* Madeleine Rosy Editha Olga Ingetrud Sabine, *b* posthumously at Krüden, Altmark 21 Jan 1944; *m* at ... 1971, Hanno von Wulffen (*b* at Dingolfing, Lower Bavaria 15 April 1940).

[*The Hill Farm, Rt. 1, Box 92, Gordonsville, Virginia 22942, U.S.A.*].

Brother of Grandfather

Issue of Gustav, Prince (Fürst) zu Sayn-Wittgenstein-Berleburg (*b* 20 May 1837; ✝ 1 April 1889) and Baroness Marie von Gemmingen-Hornberg (*b* 22 Nov 1855; *m* 24 Sept 1878; ✝ 10 Oct 1946), among whom,

Son

Prince *Wolfgang* Friedrich Max, *b* at Berleburg 13 March 1887; ✝ at Göttingen 9 Jan 1966, Col (ret), Kt of St John of Jerusalem; *m* 1stly at Baden-Baden 3 June 1916 (*m* diss by div at Munich 6 March 1924), Editha (*b* at Marienborn, Kr Neuhaldensleben 13 Oct 1888; ✝ at Cologne 27 June 1962; *m* 1stly at Shanghai, China 21 Dec 1907, Bernhard von Schweinitz; that *m* diss by div at Baden-Baden 13 Oct 1915; she *m* 3rdly at Munich 18 Dec 1924, Konrad von Gossler who ✝ at Berlin 9 Sept 1939), dau of Max von Niesewand and Charlotte von Löbbecke. He *m* 2ndly at Munich 29 Nov 1926, Baroness Lucy (*b* at Frankfurt-am-Main 3 July 1898; ✝ at Göttingen 20 June 1952; *m* 1stly at Arolsen 26 April 1922, Kurt von Griesheim; that *m* diss by div at Berlin 19 Oct 1925), dau of Ludwig, Baron von Kleydorff and Erna Kühls, and had issue by his first wife, among whom,

    1. Prince *Karl-Heinrich* Otto Max Adalbert Hermann, *b* at Kassel 31 Oct 1919; ✝ at Odenthal 11 Dec 2002, Kt Gd Cross Order of St Silvester; *m* at Schloß Gracht 16 April 1947,

Countess Monica (*b* at Haus Beck 17 Dec 1919), dau of Paul, Count Wolff Metternich zur Gracht, Proprietor of Gracht, etc, and Christine Fane, and has issue,

[*Schloß Strauweiler, 51519 Odenthal, Germany*].

> 1. Prince *Hubertus* Maximilian Casimir Thomas Maria, *b* at Bonn 21 Dec 1948, Kt of Hon Sovereign Military Order of Malta; *m* at Odenthal 8 July (civ) and at Salzburg 1 Sept (relig) 1973, Countess Irina (*b* at Salzburg 25 July 1953), dau of Friedrich-Hans, Count zu Solms-Baruth and Princess Oda zu Stolberg-Wernigerode, and has issue,
>
> [*Haus Selbach, 51519 Odenthal, Germany*].

>> 1. Prince *Christian-Albrecht* Paul Hubertus Maria, *b* at Bergisch-Gladbach 8 May 1974.
>> 2. Prince *Nicolaus* Henrich Franz Johannes Hubertus Maria, *b* at Bergisch-Gladbach 19 Aug 1975.
>> 3. Princess *Marie-Charlotte* Oda Stephanie Hildegard, *b* at Bergisch-Gladbach 28 July 1979.
>> 4. Princess *Marie-Elisabeth* Gabrielle Christine Caroline Andrea Jutta, *b* at Bergisch-Gladbach 30 Oct 1982.
>> 5. Princess *Maria-Catharina* Renata Alexandra Dorothea Theresa Ferdinanda, *b* at Bergisch-Gladbach 22 July 1985.
>> 6. Prince *Ludwig-Ferdinand* Botho Michael Eugen Hubertus Maria, *b* at Bergisch-Gladbach 24 Dec 1986.
>> 7. Princess *Marie-Sophie* Dorothee Larissa Leonille, *b* at Bergisch Gladbach 9 Nov 1988.

> 2. Princess *Stephanie* Maria, *b* 3 June 1950; *m* at Odenthal 2 Feb (civ) and 3 Feb (relig) 1973, Stephan von Watzdorf (*b* at Berlin 3 May 1942), Banker.
>
> [*Schumannstraße 8, 81679 Munich, Germany*].

> 3 Prince *Andreas* Wolfgang Josef Maria, *b* at Bonn 24 Dec 1952, Historian, Kt of Hon Sovereign Military Order of Malta.
>
> [*Friedrichstraße 3, 60323 Frankfurt-am-Main, Germany*].

> 4. Princess *Maria Christina* Therese, *b* at Bonn 20 Oct 1955, Art Dealer.

[*155 East 72nd Street, New York, N.Y. 10021, U.S.A.*].

Brother of Great-Great-Grandfather

Issue of Christian Heinrich, 1st Prince (Fürst) zu Sayn-Wittgenstein-Berleburg (*b* 12 Dec 1753; ✣ 4 Oct 1800) and Countess Charlotte von Leiningen-Westerburg (*b* 19 Aug 1759; *m* 17 April 1775; ✣ 22 Jan 1931), among whom,

Son

Prince *August* Ludwig, *b* at Berleburg 6 March 1788; ✣ there 6 Jan 1874, Imp Minister for War 1849, Gen Cavalry; *m* at Frankfurt-am-Main 7 April 1823, Franziska (*b* at Geneva 27 Oct 1802; ✣ at Weimar 30 Nov 1878), dau of Karl Franz Allesina genannt von Schweitzer, Proprietor of Sindlingen, and Augusta Wynne, and had issue,

Son

Prince *Franz* Emil Luitpold, *b* at Darmstadt 23 Nov 1842; ✣ at Munich 4 April 1909, Major Prussian Army, Kt of Hon St John of Jerusalem; *m* at Heidelberg 16 June 1877, Julie (*b* at Neuilly, nr Paris 14 May 1859; ✣ at Rottach-Egern am Tegernsee 27 Aug 1930), dau of Julio Constancio, Count de Villeneuve and Anna Maria Cavalcanti de Albuquerque, and had issue, among whom,

Son

1. Prince *Otto-Konstantin* Emil Franz, *b* at Munich 11 June 1878; ✣ at Bad Ischl 16 Nov 1955, Capt Prussian Army; *m* 1stly at Langenzell, Baden 25 Sept 1909 (*m* diss by div at Munich 13 April 1923), Princess Elisabeth (*b* at Langenzell 5 May 1890; ✣ at Frankfurt-am-Main 28 March 1953; *m* 2ndly at Frankfurt-am-Main 28 March 1930, Richard Merton who ✣ 6 Jan 1960, Industrialist), dau of Alfred, Prince zu Löwenstein-Wertheim-Freudenberg and Countess Pauline von Reichenbach-Lessonitz, and had issue, among whom,

1. Prince *Casimir* -Johannes Ludwig Otto, *b* at Frankfurt-am-Main 22 Jan 1917; *m* 1stly at Hamburg 21 April 1939 (*m* diss by div at Hamburg 18 Oct 1949), Ingrid (*b* at Hamburg 12 April 1915; ✣ at Harbarnsen, Bez Hildesheim 23 June 1966; *m* 2ndly at Hamburg 6 Dec 1950, Wilhelm-Ernst, Baron von Cramm, Proprietor of Harbarnsen), dau of Lucian Alsen and Victoria Lücken, and has issue,

1. Prince Christian *Peter* August Richard Udo Maria Casimir, *b* at Hamburg 5 Feb 1940, Kt of

Honour of St John of Jerusalem; *m* 1stly at Rabertshausen, Kr Giessen 1 July (civ) and at Graz 9 July (relig) 1967 (*m* diss by div at Munich 2 July 1974), Princess Felizitas (*b* at Mauritzen, Bez Frohnleiten, Styria 26 Oct 1946; *m* 2ndly at Munich 25 Oct 1974, Franz Clemens, Count von Schönborn-Wiesentheid who was *b* 3 Oct 1939, Bank Director), dau of Heinrich III, Prince Reuss and Baroness Franziska Mayr von Melnhof, and has issue,

    1. Prince *Carl-Constantin* Heinrich Egbert Franz Welf Casimir, *b* at Düsseldorf 2 June 1968.
    [*La Renardière, 7 Chemin de Mapraz, 1225 Chêne-Bourg, Kt. Genf, Switzerland*].
    2. Prince *Johann-Philipp* Friedrich Benedikt Heinrich Franz Richard, *b* at Munich 10 Nov 1970.
    [*La Renardière, 7 Chemin de Mapraz, 1225 Chêne-Bourg, Kt. Genf, Switzerland*].

Prince Peter *m* 2ndly at Munich 17 Jan (civ) and at Rodheim vor der Höhe, OHessen 29 Jan (relig) 1977, Judit (*b* at Budapest 27 Jan 1942), dau of István Mártonffy-Dudutz (of Hungarian nobility) and Marta Veverán, and has further issue,

[*Claudiusstraße 2, 40474 Düsseldorf, Germany*].

    3. Prince *Christian* Georg Maximilian Imre Richard István Casimir, *b* at New York 10 July 1978.
    4. Prince *Franz-Alexander* Thomas Anton Peter, *b* at New York 13 April 1981.

2. Princess *Leonille* Elisabeth Victoria Barbara Margarete, *b* at Hamburg 6 July 1941; *m* at Haubenmühle, OHessen 27 Jan (civ) and at Rodheim 28 Jan (relig) 1967, Wolfgang-Ernst, 4th Prince (Fürst) zu Isenburg and Büdingen

(*b* at Frankfurt-am-Main 20 June 1936), Dipl Business.

[*Schloß Büdingen, 63654 Büdingen, Germany*].

Prince Casimir *m* 2ndly at London 1 May 1950 (*m* diss by div at Frankfurt-am-Main 6 May 1987), Iris [*36 Ennismore Gardens Mews, London, S.W.7.*] (*b* at London 16 May 1917), dau of Edward Hewish Ryle and Anne Rhodes Moorhouse. He *m* 3rdly at Nidda, OHessen 13 Feb 1988, Beatrix (*b* at Berlin 10 July 1942; *m* 1stly ..., Alexander Schön; that m diss by div ...), dau of Otto Wolfram von Eichel and Eleonore Cainneci, and has further issue from his second wife, [*Hofgut Haubenmühle, 63667 Nidda-Unter-Schmitten, Germany*].

3. Prince *Richard* Casimir Roger William, *b* at London 21 March 1952; *m* at Kitzbühel 6 Sept 1980 (*m* diss by div at Kitzbühel 20 Dec 1989), Countess Louise (Lille) (*b* at Madrid 18 May 1956), dau of Sigmund (Zsiga), Count Batthyány de Német-Ujvár, Proprietor of Güssing, Burgenland and Maria del Carmen Escandón y Pardo. He *m* 2ndly at ..., Mary Anne (*b* at ..), dau of ... and ..., and has issue from his first wife,

1. Prince *John-Alvin* Edward Richard Zsigmond Maria-Gobertus, *b* at Bad Tölz 17 Oct 1982.

2. Princess *Ariana* Maria-Gobertina, *b* at Leawood, Kansas 23 Aug 1985.

4. Prince *Johannes* Carl Franz August, *b* at London 30 Sept 1953; *m* at Munich 3 May 1985, Bettina Elisabeth (*b* at Munich 15 Oct 1959), dau of Ernst Ludwig, Ritter von Molo and Gertraud Schlumprecht, and has issue,

1. Princess *Teresa* Elisabeth Marina Franziska, *b* at Munich 14 Oct 1988.

2. Princess *Helena* Victoria Beatrix Astrid, *b* at Hamburg 4 April 1990.

Prince Otto-Konstantin *m* 2ndly at Munich 3 June 1929, Ilse (*b* at Linz 26 Aug 1901; ✠ at Rottach-Egern 24 Aug 1983), dau of Rudolf Lampl and Anna Schausberger, and had further

issue,

> 3. Princess *Alexandra* Juliane, *b* at Rottach-Egern 2 Dec 1932; *m* at Kreuth 15 April 1955, Ortwin Beck (*b* at Karlsruhe 30 Sept 1915; ✝ at Rottach-Egern 5 Nov 1995), Dr of Med Dentistry.
> [*Südliche HauptStraße 39, 83700 Rottach-Egern, Germany*].

Second Branch - SAYN-WITTGENSTEIN-SAYN and LUDWIGSBURG-CARLSBURG

Catholic: Founded by Count Ludwig Franz (*b* 13 Dec 1694; ✝ 24 Feb 1750); (Fürst) Prince zu Sayn and Wittgenstein in Ludwigsburg for Imp Russian Field Marshal Count Ludwig Adolf *Peter* (*b* 6 Nov 1769; ✝ 11 June 1943), Prussian title with the qualification of "Durchlaucht", Berlin 1 May 1834; joined with the line of Carlsburg, issue of Karl, older brother of Count Ludwig, by virtue of a convention concluded in 1851; foundation of the fideicommis of Sayn 1861 by Prince Ludwig Adolf Friedrich (*b* 18 June 1799; ✝ 20 June 1866); confirmation of the title of "(Fürst) Prince zu Sayn-Wittgenstein-Sayn" for the Proprietor of Sayn, Berlin 23 Sept 1861; Hereditary Member of the former Prussian House of Lords 23 Sept 1861. Members of this Line bear the title of Prince or Princess or Count or Countess zu Sayn-Wittgenstein-Berleburg.

ALEXANDER Konrad Friedrich Heinrich, **7TH PRINCE (FÜRST) ZU SAYN-WITTGENSTEIN-SAYN,** *b* at Salzburg 22 Nov 1943, Kt of Hon Sovereign Military Order of Malta, son of Ludwig, 6th Prince (Fürst) zu Sayn-Wittgenstein-Sayn (*b* 4 May 1915; ✝ 9 Jan 1962) and Baroness Maria Anna Mayr von Melnhof (*b* 9 Dec 1919; *m* 12 March 1942); *m* at Keilberg 29 July (civ) and at Pommersfelden 27 Sept (relig) 1969, Countess Gabriela (*b* at Würzburg 16 Oct 1950), dau of Rudolf, Count von Schönborn-Wiesentheid and Princess Helene von Thurn and Taxis.

[*56170 Bendorf-Sayn bei Koblenz, Germany*].

Sons and Daughters

1. *Heinrich* Stanislaus Ludwig Ernst Johannes Maria Franz Josef, Hereditary Prince (Erbprinz) zu Sayn-Wittgenstein-Sayn, *b* at Munich 3 Jan 1971.

2. Princess *Alexandra* Marie Leonille Helene Elisabeth Ladislaja, *b* at Munich 20 Aug 1973; *m* at Bendorf 24 June (civ) and Sayn 26

June (relig) 1994 (*m* diss by div 2002), Carl Eugen, Hereditary Prince (Erbprinz) zu Oettingen-Wallerstein (*b* at Munich 29 April 1970).
[*Schloß, Herrenstraße 78, 86757 Wallerstein, Germany*].
3. Prince Johann *Casimir* Ludwig Karl Andreas Maria Rudolf, *b* at Koblenz 4 May 1976; *m* at London Dec 2000, Corinna Larsen (*b* at ... 1968; *m* 1stly Philip Atkins).
4. Princess Maria *Filippa* Johanna Elisabeth Fernanda Yvonne, *b* at Koblenz 23 July 1980; ✝*k* at Clevedon, Somerset 29 Sept 2001; *m* at Sayn 8 June (civ) and at Schloß Sayn 10 June (relig) 2001, Count *Vittorio* Mazzeti d'Albertis (*b* at Florence 24 Aug 1965).
5. Prince *Ludwig* Franz Ferdinand Maria Karl August Simon Theodor, *b* at Koblenz 25 Oct 1982.
6. Princess Maria *Sofia* Helene Elisabeth Edith Alberta Anna, *b* at Koblenz 21 Jan 1986.
7. Prince Christian *Peter* Maximilian Carl Ladislaus Albert Maria Salentin, *b* at Koblenz 27 June 1992.

Mother

Maria Anna, Dowager Princess zu Sayn-Wittgenstein-Sayn, *b* at Salzburg 9 Dec 1919, dau of Friedrich, Baron Mayr von Melnhof, Proprietor of Glanegg and Countess Maria-Anna von Meran; *m* at Glanegg 12 March 1942, Ludwig, 6th Prince (Fürst) zu Sayn-Wittgenstein-Sayn (*b* at Copenhagen 4 May 1915; ✝ at Sayn 9 Jan 1962), Kt of Hon Sovereign Military Order of Malta.
[*Zaubzerstraße 16, 81677 Munich, Germany; Jagdhaus Ellmau, 5330 Fuschl am See, Austria*].

Brother and Sisters

1. Princess Marie *Yvonne* Helena Walburga Anna Leonille, *b* at Glanegg 9 Dec 1942; *m* 1stly at Salzburg 21 May 1962 (*m* diss by div at Salzburg 13 Oct 1970), Alfons, Count von Coreth zu Coredo (*b* at Waizenkirchen, Austria 19 Feb 1930), Consul for the Kingdom of Thailand in Salzburg. She *m* 2ndly at Salzburg 18 June 1976, Klaus Bolzano, Edler von Kronstätt (*b* at Wels, Austria 22 May 1936), Dr of Med, Assistant Professor.
[*Nesselthaler Gasse 7, 5020, Salzburg, Austria*].
2. Princess *Elisabeth* Maria Leonilla, *b* at Glanegg 1 April 1948; ✝ at Fuschl am See 15 April 1997; *m* at Bendorf 6 April (civ) and at Fuschl am See, Austria 25 April (relig) 1970, Hasso, Baron Schuler von Senden (*b* at Zielenzig, Neumark 30 Jan 1943), Banker, Managing Director, Kt of St John of Jerusalem.

[*Prinzregentenstraße 81, 81675 Munich, Germany; Ellmau 9, 5330 Fuschl am See, Austria*].

3. Princess *Teresa* Maria Leonilla, *b* at Neuwied 25 April 1952; *m* 1stly at Bendorf 23 Aug (civ) and at Mondsee, Austria 8 Oct (relig) 1973 (*m* diss by div at Munich 7 May 1983 and annulled at New York, USA 26 May 1983), Luis Figueroa y Griffith, Count de Quintanilla (*b* at Madrid 5 Feb 1950), Businessman. She *m* 2ndly at Munich 13 June (civ) and at Sayn 15 Oct (relig) 1983, Karl-Erbo, Count von Kageneck (*b* at Blumenscheidt, near Wittlich 29 July 1947), Lawyer.

[*Sintzenichstraße 2, 81479 Munich, Germany; Top of the Hill, Clinton Corners, NY 12541, U.S.A.*].

4. Prince *Peter* Heinrich Stanislaus Maria, *b* at Neuwied 22 Jan 1954, Businessman; *m* at Munich 1 Oct (civ) and at Fuschl am See, Austria 9 Oct (relig) 1993, Sunnyi (*b* at Luxemburg 7 Oct 1958), Actress, dau of Prof Károly Melles and Judith von Rohonczy, and has issue,

[*Herterichstraße 31, 81479 Munich, Germany; Jagdhaus Ellmau, 5330 Fuschl am See, Austria*].

    1. Prince *Constantin* Victor Ludwig, *b* at Munich 1 Nov 1994.
    2. Princess *Leonille* Elisabeth Judith Maria Anna, *b* at Munich 19 Aug 1996.

Brother of Great-Grandfather

Issue of Ludwig, 2nd Fürst (Prince) zu Sayn-Wittgenstein-Berleburg in Ludwigsburg, 1st Fürst (Prince) zu Sayn-Wittgenstein-Sayn (*b* 18 Jan 1799; ✠ 20 June 1866) and his second wife, Princess Leonilla Ivanovna Bariatinska (*b* 9 May 1816; *m* 23 Oct 1834; ✠ 1 Feb 1918).

Son

Theodor Friedrich, 3rd Fürst (Prince) zu Sayn-Wittgenstein-Sayn, *b* at Berlin 3 April 1836; ✠ at Meran 19 May 1909, resigned as Head of the Family 30 Sept 1879 and was *cr* Count von Altenkirchen by the King of Prussia, 22 Dec 1897; confirmed the title of Kniasz (Fürst) with the qualification of Serene Highness by Imp Russian Ukase, 22 May 1899; *m* 1stly 16 July 1868 (*m* diss by div 18 Oct 1871), Pauline Lilienthal (*b* at Berlin; ✠ Berlin 1903). He *m* 2ndly at Biberach 19 July 1877, Wihelmine Hagen (*b* at Wiesbaden 22 Feb 1854; ✠ at Innsbruck 2 Aug 1917), and had issue by his second wife,

Son

Prince *Heinrich* Gottfried Chlodwig, *b* at Frankfurt-am-Main 29 Jan

1879; ✠ in prison at Winnitza 28 Jan 1919, Lord of Drujnoselie, Kamenka and Dokudowa; Imp Russian Chamberlain; *m* at St Petersburg 16/29 April 1900, Elizaveta Dimitrievna (*b* at St Petersburg 13/25 Sept 1877; ✠ at Bucharest 31 May 1942; *m* 2ndly at Bucharest 4 May 1930, Roman Leikmann), dau of Dimitri Nabokov and Baroness Maria von Korff genannt Schmising, and had issue, among whom,

1. Prince *Leon, b* at Tsarskoie-Selo 31 Dec 1900/13 Jan 1901; ✠ at Ottawa 24 Jan 1974; *m* at Cernauti 11 Feb 1926, Countess Eva (*b* at Olmutz 27 July 1902; ✠ at Ottawa 12 June 1969), dau of Alexander, Count Wassilko von Serecki and Baroness Eva Putz von Rolsberg, and had issue,

    1. Prince *Leon* (*Leo*), *b* at Hangu, Romania 9 Sept 1935, PhD, Consultant; *m* at Montreal, Canada 31 July 1965, Maria (*b* at Vienna 11 Aug 1941), dau of George Olsufieff and Alexandra Miloradovitch, and has issue,

        1. Prince *George* Michael, *b* at Ottawa, Canada 6 Sept 1966; *m* at Ottawa 2 Oct 1993, Audra Maria (*b* at Ottawa 30 Nov 1969), dau of Rudolf Blohon and Regina Koelmans, and has issue, [*455 Turnberry Crescent, Mississauga, Ontario L4Z 3W5, Canada*].

            1. Princess *Alexandra* Katherine Maria, *b* at Mississauga, Ontario 18 March 1996.
            2. Princess *Caroline* Eva, *b* at Mississauga, Ontario 27 Jan 1998.

        2. Prince *Alexander, b* at Ottawa 14 March 1969, Lawyer.
[*1865 West 14th Avenue, Vancouver, BC V6J 2J8, Canada*].

        3. Princess *Katherine, b* at Ottawa 29 Nov 1971, BA.
[*47 Waverley Street, Apt 4, Ottawa, Ontario K2P OT7, Canada*].

        4. Prince *Peter*, Bachelor of Applied Arts, *b* at Ottawa 6 July 1975.
[*182 Mutual Street, Toronto, Ontario, M5B 2B3, Canada*].

    2. Princess *Katherina, b* at Cernauti 10 Jan 1937, B.Sc; *m* at Ottawa, Canada 24 Sept 1960, Georg

Heinrich, Baron von Schönberg (*b* at Chemnitz 8 March 1935).

[*617 Dickinson Ave., Ottawa, Ontario K1V 7J2, Canada*].

2. Prince *Peter*, *b* at Drujnoselie 24 Jan/6 Feb 1902; ✠ at Dreieich-Buchschlag 29 Sept 1980; *m* at Bucharest 16 Jan 1938, Princess Maria-Despina (*b* at Jassy 30 Nov 1917), Dr of Law, Dipl Biology, dau of Dimitri, Prince Mavrocordato and Emanuella Gradisteanu, and had issue,

[*Weissdornweg 3, 63303 Dreieich, Germany*].

1. Princess *Margareta*, *b* at Cernauti 8 Feb 1940; *m* at Bucharest 18 July 1964, Toma Varlam (*b* at Constanza, Romania 24 March 1940).

[*An der Vogelhecke 9, 63263 Neu Isenburg, Germany*].

Brother of Great-Great-Great-Great-Grandfather

Issue of Ludwig Franz, Count zu Sayn-Wittgenstein-Berleburg in Ludwigsburg, Founder of this Line (*b* 13 Dec 1694; ✠ 24 Feb 1750) and Countess Helene Emilie zu Solms-Baruth (*b* 17 Sept 1700; *m* 17 March 1722; ✠ 21 Feb 1750), among whom,

Son

Count *Georg Ernst*, *b* at Berleburg 22 Sept 1735; ✠ (guillotined) at Paris 2 Sept 1792, French Marshal; *m* 14 May 1775, Baroness Carola Josèphe (*b* 15 July 1755; ✠ at Blois l-Église, Isère post 1839; *m* 2ndly, Louis Charles Antoine de Beaufranchet d'Ayout), dau of Jean Baptiste, Baron de Kaempfer and Anne-Françoise de Saulnois, and had issue,

Son

Count *Ludwig*, *b* at Paris 10 April 1784; ✠ at Dresden 7 July 1857, Col Prussian Army; *m* 31 Dec 1831, Countess Pauline (*b* 4 July 1803; ✠ at Dresden 18 Dec 1861), dau of Friedrich Christian, Count von Degenfeld-Schonburg and Countess Luise Charlotte Polyxene zu Erbach-Erbach, and had issue,

Son

Count *Friedrich* Ernst, *b* at Sannerz 5 June 1837; ✠ at Meran 16 April 1915, Capt Austrian Army; *m* 1stly at Dobritschan, Bohemia 6 June 1861, Baroness Therese (*b* at Dobritschan 9 Jan 1841; ✠ at Graz 1 June 1887), Dame Star Cross Order, dau of Vincenz, Baron Zessner von Spitzenberg and Countess Therese von Buquoy. He *m*

2ndly at Schloß Roth, Württemberg 16 Oct 1888, Countess Emilie (*b* at Eulbach 18 May 1852; ✠ at Bad Homburg vor der Höhe 6 Feb 1919), dau of Eberhard, Count zu Erbach-Erbach and Countess Klothilde zu Erbach-Fürstenau, and had issue, among whom, by his first wife,

Sons

1. Count *Ottokar, b* at Salzburg 22 May 1878; ✠*k* at Willern, near Belfort, Alsace 13 Aug 1914, Lt Prussian Army; *m* at Karlsruhe 11 Dec 1909, Eva (*b* at Berlin 14 Oct 1889; ✠ at Waldshut 26 May 1970), dau of Louis Richard Dahlmann and Edda Ganzer, and had issue, among whom,

1. Count *Ottokar* Günther Constantin, *b* at Bruchsal 16 Jan 1911; ✠ at Munich 27 Nov 1995, Dr of Med, Psychoanalyst; *m* at Munich 30 July 1938, Ursula (*b* at Kiel 18 Nov 1913), dau of Georg von Hase and Eleanor Heygster, and has issue,

[*Königinstraße 101, 80802 Munich, Germany*].

1. Countess *Nadja* Eva Eleanor Maria, *b* at Munich 25 March 1940; *m* at Munich 4 Feb 1965 (*m* diss by div at Munich 1 Oct 1982 since when she has reverted to her maiden name), Joachim von Prittwitz and Gaffron (*b* at Leipzig 9 Jan 1931), Lawyer.

[*St. Emmeram 8, 81925 Munich, Germany*].

2. Countess *Beatrice* Helene Gisela Maria, *b* at Kiel 13 Jan 1942; *m* at Munich 28 May 1967, Götz von Bernuth (*b* at Bethel, near Bielefeld 16 April 1935), Dr of Med, Prof of Paediatric Cardiology, Aachen.

[*Tentstraat 45A, 6291 BD Vaals, The Netherlands*].

LINE II:
SAYN-WITTGENSTEIN-HOHENSTEIN

Evangelist: Founded by Ludwig, Count of Sayn-Wittgenstein-Wittgenstein (*b* 15 March 1571; ✠ 14 Sept 1634); joined the name and arms of the Counts of Hohenstein 11 Aug 1653; Prince of the Holy Empire with the qualification of "Hochgeboren", Vienna 20 June 1801; received the qualification of "Durchlaucht" (primogeniture) by the German Diet 18 Aug 1825; Hereditary Member of the former Prussian House of Lords 12 Oct 1854.

Members of this line bear the title of Prince or Princess zu Sayn-Wittgenstein-Hohenstein with the qualification of Serene Highness.

BERNHART Otto Peter, **6TH PRINCE (FÜRST) ZU SAYN-WITTGENSTEIN-HOHENSTEIN,** *b* at Marburg 15 Nov 1962, son of Christian Heinrich, 5th Prince (Fürst) zu Sayn-Wittgenstein-Hohenstein, *b* at Berleburg 20 Sept 1908; ✠ Schwarzenau, nr Bad Berleburg 17 Aug 1983; natural son of Richard 4th Prince (Fürst) zu Sayn-Wittgenstein-Berleburg - *see above*, and Princess Dagmar Elisabeth Rosemary zu Sayn-Wittgenstein-Hohenstein (*b* at Eisenach 16 Nov 1919, ✠ at Schwarzenau 13 Feb 2002; (adopted 3 May 1927 by his kinsman August, 4th Prince (Fürst) zu Sayn-Wittgenstein-Hohenstein and succeeded him as his heir and as 5th Prince (Fürst) zu Sayn-Wittgenstein-Hohenstein); *m* at Schwarzenau, nr Bad Berleburg 31 Aug 1996, Countess Katharina (*b* at Munich 23 Dec 1963), dau of Max, Count von Podewils-Dürniz and Baroness Elisabeth von Hirschberg.
[*Schwarzenau, 57319 Bad Berleburg, Germany*].

Son

1. Prince *Wenzel* Maximilian, Hereditary Prince (Erbprinz) zu Sayn-Wittgenstein-Hohenstein, *b* at Prague 18 October 1997.

1st Wife of Father

Countess *Beatrix*, *b* at Varzin, Pommerania 20 June 1921, *m* at Berleburg 28 March 1945 (*m* diss by div at Siegen 27 Nov 1951); (she *m* 2ndly at Munich 11 Oct 1961, Kai von Mengersen who ✠ 28 April 1975), dau of Nikolaus, Count von Bismarck-Schönhausen, Proprietor of Varzin and Brigitte von Eickstedt-Peterswaldt of the Counts von Eickstedt.
[*Feichtetstraße 45, Possenhofen, 82343 Pöcking, Kr. Starnberg, Germany*]

Sister

Princess *Madeleine* Elisabeth Maria, *b* at Marburg 17 March 1961; *m* at 1stly 1987 (*m* diss by div), Burkhard Driest (*b* at ...), Actor. She *m* 2ndly at Bad Berleburg 9 Oct 1990 (civ) and 27 Sept 1991 (relig), Nicolaus Hübner (*b* at Bad Godesberg 17 Dec 1962).
[*Beim Andreas Brunner 7, 20249 Hamburg, Germany*].

Half-Sisters

1. Princess *Loretta* Augusta Brigitte Madeleine, *b* at Wittgenstein

16 June 1946; *m* 1stly at Berleburg 19 Sept 1966 (*m* diss by div at Darmstadt 17 Sept 1973 and annulled at … March 1976), Lanzo, Baron Wambolt von Umstadt (*b* at Heidelberg 2 July 1934, ✠ 4 Feb 2002), Proprietor of Umstadt and Birkenau, Hessen, Land Manager and Forester. She *m* 2ndly at … 30 Oct 1974, Juan Ramon Theler (*b* at ….).

[*Finca Rotana, Apt. postal 69, Manacor, Mallorca, Spain*].

2. Princess *Johanna* Elisabeth Margareta, *b* at Wittgenstein 22 Oct 1948; *m* 1stly at Langenstein, Baden 20 Sept 1970 (*m* diss by div at Munich 9 Jan 1974), Axel, Count Douglas (*b* at Konstanz 22 July 1943), Proprietor of Langenstein, etc, Gondelsheim, etc, Land Manager. She *m* 2ndly at Pöcking am Starnberger See 15 April 1976 (*m* diss by div at Berlin 2 Feb 1979), Gert-Rudolf Flick (*b* at Berlin 29 May 1943), Dr of Law, Industrialist. She *m* 3rdly at Las Vegas 5 Oct 1986, Axel Walter (*b* at ….1941).

[*36 Lagorce Circle, Miami Beach, FL 33141, U.S.A.*].

Brothers of 4th Prince (Fürst) zu Sayn-Wittgenstein-Hohenstein

1. Prince *Georg* Wilhelm Friedrich-Wilhelm Hermann, *b* at Wittgenstein 7 April 1873; ✠ at Marburg 17 March 1960; *m* at Marburg 22 April 1913, Marie (*b* at Altenburg 2 July 1892; ✠ at Laasphe 12 May 1975), *cr* Baroness von Freusburg at Detmold 12 Dec 1916, dau of Hilmar Rühm and Marie Beckert, and had issue (*cr* Barons and Baronesses von Freusburg and, from 1 April 1946/11 Feb 1947, authorised to bear the title of Prince or Princess of Sayn-Wittgenstein-Hohenstein, with the exception of the eldest son),

    1. *Rolf* Georg, Baron von Freusburg, *b* at Eisenach 29 March 1914.

    2. Princess *Dagmar* Elisabeth Rosemarie, *b* at Eisenach 16 Nov 1919; *m* 1stly at Eisenach 24 April 1942 (*m* diss by div at Kassel 15 June 1954), Hans Karl Zirkel (*b* at Erfurt 20 Jan 1913), Dr of Med. She *m* 2ndly at Arfeld, near Berleburg (civ) and at Schwarzenau (relig) 4 Nov 1960, Christian Heinrich, Prince zu Sayn-Wittgenstein-Hohenstein (*b* at Berleburg 20 Sept 1908; ✠ at Schwarzenau 17 Aug 1983).

    [*Herrenhaus 57319 Bad Berleburg-Schwarzenau, Germany*].

    3. Princess *Jutta* Irmgard Caroline, *b* at Eisenach 31 Jan 1923; *m* at Wittgenstein 24 April 1951, Maximilian, Count von Korff genannt Schmising (*b* at Münster, Westphalia 3 Feb 1911; ✠ at Hamburg 9 June 1984), Businessman.

[Elbchaussee 557, 22587 Hamburg - Blankenese, Germany].

4. Prince *Botho* Eberhard Ernst August Clodwig, *b* at Eisenach 16 Feb 1927, Hon President German Red Cross, President of the Standing Commission of Red Cross and Red Crescent, Hon Cmndr Kt of St John of Jerusalem, Cmdr Sovereign Military Order of Malta; *m* at Laasphe 23 May 1959, Baroness Elisabeth (*b* at Zülzendorf, Schweidnitz, Silesia 8 May 1937), dau of Hans Siegmund, Baron von Zedlitz and Leipe, Proprietor of Zülzendorf, etc and Baroness Ellinor von Durant, and has issue,

[Hof Breitenbach, 57334 Laasphe, Westfalen, Germany].

  1. Prince *Georg* Christian Sigmund Winfried Rolf, *b* at Marburg 4 April 1960, Kt of Honour of St John of Jerusalem; *m* at Oberzwieselau nr Zwiesel 23 May 1998, Benedika (*b* at Zwiesel 29 July 1961), dau of Joachim Martin, Baron von Maydell (by adoption 1987) von Wolffersdorff and Countess Barbara von Mellin.
  [Kastanienallee 9, 50968 Cologne, Germany].

    1. Princess *Pauline* Marie Ellinor Barbara Isabel, *b* at Cologne 30 Jan 1999.

  2. Princess *Friederike* Maria Monika Jutta, *b* at Marburg 21 Nov 1961, MSc, Mph (Harvard).
  [Zelterstraße 22, 49076 Osnabrück, Germany].

  3. Princess *Katharina* Viktoria Ellinor, *b* at Siegen 22 Sept 1965; *m* at Bad Laasphe 17 July 1993, Stafen Momolo Friedrich (*b* at Harbel, Monrovia, Liberia, West Africa 29 April 1961), Lawyer.
  [Weserstraße 94, 28757 Bremen, Germany].

5. Prince *Wilhelm* Richard Ludwig, *b* at Wittgenstein 6 Sept 1877; ✝ at Lugano-Castagnola 27 Nov 1958, Kt of Hon St John of Jerusalem; *m* at Wiesbaden 25 Sept 1928, Clara Schaefer (*b* at Prüm 19 April 1894; ✝ at Lugano 18 Feb 1978; *m* 1stly at Brussels 8 May 1916, Curt Michelmann; that *m* diss by div), and adopted his step-daughter,

  1. *Eva* Sabina Elisabeth Michelmann, *b* at Frankfurt-am-Main 26 Aug 1910, adopted 12 Sept 1935/22 Feb 1936, bears the name of "Princess zu Sayn-Wittgenstein-Hohenstein; *m* at Berlin Schöneberg 11 Aug (civ) and at Munich 25 Aug (relig) 1941, Helmut von Hartz (*b* at Munich 10 April 1900; ✝ at Davos-Platz 27 Dec 1966), Dipl Eng.
  [Züricherstraße 168, 8800 Thalwil, Kt. Zürich, Switzerland].

SCHAESBERG

Catholic: This family belongs to the feudal nobility of Limburg and can be authenticated to Walram van Retersbeeke (von Reitersbach) living 12 Dec 1335 who between 1400 and 1415 took the name of Schaesbergh (Schaesberg, Limburg, Netherlands); Baron of the Holy Empire, Elbersdorf 3 Oct 1637; Count of the Holy Empire with the qualification of "Hoch and Wohlgeboren", Vienna 9 Sept 1706; elevation of the Lordships of Kerpen and Lommersum into a County of the Holy Empire, Vienna 11 Feb 1712; received into the Westphalian College of Counts of the Holy Empire 4 April 1715; compensated for the loss of lands in 1801 by the Bailiwick of Thannheim, 1803; Hereditary Member of the House of Lords of Württemberg 25 Sept 1819; received the qualification of "Erlaucht" (primogeniture) by the German Diet 13 Feb 1829.

Members of the family bear the title of Count or Countess von Schaesberg with the qualification of Illustrious Highness for the Head of the Family and his wife only.

JOHANNES Friedrich Walter Alfred Josef Maria, **COUNT (GRAF) VON SCHAESBERG,** Lord of Thannheim, *b* at Munich 22 Oct 1960, Managing Partner, Kt of Hon Sovereign Military Order of Malta, son of Heinrich, Count von Schaesberg, etc (*b* 12 Feb 1922; ✠ 22 Jan 1996) and Princess Margaretha von Croÿ (*b* 11 Oct 1930; *m* 7 June 1956); *m* at Sünching 2 July 1994, Baroness Antoinette (*b* at Munich 16 Jan 1968), dau of Johann Carl, Baron von Hoenning O'Carroll and Countess Katalin Zichy.
[*An den Linden 28, 40667 Meerbusch, Germany; Schlössle, 88459 Tannheim, Germany*].

Daughters

1. Countess *Sophie, b* at Regensburg 12 Dec 1997.
2. Countess *Marie-Dorothee* Friederike Christina Henriette Kreszentia, *b* at Düsseldorf 5 April 1999.

Mother

Princess *Margaretha,* Dowager Countess von Schaesberg, *b* at Grumsmühlen 11 Oct 1930, Dame Sovereign Military Order of Malta, dau of Anton, Prince von Croÿ and Rosalie von Heyden-Linden; *m* at Grumsmühlen, nr Lingen an der Ems 7 June 1956, Heinrich, Count von Schaesberg, Lord of Thannheim (*b* at Berlin 12 Feb 1922; ✠ at Tannheim, Kr Biberach an der Riss 22 Jan 1996), adopted 17 Dec 1951/16 May 1952 by and *succ* his uncle, Joseph, Count von

Schaesberg (*b* 22 Dec 1882; ✠ 12 Nov 1963), Land Manager and Forester, Kt of Hon Sovereign Military Order of Malta.
[*88459 Tannheim, Germany*].

Brothers and Sister

1. Count *Georg* Clemens Heinrich Joseph Maria, *b* at Munich 21 June 1962, Forest Manager; *m* at Tannheim 12 Feb 1994, Princess Marie Aglaë (*b* at Munich 22 April 1966), dau of Karl Albrecht, Prince (Fürst) zu Hohenlohe-Schillingsfürst and Countess Ladislaya von Meran.
[*Woltersdorf Farms, RR2 Chapeau, Quebec J0X 1MO, Canada*].

2. Count *Christoph* Rudolf Antonius Heinrich Joseph Maria, *b* at Munich 26 June 1963, Marketing Manager; *m* at Tannheim 25 March (civ) and at St Florian, Upper Austria 6 July (relig) 1996, Countess Maria Magdalena (*b* at Vienna 5 May 1971), dau of Xaver Matz, Count von Spiegelfeld and Waltraud Stanek, and has issue,
[*88459 Tannheim, Kr. Biberach an der Riss, Germany*].

    1. Countess *Franziska* Xaveria Margarete Emilie Maria, *b* at Ochsenhausen, Württemberg 8 April 1997.

    2. Count *Camillo* Heinrich Franz Stephan Joseph Maria, *b* at Vienna 9 June 2000.

    3. Count *Tassilo* Heinrich Franz Carl Peter Joseph Maria, *b* at Vienna 8 Apr 2002.

3. Countess *Maria* Elisabeth Henriette Bernadette, *b* at Munich 12 June 1965, Librarian; *m* at Tannheim 28 Sept 1991, Eugen Heinrich Solf (*b* at Düsseldorf 18 Feb 1958), MBA, Banker.
[*Goethestraße 37, 61476 Kronberg, Germany*].

4. Count *Peter* Karl Martin Stephan Joseph Maria, *b* at Munich 7 Nov 1067, Art Historian.
[*Jakob Klarstraße 8, 80796 Munich, Germany*].

5. Count *Martin* Walter Tanguy Paulus Josef Maria, *b* at Memmingen 17 Feb 1973, Hotel Manager.
[*Schlössle, 88459 Tannheim, Germany*].

Brothers and Sisters of Father

Issue of of Walter, Count von Schaesberg (*b* 3 Sept 1890; ✠ 15 Aug 1971) and Countess Hermine von Redern (*b* 11 April 1899; ✠ 17 June 1988; *m* 22 April 1920), among whom,

1. Countess *Marie-Therese* Elisabeth Huberta, *b* at Berlin 11 Dec 1927; *m* at Engelskirchen 27 July 1955, Clemens, Prince von Croÿ

(*b* at Grumsmühlen, nr Lingen an der Ems 7 Sept 1926).
[*Holunderweg 18, 51519 Odenthal-Eberich, Germany*].
2. Count *Karl Anton* Hubertus Maria, *b* at Berlin 12 April 1934, BA;
m at Griessem, Hameln-Pyrmont 15 Oct 1976, Baroness Monica (*b* at
Schellenstein, nr Bigge 16 Dec 1939), Teacher, dau of Werner, Baron
von Canstein, Proprietor of Griessem, and Baroness Elisabeth von
Wendt, and has issue,
[*Landstraße 21, 79809 Weilheim-Bannholz, Germany*].

     1. Countess *Antonia* Victoria Maria Pia Margaretha, *b* at
     Heinsberg 4 Jan 1978.
     2. Count *Joseph* Werner Walter Heinrich Maria, *b* at
     Heinsberg 21 Sept 1979.

Brothers and Sister of Grandfather

Issue of Heinrich, Count von Schaesberg (*b* 17 Oct 1855; ✝ 27 Nov
1910); *m* 1stly 18 July 1881, Countess Elisabeth von Waldburg zu
Zeil (*b* 8 Aug 1862; ✝ 8 March 1891); *m* 2ndly 29 March 1892,
Countess Maria Theresia von Waldburg-Zeil (*b* 15 Aug 1865; ✝ 9
Feb 1952) sister of his first wife, among whom,

1. **Joseph** Ludwig Richard Petrus Hubertus Maria, **Count von
Schaesberg**, etc, *b* at Tannheim 22 Dec 1882; ✝ at Memmingen 12
Nov 1963, Kt of Hon Sovereign Military Order of Malta; *m* at
Brussels 30 Jan 1913, Countess Ghislaine (*b* at Theux 17 July 1886; ✝
at Ulm 5 Aug 1954), dau of Guy, Count de Berlaymont and Countess
Marie de Pinto, and had issue, among whom,

     1. Countess *Agathe* Anna Maria Ghislaine Josephine Ingeborg
     Huberta, *b* at Mainz 14 May 1925; *m* at Tannheim 21 Oct
     1954, Alram Karl, Count zu Ortenburg (*b* at Budapest 23 Oct
     1925), Forester.
     [*Schloß Tambach, 96479 Weitramsdorf, OFranken, Germany*].
*Joseph, Count von Schaesberg also adopted his nephew who was the
father of the present Head of the Family (see above).*
2. Count Wilhelm *Julius* Rudolf Quirinus Joseph Hubertus Maria,
b at Tannheim 30 March 1887; ✝ at Munich 12 Jan 1956, Capt
Prussian Cavalry, Kt of Hon Sovereign Military Order of Malta;
m 1stly at Melschede, Westphalia 18 Aug 1926, Baroness Irene (*b* at
Cologne 16 Dec 1906; ✝ at Birlinghoven 9 July 1939), dau of Clemens,
Baron von Wrede and Elisabeth Hagen. He *m* 2ndly at Munich 15
April 1941, Alexandra (*b* at Triest 28 Jan 1913; *m* 2ndly at Hechendorf
4 Sept 1961, Hans von Seemen who ✝ 13 July 1972; she ✝ at Munich

23 May 2002), dau of Walter Billig and Christina Schalk, and had issue by his first wife,

[*Ottostraße 6, 80333 Munich, Germany*].

    1. Countess *Christa* Elisabeth Therese Clementine Emma Maria, *b* at Melschede 18 March 1928; ✠ at Munich 18 Jan 1975; *m* at Grabenstätt, Bavaria 23 Feb 1952, Simon Ranner (*b* at Grabenstätt 22 Oct 1918).

    [*Tüttenseestraße 1, 83355 Grabenstätt, Germany*].

    2. Countess *Gabriele* Anna Maria Carola, *b* at Melschede 20 May 1929; ✠ at Traunstein, Bavaria 3 Sept 1974; *m* 1stly at Grabenstätt am Chiemsee 25 Sept (civ) and at Melschede 9 Oct (relig) 1954 (*m* diss by div at Munich 15 Nov 1955; annulled 27 Nov 1964), Albrecht, Baron von Pechmann (*b* at Stuttgart 19 March 1931), Dr of Law. She *m* 2ndly at Transtein 12 Sept 1956 (*m* diss by div at Munich 10 May 1968), Erwin Rixner (*b* at Moosburg, Bavaria 14 Feb 1930), Businessman.

3. Count Wolfgang *Rudolf* Maria Pius Michael Joseph Hubertus, *b* at Tannheim 8 May 1888; ✠ at Starnberg, Bavaria 14 April 1961, Capt Württemberg Cavalry; *m* at Berlin 7 Jan 1920, Countess Margarethe (*b* at Görlsdorf 24 Sept 1893; ✠ at Düsseldorf 24 Dec 1945), dau of Wilhelm, Count von Redern, Proprietor of Görlsdorf, and Countess Marie Karoline Lichnowsky of the Princes Lichnowsky, and had issue,

    1. Count *Karl Max* Rudolf Wilhelm Heinrich Hubertus Maria, *b* at Ingenraedt 25 June 1921, Businessman; *m* at Mülheim-Speldorf 19 April 1956, Eva Maria (*b* at Düisburg 5 Oct 1932), dau of Max Böllert and Elsbeth Leverkus, and has issue,

    [*Prinzregentenstraße 83, 81675 Munich, Germany*].

        1. Countess *Pia* Maria Margarethe Elisabeth, *b* at Mülheim an der Ruhr 6 Sept 1958, Hotel Manager; *m* at Ehrenshoven 8 April 1995, Rainer Heym (*b* at Saarbrücken 26 Sept 1958), Hotel Manager.

        [*Rückertstraße 6, 51373 Leverkusen, Germany*].

        2. Count *Rudolf Victor*, *b* at Ingenraedt 2 Sept 1922, Businessman; *m* 1stly Odonthal, Cologne 29 Jan 1955, Baroness Monica (*b* at Jacobsdorf 3 April 1927; ✠ at Cologne 26 May 1974), dau of Stephan, Baron von Thielmann, Proprietor of Jacobsdorf and Kleuschnitz, Kr Falkenberg, Upper Silesia and Baroness Julia von Schönberg. He *m* 2ndly at Nettetal 11 July (civ) and 12 July (relig) 1975, Ina-Maria (*b* at Breslau 19 March 1926; *m* 1stly at Munich 4 July 1960, Edwin, Count

von Francken-Sierstorpff; that *m* diss by div at Munich 27
Jan 1970 and annulled at Augsburg 17 Feb 1970), dau of
Maximilian Weinert and Ruth Bräuer, and has issue from his
first wife,
[*Gutenbergstraße 65, 47803 Krefeld, Germany*].

    1. Countess *Alice* Margarethe Pia Maria, *b* at Cologne
5 Nov 1955, Dr of Med; *m* at Hildesheim 22 June (civ)
and 7 July (relig) 1984, Jörg Deselaers (*b* at Düren 13
Nov 1956), Dipl Forestry.
[*Schloß Ehreshoven, 51766 Engelskirchen, Germany*].

    2. Count *Michael* Josef Heinrich Hubertus Maria, *b* at
Cologne 15 May 1958, Marketing Manager.
[*Sentilostraße 22, 81477 Munich, Germany*].

    3. Countess *Nadine* Margarethe Josephine Maria,
b Leverkusen-Schlebusch 11 Feb 1961, Dr rer Agr,
Dipl Ing agr.
[*Remscheiderstraße 9, 40215 Düsseldorf, Germany*].

    4. Count *Antonio* Josef Caspar Maria, *b* at Leverkusen-
Schlebusch 21 April 1962.
[*Gutenbergstraße 65, 47803 Krefeld, Germany*].

3. Countess *Elisabeth* Maria Therese Margarete, *b* at Berlin
29 May 1927; *m* at Munich 4 Oct 1956 (*m* diss by div at
Munich 28 Oct 1959), Pedro Botas Menéndes (*b* at ...).
[*Rheinlandstraße 8, 82319 Starnberg, Germany*].

SCHLITZ GENANNT VON GÖRTZ

**Lutheran (and Catholic): Feudal family authenticated since
Ermenoldus von Slitese living in 1116, his son Gerlachus was
appointed "vir nobilis et religiosus" 1126; Otto von Schlitz, Hereditary
Grand Marshal of Fulda circa 1200, and his great-grandson, Otto
added "von Görtz" 1218; Baron of the Holy Empire with the
qualification of "Wohlgeboren", Vienna 15 July 1677 and Passau 21
Aug 1683; Count of the Holy Empire (primogeniture) with the
qualification of "Hoch and Wohlgeboren" and ratification of arms,
Laxenburg 10 June 1726; two sons of the first Count, Friedrich
Wilhelm (✝ 1728) founded the two lines (of which only the elder line
is treated here); the elder line was received into the College of
Counts of the Holy Empire 1804; Hereditary Member of the First
Chamber of the Grand Duchy of Hesse 17 Dec 1820; received the
qualification of "Erlaucht" (primogeniture) by the German Diet 13**

Feb 1829; extended to all members of the family 7 March 1914.
Members of the family bear the title of Count or Countess von
Schlitz genannt von Görtz with the qualification of Illustrious
Highness.

RÜDIGER Maria, **COUNT and LORD (GRAF AND HERR)
VON SCHLITZ GENANNT VON GÖRTZ**, Proprietor of
Schlitz, Wegfurth and Rechberg, *b* at Richthof, nr Schlitz 4 Feb
1939, *succ* his father, son of Otto Hartmann, Count and Lord von
Schlitz genannt von Görtz, (*b* 10 Sept 1907; ✠ 10 March 1977) and
Martha Hagen (*b* at Munich 25 Nov 1903; *m* 4 Oct (civ)/18 Oct
(relig) 1928; ✠ 13 Nov 1966); *m* at Munich 31 Aug 1965, Margarete
(*b* at Halle 12 March 1940), dau of Georg Dittman and Ingeborg Reif.
[*Südstraße 1, 8451 Hahnbach über Amberg, OPfalz, Germany*].

Sister

1. Countess *Faralda* Angela, *b* at Munich 7 Dec 1933, Pilot and
Aviation Instructor.
[*Arnoldstraße 20, 50679 Cologne - Deutz, Germany*].

Step-Mother

Margarethe, Countess von Schlitz genannt von Görtz (see also
below), *b* at Berlin 28 Jan 1909, dau of Carl, Hereditary Count
(Erbgraf) von Schlitz genannt von Görtz and Princess Amélie von
Thurn and Taxis; *m* 1stly at Schlitz 26 Nov 1930, Ernst von Morgen
(*b* at Berlin 1 Feb 1893; ✠ at Grosshesselohe 8 Sept 1963); *m* 2ndly
at Schlitz 14 Aug 1967, Otto Hartmann, Count and Lord von Schlitz
genannt von Görtz (*b* at Darmstadt 10 Sept 1907; ✠ at Lucerne 10
March 1977).
[*Schloß Richthof, 36110 Schlitz, OHessen, Germany*].

Sisters of Father

Issue of Friedrich Wilhelm, Count and Lord von Schlitz genannt von
Görtz (*b* 5 Jan 1882; ✠ 30 June 1935) and Catharina (Cateau)
Riedesel, Baroness zu Eisenbach (*b* 5 Jan 1883; *m* 25 Oct 1906; ✠ 28
March 1969), among whom,

1. Countess *Alexandra* Anna Sophie Catharina Emilia Adrienne,
b at Darmstadt 24 Sept 1910; *m* at Schlitz 4 Oct 1938, Wilhelm
Ernst, Prince zu Erbach-Schönberg (*b* at König, Odenwald 4 Jan
1904; ✠*k* as a POW at Krasni-Lutsch, 27 Sept 1946), Forester, Lt.
[*Vorderburg, 36110 Schlitz, OHessen, Germany*].

2. Countess *Marie Gabriele* Franziska Lillly Christiane Johanna, *b* at Schlitz 19 Aug 1916; *m* at Schlitz 28 June 1947, Heinrich Janssen (*b* at Hameln 27 Oct 1900; ✠ there 1 April 1979), Proprietor of Behrensen (since 1932), Dr of Law.
[*Klütstraße 15, 31787 Hameln, Germany; Behrensen, 31863 Coppenbrügge, Germany*].

Brother of Grandfather

Issue of Emil, Count and Lord von Schlitz genannt von Görtz (*b* 15 Feb 1851; ✠ 9 Oct 1914) and Sophie Cavalcanti de Albuquerque de Villeneuve (*b* 5 May 1858; *m* 15 Feb 1876; ✠ 2 Nov 1902), having had issue, among whom,

Son

Carl August Constantin, Hereditary Count (Erbgraf) von Schlitz genannt von Görtz; *b* at Munich 28 Dec 1877; ✠ at Kristiania 29 Dec 1911, Lt-Col, Kt of Hon St John of Jerusalem; *m* at Vienna 29 Aug 1905, Princess Amélie (*b* at Innsbruck 9 June 1876; ✠ at Salzburg 7 Nov 1930), dau of Adolf, Prince von Thurn and Taxis and Countess Franziska Grimaud von Orsay, and had issue,

    1. Countess *Sophie* Anna Constantia Emilia Franziska, *b* at Rome 13 May 1906; *m* at Vienna 15 Sept 1931, Alfons, 6th Prince Paar (*b* at Vienna 15 Dec 1903; ✠ at Hartberg 20 April 1979).
    [*Herren Gasse1, 8230 Hartberg, Steiermark, Austria; Via Loreto 6, 6900 Lugano, Tessin, Switzerland*].
    2. Countess *Margarethe* Franziska Eleonore Karoline, *b* at Berlin 28 Jan 1909; *m* 1stly at Schlitz 26 Nov 1930, Ernst von Morgen (*b* at Berlin 1 Feb 1893; ✠ at Grosshesselohe, nr Munich 8 Sept 1963), Major. She *m* 2ndly at Schlitz 14 Aug 1967, her first cousin, Otto Hartmann, Count and Lord von Schlitz genannt von Görtz (*b* at Darmstadt 10 Sept 1907; ✠ at Lucerne, Switzerland 10 March 1977).
    [*Schloß Richthof, 36110 Schlitz, OHessen, Germany*].

SCHÖNBORN

Catholic: This Rhenish feudal family take their name from the village of Schönborn (near Lahn, Hesse-Nassau) and can be authenticated to Dyderich de Sconenburne (living 1 July 1284) and his sister

Gysell; Baron of the Holy Empire and comites palatini, Vienna 29 Jan 1663 (for Philipp-Erwin von Schönborn and his descendants); received the hereditary appointments of "Erbschenkenamt des Erzstifts", Mainz and "Erbtruchsessenamt des Hochstifts", Würzburg; acquired Reichelsberg 27 Sept 1671; Count of the Holy Empire with augmentation of arms and the privilege to mint coins, Vienna 5 Aug 1701 (for the brothers Johann-Philipp, Melchior Friedrich, and Johann Erwein); acquired the Lordship of Wiesentheid through the marriage of Count Rudolf Franz Erwin (b 28 Oct 1677; marriage contract 14 Nov 1701; ✠ 22 Sept 1754) to Marie Eleonore, Dowager Countess of Dernbach, née Countess of Hatzfeldt, 26 July 1704; inherited the Lordship of Pommersfelden 1710; instituted fideicommis 3 Jan 1711; inherited the possessions of the last Count of Buchheim and joined the name and arms of Puchaim (Puchheim, near Vöcklabruck, Upper Austria) with transfer of their hereditary appointment of "Oberst-Erbtruchsessenamt" in Austria Upper and Lower der Enns, Vienna 18 Feb 1711; Lord of Upper Austria 21 April 1711; separation of the cadet branch of Heussenstamm (Hesse, extinct 25 July 1801), 19 May 1717 by Count Anselm Franz (b 1 Jan 1681; ✠ 10 July 1726); changed the statutes of the family fideicommis 17 Nov 1722; donation of the Lordship of Munkács (Hungary), Laxenburg 4 Jan 1731; Hereditary "Obergespan" of the County of Beregh 8 July 1740; order of succession 14 Sept 1766; inherited the Lordships of Lukavic, Przichowitz, Malesitz and Dzlazkovic in Bohemia, succession of the Counts of Hatzfeldt-Gleichen 1794; the three existing lines descend from sons of Count Hugo Damian Erwein (b 28 Nov 1738; ✠ 29 March 1817).

LINE I:
SCHÖNBORN-BUCHHEIM
(formerly SCHÖNBORN-HEUSSENSTAMM)

Founded by Count Franz Philipp (b 14 Sept 1768; ✠ 18 Aug 1841) = received the qualification of "Erlaucht" (primogeniture) 22 April 1829, confirmed by the German Diet 13 Feb 1829.

Members of this line bear the title of Count or Countess von Schönborn-Buchheim with the qualification of Illustrious Highness for the Head of the Family and his wife only.

FRIEDRICH KARL, COUNT (GRAF) VON SCHÖNBORN-BUCHHEIM, b at Schloß Schönborn 30 March 1938, succ his father, son of Georg, Count von Schönborn-Buchheim (b 5 March 1906; ✠ 27 Jan 1989) and his first wife, Countess Elisabeth Orssich de Slavetich (b 3 June 1902; m 14 July 1931; ✠ 17 April 1967); m at Louveciennes, Yvelines 9 Sept (civ) and at Dreux 10 Sept (relig) 1964 Princess Isabelle (b at the Manoir d'Anjou 8 April

1932), Dame Star Cross Order, dau of Henri, Count of Paris and Princess Isabella of Orléans Bragança, and has issue,
[*Schloß Weyerburg, 2031 Eggendorf im Thale, NÖsterreich, Austria*].

Sons and Daughters

1. *Damian,* Hereditary Count (Erbgraf) von Schönborn-Buchheim, *b* at Vienna 17 July 1965, Dipl Engineer, Dr rer nat techn, Land Manager and Forester; *m* at Blessington, nr Dublin 2 Feb 2002, Deirdre Mary (*b* at Dublin 16 April 1969), dau of Matthew Ascough and Carmen Cusack.
[*Schloss Schönborn, 2013 Göllersdorf, Hollabrunn, Austria*].

2. Count *Vincenz, b* at Schönborn 28 Nov 1966, Mag biol Biology; *m* at Neulengbach, Austria 4 May 2002, Katharina Maria Christiane Martina (*b* at Vienna 30 Jan 1975), dau of Wolfgang Graf and Countess Marie-Antoinette von and zu Trauttmansdorff-Weinsberg.
[*Renn Gasse4, 1010 Vienna, Austria*].

3. Countess *Lorraine* Marie, *b* at Johannesburg, South Africa 3 Jan 1968; *m* at Berlin 26 April (civ) and at Wullersdorf, NÖsterreich 17 May (relig) 1997, Wilhelm, Count von Spee (*b* at Paderborn 10 Sept 1963), Lawyer.
[*Krummestraße 50, 10627 Berlin-Charlottenburg, Germany*].

4. Countess *Claire Marie, b* at Neuilly-sur-Seine 7 Oct 1969.
[*Schloß Weyerburg, 2031 Egendorf im Thale, NÖsterreich, Austria*].

5. Count *Melchior* Raphael, *b* at Vienna 22 Sept 1977.
[*Schloß Weyerburg, 2031 Egendorf im Thale, NÖsterreich, Austria*].

Brothers and Sisters

1. *Georg* Friedrich Karl Franz Erwin Apollonius, Hereditary Count (Erbgraf) von Schönborn-Buchheim, *b* at Vienna 18 April 1932; ✛ nr Kitzbühel 3 Feb 1973, Dipl Eng; *m* at Altaussee, Steiermark 12 June 1965, Countess and Noble Lady Elisabeth (*b* at Korneuburg, Lower Austria 25 May 1942; *m* 2ndly at Imlau, nr Werfen, Land Salzburg 7 July 1990, Matthias Kaindl), dau of Count and Noble Lord von and zu Eltz genannt Faust von Stromberg and Countess Teresita von Wilczek.
[*Chirk, Cefin-Y-Wern Clwyd, North Wales*].

2. Countess *Elisabeth* Helene Marie, *b* at Schloß Beregvár, nr Munkács (Hungary) 14 March 1934, Dr of phil; *m* at New York City 28 10 (civ)

and at Schönborn 1 Nov (relig) 1965, Roel F Karamat (*b* at Paramaribo 16 Oct 1936), Dr of Phil.
[*2020 Oberfellabrunn 72, Austria*].

3. Countess *Teresa, b* at Budapest 26 Nov 1942; *m* at Vienna 10 July (civ) and at Schönborn 14 July (relig) 1968, José Pedro de Erice y Gómez-Acebo (*b* at Oporto, Portugal 3 May 1943), Diplomat.
[*Am Kurpark 7, 53177 Bonn-Bad Godesberg, Germany*].

4. Count *Max* Eugen, *b* at Augsburg 24 Nov 1944; *m* at Kitzbühel 8 Aug 1981, Heide-Maria (Heidemarie) (*b* at Vienna 31 March 1944,) dau of Hans Jörg Leuze and Ingeborg Cavallar von Grabensprung.
[*Plössl Gasse9, 1040 Vienna, Austria; Feldweg 7, 6370 Kitzbühel, Austria; 2032 Enzersdorf im Thale, Austria*].

Stepmother

Christiana, Countess von Schönborn-Buchheim, dau of Manfred Mautner von Markhof and Marie Kupelwieser, *b* at Vienna 23 Jan 1928; *m* 1stly at Vienna 5 June 1948 (*m* diss by div at Vienna 19 Aug 1953 and annulled at Salzburg 22 March 1975), Johann Heinrich, Baron von Tinti (*b* ...; ✠ at Pöchlarn an der Donau 23 Dec 1986). She *m* 2ndly at Schönborn 19 April 1975, *Georg* Erwin Karl Peter, Count (Graf) von Schönborn Buchheim (*b* at Bogliaco, Lake Garda 5 March 1906; ✠ at Schönborn 27 Jan 1989; *m* 1stly at Weiss-Polican, Bez Neupaka, Bohemia 14 July 1931, Countess Elisabeth (Betka) Orssich de Slavetich (*b* at Baden-Baden 3 June 1902; ✠ at Vienna 17 April 1967).
[*Renn Gasse4, 1010 Vienna, Austria*].

Half Brothers and Sister of Father

Issue of Friedrich Karl, Count von Schönborn-Buchheim (*b* 23 Feb 1869; ✠ 2 March 1932) and his second wife, Donna Sofia Dentice of the Princes di Frasso (*b* 10 Jan 1889; *m* 14 Sept 1910; *m* diss by div 11 Dec 1922; ✠ 5 Aug 1968), cousin of his first wife.

1. Count *Erwein* Friedrich Karl Alois, *b* at Schönborn 2 Jan 1912, Engineer; *m* at Vienna 18 Feb (civ) and 20 Feb (relig) 1950 (*m* diss by div 24 March 1959), Christine (*b* at Seeburg an der Ybbs 16 July 1926; since their divorce she has reverted to her maiden name), dau of Leopold Bachmayr-Heyda von Lowczicz and Adele Günste, and has issue,
[*Schönborn 4, 2013 Göllersdorf, Austria*].

1. Count *Christian* Georg Karl Leopold Maria, *b* at Vienna 16
Dec 1950; *m* at Vienna ... (*m* diss by div at Vienna), Johanna
(*b* at Vienna 30 Jan 1954; *m* 2ndly 30 Oct 1990, Karl, Count
von Arco), dau of Karl Maria Wodrazka and Irma Kronberger.
2. Countess *Verena* Maria Madeleine, *b* at Vienna 15 July
1952; *m* at Vienna 8 Sept (civ) and 24 Sept (relig) 1977,
Hieronymus, Count Spannocchi (*b* at Linz an der Donau 28
March 1946) Dr of Law.
[*Schloß Sprinzenstein, 4150 Rohrbach, Upper Austria*].
2. Countess *Irma* Sophie Tiburtia, *b* at Vienna 14 April 1913;
m 1stly at Vienna 10 July 1933 (*m* diss by div at Vienna 1937), Ernst,
Count von Kesselstatt (*b* at Au 17 June 1905; ✝ at Vienna 15 Aug
1939), Dipl Forestry. She *m* 2ndly at Vienna 19 Sept 1942 (*m* diss by
div at Hildesheim 1960), Rudolf Schulze-Wengler (*b* at Ballenstedt,
Harz 10 April 1916). She *m* 3rdly at Klagenfurt 21 Jan 1961, Erwin
Crobath (*b* at Mistelbach, Lower Austria 22 May 1898; ✝ at Kagenfurt
20 Nov 1973).
[*Brahms Gasse4, 9020 Klagenfurt, Austria*].
3. Count *Friedrich Karl* Anton, *b* at Schönborn 18 Nov 1914; *m* 1stly
at Graz 4 Oct (civ) and 8 Oct (relig) 1938 (*m* diss by div at Graz 21
Nov 1945), Countess Camilla (*b* at Graz 17 April 1918; ✝ there 10
June 1961), dau of Karl, Count Chorinsky, Baron von Ledske and
Countess Helene Szögyény-Marich von Magyar-Szögyén and
Szolgaegyháza. He *m* 2ndly at Trieste 21 June (civ) and at San
Francisco 30 July (relig) 1961, Edith Carpenter (*b* at New York 5 Jan
1927), dau of Valentine Everet Macy and Lydia Bodrero, and had
issue by his first wife,
[*"Green Hill", Woods Road, P.O. Box 99, Tivoli, N.Y. 12583-099,
U.S.A.; Kriechbaumhof, 5303 Thalgauegg 14, Austria*].
   1. Countess *Camilla* Maria Helene Sofie Caroline, *b* at Graz
   29 July 1929; ✝ at Half Moon Bay, San Francisco 29 Dec
   1956.
4. Count *Maximilian* Stefan Eugen, *b* at Schloß Beregvár, nr Munkács
10 Oct 1917; ✝ at Waidhofen an der Thaya 24 Aug 1967; *m* at
Innsbruck 29 Aug 1947, Gertrude (*b* at Innsbruck 30 April 1925; ✝
at ... 4 July 1988), dau of Ignaz Bock and Aloisia Maria Haider, and
had issue, an adopted son,
   1. *Peter* Theodor Ignaz, *b* at Innsbruck 17 Feb 1946,
   (adopted), bears the name "Schönborn-Buchheim".

LINE II:
SCHÖNBORN-WIESENTHEID

Founded by Count Franz Erwein (*b* 7 April 1776; ✝ 5 Dec 1840);
Hereditary Member of Bavarian "Reichsrate" 26 May 1818; received
the qualification of "Erlaucht" (primogeniture) by the German Diet
22 April 1829; extended to all members of the family 7 March 1911.
Members of this Line bear the title of Count or Countess von
Schönborn-Wiesentheid with the qualification of Illustrious Highness.

FILIPP Erwein Anton, **COUNT (GRAF) VON
SCHÖNBORN-WIESENTHEID,** Count and Lord zu
Wiesentheid, Lord of Gaibach and Heussenstamm, *b* at Würzburg
24 July 1954, *succ* his father; (son of Friedrich *Karl* Anton Count von
Schönborn-Wiesentheid (*b* at Würzburg 14 Oct 1916, ✝ 12 Sept
1998) and Donna Graziella Álvarez Pereira de Melo (*b* at Pau 20 Dec
1929; *m* at Sintra, Portugal 21 April (civ) and at Muge, Portugal 14
June (relig) 1953); *m* at Sintra, Portugal 28 Oct 1995 (relig), Béatrice
(*b* at Neuilly-sur-Seine 5 Oct 1961), dau of Henri, Count de Castellane
of the Marquesses de Castellane-Novejean and Isabella Manuela di
Rovasenda.
[*Schloßplatz 1, 97353 Wiesentheid, UFranken, Germany;Forststraße
3, 97332 Volkach-Rimbach, Germany*].

Mother

Donna *Graziella* (*b* at Pau 20 Dec 1929), dau of Dom António,
Marquess Álvarez Pereira de Melo of the Dukes de Cadaval and Olga
Nicolis of the Counts di Robilant; *m* at Sintra, Portugal 21 April
(civ) and at Muge, Portugal 14 June (relig) 1953, Friedrich *Karl*
Anton Count von Schönborn-Wiesentheid (*b* at Würzburg 14 Oct
1916, ✝ 12 Sept 1998), Dr of Med, Kt of Hon Sovereign Military
Order of Malta.
[*Schloßplatz 1, 97353 Wiesentheid, UFranken, Germany; 96178
Pommersfelden, OFranken, Germany; Quinta da Bela Vista a
Piedade, 2710 Sintra, Portugal*].

Brother and Sisters

1. Countess *Teresa* Eleonore Ernestina Maria, *b* at Würzburg 7 Nov
1955, Travel Agent.
[*Quinta da Piedade, 2710 Sintra, Portugal*].
2. Countess *Maria* Johanna Gabriela, *b* at Würzburg 28 July 1958; *m*
at Quinta da Bela Vista á Piedade, Sintra 1 July 1983, Johann-
Friedrich, Hereditary Count (Erbgraf) zu Castell-Rüdenhausen

(*b* at Rüdenhausen 27 Jan 1948), Banker.
[*Kelterhaus, 97355 Rüdenhausen, Germany*].
3. Count *Paul* Anton, *b* at Lisbon 15 May 1962, Banker; *m* at Venice 17 April (civ) and 22 April (relig) 1989, Countess Damiana (*b* at Lima, Peru 31 March 1961), Dr of Phil, dau of Count Massimilian Lovatelli and Countess Francesca Foscari, and has issue,
[*Schloß Platz 1, 97353 Wiesentheid, Germany*].

    1. Count *Franz* Georg Filipp Paul Maria, *b* at Würzburg 2 March 1990.

    2. Count *Alexander* Maximilian, *b* at Würzburg 17 June 1991.

    3. Count *Johannes* Damian, *b* at Würzburg 17 June 1991 (twin with Count Alexander).

    4. Countess *Benedicta* Olga, *b* at Würzburg 12 April 1993.

    5. Count *Georg* Friedrich, *b* at Würzburg 31 Aug 1995.

    6. Count *Michael* Maria, *b* at Würzburg 16 Aug 1997.

Brother of Father

1. Count *Rudolf* Erwein Ernst, *b* at Würzburg 1 Oct 1918, Proprietor of Heusenstamm and Weiler, Kt of Hon Sovereign Military Order of Malta; *m* 1stly at Regensburg 18 April (civ) and 29 April (relig) 1947 (*m* annulled at Bamberg 4 Nov and at Würzburg 30 Nov 1967 and diss by div at Munich 5 Sept 1968), Princess Helene (*b* at Schloß Haus, nr Regensburg 27 May 1924; ✝ at Monte Carlo 27 Oct 1991, since their divorce she reverted to her maiden name), dau of Franz Joseph, 9th Prince (Fürst) von Thurn and Taxis and Infanta Elisabeth of Portugal and had issue,

    1. Count *Albert* Ernst Erwein Franz-Joseph Maria, *b* at Würzburg 20 Feb 1948, Dr of Law, Lawyer, Tax Consultant; *m* at St Gilgen am Wolfgangsee 15 Feb 1975 (*m* diss by div at Munich 13 Oct 1993), Ilona (*b* at Bad Driburg 13 Oct 1947; *m* 2ndly 27 Jan 1994, Emmanuel Wiemer), dau of Hans-Günther Dietrich and Christa Hahn, and has issue,
[*Vierheiligstraße 9, 81545 Munich, Germany*].

        1. Count *Moritz* Philipp Alexander, *b* at Munich 24 Feb 1977.
        [*Vierheiligstraße 9, 81545 Munich, Germany*].

        2. Count *Konstantine* Max Ferdinand, *b* at Munich 2 Oct 1979; ✝ at London 26 Nov 1998.

    2. Count Johannes (*Johann*) Philipp Gabriel Kilian Karl Maria Elisabeth, *b* at Würzburg 3 July 1949; *m* at Donaueschingen 16 April 1977 (*m* diss by div at Munich 7

March 1980), Princess Marie-Antoinette [*Ziegelstadel 9, 86911 Diessen-St. Georgen am Ammersee, Germany*] (*b* at Donaueschingen 15 May 1949; she *m* 2ndly at Pöcking 15 Dec 1980, Thomas Bagusat), dau of Joachim Egon, 10th Prince (Fürst) zu Fürstenberg and Countess Paula zu Königsegg-Aulendorf.

[*R.D.1, P.O. Box 136 Delancy, NY 13752, U.S.A.*].

3. Countess *Gabriela* Helen Elisabeth Margarethe Anna Fernanda, *b* at Würzburg 16 Oct 1950; *m* at Keilberg 29 July (civ) and at Pommersfelden 27 Sept (relig) 1969, Alexander, 7th Prince (Fürst) zu Sayn-Wittgenstein-Sayn (*b* at Salzburg 22 Nov 1943).

[*56170 Bendorf-Sayn bei Koblenz, Germany*].

4. Count *Peter* Andreas Edmund Maria Johannes, *b* at Regensburg 10 Nov 1954, Businessman; *m* at Monaco 9 April 1994, Bénédicte (*b* at Monaco 10 June 1964), dau of Jean Marie Courtin and Marie Jeanne Marquet, and has issue,

[*Villa l'Oasis, 589 Chemin du Cros, 06190 Roquebrune-Cap Martin, France*].

    1. Countess *Alana* Maria Jeanne, *b* at Monaco 4 Dec 1994.

    2. Countess *Janina* Maria Isabelle, *b* at Monaco 30 Dec 1995.

Count Rudolf *m* 2ndly at Heusenstamm 20 Nov (civ) and at Schloß Sprinzenstein 14 Dec (relig) 1969, Countess Katharina (*b* at Linz an der Donau 9 July 1943) dau of Lelio, Count Spannocchi and Countess and Baroness Gabriele von and zu Sprinzenstein and Neuhaus, and has further issue,

(*Sprinzenstein 3, 4150 Rohrbach, Upper Austria; Podere Calamassi 2, 58021 Bagno di Gavorrano, Italy*).

5. Countess *Elisabeth* Teresa Gabriela Maria, *b* at Würzburg 19 Feb 1971.

[*Sprinzenstein 3, 4150 Rohrbach, Upper Austria; Podere Calamassi 2, 58021 Bagno di Gavorrano, Italy*].

6. Count *Franz* Erwein Georg, *b* at Würzburg 15 May 1974.

[*Parkstraße 2-4, 94032 Passau, Germany*].

Brother of Great Grandfather

Issue of Clemens, Count von Schönborn-Wiesentheid, Count and Lord of Wiesentheid (*b* 8 Oct 1810; ✝ 24 Aug 1877) and Countess Irene Batthyány von Német-Ujvar (*b* 30 Dec 1811; *m* 20 Oct 1838; ✝

25 April 1891), having had issue, among whom,

Son
Count *Clemens* Philipp Erwein, *b* at Schloß Hallburg, nr Volkach
am Main 12 July 1855; ✠ at Bayrischzell, Bavaria 1 Jan 1938, Lt.-Col.
Prussian Army, Kt Sovereign Military Order of Malta; *m* at Laband,
Silesia 5 Oct 1892, Baroness Maria-Rosario (*b* at Laband 5 Oct 1873;
✠ at Bayrischzell 2 July 1943), Dame Star Cross Order, Dame
Bavarian Order of St Theresia, dau of Bernhard, Count von Welczek
and Countess Luise Hatzfeld zu Trachenberg, and had issue, among
whom,

Son
Count *Clemens* Franz Erwein Wilhelm Arthur Bonifacius, *b* at
Munich 3 April 1905; ✠ at Sofia 30 Aug 1944, Col German Airforce;
m at Iszka Szent-György, Kom Fejér, Hungary 20 April 1933,
Countess Dorothea (*b* at Iszka Szent-György 29 May 1908; ✠ at
Munich 24 Sept 1991), dau of Siegfried, Count zu Pappenheim,
Proprietor of Iszka Szent-György, and Countess Elisabeth Károlyi
de Nagy-Károly, and had issue,

> 1. Countess *Priscilla* Irene Franziska Elisabeth Maria Barbara,
> *b* at Munich 5 Feb 1934; *m* at Pommersfelden 21 June 1956,
> Franz Josef, Count von Waldburg-Zeil-Hohenems (*b* at Chur
> 7 March 1927), Proprietor of Hohenems.
> [*Schloß Platz 8, 6845 Hohenems, Vorarlberg, Austria*].
> 2. Count *Manfred* Clemens Siegfried Karl Theodor, *b* at
> Munich 19 May 1935; ✠ at Munich 4 June 1989, Kt of Hon
> and Dev Sovereign Military Order of Malta, Banker; *m* at
> Munich 28 Jan (civ) and at Vienna 19 Feb (relig) 1966,
> Princess Margit (*b* at Budapest 11 April 1934), dau of Ladislaus
> (László), Prince Esterházy von Galántha and Countess Maria
> (Marietta) Erdödy de Monyorókerék Monoszló, and has issue,
> [*Hauptplatz 8, 7442 Lockenhaus, Austria; Akademiestraße
> 2, 1010 Vienna, Austria*].

>> 1. Count *Nicolaus* Georg Clemens Eustachius, *b* at
>> Innsbruck 14 Sept 1966, Carpenter.
>> [*Akademiestraße 2, 1010 Vienna, Austria*].
>> 2. Countess *Clarissa* Marie Sophie Eleonore, *b* at
>> Vienna 14 Oct 1967, Fashion Designer; *m* at
>> Lockenhaus, Burgenland 13 Sept 1996, Léon de La

Torre Krais (*b* at Madrid 7 July 1969), Secretary to Spanish ambassador.
[*Calle Monte Esquinza 16, 28010 Madrid, Spain; Royal Spanish Embassy, Quito, Ecuador*].

3. Countess *Melinda* Katharina Margit Dorothea, *b* at Vienna 20 Oct 1970.
[*Böddigheide Weg 32, 48167 Münster, Germany*].

4. Countess *Maria-Christina* Margit Helene, *b* at Frankfurt-am-Main 19 Feb 1974, Graphic Designer; *m* at Lockenhaus 12 Aug 2000, Martin Kammerlander (*b* at ......).
[*Akademiestraße 2, 1010 Vienna, Austria*].

3. Countess *Clarissa* Rosario Luisa Dorothea, *b* at Jüterbog 14 Oct 1936; *m* at Munich 23 May (civ) and at Pommersfelden 21 June (relig) 1956, Aloysius (Alois), Count von Waldburg zu Zeil and Trauchburg (*b* at Schloß Zeil 20 Sept 1933).
[*Ratzenried, 88260 Argenbühl, Allgäu, Germany; Im Hohn 13, 53177 Bonn - Bad Godesberg, Germany*].

4. Count *Franz Clemens* Karl Alexander Hubertus, *b* at Breslau 3 Oct 1939, Bank Director; *m* 1stly at Vevey, nr Lausanne 6 Jan (civ) and 14 Jan (relig) 1964 (*m* diss by div at Zurich 21 Feb 1974 since when she has reverted to her maiden name), Princess Tatjana [*21 Chemin de la Fontanetaz, 1009 Lausanne-Pully, Switzerland*] (*b* at New York 25 July 1940), dau of Konstantin Alexandrovitch, Prince (Fürst) Gortschakov and Maria Alexandrovna Vyrubov, and has issue,

    1. Count *Clemens* Franz Alexander Constantin Eustachius, *b* at New York 29 Sept 1964.
    [*21 chemin de la Fontanetaz, 1009 Pully, Switzerland*].

    2. Count *Constantin* Manfred Sebastian Lothar-Franz, *b* at Zurich 29 March 1966.
    [*21 chemin de la Fontanetaz, 1009 Pully, Switzerland*].

    3. Countess *Alexandra* Maria Dorothea Nadine Cecilia, *b* at Zurich 2 June 1967; *m* 1stly at Pully, Switzerland 4 Nov 1989 (*m* diss by div 20 Feb 1995), Dom Pedro de Mello de Vasconcellos e Souza (*b* at Cascais 9 Aug 1965); *m* 2ndly at Geneva 17 June 2000, Prince Don Francesco of Bourbon-Two Sicilies (*b* at Ravensburg 20 June 1960), Kt Order of St Januarius.

[*21 chemin de la Fontanetaz, 1009 Pully, Switzerland*].

Count Franz Clemens *m* 2ndly at Munich 25 Oct 1974 (*m* diss by div 10 March 1992), Princess Felizitas [*La Renardière, 7 chemin de Mapraz, 1225 Chene-Bourg, Kt. Genève, Switzerland*] (*b* at Mauritzen, Bez Frohnleiten, Styria 26 Oct 1946; *m* 1stly at Rabertshausen, Kr Giessen 1 July (civ) and at Graz 9 July (relig) 1967, Peter, Prince zu Sayn-Wittgenstein-Berleburg; that *m* diss by div at Munich 3 July 1974), dau of Heinrich III, Prince Reuss and Baroness Franziska Mayr von Melnhoff, and has further issue,

[*218 East 70th Street, Apt 3B, New York, NY 10021, U.S.A.*].

    4. Count *Gregor* Franz Friedrich Karl Teilhard, *b* at Geneva 18 April 1977.

[*La Renardière, 7 chemin de Mapraz, 1225 Chene-Bourg, Kt. Genève, Switzerland*].

LINE III (Bohemian):
SCHÖNBORN

Founded by Count Friedrich Carl (*b* 2 Aug 1781; ✠ 24 March 1849); Hereditary Member of the former Austrian House of Lords since 1881.

Members of this Line bear the title of Count or Countess von Schönborn but are not entitled to the predicate of Erlaucht (Illustrious Highness).

Johann **PHILIPP** Maria Karl Herbert Ferdinand, **COUNT (GRAF) VON SCHÖNBORN**, *b* at Prague 27 Jan 1943, Photographer, *succ* his father, son of Hugo-Damian, Count von Schönborn (*b* 22 Sept 1916; ✠ 6 March 1979) and Baroness Eleonore von Doblhoff (*b* 14 April 1920; *m* 10 May 1942; *m* diss by div 1959); *m* at Altenmuhr, Franconia 10 Oct 1970, Adelheid (*b* at Berlin-Gatow 16 Sept 1938), Landscape Designer, dau of Friedrich (Fritz) von Buchwaldt and Elisabeth Charlotte (Liselotte) von Le Suire. [*Georgenstraße 4, 80799 Munich, Germany*].

Daughters

1. Countess *Johanna* Maria, *b* at Gunzenhausen 14 Nov 1972. [*91735 Muhr am See, Germany*].
2. Countess *Anna* Katharina, *b* at Gunzenhausen 7 Nov 1979. [*91735 Muhr am See, Germany*].

Brothers and Sister

2. Count *Christof* Maria Michael Hugo Damian Peter Adalbert, *b* at Skalken 22 Jan 1945, former Prof. at Fribourg university, Switzerland; Father in Dominican Order at Vienna since 27 Dec 1970, Cardinal Archbishop of Vienna.

[*Erzbischöfl. Palace, Wollzeile 2, 1010 Vienna, Austria*].

3. Countess *Barbara* Maria Anna Michaela Elisabeth, *b* at Graz 23 Sept 1947; *m* 1stly at Paris 22 March 1973 (*m* diss by div at Paris 22 Oct 1984), Daniel Manchon (*b* at Paris 21 March 1934), Photographer; *m* 2ndly at Schruns, Vorarlberg 22 Sept 1985, Maurice Dor de Lastours (*b* at Paris 17 March 1948).

[*Gruchy-Saon, 14330 Le Molay Littry, France*].

4. Count *Michael* Anatol Maria Hugo Karl, *b* at Schruns 2 Nov 1954, Actor; *m* at Hamburg 30 Aug 1995, Barbara (*b* at Bad Ischl 2 Feb 1962), dau of Heinrich Neureiter and Elisabeth ..

[*Simon von Utrechtstraße 391, 20359 Hamburg, Germany*].

Mother

Eleonore Ottilie Hilda Marie, Dowager Countess von Schönborn, *b* at Brünn 14 April 1920; Dame, Star Cross Order, dau of Herbert, Baron von Doblhoff and Gertrud von Skutezky; *m* at Prague 10 May 1942 (*m* diss by div at Feldkirch 13 March 1959), Hugo-Damian, Count von Schönborn (*b* at Lukawitz 22 Sept 1916; ✠ at Vienna 6 March 1979), Painter.

[*Monjolastraße 48, 6780 Schruns, Vorarlberg, Austria*].

Stepmother

Johanna, Countess von Schönborn, *b* at Graünd 29 Jan 1935, dau of Josef Moser und Maria Egger; *m* at Vienna 10 May 1963, Hugo-Damian, Count von Schönborn (*b* at Lukawitz 22 Sept 1916; ✠ at Vienna 6 March 1979), Painter.

[*Czerninplatz 1, 1020 Vienna, Austria*].

Sisters of Father

Issue of Karl Johann, Count von Schönborn (*b* 28 Nov 1890; ✠ 31 Aug 1952) and his 1st wife, Countess Elisabeth von Nostitz-Rieneck (*b* 18 May 1890; *m* 9 June 1914; *m* diss by div 21 June 1920; ✠ 19 March 1984), among whom,

1. Countess Maria *Johanna* Nepomucena Olga Desideria Philippa, *b* at Lukawitz 23 May 1915; *m* at Salzburg 27 Nov 1937 (*m* diss by div at Munich 28 April 1960), Ferdinand, Baron von Skal and

Gross-Ellguth (*b* at Endersdorf, Grottkau 9 July 1903; ✠ at Munich 20 Sept 1972), Proprietor of Jungferndorf and Schwarzwasser, Silesia.

[*Schwefelstraße 30, 9490 Vaduz, Liechtenstein*].

2. Countess Maria *Anna* Elisabeth Cyrilla Franziska von Paula, *b* at Prague 29 March 1919; bears the name Sister Theresia.

[*Kloster, 84539 Zangberg, Germany*].

Brother of Grandfather

Issue of Johann, Count von Schönborn (*b* 3 April 1864; ✠ 7 June 1912) and Countess Anna von Wurmbrand-Stuppach (*b* 23 April 1868; *m* 17 June 1889; ✠ 2 March 1938) among whom,

Son

Count *Heinrich* Maria Johann Adalbert Alexander Aloys, *b* at Prague 13 Feb 1895; ✠ at Neuhaus, nr Schliersee, Bavaria 11 Oct 1976, Lt.-Col., Businessman; *m* at Prague-Karolinental 7 Oct 1936, Margarethe (*b* at Graslitz 29 July 1910; ✠ at North Hollywood, California 20 Nov 1991; *m* 1stly at Prague 15 April 1933, Nikolaj R Peter who ✠ 1947; *m* diss by div at Prague 25 Feb 1936), dau of Bruno Wilhelm Gerstenberger and Josephine Riedl, and had issue,

    1. Count *Alexander* Maria Karl Heinrich Franz, *b* at Prague 29 Jan 1938, Professor; *m* 1stly at Seattle, Washington 14 June 1970 (*m* diss by div at Austin, Texas 10 April 1975), Maureen (*b* at Hollywood, California 29 Sept 1943), dau of Rosaire Honoré Dufault and Kathleen Ann McNiece. He *m* 2ndly at Corpus Christi, Texas 12 Aug 1978, Mary Leona (*b* at Mason, Texas 4 Oct 1955), dau of Gordon Grote and June L Visor, and by her has issue,

    [*3308 Crawford Street, Columbia, MO. 65203, U.S.A.*].

        1. Count *Damian* Andreas, *b* at Columbia, Missouri 14 July 1987.

    2. Countess Maria *Elisabeth* Anna Henriette Dionysia, *b* at Prague 9 Oct 1940; *m* 1stly at Los Angeles, California 27 Jan 1962 (*m* diss by div at Los Angeles 14 Nov 1978), James Christian Specht (*b* at Los Angeles 13 June 1938). She *m* 2ndly at Los Angeles 7 Feb 1979, Glen Lee Hollinger (*b* at Los Angeles 24 June 1936), Dr of Med.

    [*2040 Dublin Drive, Glendale, CA. 91206, U.S.A.*].

    3. Count Maria *Lothar Franz* Maria Hugo Damian Eduard, *b* at Prague 9 June 1943.

[*1831 Hollyvista Avenue, Los Angeles, CA. 90027, U.S.A.*].

Brothers of Great-Grandfather

Issue of Karl, Count von Schönborn (*b* 10 April 1840; ✚ 29 May 1908) among whom,

Sons

A) - by First Wife: Princess Johanna von Lobkowicz (*b* 16 June 1840; *m* 11 Sept 1861; ✚ 5 Aug 1872).

    1. Count Maria *Friedrich* Karl Johann Joseph Eugen Franz von Assisi, *b* at Malesitz 4 Oct 1865; ✚ at Vienna 23 Aug 1919, Lt Austrian Army; *m* at Prague 21 May 1898, Princess Sofie (*b* at Loham, Kr Bogen, Bavaria 11 Oct 1871; ✚ at Bad Tölz 7 Sec 1959), Dame of Hon Bavarian Order of St Theresia, dau of Constantin, Prince Cantacuzène and Victoria Nádherny von Borutin, and had issue,

        1. Count Maria *Paul* Franz von Paula Perceval Christinus Anton Demetrius Alois Joseph Theodosius, *b* at Egern 29 May 1900; ✚ at Correze 2 Jan 1984, Dr of Law. He adopted a daughter,

            1. *Alice* Gabriele Anna Weissenberger, *b* at Neuenkirchen, Lower Austria 27 Sept 1923, bears the name Schönborn, dau of Karl Weissenberger and Josefine Görner, adopted at Vienna 4 Dec 1954 and at Berlin-Charlottenburg 1955; *m* 1stly at Vienna 20 July 1944 (*m* diss by div at Vienna 19 April 1949), Hans Klitzner (*b* at Duppau, Kr Kaaden 26 Aug 1919). She *m* 2ndly at Vienna 28 Sept 1949 (*m* diss by div at Vienna 7 July 1950), Heinrich (Hainz), Count von Gudenus, adopted Ziffer (*b* at Hainfeld, Lower Austria 14 Feb 1919). She *m* 3rdly at Munich 4 May 1956, John William Scott (*b* at Ottawa, Kansas, USA 13 Oct 1903), Businessman.

        [*Hasenauerstraße 30, 1190 Vienna, Austria*].

B) - by Second Wife: Countess Zdenka von Sternberg (*b* 16 April 1846; *m* 13 Sept 1875; ✚ 16 Sept 1915):

    2. Count *Zdenko* Maria Karl Wilhelm, *b* at Prague 10 Feb 1879; ✚ at Krumbach, Schwaben 11 Feb 1960; *m* at Prague

9 May 1905, Countess Marie (*b* at Seehof 22 Feb 1886; ✝ at Rheydt 20 Jan 1940), Proprietor of Kauth-Chodenschloss, Bez. Taus, Bohemia, dau of Gerolf, Count von Coudenhove, Proprietor of Seehof, Elfershausen, etc, and Countess Gisela von Stadion-Warthausen and Thannhausen, and had issue, among whom,

    1. Count *Gerolf* Max Karl Zdenko Rudolf Heironymus Maria, *b* at Chlum 30 Sept 1915; ✝ at Wiesbaden 27 April 1991, Proprietor of Kauth-ChodenSchloß, Businessman; *m* 1stly at Munich 5 Nov 1942, Blanka (*b* at Biberach an der Riss 24 May 1916; ✝ at Seon, Kt Aargau 24 Oct 1943), dau of Alfons Knapp and Blanka Lautenschlager. He *m* 2ndly at Wiesbaden 22 Aug 1953, Johanna-Maria (*b* at Braunsweig 22 June 1924; ✝ at Ehingen, Württemberg 18 Aug 1969; *m* 1stly at Wiesbaden 18 March 1948, Udo von Oven; that *m* diss by div at Wiesbaden 27 May 1952), dau of Maximilian Alberts and Johanna von Carnap. He *m* 3rdly at Wiesbaden 17 Nov 1972, Ilse (*b* at Lübeck 30 Jan 1922), dau of Dionys Gemündt and Mathilde Beez.
[*Kirchbachstraße 34, 65191 Wiesbaden, Germany*].
    2. Count *Zdenko* Friedrich Franz Edmund Theophil Cajetan Maria, *b* at Prague 22 April 1917; ✝ at Oberstadion 18 March 1993, Proprietor of Oberstadion, near Ehingen, Württemberg; *m* 1stly at Munich 5 Dec 1939 (*m* diss by div at Munich 5 Nov 1947), Ingeborg (Inge) (*b* Munich 9 May 1918; ✝ at Munich 10 Sept 1999), dau of Nikolaus (Klaus) von Bomhard and Mathilde (Thilda) Oldenbourg. He *m* 2ndly at Oberstadion 29 Nov 1947 (*m* diss by div at Munich 13 Feb 1952), Maria Johanna (*b* at Regensburg 17 July 1922; ✝ at Kempten, Allgäu 22 April 1981), dau of Georg Hirsch and Babette Oberdorfer. He *m* 3rdly at Munich 13 Dec 1954, Katharina (*b* at Würzburg 19 March 1911; ✝ at Oberstadion 7 Feb 1967; *m* 1stly at Munich 22 May 1950, Hans Pfingstler; that *m* diss by div at Munich 15 Nov 1954), dau of Josef Märkl and Katharina Heil. He *m* 4thly at Oberstadion 21 March 1968, Margret (*b* at Therwil, Kt Basel 12 June 1927), dau of Anton Gschwind and Madelaine Beuret, and has issue by his first wife,

[89613 Oberstadion, Kr. Ehingen, Württemberg, Germany].

    1. Count *Alexander* Friedrich, *b* at Munich 5 June 1941; *m* 1stly at Schöntal an der Jagst 12 Sept 1966 (*m* diss by div at Günzberg 19 Oct 1996), Countess Mechtilde (*b* at Heidelberg 20 Oct 1937), dau of Friedrich-Hermann, Count von Zeppelin-Aschhausen, Proprietor of Aschhausen and Buchhof and Countess Elisabeth Zedtwitz von Moraván and Duppau, and has issue,

        1. Count *Johann-Philipp* Konstantin Alexander Zdenko Friedrich-Wilhelm Alfred, *b* at Munich 14 Sept 1967; *m* at Erbach 5 Sept 1998, Baroness Concordia (*b* at Ulm 5 May 1969), dau of Franz, Baron von Ulm zu Erbach and Countess Adelheid von Preysing-Lichtenegg-Moos.

        2. Count *Konstantin* Alexander Friedrich-Karl Ludolf Ludwig Burkhart Franz, *b* at Munich 7 Nov 1968.

        3. Count *Wolfgang* Georg Eugen Kurt, *b* at Munich 5 May 1973.

Count Alexander *m* 2ndly at Ziemetshausen 6 Dec 1996, Elisabeth (Sissy) (*b* at ... 24 Nov 1959), dau of Bruno Fischer and Rosalie Miller, and has further issue,

    [v. Kiechendorff-Straße 28, 80470 Thannhausen, Schwaben, Germany].

        4. Countess *Marie-Christine* Sophie Therese Elisabeth, *b* at Augsburg 2 June 1993.

        5. Count *Franz-Georg* Albrecht Eugen Alexander Friedrich Maria, *b* at Augsburg 16 April 1995.

    2. Countess Angelika (*Angela*) Elisabeth, *b* at Oberstadion 24 Aug 1942; *m* 1stly at South San Gabriel, California 6 Nov 1965 (*m* diss by div at Santa Barbara, California ... 1971), Andrzej Jan Ruttié (*b* at Posen 6 Feb 1938).

She *m* 2ndly at Oberstadion 19 Sept 1975
(*m* diss by div at Munich 13 Oct 1985), Gerwin
Franzen (*b* at Eberswalde 2 Sept 1929). She *m*
3rdly at Ziemetshausen 16 Jan 1986, Wolfgang,
Prince zu Oettingen-Oettingen and Oettingen-
Wallerstein (*b* at Munich 1 Aug 1924).
[*Schloß Seyfriedsberg, 86473 Ziemetshausen,
Germany*].

3. Count Maria *Adalbert* Erwein Karl Laurenz, *b* at Malesitz
16 Aug 1881; ✠ at Klattau 18 Jan 1946, Imp and Royal
Chamberlain; *m* 1stly at Besin 18 June 1907, Countess Rosine
(*b* at Prague 14 Oct 1880; ✠ at Skotschitz, nr Budweis 23
Sept 1926), dau of Joseph, Count Czernin von and zu
Chudenitz and Countess Maria Des Fours-Walderode. He *m*
2ndly at Prague 1 June 1941, Baroness Selina (*b* at Horka an
der Iser 8 Sept 1911; ✠ at Prague 19 Oct 1953), dau of Alfred,
Baron von Ringhoffer and Countess Maria-Anna von Nostitz-
Rieneck, and had issue by his first wife, among whom,

1. Count Maria *Carl* Zdenko Adalbert Markus, *b* at
Linz 25 April 1910; ✠ at Bad Reichenhall 26 July
1991, Dr of Law; *m* 1stly at Wuppertal-Barmen 24
April (civ) and 25 April (relig) 1935 (*m* diss by div at
Wuppertal 23 Jan 1951), Ilse (*b* at Langerfeld, nr
Wuppertal 2 Dec 1908; ✠ at Thambach, nr Mühldorf
am Inn 11 July 1990; *m* 2ndly 30 June 1951, Michael
Albert Puhris; that *m* diss by div 23 June 1954 since
when she reverted to her previous married name of
Schönborn), dau of Georg Otto Pfarr and Pauline
(Paula) Hartmann. He *m* 2ndly at Burg an der Wupper
1 Feb 1961, Annelore (*b* at Barmen 11 March 1923;
m 1stly .. Züge), dau of Julius Dicke and Cläre
Altenhain, and had issue by his first wife,
[*Wittelsbacherstraße 28, 42287 Wuppertal - Barmen,
Germany*].

1. Countess *Edda* Maria Paula Charlotte, *b* at
Wuppertal-Barmen 21 Feb 1938; *m* at Bonn 24
Sept 1955 (*m* diss by div at Hamburg 22 July
1967), Wolf van Riesenbeck (*b* at Wuppertal 8
Nov 1931). She *m* 2ndly at Munich 6 May 1975,
Klaus Wondratscheck (*b* 6 May 1938), Lt.-Col.
[*Feldmochingerstraße 24, 80992 Munich,*

Germany].

Count Carl also adopted a daughter,

> *Dagmar* ...., *b* at Wernigerode, Harz 10 March
> 1940, (adopted), bears the name "Countess von
> Schönborn"; *m* at Munich 26 Aug 1961, Karl
> Anton Grünes (*b* at ... 8 May 1930), Engineer.
> [*Göggingerstraße 93a, 86199 Augsburg,
> Germany*].

SCHÖNBURG

This Seigneural family originated in Franconia and Thuringia and can be authenticated to Ulricus de Schunenberg (Sconenberg) documented in 1130, 1157 and 1161/6 in possession of the immediate territory of Geringswalde (passed to the Elector of Saxony in 1590) circa 1182, in possession of Glauchau 1256, of Lichtenstein 1286, of Waldenburg 1378. Descent can be proved from Hermannus de Sconeburg 1212 - 24; Imperial investiture of the county of Hartenstein in 1406; Frankfurt 31 July 1442; acquired the Lordships of Penig and of Wechselburg 1543, and the Lordship of Rochsburg 1548; received the dignity of Count of the Holy Empire with the qualification of "Hoch and Wohlgeboren", Vienna 7 Aug 1700; the House of Schönburg had two Seats in the former First Chamber of the Kingdom of Saxony since 4 Sept 1831; the lines below descend from two sons of Ernest von Schönburg (*b* 1484; ✝ 1534).

A. SUPERIOR LINE (Princely)

Founded by Hugo, Lord of Schönburg zu Glauchau and Waldenburg (*b* 8 Sept 1529; ✝ 4 Feb 1585); received the qualification of "Wohlgeboren", Regensburg 26 Oct 1640; Prince of the Holy Empire with the qualification of "Hochgeboren", Frankfurt-am-Main 9 Oct 1790; partition of the family possessions in 1813 between two sons of Prince Otto Carl Friedrich (*b* 2 Feb 1758; ✝ 29 Jan 1800), from whom the two branches below descend.

First Branch: SCHÖNBURG-WALDENBURG

Lutheran. Founded by Otto Viktor, 2nd Prince von Schönburg-Waldenburg (*b* 1 March 1785; ✝ 16 Feb 1859); Bohemian Incolat, Vienna 11 June 1818; received the qualification of "Durchlaucht" (primogeniture) by the German Diet 18 Aug 1825; recognised in Austria 4 Nov 1825; extended in Saxony to all descendants 29 Oct 1878.

Members of this branch bear the title of Prince or Princess von

Schönburg-Waldenburg with the qualification of Serene Highness.

ULRICH, 7TH PRINCE (FÜRST) VON SCHÖNBURG-WALDENBURG, Count and Lord von Waldburg and zu Glauchau,

Count von Hartenstein, *b* at Dresden 9 Oct 1940, *succ* his uncle, Wolf, 6th Prince (Fürst) von Schönburg-Waldenburg (*b* 1902; ✠ 1983), son of Prince Wilhelm von Schönburg-Waldenburg (*b* 3 April 1913; ✠ 11 June 1944) and Princess Marie-Elisabeth zu Stolberg-Rossla (*b* 1 Oct 1921; *m* 27 Sept 1939; ✠ 11 July 1975); *m* at Cologne 14 July 1972, Brigitte (*b* at Ravensburg 31 March 1943), dau of Norbert Hirschle and Hildegard Lucas.

Daughter

Princess *Verena* Alexandra Natalie, *b* at Cologne 3 Nov 1971.

Brother

Prince *Wolf Christoph*, *b* at Dresden 3 April 1943; *m* at Lüneburg 6 Dec 1968, Evelin (*b* at Hindenburg 6 June 1944), dau of Werner Mente and Johanna Kutter, and has issue,

> 1. Prince *Kai* -Philipp, *b* at Hamburg 24 April 1969; *m* at Brasilia 14 Jan 1994, Isabelle (*b* at Salvador, Brazil 13 May 1966), Painter, dau of Renelson Ribeiro Sampaio and Maria Hortencia Borges.

Brothers of Father

Issue of Prince Ulrich von Schönburg-Waldenburg (*b* 25 Aug 1869; ✠ 1 Dec 1939) and Princess Pauline zu Löwenstein-Wertheim-Freudenberg (*b* 16 Oct 1881; *m* 24 Feb 1900; ✠ 24 April, among whom,

1. **Wolf** Georg Alfred, **6th Prince (Fürst) von Schönburg-Waldenburg,** *b* at Dresden 26 Nov 1902; ✠ at Siena 24 Nov 1983; *succ* his kinsman, Günther, 5th Prince (Fürst) von Schönburg-Waldenburg (*b* 1865; ✠ 1960); *m* at Asciano 16 Oct 1944, Countess Luciana (*b* at Bologna 17 Jan 1921; ✠ at Siena 26 March 1984), dau of Luigi, Marquess Bargagli-Stoffi and Giuseppina Rovatti, and had issue,

> 1. Princess *Grazia* Dorothea Guglielmina, *b* at Asciano 4 March 1946; *m* at Asciano 26 Oct 1976, Nobile Gianfranco Vailati (*b* at Offanengo 17 Oct 1937).
> [*Villa di Lappeggi, 50011 Antella, Prov. Florence, Italy*].
> 2. Princess *Alessandra* Luisa Carlotte, *b* at Asciano 18 April

1949; *m* 1981, Riccardo di Tanturri Horatio (*b* ... 1 Nov 1944), Prof, Journalist.

3. Princess *Anna-Luisa* Ermanna Pia Cecilia, *b* at Asciano 22 Nov 1952; *m* at Rome 2 April 1977, Don Fabrizio Pignatelli della Leonessa of the Princes di Monteroduni (*b* at Rome 2 Aug 1952).

[*Via di Villa Ada 10, 00199 Rome, Italy*].

2. Prince *Georg* Ulrich, *b* at Guteborn 18 Nov 1908; ✣ at Ueberackern, Upper Austria 4 Aug 1982, Proprietor of Guteborn, Kt of Hon St John of Jerusalem; *m* at Burghausen, Kr Altötting 30 April (civ) and at Munich 4 May (relig) 1935, Countess Pauline (*b* at Langenzell 5 Sept 1906), dau of Otto, Count zu Castell-Castell and Princess Amélie zu Löwenstein-Wertheim-Freudenberg, and had issue,

[*Ueberackern, 5122 Ach, Upper Austria*].

   1. Princess *Anna-Amelie* Madeleine Charlotte Marie Therese Sibylle Ulrike, *b* at Frankfurt an der Oder 22 Jan 1936; ✣ at Frankenmarkt, Austria 7 Oct 1966; *m* at Hochburg, nr Ach, Austria 26 April 1962, Franz Salvator, Archduke of Austria (*b* at Wallseee, Austria 10 Sept 1927), Engineer.

   [*3313 Schloß Wallsee bei Amstetten, Upper Austria*].

   2. Princess *Clementine* Pauline Hermine Dorothea Antonie Ottilie, *b* at Frankfurt an der Oder 22 Jan 1936 (twin with Princess Anna-Amelie).

   [*Ueberackern, 5122 Ach, Upper Austria*].

   3. Princess *Stephanie* Pauline Amelie Walpurgis Alexandrine, *b* at Gusow 22 Sept 1938; *m* at Hochburg 17 Aug (civ) and 7 Sept (relig) 1960, Ludwig, Count von Waldburg zu Wolfegg and Waldsee, Proprietor of Assumstadt, (*b* at Pähl, nr Weilheim 15 June 1934).

   [*Schloß Assumstadt, 74219 Möckmühl - Züttlingen, Germany*].

   4. Princess *Luise* Pauline Amelie Vibeke Emma, *b* at Frankfurt an der Oder 12 Oct 1943; *m* at Burghausen 9 Sept 1968, Andreas, Prince zu Hohenlohe-Langenburg (*b* at Schwäbisch Hall 24 Nov 1938), Banker.

   [*Trianstraße 18a, 81804 Munich, Germany*].

Brother of Great-Grandfather

Issue of Prince Hugo von Schönburg-Waldenburg (*b* 29 Aug 1822; ✣ 9 June 1897) and Princess Hermine Reuss (*b* 25 Dec 1840; *m* 29 April 1862; ✣ 4 Jan 1890), having had issue, among whom,

Son

Prince *Heinrich,* Proprietor of Droyssig, Szelejewo and Quesnitz, Kr Weissenfels, Kt of Hon St John of Jerusalem, *b* at Droyssig 8 June 1863; ✠ at Rheda, Wesphalia 28 Dec 1945; *m* 1stly at Langenzell 5 Oct 1898, Princess Olga (*b* at Bonn 25 Oct 1880; ✠ at Heidelberg 1 July 1961; *m* diss by div at Leipzig 20 Aug 1920; *m* 2ndly at Frankfurt-am-Main 22 Oct 1922, Wolfgang, Prince zu Löwenstein-Wertheim-Freudenberg; that *m* diss by div at Berlin 8 Feb 1938), dau of Alfred, Prince zu Löwenstein-Wertheim-Freudenberg and Countess Pauline von Reichenbach-Lessonitz, and had issue, among whom,

    1. Prince *Hugo, b* at Droyssig 15 Oct 1910; ✠k nr Knutowa 16 Jan 1942, Lt; *m* at Leipzig 4 Nov 1937, Waltraut Benedicta (*b* at Sondershausen 2 July 1918; ✠ at Munich 2 Sept 1979; *m* 2ndly at Munich 17 Sept 1954, Jürgen von Goerne), dau of Wilko von Klüchtzner and Ottilie (Tilly) Greiner, and had issue,

        1. Princess *Michaela, b* at Berlin 9 March 1940; *m* 1stly at Fuschl 7 June 1963 (*m* diss by div at Bückeburg 12 Nov 1974), Alexander, Prince (Fürst) zu Hohenlohe-Jagstberg (*b* at Haltenbergstetten, Württemberg 25 Aug 1937), Lt-Col (Res). She *m* 2ndly at Wachtberg-Berkum 14 Feb 1975; (*m* diss by div at Munich 23 Jan 1985), Wolfgang, Prince zu Oettingen-Oettingen and Oettingen-Wallerstein (*b* at Munich 1 Aug 1924), Lt (Res). She *m* 3rdly Buenos Aires, Argentina 20 Sept 1985, Alfonso von der Becke-Klüchtzner (*b* at Buenos Aires 18 March 1929), Dr of Med, Consul (Ret).

        [*Libertador 1110-6-C, 1111 Buenos Aires, Argentina*].

Prince Heinrich *m* 2ndly at Schwalenberg, Lippe 14 July 1921, Princess Adelheid (*b* at Darmstadt 14 Oct 1884; ✠ at Frankfurt-am-Main 9 March 1961), dau of Friedrich, Count zur Lippe and Princess Marie zu Löwenstein-Wertheim-Freudenberg, and had further issue,

    4. Princess *Marie, b* at Droyssig 29 March 1922; *m* at Droyssig 19 Sept (civ) and 20 Sept (relig) 1944, Wolf-Dietrich, Baron von Wolzogen and Neuhaus (*b* at Berlin-Halensee 5 June 1910).

    [*Im Kirschenwäldchen 2A, 60437 Frankfurt-am-Main, Germany*].

Brother of Great-Great-Grandfather

Issue of Otto-Viktor, 2nd Prince von Schönburg-Waldenburg (*b* 1 March 1785; ✠ 16 Feb 1859) and Princess Thekla von Schwarzburg-Rudolstadt (*b* 23 Feb 1795; *m* 11 April 1817; ✠ 4 Jan 1861), having had issue, among whom,

Son

Prince *Karl Ernst,* *b* at Waldenburg 8 June 1836; ✠ at ... 1915, Proprietor of Gauernitz in Saxony, Schwarzenbach an der Saale mit Fahrenbühl, Förbau and Bug in Bavaria, Kt of Hon St John of Jerusalem; *m* at Peterswaldau 25 Nov 1863, Countess Helen zu Stolberg-Wernigerode (*b* 11 April 1840; ✠ at Gauernitz 2 Dec 1908), having had issue, among whom,

Son

Prince Viktor *Friedrich* Ernst, *b* at Gauernitz 20 Oct 1872; ✠ at Schwarzenbach an der Saale 27 Oct 1910 (Catholic since 5 June 1895) and annulled by the Holy See 26 May 1906), Princess Alicia (*b* at Pau 29 June 1876; ✠ at Bagecchia 20 Jan 1975; *m* 2ndly 3 June 1906, Col Lino del Prete who ✠ 11 Feb 1956), dau of Don Carlos de Bórbon, Duke of Madrid (Carlist claimant to the Spanish Throne) and Princess Margarita of Bourbon-Parma. He *m* 2ndly at Bamberg 19 Nov 1907, Franziska (*b* at Graz 30 June 1874; ✠ at Belgard, Pomm 9 Aug 1942), created Countess von Bug *ad personam* at Dresden 6 Dec 1907, dau of Alois Maison von Lobenstein and Maria Bechet, and had issue, among whom from his first wife,

Son

Prince Maria *Karl Leopold* Salvator Ernst Anton Joseph Franz Xaver Friedrich Bonifacius Benno Jaime, *b* at Gauernitz 2 June 1902; ✠ at Viareggio 19 Feb 1992, Proprietor of Gauernitz in Saxony and Schwarzenbach an der Saale, Kt of Hon and Dev Sovereign Military Order of Malta; *m* 1stly at Rome 6 June 1928 (*m* annulled ,,,,,), Ornella (*b* at Rome 16 June 1904; ✠ at ...), dau of Vincenzo, Count Ravaschieri Fieschi of the Dukes di Roccapiemonte and Donna Beatrice of the Princes Spada-Veralli-Pootenziani. He *m* 2ndly at Afaahiti, Tahiti 24 Sept 1955, Varaïterai (*b* at Teahavoa, Moorea 22 May 1915), dau of Tau a Neti and Tatumareva a Naume, and had issue (who bear the name "de Schoenburg"),

    1. Maria *Marewa, b* at Papeete 9 April 1939; *m* at Escublens, Kt Waadt 11 July 1964, Albert Colelough (*b* at Lausanne 17

Nov 1938).

[*34 avenue Verdeil, 1006 Lausanne, Switzerland*].

2. *Vetea* Pierre Jaime, *b* at Papeete 1 March 1941, Chemist; *m* at Divonne-les-Bains, Dept Ain 21 April (civ) and 22 April (relig) 1965, Catherine (*b* at Chambéry, Dept Savoie 10 June 1942), dau of André Brizard and Andrée Rehm, and has issue,

[*823 rue Guy de Maupassant, 01220 Divonne-les-Bains, France*].

    1. *Vaea* Isabelle, *b* at St Julien-en-Gènevois, Dept Haute-Savoie 5 Aug 1967.

    [*Route de Divonne, 01220 Sauverny, France*].

    2. *Thomas* Charles, *b* at St Julien-en-Gènevois 17 Jan 1971.

    3. *Benjamin* Teva, *b* at St Julien-en-Gènevois 2 May 1980.

3. *Teva* Karl Manuia Pai, *b* at Papeete 13 Oct 1945, Technician; *m* at Paea 18 Oct 1969, Hinano (*b* at Papeete 9 Jan 1948), dau of Henri Bernardino and Hélène Degage, adopted dau of Clifford Ratz, and has issue,

[*Aue, PK2, 5, Faa, Tahiti*].

    1. *Ei-Arii* Sandra Purea Eva, *b* at Papeete 21 June 1971.

    2. *Tamatoa* Arri Frederik Clifford, *b* at Papeete 4 Oct 1974.

4. *Mihimana* Christine, *b* at Afaahiti 17 Aug 1947; *m* at Collonge-Bellerive, nr Geneva 21 March 1970, Jean-Luc Maurer (*b* at Paris 17 June 1948).

[*Bellaison, Les Tattes Peuteys, 74140 Douvaine, Dept Haute-Savoie, France*].

5. *Matahi* Georges Léopold, *b* at Taravaoo 11 March 1951; *m* at Papeete 19 Oct 1974 (*m* diss by div at ... 1979), Severine Tea (*b* at Papeete ... 1947), dau of ... Hirshon and ..., and has issue,

[*Tohahotu, PK 4, Tahiti*].

    1. *Manu-Ura* Lewis, b at Papeete 27 Oct 1975.

2nd Branch: SCHÖNBURG-HARTENSTEIN

Catholic: Founded by Prince Heinrich Eduard (*b* 11 Oct 1787; ✝ 16 Nov 1872); received the qualification of "Durchlaucht" (primogeniture) by the German Diet 18 Aug 1825; extended to all

members of the family 27 April 1869; recognised in Austria 9 Oct 1843; Bohemian Incolat, Vienna 26 Sept 1845; Hereditary Member of the former Austrian House of Lords, 18 April 1861.
Members of this branch bear the title of Prince or Princess von Schönburg-Hartenstein with the qualification of Serene Highness.

Karl **ALEXANDER** Oktavian Franziskus Severin Maria, **8TH PRINCE (FÜRST) VON SCHÖNBURG-HARTENSTEIN,** *b* at Hartenstein 8 Jan 1930, *succ* his brother Hieronymus, 7th Prince (Fürst) von Schönburg-Hartenstein, son of Alexander, 5th Prince (Fürst) von Schönburg-Hartenstein (*b* 28 July 1888; ✠ 20 Jan 1956), and Princess Agathe von Auersperg (*b* 6 April 1888; *m* 2 April 1913; ✠ 13 Oct 1973); *m* at Vienna 16 Feb 1950, Princess Margarethe (*b* at Weidlingau 11 Sept 1928), Dame Star Cross Order, dau of Johann (Hans), Prince zu Windisch-Graetz and Lucie Wettel, and has issue, [*Krugerstraße 16, 1010 Vienna, Austria*].

Sons and Daughters

1. *Johannes* Karl Alexander Franziskus Alfred Valentin Maria, Hereditary Prince (Erbprinz) von Schönburg-Hartenstein, *b* at Vienna 7 Jan 1951, Mag jur; *m* at Mariazell, Steiermark 18 June 1977, Countess Alexandra (*b* at Diadema, Argentina 11 Aug 1953), Dame Star Cross Order, dau of Joseph Count von Attems-Gilleis and Countess Marie-Christine (Christa) von Thurn and Valsasina-Como-Vercelli, and has issue,
[*Schwind Gasse 7, 1040 Vienna, Austria*].

    1. Princess *Aglaë* Alexandra Johanna Stephanie Franziska Gobertine Maria, *b* at Vienna 26 Dec 1977; *m* at Grossweikersdorf, Lower Austria 30 June 2001, Maximilian Salzer (*b* at St Pölten 14 Sept 1976).

    2. Princess *Johanna* Alexandra Sophie Franziska Gabrielle Maria, *b* at Vienna 15 May 1979.

    3. Prince Aloys (*Louis*) Konrad Johannes Alexander Maximilian Felix Otto Maria, *b* at Vienna 20 Nov 1982.

    4. Princess *Franziska* Sophie Margarethe Alexandra Christine Zita Maria, *b* at Vienna 27 April 1985.

2. Prince *Alfred* Alexander Josef Antonius Gabriel Victor Maria, *b* at Vienna 23 Dec 1953, Dr of Law; *m* at Zell am See, Austria 14 Oct 1978, Marie Therese (*b* at Graz 5 April 1955), dau of Hermann Kastner-Lanjus and Elfriede Tausch, and has issue,
[*Rochus Gasse 11, 1030 Vienna, Austria; Schloß Stein, 08118 Hartenstein, Germany*].

1. Prince *Alexander* Alfred Andreas Eduard Philipp Eusebius Maria, *b* at Vienna 2 Aug 1979.
2. Princess *Caroline* Theresia Luise Anna Marcesine Fidelis Maria, *b* at Vienna 24 April 1981.
3. Prince *Ferdinand* Alfred Franz Karl Alexander Willibald Maria, *b* at Vienna 7 July 1984.
4. Princess *Marieluise* Theresia Pia Eleonore Kunigunde Maria, *b* at Vienna 3 March 1991.

3. Princess *Aglaë* Lucia Agathe Gabrielle Ferdinanda Maria, *b* 30 May 1955; *m* at St Benin d'Azy, Dept Nièvre, France 7 March (civ) and at Vienna 26 May (relig) 1984, Charles R Tyser (*b* at Oxford 16 Jan 1959), Farmer.
[*Château de St Benin d'Azy, 58270 St Benin d'Azy, France*].
4. Princess *Gabrielle* Mathilde Barbara Maria, *b* at Vienna 4 Dec 1959.
[*Gumpendorferstraße 49, 1060 Vienna, Austria*].

Brothers and Sisters

1. Princess *Eleonore Maria* Johanne Agathe Gobertina Victoria, *b* at Goldegg 23 Sept 1914; ✠ at Vienna 4 July 1986; *m* at Rome 25 July 1950 (*m* diss by div at .... 1961), Thomas A Emmet (*b* at New York 14 Oct 1915).
2. *Aloys* Franz Josef Hieronymus Maria, Hereditary Prince (Erbprinz) von Schönburg-Hartenstein, *b* at Goldegg 18 Aug 1916; ✠*k* in Prague 13 May 1945; *m* at Hartenstein 31 Dec 1944 (civ) and at Aue, Saxony 1 Jan 1945 (relig), Elisabeth (*b* at Frankfurt-am-Main 7 July 1920; ✠ at Medingen 13 Dec 1994), dau of Thilo von Trotha and Princess Ida zu Isenburg and Büdingen in Wächtersbach, and had issue,

    1. Alois **(Aloys)** Alexander Franz Joseph Hieronymus Thilo Michael Maria, **6th Prince (Fürst) von Schönburg-Hartenstein**, *b* posthumously at Munich 3 Oct 1945; ✠ there 18 April 1972.

3. Prince *Carl* Alexander Hieronymus Franz Maria, *b* at Goldegg 20 Feb 1918; ✠ at ... 31 July 1938.
4. Prince *Johannes* Rupprecht Franziskus Maria, *b* at Achensee, Tyrol 13 Sept 1919; ✠*k* nr Stalingrad Feb 1943.
5. **Hieronymus** Günther Maria, **7th Prince (Fürst) von Schönburg-Hartenstein**, *b* at Hartenstein 1 Nov 1920; ✠ at Kreuth 31 Oct 1992, Dipl Eng, since 1982 known as Brother Rupert OSB in the Benedictine Monastery of St Georgenberg-Fiecht, nr Schwaz, Tyrol; *m* at Munich 29 March (civ) and at Maxensruh, nr Immenstadt,

Allgäu 2 April (relig) 1946, Countess Mathilde (*b* at Munich 20 Sept 1905; ✠ in Natal, South Africa 6 July 1981), Dame Star Cross Order, dau of Gottfried, Count von Tattenbach and Countess Maria von Quadt zu Wykradt and Isny.

6. Princess *Johanna* Aglae Eleonore Maria, *b* at Hartenstein 6 June 1922; ✠ at Ereichsdorf 2 Nov 1985, Dame Star Cross Order; *m* at Vienna 16 Feb (civ) and 18 Feb (relig) 1943, Ignaz, Count von Attems (*b* at Vienna 23 June 1918; ✠ at Ebreichsdorf 24 Feb 1986).

7. Prince *Adolf* Alexander Karl Maria, *b* at Vienna 8 Dec 1923; ✠*k* nr Schlüsselburg, Russia 2 May 1944.

8. Prince *Alfred* Karl Paul Maria, *b* at Hartenstein 27 Feb 1926; ✠*k* nr St Avold, Saar 26 Nov 1944.

9. Prince *Herward*, *b* at Hartenstein 2 Oct 1927; ✠*k* nr Othfresen, Harz 10 April 1945.

10. Princess *Karoline* Constantine Rosa Maria, *b* at Graz-Ragnitz 18 Feb 1931; *m* at Panama City 30 July (civ) and 31 July (relig) 1987 (*m* diss by div ...), Mario Laserna Pinzon (*b* at Paris 21 Aug 1923), Ambassador (Ret).

[*Schwarzenburgplatz 10, 1040 Vienna, Austria*].

11. Prince *Constantin* Rudolf, *b* at Graz-Ragnitz 11 July 1933, Dipl Eng, Architect; *m* at Vienna 4 Aug 1958, Mathilde (*b* at São Paulo 14 July 1929), dau of Juan Cayetan Hartenstein and Virginia Moyrano y Mora, and has issue,

[*Rua Nove de Julho 326, Santo Amaro, São Paulo, Brazil*].

    1. Prince *Alexander* Maria Constantin Pius Johannes, *b* at Vienna 11 March 1959, Art Director; *m* at Stainz 12 Dec 1982 (*m* diss by div at Graz 26 Aug 1984), Countess Marie Therese [*Försthaus Schöneck 64, 8510 Stainach, Austria*] (*b* at Brandhof 28 Aug 1962; *m* 2ndly 21 June 1993, Hans-Christian Hoschek; that *m* diss by div 15 April 1996), dau of Johann, Count von Meran and Ingrid Messner, and has issue,

        1. Prince *Constantin* Johann Maria Pius Alois Eduard, *b* at Graz 13 April 1983.

        [*Försthaus Schöneck 64, 8510 Stainach, Austria*].

Prince Alexander *m* 2ndly at Greenwich, Connecticut, USA 15 Sept 1990 (*m* diss by div at New York 14 July 1993), Elizabeth (*b* at New York 20 Sept 1965), dau of John J Kennedy and Rosemary Fitzgerald. He *m* 3rdly at New York 20 Feb 1995, Selma (*b* at São Paulo 19 April 1962), dau of Luiz Navarro and Evelina Simonini and, by her, has further issue,

[*Rua Tombadouro 1051, Chacara Flora, 04663-040 São Paulo,*

Brazil].

       1. Prince *Mathias* Maria Luiz Alexander Pius Herward Eduard, *b* at São Paulo 26 July 1995.

2. Prince *Michael* Maria Constantin Alois, *b* at Vienna 22 Feb 1960, BSc, MBA, Underwriter; *m* at Sant'Appiano, nr Florence 11 Oct 1997, Victoria (*b* at Rio de Janeiro 7 March 1957; *m* 1stly at Korneuburg, NÖsterreich 1 Aug 1978, Georg, Prince zu Fürstenburg; that *m* diss by div), dau of Guy Hunter Pullen and Maria Theresia Pullen.

[*Myliusstraße 31, 60323 Frankfurt-am-Main, Germany*].

3. Princess *Karoline* Mathilde Eleonore Maria Cayetana, *b* at Vienna 13 Feb 1962, Goldsmith; *m* at Bozen, STirol 10 July 1992 (civ) and at Punta del Este, Uruguay 6 March 1993 (relig), Gregor, Count Khuen von Belasi (*b* at Bozen 20 Oct 1961), Photographer.

[*Apartado 125, 07150 Andraitz, Mallorca, Spain*].

4. Princess *Christine* Mathilde Maria, *b* at São Paulo 16 Oct 1965, Goldsmith, Jewelry Designer.

[*E2 Sloane Avenue Mansions, Sloane Avenue, Chelsea, London SW3 3JJ*].

5. Prince *Eduard* Maria Constantin Heinrich Friedrich Alfred, *b* at São Paulo 1 Nov 1966, Underwriter, Kt of Hon and Dev Sovereign Military Order of Malta; *m* at São Paulo 8 April (civ) and 4 May (relig) 1996, Angela (*b* at São Paulo 9 Dec 1966), dau of Nelson Pinto e Silva and Gisela Margarethe Schifferdecker.

[*Rua Carvalho 1, Chacara Tres Caravelas, 04926-140 São Paulo, Brazil*].

6. Princess *Sophie* Mathilde Maria del Pilar Eugenia Josephine, *b* at São Paulo 15 Jan 1970.

[*Rua da Granja Julieta 9, Apt 62, 04721-060 São Paulo, Brazil*].

Brother of Grandfather

Issue of Alexander, 3rd Prince von Schönburg-Hartenstein (*b* 5 March 1826; ✝ 1 Oct 1896) and Princess Karoline von and zu Liechtenstein (*b* 27 Feb 1836; *m* 3 June 1855; ✝ 28 March 1885), having had issue, among whom,

Son

Prince *Johannes* Maria Aloys Otto Heinrich Alexander, *b* at Enzesfeld

12 Sept 1864; ✠ at Vienna 30 March 1937, Diplomat, Bailiff Gd Cross Sovereign Military Order of Malta, Kt Order of the Golden Fleece; *m* at Vienna 27 April 1897, Princess Sophie (*b* at Hlubosch 4 Oct 1878; ✠*k* at Vienna 10 Sept 1944), Dame Star Cross Order, dau of Karl, Prince (Fürst) and Herr zu Oettingen-Oettingen and Countess Ernestine Czernin von and zu Chudenitz, and had issue, among whom,

1. Prince *Aloys* Alexander, *b* at London 24 March 1906; *m* 1stly at London 20 Sept 1935, Dilys (*b* at Glamorgan, Wales 7 March 1912; ✠ at Tenby, Wales 3 Nov 1943), dau of Maj. ER Martens and Gladwys Williams, and has issue,

    1. Prince *Johannes* Carl, *b* at Linz 13 Feb 1938, Dipl Eng; *m* at Salzburg 20 July 1968, Karin (*b* at Graz 29 Nov 1937; *m* 1stly 30 Oct 1956, Peter, Ritter Seemann von Treuenwart; that *m* diss by div 3 June 1966), dau of Wolfgang Strohschneider and Charlotte von Foregger zum Greiffenthurn, and has issue,
    (*Josef Kainzstraße 8, 5020 Salzburg, Austria*].

        1. Princess *Sophie*, *b* at St Gilgen 8 Feb 1969; *m* at Salzburg 23 May 1995, Wolfgang Beindl (*b* at Salzburg 26 Jan 1966), Dr rer nat.
        [*Kleingmainer Gasse25, 5026 Salzburg, Austria*].
        2. Princess *Margarethe*, *b* at St Gilgen 17 Jan 1970.
        [*Getreide Gasse13, 5020 Salzburg, Austria*].

    2. Prince *Nikolaus* Alexander, *b* at Tenby 6 April 1940, Dr of Law; *m* at Mondsee 14 Aug 1969, Johanna (*b* at Korneuburg 4 Dec 1942), dau of August Fetter and Johanna Koch, and has issue,
    [*Bräunerstraße 7, 1010 Vienna, Austria*].

        1. Princess *Therese*, *b* at Vienna 8 Feb 1970, Mag jur; *m* at Vienna 5 Feb (civ) and 27 Feb (relig) 1993, Stephan, Ritter von Stockert (*b* at Vienna 10 Feb 1962), Dr of Law.
        [*Planken Gasse1, 1010 Vienna, Austria*].
        2. Prince *Johannes*, *b* at Vienna 20 April 1972, Mag rer oec.
        [*Bräunerstraße 7, 1010 Vienna, Austria*].

Prince Aloys *m* 2ndly at Salzburg 21 July 1949, Christine (*b* at Steeg, Austria 9 Nov 1924; *m* 1stly 4 Jan 1941, Franz

Forstinger who was ✠k 4 April 1945), dau of Wolfgang Strohschneider and Hertha Ramsauer, and has further issue, [*5351 Aigen-Voglhub bei Strobl am Wolfgangsee, Austria*].

        3. Prince *Michael* Alexander, *b* at Steeg 26 June 1950; ✠ there 10 May 1965.

        4. Prince *Alexander, b* at Bad Goisern, Austria 1 Oct 1955.

        [*5351 Aigen-Voglhub bei Strobl am Wolfgangsee, Austria*].

2. Princess Aloysia (*Louise*) Alexandra, *b* at London 24 March 1906 (twin with Prince Aloys); ✠ at Berlin 11 April 1976; *m* at Salzburg 31 Oct 1936, Otto von Simson (*b* at Berlin-Dahlem 17 June 1912; ✠ at Berlin 23 May 1993; he *m* 2ndly 27 Nov 1978, Altgräfin Marie Anne zu Salm-Reifferscheidt-Krautheim and Dyck, widow of Hon Alexander Campbell Geddes of the Barons Geddes).

3. Prince *Johannes* Maria Carl Alexander Anton, *b* at Bucharest 2 March 1908.

4. Prince *Peter* Karl Marie Anton Pius Benediktus Markus Johannes, *b* at Rome 25 April 1915; *m* 1stly at Tena, Columbia 8 Sept 1945 (*m* diss by div 1951) Lyna Elisa Clothilde [*Pelham Manor, Penfield, N.Y. 14526, U.S.A.*] (*b* at Brussels 3 June 1914), dau of Carlos Rodriguez and Carlota Maldonado, and has issue,

        1. Princess *Alexandra* Carlota Sophy, *b* at Bogotá 26 Sept 1946; *m* at New York 5 March 1981 (*m* diss by div at New York 19 March 1985), Taki Theodorakopoulos (*b* at Athens 15 Aug 1937).

        [*123 East 71st Street, New York, N.Y. 10021, U.S.A.*].

Prince Peter *m* 2ndly at Havanna 8 March 1951, Lee Russel (*b* at New York 27 Jan 1924), dau of Charles Maury Jones and Katharine Hoagland, and has further issue,

[*16 West 77th Street, New York, N.Y. 10024, U.S.A.*].

        2. Prince *Peter, b* at New York 1 March 1955, Dr of Law, Lawyer; *m* at Sandwich, New Hampshire, USA 8 Aug 1981, Jane West (*b* at Okinawa, Japan 1 April 1954), dau of David Black McGrath and Sally Carter Vincent, and has issue,

        [*1614 Bayita Lane NW, Albuquerque, NM 87107, U.S.A.*].

            1. Prince David *Johannes, b* at Albuquerque,

New Mexico 22 June 1987.
2. Prince Peter *Benjamin, b* at Albuquerque
26 May 1989.
3. Princess *Victoria, b* at New York 28 Dec 1958; *m* at
Claryville, New York 29 Aug 1987, Brian Marx Culhane
(*b* at New York 2 Sept 1954), Dr of Phil.
[*6719 Palatine Avenue N, Seattle, WA 98103, U.S.A.*].
5. Princess *Sophie* Marie Karoline Johanna Ernestine, *b* at
Vienna 19 April 1917; *m* at Bogotá, Columbia 30 July 1948,
Alberto Carillo Leiser (*b* at Barranquilla, Columbia 15 Aug
1920).
[*Carrera 9, Nr 93, Bogotá, Columbia*].

B. INFERIOR LINE (Comtale)
SCHÖNBURG-GLAUCHAU

Catholic: Founded by Wolf II, Lord of Schönburg zu Glauchau and
Waldenburg (*b* 30 Oct 1532; ✝ 8 Sept 1581), Lord (1566) of Penig,
Rochsburg and Wechselburg; his two grandsons founded the branches
below; received the qualification of "Erlaucht" (primogeniture) by
the German Diet 13 Feb 1829.
Members of this line bear the title of Count and Lord or Countess
and Lady von Schönburg-Glauchau with the qualification of
Illustrious Highness.

First Branch:
(✝ Extinct ✝)

Lutheran: Founded by Wolf Ernst, Lord (Herr) von Schönburg zu
Glauchau and Waldenburg (*b* 9 June 1589; ✝ 16 Feb 1590).

Second Branch:
Founded by Wolf Heinrich, Lord (Herr) von Schönburg zu Glauchau
and Waldenburg (*b* 7 Nov 1605; ✝ 5 Dec 1657); Hereditary Member
of the former House of Lords of the Kingdom of Saxony

ALEXANDER Georg Maria Ernst Heinrich István Ludwig Kisito
Hubertus,**COUNT and LORD VON SCHÖNBURG, COUNT
and LORD ZU GLAUCHAU AND WALDENBURG**, Lord
zu Penig, Wechselburg and Rochsburg *b* at Mogadiscio, Somalia 15
Aug 1969 (succeeded in place of his older brother as a consequence
of his brother's non-dynastic marriage - *see below*); son of Joachim,
Count and Lord von Schönburg-Glauchau (*b* 4 Feb 1929 ✝ 29 Sept

1998) and Countess Beatrix Széchenyi von Sárvár and Felsövidék (*b* 30 Jan 1930); *m* at Wolfsgarten nr Frankfurt-am-Main 22 May (relig) and at Berlin 30 April (civ) 1999, Princess *Irina* Verena (*b* at Munich 1 April 1971), only dau of Prince *Karl* Adolf Andreas of Hesse and Countess Yvonne Szápary von Muraszombath, Széchysziget and Szápar.

[*Carl-von-Ossietzky-Straße 7, 14471 Potsdam, Germany*].

Daughter

1. Countess *Maria-Letitia* Jolanta, *b* at Berlin 30 July 2001.

Brother and Sisters

1. Countess Maria-Felicitas (*Maya*) Alexandra Albertina Assunta Anna Fernanda Beatrix, *b* at Berlin-Steglitz 15 Aug 1958; *m* at Munich 29 Aug (civ) 1985 (*m* diss by div at London 15 July 1993), Friedrich Christian Flick (*b* at Sulzbach-Rosenberg 19 Sept 1944), Dr of Law.

[*Parkside House, Englefield Green, Surrey TW20 0XA*].

2. Countess *Mariae-Gloria* Ferdinanda Joachima Josephine Wilhelmine Huberta, *b* at Stuttgart-Degerloch 23 Feb 1960; *m* at Regensburg 30 May (civ) and 31 May (relig) 1980, Johannes, Prince (Fürst) von Thurn and Taxis (*b* at Schloß Höfling, nr Regensburg 5 June 1926; ✠ at Munich 14 Dec 1990).

[*Schloß Emmeramsplatz 9, 93047 Regensburg, Germany*].

3. *Carl-Alban* Maria László Gebhard Rudolf Johannes Georg Hubertus Kisito, (until 2 Sept 1995 Hereditary Count (Erbgraf) von Schönburg-Glauchau), *b* at Lomé, Togo 2 Feb 1966; *m* at London 1 Aug (civ) and at Hamburg 2 Sept (relig) 1995, Juliet (*b* at Hamburg 10 Aug 1966) dau of Nicholas Fowler and Countess Jutta von Pfeil and Klein-Ellguth, and has issue,

[*Ackermannstraße 18, 22087 Hamburg, Germany*].

    1. Count *Hubertus* Maria Joachim Nicholas Maximilian Leopold Carl Ludwig Denis, *b* at Hamburg 19 Dec 1996.

    2. Count *Benedikt* Maria Leopold Joseph Friedrich Jacob Fraanziskus Gelroy, *b* at Hamburg 7 Sept 1999.

Half-Sister

1. Countess *Anabel* Maya-Felicitas Sarah Christin, *b* at Munich 10 June 1980.

Mother

Beatrix, Countess von Schönburg-Glauchau, *b* at Hegykö, Hungary

30 Jan 1930, dau of Bálint, Count Széchenyi von Sárvár and Felsövidék and Princess Maria Pavlovna Galitzine, m at Wadersloh 21 Oct (civ) and at Münster 23 Oct (relig) 1957 (m diss by div at Munich 25 April 1986), Joachiem Heinrich Maria Carl Rudolf Franz Xaver Joseph Antonius Christopherus Hubertus, Count and Lord von Schönburg, Count and Lord zu Glauchau and Waldenburg (b at Glauchau 4 Feb 1929 ✠ at Röckmühle 29 Sept 1998), Journalist, Kt of Hon Sovereign Military Order of Malta.
[*Seybothstraße 56a, 81545 Munich 90, Germany*]

Step-Mother

Ursula, Dowager Countess von Schönburg-Glauchau, b at Gauting 30 April 1951, dau of Martin Zwicker and Dorothea Thiele; m at Munich 18 July 1986, Joachiem Heinrich Maria Carl Rudolf Franz Xaver Joseph Antonius Christopherus Hubertus, Count and Lord von Schönburg, Count and Lord zu Glauchau and Waldenburg (b at Glauchau 4 Feb 1929 ✠ at Röckmühle 29 Sept 1998), Journalist, Kt of Hon Sovereign Military Order of Malta.
[*Röcklmühle 1, 94529 Aicha vorm Wald, Germany*]

Brothers and Sisters of Father

1. Countess *Maria Franziska* Adelheid Josepha Philomena Coletta Rudolfine Octavie Theresia Dorothea Felicitax, b at Glauchau 5 March 1928.
[*Humboldstraße 10, 78166 Donaueschingen, Germany*].
2. Countess *Marie Octavie* Antonia Maximiliana Philomena Josepha Theresia Augustina, b at Wechselburg 13 June 1930; m at Stuttgart 7 June (civ) and at Heiligenberg, Baden 8 June (relig) 1953, Albert Bartels (b at Zerbst 17 Sept 1011; ✠ at Munich 1 May 1973), Dr of Med.
[*Vorder Gasse3, 55606 Bärweiler, Germany*].
3. Count *Rudolf* Maria Emil Franz Friedrich Carl Antonius Christopherus Hubertus Joseph Wenzel Michael, b at Wechselburg 25 Sept 1932, Hotel Director, Kt of Hon Sovereign Military Order of Malta, Bavarian Order of St George; m at Hechingen 19 May (civ) and at Donaueschingen 22 May (relig) 1971, Princess Marie-Louise (b at Konstanz 18 Sept 1945), Dame Star Cross Order, Pediatric Nurse, dau of Prince Victor of Prussia and Countess Marie-Antoinette Hoyos, Baroness zu Stichsenstein, and has issue,
[*Quinta Maria Louisa, Marbella, Prov. Malaga, Spain*].

    1. Countess *Sophie* Anastasia Wilhelmine Marie Antoinette,

b at Malaga 17 May 1979.

2. Count *Friedrich* Wilhelm Simeon Heinrich Dioysius Joachim Rudolf Maria Adalbert, *b* at Malaga 27 April 1985.

4. Countess *Maria Assunta* Adelheid Josepha Benedikta Philomena Theresia Pudentiana, *b* at Wechselburg 19 May 1935, Dame Star Cross Order; *m* at Heiligenberg, Baden 18 July (civ) and at Birnau am Bodensee 10 Sept (relig) 1958, Josef Ferdinand, Count von Oppersdorff (*b* at Ober-Altwaltersdorf 26 March 1922), Banker. [*Goethestraße 41, 80336 Munich, Germany*].

5. Count *Johannes* Ernst Heinrich Maria Carl Antonius Hubertus Christopherus Benedictus Georg, *b* at Wechselburg 10 June 1938, Banker, Kt of Hon Sovereign Military Order of Malta; *m* at Stuttgart 30 April (civ) and 17 May (relig) 1971 (*m* diss by div at Stuttgart 17 Jan 1986), Margarete (*b* at Schwenningen am Neckar 26 Nov 1936; she *m* 1stly at Stuttgart 18 Dec 1958, Martin Stephani; that *m* diss by div 26 Jan 1966) [*Schimmelweg 6, 7000 Stuttgart 60, Germany*], dau of Walter Bartler and Martha Grimm, and has issue, [*Karl Pfaffstraße 12B, 70597 Stuttgart, Germany*].

> 1. Countess *Marie Antonia* Josepha Huberta Margarete Beatreix, *b* at Stuttgart 30 Jan 1972, cand rer pol.
> [*Madenstraße 14, 70619 Stuttgart, Germany*].

6. Count Carl *Georg* Adam Ernst Heinrich Joseph Antonius Benedictus Christophorus Hubertus Sylvester Maria, *b* at Wechselburg 31 Dec 1940, Major, Kt of Hon Sovereign Military Order of Malta; *m* at Schwanewede 21 March (civ) and at Heggen 16 May (relig) 1970, Countess Madeleine (*b* at Ahausen, nr Finnentrop Sauerld 25 Feb 1949), dau of Ferdinand, Count von Spee, Proprietor of Ahausen and Baroness Huberta von Twickel, and has issue, [*Sandstraße 17, 71364 Winnenden-Breuningsweiler Germany; Rothenbaucherstraße 57b, 08371 Glauchau, Germany*].

> 1. Count Friedrich-*Christian* Carl Georg Hubertus Joachim Antonius Christophorus Paphnutius Timotheus Joseph Maria, *b* at Bremen 22 Aug 1971, Dipl Business Studies, 1st Lt.
> [*Sandstraße 17, 71364 Winnenden-Breuningsweiler Germany; Rothenbaucherstraße 57b, 08371 Glauchau, Germany*].

> 2. Countess *Stephanie* Maria Assunta Adelheid Madeleine Huberta Marina, *b* at Ansbach 30 Jan 1974, Banker.
> [*Sandstraße 17, 71364 Winnenden-Breuningsweiler Germany*].

> 3. Countess *Michaela* Maria Elisabeth Rudolfine Madeleine Huberta Jacoba, *b* at Würzburg 25 July 1975.

[*Sandstraße 17, 71364 Winnenden-Breuningsweiler Germany*].

4. Countess *Gabriela* Maria Octavia Walburga Huberta Madeleine Jacoba, *b* at Würzburg 25 July 1975 (twin with Countess Michaela).
[*Sandstraße 17, 71364 Winnenden-Breuningsweiler Germany*].

5. Count *Johannes*-Joachim Carl Georg Michael Wolf Heinrich Hubertus Antonius Christopherus Alban Maria, *b* at Albstadt-Ebingen 29 Sept 1976.
[*Sandstraße 17, 71364 Winnenden-Breuningsweiler Germany*].

7. Countess Maria *Josephine* Luitgarde Franziska Philomena Antonia Coletta Adelheid Gertrud Elisabeth, *b* at Wechselburg 16 Nov 1943; *m* at Lintorf, Düsseldorf 31 March (civ) and at Bad Waldsee 19 June (relig) 1971, Franz Egon, Baron von Wendt (*b* at Untermaubach 6 March 1944), Major.
[*Triftstraße 40b, 53919 Weilerswist, Germany*].

Brother and Sisters of Grandfather
Issue of Joachim, Count and Lord von Schönburg zu Glauchau and Waldenburg, etc (*b* 20 July 1873; ✠ 3 July 1943) and Countess Oktavia Chotek von Chotkowa und Wognin (*b* 5 May 1873; *m* 1 Oct 1898; ✠ 29 Nov 1946), among whom,

1. Countess *Maria Immaculata*, *b* at Wechselburg 22 Aug 1904; took the name of Sister Maria Antonia in the Benedictine Convent of St Gabriel.
[*Bertholdstein, 8350 Fehring, Steiermark, Austria*].

SCHWARZENBERG

Catholic: This family originated in Franconia and traces its descent from the Counts of Seinsheim; authenticated from Sifridus von Sowensheim (later Saunsheim, now Seinsheim, Lower Franconia, Bavaria) 1172; acquired the Lordship of Schwarzenberg (Franconia) 1405 - 1421; Baron of the Holy Empire, Pressburg 10 Oct 1429; Count of the Holy Empire with ratification of arms, Prague 5 June 1599; Bohemian Inkolat, Regensburg 25 April 1654; Hungarian Indigénat 1659; Prince of the Holy Empire (primogeniture), Vienna 14 July 1670; introduced into the Imperial College of Princes 22 Aug 1674;

Grand Palatine, Vienna 20 Oct 1671; Count of Sulz (near the Black
Forest, Württemberg) and Landgrave of Kleggau (near Schaffhouse)
through the marriage (21 May 1674) of Count Ferdinand (*b* 23 May
1652; ✠ 22 Oct 1703) to Marie Anne (*b* 24 Oct 1653; ✠ 18 July 1698),
daughter and heiress of the last Landgrave of Sulz and of Kleggau (✠
1687); joined the arms of Sulz, Vienna 8 Feb 1688; elevation of the
Landgraviate of Kleggau into a Princely Landgraviate, Vienna 20
July 1689; creation of two Majorats 22 Oct 1703 by the Testament of
Ferdinand Eusebius, 2nd Prince of Schwarzenberg; Duke of Krumau
28 Sept 1723 (inherited from the Princes of Eggenberg, 1719);
Bohemian Prince to all descendants, Vienna 5 Dec 1746; the title of
Prince of the Holy Empire was extended to all descendants, Vienna
5 Dec 1746; received the qualification of "Durchlaucht"
(primogeniture) by the German Diet 18 Aug 1825; recognised in
Austria 7 Oct 1825; this qualification was extended to all descendants
27 April 1869 (confirmed by the Ministry of the Interior 9 May
1869).
Members of the family bear the title of Prince and Princess zu
Schwarzenberg with the qualification of Serene Highness.

FIRST MAJORAT
(✠ Extinct ✠)

Founded by Josef, 6th Prince of Schwarzenberg (*b* 27 June 1769; ✠
19 Dec 1833); Hereditary Member of the former Austrian House of
Lords, Vienna 18 April 1861.
This line is now extinct in the male line; the last Prince, Joseph,
11th Prince of Schwarzenberg, was *succ* by his kinsman, Karl Johannes
7th and 12th Prince zu Schwarzenberg (2nd Majorat - see below).

✠ **JOSEPH** Maria Adolphius Pius Titus, **11TH PRINCE
(FÜRST) ZU SCHWARZENBERG,** Princely Landgraf im
Kleggau, Count zu Sulz, Duke zu Krumau, *b* at Pressburg 3 Jan
1900; ✠ at Vienna 25 Oct 1979, Kt Order of the Golden Fleece,
Bailiff Gd Cross Hon and Dev Sovereign Military Order of Malta,
succ his cousin, Adolf, 10th Prince (Fürst) zu Schwarzenberg, etc
(✠ 27 Feb 1950), son of Prince Felix zu Schwarzenberg (*b* 8 June
1867; ✠ 18 Nov 1946) and Princess Anna zu Löwenstein-Wertheim-
Rosenberg (*b* 28 Sept 1873; *m* 15 June 1897; ✠ 27 June 1936).

Brother
Prince *Heinrich* Karl Borromäus Maria Franz von Sales, Duke zu
Krumau, *b* at Pressburg 29 Jan 1903; ✠ at Vienna 18 June 1965, Dr
of Law, Kt of Hon Sovereign Military Order of Malta; adopted at
Budejovice 29 Mar 1940 by his kinsman Adolph, Prince zu

Schwarzenberg (*b* 18 Aug 1890; ✛ 27 Feb 1950); *m* at Kirchdorf 30 Nov 1946, Countess Eleonore (*b* at Micheldorf 8 June 1920; ✛ at Schloß Gusterheim 27 Dec 1994), Dame Star Cross Order, dau of Georg, Count zu Stolberg-Stolberg and Princess Regina Reuss, and had issue,

    1. Princess *Elisabeth* Regina Maria Gabriela, *b* at Vienna 1 Oct 1947; adopted at Schloß Gusterheim 24 Jan 1993 by her kinswoman Princess Amalie of Lobkowicz, née Princess zu Schwarzenberg (*b* 25 Jan 1921 - see 2nd Majorat below); *m* at Pöls, Steiermark 16 May (civ) and 31 May (relig) 1970, Rüdiger von Pezold (*b* at Würzburg 11 July 1941), Lawyer, Kt of St John of Jerusalem, Chairman of the Ducal Saxe-Coburg-Gotha Foundations.

    [*U Mlyna 24, Prague 4, Czech Republic; Schloß Gusterheim, 8761 Pöls, Steiermark, Austria*].

Prince Heinrich adopted his kinsman Karl Johannes, 7th Prince zu Schwarzenberg (*b* at Prague 10 Dec 1937) at Vienna 24 Nov 1960/12 Dec 1960 (see 2nd Majorat below).

SECOND MAJORAT

Founded by Prince Karl Philipp (*b* 15 April 1771; ✛ 13 Oct 1820), younger brother of Prince Joseph Johann (see First Majorat above); Hereditary Member of the former Austrian House of Lords, Vienna 18 April 1861.

KARL JOHANNES Nepomuk Joseph Norbert Friedrich Antonius Wratislaw Menas, **(7TH) 12TH PRINCE (FÜRST) ZU SCHWARZENBERG,** Princely Landgraf im Kleggau, Count zu Sulz, Duke zu Krumau, *b* at Prague 10 Dec 1937, Kt Order of the Golden Fleece, Kt of Hon Sovereign Military Order of Malta, Kt Constantinian Order of St George, Kt Bavarian Order of St George, son of Karl, 6th Prince (Fürst) zu Schwarzenberg (*b* 5 July 1911, ✛ 9 April 1986) and Princess Antonie zu Fürstenberg (*b* 12 Jan 1905; *m* 30 June 1904, ✛ 24 Dec 1988) adopted by his kinsman Heinrich, 11th Prince (Fürst) zu Schwarzenberg, Duke zu Krumau (*b* 1903; ✛ 1965 see 1st Majorat above); *succ* his kinsman, Joseph, 11th Prince (Fürst) zu Schwarzenberg (*b* 1900; ✛ 1979 see 1st Majorat above); *m* Seefeld, Lower Austria 22 April 1967 (*m* diss by div at Vienna 18 Oct 1988), Countess Therese (*b* at Vienna 17 Feb 1940), Dr of Med, dau of Johannes, Count zu Hardegg, Count of Glatz and im Machlande, Proprietor of Kadolz, etc and Johanna, Countess von and zu Firmian.

[*Renn Weg 2, 1030 Vienna, Austria; 8850 Schloß Murau, Steiermark, Austria; Nizbor, Sykorice-Drevíc 83, 26705 Bohemia*].

Sons and Daughter

1. *Johannes* Nepomucenus Andreas Heinrich Joseph Karl Ferdinand Johannes Evangelis die Heiligen Drei Könige Achaz Michael Maria, Hereditary Prince (Erbprinz) zu Schwarzenberg, *b* at Vienna 13 Dec 1967.

[*Renn Weg 2, 1030 Vienna, Austria*].

2. Princess *Anna Carolina* Antoinette Elisabeth Theresia Olga Adelheid Maria, *b* at Vienna 16 Dec 1968; *m* at London 28 July (civ) and at Murau 6 Sept (relig) 1997, Peter Morgan (*b* at Wimbledon 10 April 1963).

[*57 Brynmaer Road, London SW11 4EN*].

3. Prince *Karl* Philipp Ernst Ferdinand Alwig Kilian, *b* at Vienna 12 May 1979; adopted 25th Nov 1987 by Dipl Ing Thomas Prinzhorn and according the Court of Justice of the City of Vienna (Bezirksgericht Wien Innere Stadt) from 16 May 1988 ceased to be a Member of the Princely House of Schwarzenberg and bears the name of Prinzhorn.

Brother and Sisters

1. Princess *Marie Eleonore* Anna Anastasia Theresia, *b* at Prague 11 April 1936; *m* at Vienna 26 Jan 1969, Leopold-Bill von Bredow (*b* at Potsdam 2 Jan 1933), Ambassador.

[*Wundstraße 66/1, 14057 Berlin, Germany; Enten Gasse25, 5121 Ostermiething, Austria*].

2. Prince *Friedrich* Karl Joseph Johannes von Nepomuk Antonius Bartholomäus Felix Judas Thaddäus Conrad von Parzham, *b* at Prague 24 Aug 1940, Dr rer oec, Dipl Business Administration, Banker, Kt of Hon Sovereign Military Order of Malta; *m* at Zürich 12 Oct 1984, Regula Brigitta (*b* at Zürich 16 April 1956), dau of Johann Jakob Schlegel and Brigitte Brunner, and has issue,

[*Alte Landstraße 123, 8702 Zollikon, Switzerland*].

    1. Princess Marie Helene Antoinette Teresa Maximiliana, *b* at Zurich 29 April 1987.

    2. Prince Ferdinand Karl Friedrich Johannes von Nepomuk Jakob Maria Alexius, *b* at Zurich 17 July 1989.

3. Princess *Anna* Maria Karolina Ignatia Theresia, *b* at Prague 31 July 1946, Dr of Phil; *m* at Vienna 21 Dec (civ) 1979 and 19 Jan (relig) 1980, Elmar, Baron von Haxthausen (*b* at Bökerhof 20 Oct

1925), Proprietor of Vörden, Abbenburg and Bökerhof, Land Manager, Forester.
[*Abbenburg, 33034 Brakel, Germany*].

Brother of Father

Issue of Karl, 5th Prince zu Schwarzenberg (*b* 26 Feb 1886; ✝ 6 Sept 1914) and Countess Eleonore von Clam and Gallas (*b* 4 Nov 1887; *m* 5 Feb 1910; ✝ 31 May 1967; *m* 2ndly 7 June 1921, Zdenko Radslav, Count Kinsky von Wchinitz and Tettau who ✝ 1 Jan 1975), and had issue, among whom,

Son

Prince *Franz* Friedrich Maria, *b* at Prague 24 March 1913; ✝ at Unzmarkt 9 March 1992, Dr of Law, Prof of Political Science Loyola University Chicago, Kt Gd Cross Sovereign Military Order of Malta, Baillie and Kt Gd Cross of Justice Constantinian Order of St George; *m* at Dolní Berkovice 23 May 1944, Princess Amelie (*b* at Dolní Berkovice 25 Jan 1921), Dame of Hon Sovereign Military Order of Malta, dau of Leopold, Prince of Lobkowicz and Princess Franziska (Fanny) von Montenuovo, and had issue,
[*Renn Wey 2, 1030 Vienna, Austria; 26293 Nalzovice, nr Sedlcany, Czech Republic*].

    1. Princess *Ludmila* Maria de Victoria Franziska de Paula Eleonore Thaddea Leonharda Agnes de Bohemia, *b* at Prague 25 July 1945; *m* at New Hope 14 Feb 1998 (civ) and at Salebury, Pennsylvania 14 Feb 1998 (relig), Carl Barton Hess (*b* at Chicago),
    [*2 Sutton Place South, New York, NY 10022, U.S.A.*].
    2. Princess *Isabella* Eleonora Maria Franziska Romana Leonharda Thaddäa Sidonia, *b* at Rome 22 June 1946; *m* at Gräfelfing, nr Munich 15 July (civ) and at Vienna 25 July (relig) 1970, Louis von Harnier, Baron von Regendorf (*b* at Munich 3 July 1938), Dipl Phys.
    [*Scharnitzerstraße 54, 82166 Gräfelfing, Germany*].
    3. Prince *Johann* von Nepomuk Maria Heinrich Franz Leonhard Thaddäas Thomas von Aquin, *b* at Chicago 19 Feb 1957, Financial Consultant, Capt. US Naval Reserve; *m* at Unzmarkt, Steiermark 19 Sept 1982, Regina (*b* at Milford, Massachusetts, USA 22 Oct 1949; *m* 1stly 6 Sept 1975, Andrew D Paull who ✝ 22 Feb 1977), dau of Charles Henry Hogan

and Helen Mae Holden, and has issue,

[*"Skipper's Lea", 105 Kane Avenue, Middletown, R.I. 02842, USA*].

    1. Prince *Alexander, b* at Newport, Rhode Island, USA 5 April 1984.

Half-Brothers of Grandfather

Issue of Karl, 4th Prince zu Schwarzenberg (*b* 1 July 1859; ✠ 4 Oct 1913) and his 2nd wife, Ida, Countess Hoyos, Baroness zu Stichsenstein (*b* 31 Aug 1870; *m* 24 Nov 1891; ✠ 27 Jan 1946), having had issue, among whom,

Sons

1. Prince *Ernst* Johann Nepomuk Benedikt Josef Maria, *b* at Wossow 11 Oct 1892; ✠ at Písek, Czechoslovakia 18 Dec 1979, Major Czech Army; *m* 1stly at Budapest 19 Feb 1916 (*m* diss by div at Prague 20 Nov 1934), Countess Elisabeth (*b* at Vajszka 2 Aug 1895; ✠ at Erzsébet Tanja 14 Jan 1957; she *m* 2ndly at Budapest 11 Feb 1935, Tibor, Baron Collas de Ramaille et Lincour; that *m* diss by div 1 Sept 1945), dau of Emil, Count Széchényi de Sárvár-Felsövidék and Countess Marie Hunyady von Kéthely. Prince Ernst *m* 2ndly at Bernartice 12 May 1973, Mathilde (*b* at Stuttgart 22 July 1899), dau of Hans Gerber and Georgine Dietrich, and by her had issue,

    1. *Anna* Maria Agathe Margarethe, *b* at Pilsen 28 Jan 1933; *m* at St Margarethen, St Gallen 18 May (civ) and at Schwarzenberg 19 May (relig) 1956, Adolf Bucher (*b* at Ehrendorf, Kärnten 19 Nov 1918), Architect.

    [*Johann Ure Weg 10, 9020 Klagenfurt, Austria; 26281 Tochovice 1 Zamek, Czech Republic*].

2. Prince *Johann* von Nepomuk Erkinger Alfred Joseph Peter, *b* at Prague 31 Jan 1903; ✠ at Città della Pieve, Perugia 26 May 1978, Dr of Law, Director Int'l Red Cross in Geneva 1940 - 1946; Austrian Ambassador to Paris, Rome, London and Holy See, Rep in Rome of Sovereign Military Order of Malta, Kt of Hon Gd Cross Sovereign Military Order of Malta; *m* at Wespelaar, Belgium 1 Sept 1931, Kathleen (*b* at Brussels 19 May 1905; ✠ at Città della Pieve 26 May 1978), dau of Guillaume, Viscount de Spoelberch and Colienne de Neufforge, and had issue,

    1. Prince Karl *Erkinger* Thaddäas, *b* at Vienna 8 April 1933, Dr of Phil; *m* 1stly at Athens 26 July 1962 (*m* diss by div at Vienna 29 Oct 1975), Elisabeth [*Schloß Ratzenegg, Johann*

Zeno Weg 23, 9062 Moosburg, Austria] (*b* at Athens 2 Nov 1943; *m* 2ndly 29 Oct 1988, Ernst-Friedrich, Count von Goëss), dau of Konstantin Constantinides and Elisabeth Philini, and has issue,

> 1. Prince *Johannes, b* at Florence 17 Feb 1963, Dr of Phil, M Sc.
> [*Schloß Ratzenegg, Johann Zeno Weg 23, 9062 Moosburg, Austria*].
> 2. Princess Anna *Gabriella, b* at Athens 14 Sept 1964; *m* 1stly at Vienna 5 Sept 1987 (*m* diss by div at Vienna 23 March 1993), Philipp, Baron von Waechter (*b* at London 18 Oct 1959), Dr of Law. She *m* 2ndly at Klagenfurt 3 June 1995, Adam Dixon (*b* at New York 12 March 1960).
> [*Wohlleben Gasse 7/12, 1040 Vienna, Austria*].
> 3. Prince *Alexander* Konstantin, *b* at Athens 28 Aug 1971.
> [*Schloß Ratzenegg, Johann Zeno Weg 23, 9062 Moosburg, Austria*].

Prince Erkinger *m* 2ndly at San Casciano, Tuscany 13 July 1977, Countess and Lady Claudia (*b* at Fahlburg 10 May 1949), dau of Clemens, Count and Herr zu Brandis, Proprietor of Brandis, Leonburg and Fahlburg bei Meran and Irmgard Waidthaler, and has further issue,

[*L'Ugolino, Castelbonsi, 50026 San Casciano, Val di Pesa, Prov. Florence, Italy*].

> 4. Princess *Gaia* Maria, *b* at Florence 23 Feb 1978.
> 5. Princess *Ida* Letizia, *b* at Florence 9 Oct 1980.

2. Princess *Colienne* Ida Franziska Kathleen Eleonore Marie, *b* at Berlin 16 Feb 1937; *m* at Vienna 16 Sept 1961, Maximilian Josef, Count von Meran (*b* at Csákberény, Kom Fejér, Hungary 20 April 1930), Banker.

[*"Pirkerhube", Grossbuch. Str. 104, 0061 Klagenfurt-Wölfnitz, Austria*],

◆━●━◆

SOLMS

Seigneural family from Lahngau, who can be traced from Marquard de Sulmesso in 1129 (whose name was taken from the ancient castle of Solmissa, today in Oberndorf, Solmsbach); continuously documented since comes Henricus de Solmese who first appears in 1223 bearing the title of Count; Counts of Solms 1226, of Braunfels (see below) 1280; the branches below descend from two sons of Otto, Count of Solms- Braunfels (✝ 27 Oct 1409).

A: SOLMS-BRAUNFELS
(✝ Extinct ✝)

Founded by Bernard II, Count of Solms-Braunfels, Lord of Münzenberg, Braunfels, Greifenstein and Hungen (b 29 Aug 1409; ✝ 6 Aug 1459); inherited the possessions of Werner von Fulkenstein, Archbishop of Trier in 1418, viz: Braunfels and Lich; (two other branches, extinct 1693 and 1678, Braunfels and Hungen, respectively, founded by Johann-Albert I and Rheinhard - the extant branch descends from their brother Wilhelm, Count zu Solms-Greifenstein; Prince of the Holy Empire with ratification of arms and the qualification of "Hochgeboren", Frankfurt-am-Main 22 May 1742; recognised in Saxony 5 Aug 1743; the right of primogeniture was instituted 1 Feb 1635; with effect from 24 Oct 1783; Hereditary Member of the former First Chamber of the Grand Duchy of Hesse 17 Dec 1820; received the qualification of "Durchlaucht" (primogeniture) by the German Diet 18 Aug 1825; Hereditary Member of the former Prussian House of Lords 12 Oct 1854; confirmation in Hesse of the right of all members of the family to bear the qualification of Serene Highnesses, Darmstadt 22 Aug 1912. Members of the family bear the title of Prince or Princess zu Solms-Braunfels with the qualification of Serene Highness.

✝ **GEORG FRIEDRICH** Victor Heinrich Joseph Wilhelm Maria Johannes Emanuel, **7TH PRINCE (FÜRST) ZU SOLMS-BRAUNFELS**, Count zu Greifenstein, Lichtenstein and Hungen, also Tecklenburg, Crichingen and Lingen, Lord zu Münzenberg, Rheda, Wildenfels, Sonnenwalde, Püttlingen, Dorstweiler and Beaucourt, b at Frankfurt-am-Main 13 Dec 1890; ✝ at Braunfels 30 Nov 1970, son of Georg, 6th Prince (Fürst) zu Solms-Braunfels (b 18 March 1836; ✝ 3 April 1891) and Emanuela Gallone of the Princes di Tricase Moliterno (b 19 Feb 1854; m 5 Aug 1878; ✝ 26 March 1936; she m 2ndly 16 May 1895, Alexander, Prince zu Hohenlohe-Waldenburg-Schillingsfürst, Prince von Ratibor and Corvey who ✝

16 May 1924); *m* at Naples 8 May 1913, Donna Beatrice, Countess Saluzzo (*b* at Naples 29 Feb 1888; ✧ at Braunfels 23 Feb 1976), dau of Don Alfonso, 3rd Prince Saluzzo, Duke di Corigliano and Donna Margherita Caracciolo of the Princes di Forino.

Daughter

1. Princess *Maria Gabriele* Anna Josephine, *b* at Braunfels 23 Aug 1918, Dame Star Cross Order; *m* at Braunfels 15 Aug (civ) and 30 Aug (relig) 1950, Hans Georg, Count von Oppersdorff (*b* at Ober-Altwaltersdorf 27 Nov 1920), 1st Lt, known from 2 May 1969 as "Count von Oppersdorff-Solms-Braunfels".
[*Englischer Garten, 61350 Bad Homburg vor der Höhe, Germany*].

Brother of Father

Issue of Prince Wilhelm zu Solms-Braunfels (*b* 30 Dec 1801; ✧ 12 Sept 1868) and Countess Maria Kinsky von Wchinitz and Tettau (*b* 19 June 1809; *m* 8 Aug 1831; ✧ 5 Dec 1892), having had issue, among whom,

Son

Prince *Hermann* Ernst Ludwig Bernhard Wilhelm, *b* at Düsseldorf 8 Oct 1845; ✧ at Schloß Braunfels 30 Aug 1900, Major Hessian Army, Kt of St John of Jerusalem; *m* 1stly at Salzburg 30 April 1872, Princess Maria (*b* at Zinkau 26 June 1852; ✧ at Königsbrück, Saxony 23 July 1882), dau of Karl, Prince zu Solms-Braunfels and Princess Sophie zu Löwenstein-Wertheim-Rosenberg. He *m* 2ndly at Gera 17 Nov 1887, Princess Elisabeth (*b* at Gera 27 Oct 1859; ✧ at Schloß Hungen 23 Feb 1951), dau of Heinrich XIV, Prince Reuss and Duchess Agnes of Württemberg, and had issue, among whom, from his second wife,

Son

Prince *Ernst-August* Adolf Wilhelm Friedrich Hermann Albrecht Bernhard Maria, *b* at Darmstadt 10 March 1892; ✧ at Karlsruhe 24 July 1968, Dr of Law, Lawyer, Major, Kt of Justice St John of Jerusalem, Prussian Councillor of State, *m* at Dresden 15 Feb 1939, Princess Elisabeth-Caroline (*b* at Dresden-Blasewitz 23 Jan 1916), dau of Julius Ernst, Prince zur Lippe and Duchess Marie zu Mecklenburg-Strelitz, and had issue,
[*Lichtentaler Allee 100, 76530 Baden-Baden, Germany*].

    1. Princess *Maria-Angela* Elisabeth Friederike Uta Beatrice, *b* at Gera 6 Aug 1940; *m* at Baden-Baden 5 May 1963 (*m* diss

by div 1973), Werner Zawade (*b* at Repten 29 Oct 1926), Dr of
Law. She has since reverted to her maiden name.

B: SOLMS-LICH

**Founded by Johann, Count of Solms-Lich (✝ 1457), Lord of Lich,
Hohensolms and Laubach (see below); inherited Rödelheim and
Assenheim 1461; acquired Sonnewalde, Upper Lusatia 1537; the
lines below descend from two sons of Count Philipp (*b* 15 Aug 1468;
✝ 3 Oct 1544).**

I: SOLMS-HOHENSOLMS-LICH

**Founded by Field Marshal Reinhard I, Count of Solms-Lich and
Hohensolms, Lord of Lich, Butzbach, Hohensolms, Kleeberg and
Villmar (*b* 12 Oct 1491; ✝ 23 Sept 1562) whose lands were divided
with the two sons of his younger brother 9 Nov 1548; Reinhard's sons
founded two Lines in 1579; viz Solms-Lich (extinct 1718) and Solms-
Hohensolms, which inherited Lich in 1718 and took the name of
"Solms-Hohensolms-Lich"; Prince of the Holy Empire with the
qualification of "Hochgeboren", Frankfurt-am-Main 14 July 1792;
recognised by the Elector of the Bavarian Palatinate 4 Oct 1792;
received the qualification of "Durchlaucht" (primogeniture) by the
German Diet 18 Aug 1825; Hereditary Member of the former First
Chamber of the Grand Duchy of Hesse, 17 Dec 1820 and the former
Prussian House of Lords, 12 Oct 1854; Ministerial confirmation in
Hesse of the right of all family members of the Princely House to the
qualification of Serene Highness, Darmstadt 28 May 1910.**
**Members of the family bear the title of Prince of Princess zu Solms-
Hohensolms-Lich with the qualification of Serene Highness.**

PHILIPP REINHARD, 8TH PRINCE (FÜRST) ZU SOLMS-HOHENSOLMS-LICH, Count zu Tecklenburg, Crichingen and

Lingen, Lord zu Münzenberg, Rheda, Wildenfels, Sonnenwalde,
Püttlingen, Dorstweiler and Beaucourt, *b* at Lich 27 Nov 1934, *succ*
his grandfather, Reinhard, 7th Prince (Fürst) zu Solms-Hohensolms-
Lich (*b* 17 Sept 1867; ✝ 12 April 1951), son of Hermann Otto,
Hereditary Prince (Erbprinz) zu Solms-Hohensolms-Lich (*b* 12 Oct
1902; *ka* 3 July 1940), and Baroness and Dame Gertrud von Werthern
(*b* 29 Aug 1913; ✝ 27 Nov 1987; *m* 29 Dec 1933; *m* 2ndly 21 Oct 1950,
Hans Joachim Sell; *m* at Stockholm 3 Oct 1970, Marie (*b* at
Stockholm 12 Feb 1948) dau of Louis Fouché, Count d'Otrante and
Birgitta Tham (of Swedish nobility).
[*Schloß, 35423 Lich, Germany*].

Sons and Daughter

1. Princess *Caroline*, *b* at Giessen 2 Nov 1971.
2. *Carl-Christian*, Hereditary Prince (Erbprinz) zu Solms-Hohensolms-Lich, *b* at Giessen 19 March 1975.
3. Prince *Louis Philipp*, *b* at Giessen 11 July 1978.
4. Prince *Frederik* Sebastian, *b* at Giessen 23 July 1987.

Brothers and Sisters

1. Princess *Dorothea*, *b* at Lich 11 Dec 1935; *m* at Lich 17 May 1959, Andreas, Count Razumovsky von Wigstein (*b* at Schönstein, nr Troppau 15 Nov 1929; ✠ 26 July 2002), Journalist.
[*Jacquin Gasse57, 1030 Vienna, Austria; Heinrich-Neeb-Straße 1, 35423 Lich, Germany*].
2. Prince *Wilhelm*, *b* at Lich 5 Jan 1937 (Catholic), Dr of Phil, Prof of Literature; *m* at Mettlach, Saar 16 May 1964, Millicent (*b* at Mettlach 13 July 1937), dau of Luitwin von Boch-Galhau and Beatrice Dodd, and has issue,
[*Barfüsser Tor 10, 35037 Marburg, Germany; Mandlstraße 19, 80802 Munich, Germany*].
  1. Prince *Benedict* Hermann-Otto Luitwin Maria, *b* at Munich 22 Sept 1965, Underwriter.
  [*6 Cité de Varenne, 75007 Paris, France*].
  2. Princess *Cynthia* Johannetta Adeline Milicent Marka, *b* at Saarlouis 24 Nov 1967, Dipl rer sc.
  [*Grüneburg Weg 143, 60323 Frankfurt-am-Main, Germany*].
  3. Princess *Amicie* Beatrice Ségolene Milicent Maria Consuelo, *b* at Saarlouis 9 March 1972; *m* at Mettlach am Saar 22 July 2000, Johannes, Count von Thurn and Valsassina-Como-Vercelli (*b* at Klagenfurt 11 Feb 1967).
  [*Mandlstraße 19, 80802 Munich, Germany*].
  4. Prince *Christian-Lucius* Felician Anselm Maria, *b* at Zürich 25 Aug 1974, B sc oec, Investment Banker.
  [*9 Argyll Mansions, 303-333 Kings Road, London SW3 5ER*].
3. Princess *Eleonore*, *b* at Lich 20 April 1938, Teacher; *m* at Freiburg im Breisgau 9 March (civ) and at Madrid 30 March (relig) 1964, Hans-Henning von der Burg (*b* at Erfurt 8 Jan 1939), Dr of Phil, Radio Executive.
[*Hermann Sielckenstraße 68, 76530 Baden-Baden, Germany*].
4. Prince *Hermann* Otto, *b* posthumously at Lich 24 Nov 1940, Dr of Agriculture, Dipl Econ, Member German Bundestag; *m* 1stly at Frankfurt-am-Main 19 June 1969 (*m* diss by div at Frankfurt-am-

Main 14 May 1971), Margit [*Sand Weg 53, 60316 Frankfurt-am-Main, Germany*] (*b* at Würzburg 22 May 1944), dau of Albert Mayer and Erna Kunz. He *m* 2ndly at Bielefeld 1 July 1989, Christiane (*b* at Bielefeld 7 Jan 1955), dau of Horst Meyer zu Eissen and Liesel Lotte Niedergassel, and has issue by his second wife,
[*Schloß Gasse6a, 35423 Lich, Germany*].

    1. Princess *Sophie* Charlotte, *b* at Bielefeld 10 Dec 1989.
    2. Princess *Marie Christine*, *b* at Bielefeld 15 Aug 1991.
    3. Princess *Lilly* Constanza, *b* at Bielefeld 17 Feb 1993.

Brother of Father

Issue of Reinhard, 7th Prince (Fürst) zu Solms-Hohensolms-Lich (*b* 17 Sept 1867; ✝ 12 April 1951) and Countess Marka zu Solms-Sonnenwalde (*b* 20 March 1879; *m* 14 Nov 1898; ✝ 5 Dec 1965) among whom,

1. Prince *Carl* Friedrich, *b* at Potsdam 12 Nov 1903, Kt of Hon St John of Jerusalem.
[*Unterstadt 29, 35423 Lich, Germany*].

II: SOLMS-LAUBACH

Founded by Otto, Count of Solms-Lich (*b* 11 May 1496; ✝ 14 May 1522). His son, Friedrich Magnus, received Sonnewalde and Pouch from his grandfather *circa* 1540, and Rödelheim, Assenheim and Laubach (Hesse) from his uncle (see below) 9 Nov 1548. The lines below descend from two sons of Johann Georg, 1st Count of Solms-Laubach, Lord of Rödelheim and Assenheim (*b* 26 Nov 1547; ✝ 19 Aug 1600).

i) LINE OF SONNENWALDE

Founded by Heinrich-Wilhelm, Count of Solms-Laubach, Lord of Sonnenwalde and Pouch (*b* 21 March 1583; ✝ 21 March 1632). The branches below descend from two sons of Count Otto-Wilhelm (*b* 25 Aug 1701; ✝ 8 Feb 1737). Final partition of the lands between the Heads of these branches took place in 1820; the Head of this branch does not have the right to the qualification of "Erlaucht" since the possession of Lordships were not considered "Reichständisch" or "Immediate", however Members of this line were recognised as members of the Prussian Nobility 6 Feb 1886.
Members of this Line bear the title of Count or Countess zu Solms-Sonnenwalde.

1st Branch:
SOLMS-RÖSA
(✠ Extinct ✠)

Founded by Carl Georg Heinrich, Count zu Solms-Sonnenwalde (*b* 28 April 1728; ✠ 21 July 1796). Aquired Rösa in 1820.

2nd Branch:
SOLMS-SONNENWALDE

Founded by Count Viktor Friedrich (*b* 16 Sept 1730; ✠ 24 Dec 1783); inherited part of the Lordship of Alt-Pouch in 1769 and the remainder in 1818; Hereditary Member of the Prussian House of Lords 12 Oct 1854.

ALFRED Otto Friedrich, **COUNT (GRAF) ZU SOLMS-SONNENWALDE**, Proprietor of the Lordship of Weldam, *b* at Sonnewalde 4 July 1932, *succ* his father, son of Wilhelm, Count zu Solms-Sonnenwalde (*b* at 11 April 1886; ✠ 31 Dec 1981) and Countess Isabelle Bentinck (*b* 15 Nov 1889; *m* 6 Aug 1914; ✠ 21 Nov 1981); *m* at Weldam 17 Oct 1992, Christine (*b* at Westerstede 8 Feb 1964), Dr of Med, dau of Peter Hüsmert and Anne Kienle. [*Weldam, near Goor, 7475MJ Markelo, The Netherlands*].

Daughters
1. Countess *Maria* Charlotte Sophie, *b* at Weldam 24 Jul 1993.
2. Countess *Caroline* Anna Amalia, *b* at Weldam 13 Aug 1994.
3. Countess *Isabelle* Rosa Catharina, *b* at Weldam 29 Aug 1996.

Brother and Sisters
1. Countess *Marie-Helene* Luise Clementine, *b* at Potsdam 15 April 1917; *m* at Mettmann, nr Düsseldorf 21 July and at Rudenhausen 6 Sept (relig) 1951, Günther von Bünau (*b* at Dresden 3 Aug 1911; ✠ at Mettmann 10 Aug 1996), Kt of St John of Jerusalem. [*Am Sonnenhang 11, 40822 Mettmann, Germany*].
2. Countess *Rosa* Friederike Marka, *b* at Potsdam 5 April 1918; ✠ at Sonnewalde 15 Sept 1938.
3. *Otto* Wilhelm Carl Theodor, Hereditary Count (Erbgraf) zu Solms-Sonnenwalde, *b* at Wurschen 6 Sept 1921; ✠ at Sonnewalde 12 March 1931.

ii) LINE OF BARUTH

Founded by Johann Georg II, Count of Solms-Laubach, Lord of Wildenfels and Baruth (*b* 19 Nov 1591; ✝ 4 Dec 1632); inherited part of Rödelheim and Assenheim 5 Sept 1635; partition of family possessions took place between his sons who founded the lines below.

1st Branch
SOLMS-RÖDELHEIM AND ASSENHEIM

Founded by Johann August, Count zu Solms-Rödelheim (*b* 7 June 1623; ✝ 23 Nov 1680); inherited the remaining parts of Rödelheim and Assenheim 6 Aug 1676; Hereditary Member of the former First Chamber of the Grand Duchy of Hesse 17 Dec 1820; received the title of "Erlaucht" (primogeniture) 13 Feb 1829; Hereditary Member of Prussian House of Lords 12 Oct 1854.

Members of the family bear the title of Count or Countess zu Solms-Rödelheim and Assenheim.

PHILIP Moritz, **COUNT (GRAF) ZU SOLMS-RÖDELHEIM AND ASSENHEIM,** *b* at Munich 5 Feb 1964, *succ* his brother, Nikolaus (*b* 1961; ✝ 1981), son of Count Günther zu Solms-Rödelheim and Assenheim (*b* 7 Sept 1931; ✝ 10 Feb 1979) and Countess Alexandra zu Eulenburg (*b* 10 Nov 1933; *m* 10 July 1960; she *m* 2ndly 30 July 1975, Jean-Louis Sprecher).

[*Schloß Assenheim, 61194 Niddatal, Germany*].

Brother and Sister

1. **Nikolaus** Alexander, **Count zu Solms-Rödelheim and Assenheim,** *b* at Munich 14 April 1961; ✝ at Assenheim 23 March 1981; *succ* his kinsman, Markwart, Count zu Solms-Rödelheim and Assenheim (*b* 1925; ✝ 1976 - see below).

2. Countess *Antonia* Sophie Luise, *b* at Munich 27 Sept 1962; *m* at Assenheim 11 July 1992, Bernhard von Rothkirch and Panthen (*b* at Heide, Holstein 21 April 1951), Dipl Berg Ing.

[*Albert Schweitzerstraße 32, 50226 Frechen, Germany*].

Mother

Alexandra Dorothea Heather Marie Juliana Martina, Countess Günther zu Solms-Rödelheim and Assenheim, *b* at Gumbinnen, East Prussia 10 Nov 1933, dau of Carl-Elimar, Count zu Eulenburg and Dorothea von Halem; *m* 1stly at Assenheim 10 July 1960 (*m* diss by div at Munich 21 Nov 1973), Günther, Count zu Solms-Rödelheim and Assenheim (*b* at Bad Nauheim 7 Sept 1931; ✝ at Munich 10 Feb

1979), Dr of Phil. She *m* 2ndly at Munich 30 July 1975, Jean-Louis
Sprecher (*b* at Nice 23 April 1940).
[*13 Avenue Princesse Charlotte-Victoria, Monte Carlo, Monaco*].

Step-Mother

Gabriele, Countess Günther zu Solms-Rödelheim and Assenheim,
b at Breslau 4 March 1939, dau of Franz Podleska and Irmgard
Finke; *m* at Munich 18 April 1975, Günther, Count zu Solms-
Rödelheim and Assenheim (*b* at Bad Nauheim 7 Sept 1931; ✠ at
Munich 10 Feb 1979), Dr of Phil.
[*Karl Theodorstraße 34, 80803 Munich, Germany*].

Brother and Sister of Father

Issue of Count Joachim zu Solms-Rödelheim and Assenheim (*b* 13
June 1896; *m* 15 Feb 1928; ✠ 10 Sept 1978) and Countess Klara von
Bullion (*b* 12 March 1901; ✠ 6 Sept 1996; *m* 15 Feb 1928).

1. Count *Jost* Heinrich, *b* at Munich 3 Jan 1929, Bank Director; *m* at
Wuppertal-Elberfeld 22 May (civ) and 25 May (relig) 1964, Karin
(*b* at Wuppertal-Elberfeld 19 April 1936), dau of Ernst Günther
Frowein and Countess Louise-Marie von Rhoden.
[*Mürnaü-Froschhausen, Germany*].
2. Countess *Maritta,* *b* at Berlin 18 April 1940; *m* at Munich 23 July
1964, Thedel Jasper von Walmoden (*b* at Alt-Wallmoden, Kr Goslar
17 Jan 1936), Dipl Eng, Dipl Master Brewer.
[*Am Vogeltal 22, 97702 Münnerstadt, Germany*].

Brother of Grandfather

Issue of Karl Franz, Count zu Solms-Rödelheim and Assenheim (*b* 15
Dec 1864; ✠ 9 Feb 1923) and his first wife, Countess Anastasia zu
Pappenheim (*b* 9 March 1863; *m* 26 Oct 1892; ✠ 5 July 1904), having
had issue, among whom,

Son

Maximilian Ludwig, **Count (Graf) zu Solms-Rödelheim and
Assenheim,** *b* at Assenheim 24 Sept 1893; ✠ at Marburg an der
Lahn 2 Sept 1968, Dr of Phil, Prof of Sociology University of Marburg;
m 1stly at Amorbach 23 Feb 1922 (*m* diss by div 1 Oct 1937),
Princess Viktoria (*b* at Amorbach 12 May 1895; ✠ at Assenheim 9
Feb 1973), dau of Emich, Prince zu Leiningen and Princess Feodora
zu Hohenlohe-Langenburg, and had issue; *m* 2ndly at Riga 30 Oct
1937, Freda (*b* at Daugeln, Latvia 4/8 May 1901), dau of Georg von

Gersdorff and Baroness Alexandrine von Rosen, and had further
issue

    1. Count *Johann Georg,* b at Marburg an der Lahn 1 Feb
1938, Prof of Architect University of Wuppertal; m at Marburg
8 July (civ) and 11 July (relig) 1964 (m diss by div at Düsseldorf
8 Feb 1995), Gabriele [*Salier Platz 4, 40545 Düsseldorf,
Germany*] (b at Zoppot, nr Danzig 5 July 1939), Teacher, dau
of Rudolf Jahr and Elisabeth Culeman, and has issue,
[*Georg Voigtstraße 57, 35039 Marburg, Germany*].

        1. Countess *Ricarda,* b at Milan 18 April 1967, MA,
Journalist; m at Düsseldorf 7 Sept 1985 (m diss by div
1989), Udo Hoyn (b 19 Oct 1960). She has since reverted
to her maiden name.
        2. Countess *Cora,* b at Düsseldorf 3 June 1970.
[*Markengrafenstraße 27, 40545 Düsseldorf, Germany*].
        3. Countess *Hanna,* b at Düsseldorf 26 Oct 1973.
[*Markengrafenstraße 27, 40545 Düsseldorf, Germany*].

Brother of Great-Grandfather

Issue of Maximilian, Count zu Solms-Rödelheim and Assenheim
(b 14 April 1826; ✠ 15 Feb 1892) and Countess Thekla zu Solms-
Laubach (b 4 June 1835; m 1 June 1861; ✠ 17 Jan 1892), having had
issue, among whom,

Son

Count *Ernst,* b at Assenheim 8 July 1868; ✠ at Friedberg, Hesse 2
May 1920, Dr rer pol, Capt Prussian Army; m at Schönweide, Plön 2
July 1903, Countess Anna (b at Weissenhaus 14 April 1874; ✠ at
Frankfurt-Rödelheim 18 Aug 1937), dau of Carl, Count and Noble
Lord von Platen-Hallermund and Baroness Luise von Hollen, and
had issue,

    1. Count Maximilian (*Max*) Ernst Wilhelm, b at Strasbourg 16
May 1910; ✠ at Göttingen 6 June 1993, Dr rer pol, Prof of
Sociology University of Göttingen; m at Freiburg im Breisgau
4 Sept 1948, Hella (b at Freiburg im Breisgau 28 Dec 1923),
dau of Albert Gessner and Johanna Diehl, and has issue,
among whom,
[*Ludwig Beckstraße 11, 37075 Göttingen, Germany*].

        1. Countess *Florence* Anna Marie, b at Freiburg im
Breisgau 21 Aug 1949, Teacher.

[*Hainholz Weg 27, 37085 Göttingen, Germany*].

2. Countess *Caroline* Constanze Johanna, *b* at Wilhelmshaven 3 Sept 1959, Pediatric Nurse; *m* at Weiler/Allgäu 6 Oct 1989, Franz Josef Sauer (*b* at Freiburg im Breisgau 20 Nov 1961), Dr of Med.

[*Eyenbach Nr. 5, 88171 Weiler/Allgäu, Germany*].

2. Count *Wilhelm* Oskar Friedrich Eurgen, *b* at Strasbourg 24 April 1914; ✠ at Baden, nr Vienna 11 Jan 1996, Dr of Med, Psychiatrist, Prof Univ of Vienna; *m* 1stly at Vienna 21 Sept 1939 (*m* diss by div at Vienna 17 Jan 1947), Gabriele [*Piazza Navona 93, 00186 Rome, Italy*] (*b* at Vienna 2 April 1918; she *m* 2ndly, Paul Geier), dau of Rudolf Brougier and Gabriele Werther. He *m* 2ndly at Vienna 14 Oct 1953, Monica (*b* at Linz an der Donau 21 Dec 1927), dau of Leo Nagel and Nadine Testa.

[*Elisabethstraße 56, 2500 Baden bei Wien, Austria*].

2nd Branch:
LAUBACH

Founded by Johann Friedrich, Count of Solms-Laubach, Lord of Wildenfels (*b* 19 Feb 1625; ✠ 10 Dec 1696). Inherited a fifth of the Lordship of Laubach on the extinction of the first branch 6 Aug 1676; acquired the remainder of that Lordship 1696; final partition of family possessions was made between his two sons who founded the sub-branches below 15 Oct 1709.

1st Sub-Branch
SOLMS-LAUBACH

Founded by Count Friedrich-Ernst (*b* 26 March 1671; ✠ 26 Jan 1723); Hereditary Member of the First Chamber of the Grand Duchy of Hesse 17 Dec 1820, received the qualification of "Erlaucht" (primogeniture) by the German Diet 13 Feb 1829; extended by all members of the family 7 March 1914.

Members of this Branch bear the title of Count or Countess zu Solms-Laubach, with the qualification of Illustrious Highness.

KARL, COUNT (GRAF) ZU SOLMS-LAUBACH, *b* at Laubach 1 Dec 1963, Dipl Forestry, *succ* his father, son of Otto, Count zu Solms-Laubach (*b* 26 Aug 1926; ✠ 1 March 1973) and Princess Madeleine zu Sayn-Wittgenstein-Berleburg (*b* 22 April 1936); *m* at Düsseldorf 26 Aug 1991, Julia (*b* at Essen 20 Jan 1966), dau of Prof Dr Hans G Willers and Elisabeth Meyer-Rudolphi.

[*Schloß, 35321 Laubach, Germany*].

Son and Daughters

1. Countess *Emma* Margaretha, *b* at Giessen 17 July 1992.
2. *August* Otto, Hereditary Count (Erbgraf) zu Solms-Laubach, *b* at Giessen 23 Jan 1994.
3. Countess *Clara* Elisabeth, *b* at Lich 18 Oct 1996.

Brothers and Sisters

1. Countess *Tatiana, b* at London 16 Dec 1958; *m* 1stly at Laubach 22 Oct 1977 (*m* diss by div at Frankfurt-am-Main 15 Feb 1982), Christian, Count von Hochberg, Baron zu Fürstenstein of the Princes von Pless (*b* at Frankfurt-am-Main 5 April 1953; *m* 2ndly 21 Nov 1984 (civ) 2 Feb 1985 (relig), Carina Edye), Banker. She *m* 2ndly at Amöneburg 18 Aug 1986, Patrick, Count zu Saurma-Jeltsch (*b* at Neheim-Hüsten 24 Aug 1956), Proprietor of Plausdorf, Kr Marburg.
2. Countess *Ariane, b* at London 16 Dec 1958 (twin with Countess Tatiana), Sociologist; *m* 1stly at Laubach 30 March (civ) and 31 March (relig) 1979, Stephan Königs (*b* at Cologne 16 Jan 1952; ✝ at Vettweiss 26 April 1985), Dr of Med, Banker. She *m* 2ndly at Laubach 12 Dec 1987 (*m* diss by div at Giessen 10 July 1996), Hubertus von Dewitz (*b* at Berlin 27 Feb 1947), Physician. She *m* 3rdly at Laubach 15 Aug (civ) and 28 Sept (relig) 1996, Dieter Brinks (*b* at Bad Nauheim 25 Sept 1943).
[*Gartenhaus, 35321 Laubach, Germany*].
3. Countess *Anna Margareta, b* at Berleburg 29 June 1960, Interior Decorator.
[*Schloß, 35321 Laubach, Germany*].
4. Countess *Christina, b* at Frankfurt-am-Main 19 July 1962, Translator; *m* at Laubach 13 July 1990, Hans Kilian von Pezold (*b* at Coburg 7 March 1964), Lawyer.
[*Schloß, 96489 Niederfüllbach, Germany*].
5. Count *Gustav* Albrecht, *b* at Frankfurt-am-Main 22 Oct 1965, Journalist; *m* at Ilmmünster 3 Aug (civ) and at Birnau am Bodensee 26 Aug (relig) 2000, Nicola Ute (*b* at Munich 15 Apr 1969), dau of Claus Hipp and Ute ......
[*Grüneburgweg 143, 60323 Frankfurt-am-Main-am-Main, Germany*].
6. Countess *Elisabeth, b* at Frankfurt-am-Main 12 Aug 1968; *m* at Laubach 8 June 1996, Ludwig Schmucker (*b* at Munich 19 Sept 1967), Dr rer soz oec.
[*Prinzregentenstraße 87, 81675 Munich, Germany*].

7. Countess *Maria,* b at Frankfurt-am-Main 12 Aug 1968 (twin with Countess Elisabeth); m at Detmold 15 Oct 1994, Prince Stephan zur Lippe (b at Detmold 24 May 1959), Lawyer.
[*Friedrich Ebertstraße 5, 32756 Detmold, Germany*].
8. Count *Franz,* b at Giessen 2 Oct 1971, Student Economics.
[*Schloß, 35321 Laubach, Germany*].
9. Count *Ferdinand,* b at Giessen 2 Oct 1971 (twin with Count Franz); ✝ there 2 Nov 1971.

Mother

Madeleine Olga Dora Edle Benedikte, Countess zu Solms-Laubach, b at Giessen 22 April 1936, dau of Gustav Albrecht, Prince (Fürst) zu Sayn-Wittgenstein-Berleburg and Margareta Fouché d'Otrante of the Dukes d'Otrante; m at Berleburg 29 July 1958, Otto, Count zu Solms-Laubach (b at Laubach 26 Aug 1926; ✝ there 1 March 1973), Kt of Hon St John of Jerusalem.
[*Schloß, 35321 Laubach, Germany*].

Brothers and Sisters of Father

Issue of Georg Friedrich, Count zu Solms-Laubach (b 7 March 1899; ✝ 13 May 1969) and Princess Johanna zu Solms-Hohensolms-Lich (b 17 Dec 1905; m 13 Sept 1924; ✝ 7 Sept 1982).

1. Countess *Irene,* b at Laubach 25 June 1925; m at Laubach 17 Oct 1946, Siegried 4th Prince (Fürst) zu Castell-Rüdenhausen (b at Rüdenhausen 16 Feb 1916).
[*97355 Rüdenhausen, UFranken, Germany*].
2. Count *Karl,* b at Laubach 26 Aug 1926 (twin with Otto, Count zu Solms Laubach   see above); ✝ nr Küstrin 7 Feb 1945.
4. Countess *Monika,* b at Laubach 8 Aug 1929; m at Laubach 16 July (civ) and 17 July (relig) 1981, as his 2nd wife, Ernst August, Prince of Hanover, Duke of Brunswick and Lüneburg (b at Brunswick 18 March 1914; ✝ at Hanover 9 Dec 1987; he m 1stly 4 Sept 1951, Princess Örtrud zu Schleswig-Holstein-Sonderburg Glücksburg who ✝ 6 Feb 1980), Dr of Law, Lt-Col, Grand Master Hanoverian Orders of St Georg, Guelph and Ernst August, etc.
[*Calenberg, 30982 Pattensen 5-Schulenburg an der Leine, Germany; Königinvilla, 4810 Gmunden, OÖsterr., Austria*].
5. Count *Johann Friedrich,* b at Laubach 26 April 1932, Businessman; m 1stly at Arnsburg 20 June 1962 (m diss by div at Düsseldorf 4 April 1969), Countess Eleonore (b at Frankfurt-am-

Main 5 Sept 1937; ✝ 27 May 1999), dau of Ernstotto, Count zu Solms-Laubach and Margot Bertram. He *m* 2ndly at Laubach 26 March (civ) and 9 May (relig) 1987, Birgit (*b* at Schloß Neuhaus 5 July 1944), dau of Wilhelm Dallhammer and Katharina Thorweston, and has issue by his first wife,

[*Friedrichsburg, 35321 Laubach, Germany*].

> 1. Count *Maximilian* Jörg, *b* at Hilden, nr Düsseldorf, 27 Sept 1962, Businessman; *m* at Laubach 21 June (civ) and at Frauenchiemsee 3 July (relig) 1993, Usula (*b* at Munderkingen an der Donau 31 May 1962), dau of Gerold Egon Weiss and Christina Theresa Winter, and has issue,
>
> [*Schloß 2, 35321 Laubach, Germany; Dölitzerstraße 12, 04416 Markkleeberg, Germany*].
>
> > 1. Countess *Fiona* Theresa Maximiliane, *b* at Munich 27 Oct 1993.
> >
> > 2. Countess *Celina* Christina Margot Maximilianne, *b* at Munich 21 Jan 1997.

6. Count *Friedrich,* *b* at Laubach 16 June 1937, Hotelier; *m* at Schlitz, OHessen 28 Aug (civ) and at Laubach 29 Aug (relig) 1963 (*m* diss by div 1971), Countess Ulrike [*Bahnhofstraße 59, 36431 Lauterbach, Germany*] (*b* at Schlitz 13 Feb 1940; she *m* 2ndly 30 Jan 1976, Joachim Riedesel, Baron zu Eisenbach), dau of Ludwig-Christian, Count zu Stolberg-Wernigerode and Countess Anna Schlitz genannt von Görtz, and has issue,

[*Hermann Sackstraße 2, 80331 Munich, Germany*].

> 1. Countess *Katharina* Elisabeth, *b* at Würzburg 11 Feb 1964; *m* at Lauterbach 12 Sept (civ) and 13 Sept (relig) 1997, Rupert, Count Strachwitz von Gross-Zauche and Camminetz (*b* at London 16 May 1965).
>
> [*23 Greyhound Road, London W6 8NH; Burg Braunsberg, 39011 Lana, Prov. Bozen, Italy*].
>
> 2. Count Ludwig Christian, *b* at Würzburg 6 July 1965.
>
> [*Viehtriftstraße 49, 67346 Speyer, Germany*].
>
> 3. Count Georg Friedrich, *b* at Giessen 12 Aug 1971.
>
> [*Graben 47, 99423 Weimar, Germany*].

7. Countess *Andrea* Emma Alexandra, *b* at Laubach 31 July 1941.
[*35321 Laubach, Germany*].

Brothers of Grandfather

Issue of Otto, Count zu Solms-Laubach (*b* 26 May 1860; ✝ 9 Sept 1904) and Princess Emma zu Isenburg and Büdingen in Büdingen (*b* 28 Aug 1870; *m* 14 April 1898; ✠ 13 Feb 1944), having had issue, among whom,

Sons

1. Count *Bernhard Bruno*, *b* at Arnsburg, Ober Hessen 4 March 1900; ✠ at Berlin 13 March 1938, Dir of Theatre at Nollendorfplatz, Berlin; *m* at Rüdenhausen 26 Sept 1928, Countess Louise (*b* at Rüdenhausen 1 Oct 1902; ✠ at Laubach 25 Aug 1986), dau of Hugo, Count zu Castell-Rüdenhausen and Countess Clementine zu Solms-Sonnenwalde, and had issue, among whom,

    1. Countess *Ilona* Emma Clea Mechtild, *b* at Arnsburg 15 Jan 1931; *m* 1stly at Lübbenau, Spreewald 28 Aug 1954 (*m* diss by div at Lüben 13 April 1966), Heinz Otto (*b* at Chemnitz 26 May 1930), Businessman. She *m* 2ndly at Wernigerode 12 Nov 1971 (*m* diss by div at Wernigerode 1 April 1977), Wolfgang Pilz (*b* at Trautenau 11 Jan 1924), Teacher.
    [*Karl Marxstraße 46, 38855 Wernigerode, Germany*].
    2. Count *Friedrich* Ernst, *b* at Laubach 24 March 1932, Dipl Business Studies; *m* at Frankfurt-am-Main 21 May (civ) and 22 May (relig) 1958, Richardis (*b* at Frankfurt-am-Main 29 June 1929), dau of Albrecht von Roeder and Irene Roethig, and has issue,
    [*Werner von Siemensstraße 21, 63150 Heusenstamm, Germany*].

        1. Countess *Irene* Andrea Louise, *b* at Frankfurt-am-Main 27 Feb 1960, Medical Assistant.
        [*Theodor Heussstraße 31, 63150 Heusenstamm, Germany*].

    3. Count *Alexander*, *b* at Dessau 6 March 1934, Insurance Broker; *m* at Stockheim, Rhön 14 Dec 1963 (*m* diss by div at Seligenstadt 8 Oct 1983 since when she reverted to her madiden name), Ramona (*b* at Würzburg 23 April 1941), dau of Erich Heilmann and Baroness Paula von Crailsheim, and has issue, among whom,
    [*Ahornstraße 12, 63099 Rödermark-Ober-Roden, Germany*].
        1. Countess Daniela *Polli*, *b* at Laubach 12 March 1965; *m* at Rödermark 1 April 1993, Karl Ziffer (*b* at Villach, Kärnten 31 July 1968).
        [*Weiherstraße 3, 63322 Rödermark, Germany*].
2. Count *Friedrich Botho*, *b* at Laubach 23 April 1902; ✠ at Laubach 30 March 1991, Dr of Phil; *m* at Berlin 1 June 1931 (*m* diss by div at

Berlin 19 Nov 1943), Dorothea (*b* at Berlin 16 Oct 1909; ✝ at
Rosenheim 9 Aug 1988), dau of Lothar von Gohren, Vice-Adm.
German Navy and Dorothea von Tzschoppe, and has issue,

    1. Countess Ermute *Benigna*, *b* at Berlin-Schöneberg 23 April
1932; *m* at Bentheim 30 Aug (civ) and at Kloster Arnsburg,
nr Lich 14 Oct (relig) 1966, Christian-Ludwig von Maltzan,
Baron zu Wartenberg and Penzlin (*b* at Lenschow 17 Sept
1929), Dipl Eng.
[*Zweiter Rundweg 1, 48465 Schüttorf, Germany*].

    2. Countess Karola *Brigitte,* *b* at Laubach 31 July 1933; *m* at
Frankfurt-am-Main 27 April 1957, Detlev Schulte-Vieting
(*b* at Halle an der Saale 24 June 1928), Dipl Eng.
[*Eichendorffstraße 4, 60320 Frankfurt-am-Main, Germany*].

    3. Countess *Agnes* Elisabeth, *b* at Berlin-Lichtenberg 4 Dec
1935; *m* at Frankfurt-am-Main 4 Dec 1963 (civ) and 4 Jan
1964 (relig), Jürgen von Maltzan, Baron zu Wartenberg and
Penzlin (*b* at Parchim 27 Dec 1934), Banker.
[*Kälberstücks Weg 61, 61350 Bad Homburg vor der Höhe,
Germany*].

    4. Count *Ernst* Lothar, *b* at Berlin 4 Feb 1939, Doctor;
m 1stly at Marburg an der Lahn 19 March (civ) and 20 March
(relig) 1965 (*m* diss by div at Marburg 18 Feb 1970), Ursula
(Ulla) [*Teylingerhorstlaan 4, Wassenaar, The Netherlands*]
(*b* at Siegen 17 May 1937; she *m* 2ndly at Klaaswaal 31 Oct
1975, Hans Balner), Dr of Med, Pediatrician, dau of Helmut
Hartmann and Johanna Guntermann. He *m* 2ndly at Wehrda,
nr Marburg 24 April 1970 (*m* diss by div at Traunstein 9 Oct
1975), Eva Maria [*Fridolinstraße 83, 79713 Bad Säckingen,
Germany*] (*b* at Dresden 3 Aug 1937; *m* 1stly ... Kromat, that
m diss by div ..), Dr of Med, dau of ... Ritter and ...., and by
her has issue,

        1. Count *Ruppert* Botho, *b* at Bielefeld 29 July 1971,
Mechanic.
[*Erlenaustraße 35, 83024 Rosenheim, Germany*].

        2. Countess *Kristin* Madeleine, *b* at Rosenheim 20
Dec 1972.
[*Fridolinstraße 83,, 79713 Bad Säckingen, Germany*].
Count Ernst also adopted the dau of his second wife,

        3. *Angela* Maria Kromat, *b* at Berlin 6 Feb 1959, bears
the name of "Countess zu Solms-Laubach".
Count Ernst *m* 3rdly at Rosenheim 22 March 1991, Karin

(*b* at Erfurt 26 Feb 1941), dau of ... Zürbig and ..., and by her has further issue,
[*Tassilostraße 9, 83026 Rosenheim, Germany*].

    4. Count *Stephan*, *b* at Rosenheim 22 April 1976.

    [*Tassilostraße 9, 83026 Rosenheim, Germany*].

5. Countess *Oda*, *b* at Laubach 21 June 1941; *m* at Frankfurt-am-Main 4 Dec 1964 (*m* diss by div at Frankfurt-am-Main 25 Jan 1972), Hartmuth Machholz (*b* at Oels, Silesia 11 Sept 1940). She *m* 2ndly at Mühltal, nr Darmstadt 22 Nov 1994, Helmut Pest (*b* at Insterburg, Ostpreussen 5 May 1931).
[*Eberstädterstraße 20B, 64367 Mühltal, Germany*].

Brothers of Great-Grandfather

Issue of Friedrich, Count zu Solms-Laubach (*b* 23 June 1833; ✠ 1 Sept 1900) and Countess Marianne zu Stolberg-Wernigerode (*b* 6 Sept 1836; *m* 23 June 1859; ✠ 13 Aug 1910), having had issue, among whom,

Sons

1. Count Georg *Reinhard*, *b* at Arnsburg 28 Feb 1872; ✠ at Oberstdorf, Allgäu 26 Jan 1937, Major Prussian Army; *m* at Waidring 18 Sept 1921, Emma (*b* at Speyer 13 March 1888; ✠ at Munich 22 Dec 1952), dau of Alexander Kreuter and Emma Hassler, and had issue,

    1. Countess *Luitgard* Roswitha, *b* at Munich 27 Nov 1924; *m* at Munich 5 Aug 1950, Hans, Count von der Goltz (*b* at Stettin 22 Sept 1926), Lawyer, Industrialist.
    [*Westfalenstraße 4, 80805 Munich, Germany*].

    2. Count *Hans Günther*, *b* at Munich 26 June 1927, Lawyer; *m* at Essen 30 Aug (civ) and at Hummelo 31 Aug (relig) 1968, Countess Anna (*b* at Arnheim 27 Sept 1940; ✠ at Essen 12 May 1994), dau of Sweder, Count van Rechteren Limpurg, Lord of Enghuizen nr Hummelo, Gelderland and Princess Eleonore of Lippe-Weissenfeld, and has issue, among whom,
    [*Hunsrückerstraße 19, 45133 Essen - Bredeney, Germany*].

        1. Count *Georg* Alexander, *b* at Essen 31 March 1972.
        [*Hunsrückerstraße 19, 45133 Essen - Bredeney, Germany*].

Brother of Great-Great-Grandfather

Issue of Otto, Count zu Solms-Laubach (*b* 1 Oct 1799; ✠ 22 Nov 1872) and Princess Luitgarde zu Wied (*b* 4 March 1813; *m* 11 Sept 1832; ✠ 9 June 1870), having had issue, among whom,

Son

Count *Ernst, b* at Laubach 24 April 1837; ✠ at Naumburg an der
Saale 11 Aug 1908, Imp German Counsellor of State, Kt of Hon St
John of Jerusalem; *m* at Ahrensburg 31 Jan 1874, Countess Auguste
(*b* at Ahrensburg 13 June 1847; ✠ at Marburg an der Lahn 17 Jan
1921), dau of Ernst, Count Schimmelman, Proprietor of Lindenborg
and Baroness Adelaide von Lützerode, and had issue, among whom,

Son

Count *Ernstotto, b* at Strasburg 8 Nov 1890; ✠ at Frankfurt-am-
Main 2 Sept 1977, Dr of Phil, Dir Städel Gallery, Frankfurt-am-
Main; *m* at Frankfurt-am-Main (civ) and at Arnsburg (relig) 21 Aug
1935, Margot (*b* at Erfurt 28 Dec 1906; ✠ at Vallendar 25 Aug 1994),
dau of Franz Bertram and Elisabeth Escherich, and had issue,

    1. Countess *Eleonore* Elisabeth, *b* at Frankfurt-am-Main 5
    Sept 1937, ✠ 27 May 1999; *m* at Arnsburg 20 June 1962
    (*m* diss by div at Düsseldorf 4 April 1969), Count Johann
    Friedrich zu Solms-Laubach (*b* at Laubach 26 April 1932 - see
    above), Businessman.

    2. Count *Friedrich Ernst, b* at Frankfurt-am-Main 7 March
    1940, Proprietor of Schloß Dorheim, Dipl Business Studies;
    m at Erbendorf, Ober Pfalz 29 June (civ) and at Wildenreuth,
    Gmde Erbendorf 1 July (relig) 1979, Baroness Sylvia (*b* at
    Neustadt an der Waldnaab 6 April 1952), dau of Heinrich,
    Baron von Podewils and Anneliese Bode, and has issue,
    [*Schloß Dorheim, 61169 Friedberg, Germany*].

        1. Count *Moritz* Friedrich Ernst Otto Heinrich, *b* at
        Frankfurt-am-Main 26 Sept 1980.

        2. Countess *Angelina* Sylvia Anneliese Margot, *b* at
        Southampton, New York 1 Oct 1983.

        3. Count *Philipp* Friedrich Carl Ernst Nikolaus, *b* at
        Frankfurt-am-Main-am-Main 23 Sept 1985.

        4. Countess *Margarita* Sylvia Elisabeth Alexandra,
        b at Frankfurt-am-Main 4 Aug 1989.

    3. Countess *Sibylle* Adelaide Erika, *b* at Frankfurt-am-Main
    18 Feb 1942; *m* at Arnsburg 15 April 1966, Peter Thomas
    (*b* at Reine, Westphalia 12 Sept 1935; ✠ at Kuala Lumpur 19
    June 1985), Businessman.
    [*Amboni Limited, P.O. Box 117, Tanga, Tanzania,
    East Africa*].

    4. Countess *Juliane, b* at Frankfurt-am-Main 2 July 1951.

[Breiter Stein 8, 35510 Butzbach, Germany].

2nd Sub-Branch
WILDENFELS

Founded by **Heinrich Wilhelm, Count of Solms-Wildenfels** (*b* 16 May 1675; ✝ 15 Sept 1741) who purchased Sachsenfeld in 1722. The lines below descend from his sons.

A: SOLMS-WILDENFELS

Founded by **Count Heinrich Carl** (*b* 28 Feb 1706; ✝ 7 Oct 1746) who purchased Wildenfels in 1739; qualification of "Erlaucht" (primogeniture) by the German Diet 13 Feb 1829; Hereditary Member of the former First Chamber of the Kingdom of Saxony 4 Sept 1831. Members of this sub-branch bear the title of Count or Countess zu Solms-Wildenfels.

FRIEDRICH MAGNUS (VI), COUNT (GRAF) ZU SOLMS-WILDENFELS, *b* at Wildenfels 18 Jan 1927, son of Friedrich Magnus (V), Count zu Solms-Wildenfels (*b* 1 Nov 1886; ✝ 6 Sept 1945) and Princess Marie Antoinette zu Schwarzburg *b* 7 Feb 1898; ✝ 4 Nov 1984; *m* 4 Jan 1925); *m* 1stly at Esslingen am Neckar 7 Feb 1948 (*m* diss by div at 1954), Katharina (*b* at Rathenow 22 April 1923; ✝ at Bonn 14 Sept 1970), dau of Harald Eduard Duerst and Käthe Saile (Lambert). He *m* 2ndly, his 1st wife at 1966; *m* 3rdly at Bonn 30 Sept 1994, Gisela Ursula Maria Paroll (*b* at 13 Jan 1957). *[Lotharstraße 55, 53115 Bonn, Germany].*

Sons - 1st Marriage
1. Count *Michael,* *b* at Esslingen 10 Jan 1949.
2. Count *Konstantin* Alexander Georg, *b* at Esslingen 9 March 1950; *m* 1stly at Bornheim 30 March 1973 (*m* diss by div), Gabriele (*b* at Wissen an der Sieg 23 July 1951), dau of Rudolf Schaessberg and Hildegard Thois. He *m* 2ndly at Reno, U.S.A 21 March 1994 *Erica* Sieglinde (*b* at Cologne 6 Oct 1937; *m* 1stly Herbert Schmitz-Krummacher; *m* diss by div), dau of Dr Gottfried Adolf Krummacher and Marianne Schmidt.
[am Kottenforst 72, 59126 Bonn, Germany].

Brother and Sisters
1. Countess *Anne Alexandra* Irene Sophie, *b* at Wildenfels 1 Jan 1926.
[Schloß Blumenthal, 8891 Klingen, Germany].
2. Countess *Jutta* Maria, *b* at Wildenfels 12 Feb 1928, *m* at Beirut,

Lebanon 20 Dec 1957, Salim Farid Saad (*b* at Kaferakka 9 Sept 1922; ✠ March 2000).
[*Kaferakka/Koura, Lebanon*].

3. Count *Albrecht Sizzo, b* at Wildenfels 28 May 1929; *m* at Gottlieben 30 Aug 1970 (*m* diss by div at Frankfurt-am-Main 6 May 1977), Ingrid [*An den Römergarten 24, 65779 Kelkheim, Germany*] (*b* at Frankfurt-am-Main 7 July 1933; *m* 1stly 30 July/7 Sept 1962, Nikolaus Fischler, Count von Treuberg; that *m* diss by div 6 April 1966), Dr of Med, Internist, Psychotherapist, International Director of Zonta International, Holder of the Cross of the Order of Merit of the Federal Republic of Germany, dau of Arthur Gross and Ruth Krönig.
[*Nerotal 37, 65193 Wiesbaden, Germany*].

4. Countess *Kristin, b* at Wildenfels 27 May 1938; *m* at Oberhöchstadt 3 April 1971, Dieter Gross (*b* at Lissa 25 Dec 1923), Dr of Med, Radiologist.
[*Schöne Aussicht 14, 61476 Kronberg, Taunus, Germany*].

Brother of Great-Great-Grandfather

Issue of the Friedrich Magus I, Count zu Solms-Wildenfels (*b* 31 Aug 1743; ✠ 12 Feb 1801) and Princess Caroline zu Leiningen-Dachsburg-Hartenburg (*b* 4 April 1757; *m* 21 Sept 1773; ✠ 18 March 1832), having had issue, among whom,

Son

Count *Emich* Otto Friedrich, *b* at Wildenfels 4 Dec 1794; ✠ at Berlin 7 July 1834, Capt Prussian Army, Kt Order of St Vladimir; *m* at Potsdam 14 Dec 1819, Baroness Paulina (*b* 25 March 1802; ✠ at Potsdam 18 Jan 1848), dau of Jan Willem, Baron Sirtema van Grovestins and Countess Jeanette van Limburg-Stirum, having had issue, among whom,

Son

Count Karl *August* Adalbert, *b* at Potsdam 7 Sept 1823; ✠ at Berlin-Halensee 28 Feb 1918, Lt-Gen Prussian Army, Kt of St John of Jerusalem; *m* 1stly at Baruth 12 July 1862, Countess Elisabeth (*b* at Dresden 27 March 1836; ✠ at Wandsbek, nr Hamburg 27 Sept 1868), dau of Friedrich, Count zu Solms-Baruth and Countess Ida von Wallwitz. He *m* 2ndly at Ahrensburg 28 Sept 1875, Countess Fanny (*b* at Altona 20 Jan 1846; ✠ at Berlin 8 May 1918), dau of Ernst, Count Schimmelmann Lehensgreve, Proprietor of Lindeborg and Baroness Adelaid von Lützerode, and had issue, among whom by his second wife,

Sons

1. Count Friedrich *Ernst, b* at Freiburg im Breisgau 4 Aug 1877; ✠ at Zoppot 9 Feb 1945, Major Prussian Army; *m* at Reval 18 Nov/1 Dec 1904, Baroness Karin (*b* at Reval 15/27 May 1882; ✠ at Hamburg 18 March 1959), dau of Bernhard, Baron von Uexküll and Marie Rudnick (of Polish nobility), and had issue,

    1. Countess *Karin, b* at Hanover 25 March 1907; *m* at Hamburg 12 May 1953, Otto Stade (*b* at Blumenthal, Stade 8 Oct 1903).

    2. Count Ernst August *Bernhard, b* at Danzig-Langfuhr 30 July 1909, Capt; *m* at Hamburg-Altona 23 Sept 1940, Lieselott (*b* at Elmshorn 8 March 1915), dau of Willy-Ferdinand Voigt and Emma Katharina Germeck, and has issue,
    [*Martinistraße 21, 20251 Hamburg, Germany*].

        1. Count Friedrich-Ernst Peter *Bernhard, b* at Bevensen, Uelzen 29 May 1941; *m* 1stly at Frankfurt-am-Main .... Astrid (*b* at ... 10 Oct 1938; *m* diss by div ...), dau of Erich Kohlhauer, and has issue,

            1. Count *Christian, b* ...

        Count Bernhard *m* 2ndly at Garssen 8 May 1967, Karin (*b* at Schwerin 14 Sept 1943), dau of Helmut Pretsch and Eva Neumann, and has further issue,

            2. Countess *Christina, b* at Hamburg 12 Dec 1967.

            3. Countess *Sylvia* Alexa, *b* at Hamburg 20 Nov 1968.

        2. Countess Karin Lieselotte *Friedel, b* at Bevensen 28 Dec 1942; *m* at Hamburg 9 ... 1963 (*m* diss by div at Detmold July ... 1965), Victor Javier Julio Garcia y Perez (*b* at ...).
        [*Harvestehuder Weg 75, 20419 Hamburg, Germany*].

        3. Count Emich Jobst *Friedrich-Magnus, b* at Bevensen 15 May 1944.
        [*Auf der Fuchskaul 67, 45419 Essen, Germany*].

        4. Count *Alexander, b* at Bevensen 5 Oct 1945; *m* at Hamburg 3 July 1967, Hannelore (*b* at Hamburg 11 June 1952), dau of ... Tietze and Erne ..., and has issue,
        [*Am Hasenberge 14, 22335 Hamburg, Germany*].

            1. Countess *Alexandra, b* at Hamburg 15 Jan 1970.

    3. Count *Friedrich* Ernst Magnus, *b* at Reval 2 June 1911,

✠ 12 Dec 1997; *m* 1stly at Bad Godesberg 13 Dec 1952 (*m* diss by div at Cologne 30 Aug 1960), Renata [*Rennbahnstraße 153, 50737 Cologne, Germany*] (*b* at Potsdam 1 Feb 1906), dau of Theodor von Schmidt-Pauli and Bertha Schramm. He *m* 2ndly at Rodenkirchen, nr Cologne 27 Dec 1962, Maria Theresia (*b* at Bad Godesberg 1 Aug 1932), dau of Peter Hermanns and Katharina Fleischhauer, and has issue by his second wife, [*Heinrich Zillestraße 16, 50999 Cologne - Rodenkirchen, Germany*].

    1. Countess *Béatrice, b* at Bad Godesberg 28 Oct 1963.

    2. Count *Peter* Alexander, *b* at Cologne 19 June 1966.

2. Count *Karl* August, *b* at Freiburg im Breisgau 9 Aug 1879; ✠ at Ahrensburg, nr Hamburg 15 Dec 1958, Major Prussian Army; *m* at Berlin 14 Sept 1915, Maria Gans, Edle von Putlitz (*b* at Grube, Westprignitz 23 April 1892; ✠ at Ahrensburg 9 Nov 1955), dau of Busso Gans, Edler von Putlitz and Anna von Bredow, and had issue, among whom,

    1. Count *Harald* Ernst Emich Magnus, *b* at Berlin 23 Feb 1922, Businessman; *m* at Ahrensburg 2 Sept 1950, Helga (*b* at Trittau 18 Aug 1921), dau of Philipp Hamburger and Ingeborg Sommerfeldt, and has issue, [*Travemünder LandStraße 23, 23669 Timmendorferstrand-Niendorf, Germany*].

        1. Count *Niels* Siegfried Harald, *b* at Ahrensburg 9 June 1952, Sociology Educator; *m* 11 Nov 1980, Annette (*b* 12 Aug 1957), dau of Horst Jungmann and Käthe Prediger, and has issue, [*Wrangelpark 11, 22605 Hamburg, Germany*].

            1. Countess *Lisa, b* at Hamburg 27 April 1981.

            2. Countess *Janne, b* at Hamburg 24 Feb 1983.

3. Count *Emich* Hermann Werner, *b* at Münzenberg 5 Feb 1883; ✠ at Frankfurt-am-Main 12 Nov 1961, Lt-Col German Army, Jockey; *m* at Berlin 5 Dec 1910, Erika (*b* at Sagerke, Stolp 17 April 1892; ✠ at Usingen 18 Feb 1976), dau of Nikolaus von Boehn and Elisabeth von Michaelis, and had issue,

    1. Count *Emich* Nicolaus August Otto Ernst, *b* at Danzig-Langfuhr 2 Oct 1911; ✠*k* at Kuglin, Prussia 19 Jan 1945; *m* at Frankfurt-am-Main 13 April 1938, Tilly (*b* at Hofheim, Taunus 23 April 1912), dau of Josef Schmitt and Anna Söhngen, and had issue, among whom,

[*Gerhart Hauptmann Ring 236a, 60439 Frankfurt-am-Main, Germany*].

    1. Countess *Gerda* Anneliese, *b* at Frankfurt-am-Main 29 July 1941.

    2. Count *Emich* Wilhelm, *b* at Frankfurt-am-Main 8 Feb 1944; ✠ there 7 Dec 1946.

Count Emich also adopted a dau,

    4. *Alexa* Sigrid Pauly, *b* at Bad Doberan, Mecklenburg 16 Aug 1942, Businesswoman, adopted at Frankfurt-am-Main 11 June 1956/19 Nov 1956, bears the name of "Countess zu Solms-Wildenfels-Hadik-Barköczy"; *m* at Darmstadt 25 Oct 1978, Adam Berecz (*b* at Pöstyén, Neutra 22 Dec 1945), Machine Eng.

[*Arndstraße 31, 60325 Frankfurt-am-Main, Germany*].

B: SACHSENFELD
(✠ Extinct ✠)

Evangelist: Founded by Count Friedrich Ludwig (*b* 2 Dec 1708; ✠ 27 Aug 1789) who, circa 1750 purchased the lands of Sachsenfeld from his younger sister. The Head of this Branch did not have the right to the qualification of "Erlaucht" since the possession of Lordships were not considered "Reichsständisch" or "Immediate".

3rd Branch:
SOLMS-BARUTH

Founded by Count Friedrich Sigismund I (*b* 28 June 1627; ✠ 7 Jan 1696) who received half of the Lordship of Baruth in the partition of the family possessions with his brothers (see above) 30 Oct 1665, and purchased the other half 9 June 1694. Hereditary Member of the former Prussian House of Lords 12 Oct 1854; Prince of Solms-Baruth (Prussian title; primogeniture) with the qualification of "Durchlaucht", Charlottenburg 16 April 1888 (for Friedrich, Count of Solms-Baruth); however cadet members of this branch do not have the right to the qualification of "Erlaucht" since the possession of Lordships were not considered "Reichsständisch" or "Immediate". The Head of this Branch and his wife bear the title of Prince and Princess zu Solms-Baruth with the qualification of Serene Highness and the cadet members bear the title of Count or Countess zu Solms-Baruth.

FRIEDRICH Wilhelm Ferdinand Hermann Hans, **4TH PRINCE (FÜRST) ZU SOLMS-BARUTH**, *b* at Baruth 22 Dec 1926, Kt of Hon St John of Jerusalem, *succ* his father, son of Friedrich, 3rd Prince zu Solms-Baruth (*b* 25 March 1886; ✠ 12 Sept 1951) and

Princess Adelheid zu Schleswig-Holstein-Sonderburg-Glücksburg
(*b* 19 Oct 1889; *m* 1 Aug 1914; ✠ 11 June 1964); *m* 17 Aug 1963,
Baroness Birgitta (*b* at Berlin-Charlottenburg 9 Jan 1924), only dau
of Eduard, Baron von Berchem-Königsfeld and Ingrid von Horn.
[*Topcliffe, Parel Vallei, 7130 Somerset West, C.P., South Africa*].

Sons

1. Count *Friedrich* Eduard Philipp Theodor Nikodemus, *b* at
Marienthal 27 Nov 1963.
[*965 North Doheny Drive, Los Angeles, CA 90069, U.S.A.*].
2. Count *Julian* Immanuel Friedrich Christian Hubertus, *b* at
Marienthal 6 Aug 1965; *m* at Baruth 18 May (civ) and at Florence 9
June (relig) 1996, Livia (*b* at New York 28 Jan 1970), dau of Florens
Deuchler and Karin Lauke-Gernsheim.
[*Schloß, 15837 Baruth, Germany*].

Sisters

1. Countess Victoria *Friederike Louise* Karoline Mathilde Hedwig
Dorothea Rosa Helene Marka Marie, *b* at Baruth 10 Oct 1916; ✠ at
Salzburg 10 Jan 1989, Journalist.
2. Countess *Feodora* Hedwig Luise Victoria Alexandra Marie, *b* at
Baruth 5 April 1920; *m* 1stly at Flienicke, nr Potsdam 28 Nov 1942,
Gert Schenk (*b* at Charlottenburg, nr Berlin 2 July 1910; ✠ at
Vienna 23 Aug 1957), Dr of Med; *m* 2ndly at Vienna 6 Oct 1961, Karl
Adolf, 10th Prince (Fürst) von Auersperg (*b* at Goldegg 13 March
1915).
[*Prinz Eugenstraße 16, 1010 Vienna, Austria*].
3. Countess *Rosa* Cecilie Karoline-Mathilde Irene Sibylla Anna, *b* at
Baruth 15 May 1925; *m* at Stellenbosch, South Africa 3 Nov 1955,
Neville Lewis (*b* at Kapstadt 8 Oct 1895; ✠ at Stellenbosch 26 June
1972). She *m* 2ndly at Stellenbosch 9 Oct 1981, Heinrich W Weber
(*b* at Berlin ... 1926; ✠ at Stellenbosch 11 Oct 1983).
4. Countess *Caroline-Mathilde* Luise Adelheid Elisabeth, *b* at
Klitschdorf 15 April 1929, Dr of Med; *m* at Stellenbosch 12 May
1963, Johan van Stenderen (*b* at Amsterdam 8 June 1905; ✠ at
Stow-on-the-Wold 19 July 1978).
[*Barn Cottage, Blendington, Kingham, Oxon, U.K.*].

Brother of Father

Issue of Friedrich, 2nd Prince zu Solms-Baruth (*b* 24 June 1853;
✠ 31 Dec 1920) and Countess Luise von Hochberg, Baroness zu
Fürstenstein of the Princes von Pless (*b* 29 July 1863; *m* 10 Sept

1881; ✠ 7 May 1938), having had issue, among whom,

Sons

1. Count *Hermann* Franz, *b* at Klitschdorf 11 Oct 1888; ✠ at Eckart, nr Werfen, Salzburg 7 May 1961, Proprietor of Dambrau in Upper Silesia, Dr of Law; *m* at Pless 29 March 1913, Countess Anna (*b* at Pless 24 Feb 1888; ✠ at Salzburg 13 Nov 1966), dau of Hans Heinrich XI, 2nd Prince and Duke von Pless, Count von Hochberg, Baron zu Fürstenstein and Burggravine and Countess Mathilde zu Dohna-Schlobitten, and had issue, among whom,

    1. Count Wilhelm *Friedrich-Sigismund* Hans Hermann Konrad, *b* at Potsdam 26 Jan 1914; ✠ at Munich 21 Nov 1982, Businessman, Farmer; *m* at Munich 15 March 1948, Rosemarie (*b* at Verchland, Stettin 21 Sept 1918; ✠ at Munich 20 Jan 2000; she *m* 1stly at Verchland 6 June 1940, Alfred, Ritter Hentschel von Gilgenheimb who ✠ 1 Nov 1948; that *m* diss by div at Munich 29 May 1947), dau of Jakob von Wietzlow, Proprietor of Verchland, Proprietor of Cunow and Eleonore von Roennebeck, and had issue,

    [Neufeldstraße 7, 81243 Munich, Germany].

        1. Countess *Felicitas* Anna Eleonore, *b* at Munich 11 Feb 1952; *m* at Munich 19 Feb 1970 (*m* diss by div 24 April 1992 since when she reverted to her maiden name), Friedrich Karl, Baron Michel von Tüssling (*b* at Munich 10 July 1943), Lawyer.

        [Flat 1, 5 Stafford Terrace, London, W8 7BJ, U.K.].

    2. Countess *Marie-Agnes* Louise Mathilde, *b* at Potsdam 31 Dec 1916; *m* 1stly at Krakau 21 July 1938, Hans Balduin von Plessen, Proprietor of Damshagen (*b* at Damshagen, Mecklenburg 19 Sept 1907; ✠k at Le Havre 11 June 1940). She *m* 2ndly at Jeltsch 29 July 1943 (*m* diss by div at Munich 28 Oct 1948), Johannes-Heinrich, Count von Saurma, Baron von and zu der Jeltsch (*b* at Franzdorf 28 May 1909; ✠ at Graz 1 Sept 1977). She *m* 3rdly at Munich 28 June 1949, Albert Prollius (*b* at Kreuth, nr Tegernsee 18 June 1905; ✠ at Munich 31 July 1992), Businessman.

    [Karl Singerstraße 3, 81479 Munich, Germany].

2. Count *Hans* Georg Eduard, *b* at Klitschdorf 3 April 1893; ✠ at Salzburg 9 Oct 1971, Capt Prussian Army, Kt of Hon St John of Jerusalem; *m* at Glücksburg 27 May 1920, Princess Caroline-Mathilde (*b* at Grünholz 11 May 1894; ✠ at Salzburg 22 Jan 1972), dau of

Friedrich Ferdinand, Duke zu Schleswig-Holstein-Sonderburg-Glücksburg and Princess Karoline Mathilde zu Schleswig-Holstein-Augustenburg, and had issue,

1. Countess *Viktoria-Luise* Friederike Caroline-Mathilde, *b* at Casel, Nieder Lausitz 13 March 1921; *m* 1stly as Casel 21 Jan 1942 (*m* diss by div at Coburg 19 Sept 1946), Prince Friedrich Josias von Saxe-Coburg and Gotha, Duke of Saxony (*b* at Schloß Callenberg 29 Nov 1918; ✚ at Grein 23 Jan 1998), Businessman, Lt-Col; *m* 2ndly at Steinwänd, nr Werfen, Salzburg 6 Nov 1947, Richard CB Whitten (*b* at Indianapolis 9 May 1910; ✚ at Louisiana Oct 2001).

[*74210 Military Road, Covington, LA 70435, U.S.A.*].

2. Count *Friedrich-Hans* Ferdinand Wilhelm, *b* at Casel 3 March 1923, Businessman, Kt of Hon St John of Jerusalem; *m* at Werfen 21 Jan (civ) and at Luisenlust, nr Hirzenhain, Ober Hessen 30 April (relig) 1950, Princess *Oda* (*b* at Wernigerode 10 June 1925; ✚ at St Veit an der Glan 30 May 1978), dau of Botho, Prince zu Stolberg-Wernigerode and Princess Renata von Schoenaich-Carolath, and has issue,

[*Zensweg am Vogelbichl, 9300 St. Veit an der Glan, Austria*].

  1. Countess *Irina* Renata, *b* at Salzburg 25 July 1953; *m* at Odenthal 8 July (civ) and at Salzburg 1 Sept (relig) 1973, Hubertus, Prince zu Sayn-Wittgenstein-Berleburg (*b* at Bonn 21 Dec 1948).

  [*Haus Selbach 51519 Odenthal, Germany*].

  2. Count *Christian-Friedrich,* *b* at Salzburg 13 July 1954, Businessman; *m* at New York 31 Oct 1979, Melissa (*b* at Providence, RI, USA 5 May 1954), dau of Georg Anthony Buttler and Mary Margaret von Fellinger, and has issue,

  [*P.O. Box 798, 3000 Hollywood Road, Leonardtown, MD 20650, U.S.A.*].

    1. Countess *Oda-Desirée, b* at Florence 4 May 1981.

    2. Countess *Caroline* Mathilda, *b* at Providence 24 March 1987.

    3. Count *Alexander* Friedrich Christian, *b* at Washington, DC 30 May 1989.

3. Countess *Huberta* Désirée, *b* at Klagenfurt 22 Aug 1958; *m* at Frankfurt-am-Main 16 March 1982, Rafael Herrlich (*b* at Tel Aviv 18 March 1954), Photographer.

[*Bishofs Weg 7, 60598 Frankfurt-am-Main, Germany*].

3. Count *Hubertus* Conrad Ferdinand, *b* at Berlin 7 Dec 1934; ✠ at Rathmannsdorf 22 Oct 1991, Dr of Chem; *m* 1stly at Barntrup 12 Aug 1961, Elisabeth-Charlotte (Ebi) (*b* at Barntrup 3 Dec 1935; ✠ at Lemgo 6 Nov 1968), dau of Ernst von Kerssenbrock and Elisabeth-Charlotte von Klot, and had issue,

> 1. Count *Rupprecht* Caspar Friedrich, *b* at Munich 5 Aug 1963; *m* at Mainz 24 July (civ) and at Breitenbach am Herzberg 29 July (relig) 1989, Princess Henriette (*b* at Hamburg 24 April 1964), dau of Prince Heinrich XI Licco Reuss and Baroness Ulfa von Dörnberg, and has issue,
>
> [*Salzachstraße 16, 84036 Landshut, Germany*].
>
> > 1. Count *Kasimir* Friedrich August, *b* at Bad Säckingen 30 Aug 1991.
> > 2. Count *Hubertus* Caspar Friedrich, *b* at Bad Säckingen 24 April 1993.
> > 3. Count *Clemens* Friedrich Leopold, *b* at Landshut 15 Feb 1996.
>
> 2. Countess Frederike *Donata*, *b* at Friesing 23 March 1965; *m* at Lütjenburg 8 Aug (civ) and at Kirchnüchel, Kr Lütjenburg 1 Oct 1988, Christian-Jasper, Baron von Brockdorff of the Counts Kletkamp (*b* at Kiel 26 June 1960), Lawyer.
>
> [*Langhansstraße 13, 14469 Potsdam, Germany*].
>
> 3. Countess *Eilika* Sophie, *b* at Freising 8 Aug 1966; *m* at Wolfegg 28 April (civ) and at Greinburg, Upper Austria 11 May 1991, Jakob, Count von Waldburg zu Wolfegg and Waldsee (*b* at Ravensburg 9 March 1957).
>
> [*Tiche Udoli 19, 25263 Rozloke, nr Prague, Czech Republic*].

Count Hubertus *m* 2ndly at Salzburg 13 Dec 1969, Baroness Gerta (*b* at Riga 23 March 1939), dau of Fabian, Baron Stael von Holstein and Baroness Helene von der Osten genannt Sacken, and by her has further issue,

[*Sternwartstraße 7, 81679 Munich, Germany*].

> 4. Countess *Viktoria* Caroline, *b* at Hamburg 27 Aug 1971.

STARHEMBERG

Catholic: This feudal family originated in Upper Austria and can be authenticated from Gundaker von Stainpach (in Styria) 1150 whose grandson, Gundaker built the castle of Strochenberg, Upper Austria and took the name of "de Storichenberg" which later became Starhemberg; acquired the Lordships of Schaunberg, Eferding, etc in Upper Austria through the marriage (1530) of Erasmus to Countess Anne of Schaunberg; authorised to join the arms of Schaunberg, Augsburg 23 July 1559; Count of the Holy Empire, Vienna 27 Feb 1643; extended to all family Members, Vienna 3 March 1643; Bohemian Incolat, 4 Aug 1667; Hereditary Grand Marshal in Austria, Vienna 6 March 1717 (for Gundaker Thomas, Count of Starhemberg); received into the College of Counts of Franconia, 9 Nov 1719; Hungarian Indigenat 1723; Bohemian Prince (primogeniture), Vienna 13 Nov 1765; Prince of the Holy Empire (primogeniture) with the qualification of "Hochgeboren", Vienna 18 Nov 1765; received the qualification of "Durchlaucht" by the German Diet 18 Aug 1825; Hereditary Member Austrian "Reichsrate", Vienna 18 April 1861. The Head of the family and his wife bear the title of Prince and Princess von Starhemberg with the qualification of Serene Highness, while cadet members bear the title of Count or Countess von Starhemberg.

GEORG ADAM Salvator Franz Josef Ernst Rüdiger Camillo Maria, **9TH PRINCE (FÜRST) VON STARHEMBERG,** *b* at Klagenfurt 7 April 1961, Proprietor of Schaunberg, Waxenberg, Eferding, etc, adopted by (Vienna 4 July 1994) and *succ* his kinsman, Heinrich, 8th Prince (Fürst) von Starhemberg (*b* 4 Oct 1934; ✝ 30 Jan 1997), son of Count Franz Josef (*b* 18 July 1933; ✝ 28 Sept 1995) and Itha Hauniger, Noble (Edle) von Haueningen (*b* 24 Nov 1938; *m* 25 June 1960); *m* at Maissau, NÖsterreich 2 Sept (civ) and 4 Sept (relig) 1988, Countess Nadejda (*b* at Cologne-Lindenthal 29 June 1961), dau of Ernst Ferdinand, Count von Abensperg and Traun and Felicia Guépin.
[*Kirchenplatz 1, 4070 Eferding, Austria*].

Sons and Daughters
1. Countess Larissa (*Lara*) Maria Franziska Katharina, *b* at Madrid 9 Sept 1989.
2. Countess *Kalina* Maria Felicia Cecilia, *b* at Madrid 25 Jan 1991.
3. *Constantin* Franz-Josef Ernst Gundakar Maria, Hereditary Prince (Erbgraf) von Starhemberg, *b* at Vienna 17 Sept 1992.
4. Count *Ernst Ferdinand* Maria, *b* at Linz 13 Aug 1995.

Mother

Itha, Countess *Franz Joseph* von Starhemberg, *b* at Vienna 24 Nov 1938, Stage Designer, dau of Franz Hauniger, Edler von Haueningen and Maria von Raits; *m* at Maria Wörth 25 June 1960, Franz Josef, Count von Starhemberg (*b* at Bad Ischl 18 July 1933; ✠ at Moosburg 28 Sept 1995), Saw Mill Owner.
[*Gradenegg 24, 9262 Moosburg, Kärnten, Austria*].

Brother and Sisters

1. Count *Franz Josef* Johannes Salvator Clemens Maria, *b* at Klagenfurt 24 June 1963, Underwriter.
[*Viktringer Ring 11, 9020 Klagenfurt, Austria*].

2. Countess *Franziska* Sophie Benedikta Anna Agnes Maria, *b* at Klagenfurt 2 Dec 1964; *m* at Gurk, Kärnten 3 April 1993, Ernst Benedikt Hoffmann von Rumerstein (*b* at Vienna 29 Feb 1964).
[*Burghardt Gasse21, 1200 Vienna, Austria*].

3. Countess *Felicia* Friederike Camilla Bernadette Katharine Maria, *b* at Klagenfurt 6 April 1967; *m* at Moosburg 7 May 1994, Gustav Pichelmann (*b* at Vienna 12 Feb 1955), Architect.
[*Ungar Gasse47-7, 1030 Vienna, Austria*].

Sisters of Father

Issue of Count *Georg* von Starhemberg (*b* 10 April 1904; ✠ 12 Feb 1978) and Princess Anna Agnes von Isenburg (*b* 7 March 1904; *m* 17 April 1929; ✠ 5 Nov 1970).

1. Countess *Franziska* Sophie Marie Friederike, *b* at Eisenkappel 10 July 1930; *m* at Eltville 23 May 1956, Karl Theodor Mayer (*b* at Vienna 5 Feb 1924; ✠ at Oberjeserz, nr Rosegg, Kärnten 5 July 1990).
[*Kögeln Gasse12, 1130 Vienna-Lainz, Austria*].

2. Countess *Sophie* Marie Elisabeth Therese Franziska Alexandra Anna, *b* at Eisenkappel 14 Sept 1931, Dame Star Cross Order; *m* at Eisenkappel, Kärnten 14 May 1951, Alexander Muta, Count von Spiegelfeld (*b* at Graz 2 Nov 1925), Dr rer pol.
[*Hanselmayer Gasse4, 1130 Vienna, Austria*].

3. Countess *Friederike* Olivia Helene Louise Ludviga Stefanie Maria, *b* at Reichwaldau 20 Aug 1936; *m* at Eisenkappel, Kärnten 8 June 1955, Karl, Prince von Auersperg-Breunner (*b* at Goldegg, Lower Austria 26 April 1930).
[*Estancia Los Leones, RA-6614 Rivas FCNGSM, Argentina; Schloß*

Wald, 3144 Wald, Lower Austria].

4. Countess *Irene, b* at Birstein 7 March 1940; *m* 1stly at Eisenkappel 16 July 1959 (*m* diss by div at Korneuburg 11 Aug 1971), Johannes, Prince von Auersperg (*b* at Weitwörth 29 Jan 1934), Music Professor; *m* 2ndly at Vienna 1 Sept 1972 (*m* diss by div 12 April 1985), Johann Heinrich, Baron von Tinti (*b* at Pöchlarn an der Donau 2 April 1919; ✠ there 23 Dec 1986).
[Goldegg Gasse2A, 1040 Vienna, Austria].

STOLBERG

This Seigneural family originated in the Harz and can be traced from Heinricus von Vockstete (near Sangerhausen) in 1200; acquired the Lordship of Rossla in the partition of possessions between the heirs of the last Count of Beichlingen in 1341; inherited the County of Hohnstein 1417; the County of Wernigerode 3 June 1429; and the County of Königstein and Rochefort in 1535, with the Bailiwicks of Ortenberg and Gedern, authorised to bear the title and arms of the Counts of Königstein, Lords of Eppstein; ratification of arms, Augsburg 17 May 1548; joined the arms of the Counts of Hohnstein, Prague 18 April 1597; the family possessions were divided between sons of Count Chrisoph II (*b* 1 Dec 1567; ✠ 21 Nov 1638), from whom the lines below descended.

LINE I
STOLBERG-WERNIGERODE

Founded by Count Heinrich Ernst, Lord of the County of Wernigerode (*b* 20 July 1593; ✠ 4 April 1672); the right of primogeniture was instituted 21 May 1738; the dignity of Prince of the Holy Empire with the qualification of "Hochgeboren" was bestowed on Count Friedrich Carl of Stolberg-Gedern (*b* 11 Oct 1693; ✠ 28 Sept 1767), Frankfurt-am-Main 18 Feb 1742 (extinct 5 Jan 1804); Christian Friedrich, Count of Stolberg-Wernigerode 8 June 1765 inherited the Lordships of Peterswaldau, Jannowitz and Kreppelhof in Silesia from Erdmann, Count of Promnitz and his three younger sons Ferdinand, Konstantin and Anton founded the three Cadet Branches of this Line; Hereditary Member of the former House of Lords of the Grand Duchy of Hesse 17 Dec 1820; received the qualification of "Erlaucht" (primogeniture) by the German Diet 13 Feb 1829; Hereditary Member of the former Prussian House of Lords 12 Oct 1854; Family Law established 1876; received Prussian authorisation for each Head of the family of Stolberg-Wernigerode, descending from Christian-Ernst, Count of Stolberg-Wernigerode (*b* 2 April 1691; ✠ 25 Oct 1771), to bear the title of Prince, and for all descendants in the first degree of the Head of the family to bear the title of Prince or Princess with the qualification of "Durchlaucht", 22 Oct 1890 The Head of the family and his children bear the name of Prince or Princess zu Stolberg-Wernigerode with the qualification of Serene Highness, and other members of the family bear the title of Count or Countess zu Stolberg-Wernigerode with the qualification of Illustrious Highness.

PHILIPP Constantin, **5TH PRINCE (FÜRST) ZU STOLBERG-WERNIGERODE,** Count zu Königstein, Rochefort, Wernigerode and Hohenstein, Lord zu Eppstein, Münzenberg, Breuberg, Agimont, Lohra and Clettenberg, *b* at Frankfurt-am-Main 8 June 1967, *succ* his father, son of Christian-Heinrich, 4th Prince (Fürst) zu Stolberg-Wernigerode, *b* 21 Dec 1922; ✠ 4 Dec 2001); *m* at Wernige-Rode 21 April (civ) and at Wolfegg 19 May (relig) 2000, Countess Caroline (*b* at Munich 18 April 1971) dau of Count Gebhard of Waldburg of Wolfegg and Waldsee and of Birgit Riedesel, Baroness zu Eisenbach.
[*Hofgut Luisenlust, 63697 Hirzenhain OHessen, Germany*].

Mother

Maria-Elisabeth, Dowager Princess zu Stolberg-Wernigerode, *b* at Pinnow 25 July 1936, dau of Albrecht, Baron von Maltzahn, Proprietor of Pinnow and Duckow and Countess Friederike zu Dohna-Schlobitten; *m* at Hamburg-Othmarschen 19 July 1957, Christian-Heinrich, 4th Prince (Fürst) zu Stolberg-Wernigerode (*b* at Wernigerode 21 Dec 1922; ✠ at Hofgut Luisenlust nr Bad Nauheim 4 Dec 2001; *succ* his father 3 Sept 1989).
[*Hofgut Luisenlust, 63697 Hirzenhain OHessen, Germany*].

Brothers

1, Prince *Ludwig-Christian* Botho Albrecht, *b* at Würzburg 5 April 1958; *m* at Ortenberg, OHessen, 24 May (civ) and at Usenborn 3 Aug (relig) 1991, Astrid (*b* at Bad Homburg 5 Jan 1959), dau of Klaus Höhne and Hannelore Frömel, and has issue,
[*Carrer de SA Goleta 73, 07350 Binissalem Balears, Spain*].

  1. Countess *Felicitas*, *b* at Büdingen 29 March 1994.
2. Prince *Bolko* Hubertus, *b* at Würzburg 13 March 1959; *m* at Gelroy, California, USA 3 July (civ) and at Usenborn 8 July (relig) 1989, Kim (*b* at San Francisco 25 March 1959), dau of Major Kirke La

Shelle and Loritta Bonfante, and has issue,
[*665 Portofino Lane, Foster City, CA 94404, U.S.A.*].

1. Countess *Natasia* Elisabeth Joan, *b* at San Francisco 27 March 1992.

3. Prince *Georg Henrich, b* at Frankfurt-am-Main 29 Nov 1970.
[*Hofgut Luisenlust, 63697 Hirzenhain OHessen, Germany*]

Brother and Sisters of Father

1. Princess *Oda, b* at Wernigerode 10 June 1925; ✠ at St Veit 30 May 1978; *m* at Werfen, Salzburg 21 Jan (civ) and at Luisenlust, nr Hirzenhain, OHessen 4 April (relig) 1950, Friedrich Hans, Count zu Solms-Baruth (*b* at Casel, Niederlausitz 3 March 1923), Businessman.
[*Zensweg am Vogelbichl, 9300 St. Veit an der Glan, Austria*].

2. Princess *Huberta* Alexandra, *b* at Wernigerode 21 Sept 1927; ✠ at Bad Homburg vor der Höhe 21 Jan 1984; *m* at Hirzenhain 4 Sept (civ) and at Frankfurt-Preungesheim 6 Sept (relig) 1951 (*m* diss by div 18 Nov 1982), Wilhelm Dietrich, Count von Hochberg, Baron zu Fürstenstein of the Princes von Pless (*b* at Wanscha 27 Jan 1920), Lt-Col.

3. Prince *Elger, b* at Wernigerode 9 Dec 1935, Forestry Manager; *m* at Horneburg, Nieder Elbe 18 Sept (civ) and 18 Sept (relig) 1961, Baroness Maria Karin (*b* at Hamburg-Altona 8 July 1934), Proprietor of Horneburg, Psychologist, dau of Carl, Baron von Düring, Proprietor of Horneburg and Georgine (Georgette) Henrich von Omorovicza, and has issue,
[*Forsthaus Luisenlust, 63697 Hirzenhain OHessen, Germany*]

1. Countess *Carolin* Leonore, *b* at Frankfurt-am-Main 29 Sept 1962; *m* at Hamburg 17 June (civ) and 18 June (relig) 1994, Magdy Missiha (*b* at Cairo 9 Jan 1955).
[*Fischers Allee 12, 22763 Hamburg, Germany*].
[*Forsthaus Luisenlust, 63697 Hirzenhain OHessen, Germany*]

2. Countess *Nicola* Huberta Georgette, *b* at Frankfurt-am-Main 21 Sept 1965.
[*Guldeinstraße 40, 80339 Munich, Germany*]

3. Count Botho Friedrich Carl *Alexander, b* at Frankfurt-am-Main 23 Sept 1967.
[*Schloß, 63683 Ortenberg, OHessen, Germany*]

Brother of Great-Grandfather

Issue of Otto I, Prince zu Stolberg-Wernigerode (*b* 30 Oct 1837;

✠ 19 Nov 1896) and Princess Anna Reuss (b 9 Jan 1837; m 22 Aug 1863; ✠ 2 Feb 1907) having had issue, among whom,

Son

Prince Friedrich *Wilhelm* Heinrich, b at Hanover 23 July 1870; ✠ at Posen 23 Jan 1931, Dr of Law, Kt of Hon St John of Jerusalem, German Consul at Vienna 1914 - 1918; m at Schönberg, Hesse 19 Jan 1910, Princess Elisabeth (Edda) (b at Schönberg 7 July 1883; ✠ at Schlitz 12 March 1966), dau of Gustav, Prince and Count zu Erbach-Schönberg and Princess Marie von Battenberg, having had issue, among whom,

Son

Count *Ludwig-Christian* Otto Gustav Alexander Romanus, b at Rome 30 Dec 1910; ✠k at Schönbeck an der Elbe 12 April 1945, Propritor of Radenz and Galazki, Krotoschin, Lt-Col; m at Schlitz, Hesse 5 April (civ) and 8 April (relig) 1937, Countess Anna (b at Darmstadt 26 Dec 1912; ✠ at Schlitz 16 March 1999), dau of Wilhelm, Count and Lord von Schlitz genannt von Görtz and Baroness Catharina (Cateau) Riedesel zu Eisenbach, and had issue,

1. Count *Wilhelm,* b at Galazki 6 April 1938, ✠ at Friedrichsdorf 11 Jan 2001, Banker; m at Schlitz 20 March (civ) and at Kloster Arnsburg, nr Lich 22 April (relig) 1967, Baroness Marie-Agnes (b at Niederaula 15 Feb 1940), dau of Christoph, Baron von Seebach and Baroness Marie-Adelheid von Brandis, and has issue,
[*Hintergärtenweg 6, 61381 Friedrichsdorf, Germany*].

    1. Countess *Donata* Anna Uta, b at Heidelberg 5 Oct 1967; m at Schlitz 26 May (civ) and 27 May (relig) 1995 Alexander Eichstaedt (b at Eckernförde 30 June 1965), Chartered Accountant.
    [*Witts Park 14, 22587 Hamburg, Germany*].

    2. Countess *Annabel* Katharina, b at Schlitz 30 April 1969.

    3. Count *Christoph* Wilhelm, b at Frankfurt-am-Main 26 Jan 1974.

2. Countess *Ulrike,* b at Schlitz 13 Feb 1940; m 1stly at Schlitz 28 Aug (civ) and at Laubach, Giessen 29 Aug (relig) 1963 (m diss by div at Gießen 29 March 1972), Friedrich, Count zu Solms-Laubach (b at Laubach 16 June 1937), Hotelier; m 2ndly at Arnsburg 9 Jan (civ) and at Eisenbach

30 Jan (relig) 1976, Kurt-Joachim (Jockel) Riedesel, Baron zu Eisenbach (*b* at Lauterbach 29 Dec 1943), Banker.
[*Bahnhofsstraße 59, 36341 Lauterbach, Germany*].

3. Count *Gisbert, b* at Radenz 2 May 1942, Banker; *m* at Schlitz 28 Aug (civ) and at Herrnhaag, nr Büdingen 10 Sept (relig) 1967, Princess Feodora (*b* at Gera 5 Feb 1942), Kindergarten Teacher, dau of Prince Heinrich I Reuss and Duchess Woizlawa Feodora of Mecklenburg, and has issue,
[*Am Wildenstein 7, 63654 Büdingen, OHessen, Germany*].

    1. Count *Constantin* Hermann Heinrich, *b* at Frankfurt-am-Main 6 May 1969.

    2. Count *Friedrich* Christian Heinrich, *b* at Frankfurt-am-Main 5 June 1972.

4. Count *Hermann, b* at Radenz 12 Aug 1943, Advertising Executive; *m* at Bad Driburg 20 May 1977, Countess Angelina (*b* at Hildesheim 19 Aug 1949), dau of Caspar-Heinrich, Count von Oeynhausen, Proprietor of Driburg and Countess Ramona von Wedel, and has issue,
[*Frauenlobstraße 7, 60487 Frankfurt-am-Main, Germany*].

    1. Count *Moritz* Caspar, *b* at Frankfurt-am-Main 16 May 1978.

    2. Countess *Marie* Victoria Anna Ramona, *b* at Frankfurt-am-Main 17 July 1979.

    3. Count Ludwig Christian *Leopold* Emil, *b* at Frankfurt-am-Main 10 May 1982.

    4. Count Caspar *Heinrich* Damon, *b* at Frankfurt-am-Main 8 Oct 1986.

Cadet Branches
I: PETERSWALDAU

This branch descends from Count Ferdinand (*b* 18 Oct 1775; ✠ 20 May 1854) who succeeded to the Lordship of Peterswaldau in Silesia 26 May 1824; Hereditary Member of the former Prussian House of Lords 12 Oct 1854.

Ferdinand **ANTON** Maria Christian Friedrich Leopold Franz Josef Pius Gabriel, **COUNT (GRAF) ZU STOLBERG-WERNIGERODE**, *b* at Peterswaldau 4 July 1925, son of Count Franz Xaver (*b* 19 July 1894; ✠ 4 May 1947) and Princess Barbara of Bourbon-Two Sicilies (*b* 14 Dec 1902; *m* 31 May 1922; ✠ 1 Jan 1927).

Sisters

1. Countess *Elisbeth* Bona Maria Alfonsa Ferdinanda Josefa Antonie Juliane, *b* at Peterswaldau 17 April 1923; *m* at Lindau, Bodensee 26 Jan 1944, Rüdiger, Count von Stillfried and Rattonitz (*b* at Silbitz, Silesia 14 July 1923).
[*Bäuerlinshalde 13, 88131 Lindau, Germany*].
2. Countess *Maria* Josefa Gabriele Antonia Gebharda, *b* at Peterswaldau 11 May 1924; ✟ at Lindau 24 Sept 1986.
3. Countess *Sophie* Marie Antonie Henrike Thaddea Gabriele, *b* at Peterswaldau 21 Dec 1926; ✟ at Weingarten 25 Oct 1987.

Brother of Great-Grandfather

Issue of Count Ferdinand (*b* 18 Oct 1775; ✟ 20 May 1854) and Countess Marie-Agnes zu Stolberg-Stolberg (*b* 4 May 1785; *m* 25 May 1802; ✟ 16 Oct 1848), having had issue, among whom,

Son

Count *Günther,* *b* at Peterswaldau 19 June 1816; ✟ at Reinerz, Silesia 25 Oct 1888; *m* at Dessau 4 Nov 1850, Marie von Lebbin (*b* at Trampe 16 Nov 1820; ✟ at Reinerz 14 July 1857), having had issue, among whom,

Son

Count Ferdinand Anton *Leonhard,* *b* at Reinerz 6 March 1853; ✟ at Würben 1 May 1914, Capt Prussian Army, Kt of Hon St John of Jerusalem ; *m* at Schlemmin, Pommern 14 Dec 1892, Countess Bertha (*b* at Rödelheim 17 June 1869; ✟ at Leipzig 30 Dec 1939), dau of Otto, Count zu Solms-Rödelheim and Assenheim and Emma von Thun, having had issue, among whom,

Son

Count *Günther,* *b* at Glatz 27 Sept 1900; ✟ at Munich-Gladbach 24 Dec 1939, Capt German Army; *m* at Schlemmin 31 May 1923, Erna (*b* at Beeskow 31 May 1897; ✟ 25 July 1991), dau of Leo von Platen and Emma von Levetzow, and had issue, among whom,

    1. Count *Leonhard* Hans Bertram, *b* at Leipzig 27 Sept 1928; ✟ at Prince George, British Columbia, Canada 23 May 1999; *m* at Prince George, British Columbia 20 April 1956, Eleonore (*b* at Basel 18 Nov 1921; ✟ at Prince George, British Columbia, Canada 14 Jan 1976), dau of Otto Frikker and Charlotte Feldmann, and has issue,

        1. Countess *Marianne* Charlotte, *b* at Prince George 5

Nov 1956.
[*Box 616 Church Langley, V1M 2R9, Canada*].
2. Countess *Sibylle, b* at Leipzig 12 Feb 1931; *m* at Spenge,
Westfalen 30 March 1951 (*m* diss by div at Bielefeld 20 June
1960 since when she has resumed her maiden name), Rüdiger
Frommholz (*b* at ... 10 May 1925), Dr of Phil.
[*Freseniusstraße 59, 81247 Munich, Germany*].

II: JANNOWITZ

**This line descends from Count Konstantin (*b* 25 Sept 1779;
✠ 19 Aug 1817). His son, Wilhelm, succeeded to the Lordship
of Jannowitz in Silesia 26 May 1824.**

EBERHARD Georg Christian, **COUNT (GRAF) ZU
STOLBERG-WERNIGERODE,** *b* at Hirschberg, Silesia 19 June
1931, Industrialist, son of Christian Friedrich Count zu Stolberg-
Wernigerode (*b* 16 Aug 1901; ✠ 18 July 1994) and Erica zu Solms-
Sonnenwalde (*b* 4 March 1880; *m* 30 July 1900; ✠ 13 July 1970);
m 1stly at Giessen 29 Aug (civ) and at Holzhausen 21 Oct (relig)
1956 (*m* diss by div at Koblenz 29 June 1972), Baroness Anna-
Elisabeth [*33039 Nieheim-Holzhausen, Germany*] (*b* at Schönebeck
11 Jan 1935), dau of Alhard, Baron von der Borch and Ingeborg von
Rohrscheidt. He *m* 2ndly at Krailling (civ) and at Planegg, nr Munich
(relig) 9 April 1973, Barbara (*b* at Schweidnitz 6 Nov 1935; *m* 1stly 2
June (civ) and 3 June (relig) 1954, Christoph von Wiedebach and
Nostitz-Jänkendorf; that *m* diss by div at Mannheim 25 March 1970),
dau of Christoph von Lindeiner genannt von Wildau and Ruth
Stockhausen, and has issue,
[*Auf dem Rümmer 13, 56598 Rheinbrohl, Germany*].

Daughters - 1st Marriage

1. Countess *Ernestine* Ludmilla Alexandra, *b* at Giessen 6 March
1957.

[*Unterbachstraße 10, 37603 Holzminden, Germany*].

2. Countess *Huberta* Maria Annemarie, *b* at Giessen 14 Aug 1959;
m at Brakel 3 Oct 1984 (*m* diss by div at Brakel 25 Aug 1997),
Wolfgang Ziegann (*b* at ... 4 Jan 1951), from 3 Oct 1984 known as
"Count zu Stolberg-Wernigerode".

[*Van-Gogh-Platz 7, 53844 Troisdorf, Germany*].

3. Countess *Susanne* Antonie Erica, *b* at Neuwied 23 May 1962, Teacher; *m* at Nieheim 15 June 1984 (*m* diss by div Kassel 4 May 1987), Peter Schulz (*b* at ... 1948).

[*Grasweg 14b, 32657 Lemgo, Germany*].

Son - 2nd Marriage

4. Count *Constantin* Georg Christian-Friedrich, *b* at Neuwied 22 Feb 1975.

[*Auf dem Rümmer 13, 56598 Rheinbrohl, Germany*].

Brothers and Sisters of Father

1. Count *Konrad, b* at Rohrlach 24 July 1904 ✠ at Oldenburg 10 June 1993, Musician; *m* 1stly at Munich 19 May 1936, Anna Sibylle (*b* at Letting, Livld 9/22 Sept 1914; ✠ at Zurich 9 Oct 1957; *m* diss by div at Oldenburg 10 July 1946), dau of Karl Zoege von Manteuffel and Baroness Katharina (Karin) von Wolff, and had issue,

    1. Countess *Jutta, b* at Munich 6 Oct 1936; *m* 1stly at Hamburg 8 Aug 1959, Curt Rönnau (*b* at Lübeck 1 May 1928; *m* diss by div at Hamburg 4 June 1964). She *m* 2ndly at Hamburg 8 Aug 1964, Günther Hildmann (*b* at Bitterfeld 13 April 1926; ✠ at Saalbach, Austria 4 July 1980), Dipl Engineer. She *m* 3rdly at Ahrensburg 28 June 1986, Gerhart Paul Peritz (*b* at at Ahrensburg 9 Nov 1923; ✠ at Ahrensburg 9 Oct 1997).

    [*Rudolf Kinaustraße 27a, 17255 Ahrensburg, Germany*].

    2. Countess *Brilla, b* at Munich 20 Feb 1939; *m* at Munich 7 July 1967 (*m* diss by div at at Munich 1 April 1976), Friedrich-Carl von Ribbeck (*b* at Berlin 9 July 1939).

    [*Marbachweg 236, 60320 Frankfurt, Germany*].

Count Konrad *m* 2ndly at Oldenburg 27 July 1946 (*m* diss by div at Oldenburg 6 Sept 1970), Anneliese (*b* at Wandorn, Ostenburg 30 Dec 1916; she *m* 2ndly ... Wilms), dau of Emil Bergmann and Anna Trebes, and had further issue, among whom,

[*Burenkamp 4, 26127 Oldenburg, Germany*].

    3. Count *Günther* Ulrich, *b* at Berlinchen, Neumark 13 June 1944; *m* at Oldenburg 25 Aug 1967 (*m* diss by div at Oldenburg 4 May 1974), Clare Johanne (*b* at Schweieraussendeich, Wesermarch 22 Dec 1948), dau of Arthur Johann Georg

Heinrich Cordes and Ella Johanne Gerhardine Kallmeyer, and has issue,
[*Ringstraße 7, 26935 Stadland, Oldenburg, Germany*].

    1. Count *Marco*, b at Brake an der Unterweser 26 Jan 1968.
    [*......, 26919 Brake, Germany*].

4. Countess Edelgard *Imma*, b at Oldenburg 1 Feb 1946, Pediatric Nurse; m 1stly at Oldenburg 1 March 1968 (m diss by div at Münster, Westphalia 23 June 1973), Freerk Eilt de Vries (b at Kirchdorf, Aurich 21 June 1947). She m 2ndly at .... 13 Feb 1976, Peter Bonhagen (b at ...; ✝ Jan 2000).
[*Kleistraße 3, 26203 Wardenburg, Germany*].

5. Count *Hans-Udo*, b at Oldenburg 13 July 1950, Insurance Broker; m at Wardenburg 31 Aug 1973, Inge (b at Oldenburg 26 March 1953), dau of Heinz Schmidt and Hella Sander, and has issue,
[*Alter Esch 31, 26203 Wardenburg, Germany*].

    1. Countess *Melanie*, b at Oldenburg 8 Oct 1975; m at Wardenburg 12 May 2000 Hergen Brandes (b at Oldenburg 12 Dec 1971).
    [*An der Bäke 24, 26203 Wardenburg, Germany*].

    2. Countess *Nadine*, b at Oldenburg 26 April 1978.

6. Count *Wolf-Botho*, b at Oldenburg 11 Feb 1955.
[*Von Thünenstraße 12, 26131 Oldenburg, Germany*].

2. Count *Johann-Otto*, b at Jannowitz 19 May 1906 ✝ 11 May 1996, Agragarian Manager; m at Stuttgart 29 March 1956, Baroness Maria-Irmgard (b at Colmar, Alsace 3 April 1914; m 1stly at Berlin 25 May 1938, Axel von Bülow who was ✝k nr Mittenwald 21 July 1945), dau of Friedrich-Wilhelm, Baron von Willisen and Irmgard Riess von ScheurnSchloß.
[*Klopstockstraße 67, 70143 Stuttgart, Germany*].

3. Countess *Erica*, b at Jannowitz 7 Jan 1919; m 1stly at Breslau 24 Nov 1943, Friedrich-Karl Stier (b at Breslau 16 Oct 1917; ✝ at Herrsching 21 Feb 1970), Proprietor of Skarsine, Trebnitz. She m 2ndly at Munich 23 Sept 1993, Gerhard Wetzig (b at Coswig, Meissen 7 March 1911; ✝ at Munich 3 Oct 1999).
[*Heßstraße 22/69, 80799 Munich, Germany*].

Brother of Great Grandfather

Issue of Constantin, Count zu Stolberg-Wernigerode (b 8 Oct 1843; ✝ 27 May 1905) and his first wife, Countess Antonie zu Stolberg-

Wernigerode (*b* 24 March 1850; *m* 12 July 1870; ✠ 12 Dec 1878), having had issue, among whom,

Son

Count *Carl, b* at Jannowitz 14 Sept 1876; ✠ at Herrsching am Ammersee 20 April 1934, Major Prussian Army; *m* 1stly at Alt-Doebern, Nieder Lausitz 24 Sept 1903 (*m* diss by div at Berlin 5 Dec 1919), Countess Hilde (*b* at Alt-Doebern 29 March 1884; ✠ at Dierdorf, nr Selters 20 Oct 1966), dau of Heinrich, Count von Witzleben and Princess Marie Reuss. He *m* 2ndly at Herrsching 8 Oct 1931, Countess Erica (*b* at Potsdam 4 March 1880; ✠ at Hersching 13 July 1970; she *m* 1stly at Klitschdorf 30 July 1900, Eberhard, Count zu Stolberg-Wernigerode who ✠ 18 March 1929), dau of Otto, Count zu Solms-Sonnenwalde and Countess Helene zu Solms-Baruth, and had issue by his first wife, among whom,

1. Countess *Maria Antonie, b* at Várpalota, Hungary 6 Feb 1909; *m* 1stly at Neuwied 29 April 1930, Hermann, Hereditary Prince (Erbprinz) zu Wied (*b* at Potsdam 18 Aug 1899; ✠*k* at Rzeszów, Poland 5 Nov 1941), Capt, Dipl Agr. She *m* 2ndly at Strawald, nr Herrnhut, Ober Lausitz 31 Aug 1943, Edmund von Gordon (*b* at Laskowitz 3 Oct 1901; ✠ at Andernach am Rhein 22 Sept 1986), Editor.
[*Wied Runkelstraße 1, 56269 Dierdorf, Germany*].

2. Count *Dietrich* Hartmann, *b* at Alt-Doebern 1 Oct 1910; ✠ at Ranstadt 26 Oct 1988, Capt (Res), Farmer, Cmdr St John of Jerusalem; *m* at Ribbeck, Westhavelland 11 July 1942, Renate (*b* at Berlin-Schöneberg 11 May 1918), dau of Hans von Ribbeck, Proprietor of Ribbeck and Bagow and Baroness Marie-Agnes von Schele, and had issue,
[*Seniorenheim, Saarstraße 3, 61350 Bad Homburg, Germany*].

   1. Count *Christian* Carl, *b* at Nauen, Westhavelland 8 April 1943, Engineer, Technician, Businessman; *m* at Gundersheim 16 April 1977, Mechtild (*b* at Gundersheim 31 March 1945), dau of Franz Kampt and Hedwig Lawall, and has issue,
[*Hans Purrmannstraße 4, 01909 Frankenthal, Germany*].

      1. Countess Dorothee Elisabeth, *b* at Grünstadt 6 Aug 1981.

      2. Countess *Bettina, b* at Kreppelhof 13 Dec 1944; *m* at Ranstadt, Ober Hessen 2 Sept (civ) and 6 Sept

(relig) 1969, Wolf, Baron von Uslar-Gleichen (*b* at Hohenkränig 6 Sept 1943), Banker, Kt of St John of Jerusalem.

[*Kasinoweg 13, 13465 Berlin-Frohnau, Germany*].

3. Count *Alexander* Hans Heinrich, *b* at Ortenberg, Hessen 1 Jan 1947, Dr of Agr, Dipl Eng Agr, Kt of Hon St John of Jerusalem; *m* at Bonn-Bad Godesberg 7 May 1977, Victoria-Elisabeth (*b* at Warburg 5 April 1954), dau of Col Gustav Josef von Detten and Elisabeth von Wedelstaedt, and has issue,

[*Zur Hardthöhe 4, 63691 Ranstadt, Germany*].

    1. Countess *Juliane* Bettina Luise, *b* at Manus, Amazon Brazil 15 June 1978.

    2. Count *Maximilian* Hans Heimdall, *b* at Belém, Pará, Brazil 20 June 1980.

    3. Countess *Anna Donata* Elisabeth, *b* at Belém 25 Aug 1982.

4. Countess *Henriette* Marie, *b* at Ortenberg 5 Dec 1949, Schoolteacher; *m* 1stly at Nieder-Weisel, Ober Hessen 7 Oct 1978 (*m* diss by div 17 Aug 1987), Michael Deines (*b* at Hanau 10 Jan 1950), Lt (Res). She *m* 2ndly at Reiskirchen 5 Oct (civ) and at Ranstadt 29 Dec (relig) 1989, Wolf-Werner Trebeljahr (*b* at Karnkewitz, Schlawe, Pommern 30 May 1932), Dipl Forestry, Forester.

[*Limestraße 23, 61381 Köppern, Germany*].

5. Count Johannes *Constantin*, *b* at Nieder-Weisel 18 March 1958, Banker, Lt (Res), Banker; *m* at Hanover 31 Aug 1985, Catrin (*b* at Hanover 5 Nov 1959), dau of Carl Ludwig Wilkening and Birgitt Dunkel), and has issue,

[*Waldwinkel, Rannenberg, 31749 Auetal, Germany*].

    1. Countess *Marie Agnes*, *b* at Berlin 21 Nov 1987.

    2. Countess *Johanna*- Katharina, *b* at Berlin 30 Jan 1989.

    3. Countess *Josephine* Dorothea, b at London 12 Feb 1992.

    4. Countess *Irina* Amelie Magdalene, *b* at London 22 April 1995.

3. Countess *Ingeborg*, *b* at Eichbert, nr Hirschberg 22 May

1915; *m* at Norf am Rhein 20 Sept 1950, Karl-Heinrich von Waldthausen, Proprietor of Müggenburg and Vellbrüggen (*b* at Essen 11 June 1910; ✠ there 18 April 1985), Lawyer, Banker.

[*Kantorei 33, 4300 Essen 1 - Rellinghausen, Germany*].

Half-Brother and Sisters of Granfather

Issue of Constantin, Count zu Stolberg-Wernigerode and his second wife, Princess Elisabeth zu Stolberg-Wernigerode (*b* 1 May 1866; *m* 4 June 1885; ✠ 30 Jan 1928), having had issue, among whom,

1. Count *Otto*, *b* at Wernigerode 31 March 1893; ✠ at Hamburg 5 Aug 1984, Dr of Phil, Prof Univ of Munich, Editor "Neue Deutsche Biographic"; *m* at Berlin 19 April 1932, Baroness Yvonne (*b* at Jacobstadt, Kurland 22 April / 4 May 1895; ✠ at Hamburg 3 Aug 1982), dau of Bernhard, Baron von Gershau von Flotow and Baroness Sophie von Klopmann, and had issue,

    1. Count *Ulrich* Wolf Philipp, *b* at Munich 4 May 1935, ✠ at Hamburg 30 Jan 1998, Patent Lawyer, Dipl Chem, Dr rer nat; *m* at Tutzing, Bavaria 29 Aug (civ) and at Weilheim, Bavaria 30 Aug (relig) 1958, Christa (*b* at Crossen an der Oder 8 April 1937), dau of Christoph von L'Estocq and Waldtraut von Tiedemann-Behr, and has issue,

    [*Jürgensallee 27, 22609 Hamburg, Germany*].

        1. Countess *Vivica* Charlotte Natalie, *b* at Munich 14 Sept 1959, Goldsmith; *m* at Tutzing 29 Dec 1988 (civ) and at Haseldorf 27 May 1989 (relig), Jörg Mittelsten Scheid (*b* at Wuppertal 7 May 1936), Dr of Law, Lawyer.

        [*Hosfelds Katernberg 10, 5600 Wuppertal, Germany*].

        2. Count *Nikolaus* Ferdinand Constantin, *b* at Wilmington, Delaware, USA 22 June 1963, Industrialist; *m* at Hamburg 9 Aug (civ) and at Haseldorf 11 Aug (relig) 1990, Baroness Alexandra (*b* at East London, South Africa 17 April 1965), Joachim, Baron von Esebeck and Ursula von der Lühe, and has issue,

        [*Isestraße 79, 20149 Hamburg, Germany*].

            1. Countess *Antonia* Yvonne, *b* at Hamburg 25 April 1991.

            2. Countess *Theresa* Marie-Agnes, *b* at Hamburg 11 March 1993.

3. Countess *Rosanna* Naomi, *b* at Hamburg 21 Aug 1997.

3. Countess Marie Antoinette *Natalie, b* at Hamburg 28 Oct 1964, *m* at Haseldorf 30 May 1992, *Andreas* Jacobs (*b* at Bremen 27 Oct 1963), Dr of Laws.
[*Johnsallee 18, 20148 Hamburg, Germany*].

III: KREPPELHOF
This branch descends from Count Anton (*b* 23 Oct 1785; ✠ 11 Feb 1854); succeeded to the Lordship of Kreppelhof in Silesia, with Peikersdorf, 26 May 1824; succeeded to the Lordship of Diersfordt, nr Wesel in Upper Rheinland; inherited the Lordship and fideicommiss of Dönhoffstädt, Prussia 14 Dec 1884; Hereditary Members of the former Prussian House of Lords 1 Sept 1907.

SIEGFRIED, COUNT (GRAF) ZU STOLBERG-WERNIGERODE, *b* at Diersfordt 16 April 1937, Proprietor of the Lordship of Wesel, nr Diersfordt, son of Bolko, Count zu Stolberg-Wernigerode (*b* 13 Oct 1885; ✠ 15 Sept 1956) and Countess Marie-Elise zu Stolberg-Wernigerode (*b* 2 Nov 1893; ✠ 14 March 1973; she *m* 1stly 24 March 1917, Helmuth-Paul von Kulmiz who ✠ 29 Dec 1932; *m* 2ndly 26 Sept 1934, Siegfried, Count zu Stolberg-Wernigerode); *m* at Diersfordt 29 Aug 1964 (*m* diss by div at Duisburg 20 Sept 1973), Renate Marie (*b* at ... 1942), dau of Martin Luther and Marie Zach.
[*Lindenberg 1, 46487 Wesel-Diersfordt, Germany*].

Sons
1. Count *Günther, b* at Flensburg 31 Aug 1964.
[*Marienweg 53, 46483 Wesel, Germany*].
2. Count *Michael, b* at Wesel 12 Aug 1966.
[*Lindenberg 1, 46487 Wesel-Diersfordt, Germany*].

Brother of Father
Issue of Stephan, Count zu Stolberg-Wernigerode (*b* 24 Dec 1847; ✠ 7 Oct 1891) and Ordalie Nickisch von Rosenegk (*b* 6 Dec 1853; *m* 27 April 1880; ✠ 14 Oct 1916), having had issue, among whom,

Son
Count *Reinhard, b* at Oberau 29 Oct 1889; ✠ at Rahden, Westphalia 29 March 1973, Capt Prussian Cavalry, Farmer, Kt of Hon St John of Jerusalem; *m* at Schlemmin 17 Aug 1918, Countess Mariagnes (*b* at Merseburg 12 Dec 1894; ✠ at Espelkamp 9 Feb 1972), dau of

Leonhard, Count zu Stolberg-Wernigerode and Countess Bertha zu Solms-Rödelheim, and had issue, among whom,

1. Countess *Ordalie* Bertha, *b* at Schlemmin 25 May 1919 ✠ at Knellesberg 20 Oct 1992, Auxiliary Sister German Red Cross; *m* at Diersfordt 17 June 1948, Otto Gottfried von Lieres and Wilkau (*b* at Breslau 17 April 1909), Dr of Law, Farmer, Kt of St John of Jerusalem.
[*Knellesberg 1, 88074 Meckenbeuren, Germany*].

2. Countess *Antonie* - Ferdinande Auguste Viktoria, *b* at Schlemmin 26 Aug 1920; *m* at Dönhofstädt, East Prussia 1 Jan 1941, Ulrich, Baron von Mirbach (*b* at Tilsit 4 March 1914).
[*Gravensteinerstraße 9, 25704 Meldorf, Holstein, Germany*].

3. Count *Stephan-Leonhard*, *b* at Stralsund 13 Feb 1924; ✠ at Rheinberg 7 July 1990, Proprietor of Dönhoffstädt and Carlswalde, East Prussia, adopted by his kinsman Albrecht, Count zu Stolberg-Wernigerode (*b* 1886; ✠ 1948) and his wife, Countess Magna Maria zu Solms-Wildenfels (*b* 1883; ✠ 1966) to inherit Dönhoffstädt and Carlswalde, 29 Dec 1938 ratified at Barten 10 March 1939; *m* at Diersfordt 21 July 1951, Ruth (*b* at Chunking, China 4 April 1926), dau of Friedrich Jessel and Dorothea Hoffmann, and had issue,
[*Schwarzer Weg 29, 47495 Rheinberg, Germany*].

> 1. Countess *Henriette* Agnes Dorothea, *b* at Moers 10 April 1955; *m* at Kaarst 22 July 1983, Jörg Bauer (*b* at Strackholt 19 Jan 1953).
> [*Flachsbleiche 15, 41564 Kaarst, Germany*].

> 2. Count *Albrecht-Georg*, *b* at Moers 20 Oct 1956; *m* at Wesel Oct 1986 (*m diss by div 1991*), Heike Voß (*b* at ...).
> [*St Antoniusstraße 8, 47495 Rheinberg, Germany*].

> 3. Count *Robert* Heinrich Leopold, *b* at Moers 5 Feb 1958, Engineer; *m* at Xanten 15 Nov 1985, Maria Scheffers (*b* at Xanten 5 May 1959), dau of Wilhelm Scheffers and Katharina Lamberti, and has issue,
> [*Grüner Weg 26, 46519 Alpen, Germany*].

> > 1. Countess *Anja* Katharina Ruth, *b* at Xanten 30 March 1989.

> > 2. Count *Andreas* Stephan Wilhelm, *b* at Xanten 8 Oct 1990.

4. Countess *Elisabeth-Charlotte*, *b* at Moers 18 April

1962; *m* at Alpen 29 May 1987, Helmut Hackstein (*b* at Alpen 4 Jan 1963).

[*Bothenweg 2a, 46519 Alpen, Germany*].

5. Count *Claus-Günther*, *b* at Moers 19 Feb 1965.

[*Rathausstraße 62, 46519 Alpen, Germany*].

4. Count *Christian-Albrecht*, *b* at Dönhofstädt 4 April 1926; ✝ at Rösrath-Forsbach, Cologne 10 Feb 1991, Proprietor of Kreppelhof and Krausendorf in Silesia, and Udowald in der Neumark, adopted by his kinsman Albrecht Count zu Stolberg-Wernigerode (*b* 1886; ✝ 1948) and his wife, Countess Magna Maria of Solms-Wildenfels (*b* 1883; ✝ 1966) to inherit Kreppelhof and Krausendorf, 29 Dec 1938/ ratified at Barten 10 March 1939; *m* at Cologne-Marienburg 13 July 1957, Hannelore (*b* at Berlin 11 March 1934), dau of Walter Dahms and Else Joël.

5. Count *Friedrich* Wilhelm Anton, *b* at Dönhofstädt 31 Aug 1927 ✝ at Düsseldorf 5 April 1992; *m* 1stly at Kassel-Wilhelmshöhe 12 Dec 1956 (*m* diss by div at Duisburg 1 Feb 1966), Christine (*b* at Dresden 28 Feb 1936), dau of Werner Günther and Annemarie Schmidt. He *m* 2ndly at Eutin-Fissan 12 May 1972, Verena (*b* at Berlin 16 Feb 1931), dau of Dietrich von Holtzendorff and Ehrengard von Hertzberg.

[*Heinrichstraße 60a, 40239 Düsseldorf, Germany*].

LINE II

Founded by Count Johann Martin, Lord of the ancient County of Stolberg, Lord of Ortenberg and Heringen (*b* 4 Nov 1594; ✝ 22 May 1669); Partition of possessions 19 July 1706 between two sons of Count Christoph Ludwig I, Lord of Ortenberg and since 23 Aug 1684, also of Stolberg (*b* 18 June 1634; ✝ 7 April 1704), who founded the two lines below of Stolberg-Stolberg and Stolberg-Rossla.

I: STOLBERG-STOLBERG

Founded by Count Christoph Friedrich (*b* 18 Sept 1672; ✝ 22 Aug 1738); the right of primogeniture was instituted 13 May 1737; received Prussian authorisation for the Head, his wife and for all their descendants in the first degree including the children of the Hereditary Prince to bear the title of Prince or Princess with the qualification of "Durchlaucht", Berlin 22 March 1893 in accordance with the creation of Friedrich Carl of Stolberg-Gedern as a Prince of the Empire by Karl VII, 18 Feb 1742. The Lines below descend from two sons of the founder of this branch - see above.
The Head of the Family, his siblings and children all bear the title of

Prince or Princess zu Stolberg-Stolberg with the qualification of Serene Highness, while cadet members of this branch bear the title of Count or Countess zu Stolberg-Stolberg with the qualification of Illustrious Highness.

PRINCIPAL BRANCH

This branch descends from Count Christoph Ludwig II (*b* 1703; ✠ 1761); received the qualification of "Erlaucht"; 13 Feb 1829; Hereditary Member of the former Prussian House of Lords 12 Oct 1854.

JOST CHRISTIAN, 4TH PRINCE and COUNT (FÜRST AND GRAF) ZU STOLBERG, Königstein, Rochefort, Wernigerode and Hohenstein, Lord of Eppstein, Münzenberg, Breuberg, Agimont, Lohra and Clettenberg, etc, *b* at Stolberg 19 July 1940, Kt of Hon St John of Jerusalem, son of Wolff-Heinrich, 3rd Prince and Count zu Stolberg (*b* 28 April 1903; ✠ 2 Jan 1972) and Irma Erfert (*b* 28 April 1910; ✠ at Neuwied 28 June 1994); *m* at Neuwied am Rhein 7 May (civ) and Maulde, Belgium 31 May (relig) 1980, Sylviane (*b* at Brussels 9 Aug 1956), dau of Louis Janssens van der Maelen and Thérèse Plaquet.
[*Avenue de l'Armée 76, 1040 Brussels, Belgium; Jagdhaus am Schindelbruch, 06547 Stolberg, Harz, Germany*].

Son and Daughter

1. *Christoph Ludwig*, Hereditary Prince (Erbprinz) zu Stolberg, *b* at Brussels 13 May 1982.
2. Princess *Louise* Marie Juliana, *b* at Brussels 2 March 1984.
3. Count *Heinrich-Victor*, *b* at Brussels 26 June 1986.
4. Countess *Juliana* Mathilde Irina, *b* at Brussels 6 May 1995.

Sisters

1. Princess Irmgard *Sixtina* Juliana, *b* at Stolberg 4 Nov 1933, *m* at Arolsen 29 Aug (civ) and 30 Aug (relig) 1961, Georg-Friedrich, Prince zu Waldeck and Pyrmont (*b* at Hanover 22 Oct 1936), Lt.-Col.
[*An der Bullungsburg 14, 34454 Arolsen, Germany*].
2. Princess *Sophie Charlotte* Agnes, *b* at Nordhausen 4 Oct 1943, *m* at Neuwied 14 July (civ) and Burg Runkel 15 July (relig) 1967, Friedrich Wilhelm, 7th Prince (Fürst) zu Wied (*b* at Stuttgart 2 June 1931).
[*Schloß, 56564 Neuwied, Germany*].

CADET BRANCH: BRAUNA
Catholic (since 1800): Founded by Count Christian Günther (*b* 9 July 1714; ✠ 22 June 1765).

PIUS Maria Leopold Alfred Josef Petrus Paulus Johannes Evangelist Patrick Martinus Hubertus Michael, **COUNT (GRAF) ZU STOLBERG-STOLBERG,** *b* at Brauna 8 Oct 1924, Dipl Land Management, Kt Bavarian Order of St George, son of Leopold, Count zu Stolberg-Stolberg (*b* 1 July 1868; ✠ 4 Sept 1955) and Countess Maria von Spee (*b* 23 June 1895; *m* 26 April 1922; ✠ 30 Oct 1975); *m* at Frankfurt-am-Main 26 May 1962, Gudrun (*b* at Wilhelmshaven 29 Dec 1940), dau of Armin Bock and Liselotte Michels.
[*Altenrond 7, 79872 Bernau, Germany*].

Son and Daughters
1. Count *Patrick* Valentin Pius Michael Meinolf, *b* at Bensheim 27 May 1963; *m* at Sulzburg 30 March (civ) and 31 March (relig) 1990, Juliane (*b* at 16 Aug 1996), dau of Hjul Jenson and Arwide Leucke. [*Hinrichsenstraße 9, 04105 Leipzig, Germany*].
> 1. Count *Friedrich-Leopold* Patrick Valentin Clemens Maria, *b* at Freiburg 22 July 1990.
> 2. Count *Johann* Albrecht Hjul Magnus Patrick Maria, *b* at Freiburg 15 Jan 1993.
2. Countess *Stephanie* Elisabeth Maria Gabriele Mechtild, *b* at Freiburg 22 Feb 1966.
[*Santa Paissa Cala Llonga n 2, 07669 Santanyi, Mallorca, Spain*].
3. Countess *Elisabeth* Christine Maria Pia Mechtild, *b* at Freiburg 30 June 1971.
[*Am Rank 4, 79872 Bernau, Germany*].
4. Countess *Juliane* Antonia Maria Theresa, *b* at Freiburg 6 Jan 1983.

Brothers
1. Count *Friedrich-Leopold* Alfred Hermann Christian Josef Petrus Johannes Evangelist Maria, *b* at Brauna 28 Feb 1923; ✠ in a Russian POW camp at Sandar, nr Tiflis 9 Feb 1943.
2. Count *Georg* Ferdinand Aloysius Alfred Petrus Johannes Evangelist Antonius Lukas Maria, *b* at Brauna 14 Oct 1927, Forester, Kt of Hon Sovereign Military Order of Malta; *m* at Ullstadt, Neustadt an der Aisch, MFranken 25 June 1959, Baroness Marie-Gabrielle (*b* at Ullstadt 1 Aug 1931), dau of Georg, Baron von and zu

Franckenstein, Proprietor of Ullstadt and Princess Caroline (Lilly) von Schönburg-Hartenstein, and has issue, among whom,
[*Peter Griesbacher Weg 1, 94032 Passau, Germany*].

    1. Count *Christoph* Thaddäus Moritz Georg Aloysius Friedrich-Leopold Maria, *b* at Bad Reichenhall 15 June 1960; *m* at Deutschlandsberg, Steiermark 19 Nov (civ) and at Hafnerbach, Lower Austria 22 Nov (relig) 1987, Countess Elisabeth (*b* at Vienna 15 Sept 1962), dau of Albert, Count Montecuccoli-Laderchi and Barbara von Pflügl, and has issue,
[*Am Schloßpark 29, 65203 Wiesbaden-Biebrich*].

        1. Count *Maximilian* Antonius Friedrich-Leopold Gottfried Wolfgang Maria, *b* at Graz 18 May 1988.

        2. Count *Sebastian* Friedrich Leopold Albert Georg Maria, *b* at Deutschlandsberg 18 Jan 1990.

        3. Countess *Bernadette*, *b* at Graz 22 April 1991.

        4. Countess *Theresa*, Elizabeth Barbara Gabriele Maria *b* at Aschaffenburg 2 Oct 1992.

        5. Countess *Barbara* Karoline Johanna Anna Maria, *b* at Aschaffenburg 8 July 1994.

        6. Countess *Elisabeth* Anna-Katharina Gabriele Barbara Maria, *b* at Aschaffenburg 29 Dec 1996.

        7. Count *Georg* Rupert Friedrich-Leopold Joseph Christoph Maria, *b* at Aschaffenburg 18 April 2000.

    2. Count *Friedrich-Leopold* Johannes Thaddäus Franziskus Josef Maria, *b* at Salzburg 16 March 1962; *m* at Nassenfels nr Adelschlag 29 May (civ) and at Voerde-Möllen 2 June (relig) 1990, Countess *Sophie* (*b* at Duisberg 24 Aug 1959), dau of Count Wilderich von Spee and Baroness Hugoline von und zu Eltz-Rübenach.
[*Neraditz 11, 01920 Kleinhänchen, Germany*].

        1. Countess *Maria* Monica Elisabeth Agnes Theresia, *b* at Dresden 8 Dec 1993.

    3. Count *Rupert* Ferdinand Carl Thaddäus Antonius Maria, *b* at Salzburg 29 July 1970

3. Count *Alfred* Adam Friedrich-Leopold Martinus Meinrad Petrus Johanes Evangelist Bonifatius Thomas-Aquin Maria, *b* at Brauna 18 Jan 1929; ✠ at Würzburg 15 May 1980, Businessman; *m* 1stly at Wald-Michelbach, Odenwald 14 Dec 1960 (civ) and at Würzburg 14 Dec 1961 (relig) (*m* diss by div 22 Sept 1967 and annulled at Paderborn 16 July 1973), Anneliese (*b* at Ahrweiler 23 April 1926; ✠ 22 June 1998), dau of Anton Ernst and Magdalena Gruhn. He *m*

2ndly at Rome 27 Sept 1968 (*m* diss by div at Munich 5 June 1973),
Anna Anita (*b* at Christerode 19 April 1947; she *m* 2ndly at Frauenau
1 Aug 1981, Gotthard, Baron Poschinger von Frauenau), dau of
Konrad Pfaff and Anna Hellwig, and by her has issue,

> 1. Count *Michael* Thomas Maria, *b* at Frankfurt-am-Main 20
> March 1969.
> [*Mallertshofener Straße 21, 85716 Unterschleißheim,
> Germany*].

Brother of Great-Grandfather
Issue of Count Friedrich-Leopold (*b* 7 Nov 1750; ✝ 5 Dec 1819) and
his second wife, Countess Sophie von Redern (*b* 4 Nov 1765; *m* 15
Feb 1790; ✝ 8 Jan 1842, heiress of the fideicommis of Brauna),
having had issue, among whom,

Sons

A: PASKAU
1. Count *Bernard* Joseph, *b* at Münster, Westphalia 30 April 1803;
✝ at Weidenhof, Breslau 21 Jan 1859, Proprietor of Schönwitz and
Weidendorf in Silesia; *m* at Dobrau, Upper Silesia 8 Jan 1833,
Countess Charlotte Agnes (*b* at Dobrau 8 July 1809; ✝ at Marienbad
1 Aug 1878), dau of Ernst, Count von Seherr-Thoss and Baroness
Agness von Loën, and had issue, among whom,

> Sons
> 1. Count *Friedrich* Leopold Johann Heinrich Stephan Maria,
> *b* at Schönwitz 24 Dec 1836; ✝ at Brustawe 3 Oct 1904,
> Proprietor of Brustawe, Capt Austrian Army, Kt of Hon
> Sovereign Military Order of Malta; *m* at Kiowitz 14 July 1868,
> Countess Bertha (*b* at Kiowitz 25 March 1844; ✝ at Breslau
> 4 Jun 1916), dau of Theodor, Count von Falkenhayn,
> Proprietor of Kiowitz and Baroness Ida von Hauer, and had
> issue, among whom,

>> Sons
>> 1. Count *Bernhard* Joseph Theodor Friedrich Leopold
>> Cajus Raphael Maria, *b* at Brustawe 24 Oct 1872; ✝ at
>> Fürstenberg 18 Feb 1951, Proprietor of Brustawe, Capt
>> Austrian Army, Major, Kt of Hon Sovereign Military
>> Order of Malta; *m* at Berlin 5 Feb 1902, Countess
>> Antonia (*b* at Fürstenberg 2 April 1872; ✝ there 2
>> Feb 1962), dau of Joseph, Count von Westphalen zu
>> Fürstenberg and Katharina Friedberg, and had issue,

among whom,

>> 1. Countess *Maria Bertha* Agnes Katharina Hedwig Christine, *b* at Brustawe 24 July 1907; *m* at Eichensee, Silesia 19 Jan 1939, Albrecht, Baron von Keyserlingk (*b* at Gr-Lahnen 6 May 1900; ✠ 17 Dec 1997), Forester, Farmer.
>> [*Coteaux de Bordéo, 20230 San Nicola, Corsica, France*].

> 2. Count *Friedrich Theodor* Alfred Pius Franz von Sales Maria, *b* at Thomaswaldau 14 Dec 1877; ✠ at Gamburg an der Tauber 28 March 1954, Proprietor of Kiowitz, Imp Chamberlain, Senator; *m* at Drensteinfurt 29 Aug 1911, Baroness Antonie (*b* at Drensteinfurt 13 June 1877; ✠ there 29 Sept 1964), Dame Star Cross Order, dau of Ignaz, Baron von Landsberg-Velen and Princess Bertha von Croÿ, and had issue, among whom,

>> 1. Countess Maria *Regina* Pacis Bernardina Regina Antonia, *b* at Kiowitz 7 Sept 1917.
>> [*Greiteler Weg 76, 33102 Paderborn, Germany*].

2. Count *Günther* Ernst Leopold Franz Ignatius Hubertus Maria, *b* at Breslau 7 Feb 1845; ✠ at Paskau 6 Nov 1926, Proprietor of Paskau, Major, Diplomat Austro-Hungarian Service, Kt of Hon Sovereign Military Order of Malta; *m* at Koppitz 9 Oct 1879, Countess Klara (*b* at Breslau 20 Nov 1860; ✠ at Munich 16 Aug 1930), Lady-in-Waiting, dau of Hans Ulrich, Count Schaffgotsch genannt Semperfrei von und zu Kynast and Greiffenstein, Baron zu Trachenberg and Johanna Gryczik von Schomberg-Godulla, and had issue, among whom,

Sons

1. Count *Hubert* Maria Johannes Bernhard Joseph Adalbert Cyrill Matthias Franz, *b* at Vienna 24 Feb 1881; ✠ at Tutzing 11 April 1963, former Proprietor of Paskau, Diplomat Austro-Hungarian Service, Kt of Hon Sovereign Military Order of Malta; *m* at Prague 7 Jan 1911, Princess Anna (*b* at Kosten 20 July 1890; ✠ in an auto accident at Tutzing 31 March 1964), dau of Ferdinand, Prince of Lobkowicz and Countess Anna Bertha von Neipperg, and had issue,

1. Count *Ernst Günther* Maria Josef Ignatius Aloisius Hubert Flavianus Eleutherius, *b* at Munich 18 Feb 1912, ✠ there 2 March 2001; *m* at Tutzing 15 Oct (civ) and at Ettal 16 Oct (relig) 1954, Irmela (*b* at Haggers, nr Reval, Estonia 12 Aug 1929), dau of Hellmut Matthey and Ilse von Hahn, and has issue, among whom, [*Schlagintweitstraße 7, 80638 Munich, Germany*].

> 1. Countess *Angela* Maria Anna, *b* at Munich 8 April 1956.
> [*Heckenweg 36, 63743 Aschaffenburg, Germany*].

> 2. Count *Ernst Christian*, *b* at Munich 12 Dec 1960; *m* at Munich 3 Sept 1994, Sigrid Marondell (*b* at Landshut 19 July 1962), dau of Bernhard Marondell and Edith Tietz, and has issue,
> [*Baderstraße 10, 82211 Herrsching am Ammersee, Germany*].

>> 1. Countess *Elena* Sophie, *b* at Munich 23 Aug 1995.

>> 2. Count *Leon* Frederic, *b* at Herrsching 14 March 1998.

>> 3. Count *Linus* Constantin, *b* at Herrsching 10 Sept 2000.

> 3. Count *Hubertus* Johannes Hellmut, *b* at Munich 7 Sept 1963.
> [*Immanuel-Kirch-Straße 27, 10405 Berlin, Germany*].

2. Countess *Hedwig* Maria Clara Anna Josefa Ignatia Johanna Ursula, *b* at Tutzing 20 Oct 1922.
[*Eichen Weg 2, 83457 Bayerisch Gmain, Germany*].

2. Count *Friedrich-Leopold* Joseph Johannes Hubertus Maria, *b* at Paskau 27 Aug 1883; ✠ at Tutzing 19 May 1975, Dr of Law, Kt of Hon Sovereign Military Order of Malta; *m* at Berlin 11 May 1910, Countess Paula (*b* at Potsdam 9 Nov 1888; ✠ at Tutzing 26 April 1967), Dame of Hon Sovereign Military Order of Malta, dau

of Johannes Mauritius, Count von Brühl and Princess
Marianne of Lobkowicz, and had issue, among whom,

1. Count *Carl* Maria Josef Johannes Aloysius
Hilarius, *b* at Kaminietz 11 Jan 1926; ✠ at
Frankfurt-am-Main 5 Oct 1963, Kt of Hon
Sovereign Military Order of Malta; *m* 1stly at
Tutzing 15 July 1954 (*m* diss by div 5 Dec
1957), Ernie-Reno (*b* at Breda, North Brabant
7 May 1924), dau of Antonie van Gogh and
Reino van der Ploeg. He *m* 2ndly at Frankfurt-
am-Main 23 July 1958, Nora (*b* at ... 24 Nov
1920; ✠ Frankfurt 30 July 2000), dau of
Alexander Epstein and Lisbeth Lemke, and by
her had issue,

1. Countess *Alexandra* Paula Friederike
Marianne Nora, *b* at Frankfurt-am-Main
3 Jan 1959.
[*Textorstraße 54, 60594 Frankfurt-am-
Main, Germany*].

3. Count *Otto* Joseph Maria Aloysius Hubertus
Günther Thomas, *b* at Paskau 19 Dec 1888; ✠ at
Mährisch-Ostrau 16 June 1945, former Proprietor of
Paskau, Lt Austrian Army, Dr of Law; *m* at Vienna 28
June 1920, Hermine (*b* at Vienna 18 Dec 1886; ✠ at
Graz 4 Aug 1970), dau of Karl Krapfl and Katharina
Rauscher, and had issue,

1. Count *Wolfgang* Günther Hubertus Maria
Dominikus, *b* at Paskau 5 Aug 1922, ✠ at
Munich 7 Feb 1993, Banker; *m* 1stly at
Drensteinfurt 20 Feb 1954 (*m* diss by div at
Frankfurt-am-Main 12 July 1968), Baroness
Elisabeth [*Zur Wöllenbök 29, 45239 Essen-
Werden, Germany*] (*b* at Breslau 24 Oct 1927;
she *m* 2ndly at Rottach-Egern 30 Dec 1974,
Alexander-Barbu Costinescu Tataranu), dau of
Lt-Gen Mauritz, Baron von Strachwitz and
Gross-Zauche and Baroness Elisabeth von
Landsberg-Velen, and had issue,

1. Count *Otto* Hubert Friedrich Mauritz
Maria, *b* at Frankfurt-am-Main 6 March
1955, Lawyer; *m* at Moone Abbey,

Ireland 20 June 1981, Countess Stefanie (*b* at Rottweil 21 July 1957), dau of Clemens, Count von Matuschka, Baron von Toppolszan and Spaetgen and Princess Amelie zu Hohenlohe-Waldenburg-Schillingsfürst, and has issue,
[*Böhmerstraße 1, 01099 Dresden, Germany*].

1. Count Antonius Philipp Friedrich-Karl, *b* at Munich 17 Nov 1982.

2. Count *Ludwig* Clemens Anton Gabriel Maria, *b* at Munich 22 Aug 1984.

3. Count *Josef* Antonius Dietrich Maria, *b* at Munich 1 Oct 1986.

4. Count Johannes Eberhard Dieter Maria, *b* at Munich 16 March 1992.

2. Count *Clemens* Antonius Herbert, *b* at Frankfurt-am-Main 23 March 1958; *m* at Salzburg 9 Jan (civ) and at Maria Plain nr Salzburg 31 Jan (relig) 1998 (*m* diss by div Salzburg 23 March 2000), Michaela (*b* at Vienna 21 Nov 1964), dau of Gerhard Schneider, Noble (Edler) von Manns-Au and Christine Pec, and has issue,
[*Brunnhausgasse 22, 5020 Salzburg, Austria*].

1. Count *Mathias* Leopold Vinzenz, *b* at Salzburg 9 July 1998.

Count Wolfgang *m* 2ndly at Frankfurt-am-Main 17 Jan 1969 (*m* diss by div at Munich 11 July 1972), Ingrid Maria Christine [*Falkenberg 58, 80539 Moosach bei Grafing, Germany*] (*b* at Berlin 24 May 1935), dau of Georg Gewiese and Lotte Simonsen. He *m* 3rdly at Munich 29 June

1983, Elisabeth Maria (*b* at Klagenfurt 15 June 1950), dau of Walter Baumgartner and Berta Maria Pichler, and had further issue by his second wife,
[*Kohlbrennerstraße 24, 81929 Munich, Germany*].

> 3. Count *Georg* Wolfgang Dennis, *b* at Wiesbaden 12 April 1966, Private Wealth Management; *m* at Salzburg 17 Sept 1994, Nicola (*b* at Buchholz, Nordheide 3 Sept 1963), dau of Götz-Rüdiger Euler and Barbara-Christine Brigitta Sieber, and has issue,
> [*Reinacher Straße 7, 8032 Zurich, Switzerland*].

>> 1. Count *Philipp* Georg Maximilian, *b* at Munich 6 Jan 1997.
>> 2. Count *Vincent* Alexander Leopold, *b* at Zurich 1 Sept 1998.

> 4. Count *Alexander* Konstantin, *b* at Frankfurt-am-Main 11 Feb 1970.
> [*Falkenberg 28, 85665 Moosach, Germany*].

2. Count *Hubert* Maria Otto Josef Carolus Felix von Valois, *b* at Paskau 21 Nov 1923, Dr of Med, Psychiatrist; *m* at Georgshausen 21 April 1956, Margita (*b* at Wuppertal-Barmen 12 Nov 1931), dau of Hans Bremme and Beate Engelbrecht, and has issue,
(Gumbinnenstraße 12 81022 Munich, Germany).

> 1. Countess *Marie* Therese Eleonore Beatrice, *b* at Concorde, New Hampshire, USA 23 Feb 1962; *m* at Munich 16 Aug (civ) and 15 Sept (relig) 1990, Vollrat, Count Schwerin von Krosigk (*b* at Berlin-Tempelhof 19 Sept 1956), Dipl Communications, Advertising Executive.
> [*Siegrunestraße 5, 80639 Munich,*

Germany].

2. Count Nicolas (*Nicki*) Constantin Hubert Maria Georg, *b* at Princeton, New Jersey, USA 12 June 1964.

[*Baaderstraße 5, 80469 Munich, Germany*].

B: WESTHEIM

2. Count *Joseph Theodor, b* at Lüttgenbeck 12 Aug 1804; ✠ at Rumillies, nr Tournai, Belgium 5 April 1859, Proprietor of Westheim in Westfalen; *m* 1stly at Heltorf 17 Oct 1838, Countess Marie Theresia (*b* at Düsseldorf 19 June 1811; ✠ at Westheim 1 Feb 1850), dau of Franz Anton, Count von Spee and Countess Sophie von Merveldt, and had issue,

    1. Count Franz Friedrich *Leopold* Hubertus Maria, *b* at Westheim 4 April 1846; ✠ at Linsen 30 Jan 1923, of Kinsen, Militsch, Silesia; *m* at Vornholz 30 Sept 1875, Mary (*b* at Dublin 14 Nov 1845; ✠ at Reichen, Silesia 15 Dec 1926), dau of Smollett Montgomerie Eddington and Mary Jane Fleming, and had issue,

        1. Count *Bernhard* Friedrich Hubertus Aloisius Maria, *b* at Mankato, Minnesota, USA 20 Jan 1881; ✠ at Hall, Tirol 22 Sept 1952, Capt Austrian Army, Kt Order of the Golden Fleece; *m* at Schloß Wallsee 24 April 1918, Archduchess Hedwig (*b* at Ischl 24 Sept 1896; ✠ at Hall 1 Nov 1970), dau of Franz Salvator, Archduke of Austria and Archduchess Marie Valerie of Austria, and had issue,

            1. Countess *Marie Elisabeth* Valerie Josefa Anna, *b* at Innsbruck 21 May 1919; now Mother Maria Bonifacia OSB Benedictine Mission.

[*7 rue d'Issy, 92170 Vanves, France*].

            2. Count *Franz Joseph* Hubert Bernhard Stephan Martin Maria, *b* at Schloß Wallsee 30 April 1920; ✠ at Vienna 29 June 1986, Lt.-Col. Austrian Army; *m* at Kremsmünster 5 Aug 1957, Countess Elisabeth (*b* at Mähr-Kromau 16 May 1936), dau of Rudolf, Count Kinsky von Wchinitz and Tettau and Baroness Elisabeth Herring von Frankensdorf, and had issue,

[*Prinz Eugenstraße 68, 1040 Vienna, Austria*].

1. Countess *Marie-Valerie* Aglaë Hedwig Elisabeth, *b* at Vienna 6 June 1958; *m* at Bernstein, Burgenland 22 May 1982, Albert Studt (*b* at Oberbruch, Aachen 30 Dec 1953), Dipl Eng, Architect.

[*Pfeil Gasse32, 1080 Vienna, Austria*].

2. Countess Marie-*Christine* Sybille Hedwig Elisabeth, *b* at Vienna 20 July 1959; *m* at Vienna 26 Sept 1981, Franz, Baron von Waechter (*b* at Vienna 23 Feb 1955), Opera Singer.

[*Roosevelt Platz 13, 1090 Vienna, Austria*].

3. Countess Marie-*Antoinette* Mathilde Hedwig Elisabeth, *b* at Hall, Tyrolia 8 Sept 1960; *m* 1stly at Vienna 24 May 1980 (diss by div), Konrad, Count von Goëss-Saurau (*b* at Frohnleiten, Styria 9 Jan 1952), she *m* 2ndly London 8 Oct 1996, David Charles Dobie (*b* at Lugano 20 April 1960), Company Director.

[*P.O. Box 1192, Dar es Salaam, Tansania*].

4. Countess Marie-*Sophie* Elisabeth Hedwig, *b* at Hall 14 Dec 1961.

[*Pinienstraße 2, 40233 Düsseldorf, Germany*].

3. Count *Friedrich Leopold* Josef Martin Maria, *b* at Schloß Wallsee 23 May 1921; *m* at Werfen, nr Salzburg 24 March 1948, Luise (Aloysia) (*b* at Zell am See 24 July 1923), dau of Ernst, Ritter von Pachmann and Countess Elma von Galen, and has issue,

[*Grosser Sandbühel 17, 6404 Eilu, Tirol, Austria*].

1. Count *Christoph, b* at Zermatt, Switzerland 18 July 1948, Dr of Law; *m* at Graz 24 Sept 1983, Elisabeth (*b* at Graz 10 July 1952), dau of Hans Mayer-Rieckh and Renate Kohlrausch,

and has an adopted dau,
[*Veitlissen Gasse 19, 1130 Vienna, Austria*].

  1. Aglaë Marie Elisabeth Theresa, *b* at Beirut, Lebanon 18 Oct 1985, (adopted), bears the name of "Stolberg-Stolberg".

2. Countess Marie *Elisabeth* Emanuela, *b* at Hall 19 Dec 1949; *m* at Hall 7 Jan 1984, Thomas, Ritter von Mayr-Harting (*b* at Epsom, Surrey, England 22 May 1954), Dr of Law, Diplomat.
[*Avenue Franklin Roosevelt 60, 1050 Brussels, Belgium*].

3. Count *Peter* Franziskus Theodor Raphael Blasius Maria, *b* at Hall 3 Feb 1951, Businessman; *m* at Hall 13 June (civ) and at Vienna 27 June (relig) 1992, Countess Susanne (Zsuzsanna) (*b* at Budapest 14 Nov 1958), dau of Count Miklós Kornis de Goncz-Ruska and Katalin Szabolcs, and has issue,
[*Frankenberggasse 13, 1040 Vienna, Austria*].

  1. Countess *Anna* Maria Magdalena Pauline Elisabeth, *b* at Vienna 9 Sept 1998.

4. Count *Johannes* Ernst Bonifaz Maria, *b* at Hall 14 May 1952.
[*Grossen Sandbühel 17, 6424 Silz, Tirol, Austria*].

5. Count *Markus* Eugenius Bernhard Maria, *b* at Innsbruck 19 May 1953, Actor; *m* at Stuttgart 2 Jan 1995, Margit (*b* at Stuttgart 23 Jan 1974), dau of Christian Schalit and Irmeli Ranttala, and has issue,
[*Ebitzweg 5, 70374 Stuttgart, Germany*].

  1. Count *Johannes* Franziskus Benedikt, *b* at Stuttgart 8 Jan 1996.

2. Count *Benedikt* Christian Maria, *b* at Stuttgart 22 Jan 1997.

6. Countess *Eleonore*, *b* at Innsbruck 7 June 1959; *m* at Hall 8 Oct 1993, Johannes, Count von Firmian (*b* at Bolzano 4 Jan 1955; he *m* 1stly at Eppan 26 Aug 1978, Baroness Maria Michaela von Hohenbühel, *b* at Bolzano 11 Feb 1956; *m* diss by div 1985).
[*Wangergasse 95, 39100 Bozen, Italy*].

7. Countess Maria *Immaculata* Franziska Aloisia Hedwig Juliana, *b* at Innsbruck 9 Jan 1964; *m* at Stams, Tirol 6 Feb 1988, Carl-Anton, Lord and Count zu Stubenberg (*b* at Graz 23 April 1960, Architecture Student.
[*Garrach 7, 8160 Weiz, Austria*].

4. Count *Carl* Franz Josef Georg Petrus Canisius Hubert Martin Maria, *b* at Reichen, Silesia 7 June 1925, Hotelier; *m* 1stly at Maria-Wörth, Kärnten 22 Aug 1951 (*m* diss by div at Innsbruck 12 Oct 1967), Edina (*b* at Vienna 25 May 1923), dau of Adolf Winkelbauer and Countess Eduardine (Edina) von Clam and Gallas. He *m* 2ndly at Hamburg 9 Nov 1967 (*m* diss by div at Innsbruck 5 Dec 1968), Ute (*b* at Cologne 16 Aug 1939; she *m* 2ndly at Mannheim 29 May 1970, Christoph von Wiedebach and Nostitz-Jänkendorf, *m* diss by div at Mannheim 3 Nov 1995), dau of Herbert Sommerlatte and Thea Traut, and has issue by his first wife,
[*6183 Kühtai, Tirol, Austria*].

1. Count *Christian Friedrich*, *b* at Vienna 9 June 1952, Hotelier; *m* 1stly at Hamburg 10 March 1983 (*m* diss by div at Hamburg 3 Feb 1988), Baroness Marion (*b* at Mülheim an der Ruhr 29 Nov 1950; *m* 1stly at Friedelhausen 18 May 1974, Enno, Baron zu Innhausen

und Knyphausen; that *m* diss by div
...), dau of Harald, Baron von
Hardenberg and Brigitte von Freier, and
has issue,

> 1. Countess *Edina, b* at Hamburg
> 30 March 1984.

Count Christian Friedrich *m* 2ndly at
Hamburg 24 March 1988, Manuela
Patricia (*b* at Lübeck 19 Sept 1959),
dau of Friedrich Hofacker and Frauke
Schlüter, and has further issue,

> 2. Count *Maximilian* Carl Georg
> Maria, *b* at Hamburg 27 Aug
> 1988.

> 3. Countess *Marie Valerie*
> Josepha Charlotte, *b* at Hamburg
> 17 Dec 1989.

Count Christian Friedrich *m* 3rdly at
Reinbek nr Hamburg 23 Oct 1998, Hele
(*b* at Hannover 9 Dec 1965), dau of
Heinrich Herren and Tete von Seldern,
and has further issue,
[*Unterthurmstraße 118, 5412 Puch,
Austria*].

> 4. Count *Heinrich* Leopold
> Ferdinand, *b* at Reinbek 6 July
> 1999.

2. Count *Andreas, b* at Klagenfurt 8
Oct 1954; *m* at Boskovice, Czech
Republic 12 July 1997, Countess
Gertrude (*b* at Freistadt 19 March
1966), dau of Count Heinrich von
Mensdorff-Pouilly and Margarethe
Gartner, and has issue,
[*Eschenbachgasse 23, 5020 Salzburg,
Austria*].

> 1. Countess *Margarita* Hedwig
> Juliane Dorothea Maria, *b* at
> Freistadt, Austria 26 June 1999.

3. Countess *Claudia* Maria Edina
Hedwig, *b* at Hall 25 May 1956; *m* at

Kühtai, Tirol 11 April 1988, Philipp
Willport (*b* at 29 May 1953).
[*Artilleriestraße 19, 80636 Munich,
Germany*].

5. Count *Ferdinand* Maria Immaculata Josef
Martin Hubert, *b* at Reichen 8 Dec 1926; ✠ at
Vienna 7 July 1998, Dr of Law, Ambassador;
m at Bodenburg, nr Elze 23 April 1966 (*m* diss
by div at Vienna 14 June 1988), Baroness Jutta
(*b* at Berlin-Charlottenburg 15 March 1938; she
m 2ndly at New York 14 Sept 1988, Pierre
Louis Blanc, French Ambassador to UN), dau
of Adalbert, Baron von Cramm and Elfriede
(Elfi) Nieders, and has issue,
[*Quartier de Gergouven, 84560 Menerbes,
France*].

> 1. Countess *Katharina* Maria Bonifatia
> Veronica Ruth Jadwiga, *b* at Innsbruck
> 2 Jan 1968; *m* at Huy 2 May 1998,
> Jean-François Poncelet, (*b* at
> Kimuenza-Lolvanium Congo 26 Feb
> 1959).
> [*Avenue Edouard de Thibault 51/1,
> 1040 Brussels, Belgium*].
> 2. Countess *Johanna* Paula Irene
> Adelheid Maria, *b* at Hamburg 13 Aug
> 1969; *m* at Kuhtai, Tyrol 9 Apr 1994,
> Prince *Clemens* Angelus Paul
> Ferdinand Moritz zu Salm-Salm
> (*b* Düsseldorf 18 Nov 1966).
> [*Mühlbaurstraße 6, 81677 Munich,
> Germany*].
> 3. Count *Bernhard* Franz Joseph
> Heinrich Stanislaus Maria, *b* at
> Innsbruck 11 Oct 1970; *m* at
> Altenbourg 4 July 1998, Alice (*b* at
> Vienna 22 March 1971), dau of Christian
> Lippert and Andrea Haumann, and has
> issue,
> [*Sebastiansplatz 3, 80331 Munich,
> Germany*].

1. Countess *Philippa* Theresa Gea Alix Maria, *b* at Munich 5 Nov 1999.

4. Countess *Theresa* Elisabeth Anna Eva Maria, *b* at Vienna 17 May 1973; *m* at Stift Rein, Austria 13 April 2002, Alexander Tessmar-Pfohl (*b* at Gratz, Styria 11 July 1973).
[*Landstrasser Hauptstraße 6/12 A, 1030 Vienna, Austria*].

6. Countess *Anna Regina* Emanuela Maria, *b* at Bad Ischl 20 Dec 1927, ✠ at Brussels 2 May 2002; *m* at Hall 9 Oct 1954, Jacques (Jack), Chevalier de Spirlet (*b* at Woluwe-Saint-Lambert 3 April 1930), Dr of Law.
[*"La Hêtraie", Kapucijnendreef 64, 3090 Overijse, Belgium*].

7. Countess *Magdalena* Maria Mathilde Emmanuela Walpurgis, *b* at Hall 19 Dec 1930; *m* at Hall 8 Sept 1958, Martin, Baron von Kripp zu Prunberg and Krippach (*b* at Krippach 25 Dec 1924; ✠ at Innsbruck 21 May 1990), Dr of Law.
[*Ansitz Knillenberg, Dantestraße 30, 39012 Meran-Obermais, Austria*].

2. Count *Franz* Ignatius Hubertus Maria, *b* at Westheim 13 Sept 1848; ✠ at Paderborn 22 April 1912, Proprietor of Burlinghausen in Westfalen; *m* at Neubourg, nr Maastricht 30 July 1872, Countess Maria (*b* at Neubourg 15 Jan 1847; ✠ at Ascherode, Gfschaft Hohenstein 2 Oct 1922), dau of Oscar, Count von Marchant and Ansembourg and Baroness Leonie von Wendt zu Holtfeld, Proprietor of Crassenstein, etc, and had issue,

1. Count *Joseph* Oskar Franziskus Antonius Hubertus Maria, *b* at Neubourg 14 March 1874, Proprietor of Ascherode, Harz, Püth and Borlinghausen, Kt of Hon Sovereign Military Order of Malta; ✠ at Gulpen, Holland 24 Oct 1956; *m* at Kronberg, Taunus 10 Jan 1911, Baroness Theresia (*b* at Thüle 3 Feb 1890; ✠ at Schaan, Liechtenstein 30 May 1973), dau of Wilhelm, Baron von Ketteler and Baroness Luise (Ludovika)

Wambolt von Umstadt, and had issue, among whom,

  1. Count *Martin* Wilhelm Emanuel Franz Ludwig Hubertus Elger Maria, *b* at Borlinghausen 12 Nov 1911; ✠*k* at Le Havre 10 Aug 1940; *m* at Düsseldorf 31 Dec 1938, Adélaide (Ada) (*b* at Ayeneux, Belgium 22 June 1909; ✠ at Turin 19 Aug 1984; she *m* 1stly at Moncalieri, Italy 3 April 1930, Joseph, Baron von Ketteler who ✠ 1982; that *m* legally annulled at Düsseldorf 30 April 1937; she *m* 3rdly Tassilo von Strzemieczny who ✠ nr Mittenwald 2 Feb 1947), dau of Egon, Chevalier de Spirlet and Baroness Paula von Ketteler, and had issue,

    1. Count *Franz* Josef Emanuel Johannes Albertus Franziskus Antonius Hubertus, *b* at Kottgeisering, Fürstenfeldbruck, Bavaria 1 Jan 1936, Kt Constantinian Order, Com Teutonic Order, Dr of Law, Banker; *m* at Montreal, Quebec, Canada 21 Dec 1968, Jacqueline (*b* at Brussels 3 March 1942), dau of Henri Florin de Duikingberg and Lucienne Nolf, and has issue,
    [*Gaiglstraße 19, 80335 Munich, Germany; Villa Cravanzana,straße S. Brigida 18, 10024 Moncalieri, Italy*].

      1. Count *Alexander* Heinrich Martin Christoph Antonius Franziskus Xaverius Benedictus Hubertus Maria, *b* at Frankfurt-am-Main 26 Feb 1974.
      [*33 Oakley Street, London, SW3 5NT*].
      2. Count *Maximilian Christoph* Martin Egon Ludwig Friedrich Gabriel Benedictus Maria, *b* at Neuilly-sur-Seine 24 March 1976.
      3. Countess Maria *Isabella* Louise Bianca Johanna Theresia Lucia Benedikta Theophano, *b* at

Neuilly 12 July 1978.

    4. Count *Christian-Henri* Emanuel Jaroslav Konstantin Francesco Johannes Benno Theodor Maria, *b* at Munich 29 Sept 1982.

2. Countess Marie *Elisabeth* Pauline Therese Friederike Benedikta Roswitha Huberta, *b* at Mannheim 29 March 1939, Dr of Phil; *m* at Montelibretti, nr Rome 18 Feb (civ) and at Voerendaal, Limburg 27 Feb (relig) 1965, Paolo Angioni (*b* at Cagliari, Sardinia 22 Jan 1938), Lt-Col.
    [*Via Pietro Micca 20, 10122 Turin, Italy*].

2. Countess *Eugenie* Therese Aloysia Johanna Maria, *b* at Ascherode 22 June 1914; *m* at Ascherode 4 June 1935, Hanno von Halem (*b* at Schwetz an der Weichsel, West Prussia 11 June 1906, ✠ at Schaan, Liechtenstein 13 Feb 1994).
[*Haus Gamander, 9494 Schaan, Liechtenstein*].

3. Countess Ludowika (*Wika*) Adolfine Paula Josepha Hubert, *b* at Ascherode 25 Dec 1915; *m* at Nordhausen, Saxony 12 July 1938, Endre, Baron Bánffy de Losoncz, Proprietor of Aranyosgerend, Torda-Aranyos (*b* at Nagysajó, Hungary 8 Oct 1909; ✠ at Buenos Aires 22 Jan 1990), Dipl Eng.
[*Vicente Lopez 121, 1640 Martinez, Buenos Aires, Argentina*].

4. Count Franziskus (*Franz*) Wilhelm-Emmanuel Paulus Hubertus Maria Sylvester, *b* at Ascherode 30 Dec 1917, ✠ at Wiesbaden 6 April 2002, Businessman, Capt Germany Army, Kt of Hon Sovereign Military Order of Malta; *m* 1stly at Hasselburg 27 April 1949 (*m* diss by div at Lübeck 10 July 1970 and annulled at Osnabrück 20 Oct 1972), Countess Elisabeth [*Hasselburg, 23730 Altenkrempe, Ostholstein,*

Germany] (*b* at Lehmkuhlen, nr Preetz, Holstein 13 Oct 1919), dau of Carl, Count von Scheell-Plessen and Elisabeth von Bülow. He *m* 2ndly at Neustadt, Holstein 16 March 1972 (civ) and at Mainz 24 March 1973 (relig) Noble (Edle) Christiane (*b* at Gleiwitz, Silesia 11 Sept 1935), dau of Edwin, Noble (Edler) von Braunmühl and Gisela Gobiet, and had issue by his first wife,
[*Sand Weg 5, 65191 Wiesbaden, Sonnenberg, Germany*].

    1. Countess *Therese* Hedwig Scholastika Huberta Maria, *b* at Neustadt 10 Feb 1950; *m* 1stly at … 24 March 1972 (*m* diss by div 8 Nov 1973), Rainer Csizmazia (*b* at 18 May 1947); *m* 2ndly Berlin-Kreuzberg 19 Sept 1974 (*m* diss by div at Kassel 9 June 1976), Kamel Salem (*b* at Khenchela, Algeria 22 May 1948; ✝ 1976).
    [*Wörtherstraße 5b, 37085 Göttingen, Germany*].
    2. Countess *Maria-Elisabeth* Josefa Huberta, *b* at Neustadt 12 July 1952, Author; *m* at ……, René Walter Ferry Gericke (*b* at …), he took the name zu Stolberg-Stolberg-Gericke.
    [*Allee 7, 23730 Hasselburg, Germany*].
    3. Countess *Benedikta* Augusta Agnes Wilhelmine Hubert Maria, *b* at Lübeck 18 April 1955; *m* at … 14 Dec 1979 (*m* diss by div 18 Dec 1985), Hans-Christian Georgs (*b* at … 10 June 1940).
    [*Mühlenweg 1, 25813 Husum, Germany*].
    4. Countess *Huberta* Johanna Anita Ida Maria, *b* at Eutin 1 July 1960.
    [*Eisenacherstraße 23, 10781 Berlin-Schöneberg, Germany*].
    5. Countess *Ludmilla* Elisabeth Josefa Juliana

Maria, *b* at Ascherode 16 Feb 1922.
[*Gotenstraße 152, 53175 Bonn, Germany*].

6. Count *Wilhelm* Josef Oskar Friedrich Leopold Maria, *b* at Ascherode 2 June 1927, Businessman; *m* 1stly at Birstein 20 Aug (civ) and 28 Aug (relig) 1961 (*m* diss by div at Berlin 28 May 1970), Princess Irene Friederike [*63633 Schloß Birstein, über Wächtersbach, Hessen, Germany*] (*b* at Birstein 30 Sept 1940; she *m* 2ndly at Munich 1 Sept 1980, Jan ter Meer; that *m* diss by div at Munich 7 July 1986), dau of Franz-Ferdinand, Prince von Isenburg and Countess Irina (Nina) Tolstoy. He *m* 2ndly at Tondern 14 Aug 1972, Anne Marie Elisabeth (*b* at Zurich 11 Feb 1933; *m* 1stly at Zurich 22 March 1955, Hermann Hirzel who was *b* at Zurich 9 Nov 1927; that *m* diss by div at Zurich on 30 June 1972; ✝ 23 July 2002), dau of Matheus Klaas and Ida Lysse, and has issue by his first wife,
[*Kasteel Püth, Voerendaal, Prov. Limburg, The Netherlands; Casa São Cristovão, Avenida dos Eucaliptos 449, Qt Marinha, 2750-687 Cascais, Portugal*].

> 1. Count *Franz-Joseph* Johannes Wilhelm Laurentius Maria, *b* at Aachen 24 June 1962.
> [*Dirckenstraße 41, 10178 Berlin, Germany*].
>
> 2. Countess *Isabel-Juliana* Helene Therese Maria Annunciata, *b* at Aachen 7 June 1963; *m* at Lausanne 30 June (civ) and at Funchal, Madeira 9 Sept (relig) 1995, Prince and Duke Léopold-Englebert d'Arenberg (*b* at Tervuren 20 Feb 1956), Lic jur, MBA, Kt Sovereign Military Order of Malta.
> [*19 Avenue l'Avenir, 1009 Pully, Switzerland*].
>
> 3. Countess *Irina* Christiana Maria, *b* at Aachen 21 April 1964; *m* at Brussels 23

April (civ) 1994 and at Lucignano, Italy
21 May (relig) 1994, Michel, Count de
Liedekerke (*b* at Brussels 2 March 1965),
Lic jur, Banker.
[*32 Cleveland Square, London,
W2 6DD; Molendaal, 3061 Leefdaal,
Belgium*].

Count Joseph Theodor *m* 2ndly at Rumillies 25 Feb 1851, Caroline
(*b* at Rumillies, Belgium 24 Dec 1826; ✛ there 9 Jan 1882), dau of
Karl, Count von Robiano, Proprietor of Rumillies and Countess Marie
Theresia zu Stolberg-Stolberg, and had further issue,

3. Count *Hermann* Joseph Karl Hubertus Maria, *b* at
Westheim 28 Feb 1854, ✛ at Westheim 19 June 1925; *m* at
Pressburg 27 Nov 1879, Countess Maria Karoline (*b* at
Pressburg 23 Nov 1854; ✛ at Westheim 18 Jan 1918), dau of
Georg, Noble Lord (Edler) Herr von Walterskirchen, Baron
zu Wolfsthal and Countess Ida von Fries, and had issue,
among whom,

1. Count *Josef Theodor* Karl Maria Albert Hubertus,
b at Westheim 12 12 Feb 1882; ✛ at St Blasien 25 Oct
1941, Member German Colonial Office; *m* at Padberg
16 Jan 1923, Countess Helene (*b* at Padberg 23 Nov
1894; ✛ at Wunnenberg, Furstenberg 4 Oct 1997),
dau of Wilhelm, Count Droste zu Vischering,
Proprietor of Padberg and Baroness Antonia von
Wendt, and had issue,

1. Countess *Marie Antonia* Michaela Huberta
Caroline Anna Catherina, *b* at Padberg 2 Nov
1923; *m* at Westheim Westphalia 26 Aug 1947,
Klemens, Baron von Twickel (*b* at Hameren,
Coesfeld 26 April 1911; ✛ at Westheim,
Westphalia 27 May 1960), Forester.
[*Kasselerstraße 1, 34431 Marsberg - Westheim,
Westfalen, Germany*].

2. Count *Georg* Ernst Maria Karl Joseph Anton, *b* at
Westheim 25 Feb 1883; ✛ at Gusterheim, Steiermark
25 Feb 1965, Capt Prussian Army; *m* at Dresden 12
July 1916, Princess Regina (*b* Jänkendorf 4 April 1886;
✛ at Katsch an der Mur, Steiermark 31 Jan 1980), dau
of Heinrich XXIV, Prince Reuss-Köstritz and Princess
Elisabeth Reuss, and had issue, among whom,

1. Countess *Elisabeth* Maria Theresia, *b* at Vienna 2 June 1918; *m* 1stly at Micheldorf 21 Jan (civ) and 22 Jan (relig) 1941, Walter Eisenbach (*b* at Toluca, Mexico 12 Aug 1906; ✝*k* at Lukawa, nr Sandomierz 19 Aug 1944), Dr of Law, Lawyer. She *m* 2ndly at Pöls, Steiermark 1 Aug (civ) and 12 Aug (relig) 1951, Alexander, Baron von Warsberg, Proprietor of Neckarsteinach (*b* at Salzburg 3 Nov 1910; ✝ at Neckarsteinach, nr Heidelberg 2 Jan 1983), Dr of Med.
[*Domstraße 8, 55116 Mainz, Germany; Mittelburg, 69239Neckarsteinach, Germany*].

2. Countess *Maria Andrea* Ferdinande Antonia Ida, *b* at Micheldorf 24 Nov 1921; Sister Maria Walburga, Benedictine Abbey Nonnberg, Salzburg.
[*Abtei Nonnberg, 5010 Salzburg, Austria*].

3. Count *Hermann Josef* Bonifacius Petrus Heinrich Maria, *b* at Ernstbrunn, Lower Austria 4 March 1925; ✝*k* (missing in action) in Russia Jan 1945.

4. Count *Lukas* Ernst Heinrich Petrus Konrad Arnold Maria, *b* at Ernstbrunn 19 Oct 1926, Master Clock Maker; *m* at Vienna 28 Dec 1962, Noble (Edle) Lydia Maria (*b* at Vienna 24 May 1937), dau of Felix Perko, Noble (Edler) von Monshoff and Dora Mraovic de Gric, and has issue,
[*Prevenhueber Weg 3, 8047 Graz-Ragnitz, Austria*].

    1. Countess *Sophie* Elisabeth Regina Margareta, *b* at Graz 17 Oct 1963.
    [*Kohlbachgasse 7, 8047 Graz, Austria*].

    2. Countess *Regina* Dorothea Eleonore Maria, *b* at Graz 21 Nov 1964.
    [*Prevenhueber Weg 3, 8047 Graz-Ragnitz, Austria*].

    3. Count *Georg* Heinrich Felix Petrus, *b* at Graz 18 Jan 1966.
    [*Fickeygasse 6/2/6, 1110 Vienna,*

Austria].

3. Count *Christoph* Klemens Maria Joseph Johanes
Baptista, *b* at Westheim 22 Jan 1888; ✝ at Arnsberg
3 July 1968, Major-Gen German Army; *m* at Baden, nr
Vienna 27 Sept 1916, Countess Ida (*b* at Prague 25
Sept 1891; ✝ at Weilheim, Bavaria 23 Sept 1955), dau
of Maximilian, Count von Orsini and Rosenberg and
Countess Maria Anna zu Herberstein, and had issue,

> 1. Countess Maria Anna (*Marianne*) Theresia
> Ada Sofie Huberta Emanuela, *b* at Davos 20
> March 1919; *m* at Westheim 27 Jan 1947, Carl
> Friedrich Oehlmann (*b* at Münster, Westphalia
> 1 Feb 1912; ✝ there 15 Nov 1983).
> [*Hofmarkstraße 4, 85368 Wang-Hagsdorf,
> Germany*].
>
> 2. Countess *Elisabeth* Theresia Leopoldine
> Angela Maria, *b* at Berlin-Lichterfelde 2 Oct
> 1920; *m* at Bigge, Westphalia 16 April 1953
> Benno Bubert (*b* at Bisslich 1 Aug 1924, ✝ at
> Köln 22 Feb 1994), Bank Employee.
> [*Duisburgerstraße 22, 5145 Cologne - Porz,
> Germany*].

II: STOLBERG-ROSSLA
(✝ Extinct ✝)

Lutheran: Founded by Count Jost Christian (*b* 24 Oct 1676; ✝ 17
June 1739); the right of primogeniture was instituted 10 Sept 1738;
Hereditary Member of the former First Chamber of the Grand Duchy
of Hesse 17 Dec 1820; received the qualification of "Erlaucht"
(primogeniture) 13 Feb 1829; confirmed in Hesse for all members of
this branch 7 March 1914; Hereditary Member of the former Prussian
House of Lords 12 Oct 1854; received Prussian authorisation for the
Head, his wife and for all their descendants in the first degree
including the children of the Hereditary Prince to bear the title of
Prince or Princess with the qualification of "Durchlaucht", Berlin
22 March 1893.
The Head of the Family, his siblings and children all bear the title of
Prince or Princess zu Stolberg-Rossla with the qualification of Serene
Highness, while cadet members of this branch bear the title of
Count or Countess zu Stolberg-Rossla with the qualification of
Illustrious Highness.

✠ **JOHANN MARTIN, 4TH PRINCE (FÜRST) ZU STOLBERG-ROSSLA**, Count zu Königstein, Rochefort, Wernigerode and Hohnstein, Lord zu Eppstein, Münzenberg, Breuberg, Agimont, Lohra and Clettenberg, *b* at Rossla 6 Oct 1917; ✠ at Frankfurt-am-Main 10 Dec 1982, Kt of St John of Jerusalem; son of Christoph Martin, 3rd Prince (Fürst) zu Stolberg-Rossla (*b* 1 April 1888; ✠ 27 Feb 1949) and Princess Ida Reuss (*b* 4 Sept 1891; *m* 7 Nov 1911; ✠ 29 March 1977); *m* at Ortenberg 27 Jan (civ) and at Kloster Engeltal, nr Altenstadt, Hesse 28 Jan (relig) 1927 Hildegard (*b* at Hanau 5 Oct 1922), Dr of Med, dau of Oskar Sauerbier and Sofie Klaus.
[*Schloß, 63683 Ortenberg, OHessen, Germany*].

Brother of Father

Issue of Botho, 1st Prince zu Stolberg-Rossla (*b* 12 July 1850; ✠ 8 Nov 1893) by his second wife, Princess Hedwig zu Isenburg and Büdingen in Büdingen (*b* 1 Nov 1863; *m* 27 Sept 1883; ✠ 1 July 1925), having had issue, among whom,

Son

Prince *Ernst Heinrich, b* at Rossla 7 Oct 1890; ✠ at Ortenberg 22 March 1946, 1st Lt, Kt of Hon St John of Jerusalem; *m* at Thüngen 27 Oct 1922, Baroness Agnes (*b* at Thüngen 10 Feb 1884; ✠ at Munich 6 Aug 1971; *m* 1stly at Thüngen 22 Sept 1910, Maximilian, Baron von Schnurbein who was ✠*k* 28 April 1915), dau of Hans Karl, Baron von Thüngen and Countess Julia von Giech, and had issue,

> 1. Countess *Brigitta* Agnes Alexandrine, *b* at Ortenberg 20 Dec 1925; *m* at Ortenberg 11 April 1948, Wolf von Kalckreuth (*b* at Hackpfüffel, Sangerhausen 24 May 1904; ✠ at Frankfurt-am-Main 7 Oct 1995).
> [*Marbach Weg 236, 60320 Frankfurt-am-Main, Germany*].

———◆———

THURN AND TAXIS

This family originated in Lombardy and can be authenticated from Reinerius de Tasso (1117) and documented since Odonus de Taxo in the Brembana Valley north of Bergamo in 1146; Nobility of the Holy Empire with ratification of arms, Trier 31 May 1512 (for two sets of four brothers who were cousins, de Taxis); confirmation of Nobility of the Holy Empire and ratification of arms (in favour of Jean-Baptiste), Saragosse 5 Jan 1534; Grand Postmaster General to the German Empire, Prague 16 June 1595; received the dignity of Lord and Baron of the Holy Empire (for Leonard I de Taxis), Prague 16 Jan 1608; Hereditary Grand Postmaster General of the Empire in The Netherlands, Lorraine and Burgundy, Prague 27 July 1615; Count of the Holy Empire, Vienna 8 June 1624; permission to bear the name and arms of the Counts von Thurn and Valsássina, 24 Sept 1650; title of Prince de la Tour et Tassis (Spanish Netherlands), Madrid 19 Feb 1681; title of Prince of the Holy Empire extended to all descendants, Vienna 4 Oct 1695; Hereditary Grand Postmaster General of the Holy Empire, 2 July 1744; vote in the Council of Princes of the Holy Empire 30 May 1754 by virtue of the dignity of Hereditary Grand Postmaster General - see above. The lines below descend from two half-brothers, sons of Alexander Ferdinand, 3rd Prince (b 21 March 1704; ✝ 17 March 1773).

Members of the family bear the title of Prince or Princess von Thurn and Taxis with the qualification of Serene Highness.

LINE I

Catholic: Founded by Charles-Anselm, 4th Prince (b 2 June 1733; ✝ 13 Nov 1805); Hereditary Grand Postmaster General of the Holy Empire 27 Dec 1774; bought the County of Friedberg and the Lordships of Scheer, Dürmentingen and Bussen (Württemberg), Vienna 22 Oct 1785 (for 2,100,000 florins); Princely-Count of Friedberg-Sheer and ratification of arms, Vienna 16 July 1787; compensated for the loss at the Peace of Lunéville in 1801 of postal revenues from the left bank of the Rhine with Buchau, Marchtal, Neresheim, etc (Württemberg) and the elevation of these lordships into the principality of Buchau 25 Feb 1803; Hereditary Grand Postmaster of the Crown of Bavaria 1 May 1808; Hereditary Member of the Bavarian Crown "Reichsräte" 26 May 1818; Prussian title of Prince of Krotoszyn, Berlin 29 May 1819; Hereditary Member of the First Chamber of the Kingdom of Württemberg 25 Sept 1819; Bohemian Incolat 6 March 1820, received the qualification of "Durchlaucht" (primogeniture) by the German Diet 18 Aug 1825; Hereditary Member of the former Prussian House of Lords 12 Oct 1854; of the former Austrian House of Lords 5 April 1862; Duke of Worth and Donaustauf (in Bavaria - primogeniture), Munich 8 May 1899.

ALBERT Maria Lamoral Miguel Johannes Gabriel, **12TH PRINCE (FÜRST) VON THURN AND TAXIS**, Prince zu Buchau, Prince von Krotoszyn, Duke zu Wörth and Donaustauf, Princely Count zu Friedberg-Scheer, Count zu Valsássina, zu Marchtal and zu Neresheim etc, b at Regensburg 24 June 1983, son of Johannes, 11th Prince (Fürst) von Thurn and Taxis, etc (b 5 June 1926; ✝ 28 Dec 1990) and Countess and Lady Mariae Gloria von Schönburg-

Glauchau (*b* 23 Feb 1960; *m* 30/31 May 1980).
[*Schloß Emmeramsplatz 5, 93047 Regensburg, Germany*].

Sisters

1. Princess *Maria Theresia* Ludowika Klothilde Helene Alexandra, *b* at Regensburg 28 Nov 1980.
2. Princess *Elisabeth* Margarete Maria Anna Beatrix, *b* at Regensburg 24 March 1982.

Mother

Mariae Gloria Ferdinanda Joachina Josephine Wilhelmine Huberta, Dowager Princess von Thurn and Taxis, *b* at Stuttgart-Degerloch 23 Feb 1960, dau of Joachim, Count and Lord (Graf and Herr) von Schönburg, Count and Lord (Graf and Herr) zu Glauchau and Waldenburg and Countess Beatrix Széchényi von Sárvár and Felsövidék; *m* at Regensburg 30 May (civ) and 31 May (relig) 1980, Johannes, 11th Prince (Fürst) von Thurn and Taxis, etc (*b* at Schloß Höfling, nr Regensburg 5 June 1926; ✝ at Regensburg 28 Dec 1990).
[*Schloß Emmeramsplatz 5, 93047 Regensburg, Germany*].

Sisters of Father

Issue of Karl August, 10th Prince von Thurn and Taxis, etc (*b* 23 July 1898; ✝ 26 April 1982) and Infanta Maria Ana of Portugal (*b* 3 Sept 1899; *m* 18 Aug 1921; ✝ 23 June 1971).

1. Princess *Clotilde* Alberta Maria Franziska Xaveria Andrea, *b* at Regensburg 30 Nov 1922, Dame Star Cross Order; *m* at Burgweinting, nr Regensburg 1 Nov (civ) and at Regensburg 7 Nov (relig) 1944, Johann Moritz, Prince von und zu Liechtenstein (*b* at Waldstein, nr Peggau 6 Aug 1914), Dr of Law, Dipl Forestry.
[*Dietersdorf 7, 3441 Judenau, Austria*].
2. Princess *Mafalda* Theresia Franziska Josepha Maria, *b* at Regensburg 6 March 1924; *m* at Munich 22 Dec 1963 (civ) and at Andechs 16 Jan (relig) 1964, Franz, Prince von Thurn and Taxis (2nd Line - see below) (*b* at Schloß Lissa 15 April 1915; ✝ at Vienna 17 April 1997).

Brothers of Grandfather

Issue of Albert, 8th Prince (Fürst) von Thurn and Taxis, etc (*b* 8 May 1867; ✝ 22 Jan 1952) and Archduchess Margarete of Austria, Princess of Hungary (*b* 6 July 1870; *m* 15 July 1890; ✝ 2 May 1955) having had issue, among whom,

Sons

1. **Franz Joseph** Maximilian Maria Antonius Ignatius Lamoral, **9th Prince (Fürst) von Thurn and Taxis**, *b* at Regensburg 21 Dec 1893; ✠ at Schloß Haus, nr Regensburg 13 July 1972, Bailiff Gd Cross Hon and Dev Sovereign Military Order of Malta, etc; *m* at Schloß Bronnbch 23 Nov 1920, Infanta Elisabeth of Portugal (*b* at Kleinheubach 19 Nov 1894; ✠ at Regensburg 12 Jan 1970), Dame Star Cross Order, dau of Miguel, Duke of Bragança and Princess Therese zu Löwenstein-Wertheim-Rosenberg, and had issue, among whom,

    1. Princess Maria *Fernanda* Eudoxia Michaela Gabriela Raphaela, *b* at Schloß Haus 19 Dec 1927; *m* at Regensburg 15 July 1950 (*m* diss by div at Freiburg 30 Oct 1951 and annulled 7 Dec 1954 since when she reverted to her maiden name), Franz Joseph, Prince of Hohenzollern (*b* at Umkirch 15 March 1926; ✠ at Sigmaringen 13 March 1996); has issue, an adopted dau

    [*Keplerstraße 11, 8000 Munich 80, Germany*].

2. Prince *Ludwig Philipp* Maria Friedrich Joseph Maximilian Antonius Ignatius Lamoral, *b* at Regensburg 2 Feb 1901; ✠ at Schloß Niederaichbach 22 April 1933, Kt of Hon Sovereign Military Order of Malta; *m* at Schloß Hohenberg, nr Lenggries, Bavaria 14 Nov 1922, Princess Elisabeth (*b* at Luxemburg 7 March 1901; ✠ at Schloß Hohenberg 2 Aug 1950), Dame Star Cross Order, dau of Wilhelm, Grand Duke of Luxemburg, Duke of Nassau and Infanta Maria Anna of Portugal, and had issue, among whom,

    1. Princess *Iniga* Anna Margarete Wilhelmine Louisa, *b* at Schloß Niederaichbach 25 Aug 1925; *m* at Niederaichbach 18 May (civ) and at Regensburg 20 May (relig) 1948, Eberhard, Prince von Urach, Count von Württemberg (*b* at Stuttgart 24 Jan 1907; ✠ at Aufkirchen, in Starnberg 29 Aug 1969), Major.

    [*Villa Außhausen, Oberlandst. 22, 8137 Berg 2 - Aufkirchen, Germany*].

3. Prince *Raphael Rainer* Karl Maria Joseph Antonius Ignatius Hubertus Lamoral, *b* at Regensburg 30 May 1906; ✠ at Schwangau 8 June 1993, Kt of Hon Sovereign Military Order of Malta; *m* at Regensburg 24 May 1932, Princess Margarete (Rita) (*b* at Berlin 19 Oct 1913; ✠ at Füssen 16 June 1997), dau of Maximilian Theodor, Prince von Thurn and Taxis (see below) and Princess Pauline von Metternich-Winneburg, and had issue,

1. Prince *Max Emanuel* Maria Albert Paul Isabella Klemens Lamoral, *b* at Schloß Bullachberg 7 Sept 1935; *m* 1stly at Schwangau 20 May (civ) and 22 May (relig) 1969, Countess Anna Maria (Mirzl) [*87645 Hohenschwangau über Füssen, Germany*] (*b* at Heidenheim an der Brenz 1 April 1955; *m* diss by div at Kempten 1 July 1970 and annulled at Augsburg 17 Oct 1972; she *m* 2ndly at Füssen 6 Nov 1970, Walter Stanner), dau of Konrad Albert, Count von Pocci and Anna Elisabeth Hartmann. He *m* 2ndly at Schwangau 14 March (civ) and at Bullachberg 15 March (relig) 1973, Christa Ingeburg (*b* at Heidenheim an der Brenz 14 Dec 1941), dau of Erich Heinle and Ingeburg Würzner, and by her has issue, [*Kurparkweg 10, 87645 Schwangau, Germany*].

> 1. Prince *Hubertus* Raphael Franz Josef Ulrich Maria Lamoral, *b* at Füssen 22 June 1973.
> [*Kurparkweg 10, 87645 Schwangau, Germany*].
> 2. Prince *Philipp* Gabriel Franz Josef Magnus Maria Lamoral, *b* at Füssen 19 April 1975.
> [*Kurparkweg 10, 87645 Schwangau, Germany*].

4. Prince *Philipp Ernst* Maria Adalbert Joseph Maximilian Antonius Ignatius Stanislaus Lamoral, *b* at Schloß Prüfening 7 May 1908; ✠ at Schloß Hohenberg 23 July 1964, Kt of Hon Sovereign Military Order of Malta; *m* at Schloß Taxis 8 Sept 1929, Princess Eulalia (Illa) (*b* at Schloß Biskupitz 21 Dec 1908; ✠ at Hohenberg 30 Dec 1993), Dame Star Cross Order, dau of Friedrich, Prince von Thurn and Taxis (see Line II below) and Princess Eleonore de Ligne, and had issue,

> 1. Prince *Albert Friedrich* Maria Lamoral Kilian, *b* at Schloß Prüfening 5 July 1930; *m* at Seeshaupt 28 July (civ) and at Birkenstein 30 July (relig) 1962, Baroness Alexandra (*b* at Königsberg 31 Oct 1932), Actress, dau of Schweter, Baron von der Ropp and Ursula von Boetticher.
> [*Sonnenbergstraße 7, 82467 Garmisch-Partenkirchen, Germany*].
> 2. Princess *Marguerite* Eleonore Marie Franziska Antoine de Padua, *b* at Schloß Hohenberg 1 Dec 1933.
> [*Hohenberg, 82402 Seeshaupt, Upper Bavaria, Germany*].
> 3. Princess Antonia Maria Margareta Theresia vom Kinde Jesu, *b* at Schloß Hohenberg 28 Jan 1936.
> [*Hohenberg, 82402 Seeshaupt, Upper Bavaria, Germany*].

LINE II

This line descends from Prince Maximilian Joseph (*b* 28 May 1769;
✠ 15 May 1831); Bohemian Incolat, Vienna 18 Sept 1797; Bohemian
Incolat, Baden 9 July 1829; "Landmann" in Tirol, Vienna 9 Oct
1838.

LAMORAL Karl Johannes **PRINCE (FÜRST) VON THURN
AND TAXIS**, *b* at Prague 15 May 1937, son of Alexander, Prince
von Thurn and Taxis (*b* at Schloß Mzell 31 Aug 1906; ✠ 16 Dec
1992) and Countess *Marie Valerie* von Mazzuchelli (*b* at Vienna 15
April 1913; *m* at Prague 26 Oct 1935); *m* at Vienna 29 July 1961
(*m* diss by div at Vienna 19 June 1978), Dorothea Auguste (*b* at
Vienna 12 March 1942), dau of Wilhelm Karl Hornberg and Ellida
Siegmann, and has issue,
[*Ettingshauserig 8, 1190 Vienna, Austria*].

Sons

1. Prince *Max-Emanuel* Karl Lamoral, *b* at Vienna 8 June 1965,
Businessman; *m* at Vienna 14 March 1986, Carine (*b* at Vienna ...
1962), dau of ... Lackner and ...
[*Ettingshauserig 8, 1190 Vienna, Austria*].
2. Prince *Stefan* Alexander Lamoral, *b* at Vienna 7 May 1967.
[*Ettingshauserig 8, 1190 Vienna, Austria*].
3. Prince *Andreas* Patrick Lamoral, *b* at Vienna 30 March 1970; *m* at
Deutsch-Wagram, Austria Aug 1998, Nina Zeiringer (*b* at ......).
[*Wehrbrücklstraße 37, 1220 Vienna, Austria*].

Brother

2. Prince *Egmont* Erich Johann Lamoral Karl Maria Joseph Wenzel
Alexander Ferdinand Eugen Pius Antonius Hadrian Gabriel Judas
Thadeus, *b* at Prague 26 Feb 1939; *m* at Vienna 2 July 1977 (*m* diss
by div at Vienna 2 July 1981 since when she has reverted to her
maiden name), Countess Maria Christiane [*Franz-Josefs-Kai 29, 1010
Vienna, Austria*] (*b* at Vienna 2 July 1936), dau of Eugen, Count von
Waldstein, and Princess Marie Elisabeth von Croÿ.
[*Beckmann Gasse 30-34/3/3, 1140, Vienna, Austria*].

Mother

Marie Valerie Dowager Princess von Thurn and Taxis *b* at Vienna 15
April 1913, dau of Ludwig, Count von Mazzuchelli and Johanna von

Mátyás; *m* at Prague 26 March 1935, Alexander-Ferdinand, Prince
von Thurn and Taxis (*b* at Schloß Mzell 31 Aug 1906; 16 Dec 1992).
[*Heinestraße 19, 1020 Vienna, Austria*].

Brothers and Sisters of Father

Issue of Erich, Prince von Thurn and Taxis (*b* 11 Jan 1876; ✠ 20 Oct
1952) and Countess Gabriele Kinsky von Wchinitz and Tettau (*b* 28
March 1883; *m* 21 Feb 1903; ✠ 28 Oct 1970), having had issue,
among whom,

1. Prince Johann (*Hans*) von Nepomuk Emmerich Lamoral Leo
Udalrich Emmo Maria Josef Erich Gabriel Ignatius, *b* at Schloß
Mzell 28 June 1908; ✠ at Freiburg 3 April 1959, Proprietor of Lissa,
Dipl Land Management, Kt of Hon Sovereign Military Order of
Malta; *m* at Prague 26 Jan 1939, Princess Maria Julia (*b* at Prague 25
Feb 1919), Dame Star Cross Order, dau of Leopold, Prince of
Lobkowicz, Proprietor of Unterberkovic, Winteritz, etc and
Princess Franziska von Montenuovo, and had issue, among whom,
[*Mauerkircherstraße 181, 81925 Munich, Germany*].

    1. Princess Maria Alexandra (*Almerie*) Franziska Gabriele
    Leonhardine Kaspara Ursula, *b* at Prague 21 Oct 1939; *m* at
    Munich 20 Sept 1962, Rudolf, Count von Colloredo-Mannsfeld
    (*b* at Paris 10 Aug 1938), Proprietor of Sierndorf, Land
    Manager, Forester.
    [*Schloß, 2011 Sierndorf, Lower Austria*].

    2. Prince *Friedrich* Leonhard Ignatius Josef Maria Lamoral
    Balthasar, *b* at Linz an der Donau 22 June 1950, Sports
    Journalist; *m* at Munich 4 June 1977, Beata (*b* at Budapest 21
    Feb 1947), Dame Star Grand Cross Order, dau of Laszlo Béry
    (of Hungarian nobility) and Countess Paula Apponyi von
    Nagy-Apponi.
    [*Lucille Grahnstraße 39, 81675 Munich, Germany*].

    3. Prince *Karl Ferdinand* Maria Lamoral Leonhard Ignatius
    Anselm, *b* at Linz 13 April 1952; *m* at Hamburg 16 Oct 1982,
    Viola Christine (*b* at Hamburg 10 June 1960), dau of Egon
    Pauen and Laura Christine Jebe, and has issue,
    [*Birk 9, 53359 Rheinbach-Todenfeld, Germany*].

        1. Princess *Alice* Maria Stephanie, *b* at Flensburg 16
        Aug 1985.

        2. Prince *Stanislaus* Johann Franz, *b* at Flensburg 29
        April 1987.

      3. Prince *Raphael* Ferdinand Egon, *b* at Flensburg 10 March 1992.

      4. Prince *Benedikt* Nikolaus Anselm, *b* at Bonn 16 Oct 1996.

    4. Prince Maximilian (*Max*) Anselm Andreas Paulinus Leonhard Lamoral Maria, *b* at Linz 22 June 1955.

    [*Mauerkircherstraße 18, 81925 Munich, Germany*].

2. Princess *Therese* Elisabeth Karolina Johanna Stephanie Maria Alexandra Josepha Ignatia, *b* at Schloß Mzell 29 Aug 1911; *m* 1stly at ..... (*m* diss by div at ....), Karl Svoboda (*b* at ....); *m* 2ndly at Prague 23 Dec (relig) 1947 and at Baden, nr Zurich 30 Jan (relig) 1948 (*m* diss by div at Prague 26 June 1949 since when she reverted to her maiden name), Alfons Stomm-Schweizer (*b* at Chur, Switzerland 26 Aug 1900; ✠ at ...).

[*Opern Gasse24, 1040 Vienna, Austria*].

3. Prince *Rudolf* Ferdinand Lamoral Franz Joseph Maria Ignatius Adam, *b* at Schloß Lissa 23 Dec 1913; ✠ at Graz 1 June 1986, Official in Finance Dept Government of Steiermark, Dr rer pol, Dipl Business Studies, Kt of Hon Sovereign Military Order of Malta; *m* at Graz 7 Jan (civ) and at Kremsegg 10 Jan (relig) 1960, Anna Maria (Annemarie) (*b* at Klagenfurt 28 Jan 1934), dau of Otto Zhuber von Ohróg and Elsa Rauscher, and has issue,

[*Hafnerriegel 72, 8010 Graz, Austria*].

    1. Prince *Paul Ferdinand*, *b* at Graz 23 Aug 1961.

    [*Gonzaga Gasse12, 1010 Vienna, Austria*].

    2. Princess *Elisabeth* Gabriele Maria Theresia, *b* at Graz 7 March 1963.

    3. Prince *Karl Alexander*, *b* at Graz 10 Jan 1965.

4. Prince *Franz* von Assisi Josef Ferdinand Wilhelm Paulus Rudolf Emil Lamoral Alexander Ignatius Theodor Pius Maria, *b* at Schloß Lissa 15 April 1915, ✠ at Vienna 17 April 1997; *m* 1stly at Vienna 27 May 1950 (*m* diss by div at Vienna 27 March 1952 and annulled 2 Nov 1063), Beatriz Estella (*b* at Buenos Aires 27 Feb 1928), dau of Miguel Angel de Gamas and Elena Mascias. He *m* 2ndly at Munich 22 Dec (civ) 1961 and at Andechs 16 Jan (relig) 1964, Princess Mafalda (*b* at Regensburg 6 March 1924; ✠ at Munich 23 July 1989), dau of Karl August, Prince von Thurn and Taxis and Infanta Maria Anna of Portugal, and by her has issue,

    1. Princess *Daria* Maria Gabriele, *b* at Munich 6 March 1962.

    [*Knöbelstraße 26, 80538 Munich, Germany*].

5. Prince *Wilhelm* Alexander Lamoral Erich Maria Josef Ignatius

von Loyola Franciscus von Assisi Benedictus Cyrillus Quirinus, *b* at
Schloß Mzell 29 March 1919, Lt Austrian Army.
[*Vega Gasse11, 1190 Vienna, Austria*].

Brother of Grandfather

Issue of Alexander, Prince von Thurn and Taxis (*b* 1 Dec 1851; ✠ 21
July 1939) and Princess Marie zu Hohenlohe-Waldenburg-
Schillingsfürst (*b* 28 Dec 1855; *m* 19 April 1875; ✠ 16 Feb 1934),
having had issue, among whom,

Son

Prince *Alexander* Karl Egon Theobald Lamoral Johann Baptist Maria,
b at Schloß Mzell 8 July 1881; ✠ at Schloß Duino 11 March 1937
(became a naturalised Italian along with his two sons with the title
of Principi della Torre e Tasso, 1st Duke di Castel Duino with the
qualification of Serene Highness); *m* 1stly at Paris 27 Jan (civ) and
29 Jan (relig) 1906 (*m* diss by div at Mlada-Boleslaw 13 Dec 1919),
Princess Marie (*b* at Mauny 22 July 1885; ✠ at Paris 13 Jan 1971),
Dame of Hon Bav Order of St Theresia, dau of Louis, Prince de Ligne
and Elisabeth de La Rochefoucauld of the Dukes de Doudeauville.
He *m* 2ndly at Vrana 18 Oct 1932, Hellena (Ella) Holbrook (*b* at
Detroit, Michigan, USA 17 Jan 1875; ✠ at Bellagio, Italy 22 June
1959; *m* 1stly at Detroit 15 June 1897, Manfred, Count von Matuschka,
Baron von Toppolczan and Spaetgen; that *m* diss by div at Berlin 20
Oct 1925 and annulled; she *m* 2ndly at Versailles 6 Dec 1930, James
Hazen Hyde; that *m* diss by div at Paris 26 May 1932), dau of
Franklin Hiram Walker and May Holbrook, and had issue from his
first marriage,

> 1 Princess *Margarete* Marie Therese Elisabeth Friederike
> Alexandra Louise, *b* at Chateau de Beloeil, Belgium 8 Nov
> 1909; *m* at Paris 29 April 1931 (*m* diss by div at at Budapest
> 30 Aug 1940 and at Paris 24 Jan 1955), Gaetan, Prince of
> Bourbon-Parma (*b* at Pianore 11 June 1905; ✠ at Mandelieu
> 9 March 1958).
> [*Hotel Atlantico, 55042 Forte dei Marmi, Prov. Lucca, Italy*].

(see Torre e Tasso - Part III)

Brother of Great-Great-Great-Grandfather

Issue of Maximilian, Prince von Thurn and Taxis (*b* 28 May 1769;
✠ 15 May 1831) and Princess Marie-Eleonore of Lobkowicz (*b* 22
April 1770; *m* 6 June 1791; ✠ 9 Nov 1834), having had issue, among
whom,

Son

Prince *Friedrich* Hannibal, *b* at Prague 3 Sept 1799; ✠ at Venice 17 Jan 1857; *m* at Vienna 29 June 1831, Countess Aurore (*b* at Budapest 13 June 1806; ✠ at Ischl 18 Sept 1881), dau of Vincenz, Count Batthyány de Német-Ujvár and Josephine von Rudnyak, having had issue, among whom,

Son

Prince *Lamoral* Friedrich Wilhelm Maximilian Vincent Georg, *b* at Maria-Theresiopol 13 April 1832; ✠ at Pressburg (Bratislava) 9 Dec 1903, Field Marshall, Kt Sovereign Military Order of Malta; *m* at Pressburg 22 April 1871, Countess Marie Antonie (*b* at Brünn 18 July 1850; ✠ at Schloß Biskupitz 26 March 1942), Dame Star Cross Order, dau of Friedrich, Count Schaffgotsch and Countess Therese Pálffy d'Erdöd, having had issue,

Son

Prince *Friedrich* Lamoral Joseph Maria Anton, *b* at Raab 23 Dec 1871; murdered at Biskupitz 10 May 1945, Lt-Col Austrian Army; *m* at La Neuville-sous-Huy 30 Nov 1907, Princess Eléonore (*b* at Brussels 25 Jan 1877; ✠ at Hohenberg 13 Aug 1959), Lady-in-Waiting, Dame Star Cross Order, dau of Eduard, Prince de Ligne and Princess Eulalie zu Solms-Braunfels, and had issue, among whom,

    1. Prince *Georg* Lamoral Alexander Anton Joseph Maria, *b* at Schloß Biskupitz 26 April 1910; ✠ at Munich 4 Oct 1986; *m* 1stly at Berlin-Steglitz 6 Jan (civ) and 7 Jan (relig) 1943 (*m* diss by div at Johannesburg, South Africa 21 April 1954), Editha (*b* at Königsberg 9 Aug 1921; she *m* 2ndly in 1962, Horst Ganske), dau of Max Schoer and Käthe Patzig. He *m* 2ndly at Munich 13 June 1969, Anneliese [*Griechenstraße 15, 81545 Munich, Germany*] (*b* at Berlin 13 Oct 1922), dau of Willy Zerbst and Emma Meske, and had issue by his first wife,

        1 Princess *Maria Katharina* Eleonore, *b* at Brünn 22 April 1944; *m* 1stly at Rome 14 Oct 1968 (*m* diss by div at Cologne 11 July 1979), Anton Weiler (*b* at Cologne 3 Aug 1925). She *m* 2ndly at Königstein, Taunus 1 July 1981, Heinz Köster (*b* at Cologne 2 July 1931), Dr of Law.
        [*Mainblick 3, 61462 Königstein, Taunus, Germany*].

2. Prince *Hugo* Lamoral Nikolaus, *b* at Schloß Biskupitz 21
Sept 1916; ✠ at Munich 6 May 1975, Dipl Business Studies;
m 1stly at Vienna 16 Dec 1940 (*m* diss by div at Brünn 11 Dec
1945), Ingeborg (*b* at Vienna 8 Sept 1921; she *m* 2ndly 23 Dec
1985, Günther Kollmann), dau of Karl Sponer and Elisabeth
Budig, and had issue,
[*Impeuberg 7, 85567 Grafing Bei Munich, Germany*]

    1. Prince *Karl Friedrich* Lamoral Hugo, *b* at Pähl,
Upper Bavaria 20 June 1941; *m* at 1stly Hanover 30
July 1965 (*m* diss by div at Rosenheim Dec 1988),
Monika Anna (*b* at Vienna 11 April 1942), dau of
Herbert Brückner and Anna Danzinger. He *m* 2ndly
at Munich 10 Aug 1989, Nancy Brown (*b* at Keyser,
West Virginia, USA 14 June 1940), dau of Earl Kieffer
Hess and Louise Welch, and has issue by his first wife,
[*Giselastraße 6, 80802 Munich, Germany*].

        1. Princess *Beatrice* Antonie, *b* at Weingarten
5 Jan 1966.
[*Kaulbachstraße 41, 80539 Munich, Germany*].
        2. Prince *Georg* Lamoral Alexander, *b* at
Weingarten 2 Aug 1967, Sports Publicist,
Advertising Executive.
[*Frauenhoterstraße 15, 80469 Munich,
Germany*].
        3. Princess *Julia* Christina Verena, *b* at Bad
Reichenhall 17 April 1980.

    2. Prince *Friedrich* Lamoral, *b* at Kornitz, Mähren 8
Sept 1943, Dipl Business Studies; *m* at Birkfeld,
Steiermark 12 Dec 1970, Angelica (*b* at Graz 24 May
1951), dau of Gherardo, Marquess Tacoli di San
Possidonio, Proprietor of Birkenstein and Baroness
Marga Musulin de Gomirje, and has issue,
[*Fridau 2, 3200 Obergrafendorf, Austria*].

        1. Prince *Philipp* Lamoral Alfonso Thaddäus,
b at Salzburg 20 June 1971, Mag jur; *m* at
Natoye 22 Aug 1998, Countess Pauline (*b* at
Brussels 24 Aug 1974), dau of Count Arnould
d'Aspremont-Lynden and Countess Hedwig von
Thurn and Valsassina-Como-Vercelli.
[*Schmöllergasse 5, 1040 Vienna, Austria*].
        2. Princess *Olivia* Maria, *b* at Vienna 16 Feb

1973; *m* at Pomarolo nr Rovereto 19 June 1999,
Johannes Volpini de Maestri.
[*Fridau 2, 3200 Obergrafendorf, Austria*].
3. Prince *Alfonso* Lamoral Hugo Maria, *b* at
Vienna 21 July 1976.
[*Fridau 2, 3200 Obergrafendorf, Austria*].

Prince Hugo *m* 2ndly at Munich 31 July 1953, Countess
Beatrice (*b* at Bankau 17 April 1925; ✠ at Perlach, nr Munich
13 Dec 1954), dau of Otto, Count von Bethusy-Huc and Sibylle
von Gersdorff. Prince Hugo *m* 3rdly at Munich 29 Dec 1961,
Dorothea [*Ottilienstraße 82, 81827 Munich, Germany*] (*b* at
Dessau 29 Oct 1931), dau of Wolfgang van der Elst and Luise
Ebermaier, and by her had further issue,

3. Princess *Marie-Luise, b* at Munich 30 July 1963,
Dipl Engineer, Architect.
[*Ottilienstraße 82, 81827 Munich, Germany*].
4. Princess *Eleonore* Melanie, *b* at Munich 2 March
1965, Dr of Med; *m* at Berlin 11 Aug (civ) and at
Altenmarkt 16 Sept (relig) 1995, Hubertus von der
Schulenburg (*b* at Erlangen 24 March 1966).
[*Lützowstraße 81, 10785 Berlin, Germany*].

TOERRING

Catholic: Feudal family of Upper Bavaria which can be traced from
Adalram and Odalchalch von Toerring, living 16 Sept 1158; acquired
Jettenbach ca 1200; Baron of the Holy Empire, Augsburg 3 June
1566; "Erboberstjägermeister" Hereditary Chief Master of the Hunt
of the Duchy of Bavaria, Munich 18 July 1607; Hereditary
Chamberlain of the Duchy of Salzburg, 1618; Count of the Holy
Empire, Regensburg 21 Oct 1630; Hereditary Member of the Bavarian
"Reichsräte" 26 May 1818; joined the names and arms of Minucci 10
April 1824; Count Clemens zu Toerring-Jettenbach (✠ 22 Oct 1826;
✠ 12 Nov 1891) was recognised in Württemberg as successor to the
extinct branch of Toerring-Gutenzell (extinct 30 April 1860) and
authorised to use the qualification of "Erlaucht" for the Head of the
Family 9 Oct 1888 in accordance with the decision of the German
Diet 13 Feb 1829; the qualification of Illustrious Highness was extended
to all Members of the family, Bavaria 7 March 1911.
Members of the family bear the title of Count or Countess zu Toerring-
Jettenbach with the qualification of Illustrious Highness.

HANS VEIT Kaspar Nikolaus, **COUNT (GRAF) ZU TOERRING-JETTENBACH,** Count zu Gutenzell, Baron von Seefeld, Lord von Pörnbach-Pertenstein-Jettenbach and Gutenzell, *b* at Munich 11 Jan 1935; son of Carl Theodor, Count zu Toerring-Jettenbach (*b* 22 Sept 1900; ✠ 14 May 1967) and Princess Elisabeth of Greece and Denmark (*b* 24 May 1904; *m* 9 Jan (civ) / 10 Jan (relig) 1934; ✠ 11 Jan 1955); *m* at Bartenstein, Württemberg 22 March (civ) and 20 April (relig) 1964, Princess Henriette (*b* at Bartenstein 23 Aug 1938), dau of Karl, Prince zu Hohenlohe-Bartenstein and Baroness Clara von Meyern-Hohenberg.
[*Cuvilliésstraße 8, 81679 Munich, Germany; Steubstraße 12, 81925 Munich, Germany*].

Sons and Daughter

1. Countess *Clarissa* Beatrix Eleonore Maria, *b* at Munich 31 March 1965; *m* at Tulln, Austria 8 June (civ) and at Winhöring 4 July (relig) 1999, Prince Tassilo von Ratibor und Corvey, Prince zu Hohenlohe-Schillingsfürst-Breunner-Enkevoirth (*b* at Vienna 24 Oct 1965).
[*Schloß Grafenegg, 3485 Haitzendorf, Austria*].
2. *Ignatius* Maximilian Karl Veit, Hereditary Count (Erbgraf) zu Toerring-Jettenbach, *b* at Munich 30 March 1966.
[*Cuvilliésstraße 8, 81679 Munich, Germany; Steubstraße 12, 81925 Munich, Germany*].
3. Count *Carl Theodor* Ferdinand, *b* at Munich 17 Feb 1969.
[*Cuvilliésstraße 8, 81679 Munich, Germany; Steubstraße 12, 81925 Munich, Germany*].

Sister

Countess *Helen* Marina Elisabeth, *b* at Winhöring 20 May 1937, Dame Star Cross Order; *m* at Munich 6 April (civ) and at Schloß Seefeld 10 April (relig) 1956, Archduke Ferdinand of Austria (*b* at Vienna 6 Dec 1918), Kt Order of the Golden Fleece.
[*20 Friston Street, London SW6 3AT; 5081 Anif bei Salzburg, Austria*].

Brother and Sister of Father

Issue of Hans Veit, Count zu Toerring-Jettenbach, etc (*b* 7 April 1862; ✠ 29 Oct 1929) and Duchess Sophie in Bavaria (*b* 22 Feb 1875; *m* 26 July 1898; ✠ 4 Sept 1957).

1. Count *Hans Heribert* Wilhelm Veit Adolf, *b* at Winhöring 25 Dec

1903; ✠ at Murnau, Bavaria 16 March 1977, Proprietor of Seefeld; *m* 1stly at Munich 19 Oct (civ) and 20 Oct (relig) 1938 (*m* annulled 23 Oct 1947), Victoria (*b* at Frankfurt-am-Main 13 Feb 1918; ✠ at Tegernsee 29 April 1965; she *m* 2ndly at Tegernsee 12 Dec 1947, Rudolf Hantschel who ✠ 18 March 1985, Businessman), dau of Paul Lindpaintner and Maria Wegemann. He *m* 2ndly at Oberalting-Seefeld 10 Dec 1947, Baroness Maria Immaculata (*b* at Harmashutta 27 July 1921), dau of Friedrich Heinrich, Baron Waldbott von Bassenheim and Archduchess Marie Alice of Austria, and by her had issue, among whom,

[*Schloß Plöcking 1, 84326 Falkenberg, Germany*].

1. Countess *Alice* Maria Immaculata Sophie Isabella, *b* at Munich 5 June 1949.

[*Schloß Seefeld, 82229 Seefeld, Germany*].

2. Countess Maria Josefa *(Marie-José)* Gabriele Stefanie, *b* at Munich 27 Oct 1950.

[*Engelhardstraße 32, 81927 Munich, Germany*].

3. Count *Hans-Caspar* Heribert Veit Friedrich, *b* at Munich 22 July 1953, Kt Bav Order of St George; *m* at Zeil 30 April (civ) and 23 May (relig) 1980, Countess Elisabeth (*b* at Glashütte, nr Wengen 6 Jan 1954), dau of Konstantin, Count von Waldburg zu Zeil and Trauchburg and Princess Eleonore of Bavaria, and has issue,

[*Dünzelbach 89, 82272 Moorenweis, Germany*].

1. Countess *Maria Antonia* Sophie Immaculata, *b* at Munich 22 June 1981.

2. Countess *Eleonore* Gabriele Isabelle, *b* at Toronto, Canada 16 Feb 1984.

3. Countess *Fernanda* Maria Alice, *b* at Munich 17 Dec 1985.

4. Count *Cajetan* Anton Gaudenz Tassilo, *b* at Munich 29 Dec 1986

5. Count *Georg* Clemens Friedrich, *b* at Munich 3 Nov 1989.

4. Countess *Sophie* Maria Antonia Eleonore, *b* at Munich 26 March 1957.

[*Knöbelstraße 24, 80538 Munich, Germany*].

TRAUTTMANSDORFF

Catholic: A feudal family from Styria who take their name from their principal manor of Trauttmansdorf, near Feldbach and can be traced from Herrand von Trauttmansdorf, 1308 - 25; Baron, Prague 12 March 1598, with the qualification of "Wohlgeboren", Vienna 13 Oct 1620; Count of the Holy Empire (primogeniture) with the qualification of "Wohlgeboren", Regensburg 15 March 1623 (for the brothers Sigmund Friedrich Johan David and their cousin Adam Maximilian) a title confirmed in Bohemia, Ödenburg 25 Nov 1625; Hungarian Indignat 1625; received into the Swabian College of Counts of the Holy Empire (for the Head of the Family) 1631; inherited the Lordships of Weinsberg and Neuenstadt am Kocher in Württemberg, 1635 which were returned to Württemberg after the Peace of Westphalia; authorised to add the name of Weinsberg, Vienna 31 July 1639; received again into the Swabian College of Counts of the Holy Empire (for all descendants of Count Maximilian - b 1584; ✝ 1650), 1778. The lines below descend from two sons of the above-mentioned Count Maximilian.

LINE I

Founded by Count Adam Mathias (b 1617; ✝ 2 Nov 1684). Bohemian Incolat 21 May 1667; Lord of Upper Austria 20 Sept 1712; reintroduced into the College of the Counts of Holy Empire 1778 (for all descendants of Count Maximilian who ✝ 1650); acquired the Lordship of Umpfenbach (Upper Franconia, Bavaria) 6 Jan 1805 (sold 1812); Prince of the Holy Empire (primogeniture) with ratification of arms, qualification of "Hochgeboren" and elevation of the Lordship of Umpfenbach into a Princely County of the Holy Empire, Vienna 12 Jan 1805; Bohemian Prince (primogeniture), Vienna 10 April 1805; qualification of "Durchlaucht" (primogeniture) by the German Diet 18 Aug 1825; confirmed in Austria 7 Oct 1825; Hereditary Member of the former Austrian House of Lords 18 April 1861.
The Head of the family and his wife bear the title of Prince and Princess von and zu Trauttmansdorff-Weinsberg with the qualification of Serene Highness, and cadet members bear the title of Count or Countess von and zu Trauttmansdorff-Weinsberg.

CARL-WOLFGANG, 7TH PRINCE (FÜRST) VON AND ZU TRAUTTMANSDORFF-WEINSBERG and Neustadt am Kocher, Princely Count zu Umpfenbach, Baron auf Gleichenberg, Negau, Burgau and Totzenbach, b at Vienna 11 Sept 1965, Mag jur, son of Rudolf, 6th Prince (Fürst) von and zu Trauttmansdorff-Weinsberg (b 18 Nov 1923; ✝ 12 April 1994) and Countess Sybilla Wolff Metternich zur Gracht (b 12 Aug 1930; m (civ) 27 Aug 1958

and (relig) 5 Feb 1959).
[*Formanek Gasse50, 1190 Vienna, Austria*].

Sisters

1. Countess *Stefanie* Sophie, *b* at Vienna 15 Sept 1959; *m* at Vienna 30 Jan 1994, Noble Giulio Superti Furga (*b* at Milan 17 May 1962).
[*Am Neckarhangweg 1, 69118 Heidelberg, Germany; 16 Via Niccolò Machiavelli, 20145 Milan, Italy*].
2. Countess *Fiona* Marie-Adelheid, *b* at Vienna 1 Aug 1961; *m* at Vienna April 21 2001, Francesco de Medici (*b* at ......).
[*Untere Viadukt Gasse43, 1030 Vienna, Austria; Liechtensteinstraße 52, 1090 Vienna, Austria*].

Mother

Sybilla, Princess (Fürstin) von and zu Trauttmansdorff-Weinsberg, *b* at Göttingen 12 Aug 1930, Dame Star Cross Order, dau of Wolfgang, Count Wolff Metternich zur Gracht, Proprietor of Vinsebeck and Kreuzberg, nr Bonn and Adelheid von Adelebsen, adopted dau of Heinz von Gerdorff; *m* at Vinsebeck, nr Steinheim, Westphalia (civ) 27 Aug 1958 and (relig) 5 Feb 1959, Rudolf 6th Prince (Fürst) von and zu Trauttmansdorff-Weinsberg (*b* at Bischofteinitz 18 Nov 1923; ✠ at Vienna 12 April 1994).
[*Formanek Gasse50, 1190 Vienna*].

Brothers of Father

Issue of Joseph, 5th Prince von and zu Trauttmansdorff-Weinsberg (*b* 10 March 1897; ✠ 3 June 1976) and Countess Johanna Kinsky von Wchinitz and Tettau (*b* 24 Aug 1902; *m* 16 Aug 1921; ✠ 16 Nov 1964) and had issue among whom,

1. Count *Friedrich*, *b* at Bischofteinitz 21 June 1926, Farmer; *m* 1stly at Assen, Soest, Westphalia 18 Oct 1955 (*m* diss by div 1972), Countess Pauline (*b* at Neuengraben 29 June 1932), dau of Bernhard, Count von Galen and Countess Marie Sophie Kinsky von Wchinitz and Tettau. He *m* 2ndly at St Catharines, Ontario, Canada 20 Dec 1974 (*m* diss by div 1983), Nora Dethune (*b* at Kitchener, Ontario 6 July 1932), dau of John Goldie and Mary Larratt-Smith. He *m* 3rdly at Toronto, Ontario 4 Feb 1984, Brenda Clara (*b* at Toronto 25 Nov 1939), dau of Clarence Northey and Mary Margaret Despard, and has issue from his first wife,
[*R.R.3. Beamsville, Ontario L0R 1B0, Canada*].

  1. Countess *Marie Therese*, *b* at Hamilton, Ontario 28 July

1956; *m* at Beamsville, Ontario 31 July 1982, Stephen Stanley Jones (*b* 27 Jan 1954).

[*145 Brixham Crescent, London, Ontario N6K 1K9, Canada*].

2. Count *Ferdinand, b* at Hamilton, Ontario 1 Nov 1957; *m* at Toronto 27 Aug 1983, Christine Eleonore (*b* 16 March 1959), dau of David Miller Brown and Eleonore Martin.

[*19 Keppler Crescent, Nepan, Ontario K2H 5S3, Canada*].

3. Count *Andreas, b* at Hamilton 15 Oct 1962.

[*345 Lonsdale Road, Apt. 308, Toronto, Ontario M5P 1R5, Canada*].

2. Count *Johannes* Maximilian, *b* at Vienna 20 Feb 1929, Businessman; *m* at Wald 2 Sept 1959, Princess Johanna (*b* at Ainödt 4 May 1934), dau of Karl, Prince von Auersperg-Breunner, Proprietor of Ainödt and Countess Henriette von Meran, and has issue,

[*Taubstummen Gasse 2, 1140 Vienna, Austria*].

    1. Count Johannes *Markus, b* at Vienna 23 Nov 1960, Dr of Law, Lt, Management Consultant; *m* at Vienna 19 March 1988, Countess Natalie (*b* at Johannesburg, South Africa 26 Feb 1966), dau of Peter, Count von Hartig and Camilla, Noble (Edle) von Hackenschmidt, and has issue,

[*Defreggerstraße 3, 81445 Munich, Germany*].

        1. Count *Paul* Vinzenz Georg Antonius Maria Judas Thaddäus, *b* at Munich 4 Jan 1989.

        2. Count *Benedict* Markus Dominik Maria Judas Thaddäus, *b* at Munich 14 Sept 1990.

        3. Countess *Elena* Katerina, *b* at Munich 28 June 1992.

        4. Count *Anton* Johannes, *b* at Munich 3 May 1995.

        5. Count *Johannes* Hubertus, *b* at Munich 25 Oct 1996.

    2. Countess *Désirée* Theresia, *b* at Vienna 4 March 1962, Assistant Medical Technician; *m* at Wald 1 Aug 1987, Alberich, Count zu Lodron-Laterano and Castelromano (*b* at Klagenfurt 1 Aug 1961).

[*Weingartenhaus, 9562 Himmelberg 83, Kärnten, Austria*].

    3. Countess Johanna *Daria, b* at Vienna 23 Oct 1963; *m* at Wald 25 April 1987, Vinzenz, Count von Thurn and Valsassina-Como-Vercelli (*b* at Klagenfurt 11 Sept 1963), Farmer, Forester.

[*Schloß, 9150 Bleiburg, Kärnten, Austria*].

4. Count *Thomas* Friedrich, *b* at Vienna 23 March 1965, Mag soc oec.

[*Mailingerstraße 34/3, 80636 Munich, Germany*].

5. Countess *Huberta* Margareta, *b* at Vienna 13 April 1966; *m* at Maria Loretto 6 May 1995, Count Matthias von Orsini and Rosenberg (*b* at Klagenfurt 8 Aug 1955; *m* 1stly 9 June 1985, Brigitte Nagele; that *m* diss by div 1987 and annulled 1992; *m* 2ndly 1992, Michaela Lang who ✠ 19 June 1993), Forester.

[*Gut Höhenbergen, 9121 Tainach, Kärnten, Austria*].

3. Count *Carl-Mathias, b* at Bischoftenitz 16 May 1937; *m* 1stly at Bogotá, Columbia 8 Feb 1964 (*m* diss by div 1973), Grete [*Transversal 19, N-121-50, Santafé de Bogotá, Columbia*] (*b* at Bogotá 23 June 1939), dau of Hans-Dietrich Streubel and Cecilia Gutiérres, and has issue,

1. Count *Felipe* Mathias, *b* at Medellin 30 July 1968.

[*Transversal 19, N-121-50, Santafé de Bogotá, Columbia*].

2. Count *Andres* Mathias, *b* at Bogota 7 April 1972.

[*Transversal 19, N-121-50, Santafé de Bogotá, Columbia*].

Count Carl-Mathias *m* 2ndly at Santa Cruz 2 Feb 1975, Thea Ellen (*b* at Bremen 1 Feb 1941), dau of Carl Degenhardt and Hildegard Betke, and has further issue,

[*32 West Hills Road, Ivorton, CT 06442, U.S.A.*].

3. Countess *Isabella* Maria, *b* at São Paulo 5 Aug 1976.

4. Count *Michael* Johannes, *b* at Prague 16 Sept 1940; ✠ at Toronto, Ontario, Canada 12 Oct 1971; *m* at Seeon, Bavaria 24 June 1967, Gabrielle (*b* at Neujasenitz 6 Sept 1944; *m* 2ndly at Glentorf 21 June 1975, Heinz Walter Löhr, Dr of Med), dau of Wilhelm Retzdorff and Alexa Werth, and had issue,

[*Strähler Weg 21, 76227 Karlsruhe - Durlach, Germany*].

1. Count *Johannes* Maximilian, *b* at Toronto 7 July 1969; *m* at Stevenage, Herts 16 Aug 1997, Alison (*b* at Hitchin, Herts 10 Dec 1970), MBA, dau of William Vernon Davies and Elisabeth Anderson Crosbie.

[*Alte Schulstraße 95a, 61091 Bad Nauheim-Steinfurth, Germany*].

2. Countess *Felicia* Alexandra, *b* at Toronto 1 March 1971, Architect; *m* at Grundlsee 24 Aug 2002, Count Georg de la Fontaine und d'Harnoncourt-Unverzagt (*b* at ......).

[*Bambergerstraße 27, 10779 Berlin, Germany*].

Brothers of Father

Issue of Ferdinand Alfons, Hereditary Count von and zu Trauttmansdorff-Weinsberg (*b* 14 Jan 1871; ✠ 18 Sept 1915) and Princess Maria zu Schwarzenberg (*b* 2 Oct 1869; *m* 23 Jan 1895; ✠ 20 March 1931), having had issue, among whom,

Sons

1. Count *Ferdinand* Johann, *b* at Kaaden 10 March 1897; ✠ at Klagenfurt 14 May 1958, Papal Chamberlain, Kt of Hon and Dev Sovereign Military Order of Malta, Kt of Justice Constantinan Order of St George; *m* at Prague 15 June 1921, Countess Johanna (Hanna) (*b* at Vienna 2 April 1891; ✠ at Feldkirch 15 May 1984; *m* 1stly at Vienna 6 July 1914, Aloysius, Count Esterházy de Galántha who was *ka* at Sósmezö, Ojtoz-Pass, Háromszék, Hungary 24 Oct 1916), Dame Star Cross Order, dau of Zdenko, Count Kinsky von Wchinitz and Tettau and Countess Georgine Festetics de Tolna, and had issue,

    1. Count Karl *Norbert*, *b* at Prague 13 Sept 1922; ✠ at Grabs 26 Aug 1990; *m* 1stly at Lucca, Toscana 14 July 1948 (*m* diss by div 1962), Ortensia [*Via Gallitassi 69, 55100 Lucca, Italy*] (*b* at Lucca 11 Sept 1926), dau of Piero, Count Minutoli Tegrim and Tecla Gulinelli of the Counts Gulinelli, and has issue,

        1. Countess *Benedetta* Ottavia, *b* at Rome 9 July 1949; *m* at Edmonton Alberta, Canada 17 Oct 1975, Massimo de Vito Piscicelli, Count di Collesano (*b* at Lucca 15 Jan 1943), Dr of Engineering, Kt of Dev Sovereign Military Order of Malta.
        [*Villa Piscicelli, Monte San Quirico, 55100 Lucca, Italy*].

        2. Count *Herrand* Ferdinand, *b* at Milan 17 Aug 1951; *m* at Feldkirch, Vorarlberg 1 June 1973, Monika (*b* at Judenburg 11 March 1949), dau of Walter Russheim and Monika Wieland, and has issue,
        [*Via Camugliano 18, 56038 Ponsacco, Prov. Pisa, Italy*].

            1. Countess *Sandra*, *b* at Chur 3 Nov 1974.
            2. Countess *Ilona*, *b* at Barga 10 Sept 1981.

        3. Count *Hektor* Heinrich, *b* at San Antonio Abad, Ibiza, Balearic Islands 22 May 1955, Hotelier.
        [*Pantzer Gasse10, 1190 Vienna, Austria; Glaser Gasse5, 1090 Vienna, Austria*].

Count Norbert *m* 2ndly at Innsbruck 1963 (*m* diss by div at

Frankfurt-am-Main 20 Sept 1988), Theda [*Hauptstraße 42, 61194 Niddatal-Assenheim, Germany*] (*b* at Schaan, Liechtenstein 9 Jan 1940), dau of Hanno von Halem and Countess Eugénie zu Stolberg-Stolberg, and has further issue,

> 4. Count *Franz-Martin, b* at London 16 Feb 1964, Silversmith; m at Brooklyn, New York 28 Sept 1999, Princess Margaretha Patricia (*b* at St Johann, Tyrol 22 Dec 1964), dau of Prince Anton of Croÿ and Margriet Krayenbrink.
> [*Unterfeld 551, 9495 Triesen, Liechtenstein*].
> 5. Countess *Alexandra* Maria della Vittoria, *b* at Heilbronn 29 Jan 1966; m at Paris 18 April 1992, François Neel (*b* at ... 5 Nov 1966).
> [*7 rue Saulnier, Paris 27009, France*].

Count Norbert m 3rdly at Alpbach, Tirol 29 March 1989, Gertraud Straumer (*b* at Villach, Kärnten 7 Oct 1946), and has further issue,
[*Albblick 18, 73730 Esslingen, Germany*].

> 6. Countess *Nancy* Natalie, *b* at Esslingen am Neckar 22 Dec 1972.
> [*Albblick 18, 73730 Esslingen, Germany*].

2. Count *Maximilian* Karl, *b* at Kalsburg 13 Sept 1900; ✝ at Innsbruck 25 June 1965, Dr of Law, Kt of Dev Sovereign Military Order of Malta, Kt Order of St George, Papal Chamberlain; m 1stly at Berlin 6 May 1933 (*m* diss by div 1939), Baroness Elisabeth (*b* at Potsdam 23 Aug 1902; ✝ at Brunswick 28 July 1965), dau of Eberhard, Baron von Schrötter and Elisabeth Gleichmann. He *m* 2ndly at Berlin 1 Sept 1939 (*m* diss by div 1944), Gabriele Tielsch (*b* at Ratibor 21 Oct 1908; *m* 1stly ... Kennedy, that *m* diss by div. He *m* 3rdly at Friedenau 17 Sept 1944 (*m* diss by div at Bonn June 1954), Sibylle (*b* at Friedenau 20 Aug 1923; she *m* 2ndly at Bad Godesberg 21 Dec 1957, Hanns Joachim Proske), dau of Ewald von Kries, Proprietor of Friedenau and Baroness Catharina von Beschwitz. He *m* 4thly at Koblenz 28 May 1965, Antonia Fisher (*b* at ....), and with his second wife adopted a son,

> 1. Klaus Jürgen Weingarten, *b* at Berlin-Schmargendorf 5 Oct 1940; adopted .... 1943, bears the name "Trauttmansdorff"; *m* at Bergheim an der Erft, Cologne 27 Oct 1967, Ingrid (*b* at Bedburg 25 Feb 1947), dau of ... Kramm and ...
> [*Hermann Lönsstraße 41, 5010 Bergheim-Quadrath-*

Ichendorf, Bez. Cologne, Germany].

Brother of Grandfather

Issue of Karl, 4th Prince (Fürst) von and zu Trauttmansdorff-
Weinsberg (*b* 5 Sept 1845; ✠ 9 Nov 1921) and Margravine Josephine
von Pallavicini (*b* 22 Jan 1849; *m* 29 April 1969; ✠ 14 July 1923),
having had issue, among whom,

Son

Count *Karl, b* at Ober-Waltersdorf 5 May 1872; ✠ at Weissenegg 1
April 1951, Imp and Royal Chamberlain, Kt Order of the Iron Crown
(3rd Cl), Kt Order of Leopold; *m* at Vienna 2 May 1905, Princess
Marie (*b* at Vienna 15 Jan 1880; ✠ 6 May 1960), Lady-in-Waiting,
Dame Order of the Star Cross, dau of Franz Joseph, Prince (Fürst)
von Auersperg and Countess Wilhelmine Kinsky von Wchinitz and
Tettau, and had issue, among whom,

    1. Count *Joseph* Karl, *b* at Berlin 8 April 1906; ✠ at Vienna
    15 Feb 1985, Dr of Law; *m* at Kitsee, Wieselburg 19 July 1936,
    Countess Blanka (*b* at Kitsee 23 June 1911; ✠ 18
    Dec 1998), Dame Star Cross Order, dau of Ladislaus, 3rd
    Prince (Fürst) Batthyány von Német-Ujvár, Proprietor of
    Güssing, Eisenburg, Kitsee, etc, and Countess Maria Theresia
    Coreth zu Coredo and Starkenberg, and had issue,
    [*Dornau, 2544 Leobersdorf, Austria*].

        1. Count *Matthias* Franz Joseph, *b* at Vienna 9 June
        1937, Farmer; *m* at Munich 31 May 1961, Countess
        Amélitta (Amélie) (*b* at Breslau 5 Nov 1934), Dame
        Star Cross Order, dau of Alexander, Count von Wallwitz
        and Anna Maria Schuster, and has issue,
        [*Lanzendorferstraße 8, 2325 Pellendorf, Austria*].

            1. Count *Alexander, b* at Vienna 8 March 1962,
            Mag soc oec; *m* at Nice 7 Jan 1989, Countess
            Maria Theresia (*b* at Regensburg 22 May 1963),
            dau of Ferdinand, Count Kinsky von Wchinitz
            and Tettau and Countess Hedwig von
            Ballestrem, and has issue,
            [*6295 Ginzling, Tirol, Austria*].

                1. Countess *Marie-Catherine, b* at
                Munich 20 Jan 1990.
                2. Countess *Johanna* Maria, *b* at Muich
                7 June 1991.

3. Count *Augustinus* Franziskus, *b* at Munich 30 Aug 1993.

4. Countess *Anna* Benedikta, *b* at Munich 29 Dec 1994.

2. Count *Maximilian, b* at Vienna 15 Feb 1964, Dipl Engineer; *m* at Pianezza, Prov Turin 3 June 1990, Lidia (*b* at Turin 30 Aug 1963), dau of Ernesto, Count Rossi di Montelera and Emanuela San Martino d'Agliè of the Marquesses di Fontanetto con San Germano, and has issue,

[*Gusshausstraße 17, 1040 Vienna, Austria*].

1. Countess *Luisa* Maria, *b* at Vienna 27 June 1991.

2. Countess *Maria* Amelie, *b* at Vienna 20 April 1993.

3. Countess *Elisabeth* Marie, *b* at Vienna 29 Sept 1995.

2. Count *Peter, b* at Vienna 5 Dec 1938, Major; *m* at Laxenburg 22 Sept 1966, Jutta (*b* at Vienna 22 Oct 1939), dau of Hermann Khaelss von Kaelsberg and Leopoldine Fuhrmann, and has issue,

[*Klausen Gasse12, 2331 Vösendorf, Austria*].

1. Countess *Blanka, b* at Vienna 19 July 1967; *m* at Vösendorf 14 Aug 1994, Josep Ferrer (*b* at ....).

[*Calle Copérnico 28, 08021 Barcelona, Spain*].

2. Countess *Sophie, b* at Vienna 7 April 1973.

[*Klausen Gasse12, 2331 Vösendorf, Austria*].

3. Count *Christoph, b* at Vienna 6 April 1941, Garden Designer.

[*Dornau, 2544 Leobersdorf, Austria*].

4. Count *Alfred, b* at Elatinon 27 July 1943, Agr Eng; *m* at Scheibbs, Austria 6 Sept 1969, Isabella (*b* at Vienna 5 Jan 1949), dau of Gustav von Herrmann and Countess Silvia von Schönfeldt, and has issue,

[*Dornau, 2544 Leobersdorf, Austria*].

1. Count *Ferdinand, b* at Vienna 24 Sept 1970; *m* at Vaduz 2 June (civ) and at Dellach bei Moosburg, Carinthia 10 June (relig) 2000, Princess Maria Ileana (*b* at Klagenfurt 20 July

1974), dau of Prince Eugen of Liechtenstein and Countess Maria Theresia von Goëß.

2. Countess *Josefine, b* at Vienna 16 Sept 1972.

3. Countess Anna *Isabella, b* at Vienna 26 July 1974.

4. Countess *Johanna, b* at Vienna 25 June 1978.

5. Count *Georg, b* at Graz 23 May 1946, Technician; *m* at Lichendorf 23 June 1973, Denyse (*b* at Graz 2 Sept 1950), dau of Georg Lippit and Elisabeth Trummer, and has issue,

[*Schimmel Gasse21, 1030 Vienna, Austria*].

    1. Countess *Stephnie, b* at Vienna 24 Oct 1974.

    2. Countess *Valerie, b* at Vienna 24 Nov 1976.

2. Count *Michael, b* at Vienna 16 March 1915; ✝ at Weissenegg 1 July 1978, Proprietor of Weissenegg; *m* at Neudau East Styria 15 Feb (civ) and at Fürstenfeld, Styria 16 Feb (relig) 1954, Countess Maria Sidonia (*b* at Munich 4 June 1931), dau of Friedrich, Count von Mensdorff-Pouilly and Countess Gabriele (Elly) von Schönborn, and had issue,

[*Dunlea Farm, 400 Field Road, Jerseyville, Ontario L0R 1R0, Canada*].

    1. Count *Friedrich Carl, b* at Graz 18 Dec 1954, Proprietor of Weissenegg; *m* at Graz 29 Nov 1980, Gisela (*b* at Graz 15 Sept 1954), dau of Walther Christiane and Christa Schmid von Schmidsfelden, and has issue,

    [*Dunlea Farm, 400 Field Road, Jerseyville, Ontario L0R 1R0, Canada*].

        1. Count *Michael, b* 25 July 1982.

        2. Count *Thomas, b* 29 Aug 1984.

2. Count *Josef, b* at Graz 31 March 1956, Dr of Biology.

[*3422 Greifenstein, NÖsterreich, Austria*].

3. Countess *Marie Gabrielle, b* at Graz 13 April 1957; *m* at Fernitz, nr Graz 13 June 1981, Gerhard Kordon (*b* at Graz 16 Sept 1956), Dipl Architect.

[*Glacisstraße 35, 8010 Graz, Austria*].

4. Countess *Bernadette, b* at Graz 11 June 1958; *m* at Graz 3 Oct 1987, Heribert, Baron Seyffertitz (*b* at Ehingen 27 May 1959).

[*Moserwald Weg 15, 8040 Graz, Austria*].

5. Countess *Elisabeth, b* at Graz 7 Jan 1964; ✝ at

Coburg 11 April 1989; *m* at Lynden, Ontario, Canada
15 Sept 1982, Alexander, Count Mailáth de Székhely
(*b* at Toronto, Ontario 18 July 1959).
[*R.R.5, Coburg, Ontario K0A 4J8, Canada*].
6. Countess *Franziska, b* at Graz 16 June 1965.
[*400 Field Road, Jerseyville, Ontario L0R 1R0,
Canada*].

Brother of Great-Grandfather
Issue of Ferdinand, 3rd Prince von and zu Trauttmansdorff-Weinsberg
(*b* 11 June 1803; ✝ 31 March 1859) and Princess Anna von and zu
Liechtenstein (*b* 25 Aug 1820; *m* 17 July 1841; ✝ 17 March 1908),
having had issue, among whom,

Son
Count *Ferdinand, b* at Vienna 7 Dec 1855; ✝ at Hösting, Mähren 4
Feb 1928; *m* at Vienna 4 Sept 1893, Bertha (*b* at Mädiswil, Kt Bern
5 March 1870; ✝ at Offenbach am Main 23 Jan 1956), dau of Gottlieb
Fischer and Elisabeth Lehmann, and had issue, among whom,

Sons
1. Count *Viktor, b* at St Jean, France 16 May 1895; ✝ at Salzburg 3
Aug 1969, Capt Austrian Cavalry; *m* at Vienna 12 July 1922,
Princess Eduarda (Edina) (*b* at Salzburg 16 Oct 1903; *m* 2ndly at
Maria-Kirchenthal, nr Lofer 20 Aug 1975, Alexander, Count and
Lord zu Pappenheim who ✝ at Salzburg 6 April 1995), dau of
Eduard, Prince von and zu Liechtenstein and Countess Olga von
Pückler and Limpurg, and had issue, among whom,
[*Anton Hochmuthstraße 4, 5020 Salzburg, Austria*].

    1. Countess *Gabrielle* Olga Irma Berta Eduarda, *b* at Hösting
24 Aug 1924; *m* 1stly at Weyregg 24 April 1946 (*m* diss by div
1968), Max Domenig (*b* at Hallein 17 April 1917; ✝ at Hallein
.. 1994), Dr of Med. She *m* 2ndly at Kitzbühel 15 Sept 1975,
Herbert Kuhlmann (*b* at Linz 1 May 1916), Dr of Law.
[*Schloß Urstein, 5412 Puch bei Hallein, Austria*].

    2. Countess *Elisabeth* Anna Berta Eduarda Maria, *b* at Hösting
29 Dec 1927; *m* at Loosdorf, Austria 12 Sept 1953,
Franz-Eugen, Count von Walderdorff (*b* at Anzbach 11 April
1925), Dipl of Engineering.
[*Schloß Ennsegg, 4470 Enns, Upper Austria*].

2. Count *Rudolf, b* at Mödling, nr Vienna 3 Nov 1896; ✠ at Vienna 20 June 1980, Dr of Law; *m* at Vienna 15 Feb 1921, Helene (*b* at Constantinople 8 Sept 1896; ✠ at Vienna 6 March 1980), dau of Leonardo Dassira and Catharina Filippuci, having had issue, among whom,

> 1. Countess Maria Magdalena (*Madeleine*) Anna Katharina, *b* at Vienna 11 May 1925, Dentist.
> [*Radetzkystraße 45, 2500 Baden bei Wien, Austria*].

Brother of Great-Great-Grandfather

Issue of Ferdinand, 1st Prince (Fürst) von and zu Trauttmansdorff-Weinsberg (*b* 12 Jan 1749; ✠ 27 Aug 1827) and Countess Caroline von Colloredo (*b* 14 Feb 1752; *m* 18 May 1772; ✠ 20 Sept 1852), having had issue, among whom,

Son

Count *Joseph, b* at Brussels 19 Feb 1788; ✠ at Obristvi 22 Aug 1870, Imp and R Chamberlain, Life Member Austrian House of Lords, Ambassador to Berlin, Munich and Schwerin; *m* at Prague 16 Oct 1821, Countess Josephine Károlyi de Nagy-Károly (*b* at Vienna 7 Nov 1803; ✠ 9 May 1863), Dame Star Cross Order, having had issue, among whom,

Son

Count *Ferdinand, b* at Vienna 27 June 1825; ✠ at Schloß Friedau, nr St Pölten 12 Dec 1896, Kt Orders of the Golden Fleece, Black Eagle and Sovereign Military Order of Malta, Imp and Royal Chamberlain, Life Member and Pres Austrian House of Lords; *m* at Vienna 29 Oct 1860, Princess Marie (*b* at Schloß Liechtenstein 20 Sept 1834; ✠ at Vienna 1 Dec 1909), Dame Star Cross Order, Dame Sovereign Military Order of Malta, dau of Alois, Prince von and zu Liechtenstein and Countess Franziska Kinsky, having had issue, among whom,

Son

Count *Karl* Ferdinand, *b* at Vienna 24 March 1864; ✠ at Pressbaum 4 Jan 1910, 1st Lt; *m* at Vienna 25 April 1892, Countess Marie Therese (*b* at Dobris 5 Aug 1869; ✠ at Vomp, Tirol 27 Feb 1960; she *m* 2ndly at Prague 5 Aug 1911, Adolf, Count von and zu Trauttmansdorff-Weinsberg who was ✠*k* nr Jaroslawice, Galizia 21 Aug 1914), Dame Star Cross Order, dau of Hieronymus, Count von Colloredo-Mannsfeld and Countess Aglaë Festetics de Tolna, having had issue, among whom,

Sons

1. Count *Ferdinand* Joseph, *b* at Koritschan, Gaya, Mähren 20 Feb 1893; ✠ at St Pölten, Austria 24 Nov 1932, 1st Lt; *m* at Prague 30 April 1921, Princess Marie (*b* at Wossow 8 June 1896; ✠ at Pettenbach Austria 13 Dec 1945; she *m* 2ndly at Budapest 18 Feb 1938, Andor Pál Somssich de Sáard who ✠ at St Pölten 24 Sept 1963), dau of Karl, Prince zu Schwarzenberg and Countess Ida Hoyos, and had issue, among whom,

    1. Countess *Maria Theresia* Ida Eleonore Wilhelmine Tadea Benedikta, *b* at Prague 1 Aug 1922, Dame Star Cross Order; *m* at Kremsmünster 26 June 1954, Christian, Prince of Lobkowicz (*b* at Krimitz, nr Pilsen, Bohemia 12 June 1924; ✠ 2 Sept 2001).

    [*70 chaussée de Charleroi, 1060 Brussels, Belgium*].

    2. Count *Adolf* Karl Josef Hieronymus Ernst, *b* at Prague 1 June 1925, Businessman; *m* at Tannenmühle, Austria 9 June 1946, Countess Sophie (*b* at Munich 15 Dec 1922; ✠ at Vienna 22 Oct 1994), Dame Star Cross Order, dau of Joseph, Count von Arco-Zinneberg and Countess Christiane von Clam and Gallas. He *m* 2ndly at Pfaffstätten, NÖsterreich 21 Sept 1996, Eva Katharina (*b* at Vienna 29 June 1941), dau of Friedrich Dolp and Eva Nadler, and has issue from his first wife among whom,

    [*Czapka Gasse15, 1030 Vienna, Austria*].

        1. Countess Marie *Wilhelmine* Therese Ida Christiane, *b* at Vienna 3 Feb 1947; *m* at Ising am Chiemsee 28 May 1900, Philipp Riccabona von Riechenfels (*b* at Vienna 15 Nov 1949), Dr of Phil.

        [*Trogerstraße 38, 81675 Munich, Germany*].

        2. Countess *Marie-Antoinette* Ida Gertrude Eugeni Eva, *b* at Nussbach 24 Dec 1953; *m* at Brand-Laaben 19 Aug 1974, Wolfgang Graf (*b* at Vienna 5 Jan 1949), Dr rer soc oec.

        [*Schönfeld 31, 3061 Ollersbach, Austria*].

    4. Count *Josef* Adolf Engelbert, *b* at Altlengbach 10 Nov 1958.

    [*Czapka Gasse15, 1030 Vienna, Austria*].

4. Count *Karl Ernst* Hieronymus Bruno Ulrich, *b* at Pottenbrunn, Lower Austria 6 Oct 1927, ✠ at Auf der Pack

23 Mar 2000; *m* at Stainz 12 Oct 1949, Countess Maria Cäcilia (Maritzi) (*b* at Vienna 3 Dec 1924), dau of Franz, Count von Meran and Princess Wilhelmine von Auersperg, and has issue,
[*Pack 114, 8583 Edelschrott, Austria; Libellen Weg 6-8/2, 8042 Graz, Austria; Franckstraße 28, 8042 Graz, Austria*].

1. Count *Ferdinand* Karl Josef Franz Viktor, *b* at Graz 28 July 1950, Dr of Law; *m* at Munich 1 July 1978, Margrit Gabriele (*b* at Wittlich, Eifel 27 Nov 1952), dau of Dominik Scholtz-Rautenstrauch and Ute Braun, and has issue,
[*Bundesministerium f. ausw. Angelegenheiten (Kurierleitung), Ballhausplatz 2, 1014, Vienna, Austria; Linke Wienzeile 34, 1060 Vienna, Austria*].

    1. Countess *Anna* Andrea Monika, *b* at Vienna 1 Oct 1980.

    2. Countess Maria *Magdalena* Felicitas, *b* at Vienna 8 Jan 1982.

    3. Count Mathäus Nikolaus Karl Dominik Josef, *b* at Vienna 23 July 1986.

2. Count *Andreas* Otto Michael Franz, *b* at Graz 17 Nov 1951, Hotel Manager; *m* at Salzburg 27 Nov 1976, Dominique Isabella Wilhelmine (*b* at Geneva 15 Jan 1954), dau of Theodor, Ritter von Pachmann and Huguette von Graffenried, and has issue,
[*16 Terragon Place, Forest Lake, 4078 Queensland, Australia*].

    1. Countess *Theresa* Elisabeth Wilhelmine, *b* at Salzburg 7 Oct 1977.

    2. Countess *Anna-Maria* Henriette Elisabeth, *b* at Salzburg 16 June 1979.

    3. Count *Clemens* Franz Thadäus Ferdinand Heinrich, *b* at Graz 5 Dec 1980.

    4. Count *Paul,* *b* at Sydney, Australia April 1985.

3. Countess *Isabella* Wilhelmine, *b* at Graz 8 July 1953; *m* at Gollrad, Styria 10 May 1975 (*m* diss by div 1984), Wolfgang Freisleben (*b* at Bad Aussee 17 Sept 1947), Dr rer pol, Journalist. Countess Isabella has since reverted to her maiden name.
[*Zierer Platz 9/10, 1030 Vienna, Austria*].

4. Countess *Charlotte* (Lotti) Maria Josefa, *b* at Graz

24 Aug 1955; *m* at Gusswerk 25 June 1977 (*m* diss by div at ...), Peter Bruno, Baron von Löwenthal-Maroicic von Madonna del Monte (*b* at Graz 1 Oct 1954).

5. Countess *Marie* Theresia, *b* at Graz 28 Aug 1960; *m* at Lilongwe, Malawi 8 Dec 1989 (civ) and at Stainz 25 March 1990 (relig), Busso von Alvensleben (*b* at Hamburg 6 Feb 1957).
[*Wolffson Weg 16, 22297 Hamburg, Germany*].

6. Countess *Eleonore* Sophie, *b* at Graz 26 May 1962; *m* at St Ilgen 12 Sept 1998, Stefan Schindele (*b* at Munich ....).
[*Mitterberg Gasse16/19, 1180 Vienna, Austria*].

2. Count *Josef* Hieronymus, *b* at Friedau 30 June 1894; shot by retreating Nazis at St Pölten 13 April 1945, 1st Lt; *m* at Trieste 15 Oct 1932, Baroness Helen (Ellie) (*b* at London 1 June 1908; shot by retreating Nazis at St Pölten 13 April 1945), dau of Dimitri, Baron Economo von San Serff and Eugenie Ralli of the Barons Ralli, having had issue,

1. Countess *Monika* Eugenie Therese, *b* at Vienna 27 June 1933; *m* at Vienna 8 Feb 1956, Michel, Count Didisheim (*b* at Wimbledon 18 April 1930), Capt Belgian (Res), Hon Principal Private Secretary to HM King Albert II of Belgium (ret).
[*25 Drève du Sénéchal, 1180 Brussels, Belgium*].

2. Count *Johannes* Demetrius Ferdinand Joachim, *b* at Pottenbrunn 16 Aug 1934, Dr of Law, Proprietor of Pottenbrunn, Bez St Pölten, NÖsterreich; *m* at Maria Plain 2 Sept 1967, Countess Maria Christina (*b* at Vienna 13 March 1943), dau of Johannes, Count Czernin von and zu Chudenitz and Baroness Österheldis von der Lippe, and has issue,
[*Schloß, 3140 Pottenbrunn, Austria*].

1. Countess *Helene* Monika, *b* at Vienna 18 July 1968; *m* at Jeutendorf 24 June 1995, Michael, Count Bubna and Litic (*b* at St Pölten 15 Feb 1967)
[*3485 Donaudorf 8, Austria; Neusiedl 13, Nussdorf an der Traisen, 3133 Traismauer, Austria*].

2. Countess Gabrielle Eleonore, *b* at Vienna 11 July 1969; *m* at Jeutendorf 9 July 1988, Dr Georg Erd (*b* at Vienna 11 Sept 1964), Dr of Med.
[*Statz 61, 6143 Matrei, Tirol, Austria; Innsbruckerstraße 34, 6176 Völs, Austria.*

3. Count *Johannes* Paul, *b* at Vienna 12 Dec 1970;

m at St Erhard 25 June 1994, Dorothea (*b* 31 March 1971), dau of Werner Tessmar-Pfohl and Marie Juliane Altmann-Althausen, and has issue,

> 1. Countess Marie *Aglae*, *b* at Vienna 23 November 1994.
>
> 2. Count *Johannes* Nepomuk, *b* at Vienna 26 Oct 1996.
>
> 3. Count *Dimitri*, *b* at ... 26 Feb 2000.

4. Countess *Elisabeth* Nathalie, *b* at Vienna 30 May 1979.

3. Countess Eleonore (*Nora*) Marie Therese Aglaë, *b* at Pottenbrunn 8 Feb 1938; *m* at Vienna 5 Sept 1964, Johannes, Count Kinsky von Wchinitz and Tettau (*b* at Prague 22 March 1937), Eng, Farmer.

[*Schloß Stadl, 8181 St. Ruprecht an der Raab, Steiermark, Austria*].

3. Count *Karl* Josef, *b* at Koritschan 19 Nov 1897; ✝ at Vienna 23 March 1970, Dr of Law, Lawyer, Kt Order of the Golden Fleece and of the Polar Star; *m* at Sigmundslust, nr Schwaz, Ryrol 4 Sept 1924, Baroness Maria Gertrud (Gerda) (*b* at Vienna 28 Nov 1892; ✝ there 24 Feb 1964), dau of Maximilian, Baron von Biegeleben and Baroness Maria Rivalier von Meysenbug, and had issue,

1. Count *Ferdinand* Maximilian, *b* at Pottenbrunn 1 Feb 1928; *m* at Vienna 18 Jan 1958 (*m* diss by div at Vienna .. Feb 1969), Marie Frédérique Isabell (Tanja) [*Metternich Gasse5, 1030 Vienna, Austria*] (*b* at Utrecht 6 Dec 1934), dau of Ambassador Eduard Star Busmann and Baroness Adriana Röell. He *m* 2ndly at Vienna 12 Oct 1979, Elisabeth [*Ashberg, 3051 St. Christophen, Austria*] (*b* at Sünching 22 Sept 1945; *m* 1stly at Vienna 7 Oct (civ) and 8 Oct (relig) 1966, Nicholas Meinertzhagen; that *m* diss by div at Vienna 29 Aug 1978), dau of Janos Kenyeres de Homoród-Almás and Dálnok and Countess Éva Tholdalgi von Nagy-Ertse and Gelencze, and had issue from his first wife,

[*Tobaj, 7540 Güssing, Austria*].

> 1. Countess Maria *Victoria*, *b* at Vienna 8 Sept 1960; *m* at Klein Zwettl, Austria 20 Aug 1989, Wolf-Dietrich Sprenger (*b* at Zeitz 11 Oct 1942).
>
> [*Heinrich Hertzstraße 21, 22085 Hamburg, Germany*].
>
> 2. Countess Maria *Katharina*, *b* at Vienna 1 May 1963.
>
> [*Metternich Gasse5, 1030 Vienna, Austria; Pietralata,*

50024 Mercatale, Italy].

3. Count Maximilian *Octavian*, *b* at Vienna 12 Aug 1965.

[*Markt Gasse 5, 1030 Vienna, Austria*].

LINE II
(✝ Extinct ✝)

Founded by Count Georges-Sigismund (*b* 22 Aug 1638; ✝ 16 Oct 1702); Hereditary Grand Master of the Court in Styria 1704, Hereditary Member of the former Austrian House of Lords 1881.

WALDBOTT VON BASSENHEIM

Catholic: A feudal family from Rhineland traceable from the brothers Siegefridus, Gebehardus and Fridericus von Waltmaneshusen (near Hadamar), liberi milites, 1138; acquired Bassenheim (near Koblenz) *ca* 1300; acquired the Lordship of Olbrück (near Andernach) *ca* 1480 and 1555, through the marriage (1477) of Otto Waldpott von Bassenheim (✝ 1498) to Appollonia, daughter and heiress of Burggrave Godard von Drachenfels; Baron of the Holy Empire with the qualification of "Wohlgeboren", Vienna 16 April 1638 (for Johann Lothar Waldbott von Bassenheim); acquired the Lordship of Pyrmont in the Eifel 1652 and 1711; title of Baron of the Holy Empire confirmed to all members of the family Regensburg 10 Jan 1664; Count of the Holy Empire with the qualification of "Hoch and Wohlgeboren", Laxenburg 23 May 1720 (for the brothers Franz Emeric Wilhelm and Casimir Ferdinand Adolf Waldbott von Bassenheim; Hereditary Knights of the Teutonic Order (primogeniture) 28 Sept 1764; lost Olbrück and Pyrmont in 1801 and compensated (with title indemnified) with the Abbey of Heggbach in Württemberg 1803; inherited the County of Buxheim (from the Counts von Ostein) and acquired the Burggraviate of Winterrieden (both properties in Swabia, Bavaria) 1810; Hereditary Member of the Bavarian "Reichsräte" 26 May 1818; qualification of "Erlaucht" (primogeniture) by the German Diet 13 Feb 1829, recognised in Bavaria 22 April 1829; this qualification was extended to all family members, 7 March 1911.

Members of the family bear the title of Count or Countess Waldbott von Bassenheim with the qualification of Illustrious Highness.

CARL LUDWIG, COUNT (GRAF) WALDBOTT VON BASSENHEIM, Count zu Buxheim, Princely Burggraf zu Winterrieden, Lord zu Beuren and of Ober-and-Nieder Waldbach, *b* at Dessau 23 Oct 1938; son of Carl Maria, Count Waldbott von

Bassenheim (*b* 15 Sept 1913; ✝ 27 March 1939) and Maria von Alvensleben (*b* 14 March 1918; *m* 18 Oct 1937; ✝ 16 Dec 1984); *m* at Bonn 18 Sept 1965, Sigried (*b* at Bonn 8 Oct 1941), dau of Johannes Plümacher and Helene Müller.
[*Domstraße 1, 83047 Regensburg, Germany*].

Daughter

Countess *Iris* Annares, *b* at Regensburg 14 July 1970.

Brothers and Sister of Father

Issue of Ludwig, Count Waldbott von Bassenheim (*b* 1 May 1876; ✝ 23 Aug 1926) and Baroness Marie von Godin (*b* 3 Nov 1882; *m* 15 June 1903; ✝ 23 April 1967), having had issue, among whom,

1. Hugo **Franz** Maria Heinrich Ludwig Irenäus, **Count Waldbott von Bassenheim**, *b* at Freising 4 July 1907; ✝ at Munich 4 Nov 1981, Technician, *succ* his father as Head of House; renounced his rights in favour of his brother, Ludwig (see below) on 14 July 1928; *m* 1stly at Tegernsee 20 Jan 1932 (*m* diss by div at Munich 20 April 1949), Charlotte (Lotte) [*Meistersingerstraße 28, 70597 Stuttgart, Germany*] (*b* at Pforzheim 13 Dec 1910; she *m* 2ndly at Stuttgart 1 June 1950, Erwin Scheuermann), dau of Albert Hienerwadel and Julie Heckmann. He *m* 2ndly at Munich 13 May 1949, Gerda [*Hengelerstraße 4, 80637 Munich, Germany*] (*b* at Thorn 16 May 1919), dau of Wilhelm Eimecke and Gertrud Sablowski, and had issue by his first wife,

    1. Count *Clemens* Adolf, *b* at Tegernsee 26 May 1932, Jeweller; *m* at Essen-Bredeney 7 May 1955, Anna (*b* at Villavicencio, nr Bogotá, Columbia 25 Feb 1933), dau of Gustav Burkhardt and Marta Reinmann, and has issue,
    [*Franzensbaderstraße 6/1, 14193 Berlin - Grunewald, Germany*].

        1. Countess *Ulrike*-Henriette, *b* at Essen 15 Oct 1955, Secretary.
        [*Franzensbaderstraße 6/1, 14193 Berlin - Grunewald, Germany*].

        2. Count *Michael* Heinrich, *b* at Essen 9 March 1957, Goldsmith and Jeweller.
        [*Franzensbaderstraße 6/1, 14193 Berlin - Grunewald, Germany*].

        3. Count *Joachim* Heinrich, *b* at Bogota 10 April 1959,

Banker.
[*Franzensbaderstraße 6/1, 14193 Berlin - Grunewald, Germany*].

2. Countess Maria *Ludovika* Franziska Xavieria Irene Henriette, *b* at Buxheim 20 Feb 1911; *m* at Munich 2 June 1936, Herbert von Hartz (*b* at Ingolstadt 20 April 1905), Lt-Col, Engineer.
[*Hindelangerstraße 8, 86163 Augsburg, Germany*].

Brothers of Grandfather

Issue of Friedrich, Count Waldbott von Bassenheim (*b* 19 July 1844; ✠ 31 Jan 1910) and Rosa Schürch (*b* 9 Sept 1855; *m* 30 May 1875; ✠ 25 Feb 1904), having had issue, among whom,

Sons

1. Count *Felix* Maria Carl Benedikt Thomas Heinrich, *b* at St André 7 March 1884; ✠ at Buenos Aires 30 Jan 1946; *m* at Buenos Aires 7 Dec 1917, Iris (*b* at Rome 17 March 1894; ✠ at Buenos Aires 29 Nov 1966), dau of Filiberto de Romaro de Turetta and Amalie Agostini, and had issue,

> 1. Countess *Iris* Maria Rosa Melia Huguette Alexandrine Renata, *b* at Lomas de Zamora, Argentina 8 Jan 1919; *m* at Buenos Aires 9 Dec 1946, Rodolfo Rernando Bertoldi-Hepburn (*b* at Buenos Aires 11 Oct 1922).
> [*59 - 1353 Necochea, Buenos Aires, Argentina*].

> 2. Count *Karl* Fillbert Maria Emil Hugo Rudolf Johann Felix, *b* at Lomas de Zamora 22 April 1920; ✠ at Buenos Aires 17 Oct 1967, Dr of Med; *m* at Buenos Aires 22 May 1950, Olga (*b* at Buenos Aires 18 April 1926; she *m* 2ndly ...), dau of Prof Dr Lanfranco Ciampi and Matilde Flairoto, having had issue, [*José Bonifacio 1093, Buenos Aires, Argentina*].

>> 1. Count *Carlos* Gustavo Felix, *b* at Buenos Aires 18 April 1954; *m* at ......, Adriana Alicia Amato (*b* at Buenos Aires 14 June 1960), and has issue,
>> [*José Bonifacio 1099, Buenos Aires, Argentina*].

>>> 1. Count *Carlos* Federico, *b* at Buenos Aires 4 March 1982.

>>> 2. Count *Gustavo* Hernán, *b* at Buenos Aires 13 Dec 1985.

>>> 3. Count *Fernando* Martin, *b* at Buenos Aires 28 Feb 1990.

>>> 4. Count *Patricio* Alejandro, *b* at Buenos Aires

28 Feb 1990 (twin with Count Fernando).

    2. Countess *Christina* Isabel, *b* at Buenos Aires 6 Jan 1959; *m* at ......, Daniel Nuñez (*b* at ......).

3. Countess *Eleonore* Maria Iris Nerina Fernanda Blanca Nelda Lucia, *b* at Buenos Aires 10 Aug 1922, Dr of Phil, Chemist.
[*Melo 3081, Buenos Aires, Argentina*].

4. Count *Johann* Maria Rudolf Felix Lothar, *b* at Buenos Aires 27 April 1928; ✝ there 29 Jan 1974, Engineer; *m* at Buenos Aires 12 Dec 1953, Maria (*b* at Buenos Aires 15 Jan 1926), dau of Guillermo Castex Lainfor and Margarita Colombi, and has issue,
[*Jerbal 2365, Buenos Aires, Argentina*].

    1. Count *Guillermo* Felix Maria Enrique Alejandro, *b* at Buenos Aires 8 Jan 1955; *m* at Buenos Aires 12 Nov 1983, Silvia Buezzalino (*b* ..), and has issue,
    [*Jerbal 2365, Buenos Aires, Argentina*].

        1. Countess *Carolina* Ines Maria, *b* at ... 23 Nov 1990.
        2. Countess *Daniela* Maria Sofia, *b* at ... 27 July 1996.

    2. Count *Gustav* Marcelo Maria Hugo Rodolfo, *b* at Buenos Aires 16 Nov 1957; *m* at Buenos Aires 2 July 1983, Maria Christina Gnecco (*b* at ... 29 Nov 1957), and has issue,
    [*Jerbal 2365, Buenos Aires, Argentina*].

        1. Count *Agustin* Tomás Maria, *b* at 16 Nov 1984.
        2. Count *Santiago* Juan Maria, *b* at 30 Nov 1987.
        3. Countess *Josefina* Ines Maria, *b* at 3 March 1992.

    3. Count *Johann* Maria Rodolfo, *b* at Buenos Aires 9 July 1962.
    [*Jerbal 2365, Buenos Aires, Argentina*].

5. Countess *Isabella* Wilhelmine Maria Iris Amalia Felicitas Albertine, *b* at Buenos Aires 17 March 1930, Pianist; *m* at Buenos Aires 1 April 1965, Jorge Enrique Bachella (*b* at Buenos Aires 28 Sept 1924), Dr rer pol.
[*Colombres 1140, Buenos Aires, Argentina*].

2. Count *Rudolf* Maria Anton Friedrich Joseph Heinrich, *b* at St André 17 May 1886; ✝ at Berlin-Wilmersdorf 26 April 1930; *m* at

Schloß Frauenau, nr Zwiesel 14 Oct 1929, Baroness Sofie-Anna (*b* at Dresden 13 March 1903; ✠ at Bad Tölz 24 Dec 1957), Dame of Hon Bavarian Order of St Theresia, dau of Eduard, Baron Poschinger von Frauenau, Proprietor of Frauenau and Moosau, and Countess Elisabeth von Bray-Steinburg, and had issue,

> 1. Countess *Elisabeth Rudolphine* Rosa Friederika Benedicta Henrietta Renata Maria, *b* posthumously at Berlin 2 Aug 1930; *m* at Irlbach, Bavaria 26 May 1957, Carl Werner Sanne (*b* at Stuttgart 13 Oct 1923; ✠ at Bonn 4 July 1981), Dr of Law.
>
> [*Horionstraße 32a, 53177 Bonn - Bad Godesberg, Germany*].

WALDBURG

Catholic: This feudal family originated in Swabia and can be traced from Ebirhardus von Tanne (Alttann, near Wolfegg in Württemberg) living circa 1170; acquisition of Wolfegg *circa* 1200; acquired Waldsee 1240, Trauchburg 1306; and Zeil 1337; Baron of the Holy Empire, Ulm 4 July 1502; "Truchsess" of Waldburg 1419; Hereditary Grand Seneschal of the Empire "Erbtruchsess" 1525 (confirmed 1594); Hereditary Grand Master of the Royal Court of Württemberg 23 July 1808.

LINE I: WOLFEGG and WALDSEE

This line descends from Heinrich, Baron of Waldburg, Lord of Wolfegg and Waldsee (*b* 8 March 1568; ✠ 16 Aug 1637); Count of the Holy Empire as Count zu Wolfegg with ratification of arms and qualification of "Hoch and Wohlgeboren" and the elevation of Wolfegg into a County, Prague 29 Feb 1628; Prince of the Holy Empire (primogeniture) with the qualification of "Hochgeboren", Vienna 21 March 1803 (for Joseph Anton Xavier, Count of Waldburg in Wolfegg and Waldsee); Hereditary Member of the former First Chamber of the Kingdom of Württemberg 25 Sept 1819; received the qualification of "Durchlaucht" (primogeniture) by the German Diet, 18 Aug 1825.

The Head of the Family and his wife bear the title of Prince and Princess von Waldburg zu Wolfegg and Waldsee with the qualification of Serene Highness and cadet members bear the title of Count or Countess von Waldburg zu Wolfegg and Waldsee with the qualification of Illustrious Highness.

JOHANNES Franz Xaver Willibald Maria Josef Philipp Jeningen Leonhard, **7TH PRINCE (FÜRST) VON WALDBURG ZU**

WOLFEGG AND WALDSEE, *b* at Ravensburg 9 March 1957, Lic oec, Kt of Hon Sovereign Military Order of Malta, Kt Bavarian Order of St George; son of Maximillian Willibald, 6th Prince (Fürst) von Waldburg zu Wolfegg and Waldsee (*b* 22 June 1924 ✝ at Wolfegg 5 Sept 1998) and Countess Ida Franziska (*b* at Prague 1 May 1928; ✝ at Wolfegg 6 June 1987), Dame of Hon and Dev Gd Cross Sovereign Military Order of Malta, *m* at Florence 29 April 1989, Viviana (*b* at Florence 11 Feb 1963), dau of Vittorio Emmanuele of the Counts Rimbotti and Donna Maria Vittoria Colonna of the Princes di Summonte, and has issue,
[*Schloß Wolfegg, 88364 Wolfegg, Germany*].

Sons and Daughters

1. Count *Ludwig* Franz Willibald Maria Josef Leonhard, Hereditary Count (Erbgraf) von Waldburg zu Wolfegg and Waldsee, *b* at Ravensburg 12 July 1990.
2. Countess *Vittoria* Ida Walburga Maria Josefa Leonharda, *b* at Ravensburg 4 April 1992.
3. Count *Leonardo* Maximilian Wunibald Maria Josef Bruno, *b* at Ravensburg 6 Oct 1995.

Step-Mother

Elisabeth Anne-Laure Veronica Marie Hildegard Merey (*b* at Hartfield, East Sussex 12 Aug 1948; *m* 1stly at Neuheim, Switzerland 12 Aug 1972, Baron Maximilian Wiedersperger von Wiedersperg), dau of Georg Merey von Kaposmere and Kisdovoran and Baroness Elisabeth Ullmann von Baranyavar.
[*Burgweitherweg 1, 88339 Bad Waldsee, Germany*].

Brothers and Sisters

1. Countess *Maria Katharina* Walburga Ida Oktavia Leonarda Theresia vom Kinde Jesu Johanna, *b* at Ravensburg 18 March 1956, Attorney-at-Law, Dame of Hon Sovereign Military Order of Malta; *m* at Wolfegg 2 May (civ) and 3 May (relig) 1983, Valentin, Baron Heereman von Zuydtwyck (*b* at Misburg, Hanover 22 Nov 1942), Dipl Business Studies, MBA, Entrepreneur, Kt of Hon Sovereign Military Order of Malta, Order of Merit Fed Rep Germany (1985), 1st Class (1992), Spl Hon Cross of State of Berlin (1986), Cmdr Cross of Merit Sovereign Military Order of Malta.
[*Landauerstraße 11, 14197 Berlin, Germany*].
2. Count *Jakob* Heinrich Wunibald Maria Josef Rupert Leonhard, *b* at Ravensburg 9 March 1957 (twin with Count Johannes), Kt of

Hon Sovereign Military Order of Malta; *m* at.. 28 April (civ) and at Grein 11 May (relig) 1991, Countess Eilika (*b* at Freising 8 Aug 1966), dau of Hubertus, Count zu Solms-Baruth and Baroness Elisabeth-Charlotte von Kerssenbrock, and has issue,

[*Luise-Benger-Straße 13, 70329 Stuttgart, Germany*].

    1. Countess *Lioba* Maria Walburga Nina Elisabeth, *b* at Frankfurt-am-Main 14 Oct 1994.

    2. Count *August* Wilhelm Wunibald Maria Joseph Adalbert Basilius, *b* at Prague 2 Jan 1997.

    3. Count *Theodor* Johannes Nepomuk Willibald Maria Joseph Richard Hubertus, *b* at Prague 9 June 1998.

    4. Countess *Laetitia* Maria Walburga Viktoria Andrea, *b* at Esslingen am Neckar 8 Oct 2000.

3. Count *Thomas* Georg Willibald Maria Johannes Vianney Leonhard, *b* at Ravensburg 28 July 1960, Dr of Med, Kt of Hon Sovereign Military Order of Malta; *m* at La Forge Roussel/Florenville 10 Oct 1991, Baroness Charlotte (*b* at Katana-Kiwu 15 Jan 1958), dau of Michel, Baron de Mevius and Françoise LeBoeuf, and has issue,

[*Welriedende Dreef 23, 3090 Overijse, Belgium*].

    1. Countess *Sophie* Walburga Johanna Barbara, *b* at Ravensburg 1 Sept 1992.

    2. Count *Gregor* Josef Willibald, *b* at Uccle, Belgium 16 March 1994.

4. Countess Maria *Adelheid* Franziska Josefa Leonharda Walburga, *b* at Ravensburg 31 Aug 1963; *m* at Wolfegg 14 Oct (civ) and there 19 Oct (relig) 1991, Eberhard, Baron von Gemmingen-Hornberg (*b* at Bamberg 8 Dec 1957).

[*Köhlerlohe 3, 95688 Friedenfels, Germany*].

5. Count *Andreas* Maria Wunibald Johannes Leonhard Josef Bernhard, *b* at Ravensburg 30 Jan 1966, M.A., Kt Bavarian Order of St George, Lt (res).

[*155 Riverside Drive, Apt. 12D, New York, NY 10024, U.S.A.*].

Brothers and Sisters of Father

1. Countess Maria *Oktavia* Monika Coletta Christophora Sophie Johanna Walburga, *b* at Wechselburg 1 Aug 1926, Dame Star Cross Order; *m* at Bad Waldsee 5 May (civ) and 6 May (relig) 1958, Dietrich Georg, Count von Brühl (*b* at Königsberg 1 Dec 1925), former German Ambassador in Austria.

[*Rettenschöß 12, 6342 Niederndorf, Tirol, Austria; Josefstädterstraße 66/41, 1080 Vienna, Austria*].

2. Count *Otto* Joachim Maria Josef Wunibald Petrus Canisius Georg Christophorus Felix, *b* at Waldsee 30 May 1928.
[*Seidenstraße 5, 88339 Bad Waldsee, Germany*].

3. Countess Maria *Sidonia* Josefa Walburga Ignatia Coletta Ursula, *b* at Waldsee 20 Oct 1929, Dame Star Cross Order; *m* at Waldsee 27 Sept (civ) and 28 Sept (relig) 1955, Leopold, Count von Walderdorff (*b* at Kürn 7 April 1928), Kt of Hon and Dev Sovereign Military Order of Malta, Dipl of Agr.
[*Schloßstraße 4, Hauzenstein, 93173 Wenzenbach, Germany*].

4. Count *Gebhard* Heinrich Maria Willibald Benedikt Eucharius, *b* at Waldsee 8 Dec 1930; *m* at Bad Waldsee 31 Aug (civ) and at Fulda 14 Sept (relig) 1968, Baroness Birgit (*b* at Hanover 12 March 1942), dau of Max Riedesel, Baron zu Eisenbach and Claire Kück, and has issue,
[*Hölderlin Weg 15, 88339 Bad Waldsee, Germany*].

    1. Countess *Caroline* Antoinette Franziska Maria Walburga, *b* at Munich 18 April 1971; *m* at Wernigerode 21 April (civ) Wolfegg 19 May (relig) 2001, Prince Philipp zu Stolberg-Wernigerode (*b* at Frankfurt 8 June 1967).
    [*Hofgut Luisenlust, 63697 Hirzenhain, OHessen, Germany*].

    2. Count *Moritz* Rudolf Joachim Maria Willibald Gabriel, *b* at Munich 24 March 1973.

5. Count *Ferdinand* Ludwig Josef Maria Wunibald Konrad von Parzha Christophorus, *b* at Waldsee 17 Dec 1933, ✠ at Kitzbühel 12 Jun 2001, Kt Bavarian Order of St George; *m* at Munich 20 May (civ) and at Aurach, nr Kitzbühel 8 June (relig) 1964, Princess Emma (*b* at Sutton, Sussex, England 30 Dec 1943), dau of Alexander, Prince von Croÿ and Anne Campbell, and has issue,
[*Waldtruderinger Straße 60, 81827 Munich, Germany*].

    1. Count *Richard* Heinrich Gebhard Wunibald Bernhard, *b* at Augsburg 20 May 1965, B.Sc., M.B.A., Kt Bavarian Order of St George.
    [*Ulmenstraße 37, 60325 Frankfurt-am-Main, Germany*].

    2. Count *Sebastian* Willibald Dietrich Florian, *b* at Augsburg 19 Jan 1967, M.A., M.B.A., Kt Bavarian Order of St George; *m* at Barcelona 25 June 1998, Teresa (*b* at Barcelona 8 Sept 1972) dau of Francesco Guardans and Marisa Hontoria Gaya.
    [*Muntaner 307, 08021 Barcelona, Spain*].

    3. Countess *Camilla* Miriam Walburga Ludovica Elisabeth, *b* at Munich 30 May 1976, B.A.
    [*Waldtruderingerstraße 60, 81827 Munich, Germany*].

Brothers and Sisters of Grandfather

Issue of Maximilian, 4th Prince von Waldburg zu Wolfegg and Waldsee (*b* 13 May 1863; ✠ 27 Sept 1950) and Princess Sidonie of Lobkowicz (*b* 12 Aug 1869; *m* 26 July 1890; ✠ 24 July 1941), among whom,

1. Count *Johannes Nepomuk* Maria Wunibald Anton Laurentius, *b* at Waldsee 10 Aug 1904; ✠ at Kisslegg, Allgäu 17 May 1966, Dr of Phil, Kt Bavarian Order of St George; *m* at Milleschau am Donnersberg 19 Sept 1938, Countess Franziska (*b* at Milleschau 18 June 1913), dau of Eugen, Count von Ledebur-Wicheln and Countess Eleonore Larisch von Moennich, having had issue, among whom,
[*Rotes Haus, 88353 Kißlegg, Allgäu, Germany*].

    1. Countess *Eleonore* Henriette Walburga Therese Maria, *b* at Petersburg, Karlsbad 15 July 1939; *m* at Kisslegg 15 May 1962, Mario, Count von Matuschka, Baron von Toppolczan and Spaetgen (*b* at Oppeln 27 Feb 1931), Dr of Law, Kt Sovereign Military Order of Malta, Ambassador and Perm Rep of Germany to OECD.
    [*Drachenfelsstraße 45, 53757 St Augustin, Germany*].

    2. Count Eugen *Wunibald* Hubert Augustinus Lukas Maria, *b* at Krzemusch, nr Dux, Bohemia 18 Oct 1943, Proprietor of Kisslegg, Allgäu; *m* at Munich 8 June 1974, Michaela (*b* at Hamburg 11 July 1948), dau of Joachim von Oertzen and Gerda von Siemens, and has issue,
    [*Fürst-Maximilian Straße 8, 88353 Kißlegg, Allgäu, Germany*].

        1. Countess *Sophie* Margarete Walburga, *b* at Wangen, Allgäu 10 Dec 1975.

        2. Countess *Isabelle* Katharina, *b* at Wangen 31 Jan 1978.

        3. Count *Ferdinand* Georg Wunibald, *b* at Tettnang 30 July 1981.

3. Count *Franz* Willibald Ignatius omnes sancti, *b* at Wolfegg 1 Nov 1946, Dr of Eng, Architect, *m* at Gutenstein, Austria 12 June 1983, Countess Veronika (*b* at Petropolis, Rio de Janeiro, Brazil 10 July 1955), Goldsmith, dau of Heinrich, Count Hoyos, Baron zu Stichsenstein, Proprietor of Gutenstein and Baroness Therese Mayr von Melnhof, and has issue,
[*Dorfing 1, 06618 Pauscha, Germany*].

1. Count *Anton* Friedrich Willibald Maria, *b* at Munich 25 May 1984.

2. Countess *Clara* Maria Johanna Hemma, *b* at Munich 6 Oct 1985.

3. Count *Lorenz* Maria Thomas Paul, *b* at Munich 8 March 1992.

4. Countess *Elisabeth* Marie Walburga Magdalena Rosa, *b* at Wolfegg 19 Feb 1948, Dipl of Psychology; *m* at Kisslegg 9 Sept 1972, Wendelin, Count von Kageneck (*b* at Freiburg 9 July 1943), Lawyer.

[*Schloßbuck 9, 79112 Freiburg-Munzingen, Germany*].

5. Countess *Maria* Sidonia Walburga Katharina Anna, *b* at Wolfegg 19 Feb 1948 (twin with Countess Elisabeth), Journalist; *m* at Kisslegg 27 June 1981, Benedikt, Baron von Perfall (*b* at Hamburg 4 April 1947).

[*Schloß, 86926 Greifenberg, Ammersee, Germany; Montsalvatstraße 1b, 80804 Munich, Germany*].

6. Countess *Monika* Maria Anna Antonia Walburga, *b* at Kisslegg 2 Feb 1952; *m* at Kisslegg 25 Oct 1975, Ferreol Jay von Seldeneck (*b* at Baden-Baden 4 Nov 1943), Lawyer, Notary.

[*Sophie Charlottestraße 18, 14169 Berlin, Germany*].

2. Count *Heinrich* Maria Willibald Benedikt Albrecht Philipp Ulrich, *b* at Wolfegg 16 Sept 1911; ✢ at Stuttgart 25 May 1972, Kt of Hon Sovereign Military Order of Malta; *m* at Sigmaringen 4 Jan 1942, Princess Maria Antonia (*b* at Sigmaringen 19 Feb 1921), Dame Gd Cross Sovereign Military Order of Malta, Dame Star Cross Order, dau of Friedrich, Prince of Hohenzollern and Princess and Duchess Margarete of Saxony, and had issue, among whom,

[*Karl Anton Platz 3, 72488 Sigmaringen, Germany*].

1. Countess Maria *Sidonia* Margarete Elisabeth Walburga Caspara Meinrad Barbara, *b* at Freiburg 4 Dec 1942, Interior Decorator; *m* at Eberhardzell 12 Sept (civ) and at Heinrichsburg 10 Oct (relig) 1970, Alexander (Sándor), Count Esterházy de Galántha (*b* at Budapest 15 July 1943), Bank Director.

[*20 chemin du Prépoiset, 1253 Vandoevres, Switzerland*].

2. Countess Maria *Sophie* Theresia Victoria Walburga Elisabeth, *b* at Krauchenwies 9 July 1946, Picture Restorer; *m* at Heinrichsburg 5 Oct 1968, Matthäus Lill-Rastern von Lilienbach (*b* at Krumbach, Schwaben 16 Jan 1947), Dr of

Law, Businessman.

[*Falkstraße 16, 6020 Innsbruck, Austria*].

3. Count Maria *Josef* Anton Wunibald Fidelis Petrus Canisius, *b* at Heinrichsburg 15 Dec 1950, Advertising Executive; *m* at Rottach-Egern 9 Dec 1985 (*m* diss by div 11 July 1989), Claudia Isabelle (*b* at Büderich 9 Dec 1959), Journalist, dau of Klaus Dyckerhoff and Edith Gatzke.

[*Kuglmüllerstraße 19, 80638 Munich, Germany*].

4. Countess Maria *Margarete* Theresa Walburga Dionysia, *b* at Heinrichsburg 26 Feb 1953, BA, Illustrator.

[*Prinzenstraße 117, 80637 Munich, Germany*].

5. Countess Maria *Anna* Adelheid Jacobe Walburg Petrusa Bernhardine, *b* at Heinrichsburg 20 Aug 1954, Dipl Agr Eng; *m* at Hohenstein, Holstein 12 July 1980, Hubertus Neuschäffer (*b* at Pfaffengrund, Hirschberg 9 Sept 1944), Dr of Phil.

[*Seekamp, 24306 Plön, Germany*].

6. Count Maria *Hubert* Willibald Pius Johannes Nepomuk, *b* at Heinrichsburg 25 June 1956, Nurse.

[*Schulstraße 1, 88410 Bad Wurzach, Germany*].

7. Countess *Maria Theresia* Viktoria Walburga Franziska Epiphania, *b* at Heinrichsburg 8 Jan 1958, Textile Restorer; *m* at Munich 20 July 1991 (*m* diss by div at Landberg Feb 2001), Manfred Kramer (*b* at Legau 30 Aug 1955).

[*Raiffeisenweg 10, 86920 Epfach, Germany*].

8. Countess Maria *Jakobe* Walburga Meinrada Sebastiana, *b* at Heinrichsburg 20 Jan 1960, Goldsmith; *m* at Graz 23 April (civ) and 8 Oct (relig) 1988, Michael Seidl (*b* at Graz 29 July 1954), Mag jur.

[*Wastler Gasse 1, 8010 Graz, Austria*].

9. Countess *Ludmila* Walburga Martha Ida Johanna Vianney, *b* at Biberach an der Riss 29 July 1964; *m* at Steinhausen 16 July 1988, Matthias Matz, Count von Spiegelfeld (*b* at Vienna 27 Dec 1960), Manager.

[*Remete ut. 16, 1121 Budapest, Hungary*].

Brothers of Great-Grandfather

Issue of Franz, 3rd Prince von Waldburg zu Wolfegg and Waldsee (*b* 11 Sept 1833; ✠ 14 Dec 1906) and Countess Sophie Leopoldine von Arco-Zinneberg (*b* 14 Nov 1836; *m* 19 April 1860; ✠ 21 Dec 1909), having had issue, among whom,

Sons

1. Count *Ludwig* Maria Josef Wunibald Petrus Pius, *b* at Waldsee 27 Oct 1871; ✝ at Baden-Baden 24 June 1906, Kt Bav Order of St George; *m* at Salzburg 17 April 1902, Countess Anna (*b* at Meran 17 Nov 1881; ✝ at Tagmersheim 22 June 1970; *m* 2ndly at Obenhause, nr Illertissen 2 May 1916, Karl, Count von Moy de Sens who ✝ at Saulgau 29 April 1950), Dame Star Cross Order, dau of Hubert, Count von Galen and Countess Therese von Bocholtz-Asseburg, and had issue, among whom,

    1. Count *Hubertus* Maria Aloysius Wunibald Pius, *b* at Kisslegg 7 Jan 1906; ✝ at Möckmühl 30 Jan 1976, Proprietor of Assumstadt, Heilbronn, Dir of the Fugger Foundation, Augsburg, Kt of Hon Sovereign Military Order of Malta; *m* at Adldorf, Bavaria 12 Sept 1933, Countess Anna-Elisabeth (Annalies) (*b* at Adldorf 10 Aug 1909; ✝ at Marquartstein 31 Dec 1981), Dame Star Cross Order, dau of Maximilian, Count von Arco, Proprietor of Valley and Baroness Adelheid von Aretin, and had issue,

        1. Count *Ludwig* Karl Maximilian Hubert Willibald Modestus, *b* at Pähl, nr Weilheim 15 June 1934, Proprietor of Assumstadt, Farmer, Kt of Hon Sovereign Military Order of Malta, Kt Bavarian Order of St George; *m* at Hochburg 17 Aug (civ) and 7 Sept (relig) 1960, Princess Stephanie (*b* at Gusow, Mark, 22 Sept 1938), dau of Georg, Prince von Schönburg-Waldenburg and Countess Pauline zu Castell-Castell, and has issue,
[Schloß Assumstadt, 74219 Möckmühl-Züttlingen, Germany].

            1. Countess *Elisabeth* Pauline Anna Amelie Maria Walburga, *b* at Möckmühl 7 June 1962; *m* at Kreuzwertheim am Main 4 Aug (civ) and Züttlingen, nr Möckmühl 12 Sept (relig) 1987, Ludwig, Hereditary Prince (Erbprinz) zu Löwenstein-Wertheim-Freudenberg (*b* at Kreuzwertheim 24 May 1951), Dipl Business Studies.
[Schloß Hauptstraße 37, 97892 Kreuzwertheim am Main, Germany].

            2. Count *Hubertus* Georg Karl Maria Willibald Johannes, *b* at Möckmühl 15 May 1964, Farmer,

Forester; *m* at Möckmühl 7 June (civ) 1993
and at Hochosterwitz 19 June (relig) 1993,
Countess Melanie (*b* at Madrid 22 April 1967),
dau of Maximillian, Prince (Fürst) von
Khevenhüller-Metsch and Countess Wilhelmine
Henckel von Donnersmarck.
[*Schloß Assumstadt, 74219 Möckmühl-
Züttlingen, Germany*].

1. Countess Marie *Isabel* Walburga Anna
Clementine Leonhardine Henriette,
b at Öhringen 18 Jan 1996.
2. Countess *Anna* Walburga Lavinia
Stefanie Wilhelmine Franziska
Henriette, *b* at Öhringen 26 Oct 1997.
3. Count *Georg* Maria Willibald
Karl-Eugen Leonard Heinrich, *b* at
Öhringen 9 Jan 2000.

2. Count *Maximilian* Otto Wunibald Maria Hubert
Agapitus, *b* at Adldorf 18 Aug 1935, Architect; *m* at
Unsleben 16 July 1960, Baroness Henriette (*b* at
Würzburg 8 Nov 1937), dau of Hugo, Baron von
Habermann and Johanna Thomberg, and has issue,
[*Romenthal, 86911 Diessen am Ammersee, Germany*].

1. Count *Christoph* Hubertus Willibald Maria
Maximilian Eusebius, *b* at Munich 2 Dec 1961;
m at Heimerzherim 11 March 2000, Baroness
Viktoria (*b* at Bremen 11 July 1969), dau of
Adalbert, Baron von Rosenberg and Heidi
Zimmer, and has issue,
[*Kolberger Straße 13, 81679 Munich, Germany;
Schloß, 97618 Unsleben, Germany*].

1. Countess *Juliane* Viktoria Walburga
Rosa Ita Maria, *b* at Dortmund 15 Jan
2001.

2. Count *Ludwig* Niklas Maria Wunibald
Maximilian Bernhard, *b* at Munich 20 Aug 1971.
[*Muskauerstraße 43, 10997 Berlin, Germany*].

3. Count *Franz Ferdinand* Maria Hubert Willibald
Johannes, *b* at Augsburg 8 Feb 1939, Farmer; *m* at
Dublin 21 Dec 1974, Sara Louise (*b* at Dublin 10 May
1955), dau of Brian Freeman and Helene Mitchell,

and has issue,

[*Ballyshemane House, Rathdrum, County Wicklow, Ireland*].

    1. Countess *Anna* Elisabeth Maria, *b* at Dublin 30 April 1976, Public Relations Manager.

    2. Count *Hubert* Brian Willibald, *b* at Dublin 1 Jan 1978.

    [*10 Carmans Court, Dublin 8, Ireland*].

    3. Count *Maximilian* Douglas, *b* at Dublin 18 March 1981.

4. Count *Karl* Ernst Maria Hubert Wunibald Dionys, *b* at Augsburg 17 Nov 1940, Farmer; *m* at Mettlach an der Saar 16 Sept 1967 (*m* diss by div at Dublin 3 Feb 1984), Dorothea [*Baron Voghtstraße 61, 22609 Hamburg, Germany*] (*b* at Mettlach 15 June 1941; she *m* 2ndly 16 Oct 1987, Bernhard von Hohberg and Buchwald), dau of Franz Egon von Boch-Galhau and Countess Agnes von Montgelas, and has issue,

[*Belcamp Hutchinson, Balgriffin, Dublin 17, Ireland*].

    1. Countess *Lavinia* Isabelle Christiane Walburga Maria Monika, *b* at Dublin 25 Dec 1969, Landscape Architect.

    [*Baron-Voght-Straße 61, 22609 Hamburg, Germany*].

    2. Count *Georg* Friedrich Karl Christian Hubertus Maria, *b* at Dublin 10 Jan 1972.

    [*64 Ladbroke Grove, Flat 4, Notting Hill Gate, London W11 2PB*].

5. Countess *Maria Assunta* Walburga Adelheid Anna Huberta, *b* at Tagmersheim 1 Nov 1950; *m* at Züttlingen 17 Oct 1980, Hans Georg Wolfhard (*b* at Heilbronn 18 Dec 1934), Veterinarian.

[*Brombacherstraße 62, 69434 Brombach, Germany*].

LINE II: ZEIL

This line descends from Baron Froben, Lord of Zeil (*b* 19 Aug 1569; ✝ 4 May 1614); Count of the Holy Empire with ratification of arms and the qualification of "Hoch and Wohlgeboren" and elevation of Zeil into a County of the Holy Empire, Vienna 7 Sept 1628; Grand Palatine 1745; inherited Trauchburg at the extinction of that line 9 July 1772; received the title of Prince of the Holy Empire and of Waldburg zu Zeil and Trauchburg (primogeniture) with the

qualification of "Hochgeboren", Vienna 21 March 1803 (for Count Maximilian Wunibald); received the qualification of "Durchlaucht" (primogeniture) by the German Diet 18 Aug 1825; inherited Wurzach-Kisslegg at the extinction of the branch of Zeil-Wurzach, 1 Aug 1903.

The Head of the Family and his wife bear the title of Prince and Princess von Waldburg zu Zeil and Trauchburg with the qualification of Serene Highness and cadet members bear the title of Count or Countess von Waldburg zu Zeil and Trauchburg with the qualification of Illustrious Highness.

Maria **GEORG** Konstantin Ignatius Antonius Felix Augustinus Wunibald Kilian Bonifacius Reichserbtruchsess, **7TH PRINCE (FÜRST) VON WALDBURG ZU ZEIL and TRAUCHBURG**, *b* at Würzburg 5 June 1928, Dipl Econ, Kt of Hon Sovereign Military Order of Malta, Kt Order of the Golden Fleece, Hon Senator University of Ulm, son of Erich August, 6th Prince (Fürst) von Waldburg zu Zeil and Trauchburg (*b* 21 Aug 1899; ✝ 24 May 1953) and Princess Monika zu Löwenstein-Wertheim-Rosenberg (*b* 25 Feb 1905; *m* 5 April (civ) and 6 April (relig) 1926; ✝ 28 Dec 1992); *m* at Munich-Nymphenburg 23 Oct 1957, Princess Marie Gabrielle (*b* at Munich 30 May 1931), Dame of Hon Bavarian Orders of St Theresia and St Elisabeth, dau of Albrecht, Duke of Bavaria and Countess Maria (Marita) Draskovich von Trakostjan.
[Schloß Zeil, 88299 Leutkirch im Allgäu, Germany].

Son and Daughters

1. Countess Maria *Walburga* Monica Charlotte Matthäa, *b* at Ravensburg 21 Sept 1958; *m* at Schloß Zeil 30 June (civ) and 24 Aug (relig) 1986, Carl, Baron von Lerchenfeld (*b* at Bamberg 26 April 1958), Farmer and Forester.
[Schloß Frankenberg, 97215 Weigenheim, Germany].

2. Countess Maria *Gabriele* Walburga Cäcilia Theresia, *b* at Ravensburg 22 Nov 1959.
[Kaulbachstraße 104, 80802 Munich, Germany].

3. Countess Maria *Monika* Sofie Walburga Nikoletta, *b* at Ravensburg 22 March 1961; *m* at Leutkirch 29 May (civ) and Schloß Zeil 6 Sept (relig) 1987, Christoph Schenk, Count von Stauffenberg (*b* at Bamberg 1 Aug 1950), Lic oec, Tax Consultant, Kt Sovereign Military Order of Malta and Bavarian Order of St George.
[Schloß Burggrub, 91332 Heiligenstadt, Germany].

4. Maria *Erich* Wunibald Aloysius Georg, Hereditary Count (Erbgraf) von Waldburg zu Zeil and Trauchburg, *b* at Ravensburg 21 Nov

1962, Kt of Hon Sovereign Military Order of Malta; *m* at Altshausen, Ravensburg 17 Nov (civ) and 19 Nov (relig) 1988, Duchess Mathilde (*b* at Friedrichshafen 11 July 1962), dau of Carl, Duke of Württemberg and Princess Diane of France, and has issue,

[*Schloß Rimpach, 88299 Leutkirch im Allbäu, Germany*].

    1. Countess *Marie-Thérèse* Walburga Gabrielle Diane Georgina Franziska, *b* at Memmingen 4 Oct 1989.

    2. Countess Maria *Elisabeth* Walburga Apollonia Alexandra Frederike, *b* at Ravensburg 31 Dec 1990.

    3. Countess *Marie Charlotte* Walburga Antonia Adelheid Viktoria Henriette, *b* at Ravensburg 10 May 1992.

    4. Countess *Maria Hélène* Walburga Yolande Christiana Michaela, *b* at Ravensburg 29 Nov 1993.

    5. Countess *Marie Gabrielle* Walburga Angelika Antonia Friederike Fleur, *b* at Ravensburg 29 Nov 1996.

5. Countess Maria *Adelheid* Walburga Rufina, *b* at Ravensburg 28 Nov 1964; *m* at Schloß Zeil 30 Dec 1988 (civ) and 8 April 1989 (relig), Max Emanuel, Count von Rechberg and Rothenlöwen zu Hohenrechberg (*b* at Munich 25 Sept 1959), Proprietor of Elkofen, Capt (Res).

[*Schloß Elkofen, 85567 Grafing, Germany*].

6. Countess Maria *Elisabeth* Walburga Priscilla Wiltrud, *b* at Ravensburg 30 July 1966; *m* at Schloß Zeil 16 April (civ) and 7 July (relig) 1990, Engelbert, Prince von Croÿ (*b* at Leverkusen-Schlebusch 5 June 1962), Industrialist.

[*Zur Amtsschlade 43, 58802 Balve, Germany*].

Brothers and Sisters

1. Countess Maria Immakula *Josefine* Walburga Theresia Lucia Coletta, *b* at Munich 13 Dec 1929, ✞ at Munich 12 March 1999; *m* at Reichenhofen 11 July (civ) and at Schloß Zeil 28 Aug (relig) 1953, Nikolaus, Prince of Lobkowicz (*b* at Prague 9 July 1931), Dr of Phil, Dr hc mult, o, Prof of Political Theory and Phil Univ of Munich, Pres Catholic Univ of Eichstätt, Kt Order of the Golden Fleece.

[*Am Kirchberg 6, 91804 Mörnsheim-Ensfeld, Germany*].

2. Countess Maria *Theresia* Walburga Elisabeth Antonia, *b* at Schloß Zeil 8 Aug 1931, Dame Star Cross Order; *m* at Schloss Zeil 7 Aug (civ) and 12 Sept (relig) 1962, Alois, Count von Nostitz-Rieneck (*b* at Vienna 12 Aug 1925), Kt Sovereign Military Order of Malta.

[*Schloß Geyregg, 8790 Eisenerz, Steiermark, Austria*].

3. Count Maria Aloyusius (*Alois*) Willibald Eustachius Matthäus

Franziskus vom Kreuz, *b* at Schloß Zeil 20 Sept 1933; *m* at Munich 23 May (civ) and at Pommersfelden 21 June (relig) 1956, Countess Clarissa (*b* at Jüterbog 14 Oct 1936), dau of Clemens, Count von Schönborn-Wiesentheid and Countess Dorothea zu Pappenheim, and has issue, among whom,

[*Schloßhalde 1, Ratzenried, 88260 Argenbühl, Allgäu, Germany*].

    1. Countess Maria *Monika* Walburga Dorothea Gabriele, *b* at Munich 26 May 1957; *m* at Eisenharz 14 March (civ) and at Ratzenried 29 April (relig) 1978, Franz Joseph, Count Wolff Metternich zur Gracht (*b* at Heppingen, Ahrweiler 7 Oct 1947), Lawyer.

    [*Burgstraße 30, 53474 Heppingen, Bad Neuenahr-Ahrweiler, Germany*].

    2. Count Maria *Clemens* Franz Erich Thomas Wunibald, *b* at Munich 13 April 1960, Dipl Business Studies, Lt-Col (Res), Finance Director des Erzbistums Berlin; *m* at Vaduz 10 Oct (civ) and at Friedrichshafen 23 Nov (relig) 1985, Princess Georgina (*b* at Vienna 13 Nov 1962), dau of Georg, Prince von and zu Liechtenstein and Duchess Marie Christine of Württemberg, and has issue,

    [*Kleinaustraße 16, 14169 Berlin-Zehlendorf, Germany*].

        1. Countess *Maria-Annunciata* Florentine Georgina Michaela Alexandra Antonia Walburga, *b* at Tübingen 24 Sept 1988.

        2. Countess *Maria-Assunta* Christiana Katharina Monika Antonia Walburga, *b* at Stuttgart 11 April 1990.

        3. Count *Maximilian* Aloysius Anselm Franz Joseph Andreas Antonius Wunibald, *b* at Stuttgart 10 Feb 1992.

        4. Count *Constantin* Maria Carl Christoph Raimund Teresianus Antonius Willibald, *b* at Berlin-Wilmersdorf 7 Aug 1994.

        5. Countess *Philippa* Margarita Maria Theresia Birgitta Andrea Antonia Walburga, *b* at Berlin 26 March 1996.

    3. Countess Maria *Teresa* Walburga Domitilla Adelheid, *b* at Munich 31 July 1962; *m* at Esslingen 8 Feb (civ) and at Ratzenried 6 April (relig) 1991, Dr Andreas Lenhart (*b* at Stuttgart 7 Sept 1960).

    [*Podbielskiallee 81, 14195 Berlin, Germany*].

4. Count Maria *Karl* Wunibald Josef Friedrich Franz, *b* at Schloß

Zeil 10 Jan 1936; *m* at Schloß Zeil 15 May 1965, Doña Maria Victoria (*b* at Barcelona 12 Feb 1936), dau of Don Francisco de Verdugo y Sanmartin and Sara Peña y de Freixas, and has issue,
[*Calle Principe de Vergara 83-7 °, 28006 Madrid, Spain*].

    1. Count *Raphael* Maria Erich Franziskus Karl Josef Wunibald Alexander Oskar, *b* at Basel 19 July 1966; *m* at Madrid 29 Jan 1997, *Sonia* (*b* at Madrid 16 Feb 1966) dau of N Montero y Varga-Zuniga and Maria Trenor y Dicenta.
    [*Maldonado 26-1d, 28006 Madrid, Spain*].

5. Countess Maria Magdalena *Sophie* Walburga Elisabeth Notburga Monika, *b* at Schloß Zeil 17 Nov 1938; *m* at Schloß Zeil 15 May 1965 (*m* diss by div at Rüdesheim 23 Nov 1983), Erwein, Count von Matuschka, Baron von Greiffenclau von Toppolczan and Spaetgen (*b* at Würzburg 14 Nov 1938; ✝ at Vollrads 19 Aug 1997; *m* 2ndly Sabine Neggert, ✝ 1995), Proprietor of Vollrads, Rheingau.
[*Armenruhstraße 20, 65203 Wiesbaden-Biebrich, Germany*].

6. Count Maria *Eberhard* Willibald Konstantin Josef Franz Konrad, *b* at Schloß Zeil 30 April 1940; *m* at Vienna 10 Sept 1966, Countess Johanna (*b* at Königgrätz 10 July 1944), dau of Johann, Count von Harrach zu Rohrau and Thannhausen, Proprietor of Prugg and Rohrau, Lower Austria and Countess and Noble Lady Stephanie von and zu Eltz genannt Faust von Stromberg, and has issue,
[*Schloß Rohrau, 2471 NÖsterreich, Austria*].

    1. Countess *Stephanie* Elisabeth Maria Monika Walburga, *b* at Vienna 9 Oct 1967.
    2. Countess *Maria* Theresa Walburga, *b* at Vienna 28 Oct 1972; *m* at Bruch an der Leitha 6 Aug (civ) and there 28 Aug (relig) 1999, Philipp Hammer-Purgstall von Bernd (*b* at Vienna 14 March 1968).
    [*Weinbach 6, 5351 Aigen-Voglhub, Austria*].
    3. Count *Johannes* Alois Wunibald Erich Josef, *b* at Vienna 13 May 1975.
    4. Count *Karl* Erwein Alexander Maria Willibald, *b* at Vienna 22 Feb 1979.

Brother and Sister of Father

Issue of Georg, 5th Prince von Waldburg zu Zeil and Trauchburg (*b* 29 May 1867; ✝*k* 2 Sept 1918) and Altgravine Marie Therese zu Salm-Reifferscheidt-Raitz (*b* 31 Oct 1869; *m* 8 May 1897; ✝ 27 Aug 1930) among whom,

1. Count Maria *Konstantin* Friedrich Georg Wunibald Wilhelm Josef Anton, *b* at Schloß Zeil 15 March 1909; ✠ at Feldafine 27 Feb 1972, Kt of Hon Sovereign Military Order of Malta; *m* at Munich-Nymphenburg 14 Aug 1951, Princess Eleonore (*b* at Nymphenburg 11 Sept 1918), Dame of Hon Bavarian Orders of St Theresia and St Elisabeth, dau of Franz, Prince of Bavaria and Princess Isabella von Croÿ, and had issue,

[*Dünzelbach 89, 82272 Moorenweis, Germany*].

    1. Count Maria *Erich* Franz Georg Wunibald, *b* at Glashütte, nr Wengen 25 Sept 1952, Dipl Eng rer oec; *m* at Andechs 4 June 1982 (*m* diss by div 17 Dec 1993), Antonia (*b* at Viareggio 10 June 1952), dau of Tito Brunetti and Princess Editha of Bavaria, and has issue,

    [*Rathausgasse 2/IV, 81241 Munich, Germany*].

        1. Countess Maria *Sophie* Eleonore Editha Walburga, *b* at Tettnang 2 May 1984.

        [*Ladestraße 12, 88131 Lindau, Germany*].

    2. Countess Maria *Elisabeth* Therese Eleonore Walburga Monika, *b* at Glashütte 6 Jan 1954; *m* at Zeil 30 April (civ) and 23 May (relig) 1980, Hans-Caspar, Count zu Toerring-Jettenbach (*b* at Munich 22 July 1953).

    [*Dünzelbach 89, 82272 Moorenweis, Germany*].

    3. Count Maria *Georg* Konstantin Franz Wunibald Ulrich, *b* at Munich 1 May 1955, Textile Businessman; *m* at Oberarth, Switzerland 16 Oct 1976, Gabriele (*b* at Frankfurt-am-Main 23 Aug 1957), dau of Emil Schmidt and Angela Wedderhoff, and has issue,

    [*Rickenbachstraße 87, 6430 Schwyz, Switzerland*].

        1. Count Maria *Hendrik* Wunibald, *b* at Glarus 2 May 1977, Student of Veterinary Medicine.

        2. Count Maria *Alexander* Wunibald, *b* at Lucerne 3 Nov 1979.

    4. Countess Maria *Eleonore* Gabriele Theresia Walburg Elisabeth, *b* at Munich 22 Feb 1957; *m* at Munich 11 Oct 1980, Joseph Dichgans (*b* at Überlingen 18 March 1952), Lawyer.

    [*Süßenmühle 8, 78354 Sipplingen, Germany*].

    5. Count Maria *Konstantin* Karl Ludwig Willibald Georg, *b* at Munich 30 July 1958, Artist; *m* at Sutton, Quebec, Canada 4 Aug 1990, Claudia (*b* at Montreal, Quebec 13 Feb 1961), Businesswoman, dau of Erhard von Glasow and Inge Scherer,

and has issue,
[*548 Dainry Crescent, Cobourg, Ontario K9A 4Y3, Canada*].

    1. Countess *Louisa* Theresa Walburga, *b* at Peterborough, Ontario, Canada 3 Sept 1992.

    2. Countess *Caroline* Sophie Walburga, *b* at Peterborough 8 Nov 1994.

    3. Count *Christoph* Erhard, *b* at Cobourg, Ontario 3 Nov 1996.

6. Countess Maria Theresia (*Therese*) Monika Walburga, *b* at Munich 19 Jan 1960; *m* at Grünwald, nr Munich 23 July (civ) and at Schloß Zeil 6 Sept (relig) 1980, Friedrich-Wilhelm von Hesler (*b* at Munich 16 Jan 1952), Dr of Med.
[*Türksteinweg 20, 14167 Belin, Germany*].

2. Countess Maria *Gabriele* Anna Georgine Walburga Antonia Josepha, *b* at Schloß Zeil 26 April 1910; *m* at Schloß Zeil 20 June 1940, Karl Gero, Duke von Urach, Count von Württemberg (*b* at Lichtenstein 19 Aug 1899; ✝ there 15 Aug 1981), Major (Ret), Dipl Eng.
[*Schloß Lichtenstein, 72805 Lichtenstein, Germany*].

Half-Brother of Grandfather

Issue of Wilhelm, 4th Prince von Waldburg zu Zeil and Trauchburg (*b* 26 Nov 1835; ✝ 20 July 1906) and his second wife, Princess Marie Georgine von Thurn-und-Taxis (*b* 25 Dec 1857; *m* 23 May 1889; ✝ 13 Feb 1909), having had issue, among whom,

Son

Count Maria *Wilhelm* Karl Maximilian, *b* at Schloß Zeil 19 Jan 1890; ✝*k* in a car accident on the Oberalpstrasse (Graubünden) 28 July 1927, Capt Württemberg Army; *m* at Vienna 28 Sept 1921, Altgravine Marie Therese (*b* at Vienna 28 Feb 1896; ✝ at Rimpach, Württemberg 17 Jan 1985), Dame Star Cross Order, dau of August, Altgrave zu Salm-Reifferscheidt-Raitz and Baronesse Gabrielle Perényi de Perény, and had issue,

    1. Countess Marie *Gabrielle* Therese Karoline Augusta Walburga, *b* at Schloß Zeil 1 Sept 1922, Dame Star Cross Order; *m* at Schloß Zeil 12 Sept 1949, Georg Sigmund, Count Adelmann von Adelmannsfelden (*b* at Bitburg, Eifel 29 Nov 1913; ✝ at Ludwigsburg 26 Oct 1991), Dr of Phil, Kt Sovereign Military Order of Malta, former Pres of the Dept of Public Monuments in Baden-Württemberg.

[Mömpelgardstraße 18, 71640 Ludwigsburg, Germany].

2. Countess *Elisabeth* Maria Karolina Gabriele Therese Antonia
Walburga, *b* at Rimpach 26 Feb 1925, Dipl Land Management,
Dame Star Cross Order.

[Schloß Zeil, Orangerie, 88299 Leutkirch, Allgäu, Germany].

Brother of Great-Great-Great-Grandfather

Issue of Maximilian-Wunibald, 1st Prince von Waldburg zu Zeil and
Trauchburg (*b* 20 Aug 1750; ✝ 16 May 1818) and his second wife,
Countess Marie-Anne von Waldburg zu Wolfegg (*b* 11 Jan 1772; *m* 18
Feb 1798; ✝ 6 July 1835), having had issue, among whom,

Son

Count *Maximilian-Clemens*, *b* at Mattsies 8 Oct 1799; ✝ at Hohenems
29 May 1868 (inherited the fidéicommis of Lustnau and the Lordship
of Hohenems from his father's brother, Count Clemens in 1817), Imp
and Royal Chamberlain, Capt Austrian Army; *m* at Mühlheim,
Württemberg 25 Nov 1841, Baroness Josepha (*b* at Mühlheim 13
June 1814; ✝ at Bregenz 17 Aug 1892), dau of Leopold Nikolaus,
Baron von Enzberg and Countess Josephine von Waldburg zu Zeil
and Trauchburg, and had issue,

Son

Count *Clement* Maximilian Sigismund Ferdinand, *b* at Mattsies 21
Oct 1842; ✝ at Hohenems 13 Aug 1904, Possessor of the Lordships of
Lustnau and Hohenems, Lt-Col Austrian Army; *m* at Munich 22 Feb
1870, Princess Klementine (*b* at Oettingen 23 Sept 1844; ✝ at
Hohenems 6 March 1894), Dame Bavarian Orders of St Theresa, dau
of Otto Carl, Prince zu Oettingen-Oettingen and Oettingen-Spielberg
and Countess Georgine zu Königsegg-Aulendorf, and had issue, among
whom,

Sons

1. Count *Georg* Julius Kaspar Konrad, *b* at Hohenems 7 Jan 1878;
✝ at Syrgenstein, Allgäu 26 Oct 1955, Lord of Lustnau and Hohenems
1930, Imp and Royal Chamberlain, Capt Austrian Army, Kt Order of
the Golden Fleece; *m* 1stly at Niederwallsee 19 Sept 1912, Archduchess Elisabeth (*b* at Vienna 27 Jan 1892; ✝ at Syrgenstein 29 Jan
1930), Dame Star Cross Order, dau of Franz Salvator, Archduke of
Austria and Archduchess Marie Valerie of Austria, and had issue
among whom,

    1. Countess *Marie Valerie* Klementine Franziska Elisabeth

Walburga, *b* at Wallsee 28 June 1913, Dame Star Cross Order; *m* at St Gilgen am Abersee 29 April 1936, Georg, Archduke of Austria (*b* at Parsch, nr Salzburg 22 Aug 1905; ✠ at Altshausen 21 March 1952).

[*Schwarzenberg Promenade 28, 5026 Salzburg, Austria*].

2. Count *Franz Josef* Vitus Xaver Georg Wunibald, *b* at Chur 7 March 1927, Count von Waldburg zu Zeil-Hohenems, Proprietor of the Lordships of Lustnau and Hohenems, Kt of Hon and Dev Sovereign Military Order of Malta; *m* at Pommersfelden 21 June 1956, Countess Priscilla (*b* at Munich 5 Feb 1934), dau of Clemens, Count von Schönborn-Wiesentheid and Countess Dorothea zu Pappenheim, and has issue,

[*Schloß Platz 8, 6845 Hohenems, Vorarlberg, Austria*].

    1. Countess *Maria Rosario* Clara Dorothea Walburga, *b* at Hohenems 2 April 1957; *m* at Hohenems 8 Jan (civ) and at St Christoph 12 Jan (relig) 1980, José Angel Villalón-Alonso (*b* at Leon 29 Oct 1953), Dipl Eng.

    [*La Sacedilla 3/1, 28220 Majadahonda, Prov. Madrid, Spain*].

    2. Countess *Carolina* Josepha Graziella Maria Walburga, *b* at Hohenems 15 Dec 1958.

    [*Schloß Platz 8, 6845 Hohenems, Vorarlberg, Austria*].

    3. Count *Franz-Clemens* Maria Josef Willibald, *b* at Hohenems 5 March 1962, Furniture Restorer; *m* at Langenstein/Baden 8 March (civ) and 4 May (relig) 1991, Countess Stefanie (*b* at Konstanz 2 June 1966), dau of Rudolf Adolf, Count von Blanckenstein and Countess Béatrice Douglas, and has issue,

    [*Schloß Platz 8, 6845 Hohenems, Vorarlberg, Austria*].

        1. Countess *Tatjana* Priscilla Walburga Marie, *b* at Hohenems 30 April 1992.

        2. Countess *Cecilia* Béatrice Natalie Walburga Marie, *b* at Hohenems 11 March 1994.

        3. Countess *Leonie* Alexandrine Maria Walburga, *b* at Hohenems 22 Aug 1997.

        4. Countess *Sophie* Maxima Philippa Walburga Marie, *b* at Hohenems 29 June 2000.

    4. Count *Stephan-Georg* Manfred Rupert Wunibald, *b* at Hohenems 3 Aug 1963, Businessman; *m* at Vienna

26 Feb (civ) and St Jakob im Walde, Steiermark 26 May (relig) 1990, Countess Diana-Maria (*b* at Vienna 1 March 1967), dau of Georg, Count zu Lodron-Laterano and Castelromano and Baroness Alice von Steeb, and has issue,

[*Krummgasse 3, 88131 Lindau, Germany*].

        1. Count *Georg* Maria Franz-Josef Wolfgang Willibald, *b* at Hohenems 6 Nov 1992.

        2. Count *Maximilian* Maria Kaspar Christian Wunibald, *b* at Hohenems 15 June 1996.

    5. Countess *Philippa* Charlotte Gertrud Walburga Maximiliana, *b* at St Gallen 2 Dec 1968; *m* at Königseggwald, nr Aulendorf, Württemberg 23 May (civ) and Hohenems 14 July (relig) 1990, Markus, Count zu Königsegg-Aulendorf (*b* at Munich 16 May 1963), Dipl Land Management.

[*Parkstraße 4, 7131 Halbturn, Burgenland, Austria*].

    6. Count *Maximilian* Kaspar Ignatius Wunibald, *b* at St Galen 14 Nov 1976.

Count Georg *m* 2ndly at Bad Ischl 29 Dec 1931, Archduchess Gertrud (*b* at Schloß Wallsee 19 Nov 1900; ✠ at Ravensburg 20 Dec 1962), Dame Star Cross Order, sister of his first wife, and had further issue,

    3. Countess Marie *Sophie* Josepha Elisabeth Walburga, *b* at Innsbruck 5 Dec 1932; *m* at Maria-Thann, nr Hergatz 7 May 1957, Wessel, Baron von Loë of the Counts von Loë (*b* at Wissen 8 Aug 1928), Farmer, Forester.

[*Burg Adendorf, 53343 Wachtberg-Adendorf, Germany*].

    4. Count *Josef* Klemens Georg Vitus Willibald Konrad von Parzham, *b* at Syrgenstein 12 April 1934, Dr of Law, *m* at Hütting 8 May (civ) and at Bergen, nr Neuburg an der Donau 21 May (relig) 1960, Baroness Maria Benedikta (*b* at Wertheim am Main 12 April 1937), Dame Star Cross Order, dau of Alfons, Baron von Redwitz and Countess Helga von Moy, and has issue,

[*Trogerstraße 56/4, 81675 Munich, Germany; Schloß Syrgenstein, 88260 Argenbühl-Eglofs über Wangen, Allgäu, Germany*].

        1. Count *Vitus Franziskus* Rupert Benedikt Josef Wunibald Maria, *b* at Munich 17 March 1961, Capt (Res), Kt of Hon and Dev Sovereign Military Order of Malta; *m* at Kitzbühel 9 March (civ) and Vienna 28

April (relig) 1990, Countess Marie-Thérèse (*b* at Vienna 23 July 1965), Mag Phil, Dame Star Cross Order, dau of Franz, Count Nemes von Hidvég and Oltszem and Countess Maria-Antonia (Marie-Antoinette) von Thun and Hohenstein, and has issue,

[*Auf der Haid 47, 79114 Freiburg i.Br, Germany*].

     1. Countess *Marie-Valerie* Thérèse Benedikta Antonia Josefa Walburga, *b* at Stuttgart 19 March 1991.

     2. Count *Benedikt* Vitus Franz Josef Nikolaus Maria Wunibald, *b* at Munich 8 June 1992.

     3. Count *Antonius* Vitus Georg Leo Sebastian Maria Willibald, *b* at Munich 29 Dec 1995.

     4. Countess *Maria-Leopoldina* Thérèse Aloisia Gertrud Viola Walburga, *b* at Freiburg 4 July 1998.

2. Countess *Marie-Christine* Sophie Eugenie Walburga Benedikta Josefa, *b* at Ravensburg 2 July 1962, Philosophy Student; *m* at Vaduz 10 March (civ) and Maria-Thann 20 May (relig) 1989, Christian, Prince von and zu Liechtenstein (*b* at Klagenfurt 14 Nov 1961), Dr of Med.

[*Moosburger Straße 21, 9210 Pörtschach, Kärnten, Austria*].

3. Count *Alois* Willibald Johann Baptist Paul Maria, *b* at Ravensburg 23 June 1963, Dr of Law, Assessor; *m* at Schloß Syrgenstein 6 Aug (civ) and at Mariakirchen 10 Sept (relig) 1994, Countess Maria-Christina (*b* at Arnstorf 31 July 1968; ✝*k* in car accident nr Buchloe 28 May 2000), dau of Ferdinand, Count von Deym, Baron von Stritez and Waltraud Kathrein von Andersill.

[*Trogerstraße 56/IV, 81675 Munich, Germany*].

     1. Count *Clemens* Leonhard Wunibald Josef, *b* at Munich 7 July 1997.

     2. Count *Ludwig* Willibald Berthold Maria, *b* at Munich 2 Nov 1999, ✝*k* in car accident 28 May 2000.

4. Countess Maria *Josefa* Gabriele Philippa, *b* at Ravensburg 29 Aug 1964, Mag Phil, Editor; *m* at Kirchlauter 19 Aug (civ) and at Maria-Thann 2 Sept

(relig) 1995, Hans Caspar Schenk, Count von Stauffenberg (*b* at Munich 3 March 1966), BA, Dipl Business Administration.
[*Römerstraße 17 1/2, 82131 Gauting, Germany*].

5. Count *Nikolaus* Maria Ludwig Georg Alfons Engelbert Wunibald, *b* at Kempten 8 Aug 1970; *m* at Achstetten 9 Sept (civ) and at Dellmensingen 11 Sept (relig) 1999, Countess Maria Theresia (*Thesy*) Reuttner (*b* at Boskowstein 8 March 1976), stud. Phil., dau of Count David Reuttner von Weyl-Mynett and Katharina (Kitty) Radda von Boskowstein, adopted Countess Reuttner von Weyl.
[*Garvald Farmhouse, Heriot, Mid Lothian, EH38 5YE, Scotland*].

WIED

Evangelical: Seigneural family from Lahngau, whose lands were divided between the two sons of Sigfrid (Sigfrid and Dietrich - from whom the present Line descends); Lord of Runkel and of Westerburg, by a treaty of partition in 1226; inherited half of the county of Wied in 1462 through the marriage of Dietrich IV of Runkel (✝ post 22 Feb 1462) to Anastasia, dau and heiress of Johann II, Count of Isenburg-Wied (✝ 1454); division of territory between Maximilian Heinrich, Lord of Runkel (ancestor of the extinct Princes of Wied Runkel) and Friedrich Wilhelm, Lord of Neuwied, grandson and son, respectively, of Friedrich, Count of Wied (*b* 1618; ✝ 1698), Lord of Runkel, Braunsberg, Isenburg and Neuwied; Prince of the Holy Empire, Prince of Wied, Count of Isenburg, Lord of Runkel and Neuerburg with the qualification of "Hochgeboren", Vienna 29 May 1784 for Johann Friedrich Alexander, Count of Wied-Neuwied (*b* 1706, ✝ 1791); Johann August Karl, 3rd Prince of Wied-Neuwied (*b* 1779; ✝ 1836) inherited Runkel in 1824; received the qualification of "Durchlaucht" (primogeniture) by the German Diet 18 Aug 1825; Hereditary Member of the former Prussian House of Lords 12 Oct 1854.
Members of the family bear the title of Prince or Princess zu Wied with the qualification of Serene Highness.

Johann Friedrich **ALEXANDER** Hermann Josias Wilhelm, **8TH PRINCE (FÜRST) ZU WIED**, Count zu Isenburg, Herr zu Runkel and Neuerburg, *b* at Neuwied 29 Sept 1960, son of Friedrich

Wilhelm, 7th Prince (Fürst) zu Wied (*b* 2 June 1931; ✠ 28 Aug 2000).

[*Schloß, 56564 Neuwied, Germany*].

Brother

1. Prince Friederich August Maximilian Wilhelm *Carl*, *b* at Neuwied 27 Oct 1961; *m* at Birstein 25 April 1998, Princess Isabelle (*b* at Frankfurt-am Main 26 April 1973), dau of Prince Franz-Alexander, 8th Prince (Fürst) von Isenburg and Countess Christiane von Saurma, Baroness von and zu der Jeltsch, and has issue,

[*Schloß, 56564 Neuwied, Germany*].

    1. Prince Franz Alexander Friedrich Wilhelm *Maximilian*, *b* at Neuwied 10 Aug 1999.

    2. Prince Franz Alexander Heinrich Konstantin *Friedrich*-Wilhelm, *b* at Neuwied 12 June 2001.

Half-Brother and Sister

2. Princess *Christina* Elisabeth Sophie Wilhelmine Friederike, *b* at Neuwied 9 June 1970; *m* at Neuwied 8 June 1996, Wolf-Eckart, Baron von Gemmingen-Hornberg (*b* at Bamberg 21 Oct 1959), Dipl Business Studies.

[*Schloß Babstadt, 74906 Bad Rappenau, Germany*].

3. Prince *Wolff-Heinrich* Friedrich Wilhelm Ello, *b* at Neuwied 12 Feb 1979.

Mother

Princess *Guda*, *b* at Arolsen 22 Aug 1939, dau of Josias, Prince of Waldeck and Pyrmont and Duchess Altburg of Oldenburg; *m* 1stly at Arolsen 31 Aug (civ) and 9 Sept (relig) 1958 (*m* diss by div at Neuwied 3 Jan 1967), Friedrich Wilhelm, 7th Prince (Fürst) zu Wied (*b* at Stuttgart 2 June 1931; ✠ at Salmon Arm, British Columbia 28 Aug 2000), Kt of St John of Jerusalem, Kt Teutonic Order. She *m* 2ndly at Schaumburg, nr Diez an der Lahn 4 March (civ) and 9 March (relig) 1968, Horst Dierkes (*b* at ......), MD.

[*Am Carmen-Sylva-Garten 3, 5450 Neuwied 1, Germany*].

Grandmother

Countess *Maria Antonia*, *b* at Várpalota, Hungary 6 Feb 1909, dau of Carl, Count zu Stolberg-Wernigerode and Hilde von Witzleben; *m* 1stly at Neuwied 29 April 1930, Hermann, Hereditary Prince zu Wied (*b* at Potsdam 18 Aug 1899; ✠ at Rzeszów, Poland 5 Nov 1941), Dipl Agr, Capt German Army, Kt of Hon St John of Jerusalem. She

m 2ndly at Strahwalde, nr Hernhug 31 Aug 1943, Edmund von Gordon (*b* at Laskowitz 3 Oct 1901; ✠ at Andernach am Rhein 22 Sept 1986).
[*Wied Runkelstraße 1, 56269, Germany*].

Brother and Sister of Father

1. Prince *Metfried* Alexander Wilhelm Friedrich, *b* at Stuttgart 25 April 1935, Kt of Hon St John of Jerusalem; *m* at Andernach 12 Feb (civ) and at Neuwied 17 Feb (relig) 1968, Baroness Felicitas (*Fe*) (*b* at Linnich, Jülich 31 Dec 1948), dau of Georg, Baron von der Pahlen and Irmgard von Mitzlaff, and has issue,
[*65594 Burg Runkel bei Limburg an der Lahn, Germany*].

> 1. Prince Friedrich *Christian* Hermann Wilhelm Alexis, *b* at Waldbröl 5 Aug 1968; *m* at Runkel 29 June (relig) 2002, Sibylle Garbe (*b* at Freiburg 29 June 1972), dau of Günter Garbe and of Karin Butzin.
> [*65594 Burg Runkel bei Limburg an der Lahn, Germany*].
> 2. Prince *Magnus* Alexander Wilhelm Friedrich, *b* at Waldbröl 6 June 1972.
> [*65594 Burg Runkel bei Limburg an der Lahn, Germany*].

2. Princess Wilhelmine Friederike Elisabeth Henriette Anastasia *Osterlind*, *b* at Stuttgart 8 April 1939; *m* at Neuwied 5 Sept (civ) and 7 Sept (relig) 1964, Werner von Klitzing (*b* at Hanover 3 Aug 1934), Lawyer.
[*65594 Burg Runkel bei Limburg an der Lahn, Germany*].

Brother of Grandfather

Issue of Friedrich, 6th Prince (Fürst) zu Wied (*b* 27 June 1872; ✠ 18 June 1945) and Princess Pauline of Württemberg (*b* 10 Dec 1877; *m* 29 Oct 1898; ✠ 7 May 1965), having had issue, among whom,

Son

Prince *Dietrich* Wilhelm Friedrich Karl Paul, *b* at Potsdam 31 Oct 1901; ✠ at Ludwigsburg 8 Jan 1970, *m* at Berlin 10 July 1928, Countess Antoinette (*b* at Berlin 9 Oct 1902; ✠ at Ludwigsburg 17 Feb 1988), dau of Otto, Count Grote and Alice van Bergen, and had issue,

> 1. Prince Wilhelm Friedrich Otto Hermann *Maximilian*, *b* at Hanover 30 May 1929.
> [*Schloßbergstraße 13, 78476 Allensbach-Hegne, Germany*].
> 2. Prince Wilhelm Friedrich *Ulrich*, *b* at Stuttgart 12 June

1931; *m* at Munich 2 Dec 1968, Ilke (*b* at Bonn 9 Dec 1936), dau of Dr Gottfried Fischer and Maria Mühlenbein, and has issue,
[*Zühzagl, 83697 Rottach-Egern, Germany; Marienwahl, 71634 Ludwigsburg, Germany*].

> 1. Prince *Wilhelm* Friedrich Ulrich, *b* at Munich 26 June 1970; *m* at Fladbury, Worcestershire 1 July 2000, Clarissa Elizabeth (*b* at Evesham 8 July 1971), dau of George Makepeace-Massingham and ......, and has issue,
>> 1. Prince Wilhelmn *Friedrich* Ulrich Maximilian Georg, *b* at London 9 May 2001.
> 2. Princess Wilhelmine Friederike Pauline Elisabeth *Marie,* *b* at Munich 27 Dec 1973; *m* at Schloß Altshausen 11 Oct 1993, Friedrich, Hereditary Prince of Württemberg (*b* at Friedrichshafen 1 June 1961).
> [*Schloß Friedrichshafen, 88045 Friedrichshafen, Württemberg*].

3. Prince Wilhelm Friedrich Dietrich *Ludwig-Eugen,* *b* at Stuttgart 27 Aug 1938, ✠ at Munich 11 May 2001; *m* at Munich 30 May (civ) and 8 June (relig) 1966, Helga (*b* at Sorau, 7 May 1941), dau of Hans Gemeinert and Anneliese Kopsch, and has issue,
[*Trogerstraße 17, 81675 Munich, Germany*].

> 1. Prince Wilhelm Friedrich Dietrich Ludwig *Karl Eduard,* *b* at Munich 16 Jan 1968.
> [*Trogerstraße 17, 81675 Munich, Germany*].

Brothers of Great-Grandfather
Issue of Wilhelm, 5th Prince (Fürst) zu Wied (*b* 22 Aug 1845; ✠ 22 Oct 1907) and Princess Marie of the Netherlands (*b* 5 July 1841; *m* 18 July 1871; ✠ 22 June 1910), having had issue, among whom,

Sons
1. Prince *Wilhelm* Friedrich Heinrich, *b* at Neuwied 26 March 1876; ✠ at Predeal, nr Sinaia, Rumania 18 April 1945, former Prince of Albania (accepted the Crown 6 Feb 1914 but was only in Albania from 7 March to 5 Sept 1914 when he left the country having reserved his rights), assumed the qualification of Highness, Major Prussian Army, Kt of Hon St John of Jerusalem; *m* at Waldenburg, Saxony 30 Nov 1906, Princess Sophie (*b* at Potsdam 21 May 1885; ✠ at Fontaneli, Moldavia 3 Feb 1936), dau of Victor, Hereditary Prince (Erbprinz)

von Schönburg-Waldenburg and Princess Lucie zu Sayn-Wittgenstein-Berleburg, and had issue among whom,

    1. *Karl Viktor* (Carol Victor) Wilhelm Friedrich Ernst Günther, Hereditary Prince of Albania, Prince zu Wied, with the qualification of Highness, *b* at Potsdam 19 May 1913; ✠ at Munich 8 Dec 1973, Dr of Law; *m* at New York 8 Sept 1966, Eileen (*b* at Chester 3 Sept 1922; *m* 1stly at New York 6 Nov 1943, André de Coppet who ✠ at Lausanne 1 Aug 1953, Stockbroker), dau of George Johnston and Alice Percival.

[*7 Shrewsbury House, Cheyne Walk, London S.W.3*].

WINDISCH-GRAETZ

Catholic: Feudal family, probably a branch of the "von Diengen" who originated from the county of Wolfratshausen and moved to Austria as officials of the Counts of Andechs, whose property included Windisch-Graetz; the family can be reliably traced from Wernhardus de Graeze, flourishing in 1218 - 1222; Windisch-Graetz passed to the Patriarchate of Aquileja in 1251 and the family followed; Conrad of Windisch-Graetz 1299 (✠ 1339) was Regent of Styria 1323; Baron of the Holy Roman Empire with "zu Waldstein and im Thal" 7 July 1551; ratification of arms, Vienna 21 Nov 1557; "Erbstallmeister" Hereditary Master of the Horse in the Duchy of Styria 27 June 1565 (primogeniture); Bohemian Incolat 12 June 1574; Hungarian Indigenat 19 July 1655; Count of the Holy Roman Empire, Frankfurt-am-Main 2 Aug 1658; received into the Franconian College of Counts of the Holy Roman Empire 28 Jan 1684 (for the Head of the Family only), the lines below descend from two sons of Count Joseph Nikolas (*b* 6 Dec 1744; ✠ 24 Jan 1802).

LINE I

This line descends from Prince Alfred (*b* 11 May 1787; ✠ 21 March 1862); acquired the Lordships of Egloffs and of Siggen (Württemberg) 3 April 1804; Prince of the Holy Empire (primogeniture) with ratification of arms, qualification of "Hochgeboren" and the elevation of the Lordships of Egloffs and Siggen into a Principality of the Holy Roman Empire, under the name of Windisch-Graetz, Vienna 14 May 1804; Hereditary Member of the former First Chamber of the Kingdom of Württemberg 25 Sept 1819; the title of Prince was extended to all descendants of the first Prince of the Holy Empire, Vienna 18 May 1822; received the qualification of "Durchlaucht" (primogeniture) by the German Diet 18 Aug 1825, recognised in

Austria 7 Oct 1825; title extended to all descendants 27 April 1869; Hereditary Member of the Austrian House of Lords 18 April 1861. Members of the family bear the title of Prince or Princess zu Windisch-Graetz with the qualification of Serene Highness.

Ludwig **ANTON, 5TH PRINCE (FÜRST) ZU WINDISCH-GRAETZ,** Baron von Waldstein and im Thal, *b* at Vienna 12 Jan 1942, Businessman, Director, son of Ludwig Aladar, 5th Prince (Fürst) zu Windisch-Graetz (*b* 4 Dec 1908; ✠ at 3 May 1990) and Christine Ebert (*b* 21 Oct 1905; *m* 29 July 1936; *m* 17 June 1926, Theodor, Baron von Fries who ✠ 7 July 1963; that *m* diss by div ... and annulled 25 May 1936); *m* at New York, NY, USA 9 May 1981, Angelika (*b* at Cologne 15 March 1943), dau of Heinrich Bovenschen and Gisela Horten.

[*Pienzenauerstraße 162, 81925 Munich, Germany*].

Brother

1. Prince *Alfred, b* at Vienna 1 June 1939, renounced his rights of succession 18 July 1966, Businessman; *m* at Kitzbühel 30 Sept 1978, Monika (*b* at Vienna 3 March 1954; ✠ at Bern 11 March 1991), dau of Helmuth Rasper and Baroness Maily Jacobs von Kantstein, and has issue,

[*Kaasgraben Gasse2, 1190 Vienna, Austria*].

    1. Princess Marie-Christine *Alexandra, b* at Kitzbühel 30 July 1980.

    2. Princess *Natalie, b* at Kitzbühel 8 Jan 1983.

    3. Prince *Maximilian* Ludwig Wilhelm, *b* at Kitzbühel 30 July 1984.

Brother and Sisters of Father

Issue of of Ludwig, 4th Prince (Fürst) zu Windisch-Graetz (*b* 20 Oct 1882; ✠ 3 Feb 1968) and Countess Marie Széchényi de Sárvár-Felsövidék (*b* 8 Sept 1887; *m* 18 Nov 1907; ✠ 3 Feb 1972) among whom,

1. Princess *Maria Magdalene* Valerie Paula Georgine Justine Karolina, *b* at Sárospatak 26 Sept 1911; *m* at Sárospatak 8 July 1930, Stephan, Count Károlyi de Nagy-Károly (*b* at Fóth, Pest-Pilis-Solt-Kiskun, Hungary 9 Dec 1898; ✠ at Villa Gesell, Buenos Aires, Argentina 2 June 1967), Dr of Econ, Lt.

[*4836 Reservoir Road NW, Washington, DC 20007, U.S.A.*].

2. Prince *Vincenz* Alfred Karl Ludwig Valerian Maria Gabriel, *b* at

Sárospatak 14 Sept 1913, Dipl Business Studies, Director (Retired); *m* at Kammer am Attersee 15 April 1945 (civ) and at Cairo 14 May 1960 (relig), Marta (*b* at Nagy-Szöllös 28 Oct 1910; *m* 1stly at Budapest 1929, Paul Morvay (of Hungarian nobility); that *m* diss by div 1935; *m* 2ndly at Budapest 1935, Georg, Baron Prónay de Tót Próna et Blathnicza who ✠ 1972; that *m* diss by div 1945), dau of Emil Becsky de Tasnádszántó and Ilona Rabár de Koját.

[*Ziehrer Platz 4/22, 1030 Vienna, Austria*].

3. Princess *Natalie* Juliane Sofie Maria Viktoria, *b* at Sárospatak 21 Aug 1917, Dame Star Cross Order.

[*Laimgruben Gasse4/5, 1050 Vienna, Austria*].

4. Princess *Elisabeth* Mathilda Zita Carola Rosalia Maria, *b* at Sárospatak 4 Sept 1923; *m* 1stly at Budapest 12 Jan 1944 (*m* diss by div at Budapest 22 June 1949), Joseph, Count Esterházy de Galántha (*b* at Salgócska, Neutra 8 Sept 1917; ✠ at Vienna 21 Jan 1980), Businessman. She *m* 2ndly at Geneva 30 Dec 1949 (civ) and at Chambésy, Geneva 28 Feb 1980, Friedrich (Fred) Dusendschön (*b* at London 6 Aug 1911; ✠ at Geneva 20 Nov 1986).

[*32 Crêts de Champel, 1206 Geneva, Switzerland*].

Brother of Great-Grandfather

Issue of Alfred, 1st Prince zu Windisch-Graetz (*b* 11 May 1787; ✠ 21 March 1862) and Princess Marie-Eleonore zu Schwarzenberg (*b* 21 Sept 1796; *m* 15 June 1817; ✠ 12 June 1848), having had issue, among whom,

1.Prince *Joseph* Aloys Nikolaus Paul Johann, *b* at Prague 23 June 1831; ✠ at Vienna 18 Oct 1906, Lt-Field Marshal Austrian Army; *m* at Berlin 24 Sept 1866, Marie Taglioni (*b* at Berlin 27 Oct 1833, ✠ at Neu-Aigen, nr Tulln, Upper Austria 27 Aug 1891), and had issue,

    1.Prince *Franz* Seraphim Joseph Nikolaus, *b* at Klattau, Bohemia 3 July 1867; ✠ at St Martin, Innkr, Upper Austria 13 Oct 1947, Dr of Law; *m* at Vienna 2 Feb 1893, Countess Margarete (*b* at Vienna 18 May 1870; ✠ at Neu-Pernstein 11 Jan 1935), dau of Johann, Count von Harrach zu Rohrau and Thannhausen and Princess Maria of Lobkowicz, and had issue among whom,

        1. Prince *Johann* Nepomuk Franz Joseph Liberatus Hubertus Maria, *b* at Rohrau 17 Aug 1897; ✠ at Vienna 19 July 1958; *m* at Vienna 28 Dec 1927, Lucie (*b* at

Versecz 1 Nov 1903; ✠ at Vienna 22 July 1986), dau of
Wilhelm Wettel and Marie Lukits, and had issue,

    1. Princess *Margarethe* Maria Mathilde
Franziska Johannes Theresia, *b* at Weidlingau
11 Sept 1928, Dame Star Cross Order; *m* at
Vienna 16 Feb 1950, Alexander, 8th Prince
(Fürst) von Schönburg-Hartenstein (*b* at
Hartenstein 8 Jan 1930).
[*Kruger Strasse 16, 1010 Vienna, Austria*].

2. Prince Otto *Franz* Maria Eleonore Telesforus, *b* at Zurich
5 Jan 1913, Dr of Phil, Art Historian, Kt of Hon and Dev
Sovereign Military Order of Malta; *m* at Litschau 14 Feb
1952, Countess Ida (*b* at Manetin, Bohemia 31 Jan 1919),
Dame Star Cross Order, dau of Joseph, Count von Seilern
and Aspang and Countess Theresia (Therese) Lazansky,
Baroness von Bukowa, and has issue,

(Jacquin Gasse21/5, 1030 Vienna, Austria).

    1. Prince *Johann-* Nepomuk *Martin* Maria Franz Josef
Heinrich Johannes Chrysostomus, *b* at Vienna 27 Jan
1953, Dr of Law, Diplomat, Kt of Hon and Dev
Sovereign Military Order of Malta.
[*Jacquin Gasse21/5, 1030 Vienna, Austria*].

LINE II

This line descends from Count Weriand (*b* 31 May 1790; ✠ 27 Oct
1867); the dignity of Prince of the Empire and Austrian Prince,
which was conferred on his elder brother in 1804 (see above), was
extended to Count Weriand and all descendants, Vienna 18 May
1822; received the qualification of Serene Highness, Vienna 12 Jan
1902; Hereditary Member of the former Austrian "Reichsrate" 26
Feb 1912.
Members of the family bear the title of Prince or Princess zu
Windisch-Graetz with the qualification of Serene Highness.

MARIANO HUGO, PRINCE (FÜRST) ZU WINDISCH-GRAETZ, *b* at Trieste 27 July 1955, Industrialist, Kt of Hon and
Dev Sovereign Military Order of Malta, Kt of Justice Constantinian
Order of St George, son of Maximilian, Prince zu Windisch-Graetz
(*b* 1 Sept 1914; ✠ 1 Nov 1976) and Maria Luisa (Marlise) Serra di
Gerace of the Princes di Gerace (*b* 30 July 1921; *m* 11 Nov 1946);
m at Salzburg 31 Jan (civ) and 11 Feb (relig) 1990, Archduchess
Sophie (*b* at Boulogne-sur-Seine 19 Jan 1959), dau of Ferdinand,

Archduke of Austria and Countess Helene zu Toerring-Jettenbach.
[*Il Palazzo, 81017 Sant Angelo d'Alife, Prov. Caserta, Italy; Via Monte Gordano 36, 00186, Italy*].

Sons and Daughter

1. Prince *Maximilian* Hugo, Hereditary Prince (Erbpriz) zu Windisch-Graetz, *b* at Salzburg 4 Aug 1990.
2. Prince *Alexis* Ferdinando, *b* at Rome 7 December 1991.
3. Princess *Larissa* Maria Luisa Christina Maria Grazia Leontina Hellena Franziska, *b* at Rome 11 Dec 1997.

Brother and Sisters

1. Princess Irma *Christiana* Leontine Maximiliane, *b* at Trieste 1 July 1951, Dame of Hon and Dev Sovereign Military Order of Malta; *m* at Sant'Angelo d'Alife, Caserta 21 June 1980, Don Augusto Ruffo di Calabria of the Princes Ruffo di Calabria (*b* at Turin 1 Oct 1955), Businessman.
[*Via Bigli 4, 20121 Milan, Italy*].
2. Princess *Maximiliane* Gatia Maria Leontine Friederika, *b* at Trieste 16 Nov 1952; *m* at Rome 11 Nov 1976, Heinrich, Hereditary Prince (Erbprinz) zu Fürstenberg (*b* at Schloß Heiligenberg 17 July 1950).
[*78166 Schloß Donaueschingen, Germany*].
3. Prince *Manfred*, *b* at Trieste 1 April 1963, Kt of Hon and Dev Sovereign Military Order of Malta, Kt of Justice Constantinian Order of St George; *m* at Marino 12 Oct 1996, Maria Vittoria (*b* at Rome 22 Feb 1970), dau of Guiseppe Lepri of the Marquesses Lepri di Rota and Maria Luisa Cavallini, and has issue,
[*Via Piave 66, 00187 Rome, Italy*].
    1. Prince *Nicolo*, *b* at Rome 4 Nov 1997.
    2. Princess *Olimpia*, *b* at Rome, ... March ...

Mother

Maria Luisa (*Marlise*), Dowager Princess zu Windisch-Graetz, *b* at Vienna 30 July 1921, Dame Grand Cross Hon and Dev Sovereign Military Order of Malta, Dame of Justice Constantinian Order of St George, adopted dau of Don Giovan Battista Serra di Gerace, 12th Prince di Gerace; *m* at Cortina d'Ampezzo 11 Nov 1946, Maximilian, Prince zu Windisch-Graetz (*b* at Donaueschingen 1 July 1914; ✠ at Rome 1 Nov 1976), Lt-Col (Res) Italian Airforce, Kt of Hon and Dev Gd Cross Sovereign Military Order of Malta.
[*Piazza SS. Apostoli 81, 00187 Rome, Italy*].

Brothers and Sister of Father

Issue of Hugo, Prince zu Windisch-Graetz (*b* 30 July 1887; ✠ 26 May 1959) and Princess Leontine zu Fürstenberg (*b* 16 June 1892; *m* 26 Nov 1912; ✠ 7 Oct 1979), among whom,

1. Prince *Friedrich* Karl Hugo Maximilian Maria Cyrillus Felix Hubertus, *b* at Heiligenberg, Baden 7 July 1917, ✠ at Gersau, Switzerland, 29 May 2002, Businessman, 1st Lt, Kt of Hon and Dev Sovereign Military Order of Malta; *m* at Schliersee, Bavaria 31 March (civ) and at Munich 1 April (relig) 1959, Princess Dorothea (*b* at Panker, Holstein 24 July 1934), dau of Christoph, Prince of Hesse and Princess Sophie of Greece and Denmark, and has issue,
[*Ruetlistraße 34, 6442 Gersau, Switzerland*].

> 1. Princess *Marina* Margarita Sophia Leontina Christina, *b* at Milan 3 Dec 1960, Furniture Restorer.
> [*Ruetlistraße 34, 6442 Gersau, Switzerland*].
> 2. Princess *Clarissa* Elisabeth Fiore, *b* at Erba, Como 6 Aug 1966; *m* at Alserio Como 16 Nov 1985, Eric de Waele (*b* at Brussels 6 Jan 1961), Industrialist.
> [*Ruetlistraße 34, 6442 Gersau, Switzerland*].

Brothers and Sister of Grandfather

Issue of Hugo, Prince zu Windisch-Graetz (*b* 17 Nov 1854; ✠ 15 May 1920) and Princess Christiane von Auersperg (*b* 26 Feb 1866; *m* 16 May 1885; ✠ 12 July 1962) among whom,

Sons

1. Prince *Alfred* Veriand, *b* at Gonobitz 12 March 1890; ✠ at Weikersheim, Württemberg 7 March 1972, Capt Austrian Army; *m* at Vienna 29 April 1919, Princess Isabella (*b* at Rothenhaus, Bohemia 30 May 1891; ✠ at Bad Mergentheim 10 Sept 1982), dau of Gottfried, Prince zu Hohenlohe-Langenburg and Countess Anna von Schönborn-Buchheim, and had issue, among whom,

> 1. Prince *Gottfried* Maximilian Weriand Antonius Maria Piedad, *b* at Vienna 5 April 1927; *m* at ... Claudia (*b* at ...), dau of ... and ...
> [*Commodore Plaza, Suite 313, 3138 Coconut Grove Drive, Miami, FL 33134, U.S.A.*].
> 2. Prince Hugo *Weriand* Antonius Franziskus Thomas Maria, *b* at Dresden 29 Dec 1929; *m* 1stly at London 21 Oct 1961 (*m* diss by div at Mexico 28 Aug 1967), Caroline Jane (*b* at

Ascot, England 30 Oct 1939), dau of Dudley Knott and Joan Sarel. He *m* 2ndly at New York 20 June 1980, Baroness Katalin Ladislaya Maria [*Ferenchegyi ut. 33, 1025 Budapest, Hungary*] (*b* at Budapest 30 Dec 1947), dau of Josef, Baron Hatvany de Hatvan and Irene Maria Halász, and had issue by his first wife,

[*La Hoya, 29600 Marbella-Montaña, Spain*].

> 1. Prince *Constantin* Weriand Alfred Maria, *b* at New York 9 July 1962.
>
> [*363 17th Street, Santa Monica, CA 90402, U.S.A.*].
>
> 2. Prince *Franziskus Charles* Weriand Gottlieb Albrecht Maria, *b* at Würzburg 22 Aug 1964.
>
> [*835 North Sierra Bonita, Los Angeles, CA 90046, U.S.A.*].

2. Prince *Eduard* Vincenz Heinrich, *b* at Gonobitz 15 July 1891; ✠ at Eybach 15 Feb 1976, Dipl Eng, Lt Austrian Army; *m* at Birstein 4 June (civ) and 14 June (relig) 1923, Princess Alexandra (*Alix*) (*b* at Birstein 21 Dec 1899; ✠ at Barcola, nr Trieste 22 Dec 1945), Dame Star Cross Order, dau of Franz Joseph, Prince von Isenburg and Princess Friederike zu Solms-Braunfels, and had issue,

> 1. Princess *Maria Friederike* Christiane Antoinette Elisabeth Modesta Gertrudis, *b* at Birstein 13 March 1924; ✠ at London 17 Dec 1972; *m* at Johannesburg 10 May 1950, Thomas (Tom) Weston-Baker (*b* at London 26 Feb 1919), Major British Army (Retired), Banker.
>
> [*1 Cambridge House, Cambridge Gardens, Tunbridge Wells, Kent TN2 4SB*].
>
> 2. Princess Leontine (*Lotti*) Christiane Alexandra Louise Elisabeth Olga Wilhelmine Gabriele Marie Antonette, *b* at Birstein 11 July 1925; *m* at Trieste 18 Feb 1947, Robert Anthony Henley (*b* at Sheffield, England 17 May 1921), Major British Army.
>
> [*51 Wetherby Mansions, Earls Court Square, London, SW10 B71*].
>
> 3. Princess *Wilhelmine* Gabriele Elisabeth Sophie Maria Christine, *b* at Graz 2 June 1930, Dame Star Cross Order; *m* at Trieste 19 Sept 1957, Gottfried (*Götz*), Count von Degenfeld-Schönburg (*b* at Würzburg 3 April 1925), Proprietor of Eybach, Lic phil, Forester.
>
> [*Schloß Eybach, 73312 Geislingen an der Steige, Württemberg, Germany*].

4. Princess *Olga* Irma Theresia vom Kinde Jesu Gabrielle Wolfgang, *b* at Graz 26 Oct 1934; *m* at Trieste 16 May 1961, Karl Anton von Riedemann (*b* at Samaden, Engadin 3 Oct 1931).

[*5815 Angus Drive, Vancouver, B.C. V0L 1B0, Canada*].

Brother of Great-Great-Grandfather

Issue of Weriand, Prince zu Windisch-Graetz (*b* 1 June 1790; ✥ 27 Oct 1867) and Princess Marie-Eleonore of Lobkowicz (*b* 28 Oct 1795; *m* 11 Oct 1812; ✥ 10 March 1876), having had issue, among whom,

Son

Prince *Ernst* Ferdinand Weriand, *b* at Winteritz 27 Sept 1827; ✥ at Vienna 22 Nov 1918, Col Austrian Army, Imp and Royal Chamberlain, Kt Order of the Golden Fleece, Kt Bavarian Order of St George; *m* at Munich 17 May 1879, Princess Kamilla (*b* at Oettingen 20 Sept 1845; ✥ at Vienna 11 Nov 1888), Dame Star Cross Order, dau of Otto, Prince zu Oettingen-Oettingen and Oettingen-Spielberg and Countess Georgine von Königsegg-Aulendorf, and had issue, among whom,

Sons

1. Prince *Otto* Weriand Hugo Ernst, *b* at Graz 7 Oct 1873; ✥ at Lugano 25 Dec 1952, Kt Gd Cross Swedish Order of the Northern Star; *m* at Vienna 23 Jan 1902 (*m* diss by div at Vienna 26 March 1924), Archduchess Elisabeth (*b* at Laxenburg 2 Sept 1883; ✥ at Vienna 22 March 1963; she *m* 2ndly at Vienna 4 May 1928, Leopold Petznek who ✥ at Vienna 27 July 1956), dau of Crown Prince Rudolf of Austria and Princess Stephanie of Belgium, and had issue, among whom,

> 1. Prince *Franz Joseph* Marie Otto Antonius Ignatius Oktavianus, *b* at Prague 22 March 1904; ✥ at Nairobi, Kenya 1 Jan 1981; *m* at Brussels 3 Jan 1934, Countess Ghislaine (*b* at Ixelles 10 March 1912; ✥ at Namur 6 March 1997), dau of Guillaume, Count d'Arschot Schoonhoven and Eva Nubar, and had issue,
>
>> 1. Princess *Stephanie* Marie Eva, *b* at Brussels 17 Jan 1939; *m* at London 16 Feb 1967 (*m* diss by div at London 1973 since when she reverted to her maiden name), Dermot Blundell-Hollinshead-Blundell (*b* at London 18 Oct 1935), Major British Army.

[65 avenue Louis Lepoutre, 1060 Brussels, Belgium].
2. Prince *Guillaume* Franz Josef Maria, *b* at Nairobi
19 Nov 1950.
[116 avenue Louis Lepoutre, 1060 Brussels, Belgium].
2. Prince *Ernst Weriand* Maria Otto Antonius Expeditus
Anselmus, *b* at Prague 21 April 1905; ✝ at Vienna 23 Dec
1952, Painter; *m* 1stly at Vienna 17 Oct 1927 (*m* diss by div 17
June 1938 and anulled at 1940), Helena (*b* at Scheibbs, Lower
Austria 6 April 1906; ✝ at Vienna 11 May 1982; she *m* 2ndly
1940, Peter Werfft), dau of Henry Skinner and Mary
Obermüller, and had issue,

  1. Prince *Otto* Ernst Wilhelm, *b* at Vienna 5 Dec 1928,
  Photographer; *m* 1stly at Vienna 27 April 1957
  (*m* diss by div at Vienna 4 Dec 1969), Countess Johanna
  [Mariahilferstraße 27, 1060 Vienna, Austria] (*b* at
  Budapest 25 May 1936; she *m* 2ndly at Bad Aussee 23
  July 1974, Gangolf Bernthaler), dau of Franz, Count
  von Wimpffen and Katharina (Käthe) Schiffer, and
  has issue,

    1. Princess Henriette Raphaela, *b* at Salzburg
    31 Jan 1958; *m* at Vienna 29 Nov 1996 (civ) and
    at Seeboden, Kärnten 9 May 1997 (relig),
    Wilhelm Böhm von Bawerk (*b* at Vienna 5 June
    1945).
    [Kupelwicscr Gassc55, 1130 Vienna, Austria].
    2. Princess *Désirée* Eleonore Maria Felicitas,
    b at Salzburg 1 July 1959; *m* at Vienna 1 Feb
    1986, Marin, Count zu Herberstein (*b* at Vienna
    1 Feb 1961, ✝ at Vienna 10 Dec 1992).
    [Türkenstraße 8, 1090 Vienna, Austria].
    3. Prince Philipp Amadeus Otto Ernst, *b* at
    Salzburg 22 Oct 1960, Farmer; *m* at Vienna 1
    Feb 1986, Andrea (*b* at Vienna 2 Aug 1956),
    dau of Friedrich Krejci and Rosa Maria
    Hamper, and has issue,
    [Drosseramt 3, 3552 Dross, Austria].
      1. Prince *Franz Josef* Otto Weriand,
      b at Vienna 23 Sept 1986.
      2. Prince *Maximilian* Konstantin
      Weriand, *b* at Vienna 27 April 1988.
      3. Prince *Konstantin* Gideon Otto

Maria, *b* at Vienna 22 Jan 1990.

4. Princess *Melanie* Louise Anastasia,
b at Vienna 11 Nov 1991.

5. Prince *Alexander* Sebastian, *b* at
Vienna 21 April 1993.

4. Prince *Ernst* Albrecht, *b* at Vienna 25 Sept
1962; *m* at Vienna 27 June 1992, Michaela (*b* at
Vienna 12 April 1967), Dr of Law, dau of Elmar
Puck and Karin Rom, and has issue,

[*Börse Gasse10, 1010 Vienna, Austria*]

1. Prince *Benedikt* Veriand Otto Elmar,
b at Vienna 23 April 1998.

5. Princess *Dominique*, *b* at Vienna 22 April
1966; *m* at Vienna 12 May 1990, Andreas, Baron
Dóczy de Német-Kersztúr (*b* at Vienna 10
March 1960), Paediatrician.

[*Schlössel Gasse11, 1080 Vienna, Austria*]

Prince Otto *m* 2ndly at Vienna 22 Dec 1969, Maria
Magdalena (*b* at Meran 7 Nov 1932), Dr of Law, dau of
Hans Gamper and Sophie Ladurner, and has further
issue,

[*Wickenburg Gasse10, 1080 Vienna, Austria*].

6. Prince *Johannes* Hubertus Maria, *b* at
Vienna 7 Feb 1971.

[*Wickenburg Gasse10, 1080 Vienna, Austria*].

7. Princess *Sophie* Eléonore, *b* at Vienna 14
Dec 1972; *m* at Vienna 29 Sept 2001, Hubertus
Wilhelm Martin Maria Franz von Löbbecke
(*b* at Vienna 20 Nov 1966).

[*Wickenburg Gasse10, 1080 Vienna, Austria*].

2. Princess *Stefanie* Maria Magdalena, *b* at Vienna 21
Jan 1933; *m* at Mariazell, Lower Austria 14 May 1956
(*m* diss by div at Salzburg 1964), Josef Christoforetti
(*b* at Kurtatsch, nr Bozen 27 Jan 1919), Mechanic and
Locksmith, Travel Agent.

[*Mitterb 8, 5211 Friedburg, Austria*].

Prince Ernst Weriand *m* 2ndly at Schwarzenbach an der
Pielach, Lower Austria 11 May 1947, Baroness Eva (*b* at Vienna
5 April 1921), dau of Lothar, Baron von Isbary, Proprietor of
Fridau, Kirchberg, etc and Baroness Aloisia Klepsch-Kloth
von Roden, and had further issue,

[*Fillgrader Gasse12, 1060 Vienna, Austria*].

      3. Princess *Eleonore* Aloysia Elisabeth Maria, *b* at Vienna 25 Aug 1947; *m* at Vienna 21 March 1968, Friedrich Johan, Count zu Hardegg, Proprietor of Glatz and im Machlande (*b* at Vienna 5 Jan 1944), Dr of Law.
[*Schotten Gasse7, 1010 Vienna, Austria*].

      4. Princess *Elisabeth* Maria Eva Margarita, *b* at Vienna 24 Oct 1951; *m* at Kirchberg an der Pielach, Lower Austria 28 Aug 1982, Christian Anton, Count von Attems-Gilleis (*b* at Diadema, Argentina 2 Oct 1954), Lawyer.[*Stallburg Gasse4, 1010 Vienna, Austria*].

3. Princess *Stephanie* Eleonore Maria Elisabeth Kamilla Philomena Veronika, *b* at Ploschkowitz 9 July 1909; *m* 1stly at Brussels 22 July 1933, Pierre, Count d'Alcantara de Querrieu (*b* at Bachte-Maria-Leerne, Belgium 2 Nov 1907; ✝ in a Concentration Camp at Oranienburg 14 Oct 1944), Dr of Law, Lt Belgian Army. She *m* 2ndly at Boitsfort, Brussels 14 Nov 1945, Carl Axel Björklund (*b* at Högsjö, Sweden 21 Dec 1906; ✝ at Anderlecht, Belgium 26 Feb 1986), Businessman.
[*42 Avenue Gustave, 1640 Rhode-Saint-Genese, Belgium*].

<hr>

WURMBRAND-STUPPACH

Catholic: Feudal family from Lower Austria, which first appeared with Leupold der Wurmprant in 1194, authentically traced from Helmwig Wurmbrand von Salloder (near Gloggnitz, District of Neunkirchen, Lower Austria) in 1322 and his brother Heinrich Wurmbrand; "Erbküchenmeister" Hereditary Grand Master of the Kitchens in the Duchy of Styria 8 Jan 1578; inherited the Lordship of Reitenau and joined the arms of Zebingen circa 1580 through the marriage of Matthias I (✝ 1601) to Sybilla van Zebingen (the two lines below descend from sons of this marriage); Baron in Austria and Hereditary Austrian Territory, Prague 17 Dec 1607 (for the brothers Ehrenreich, Friedrich, Rudolf and Matthias and their cousins Melchior and Wolfgang Leonhard Wurmbrand); Lord in Lower Austria 1607; Hungarian Indigenat 18 Jan 1682; Hungarian Count (confirmed in Hereditary States of Austria 20 May), Vienna 21 March 1682; Count of the Holy Empire with the qualification of "Hoch and Wohlgeboren", Vienna 31 Aug 1701, confirmed 2 May

1709; received in to the Franconian College of Counts of the Holy Empire (ad personam) 24 May 1726; Bohemian Incolat 18 Sept 1748; received the qualification of "Erlaucht" (primogeniture) by the German Diet 13 Feb 1829; recognised in Austria 9 Oct 1829; Lord in Bohemia, Moravia and Silesia 6 April 1836; Hereditary Member of the Austrian "Reichsrate" 26 Feb 1912.

Members of the family bear the title of Count or Countess von Wurmbrand-Stuppach with the qualification of Illustrious Highness for the Head of the Family only.

Ernst **GUNDACCAR** Maria Rudolf, **COUNT (GRAF) VON WURMBRAND-STUPPACH**, Baron von Steyersberg, Stickelberg, Reitenau and Neuhaus, *b* at Wiener Neustadt 1 June 1946, *succ* his kinsman, Degenhart, Count von Wurmbrand-Stuppach (*b* 17 July 1893; ✠ 12 Nov 1965 - see below), son of Paul, Count von Wurmbrand-Stuppach (*b* 24 June 1891; ✠ 7 Sept 1962) and Donna Bianca Massimo of the Princes di Roviano (*b* 16 April 1906; *m* 8 Feb 1943 ✠ 22 Jan 1999); *m* at Schwarzau am Steinfeld 12 April 1969, Elisabeth (*b* at Aspang 18 July 1947), dau of Gottfried Kahofer and Maria Holzer.

[*Frohsdorf, 2821 Lanzenkirchen, Lower Austria*].

Sons and Daughter

1. Countess Maria de las *Mercedes* Bianca, *b* at Neunkirchen, Lower Austria 18 Aug 1969.
[*Frohsdorf, 2821 Lanzenkirchen, Lower Austria*].
2. *Helmwig* Paul Ernst, Hereditary Count (Erbgraf) von Wurmbrand-Stuppach, *b* at Neunkirchen 23 Dec 1970.
[*Frohsdorf, 2821 Lanzenkirchen, Lower Austria*].
3. Count *Gundaccar* Ernst Robert, *b* at Neunkirchen 21 Dec 1977.
[*Frohsdorf, 2821 Lanzenkirchen, Lower Austria*].
4. Count *Paul* Rüdiger Friedrich, *b* at Neunkirchen 31 Dec 1984.

Brothers of Great-Grandfather

Issue of Heinrich Gundaccar, Count von Wurmbrand-Stuppach (*b* 30 May 1762; ✠ 21 April 1847) and his second wife, Baroness Sidonie von Ledebur-Wicheln (*b* 12 Oct 1774; *m* 7 April 1801; ✠ 28 April 1833), having had issue, among whom,

Sons

1. *Ernst,* Hereditary Count (Erbgraf) von Wurmbrand-Stuppach, *b* at Vienna 12 March 1804; ✠ at Schwarzau 9 Dec 1846, Imp and Royal Chamberlain, Major Austrian Army; *m* at Vienna 25 Sept

1834, Countess Rose (*b* at Soromberke, Hungary 18 Oct 1818; ✝ at Golssen, Lusatia 30 June 1890; *m* 2ndly 1 Nov 1851, Friedrich, 1st Prince zu Solm-Baruth), dau of Franz, Count Teleki de Szék and Baroness Elise Banffyde Losoncz, and had issue, among whom,

    1.**Ferdinand, Count von Wurmbrand-Stuppach,** etc, *b* at Saromberke, Transylvania 23 July 1835; ✝ at Pürkersdorf 22 May 1896; *m* 21 Oct 1861 (*m* diss by div 1876), Countess Gabrielle (*b* 20 Feb 1836; ✝ at Pöchlarn an der Donau 8 Aug 1904; *m* 1stly Emeric, Baron Redl von Rottenhausen who ✝ ...), Proprietor of Thalheim and Rassny, Dame Star Cross Order, dau of Marc-Laurent, Comte de Bussy-Mignot and Katherine Buss von Bartenstein, and had issue, among whom,

        1.**Wilhelm** Ernst Maria Friedrich Gundaccar, **Count von Wurmbrand-Stuppach,** etc, *b* at Wels 6 May 1862; ✝ nr Wartmannstetten 7 Dec 1927, Proprieter of Steyersberg, etc, Imp and Royal Chamberlain and Privy Counsellor, Kt Sovereign Military Order of Malta, Major Austrian Army; *m* at Vienna 27 May 1891, Margarethe (*b* at Vienna 25 Nov 1872; ✝ at Prague 19 May 1957), dau of Adolf, Ritter von Schenk and Johanna von Heiligenstädt, and had issue, among whom,

            1.**Degenhart** Adolf Gundaccar Maria, **Count von Wurmbrand-Stuppach,** etc, *b* at Krummnussbaum 17 July 1893; ✝ at Vienna 12 Nov 1965, Proprietor of Steyersberg and Stickelberg, 1st Lt Austrian Army; *m* 1stly at Paris 15 May 1926 (*m* diss by div 1936), Lawton Filer (*b* at Salt Lake City, Utah, USA 1 March 1903; she *m* 2ndly at Reno, Nevada, USA, ... Walter). He *m* 2ndly in 1956 (*m* diss by div), Florence Marly [*15 Woodgate Court, Burlingame, CA 94010, USA*] (*b* at ..., ...). He *m* 3rdly at Reno, Nevada ...., Juliana [*533 Moreno Avenue, Los Angeles CA 90049, USA; Schloß Steyersberg, 2831 Warth, Lower Austria*] (*b* at ...), and had issue by his first wife,

                1. Countess Leonora (*Lori*) Huberta Maria, *b* at New York 11 April 1927; *m* 1stly at San Francisco 1947 (*m* diss

by div at San Francisco), Robert Miller,
Lawyer. She m 2ndly at London 21 Dec
1965, Thomas-Alfred Wertheimer, Edler
von Wertheimstein, Capt British
Cavalry (b at Vienna 24 Feb 1922).
[*Schlos Steyersberg, 2831 Warth, Lower
Austria; Largo Passos Vella 12, Cascais,
Cascais, Portugal; 18 rue du Général Appert,
75116 Paris, France*].

2. Count *Ferdinand* Heinrich August Gaspard Eduard Joseph, b at
Vienna 15 Oct 1807; ✠ at Ischl 25 May 1886, Imp and Royal
Chamberlain and Privy Counsellor, Maj.-Gen. Austrian Army;
m 1stly at Vienna 29 Oct 1833, Countess Maria-Aloysia (b at
Ödenburg, Sopron 21 Dec 1807; ✠ 3 March 1842), Dame Star Cross
Order, dau of Ludwig, Count Széchényi de Sárvár-Felsövidék and
Countess Aloysia von Clam-Gallas. He m 2ndly at Vienna 16 July
1846, Countess Alexandra (b 8 July 1816; ✠ at Salzburg 5 Dec 1894),
Dame Star Cross Order, dau of Franz Seraphin, Count Amadée de
Várkony and Countess Josepha von Payersberg, and had issue, among
whom from his first wife,

1.Count *Heinrich* Gundaccar Franz von Paula Alois
Ferdinand, b at Prestitz 5 Dec 1834; ✠ at Graz 4 March 1887,
Imp and Royal Chamberlain, Capt Austrian Army, Proprietor
of Ankenstein; m at Vienna 17 March 1862, Countess Eugenie
(b at Szárvás 11 Feb 1841; ✠ at Graz 4 May 1885), Dame Star
Cross Order, dau of Karl, Count von Schönborn-Buchheim
and Countess Anna Bolza, and had issue, among whom,

1. Count *Friedrich* Karl Heinrich Eugen, b at Graz 22
Feb 1865; ✠ at Vienna 1 Feb 1938, Col. Austrian
Dragoons, Gd Master of the Household of Archduchess
Maria Annunziata; m at Prague 14 June 1892, Baroness
Oktavia (b at Crakau 13 Nov 1864; ✠ at Vienna 28
March 1951), dau of Joseph, Baron von Mensshengen
and Adelheid (Adele) von Merkl, and had issue,

1. Count *Friedrich* Karl Gundaker Maria, b at
Kolomea 6 March 1904; ✠ at Vienna 24 June
1997; m 1stly at Vienna 14 April 1929 (m diss
by div at Vienna 3 March 1938), Claire Stevens
[*Via Terza Armata, 34135 Trieste, Italy*]
(b ...; she m 2ndly, 1944, Dario Doria). He m
2ndly at Saltsjöbaden, nr Stockholm 3 Aug 1939

(*m* diss by div 1945), Baroness Mignon (*b* at
Vienna 10 Nov 1917; ✠ at Paris 28 Nov 1958),
dau of Max, Baron von Berg, Proprietor of
Röjtök, Bánfálu and Palást in Hungary and
Hedwig Thyssen. He *m* 3rdly Marianne (*b* at
Prague 13 Sept 1919; *m* 1stly, Bela Kossuth de
Udvard et Kossut; that *m* diss by div), dau of
Gyula Hirmann and Marianne Polonyi, and had
issue from his first wife among whom,
[*Mommsen Gasse6, 1040 Vienna, Austria*].

> 1. Count Johann *Friedrich,* *b* at Vienna
> 20 July 1931; ✠ at Arezzo 6 Aug 1993;
> *m* 1957, Adriana Colle (*b* at .....), and
> has issue,
> [*Il Mulino di Tavernelle, 52031
> Anghiari, Prov. Arezzo, Italy*].
>
>> 1. Countess *Giovanna,* *b* at
>> Cortina d'Ampezzo 5 Dec 1957.
>> [*Il Mulino di Tavernelle, 52031
>> Anghiari, Prov. Arezzo Italy*].
>> 2. Count Federico Giovanni,
>> *b* at Paris 22 Oct 1964.
>> [*Il Mulino di Tavernelle, 52031
>> Anghiari, Prov. Arezzo, Italy*].

2. Count *Ferdinand,* *b* at Pressburg 12 April 1879;
✠ at Vienna 20 Dec 1933, Imp and Royal Chamberlain;
m at Vienna 9 March 1909 (*m* diss by div at Vienna 20
Jan 1918), May (*b* at Napajedl 9 March 1885; ✠ at
Monte Carlo, Monaco Oct 1981), dau of Aristides
Baltazzi and Countess Maria Theresia von Stockau,
and had issue,

> 1. Countess *Maria* Anna Paula Ferdinandine,
> *b* at Vienna 3 Feb 1914; *m* at New York 20 Feb
> 1934 (*m* diss by div at 1935 and annulled at
> New York 20 Oct 1941), Clendenine Ryan (*b* at
> New York 1905; ✠ 12 Sept 1957), Businessman.
> She *m* 2ndly at Pressburg 19 Nov 1935 (*m* diss
> by div 21 Dec 1937), Franz de Paula (Paul),
> Count Pálffy von Erdöd (*b* at Vienna 12 Feb
> 1890; ✠ at Munich 11 Oct 1968), Proprietor of
> Pudmerice in Slovakia, 1st Lt Hungarian Army.

She *m* 3rdly at Budapest 5 March 1938 (*m* diss
by div Aug 1944), Thomas, Count Esterházy
de Galántha (*b* at Totis, Komorn 25 Dec 1901;
✣ at Schruns, Vorarlberg 6 Dec 1964). She *m*
4thly at Ödenburg 20 Sept 1944 (*m* diss by div
at Vienna 14 Oct 1949), Sigismund (Zsiga),
Count von Berchtold, Baron von and zu
Ugarschütz, Fratting and Pullitz (*b* at Buchlau,
Mähren 14 April 1900; ✣ at Vienna 20 July
1979), Dr of Agr. She *m* 5thly at Chicago 1949
(*m* diss by div at Mexico 1951), William Deering
Davis (*b* at Chicago ..; ....). She *m* 6thly at
London 12 June 1954 (civ) and at Rome 11 Jan
1958 (relig) (*m* diss by div), Arpád Plesch (*b* at
Budapest 25 March 1889; ✣ at London 16 Nov
1974), former Hungarian Consul.
[*Villa Leonina, 06310 Beaulieu-sur-Mer, Alpes
Maritimes, France*].

———◆◆◆———

THE MOST VENERABLE ORDER OF
THE HOSPITAL OF ST JOHN OF JERUSALEM
(ORDER OF ST JOHN)

This institution is a Royal Order of Chivalry, by Charter of Queen
Victoria in 1888. But its traditions go back to Jerusalem in the late
eleventh century. The Hospitallers were recognised as an Order by
Pope Paschal II in 1113. It has two major charitable Foundations,
the St John Ambulance (Association founded in 1877) and the St
John Eye Hospital in Jerusalem (founded in 1882).

   With the Catholic Sovereign Military Hospitaller Order of Saint
John of Jerusalem, of Rhodes and of Malta (see: Order of Malta), the
four non-Catholic Orders of St John (Germany: Johanniterorden;
Dutch: Johanniter Order; Swedish: Johanniterorde and the
Venerable Order) provide a common devotion to the lordship of the
sick and the poor and collaborate mutually in addition to independent
work. The Venerable Order and its three non-Catholic associates are
linked through the Alliance of the Orders of St John and are
distinguished from all other Orders by being Orders of Chivalry,
recognised as legitimate by the Sovereigns of the States in which
they were founded and in the case of the Johnaniterorder in Germany,
by the Federal German Republic, and by their Christian Faith.

The Most Venerable Order of the Hospital of St John of Jerusalem has eight priories, two Commanderies and over 30 St John National Councils throughout the English-speaking world.

HM **QUEEN ELIZABETH II** Alexandra Mary **QUEEN OF THE UNITED KINGDOM OF GREAT BRITAIN AND NORTHERN IRELAND**... *etc*, **SOVEREIGN HEAD**, (*see* - Great Britain and Northern Ireland)
[*Buckingham Palace, London, SW1A 1AA*].

Grand Prior, HRH Prince *Richard* Alexander Walter George, 2nd Duke of Gloucester... *etc*, (*see* - Great Britain and Northern Ireland)
[*Kensington Palace, London, W8 4PU*]

Commander-in-Chief (Nursing) St John Ambulance: [*Vacant*]; **Commander-in-Chief (Ambulance and Nursing Cadets)**: HRH The Princess Royal... *etc*; **Grand President (St John Ambulance)**: [*Vacant*]; **Deputy Commander-in-Chief (Nursing) St John Ambulance**: HRH Princess Alice, Duchess of Gloucester... *etc*; **Commandant St John Ambulance in Wales**: HRH The Duchess of Gloucester... *etc*.
(*For each see* - Great Britain and Northern Ireland).

Lord Prior: Eric L Barry; **Prelate**: The Rt Rev J Waine; **Deputy Lord Prior**: Professor A R Mellows; **Sub Prior**: Mr J A Strachan

Priory for England and the Islands: *Prior*, The Lord Slynn of Hadley (*Chief Commander and Chancellor*); Sir John Wheeler: **Priory for Scotland**: *Prior*, Colonel James Stirling of Garden; *Chancellor*, Mr John A Ford: **Priory of Wales**: *Prior*, Captain Norman Lloyd-Edwards; *Chancellor*, Mr D Hugh Thomas: **Priory of South Africa**: *Prior and Chancellor*, Bishop Mvume Dandala: **Priory in New Zealand**: *Prior*, HE The Hon Dame Silvia Cartwright; *Chancellor*, Mr Neville Darrow: **Priory of Canada**: *Prior*, HE The Rt Hon Adrienne Clarkson; *Chancellor*, Mr Jeffery Gilmour: **Priory in Australia**: *Prior*, HE The Rt Rev Dr Peter John Hollingworth; *Chancellor*, Professor Villis Marshall: **Priory in the United States of America**: *Prior*, Mr John R Drexel IV; *Chancellor*, Dr Joseph Walsh: **Commandery in Western Australia**: *Knight Commander*, HE Lieutenant General John Sanderson AC: **Commandery of Ards in Northern Ireland**: *Knight Commander*, Mr David Kingan:

Secretariat: *Secretary General*, Sir Anthony Goodenough
[Priory House, 25 St John's Lane, London, EC1M 4PP]

———◆———

BAILIWICK OF BRANDENBURG
OF THE ORDER OF ST JOHN
(JOHANNITER ORDER)

The Bailiwick of Brandenburg of the Knightly Order of St. John of the Hospital at Jerusalem is that part of the Order of St John (Order of Malta) in Germany which accepted the Reformation of the Church in the 16th Century. It is known and referred to as the Order of St John and in the German language as the Johanniter Order.

The Order of St John was founded during the time of the First Crusade in the Year 1099 in Jerusalem. A hospital has existed there, operated by a Christian brotherhood, since at least 1050 A.D. The hospital and brotherhood was given a separate ecclesiastical existence by a Papal Bull of 1113 A.D. The lay fraternity serving the hospital became known as the Order of St John.

The Bailiwick of Brandenburg of the Order of St John in North-Eastern Germany achieved special recognition within the overall Order of St John by the Accord of Heimbach in 1382. From the Bailiwick of Brandenburg evolved this distinct branch of the Order of St John. The *Treaty of Osnabruck*, which was concluded on 24 October 1648, was part of the Peace of Westphalia and ended the Thirty Years War. That treaty confirmed and recognized "the Elector of Brandenburg" as Patron" ... "of the Order of St. John of Jerusalem". This treaty effectively recognized the Bailiwick of Brandenburg, and was agreed to by every State of Europe as a party, Turkey alone excepted. The Bailiwick of Brandenburg of the Order of St John historically drew its knights from the traditional landed families of Northern and Central Europe which enjoyed tenure of land under the feudal system by right of military service. In the 18th Century, over 70% of the knights of the Bailiwick of Brandenburg were Prussian military officers. The remainder were chiefly government officials, courtiers, or land owners. Until 1948 the Order had a requirement of nobility for members.

Prior to the Reformation, Knights in the Bailiwick, like other knights of St John, were required to be unmarried. Although the Elector of Brandenburg converted to Lutheranism in 1538, the Herrenmeister (master of the Knights) of that time remained Roman Catholic. However, that Herrenmeister did not resist the conversion of the Bailiwick of Brandenburg to Protestantism. Generally after 1545 in areas of Germany in which the Commander married, that Commandery had become Protestant. By 1624, there were no remaining Roman Catholic knights under the Herrenmeister in the Bailiwick of Brandenburg and it has remained exclusively Protestant.

Being the elite of Protestant Christianity on the European continent, the Knights of St John of the Bailiwick of Brandenburg were not large in number prior to the 19th Century. In the 268 years from 1545 until 1812, there were only a total of 784 Knights entering the Bailiwick of Brandenburg, all of whom were Knights of Justice. During the period 1812 to 1852, the Bailiwick of Brandenburg went into abeyance, being temporarily succeeded by the secular Prussian Royal Order of St John. There was a total of over 1800 royal appointments from 1812 to 1852 to the Prussian Royal Order of St John. However, the suspension of the Bailiwick was abrogated in 1852 and the Bailiwick was re-established by the Crown of Prussia with the few surviving knights of the pre-1812 original foundation. The 1859 Roll of the Bailiwick listed 1488 Knights, of whom 884 were on the roll by virtue of being awarded membership in the Royal Prussian Order of St. John from 1812 to 1852. From 1852 to 1931, a total of 10,398 Knights were accepted into the Order, with the Order having a membership of 4,751 in 1931. At the outbreak of the Second World War, members were prohibited from wearing their badge on German military uniforms and a number of members of the order were martyred for their involvement in the attempt to assassinate Hitler. The Dutch and Swedish Bailiwick of Brandenburg members formed independent Orders of St John under the protection of their respective sovereigns after the Second World War. In 1953 the membership was down to approximately 2,175 due to war time casualties, persecution of the members of the Bailiwick by the Nazis, loss of the Dutch and Swedish members, and postwar dislocations. After 1953, the membership remained static for twenty years. However, in 2000 there were 3,488 knights. The purpose of the Order of St John and its goal throughout its 900 year history has been to defend the Christian faith, to care for the sick, and to help the poor.

The Order is commanded by the Herrenmeister (Master of the Knights) with the support of the Chapter of the Order and the Government of the Order. The Chapter, composed of the Commanders representing the regional Associations, elects the Herrenmeister. The seat of the Order is in Berlin, where the institutions of the Order have their headquarters.

The regional commanderies in Germany generally correspond to today's federal German states. There are additional German commanderies whose members come from a number of other historic provincial associations.

Five non-German commanderies are located in Finland, France, Austria, Switzerland and Hungary. Knights who reside abroad permanently or for extended periods are organized directly in a separate Balley Commandery. The Balley Commandery includes subcommanderies in the United States of America, in Canada, in South Africa, in Namibia and in Belgium.

The Chapter supervises 20 hospitals, 7 day clinics, 31 nursing homes. It also jointly supervises two houses with the Sovereign Military Order of Malta.

HRH WILHELM-KARL Adalbert Erich Detloff **PRINCE OF PRUSSIA**... etc, **PROTECTOR**, elected 1999, *(see - Prussia)* [*Einbeckerstrasse in 21, 37603 Holzminden, Germany*]

[Note: The title of "Protector", although not currently established by the Order's statutes, is an honour which was granted to Prince Wilhelm-Karl after his retirement from more than forty years as Herrenmeister. He is the first Protector of the Order since the death on 4 June 1941 of Wilhelm II, Emperor of Germany.]

Herrenmeister, HRH Prince Dr Oskar Hans Karl Michael of Prussia, 37th Master of the Knights (Herrenmeister), *(see - Prussia)* [*Lietzenscufer 94, 14057 Berlin, Germany*].

The Chapter: **The Herrenmeister**: [*see above*]; **Governor**: Count Wilhelm von Schwerin von Schwanenfeld; **Chancellor**: Hans-Dieter von Meibom; **Treasurer**: Wilko H Börner; **General Secretary**: Baron Egon von Knobelsdorff; **Head of Aid Association**: Baron Christoph von Hammerstein-Gesmold; **President Rescue Service**: Count Wilhelm von Schwerin von Schwanenfeld; **Head of Sisterhood**: Andrea Trenner; **23 Governing Commanders**; **Captain of the Order**: Kolja von Bismarck.
Secretariat: General Secretary, Baron Egon von Knobelsdorff [*Lietzenseeufer 94, 14057 Berlin, Germany*]

ORDER OF ST JOHN IN THE NETHERLANDS
(JOHANNITER ORDE IN NEDERLAND)

The full name of the Order is *Johanniter Orde in Nederland, Nederlandse tak van de aloude Orde van het Hospitaal van Sint Jan te Jeruzalem* (Order of St. John in the Netherlands, Dutch branch of the ancient Order of the Hospital of St. John of Jerusalem). The Order's traditions go back to Jerusalem into the late eleventh century, when a hospital was founded dedicated to Saint John the Baptist, by 1080. The hospital developed into a Hospitaller Order for the care of the sick and poor, before the capture of Jerusalem in 1099. The Order was recognised by Pope Paschal II in 1113.
    The Hospitallers were mentioned in the Netherlands for

the first time in 1122 in Utrecht as *Jerosolimitani*. The Bailiwick of
Utrecht of the Hospitaller Order of St John had from that time
hospitals and commanderies all over the Netherlands. The Bailiwick
was part of the German Langue. After the Reformation the Dutch
Johanniter Knights came under the Order s Bailiwick of
Brandenburg, after this Bailiwick became protestant *(c.1550)*.

On the instigation of HRH Prince Hendrik of the
Netherlands, consort of HM Queen Wilhelmina, a Dutch
Commandery of the Bailiwick of Brandenburg was created called
Commenderij Nederland of which all Dutch Knights became part. It
was instituted by Royal Decree of 30 April 1909.

After the World War II the Dutch branch became
independent of the Bailiwick of Brandenburg by Royal Decree of 5
March 1946.

The Order is ruled by the Chapter, headed by the
Landcommandeur. Membership of the Order is limited to the
Protestant Dutch nobility and is divided into three classes: Honorary
Knights and Dames of the Chapter, Knights and Dames of Justice
and Knights and Dames of Grace.

The Order continues its ancient charitable and hospitaller
mission supporting several hospitals and hospices. In 1974 the Order
founded together with the Knightly Teutonic Order, Bailiwick of
Utrecht, a foundation called *Stichting Werken van de Johanniter Orde in
Nederland en der Ridderlijke Duitsche Orde, Balije van Utrecht*. The
activities of the Johanniter volunteers are coordinated within this
foundation. There is a close cooperation with the Dutch branch of
the Sovereign Military Order of Malta. A joint Association for young
aspirant Johanniter and Maltese Knights and Dames is also active.
The Order is a member of the International Alliance of the Orders
of St. John.

HM QUEEN BEATRIX Wilhelmina Armgard of **THE
NETHERLANDS**, Princess of Oranje-Nassau, Princess of Lippe-
Biesterfeld ...*etc*, **COMMANDER OF HONOUR**, *(see - The
Netherlands)*
[*Paleis Huis ten Bosch, Bezuidenhoutseweg 10, 2594 AV, The Hague,
The Netherlands*].

Knight of Justice, HRH Prince *Willem-Alexander* Claus Georg
Ferdinand, Crown Prince of The Netherlands, Prince of Orange,
Prince of Oranje-Nassau, Jonkheer van Amsberg.
[*Noordeinde 66, 2514 GL The Hague, The Netherlands*].

The Chapter: The Landcommmander: HRH Prince Bernhard of
the Netherlands, Prince of Lippe- Biesterfeld ...*etc*; **The Coadjutor:**

Frits C.C. Baron van Tuyll van Serooskerken: **The Commander:**
Elsabé M Kalsbeek-Baroness Schimmelpenninck van der Oye, MA;
The First Hospitaller: Jonkvrouwe Corinne G Elias; **The Second
Hospitaller:** Prof. Jonkheer Juriy W Wladimiroff; **The Chancellor:**
Jonkheer J. Pieter de Savornin Lohman, LLD; **The Treasurer:**
Jonkheer Paul F. de Ranitz; **The First Dame of the Chapter:**
Matthea J.M.M. Diepenhorst-née Jonkvrouwe Sandberg tot
Essenburg; **The Second Dame of the Chapter:** C.C. Elisabeth
Kolff-née Jonkvrouwe Gevers Deynoot; **The Knight of the Chapter:**
Jonkheer Pieter P de Savornin Lohman; **Honorary Knigts and
Dames of the Chapter:** Jonkheer Cees C van Lidth de Jeude van
de Souburgen; Digna van den Wall Bake-née Jonkvrouwe Snouck
Hurgronje; Prof. Jonkheer Volker H. de Villeneuve; Jonkheer P
Huibert G Nahuys, LLD; Jonkheer Pieter A C Beelaerts van Blokland,
MA; Gub Baron Krayenhoff; J Madeleine C Nagtzaam-née
Jonkvrouwe van Valkenburg; Jonkheer Henk J van der Does, LLD;
Madeline M Baroness van Heemstra-née Jonkvrouwe de Brauw;
Jonkheer Klaus H A von Chrismar, LLD; Antoinette van Walré de
Bordes-née Jonkvrouwe Flugi van Aspermont; W J H (Pim) Count
van Limburg Stirum, LLD.
Chancery: *Secretary General:* Fernand W. Th. Pahud de Mortanges,
LLD.
[*Lange Voorhout 48, 2514 EG Den Haag, The Netherlands*]

THE ORDER OF ST JOHN IN SWEDEN
(JOHANNITERORDEN I SVERIGE)

The full name of the Order is *Johanniterorden i Sverige*. The Order of
St. John in Sweden traces it s origin from the establishment of a
hospital in the Holy Land in the 11th century. Pope Paschall II
eventually transferred the institution into a Religious Order in 1113.
The Bailey Brandenburg instituted in the 12th century in
Scandinavia the priory Dacia, which in Sweden provided
humanitarian aid from three monasteries until the reformation took
place in the beginning of the 15th century. The Bailey Brandenburg
however continued after the reformation its activity uninterruptedly
and through all the years Swedish subjects became members of the
Order even though the Order was not active in Sweden.

Under the guidance of HM King Gustaf V, King of Sweden,
the Order was re-established in 1920 as a priory of Bailey
Brandenburg. Following an agreement between the Bailey

Barndenburg and the Swedish priory an independent Swedish Order (Johanniterorden i Sverige) was established in 1945.

The Order provides charity work mainly as contribution to individuals, supporting organisations and for research.

HM KING CARL XVI GUSTAF, Folke Hubertus, **KING OF SWEDEN**... etc, **HIGH PROTECTOR**, *(see - Sweden)*
[Royal Palace, 11130 Stockholm, Sweden].
Dame and First Honorary Member: HM Queen Silvia Renate of Sweden

Commander: Associate Prof. Thomas Ihre; **Deputy Commander**: Count Gustaf Lagerbjelke; **Chaplain**: Prof. Carl Reinhold Bråkenhielm; **Chancellor**: Baron Otto von Schwerin; **Hospitaller**: Mr Björn Lilliehöök.
Chancellery: Chancellor, Baron Otto von Schwerin
[Riddarhuset, Box 2022, S-103 11 Stockholm, Sweden]

SOVEREIGN MILITARY HOSPITALLER ORDER OF MALTA
(ORDER OF MALTA)

This unique institution, whose full name is the "Sovereign Military Hospitaller Order of Saint John of Jerusalem, of Rhodes and of Malta", was established as a hospital for pilgrims under the authority of the Benedictine Abbot of Santa Maria Latina in Jerusalem, *ca* 1080. By Pope Paschal II's Bull *Pie Postulatio Voluntatis* of 15 Feb 1113, it was transformed into a Religious Order, under the rule of Saint Augustine, dedicated to Saint John the Baptist and to service to the Poor and Sick. Between 1126 and 1140 it assumed a military function, formalised in a fourth addition to the monastic vows "to defend the Holy Sepulchre to the last drop of blood and fight the unfaithful wherever they be". By the end of the 12th century, Langues, or national groups, had been established in France, Spain (divided into two 1462), Italy, Germany, Provence, Auvergne and England, with one of the great officers drawn from each. The Mastership of the Order was the oldest office, established even before the capture of Jerusalem in 1099; by the late 15th century this title had become Grand Master. The Order founded Grand Priories, Priories and Commanderies across Europe and, by 1309, had established its sovereign rule over the Island of Rhodes. At the same time its properties were considerably enlarged by the addition of most of the benefices of the Templar Order, by a Papal Bull of 2 May 1312. In 1489 it was enlarged further by the addition of the properties of the Order of Saint Lazarus and the Canons of the Holy Sepulchre, whose Magisteries were merged with the Magistery of Saint John. In 1523 the Order lost possession of Rhodes but not its sovereign character, recovering territorial sovereignty of the Islands of Malta, Gozo and Comino by the grant of the Emperor Charles V, as a feudatory of the Kingdom of Sicily, on 24 March 1530. Possession of the Maltese islands lost to France 11 June 1798. Czar Paul I was elected *de facto* Grand Master in breach of Canon Law by a portion of the Knights on 7 Nov 1798, but following his death 23/4 March 1801, Tsar Alexander I acknowledged the government of the Order in Messina. On 25 April 1803 the Council in St Petersburg formally resigned its powers to the new Grand Master, Giovanni-Battista Tommasi (who had held the post since 9 Feb 1803). The properties of the two Russian Grand Priories founded by Czar Paul were suppressed 2 Dec 1811 and no further admissions were made after that date. Following the death of Tommasi in 1805, he was *succ* by a Lietenant of the Grand Magistery, Innico Guevara-Suardo, elected 15 June 1805 (recognized by the Russian Grand Priories 5 April 1806), and the Order continued to be governed by Lieutenants until the election of Giovanni-Battista Ceschi a Santa Croce in 1871. The office of Grand Master was revived for Ceschi by Apostolic Brief 28 March 1879, *cf* in the Bull *Inclytum antiquitate originis* of 12 June 1888. Since 1630 the Grand Master has enjoyed at the Vatican the honours of Cardinal, with the title Eminence (but not membership of the Sacred College), and was elevated to the rank of Reichsfürst (Prince of the Holy Roman Empire) in 1607, *cf* in 1620, and Austrian Prince with the qualification of Serene Highness by grant of 27 Dec 1880, *cf* 1889 and 1905. Since the early 17th century these titles were combined into "Most Eminent Highness" which was recognized by Italian Royal Decree of 1927. The Grand Master is elected for life from among the professed Knights of Justice who have entered the Order as a Knight of Honour and Devotion by the Council Complete of State, composed of the professed Bailiffs, and representatives of the Grand Priories and National Associations. The Order is governed by the Sovereign Council, presided over by the Grand Master with the four Great-Officers - Grand Commander, Grand Chancellor, Hospitaller and Receiver of the Common Treasure - four councillors and two supplementary councillors. The Grand Chancellor, assisted by a Councillor for Special Affairs, Secretaries of Foreign Affairs, Internal Affairs and Communications administers the Order. Other Officers include the Master of Ceremonies, the Superintendant of Post and Money, and the State Advocate. There is a seven member Chamber of Accounts, a Juridical Council and Tribunals of First Instance and of Appeal, a committee of Special Consultants to the Sovereign Council, and three Heraldic Councillors. The Holy See is represented by a Cardinal Patron, and there is a Prelate of the Order. There are three Italian Grand Priories - Rome, Lombardy and Venice, and Naples and Sicily, Grand Priories of Bohemia, Austria and England, and Sub-Priories of Saint Michael (Germany), Saint Oliver Plunkett (Ireland), and Saint George and Saint James (Spain). There are 40 National Associations including: Argentinian, Australian, Belgian, Brazilian-Rio de Janeiro, Brazilian-Meridional-São Paulo, Brazilian-Septentrional, British, Canadian, Chilean, Colombian, Cuban, Dominican, Salvadoran, Equadorian, French, German, Guatemalan, Honduran, Hungarian, Irish, Italian, Lebanese, Maltese, Mexican, Monegasque, Nicaraguan, Netherlandish, Peruvian, Philippine, Polish, Portuguese, Romanian, Scandinavian, Spanish, Swiss, Uruguayan, US-American, US-Western, US-Federal, Venezuelan and a Senegalese National Committee. The Order exchanges diplomatic relations with 80 sovereign states, and has postal agreements with 48 states. It sends Delegations to the International Organizations at Geneva, and UNESCO, and is an Observer at the UN. Membership in the Order is limited exclusively to Roman Catholics in good standing and is divided into three classes: (1) Professed, (2) Obedience (prior to 8 Nov 1997 limited to Knights who had submitted proofs of Nobility, subsequently open to all Knights and Dames), (3) Honour - of which there are six divisions: Honour and Devotion (proof of nobility), Conventual Chaplains "ad honorem", Grace and Devotion (proof of nobility), Chaplains of Magistral Obedience, Magistral Grace and Donat. The Highest Rank, Bailiff, is confined to the 1st and 2nd Class and the 1st Division of the 3rd Class. The ranks of Grand Cross and Knight exist in all three classes. Grand Cross with Riband only in the 3rd and 5th divisions of the 3rd Class. Commanderies may exist in all three classes. Ladies are eligible for membership of the 2nd and 3rd class. The Order also has the Order of Merit "Pro Merito Melitense", with a Military and Civil division, open also to non-Catholic men and women, of which the rank of Collar is given exclusively to Heads of State, and of which there are classes of Grand Cross (with gold or silver star), Grand Officer, Commander, Officer and Knight or Dame. The SMHOM has signed several agreements with the Alliance of Orders of Saint John, comprising all the recognized Orders of Saint John (the British Most Venerable Order of St John, and the German, Dutch and Swedish Kt of St John of Jerusalems).

IIMDmII FRÀ ANDREW Willoughby Ninian BERTIE, 78TH PRINCE and GRAND MASTER, elected 8 April 1988, b at London 15 May 1929, eldest son of the Hon James Bertie of the Earls of Lindsey and Abingdon and Lady Jean Crichton-Stuart of the Marquesses of Bute, admitted as a Kt of Hon and Dev 14 May 1956, Kt of Obedience 31 March 1968, Novice Kt of Justice 7 Feb 1975, Professed Kt of Justice 20 May 1981, Kt of the Golden Fleece

(Habsburg 1993), Kt of the Annunziata (Savoy 1988, with Star of Sts Maurice and Lazarus), Kt of St Andrew (Romanov, with Stars of St Alexander Nevsky, the White Eagle, St Ann and St Stanislas 1994), Kt of St Januarius (Bourbon-Two Sicilies 1993), Bailiff Gd Cross with Collar Constantinian Order of St George (Bourbon-Two Sicilies 1988), Gd Cross of White Eagle (Karageorgevich 1989), Gd Cross Star of Karageorgevich (1997), Gd Cross of St Charles (Monaco 1997), Gd Cordon of Ouissam Al Arch (Morocco 1995), Gd Cross Legion of Honour (France 1989), Gd Cross of Merit (Italy 1990), Collar of the Order of the Liberator (Venezuela 1988), Collar of Andrés Bella (Venezuela 1995), Collar of Infante Dom Henry the Navigator (Portugal 1989), Collar of National Merit Order (Malta 1995), Collar of Order of Merit (Chile 1990), Collar of the Liberator San Martin (Argentina 1990), Gd Cross of Merit (Germany 1992), Collar of the Southern Cross (Brazil 1990), etc, Doctor (hc) Medicine and Surgery (Bologna 1992), Doctor (hc) Jurisprudence (Malta 1993), Doctor (hc) Humanities (Santo Domingo 1995), etc.
[*Palazzo Malta, 68 Via Condotti, 00187 Rome, Italy*].

Sovereign Council (Excellencies): **Grand Commander** - Ven Bailiff Frà Ludwig Hoffmann von Rumerstein. **Grand Chancellor** - Bailiff Gd Cross Obed Ambassador Count Carlo Marullo di Condojanni, Prince of Casalnuovo. **Grand Hospitaller** - Bailiff Gd Cross Obed Albrecht, Baron von Boeselager. **Receiver of the Common Treasure** - Bailiff Gd Cross Obed Gian Luca, Marchese Chiavari. **Councillors** - Ven Bailiff Frà Carl E Paar; Comm Frà Caro Arditi di Castelvetere; Cav. Frà Giacomo Dalla Torre de Tempio di Sanguinetto; Cav. Frà John Alexander MacPherson; Kt Obed Richard J Dunn; Kt ObedJean Pierre Mazery.

Grand Priors (Excellencies): **Rome** - Ven Bailiff Frà Franz von Lobstein. **Lombardy and Venice** - Frà Roggero Caccia Dominioni. **Naples and Sicily** - Frà Antonio Nesci. **Bohemia** - Frà Heinrich Schlik. **Austria** - Frà Wilhelm of Liechtenstein. **England** - Frà Matthew Festing.

ALMANACH

DE

GOTHA

2003
MMIII

186th Edition

(Volume I)

Diplomatic & Statistics
(Annuaire Diplomatique Et Statistique)

The Annual Diplomatic & Statistical

Record of Gotha Part I States

& The United States of America

ALBANIA
Republika e Shqipërisë

AREA – 11,099 sq. miles (28,748 sq. km). Neighbours: Montenegro (north), Kosovo and Macedonia (east), Greece (south)
POPULATION – 3,731,000 (1997 UN estimate). Muslim (70 per cent), Greek Orthodox (20 per cent), Roman Catholic (10 per cent). The language is Albanian.
CAPITAL – Tirana (population 244,153, 1990)
CURRENCY – Lek (Lk) of 100 qindarka
NATIONAL ANTHEM – Rreth flamurit të për bashkuar (The flag that united us in the struggle)
NATIONAL DAY – 28 November
NATIONAL FLAG – Black two-headed eagle on a field
LIFE EXPECTANCY (years) – male 70.9; female 76.7
POPULATION GROWTH RATE – 3.7 per cent (1999)
POPULATION DENSITY – 108 per sq. km (1999)
ENROLMENT (percentage of age group) – primary 100 per cent (1997); tertiary 12 per cent (1997)

HISTORY AND POLITICS

Albania was under Turkish suzerainty from 1468 until 1912, when independence was declared. After a period of unrest, a republic was declared in 1925 and in 1928 a monarchy. The King went into exile in 1939 when the country was occupied by the Italians; Albania was liberated in November 1944. Elections in 1945 resulted in a Communist-controlled Assembly; the King was deposed in absentia and republic declared in January 1946.

From 1946 to 1991 Albania was a one-party, Communist state. In March 1991 multiparty elections took place. Rioting broke out in January 1997 following the collapse of several pyramid investment schemes. Anti-government protests, taking the form of armed rebellion, spread throughout the country.

Following the abandonment of the Rambouillet peace talks on the future of Kosovo, NATO commenced air operations against Yugoslavia in March 1999. Yugoslavia responded by actively expelling hundreds of thousands of Kosovar Albanians, with the majority fleeing to Albania. In April 1999, Albania granted NATO unrestricted access to Albania's airspace, ports and military infrastructure. There were several incursions into Albanian territory by Serb troops. By mid-May 1999, over 400,000 Kosovar Albanians had taken refuge in Albania and over 10,000 NATO troops were stationed there. In June 1999 the refugees began returning home following the end of air operations and the entry of NATO forces into Kosovo. By the end of 1999, nearly all of the refugees had left Albania and the number of NATO troops stationed in the country had fallen to 2,000.

The most recent general election took place on 24 June and 8, 22 and 29 July 2001; resulted in the Socialist Party of Albania (SP) winning 70 seats and the Democratic Alliance Party (DAP) winning 36 seats in the 140 member People's Assembly.

HEAD OF STATE

President: Prof. Rexhep Mejdini, *elected by parliament* 24 July 1997.

COUNCIL OF MINISTERS *as at July 2002*

Prime Minister: Pandeli Majko (SP); **Deputy PM, Labour and Social Affairs:** Skender Gjinushi (SDP); **Agriculture and Food:** Agron Duka (SP); **Culture, Youth and Sport:** Agron Tato (SP); **Defence:** Luan Rama (SP); **Environment:** Lufter Xhuveli (AP); **Economic Co-operation and Trade:** Ermelinda Meksi (SP); **Education and Science:** Luan Memushi (SP); **Finance:** Kastriot Islami (SP); **Foreign Affairs:** Arta Dade (SP); **Health:** Mustafa Xhani (SP); **Interior:** Stefan Cipa (SP); **Justice:** Spiro Peci (HRUP); **Local Government and Decentralisation:** Ethem Ruka (SP); **Ministers of State:** Viktor Doda (SP) (*Industry and Energy*); Marko Bello (DAP) (*Integration*); Ndri Legisi (SP) (*Prevention of Corruption*); **Public Works and Tourism:** Fatmir Xhafa; **Transport:** Maqo Lakori (SP)

AP Agrarian Party; DAP Democratic Alliance Party; HRUP Human Rights Union Party; SP Socialist Party; SDP Social Democratic Party

---

ANDORRA
PRINCIPAT D'ANDORRA

AREA – 181 sq. miles (468 sq. km). Neighbours: Spain and France
POPULATION – 65,971 (1999); less then one-quarter of the population are native Andorrans. The official language is Catalan, but French and Spanish (Castilian) are also spoken. The established religion is Roman Catholicism
CAPITAL – Andorra la Vella (population, 21,189, 1999)
CURRENCY – Euro of 100 cents
NATIONAL ANTHEM – El gran Carlemany, mon pare (Great

Charlemagne, My father)
NATIONAL DAY – 8 September
NATIONAL FLAG – Three vertical bands, blue, yellow, red;
Andorran coat of arms frequently imposed on central (yellow) band
but not essential
POPULATION GROWTH RATE – 3.9 per cent (1999)
POPULATION DENSITY – 160 per sq. km (1999)
URBAN POPULATION – 93.0 per cent (2000 estimate)

HISTORY AND POLITICS

Andorra is a small, neutral principality formed by a treaty in 1278.
The first elections under the new constitution were held in
December 1993, and on 20 January 1994 the first sovereign
government of Andorra took office.

POLITICAL SYSTEM

Under a new constitution promulgated in May 1993, Andorra
became an independent, democratic parliamentary co-principality,
with sovereignty vested in the people rather than in the two co-
princes, as had previously been the case. The constitution enables
Andorra to establish an independent judiciary and to carry out its
own foreign policy, whilst its people may now join trade unions and
political parties. The two co-princes, the President of the French
Republic and the Spanish Bishop of Urgel, remain heads of state
but now only have the power to veto treaties with France and Spain
which affect the state's borders and security. The co-princes are
represented by Permanent Delegates of whom one is the French
Prefect of the Pyrénées Orientales department at Perpignan and
the other is the Spanish Vicar-General of the diocese of Urgel.

Andorra has a unicameral legislature of 28 members known
as the *Consell General de las Valls d Andorra* (Valleys of Andorra
General Council). Fourteen members are elected on a national list
basis and 14 in seven dual-member constituencies based on
Andorra's seven parishes. The Council appoints the head of the
executive government, who designates the members of his
government.

Permanent French Delegate: Frederic de Saint-Sernin
Permanent Episcopal Delegate: Nemsi Marqués Oste

EXECUTIVE COUNCIL *as at July 2002*

President: Marc Forné Molné; **Agriculture and the
Environment:** Olga Adellach Coma; **Chief de Cabinet:** Jordi
Guillamet Anton; **Economy:** Miquel Alvarez Marfany; **Education,
Youth and Sports:** Pere Cervós Cardona; **Finance:** Mireia Maestre

Cortadella; **Foreign Affairs:** Juli Minoves Triquell; **Health and Welfare:** Mònica Codina Tort; **Justice and Interior:** Jordi Visent Guitart; **Secretary-General:** Joaquima Sol Ordis; **Territorial Planning:** Jordi Serra Malleu; **Tourism and Culture:** Enric Pujal Areny

---

AUSTRALIA
THE COMMONWEALTH OF AUSTRALIA

AREA – 2,988,902 sq. miles (7,741,220 sq. km)

POPULATION – 19,603,500 (2001 estimate): 410,000 of Aboriginal and Torres Strait Islander origin (2001 estimate). The language is English

CAPITAL – Canberra, in the Australian Capital Territory (population, 313,900, 2001 estimate). It has been the seat of government since 1927

MAJOR CITIES – Adelaide (1,100,100); Brisbane (1,656,700); Hobart (194,400); Melbourne (3,522,000); Perth, including Fremantle (1,400,500); Sydney (4,140,800), 2001 estimates

CURRENCY – Australian dollar of 100 cents

NATIONAL ANTHEM – Advance Australia Fair

NATIONAL DAY – 26 January (Australia Day)

NATIONAL FLAG – The British Blue Ensign with five stars of the Southern Cross in the fly and the white Commonwealth Star of seven points beneath the Union Flag

LIFE EXPECTANCY (years) – male 76.6; female 82.0

POPULATION GROWTH RATE – 1.3 per cent (2001)

POPULATION DENSITY – 2.5 per sq. km (2001)

URBAN POPULATION – 84.7 per cent (2000 estimate)

Australia is a continent in the southern hemisphere. The highest point is Mt. Kosciusko (2,228m) and the lowest, Lake Eyre (-15m). Climatic conditions range from the alpine to the tropical. Two-thirds of the continent is arid or semi-arid although good rainfalls (over 800 mm annually) occur in the northern monsoonal belt and along the eastern and southern highland regions.

HISTORY AND POLITICS

Australia was discovered by Europeans in the 17th century. Its eastern coast was claimed by Capt. James Cook on behalf of Britain in 1770 and became a penal colony; Tasmania, Western Australia, South Australia, Victoria and Queensland were established as colonies between 1825 and 1859. The colonies were federated as the Commonwealth of Australia on January 1901, at which time Australia gained dominion status within the British Empire. Australia became independent within the British Commonwealth by the 1931 Statute of Westminister. Following a referendum in 1967, the Aboriginal population was granted full political rights. In 1986, the Australia Act was passed, which abolished the remaining legislative, executive and judicial links to the UK, while retaining the British monarch as head of state.

On 13 February 1998, the Constitutional Convention voted by 89 votes to 52 to sever constitutional links with the United Kingdom monarchy. A national referendum was held on the issue on 6 November 1999; the proposition to make Australia a republic was defeated, with 45.3 per cent voting in favour and 54.7 per cent against.

The general election on 10 November 2001 was won by the ruling Liberal Party-National Party Coalition.

POLITICAL SYSTEM

The government is that of a federal commonwealth within the Commonwealth, the executive power being vested in the Sovereign (through the Governor-General), assisted by a federal government. Under a constitution the powers of the federal government are defined, and residuary legislative power remains with the states. The right of a state to legislate on any matter is not abrogated except in connection with matters exclusively under federal control, but where a state law is inconsistent with a law of the Commonwealth the latter prevails to the extent of the inconsistency.

Parliament consists of Queen Elizabeth II, the Senate and the House of representatives. The constitution provides that the number of members of the House of Representatives shall be, as nearly as practicable, twice the number of senators. Members of the Senate are elected for six years by universal suffrage, half the members retiring every third year, except in the Australian Capital Territory and the Northern Territory, where members are elected for a three-year term. Each of the six states returns 12 senators, and the Australian Capital Territory and the Northern Territory two each. The House of Representatives, similarly elected for a maximum of three years, contains members proportionate to the population, with a minimum of five members for each state. There are now 148 members in the House of Representatives, including one member of the Northern Territory and two for the Australian Capital Territory.

The High Court exercises jurisdiction over all matters arising under the constitution, all matters arising between the states and between residents of different states, matters to which the Commonwealth of Australia is a party, matters arising under any treaty, and matters affecting foreign representatives in Australia.

The High Court also hears appeals from the Federal Court and from the Supreme Courts of states and territories.

The Federal Court of Australia has jurisdiction over important industrial, trade practices, intellectual property, administrative law, admiralty law and bankruptcy matters. It also acts as a court of appeal for decisions from the Australian Capital Territory Supreme Court and certain decisions of state Supreme Courts exercising federal jurisdiction. Each state has its own judicature of supreme, superior and minor courts for criminal and civil cases.

FEDERAL STRUCTURE

In the states, executive authority is vested in a Governor (appointed by the Crown), assisted by a Council of Ministers of Executive Council. Each state has a legislature comprising a Legislative Council and a Legislative Assembly or House of Assembly which are elected for four-year terms, except Queensland, which has a Legislative Assembly only.

The Northern Territory and Australian Capital Territory have a Legislative Assembly only.

STATES AND TERRITORIES

Area & Resident Population (sq. km)	Capital	Governor
Australian Capital Territory (ACT)		
2,349 / 322,600	Canberra	-
New South Wales (NSW)		
801,352 / 6,642,900	Sydney	HE Prof. Marie Bashir, AO
Northern Territory (NT)		
1,352,212 / 199,900	Darwin	John Anictomatis, OAM
Queensland (Qld)		
1,734,190 / 3,670,500	Brisbane	HE Maj.-Gen. Peter Arnison, AO
South Australia (SA)		
985,324 / 1,518,900	Adelaide	Marjorie Jackson-Nelson, AC, MBE
Tasmania (Tas.)		
67,914 /473,300	Hobart	HE Sir Guy Green, AC, KBE, CVO
Victoria (Vic.)		
227,590 / 4,854,100	Melbourne	HE John Landy, AC, MBE
Western Australia (WA)		
2,532,422 / 1,918,800	Perth	HE Lt.-Gen. John M. Sanderson, AC

HEAD OF STATE

HM by the Grace of God of the United Kingdom, Australia and Her other Realms and Territories Queen, Head of the Commonwealth, Defender of the Faith, Head of the Commonwealth, Defender of the Faith, **Queen Elizabeth II**, *succeeded* 6 February 1952; *crowned* 2 June 1953

Heir, HRH The Prince of Wales (Prince Charles Philip Arthur George), KG, KT, GCB and Great Master of the Order of Bath, OM, AK, QSO, PC, ADC(P)

GOVERNOR-GENERAL

Governor-General: HE The Rt. Revd Dr Peter Hollingworth, AC, OBE, *assumed office* 29 June 2001

CABINET as at July 2002

Prime Minister: John Howard (LP); **Deputy Prime Minister, Transport and Regional Development:** John Anderson (NP); **Agriculture, Fisheries and Forestry:** Warren Truss (NP); **Attorney-General:** Daryl Williams (LP); **Communications, Information Technology and the Arts:** Sen. Richard Alston (LP); **Defence:** Robert Hill (LP); **Education, Science and Training:** Brendan Nelson (LP); **Employment, Workplace Relations and Small Business, Leader of the House:** Tony Abbott (LP); **Environment and Heritage, Leader of the Government in the Senate:** Sen. David Kemp (LP); **Family and Community Services:** Amanda Vanstone (LP); **Finance and Administration:** Nick Minchin (LP); **Foreign Affairs:** Alexander Downer (LP); **Health and Aged Care:** Kay Patterson (LP); **Immigration and Multicultural Affairs, Aboriginal and Torres Strait Islander Affairs:** Philip Ruddock (LP); **Industry, Tourism and Resources:** Ian MacFarlane (LP); **Trade:** Mark Vaile (NP); **Treasurer:** Peter Costello (LP); **President of the Senate:** Sen. Margaret Reid (LP); **Speaker, House of Representatives:** Neil Andrew (LP)

LP Liberal Party; NP National Party

EXTERNAL TERRITORIES

CHRISTMAS ISLAND – **Administrator:** W. Taylor
COCOS (KEELING) ISLANDS – **Administrator:** W. Taylor
NORFOLK ISLAND – **Administrator:** A. J. Messner

AUSTRIA
REPUBLIC ÖSTERREICH

AREA – 32,378 sq. miles (83,859 sq. km). Neighbours: the Czech Republic and Slovakia (north), Italy and Slovenia (south), Hungary (east), Germany (north-west), Switzerland and Liechtenstein (west)

POPULATION – 8,110,244 (2000 census). The language is German, but the rights of the Slovene, Croat, Hungarian, Czech, Slovak, Roma and Sinti minorities are protected. The predominant religion is Roman Catholicism

CAPITAL – Vienna, on the Danube (population, 1,608,656, 2000 census)

MAJOR CITIES – Graz (240,967); Innsbruck (111,752); Klagenfurt (91,149); Linz (188,022); Salzburg (144,247)

CURRENCY – Euro of 100 cents

NATIONAL ANTHEM – Land Der Berge, Land Am Strome (Land Of Mountains, Land On The River)

NATIONAL DAY – 26 October

NATIONAL FLAG – Three equal horizontal stripes of red, white, red

LIFE EXPECTANCY (years) – male 75.4; female 81.5

POPULATION GROWTH RATE – 0.4 per cent (1999)

POPULATION DENSITY – 98 per sq. km (1999)

HISTORY AND POLITICS

The Austrian state dates back to the eighth century AD when Emperor Charlemagne conquered the territory and founded the Ostmark, the eastern march of the Holy Roman Empire. The Habsburg dynasty established an empire which united much of central Europe, including present-day Austria and Hungary. The Republic of Austria was established in 1918 on the break-up of the Austro-Hungarian Empire. In March 1938 Austria was incorporated into Nazi Germany under the name Ostmark. After the liberation of Vienna in 1945, the Republic of Austria was reconstituted within the 1937 frontiers and a freely elected government took office in December 1945. The country was divided into four zones occupied respectively by the UK, USA, USSR and France, while Vienna was jointly occupied by the four Powers. In 1955 the Austrian State Treaty was signed by the foreign ministers of the four Powers and of Austria. This treaty recognised the re-establishment of Austria as a sovereign, independent and democratic state, having the same frontiers as on 1 January 1938. Austria acceded to the European Union on 1 January 1995.

After the general election of 17 December 1995 the Social

Democrats and the People's Party formed a coalition government. In the general election of 3 October 1999, the Social Democrats won 65 seats and the People's Party and the Freedom Party won 52 seats each. Attempts to form a coalition between the Social Democrats and the People's Party were unsuccessful. A coalition government between the People's Party and the Freedom Party, which has stood on an anti-immigration platform and whose leader, Jörg Haider, had expressed support for some aspects of the wartime Nazi regime, was sworn in on 5 February 2000 after the signing by both parties of a document expressing the commitment of the new government of the European Union and condemning discrimination and intolerance. International opposition to the inclusion of the Freedom Party in the government resulted in the suspension of bilateral relations between the governments of the other EU members and Austria. On 1 May Jörg Haider resigned as leader of the Freedom Party in an attempt to calm the situation. The suspension of relations between the EU members and Austria was lifted in September 2000 following an investigation into the Austrian government which cleared it of any wrong-doing.

POLITICAL SYSTEM

There is bicameral national assembly; the lower house (*Nationalrat*) has 183 members and the upper house (*Bundesrat*) has 64 members. There is a 4 per cent qualification for parliamentary representation.

FEDERAL STRUCTURE

There are nine provinces:

Provinces	Area (sq. km)	Population	Capital
Burgenland	3,965	277,962	Eisenstadt
Carinthia	9,533	563,207	Klagenfurt
Lr. Austria	19,174	1,542,393	St Pölten
Salzburg	7,154	517,096	Salzburg
Styria	16,388	1,202,275	Graz
Tirol	12,648	669,710	Innsbruck
Upr. Austria	11,980	1,379,524	LinzVienna
Vienna	415	1,608,656	Vienna
Vorarlberg	2,601	340,421	Bregenz

HEAD OF STATE

President of the Republic of Austria: Dr Thomas Klestil, *took office* 8 July 1992, *re-elected* 19 April 1998

CABINET *as at July 2002*

Chancellor: Wolfgang Schüssel (ÖVP); **Vice-Chancellor, Public Affairs and Sport:** Susanne Riess-Passer (FPÖ); **Agriculture and Forestry; Environment and Water Management:** Wilhem Molterer (ÖVP); **Economic Affairs and Labour:** Martin Bartenstein (ÖVP); **Education, Science and Cultural Affairs:** Elisabeth Gehrer (ÖVP); **Finance:** Karl-Heinz Grasser (FPÖ); **Foreign Affairs:** Benita Ferrero-Waldner (ÖVP); **Interior:** Ernst Strasser (ÖVP); **Justice:** Dieter Böhmdorfer (Ind.); **National Defence:** Herbert Scheibner (FPÖ); **Social Security and Generations:** Herbert Haupt (FPÖ); **Transport, Innovation and Technology:** Matthias Reichhold (FPÖ)

ÖVP Peoples Party; FPÖ Freedom Party; Ind. Independent

━━━◆━━━

BELGIUM
KONINKRIJK BELGIË

AREA – 11,787 sq. miles (30,528 sq. km). Neighbours: the Netherlands (north), France (south), Germany and Luxembourg (east).

POPULATION – 10,239,085 (2000 estimate). Greater Brussels 959,318; Flanders 5,940,251; Wallonia 3,339,516. Roman Catholicism is the religion of 86 per cent of the population. The official languages are Flemish, French and German.

CAPITAL – Brussels (population, 959,318 2000 estimate)

MAJOR CITIES – Antwerp, the chief port (931,718); Bruges (269,158); Charleroi (424, 515); Ghent (493,329); Liège (588,312); Leuven (453,772); Mons (250,748); Namur (279,675), 1998 estimates

CURRENCY – Euro of 100 cents

NATIONAL ANTHEM – O Vaderland, O Edel Land Der Belgen (Oh Fatherland, Oh Noble Land Of The Belgians)

NATIONAL DAY – 21 July (Accession of King Leopold I, 1831)

NATIONAL FLAG – Three vertical bands, black, yellow, red

LIFE EXPECTANCY (years) – male 75.7; female 81.9

POPULATION GROWTH RATE – 0.3 per cent (1997)

POPULATION DENSITY – 333 per sq. km (1999)

URBAB POPULATION – 97.3 per cent (2000)

The Maas and its tributary, the Sambre, divide Belgium into two distinct regions, that in the west being generally level and fertile, while the tableland of the Ardenns in the east, has mostly poor soil. The polders near the coast, which are protected by dykes against floods, cover an area of 193 sq. miles. The principal rivers are the Schelde and the Maas.

Belgium is divided between those who speak Dutch (the Flemings) and those who speak French (the Walloons). Dutch is recognised as the official language in the northern areas and French in the southern (Walloon) area and there are guarantees for the respective linguistic minorities. Brussels is officially bilingual. There is a small German-speaking area (Eupen and Malmédy) along the German border, east of Liège.

HISTORY AND POLITICS

The kingdom formed part of the Low Countries (Netherlands) from 1815 until 14 October 1830, when a National Congress proclaimed its independence. Belgium was invaded by Germany in 1914 and Eupen and Malmédy were ceded to Belgium by Germany under the Versailles Treaty of 1919. The kingdom was again invaded by Germany in 1940 and was occupied by Nazi troops until liberated by the Allies in September 1944. In 1977 Belgium was divided into three administrative regions: Flanders, Wallonia and Brussels.

The last general election was held on 13 June 1999. The results were as follows (seats):

Chamber of Deputies: Christian Social Party (CVP)(Flemish) 22; Socialist Party (PS)(Francophone) 19; Flemish Liberals and Democrats (VLD) 23; Socialist Party (SP) (Flemish) 14; Liberal reform Party-Democratic Front (PRL-FDF) (Francophone) 18; Christian Social Party (PSC) (Francophone) 10; Vlaams Blok (Flemish Nationalist Party) 15; Ecolo (Francophone Ecology Party) 11; Agalev (Flemish Environmental Party) 9; Flemish People's Union (VU) 8; Front National (FN) 1.

Senate: of the 40 seats directly elected, CVP 6; SP 4; VLD 9; PRL-FDF 5; PS 4; PSC 3; Vlaams Blok 4; VU 2; Ecolo 3; Agalev 3. A further 31 Senators are indirectly elected or co-opted. The next elections are planned for June 2003.

POLITICAL SYSTEM

Belgium is a constitutional representative and hereditary monarchy with a bicameral legislature, consisting of the King, the Senate and the Chamber of Deputies. The parliamentary term is four years. Amendments to the constitution enacted since 1968 have devolved power to the regions. The national government retains competence only in foreign and defence policies, the national budget and monetary policy, social security, and the judicial, legal and penal systems. The Senate has 71 seats, of which 40 are directly elected, 21 indirectly elected and ten co-opted by the Flemish and Francophone Communities. The Chamber of Deputies has 150 seats.

There are four levels of sub-national government: community, regional, provincial, and communal.

FEDERAL STRUCTURE

There are three communities: Flemish; Francophone; Germanophone. Each community has its own assembly, which elects the community government. At this level, Flanders is covered by the Flemish Community Assembly; most of Wallonia is covered by the Francophone Community Assembly, and the areas of Wallonia in the German-speaking communities of Eupen and Malmédy are covered by the Germanophone Community Assembly; Brussels is covered by a Joint Community Commission of the Flemish and Francophone Community Assemblies.

At regional level, Belgium is divided into the three regions of Wallonia, Brussels and Flanders. Each region has its own assembly and government.

There are ten provinces; five French-speaking in Wallona (Hainaut, Liège, Luxembourg, Namur and French Brabant); and five Dutch-speaking in Flanders (Antwerp, East Flanders, West Flanders, Limburg and Flemish Brabant). In addition, Belgium has 589 communes as the lowest level of local government.

Minister – President of the Flemish Government: Patric Dewael (VLD)
Minister – President of the Walloon Regional Government: Jean-Claude Van Cauwenberghe (PS)
Minister – President of the German-Speaking Community: Karl-Heinz Lambertz (SP)
Head of City Government in Brussels: Francois-Xavier de Donnéa

Province	Area (sq. km)	Pop. (2000)	Main Town	Pop. (1998)
FLANDERS				
Antwerp	2,867	1,643,972	Antwerp	931,718
East Flanders	2,982	1,361,623	Ghent	493,329
Fl. Brabant	2,106	1,014,704	Leuven	453,772
Limburg	2,422	791,178	Hasselt	67,456
West Flanders	3,144	1,128,774	Bruges	269,158
WALLONIA				
Hainaut	3,786	1,279,467	Mons	92,260
Liège	3,862	1,019,442	Liège	588,312
Luxembourg	4,440	246,820	Arlon	15,000
Namur	3,666	443,903	Namur	279,675
Walloon Brab.	1,091	349,884	Wavre	27,000

HEAD OF STATE

ALBERT II Felix Humbert Theodor Christian Eugène Marie, **KING OF THE BELGIANS**, Dr h c University of Löwen, Gent, Brussels, Mons and St Louis (Philippines), Grand Master Order of Leopold, Kt Order of the Golden Fleece (*Austria and Spain*), Bailiff Gd Cross Hon and Dev Sovereign Military Order of Malta, *succeeded* his brother, Baudouin I, King of the Belgians, son of Leopold III, King of the Belgians 9 August 1993

Heir, HRH Prince *Philippe* Léopold Louis Marie, Duke of Brabant, Gd Cross Sovereign Military Order of Malta

CABINET *as at July 2002*

Prime Minister: Guy Verhofstadt (VLD); **Deputy PM, Budget, Social Integration and Social Economy:** Johan Vande Lanotte (SP); **Deputy PM, Foreign Affairs:** Louis Michel (PRL); **Deputy PM, Labour and Equal Opportunities:** Laurette Onkelinx (PS); **Deputy PM, Mobility and Transport:** Isabelle Durant (Ecolo); **Civil Service and Modernisation of Public Administration:** Luc Van Den Bossche (SP); **Consumer Protection, Public Health and Environment:** Magda Aelvoet (Agalev); **Defence:** André Flahaut (PS); **Economic Affairs and Scientific Research:** Charles Picqué (PS); **Finance:** Didier Reynders (PRL); **Interior:** Antonie Duquesne (PRL); **Justice:** Mark Verwilghen (VLD); **Minister attached to the Ministry of Foreign Affairs and in charge of Agriculture:** Annemie Neyts; **Social Affairs and Pensions:** Frank Vandenbroucke (SP); **Telecommunications, Public Enterprises and Participation:** Rik Deams (VLD)

Agalev Green Party (Flemish); Ecolo Green Party (Francophone); PS Socialist Party (Francophone); SP Socialist Party (Flemish); PRL Liberal Reform Party (Francophone); VLD Liberal Democrats (Flemish)

BRAZIL
República Federativa do Brasil

AREA – 3,300,171 sq. miles (8,547,403 sq. km).
Neighbours: Guyana, Suriname, French Guiana, Colombia and Venezuela (north), Peru, Bolivia, Paraguay and Argentina (west), Uruguay (south)

POPULATION – 159,884,000 (2000 census). Portuguese is the national language. Spanish and English are widely spoken
CAPITAL – Brasilia (population, 1,737,813, 2000 census)
MAJOR CITIES – Belo Horizonte (2,232 747); Fortaleza (2,138,234); Porto Alegre (1,360,033); Recife (1,421,993); Rio de Janeiro (5,851,914), the former capital; Salvador (2,440,828); São Paulo (10,405,867)
CURRENCY – Real of 100 centavos
NATIONAL ANTHEM – Ouviram do Ipiranga às Margens Plácidas (From Peaceful Ypiranga's Banks)
NATIONAL DAY – 7 September (Independence Day)
NATIONAL FLAG – Green with a yellow lozenge containing a blue sphere studded with white stars, and crossed by a white band with the motto Ordem e Progresso
LIFE EXPECTANCY (years) – male 64.7; female 72.6
POPULATION GROWTH RATE – 1.5 per cent (1999)
POPULATION DENSITY – 19 per sq. km (1998)

The north is mainly wide, low-lying, forest-clad plains. The central areas are principally plateau land and the east and south are traversed by successive mountain ranges interspersed with fertile valleys. The principal ranges are the Serra do Mar, the Serra da Mantiqueira and the Serra do Espinhaco along the east coast. The River Amazon flows from the Peruvian Andes to the Atlantic.

HISTORY AND POLITICS

Brazil was discovered by the Portuguese navigator Pedro Alvares Cabral in 1500 and colonised by Portugal in the early 16th century. In 1822 it became independent under Dom Pedro I, son of King João VI of Portugal, who had been forced to flee to Brazil during the Napoleonic Wars. In 1889, Dom Pedro II was dethroned and a republic was proclaimed. In 1985 Brazil returned to democratic rule after two decades of military government.

Fernando Henrique Cardoso of the Social Democratic Party won the presidential election of October 1994 and was returned for a second term on 4 October 1998. In simultaneous legislative elections, the five-party coalition which supported him won 377 seats in the Chamber of Deputies and 21 state governorships. The coalition ceased to be the largest block in the legislature when the Brazilian Labour Party left the coalition in August 2000, but remained in power.

Legislative and presidential elections were due in October 2002.

POLITICAL SYSTEM

The federative republic of Brazil is composed of the federal district and 26 states. Under the 1988 constitution the president, who heads the executive, is directly elected for a four-year term; in June 1997 the constitution was amended to allow the president to stand for a second term. The Congress consists of an 81-member Senate (three senators per state elected for an eight-year term) and a 513-member Chamber of Deputies which is elected every four years; the number of deputies per state depends upon the state's population. Each state has a Governor, and a Legislative Assembly with a four-year term.

FEDERAL STRUCTURE

Federal Unit	Area (sq. km)	Pop. (2000 census)	Capital
Central west		11,616,745	
Distrito Federal	5,822	2,043,169	Brasília
Goiás	341,290	4,996,439	Goiânia
Mato Grosso	906,807	2,502,260	Cuiabá
Mato Grosso do Sul	358,159	2,074,877	Campo Grande
North		12,841,299	
Acre	153,150	557,226	Rio Branco
Amapá	143,454	423,581	Macapá
Amazonas	1,577,820	2,813,085	Manaus
Pará	1,253,165	6,189,550	Belém
Rondônia	238,513	1,377,792	Pôrto Velho
Roraima	225,116	324,152	Boa Vista
Tocantins	278,421	1,155,913	Palmas
North-east		47,693,254	
Alagoas	27,933	2,819,172	Maceió
Bahia	567,295	13,066,910	Salvador
Ceará	146,348	7,418,476	Fortaleza
Maranhão	333,366	5,642,960	São Luís
Paraíba	56,585	3,439,344	João Pessoa
Pernambuco	98,938	7,911,937	Recife
Piauí	252,378	2,841,202	Teresina
Rio Grande do Norte	53,307	2,771,538	Natal
Sergipe	22,050	1,781,714	Aracajú

South		25,089,783	
Paraná	199,709	9,558,454	Curitiba
Rio Grande do Sul	282,062	10,181,749	Pôrto Alegre
Santa Catarina	95,443	5,349,580	
Florianópolis			
South-east		72,297,351	
Espírito Santo	46,184	3,094,390	Victória
Minas Gerais	588,384	17,866,402	Belo Horizonte
Rio de Janeiro	43,910	14,367,083	Rio de Janeiro
São Paulo	248,809	36,969,476	São Paulo

HEAD OF STATE

President: Fernando Henrique Cardoso, *sworn in* 1 January 1995;
Vice-President: Marco Maciel

CABINET *as at July 2002*

Agrarian Development: José Abrão; **Agriculture, Livestock and Supply:** Marcus Vinícius Pratini de Moraes; **Civilian Household of the Presidency:** Pedro Parente; **Communications:** Juarez Martinho Quadros do Nascimento; **Culture:** Francisco Corrêa Weffort; **Defence:** Geraldo Magela da Cruz Quintão; **Development, Industry and Foreign Trade:** Sérgio Amaral; **Education:** Paulo Renato Souza; **Energy and Mines:** Francisco Gomide; **Environment:** José Carlos Carvalho; **External Relations:** Celso Lafer; **Finance:** Pedro Sampaio Malan; **Foreign Affairs:** Celso Lafer; **Health:** Barjas Negri; **Justice:** Miguel Reale; **Labour and Employment:** Paulo Jobim Filho; **Military Household of the Presidency:** Gen. Alberto Cardoso; **National Integration:** Mary Dayse Kinzo; **Planning, Budget and Management:** Gulherme Gomes Dias; **Presidential Spokesman:** Georges Lamazière; **Science and Technology:** Ronaldo Mota Sardenberg; **Secretariat of the Presidency:** Arthur Virgilio; **Social Security and Assistance:** José Cechin; **Sport and Tourism:** Caio Luiz de Carvalho; **Transport:** Joyão Henrique de Almeida Sousa

BULGARIA
REPUBLIKA BALGARIJA

AREA – 42,823 sq. miles (110,912 sq. km). Neighbours: Romania (north), Serbia and the Former Yugoslav Republic of Macedonia (west), Greece and Turkey (south)

POPULATION – 8,306,000 (1997 estimate); 85.7 per cent Bulgarian, 9.4 per cent Turkish, 3.7 per cent Roma, 1.2 per cent others. The language is Bulgarian, a Southern Slavonic tongue closely allied to Serbo-Croat and Russian with local admixtures of modern Greek, Albanian and Turkish words. The alphabet is Cyrillic. The predominant religion is the Bulgarian Orthodox Church (85.7 per cent of the population); Islam is the second largest religion (13.1 per cent).

CAPITAL Sofia (population, 1,192,735, 1997 estimate)

MAJOR CITIES – Burgas (212,369); Plovdiv (340,142); Varna (305,516), 1997 estimates

CURRENCY – Lev of 100 stotinki

NATIONAL ANTHEM – Gorda Stara Planina (Proud And Ancient Mountains)

NATIONAL DAY – 3 March

NATIONAL FLAG – Three horizontal bands, white green, red

LIFE EXPECTANCY – (years) – male 67.1; female 74.8

POPULATION GROWTH RATE – 0.6 per cent (1999)

POPULATION DENSITY – 74 per sq. km (1999)

URBAN POPULATION – 67.7 per cent (1994)

HISTORY AND POLITICS

A principality of Bulgaria was created by the Treaty of Berlin in 1878, and in 1908 the country was declared an independent kingdom. A coup d'état in September 1944 gave power to the Fatherland Front, a coalition of Communists, Agrarians and Social Democrats. In August 1945, the main body of Agrarians and Social democrats left the government. A referendum in September 1946 led to the abolition of the monarchy and the establishment of a republic.

The post-war period was dominated by the Communist Party (BCP), led by Todor Zhivkov. In January 1990 the National Assembly voted to abolish the BCP's constitutional guarantee of power and establish a multiparty democracy.

In November 1996 the Union of Democratic Forces' (UDF) candidate, Petar Stoyanov, became president. The general election held on 17 June 2001 was won by the National Movement for Simeon

II, a movement founded in April 2001 by the former king, which won 43.74 per cent of the vote and 120 of the 240 seats in the legislature.

POLITICAL SYSTEM

A new constitution enshrining democracy and the free market was adopted in 1991. It provides for a directly elected president who serves for no more than two five-year terms. The chief executive is the prime minister who is appointed by the president, and is usually the leader of the largest party in the legislature. There is a unicameral National Assembly of 240 members who are directly elected by proportional representation for four-year terms.

HEAD OF STATE

President: Georgi Parvanov (BSP), *elected* 2002, *elected* November 18, 2001, *took office* 19 January 2002; **Vice President:** Angel Martin (BSP)

COUNCIL OF MINISTERS *as at July 2002*

Prime Minister: Simeon Borisov Saxe-Coburg-Gotha (*HM King Simeon II of the Bulgarians*); **Deputy PM, Economy:** Nikolai Vasilev; **Deputy PM, Labour and Social Policy:** Lidia Šuleva; **Deputy PM, Regional Development and Public Works:** Kostadin Paskalev; **Agriculture and Forestry:** Mekhmed Dikme; **Civil Service:** Dimitar Kalchev; **Culture:** Bujidar Abrašev; **Defence:** Nikolay Svinarov; **Education and Science:** Vladimir Atanassov; **Energy and Energy Resources:** Milko Kovachev; **Environment and Water:** Dolores Arsenova; **European Affairs:** Meglena Kuneva; **Finance:** Milen Velchev; **Foreign Affairs:** Solomon Passy; **Health:** Bojidar Finkov; **Internal Affairs:** Georgi Petkanov; **Justice:** Anton Stankov; **Transport and Communications:** Plamen Petrov; **Without Portfolio:** Nezhdet Mollor

---

CANADA

AREA – 3,849,674 sq. miles (9,970,610 sq. km). Neighbours: USA (south), Alaska (USA) (west)

POPULATION – 30,871,975 (2001 estimate). The languages are English and French

MAJOR CITIES – Calgary (885,130); Edmonton (899,466); Hamilton (663, 587); Montréal (3,384,233); Québec (700,197);

Toronto (4,511,966); Vancouver (1,927,998); Winnipeg (677,291), 1997 estimates

CURRENCY – Canadian dollar of 100 cents

NATIONAL ANTHEM – O Canada

NATIONAL DAY – 1 July (Canada Day)

NATIONAL FLAG – Red maple leaf with 11 points on white square, flanked by vertical red bars one-half the width of the square

LIFE EXPECTANCY (years) – male 76.2; female 81.8

POPULATION GROWTH RATE – 1.0 per cent (1999)

POPULATION DENSITY – 3 per sq. km (1999)

URBAN POPULATION – 76.7 per cent (1995)

Canada occupies the whole of the northern part of the North American continent, with the exception of Alaska. In eastern Canada, the southernmost point is Middle Island in Lake Erie. Canada has six main physiographic divisions: the Appalachian-Acadian region, the Canadian shield, which comprises more than half the country, the St Lawrence-Great Lakes lowland, the interior plains, the Cordilleran region and the Arctic archipelago.

The climate of the eastern and central portions presents greater extremes than in corresponding latitudes in Europe, but in the south-western portion of the prairie region and the southern portions of the Pacific slope the climate is milder.

HISTORY AND POLITICS

Canada was originally discovered by Cabot in 1497 and the French took possession of the country in 1534. The first permanent settlement at Port Royal (now Annapolis), Nova Scotia, was founded in 1605, and Québec was founded in 1608. In 1759 Québec was captured by British forces General Wolfe and in 1763 the whole territory of Canada became a possession of Great Britain by the Treaty of Paris 1763. Nova Scotia was ceded in 1713 by the Treaty of Utrecht, the provinces of New Brunswick and Prince Edward Island being subsequently formed out of it. British Columbia was formed into a Crown colony in 1858, having previously been a part of the Hudson Bay Territory, and was united to Vancouver Island in 1866.

The constitution of Canada has its source in the British North America Act of 1867 which formed a Dominion, under the name of Canada, of the four provinces of Ontario, Québec, New Brunswick and Nova Scotia. To this federation the other provinces and territories have subsequently been admitted: Manitoba and Northwest Territories (1870), British Columbia (1871), Prince Edward Island (1873), Yukon (1898), Alberta and Saskatchewan (1905) and Newfoundland (1949). In 1982, the constitution was patriated (severed from the British parliament) with the approval of all provinces except Québec. In 1985, the federal prime minister and the provincial premiers concluded the Meech Lake Accord which provided for Québec to be recognised as a distinct society within Canada. However, two provincial legislatures withheld approval and the accord did not come into force. In Québec, a referendum calling for sovereignty and a new political and economic partnership was defeated in October 1995. In September 1997 Québec was recognised as having a 'unique character' by leaders of the other provinces and territories. A new territory, Nunavut, which means 'our land' in the Inuit language of Inuktitut, was created on 1 April 1999 by partitioning the Northwest Territories.

In the federal election on 27 November 2000 the Liberal Party won a third consecutive term of office. The state of parties in the House of Commons following the election was Liberals 172, Canadian Alliance 66, Bloc Québécois 38, New Democrats 13, and Progressive Conservatives 12.

POLITICAL SYSTEM

Executive power is vested in a Governor General appointed by the Sovereign on the advice of the prime minister. Parliament consists of a Senate and a House of Commons. The Senate consists of 105 members, nominated by the Governor General on the advice of the prime minister, the seats being distributed between the various provinces. The House of Commons has 301 members directly elected for a five-year term. Representation is proportional to the population of each province.

The judicature is administered by judges following the civil law in Québec province and common law in other provinces. Each province has a Court of Appeal. All superior, country and district court judges are appointed by the Governor General, the others by the Lieutenant-Governors of the provinces.

The highest federal court is the Supreme Court of Canada, which exercises general appellate jurisdiction throughout Canada in civil and criminal cases. There is one other federally constituted court, the Federal Court of Canada, which has jurisdiction on appeals from its trial division, from federal tribunals and reviews of decisions and references by federal boards and commissions.

FEDERAL STRUCTURE

Provinces or Territories (official contractions)	Area (sq. km)	Population (1 Jan 2001)	Capital
Alberta (AB)	661,848	3,022,861	Edmonton
British Colombia (BC)	944,735	4,077,369	Victoria
Manitoba (MB)	647,797	1,149,220	Winnipeg
New Brunswick (NB)	72,908	757,267	Fredericton
Newfoundland and Labrador (NF)	405,212	537,797	St John's

Northwest Territories(NT)	1,346,106	42,105	Yellowknife
Nova Scotia (NS)	55,284	942,322	Halifax
Nunavut (NT)	2,093,190	27,978	Iqaluit
Ontario (ON)	1,076,395	11,741,793	Toronto
Prince Edward Island (PE)	5,660	139,078	Charlottetown
Québec (QC)	1,542,056	7,383,300	Québec
Saskatchewan (SK)	651,036	1,020,650	Regina
Yukon Territory (YT)	482,443	30,194	Whitehorse

HEAD OF STATE

HM by the Grace of God of the United Kingdom, Canada and Her
other Realms and Territories Queen, Head of the Commonwealth,
Defender of the Faith, Head of the Commonwealth, Defender of the
Faith, **Queen Elizabeth II**, *succeeded* 6 February 1952; *crowned* 2
June 1953

Heir, HRH The Prince of Wales (Prince Charles Philip Arthur
George), KG, KT, GCB and Great Master of the Order of Bath, OM,
AK, QSO, PC, ADC(P)

GOVERNOR GENERAL

Governor general and Commander-in-Chief: HE the Rt Hon
Adrienne Clarkson

FEDERAL CABINET *as at July 2002*

Prime Minister: Jean Chrétien; **Deputy Prime Minister,
Finance and Infrastructure:** John Manley; **Agriculture and
Agri-Food:** Lyle Vanclief; **Citizenship and Immigration:** Denis
Coderre; **Environment:** David Anderson; **Fisheries and Oceans:**
Robert Thibault; **Foreign Affairs:** William Graham; **Health:** Anne
McLellan; **Heritage:** Sheila Copps; **Human Resource
Development:** Jane Stewart; **Indian Affairs and Northern
Development:** Robert Nault; **Industry:** Allan Rock;
Intergovernmental Affairs, President of the Privy Council:
Stéphane Dion; **International Co-operation:** Susan Whelan;
International Trade: Pierre Pettigrew; **Justice and
Attorney-General:** Martin Cauchon; **Labour:** Claudette Bradshaw;
Leader of the Government in the House of Commons: Ralph
Goodale; **Leader of the Government in the Senate:** Sharon
Carstairs; **National Defence:** John McCallum; **National Revenue:**
Elinor Caplan; **Natural Resources:** Herb Dhaliwal; **Public Works
and Government Services:** Don Boudria; **Solicitor-General:**
Lawrence MacAulay; **Transport:** David Collenette; **Veterans'

Affairs, Secretary of State for Science, Research and Development: Rey Pagtakhan

———————◆———————

DENMARK
KONGERIGET DANMARK

AREA – 16,639 sq. miles (43,094 sq. km). Neighbour: Germany (south)

POPULATION – 5,284,000. The majority of the population is Lutheran. The language is Danish

CAPITAL – Copenhagen (population, 1,362,264, 1998 projection)

MAJOR CITIES – Ålborg (160,937); Århus (283,673); Odense (183,584), 1997 UN estimates

CURRENCY – Danish krone of 100 øre

NATHIONAL ANTHEMS – Kong Kristian stod ved højen mast (King Christian Stood By The Lofty Mast); Det er et yndigt land (There Is A Lovely Land)

NATIONAL DAY – 5 June (Constitution Day)

NATIONAL FLAG – Red, with white cross

LIFE EXPECTANCY (years) – male 74.2; female 79.1

POPULATION GROWTH RATE – 0.5 per cent (1999)

POPULATION DENSITY – 124 per sq. km (1999)

Denmark is a kingdom, consisting of the islands of Zealand (Sjælland), Funen (Fyn), Lolland, etc., the peninsula of Jutland (Julland), the outlying island of Bornholm in the Baltic, and the Færøes and Greenland.

HISTORY AND POLITICS

The Danes were at the forefront of Viking expansionism and briefly united England and Scandinavia under Knut (Canute) (995 – 1035). The Union of Kalmar (1397) brought Norway and Sweden (including Finland) under Danish rule. Danish power waned during the 16th century, however, enabling Sweden to re-establish its independence in 1523. In the 19th century Norway was ceded to Sweden under the Treaty of Kiel (1814) and both Schleswig and Holstein, which had been subsumed in 1460, were surrendered to Germany.

Denmark remained neutral during the First World War, and in a plebiscite held in accordance with the Versailles Treaty (1919), northern Schleswig voted to return to Danish sovereignty. In 1939 Denmark signed a non-aggression pact with Germany but was invaded on 9 April 1940 and coerced into contributing to the

German war effort. Iceland declared its independence from Denmark in 1944 and the Færøe Islands were granted home rule in 1948. Greenland, which had had to status of a colony, was integrated into Denmark in 1953 and granted home rule in 1979. Social Democrat-led coalitions dominated the post-war era until 1982 when a right-wing government was elected. Denmark joined the European Community in 1973.

A referendum was held on 28 September 2000 on membership of the European single currency. Membership was rejected by 53.1 per cent of those who voted.

The most recent legislative elections were held on 20 November 2001 and the Liberal Party became the largest party in Parliament. A coalition government was formed on 27 November 2001 by Anders Fogh Rasmussen between the Liberal Party and the Conservative People's Party.

POLITICAL SYSTEM

The legislature consists of one chamber, the Folketing, of 179 members, including two for the Færøes and two for Greenland, which is elected for a four-year term. The voting age is 18 with voting based on a proportional representation system with a 2 per cent threshold for parliamentary representation.

HEAD OF STATE

MARGRETHE II Alexandrine Thorhildur Ingrid, **QUEEN OF DENMARK**, *succeeded* 14 January 1972

Heir, HRH Crown Prince *Frederik* André Henrik Christian

CABINET *as at May 2002*

Prime Minister: Anders Fogh Rasmussen (V); **Culture:** Brian Mikkelsen (KF); **Defence:** Svend Aaga Jensby (V); **Ecclesiastical Affairs:** Tove Fergø; **Economy, Industry, Trade and Nordic Co-operation:** Bendt Bendtson (KF); **Education:** Ulla Toernaes (V); **Employment:** Claus Hjort Frederiksen (V); **Environment and Energy:** Hans Christian Schmidt (V); **Finance:** Thor Pedersen (V); **Food, Agriculture and Fisheries:** Mariann Fischer Boel (V); **Foreign Affairs:** Per Stig Moeller (KF); **Interior and Health:** Lars Loekke Rasmussen (V); **Justice:** Lene Esperson (KF); **Refugees, Immigrants and Integration; Minister without portfolio responsible for European Affairs:** Bertel Haarder (V); **Science, Technology and Development:** Helge Saner (V); **Social Affairs and Equality:** Henriette Kjaer (KF); **Taxation:** Svend Erik Hovmand (KF); **Transport:** Jacob Buksti (SD)

V Liberal Party; KF Conservative People's Party

HOUSEHOLD OF HM THE QUEEN

Lord Chamberlain: Maj.-Gen. Søren Haslund-Christensen (*Chamberlain*); **Master of Ceremonies:** Lt.-Col. Christian Eugen-Olsen (*Chamberlain*); **Treasurer of the Royal Household:** Søren Kruse; **Deputy Head of Division:** Susanne Brix; **Principal of the Household:** Steen Kudsk Larsen; **Ladies-in-Waiting:** Wava Kitty, Countess Armfelt (*Chamberlaine*); Marianne Boel; Ulla Gorwetz Obel; Camilla Castenskiold; Annette de Scheel; **Lady-in-Waiting to HRH Princess Alexandra:** Annick Boel; **Personal Secretary to HM the Queen:** Karen Clausen; **Chief of HRH the Prince Consort's Secretariat:** Col. Mogens Christensen (*Chamberlain*); **Private Secretary to HM the Queen:** Niels Eilschou Holm, LL.D (*Chamberlain*); **Deputy Private Secretary to HM the Queen:** Henrik Gam; **Chief of HM the Queen's Military Household:** Col. Kurt Bache; **Aide-de-Camps to HM the Queen:** Maj. Ernst Højgaard Clausen; Cdr. Bo Lund-Hansen; Maj. Hans Jørgen Andersen; Maj. Thomas Nymand Bork; Cdr. Jens Vester; Maj. Michael de Voss; **Chief of HM the Queen's Naval Household:** Capt. Steen Vestergaard Andersen; **Master of the Royal Orders:** HE Ambassador Paul Fischer, LL.D (*Chamberlain*); **Historiographer of the Royal Orders of Chivalry:** Prof. Knud J. V. Jespersen, D.Phil; **Secretary to the Chancery of the Royal Danish Orders of Chivalry:** Per Thornit (*Chamberlain*); **Palace Steward of Amalienborg and Christiansborg Palaces:** Col. Ole Nørring (*Chamberlain*); **Palace Steward of Fredensborg Palace:** Col. Niels Christian Eigtved (*Chamberlain*); **Master of the Royal Stables:** Maj. Michael Mentz; **Master of the Royal Vehicles:** Maj. Bjarne Sørensen; **Master of the Royal Hunt, State Forest Supervisor:** Klaus Waage Sørensen; **The Queen's Chaplain:** Prof. Christian Thodberg, D.Phil; **Librarian to HM the Queen:** Klaus Kjølsen, D.Phil; **Registrar of Gold and Silver to HM the Queen:** Ole Willumsen Krog; **Surveyor of Royal Household Furniture:** Ole Priskorn

HOUSEHOLD OF HRH THE CROWN PRINCE

Chief of the Household: Per Thornit (*Chamberlain*)

HOUSEHOLD OF HRH PRINCESS BENEDIKTE

Private Secretary: Col. Peter A. Lauritzen (*Chamberlain*); **Lady-in-Waiting:** Countess Karin af Rosenborg

EXTERNAL TERRITORIES
THE FÆRØE ISLANDS – **Prime Minister:** Anfinn Kallsberg
GREENLAND – **Prime Minister:** Jonathan Motzfeldt

FRANCE
La République Français

AREA – 212,935 sq. miles (551,500 sq. km). Neighbours: Belgium and Luxembourg (north-east), Germany, Switzerland and Italy (east), Spain and Andorra (south-west)

POPULATION – 59,551,227 (2001 estimate); 57,218,000 (Metropolitan France), and 58,754,000 including overseas departments (1992 official estimate): 72 per cent Catholic, 8 per cent Muslim, 2 per cent Jewish. The language is French; there are several regional languages including Basque, Breton, Catalan, Corsican, Dutch, German and Occitan.

CAPITAL – Paris (population, 9,319,367, 1990), on the Seine

MAJOR CITIES – Bordeaux (696,819); Grenoble (404,837); Lille (959,433); Lyon (1,262,342); Marseille (1,230,871); Nantes (495,229); Nice (517,291); Strasbourg (388,466); Toulon (437,825); Toulouse (650,311). The chief towns of Corsica are Ajaccio (58,315) and Bastia (52,446)

CURRENCY – Euro of 100 cents

NATIONAL ANTHEM – La Marseillaise

NATIONAL DAY – 14 July (Bastille Day 1789)

NATIONAL FLAG – The tricolour, three vertical bands, blue, white, red (blue next to flagstaff)

LIFE EXPECTANCY (years) – male 75.2; female 82.8

POPULATION GROWTH RATE – 0.4 per cent (1999)

POPULATION DENSITY – 107 per sq. km (1998)

HISTORY AND POLITICS

Gaul, the area which is now France, was conquered by Julius Caesar in the 1st century BC and remained a part of the Roman Empire until the Frankish invasions in the 6th and 6th centuries. The Treaty of Verdun (AD 843) divided the Frankish Empire into three parts, of which the western part, *Francia Occidentalis*, became the basis for modern France.

France established itself as the dominant country in Europe in the 17th century. As a result of the French Revolution, a republic was declared in 1792 and the king Louis XVI, was executed.

The republic was overthrown by Napoléon Bonaparte, who established the first French Empire, which ended in 1815. The ensuing Congress of Vienna restored the monarchy, but in 1848 the Second Republic was declared, which lasted only until 1852, when the Second Empire was proclaimed under Napoléon III. He was forced to abdicate after the defeat of France in the Franco-Prussian war (1870-1871) and the Third republic was established.

In 1940, Germany invaded France, occupying most of the country and establishing a pro-German government in the south. France was liberated in 1944, a provisional government was established under Gen. Charles de Gaulle, and the Fourth Republic was declared in 1946. In 1958, the threat of military coup following a rebellion in Algeria resulted in the assembly inviting Gen. De Gaulle was elected president. France granted its colonies independence between 1954 and 1962.

President Jacques Chirac, the candidate of the Rally for the Republic (PRP), was elected in May 1995. The state of the parties in the Senate at September 2001 was: RPR 83; Socialist Party (PS) 68; Centrist Union (UDC) 37; Republican and Independent Union (RI) 35; Democratic and European Rally (RDE) 16; Communists (PCF) 16; Independents 5; Others 60.

In the first round of the Presidential elections on 21 April 2002, National Front leader Jean-Marie Le Pen gained just under 200,000 more than Prime Minister Lionel Jospin. Jacques Chirac won the second round on 5 May with 82.2 per cent of the vote.

POLITICAL SYSTEM

The head of state is a directly elected president, whose term of office has hitherto been seven years, but will be five years with effect from the presidential election due to be held in March 2002. The legislature consists of the National Assembly of 577 deputies (555 for Metropolitan France and 22 for the overseas departments and territories) and the Senate of 321 Senators (296 for Metropolitan France, 13 for the overseas departments and territories and 12 for French citizens aboard). Deputies in the National Assembly are directly elected for five- year term. One-third of the Senate is indirectly elected every three years.

The prime minister is appointed by the president, as is the Council of Ministers on the prime minister's recommendation. They are responsible to the legislature, but as the executive is constitutionally separate from the legislature, ministers may not sit in the legislature and must hand over their seats to a substitute.

France is divided into 22 metropolitan regions and 96 metropolitan and four overseas departments, which are also regions. There are also four overseas territories and two territorial collectivities.

HEAD OF STATE

President of the French Republic: Jacques Chirac, *elected* 7 May 1995, *re-elected* 5 May 2002

COUNCIL OF MINISTERS *as at July 2002*

Prime Minister: Jean-Pierre Raffarin (RPR); **Agriculture, Food, Fisheries and Rural Affairs:** Hervé Gaymard (RPR); **Capital Works, Transport, Housing, Tourism and the Sea:** Gilles de Robien (UDF); **Civil Service, Administrative reform and Town and Country Planning:** Jean-Paul Delevoye (RPR); **Culture and Communications:** Jean-Jacques Aillagon (RPR); **Defence, War Veterans:** Michèle Alliot-Marie (RPR); **Ecology and Sustainable Development:** Roselyne Bachelot-Narquin (RPR); **Economy, Finance and Industry:** Francis Mer; **Employment and Solidarity:** François Fillon (RPR); **Foreign Affairs Co-operation and Francophony:** Dominique de Villepin (RPR); **Health, the Family and the Disabled:** Jean-François Mattéi (DL); **Interior, Internal Security and Local Freedoms:** Nicolas Sarkozy (RPR); **Justice, Keeper of the Seals:** Dominique Perben (RPR); **Overseas France:** Brigitte Girardin; **Sport:** Jean-François Lamour; **Youth, National Education and Research:** Luc Ferry

RPR Rally for the Republic; UDF Union for French Democracy; DL Liberal Democracy

OVERSEAS DEPARTMENTS

FRENCH GUIANA – Prefect: Henri Masse
GUADELOUPE – Prefect: Jean-Françoise Carenco
MARTINIQUE – Prefect: Michel Cadot
RÉUNION Prefect. Gonthier Friederici

TERRITORIAL COLLECTIVITIES

MAYOTTE – Prefect: Philippe de Mester
ST PIERRE AND MIQUELON – Prefect: Jean-François Tallec

OVERSEAS TERRITORIES

FRENCH POLYNESIA – High Commissioner: Michel Mathieu
NEW CALEDONIA – High Commissioner: Thierry Lataste
SOUTHERN AND ANTARTIC TERRITORIES – Administrator: François Garde
WALLIS AND FUTUNA ISLANDS – Administrator: Alain Waquet

GERMANY
BUNDESREPUBLIK DEUTSCHLAND

AREA – 137,846 sq. miles (357,022 sq. km). Neighbours: Denmark (north), Poland (east), Czech Republic (east and south-east), Austria (south-east and south), Switzerland (south), France, Luxembourg, Belgium and the Netherlands (west).

POPULATION – 83,029,536 (2001 estimate).

Approximately 80 per cent of the population live in the former West Germany. In 1994 there were 28,197,000 Protestants, 27,909,797 Roman Catholics, 2,700,000 Muslims and 53,797 Jews. The language is German; there are Danish – and Frisian-speaking minorities in Schleswig-Holstein and Sorbian-speaking minority in Saxony

CAPITAL – Berlin (population 3,472,009, 1997 estimate). The seat of government and parliament was transferred from Bonn to Berlin in 2000

MAJOR CITIES – Bremen (546,968); Cologne (964,311); Dortmund (594,866); Dresden (459,222); Duisburg 9529,062); Düsseldorf (570,969); Essen (608,732); Frankfurt am Main (643,469); Hamburg (1,704,731); Hannover (520,670); Leipzig (446,491); Munich (1,205,923); Nuremberg (489,758); Stuttgart (585,274) 1998 estimates

CURRENCY – Euro of 100 cents

NATIONAL ANTHEM – Einigkeit Und Recht Und Freiheit (Unity And Right And Freedom)

NATIONAL DAY – 3 October (Anniversary of 1990 Unification)

NATIONAL FLAG – Horizontal bars of black, red and gold

LIFE EXPECTANCY (years) – male 75.0; female 81.1

POPULATION GROWTH RATE – 0.1 per cent (1999)

POPULATION DENSITY – 230 per sq. km (1999)

HISTORY AND POLITICS

The first German realm was the Holy Roman Empire, established in AD 962 when Otto I of Saxony crowned Emperor. The Empire endured until 1806, but the achievement of a national state was prevented by fragmentation into small principalities and dukedoms.

The Empire was replaced by a loose association of sovereign states known as the German Confederation, which was dissolved in 1866 and replaced by the Prussian dominated North German Federation. The south German principalities united with the northern federation to form a second German Empire in 1871 and the King of Prussia was proclaimed Emperor.

Defeat in the First World War led to the abdication of the

Emperor, and the country became a republic. The Treaty of Versailles (1919) ceded Alsace-Lorraine to France, and large areas in the east were lost to Poland. The world economic crisis of 1929 contributed to the collapse of the Weimar Republic and the subsequent rise to power of the National Socialist movement of Adolf Hitler, who became Chancellor in 1933.

After concluding a Treaty of Non-Aggression with the Soviet Union in August 1939, Germany invaded Poland (1 September 1939), precipitating the Second World War, which lasted until 1945. Hitler committed suicide on 30 April 1945. On 8 May 1945, Germany unconditionally surrendered.

The Post-War Period

Germany was divided into American, French, British and Soviet zones of occupation. The territories to the east of the Oder and Neisse rivers were placed under Polish and Russian administration and some 7.75 million Germans were deported.

The Federal Republic of Germany (FRG) was created out of the three western zones in 1949. A Communist government was established in the Soviet zone (henceforth the German Democratic Republic (GDR)). In 1961 the Soviet zone of Berlin was sealed off, and the Berlin Wall was built along the zonal boundary, partitioning the western sectors of the city from the eastern.

Soviet-initiated reform in eastern Europe during the late 1980s led to unrest in the GDR, culminating in the opening of the Berlin Wall in November 1989 and the collapse of Communist government. The 'Treaty on the Final Settlement with Respect to Germany', concluded between the FRG, GDR and the four former occupying powers in September 1990, unified Germany with effect from 3 October 1990 as a fully sovereign state. Economic and monetary union preceded formal union on 1 July 1990. Unification is constitutionally the accession of Berlin and the five reformed Länder of the GDR to the FRG, which remains in being. Berlin was declared to be the capital of the unified Germany and parliament and government departments were transferred from Bonn.

A general election took place on 22 September 2002 with results announced on 23 September 2002. Chancellor Gerhard Schroeder's Social Democratic Party (SPD) and the Green Party won 47.1 per cent of the vote = 606 seats in the Bundestag. The conservative opposition of CDU/CSU led by Edmund Stoiber won 38.5 per cent of the vote. The Free Democratic Party (FDP) won 7.4 per cent of the vote and the Party of Democratic Socialism (PDS) 4 per cent.

POLITICAL SYSTEM

The Basic Law provides for a president, elected by a Federal Convention (electoral college) for a five-year term, a lower house (*Bundestag*) of 669 members elected by direct universal suffrage for a four-year term of office, and an upper house (*Bundesrat*) composed of 69 members appointed by the governments of the *Länder* in proportion to *Länder* populations, without a fixed term of office.

Judicial authority is exercised by the Federal Constitutional Court, the federal courts provided for in the Basic Law and the courts of the *Länder*.

FEDERAL STRUCTURE

Germany is a federal republic composed of 16 states (*Länder*) (ten from the former West, five from the former East and Berlin). Each *Land* has its own directly elected legislature and government led by Minister-Presidents (prime-ministers) or equivalents. The 1949 Basic Law vests executive power in the *Länder* governments except in those areas reserved for the federal government.

Land	Area (sq. km)	Pop. (1998)	Capital
Baden-Württemberg	35,752	10.4m	Stuttgart
Bavaria	70,548	12.1m	Munich
Berlin	891	3.4m	-
Brandenburg	29,476	2.6m	Potsdam
Bremen	404	0.7m	-
Hamburg	755	1.7m	-
Hesse	21,115	6.0m	Weisbaden
Lower Saxony	47,613	7.9m	Hannover
Mecklenburg	23,170	1.8m	Schwerin
N. Rhine-Westphalia	34,079	18.0m	Düsseldorf
Rhineland-Palatinate	19,847	4.0m	Mainz
Saarland	2,570	1.1m	Saarbrücken
Saxony	18,412	4.5m	Dresden
Saxony-Anhalt	20,447	2.7m	Magdeburg
Schleswig-Holstein	15,770	2.8m	Kiel
Thuringia	16,172	2.5m	Erfurt

HEAD OF STATE

Federal President: Johannes Rau, *elected* 24 May 1999

CABINET *as at July 2002*

Federal Chancellor: Gerhard Schröder (SPD); **Federal Vice-Chancellor, Foreign Affairs:** Joscha Fischer (Greens); **Commissioner for Media and Cultural Affairs:** Julian Nida-Rümelin (SPD); **Consumer Protection, Nutrition and Agriculture:** Renate Künast (Greens); **Defence:** Rudolf Scharping (SPD); **Economic Co-operation and Development:** Heidemarie Wieczorek-Zeul (SPD); **Economics and Technology:** Werner Müller

(Ind.); **Education and Research:** Edelgard Bulmahn (SPD); **Environment, Nature Conservation and Reactor Safety:** Jürgen Trittin (Greens); **Family, Pensioners, Women and Youth:** Dr Christine Bergmann (SPD); **Finance:** Hans Eichel (SPD); **Head of Chancellery:** Frank-Walter Steinmeier (SPD); **Health:** Ulla Schmidt (SPD); **Interior:** Otto Schily (SPD); **Justice:** Herta Däubler-Gmelin (SPD); **Labour and Social Affairs:** Walter Riester (SPD); **Ministers of State:** Cristoph Zöpel (SPD); **Transport, Construction and Housing:** Kurt Bodewig (SPD)

SPD Social Democratic Party; Ind. Independent

GREAT BRITAIN AND NORTHERN IRELAND
UNITED KINGDOM OF GREAT BRITAIN AND NORTHERN IRELAND

AREA – 93,784 sq. miles (242,900 sq. km), of which England 50,351 sq. miles (130,410 sq. km), Wales 8,015 sq. miles (20,758 sq. km), Scotland 30,420 sq. miles (78,789 sq. km), Northern Ireland 5,467 sq. miles (14,160 sq. km). Neighbour: Republic of Ireland (south and west)

POPULATION – 59,647,790 (2001 estimate); England 48,903,000, Wales 2,917,000, Scotland 5,137,000, Northern Ireland 1,649,000 (1996 UN estimates). The language is English, of West Germanic origin, with a vocabulary heavily influenced by French, Latin and Greek. Welsh is spoken by 18.7 per cent of the population of Wales, Scots is spoken by 30 per cent of the population of Scotland; there are also small numbers of Scottish and Irish Gaelic speakers. There are 39.4 million Christians (of which 26.1 million Anglicans, 5.7 million Roman Catholics and 2.6 million Presbyterians), nearly 2 million Muslims, 400,000 Sikhs, 380,000 Hindus, 285,000 Jews, 25,000 Buddhists and 25,000 Jains

CAPITAL – London (population, 7,285,000 1999 estimate) (capital of the UK and England)

MAJOR CITIES – Belfast (297,300) (capital of Northern Ireland); Birmingham (population 861,041); Bradford (457,344); Bristol (399,600); Cardiff/Caerdydd (315,040) (capital of Wales); Dudley (304,615); Edinburgh (452,806) (capital of Scotland); Glasgow (611,440); Leeds (680,722); Liverpool (452,450); Manchester (404,861);

Sheffield (501,202); Wakefield (310,915); Wigan (306,521), 1996 estimates

CURRENCY – Pound sterling of 100 pence

NATIONAL ANTHEM – God Save The Queen

NATIONAL DAY – St David's Day (Wales only) 1 March, St Patrick's Day (N. Ireland only) 17 March, St George's Day (England only) 23 April, St Andrew's Day (Scotland only) 30 November

NATIONAL FLAG – A red cross and a red diagonal cross on a white cross and a white diagonal cross on a blue ground

LIFE EXPECTANCY (years) – male 75.7; female 80.7

POPULATION GROWTH RATE – 0.2 per cent (2001)

POPULATION DENSITY – 242 per sq. km (1999)

URBAN POPULATION – 89.5 per cent (2000) estimate

The United Kingdom consists of Great Britain (formed of Scotland in the north, Wales in the west of the central portion of the island, and England, which occupies the rest of the island), the north-eastern part of the island of Ireland, and the Hebrides, Orkney and Shetland Islands, the Isle of Wight, Anglesey and the Isles of Scilly. The United Kingdom is bounded on the south by the English Channel, on the east by the Straits of Dover and the North Sea, and on the north and west by the Atlantic Ocean. The North Channel and the Irish Sea separate Northern Ireland from Great Britain.

HISTORY AND POLITICS

The United Kingdom is formed of four constituent nations: England, Wales, Scotland and Northern Ireland. The Normans, who had invaded England in 1066, established control over Wales by 1300; Wales was politically assimilated to England under the Act of Union of 1535.

Following the death of Queen Elizabeth I, James VI of Scotland succeeded to the English throne as James I of England in 1603; an Act of Union was proclaimed in 1707, under which the seat of Scottish Government was transferred to London.

The Norman English had established control over most of Ireland in the 12th century, but their influence waned. King Henry VIII re-established English control over Ireland and was declared king of Ireland by a parliament summoned in Dublin in 1541. The United Kingdom of Great Britain and Ireland was established by the Act of Union in 1801.

By the early Twentieth century, the United Kingdom had acquired a substantial empire, which included Australia, Canada, the Indian subcontinent, Malaysia, New Zealand, and extensive territories in Africa, the West Indies and the Pacific.

Ireland was partitioned in 1921 and the Irish Free State became a republic in 1949. Northern Ireland remained part of the

United Kingdom, governed by a Northern Ireland parliament.

Beginning with the independence of India and Pakistan in 1947, a process of decolonisation began.

The Labour government elected in 1945 nationalised iron and steel, transport and the utilities. Prime Minister Margaret Thatcher, who was in power from 1979 to 1990, broke the post-war consensus. Her Conservative government privatised state-owned industries and reduced the influence of the trade unions. The Labour Party won the general election held on 1 May 1997 and retained power in the general election held on 7 June 2001 winning 413 seats; the Conservative Party won 166 seats, the Liberal Democrats 52 seats, the Ulster Unionist Party six seats, the Scottish Nationalist Party and the Democratic Unionist Party five seats each, Plaid Cymru and Sinn Féin four seats each, the Social and Democratic Labour Party three seats, and the Kidderminster Hospital and Health Concern won one seat and one seat was held by the Speaker.

Referendums held in Scotland and Wales in September 1997 produced majorities in favour of devolution. The first elections to the Scottish Parliament and the Welsh National Assembly took place in May 1999.

NORTHERN IRELAND

Following the partition of Ireland in 1921, the Protestant Unionists held a permanent majority in the government and administration of Northern Ireland. A Roman Catholic civil rights campaign in the late 1960's led to rioting, sectarian violence and terrorist activity conducted by the Irish Republican Army (IRA), an Irish nationalist paramilitary organisation, and several Protestant paramilitary organisations. Following the resignation in 1972 of the Northern Ireland government, the Northern Ireland parliament was abolished and replaced with direct rule from London.

Several attempts were made by successive governments to restore power to a devolved government which was acceptable to both the Catholic and Protestant communities.

In November 1985 the governments of the UK and the Republic of Ireland signed the Anglo-Irish Agreement, under which both parties agreed to improve cross-border co-operation and that Northern Ireland should remain part of the UK for as long as the majority of the population wished it to remain so.

The 'Good Friday Agreement', which proposed the establishment of a Northern Ireland Assembly, along with a cross-border ministerial council and a consultative body of ministers from the UK, the Republic of Ireland and the Northern Irish, Scottish and Welsh assemblies, was put to a referendum in May 1998 and was endorsed by the electorate. At the same time, a referendum was held in the Republic of Ireland to repeal its constitutional claim to Northern Ireland; this was also endorsed by voters. The first election for the Northern Ireland Assembly was held in June 1998. Power was devolved to the Northern Ireland Assembly in December 1999. The Assembly was suspended in February 2000 owing to the lack of progress made in talks with the IRA on decommissioning its weaponry, but it was reinstated in May 2000 following further negotiations. On 8 April 2002, the IRA released a statement on decommissioning in a further initiative to put arms beyond use.

POLITICAL SYSTEM

Parliament consists of the House of Commons and the House of Lords. The House of Commons has 659 directly-elected members, whose term of office is a maximum of five years. The House of Lords is appointed and consists of 92 hereditary peers, over 500 life peers, certain senior judges, and 26 bishops of the Church of England.

HEAD OF STATE

HM by the Grace of God, of the United Kingdom of Great Britain and Northern Ireland and of her other Realms and Territories Queen, Head of the Commonwealth, Defender of the Faith, **Queen Elizabeth II**, *succeeded* 6 February 1952; *crowned* 2 June 1953

Heir, HRH The Prince of Wales (Prince Charles Philip Arthur George), KG, KT, GCB and Great Master of the Order of Bath, OM, AK, QSO, PC, ADC(P)

CABINET *as at November 2002*

Prime Minister, First Lord of the Treasury, Civil Service: Tony Blair; **Deputy Prime Minister, First Secretary of State (responsible for the Regions):** John Prescott; **Chancellor of the Exchequer:** Gordon Brown; **Chief Secretary to the Treasury:** Paul Boateng; **Culture, Media and Sport:** Tessa Jowell; **Defence:** Geoff Hoon; **Education and Skills:** Charles Clarke; **Environment, Food and Rural Affairs:** Margaret Beckett; **Foreign and Commonwealth Affairs:** Jack Straw; **Health:** Alan Milburn; **Home Office:** David Blunkett; **International Development:** Clare Short; **Lord Chancellor:** Lord Irvine of Lairg; **Lord Privy Seal, Leader of the House of Lords:** Lord Williams of Mostyn; **Northern Ireland:** John Reid; **Parliamentary Secretary, Treasury, Chief Whip:** Hilary Armstrong; **President of the Council of the Leader of the House of Commons:** Robin Cook; **Scotland:** Helen Liddell; **Trade and Industry:** Patricia Hewitt; **Transport:** Alistair Darling; **Wales:** Paul Murphy; **Without Portfolio, Labour Party**

Chair: Charles Clarke; **Work and Pensions:** Andrew Smith

HOUSEHOLD OF HM THE QUEEN
Lord Great Chamberlain: The Marquess of Cholmondeley; **Earl Marshall:** The Duke of Norfolk; **Lord Steward:** The Duke of Abercorn, KG; **Lord Chamberlain:** The Rt. Hon. the Lord Luce, KCVO; **Master of the Horse:** The Lord Vestey; **Keeper of the Privy Purse and Treasurer:** Alan Reid; **The Comptroller:** Lt.-Col. Sir Malcolm Ross, KCVO, OBE; **Vice-Chamberlain:** Gerry Sutcliffe, MP; **Private Secretary to the Queen:** The Rt. Hon. Sir Robin Janvrin, KCVO, CB; **Private Secretary to the Duke of Edinburgh:** Brig. Miles Hunt-Davis, CVO, CBE; **Master of the Household:** Vice-Adm. Tom Blackburn; **Crown Equerry:** Lt.-Col. Sir Seymour V. Gilbart-Denham, KCVO; **Marshall of the Diplomatic Corps:** Vice-Adm. Sir James L. Weatherall, KCVO, KBE

HOUSEHOLD OF HRH THE PRINCE OF WALES
Private Secretary: Sir Michael C. G. Peat, KCVO

COLLEGE OF ARMS
Kings of Arms: Peter L Gwynn-Jones, CVO (*Garter Principal*); David H B Chesshyre, LVO, FSA (*Clarenceux*); Thomas Woodcock, LVO, FSA (*Norroy and Ulster*); **Heralds:** Patric L Dickinson (*Richmond*); Henry E Paston-Bedingfeld (*York*); Timothy H S Duke (*Chester*); Robert J B Noel, Ph.D (*Lancaster*); William G Hunt, TD (*Windsor*); **Pursuivants:** David V White (*Rouge Croix*); Clive E A Cheesman, Ph.D (*Rouge Dragon*); **Herald Extraordinarys:** Francis S Andrus, LVO (*Beaumont*); John M Robinson, D.Phil (*Maltravers*); Phillip P. O'Shea, LVO (*New Zealand*), Michael P. Siddons (*Wales*); David Rankin-Hunt, MVO, MBE, TD (*Norfolk*); Alan R. Dickins (*Arundel*); **Fitzalan Pursuivant Extraordinary:** Alastair A B R Bruce of Crionaich

COURT OF THE LORD LYON
Lord Lyon King of Arms: R. O. Blair, LVO, WS; **Heralds:** J. A. Spens, MVO, RD, WS (*Albany*); Sir Crispin Agnew of Lochnaw, Bt., QC (*Rothesay*); C. J. Burnett, FSA Scot. (*Ross*); **Pursuivants:** Alastair Campbell of Airds (*Unicorn*); Mrs C. G. W. Roads, MVO (*Carrick*); W. D. H. Sellar (*Bute*)

CROWN DEPENDENCIES

*ALDERNEY – **President of the States:** Sir Norman Browse

*GUERNSEY – **Lt.-Governor and Cdr-in-Chief:** HE Lt.-Gen. Sir John Foley, KCB, OBE, MC, *apptd* 2000; **Bailiff:** de V. G. Carey

THE ISLE OF MAN – **Lt.-Governor:** HE Air-Marshal I. MacFadyen, CB, OBE; **President of the Tynwald:** The Hon. N. Q. Cringle

*JERSEY – **Lt.-Gov. and Cdr-in-Chief:** Chief Marshall Sir John Cheshire, KBE, CB, *apptd* 2001; **Bailiff:** Sir Philip Bailhache, Kt.

*SARK – **Seigneur of Sark:** J. M. Beaumont, OBE; **The Seneschal:** Lt.-Col. R. J. Guille, MBE

* *Dukedom of Normandy*

UK OVERSEAS TERRITORIES

ANGUILLA – **Governor:** HE Peter Johnson, *apptd* 2000; **Deputy Governor:** Roger Cousins, OBE, *apptd* 1997; **Chairman of the Executive Council, Chief Minister:** Osbourne Fleming

BERMUDA – **Governor and Commander-in-Chief:** HE Sir John Vereker, KCB, *apptd* 2002, 1997; **Deputy Governor:** Tim Gurney; **Premier:** Jennifer Smith

THE BRITISH ANTARTIC TERRITORY – **Commissioner** (*non-resident*)**:** Alan Edden Huckle, *apptd* 2001

THE BRITISH INDIAN OCEAN TERRITORY – **Commissioner:** Alan Edden Huckle, *apptd* 2001; **Administrator:** Louise Savill, *apptd* 1996

BRITISH VIRGIN ISLANDS – **Governor:** HE Frank Savage, CMG, OBE, LVO, *apptd* 1998; **Deputy Governor:** Elton Georges, OBE; **Chairman of the Executive Council:** The Governor; **Chief Minister and Minister of Finance:** Ralph O'Neal, OBE

CAYMAN ISLANDS – **Governor:** HE Bruce Dinwiddy, *apptd* 2002; **President:** The Governor; **Chief Secretary, Internal and External Affairs:** James Ryan, MBE

FALKLAND ISLANDS – **Governor and Chairman of the Executive Council:** HE Howard Pearce, *apptd* 2002; **Chief Executive:** Dr Michael D Blanch

GIBRALTAR – **Governor and Commander-in-Chief:** HE the Rt Hon David Durie, CMG; **Deputy Governor:** D Blunt

MONTSERRAT – **Governor:** HE Anthony Longrigg, CMG, *apptd* 2001; **President:** The Governor; **Chief Minister and Minister of Finance and Economic Development:** Dr John Osborne

PITCAIRN ISLANDS – **Governor of Pitcairn, Henderson,**

Ducie and Oeno Islands: HE Richard Fell, CVO (*British High Commissioner to New Zealand*); **Island Mayor:** Steve Christian
ST HELENA AND DEPENDENCIES – **Governor:** HE David Hollamby, *apptd* 1999
ASCENSION ISLAND – **Administrator:** Geoffrey Fairhurst, *apptd* 1999
TRISTAN DA CUNHA – **Administrator:** Bill Dickson, *apptd* 2001
SOUTH GEORGIA AND THE SOUTH SANDWICH ISLANDS – **Commissioner for South Georgia and the South Sandwich Islands:** Donald Lamont, *apptd* 1999
TURKS AND CAICOS ISLANDS – **Governor:** HE Mervyn T Jones, *apptd* 2000; **President:** The Governor

OTHER REALMS OF HM QUEEN ELIZABETH II
ANTIGUA AND BARBUDA – **Governor-General:** HE Sir James Carlisle, GCMG; **Prime Minister:** Lester Bird
THE BAHAMAS – **Governor-General:** HE Dame Ivy Dumont; **Prime Minister:** Perry Christie
BARBADOS – **Governor-General:** HE Sir Clifford Husbands, GCMG, KA, *apptd* 1996; **Prime Minister:** Owen Arthur
BELIZE – **Governor-General:** HE Sir Colville Norbert Young, GCMG, *apptd* 17 November 1993; **Prime Minister:** Said Musa
GRENADA – **Governor-General:** HE Sir Daniel Williams, GCMG, QC, *apptd* 1996; **Prime Minister:** Keith Mitchell
JAMAICA – **Governor-General:** HE Sir Howard Felix Hanlon Cooke, GCMG, GCVO, *Apptd* 1991; **Prime Minister:** Percival J. Patterson, QC
PAPUA NEW GUINEA – **Governor-General:** HE Sir Silas Atopare, GCMG, *apptd* 14 November 1997; **Prime Minister:** Sir Michael Somare
ST CHRISTOPHER AND NEVIS – **Governor-General:** HE Sir Cuthbert Montraville Sebastian, GCMG, OBE, *apptd* 1996; **Prime Minister:** Denzil Douglas
ST LUCIA – **Governor-General:** HE Dame Pearlette Louisy, *apptd* 1997; **Prime Minister:** Kenny Anthony
ST VINCENT AND THE GRENADINES – **Governor-General:** Monica Deacon (*acting*), *sworn in* 5 October 2001; **Prime Minister:** Ralph Gonsalves
SOLOMON ISLANDS – **Governor-General:** HE John Lapli, GCMG, *apptd* 1999; **Prime Minister:** Sir Allan Kemakesa

TUVALU – Governor-General: Sir Tomasi Puapua; **Prime Minister:** Saufatu Sopoanga

---

GREECE
ELLINIKI DIMOKRATIA

AREA – 50,949 sq. miles (131,957 sq. km). Neighbours: Albania, Bulgaria and Macedonia (north), Turkey (east)

POPULATION – 10,623,835 (2001 estimate): 98 per cent Greek Orthodox, 1 per cent Catholic, 1 per cent Muslim. The language is Greek

CAPITAL – Athens (population 3,072,922, 1991); including Piraeus and suburbs, 3,096,775 (1991 census)

MAJOR CITIES – Iráklion (Heraklion) (132,117); Lárisa (113,090); Pátrai (Patras) (170,452); Thessaloníki (Salonika) (749,048); Vólos (116,031), 1991

CURRENCY – Euro of 100 cents

NATIONAL ANTHEM – Imnos Eis Tin Eleftherian (Hymn To Freedom)

NATIONAL DAY – March 25 (Independence Day)

NATIONAL FLAG – Blue and white stripes with a white cross on blue in the canton

LIFE EXPECTANCY (years) – male 75.9; female 81.2

POPULATION GROWTH RATE – 0.4 per cent (1999)

POPULATION DENSITY – 81 per sq. km (1999)

URBAN POPULATION – 60.1 per cent (2000 estimate)

The main areas are: Macedonia, Thrace, Epirus, Thessaly, Continental Greece, Crete and the Peloponnese. The main island groups are the Sporades, the Dodecanese or Southern Sporades, the Cyclades, the Ionian Islands, and the Aegean Islands (Chios, Lesbos, Limnos and Samos). In Crete from about 3000 to 1400BC a civilisation flourished which spread its influence throughout the Aegean, and the ruins of the place of Minos at Knossos afford evidence of astonishing comfort and luxury.

HISTORY AND POLITICS

Greece was under Turkish rule from the mid-15th century until a war of independence (1821-7) led to the establishment of a Greek kingdom in the Peloponnese in 1829. The remainder of Greece gradually became independent until the Dodecanese were returned by Italy in 1947. After the Nazi German occupation of 1941-4, a civil war between monarchist and Communist groups lasted from 1946 to

1949, and tension between right-wing and radical groups continued after 1949. In 1967 right-wing elements in the army seized power and established a military regime (the 'Greek Colonels'). The King went into voluntary exile in 1967. Unrest in Athens in 1973-4 intensified after the government was involved in the overthrow of President Makarios of Cyprus in July 1974, and led the Colonels to surrender power. Konstantininos Karamanlis (prime minister 1955-63) returned from exile to form a provisional government, and the first elections for ten years were held in 1974. The restoration of the monarchy was rejected by referendum on 8 December 1974 and Greece became a republic.

The most recent general election was held on 9 April 2000 with the Panhellenic Socialist Party (PASOK) winning 158 seats, the New Democracy Party (Christian Democrats) 125 seats, the Communist Party 11 seats, and the Coalition of the Left and Progress six seats.

POLITICAL SYSTEM

In 1986 most executive power was transferred from the president to the government. The unicameral 300-member Chamber of Deputies (*Vouli*) is elected for a four-year term by universal adult suffrage under a system of proportional representation, with a three per cent threshold for parliamentary representation.

HEAD OF STATE

President of the Hellenic Republic: Constantine Stephanopoulos, *elected by parliament* 1995, *re-elected* 10 March 2000

CABINET *as at July 2002*

Prime Minister: Costas Simitis; **Aegean:** Nicos Sifounakis; **Agriculture:** Georgios Drys; **Culture:** Evangelos Venizelos; **Development:** Apostolos-Athanassios Tsohatzopoulos; **Education and Religious Affairs:** Petros Ephthimiou; **Environment, Town Planning and Public Works:** Vasso Papandreou; **Foreign Affairs:** George Papandreou; **Health and Welfare:** Constantine Stefanis; **Interior, Public Administration and Decentralisation:** Costas Skandalidis; **Justice:** Philippos Petsalnikos; **Labour and Social Affairs:** Dimitrios Reppas; **Macedonia and Thrace:** George Pashalidis; **Merchant Marine:** Georgios Anomeritis; **Minister of State, Office of the Prime Minister:** Stefanos Manikas; **National Defence:** Yiannos Papantoniou; **National Economy and Finance:** Nikolaos Christodoulakis; **Press and Media, Government Spokesman:** Christos Protopapas; **Public Order:** Michalis Chrysohoidos; **Transport and Communications:** Christos Verelis

ITALY
Repubblica Italiana

AREA – 116,339 sq. miles (301,318 sq. km). Neighbours: Switzerland and Austria (north), Slovenia (east), France (west)

POPULATION – 57,523,000 (2001 estimate): 83 per cent Catholic. The language is Italian, a Romance Language derived from Latin. There are several regional languages including Sardinian and Catalan in Sardinia, Friulian in Friuli, German and Ladin in the South Tyrol, French in the Valle d'Aosta, and Slovene in parts of Gorizia.

CAPITAL – Rome (population 2,648,843, 1995 estimate). The Eternal City was founded, according to legend, by Romulus in 753 BC. It was the centre of Latin civilisation and capital of the Roman Republic and Roman Empire

MAJOR CITIES – Bologna (385,813); Florence (381,762); Genoa (655,704); Milan (1,305,591); Naples (1,046,987); Turin (921,485); Sicily, Palermo (689,349); Sardinia, Cagliari (173,564), 1995 estimates

CURRENCY – Euro of 100 cents

NATIONAL ANTHEM – Inno di Mameli (Hymn Of Mameli)

NATIONAL DAY – 2 June

NATIONAL FLAG – Vertical stripes of green, white and red

LIFE EXPECTANCY (years) – male 75.5; female 81.9

POPULATION GROWTH RATE – 0.1 per cent (1999)

POPULATION DENSITY – 190 per sq. km (1999)

Italy consists of a peninsula, the islands of Sicily, Sardinia, Elba and about 70 other small islands. The peninsula is for the most part mountainous, but between the Apennines, which form its spine, and the eastern coastline are two large fertile plains: Emilia-Romagna in the north and Apulia in the south. The Alps divide Italy from France, Switzerland, Austria and Slovenia. Partly within the Italian borders are Monte Rosa (15,217 ft), the Matterhorn (14,780ft) and several peaks from 12,000 to 14,000ft. The chief rivers are the Po (405 miles), flowing through Piedmont, Lombardy and the Veneto; the Adige (Trentino and Veneto); The Arno (Florentine plain); and the Tiber (flowing through Rome to Ostia).

HISTORY AND POLITICS

Italian unity was accomplished under the House of Savoy after a struggle from 1848 to 1870 in which Mazzini (1805-72), Garibaldi (1807-82) and Cavour (1810-61) were the principal figures. It was completed when Lombardy was ceded by Austria in 1859 and Venice in 1866, and through the evacuation of Rome by the French in 1870.

In 1871 the King of Italy entered Rome, and that city was declared to be the capital.

A fascist regime came to power in 1922 under Benito Mussolini, known as *Il Duce* (The Leader), who was prime minister from 1922 until 25 July 1943, when the regime was abolished. Mussolini was captured by Italian partisans while attempting to escape across the Swiss frontier and killed on 28 April 1945.

Italy became a republic following a referendum on the future of the monarchy in June 1946.

Political instability and corruption led to public disenchantment with the major political parties, whose support collapsed in the 1992 general election. The so-called 'clean hands' investigation into corruption and Mafia links that began in 1992 has led to the arrest by magistrates of thousands of politicians and businessmen.

The general election on 21 April 1996 was won by the left-wing Olive Tree alliance led by the Democratic Party of the Left, whose leader, Romano Prodi, became prime minister. The government collapsed on 9 October 1998 after the Communist Refoundation party, on whose support it had been dependent, refused to vote for the 1999 budget. Massimo d'Alema was invited by the president to form a new government on 20 October. On 19 December 1999, the government collapsed, but Massimo d'Alema was asked to form a new government the following day; he resigned as prime minister on 17 April 2000 following the defeat of his centre-left coalition in regional elections on 16 April. President Ciampi invited Giuliano Amato to form a new government and Amato was sworn in as prime minister on 26 April 2000.

The general election held on 13 May 2001 was won by the centre-right House of Freedom alliance, which obtained 368 seats. The alliance was led by Forza Italia and also comprised the Christian Democratic Centre, the Christian Democratic Union, the National Alliance, the New Italian Socialist Party and the Northern League. Silvio Berlusconi, the Forza Italia leader, was sworn in as prime minister.

POLITICAL SYSTEM

The constitution provides for the election of the president for a seven-year term by an electoral college which consists of the two houses of the parliament (the Chamber of Deputies and the Senate) sitting in joint session, together with three delegates from each region (one in the case of the Valle d'Aosta). The president, who must be over 50 years of age, has the right to dissolve one or both houses after consultation with the Speakers. Members of both houses were elected wholly by proportional representation. There is a variable number of life senators, who are past president and senators appointed by incumbent presidents. In the Chamber of Deputies 75 per cent (472) of seats are elected on a first-past-the-post basis, and 25 per cent (158) by proportional representation, with a 4 per cent threshold for parliamentary representation. A referendum on 18 April 1999 on abolishing the seats elected by proportional representation foundered when less than the required 50 per cent of the electorate participated.

HEAD OF STATE

President: Carlo Azeglio Ciampi, *elected by electoral college* 13 May 1999

COUNCIL OF MINISTERS *as at July 2002*

Prime Minister, Foreign Affairs: Silvio Berlusconi (FI); **Deputy Prime Minister:** Gianfranco Fini (AN); **Agriculture and Forestry:** Giovanni Alemanno (AN); **Culture:** Giuliano Urbani (FI); **Defence:** Antonio Martino (FI); **Economy and Finance:** Giulio Tremonti (FI); **Education, Higher Education and Scientific Research:** Letizia Moratti (Ind.); **Employment and Social Welfare:** Roberto Maroni (LN); **Environment:** Altero Matteoli (AN); **Health:** Gerolamo Sirchia (Ind.); **Industry:** Antonio Marzano (FI); **Infrastructure and Transport:** Pietro Lunardi (Ind.); **Interior:** Giuseppe Pisanu (FI); **Justice:** Roberto Castelli (LN); **Telecommunications:** Maurizio Gasparri (AN)

AN National Alliance; FI Forza Italia; LN Northern League; Ind. Independent

---

LIECHTENSTEIN
FÜRSTENTUM LIECHTENSTEIN

AREA – 62 sq. miles (160sq.km). Neighbours: Austria, Switzerland
POPULATION – 32,528 (2001 estimate). The language of the principality is Standard German. An Alemannic dialect is in general use. About 65.4 per cent of the population are Liechtensteiners, the remainder being mainly Swiss, Austrians and Germans. Roman Catholicism is the religion of 80.4 per cent of the population; there is a Protestant minority
CAPITAL – Vaduz (population 5,106, 1998)
CURRENCY – Swiss franc of 100 rappen (or centimes)
NATIONAL ANTHEM – Oben Am Jungen Rhein (Up On The Young Rhine)
NATIONAL DAY – 15 August

NATIONAL FLAG – Equal horizontal bands of blue over red; gold crown on blue band near staff
LIFE EXPECTANCY (years) – male 66.1; female 72.9
POPULATION GROWTH RATE – 1.0 per cent (1999)
POPULATION DENSITY – 200 per sq. km (1999)

HISTORY AND POLITICS

The region was settled in the fifth century AD by the West Germanic Alemanni. The Principality of Liechtenstein was established by Emperor Charles VI in 1719. Following the First World War, Liechtenstein served its ties with Austria and began its association with Switzerland, taking up the Swiss currency in 1921.

In November 1999, the European Court of Human Rights fined Prince Hans Adam II for abusing his subjects' freedom of speech, a development which prompted a constitutional crisis in the principality.

In February 2000, Prince Hans Adam announced that he wished to hold a referendum on constitutional reform, and threatened to abdicate if his proposals were rejected by the electorate.

The Patriotic Union (VU) and the Progressive Citizens' Party (FBP) governed the country in coalition from 1938 until March 1997. The 1997 general election was won by the VU, which lost power to the FBP, who won 13 seats in the general election held on 9 and 11 February 2001. The new government took office on 5 April.

POLITICAL SYSTEM

Liechtenstein is a constitutional monarchy. The Cabinet is appointed by the Prince on the advice of parliament and consists of a head of government and four ministers. The 25-member *Landtag*, the unicameral parliament, has a four-year term. There is a threshold of 8 per cent for parties to gain representation.

HEAD OF STATE

Johannes **(HANS)-ADAM II** Ferdinand Alois Josef Maria Marko d'Aviano Pius, **PRINCE OF LIECHTENSTEIN**, Duke of Troppau and Jägerndorf, Count of Rietberg, *succeeded* 13 November 1989

Heir, HSH Hereditary Prince *Alois* Philipp Maria of Liechtenstein

CABINET *as at July 2002*

Head of Government, Construction, Family Affairs and Equal Opportunities, Finance, General Government Affairs: Otmar Hasler; **Deputy Head of Government, Education, Justice,**

Transport: Rita Kieber-Beck; **Culture and Sports, Environment, Interior:** Alois Ospelt; **Economy, Health, Social Matters:** Hansjörg Frick; **Foreign Affairs:** Ernst Walch

———◆◆———

LUXEMBOURG
GROUSSHERZOGTOM LËTZEBUERG / GRAND-DUCHÉ DE LUXEMBOURG / GROSSHERZOGTUM LUXEMBOURG

AREA – 998 sq. miles (2,586sq. km). Neighbours: Germany (east), Belgium (west and north), France (south)

POPULATION – 442,972 (2001 estimate), nearly all Roman Catholic. The officially designated 'national language' is Lëtzebuergesch (Luxembourgish), a mainly spoken language. French and German are the official languages for written purposes, and French is the language of administration.

CAPITAL – Luxembourg (population, 77,400, 1996)

CURRENCY – Euro of 100 cents

NATIONAL ANTHEM – Ons Hémécht (Our Homeland)

NATIONAL DAY – 23 June

NATIONAL FLAG – Three horizontal bands, red, white and blue

LIFE EXPECTANCY (years) – male 74.6; female 80.9

POPULATION GROWTH RATE – 1.2 per cent (1999)

POPULATION DENSITY – 166 per sq. km (1999)

ENROLMENT – (percentage of age group) – primary 81 per cent (1985); secondary 64 per cent (1994); tertiary 10 per cent (1996)

HISTORY AND POLITICS

Established as an independent state under the sovereignty of the King of the Netherlands as Grand Duke by the Congress of Vienna in 1815, Luxembourg formed part of the Germanic Confederation from 1815 to 1866, becoming neutral in 1867.

The territory was invaded by Germany in 1914 but was liberated in 1918. By the Treaty of Versailles (1919), Germany renounced its former agreements with Luxembourg and in 1921 an economic union was formed with Belgium. The Grand Duchy was again invaded and occupied by Germany in 1940, and liberated in 1944.

The constitution was modified in 1948 and the stipulation of permanent neutrality was abandoned.

POLITICAL SYSTEM

There is Chamber of 60 deputies, elected by universal suffrage for five years. Legislation is submitted to the Council of State. The last general election was held on 13 June 1999 and a coalition government was installed. In March 1998, Grand duke Jean passed certain constitutional powers on to his son and heir, Prince Henri, and announced on 25 December 1999 that he would abdicate in favour of Prince Henri in September 2000.

HEAD OF STATE

HENRI Albert Gabriel Felix Marie Guillaume, **GRAND DUKE OF LUXEMBOURG,** Duke of Nassau, Prince of Bourbon-Parma, Count Palatine of the Rhine, Count of Sayn, Königstein, Katzenelnbogen and Dietz, Burggrave of Hammerstein, Lord of Mahlberg, Wiesbaden, Idstein, Merenberg, Limburg and Eppstein, *succeeded* (on the abdication of his father) 7 October 2000

Heir, HRH Crown Prince *Guillaume* Jean Joseph Marie, Hereditary Grand Duke of Luxembourg, Prince of Nassau, etc, Kt of the Golden Lion of the House of Nassau.

CABINET *as at July 2002*

Prime Minister, Finance: Jean-Claude Juncker (CSP); **Deputy PM, Foreign Affairs, Trade, Civil Service and Administrative Reform:** Lydie Polfer (DP); **Agriculture, Viticulture, Rural Development, Small Businesses, Housing and Tourism:** Fernand Boden (CSP); **Culture, Higher Education and Research, Public Works:** Erna Hennicot-Schoepges (CSP); **Development Aid and Defence, Environment:** Charles Goerens (DP); **Economy, Transport:** Henri Grethen (DP); **Employment, Religion, Parliamentary Relations:** François Biltgen (CSP); **Family, Social Solidarity and Youth, Advancement of Women:** Marie-Josée Jacobs (CSP); **Health and Social Security:** Carlo Wagner (DP); **Home Affairs:** Michel Wolter (CSP); **National Education, Vocational Training and Sports:** Anne Brasseur (DP); **Secretaries of State:** Joseph Schaack (DP) (*Civil Service and Administrative reform*); Eugène Berger (DP) (*Environment*); **Treasury and Budget, Justice:** Luc Frieden (CSP)

CSP Christian Social Party; DP Democratic Party

HOUSEHOLD OF HRH THE GRAND DUKE

Marshal of the Court: Henri Ahlborn; **Head of the Grand**

Duke's Cabinet and Chamberlain in ordinary service: Albert Hansen; **Secretaries to HRH the Grand Duchess:** Chantal Brück; Anne Masotti; **Ladies-in-Waiting:** Dita Dupong-Schackmann; Aline Schleder-Leuck; Valérie Krieps-Dupong; Rita Krombach-Meyer; Marie-Paule Prost-Heinisch; Maggy Schmit-Molitor; Marianne Tholl-Hoesdorff; **Chamberlains Extraordinary:** Hubert Clasen; Marc Elvinger; Paul Lesch; François Tesch; **Aide-de-Camp:** Lt.-Col. Henri Chrisnach; **Court Chaplain:** Revd. Canon Georges Vuillermoz; **Court Physicians:** Dr Jules Hoffelt; Dr Robert Berwick; **Honorary Marshals of the Court:** Guy de Muyser; Roger Hastert; Marcel Mart; **Honorary Ladies-in-Waiting:** Anne-Marie Reuter-Jörg; Andrée Neuman-Simons; Manette Meyers-Turk; **Honorary Chamberlains:** Jacques Loesch; Gérard Rasquin; Georges Als; Jean Petit; **Honorary Aide-de-Camp to HRH the Grand Duke:** Col. (hon) Eugène Meunier; **Honorary Court Physicians:** Dr André Beissel; Dr Emile Gretsch; **Court Intendent:** Guy May; **Librarian:** Gast Mannes; **Steward of the Palace of Luxembourg:** Pascal Konz

HOUSEHOLD OF HRH GRAND DUKE JEAN

Ladies-in-Waiting: Marie-Anne Konsbruck-Raus; Marianne Hamilius-Thill; **Chamberlains in ordinary service:** Col. (hon) Germain Frantz; Lt.-Col. (hon) Léandre Mignon; **Chamberlain Extraordinary:** Jean-Luc Koltz; **Aide-de-Camp:** Lt.-Col. Fernand Brosius

---

MONACO
PRINCIPAUTÉ DE MONACO

AREA – 0.4 sq. miles (1sq. km). Neighbour: France

POPULATION – 31,842 (2001 estimate). Only 7,175 residents have full Monégasque citizenship and thus the right to vote. The official language is French. Monégasque, a mixture of Provençal and Ligurian, is also spoken

CAPITAL – Monaco

CURRENCY – Euro of 100 cents

NATIONAL ANTHEM – Hymne Monégasque

NATIONAL DAY – 19 November

NATIONAL FLAG – Two equal horizontal stripes, red over white

LIFE EXPECTANCY (years) – male 74.7; female 83.6

75 members, elected for four years by the Provincial Council; and the *Tweede Kamer* (Second Chamber) of 150 members, elected for four years by votes of 18 years and upwards. Members of the *Tweede Kamer* are paid.

HEAD OF STATE

BEATRIX Wilhelmina Armgard, **QUEEN OF THE NETHERLANDS,** Gd Mistress Mil Willems Order, Order of the The Netherlands Lion, Order of Orange-Nassau, of the House of Orange, and House Order Golden Lion of Nassau, Lady of the Order of the Garter (1989), Royal Victorian Chain (1982), GCVO (1958), etc, *succeeded* 30 April 1980

Heir, HRH Crown Prince *Willem-Alexander* Claus Georg Ferdinand of The Netherlands, Prince of Orange, Prince of Orange-Nassau, Jonkheer van Amsberg

CABINET *as at August 2002*

Prime Minister, General Affairs: Jan Peter Balkenende (CDA); **Deputy Prime Minister, Health, Welfare and Sport:** Eduard Bomhoff (LPF); **Deputy Prime Minister, Interior and Kingdom Relations:** Johan Remkes (VVD); **Agriculture, Nature Management and Fisheries:** Kees Veerman (CDA); **Defence:** Benk Korthals; **Economic Affairs:** Herman Heinsbroek (LPF); **Education, Cultural Affairs and Science:** Maria van der Hoeven (CDA); **Finance:** Hans Hoogervorst (VVD); **Foreign Affairs:** Jaap de Hoop Scheffer (CDA); **Housing, Spatial Planning and Environment:** Henk Kamp (VVD); **Immigration and Integration:** Hilbrand Nawijn (LPF); **Justice:** Piet Hein Donner (CDA); **Social Affairs and Employment:** Aart Jan de Geus (CDA); **Transport and Public Works and Water Management:** Roelf de Boer (LPF)

CDA Christian Democratic Party; LPF List Pim Fortuyn; VVD People's Party for Freedom and Democracy

HOUSEHOLD OF HM THE QUEEN

Grand Master of the Royal Household: HE P.W. Waldeck; **Mistress of the Robes:** HE Mrs M. L. A. van Loon-Labouchere; **Adjutant-General and Chief of the Military Household:** HE Lt.-Gen. A. J. G. M. Blomjous; **Principal Secretary:** H. A. C. van der Zwan; **Treasurer:** J. Baars; **Chamberlains:** E. ten Cate; Prof. Dr. D. W. Erkelens; Baron G. W. van der Feltz; Prof. Dr. C. M.

POPULATION GROWTH RATE – 1.1 PER CENT (1999)
A small principality on the Mediterranean, with land frontiers joining France at every point, Monaco is divided into the districts of Monaco-Ville, La Condamine, Fontvielle and Monte Carlo.

HISTORY AND POLITICS

The principality, ruled by the Grimaldi family since 1297, was abolished during the French Revolution and re-established in 1815 under the protection of the kingdom of Sardinia. In 1861 Monaco came under French protection.

The 1962 constitution, which can be modified only with the approval of the National Council, maintains the traditional hereditary monarchy and guarantees freedom of association, trade union freedom and the right to strike. Legislative power is held jointly by the Prince and a unicameral, 18-member National Council elected by universal suffrage. In the most recent legislative election on 1 and 8 February 1998, all 18 seats were won by the National and Democratic Union. Executive power is exercised by the Prince and a four-member Council of Government, headed by a Minister of State, who is nominated by the Prince from a list of three French diplomats submitted by the French government. The judicial code is based on that of France. The next election is due to be held in February 2003.

HEAD OF STATE

RAINIER III Louis Henri Maxence Bertrand, **SOVEREIGN PRINCE OF MONACO,** Duke of Valentinois, Marquis des Baux, Comte de Carladès, Baron du Buis, Seigneur de Saint-Remy, Sire de Matignon, Comte de Torigni, Baron de Saint-Lô, Baron de la Luthumière, Baron de Hambye, Duc d'Estouteville, de Mazarin et de Mayenne, Prince de Château-Porcien, Comte de Ferrette, de Belfort, de Thann et de Rosemont, Seigneur d'Isenheim, Marquis de Chilly, Comte de Longjumeau, Baron de Massy, Marquis de Guiscard, founded Order of Cultural Merit 1952, Order of the Grimaldi 1954, and Order of the Crown of Monaco 1960, *succeeded* 9 May 1949

Heir, HSH Hereditary Prince *Albert* Alexandre Louis Pierre of Monaco, Marquis des Baux, Grand Officer of the Lion of Senegal National Order, Grand Cross of the Order of St. Charles, Grand Officer of the Legion of Honor of France, Kt Sovereign Military Order of Malta

COUNCIL OF MINISTERS

President of the Crown Council: Charles Ballerio; **President of**

the National Council: Dr Jean-Louis Campora; **President of the State Council:** Patrice Davost; **Minister of State:** Patrick Leclercq; **Finance and Economy:** Franck Biancheri; **Interior:** Philippe Deslandes; **Public Works and Social Affairs:** José Badia

HOUSEHOLD OF HSH THE SOVEREIGN PRINCE

Chamberlain: Col. Serge Lamblin; **Lady-in-Waiting:** Mrs Paul Gallico; **The Prince's Cabinet:** Georges Grinda (*Head Councillor*); Raymond Biancheri (*Councillor*); Robert Projetti (*Councillor*); Philippe Blanchi (*Councillor*); **Personal Secretary:** Francine Siri; **Private Secretary:** Jean-Pierre Diter; **Private Secretary to the Princess of Hanover:** Judith Mann; **Private Secretary to Princess Stéphanie:** Christine Barca; **Curator of the Archives and Library:** Régis Lecuyer

HOUSEHOLD OF HSH HEREDITARY PRINCE ALBERT

Principal Private Secretary: Robert Projetti; **Principal Secretary:** Mireille Viale; **Aides-de-Camp:** Lt.-Col. Luc Fringant; Lt.-Col. Thierry Jouan; Cdr. Bruno Philipponnat

---

THE NETHERLANDS
KONINKRIJK DER NEDERLANDEN

AREA – 16,033 sq. miles (41,526 sq. km). Neighbours: Belgium (south), Germany (east)

POPULATION – 15,981,472 (2000 estimate): 36 per cent Catholic, 27 per cent Reformed Church, 8 per cent Muslim. The language is Dutch, a West Germanic language of Low Franconian origin closely akin to Old English and Low German. It is spoken in the Netherlands and the northern part of Belgium (Flanders). Frisian is spoken in Friesland. Dutch is the official language in the Netherlands Antilles and Aruba; Papiamento, a mixture of Dutch and Spanish, is the vernacular

CAPITAL – Amsterdam (population 1,102,323, 1996 estimate)

SEAT OF GOVERNMENT – The Hague (Den Haag or, in full, 's-Gravenhage), population 695,815, 1996 estimate

MAJOR CITIES – Eindhoven (399,756); Groningen (209,051); Haarlem (211,124); Rotterdam (1,077,818); Tilburg (239,057); Utrecht (549,773), 1996 estimates

CURRENCY – Euro of 100 cents

NATIONAL ANTHEM – Wilhelmus van Nassouwe (William of Nassau)

NATIONAL FLAG – Three horizontal bands of red, white and blue

LIFE EXPECTANCY (years) – male 75.6; female 81.0

POPULATION GROWTH RATE – 0.6 per cent (1999)

POPULATION DENSITY – 381 per sq. km (1999)

URBAN POPULATION – 61.0 per cent (1996)

The Kingdom of the Netherlands is a maritime country of western Europe, situated on the North Sea, consisting of 12 provinces (Eastern and Southern Flevoland being amalgamated to form the twelfth province). The land is generally flat and low, intersected by numerous canals and connecting rivers. The principal rivers are the Rhine, Maas, Ijssel and Schelde.

HISTORY AND POLITICS

Following a revolt against Spanish rule under the leadership of William of Orange, the northern provinces were united by the Union of Utrecht (1579) and in 1581 independence was declared. Dutch economic and military power flourished in the 17th and 18th centuries.

The Netherlands were overrun by France in the late 18th century, becoming part of the French Empire until 1814, when the northern and southern Netherlands were united into one kingdom. In 1830 the southern provinces seceded to form Belgium. The Duchy of Luxembourg was made an independent state in 1867.

The Netherlands remained neutral during the First World War but were invaded by Germany during the Second World War and occupied until the war ended. The Netherlands joined the Benelux economic union with Belgium and Luxembourg in 1948 and became a member of NATO in 1949. The Dutch East Indies gained independence as Indonesia in 1949.

In 2001, the Netherlands became the first country in the world to legalise euthanasia and to allow same sex marriages.

On 6 May 2002, right-wing politician Pim Fortuyn, leader of the List Pim Fortuyn (LPF) party, was assassinated, nine days before the general elections on 15 May in which the Christian Democratic Appeal (CDA) gained 43 of the 150 seats in the second chamber. The state of the parties as at May 2002 was: CDA 43; LPF 26; People's Party for Freedom and Democracy 66 7; others 8. A coalition government headed by CDA leader Jan Peter Balkenende and comprising the CDA, LPF and VVD was sworn in on 22 July.

POLITICAL SYSTEM

The States-General consists of the *Eerste Kamer* (First Chamber) of

Karssen; C. Kostense; C. L. M. de Quay; A. Robaard; Baron C. O. A. Schimmelpenninck van der Oijec; R. E. Selman; Baron E. H. van Tuyll van Serooskerken; G. Vlieghuis; L. E. H. Vredevoogd; R. S. Wegener Sleeswijk; **Master of Ceremonies:** G. H. A. Monod de Froideville; **Marshal of the Court:** J. W. S. van Eenennaam; **Comptroller of the Royal Palaces:** Baron B. W. Bentinck tot Buckhorst; **Crown Equerry:** Col. G. E. Wassenaar; **Ladies-in-Waiting:** Mrs. M. P. van Karnebeek; Mrs. M. J. Boellaard; Mrs. J. Jeekel; Mrs. O. A. Gaarlandt; Mrs. R. D. de Blocq van Scheltinga; **Director of Personnel:** K. W. Ruijg; **Director of the Royal Archives:** B. Woelderink; **Master Forester:** Dr. J. H. Kuper; **Private Secretaries:** W. H. B. van Rossem; Mrs A. M. Leendertse; **Private Secretary to T.R.H. Princes Friso and Constantijn:** Baroness M. C. A. Taets van Amerongen tot Woudenberg; **Aides-de-Camp:** Lt.-Col. B. W. Valk; Lt. Col. Mrs W J. M. Wiersma; Lt.-Col. P. W. E. Whittle; Lt.-Col. Ms. A. M. H. Vranken; Lt.-Col. J. van Leeuwen; Lt.-Col. W. Baron; Lt.-Col. J. A. Dijkstra; Cdr. J. P. D. van Zaalen

HOUSEHOLD OF HRH THE PRINCE OF ORANGE
Private Secretary: J. W. Leeuwenburg; **Assistant Private Secretary:** Th. A. van der Werf

NEW ZEALAND

AREA – 104,454 sq. miles (270, 534 sq. km)
POPULATION – 3,864,129 (2001 estimate): 79 per cent European stock, 13 per cent Maori, 5 per cent other Pacific islanders. The main religion is Christianity. In 1991 the principal denominations were Anglican 22.1 per cent, Presbyterian 16.3 per cent, Roman Catholic 15 per cent, Methodist 4.2 per cent, Baptist 2.1 per cent. The official languages are English and Maori

Islands	Area (sq. miles)	Population (census 1996)
North Island	44,281	2,749,788
South Island	58,093	930,824
Other islands	1,362	934
Total	103,736	3,681,546
Territories		
Tokelau	5	1,487

Niue	100	1,708
Cook Islands	93	18,008
Ross Dependency	175,000	-

CAPITAL – Wellington (population, 346,700, 1999 estimate)
MAJOR CITIES – Auckland (1,105,700); Christchurch (342,100);
Dunedin (111,700); Hamilton (170,900); Napier-Hastings (114,500),
2000 estimates
CURRENCY – New Zealand dollar of 100 cents
NATIONAL ANTHEM – God Save The Queen/God defend New
Zealand
NATIONAL DAY – 6 February (Waitangi Day)
NATIONAL FLAG – Blue ground, with Union Flag in top left
quarter, four five-pointed red stars with white borders on the fly
LIFE EXPECTANCY (years) – male 75.3; female 80.7
POPULATION GROWTH RATE – 1.0 per cent (1999)
POPULATION DENSITY – 14 per sq. km (1999)
URBAN POPULATION – 85.4 per cent (1996)

New Zealand consists of a number of islands in the South Pacific
Ocean, and also has administrative responsibility for the Ross
Dependency in Antarctica. The two larger islands, North Islands
and South Islands, are separated by a relatively narrow strait. The
remaining islands are much smaller and widely dispersed.

Much of the North and South Islands is mountainous. The
principal range is the Southern Alps, extending the entire length of
the South Islands and having its culminating point in Mount Cook/
Mount Aoraki (3,754 m/12,349 ft). The North Islands mountains
include several volcanoes, two of which are active. Of the numerous
glaciers in the South Island, the Tasman (18 miles long), the Franz
Josef and the Fox are the best known. The more important rivers
include the Waikato (425 km/270 miles in length), Wanganui (180
miles), and Clutha (210 miles) and lakes include Taupo, 234 sq.
miles in area; Wakatipu, 113; and Te Anau, 133.

New Zealand includes, in addition to North and South
Islands: Chatham Islands (Chatham, Pitt, South East Islands and
some rocky islets, combined area, 965 sq. km (373 sq. miles), largely
uninhabited); the Kermadec Group (Raoul or Sunday, Macauley,
Curtis Islands, L'Esperance, and some islets; population 9-10, all
government employees at a meteorological station); Campbell
Island, used as a weather station; the Three Kings (discovered by
Tasman on the Feast of the Epiphany); Auckland Islands;
Antipodes Group; Bounty Islands; Snares Islands and Solander.

New Zealand has a temperate marine climate, but with
abundant sunshine. The mean temperature ranges from 15 C in the
north to about 9 C in the south. Rainfall in the North Island ranges

from 35 to 70 inches and in the South Island from 25 to 45 inches.

HISTORY AND POLITICS

The discoverers and first colonists of New Zealand were Polynesians, ancestors of the modern-day Mâori, who settled the islands between the ninth and 14th centuries. The Dutch navigator, Abel Tasman, sighted the coast in 1642 but did not land, but the British explorer James Cook circumnavigated New Zealand and landed in 1769. Largely as a result of increased British emigration, the country was annexed by the British government in 1840. The British Lieutenant-Governor, William Hobson, proclaimed sovereignty, over the North Island by virtue of the Treaty of Waitangi, signed by him and many Mâori chiefs, and over the South Island and Stewart Island by right of discovery.

In 1841 New Zealand was created a separate colony distinct from New South Wales. In 1907 the designation was changed to 'The Dominion of New Zealand'.

Following the general election of 27 July 2002, the state of the parties in the House of Representatives was: Labour Party (LP) 52 seats, National Party 27, New Zealand First 13, ACT New Zealand 9, Green Party 9, United Future 8; Jim Anderton's Progressive Coalition (PC) 2. The Labour Party and the Progressive Coalition formed a minority administration.

POLITICAL SYSTEM

The executive authority is entrusted to a Governor-General appointed by the Crown and aided by an Executive Council, within a unicameral legislature, the House of Representatives. A non-binding referendum, held simultaneously with the general election in November 1999, approved a reduction in the number of members to 100 in future parliaments. There is no written constitution. The judicial system comprises a High Court, a Court of Appeal and district courts having both civil and criminal jurisdiction.

HEAD OF STATE

HM by the Grace of God of the United Kingdom, New Zealand and Her other Realms and Territories Queen, Head of the Commonwealth, Defender of the Faith, **Queen Elizabeth II**, *succeeded* 6 February 1952; *crowned* 2 June 1953

Heir, HRH The Prince of Wales (Prince Charles Philip Arthur George), KG, KT, GCB and Great Master of the Order of Bath, OM, AK, QSO, PC, ADC(P)

GOVERNOR-GENERAL

Governor-General and Commander-in-Chief: HE Dame Silvia

Cartwright, *sworn* in April 2001

THE EXECUTIVE COUNCIL *as at August 2002*

The Governor-General; Prime Minister, Arts, Culture and Heritage: Helen Clark (LP); **Deputy Prime minister, Finance and Revenue:** Dr Michael Cullen (LP); **Attorney-General, Courts, Labour, treaty of Waitangi Negotiations:** Margaret Wilson (LP); **Agriculture, Biosecurity, Forestry and Trade Negotiations:** Jim Sutton; **Commerce:** Lianne Dalziel; **Conservation, Local Government:** Chris Carter (LP); **Corrections, Housing, Pacific Island Affairs, Racing:** Mark Gosche (LP); **Defence, State-owned Enterprises, Tourism:** Mark Burton (LP); **Economic Development, Industry and Regional Development:** Jim Anderton (PC); **Education, State Services, Sport and Recreation:** Trevor Mallard (LP); **Energy, Fisheries, Research, Science and Technology, Crown Research Institutes:** Pete Hodgson (LP); **Environment, Disarmament and Arms Control:** Marian Hobbs (LP); **Foreign Affairs and Trade, Justice:** Phil Goff (LP); **Health and Food Safety:** Annette King (LP); **Māori Affairs:** Parekura Horomia (LP); **Police, Civil Defence, Internal Affairs, Veteran's Affairs:** George Hawkins (LP); **Social Services, Employment, Broadcasting:** Steve Maharey (LP); **Transport, Communications and Information Technology:** Paul Swain (LP); **Women's Affairs:** Ruth Dyson (LP); **Youth Affairs, Land Information and Statistics:** John Tamihere (LP)

TERRITORIES

TOKELAU (OR UNION ISLANDS) – Administrator: Lindsey Watt; **Ula-o-Tokelau** (2002): Pio Tuia

COOK ISLANDS – HM Representative: Frederick Goodwin; **Prime Minister:** Dr Robert Woonton; **New Zealand High Commissioner:** Kurt Meyer

NIUE – New Zealand High Commissioner: John Bryan

NORWAY
KONGERIKET NORGE

AREA – 125,050 sq. miles (323,877 sq. km) of which Svalbard and Jan Mayen have a combined area of 24,355 sq. miles (63,080 sq. km).

Neighbours: Sweden, Finland, Russia (east)

POPULATION – 4,504,000 (2001 estimate). The language is Norwegian and has two forms: Bokmål and Nynorsk. Sami is spoken in the north of the country. The state religion is Evangelical Lutheran

CAPITAL – Oslo (population, 508,726, 2001)

MAJOR CITIES – Bergen (230,948); Kristiansand (73,087); Stavanger (108,848); Trondheim (150,166), 2001

CURRENCY – Krone of 100 øre

NATIONAL ANTHEM – Ja, Vi Elsker Dette Landet (Yes, We Love This Country)

NATIONAL DAY – 17 May (Constitution Day)

NATIONAL FLAG – Red, with white-bordered blue cross

LIFE EXPECTANCY (years) – male 76.0; female 81.9

POPULATION GROWTH RATE – 0.6 per cent (1999)

POPULATION DENSITY – 14 per sq. km (1999)

The coastline is deeply indented with numerous fjords and fringed with rocky islands. The surface is mountainous, consisting of elevated and barren tablelands separated by deep and narrow valleys. At the North Cape the sun does not appear to set from about 14 May to 29 July, causing the phenomenon known as the Midnight Sun; conversely, there is no apparent sunrise from about 18 November to 24 January. During the long winter nights are seen the Northern Lights or Aurora Borealis.

HISTORY AND POLITICS

Norway was unified under Harald I Fairhair c.AD 900 and participated in the Viking expansion from the ninth to the 11th centuries. The accession of Magnus VII (1319) unified the Norwegian and Swedish crowns until his son became King Håkon VI of Norway in 1343. The Norwegian and Danish crowns were united in 1380 and confirmed by the Union of Kalmar (1397) which also brought Sweden under the rule of Queen Margrethe of Denmark. Norway remained a Danish province until transferred to Sweden under the Treaty of Kiel (1814). The union with Sweden was dissolved on 7 June 1905 when Norway regained complete independence.

Norway remained neutral during the First World War and on the outbreak of the Second World War but was invaded by Germany in 1940. Neutrality was abandoned when Norway joined NATO in 1949. Norway became a founder member of EFTA in 1960. The Labour Party governed from 1945 to 1965 when the extensive welfare state system was build. A referendum in 1972 rejected membership of the EC.

The ruling centre-right coalition collapsed in October 1990

over the question of EC membership and was replaced by a minority
Labour government. This was returned to power in the general
election held on 13 September 1993. A general election was held on
15 September 1997, in which no party won an outright majority.
The Labour Party has the largest number of seats (65) but a
government was formed by a minority coalition of the Christian
Democratic People's Party, the Centre Party and the Liberal Party,
led by Kjell Magne Bondevik, which resigned on 9 March 2000 after
being defeated in confidence vote. The Labour Party was invited to
form a government the following day and appointed its Cabinet on
17 March. A general election was due to be held on 10 September
2001.

FOREIGN RELATIONS

The Storting voted in November 1992 to apply to join the European
Community. Negotiations with the EU concluded on 1 March 1994
with a proposed accession date of 1 January 1995, subject to
parliamentary and national referendum ratifications. However, in a
national referendum on 28 November 1994 the electorate voted
against joining the EU by 52.4 per cent to 47.6 per cent.

POLITICAL SYSTEM

Under the 1814 constitution, the 165 member unicameral
legislature, the *Storting*, elects one-quarter of its members to
constitute the *Lagting* (Upper Chamber), the other three-quarters
forming the *Odelsting* (Lower Chamber), dividing when legislative
matters are under discussion.

HEAD OF STATE

HARALD V, KING OF NORWAY, Gd Master of the Royal
Norwegian Order of St Olav, Gd Master Royal Norwegian Order of
Merit, St Olav's Medal, Kt Gd Cross Order of Leopold (Belgium), Kt
Gd Cross Order of the Southern Cross (Brazil), Kt Order of the
Elephant (Denmark), Gd Cmdr "with diamonds" Order of the
Dannebrog (Denmark), Kt Gd Cross with Collar Order of the White
Rose (Finland), Olympic Cross of Merit 1st Class (Finland), Kt Gd
Cross Legion of Honour (France), Kt Gd Cross Order of the Saviour
(Greece), The Hundredth Anniversary Memorial Medal of the Greek
Royal House, Golden Olympic Order, Kt Gd Cross with Collar
Icelandic Order of the Falcon, Kt Gd Cross Italian Order of Merit,
Kt Gd Cross Order of Chrysanthemum (Japan), Yugoslavian Grand
Star, Kt Gd Cross Civ and Mil Order of Merit of Adolph of Nassau
(Luxembourg), Commemoration Medal - Wedding (Luxembourg),
Kt Gd Cross Crown Order of the Family Order of Orange
(Netherlands), Cmdr Order of the Golden Ark (Netherlands), Queen

Beatrix' Coronation Medal 1980 (Netherlands), Kt Gd Cross Order of the White Eagle (Poland), Kt Gd Cross Order of Aviz (Portugal), Kt Gd Cross Order of Carlos III (Spain), Order del Loison de Oro - Chain (Spain), Kt Gd Cross Royal Victorian Order, The Royal Victorian Chain, Kt Most Noble Order of the Seraphim with Collar (Sweden), King Gustav V's 90th Anniversary Medal (Sweden), Kt Most Noble Family Order with Collar (Thailand), Kt Gd Cross 1st Class Order of Merit of the Federal Republic of Germany, The Decoration of Honour for Merit - Grand Star (Austria), *succeeded* 21 Sept 1957

Heir, Crown Prince *Haakon Magnus* of Norway, Kt Gd Cross with Collar Order of St Olav, Kt Gd Cross Royal Norwegian Order of Merit, Kt Order of the Elephant (Denmark), Kt Most Noble Order of the Seraphim (Sweden)

CABINET *as at July 2002*

Prime Minister: Kjell Magne Bondevik (KrF); **Agriculture:** Lars Sponheim (V); **Children and Family Affairs:** Laila Daavøy (KrF); **Church and Cultural Affairs:** Valgerd Svarstad Haugland (KrF); **Defence:** Kristin Krohn Devold (H); **Education and Research:** Kristin Clemet (H); **Environment:** Børge Brende (H); **Finance:** Per-Kristian Foss (H); **Fisheries:** Svein Ludvigsen (H); **Foreign Affairs:** Jan Petersen (H); **Health:** Dagfinn Høybraaten (KrF); **Industry and Trade:** Ansgar Gabrielsen (H); **International Development:** Hilde Frafjord Johnson (KrF); **Justice and Police:** Odd Einar Dørum (V); **Labour and Government Administration:** Victor Danielsen Norman (H); **Local Government and Regional Development:** Erna Solberg (H); **Petroleum and Energy:** Einar Steensnaes (KrF); **Social Affairs:** Ingjerd Schou (H); **Transport and Communications:** Torild Skogsholm (V)

HOUSEHOLD OF HM THE KING

Lord Chamberlain: Lars Petter Forberg; **Grand Marshal:** Arne Omholt; **Private Secretary:** Berit Tversland; **Master of the Household:** Lise Harlem; **Equerry:** Brig. Bjørn Ruud; **Court Architect:** Ragnar Osnes; **Master of the Royal Court:** Ellen Jøldal; **Deputy Private Secretary:** Vigdis Wiesener Jorge; **Lady-in-Waiting:** Lise Blom; **Aides-de-Comp:** Cdr. Tor Arne Moe; Maj. Anders Rangul; **Personal Secretary:** Hilde Haraldstad

HOUSEHOLD OF HRH THE CROWN PRINCE
Aides-de-Comp: Andes Flogen

OVERSEAS TERRITORIES
ARUBA – **Governor:** Olindo Koolman; **Prime Minister:** Nelson O Oduber
NETHERLANDS ANTILLES – **Governor:** Frits Goedgedrag; **Prime Minister:** Etienne Ys

---

PORTUGAL
REPÚBLICA PORTUGUESA

AREA – 35,514 sq. miles (91,982 sq. km). Neighbour: Spain (north and east)

POPULATION – 10,066,253 (2001 estimate); 9,833,014 (excluding the Azores and Madeira). 94 per cent of the population are Catholic. The language is Portuguese

CAPITAL – Lisbon (population, 2,561,225, 1991)

MAJOR CITIES – Oporto (1,683,000)

CURRENCY – Euro of 100 cents

NATIONAL ANTHEM – A Portuguesa

NATIONAL DAY – 10 June

NATIONAL FLAG – Divided vertically into unequal parts of green and red with the national emblem over all on the line of division

LIFE EXPECTANCY (years) – male 72.6; female 79.6

POPULATION GROWTH RATE – 0.2 per cent (1999)

POPULATION DENSITY – 109 per sq. km (1999)

HISTORY AND POLITICS

Portugal was a monarchy from the 12 century until 1910, when an armed rising in Lisbon drove King Manuel II into exile and a republic was set up. A period of political instability ensued until the military stepped in and abolished political parties in 1926. The constitution of 1933 gave formal expression to the corporative 'Estado Novo' (New State) which was personified by Dr Antonio Salazar, Prime Minister 1932-68. Dr Caetano succeeded Salazar as Prime Minister in 1968 but his failure to liberalise the regime or to conclude the wars in the African colonies resulted in his government's overthrow by a military coup on 25 April 1974. There was great political turmoil between April 1974 and July 1976, a period in which most of the colonies gained their independence, but with the failure of an attempted coup by the extreme left in November 1975 the situation stabilised. Full civilian Government was restored in 1982.

In the general elections held on 10 October 1999, the Socialist Party was re-elected, winning 115 seats, just one seat short of a majority.

Macao, which had been a Portuguese colony since 1557, was transferred to Chinese sovereignty on 19 December 1999.

In the presidential election held on 14 January 2001, Jorge Sampaio was re-elected, gaining 55.8 per cent of the votes cast. In the general election held on 17 March 2002, the Social Democratic Party (PSD) became the largest party in the Assembly winning 102 seats. José Manuel Durão Barroso of the PSD was sworn in as prime minister on 6 April, leading a coalition government of the PSD and the People's Party (PP).

POLITICAL SYSTEM

Under the 1976 constitution, amended in 1982 and 1989, the President is elected for a five-year term by universal adult suffrage. The Prime Minister is designated by the largest party in the legislature. Legislative authority is vested in the 230-member Assembly of the Republic, elected by a system of proportional representation every four years. The President retains certain limited powers to dismiss the government, dissolve the Assembly or veto laws.

HEAD OF STATE

President of Republic: Jorge Sampaio, *elected* 14 January 1996, *inaugurated* 9 March 1996, *re-elected*, 14 January 2001

COUNCIL OF MINISTERS *as at July 2002*

Prime Minister: José Manuel Durão Barroso; **Agriculture, Rural Development and Fisheries:** Armando José Cordeiro Sevinato Pinto; **Assistant to the Prime Minister:** José Luis Fazenda Arnaut Duarte; **Culture:** Pedro Manuel da Cruz Roseta; **Economy:** Carlos Manuel Tavaras da Silva; **Education:** José David Gomes Justino; **Foreign Affairs and Portuguese Communities Abroad:** António Manuel de Mendonça Martins da Cruz; **Health:** Luis Filipe da Conceição Pereira; **Internal Administration:** António Jorge de Figueiredo Lopes; **Justice:** Maria Celeste Ferreira Lopes Cardona; **Minister of State for Finance:** Maria Manuela Dias Ferreira Leite; **Minister of State for National Defence:** Paulo Sacadura Cabral Portas; **Parliamentary Affairs:** Luís Manuel Gonçalves Marques Mendes; **Presidency:** Nuno Albuquerque Morais Sarmento; **Public Works, Transport and Housing:** Luís Francisco Valente de

Olìveira; **Science and Higher Education:** Pedro Augusto Lynce de Faria; **Social Security and Work:** António José de Castro Bagão Félix; **Towns, Territorial Planning and Environment:** Isaltino Afonso de Morais

---

ROMANIA
ROMÂNIA

AREA – 92,043 sq. miles (238,391 sq. km). Neighbours: Ukraine (north and east), Moldova (east), Bulgaria (south), Yugoslavia (south-west), Hungary (north-west)

POPULATION – 22,430,457 (2001 estimate); 22,810,035 (1992 census): 89.4 per cent Romanian, 7.1 per cent Hungarian, 1.7 per cent Romany, 0.5 per cent German, 0.3 per cent Ukrainian, 0.04 per cent Jews and others. Religious affiliation: Orthodox 86.8 per cent, Roman Catholic 5 per cent, Reformed 3.5 per cent, Greek Catholic 1 per cent. Romanian is a Romance language with many archaic forms and with admixtures of Slavonic, Turkish, Magyar and French words

CAPITAL – Bucharest (population, 2,066,723, 2001 estimate)

MAJOR CITIES – Brasov (324,104); Constanta (348,985); Cluj-Napoca (321,850); Craiova (303,033); Galati (324,234); Iasi (337,643); Oradea (221,559); Ploiesti (254,304); Timisoara (325,359), 2001 estimates

CURRENCY – Leu (Lei) of 100 bani

NATIONAL ANTHEM – Desteaptate, Române, Din Somnul Cel De Moarte (Awake Ye, Romanians, From Your Deadly Slumber)

NATIONAL DAY – 1 December

NATIONAL FLAG – Three vertical bands, blue yellow, red

LIFE EXPECTANCY (years) – male 66.5; female 73.3

POPULATION GROWTH RATE – 0.2 per cent (1999)

POPULATION DENSITY – 94 per sq. km (1999)

URBAN POPULATION – 54.9 per cent (1996)

HISTORY AND POLITICS

Romania has its origin in the union of the Danubian principalities of Wallachia and Moldavia in 1859. In 1918 Bessarabia, Bukovina, Transylvania and Banat were united with Romania.

In 1947 Romania became 'The Romanian People's Republic' under the leadership of the Romanian Communist Party. A revolution in December 1989 led to the overthrow of Nicolae Ceausescu, president since 1965. A provisional government abolished the leading role of the Communist Party and held free elections in May 1990.

In the elections held on 26 November 2000 the Social Democratic Party of Romania (SDPR) gained 155 seats in the Chamber of deputies and 65 seats in the Senate, becoming the largest party in both houses. The SDPR presidential candidate, Ion Iliescu, obtained 36.35 per cent of the vote in the first round of the presidential election. He won the second round, held on 10 December, obtaining 66.83 per cent of the vote. On 27 December, the SDPR reached an agreement with other centre-right parties to enable it to form a workable minority government.

POLITICAL SYSTEM

The constitution of 1991 formally makes Romania a multiply democracy and endorses human rights and a market economy. The parliament comprises the Chamber of Deputies with 345 seats, of which 18 are reserved for ethnic minorities, and the Senate with 140 seats. Both houses are elected for four-year terms.

HEAD OF STATE

President of the Republic: Ion Iliescu, *elected* 10 December 2000

CABINET *as at August 2002*

Prime Minister: Adrian Nastase; **Agriculture, Food and Forestry:** Ilie Sârbu; **Communications and Information Technology:** Dan Nica; **Culture and Religious Affairs:** Razvan Theodorescu; **Defence:** Ioan Mircea Pascu; **Development and Forecasts:** Gheorghe Cazan; **Education and Research:** Ecaterina Andronescu; **European Integration:** Hildegard Puwak; **Finance:** Mihai Tanasescu; **Foreign Affairs:** Mircea Geoana; **Health and Family:** Daniela Bartos; **Industry and Resources:** Ioan Dan Popescu; **Interior:** Ioan Rus; **Justice.** Mihaela Rodica Stanoiu; **Labour, Social Solidarity:** Marian Sarbu; **Minister-Delegate, Ministry for Education and Research:** Serban Constantin Valeca; **Minister-delegate to the Prime Minister, Chief EU Negotiator:** Vasile Puscas; **Parliamentary Relations:** Acsinte Gaspar; **Privatisation:** Ovidiu Musetescu; **Public Administration:** Octav Cozmânca; **Public Information:** Vasile Dâncu; **Public Works, Transport and Housing:** Miron Mitrea; **Secretary-General of the Government:** Petru Serban Mihailescu; **Small and Medium Enterprises and Co-operatives:** Silvia Ciornei; **Tourism:** Matei Agathon Dan; **Water and Environment:** Petru Lificiu; **Youth and Sports:** Georgiu Gingaras

RUSSIA
Rossiiskaya Federatsiya

AREA – 6,592,850 sq. miles (17,075,400 sq. km). Neighbours: Norway, Finland, Estonia, Latvia, Belarus, and Ukraine (west), Georgia, Azarbaijan, Kazahstan, China, Mongolia and North Korea (south). The Kaliningrad enclave borders Lithuania and Poland.

POPULATION – 144,200,000 (2001 estimate): 87.5 per cent Russian, 3.5 per cent Tatar, 2.7 per cent Ukrainian, 1.3 per cent ethnic German, 1.1 per cent Chuvash, 0.9 per cent Bashkir, 0.7 per cent Belarusian and 0.7 per cent Mordovian. There are another six minorities with populations of over half a million and more than 130 nationalities in total. The Russian Orthodox Church is the predominant religion, though the Tatars and many in the north Caucasus are Muslims and there are Jewish communities in Moscow and St Petersburg. The language is Russian.

CAPITAL – Moscow (population 8,539,000, 2001 estimate), founded about 1147, became the centre of the rising Moscow principality and inn the 15th century the capital of the whole of Russia (Muscovy). In 1325 it became the seat of the Metropolitan of Russia. In 1703 Peter the Great transferred the capital to St Petersburg, but on 14 March 1918 Moscow was again designated as the capital.

MAJOR CITIES – St Petersburg (4,660,800, 2001), from 1914 to 1924 Petrograd and from 1924 to 1991 Leningrad. Other cities: Chelyabinsk (1,111,000); Kazan (1,077,750); Nizhny-Novgorod/Gorky (1,380,100); Novosibirsk/Novonikolayevsk (1,398,350); Omsk (1,785,000); Perm/Molotov (1,050,950); Rostov-on-Don (1,013,635); Samara/Kuibyshev (1,215,050); Ufa (1,098,150); Yekaterinburg/Sverdlovsk (1,275,000), 1997 estimates

CURRENCY – Rouble of 100 kopeks

NATIONAL ANTHEM – Russia, Sacred Our Empire (the former Soviet national anthem, with new lyrics)

NATIONAL DAY – 12 June (Independence Day)

NATIONAL FLAG – Three horizontal stripes of white, blue, red

LIFE EXPECTANCY (years) – male 60.0; female 72.5

POPULATION GROWTH RATE – 0.4 per cent (1999)

POPULATION DENSITY – 9 per sq. km (1999)

ILLITERACY RATE – 0.4 per cent (2002)

Russia occupies three-quarters of the land area of the former Soviet Union.

The Russian Federation comprises 89 members: 49 regions

(*oblast*) – Amur, Arkhangelsk, Astrakhan, Belgorod, Bryansk, Chelyabinsk, Chita, Irkutsk, Ivanovo, Kaliningrad, Kaluga, Kamchatka, Kemerovo, Kirov, Kostroma, Kurgan, Kursk, Leningrad, Lipetsk, Magadan, Moscow, Murmansk, Nizhny-Novgorod, Novgorod, Novosibirsk, Omsk, Oreal, Orenburg, Penza, Perm, Pskov, Rostov, Ryazan, Sakhalin, Samara, Saratov, Smolensk, Sverdlovsk, Tambov, Tomsk, Tula, Tver, Tyumen, Ulyanovsk, Vladimir, Volgograd, Vologda, Voronezh, Yaroslavl; six autonomous territories (krai) – Altai, Khabarovsk, Krasnodar, Krasnoyarsk, Primorye, Stavropol; 21 republics – Adygeia, Altai, Bashkortostan, Buryatia, Chechnya, Chuvash, Daghestan, Ingush, Kabardino-Balkar, Kalmykia, Karachai-Cherkessia, Karelia, Khakassia, Komi, Mari-El, Mordovia, North Ossetia (Alania), Sakha, Tatarstan, Tyva, Udmurt; ten autonomous areas – Aga-Buryat, Chuckchi, Evenki, Khanty-Mansi, Komi-Permyak, Koryak, Nenets, Taimyr, Ust-Orda-Buryat, Yamal-Nents; two cities of federal status – Moscow, St Petersburg; and one autonomous Jewish region, Birobijan.

There are three principal geographic areas: a low-lying flat western area stretching eastwards up to the Yenisei and divided in two by the Ural ridge; the eastern area between the Yenisei and the Pacific, consisting of a number of tablelands and ridges; and a southern mountainous area. Russia has a very long coastline, including the longest Arctic coastline in the world (about 17,000 miles).

The most important rivers are the Volga, the Northern Dvina and the Pechora, the Neva, the Don, and the Kuban in the European part, and in the Asiatic part, the Ob, the Irtysh, the Yenisei, the Lena, and the Amur, and, further north, Khantanga, Olenek, Yana, Indigirka, Kolyma and Anadyr. Lake Baikal in eastern Siberia is the deepest lake in the world.

HISTORY AND POLITICS

The Gregorian calendar was not introduced until 14 February 1918. For the events surrounding the 1917 revolutions the dates given here are the Gregorian calendar dates in use in the rest of the world at the time, with the dates in the Julian calendar (OS) in parenthesis.

Russia was formally created from the principality of Muscovy and its territories by Tsar Peter I (The Great) (1682-1725), who initiated its territorial expansion, introduced Western ideas of government and founded St Petersburg. By the end of Peter the Great's reign, the Baltic territories (modern-day Estonia and Latvia) had been annexed from Sweden, and Russia had become the dominant military power on north-eastern Europe. In the 18th century the partitions of Poland and wars with Turkey brought the territories of modern-day Lithuania, Belarus, Ukraine and the Crimea under Russian control, and the colonisation of Siberia east of the Urals began in earnest. Russia overran the Caucasus region (modern-day Armenia, Azerbaijan and Georgia) in the early 19th century, seized Finland from Sweden in 1809 and Bessarabia from Turkey in 1812. Throughout the remainder of the 19th century Russia subdued and annexed the independent Muslim states which later formed the five Central Asian republics.

Discontent caused by autocratic rule, the poor conduct of the military in the First World War and wartime privation led to a revolution which broke out on 12 March (27 February OS) 1917. Tsar Nicholas II abdicated three days later and a provisional government was formed; a republic was proclaimed on 14 September (1 September OS) 1917. A power struggle ensued between the provisional government and the Bolshevik Party which controlled the Soviets (councils) set up by workers, soldiers and peasants. This led to a second revolution on 7 November (25 October OS) 1917 in which the Bolsheviks, led by Lenin, seized power.

Armed resistance to Communist rule developed into an all-out civil war between 'red' Bolshevik forces and 'white' monarchist and anti-Communist forces which lasted until the end of 1922. During the civil war, Russia had been declared a Soviet Republic and other Soviet republics had been formed Ukraine, Byelorussia and Transcaucasia. These four republics merged to form the Union of Soviet Socialist Republics (USSR) on 30 December 1922.

The Nazi-Soviet pact of August 1939 and the Second World War resulted in further territorial expansion, regaining much of the territory lost in or after 1918, as well as extending Soviet influence to the countries of eastern Europe liberated by Soviet troops. The USSR lost 27 million combatants and civilians in the war.

Joseph Stalin introduced a policy of rapid industrialisation under a series of five-year plans, brought all sectors of industry under government control, abolished private ownership and enforced the collectivisation of agriculture.

Mikhail Gorbachev became Soviet leader in March 1985 and introduced the policies of *perestroika* (complete restructuring) and *glasnost* (openness) in order to revamp the economy, which had stagnated since 1970s, to root out corruption and inefficiency, and to end the Cool War and its attendant arms race. The retreat from total control by the Communist Party unleashed ethnic and nationalist tensions.

On 19 August 1991 a coup was attempted by hardline elements of the Communist Party, but was defeated by reformist and democratic political groups under the leadership of Russian President Yeltsin. Effective political power was now in the hands of the republican leaders, especially Russian President Yeltsin, and the Soviet Union began to break up as the constituent republics declared their independence. Gorbachev resigned as Soviet President on 25 December 1991 and on 26 December 1991 the USSR formally ceased to exist.

Russia was recognised as an independent state by the EC

and USA in January 1992; it took over the Soviet Union's seat at the UN in December 1991.

A new Russian Federal Treaty was signed on 13 March 1992 between the central government and the autonomous republic. Tatarstan and Bashkortostan initially declared themselves independent, but signed the treaty in 1994 after securing considerable legislative and economic autonomy.

The state of the parties in the State *Duma* following the election on 19 December 1999 was: Communist Party 113 seats; Unity 72; Fatherland-All Russia 67; Union of Rightist Forces 29; Yabloko 21; Zhirinovski's Bloc 17; Our Home is Russia 7; DPA 2; Russian All People Unity 2; others 5.

In the presidential election held on 26 March 2000, Vladimir Putin won 52.94 per cent of the vote, in which the turnout was 68.88 per cent, and was formally inaugurated on 7 May 2000.

POLITICAL SYSTEM

The 1993 constitution enshrines the right to private ownership and the freedoms of press, speech, association, worship and travel, and states that Russia is a multiparty democracy. The President is directly elected for a maximum of two four-year terms. The Prime Minister takes over from the President in the event that he is unable to fulfil his duties.

Legislative power is vested in the Federal Assembly, comprising the Federation Council (upper house) of 178 members, two elected by each of the 89 members of the Russian Federation; the State Duma (lower house) of 450 members, of which 225 are elected by constituencies on a first-past-the-post basis and 225 by proportional representation, with a five per cent threshold for representation. The Council is composed of two representatives from each constituent territory of the Federation: the head of legislative and the head of the executive body. From 2002 the governments and the legislatures of the constituent territories will each elect one representative.

The judicial system consists of a Constitutional Court of 19 members appointed for a 12-year term which protects and interprets the constitution and decides if laws are compatible with it. The Supreme Court adjudicates in criminal and civil laws cases. The Arbitration Court deals with commercial disputes between companies.

INSURGENCIES

The Chechen republic declared its 'independence' in November 1991 after a nationalist coup in the republic. Chechnya refused to sign the Russian Federal Treaty in March 1992. Civil war began in early 1994 between the Chechen government and armed opposition forces of the 'Provisional Chechen Council' tacitly supported by the Russian government. On 9 December 1994 President Yeltsin ordered the Russian military to retake the republic. Chechen forces were finally forced out of Grozny in early February 1995.

Russian troops were withdrawn in January 1997 when presidential and legislative elections were also held in Checnya. A treaty renouncing the use of force to resolve Chechnya's status was signed between Presidents Maskhadov and Yeltsin in May 1997.

Following an incursion by Islamic militants into Dagestan on 10 August 1999, Russian forces launched airstrikes and Russian ground troops entered the territory. Russian forces captured the Chechen capital, Grozny, on 6 February 2000 and captured the last Chechen-held town on 29 February, but Chechen guerrilla attacks on Russian targets continued. On 8 June 2000, President Putin imposed temporary direct presidential rule on Chechnya.

FOREIGN RELATIONS

A union treaty was signed by the presidents of Russia and Belarus in April 1997. Both countries will retain sovereignty and territorial integrity although citizens of the two countries will also be citizens of the Union. The presidents of the two countries decided in December 1998 to effect a currency union.

A Founding Act was signed by Russia and NATO in May 1997 which lays down the principles of post-Cold War co-operation. A joint permanent council is to be set up.

HEAD OF STATE

President: Vladimir Putin, *elected* 26 March 2000, *inaugurated* 7 May 2000

GOVERNMENT *as at August 2002*

Chair, Atomic Energy, Property Relations, Science, Industry and Technology, Customs: Mikhail Kasyanov; **Deputy Chairs:** Aleksey Gordeyev (*Agriculture and Food, Fisheries, Cartography and Land Survey*); Aleksey Kudrin (*Finance, Economic Development and Trade*); Viktor Khristenko (*Energy, Natural Resources, Communications, Railways, Housing and Construction*); Valentina Matviyenko (*Labour, Health, Education, Culture and Media, Sport*); **Anti-Monopoly and Entrepreneurial Affairs:** Ilya Yuzhanov; **Atomic Energy:** Aleksandr Rumyantsev; **Culture:** Mikhail Shvydkoi; **Defence:** Sergey Ivanov; **Director of the Federal Security Services:** Nikolai Patrushev; **Economic Development and Trade:** German Gref; **Education:** Vladimir Filippov; **Emergencies, Civil Defence, Natural Disasters:** Sergei Shoigu; **Employment and Social Development:** Aleksandr Pochinok; **Energy:** Igor Yusufov; **Foreign Affairs:** Igor Ivanov; **Head of Government Administration:** Igor Shuvalov; **Health:**

Yuri Shevchenko; **Interior:** Boris Gryzlov; **Justice:** Yuri Chaika; **Nationalities Policy:** Vladimir Zorin; **Natural Resources:** Vitaly Artyukhov; **Press, Broadcasting and Mass Communications:** Mikhail Lesin; **Privatisation:** Farid Gazizullin; **Railways:** Nikolai Aksenenko; **Secretary of the Security Council:** Vladimir Rushailo; **Social and Economic Development of Chechnya:** Vladimir Yelagin; **Tax and Levy Collection:** Gennady Bukayev; **Telecommunications and Information:** Leonid Reyman; **Transport:** Sergei Frank

---

SERBIA AND MONTENEGRO
(Republika Srbija i Crna Gora)

See also - (Yugoslavia)
Savezna Republika Jugoslavija

REPUBLIC OF MONTENEGRO

MONTENEGRIN NATIONAL DAY – 13 July.

NATIONAL FLAG – Three horizontal stripes of blue, white red with Montenegrin Coat of Arms.

AREA – 5,331 sq. miles (13,812 sq. km)

POPULATION – 615,000: 62 per cent Montenegrin, 14.5 per cent Bosniac, 6.5 per cent Albanian and 3 per cent Serb

CAPITAL – Podgorica (population 117,875, 1991)

The last presidential election was won by Milo Djukanovic, a reformist candidate favouring independence for the province. Elections to the 85-seat Republican Assembly held on 22 April 2001 were won by the Victory Belongs to Montenegro coalition who gained 36 seats with Together for Yugoslavia winning 36 seats. A coalition government was approved by parliament on 2 July 2001, followed by new elections on 20 October 2002. By 25 November 2002 (at time of going to press) an new Government had yet to be announced, and the old Government remained in office. In the most recent elections the group allied to Montenegrin President, Milo Djukanovic, achieved an absolute majority, and the President announced that he would relinquish his post and take up the premiership of Montenegro, a post he has previously held. Elections for the post of President of Montenegro were in any case scheduled for 22nd December 2002.

President: *Milo Djukanovic, elected 19 October 1997; **Prime Minister:** *Filip Vujanovic; **Deputy Prime Minister:** *Branislav Gvozdenovic and *Zarko Rakcevic (SDP); Foreign Minister *Branko Lukovac (Ind). *The outgoing Government remains in office at the time of going to press, one month after the elections of 20 October 2002.

REPUBLIC OF SERBIA

AREA – 34,175 sq. miles (88,538 sq. km)

POPULATION – 9,300,000, of whom 66 per cent are Serbs

CAPITAL – Belgrade (population, 1,338,856, 1997 estimate)

Serbia includes the provinces of Kosovo (population 1.6 million), of great historic importance to Serbs, and Vojvodina (population 2 million); the autonomy of both was ended in September 1990. Vojvodina, with its capital at Novi Sad, has a large Hungarian minority (21 per cent). Kosovo, with its capital at Priština, is predominantly Albanian (90 per cent). Following the conflict in Kosovo, more than 200,000 people have been left homeless and entire villages have been destroyed.

The reformist Democratic Opposition of Serbia (DOS) won the parliamentary elections to the National Assembly held on 24 December 2000, gaining 176 of the 250 seats. Serbia's Presidential elections were held on 29 September 2002. The second round was held on 13 October 2002 but failed due a boycott by supporters of candidates eliminated in the first round of voting, resulting in the minimum quorum of the voting electorate not being achieved. The second round of the elections were abandoned and a complete new election was ordered under the constitution of Serbia. The new elections were ordered for 8 December 2002, but they in turn failed when less than 50% of the electorate eligible to vote took part, prompting a constitutional crisis.

President: Milan Milutinovic; **Prime Minister:** Zoran Djindjic

SERBIAN NATIONAL DAY – 29 October (Republic Day)

NATIONAL FLAG – Three horizontal stripes of blue, white red with Serbian Coat of Arms.

AREA – 39,449 sq. miles (102,173 sq. km). Neighbours: Hungary (north), Romania and Bulgaria (east), the Former Yugoslav republic of Macedonia and Albania (south), Bosnia-Hercegovina and Croatia (west)

POPULATION – 10,677,290 (2001 estimate): 67.6 per cent Serb and Montenegrin, 16.5 per cent Albanian, 3.2 per cent Muslim Slavs, 3.3 per cent Hungarian, with smaller numbers of Romanies, Croats,

Slovaks and Bulgarians. The majority religion is Serbian Orthodox, with significant Muslim and small Roman Catholic minorities. The main language is Serbian (74 per cent), with Albanian and Hungarian minorities. Serbian is a South Slav language written in the Cyrillic script

The climate is continental. Montenegro and southern Serbia are extremely mountainous, while the north is dominated by the low-lying plains of the Danube. The major rivers are: the Danube, which flows through the north of Serbia to Romania and Bulgaria; the Sava, which flows eastwards from Bosnia to join the Danube at Belgrade; the Drina, which flows along most of the Serbian-Bosnian border to join the Sava; and the Morava, which flows from the extreme south to join the Danube in the north.

HISTORY AND POLITICS (Republics & Federation)

The history of the Montenegro state began in the ninth century with the emergence of Duklja, a vassal state of Byzantium. In 1042 following a decisive battle near Bar against Byzantium, Duklja became independent. Duklja s power and prosperity reached their zenith under King Vojislav s son, King Mihailo (1046-81), and his son King Bodin (1081-1101).

The territory of Duklja comprised much of the southern Adriatic coast, most of present-day Montenegro

Montenegro s ruler, Mihailo received royal insignia from the Pope in 1077, referring to *Michaeli Sclavorum Regi* (Mihailo, King of Slavs).

Later the institution of a theocratic sovereign became key to Montenegro s independence, and under the Prince Bishops, in the seventeenth century, Montenegrins increasingly fought against the Turkish armies.

In 1910, the parliament proclaimed Montenegro a constitutional monarchy

Events during and after World War I led to the end of Montenegro as an independent country and kingdom.

Serbia had emerged from the rule of the Byzantine Empire in the 13th century to form a large and prosperous state in the Balkans. Defeat by the Turks in 1389 led to almost 500 years of Turkish rule. After gaining autonomy within the Ottoman Empire in 1815, Serbia became fully independent in 1878 and a kingdom in 1881. Montenegro remained independent during the Ottoman period and was recognised at the Congress of Berlin on 13 July 1878 (Montenegrin National Day). At the end of the First World War Serbia annexed Montenegro and orchestrated the deposing and exile of the Royal House of Montenegro. The new territory was combined with the former Austro-Hungarian provinces of Slovenia, Croatia and Bosnia-Hercegovina to form the 'Kingdom of Serbs, Croats and Slovenes' which was renamed Yugoslavia in 1929. Yugoslavia was occupied by

Axis forces in 1941 and reformed as a Communist federal republic under the presidency of partisan leader Josip Broz Tito in 1945, who orchestrated the deposing and exile of the Royal House of Yugoslavia.

Tito died in 1980 and was succeeded by a rotating federal presidency which was unable to contain the growing nationalist movements. Efforts by the six republican presidents to negotiate a new federal or confederal structure for the country failed in 1991. On 25 June 1991 Slovenia and Croatia declared their independence from Yugoslavia.

In Croatia the ethnic Serb minority refused to accept Croatia's independence and fighting began in July 1991 between Croat Defence Forces and indigenous Serbs backed by the Yugoslav National Army (JNA). By September 1991 this had escalated into war between the Croatian province and the Federal Republic. The war in Croatia continued until January 1992 when there was an EU and UN sponsored cease-fire.

Macedonia declared its independence on 18 September 1991.

Bosnia-Hercegovina declared its independence on 1 March 1992. Independence was supported by the Bosniacs (Muslims) and Croats but rejected by the ethnic Serbs and fighting between Bosniacs and Serbs broke out in March 1992 and later between the Croats and Bosniacs in March 1993 plus some intra-Bosnian Muslim fighting between the Army of President Izetbegovic (Bosnian Army) and the Abdic forces in Cazinska Krajina/Western Bosnia. The JNA intervened against the Bosniacs but in May 1992 withdrew to Serbia and Montenegro.

On 27 April 1992 the two remaining republics of the former Socialist Federal Republic of Yugoslavia, Serbia and Montenegro, announced the formation of a new Yugoslav federation, which they invited Serbs in Croatia and Bosnia-Hercegovina to join. Subsequently Montenegro has declared that it will hold a referendum on independence, having abandoned the Federal Republic de facto, introducing its own legislative and fiscal structures, and abolishing the Yugoslav Dinar in favour of the German Mark, and as of 1 Jan 2002, becoming part of the Euro Zone.

Legislative elections were held in Montenegro in May 1998 and October 2002 and were won by reformists led by President Djukanovic, whose party stood on a platform of Independence for Montenegro and the restoration of a Sovereign State.

Kosovo has been under UN administration since June 1999.

Federal Yugoslav Presidential and legislative elections were held on 24 September 2000, but were largely boycotted in Montenegro after its government had urged the population not to vote. The Democratic Opposition of Serbia (DOS) became the largest party in both chambers of parliament. In the presidential election, the Federal Election Commission announced that President Slobodan Miloševic of the Socialist Party of Serbia (SPS), had obtained 40.23 per cent of votes and his rival, Vojislav Koštunica of the DSS, had won 48.22 per cent, just short of the 50 per cent necessary to win without a second round, although an independent monitoring organisation had given Koštunica a clear majority. Koštunica denounced the official result as fraudulent and refused to participate in the second round, scheduled for 8 October. Tension grew and on 28 September, the Serb Orthodox Church declared that Koštunica was the elected president and the Yugoslav Army guaranteed that it would not involve itself in politics. The next day, the Serbian Radical Party (SRP), one of the coalition partners in the Miloševic regime, declared its support for Koštunica. A general strike began on 2 October. On 5 October, opposition supporters stormed the parliament building and took over the television station and the state news agency and by evening the media organizations were declaring Koštunica to be the elected president. Miloševic accepted his defeat on 6 October and Koštunica was sworn in the following day. Following a period of uncertainty, the DOS and the SPS agreed to dissolve parliament and form a transitional government until a fresh election could be held for the Serbian Parliament. In the Federal parliament, the DOS, who had won 138 seats, formed a coalition government with the Socialist People's Party of Montenegro (SPP), who had 28 seats.

An election to the Serbian Parliament was held on 23 December 2000, in which the DOS won an overwhelming victory, obtaining 176 of the 250 seats. The SPS won 37, the SRP won 23 and the Party of Serbian Unity won 14.

In Montenegro, which had steadily removed itself from the influence of Serbia, the government coalition collapsed on 29 December 2000. A legislative election was held 22 April 2001, in which the pro-independence Victory Belongs to Montenegro (VBM) alliance, led by the Democratic Party of Socialists (DPS), won 36 of the 77 seats. The VBM alliance formed a coalition government with the pro-independence Liberal League, which had six seats.

Former President Slobodan Miloševic was arrested in Belgrade on 1 April 2001 and on 28 June, he was handed over to the UN International Criminal Tribunal for the Former Yugoslavia, which in May 1999 had indicted him on charges of crimes against humanity. A legal challenge was begun on 23 August 2001 by lawyers acting for Miloševic, against the UN International Criminal Tribunal for the Former Yugoslavia in a Dutch court. On 23 November, Miloševic was charged with genocide for atrocities committed by forces under his command during the Bosnian war. On 9 October fresh charges were imposed upon Miloševic for 'ethnic cleansing' in Croatia in 1991-92, to which he refused to plead. The trial opened in The Hague in the Netherlands on 13 February 2002.

On 14 March 2002 the leaders of Serbia, Montenegro and the Federal Republic of Yugoslavia signed an agreement to maintain a joint state under the name of Serbia and Montenegro, while the question of Montenegro's independence was reserved for two years. Yugoslav president Vojislav Koštunica would remain president of the joint state and a new constitution would be drafted with legislative elections expected to take place before the end of 2002. Vojislav Koštunica subsequently became a candidate in the failed Serbian Presidential elections on 29 September 2002 and has announced his candidacy for the re-run on 8 December 2002. Yugoslav president Vojislav Koštunica is expected to resign that office, if, as anticipated, he emerges the victor in the Serbian Presidential Elections in December 2002.

INSURGENCIES

The province of Kosovo in the south of Serbia is now more than 90 per cent ethnically Albanian. In 1989, Slobodan Miloševic, then leader of the League of Communists of Serbia, revoked Kosovo's autonomous status, resulting in progressive exclusion of the Albanian majority from public life. Following clashes between ethnic Albanians and Serbian police in February and March 1998, the Serbian military were accused of attacking civilians in the province on the pretext of eliminating support for the Kosovo Liberation Army (KLA), an ethnic Albanian paramilitary organisation fighting for independence for the province. The international community condemned the brutality of the Serbian forces and a UN arms embargo was imposed on Yugoslavia, but the situation deteriorated with clashes between the KLA and security forces becoming commonplace. International organisations detailed widespread human rights abuses by the security forces; NATO and Russia ordered both sides to attend a peace conference in Paris on 6 February 1999, which was unsuccessful. Following warnings to the Yugoslav authorities, NATO commenced air strikes against military targets in Yugoslavia on 24 March 1999. Over eight hundred thousand people fled or were forced to leave their homes and sought refuge in Albania, Macedonia or Montenegro, which although part of the Yugoslav Federation, had refused to become involved in the fighting; more than five hundred thousand people were displaced within Kosovo. NATO intensified its bombing campaign, now targeting industrial, communications, TV and Radio and power links and main cities and towns in Serbia, away from the Kosovo conflict.

On 27 May 1999, the UN War Crimes Tribunal indicted President Miloševic of Yugoslavia, President Milutinovic of Serbia, and other senior Yugoslav officials for crimes against humanity.

On 3 June President Miloševic accepted a peace plan agreed by NATO and Russia and on 10 June Yugoslav forces began to withdraw; NATO air operations were immediately suspended and NATO and Russian forces entered Kosovo the following day. By 20 June all Yugoslav forces had been withdrawn from Kosovo and the Koso refugees began to return. Since the Yugoslav withdrawal,

Kosovo has been under the administration of the UN's Interim Administration Mission in Kosovo (UMNIK), who have established the Kosovo Transitional Council composed of four UN and four Kosovar representatives. The NATO-led Kosovo Force (KFOR) has established five command sectors, administered by UK, US, French, German and Italian troops respectively. In addition, parts of the French, German and US sectors are patrolled by Russian troops. KFOR has facilitated the disarming of the KLA and the return of over 850,000 Kosovar Albanian refugees, but at least 200,000 Kosovar Serbs have fled and been displaced in fear of reprisal attacks, which have frequently occurred.

In May 2001, the UN Interim Administration Mission in Kosovo (UMNIK) announced that elections to a legislative assembly would be held on 17 November 2001. The assembly would have powers over health, education and the environment, but UMNIK would retain final authority.

Armed fighters belonging to the ethnic Albanian Liberation Army of Preševo, Medvedja and Bujanovac (UCPMB) launched attacks on Serbs in Albanian populated areas of southern Serbia in November 2000. The rebels wanted to annex these areas into Kosovo. A cease-fire was negotiated by KFOR on 27 November, but it collapsed on 1 December. A further cease-fire was signed on 12 March 2001 after NATO agreed to permit Yugoslav forces to enter the demilitarised buffer zone which had been established on the Serbian side of the border with Kosovo in 1999.

SPAIN
Reino de España

AREA – 195,365 sq. miles (505,992). Neighbours: Portugal (west), France (north)

POPULATION – 40,037,995 (2001 estimate): 96 per cent Catholic, 1 per cent Muslim. Castilian Spanish is the official language, although Basque, Catalan, Galician and Valencian, a dialect of Catalan, are spoken and have official status in the autonomous regions where they are spoken

CAPITAL – Madrid (population 3,084,673, 1996)

MAJOR CITIES – Barcelona (4,748, 236); Valencia (2,200,319); Málaga (1,224,959); Sevilla (1,719,446); Zaragoza (852,322), 1995

CURRENCY – Euro of 100 cents

NATIONAL ANTHEM – Marcha Real Espanola (Spanish Royal March)

NATIONAL DAY – 12 October

NATIONAL FLAG – Three horizontal stripes of red, yellow, red with the yellow of double width
LIFE EXPECTANCY (years) – male 75.4; female 82.3
POPULATION GROWTH RATE – 0.1 per cent (1999)
POPULATION DENSITY – 78 per sq. km (1999)

The interior of the Iberian peninsula consists of an elevated tableland surrounded and traversed by mountain ranges: the Pyrenees, the Cantabrian Mountains, the Sierra de Guadarrama, Sierra Morena, Sierra Nevada, Montes de Toledo, etc. The principal rivers are the Duero, the Tajo, the Guadiana, the Guadalquivir, the Ebro and the Mino.

HISTORY AND POLITICS

The kingdoms of Castile and Argón were united in 1479; they captured Granada, the last region of Spain under Moorish rule, in 1492 and conquered Navarra in 1512. In 1492 Columbus reached the Americas on behalf of Spain and began the process of colonisation which led to most of central and south America coming under Spanish rule until their independence in the 19th century. A republic was proclaimed in 1931 and in February 1936 the Popular Front, a left-wing coalition, was elected. In July 1936 a counter-revolution broke out in military garrisons in Spanish Morocco and spread throughout Spain. Civil war ensued until March 1939, when the Popular Front governments in Madrid and Barcelona surrendered to the Nationalists (as Gen. Franco's followers were then named). Gen. Franco became president and ruled the country until his death in 1975, when, according to his wishes, he was succeeded as head of state by Prince Juan Carlos of Bourbon (grandson of Alonso XIII) and Spain again became a monarchy. The first free election was held on 15 June 1977. The general election of 12 March 2000 was won by the Popular Party (PP), which won 183 seats in the Congress of Deputies.

INSURGENCIES

The Basque separatist organisation ETA (*Euzkadi ta Azkatasuna* – Basque Nation and Liberty) has since its formation in 1959 carried out a terrorist campaign of bombings, shootings and kidnappings against the Spanish state and its security forces in an attempt to gain independence for the Basque country. ETA rejected regional autonomy for the Basque country in 1979 as insufficient and continued its campaign, but increased cooperation between French and Spanish security forces had greatly weakened ETA by the early 1990s. On 16 September 1998, ETA announced an indefinite truce, but ended the truce on 28 November 1999. On 23 January 2000, over a million people demonstrated in Madrid against the resumption of ETA terrorist attacks following a car bomb explosion in Madrid on 21 January, in which one person died. The ETA campaign was stepped up in July 2000 and ETA announced in June 2001 that it would continue its terrorist attacks.

POLITICAL SYSTEM

Under the 1978 constitution there is a bicameral *Cortes Generales* comprising a 350-member Congress of Deputies (*Congreso de los Diputatos*) elected for a maximum term of four years, which elects the prime minister; and a Senate (*Senado*) consisting of 208 directly elected representatives and 51 representatives appointed by the assemblies of the autonomous regions.

Since the promulgation of the 1978 constitution, 19 autonomous regions have been established, with their own parliaments and governments. These are Andalucía, Aragón, Asturias, Balearics, the Basque country, Canaries, Cantabria, Castilla-La Mancha, Castilla y León, Catalunya, Ceuta, Extemandura, Galicia, Madrid, Melilla, Murcia, Navarra, La, Rioja and Valencia.

HEAD OF STATE

HM The King of Spain, **King Juan Carlos I de Borbón, KG, GCVO,** *acceded to the throne* **22 November 1975**

Heir, **HRH The Prince of the Asturias (Prince Felipe Juan Pablo Alfonso y Todos los Santos)**

CABINET *as at August 2002*

Prime Minister: José Maria Aznar López; **First Deputy Prime Minister, Cabinet Office, Interior:** Mariano Rajoy Brey; **Second Deputy Prime Minister, Economy:** Rodrigo de Rato y Figaredo; **Agriculture, Food and Fisheries:** Miguel Arias Cañete; **Defence:** Federico Trillo-Figueroa y Martínez Conde; **Development:** Francisco Alvárez-Cascos Fernández; **Education, Culture and Sport:** Pilar del Castillo Vera; **Environment:** Jaime Matas Palou; **Foreign Affairs:** Ana Palacio; **Government Spokesman, Presidency:** Mariano Rajoy Brey; **Health and Consumer Affairs:** Ana María Pastor; **Justice:** José Maria Michavilla; **Labour and Social Affairs:** Eduardo Zaplana; **Public Administration:** Javier Arenas; **Science and Technology:** Joseph Piqué i Camps; **Treasury:** Cristóbal Montoro Romero

SWEDEN
KONUNGARIKET SVERIGE

AREA – 173,732 sq. miles (449,964 sq. km). Neighbours: Norway (west), Finland (east)

POPULATION – 8,875,053 (2001 estimate): 8,745,109 (1993 census). The state religion is Lutheran Protestant, to which over 95 per cent officially adhere. The language is Swedish; in the north there are both Finnish – and Lapp-speaking communities

CAPITAL – Stockholm (population, 1,148,953, 1995)

MAJOR CITIES – Gothenburg (Göteborg) (454,016); Malmö (248,007); Uppsala (184,507), 1996 estimates

CURRENCY – Swedish krona of 100 öre

NATIONAL ANTHEM – Du Gamla, Du Fria (Thou Ancient, Thou Freeborn)

NATIONAL DAY – 6 June (Day of the Swedish Flag)

NATIONAL FLAG – Yellow cross on a blue ground

LIFE EXPECTANCY (years) – male 77.6; female 82.6

POPULATION DENSITY – 20 per sq. km (1999)

HISTORY AND POLITICS

Sweden takes its name from the Svear people who inhabited the region during the seventh century AD. The Swedes participated in the Viking expansion during the ninth to 11th centuries and established sovereignty over Finland in the 13 century. The Union of Kalmar (1397) brought Sweden and Norway under Danish rule. Northern Sweden regained its independence following a rebellion by noblemen in 1521 which resulted in the election to the Swedish throne of Gustav I of the house of Vasa.

Sweden's power climaxed in the 17th century under Gustavus II Adolf. The Danes were driven out of southern Sweden, the Baltic coast of Russia was seized and the Swedish army pushed into Germany after vanquishing the Catholic League. Swedish power wanted in the 17th and 18th centuries. Finland was lost to Russia in 1809; Norway was ceded to Sweden under the Congress of Vienna (1814-15) but seceded in 1905.

Sweden remained neutral during both World Wars. Post-war party politics was dominated by Social Democrat-led coalitions which established a mixed economy and a generous welfare state. Right-wing and centrist parties held power from 1976-82 and 1991-4. Sweden applied for EU membership in July 1991 and acceded to the EU on 1 January 1995.

In the general election held on 15 September 2002 the Social Democrats remained the largest party in the legislature.

POLITICAL SYSTEM

Sweden is a constitutional monarchy, with the monarch retaining purely ceremonial functions as head of state. Under the Act of Succession 1810 (with amendments) the throne is hereditary in the House of Bernadotte. The constitution is based upon the Instrument of Government 1974, which amended the 1810 Act and removed from the monarch the roles of appointing the prime minister and signing parliamentary bills into law. A 1979 amendment vested the succession in the monarch's eldest child irrespective of sex.

Executive power is vested in the prime minister and Council of Ministers. There is a unicameral legislature (*Riksdag*) of 349 members elected by universal suffrage on a proportional representation basis (with a 4 per cent threshold for representation) for four years. The Council of Ministers (*Statsråd*) is responsible to the *Riksdag*. Sweden is divided into 25 counties (*län*) and 288 municipalities (*kommun*).

HEAD OF STATE

HM The King of Sweden, Carl XVI Gustaf, KG, *succeeded* 15 September 1973

Heir, HRH Crown Princess Victoria Ingrid Alice Désirée, Duchess of Västergötland

CABINET *as at August 2002*

Prime Minister: Göran Persson; **Deputy Prime Minister:** Lena Hjelm-Wallén; **Agriculture, Food and Fisheries, Gender Equality Affairs:** Margareta Winberg; **Culture:** Marita Ulvskog; **Defence:** Björn von Sydow; **Education and Science, Schools and Adult Education:** Thomas Östros; **Environment** (*acting*)**:** Lena Sommestad; **Finance:** Bosse Ringholm, **Foreign Affairs:** Anna Lindh, **Health and Social Affairs:** Lars Engqvist; **Industry, Employment and Communications:** Björn Rosengren; **Justice:** Thomas Bodström, **Ministers Delegate:** Jan Karlsson (*Development Co-operation, Migration and Asylum Policy*); Ingela Thalen (*Social Security*); Leif Pagrotsky (*Trade*)

HOUSEHOLD OF HM THE KING

The King's Council for the Royal Court: Erik Norberg; Bo Ramfors; Lars Löfgren; Prof. Erling Norrby; **The Marshal of the Realm:** HE Gunnar Brodin; **The Mistress of the Robes:** Countess Alice Trolle-Wachtmeister; **Gentlemen of the Chamber:** Gösta Westring; Baron August Trolle-Löwen; Johan af

Petersens; Ulf Janson; Baron Ninian Ramel; **The First Marshal of the Court:** Johan Fischarström; **The First Mistress of the Court:** Louise Lyberg; **Private Secretary to HM The Queen:** Margareta Lilhehöök; **Crown Equerry:** Jörn Beckmann; **Master of the Royal Hunt:** Baron Johan T. Adelswärd; **Lord Chamberlain:** Christer E. Lignell; **Principal Secretary:** Anna-Stina Swenson; **Grand Master of Ceremonies:** HE G. Christer Sylvén; **Master of Ceremonies:** S. D. Bertil Daggfeldt; **Court Auditor:** Bengt Ljungqvist; **Director of Information and the Press Department:** Elisabeth A. B. Tarras-Wahlberg

OFFICE OF HRH THE CROWN PRINCESS
Secretary: Ursula Wohlfahrt

TURKEY
TÜRKIYE ÇUMHURIYETI

AREA – 314,508 sq. miles (814,578 sq. km). Neighbours: Greece (west), Bulgaria (north), Georgia, Armenia, Nakhichevan (Azerbaijan) and Iran (east), Syria and Iraq (south)

POPULATION – 66,493,970 (2001 estimate). Islam ceased to be the state religion in 1928 but 98.99 per cent of the population are Muslim. The main religious minorities, which are concentrated in Istanbul and on the Syrian frontier, are Greek Orthodox, Armenian, Syrian Christian and Jewish. The language is Turkish; Kurdish is widely spoken in the south-east of the country.

CAPITAL – Ankara (Angora), in Asia (population, 3,258,026, 1997 estimate). Ankara (or Ancyra) was the capital of the Roman Province of *Galatia Prima*, and a marble temple (now in ruins), dedicated to Augustus, contains the *Monumentum* (*Marmor*) *Ancyranum*, inscribed with a record of the reign of Augustus Caeesar

MAJOR CITIES – Adana (1, 682,483); Bursa (1,958,529); Gaziantep (1,127,686); Istanbul (9,198,809); Izmir (3,114,859); Konya (1,931,773), 2000 estimates. Istanbul, in Europe, is the former capital. The Roman city of Byzantium, it was selected by Constantine the Great as the capital of the Roman Empire about AD 328 and renamed Constantinople. Istanbul contains the celebrated church of St Sofia, which after becoming a mosque, was made a museum in 1934. It also contains Topkapi, former palace of the Ottoman Sultans, which is also a museum

CURRENCY – Turkish lira (TL) of 100 kurus
NATIONAL ANTHEM – Istiklal Marsi (The Independence March)
NATIONAL DAY – 29 October (Republic Day)
NATIONAL FLAG – Red, with white crescent and star
LIFE EXPECTANCY (years) – male 68.0; female 73.2
POPULATION GROWTH RATE – 1.5 per cent (1999)
POPULATION DENSITY – 83 per sq. km (1999)
URBAN POPULATION – 73.1 per cent (2001)

Turkey in Europe consists of Eastern Thrace, including the cities of Istanbul and Edirne, and is separated from Asia by the Bosporus at Istanbul and by the Dardanelles (about 40 miles in length with a width varying from one to four miles). Turkey in Asia comprises the whole of Asia Minor or Anatolia.

HISTORY AND POLITICS

On 29 October 1923 the National Assembly declared Turkey a republic and elected Gazi Mustafa Kemal (later known as Kemal Atatûrk) president. In 1945 a multiparty system was introduced but in 1960 the government was overthrown by the armed forces. A new constitution was adopted in 1961 and a civilian government took office. Civilian governments remained in power until September 1980 when mounting problems with the economy and terrorism led to a military takeover.

Following the general election in November 1983 the military leadership handed over power to a civilian government.

Following elections on 18 April 1999, the Democratic Left Party (DPS) won the most seats and formed a coalition with the Nationalist Action Party (MHP) and the Motherland Party (ANAP). Hadep, the pro-Kurdish People's Democracy Party, won control of several towns in south-eastern Turkey in simultaneous local elections.

INSURGENCIES

Since 1984 Turkey has been fighting armed guerrillas of the Marxist Kurdistan Worker's Party (PKK) in the south-east of the country where Kurds are the majority population. The leader of the PKK Abdullah Öçalan was captured by Turkish authorities in February 1999 in Kenya and returned to Turkey to stand trial, where he was found guilty of treason on 31 May and sentenced to death on 29 June 1999. The Turkish government announced on 12 January 2000 that it would suspend the execution, pending an appeal. The PKK announced on 8 February 2000 that it had renounced violence and removed the world 'Kurdistan', which is illegal in Turkey, from its title.

POLITICAL SYSTEM

A new constitution, extending the powers of the president, was approved in 1982. It provided for the separation of powers between the legislature, executive and judiciary, and the holding of free elections to the unicameral Grand National Assembly, which now has 550 members elected every five years.

HEAD OF STATE

President: Ahmet Necdet Sezer, *elected* by parliament for a seven-year term 5 May 2000, *took office* 16 May 2000

CABINET *as at September 2002*

Prime Minister: Bülent Ecevit (DSP); **Deputy Prime Minister, EU Relations:** Mesut Yilmaz (ANAP); **Deputy Prime Minister, Foreign Affairs:** Sükrü Sina Gürel (DSP); **Deputy Prime Minister, Minister of State:** Devlet Bahçeli (MHP); **Agriculture and Rural Affairs:** Hüsnü Yusuf Gökalp (MHP); **Culture:** Burhan Suat Çaglayan; **Education:** Necdet Tekin; **Energy and Natural Resources:** Zeki Çakan (ANAP); **Environment:** Fevzi Aytekin (DSP); **Finance:** Sümer Oral (ANAP); **Forestry:** Nami Çagan (DSP); **Health:** Osman Durmus (MHP); **Interior:** Muzaffer Ecemis (ANAP); **Justice:** Aysel Çelikel; **Labour and Social Security:** Nejat Arseven; **National Defence:** Sabahattin Çakmakoglu (MHP); **Public Works and Housing:** Abdülkadir Akcan; **Tourism:** Mustafa Tasar (ANAP); **Trade and Industry:** Ahmet Kenan Tanrikulu (MHP); Transport: Naci Kinacioglu

ANAP Motherland Party; DSP Democratic Left Party; MHP Nationalist Action Party

---

UNITED STATES OF AMERICA

AREA – 3,615,275 sq. miles (9,363,520 sq. km).
POPULATION – 281,421,906 (2000 census). The language is English. There is a significant Spanish-speaking minority
CAPITAL – Washington DC (population, 4,923,153, 2000 census). The area of the Disctrict of Columbia (with which the City of Washington is considered co-extensive) is 61 sq. miles, with a resident population (2000 census) of 572,059. The District of Columbia is governed by an elected mayor and City Council
MAJOR CITIES – Chicago (2,896,016); Dallas (1,188,580);

Detroit (951,270); Houston (1,953,631); Los Angeles (3,694,820); New York (8,008,278); Philadelphia (1,517,550); Phoenix (1,321,045); San Antonio (1,144,646); San Diego (1,223,400), 2000 census

CURRENCY – US dollar of 100 cents

NATIONAL ANTHEM – The Star-Spangled Banner

NATIONAL DAY – 4 July (Independence Day)

NATIONAL FLAG – Thirteen horizontal stripes, alternately red and white, with blue canton in the hoist showing 50 white stars in nine horizontal rows of six and five alternately (known as the Star-Spangled Banner)

LIFE EXPECTANCY (years) – male 74.6; female 80.4

POPULATION GROWTH RATE – 0.9 per cent (1999)

POPULATION DENSITY – 29 per sq. km (1999)

The coastline has a length of about 2,069 miles on the Atlantic, 7,623 miles on the Pacific, 1,060 miles on the Arctic, and 1,631 miles on the Gulf of Mexico. The principal river is the Mississippi-Missouri-Red (3,710 miles long), traversing the whole country to its mouth in the Gulf of Mexico. The chain of the Rocky Mountains separates the western portion of the country from the remainder. West of these, bordering the Pacific coast, the Cascade Mountains and Sierra Nevada form the outer edge of a high tableland, consisting in part of stony and sandy desert and partly of grazing land and forested mountains, and including the Great Salt Lake, which extends to the Rocky Mountains. In the eastern states large forests still exist, the remnants of the forests which formerly extended over all the Atlantic slope. The highest point is Mount McKinley (20,320 ft) in Alaska, and the lowest point of dry land is in Death Valley (Inyo, California), 282 ft below sea level.

HISTORY AND POLITICS

The area which is now the USA was first inhabited by nomadic hunters who probably arrived from Asia c.30,000 BC. The first (failed) European colony was founded by Sir Walter Raleigh in 1585. By 1733 there were 13 British colonies, composed largely of religious non-conformists who had left Britain to escape persecution; the French and Spanish had also founded colonies.

The War of Independence broke out in 1775 largely because of the colonists' objection to being taxed by, but having no representation in, the British Parliament. The forces of the British government were defeated with French, Spanish and Dutch assistance. The Declaration of Independence which inaugurated the United States of America was signed on 4 July 1776; Britain recognised American sovereignty in 1783. The first federal constitution was drawn up in 1787; ten amendments, termed the Bill of Rights, were added in 1791. The 13 original states of the

Union ratified the constitution between 1787 and 1790. Vermont, Kentucky and Tennessee were admitted in the 1790s but most of the states acceded in the 19th century as the opening up of the centre and west led to the creation of new states and European or neighbouring countries ceded or sold their territories to the USA.

The Civil War (1861-5) was fought over the issue of slavery, which was integral to the economy of the southern states but was opposed by the northern states. The northern states defeated the Confederacy of southern states (South Carolina, Georgia, Alabama, Florida, Mississippi, Louisiana).

The USA emerged as a world economic and military super-power in the 20th century and played a decisive role in the two world wars. Its economic and military (including nuclear) supremacy gave the USA a key role in shaping the post-war world.

11 SEPTEMBER 2001

On 11 September 2001, four passenger aircraft were hijacked and two of them were deliberately flown into the 'twin towers' of New York's World Trade Center. The third aircraft was flown into the Pentagon in Washington DC and the fourth crashed in Pennsylvania. Over 3,000 people were killed in the attacks, the most serious attack on the USA since the Second World War.

POLITICAL SYSTEM

By the constitution of 17 September 1787 (to which amendments were added in 1791, 1798, 1804, 1865, 1868, 1870, 1913, 1920, 1933, 1951, 1961, 1964, 1967, 1971 and 1992), the government of the United States is entrusted to three separate authorities: the executive (the president and Cabinet), the legislature (Congress) and the judiciary.

The president is indirectly elected by an electoral college every four years. There is also a vice-president, who, should the president die, becomes president for the remainder of the term. The tenure of the presidency is limited to two terms.

The president, with the consent of the Senate, appoints the Cabinet officers and all the chief officials. He makes recommendations of a general nature to Congress, and when laws are passed by Congress he may return them to Congress with a veto. But if a measure so vetoed is again passed by both Houses of Congress by two-thirds majority in each House, it becomes law, notwithstanding the objection of the president. The president must be at least 35 years of age and a native citizen of the United States.

PRESIDENTIAL ELECTIONS

Each state elects (on the first Tuesday after the first Monday in November of the year preceding the year in which the presidential term expires) a number of electors (members of the electoral college), equal to the whole number of Senators and Representatives to which the state may be entitled in the Congress. The electors for each state meet in their respective states on the first Monday after the second Wednesday in December following, and vote for a president by ballot. The ballots are then sent to Washington, and opened on 6 January by the President of the Senate in the presence of Congress. The candidate who has received a majority of the whole number of electoral votes cast is declared president for the ensuing term. If no one has a majority, then from the highest on the list (not exceeding three) the House of Representatives elects a president, the votes being taken by states, the representation from each state having one vote. A presidential term begins at noon on 20 January.

THE STATES OF THE UNION

State	Land Area	Pop. (2002 census)	Capital
Alabama (AL)	131,443	4,447,100	Mtg'mery
Alaska (AK)	1,477,268	626,932	Juneau
Arizona (AZ)	294,333	5,130,632	Phoenix
Arkansas (AR)	134,875	2,673,400	Little Rock
California (CA)	403,971	33,871,648	Sacramento
Colorado (CO)	268,658	4,301,261	Denver
Connecticut (CT)	12,550	3,405,565	Hartford
Delaware (DE)	5,063	783,600	Dover
Florida (FL)	139,853	15,982,378	Tallahassee
Georgia (GA)	150,010	8,186,453	Atlanta
Hawaii (HI)	16,637	1,211,537	Honolulu
Idaho (ID)	214,325	1,293,953	Boise
Illinoise (IL)	143,987	12,419,293	Springfield
Indiana (IN)	92,904	6,080,485	Ind'polis
Iowa (IA)	144,716	2,926,324	Des Moines
Kansas (KS)	211,922	2,688,418	Topeka
Kentucky (KY)	102,907	4,041,769	Frankfort
Louisiana (LA)	112,836	4,468,976	Baton Rouge
Maine (ME)	79,939	1,274,923	Augusta
Maryland (MD)	25,316	5,296,486	Annapolis
Massachusetts (MA)	20,300	6,349,097	Boston
Michigan (MI)	147,136	9,938,444	Lansing
Minnesota (MN)	206,207	4,919,479	St Paul
Mississippi (MS)	121,506	2,844,658	Jackson
Missouri (MO)	178,446	5,595,211	Jefferson City
Montana (MT)	376,991	902,195	Helena
Nebraska (NE)	199,113	1,711,263	Lincoln
Nevada (NV)	284,396	1,998,257	Carson City
New Hampshire (NH)	23,231	1,235,786	Concord
New Jersey (NJ)	19,215	8,414,350	Trenton

New Mexico (NM)314,334	1,819,046	Santa Fé
New York (NY) 122,310	18,976,457	Albany
North Carolina (NC)126,180	8,049,313	Raleigh
North Dakota (ND)178,695	642,200	Bismarck
Ohio (OH) 106,067	11,353,140	Columbus
Oklahoma (OK) 177,877	3,450,654	Oklahoma City
Oregon (OR) 248,646	3,421,399	Salem
Pennsylvania (PA)116,083	12,281,054	Harrisburg
Rhode Island (RI)2,707	1,048,319	Providence
South Carolina (SC)77,988	4,012,012	Columbia
South Dakota (SD)196,571	754,844	Pierre
Tennessee (TN) 106,759	5,689,283	Nashville
Texas (TX) 678,358	20,851,820	Austin
Utah (UT) 212,816	2,233,169	Salt Lake City
Vermont (VT) 23,956	608,827	Montpelier
Virginia (VA) 102,558	7,078,515	Richmond
Washington (WA)172,445	5,894,121	Olympia
West Virginia (WV)62,384	1,808,344	Charleston
Wisconsin (WI) 140,672	5,363,675	Madison
Wyoming (WY) 251,501	493,782	Cheyenne
Dist. of Columbia (DC)159	572,059	-

HEAD OF STATE

President of the United States: George Walker Bush, *born* 6 July 1946, *elected* 7 November 2000, *sworn in* 20 January 2001. Republican; **Vice-President:** Richard B. Cheney, *born* 30 January 1941

THE CABINET *as at August 2002*

Agriculture: Ann Veneman; **Attorney-General:** John Ashcroft; **Commerce:** Don Evans; **Defence:** Donald Rumsfeld; **Education:** Rod Paige; **Energy:** Spencer Abraham; **Health and Human Services:** Tommy Thompson; **Housing and Urban Development:** Mel Martinez; **Interior:** Gale Norton; **Labour:** Elaine Chao; **Representative for Trade Negotiations:** Robert Zoellick; **Secretary of State:** Colin Powell; **Transportation:** Norman Mineta; **Treasury:** Paul O'Neill; **Veteran's Affairs:** Anthony Principi; **Director, Office of Homeland Defence:** Tom Ridge; **Director, Office of Management Agency:** Joseph Allbaugh; **National Security Advisor:** Condoleezza Rice; **President's Counsellor:** [*vacant*]; **Special White House Advisor on Cyberspace Security:** Richard Clarke; **White House Counsel:** Alberto Gonzales

US TERRITORIES
THE COMMONWEALTH OF PUERTO RICO –
Governor: Sila Maria Calderon
GUAM – **Governor:** Carl Gutierrez
AMERICAN SAMOA – **Governor:** Pita Sunia
THE UNITED STATES VIRGIN ISLANDS – **Governor:**
Charles Wesley Turnbull
NORTHERN MARIANA ISLANDS – **Governor:** Juan N.
Babauta

VATICAN CITY STATE
Status Civitatus Vaticanae / Stato della Città del Vaticano

AREA – 0.2 sq. miles (0.44 sq. km). Neighbour: Italy
POPULATION – 890 (2001 estimate). No national language; any
language may be used
CAPITAL – Vatican City (population 766, 1998)
CURRENCY – Euro of 100 cents
NATIONAL DAY – 22 October (Inauguration of present
Pontiff)
NATIONAL FLAG – Square flag; equal vertical bands of yellow
(next staff), and white; crossed keys and triple crown device on
white band
POPULATION GROWTH RATE – 0.0 per cent (1997)
POPULATION DENSITY – 2,273 per sq. km (1997)
GDP – US$10 million (1998); US$20,650 per capita (1998)
ANNUAL AVERAGE GROWTH OF GDP – 1.3 per cent
(1998)

The office of the ecclesiastical head of the Roman Catholic Church
(Holy See) is vested in the Pope, the Sovereign Pontiff. For many
centuries the Sovereign Pontiff exercised temporal power but by
1870 the States of the Church had become part of unified Italy. The
temporal power of the Pope was in suspense until the Lateran
Treaties of 1929 which recognised the full and independent
sovereignty of the Holy See in the City of the Vatican.

HEAD OF STATE
Sovereign Pontiff: His Holiness Pope John Paul II (Karol Wojtyla),
elected Pope in succession to Pope John Paul I, 16 October 1978

SECRETARIAT OF STATE *as at November 2002*

Secretary of State: H.E. Cardinal Angelo Sodano, *apptd* December 1990; **First Assistant:** Archbishop Leonardo Sandri; **Secretary for Relations with States:** Archbishop Jean-Louis Tauran; **Prefect to the Congregation for the Doctrine of the Faith:** H.E. Cardinal Joseph Ratzinger; **Prefect to the Congregation for Oriental Churches:** H.E. Cardinal Patriarch Ignace Moussa I; **Prefect to the Congregation for Divine Cult and Discipline of Sacraments:** H.E. Cardinal Francis Arinze; **Prefect to the Congregation for Causes of Saints:** H.E. Cardinal José Saraiva Martins; **Prefect to the Congregation for Bishops:** H.E. Cardinal Giovanni B. Re; **Prefect to the Congregation for Evangelisation of Peoples:** H.E. Cardinal Crescenzio Sepe; **Prefect to the Congregation for Clergy:** H.E. Cardinal Darío Castrillón Hoyos; **Prefect to the Congregation for Consecrated Life:** H.E. Cardinal Eduardo Martínez Somalo; **Prefect to the Congregation for Catholic Education:** H.E. Cardinal Zenon Grocholewski; **Pro-Major Penitentiary to the Apostolic Penitentiary:** Archbishop Luigi De Magistris; **Prefect to the Supreme Tribunal of the Apostolic Signature:** H.E. Cardinal Mario F. Pompedda; **Dean of the Roman Rota:** H.E. Mgr. Raffaello Funghini; **President to the Pontifical Council for the Laity:** H.E. Cardinal James F. Stafford; **President to the Pontifical Council for Union of Christians:** H.E. Cardinal Walter Kasper; **President to the Pontifical Council for the Family:** H.E. Cardinal Alfonso López Trujillo; **President to the Pontifical Council for Justice and Peace:** Archbishop Renato R. Martino; **President to the Pontifical Council Cor Unum:** Archbishop Paul J. Cordes; **President to the Pontifical Council for Migrants and Itinerants:** Archbishop Stephen Fumio Hamao; **President to the Pontifical Council for Sanitary Operators:** Archbishop Javier Lozano Barragán; **President to the Pontifical Council for Legislative Texts:** Archbishop Julián Herranz; **President to the Pontifical Council for Interreligious Dialogue:** Archbishop Michael L. Fitzgerald; **President to the Pontifical Council for Culture:** H.E. Cardinal Paul Poupard; **President to the Pontifical Council for Social Communications:** Archbishop John P. Foley

APOSTOLIC CAMERA

Camerarius of the Holy Roman Church: H.E. Cardinal Eduardo

Martinez Somalo; **Dean of the Apostolic Camera:** Mgr. Karel Kasteel; **Prefecture for the Economic Affairs:** H.E. Cardinal Sergio Sebastiani (*President*); **Patrimony of the Apostolic See:** Archbishop Attilio Nicora (*President*); **Almoner of His Holiness:** Archbishop Oscar Rizzato

HOUSEHOLD OF HIS HOLINESS THE POPE

Prefect of the Papal Household: Bishop James M Harvey; **Joint Prefect:** Bishop Stanislas Dziwisz; **Regent of the Prefecture:** Mgr. Paolo De Nicolò; **Master of Liturgical Celebrations:** Bishop Piero Marini; **Theologian of the Papal Household:** Father Georges Cottier, O.P.; **Dean of the Participating Apostolic Protonotaries:** Mgr. Marcello Rossetti; **Preacher of the Papal Household:** Father Raniero Cantalamessa, O.F.M.Cap.; **Prince Assistant to the Papal Throne:** Prince Don Alessandro Torlonia, Prince of Civitella Cesi, *etc.*; **Master of the Music:** Mgr. Giuseppe Liberto; **Dean of the Consistorial Advocates:** Dr. Vittorio Trocchi; **General Councillor of the State of Vatican City:** Marquess Don Giulio Sacchetti; **Commander of the Pontifical Swiss Guards:** Capt. Elmar Theodor Mäder; **President of the Pontifical Academy of Sciences:** H.E. Prof. Nicola Cabibbo; **Hereditary Quartermaster General and Delegate of the State of the City of the Vatican:** Marquess Giulio Sacchetti, Marques of Castel Romano; **Hereditary Superintendant of the stables of the Palaces:** Marquess Dr Gregorio Serlupi Crescenzi; **Hereditary Superintendant of the Posts:** Prince Don Filippo Massimo, Prince and Lord of Arsoli, Duke of Anticoli Corrado; **Hereditary Marshal of the Holy Roman Church and Sacred Conclave:** Prince Don Agostino Chigi Albani della Rovere, Prince of the Holy Roman Empire, Prince of Farnese, Campagnano, and Soriano, Duke of Ariccia and Formello, *etc.*; **Hereditary Grand Master of the Sacred Apostolic Hospice:** Prince Don Alessandro Ruspoli, Prince of Cerveteri; **Captain Commander of the Noble Guard:** Lt.-Gen. Princes Altieri, Aldobrandini, Barberini, Rospigliosi; **Hereditary Standard Bearer of the Holy Roman Church:** Lt.-Gen. Marquess Patrizio Patrizi Naro Montoro, Marquess of the Baldacchino; **Gentlemen of His Holiness:** members of Roman Patriciate and Nobility and others; **Dean of Procurators of the Apostolic Palaces:** Dr. Ludovico Valletta; **Dean of Chamberlains:** Pier Franco Valle; **Dean of the Papal Antechamber:** Dr. Adalberto M. Leschiutta; **Director of the Press Office of the Holy See:** Dr.

Joaquín Navarro-Valls; **President to the Pontifical Commissions for Cultural Properties of the Church and for Sacred Archaeology:** Archbishop Francesco Marchisano; **President to the Pontifical Biblical Commission and International Theological Commission:** H.E. Cardinal Joseph Ratzinger; **President to the Pontifical Commission Ecclesia Dei:** H.E. Cardinal Darío Castrillón Hoyos; **President to the Pontifical Committee for International Eucharistic Congresses:** H.E. Cardinal Jozef Tomko; **President to the Pontifical Committee for Historic Sciences:** Mgr. Brandmüller; **Secret Vatican Archives and Apostolic Vatican Library:** H.E. Cardinal Jorge M. Mejía; **General Director Vatican Printing Offices:** Revd. Elio Torrigiani, S.D.B.; **Director L'Osservatore Romano:** Prof. Mario Agnes; **President of the Vatican Publishing and Printing Services:** Archbishop Giovanni De Andrea; **General Director Vatican Radio:** Father Pasquale Borgomeo, S.J.; **President of the Vatican Television Centre:** Dr. Emilio Rossi; **President Saint Peter's Fabric:** Archbishop Francesco Marchisano; **President Labour Office of the Apostolic See:** H.E. Cardinal Jan Schotte; **Papal Administrator of Saint Paul's Patriarchal Basilica:** Archbishop Francesco Gioia; **President of the Pontifical State Commission of the State of the Vatican City:** H.E. Cardinal Edmund C. Szoka; **General Director Pontifical Monuments, Museums and Galleries:** Dr. Francesco Buranelli; **Director Pontifical Villas of Castel Gandolfo:** Dr. Saverio Petrillo; **Inspector General Pontifical Gendarmerie:** Gen. Camillo Cibin

---

YUGOSLAVIA FEDERATION
(SERBIA AND MONTENEGRO)
SAVEZNA REPUBLIKA JUGOSLAVIJA

(SEE ALSO SERBIA AND MONTENEGRO)

FEDERAL HEAD OF STATE
Federal President: Vojislav Koštunica, *elected* 24 September 2000

FEDERAL GOVERNMENT *as at December 2002*
Prime Minister: Dragiša Pešic (SNP); **Deputy Prime minister:**

Josef Kasa, Dr. Zarko Korac, Dušan Mihailovic, Dr. Nebojša Covic, Miodrag Isakov; **Foreign Affairs:** Goran Svilanovic (DOS); **Foreign Trade Relations:** Miroljub Labus (DOS); **Defence:** Velimir Radojevic (SNP); **Economy and Internal Trade:** Petar Trojanovic; **Finance** *(acting)*: Veroljub Dugalic; **Interior:** Zoran Zivkovic; **Justice:** Savo Markovic; **National and Ethnic Communities:** Rasim Ljajic (DOS); **Transportation and Telecommunications:** Bozidar Milovic.

FEDERAL CAPITAL – Belgrade (population 1,338,856, 1997 estimate)

MONTENEGRIN CAPITAL - Podgorica (162,172).

SERBIAN CAPITAL - Belgrade (population 1,338,856.

MAJOR CITIES – Kragujevac (181,061); Niš (250,104); Novi Sad (178,896); Podgorica (162,172), the capital of Montenegro; Priština (241,565); Subotica (146,075), 1997 estimates

SERBIAN CURRENCY – New dinar of 100 paras

MONTENEGRIN CURRENCY - EU Euro of 100 Cents

FEDERAL NATIONAL ANTHEM – Hej, Sloveni, Jošte Zivi Rec Naših Dedova (Oh! Slavs, Our Ancestors' Words Still Live)

FEDERAL NATIONAL DAY – 27 April

FEDERAL FLAG – Three horizontal stripes of blue, white red

LIFE EXPECTANCY (years) – male 70.9; female 75.6

POPULATION GROWTH RATE – 0.2 per cent (1999)

POPULATION DENSITY – 104 per sq. km (1999)

MILITARY EXPENDITURE – 10.0 per cent of GDP (2000)

MILITARY PERSONNEL – 105,500: Army 79,000, Navy 7,000, Air Force 19,500; Paramilitaries 93,000

CONSCRIPTION DURATION – 12-15 months

ENROLMENT – (percentage of age group) – primary 69 per cent (1997); secondary 62 per cent (1997); tertiary 22 per cent (1997)

DOS Democratic Opposition of Serbia; SNP Montenegrin Socialist National Party

POLITICAL SYSTEM

The Federal republic has a bicameral parliament with a 138-seat (100 Serbian, 38 Montenegrin) lower house, the Chamber of Citizens, and a 40-seat (20 Serbian, 20 Montenegrin) upper house, the Chamber of Republics. Both houses are directly elected and serve four-year terms. Executive power is vested in a federal president and government.

Both Serbia and Montenegro have parliaments recognised by the Federal bodies. *(See also* **SERBIA AND MONTENEGRO**).

APPENDIX I

Gotha Format

Germanic & Other Titles
and Prefixes.

Abbreviations.

ALMANACH DE GOTHA 2003 (*186th Edition*)
FORMAT

The format of the 2003 (*186th*) Edition, *Almanach de Gotha*, follows the broad tradition of this Almanac; it is a list of the living lines of the reigning and formerly reigning royal and princely houses of Europe and of South America and of the Mediatized houses of the Holy Roman Empire.

The 1998 (*182nd*) Edition was unique in that it included, within each family entry, a number of genealogical lines which had become extinct. However readers will be aware that between the years of 1944 and 1998 publication of the Gotha was suspended. It was decided to include all those who had been living, at any time during that abeyance.

Not to have done so would have seen some family members disappear from this historic record altogether.

Having successfully charted the births and deaths of members of Gotha royal and princely Houses since 1763, it was decided that this would have been an omission. More so since a number of Gotha entrants had been born, and subsequently died, between the years 1944-1998, leaving no issue.

The 1999 edition was truncated and followed the original form, including only those lines where living issue remained, regardless of generation. Readers should note therefore that where an entrants biographical details conclude with the term "*and had issue, among whom*", the term donates that the issue recorded represents only *living* issue.

In such cases, the numbering of all issue, beginning with 1., denotes the order of birth of *surviving* issue, not necessarily the order of birth of all issue.

Where an entrants biographical details ends with the term "*and has/ had issue*" this indicates that *all* issue, the complete line of descendants, is listed in full.

This rule is followed in all cases with the exception of the sons and daughters of a living head of a family and their issue; and the brothers and sisters of a living head of a family. These are all listed fully, living or deceased.

Readers who require particulars of extinct lines should refer to earlier editions of the *Almanach de Gotha*, as has been the practice when using this annual publication in the past.

Once referred to as *"The ultimate Power Register of the Ruling Classes"* the *Gotha* was intended as a chronicle of living members of its qualifying families. The Publishers are none the less working on a *Complete Gotha* which will list all members of each dynasty, both living and deceased, from the earliest times. This compete genealogy will satisfy those who have a need to check the relationships between current members and their historical forebears.

Finally, it should be noted that the *Gotha* records genealogies in the malc line, and under the principle family. Entrants are listed under their father and mother (in that order). Thus following marriage the issue of a female member is listed as part of the fathers family. If the father family is not part of the *Gotha* the subsequent issue is not recorded in this volume.

ALMANACH DE GOTHA,
London, 2nd January 2003.

GERMANIC & OTHER TITLES AND PREFIXES

Altgraf/Altgraefin: Comital title indicating feudal (alt = old) origin. A style of specific Houses or lines *(Salm-Reifferscheidt)*.

Briefadel: *"Nobility by the Letter"* as opposed to *"Uradel"* or the ancient nobility. Traditionally titles granted after c.15th or 16th century but often referring to more recent (19th and 20th century) nobility.

Edler von/Edle von; Edler Herr von: *"Noble of"*; Austrian/ Austrian-Hungarian title usually indicating *"Briefadel"* and ranking below *Freiherr/Baron*.

Erb-: Prefix (= hereditary) used to denote the senior heir of (to) a mediatized comital house *(Erbgraf)*. For royalty the prefix is Kron- (= crown) as in *Kronprinz/Kronprinzessin*.

Freiherr/Freifrau: German Baron/Baroness. The unmarried daughter of a Freiherr is titled Freiin. The style *"Baron"* is used in social address. Hungarian and Polish nobility (with German or Austrian title) of this rank are usually titled Baron rather than Freiherr.

Durchlaucht and Erlaucht: *See next Article (Appendix II)*

Fürst/ Fürstin: The title of a reigning Prince; the senior or head of princely House (others titled *Prinz/Prinzessin*)or in a princely primogeniture/comital House (others titled *Graf/Graefin*, as in *Starhemberg*).

Graf/Graefin: Count/Countess

Herzog/Herzogin: Duke/Duchess

Landgraf: *"Landgrave"*, an accessory feudal comital title style reserved for the head of different lines of Hesse and by the *Fürst zu Fürstenberg*.

Markgraf/Markgraefin: "Margrave/Margravine," equivalent to Marquess. Title of imperial counts who ruled the border territories or marches. A rank between Count and Duke.

Proprietor: The lord of the estate or territory.

Reichsfürst; Reichsgraf; Reichsfreiherren; Reichsritter: Style variation of the basic rank (*Fürst, Graf*, etc.) indicating that the title was granted prior to 1806 by the Holy Roman Emperor. Not intended as a higher rank. It has not been a popular or subsequently much utilized style.

Ritter von: *"Knight of"* (no female equivalent, Wife and daughter usually *Edle von or von*); Ancient title. In modern times an Austrian/Austrian-Hungarian *"Briefadel"* title usually conferred on military men. Like the knighthood of the British Baronet, it is hereditary and a title of nobility (*except that British Baronetcies are held in the person only, by male primogeniture and not extended to simultaneous living issue*).

von: The most basic title-particle of German(ic) nobility, translates into English as *"of"* and can be equated to the French/Spanish/Latin *"de, dela, du"*, Italian *"di"* and the Polish suffix *"-ski* or - *cki"*, and like those, not strictly an indicator of nobility. *Von* may also appear as part of a non-noble family name. To differentiate the two forms, it has been German-language practice among the nobility to abbreviate the noble *"von"* as *"v"*.

zu: Literally meaning *"to"*, the original use of *"zu"* rather than *"von"* in the titles of high nobility (princely and comital houses) indicated that the ancestral property which served as the basis for the name was still in the possession of the House (*Fuerst zu Stolberg*). Often it forms an accessory style (*Graf von Harrach zu Rohrau und Thannhausen*). *"Zu"* is also used with *"von"* to indicate the duality of origin and possession/rule (*Fürst von und zu Liechtenstein*). The common belief that *"zu"* was a higher or more valued title-particle than *"von"* has no basis.

Knjez: Prince. Russian and Slavic form, in some cases a military title.

Vojvoda: Duke. Russian and Slavic form, in some cases a military title.

Veliki Vojvoda: Grand Duke. Russian and Slavic form, in some cases a military title.

b, (Born), *m,* (Married), *m,* diss by div (Divorced), *k,* (Killed) **1stly** (Firstly) **2ndly** (Secondly etc)

APPENDIX II

History

The Mediatized Sovereign Houses

of The Holy Roman Empire

MEDIATIZED SOVEREIGN HOUSES

This designation may be applied only to certain families that occupied territories within the Holy Roman Empire and its successor states in what is now modern Germany and Austria. The Latin root of the word "Mediatised" is "media", meaning "between", and its use comes from the number of layers of allegiance (in a feudal sense) between a nobleman and his suzerain. In the Holy Roman Empire, the ultimate feudal superior was the Emperor, elected by the great Electors.[1] An "immediate" fief was held by feudal tenure directly from the Emperor, with no intervening superior Lord. When such a fief was placed under the authority of a feudal superior other than the Emperor and that superior was himself a tenant within the Empire, this fief was thereby "mediatised".

Germany did not become a single unified nation until the end of World War I and the foundation of the Weimar republic in 1919. The 1871 "German Empire" was a voluntary federation of sovereign states with each of the surviving German Kingdoms, Grand Duchies, Duchies and Principalities retaining their rulers and governments.[2]

Several hundred such "immediate" states existed under the Holy Roman Empire, but they did not all enjoy equal degrees of sovereignty. Duke and Prince Jean Engelbert d'Arenberg,[3] has explained this as follows:

"The Imperial States (Reichsstände) were the real pillars of the Holy Roman Empire. They consisted mainly of the Princes and Counts of the Empire who possessed immediate territories therein; i.e., fiefs which were held directly of the Emperor himself, and who had, each of them, a vote and a seat in the Imperial Diet.[4] The holders of these Imperial States and all those who were of equal birth with them constituted the High Nobility (Hoheradel).

"The dignity of States of the Empire was in general attached not to the person but to the fief. Such a territory had to enjoy sovereign rights under the suzerainty of the Empire. ... The States of the Empire accordingly exercised sovereignty over various Imperial Territories. But the fact of sovereignty under the suzerainty of the Emperor was not in itself sufficient to constitute a State of the Empire. Of equal importance was the fact of having a vote and a seat in the Imperial Diet. Still another requirement was the recognition of the quality of a State of the Empire either by usage or by special legal authorisation. In a few cases this authorisation was granted to persons even without an immediate territory. The following legal requirements were met by all Imperial States, except by those who had received that dignity for their person and not for their territory:

"(1) The possession of an immediate Principality, County or Lordship invested with the right of Sovereignty (*Landeshoheit*); (2) The consent of the Emperor and of all the Councils of the Imperial Diet, in the case of an Electorate; the consent of the Emperor, of the Council of Electors and of the Council of Princes in all other cases; (3) The assumption of an appropriate share in supplying the financial, military and other needs of the Empire; (4) The membership of one of the ten Imperial Circles.

"These Imperial Circles had been set up by Emperor Maximilian I, and were for military purposes. ... In the Council of Princes (*Reichsfürstlicheskollegium*) of the Imperial Diet (*Reichstag*) of 1792 there were one hundred and eight seats and votes (voting in this order), allocated as follows, with the name of the dynasty holding the seat given in parentheses:

"Three ecclesiastical Electors: *Mainz; Trier; Cologne.*

"Five secular Electors: *Bohemia (Habsburg-Lorraine); Palatinate (Wittelsbach); Electoral Saxony (Electoral Saxony, i.e., Wettin); Brandenburg (Electoral Brandenburg, i.e., Hohenzollern-Prussia); Hanover (Brunswick-Guelf-Hanover).* Thirty-three ecclesiastical Princes (not described here in detail);

"Sixty secular Princes: "Old Princes". *Austria (Habsburg-Lorraine); Burgundy (Habsburg-Lorraine); Bavaria (Wittelsbach); Palatinate-Lautern (Palatinate-Wittelsbach); Palatinate-Simmern (Palatinate-Wittelsbach); Palatinate-Neuburg (Palatinate-Wittelsbach); Palatinate-Zweibrücken (Zweibrücken-Wittelsbach); Palatinate-Veldenz (Palatinate-Wittelsbach); Saxe-Weimar (Wettin-Saxe-Weimar); Saxe-Eisenach (Wettin-Saxe-Weimar); Saxe-Coburg (Wettin-Saxe-Coburg); Saxe-Gotha (Wettin-Saxe-Gotha); Saxe-Altenburg (Wettin-Saxe-Gotha); Brandenburg-Ansbach (Hohenzollern-Prussia); Brandenburg-Bayreuth (Hohenzollern-Prussia); Brunswick-Celle (Brunswick-Guelf-Hanover); Brunswick-Kalenberg (Brunswick-Guelf-Hanover); Brunswick-*

Grubenhagen (Brunswick-Guelf-Hanover); Brunswick-Wolfenbüttel (Brunswick-Guelf-Wolfenbüttel); Pomerania-Wolgast (Sweden); Pomerania-Stettin (Hohenzollern-Prussia); Mecklenburg-Schwerin (Mecklenburg-Schwerin); Mecklenburg-Güstrow (Mecklenburg-Schwerin); Würtemberg (Würtemberg); Hesse-Kassel (Hesse-Kassel); Hesse-Darmstadt (Hesse-Darmstadt); Baden-Baden (Baden); Baden-Durlach (Baden); Baden-Hochberg (Baden); Holstein-Glückstadt (Oldenburg-Denmark); Holstein-Gottorp (Oldenburg-Holstein-Gottorp); Saxe-Lauenburg (Brunswick-Guelf-Hanover); Savoy (Savoy-Sardinia); Leuchtenberg (Palatinate-Wittelsbach); Anhalt (Bernburg, Köthen, Zerbst, and Dessau branches); Henneberg (all branches of the House of Saxony-Wettin); Lorraine-Nomeny (Habsburg-Lorraine); Montbeliard (Würtemberg); Arenberg (Ligne-Arenberg).

"Secularized ecclesiastical territories: *Magdeburg (Hohenzollern-Prussia); Bremen (Brunswick-Guelf-Hanover); Halberstadt (Hohenzollern-Prussia); Verden (Brunswick-Guelf-Hanover); Minden (Hohenzollern-Prussia); Schwerin (Mecklenburg-Schwerin); Kamin (Hohenzollern-Prussia); Ratzenburg (Mecklenburg-Strelitz); Hersfeld (Hesse-Kassel)*

'"New Princes": *Zollern (Hohenzollern-Hechingen); Sternstein (Lobkowicz); Salm (Salm-Salm and Salm-Kyrburg); Trasp in Tyrol (Dietrichstein); Nassau-Hadamar (Nassau-Dietz-Orange); Nassau-Dillenburg (Nassau-Dietz-Orange); Wels (Auersperg); East Frisia (Hohenzollern-Prussia); Stühlingen (Fürstenberg); Schwarzenberg (Schwarzenberg); Schellenberg and Vaduz (Liechtenstein); Schwarzburg (Schwarzburg); Friedberg (Thurn und Taxis)*

Four seats representing the Councils of the Counts of the Empire: *Council of the Counts of the Wetterau (representing twelve Houses); Council of the Counts of Suabia (representing twenty-three Houses); Council of the Counts of Franconia (representing seventeen Houses); Council of the Counts of Westphalia (representing thirty-two Houses).* Two other seats, representing the Free Cities.

Several points can be made about this list. First, there were substantial territories held by Imperial Princes which were not part of the Empire.[5] Second, a few houses had multiple voting rights, for example the Palatine Elector had six votes and the Elector of

Hanover had seven. The Elector of Hanover was, at that time (1792), also King of Great Britain, illustrating how many non-German sovereigns played a role in the Empire (on the other hand the Kings of Sardinia, while they had a seat in the Diet, seldom bothered even to send a representative).

There was also an important distinction between "Old Princes" and "New Princes". All of the "Old Princes" were present in the Diet of 1582, while the "New Princes" were admitted subsequently. From 1641 during the 30 years war, the Emperor conferred the title of "*Reichsfürst*" (Prince of the Empire) on those persons or Houses he thought worthy and if the recipient satisfied the other requirements, he was admitted to the Diet. Most though not all creations of *Reichsfürst* were for individuals or Houses that already possessed a territory and a function within the Empire. Those Houses which held immediate fiefs and had received the title of *Reichsfürst*, but had not fulfilled the other requirements for membership of the Diet, became members of the Councils of the Counts of the Empire. These Councils comprised, as of around 1792, the following members:

Council of the Counts of the Wetterau: *Princes and Counts of Solms-Braunfels, Solms-Hohensolms, Solms-Rödelheim, and Solms-Laubach; Princes and Counts of Nassau-Usingen, Nassau-Weilburg, and Nassau-Saarbrücken; Princes and Counts of Isenburg-Birstein, Isenburg-Büdingen, Isenburg-Meerholz, and Isenburg-Waechtersbach; Counts of Stolberg-Gedern-Ortenburg, Stolberg-Stolberg, and Stolberg-Wernigeröde; Princes and Counts of Sayn-Wittgenstein-Berleburg and Sayn-Wittgenstein-Wittgenstein; Counts of Salm (Wild und Rheingrafen zu Grumbach, and Wild-und Rheingraf zu Rheingrafenstein), Princes and Counts of Leiningen-Hartenburg and Leiningen-Heidesheim; Counts of Westerburg; Prince of Schönburg; Count of Wied-Runkel as Count of Criechingen; Count of Ortenburg; Count of Reuss zu Plauen*

Council of the Counts of Swabia: *Prince of Fürstenberg as Count of Heiligenberg; Abbess of Buchau; Commander of the Teutonic Knights as Count of Alschhausen; Prince of Oettingen; House of Habsburg-Lorraine for the Count of Montfort; Elector of Bavaria as Count of Helfenstein; Prince of Schwarzenberg as Count of Klettgau and Sulz; Count of Königsegg; Count of Waldburg; Margrave of Baden-Baden as Count of Eberstein; Count von der Leyen as Lord of Hohengeroldseck; Counts of Fugger; House of Habsburg-Lorraine as Lords of Hohenems; Count of Traun as Lord of Eggloff; Prince-Abbot of St. Blase as Count of Bonndorf; Count of Stadion as Lord of Thannhausen; Prince of Thurn und Taxis as Lord of Eglingen; Count of Khevenhüller; Count of Küfstein; Prince of Colloredo; Count of Harrach; Count of Sternberg; Count of Neipperg*

Council of the Counts of Franconia; *Princes and Counts of Hohenlohe; Counts of Castell; Counts of Erbach; Princes and Counts of Löwenstein as Counts of Wertheim; Heirs to the Counts of Limpurg; Counts of Nostitz as Counts of Rieneck; Prince of Schwarzenberg as Lord of Seinsheim; Heirs to the Counts of Wolfstein; Counts of Schönborn as Lords of Reichelsberg; Counts of Schönborn as Lords of Wiesentheid; Counts of Windischgraetz (personal); Count Orsini von Rosenberg (personal); Counts of Starhemberg (elder line); Count of Wurmbrand (personal); Counts of Giech (personal); Counts of Graevenitz (personal); Count of Pückler (personal)*

Council of the Counts of Westphalia: *King of Great Britain as Lord of Sayn-Altenkirchen; King of Great Britain as Count of Hoya; King of Great Britain as Count of Spiegelberg; King of Great Britain as Count of Diepholz; Duke of Holstein-Gottorp; Elector of Brandenburg as Count of Tecklenburg; Duke of Arenberg as Count of Schleiden; Duke of Arenberg as Lord of Kerpen; Duke of Arenberg as Count of Saffenburg; Prince of Wied-Runkel as Count of Wied; Prince of Wied-Neuwied as Chairman of the Council; Landgrave of Hesse-Kassel and Count of Lippe-Bückeburg as Count of Schaumburg; Counts of Lippe; Counts of Bentheim; Princes and Counts of Löwenstein as Counts of Virneburg; Prince of Kaunitz as Lord of Rietberg; Prince of Waldeck as Count of Pyrmont; Count of Törring as Count of Gronsfeld; Count of Aspremont as Count of Reckheim; Princes of Salm as Lords of Anholt; Count of Metternich as Lord of Winnenburg; Prince of Anhalt-Bernburg-Schaumberg as Count of Holzapfel; Counts of Plettenberg as Lords of Witthem; Counts of Limburg-Stirum as Lords of Gehmen; Count of Wallmoden as Lord of Gimborn; Count of Quadt as Lord of Wyckradt; Counts of Ostein as Lords of Mylendonk; Counts of Nesselrode as Lords of Reichenstein; Counts of Salm-Reifferscheidt as Lords of Dyck; Counts of Platen (personalit); Counts of Sinzendorf as Lords of Rheineck; Prince of Ligne as Count of Fagnolles.*[6]

Those nobles listed above controlled territories vastly different in scale and wealth, but all had a voice, although often a small one, in the Imperial decision-making process. These nobles were far from being the only titled persons in the Empire. They were not the only immediate or non-immediate feudal tenants of the Empire, nor did they comprise all those who enjoyed membership of the ten Imperial Circles.

By the time of the 1792 Diet, the Empire's western neighbour, France, had been devastated by revolution. France achieved some measure of stability under the Republic and the Directorate, and its armies, notably under the command of Bonaparte, won major victories against the Empire. By the terms of the Treaty of Lunéville (9 Feb 1801), the Empire lost some twenty-five thousand square miles of territory. To compensate the dispossessed Princes, the Emperor seized the remaining ecclesiastical territories, which were more vulnerable to spoliation. An Imperial Delegation published on 25 February 1803 the *Reichsdeputationshauptschluss*, which reorganised the Empire and the Imperial Diet. The Diet ratified this decision on 24 March 1803, and the Emperor confirmed it on 27 April 1803, while excluding Paragraph 32, which dealt specifically with the reorganisation of the Diet. The Emperor's objections were never overcome, thus the reorganisation of the Diet based on the *Reichsdeputationshauptschluss* cannot be considered strictly lawful, even though a tentative list of seats was drawn up. What little business the Diet transacted between 1803 and its dissolution in 1806 was based on this list, part of which (the Council of Princes) has been reproduced by Arenberg[7] and is given here, territory first with name of the dynasty in (parentheses):

Austria (Habsburg-Lorraine); Upper Bavaria (Wittelsbach); Styria (Habsburg-Lorraine); Magdeburg (Brandenburg); Salzburg (Lorraine-Tuscany); Lower Bavaria (Wittelsbach); Regensburg (Elector of Mainz); Sulzbach (Wittelsbach), The Teutonic Knights; Neuburg (Wittelsbach);Bamburg (Wittelsbach); Bremen (Brunswick-Guelf-Hanover); Meissen (Wettin-Saxony); Berg (Wittelsbach); Würzburg (Wittelsbach); Carinthia (Habsburg-Lorraine); Eichstaedt (Lorraine-Tuscany); Coburg (Wettin-Saxe-Coburg); Bruchsal-Speier (Zaehringen-Baden); Gotha (Wettin-Saxe-Coburg); Ettenheim-Strassburg (Zaehringen Baden); Altenburg (Wettin-Saxe-Altenburg); Constanz (Zaehringen-Baden); Weimar (Wettin-Saxe-Weimar); Augsburg (Wittelsbach); Eisenach (Wettin-Saxe-Eisenach); Hildesheim (Brandenburg); Ansbach (Brandenburg); Paderborn (Brandenburg); Bayreuth (Brandenburg); Freising (Wittelsbach); Wolfenbüttel (Brunswick-Guelf-Wolfenbüttel); Thuringia (Wettin-Saxony, Saxe-Weimar, and Saxe-Gotha); Celle (Brunswick-Guelf-

Hanover); Passau (Wittelsbach); Calenberg (Brunswick-Guelf-Calenberg); Trent (Habsburg-Lorraine); Grubenhagen (Brunswick-Guelf-Grubenhagen); Brixen (Habsburg-Lorraine); Halberstadt (Brandenburg); Carniola (Habsburg-Lorraine); Baden (Zaehringen-Baden); Teck (Würtemberg); Durlach (Zaehringen-Baden-Durlach); Osnabrück (Brunswick-Guelf-Lüneburg); Verden (Brunswick-Guelf-Hanover); Münster (Brandenburg); Hochberg (Zaehringen-Baden); Lübeck (Oldenburg-Holstein); Würtemberg (Würtemberg) Hanau (Louvain-Hesse-Kassel); Glückstadt (Oldenburg-Holstein-Glückstadt); Fulda (Nassau-Orange); Oldenburg-Gottorp (Oldenburg-Holstein-Gottorp); Kempten (Wittelsbach); Schwerin (Mecklenburg-Schwerin); Ellwangen (Würtemberg); Güstrow (Mecklenburg-Güstrow); The Knights of St. John; Darmstadt (Louvain-Hesse-Darmstadt); Berchtesgaden (Lorraine-Tuscany); Kassel (Louvain-Hesse-Kassel); Westphalia (Louvain-Hesse-Darmstadt); Pomerania (Sweden); Plön (Oldenburg-Holstein); Thither Pomerania (Brandenburg); Breisgau (Habsburg-Lorraine); Lauenburg (Brunswick-Guelf-Hanover); Corvey (Nassau-Orange); Minden (Brandenburg); The Burggraviate of Meissen (Wettin-Saxony); Leuchtenberg (Wittelsbach); Anhalt (Anhalt); Henneberg (Wettin - all Saxon houses); Schwerin (Mecklenburg-Schwerin); Camin (Brandenburg); Ratzeburg (Mecklenburg-Strelitz); Hersfeld (Louvain-Hesse-Kassel); Tyrol (Habsburg-Lorraine); Tübingen (Würtemberg); Querfurt (Wettin-Saxony); Arenberg (Ligne-Arenberg) Hechingen (Hohenzollern-Hechingen); Fritzlar (Louvain-Hesse-Kassel); Sternstein (Lobkowicz); Salm (Salm); Dietrichstein (Dietrichstein); Hadamar (Nassau-Orange); Zwiefalten (Würtemberg); Dillenburg (Nassau-Dietz); Auersperg (Auersperg); Starkenburg (Louvain-Hesse-Darmstadt); East Frisia (Brandenburg); Fürstenberg (Fürstenberg); Schwarzenberg (Schwarzenberg); Göttingen (Brunswick-Guelf-Hanover); Mindelheim (Wittelsbach); Liechtenstein (Liechtenstein); Thurn und Taxis (Thurn und Taxis); Schwarzburg (Schwarzburg); Ortenau (Habsburg-Lorraine); Aschaffenburg (Elector of Mainz); Eichsfeld (Brandenburg); Blankenburg (Brunswick-Guelf-Wolfenbüttel); Stargard (Mecklenburg-Strelitz); Erfurt (Brandenburg); Usingen (Nassau-Usingen); Weilburg (Nassau-Weilburg); Sigmaringen (Hohenzollern-Sigmaringen); Kyrburg (Salm-Kyrburg); Baar and Stuhlingen (Fürstenberg); Klettgau (Schwarzenberg); Buchau (Thurn und Taxis); Waldeck (Waldeck); Löwenstein-Wertheim (Löwenstein-Wertheim); Oettingen-Spielberg (Oettingen-Spielberg); Oettingen-

Wallerstein (Oettingen-Wallerstein); Solms-Braunfels (Solms-Braunfels); Hohenlohe-Neuenstein (Hohenlohe-Neuenstein); Hohenlohe-Waldenburg-Schillingsfürst (Hohenlohe- Waldenburg-Schillingsfürst); Hohenlohe-Waldenburg-Bartenstein (Hohenlohe-Waldenburg-Bartenstein); Isenburg-Birnstein (Isenburg-Birnstein); Ritberg (Kaunitz); Plauen-Greiz (Reuss-Plauen-Greiz); Leiningen (Leiningen); Edelstetten (Ligne); Looz-Wolbeck (Looz-Corswarem).

Added to which were the Council of the Counts of Swabia; the Council of the Counts of the Wetterau; the Council of the Counts of Franconia; and the Council of the Counts of Westphalia. In all, one hundred and thirty-one seats in the Council of Princes, after the proposed reorganisation of the Diet, based on the *Reichsdeputationshauptschluss* of 1803.

The Princes who would have benefited from this reorganisation by finally gaining a seat in the Diet, such as Leiningen and Waldeck, started acting as though they had become sovereign (though still under the suzerainty of the Emperor), and have continued to be credited as having achieved sovereignty by virtue of the *Reichsdeputationshauptschluss*, even though the 1803 reorganisation of the Diet cannot be considered entirely lawful. The number of secular Electors was almost doubled in 1803, from five - Bohemia, Palatinate, Electoral Saxony, Brandenburg, and Hanover - to nine, with the addition of Baden, Hesse-Kassel, Würtemberg, and Salzburg (and after 1807) Würzburg, held by the former Grand Duke of Tuscany, and two of the three Ecclesiastical Electors (Trier, and Cologne) were eliminated leaving only Mainz.

After Bonaparte proclaimed himself Emperor of the French on 18 May 1804, the (Holy Roman) Emperor proclaimed himself Emperor of Austria on 11 August 1804. The Electors of Bavaria and Würtemberg thereupon took advantage of the confusion and lack of Imperial control to proclaim themselves Kings, and started gobbling up smaller states, beginning with Fürstenberg, annexed by Würtemberg on 19 November 1805. The formal end of the Empire was signalled on 13 January 1806, when the King of Sweden refused to send a representative to the Imperial Diet because of the violations of the Imperial constitution by its members.

After his victory at Austerlitz (2 Dec 1805), Bonaparte tried to break up the Empire by driving a wedge between Brandenburg (the principal northern German power) and Austria (the largest power in the south), by offering to set up a federation of the German states under his protection. Those states that left the Empire and joined the federation were enabled to increase their territories at the expense of those states that did not. On 12 July 1806 the Treaty of the Confederation of the Rhine was signed, bringing this Confederation into legal existence. Those states which initially joined the Confederation, their dynasties and their date of joining were as follows: *King of Bavaria (Wittelsbach) 12 July 1806; King of Würtemberg (Würtemberg) 12 July 1806; Grand Duke of Baden (Zaehringen) 12 July 1806; Grand Duke of Frankfurt (Dalberg, non hereditary) 12 July 1806; Grand Duke of Cleves and Berg (Murat) 12 July 1806; Grand Duke of Hesse-Darmstadt (Hesse) 12 July 1806; Duke of Nassau-Usingen (Nassau) 12 July 1806; Prince of Nassau-Weilburg (Nassau) 12 July 1806; Principality of Hohenzollern-Sigmaringen (Hohenzollern) 12 July 1806; Principality of Hohenzollern-Hechingen (Hohenzollern) 12 July 1806; Prince of Salm-Salm (Salm) 12 July 1806; Prince of Salm-Kyrburg (Salm) 12 July 1806; Prince of Isenburg-Birstein (Isenburg) 12 July 1806; Duke of Arenberg (Ligne-Arenberg) 12 July 1806; Prince of Liechtenstein (Liechtenstein) 12 July 1806; Prince von der Leyen (Leyen) 12 July 1806.* Several of these dynasties elevated their titles when they joined the Confederation.

Articles 13-25 of the Treaty of the Confederation of the Rhine described in detail the territorial exchanges between the states which joined the Confederation and the annexations by the member states of the territories of those Princes and Counts which did not join. The Princes and Counts whose territories were annexed, and who were thus "mediatised" on 12 July 1806, under the terms of Articles 13-25 of the Treaty of the Confederation of the Rhine, were as follows:

The Prince of Auersperg; Duke of Croy-Solre; Prince of Dietrichstein; Prince of Esterhazy; Prince of Fürstenberg; Prince and Counts of Fugger; Princes of Hohenlohe (seven branches in all); Prince/Count of Leiningen; Prince of Lobkowicz; Prince and Count of Löwenstein-Wertheim; Duke of Looz-Corswarem; Prince of Metternich; Prince of Nassau-Orange (Dillenburg, Siegen, etc); Princes of Oettingen; Prince of Salm-Reifferscheidt; Prince of Sinzendorf; Princes/Counts of Solms; Prince of Thurn und Taxis; Prince and Counts of Truchsess-Waldburg; Prince of Wied; Count of Aspremont; Count of Bassenheim; Count of Bentheim-Steinfurt; Count of Castell; Count of Erbach; Count of Hatzfeld; Landgrave of Hesse-Homburg; Counts of Isenburg; Count of Königsegg-Aulendorf; Count of Limburg; Count of Nostitz; Count of Ostein; Count of

Plettenberg; Count of Quadt; Count of Rechteren-Limpurg; Count of Salm-Horstmar; Counts of Sayn-Wittgenstein; Count of Schaesberg; Count of Schönborn; Count of Stadion; Count of Sternberg; Count of Törring; Count of Traun; Count of Wallmoden; Count of Wartenberg; Baron of Bömelburg; Baron of Riedesel; Baron of Wendt; Prince of Anhalt as Count of Holzapfel; Prince of Stolberg-Gedern as Count of Königstein; The Knights of the Empire in Franconia; The Knights of the Empire in Swabia; The Knights of the Empire in Westphalia.

These Princes and Counts had held immediate fiefs that were mediatised by the annexations described in Articles 13-25 of the Treaty of the Confederation of the Rhine. Some of these Princes and Counts had had a seat and a vote in the Council of Princes (before or after the 1803 reorganisation of the Imperial Diet), some of these Princes and Counts had had a seat and a vote in one of the Councils of the Counts of the Empire, and some of them had had neither seats nor votes. Mediatisation of a fief refers only to the degrading of the immediacy of that fief, and does not imply anything else about its holder. Mediatisation as applied by the Confederation of the Rhine was slightly different from mediatisation under the Empire, because of the levels of feudal tenure involved.

On 1 August 1806, ten states (Bavaria, Würtemberg, the Arch-Chancellor, Baden, Hesse-Darmstadt, Hohenzollern-Sigmaringen, Hohenzollern-Hechingen, Salm-Salm, Salm-Kyrburg, and Isenburg) presented a note to the Imperial Diet stating that they were seceding from the Empire and the Diet. Two weeks later Arenberg, von der Leyen, Nassau-Usingen and Nassau-Weilburg added their names to the note, but by then the Emperor had abdicated and the Empire dissolved (6 August 1806).

More states now joined the Confederation: *Grand Duke of Würzburg (Habsburg-Lorraine-Tuscany) 25 Sept 1806; King of Saxony (Wettin) 11 Dec 1806; Duke of Saxe-Weimar (Wettin) 15 Dec 1806; Duke of Saxe-Gotha (Wettin) 15 Dec 1806; Duke of Saxe-Meiningen (Wettin) 15 Dec 1806; Duke of Saxe-Hildburghausen (Wettin) 15 Dec 1806; Duke of Saxe-Coburg (Wettin) 15 Dec 1806; Prince of Schwarzburg-Rudolstadt (Schwarzburg) 18 Apr 1807; Prince of Schwarzburg-Sondershausen (Schwarzburg) 18 Apr 1807; Duke of Anhalt-Bernburg Anhalt18 Apr 1807; Duke of Anhalt-Dessau (Anhalt) 18 Apr 1807; Duke of Anhalt-Köthen (Anhalt) 18 Apr 1807; Prince of Lippe-Detmold (Lippe) 18 Apr 1807; Prince of Schaumburg-Lippe (Lippe) 18 Apr 1807; Prince of Waldeck (Waldeck) 18 Apr 1807; Prince of Reuss-GreizReuss18 Apr 1807; Prince of*

Reuss-Schleiz (Reuss) 18 Apr 1807; Prince of Reuss-Lobenstein (Reuss) 18 Apr 1807; Prince of Reuss-Ebersdorf (Reuss) 18 Apr 1807; King of Westphalia (Bonaparte) 7 Dec 1807; Duke of Mecklenburg-Strelitz (Mecklenburg) 18 Feb 1808; Duke of Mecklenburg-Schwerin (Mecklenburg) 22 Mar 1808; Duke of Oldenburg (Oldenburg)14 Oct 1808; Grand Duke of Cleves and Berg (Bonaparte) 3 March 1809; (Murat had abdicated on 1 Aug 1808)

Napoleon's military demands constantly increased. Until 13 December 1810 Napoleon maintained the appearance of legality in his dealings with the states of the Confederation. Then, without pretext, the French Emperor incorporated the Duchy of Oldenburg, the Duchy of Arenberg, the Principalities of Salm-Salm and Salm-Kyrburg, and large parts of the Grand Duchy of Cleves and Berg, of the former Electorate of Hanover, and of the Kingdom of Westphalia, into France. This followed his absorption of Holland (9 July 1810). These actions were later cited by Alexander I of Russia (brother-in-law of the Duke of Oldenburg) as one of the reasons why he joined the Great Coalition against Napoleon.

The Confederation started unravelling after the Treaty of Kalisch (28 February 1813), which provided that the Confederation should be dissolved after an Allied victory. The Mecklenburg Dukes promptly quit the Confederation and joined the Allies, followed by the Anhalt Dukes and most of the remainder. Among the last to leave were the Princes of Hohenzollern on 24 November 1813, leaving behind the King of Saxony, the Grand Duke of Frankfurt, Prince von der Leyen, and the Prince of Isenburg, but by then the Confederation of the Rhine was effectively defunct.

The Congress of Vienna was charged with bringing some sort of order to Europe after the fall and exile of Napoleon. This led to the German Federal Act (*Deutschen Bundesakte*) of 8 June 1815, which dealt with the mediatised houses in Article 14. In this, the mediatised Houses were counted among the highest nobility with the right of equality with the reigning houses (*Ebenbürtigkeit*), the heads of the mediatised houses were the first vassals (*Standesherren*) of those states in which their former territories were located, they were exempt from military service, and accorded civil and penal jurisdiction at the lowest level, among other privileges, but always within the framework of the laws and supervision of the government of the new state. Many of the mediatised houses protested violently against the terms of this Article, but they were powerless to prevent it. At no point, though, did the Congress of Vienna decide exactly which Houses had been mediatised, and thus deserving of these higher privileges, leaving that up to the discretion of the individual states.

Those Houses which had a seat and vote in the Council of Princes of the Imperial Diet both before and after the *Reichsdeputationshauptschluss*, and those Houses which either joined the Confederation of the Rhine, or whose territories were mediatised by the Treaty of the Confederation of the Rhine, bear little or no relation to the list of families usually referred to as "mediatised". After the Congress of Vienna, Europe settled down. The sovereign states in the area that used to be the Holy Roman Empire were the states that are familiar to us, remaining sovereign until at least 1848 and even until 1918. These were the: *Empire of Austria; Kingdom of Bavaria; Kingdom of Hanover; Kingdom of Prussia; Kingdom of Saxony; Kingdom of Würtemberg; Duchy of Anhalt-Dessau; Duchy of Anhalt-Bernburg; Duchy of Anhalt-Köthen; Grand Duchy of Baden; Duchy of Brunswick; Electorate of Hesse; Grand Duchy of Hesse and by Rhine; Principality of Hohenzollern-Hechingen; Principality of Hohenzollern-Sigmaringen; Holstein (Denmark); Principality of Liechtenstein; Principality of Lippe-Detmold; Grand Duchy of Mecklenburg-Schwerin; Grand Duchy of Mecklenburg-Strelitz; Principality (Duchy) of Nassau-Usingen; Principality (Duchy) of Nassau-Weilburg; Grand Duchy of Oldenburg; Principality of Reuss-Greiz; Principality of Reuss-Schleiz; Principality of Reuss-Lobenstein; Principality of Reuss-Ebersdorf; Grand Duchy of Saxe-Weimar-Eisenach; Duchy of Saxe-Gotha; Duchy of Saxe-Meiningen; Duchy of Saxe-Hildburghausen (later Saxe-Altenburg); Duchy of Saxe-Saalfeld-Coburg; Principality of Schaumburg-Lippe; Principality of Schwarzburg-Sondershausen; Principality of Schwarzburg-Rudolstadt; Principality of Waldeck-Pyrmont.*

Several of these states acknowledged various *Standesherren* among the nobility in their country, under the terms of Article 14 of the *Deutsches Bundesakte*, and on 18 August 1825, the German Diet recognised the qualification of "Most Serene Highness" (*Durchlaucht*) for the Heads of those Princely Houses that were recognised as *Standesherren*, and later on 13 February 1829 the Diet recognised the qualification of "Most Illustrious Highness" (*Erlaucht*) for the Heads of those County Houses that were recognised as *Standesherren*.

The *Standesherren* were treated as the highest nobility in their countries, and these qualifications of "Durchlaucht" and

"Erlaucht" denoted nothing more than their social status within Germany. The *Almanach de Gotha* until the 1835 edition had divided its genealogical pages into two parts: Part I showing the reigning Sovereign Houses, and Part II showing German and some non-German non-sovereign Princely and Ducal houses. The editors added a Part III in the 1836 issue. This Part III, "*Princely and Countly Houses*", included those Princes and Counts who had been recognised as *Standesherren*, with the qualifications of "*Durchlaucht*" and "*Erlaucht*", and indicating the states in which the Standesherren had been recognised: Princes (*Durchlaucht*) as of 18 August 1825: *Arenberg (Austria, Prussia, Hanover); Auersperg (Austria); Bentheim-Bentheim (Austria, Prussia, Hanover); Bentheim-Steinfurt (Austria, Prussia, Hanover); Bentheim-Tecklenburg-Rheda (Austria, Prussia, Hanover); Colloredo-Mannsfeld (Austria, Würtemberg); Croy-Dulmen (Austria, Prussia); Dietrichstein (Austria, Würtemberg); Esterhazy v Galantha (Hungary, Bavaria); Fürstenberg (Austria, Würtemberg, Baden, Hohenzollern-Sigmaringen); Fugger-Babenhausen (Austria, Bavaria); Hohenlohe-Langenburg (Austria, Würtemberg); Hohenlohe-Oehringen (Austria, Würtemberg); Hohenlohe-Kirchberg (Austria, Würtemberg); Hohenlohe-Waldenburg-Bartenstein (Austria, Würtemberg); Hohenlohe-Waldenburg-Bartenstein-Jagstberg (Austria, Würtemberg); Hohenlohe-Waldenburg-Schillingsfürst (Austria, Bavaria, Würtemberg); Isenburg-Birstein (Austria, Electoral Hesse, Grand Duchy of Hesse); Kaunitz-Rietberg (Austria, Prussia); Khevenhuller-Metsch (Austria); Leiningen (Austria, Bavaria, Baden, Grand Duchy of Hesse); Leyen (Austria, Baden); Lobkowicz (Austria); Löwenstein-Wertheim-Freudenberg (Austria, Bavaria, Würtemberg, Baden, Grand Duchy of Hesse); Löwenstein-Wertheim-Rosenberg (Austria, Bavaria, Würtemberg, Baden, Grand Duchy of Hesse); Looz-Corswarem (Austria, Prussia, Hanover); Metternich (Austria); Oettingen-Spielberg (Austria, Bavaria, Würtemberg); Oettingen-Wallerstein (Austria, Bavaria, Würtemberg); Orsini and Rosenberg (Austria); Salm-Salm (Austria, Prussia); Salm-Kyrburg (Austria, Prussia); Salm-Horstmar (Austria, Prussia); Salm-Reifferscheidt-Krautheim (Austria, Baden); Salm-Reifferscheidt-Raitz (Austria); Sayn-Wittgenstein-Berleburg (Austria, Prussia); Sayn-Wittgenstein-Hohenstein (Austria, Prussia, Würtemberg); Schönburg-Waldenburg (Austria, Kingdom of Saxony); Schönburg-Hartenstein (Austria, Kingdom of Saxony); Schwarzenberg (Austria, Bavaria, Würtemberg); Solms-Braunfels*

*(Austria, Prussia, Würtemberg, Grand Duchy of Hesse);
Solms-Lich (Austria, Prussia, Würtemberg, Grand Duchy of Hesse);
Starhemberg (Austria); Thurn und Taxis (Austria, Bavaria,
Würtemberg, Hohenzollern-Sigmaringen); Trauttmansdorff
(Austria); Waldburg-Wolfegg-Waldsee (Austria, Würtemberg);
Waldburg-Zeil-Trauchburg (Austria, Bavaria, Würtemberg);
Waldburg- Zeil-Wurzach (Austria, Bavaria, Würtemberg); Wied
(Austria, Prussia, Nassau); Windisch-Graetz (Austria, Würtemberg).*

Counts (*Erlaucht*) as of 13 February 1829: *Castell-Remlingen
(Bavaria); Castell-Rüdenhausen (Bavaria); Erbach-Erbach (Bavaria,
Würtemberg, Grand Duchy of Hesse); Erbach-Wartenberg-Roth
(Bavaria, Würtemberg, Grand Duchy of Hesse); Fugger-Kirchberg-
Weissenhorn (Würtemberg); Fugger-Glött (Bavaria); Fugger-
Kirchheim (Bavaria); Fugger-Nordendorf (Bavaria, Würtemberg);
Giech (Bavaria); Görtz, Schlitz gennant von (Grand Duchy of Hesse);
Harrach (Austria); Isenburg-Philippseich (Grand Duchy of Hesse);
Isenburg-Büdingen (Electoral Hesse, Grand Duchy of Hesse);
Isenburg-Büdingen-Meerholz (Würtemberg, Electoral Hesse, Grand
Duchy of Hesse); Königsegg-Aulendorf (Würtemberg); Küfstein
(Austria); Leiningen-Billigheim (Baden); Leiningen-Neudenau
(Baden); Leiningen-Alt-Westerburg (Grand Duchy of Hesse);
Leiningen-Neu-Westerburg (Nassau); Neipperg (Würtemberg);
Ortenburg (Bavaria); Pappenheim (Bavaria); Platen-Hallermund
(Hanover); Plettenberg-Mietingen (Würtemberg); Pückler-Limpurg
(Würtemberg); Quadt-Isny (Würtemberg); Rechberg (Würtemberg);
Rechteren-Limpurg (Bavaria); Schaesberg-Thannheim (Würtemberg);
Schönborn-Wiesentheid (Bavaria); Schönborn-Buchheim (Austria,
Bavaria); Schönburg-Hinterglauchau (Kingdom of Saxony);
Schönburg-Rochsburg (Kingdom of Saxony); Schönburg-Wechselburg
(Kingdom of Saxony); Solms-Laubach (Grand Duchy of Hesse);
Solms-Rödelheim (Electoral Hesse, Grand Duchy of Hesse); Solms-
Wildenfels (Grand Duchy of Hesse); Stadion (Austria, Wurtemberg);
Stadion-Thannhausen (Bavaria); Sternberg-Manderscheid (Austria,
Würtemberg); Stolberg-Wernigeröde (Prussia, Hanover, Grand
Duchy of Hesse); Stolberg-Stolberg (Prussia, Hanover); Stolberg-
Rossla (Prussia, Grand Duchy of Hesse); Törring Gutenzell
(Würtemberg); Waldbott-Bassenheim (Würtemberg, Bavaria,
Nassau); Waldeck-Pyrmont (Würtemberg); Wallmoden-Gimborn
(Mecklenburg); Wurmbrand (Austria).*

Some have argued that the list of Houses selected by the
German Diet as Mediatised is at odds with the historical record.

Since the decisions as to which Prince or Count was to be recognised as a *Standesherr* was left up to the individual states, there was no reason for the states to be overly concerned about what had happened earlier. The major change for these mediatised houses was that they now had a new qualification (*Durchlaucht* or *Erlaucht*) by which they should be addressed. Even these honours were lightly given, as on 12 June 1845 the German Diet extended the recognition of "*Erlaucht*" to the Count of Bentinck, whose family had never been *Standesherren* in any of the German States (though Oldenburg later created the Count of Bentinck a *Standesherr*).

The divisions of the genealogical section of the *Almanach de Gotha* into Part I Sovereign houses reigning since 1815, Part II non-Sovereign Princely and Ducal houses, and Part III the Standesherren of the German States, continued until the Franco-Prussian War of 1870 following which the King of Prussia became German Emperor (1871). After this the *Almanach de Gotha*, placed the *Standesherren* Countly families in Part II along with non-mediatised Princely houses.

In the Preface of the 1876 edition, the editors stated they had done this as some of the houses in Part III belonged to the same dynasty as those in Part II (i.e. Fugger, Isenburg, and Leiningen), and it would be easier for the reader to deal with these houses when they were combined into a single section. In the 1877 *Almanach de Gotha*, the new Part II was divided into two sub-Parts, A and B: Part II A was for the mediatised German Princes and Counts, and Part II B was for the other German Princes and the non-German Princes. The criteria used for inclusion in Part II A were listed on page 90 of the 1877 edition, and reflected the decisions of the German Diet of 18 August 1825, 13 February 1829, and 12 June 1845 concerning the qualifications of *Durchlaucht* and *Erlaucht*. This decision of the editors of the *Almanach de Gotha* implied that the mediatised Counts were not simply equivalent in rank to the great Princely families such as Rohan, Kinsky and Chigi-Albani, but were their superior. The 1890 edition changed the name of Part II A to Part II, and the name of Part II B to Part III, but other than that there has been no alteration in the structure of either the *Almanach de Gotha* or other subsequent publications which have mimicked it.

None of the Princes of the Holy Roman Empire, with the exception of "the Emperor, the Elector of Brandenburg in his capacity as King of Prussia, the Elector of Hanover in his capacity as King of England and a few other Princes in similar positions, were full-fledged sovereigns, because they recognised the suzerainty of the Empire over their territories. The personification of this suzerainty was the Emperor, who was for his own hereditary territories Sovereign and Suzerain at the same time. But this situation changed with the establishment of the Confederation of the Rhine. The Sovereigns of the Confederation announced their secession from the Empire and the assumption of full sovereignty. That act, in itself, could of course never constitute a legal termination of the Suzerainty of the Emperor. But Francis II, in his proclamation of August 6, 1806, abdicated for himself and for his descendants, releasing the officials of the Empire from their oaths and effectuating the dissolution of the Holy Roman Empire. The position of the Emperor had legally never been that of an hereditary monarch. The imperial dignity was elective, and, therefore, contingent upon a sort of contract between the Electoral States of the Empire and one particular State to whom they wished to transfer the supreme authority. With much more justice than in the case of the German Empire as created by Bismarck, one can say of the Holy Roman Empire that it was a Republic of Princes with one of them as elected chairman. The Sovereigns of the Confederation of the Rhine constituted a minority of the total number of the States of the Empire, and their secession, therefore, could not become legal until the elected chairman agreed to bring about the end of the whole system. But once this was done, the Princes of the Confederation became independent by virtue of both their own act and of the renunciation of their legal Suzerain." [8]

Some may argue in favour of considering the *Reichsstände* of the Holy Roman Empire, (that is those Princes who held a seat and vote in the Imperial Diet before the non-lawful reorganisation of the Diet in 1803), as "former sovereign Houses". The case for including those families which had never enjoyed voting rights in the Imperial Diet their equal. Nonetheless, the Almanach de Gotha's reputation and position was such that the prevailing view came to be accepted by most comparable publications, and by those charged with determining protocol in many of the European states before World War I. The post 1998 Gothas' retain the pre-1944 structure of out of respect for the standing of the historic Almanach de Gotha.

[1] The Emperor was elected for life, although the Imperial Crown remained the heritage of the Houses of Habsburg and Habsburg-Lorraine (with the exception of one brief period in the mid-18th century) from 1438 until the Empire's dissolution in

1806.

[2] Even though the Imperial German government took responsibility for the conduct of Defence and Foreign Affairs (Bavaria alone retaining full right of legation).

[3] The Lesser Princes of the Holy Roman Empire in the Napoleonic Era , dissertation, Washington, D.C., 1950, republished as Les Princes du St-Empire à l'époque napoléonienne, Louvain, 1951, pp. 15ff.

[4] This Assembly met irregularly, but as the first permanent council of sovereign states was in a sense the precursor of the modern Council of the European Union and the United Nations General Assembly.

[5] For example Hungary and Moravia held by the Habsburgs, and Prussia, of which the Hohenzollern Elector of Brandenburg was also King. Moreover there were non-German families (mainly Italian and Polish) who were given the title of Reichfürsten without either possessing immediate fiefs or being Imperial States.

[6] Those who are shown as (personal) held personal rather than hereditary membership of their Council.

William Addams-Reitwiesner
for Almanach de Gotha

APPENDIX III

Lines of Succession of the
Ten Reigning Houses of Europe.

The Kingdoms & Principalities
of Europe & the European Union
and the Grand Duchy of Luxembourg.

LINES OF SUCCESSION
THE TEN REIGNING
HOUSES OF EUROPE

Belgium

1. Prince *Philippe* Leopold Louis Marie, Duke of Brabant, *b* 14 April 1960.

2. Princess *Elisabeth* Thérèse Marie Hélène, *b* 25 Oct 2001.

3. Princes *Astrid*, Archduchess of Austria & Austria Este, *b* 5 June 1962.

4. Prince & Archduke *Amédéo* Maria Josef Carl Pierre Philippe Paola Marcus d'Aviano, Prince of Belgium & Archduke of Austria, *b* 21 Feb 1986.

5. Princess *Maria Laura* Zita Beatrix Gerhard, Princess of Belgium & Archduchess of Austria, *b* 26 Aug 1988.

6. Prince *Joachim* Carl Maria Nikolaus Isabelle Marcus d'Aviano, Prince of Belgium Archduke of Austria, 9 Dec 1991.

7. Princess *Luisa Maria* Anna Martine Pilar, Princess of Belgium & Archduchess of Austria, *b* 11 Oct 1995.

8. Prince *Laurent*, *b* 19 Oct 1963.

Denmark

1. Crown Prince *Frederik* André Henrik Christian, Crown Prince of Denmark, *b* 26 May 1968.

2. Prince *Joachim* Holger Valdemar Christian, *b* 7 June 1969.

3. Prince *Nicolai* William Alexander Frederik, *b* 28 Aug 1999.

4. Prince *Felix* Henrik Valdemar Christian, *b* 22 July 2002.

5. Princess *Benedikte* Astrid Ingeborg Ingrid, b 29 April 1944.

6. Princess *Elisabeth*, b 8 May 1935.

Great Britain & Northern Ireland

1. Prince *Charles* Philip Arthur George, Prince of Wales, *b* 14 Nov 1948.

2. Prince *William* Arthur Philip Louis of Wales, *b* 21 June 1982.

3. Prince Henry *(Harry)* Charles Albert David of Wales, *b* 15 Sept 1984.

4. Prince *Andrew* Albert Chris-

tian Edward, Duke of York, *b* 19 Feb 1960.

5.Princess *Beatrice* Elizabeth Mary, *b* 8 Aug 1988.

6. Princess *Eugenie* Victoria Helena, *b* 23 March 1990.

7. Prince *Edward* Antony Richard Louis, Earl of Wessex, *b* 10 March 1964.

8. Princess *Anne* Elizabeth Alice Louise, The Princess Royal, *b* 15 Aug 1950.

9. Mr *Peter* Mark Andrew Phillips, *b* 15 Nov. 1977.

10. Miss *Zara* Anne Elizabeth Phillips, *b* 15 May 1981.

———❖———

Liechtenstein

1.Prince (Hereditary) *Alois* Philipp Maria, *b* 11 June 1968.
2. Prince *Joseph* Wenzel Maximilian Maria, *b* 24 May 1995.

3. Prince *Georg* Antonius Constantin Maria, *b* 20 April 1999.

4. Prince *Nikolaus* Sebastian Alexander Maria, *b* 6 Dec 2000.

5. Prince *Maximilian* Nikolaus Maria, *b* May 1969.

6. Prince *Alfons* Constantin Maria, *b* 18 May 2001.

7. Prince *Constantin* Ferdinand Maria, *b* 15 March 1972.

8. Prince *Philipp Erasmus* Alois Ferdinand Maria Sebaldus, *b* 19 Aug 1946.

9. Prince *Alexander,* *b* 19 May 1972.

10. Prince *Wenzeslaus,* *b* 12 May 1974.

———❖———

Luxembourg

1. Crown Prince *Henri* Albert Gabriel Felix Marie Guillaume, *b* 16 April 1955.

2. Prince *Guillaume* Jean Joseph Marie, *b* 11 Nov 1981.

3. Prince *Felix* Léopold Marie Guillaume, *b* 3 June 1984.

4. Prince *Louis* Xavier Marie Guillaume, *b* 3 Aug 1986.

5. Princess *Alexandra* Joséphine Teresa Charlotte Marie Wilhelmine, *b* 16 Feb 1991.

6. Prince *Sébastien* Henri Marie

Guillaume, *b* 16 April 1992.

7. Prince *Guillaume* Marie Louis Christian, *b* 1 May 1963.

8. Prince *Paul-Louis* Jean Marie Guillaume, *b* 4 March 1998.

9. Princess *Marie* Astrid Charlotte Léopoldine Wilhelmine Ingebourg Antonia Elizabeth Anne Alberta, *b* 17 Feb 1954.

<hr>

Monaco

1.Prince (Hereditary) *Albert* Alexandre Louis Pierre, Marquis des Baux, *b* 14 March 1958.

2. Princess *Caroline* Louise Marguerite, *b* 23 Jan 1957.

3. Mlle. *Andrea* Albert Pierre Casiraghi, *b* 8 June 1984.

4. Mlle. *Charlotte* Marie Pomeline Casiraghi, *b* 3 Aug 1986.

5. M. *Pierre* Rainier Stefano Casiraghi, *b* 5 Sept 1987.

6.Princess *Stéphanie* Marie Elisabeth, *b* 1 Feb 1965.

7. M. *Louis* Robert Paul Ducruet, *b* 26 Nov 1992.

8. Mlle. *Pauline* Grace Maguy Ducruet, *b* 4 May 1994.

9. Princess *Antoinette* Louise Alberte Suzanne, Baroness de Massy, *b* 28 Dec 1920.

10. Baron *Christian* Louis de Massy, *b* 17 Jan 1949.

<hr>

The Netherlands

1. Crown Prince *Willem-Alexander* Claus Georg Ferdinand, Prince of Orange, *b* 27 April 1967.

2. Prince Johan *Friso* Berhard Christian David, *b* 25 Sept 1968.

3. Prince *Constantijn* Christof Frederik Aschwin, *b* 11 Oct 1969.

4. Princess *Eloise* Sophie Beatrix Laurence, *b* 8 June 2002.
5. Princess *Margriet* Francisca, *b* 19 Jan 1943.

6. Prince *Maurits* Willem Pieter Hendrik, *b* 17 April 1968.

7. Princess Anastasia (*Anna*) Margriet Joséphine van Lippe-Biesterfeld van Vollenhoven, *b* 15 April 2001.

8. Prince *Lucas* Maurits Peter Henri van Lippe-Biesterfeld van Vollenhoven, *b* 26 Oct 2002.

9. Prince *Bernhard* Lucas Emmanuel, *b* 25 Dec 1969.

10. Princess *Isabella* Lily Juliana van Vollenhoven, *b* 14 May 2002.

Norway

1. Crown Prince *Haakon Magnus*, *b* 20 July 1973.
2. Princess *Ragnhild* Alexandra, *b* 9 June 1930.
3. Princess *Astrid* Maud Ingeborg, *b* 12 Feb 1932.

Spain

1. Don *Felipe* Juan Pablo Alfonso y Todos los Santos, Prince of the Asturias, *b* 30 Jan 1968.

2. Infanta Doña *Elena* Maria Isabel Dominga, Duchess of Lugo, *b* 20 Dec 1963.

3. HE Don *Felipe* Juan Froilán de Marichalar y Borbon, *b* 16 July 1998.

4. HE Doña *Victoria* Federica de Marichalar y de Borbón, *b* 9 Sept 2000.

5. Infanta Doña *Cristina* Federica Victoria Antonia, Duchess of Palma de Mallorca *b* 13 June 1965.

6. HE Don *Juan* Valentin de Todos los Santos Urangarin y de Borbon, *b* 29 Sept 1999.

7. HE Don *Pablo* Nicolás Urdangarín y de Borbón, *b* 6 Dec 2000.

8. HE Don *Miguel* Urdangarín y de Borbón, *b* 30 April 2002.

Sweden

1. Crown Princess *Victoria* Ingrid Alice Désiree, Duchess of Västergötland, *b* 14 July 1977.

2. Prine *Carl Philip* Edmund Bertil, Duke of Värmland, *b* 13 May 1979.

3. Princess *Madeleine* Thérèse Amelie Josephine, Duchess of Hälsingland and Gästrikland, *b* 10 June 1982.

APPENDIX IV

Complete List of the Sovereign Pontiffs

of the Holy See

—◆—

*All those before Pope Saint Sylvester I (314-335) are considered
Saints and Martyrs; from Saint Sylvester I to Pope Saint Felix IV
(526-530) all are considered Saints. Since that date formal
beatifications or canonizations was required for these titles.*

1. **SAINT PETER**,
2. **Saint Linus**,
from Tuscany 67-76.
3. **Saint Anacletus Cletus**,
Roman 76-88.
4. **Saint Clement I**,
Roman 88-97.
5. **Saint Evarist**,
Greek 97-105.
6. **Saint Alexander I**,
Roman 105-115.
7. **Saint Syxtus I**,
Roman 115-125.
8. **Saint Telesphorus**,
Greek 125-136.
9. **Saint Hyginus**,
Greek 136-140.
10. **Saint Pius I**,
from Aquileia 140-155.
11. **Saint Anicetus**,
Syrian 155-166.
12. **Saint Soter**,
from Campania 166-175.
13. **Saint Eleutherius**,
*from Nicopolis in Epyrus
175-189.*
14. **Saint Victor I**,
African 189-199.
15. **Saint Zephyrinus**,
Roman 199-217.
16. **Saint Calixtus I**,
*Roman 217-222 (Saint
Hippolytus in exile 217-235).*
17. **Saint Urban I**,
Roman 222-230.
18. **Saint Pontianus**,
Roman 230-235.
19. **Saint Anterus**,
Greek 235-236.
20. **Saint Fabian**,
Roman 236-250.

21. **Saint Cornelius**,
Roman 251-253.
22. **Saint Lucius I**,
Roman 253-254.
23. **Saint Stephen I**,
Roman 254-257.
24. **Saint Syxtus II**,
Greek 257-258.
25. **Saint Dyonisius**,
259-268
26. **Saint Felix I**,
Roman 269-274.
27. **Saint Eutichian**,
from Luni in Liguria 275-283.
28. **Saint Caius**,
from Dalmatia 283-296.
29. **Saint Marcellinus**,
Roman 296-304.
30. **Saint Marcellus I**,
Roman 308-309.
31. **Saint Eusebius**,
Greek 309.
32. **Saint Melchias**,
African 311-314.
33. **Saint Sylvester I**,
Roman 314-335.
34. **Saint Marc**,
Roman 336.
35. **Saint Julius I**,
Roman 337-352.
36. **Liberius, Roman**,
352-366.
37. **Saint Damasus I**,
from Spain 366-384.
38. **Saint Syricius**,
Roman 384-399.
39. **Saint Anastiasius I**,
Roman, 399-401.
40. **Saint Innocent I**,
*from Albano in the Latium
401-417.*

41. **Saint Zosymus,**
Greek 417-418.

42. **Saint Boniface I,**
Roman 418-422.

43. **Saint Celestine I,**
from Campania 422-432.

44. **Saint Syxtus III,**
Roman 432-440.

45. **Saint Leo I** (called the Great),
from Tuscia 440-461.

46. **Saint Hilarus,**
from Sardinia 461-468.

47. **Saint Simplicius,**
from Tivoli in the Latium 468-483.

48. **Saint Felix III,**
Roman 483-492.

49. **Saint Gelasius I,**
African 492-496.

50. **Anastasius II,**
Roman, 496-498.

51. **Saint Symmacus,**
from Sardinia 498-514.

52. **Saint Hormisdas,**
from Frosinone in the Latium 514-523.

53. **Saint John I,**
from Tuscia, Martyr 523-526.

54. **Saint Felix IV,**
from the Sannium 526-530.

55. **Boniface II,**
Roman 530-532.

56. **John II,**
Roman 533-535.

57. **Saint Agapitus,**
Roman 535-536.

58. **Saint Sylverius,**
from Campania, Martyr 536-537.

59. **Vigilius,**
Roman 537-555.

60. **Pelagius I,**
Roman 556-561.

61. **John III,**
Roman 561-574.

62. **Benedict I,**
Roman, 561-574.

63. **Pelagius II,**
Roman, 579-590.

64. **Saint Gregory I** (the Great),
Roman 590-604.

65. **Sabinianus,**
from Blera in Tuscia 604-606.

66. **Boniface III,**
Roman 607.

67. **Saint Boniface IV,**
from the Marsi 608-615.

68. **Saint Deusdedit I** [Adeodatus],
Roman, 615-618.

69. **Boniface IV,**
from Naples 619-625.

70. **Honorius I,**
from Campania 625-638.

71. **Severinus,**
Roman 640.

72. **John IV,**
from Dalmatia 640-642.

73. **Theodore I,**
Greek, 642-649.

74. **Saint Martin I,**
from Tuderte in Umbria, Martyr 649-655.

75. **Saint Eugene I,**
Roman 654 657.

76. **Saint Vitalianus,**
from Segni in the Latium 657-672.

77. **Saint Vitalianus,**
Roman 672-676.

78. **Donus**,
Roman, 676-678.
79. **Saint Agatho**,
from Sicily 678-681.
80. **Saint Leo II**,
from Sicily 682-683.
81. **Saint Benedict II**,
Roman 684-685.
82. **John V**,
from Syria 685-686.
83. **Conon**,
considered from Sicily 686-687.
84. **Saint Serge I**,
from Syria 687-701.
85. **John VI**,
Greek 701-705.
86. **John VII**,
Greek 705-707.
87. **Sisinnius**,
from Syria 708.
88. **Constantine**,
from Syria 708-715.
89. **Saint Gregory II**,
Roman, 715-731.
90. **Saint Gregory III**,
from Syria 731-741.
91. **Saint Zacharias**,
from Greece 741-752.
92. **Stephen II**,
Roman 752-757.
93. **Saint Paul I**,
Roman 757-767.
94. **Stephen III**,
from Sicily 768-772.
95. **Hadrian I**,
Roman 772-795.
96. **Saint Leo III**,
Roman 795-816.
97. **Stephen IV**,
Roman 816-817.
98. **Saint Paschal I**,

Roman 817-824.
99. **Eugene II**,
Roman 824-827.
100. **Valentine**,
Roman, 827.
101. **Gregory IV**,
Roman, 827-844.
102. **Serge II**,
Roman 844-847.
103. **Saint Leo IV**,
Roman 847-855.
104. **Benedict III**,
Roman 855-858.
105. **Saint Nicholas I**, *(called the Great)*
858-867.
106. **Hadrian II**,
Roman 867-872.
107. **John VIII**,
Roman 872-882.
108. **Marinus I**,
from Gallese in the Latium 882-884.
109. **Saint Hadrian III**,
Roman 884-885.
110. **Stephen V**,
Roman 885-891.
111. **Formosus**,
from Porto 891-896.
112. **Boniface VI**,
Roman 896.
113. **Stephen VI**,
Roman 896-897.
114. **Roman**,
from Gallese in the Latium 897.
115. **Theodore II**,
Roman 897.
116. **John IX**,
from Tivoli in the Latium 898-900.

117. **Benedict VI**,
Roman 900-903.

118. **Leo V**,
from Ardea in the Latium 903.

119. **Serge III**,
Roman 904-911.

120. **Anastiasius III**,
Roman 911-913.

121. **Lando**,
from Sabina 913-914.

122. **John X**,
*from Tossignano in the
Romagna 914-928.*

123. **Leo VI**,
Roman 928.

124. **Stephen VII**,
Roman 928-931.

125. **John XI**,
Roman 931-935.

126. **Leo VII**,
Roman 936-939.

127. **Stephen VIII**,
Roman 939-942.

128. **Marinus II**,
Roman 942-946.

129. **Agapitus II**,
Roman 946-955.

130. **John XII**,
*from the Counts of Tusculum
955-964.*

131. **Leo VIII**,
Roman 963-965.

132. **Benedict V**,
Roman 964-966.

133. **John XIII**,
Roman 965-972.

134. **Benedict VI**,
Roman 973-974.

135. **Benedict VII**,
Roman 974-983.

136. **John XIV**,

*from Pavia in Lombardy 983-
984.*

137. **John XV**,
Roman 985-996.

138. **Gregory V**,
*of the Dukes of Carinthia 996-
999.*

139. **Sylvester II**,
from Auvergne 999-1003.

140. **John XVII**,
Roman 1003.

141. **John XVIII**,
Roman 1004-1009.

142. **Serge IV**,
Roman 1009-1012.

143. **Benedict VIII**,
*of the Counts of Tusculum
1012-1024.*

144. **John XIX**,
*of the Counts of Tusculum
1024-1032.*

145. **Benedict IX**,
*of the Counts of Tusculum
1032-1045.*

146. **Sylvester III**,
Roman 1045.

147. **Gregory VI**,
Roman 1045-1046.

148. **Clement II**,
*of the Lords of Morsleben and
Hornburg 1046-1047.*

149. **Benedict IX** (again)
1047-1048.

150. **Damasus II**,
from Bavaria 1048.

151. **Saint Leo IX**,
*of the Counts of Egilsheim-
Dagsburg 1049-1054.*

152. **Victor II**,
*of the Counts of Dollstein-
Hirschberg 1055-1057.*

153. **Stephen IX**,
*of the Dukes of Lorraine 1057-
1058.*

154. **Nicholas II**,
from Burgundy 1059-1061.

155. **Alexander II**,
from Milan 1061-1073.

156. **Saint Gregory VII**,
from Tuscia 1073-1085.

157. **Blessed Victor III**,
from Benevento 1086-1087.

158. **Blessed Urban II**,
from France 1088-1099.

159. **Paschal II**,
from Ravenna 1099-1118.

160. **Gelasius II**,
*Giovanni Caetani from Gaeta
1118-1119.*

161. **Calixtus II**,
from Burgundy 1119-1124.

162. **Honorius II**,
from Imola 1124-1130.

163. **Innocent II**,
*Roman, Gregorio Papareschi
1130-1143.*

164. **Celestine II**,
from Umbria 1143-1144.

165. **Lucius II**,
*Gerardo Caccianemici from
Bologna 1144-1145.*

166. **Blessed Eugene III**,
from Pisa 1145-1153.

167. **Anastasius IV**,
Roman 1153-1154.

168. **Hadrian IV**,
*Nicholas Breakspeare, from
England 1154-1159.*

169. **Alexander III**,
*Rolando Bandinelli from Siena
1159-1181.*

170. **Lucius III**,

*Ubaldo Allucingoli from Lucca
1181-1185.*

171. **Urban III**,
*Uberto Crivelli from Milan
1185-1187.*

172. **Gregory VIII**,
*Alberto de Morra from
Benevento 1187.*

173. **Clement III**,
*Roman, Paolo Scolari 1187-
1191.*

174. **Celestine III**,
*Roman, Giacinto Bobone
1191-1198.*

175. **Innocent III**,
*Roman, of the Counts of
Segni 1198-1216.*

176. **Honorius III**,
*Roman, Cencio Savelli 1216-
1227.*

178. **Gregory IX**,
*from Anagni, of the Counts of
Segni 1227-1241.*

179. **Celestine IV**,
*Goffredo Castiglioni from
Milan 1241.*

180. **Innocent IV**,
*Sinibaldo Fieschi from Genoa
1243-1254.*

181. **Alexander IV**,
*Roman, of the Lords of Ienne
1254-1261.*

182. **Urban IV**,
*Jacques Pantaléon from
Troyes 1261-1264.*

183. **Clement IV**,
*Guy Fulcodi from France 1265-
1268.*

184. **Blessed Gregory X**,
*Tebaldo Visconti from
Piacenza 1271-1276.*

185. **Blessed Innocent V**,
*Peter of Tarantaise from the
Savoy 1276.*

186. **Hadrian V**,
*Ottobono Fieschi from Genoa
1276.*

187. **John XXI**,
*Pietro Iuliani called Hispanus
1276-1277.*

188. **Nicholas III**,
*Roman, Giovanni Gaetano
Orsini 1277-1280.*

189. **Martin IV**,
*Simon de Brion from France
1281-1285.*

190. **Honorius IV**,
*Roman, Giacomo Savelli 1285-
1287.*

191. **Saint Celestine V**,
*Pietro del Murrone from the
Molise 1294.*

192. **Boniface VIII**,
*Benedetto Caetani from
Anagni 1294-1303.*

193. **Blessed Benedict IX**,
*Niccolò Boccasini from Treviso
1303-1304.*

194. **Clement V**,
*Bertrand de Got from France
1305-1314.*

195. **John XXII**,
*Jacques Duèse from Cahors
1316-1334.*

196. **Benedict XII**,
*Jacques Fournier from France
1334-1342.*

197. **Clement VI**,
*Pierre Roger from France
1342-1352.*

198. **Innocent VI**,
Étienne Aubert from France

1352-1362.

199. **Blessed Urban V**,
*Guillaume de Grimoard from
France 1378-1389.*

200. **Gregory XI**,
*Pierre Roger de Beaufort from
France 1371-1378.*

201. **Urban VI**,
*Bartolomeo Prignano from
Naples 1378-1389.*

202. **Boniface IX**,
*Pietro Tomacelli from Naples
1389-1404.*

203. **Innocent VII**,
*Cosma Migliorati from
Sulmona 1404-1406.*

204. **Gregory XII**,
*Angelo Correr from Venice
1406-1415.*

205. **Martin V**,
*Roman, Oddone Colonna
1417-1431.*

206. **Eugene IV**,
*Gabriele Condulmer from
Venice 1431-1447.*

207. **Nicholas V**,
*Tommaso Parentucelli from
Sarzana 1447-1455.*

208. **Calixtus III**,
*Alonso de Borja from
Valencia 1455-1458.*

209. **Pius II**,
*Enea Silvio Piccolomini from
Siena 1458-1464.*

210. **Paul II**,
*Pietro Barbo from Venice
1464-1471.*

211. **Syxtus IV**,
*Francesco della Rovere from
Savona 1471-1484.*

212. **Innocent VIII**,

*Giovanni Battista Cibo from
Genoa 1484-1492.*

213. **Alexander VI**,
*Rodrigo de Borja from
Valencia 1492-1503.*

214. **Pius III**,
*Francesco Todeschini-
Piccolomini from Siena 1503.*

215. **Julius II**,
*Giuliano della Rovere from
Savona 1503-1513.*

216. **Leo X**,
*Giovanni dei Medici from
Florence 1513-1521.*

217. **Hadrian VI**,
*Adriaan Florenszoon from
Utrecht 1522-1523.*

218. **Clement VII**,
*Giulio dei Medici from
Florence 1523-1534*

219. **Paul III**,
*Roman, Alessandro Farnese
1534-1549.*

220. **Julius III**,
*Roman, Giovanni Maria
Ciocchi del Monte 1550-1555.*

221. **Marcellus II**,
*Marcello Cervini from
Montepulciano in Tuscany
1555.*

222. **Paul IV**,
*Gian Pietro Carafa from
Naples 1555-1559.*

223. **Pius IV**,
*Giovan Angelo dei Medici
from Milan 1559-1565.*

224. **Saint Pius V**,
*Antonio Ghislieri from the
Piedmont 1566-1572.*

225. **Gregory XIII**,
Ugo Boncompagni from

Bologna 1572-1585.

226. **Syxtus V**,
*Felice Perretti from the
Marches 1585-1590.*

227. **Urban VII**,
*Roman, Giambattista
Castagna 1590.*

228. **Gregory XIV**,
*Niccolò Sfondrati from
Cremona 1590-1591.*

229. **Innocent IX**,
*Giovan Antonio Facchinetti
from Bologna 1591.*

230. **Clement VIII**,
*Ippolito Aldobrandini from
Florence 1592-1605.*

231. **Leo XI**,
*Alessandro dei Medici from
Florence 1605.*

232. **Paul V**,
*Roman, Camillo Borghese
1605-1621*

233. **Gregory XV**,
*Alessandro Ludovisi from
Bologna 1621-1623.*

234. **Urban VIII**,
*Maffeo Barberini from
Florence 1623-1644.*

235. **Innocent X**,
*Roman, Giovanni Battista
Pamphilj 1644-1655.*

236. **Alexander VII**,
*Fabio Chigi from Siena 1655-
1667.*

237. **Clement IX**,
*Giulio Rospigliosi from
Pistoia, 1667-1669.*

238. **Clement X**,
*Roman Emilio Altieri 1670-
1676.*

239. **Blessed Innocent XI**,

Benedetto Odescalchi from Como 1676-1689.

240. **Alexander VIII**, *Pietro Ottoboni from Venice 1689-1691.*

241. **Innocent XII**, *Antonio Pignatelli from Venosa 1691-1700.*

242. **Clement XI**, *Giovanni Francesco Albani from Urbino 1700-1721.*

243. **Innocent XIII**, *Roman, Michelangelo dei Conti 1721-1724.*

244. **Benedict XIII**, *Pietro Francesco Orsini from Gravina 1724-1730.*

245. **Clement XII**, *Lorenzo Corsini from Florence 1730-1740.*

246. **Benedict XIV**, *Prospero Lambertini from Bologna 1740-1758.*

247. **Clement XIII**, *Carlo Rezzonico from Venice 1758-1769.*

248. **Clement XIV**, *Giovanni Vincenzo Antonio Ganganelli from Rimini 1769-1774.*

249. **Pius VI**, *Giannangelo Braschi from Cesena 1775-1799.*

250. **Pius VII**, *Barnaba Chiaramonti from Cesena 1800-1823.*

251. **Leo XII**, *Annibale della Genga from the Marches 1823-1829.*

252. **Pius VIII**, *Francesco Saverio Castiglioni from the Marches 1929-1830.*

253. **Gregory XVI**, *Bartolomeo Mauro Cappellari from Belluno 1831-1846.*

254. **Pius IX**, *Giovanni Maria Mastai Ferretti from Senigallia 1846-1878.*

255. **Leo XIII**, *Gioacchino Pecci from Carpineto in the Latium 1878-1903.*

256. **Saint Pius X**, *Giuseppe Sarto from Riese 1903-1914.*

257. **Benedict XV**, *Giacomo della Chiesa from Genoa 1914-1922.*

258. **Pius XI**, *Achille Ratti from Desio in Lombardy 1922-1939.*

259. **Pius XII**, *Roman, Eugenio Pacelli 1939-1958.*

260. **John XXIII**, *Angelo Roncalli from Bergamo 1958-1963.*

261. **Paul VI**, *Giovanni Battista Montini from Brescia 1963-1978.*

262. **John Paul I**, *Albino Luciani from Belluno 1978*

203. John Paul II, *(Karol Wojtyia)* from Wadowice, Poland, 1978, Universal Shepherd of the Church.

THE PAPAL FAMILIES

Members of all recognised Papal Families *(families that have given one or more Popes to the Church and many still with representatives)* are *ipso iure* Roman Nobles *(hereditary through the male lines ex fratribus Summi Pontificis if the family name is kept)* in accordance with the extant Bull *Urbem Romam* of Pope Benedict XIV (1740-1758). This important nobility is also part of the Italian Nobility and should not be confused with additional titles, dignities or grants conferred upon the Heads of or members of Papal Families by Popes, Emperors, Kings or other *fontes honorum*. Special grants of further nobility were made this century to the Papal Families of *Ratti di Désio* (Pope Pius XI 1922-1939) who were created Counts, *Pacelli* (Pope Pius XII 1939-1958), who were created Papal Marchesi and Italian Princes, while the Papal Family *Della Chiesa* (Pope Benedict XV 1914-1922) already were marchional. These all have heirs. There are no direct relatives alive of the reigning Supreme Pontiff.

APPENDIX v

The French Succession

and the House of Bourbón.

THE FRENCH SUCCESSION

The debate amongst French Royalists between "*Legitimists*" and "*Orleanists*", while ostensibly dealing with genealogical questions, derives much of its momentum from an historical and ideological dispute. Opinion on the political structure of a restored French Monarchy, the place of the Catholic Church therein, and the parts played by various political figures of the past in revolutionary history, have all play their part, and charge the issue with great emotion.

All apparently agree that Charles X's ascent to the throne in 1824 was in accordance with the fundamental laws of succession to the French Crown, which, in a some what altered form, dates back to the passing of the Crown to Hughes Capet in the 10th century.

It is following King Charles's accession that alternative opinion forms. The State over which Charles X presided was a hybrid, a compromise between institutions for the most part spawned by the revolution, and perfected by Napoleon, and the spirit of the Ancien Regime. Those who wished the latter to conform to the former rallied to the King; those who looked to a Monarchy like Great Britain's looked instead to the King's cousin, Louis-Philippe, the Duke of Orleans.

Much as with the dynastic struggle in Great Britain after 1688, the questions involved were purely ideological; just as no one could claim that William III and Mary II had a better right to the three Kingdoms than did James II in terms of pure legitimacy, so too could there be no question that Charles X had the right of inheritance over Louis Philippe. Nevertheless, the Duke of Orleans accepted the throne at the revolution of July 1830. It was in both cases not a question of pedigree, but of vision: vision of how the Crown itself should operate. Hence, Louis Philippe was not, like Charles X, "*by the Grace of God, King of France and Navarre*", but, "*by the Grace of God and the Will of the People, King of the French*".

A further indication of the place of heredity under the "Citizen-King" was the abolition of the hereditary peerage, although a body called the Chamber of Peers continued to meet in the Luxembourg Palace.

It was here that the current division between Legitimists and Orleanists finds its origin. On the one hand, Legitimists were mindful of the part played by Louis Philippe's father Philippe Egalite in the revolution and the murder of Louis XVI; and they pondered Louis XVIII's and Charles X's forgiveness of Louis Phillipe for this and their restoration of him to his place as a Prince of the Blood Royal. To them the Citizen-King seemed the worst sort of traitor and opportunist. Given this fact and the record of his father, Legitimists writings of the period seem to imply that the Orleans blood itself was somehow tainted with treason.

To Orleanists, on the other hand, Charles X and his supporters appeared to be hopeless romantics, whose attempts to undo the revolution would end only in the ruin of the State and the establishment of a republic. For them, the proper model of a modern King could be found in the British Monarchy, with the Sovereign reigning rather than ruling, serving as focus of loyalty above politics, and behaving in a sense as a national totem.

The overthrow of Louis Philippe himself changed the situation considerably. With both heads of both branches of the dynasty in exile, a certain opportunity for rapprochement was opened up, although it would not bear fruit for several decades. Charles X's grandson, the Count de Chambord, de jure Henry V, in time was recognised even by Louis Philippe's son of the same name, called the Count of Paris. Legitimists and Orleanists, together with a few complaisant Bonapartists had a majority in the French Parliament after the downfall of Napoleon III in 1870. In the first years of the Third Republic, it appeared that the throne was Henry V's for the asking; he refused to ascend it, if this meant he must accept the tricolour in place of the lily flag. For Legitimists, this was a principled symbolic gesture of refusal to be a Liberal "King of the French;" to Orleanists, it was yet another sign of unrealistic behaviour on the part of a senior heir.

In any case, upon the death of Henry V, childless, in 1883, the Count of Paris, who was recognised as the late claimants' legal heir, was accepted by the vast majority of Royalists as Philippe VII; this included the Parliamentary party. Moreover, in his political opinions he appeared to be more an heir to Henry V than to Louis Philippe. This was true also of his son, likewise called Louis Philippe, style Duke of Orleans, and hailed as Philippe VIII upon his father's death in 1894. This rightward shift on the part of the House of Orleans was underscored by the adherence of Charles Maurras' Action Francaise, itself bitterly opposed to post-revolutionary democracy.

Nevertheless, a small group, the so-called "blancs

d'Espagne," declared that the Carlist claimant to the Spanish throne, Don Juan, as the senior member of the House of Bourbón, was rightfully King of France. Thus was born the renewed rift between Legitimists and Orleanists which has become much more apparent in recent years.

The strictly dynastic question involved centred around three points: was the renunciation of the French throne for himself and his descendants by Louis XIV's grandson Felipe V at the 1713 Treaty of Utrecht really binding upon the French fundamental laws of succession?; did the residence outside of France or acceptance of non-French nationality for a period of time by a branch of the Royal Family invalidate that branch's rights of succession?; and could Henry V's legal adoption of the Count of Paris confer on him the right to the throne? The Legitimists argued no, the Orleanists argued yes. Both sides cited many authorities to prove their own interpretation of the fundamental laws. The "integral nationalist" concerns of the Action Francaise gave this largest group of Royalists a particular concern with upholding the rights of the Orleans—a task made easier by the ideological agreement with them of the Orleans princes of the time.

The Carlists, themselves adherents of the senior line of the Bourbóns of Spain, were engaged through the 19th century in periodic armed struggles to put their Prince upon the Spanish throne. In close parallel to the French situation, they were advocates of the pre-revolutionary Spanish Monarchy, where their Alfonsino opponents were liberals of the Orleanist mould. Interestingly enough, when this particular problem arose, thanks to Fernando VII's setting aside of his brother's rights in favour of his daughter, Charles X condemned the action—not as King of France, but as Head of the House of Bourbón. Their hands full with Spain, however, the successive Carlist Princes made little active claim to the throne of France. This, combined with the ideological contentment of most French Royalists with the Orleans princes, ensured that Legitimists would remain a minority for quite some time.

This situation changed dramatically in the 1930s, however. In 1931, Alfonso XIII of Spain went into exile; in the same year, the Carlist heir, Don Jaime, died. He was succeeded in his claims to France and Spain by his uncle, Don Alphonso Carlos. When the latter died in 1936, many of the Carlists (by that time militarily involved on the future victorious side in the Spanish Civil War) recognised Alfonso XIII as next in line to the Crown of Spain.

The French Legitimists accepted him as Alphonse I of France. Upon his death in 1941, his eldest surviving son, Don Jaime, Duque de Segovia, inherited Alfonso's French rights, having renounced his Spanish heirship in favour of his younger brother, Don Juan (father of the present King Don Juan Carlos I). The Duke of Segovia assumed the title of Duke of Anjou, and was hailed by Legitimists as Jacques-Henri VI. He in turn died in 1975, to be succeeded by his eldest son, who took the title Alphonse II, Head of the House of Bourbón, and Duke of Anjou and Cadiz.

However, due to a Spanish dynastic law, which stripped any junior branch of the Royal family who had taken up arms against the reigning line of their rights of succession, a number of Carlists refused to accept Alfonso XIII as rightful King of Spain. These turned to the head of the House of Bourbón-Parma, Enrico I (✠ 1939), his son Giuseppe I (✠ 1950), and his grandson Elie I (✠ 1977). The eldest son of the latter, Don Carlos Hugo, de jure Duke of Parma, was recognised in turn as heir to the Spanish throne by many of the remaining Carlists. But disenchantment with his politics lost him many of the Carlists, who turned to his younger brother, Don Sixto Enrique. He also attracted a few French Legitimists followers, who accepted the Spanish law as somehow barring the descendants of Alfonso XIII from the throne of France as well as Spain.

In the Orleanist camp, the 1930s ushered in many changes as well. The 1926 Papal condemnation of Action Francaise had begun a break between that organisation and Jean, Duke of Guise (called Jean III by his adherents), who had succeeded the Orleanists' Philippe VIII in that year. His son, Henri, Count of Paris, disagreed violently with Maurras, a disagreement which led to an open condemnation by the claimant's heir of Action Francaise after 1934. Despite this, Maurras and his followers hailed the Count of Paris as Henri VI after the death of the latter's father in 1940. The successors of the movement continued their adherence after the Count's vigorous acceptance of De Gaulle in 1958.

Nevertheless, the Count's actions created a climate wherein many Royalists were willing to look again at the Legitimists claims. These have been reinforced in recent years by the difficulties involving the Count of Paris, his eldest son Henri, Count of Clermont (whom, due to the latter's divorce, has been stripped of his succession rights only to be reconciled with his father and reinstated), and his grandson Jean, Duke of Vendome (himself due to the foregoing matter having replaced, and then been replaced by, his father). When the Duke of Anjou and Cadiz died in 1989, his son was proclaimed Head of the House of Bourbón and Duke of Anjou; Legitimists call him Louis XX. The Count of Paris took legal action to prevent him from using the title of Duke of Anjou and the undifferentiated Arms of France, but the case was lost.

Thus, stands the claim of, Louis, Duke of Anjou (called Louis XX), as pretender to the headship of the House of Bourbón in all its Spanish, French, Neapolitan, and Parmesan branches. The *Gotha* cannot be judge to the specific rights to the French throne, and the Duke of Anjou is listed amongst the Bourbóns of Spain in this volume, as a Prince of Bourbón, by descent through the principle line. By the same token, the Count of Paris, called Henri VI, is listed under France, as head of the senior branch of the House of Bourbón.

APPENDIX VI

Almanach de Gotha
Research Committee

ALMANACH DE GOTHA 2003
RESEARCH COMMITTEE

John G Kennedy - **Managing Editor**

John E James - **Associate Editor**

Robert M Clark Jr. Esq

Noel Cox Esq (*Barrister - NZ*)

Charles A Coulombe Esq

Prof. Dr. Robert von Dassanowsky Esq

Nob. Dr Pier Felice degli Uberti

Donald Foreman Esq

Michael G Heenan

The Right Reverend Monsignor Karel Kasteel

Andrew P Loughrey Esq

Richard Thornton Esq

Robin J Wheatley Esq

ALMANACH

DE

GOTHA

COMPLETE INDEX

2003
MMIII

ONE HUNDRED AND EIGHTY SIXTH EDITION

LONDON
ALMANACH DE GOTHA LTD

ALMANACH

DE

GOTHA

———◆———

NOTES

2003
MMIII

ONE HUNDRED AND EIGHTY SIXTH EDITION

LONDON
ALMANACH DE GOTHA LTD